COOKING
AT HOME

WILLIAMS-SONOMA
COOKING AT HOME

CHUCK WILLIAMS

Founder and Director Emeritus
Williams-Sonoma

with

KRISTINE KIDD
and The Editors of Williams-Sonoma

Contents

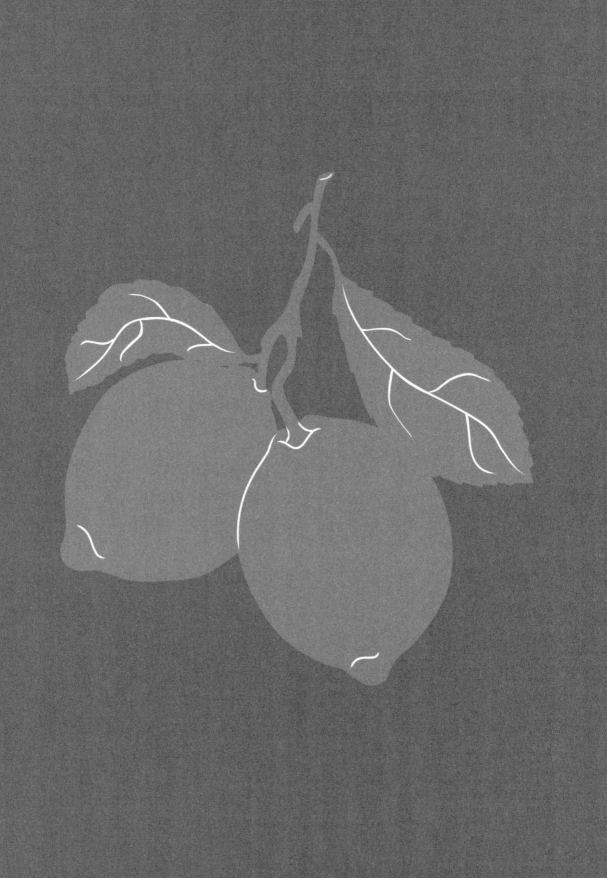

The dishes we cook and eat in our own homes, in the company of family and friends, have a unique power to soothe, satisfy, and nurture, to spark good conversation, and to conjure and create memories. Whether home cooking to you means fried chicken with mashed potatoes or a bowl of pasta with meat sauce, a simply grilled piece of fish or a slowly braised beef brisket, these are the kinds of recipes everyone would love to know how to make well—and share with others.

When I founded Williams-Sonoma in 1956, having a basic knowledge of home-style cooking was something many people took for granted. Two generations ago, almost everyone who knew how to cook first learned under the patient guidance of a parent or grandparent who passed down family recipes and time-honored techniques like how to simmer and skim a soup or stew; pare fresh vegetables and fruits; stuff and truss a holiday turkey; roast and carve large cuts of meat; or mix and roll out pie dough. Life moved at a slower pace back then, and it seemed as if there was plenty of time to learn everything one needed to know about cooking.

Today, of course, things are much different. It's true that many people may be looking for a quick fix, intrigued by what's posted on a popular Internet food site or televised on a cooking show. While I occasionally encounter those people, more often I meet customers whose primary goal, despite their busy lives, is to recreate the kind of delicious, satisfying meals they recall from childhood. Women and men alike, many of whom never learned to cook alongside a loved one, have rediscovered a strong desire to cook for their families and friends, whether it's a quick weeknight meal or a relaxed weekend dinner party. And even as they are buying good-quality pots and pans, kitchen knives, or bakeware, these same people ask questions like: "How do you poach an egg?" or "What's the best way to make birthday cake?" or "Do you know a really great recipe for roast chicken?" In these instances, I love to share every bit of knowledge I can. But there is only so much one can do in such casual and brief encounters.

Cooking at Home aims to fill the gap between then and now, offering an abundance of recipes and kitchen wisdom for home-cooked meals of all kinds. From everyday breakfasts and weekend brunches; to lunchtime salads and sandwiches; wholesome dinners you can put together in minutes; lavish slow-cooked roasts and braises; classic cakes, pies, pastries, and cookies; and refreshing frozen desserts; this book brings together more than 1,000 of our favorite, kitchen-tested recipes.

Before you explore this wonderful collection, be sure to read the introductory pages of the first chapter, which offer a primer on how to outfit a kitchen as well as ideas on how to round out what's missing. There you will also find tips for following a recipe, stocking your kitchen with food staples, fundamental knife skills and cooking techniques, hints on building flavor, and the basics of wine and spirits. Next are recipes for cooking staples such as stocks, flavored oils, breadcrumbs, and basic doughs—the building blocks that are called for multiple times throughout the book.

Twenty-two chapters of delectable recipes follow, organized by mealtime (breakfast and brunch); course (appetizers and first courses, dessert basics); featured ingredients (fish and shellfish, poultry, meat, vegetables, fruit desserts); or type of dish (sandwiches and pizzas, cakes and cheesecakes, frozen desserts). Each chapter, in turn, begins with several pages of detailed instructions relevant to the topic and to the recipes that follow, such as fundamental techniques, key ingredients, cooking methods, and reference charts.

As you'll discover, the recipes in this book are accompanied by a wealth of informative side notes. These include concise tips that give you an edge in preparing them perfectly; variations that help you adjust the recipe to your own personal taste; interesting facts about the ingredients used therein; or ideas for using the recipe in another preparation. Think of these as the informative nuggets that a friend standing by your side in the kitchen might have offered you long ago.

In short, we have packed a lot of information into these pages to create a complete cooking reference book you can use every day, whatever you are in the mood for and whatever the occasion. We hope it's a book you will return to and cook from often, and one you will want to share with others, to spread the pleasures of cooking at home.

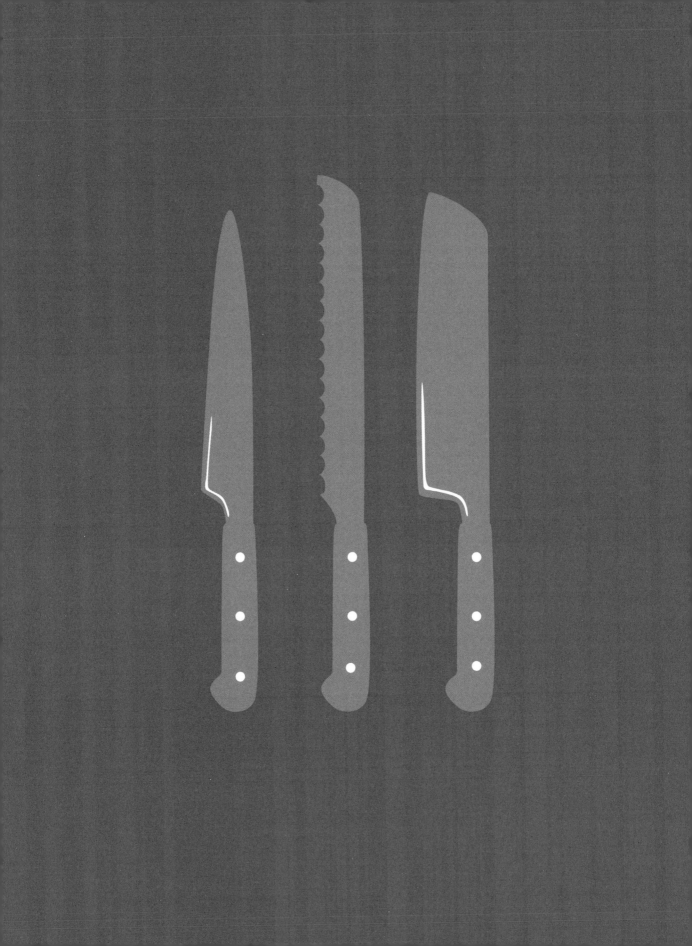

Cooking BASICS

Cooking Basics

When preparing meals at home, you'll be able to cook the widest range of dishes if you start out well prepared. On the following pages, you'll find a wealth of information on everything from how to stock your kitchen with equipment and pantry staples to how to cut and prep basic ingredients, from how to sauté, grill, and steam to how to poach, fry, and roast, from how to season dishes to how to pair food and wine.

Outfitting Your Kitchen

RECIPE ASSUMPTIONS

To ensure the best results in cooking from this book, we've made the following assumptions, unless otherwise specified in individual recipes:

Ingredients: Pantry

- Purchased broth is low sodium.

- Flour is unsifted.

- Nonstick cooking spray, also called cooking spray or vegetable spray, will be in the pantry, and may be called for although not listed in ingredients.

- Pepper is freshly ground just before using.

- Salt is fine sea salt. If you opt for kosher salt, you may find you need to add a bit more to suit your taste.

- Sugar is granulated.

Ingredients: Refrigerated

- Butter is unsalted.

- Eggs are large. This is most crucial in baking recipes.

- Milk is whole.

It's rare that you'll have all the kitchen equipment you need—or want. But even if you have a lot of gaps to fill in, don't worry. Experienced cooks know it's best to outfit a kitchen as the need arises, following a simple strategy.

BUY THE BEST YOU CAN AFFORD   You don't need a matched set of cookware. In fact, different materials are often best for different types of pots, pans, and tools. The only rule is to buy the best equipment you can afford, because good-quality pieces will last longer and will make cooking easier, and your food will turn out better. This is especially true of pans: a good heavy-gauge, thick-bottomed pan will heat evenly and prevent food from burning.

COOKWARE MATERIALS   When choosing cookware, you'll be faced with many choices of materials. For everyday pots and pans, two good choices are stainless steel and anodized aluminum. Steel heats up more slowly and less evenly than aluminum, but is more sturdy and long lasting and is nonreactive to acidic ingredients. Some steel pans have aluminum cores to help them heat quickly and evenly. Anodized aluminum has been treated to strengthen it and to prevent the aluminum from reacting with acidic foods or eggs.

Copper is the best conductor of heat and an excellent choice for cookware, but requires more maintenance and can be costly. It will also react with acidic foods unless it is lined, usually with tin. Cast iron is used for some pans, and although it reacts mildly with acidic foods, it heats up evenly and holds heat well. Enameled cast-iron cookware is good for long-simmered dishes, and the enamel coating makes the pan nonreactive. Pans with nonstick surfaces are handy for cooking a variety of items that can easily stick, such as omelets, or when you want to reduce the amount of cooking fat in your diet.

BAKEWARE MATERIALS   The greatest advancement in bakeware over the past half century has been the development and continued improvement of materials that help keep food from sticking to the pan during baking.

Traditional nonstick bakeware ensures the easy release of baked goods and quick cleanup thanks to coatings of synthetic chemical compounds that are so smooth and slick that food seldom sticks to it. Choose products made with two coats of nonstick finish, rather than a single one, to ensure top performance and durability, and avoid using metal utensils that could scratch the coating. A recent advance in nonstick surfaces is bakeware featuring two layers of a ceramic-reinforced nonstick coating ten times as resistant to scratching as traditional nonstick compounds. Another recent development is molded silicone, an extremely slick, rubber-based compound formed into molds for baking a variety of items, as well as pressed into textured nonstick baking mats. Silicone does not conduct heat as well as metal, however, so it's a good idea to support silicone pans with a metal baking sheet.

Following a Recipe

A well-written recipe should be easy for a cook of any experience level to follow, but you'll always get the best results if you approach every recipe in a simple, deliberate way.

READ THE RECIPE It may seem obvious, but it's worth saying anyway: before you do anything else, the first step to using any recipe is to read it, start to finish. This prevents unpleasant surprises—like realizing you don't have a key piece of equipment on hand, or discovering one hour before dinnertime that the meat you planned to cook needs to marinate for two hours before you can put it on the grill.

MAKE A LIST Review both the ingredients list and the cooking method, then make a shopping list. If you have already stocked your pantry with plenty of commonly used staples, your grocery shopping list won't be too long. And if you've made sure to supply your kitchen with at least a basic range of all-purpose equipment, you will know at a glance whether you have the right pieces on hand. (Even if you don't, think creatively and you may be able to come up with a substitute.)

Once you have all your ingredients and tools, it's time to set up what chefs call *mise en place* (meez-on-plahs). This French phrase, which translates as "putting in place," means preparing and measuring out your ingredients in advance according to the ingredients list and preparing your equipment according to the recipe method. Once all the ingredients are measured and cut as described and arranged in piles or in bowls, your oven is preheated, and your pans are greased, you're ready to start cooking without any sudden interruptions because you are unprepared.

PREPARING INGREDIENTS A recipe's ingredients list usually includes information about how each ingredient should be prepared before cooking: peeled, trimmed, chopped. (Some of these fundamental techniques are explained in detail on page 16.)

If you read the ingredients list carefully, you'll notice that the order of such words varies. The placement of the word *chopped* is as essential as the word itself. For example: "1 cup walnuts, finely chopped" tells you to measure out 1 cup walnuts, then chop them finely *after* measuring. However, "1 cup finely chopped walnuts" means that you should finely chop the nuts *before* you measure them. Since more of an ingredient fits into a cup after it's been chopped, each of these hypothetical ingredient lines calls for a different amount of walnuts. And that small difference in the amount of a single ingredient can make a big difference in how your recipe turns out. Here's another example: In a baking recipe, 1 cup all-purpose (plain) flour, sifted, and 1 cup sifted all-purpose (plain) flour are very different measurements; using the wrong one could affect the outcome of your baked goods.

USING YOUR SENSES Some people feel more secure cooking "by the numbers," paying careful attention to specific times and temperatures. Others prefer to trust their senses, judging food's doneness by how it looks, feels, smells, tastes, or even sounds. For this reason, the recipes in this book provide information for both kinds of cooks, linking sensory cues to corresponding times or temperatures. Remember that in the end, the success of a dish lies with the person who is eating it. Get in the habit of tasting your food often. Think about how it tastes to you, and then add salt, pepper, or other flavorings in small increments according to your personal preference.

Ingredients: Produce

- Citrus juice is freshly squeezed.

- Fresh herbs, greens, and lettuces are washed, then spun or patted dry with paper towels before use.

- Garlic, onions, and fresh ginger are peeled before use

- Onions are yellow.

- Mushrooms are brushed clean with a damp paper towel before using.

- Vegetables are medium in size.

- Vegetables are trimmed and, when necessary, peeled before cutting.

Cooking Instructions

- Ingredients are at room temperature before cooking begins. Food that has been refrigerated has sat at room temperature for 20 minutes to take off the chill.

- Cooking vessels are medium in size.

- When sautéing or pan-frying, the pan and the cooking fat have been heated to the specified level before adding the food to be cooked.

- Food is baked or roasted on the center rack of the oven.

- Adjust the seasonings to taste toward the end of cooking, after flavors have concentrated.

Store the items listed below in a pantry or cupboard at cool room temperature:

Cans Beans (black, cannellini, chickpea/garbanzo); fish, canned (anchovy fillets, tuna); broth (chicken, vegetable); tomatoes (diced, paste, purée, whole).

Bottles and jars Artichoke hearts, capers, honey, molasses (light, dark); hot-pepper sauce; vinegar (balsamic, cider, distilled white, red wine, white wine); wine (dry red, dry white); Worcestershire sauce.

Oils Canola oil, nonstick cooking spray, olive oil (pure, extra-virgin), peanut oil.

Baking ingredients Baking powder; baking soda (bicarbonate of soda); chocolate (bittersweet, semisweet/plain chips, unsweetened, cocoa powder); cornstarch (cornflour); extracts (almond, vanilla); flour, all-purpose (plain); sugar (brown, granulated, confectioners'/icing); yeast (active dry, quick rise).

Dried and milled foods Beans (black, cannellini, chickpea/garbanzo, kidney, navy, lentils); bread crumbs, fine; cornmeal and polenta; fruits (apricots, dates, figs, raisins); garlic; herbs and spices (*see pages 18–19*); onions; pasta; potatoes (starchy baking or russet, waxy white or red boiling); rice (long-grain white and brown), shallots.

Stocking Your Kitchen

Having staple ingredients on hand in your kitchen will make it possible to prepare many things with minimal shopping. The modern notion of a kitchen pantry includes not just cupboard essentials such as those listed at left, but also ingredients listed opposite that are stored in the refrigerator or freezer.

PANTRY STORAGE Many essential food items keep well for long periods at cool room temperature. These include a wide range of foods preserved in unopened cans, jars, and bottles; dried foods such as pastas, beans, and rice; baking ingredients; oils and vinegars; and even some vegetables, such as onions, garlic, and potatoes.

Even though such ingredients present few storage concerns, smart cooks stay aware of what their pantries hold. Don't let ingredients linger there too long. Some items, such as baking powder, for example, lose their effectiveness over time; others, like dried seasonings, diminish in flavor. Still others, such as flour or pasta, can begin to take on a stale taste. Also, dried items will get even drier and harder, taking longer to cook. This is true of beans, for example. If it helps you, write the date of purchase on a package. Rotate your canned goods, too, putting newer purchases behind older ones so you'll use the cans you've had the longest first.

THE SCIENCE OF REFRIGERATION Storing foods in cold conditions slows down the process of spoilage by slowing down the activity of the microbes or the food's own enzymes that cause it. Foods do continue to deteriorate in the refrigerator and even the freezer, but at a much slower rate than they do when held at room temperature.

The reason food should be carefully wrapped before you put it in cold storage is to prevent the dry air of the refrigerator or freezer from drying out the food by depleting its moisture. Wrappers also provide the benefit of giving you a surface on which to jot down the date you purchased an item or put it into storage, to help you use ingredients in a timely way.

REFRIGERATOR STORAGE Combined with pantry ingredients, the items you keep in regular supply in your refrigerator and freezer will make it easier for you to put together a square meal on short notice. Another good reason to keep a well-stocked refrigerator is because the appliance works more efficiently when full than it does empty. Cold foods help keep their neighboring foods cold, too.

When putting things away, bear in mind that the chilliest areas of the refrigerator are usually the rear and the lowest shelf. The warmest spot is the door. Keep dairy, eggs, and meats in the coldest spots, cheeses and oils in the warmest. A refrigerator thermometer will help you make sure you are keeping foods cold enough: 35° to 38°F (2° to 3°C) is ideal.

Although they may seem like cupboard items, nuts, whole grains, and whole-grain flours all contain oils that will eventually go rancid, so keep them in the refrigerator or freezer for longer storage.

REFRIGERATING FRESH FRUITS AND VEGETABLES Although some people prefer the flavor of fresh produce served at room temperature, the refrigerator will keep most fruits and vegetables in optimum condition for the longest period of time. For this reason, many refrigerators include pull-out fruit and vegetable bins at the bottom, their coldest areas. Leafy vegetables should be put in plastic bags before they go into the refrigerator. Cut off the leaves of root vegetables before storing them.

Resist the urge to wash produce before you refrigerate it. The added moisture from washing can promote spoilage. Instead, wash fruits and vegetables just before you eat or prepare them.

Some fruits should not go straight into the refrigerator, however. Apricots, peaches, pears, and melons ripen best at room temperature; once ripe, they can go into the refrigerator. Tomatoes keep their flavor and texture best at room temperature; once they are fully ripe, store them as briefly as possible in the refrigerator. Bananas should never go into the refrigerator; they ripen properly only at room temperature and should be eaten soon after ripening.

FREEZER STORAGE One of the most useful items to keep on hand in the freezer is homemade stock (pages 22–26). You can make your own on a free afternoon, divide it into useful portions of 1 cup (8 fl oz/250 ml) or 1 quart (1 l), and freeze it for up to 3 months. Some markets sell freshly made stock. Or, look for good-quality frozen stock concentrate. (If you don't have the time or inclination to make stock, however, good-quality broth, in cans or aseptic packages, is always a reasonable substitute. Look for a product labeled "low sodium," so you can more easily control the seasoning of the dish to which you are adding it. This is particularly important for long-simmered dishes in which the liquid reduces, concentrating the salt it contains.)

Butter, meat, and poultry freeze well for longer storage. Slip these foods into the freezer—they'll keep for 6 to 8 months—and you'll always be able to make a satisfying pantry meal.

If part of a loaf of bread goes stale, process it into crumbs in the food processor and freeze the crumbs for later use. If your fresh herbs are in danger of wilting, chop them and combine with softened butter in a food processor or by hand to make an herb butter. Then shape the butter into a log, wrap securely in plastic wrap, and freeze to use for flavoring meats or vegetables.

FREEZING AND THAWING FOODS Wrap foods for freezing in freezer-weight plastic wrap or in several layers of regular plastic wrap, aluminum foil, or freezer paper. If the surface of the food is exposed to the cold air of the freezer, it will develop a condition called freezer burn, which leaves the food dry and unpalatable. This is especially true for meat and poultry. Liquids can be frozen in freezer-safe containers. Label and date the items you freeze; they may not be clearly identifiable in a few weeks.

When a food is frozen, the water in its cells is converted to ice crystals, whose sharp edges pierce the cell walls and soften the texture of the food. This is one reason that foods should not be thawed and refrozen, because the food's texture worsens with each freezing. To minimize further damage to the texture and in the interest of food safety, frozen foods should be thawed slowly in the refrigerator, not at room temperature or in a bowl of warm water. Thawing foods in the refrigerator may take from several hours for chicken breasts or fish fillets to as long an entire day for a whole roasting chicken or several days for a large turkey.

THAWING FOODS IN THE MICROWAVE OVEN You can also use the microwave for a quick defrost of smaller food items, but the food will lose some of its moisture and must be watched carefully. Wrap the frozen food in waxed paper and microwave it on low power for 5-minute increments; let the food stand for 5 minutes after each increment, and then check to see if it has thawed. Repeat as necessary until the food is barely thawed. (Some microwave ovens include special buttons that activate helpful timed thawing functions, but you should still keep a close eye on the process from start to finish.) Always cook food thawed in a microwave oven immediately.

REFRIGERATOR STAPLES

Keep these regularly used items on hand in the refrigerator for easy meals:

Condiments Dijon mustard, mayonnaise, salsa, soy sauce, tomato ketchup.

Dairy Butter, unsalted; buttermilk; cheeses (blue, Cheddar, mozzarella, Parmesan); cream, heavy (double); eggs, large; milk; sour cream; yogurt, plain.

Fresh herbs Basil, chives, dill, parsley, rosemary, thyme.

Fruit Apples, citrus fruits (lemons, limes, oranges).

Preserves Orange marmalade, apricot jam, raspberry jam, strawberry jam.

Preserved meats, poultry, seafood Bacon, ham, pancetta, prosciutto, sausages, smoked salmon.

Vegetables Bell peppers, carrots, celery, chiles, cucumbers, lettuces.

FREEZER STAPLES

Keep these essentials on hand in the freezer for longer storage:

Breads Loaves, rolls, tortillas.

Dairy Butter, unsalted.

Doughs Filo, pie, puff pastry.

Fruits Blueberries, cranberries, peaches, raspberries, strawberries.

Meats Ground beef, chops, steaks.

Poultry Chicken and turkey breasts and thighs.

Nuts Almonds, hazelnuts, peanuts, pine nuts, walnuts.

Vegetables Broccoli, carrots, corn, peas, spinach.

Good knives are critical to good cooking, and they require particular care.

Cleaning Knives

Wash knives by hand in hot soapy water as soon as you are finished using them. Like wooden tools, they should not be soaked in water, which can cause the handles to swell and loosen.

Storing Knives

Store knives in a wooden knife block or hung from a magnetic strip rather than loose in a drawer, where they can be nicked and will be a danger to anyone reaching into the drawer.

Honing Knives

Get in the habit of honing your knives often to keep their edges sharp. The best home tool for honing is a sharpening steel, available wherever good-quality knives are sold. Swipe each side of the blade's cutting edge across and along the length of the steel, holding the blade at about a 15-degree angle on the long metal rod. Repeat to swipe each side three times.

Sharpening Knives

Even with regular honing, the edge of a knife gradually dulls over time. As soon it becomes noticeable, have the knife professionally sharpened. Check with the shop where you bought it or with a butcher shop or food-store meat department. The personnel can sometimes do it for you, or they will recommend a professional who can bring your knives back to razor sharpness at a reasonable cost.

Knife Techniques

Knives are the most fundamental and versatile of cooking tools. With a well-made, keenly sharpened blade of the right size and shape, you can easily and efficiently complete almost any kitchen task.

HOLDING A KNIFE Whatever the cutting task you face, begin by making sure the knife is very sharp (see left), as cutting with a dull blade can be dangerous. The knife handle should feel comfortable and secure in your grip. If desired, extend your index finger onto the top part of the blade to help steady the knife. Some cooks hold the knife a little higher on the handle, with the index finger and thumb of the cutting hand on the bottom part of the blade, a position that might be more comfortable for cutting certain foods.

STEADYING FOOD Whenever you are cutting most foods with a downward slicing motion, use your other hand to steady the food, always taking care to curl your fingertips under to keep them safely turned away from the edge of the blade. With experience, you can move your knuckles directly against the side of the blade to help guide it and gauge the width of each cut.

When making a horizontal cut in a piece of food, however, place your noncutting hand flat on top of the food, parallel to both the work surface and the blade itself. Keeping the fingers of your free hand outstretched from your palm will also help keep them well out of the way of the knife.

USING A TWO-PART SLICING MOTION To create slices, cut straight down through the food your are steadying, letting the tip of the knife touch the cutting board first. Then, gently but firmly pull the knife downward and back toward you to complete the cut.

USING A ROCKING MOTION For chopping or mincing ingredients such as fresh herbs, place your noncutting hand on the top edge of the knife blade to steady and help guide the knife. Then, rock the blade back and forth and up and down along its curved sharp edge on the cutting board as you move it over the food to cut it into smaller pieces.

CUTTING UP VEGETABLES Cutting vegetables into relatively uniform pieces helps them cook evenly and contributes to attractive results. Begin by using a chef's knife to cut the vegetables lengthwise into even slices, discarding or saving irregular pieces for stock. Next, stack 2 or 3 slices at a time and cut down through the stack lengthwise to make sticks that are the same width as the thickness of the slices.

To dice vegetables: gather a few sticks at a time into a compact bundle and cut the sticks crosswise into pieces the same length as the width of the sticks. The result should be evenly sized cubes.

To julienne vegetables: follow the process described above for cutting slices and sticks, making the initial slices very thin.

To mince vegetables: gather julienne strips into small bundles. Then, cut the bundles crosswise into very small pieces, or mince. Since the pieces are very small, you don't need to worry about being precise when cutting.

CUTTING UP ROUND ITEMS Ingredients with curved surfaces can be hard to steady on a cutting board for neat, safe slicing. First, use a chef's knife to carefully cut a thin slice from the ingredient, then place it on the flat area on the cutting board, using the fingers of your other hand to hold it steady. The ingredient can now be safely cut into smaller pieces as needed for the recipe.

Basic Cooking Techniques

Learning basic cooking tasks is an important step to recipe success. The following eight fundamental techniques are used throughout this book. Knowing them will give you increased confidence in the kitchen.

SAUTÉING This method most classically involves moving a pan briskly back and forth while lifting slightly on the backward motion to make the contents jump from the pan's surface. But sautéed food can just as easily be stirred as tossed, as long as it is cooked quickly, usually over medium or medium-high heat, in a small amount of fat. Foods to be sautéed should be naturally tender and cut into small pieces or fairly thin slices so they can cook quickly.

FRYING Ordinary frying, also called panfrying, is cooking food in a pan over medium heat with a moderate amount of fat or oil. It works well for thick but tender pieces of meat and poultry, and for firm vegetables.

In deep-frying, the food is immersed in a greater amount of fat and cooks for a shorter time, yielding crisp, golden brown results, whether the food is deep-fried plain, or coated with a batter, bread crumbs, or seasoned flour. The oil should usually be deep enough to cover the food by at least ¾ inch (2 cm). Use a heavy, relatively deep pan and never fill it more than one-third full.

BAKING This term is used for food cooked in the dry heat of the oven. It most often refers to the cooking of breads, cakes, cookies, pastries, and pies. When making any of these baked goods, read the recipe thoroughly and then measure and otherwise prepare ingredients carefully, as success often depends on precision. Baking is also sometimes used to describe the cooking of uniform pieces of meat, poultry, or seafood with a small amount of fat or liquid in an open pan or dish in the oven. When large pieces of food are cooked alone in the oven, however, the process is usually called roasting.

ROASTING This involves cooking foods in the dry heat of an oven using a relatively high temperature. Choose a heavy pan to keep the bottom of the item being roasted and the pan juices from burning. A metal rack will keep the food from stewing in the drippings and sticking to the pan. You can also place meat or poultry on a bed of chopped aromatic vegetables in place of a rack. Doneness is best judged by inserting an instant-read thermometer into the thickest part of the item not touching bone.

BRAISING This cooking method calls for simmering food slowly in a moderate amount of liquid. Relatively tough cuts of meat and fibrous vegetables are excellent candidates. Before meat is braised, it is generally browned in fat to give it color and enhance its flavor. It is then cooked in a tightly closed pot on the stove top over medium-low to medium heat or in a moderately hot oven.

STEWING A stew is made by slowly simmering pieces of meat, poultry, fish, or vegetables in liquid. It is similar to a braise, although stews generally use more liquid and the food is cut into smaller pieces. A stew can be cooked on the stove top, or in a low oven.

POACHING This technique involves gently cooking foods in not-quite-simmering water or other seasoned liquid. Poaching is ideal for delicate foods that need careful treatment to avoid breaking apart or overcooking, such as eggs, fish, chicken, and fruits such as pears.

GRILLING See four main griling techniques on the following page.

BASIC INGREDIENT TECHNIQUES

You'll find yourself using the following simple techniques again and again when preparing the recipes in this book.

Grating Citrus Zest
Use a rasp grater or the small holes of a grater-shredder to remove only the colored portion of the peel, leaving the bitter white pith beneath the peel behind.

Juicing Citrus Fruit
Press and roll the whole citrus fruit firmly against a work surface to break some of the membranes. Then, cut the fruit in half crosswise. Cup a half in one hand and, with your other hand, push and turn a handheld reamer against the flesh to extract the juice. Catch the juice in a bowl and then strain it to remove the seeds.

Toasting Nuts or Seeds
Toast the nuts or seeds in a dry frying pan over medium heat, stirring, until golden brown, 2 to 3 minutes. Transfer them to a plate to cool and crisp.

Toasting Spices
Toast spices in a dry frying pan over medium heat, stirring, until fragrant and deepened slightly in color, about 1 minute. Transfer the cooled spices to an electric spice grinder and grind.

Pitting Olives
Place olives in a zippered plastic bag, force out excess air, and seal. Using a meat pounder or rolling pin, gently pound the olives to loosen the pits. With your fingertips, separate the pits from the flesh. Use a paring knife to cut the flesh from the pits of any stubborn olives.

Allspice
Tastes like a blend of cloves, cinnamon, and nutmeg.

Cardamom
Intense, highly aromatic spice used in curries, fruit dishes, and baked goods.

Cayenne
Very hot ground red spice made from dried chiles.

Cinnamon
Highly aromatic sweet spice sold ground or in stick form.

Clove
Adds strong, sweet, peppery flavor to recipes.

Coriander seed
Whole or ground seeds with a flavor reminiscent of lemon, sage, and caraway.

Cumin
Sharp, strong, earthy spice favored in a variety of ethnic cuisines.

Ginger
Warm, sweetly perfumed, and peppery spice.

Mustard
Pungent, hot seeds used whole and ground.

Nutmeg
Warm, sweet, spicy flavor.

Paprika
Ground dried red peppers, ranging from mild and sweet, to half-sweet, to hot.

Pepper
Best freshly ground. White peppercorns are slightly milder than black.

Saffron
Gives a unique flavor and vibrant yellow color to dishes.

Grilling Techniques

While there are many models of grills on the market, there are only two basic methods for cooking on a grill: direct and indirect heat. Occasionally, a hybrid of the two methods is used. Follow these guidelines for the best results.

STARTING A FIRE Regardless of your grilling method, the process begins with starting a fire. For a gas grill, all you need is a long match or gas wand to light the burners (some models come with built-in spark igniters), following the manufacturer's directions.

For charcoal grills, a chimney starter is a safe, efficient, and environmentally friendly way to start the fire. A metal cylinder with vents on the bottom and a handle on the side, it should be chosen in a size to accommodate an amount of charcoal large enough to fill your grill. A 5-quart (5-l) chimney (about 7½ inches/19 cm in diameter and 12 inches/30 cm tall) holds enough charcoal to make a medium-hot fire in a medium kettle grill. To use the chimney, stuff newspaper into the bottom to create kindling, then top with briquettes or hardwood charcoal chunks and ignite the newspaper. The flame will burn upward inside the chimney, igniting the charcoal. When the charcoal is fully ignited, pour it onto the fire bed. Add more briquettes or chunks to the bed if needed, and in about 20 minutes the fire will be ready to use.

DIRECT-HEAT GRILLING This intense, high-heat method is used for searing and for cooking small or thin food items that are ready in 25 minutes or less. Foods are placed directly over the hot coals of a charcoal grill, or directly over the preheated heat elements of a gas grill. The surface of the food sears and caramelizes over the high heat, sealing the juices inside. Although direct-heat grilling is usually done with an uncovered grill, some cooks prefer to cover the grill to prevent flare-ups and to control temperatures. Ideal candidates for direct-heat grilling include steaks, chops, butterflied meats and poultry, pork tenderloins, burgers, sausages, boneless poultry pieces, fish fillets and steaks, small whole fish, shellfish, all types of kebabs, most vegetables, and fruits.

INDIRECT-HEAT GRILLING Indirect heat cooks foods by reflected heat, much like roasting in an oven. This method is used for cooking larger pieces of food, such as a roast or a whole bird, that take longer than 25 minutes to cook. Indirect heat is also used for smoking and barbecuing.

For indirect-heat grilling, the fire bed, whether charcoal or gas, is arranged underneath only part of the cooking grid, and the food is placed on the portion of the grid away from the fire, often with a drip pan beneath it in a charcoal grill. Once the grill is covered, the heat circulates inside to surround the food, cooking it slowly and evenly. The food can be left unattended for much of the time, but you may need to turn the food partway through the grilling time to ensure uniform doneness, or several times when barbecuing foods. Foods ideal for cooking by indirect heat include bone-in roasts, whole poultry, large whole fish, and large fish fillets, as well as such barbecue-style meats.

HYBRID GRILLING Some foods benefit from using a combination of direct and indirect heat, and/or from using two or three levels of heat. This can be accomplished in a charcoal grill by creating different heat zones, or in a gas grill by setting the heat elements at different levels.

Three levels of heat are useful for grilling very large items or for grilling two or more menu items for a single meal. For example, foods can be seared quickly over high heat. Moved to lower heat, or to the area with no heat, they finish cooking directly over lower heat or indirectly over the no-heat zone.

Building Flavor

A good recipe, carefully prepared, can seem like far more than the sum of its parts. With experience and knowledge, home cooks can learn to add their own subtle touches to make the dishes they cook uniquely their own.

SEASONING TO TASTE A recipe will tell you when to season food as you cook it, but you should also learn to rely on your own judgment. Taste and season with salt, pepper, herbs, and spices at various points throughout the cooking process to achieve the deepest and most complex flavor. (Of course, exercise caution when a recipe you are following includes raw egg or raw meat, poultry, or seafood, and practice common sense when working with raw flour. Until these items are cooked through, you will want to season without tasting.)

Much of the satisfaction of cooking comes from learning which flavors you like to bring together. Keep an assortment of spices and herbs on hand and experiment by replacing the seasonings called for in different dishes or changing the amounts. (Those seasonings listed here to the left and right are suggested pantry essentials, but they by no means exhaust the wide range of options.) Start out with a small amount of a new seasoning, and learn how much of it you like as you grow more familiar with it.

Always give a dish a final taste and adjust the seasoning to your liking just before you serve it. If you watch professional cooks seasoning a dish, you may be amazed at their liberality with salt and pepper, not to mention lemon juice, vinegar, fresh herbs, and spices. Their goal, as yours should be, is to achieve a pleasing balance of flavors.

MAKING ADDITIONS AND SUBSTITUTIONS When you're a novice cook, following ingredients lists and cooking instructions precisely can help you learn to develop your cooking skills. Once you have grown more comfortable in the kitchen, and your favorite recipes or styles of cooking have become second nature to you, you're ready to try experimenting. At that point, feel free to add an ingredient you think might enhance a dish. Add nuts to your favorite cookie recipe, for example, or top a green salad recipe with grilled shrimp to transform it from an appetizer into a light main dish. Or, you might want to replace a distinctive ingredient in a recipe with another similar one: lime juice for lemon in a marinade, or shallot for onion in the seasoning base for a sauté or braise. Some of the recipes in this book include suggested variations to help you develop your ability to improvise.

EXPLORING OTHER COOKING TRADITIONS Often, some of the happiest cooking discoveries come from exploring cooking traditions that may be less familiar to you. Use the recipes in this book inspired by other cuisines as a starting point for expanding your knowledge of how to build complex, pleasing flavors as you cook.

Many French recipes, for example, begin with a mirepoix, a mixture of diced onions, carrots, and celery that flavors stocks, stews, and sauces, and also serves as a bed for roasting meat. Similarly, many recipes for foods from the Mediterranean region and Latin America build flavor on a base—called *soffritto* in Italy and *sofrito* in Spain, Cuba, Puerto Rico, and other Spanish-speaking countries. By contrast, many Asian recipes begin with a highly fragrant mixture of garlic, ginger, and green (spring) onions, then add extra dimensions of flavor with such ingredients as boldly flavored soy sauce, miso, or fish sauce. By staying open to such influences, dining out adventurously, exploring ethnic markets, and trying new cuisines at home, you, too, can give your cooking repertoire a global accent.

ESSENTIAL HERBS

Herbs contribute bold or delicate flavors to the foods they season. Choose fresh herbs, which are generally added toward the end of cooking, or dried herbs, which are usually added near the start of cooking.

Basil
Large green leaves taste faintly of anise.

Bay
Elongated gray-green leaves with a citrusy, nutty flavor.

Chives
Slender, bright green stems impart a mild oniony flavor.

Cilantro (Fresh Coriander)
Medium, serrated leaves with an assertive flavor.

Dill
Fine, feathery leaves with a distinctively aromatic flavor.

Flat-Leaf (Italian) Parsley
Medium, serrated leaves with a pleasing peppery taste.

Marjoram
A milder cousin of oregano; best used fresh.

Mint
Medium green leaves with a distinct refreshing flavor.

Oregano
Aromatic and pungent; small leaves on branched stems.

Rosemary
Strong, fragrant herb, great with chicken or lamb.

Sage
Medium gray-green leaves with a sweet, woodsy scent.

Tarragon
Long, thin leaves with a flavor recalling anise.

Thyme
Floral, earthy-tasting herb with small leaves.

The following types of spirits play the most frequent roles in a well-stocked kitchen. For the liqueurs, look below for the flavor you seek, then find a corresponding liqueur.

Liquors

Bourbon Complex, slightly sweet-tasting American whiskey produced from at least 51 percent corn.

Gin A bracing spirit distilled with botanical ingredients, primarily juniper berries.

Rum Distilled from molasses or sugarcane, it has a unique, almost fruity flavor with a hint of sweetness; both light and dark rum is used.

Scotch whisky Made from a fermented mash of malted barley dried over smoldering peat, which lends smokiness.

Tequila Made from a fermented mash of blue agave, ranging from sharp, clear unaged or briefly aged *blanco* (also called white or silver) to dark, complex, soft long-aged *añejo*.

Vodka A clear spirit with usually no distinctive flavor, generally distilled from a fermented mash of grains.

Liqueurs

Almond: amaretto, crème d'amandes.

Anise: anisette, ouzo, pastis, Pernod, sambuca.

Black currant: crème de cassis.

Chocolate: crème de cacao.

Coffee: Kahlúa, Tia Maria.

Hazelnut: Frangelico.

Orange: Cointreau, Curaçao, Grand Marnier, Triple Sec.

Peppermint: crème de menthe.

Wine Basics

For many fine meals, whether casual or special occasion, wine is as indispensable an element as good bread or a crisp salad. Wine balances the food, aids in digestion, and gives any get-together a convivial feel.

WINE VARIETIES   The differences among wines begin with the grape variety or varieties from which each is made. Each type of grape bestows its unique characteristics of flavor, body, and color on the finished wine. The geographical region in which the grapes are grown and made into wine also contributes to a wine's character.

While European wines are labeled according to the geographical region in which they are produced, most wines bottled in the Americas, Australia and New Zealand, and South Africa are made and labeled as varietals. This makes understanding wines a bit challenging, but the chart at right will help illuminate those differences.

COLOR, BODY, AND SWEETNESS   The simplest way to start making sense of wine is to focus on the color and the body. *Body* refers to how a wine feels in the mouth—light or heavy. In simplest terms, white wines, which are made either from white grapes or from red ones with the skins removed at an early stage in the process, have lighter body than reds. Among both white and red wines, a range of styles is available. It's up to you to decide what types you like to drink, and when. Another primary consideration is sweetness. *Dry* refers to a wine low in sugar. *Off dry* is a little sweet. *Sweet* explains itself.

COOKING WITH WINE   You might think that wine for cooking calls for a less expensive bottle. While it's true that you would not want to cook with a fine old vintage, neither should wine you cook with be undrinkable. A bad wine is not going to be improved by cooking. Never buy anything labeled "cooking wine"; such products are generally inferior and may be preseasoned in ways that won't help a recipe. If you're braising a chicken in wine or otherwise using a lot of wine in a dish, you would do well to choose the same varietal to drink at the table, though not necessarily the same bottle or producer.

PAIRING WINE WITH FOOD   Forget the stiff old rules about pairing reds with meat or whites with fish. Matching wine with food is ultimately a personal choice. Of course, some tried-and-true combinations that seem made for each other exist *(right),* but it's ultimately a matter of personal taste, the mood of the moment, or simply what you have on hand. Try different combinations of varietals with the same dish, and be aware of aromas and flavors that please you. Don't worry about which wine is the "correct" one. The goal is to eat foods you like with wines you like.

When you taste a wine or discuss it with a wine merchant, keep in mind four basic qualities: body (Does the wine feel light or heavy on the tongue?); intensity (Is it bold and assertive, or delicate and mild?); general flavor (What kinds of tastes and aromas does it bring to mind, such as citrus, berry, apple, or oak?); and flavor characteristics (Is it dry or fruity; what are its levels of acidity and astringent tannins?).

Now think about the foods you want to serve. A wine can work with a dish either by mirroring it or contrasting with it. Delicately flavored foods like sole or halibut are complemented by a delicate, fruity white like Pinot Grigio. A rich, oily salmon may contrast well with a slightly acidic, medium-bodied Pinot Noir—and this fish won't be overwhelmed by this red wine. A spicy chicken stir-fry may overpower a buttery white, but be complemented by the

WINE REGIONS AND GRAPE VARIETIES

When you see the following European regions on a wine label, here's the grape that is used. See the lists of red and white varietal wines that follow for the characteristics of each grape featured in the European regions.

EUROPEAN WINE REGIONS

Beaujolais *Gamay*
Bordeaux *Cabernet Sauvignon and Merlot*
Burgundy *Pinot Noir*
White Burgundy, Chablis *Chardonnay*
Côtes du Rhône *Grenache*
Sancerre *Sauvignon Blanc*
Vouvray *Chenin Blanc*
Barolo *Nebbiolo*
Chianti *Sangiovese*
Rioja *Tempranillo*
Ribera del Duero *Tempranillo, Cabernet Sauvignon, and Merlot*

SPARKLING WINES

French Champagne *yeasty*
California sparkling wine *toasty*
Italian Prosecco *crisp, fruity*
Spanish cava *fruity, high in acid*

ROSÉ WINES

Bordeaux *dry, crisp*
Bandol (Mourvèdre) *dry, crisp*
Languedoc *dry, crisp to fruity, full bodied*
Rosado (Spanish) *full bodied, fruity*
Syrah/Shiraz *full bodied, fruity, spicy*

WHITE WINE GRAPE VARIETIES

Sauvignon Blanc *light bodied, high acid*
Pinot Grigio/Gris *light bodied, fruity, low alcohol*
Riesling *medium bodied, fruity to off dry, low alcohol*
Gewürztraminer *medium bodied, fruity to off dry, low alcohol*
Chardonnay *medium to full bodied, crisp-tart to oaky*
Chenin Blanc *crisp and acidic to full bodied and lush*
Viognier *full bodied, aromatic, and lush*
Sémillon *full bodied, aromatic, and lush*

RED WINE GRAPE VARIETIES

Gamay *light bodied, fruity*
Grenache *light bodied to medium bodied*
Pinot Noir *medium bodied, can be fruity, low alcohol*
Sangiovese *light bodied to medium bodied, high acid*
Merlot *medium bodied to full bodied (if oaked)*
Tempranillo *medium bodied to full bodied, spicy*
Syrah/Shiraz *full bodied, strong*
Zinfandel *full bodied, fruity, high acid*
Nebbiolo *full bodied, dark fruit*
Cabernet Sauvignon *full bodied, herbal*

DESSERT WINES

Eiswein/ice wine *sweet and crisp*
Late-harvest wines *sweet, honeyed*
Muscat *sweet, floral*
Sauternes *sweet, lush*
Vin santo *fortified, sweet*
Port *fortified, fruity or sweet, range of styles*
Sherry *fortified, dry to sweet styles*

WINE-PAIRING SUGGESTIONS

Consider the following classic examples for pairing food and wine.

Salty snack foods

Choose sparkling wines such as Champagne, California sparkling wine, Italian Prosecco, or Spanish cava.

Spicy dishes

Choose fruity, low-alcohol, or spicy wines such as Riesling, Pinot Gris, Pinot Noir, or Zinfandel.

Rich or fatty dishes

Choose full-bodied wines such as Chardonnay, Merlot, Cabernet Sauvignon, Syrah, or Zinfandel.

Acidic dishes (tomato, citrus, goat cheese)

Choose high-acid wines such as Sauvignon Blanc, Chianti, or Zinfandel.

Salty or smoked dishes

Choose fruity, low-alcohol wines such as Riesling, Gewürztraminer, Pinot Gris, or Pinot Noir.

Sweet fruit or dessert

Choose sweet wines, with the wine being at least as sweet as the dish.

Classic pairings

Caviar with sparkling wine.

Oysters, lobster, or crab with Chardonnay.

Goat cheese with Sauvignon Blanc.

Roast lamb with Cabernet Sauvignon.

Grilled steak with Zinfandel.

Stilton cheese with vintage Port.

spicy flavor of red Syrah or a sweet, light white like Riesling. A rich, meaty braise will need a powerful red like Cabernet Sauvignon.

Also, what is the weather like? You might prefer a refreshing Chablis or sparkling Prosecco on a hot day, and a bold Cabernet or Merlot may be just the thing to pour on a blustery winter evening.

As a general rule, when you plan to serve several different wines at a meal, they are better appreciated when they progress from light to heavy, with whites served before reds, and dry wines before sweet wines.

BEEF STOCK

A generous mix of marrowbones and beef shins, two cuts good butchers traditionally carry, gives this stock a mild, aromatic flavor and light body. Use it as an all-purpose stock to make soups, stews, and sauces that use or accompany beef.

Place the marrowbones, beef shin, carrots, celery, onion, parsley, bay leaf, and peppercorns in a heavy, large stockpot and add water just to cover by 1 inch (2.5 cm). Place over medium-high heat and bring slowly to a boil without stirring.

As soon as you see large bubbles begin to form, reduce the heat to low and let the stock simmer. Use a large slotted spoon to skim off the grayish foam that rises to the surface during the first 10 minutes of cooking. Then continue to simmer, uncovered, for 3–4 hours. Do not stir, but continue to skim the surface every 30 minutes or so. Add more water, if necessary, to keep the ingredients just covered.

Remove from the heat and remove the larger solids. Line a fine-mesh sieve with 3 layers of dampened cheesecloth (muslin), place over a large heatproof bowl, and pour the stock through the sieve. Discard the solids.

Use a large metal spoon to skim the clear yellow fat from the surface of the strained stock and use the stock right away. Alternatively, let cool to room temperature, transfer to airtight containers, and store for up to 3 days in the refrigerator or up to 3 months in the freezer. Lift off the fat solidified on the surface before using.

Using canned broth

Canned broth of any variety (beef, chicken, vegetable) can often be a valuable time-saver. It does, however, tend to be salty. Use low-sodium products, and once you add the broth to a dish, taste the dish before adding any seasoning.

3 lb (1.5 kg) beef marrowbones, cracked by the butcher

2 thick slices meaty beef shin, about 1 lb (500 g) each

2 large carrots, peeled and cut on the diagonal into ½-inch (12-mm) pieces

2 celery stalks with leaves, cut into ½-inch (12-mm) pieces

1 large yellow onion, cut into 1-inch (2.5-cm) cubes

3 or 4 fresh flat-leaf (Italian) parsley sprigs

1 bay leaf

8–10 peppercorns

MAKES ABOUT 2 QT (8 CUPS/2 L)

BROWN BEEF STOCK

This especially deep, rich stock is achieved by browning the bones and vegetables in the oven, which deepens the flavor and color of the ingredients, before simmering them in water on the stove top. Use it when you want an especially rich color and flavor in a soup or sauce.

Position a rack in the upper third of the oven and preheat to 400°F (200°C). Lightly oil a roasting pan and spread the marrowbones, beef shin, carrots, celery, and onion evenly in the pan. Roast, turning the ingredients once or twice, until they are a deep brown, about 45 minutes. Transfer the meat and vegetables to a heavy, large stockpot.

Pour the fat out of the roasting pan and place on the stove top over 2 burners. Turn on the heat to low, add 2 cups (16 fl oz/ 500 ml) water, and deglaze the pan, scraping up the browned bits from the pan bottom with a wooden spatula.

Pour the contents of the roasting pan into the pot and add the parsley, bay leaf, and peppercorns. Add water just to cover the ingredients by 1 inch (2.5 cm), and place over medium-high heat. Bring slowly to a boil without stirring.

Quick brown beef stock

If you don't have time to make Brown Beef Stock from scratch, roast the bones as directed and then deglaze the roasting pan with 2 cups (16 fl oz/ 500 ml) low-sodium beef broth instead of water. Add an additional 2 qt (2 l) beef broth to the pot with the browned bones and proceed with the recipe, but simmering just for an hour or so.

Canola oil for pan

3 lb (1.5 kg) beef marrowbones, cracked by the butcher

2 thick slices meaty beef shin, about 1 lb (500 g) each

2 large carrots, peeled and cut on the diagonal into ½-inch (12-mm) pieces

2 celery stalks with leaves, cut into ½-inch (12-mm) pieces

1 large yellow onion, cut into 1-inch (2.5-cm) cubes

3 or 4 fresh flat-leaf (Italian) parsley sprigs

1 bay leaf

8–10 peppercorns

MAKES ABOUT 2 QT (8 CUPS/2 L)

As soon as you see large bubbles begin to form, reduce the heat to low and let the stock simmer. Use a large slotted spoon to skim off the grayish foam that rises to the surface during the first 10 minutes of cooking. Then continue to simmer, uncovered, for 3–4 hours. Do not stir, but continue to skim the surface every 30 minutes or so. Add more water, if necessary, to keep the ingredients just covered.

Remove from the heat and remove the larger solids. Line a fine-mesh sieve with 3 layers of dampened cheesecloth (muslin), place over a large heatproof bowl, and pour the stock through the sieve. Discard the solids.

Use a large metal spoon to skim the clear yellow fat from the surface of the strained stock and use the stock right away. Alternatively, let cool to room temperature, transfer to airtight containers, and store for up to 3 days in the refrigerator or up to 3 months in the freezer. Lift off the fat solidified on the surface before using.

Easy degreasing

If time allows, chill the stock before removing the fat. Fill a large bowl partway with ice and water and set the bowl of stock in the ice bath to cool it to room temperature, stirring occasionally. Cover the stock and refrigerate overnight. The fat will rise and solidify on top, making it easy to lift off with a spoon.

CHICKEN STOCK

Chicken stock is a staple for many soups, stews, and sauces and is an essential ingredient for risotto. Although making any stock takes time, you can double or triple a recipe and freeze it in serving-size containers for later use; thaw before using.

6 lb (3 kg) chicken backs and necks

1 large carrot, peeled and cut into 1-inch (2.5-cm) pieces

1 large celery stalk with leaves, cut into 1-inch (2.5-cm) pieces

1 clove garlic, peeled but left whole

1 large or 2 medium yellow onions, quartered

3 or 4 fresh flat-leaf (Italian) parsley sprigs

1 bay leaf

8–10 peppercorns

MAKES ABOUT 4 QT (16 CUPS/4 L)

Place the chicken, carrot, celery, garlic clove, onion quarters, parsley, bay leaf, and peppercorns in a heavy, large stockpot and add water just to cover by 1 inch (2.5 cm). Place over medium-high heat and bring slowly to a boil without stirring.

As soon as you see large bubbles begin to form, reduce the heat to low and let the stock simmer. Use a large slotted spoon to skim off the grayish foam that rises to the surface during the first 10 minutes of cooking. Then continue to simmer, uncovered, for 2–2½ hours. Do not stir, but continue to skim the surface every 30 minutes or so. Add more water, if necessary, to keep the ingredients just covered.

Remove from the heat and remove the larger solids. Line a fine-mesh sieve with 3 layers of dampened cheesecloth (muslin), place over a large heatproof bowl, and pour the stock through the sieve. Discard the solids.

Use a large metal spoon to skim the clear yellow fat from the surface of the strained stock and use the stock right away. Alternatively, let cool to room temperature, transfer to airtight containers, and store for up to 3 days in the refrigerator or up to 3 months in the freezer. Lift off the fat solidified on the surface before using.

Skimming stocks

The grayish foam, sometimes called scum, that rises to the surface of simmering stocks is the result of collagen and gelatin being released from the bones and meat. If not removed, it will cloud the stock.

BROWN CHICKEN STOCK

This stock is a kitchen workhorse, good for sauces, gravies, and more. Browning the chicken pieces in the oven before simmering them with an array of vegetables creates a more robust flavor and deeper color than regular chicken stock.

Preheat the oven to 425°F (220°C). Spread the chicken pieces in a single layer in a large roasting pan. Roast for 30 minutes. Turn over the pieces and continue roasting until deeply browned, about 20 minutes longer.

In a large stockpot or Dutch oven over medium heat, warm the oil. Add the onion, carrot, and celery and cook, stirring occasionally, until the vegetables begin to brown, about 6 minutes. Remove from the heat. Remove the roasting pan from the oven and use tongs to transfer the chicken pieces to the stockpot.

Pour the fat out of the roasting pan and place it on the stove top over 2 burners. Turn the burners on to medium-high. Add 1 cup (8 fl oz/250 ml) water and stir with a wooden spatula to dislodge any browned bits from the pan bottom.

Pour the contents of the roasting pan into the stockpot, add water just to cover the ingredients, and place over high heat. Add the thyme, peppercorns, and bay leaf, bring just to a boil, and then reduce to a simmer. Simmer uncovered, regularly skimming off any foam from the surface of the stock, for at least 3 hours or up to 6 hours.

Remove from the heat and remove the larger solids. Line a fine-mesh sieve with 3 layers of dampened cheesecloth (muslin), place over a large heatproof bowl, and pour the stock through the sieve. Discard the solids.

Use a large metal spoon to skim the clear yellow fat from the surface of the strained stock and use the stock right away. Alternatively, let cool to room temperature, transfer to airtight containers, and store for up to 3 days in the refrigerator or up to 3 months in the freezer. Lift off the fat solidified on the surface before using.

3 lb (1.5 kg) chicken backs and/or wings, chopped with a heavy cleaver into 2–3 inch (5–7.5 cm) pieces

2 tablespoons canola oil

1 small yellow onion, coarsely chopped

1 small carrot, coarsely chopped

1 small celery stalk with leaves, coarsely chopped

4 fresh thyme sprigs, or ½ teaspoon dried thyme

6 peppercorns

1 small bay leaf

MAKES ABOUT 2 QT (8 CUPS/2 L)

Brown turkey or duck stock

Follow the directions for Brown Chicken Stock, replacing the chicken parts with turkey or duck wings, cut into 3-inch (7.5-cm) pieces. For additional flavor, add the giblets from 1 turkey or duck, including the neck, heart, and gizzard, but not the liver, to the roasting pan with the wings.

Quick brown chicken stock

If you don't have time to make Brown Chicken Stock from scratch, roast the bones as directed and then deglaze the roasting pan with 2 cups (16 fl oz/500 ml) low-sodium chicken broth instead of water. Add an additional 2 qt (2 l) chicken broth to the pot with the browned bones and proceed with the recipe, simmering just for an hour or so.

TURKEY STOCK

Make this stock whenever you have a leftover turkey carcass, such as after your Thanksgiving dinner. Use the stock and any leftover meat to make the turkey soup on page 132. If you don't have a carcass, try the turkey variation noted beside the Brown Chicken Stock (left).

Carcass from roast turkey

1 large yellow
onion, chopped

2 carrots, peeled
and chopped

1 celery stalk, chopped

4 fresh parsley sprigs

3 fresh thyme sprigs

1 bay leaf

MAKES ABOUT 2 QT
(8 CUPS/2 L)

With your hands, break the carcass into big pieces and place them in a large stockpot with water to cover (about 3–3½ qt/ 3–3.5 l). Bring to a boil, skimming off any grayish foam that forms on the surface. Reduce the heat to low, cover, and simmer for about 1 hour, skimming as needed. Add the onion, carrots, celery, parsley, thyme, and bay leaf. Cover partially and continue to simmer for about 1½ hours longer.

Remove from the heat and remove the larger solids. Line a fine-mesh sieve with 3 layers of dampened cheesecloth (muslin), place over a large saucepan, and pour the stock through the sieve. Return to high heat, bring to a boil, and adjust the heat to maintain a gentle boil. Cook uncovered, skimming the surface if necessary, until reduced to about 2 qt (2 l), about 1 hour.

Remove from the heat. Use a large metal spoon to skim the clear yellow fat from the surface of the stock. Use the stock right away, or alternatively, let cool to room temperature, transfer to airtight containers, and store for up to 3 days in the refrigerator or up to 3 months in the freezer. Lift off the fat solidified on the surface before using.

Salt-free stocks

Keep in mind that some people might like more or less salt in their dishes than you do. Take that into account when preparing stocks, the building blocks for many dishes. You can always add more salt to a recipe, but you can't take out excess.

COURT BOUILLON

This is a simple stock, ready in under an hour. (*Court* is French for "short.") Cooking crabs, lobsters, and other shellfish—as well as vegetables—in this delicate, fragrant liquid enhances their individual flavors. The acid in the wine keeps poached fish firm.

1 bottle (3 cups/24 fl oz/
750 ml) dry white wine

2 carrots, peeled and
coarsely chopped

2 yellow onions,
coarsely chopped

6 fresh flat-leaf (Italian)
parsley stems

Pinch of fresh or
dried thyme

4 bay leaves

10 peppercorns

Salt

MAKES ABOUT 2 QT
(8 CUPS/2 L)

In a stockpot over high heat, combine the wine, carrots, onions, parsley stems, thyme, bay leaves, peppercorns, 1 tablespoon salt, and 2 qt (2 l) water and bring to a boil. Reduce the heat to low and simmer to devlop the flavors, about 40 minutes.

Remove the bouillon from the heat and strain through a fine-mesh sieve. Use right away, or cover and refrigerate for up to 1 week or freeze for up to 2 months.

**Substituting
vegetable stock**

Court bouillon can be used in any recipe that calls for vegetable stock. On the other hand, if you are using vegetable stock to cook fish, add a dash of fresh lemon juice.

FISH STOCK

Bones for fish stock

When making fish stock, always use the bones and heads from firm, white-fleshed, nonoily fish. Parts from oily, fatty fish, such as salmon, mackerel, or tuna, would give the stock a strong flavor.

You need at least one fish head and a couple of fish frames, or skeletons, all carefully cleaned, to impart the desired flavor to fish stock. Cleaning them well will ensure a clean-tasting stock, which is essential for making fish soups and sauces.

Rinse the cleaned fish parts thoroughly under running cold water. With kitchen scissors, break the spine of each frame into at least 2 pieces. Place the head(s) and frames in a large bowl and add the salt and cool water to cover. Refrigerate for 1 hour, covered. Drain, rinse, and repeat the 1-hour soak without the salt.

Drain the fish pieces, place in a heavy, large stockpot, and add water to cover by 1 inch (2.5 cm). Place the pot over medium-high heat and bring slowly to a boil without stirring. Reduce the heat to medium-low and simmer, using a slotted spoon to skim off the grayish foam that rises to the surface. When the foam stops forming, add the wine, onion, celery, parsley, thyme, bay leaf, and peppercorns and simmer gently until the liquid has a nice fish flavor, about 30 minutes.

Remove from the heat. Line a sieve with 3 layers of dampened cheesecloth (muslin), place over a large heatproof bowl, and pour the stock through the sieve. Discard the solids.

Use right away, or let cool to room temperature, transfer to airtight containers, and store for up to 2 days in the refrigerator or up to 2 months in the freezer.

4 lb (2 kg) fish head(s) and frames from nonoily fish such as flounder, cod, sea bass, or snapper, cleaned

¼ cup (2 oz/60 g) plus 1 tablespoon kosher salt

½ cup (4 fl oz/125 ml) dry white wine

1 yellow onion, thinly sliced

1 celery stalk, thinly sliced

2 fresh flat-leaf (Italian) parsley sprigs

1 fresh thyme sprig

1 bay leaf

8–10 peppercorns

MAKES ABOUT 2 QT (8 CUPS/2 L)

VEGETABLE STOCK

Thawing frozen stock

To thaw frozen stock, refrigerate for 24 hours, or transfer the frozen block of stock to a saucepan and melt slowly over low heat, covered, until liquefied.

Vegetable stock can flavor a wide range of vegetarian dishes, but it also makes an aromatic base for meat-based recipes or sauces. For a deeper, more "meaty" flavor, add 6 ounces (185 g) fresh white mushrooms, brushed clean and sliced, when browning the vegetables.

Tie together the herb sprigs with kitchen string; set aside.

In a stockpot over medium heat, warm the oil. Add the onion, carrot, and celery and sauté until browned, 5–8 minutes. Raise the heat to high, pour in the wine, and deglaze the pan, scraping up any browned bits from the pan bottom. When the wine is almost fully evaporated, add 4 qt (4 l) water, the herb bouquet, and the peppercorns and bring to a boil.

Reduce the heat to medium and simmer gently, uncovered, for at least 45 minutes, then remove from the heat. For rich stock, raise the heat to medium-high and boil until reduced by half, 1¼–1½ hours longer, then remove from the heat.

Place a sieve over a large heatproof bowl and pour the stock through the sieve. Discard the solids. Use the stock right away, or let cool to room temperature, transfer to airtight containers, and store for up 1 week in the refrigerator or up to 6 months in the freezer.

1 *each* fresh flat-leaf (Italian) parsley sprig, fresh thyme sprig, and bay leaf

¼ cup (2 fl oz/60 ml) extra-virgin olive oil

1 yellow onion, coarsely chopped

1 carrot, chopped

2 celery stalks, chopped

½ cup (4 fl oz/125 ml) dry white wine

4 or 5 peppercorns

MAKES ABOUT 3 QT (12 CUPS/3 L) STOCK OR 2 QT (8 CUPS/2 L) RICH STOCK

OLIVE OIL WITH LEMON AND BAY LEAF

Flavored oils have many uses. Consider brushing this lemon-scented oil on toasted Italian bread, pairing it with grated pecorino for tossing with pasta, or using it to dress a salad. Highly aromatic California bay leaves are preferred for this recipe.

1 large lemon

1 cup (8 fl oz/250 ml) extra-virgin olive oil

1 bay leaf

¼ teaspoon peppercorns

MAKES ABOUT 1 CUP (8 FL OZ/250 ML)

Scrub the lemon with an abrasive sponge to remove all surface impurities. Rinse thoroughly and dry well.

Pour the olive oil into a small, heavy saucepan. Using a zester and working directly over the pan, remove the zest from the lemon, letting it fall into the oil. Add the bay leaf and peppercorns. Clip a candy thermometer onto the side of the pan, place the pan over medium-low heat, and heat the oil until the thermometer registers 200°F (93°C). Cook at 200°–225°F (93°–107°C) for 10 minutes. Remove from the heat and let cool slightly.

Sterilize a 1-cup (8–fl oz/250-ml) bottle (see note, right).

Carefully transfer the oil to the hot sterilized bottle. Cover tightly. Store at room temperature for up to 2 months.

Sterilizing bottles

If you are keeping flavored oils, preserves, or similar items for long storage, it's a good idea to sterilize the bottle or jar you are packing them in before use. Run the bottle or jar with its cap through a full dishwashing cycle. Or, boil the item on a rack in a tall pot in water to cover for 10 minutes. Fill the vessel while it is still hot.

27

CHILE OIL

Use this oil as a seasoning for cooking and as a table condiment. If you like, leave the pepper flakes in the oil; they will make it hotter the longer it stands. The chile oil will keep in a small, tightly capped glass jar in the refrigerator indefinitely.

¼ cup (1 oz/30 g) red pepper flakes

1 cup (8 fl oz/250 ml) peanut, canola, or safflower oil

MAKES 1 CUP (8 FL OZ/250 ML)

In a small saucepan over medium heat, combine the red pepper flakes and oil. Bring almost to a boil, then turn off the heat and set aside to cool.

Sterilize a 1-cup (8–fl oz/250-ml) bottle (see note, above right). Carefully strain the oil through a fine-mesh sieve (or pour without straining) into the hot sterilized bottle and cover tightly. Use sparingly as a seasoning or condiment.

No tears tip

Do not lean directly over the pan as the oil heats, because the red pepper flakes release very pungent fumes that may irritate your eyes.

CLARIFIED BUTTER

Cooking with clarified butter

For sautéing over high heat, use clarified butter instead of regular butter. Lacking the milk solids, the clear, yellow liquid can be cooked to a higher temperature than regular butter without smoking .

Butter is often clarified—that is, its milk solids and water are removed—when used for cooking at high temperatures, for making such classic butter-based sauces as béarnaise, and for serving with cooked lobster or crab for dipping, when it is typically labeled "drawn butter."

Melt the butter in a small, heavy saucepan over medium-low heat, watching closely to avoid burning. When the butter has fully melted and starts to bubble, reduce the heat to low and cook for about 1 minute. Remove from the heat and let stand for about 2 minutes, to allow the milk solids to settle to the bottom of the pan.

Using a spoon, skim off and discard the foam from the surface, then carefully pour off the clear yellow liquid, which is the butterfat, into a clean container. Discard the milky solids and water left behind in the pan. Use the clarified butter right away, or cover tightly for storing. Store in the refrigerator for up to 1 month or in the freezer for up to 2 months. Warm the clarified butter gently before using.

2 cups (1 lb/500 g) unsalted butter

MAKES ABOUT 1½ CUPS (12 FL OZ/375 ML)

ROASTED BELL PEPPERS IN OLIVE OIL

Small dried chiles

Thai chiles, sometimes known as bird chiles or Thai bird chiles, are a good choice for this recipe. Bright red and about 1 inch (2.5 cm) long, they'll add just the right touch of heat to the bell peppers. You can also use chiles labeled "pequin."

The red and yellow peppers are especially attractive when arranged in alternating layers in a glass jar. Add them to salads, pizzas, sandwiches, or crostini. Packed into sterilized jars, they also make great host gifts or holiday presents for friends.

Cut the peppers lengthwise into strips ½ inch (12 mm) wide. Layer half of the red pepper strips in a 1-pt (16-fl oz/500-ml) jar with a lid. Sprinkle with ½ teaspoon each rosemary and thyme and then sprinkle with ground pepper. Top with 2 lemon slices. Layer half of the yellow pepper strips on top, and season the same way, ending with 2 lemon slices. Repeat the layers. Top with the dried chile. Add enough olive oil to cover the peppers and chile.

Cover and store in the refrigerator for at least 1 day before using to allow the flavors to blend. The peppers will keep in the refrigerator for up to 1 week.

2 large bell peppers (capsicums), 1 red and 1 yellow, roasted, peeled, and seeded (see page 333)

2 teaspoons chopped fresh rosemary

2 teaspoons fresh thyme leaves

Ground pepper

8 thin lemon slices

¾ cup (6 fl oz/180 ml) extra-virgin olive oil, or as needed

1 small dried chile

MAKES ABOUT 1 PT (16 FL OZ/500 ML)

PRESERVED LEMONS

You need to put up these Moroccan salt-cured lemons at least 3 weeks before using them in a recipe, such as for the braised lamb shanks on page 285. Preserved lemons, if completely submerged in their acidic brine, will keep for up to 6 months in the refrigerator.

8 lemons (about 2 lb/1 kg), preferably organic

10 tablespoons (5 oz/155 g) coarse salt

Fresh lemon juice as needed to cover

MAKES 8 PRESERVED LEMONS

Scrub the lemons under running cold water, then place in a large jar. Add water to cover and let stand for 3 days, changing the water at least once a day or up to 6 times a day.

Drain the lemons and slice each lemon lengthwise into quarters, leaving the quarters attached at the stem end. Have ready 2 hot sterilized jars (see page 27), each large enough to hold 4 lemons. Spoon 1 tablespoon salt into the center of each lemon. Place 1 tablespoon salt into each hot jar and pack the lemons into the jars. Add lemon juice to cover, then cap tightly. Store in a cool dry place for 3–4 weeks. Do not worry if a white film forms on the lemons; it will rinse off easily under running cold water.

To use the lemons, remove as many as you need from the jar and rinse well. Cut apart the wedges, squeeze out and discard the juice, and remove and discard the pulp. Cut the peel as directed in individual recipes.

Using preserved lemons

Next to olives, preserved lemons are one of the best-known ingredients in Moroccan cuisine. Use the finely chopped peel (discard the too-salty pulp) to flavor braised meats or poultry, or vegetable dishes.

29

ROASTED GARLIC PURÉE

Roasted garlic has a mellow, nutty flavor that complements a wide range of other foods. Spread this rich purée on slices of crusty bread, for example, or swirl it into mashed potatoes or other creamy root vegetable purées.

2 whole heads garlic

Olive oil for drizzling

MAKES ABOUT 2 TABLESPOONS

Preheat the oven to 425°F (220°C).

Using a sharp knife, cut off the top one-fourth of each garlic head. Gently score the head around its middle, cutting through a few layers of the papery skin. Pull off any loose skin from the top half of the head, trying not to remove every shred. (This will make it easier to squeeze out the softened cloves later.) Drizzle lightly with olive oil and tightly wrap each head in a piece of aluminum foil. Place in a small baking dish or directly on the oven rack.

Bake until the garlic cloves are soft when pierced with a knife, 45–60 minutes. Remove from the oven and let cool completely. Using your fingers, squeeze the soft garlic pulp into a small bowl. Use right away, or store tightly covered in the refrigerator for up to 3 days.

Working with roasted garlic

To squeeze the most garlic from the head, do it systematically, squeezing each clove from the base to the top, like a tube of toothpaste, to separate all the pulp from the skins.

TOASTED BREAD CRUMBS

Good bread, good crumbs

Country bread refers to any full-bodied, usually free-form yeast bread. This usually means buying it from a local bakery or specialty-foods market, rather than picking up a loaf wrapped in cellophane on a supermarket shelf.

In the Mediterranean, bread is routinely converted into crunchy crumbs that are sprinkled liberally on vegetables before baking, stirred into pasta, or used as a topping for gratins. This is an ideal way to use stale or leftover bread.

Preheat the oven to 350°F (180°C).

Break up the bread into chunks and place in a food processor. Pulse until coarse crumbs form. Spread the crumbs on a rimmed baking sheet. In a bowl, stir 1 teaspoon each salt and pepper into the butter and drizzle over the crumbs.

Bake, stirring occasionally for even browning, until golden, about 20 minutes. Remove from the oven and let cool completely. Store in an airtight container at room temperature for up to 2 days.

1 loaf coarse country bread, 1½ lb (750g), crusts removed

Salt and ground pepper

½ cup (4 oz/125g) unsalted butter, melted, or ½ cup (4 oz/125 ml) olive oil

MAKES 1½ CUPS (6 OZ/185 G)

HERBED BREAD CRUMBS

The best bread for herbed crumbs

The ideal bread to use for these tasty bread crumbs is a coarse-textured white bread, usually baked in 1- or 1½-pound (500- or 750-g) loaves and sold presliced.

These bread crumbs benefit from the flavor of fresh herbs. If the recipe calls for *dried* herbed bread crumbs, make the crumbs as directed, then spread on a baking sheet and toast in a preheated 325°F (165°C) oven, stirring several times, until golden, about 5 minutes.

Cut the crusts off the bread and discard. Tear the bread into pieces. In a blender or food processor, combine the bread and a pinch each salt and pepper. Process until coarse crumbs form. Add the thyme and rosemary and pulse a few times just until well mixed.

Use the bread crumbs right away, or store in an airtight container in the freezer for up to 1 week.

4 slices white bread

Salt and ground pepper

¼ teaspoon *each* chopped fresh thyme and rosemary

MAKES ABOUT 1 CUP (2 OZ/60 G)

CORN BREAD STUFFING

Stuffing safety

To prevent contamination, prepare the stuffing just before roasting and cool it almost to room temperature. Roast a stuffed bird as soon as possible after stuffing and be sure the stuffing reaches 165°F (74°C) before serving.

For many people, a holiday dinner isn't complete without stuffing, especially a traditional corn bread stuffing like this one. For the best results, bake the corn bread the day before you make the stuffing. It will have a better texture and fuller flavor.

In a large frying pan over medium heat, melt the butter. Add the onion, apple, and celery and cook, stirring occasionally, until the vegetables are softened, about 5 minutes.

Add the pecans to the pan and cook, stirring, until golden, about 5 minutes. Add the crumbled corn bread, cinnamon stick, 1 teaspoon salt, and a generous amount of of pepper.

To bake the stuffing in a turkey, loosely fill the cavities with the stuffing and truss (see page 235); increase the roasting time for the turkey by 30 minutes.

4 tablespoons (2 oz/60 g) unsalted butter

2 cups (8 oz/250 g) chopped Vidalia or other sweet onion

1½ cups (6 oz/185 g) peeled, cored, and chopped apple

1 cup (5 oz/155 g) chopped celery

1 cup (4 oz/125 g)
chopped pecans

**Buttermilk Corn Bread
(page 430), baked, cooled,
and crumbled**

1 cinnamon stick, about
2 inches (5 cm)

Salt and ground pepper

**MAKES ABOUT 10 CUPS
(4 LB/2 KG)**

To bake the stuffing in a dish, preheat the oven to 325°F
(165°C). Butter a 9-by-13-by-2-inch (23-by-33-by-5-cm) baking
dish and spoon the stuffing into it; cover with aluminum foil.
Bake for 30 minutes. Uncover and continue to bake until the
top is crisp, about 30 minutes longer.

To serve, if needed, use a large spoon to transfer the stuffing
from the turkey cavity to a serving dish. Remove the
cinnamon stick and serve hot.

SAUSAGE, APPLE, AND CHESTNUT STUFFING

A Thanksgiving tradition, this stuffing is a classic accompaniment to a roast turkey, whether
cooked inside the bird or alongside it as a dressing. You can substitute 2 cups (about 10 oz/
315 g) vacuum-packed chestnuts, which have already been peeled, for the fresh chestnuts.

**1 lb (500 g) sourdough or
white coarse country bread,
crusts removed and cut
into ½-inch (12-mm) cubes**

¾ lb (375 g) bulk
pork sausage

4 tablespoons (2 oz/60 g)
unsalted butter

1 large yellow onion,
chopped

3 large celery stalks,
chopped

2 large tart apples such
as pippin or Granny Smith,
peeled, cored, and chopped

3 tablespoons chopped
fresh thyme, or 1 tablespoon
dried thyme

¾ cup (6 fl oz/180 ml)
chicken stock

1 lb (500 g) chestnuts,
roasted and peeled
(see note, right), then
coarsely chopped

½ cup (¾ oz/20 g)
chopped fresh flat-leaf
(Italian) parsley

Salt and ground pepper

2 eggs, beaten

**MAKES ABOUT 12 CUPS
(5 LB/2.5 KG)**

Preheat the oven to 400°F (200°C). Spread the bread cubes
in a single layer in a large rimmed baking pan. Bake, stirring
occasionally, until lightly golden, 12 minutes. Transfer the
bread cubes to a large bowl.

In a large frying pan over medium-high heat, cook the
sausage meat, crumbling with a fork, until browned, about
10 minutes. Transfer to the bowl with the bread. Add the
butter to the pan and reduce the heat to medium, and when
the butter has melted, add the onion and celery and sauté
until tender, about 8 minutes. Add the apples and thyme and
sauté until for 1½ minutes to blend well. Add to the bread.
Add the stock to the pan, bring to a boil, and deglaze the pan,
stirring to dislodge any browned bits from the pan bottom.
Add to the bread. Mix in the chestnuts and parsley, and
season with salt and pepper. Finally, mix in the eggs.

To bake the stuffing in a turkey, loosely fill the cavities with
the stuffing and truss (see page 235); increase the roasting
time for the turkey by 30 minutes.

To bake the stuffing in a dish, preheat the oven to 325°F
(165°C). Butter a 9-by-13-by-2-inch (23-by-33-by-5-cm) baking
dish and spoon the stuffing into it; cover with aluminum foil.
Bake for 30 minutes. Uncover and continue to bake until the
top is crisp, about 30 minutes longer.

To serve, if needed, use a large spoon to transfer the stuffing
from the turkey cavity to a serving dish and serve hot.

**Roasting and
peeling chestnuts**
*Use a sharp knife
to score an X in the
shell on the flat side
of each chestnut.
Place in a single
layer in a baking pan
with ½ cup (4 fl oz/
125 ml) water and
roast in a preheated
400°F (200°C) oven
until the shells begin
to peel back at the
X, about 20 minutes.
Peel off the outer
shells and the thin,
beige inner skin
while the nuts are
still warm.*

31

CARAMELIZED ONION AND MUSHROOM STUFFING

Planning stuffing quantities

When making stuffing, figure on ½ cup of the mixture for each pound of meat. Using this logic, the recipe at right would be enough to stuff a 24-lb (11 kg) bird. You can add any leftover stuffing to a buttered baking dish, cover, and bake alongside the bird for the last 30 minutes of roasting. Then, uncover and continue to cook until browned on top and heated through while the bird rests.

For a change of pace, try this satisfying stuffing made from browned sweet onions and meaty sautéed mushrooms. Choose buttermilk bread if you want a bit of extra tang to offset the richness of the stuffing. Fresh herbs instead of dried will also cut the richness.

Preheat the oven to 400°F (200°C).

Spread the bread cubes in a single layer in a large baking pan. Bake, stirring occasionally, until golden brown, about 10 minutes. Transfer to a large bowl.

In a large, heavy frying pan over medium-high heat, melt the butter. When hot, add the onions and sauté until golden brown, about 20 minutes. Reduce the heat to medium. Add the mushrooms and celery and sauté until tender, about 8 minutes. Add to the bread cubes, along with the tarragon and parsley. Add the stock to the pan, bring to a boil, and deglaze the pan, stirring to dislodge any browned bits from the pan bottom. Add to the bread and season with salt and pepper. Finally, mix in the eggs.

To bake the stuffing in a turkey, fill the cavities with the stuffing and truss (see page 235); increase the roasting time for the turkey by 30 minutes.

To bake the stuffing in a dish, preheat an oven to 325°F (165°C). Butter a 9-by-13-by-2-inch (23-by-33-by-5-cm) baking dish and spoon the stuffing into it. Cover with aluminum foil and bake for 30 minutes. Uncover and continue to bake until the top is crisp, about 30 minutes longer.

To serve, if needed, use a large spoon to transfer the stuffing from the turkey cavity to a serving dish and serve hot.

1 lb (500 g) buttermilk bread or egg bread, cut into ½-inch (12-mm) cubes

6 tablespoons (3 oz/90 g) unsalted butter

2 large yellow onions, chopped

1 lb (500 g) fresh white mushrooms, brushed clean and sliced

3 celery stalks, chopped

2 tablespoons chopped fresh tarragon, or 2 teaspoons dried tarragon

½ cup (¾ oz/20 g) chopped fresh flat-leaf (Italian) parsley

¾ cup (6 fl oz/180 ml) chicken stock

Salt and ground pepper

2 eggs, beaten

MAKES ABOUT 12 CUPS (4½ LB/2.25 KG)

BASIC PIZZA DOUGH

Whole-wheat pizza dough

For whole-wheat dough, substitute 1 cup (5 oz/155 g) of all-purpose (plain) flour in this recipe with 1 cup (5 oz/ 155 g) whole-wheat (wholemeal) flour. Or, if you prefer, use whole-wheat flour for the full amount. The more whole-wheat flour you use, the denser and chewier the crust will be.

This easy recipe makes enough dough for a 12-inch (30-cm) thin-crust pizza or a 9-inch (23-cm) thick-crust pizza. If you like, stir 2 tablespoons minced mixed fresh herbs (or 1 tablespoon dried) into the flour. For more flavor variations, see left and opposite.

In a small bowl, combine the yeast and the lukewarm water and let stand until bubbles start to rise, about 5 minutes.

In a bowl, stir together the flour and salt and form into a mound. Make a well in the center, and add the yeast mixture to the well. Using a fork and stirring in a circular motion, gradually pull the flour into the yeast mixture. Continue stirring until a rough dough forms.

Transfer the dough to a lightly floured work surface. Knead until smooth and elastic, about 10 minutes. As you work, sprinkle additional flour on the work surface, 1 tablespoon at a time, only if needed to prevent sticking. Form the dough into a ball. Oil a clean bowl with the oil, place the dough in

1 tablespoon active dry yeast

¾ cup plus 2 tablespoons (7 fl oz/210 ml) lukewarm water (110°F/43°C)

2¾ cups (14 oz/440 g) all-purpose (plain) flour

1 teaspoon salt

1 tablespoon extra-virgin olive oil

MAKES 1⅓ LB (650 G) DOUGH

it, and turn to coat all sides. Cover the bowl with plastic wrap and let the dough rise in a warm place until the dough is doubled in volume, 1–2 hours.

To shape the dough, turn it out onto a lightly floured work surface and press flat. Using your hands, begin to press it out gently into the desired shape. Then place one hand in the center of the dough and pull, lift, and stretch the dough with the other hand, gradually working your way all around the edge, until it is the desired thickness, about ¼ inch (6 mm) for a crusty pizza base and ½ inch (12 mm) for a softer one. Flip the dough over from time to time as you work with it. Alternatively, roll out the dough with a rolling pin. The dough should be slightly thinner in the middle than at the edge. Lift the edge of the pizza to form a slight rim.

Transfer the dough to a baker's peel or a baking sheet, cover with a kitchen towel, and let the dough rise again until almost doubled, about 20 minutes. Top and bake as directed in individual recipes.

POTATO PIZZA DOUGH

The moisture content of potatoes varies, so keep an eye on how much water you add to this dough: hold a little back if your dough seems too moist, or add a little more if it is too dry. The recipe makes enough for a 12-inch (30-cm) thin-crust or a 9-inch (23-cm) thick-crust pizza.

1 boiling potato,
5 oz (155 g)

1 tablespoon active
dry yeast

¾ cup plus 2 tablespoons
(7 fl oz/220 ml) lukewarm
water (110°F/43°C)

2½ cups (12½ oz/390 g)
all-purpose (plain) flour

1 teaspoon salt

1 tablespoon extra-virgin
olive oil

MAKES 1½ LB (750 G) DOUGH

In a saucepan, combine the potato with water to cover. Bring to a boil and cook until tender, 20–25 minutes. Drain and peel while still hot.

Meanwhile, in a small bowl, combine the yeast and the lukewarm water and let stand until bubbles start to rise, about 5 minutes.

In a large bowl, stir together the flour and salt. Pass the hot peeled potato through a ricer or sieve into the bowl and stir to combine. Form the mixture into a mound. Make a well in the center, and add the yeast mixture to the well. Using a fork and stirring in a circular motion, gradually pull the flour and potato into the yeast mixture. Continue stirring until a medium-firm dough forms.

Transfer the dough to a lightly floured work surface. Knead until smooth and elastic, about 10 minutes. As you work, sprinkle additional flour on the work surface, 1 tablespoon at a time, only if needed to prevent sticking. Form the dough into a ball. Oil a clean bowl with the oil, place the dough in it, and turn to coat all sides. Cover the bowl with plastic wrap and let the dough rise in a warm place until the dough is doubled in volume, 1–2 hours.

Shape and bake the dough as for Basic Pizza Dough, above.

Cornmeal pizza dough

For cornmeal pizza dough, use fine-grind cornmeal. Replace the 2¾ cups all-purpose (plain) flour in this recipe with 2½ cups (12½ oz/390 g) all-purpose flour plus ⅓ cup (2 oz/ 60 g) cornmeal.

Rosemary-potato dough

For added flavor, add up to 2 tbsp chopped fresh rosemary to the flour and salt mixture. It's especially good for pizzas featuring roasted vegetables.

33

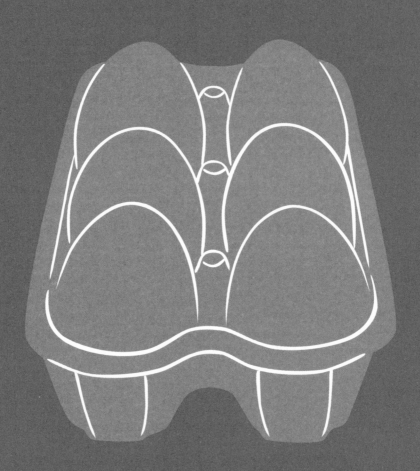

Breakfast
& BRUNCH

Breakfast & Brunch

Some people skip breakfast, and others would happily eat "breakfast food" all day. But savvy eaters know that a healthful morning meal ensures you'll work and play better throughout the day. That may mean muesli on a weekday, pancakes with the kids on Saturday, or an elegant mid-Sunday quiche for guests. Master the basics of breakfast and brunch and you'll be able to whip up endless variations with one eye still closed.

Egg Basics

Nutritional value
Eggs are nutritional powerhouses, supplying protein; vitamins A, D, and E; and minerals such as phosphorus, magnesium, iron, calcium, and zinc.

Fat versus protein
Egg whites are low in fat and high in protein, making them healthful additions to the diet. Egg yolks, in contrast, contain fat and cholesterol but also the most flavor.

Egg substitutes
Sold in cartons, liquid egg substitutes are popular with people trying to avoid the fat and cholesterol in egg yolks. They are made mainly from egg whites and thus lack the rich flavor of whole eggs. Egg substitutes can be used for scrambled eggs, for making sauces, and in other recipes. In general, substitute ¼ cup (2 fl oz/60 ml) liquid egg substitute for 1 whole large egg.

Calculating egg volume
For recipes calling for eggs by volume, 1 cup (8 fl oz/250 ml) is equal to 5 whole large eggs, the whites of 7 large eggs, or the yolks of 14 large eggs.

Scrambled, fried, poached, boiled, baked, or mixed into batters or doughs, eggs are fundamental to breakfast and brunch. The following guidelines will help you choose and store them wisely.

BUYING EGGS Chicken eggs are graded by quality and size. Quality refers to the shape and condition of the shell and the appearance of the yolk and albumen, and the size of the air cell (the area between the inner and outer shell membrane), rather than nutrition. The highest-quality eggs, grade AA, have thick whites, firm, plump yolks, and a small air cell. Grade A eggs are only slightly lower in quality. In terms of size, eggs for retail sale in the United States are labeled jumbo (2¼ oz/67 g), extra-large (2 oz/60 g), large (1¾ oz/50 g), medium (1½ oz/45 g), and small (1⅓ oz/40 g). (Medium, small, and low-quality grade B eggs rarely make it to the retail market.) Unless otherwise noted, the recipes in this book (and most others) are based on large eggs. For recipes in which eggs are fried or poached, buy grade AA eggs if possible, because they hold their shape better; grade A eggs are fine for scrambling or for use in dishes in which they are beaten.

Eggs destined for sale in grocery stores are carefully washed and coated with a natural mineral oil to seal out bacteria. When selecting a carton of eggs, first check the sell-by date, which should be as distant as possible, then open the carton to inspect the eggs. Don't buy a carton that contains a dirty or cracked egg, or an egg that is stuck to the carton, as it is likely to break when you try to remove it.

STORING EGGS A day spent on a countertop ages an egg as much as a week spent in the refrigerator. Keep eggs as cold as possible, and they'll stay fresh longer. Store eggs in the coolest part of your refrigerator and in their original carton, which helps insulate them from temperature fluctuations and protects them from refrigerator odors. (Note that they are packaged with their broad ends up, which keeps the yolks centered.) Stored this way, eggs will keep for 3 to 4 weeks past their sell-by date. As they age, the whites will thin and become more transparent and the yolks will flatten, but the nutritional value will not be diminished. Fresher eggs are good for making emulsified sauces, such as hollandaise and mayonnaise. Reserve older eggs for baking; older whites whip up better than fresher whites.

Recipes sometimes call for egg whites or egg yolks only, leaving you with leftovers. Refrigerate uncooked egg whites in a tightly sealed glass or plastic container for up to 5 days. Refrigerate uncooked egg yolks covered with a little water and sealed in a glass or plastic container for up to 2 days. Uncooked whole eggs out of the shell can be stored in the same way and for the same length of time as egg yolks, without the water.

TOPPINGS AND FILLINGS

For a fresh spin on pancakes, waffles, French toast, and crepes,
try the following fillings and toppings.

Bing Cherry Syrup

In a saucepan over high heat, combine ½ cup (3½ oz/105 g) firmly packed light brown sugar, ½ cup (4 oz/125 g) granulated sugar, and 1 cup (8 fl oz/250 ml) water and bring to a boil, stirring to dissolve the sugar. Boil for 5 minutes, stirring constantly. Add 1½ cups (9 oz/280 g) pitted Bing cherries, reduce the heat to medium-low, and simmer until the cherries are cooked, 8–10 minutes. Stir in 1 teaspoon pure almond extract and simmer for 2 minutes longer. Let cool. Use on pancakes, waffles, or French toast, or wrap the drained cherries in crepes and drizzle with the syrup.

Maple-Cranberry Butter

Bring 1 cup (8 oz/250 g) unsalted butter to room temperature. In a saucepan over low heat, combine ½ cup (2 oz/60 g) fresh or thawed frozen cranberries and ¼ cup (2 fl oz/ 60 ml) pure maple syrup. Cook, stirring, until the cranberries have softened and "popped," about 5 minutes. Let cool completely. Transfer to a bowl, add the butter, and beat with a wooden spoon to combine. Spoon the flavored butter onto a sheet of waxed paper and shape it into a log. Wrap tightly in the waxed paper and refrigerate until firm. Slice for use on top of pancakes, waffles, or French toast.

Maple-Pear Sauce

Slice 4 Anjou or Bartlett (Williams') pears and toss with the juice of 1 lemon. In a saucepan over medium heat, melt 4 tablespoons (2 oz/60 g) unsalted butter. Add the pears and sauté for 2 minutes. Add ¼ cup (2 fl oz/60 ml) water, the grated zest of ½ lemon, and 1 cup (8 fl oz/250 ml) pure maple syrup and simmer until the pears are tender, about 6 minutes. Using a slotted spoon, remove the pears and keep warm. Raise the heat to high and cook until the liquid is reduced to a syrup, about 10 minutes. Return the pears. Use on pancakes, waffles, or French toast, or as a crepe filling.

Nectarine-Apricot Sauce

In a saucepan over high heat, combine ½ lb (250 g) dried apricots, 2 cups (16 fl oz/ 500 ml) water, ½ cup (4 oz/125 g) sugar, and 2 tablespoons fresh lemon juice. Bring to a boil, stirring often. Reduce the heat to low, cover, and simmer until tender, about 35 minutes. Transfer to a blender and process until smooth. Pour into a measuring pitcher; add ½ teaspoon grated lemon zest and enough water to measure 3½ cups (28 fl oz/875 ml) total. Pit and thinly slice 3 large nectarines. Return the sauce to a simmer over low heat; stir in the nectarines. Remove from the heat and let stand for 5 minutes. Use on pancakes, waffles, or French toast, or wrap the drained nectarines in crepes and drizzle with the sauce.

Sautéed Bananas with Nuts

Slice 3 bananas into rounds ¼ inch (6 mm) thick. In a sauté pan over medium-high heat, melt 1 tablespoon unsalted butter. Add the bananas and sauté until warm, about 1 minute. Top pancakes, waffles, or French toast with the bananas, toasted pecans, and warmed pure maple syrup. Or, wrap the bananas and toasted pecans in sweet crepes and drizzle with the warmed syrup.

SEE ALSO:

- Blueberry Sauce, *page 463*
- Citrus Curd, *page 452*
- Orange Marmalade–Raspberry Sauce, *page 463*
- Raspberry Sauce, *page 462*

Using leftover whites
If you end up with a surplus of egg whites, use them to make Meringue Pie Topping (page 454), Basic Baked Meringues (page 455) Angel Food Cake (page 504), or healthful egg-white omelets.

Using leftover yolks
If you end up with a surplus of yolks, use them to make ice cream (pages 604–11), Mayonnaise (page 386), or Chocolate Mousse (page 586).

Freezing whole eggs
To freeze eggs, break them into a bowl and stir just to break the yolks. Transfer to a rigid container just large enough to hold them (less than ½-inch/ 12-mm headspace), and cover tightly. Freeze the eggs for up to 9 months. Thaw them in the refrigerator and use in baking or omelet recipes.

Freezing whites and yolks
For egg whites alone, follow the procedure for whole eggs; freeze for up to 1 year. For yolks alone, add a pinch of salt; freeze for up to 9 months. When brought to room temperature, previously frozen whites will whip up more easily than fresh ones.

RAW EGGS AND BACTERIA

Eggs are used raw or partially cooked in some recipes. Salmonella or other bacteria can be found on eggs, which may lead to food poisoning, though incidence of such contamination is rare. This risk is of most concern to young children, elderly people, pregnant women, and anyone with a compromised immune system. If you have health and safety concerns, you may wish to avoid foods made with raw eggs.

BREAKFAST BREADS

Bread is an important element of any breakfast. To bake your own, see chapters 14 and 15.

Toast

Made from all kinds of yeast-leavened loaves, toast is a classic companion to eggs and/or breakfast meats. Top with butter, preserves, or soft cheese.

Bagels

These doughnut-shaped breads (page 417) gain extra-chewy texture from being boiled before baking. Slice bagels in half, toast, and accompany with cream cheese or butter.

English Muffins

With their myriad tiny holes that soak up melted butter, these traditional English-style griddle-baked breads are often enjoyed on their own, though their texture and shape also make them the ideal platform for Eggs Benedict (page 40).

Biscuits

Quickly and simply prepared, tender biscuits (page 436) make irresistible breakfast breads, whether served on the side with butter and jam, smothered in gravy, or filled with eggs and meats for morning sandwiches.

Rolls

Fashioned from bread dough (page 415–16) or layered with butter and shaped into flaky croissants, warm rolls are morning-table favorites.

Quick Breads

Thick batters yield a wide variety of sweet and savory breads, from moist muffins to flavorful quick breads to pans of sweet coffee cake cut into generous squares.

Egg Cooking Techniques

BOILING Soft-boiled eggs have a fully cooked white and a thickened but still slightly runny yolk. They are commonly served in eggcups, with only the tip of the shell removed, accompanied by strips of buttered toast for dipping into the yolk. Hard-boiled eggs have a fully cooked white and a firm yolk and are peeled before serving or chopped and incorporated into a dish.

To boil eggs, fill a saucepan with water to cover the eggs and bring to a rolling boil over high heat. With a slotted spoon, gently lower the eggs into the water, then reduce the heat to low. Simmer for 4 minutes for eggs with runny yolks, 6 minutes for medium-firm yolks, or 8 minutes for firm yolks. To peel hard-boiled eggs, transfer the eggs to an ice bath to stop the cooking. When cool enough to handle, remove each egg from the water, firmly tap against a countertop to crack the shell all over, then peel and discard the shell.

POACHING Eggs poached in water until the white is firm and the yolk is still runny are usually served atop something, such as an English muffin (crumpet), a mound of corned beef hash, or a salad. For neatly poached eggs, use grade AA eggs, the fresher the better. Adding a teaspoon of distilled white vinegar or fresh lemon juice to the poaching water helps the whites coagulate into a nicely rounded shape.

To poach eggs, half fill a large sauté pan with water, add the vinegar and a little salt for flavor, and bring to a boil over high heat; reduce the heat to maintain a bare simmer. One at a time, break an egg into a small cup or ramekin, then gently slip the egg into the water. Allow to cook, basting once or twice with the simmering water and using a slotted spoon to keep multiple eggs separate, until the whites are completely set and the yolks look glazed but are still soft, 3–4 minutes for runny yolks or up to 5 minutes if you prefer firmer yolks. Using a slotted spoon, transfer each egg to a cutting board and use a knife to trim the ragged edges. Serve warm.

Eggs can be poached up to 12 hours in advance, submerged in a bowl of ice water, and kept in the refrigerator. Reheat in a sieve lowered into simmering water for 30 seconds.

BAKING Eggs cracked into individual buttered ramekins bake to a smooth, rich consistency. The ramekins can be lined with cooked chard, spinach, or another vegetable, then seasoned with salt and pepper and sometimes drizzled with a little heavy (double) cream.

To bake eggs, preheat the oven to 350°F (180°C). Carefully crack the eggs into the ramekins, taking care not to break the yolks. Add seasoning, cream, and any other ingredient specified in the recipe, place the ramekins on a rimmed baking sheet, and bake the eggs until the whites are set and the yolks are still runny, 10–15 minutes.

FRYING Panfrying is one of the most traditional ways to prepare eggs. Fried eggs are typically served alongside potatoes, sandwiched between slices of bread, set on top of buttered toast, or partnered with bacon, sausage, or ham.

To fry an egg, heat a nonstick frying pan over medium heat and add about 1½ teaspoons unsalted butter or other fat. Crack an egg into a small bowl, taking care not to get any shell fragments in the bowl. When the butter is melted and beginning to foam, carefully slide the egg into the pan. Reduce the heat to low and cook until the white is firm and the yolk has begun to thicken, about 3 minutes. For sunny-side up (an intact, runny yolk), tilt the pan slightly and, with a tablespoon, baste the egg with a little of the butter before carefully removing it from the pan and serving. For over easy (a lightly set yolk) or over hard (a fully cooked yolk), carefully flip the egg with a nonstick spatula and continue cooking for about 20 seconds longer for over easy or 1–1½ minutes longer for over hard.

SCRAMBLING Beaten in a bowl until the whites and yolks are well blended, and then cooked gently in butter or some other fat, scrambled eggs can be served plain or mixed with an array of other ingredients, most often shredded or crumbled cheese, diced meats, or chopped vegetables.

To scramble eggs, first break them into a bowl, being careful they are free of shell bits. Season lightly with salt and pepper and add any other ingredients called for in a recipe, such as a little cream, milk, or water. With a fork or a wire whisk, briskly beat the eggs until pale yellow and lightly frothy.

Heat a nonstick frying pan over medium heat and add a little unsalted butter. When the butter has melted and is beginning to foam, reduce the heat to low and add the beaten eggs. As they cook, gently stir and scrape with a silicone or wooden spatula, pushing curds of cooked egg from the sides toward the center. Stir often for smaller curds, less often if you prefer larger curds. Cook until done to your liking, 4–5 minutes for soft, moist eggs, 7–8 minutes for firmer, drier eggs.

MAKING OMELETS Omelets take many forms, including the traditional folded omelet, where the egg is cooked in a pan and then folded over fillings, and the flat omelet, such as the Italian frittata or the similar Spanish *tortilla* (page 74). For flat omelets, the filling is either mixed into the beaten egg or cooked in the pan before the egg is added to the pan.

To make a folded omelet, break 3 or 4 eggs into a bowl, season with salt and pepper, then beat lightly with a fork. Heat a 10-inch (25-cm) omelet pan or frying pan over medium heat and add 1 tablespoon unsalted butter. As the butter melts, swirl the pan to coat the bottom and part of the sides. When the butter is hot, add the beaten eggs. As the eggs begin to set along the edges, use a spatula to push the edges toward the center, tilting the pan to let the uncooked egg flow to the edges and maintaining an even layer. When the eggs have just set, spoon any prepared filling over half of the omelet, then use the spatula to fold the other half over the filling. Let the omelet cook for about 30 seconds longer, then slide it out onto a plate.

To make a flat omelet, preheat the oven to 350°F (180°C). Heat oil or unsalted butter in an ovenproof nonstick frying pan over medium heat. Add any filling ingredients that require sautéing, such as diced onion or other vegetables. Then, pour in beaten eggs and any other ingredients, such as cheeses, crumbled crisp bacon, chopped ham, or fresh herbs. Reduce the heat to low and cook, stirring slowly, until the eggs begin to set, 1–2 minutes. Transfer the pan to the oven and continue cooking until the omelet has gently risen and set, 8–12 minutes.

MAKING QUICHES Traditionally served as brunch or lunch dishes, quiches are savory single-crust pies with a filling based on a custard mixture of seasoned eggs beaten with cream or milk. To make a quiche, first prepare any other filling ingredients, such as cooking bacon for a classic Quiche Lorraine (page 48). Spread the ingredients evenly over the prebaked crust (page 518). Whisk together the eggs and other custard ingredients, according to the recipe, and strain the mixture through a medium-mesh sieve to eliminate any membranes or shell bits. Pour the custard into the crust, dot with butter if called for in the recipe, and bake in a preheated 350°F (180°C) oven until the quiche is browned and barely set, 40–45 minutes. Let cool on a wire rack for about 5 minutes before cutting into wedges to serve.

BREAKFAST DRINKS

Beverages that give you a lift, nutritionally or otherwise, are especially welcome with a morning meal.

Juices
In addition to common juices like orange, grapefruit, apple, and cranberry, exotic juices, such as papaya, mango, and various tropical blends, are regularly stocked in many markets. For the best juice, squeeze your own in-season fresh fruits.

Smoothies
These blender-made treats, such as the one on page 53, combine a variety of fruits with fruit juice, yogurt or milk, and sometimes a sweetener like honey. Ripe bananas are a common starting point. Some people add ice to the blender; some use protein powder or other nutritional supplements.

Coffee
However you take it, coffee is the ritual morning drink for many people. Regardless of your chosen brewing method, start with freshly roasted coffee beans that you grind yourself just before brewing.

Tea
Whether you prefer pale, brisk green teas; dark Ceylon or oolong varieties; flavored tea blends; or caffeine-free herbal infusions, use good-quality products and store them in airtight containers in a cool, dark place.

Morning Cocktails
At a weekend breakfast or brunch, it's nice to indulge with drinks that include spirits or wine, such as Bloody Marys (page 42) or Mimosas (page 438).

EGGS BENEDICT

Poaching savvy

If you don't have a sauté pan large enough to poach all the eggs at once without crowding, use 2 pans. You can also poach the eggs up to 2 hours in advance and reheat in simmering water.

With its popular building blocks of English muffins, Canadian bacon, and poached eggs, this classic brunch dish never goes out of style. When tomatoes are in season, top the ham with a broiled tomato slice before crowning it with the egg and the hollandaise.

Preheat the boiler (grill).

Prepare the Hollandaise Sauce and transfer to a heatproof bowl. Place the bowl over (but not touching) barely simmering water in a saucepan.

Lightly spread the cut sides of the muffins with 2 teaspoons of the butter and place, cut sides up, on a rimmed baking sheet. Broil (grill) until browned, about 6 minutes. Turn off the broiler, cover the muffins with aluminum foil, and keep warm in the oven.

Meanwhile, in a small sauté pan over medium-high heat, melt the remaining 1 teaspoon butter. Add the Canadian bacon and cook, turning once, until sizzling and beginning to brown, about 4 minutes total. Transfer to a baking sheet and keep warm in the oven.

Half fill a large sauté pan with water, add the vinegar and ½ teaspoon salt, and bring to a boil over high heat; reduce the heat to maintain a bare simmer. Break 1 egg into a small cup, then gently slip the egg into the water. Working quickly, repeat with the remaining eggs. Allow to cook, basting once or twice with the simmering water and using a slotted spoon to keep the eggs separate, until the whites are completely set and the yolks look glazed but are still soft, 3–4 minutes for runny yolks or up to 5 minutes for firmer yolks. Using a slotted spoon, transfer the eggs to a cutting board and use a knife to trim the ragged edges.

Place each muffin half on a warmed plate. Top with a slice of Canadian bacon and then a poached egg. Divide the hollandaise sauce evenly among the servings, spooning it over the tops. Serve right away.

Hollandaise Sauce
(page 385)

4 English muffins, split

1 tablespoon
unsalted butter

8 slices Canadian bacon

1 teaspoon distilled
white vinegar

Salt

8 eggs

MAKES 8 SERVINGS

Canadian bacon

Cut from the loin of the hog and cured but not always smoked, Canadian bacon is lean and has a mild, meaty flavor, qualities that make it more reminiscent of ham than bacon.

40

POACHED EGGS IN CHARD NESTS

Salt water

Adding salt to the simmering water in which eggs are poached helps season them all the way through, in the same way that salted water seasons pasta as it boils.

Swiss chard has large, dark leaves on red, white, or yellow stems. It's typical for the thick stems to be separated from the leaves and cooked a bit before the leaves are added. You can substitute any other dark greens, such as spinach or mustard greens.

Cut the center stems from the chard leaves. Cut the stems crosswise into thin slices; chop the leaves coarsely. Keep the leaves and stems separate.

In a large frying pan over medium-low heat, melt half of the butter with the oil. Add the stems and sauté, stirring, for 5 minutes. Add the leaves and continue to sauté, stirring

2 lb (1 kg) Swiss chard,
rinsed and drained

4 tablespoons (2 oz/60 g)
unsalted butter

2 tablespoons olive oil

Salt and ground pepper

1 teaspoon distilled
white vinegar

4 eggs

MAKES 4 SERVINGS

often, until wilted, about 2 minutes longer. Add ½ cup (4 fl oz/ 125 ml) water and a pinch of salt, cover, reduce the heat to low, and simmer until tender, 10–15 minutes. Drain the chard and return it to the pan. Season with salt and pepper. Cover the pan to keep the chard warm.

Half fill a large sauté pan with water, add the vinegar and ½ teaspoon salt, and bring to a boil over high heat; reduce the heat to maintain a bare simmer. Break 1 egg into a small cup, then gently slip the egg into the water. Working quickly, repeat with the remaining eggs. Allow to cook, basting once or twice with the simmering water and using a slotted spoon to keep the eggs separate, until the whites are completely set and the yolks look glazed but are still soft, 3–4 minutes for runny yolks or up to 5 minutes for firmer yolks.

Meanwhile, cut the remaining butter into small bits and stir into the chard, tossing to coat evenly. Divide among 4 warmed plates and make a nest in the center of each mound.

When the eggs are ready, using a slotted spoon, transfer them to a cutting board and use a knife to trim the ragged edges. Place an egg in each chard nest and serve right away.

Rainbow chard

For a wildly colorful presentation, use rainbow chard for this dish, which offers red-, yellow-, and white-stemmed Swiss chard in every bunch.

CODDLED EGGS WITH CHIVES AND CREAM

Coddling is a gentle method that uses simmering water to insulate food from the direct heat of the stove, allowing for slow, even cooking. It yields eggs that are just past raw but extremely soft—a perfect match for warm buttered toast.

2 tablespoons heavy
(double) cream

1½ tablespoons minced
spinach leaves

1 teaspoon minced
cooked ham, optional

Fine sea salt and
ground pepper

2 eggs

1 teaspoon finely snipped
fresh chives

MAKES 2 SERVINGS

Pour water to a depth of 1½ inches (4 cm) into a wide, deep saucepan and bring to a boil over high heat.

Meanwhile, divide the cream evenly between 2 egg coddlers (see note, right), and then swirl the cream to coat about halfway up the sides. Divide the spinach and ham (if using) evenly between the coddlers. Sprinkle the contents of each coddler with a tiny pinch each of salt and pepper. Break an egg into each coddler, being careful not to break the yolk, and cover the coddlers.

Carefully place the coddlers in the saucepan of boiling water. Reduce the heat so the water simmers briskly, cover the saucepan, and simmer for 6 minutes.

Using an oven mitt, transfer the coddlers to individual plates. Remove the lids from the coddlers, and sprinkle with the chives. Serve right away.

Coddling vessels

Egg coddlers, porcelain or heatproof glass cups with tight-fitting lids, are made especially for this technique, but you can also coddle eggs in standard ramekins covered with aluminum foil.

STEAK AND EGGS WITH CARAMELIZED ONIONS

Bloody Marys

In a pitcher, whisk together 2½ cups (20 fl oz/625 ml) each cold tomato juice and vegetable juice cocktail, 1½ cups (12 fl oz/ 375 ml) vodka, ¼ cup (2 fl oz/60 ml) fresh lime juice, 2 tsp Worcestershire sauce, and ½ tsp hot pepper sauce. Season to taste, strain into ice-filled glasses, and garnish each glass with a celery stalk.

Guests with hearty appetites will love this satisfying dish, no matter what time of day you serve it. Accompany with Mixed Potato Sauté (page 365) and have the makings for Bloody Marys (see note, left) on hand.

Preheat the oven to 375°F (190°C). Combine the garlic and broth in a small baking dish, and drizzle about 2 tablespoons of the oil over the garlic. Cover and bake until the garlic is soft, about 35 minutes. Let stand, covered, for 10 minutes. Uncover and let cool, then peel and slice the garlic; set aside.

Meanwhile, brush 2 large, rimmed baking sheets with oil, using 2 tablespoons for each pan. Divide the onions evenly between the pans, and season with salt and pepper. Sprinkle 1½ tablespoons of the sugar evenly over both pans of onions, then drizzle about 2 tablespoons oil over each pan. Bake, stirring every 15 minutes, until the onions are golden brown, about 45 minutes.

Remove from the oven and stir in the garlic. In a small bowl, stir together the vinegar, cayenne pepper to taste, and the remaining 2½ tablespoons sugar, then drizzle over all the onions. Return to the oven and bake until evenly browned and caramelized, about 20 minutes longer. Transfer to a bowl, then taste and adjust the seasoning; keep warm.

While the onions are cooking, score the edges of the steaks every inch (2.5 cm) or so. Rub coarse pepper on both sides of the steaks, using about 1 teaspoon total, and let the steaks stand for 5–10 minutes.

Place a large, well-seasoned cast iron or nonstick frying pan (or 2 pans if necessary to avoid crowding) over high heat and sprinkle the bottom with a dusting of coarse salt. When very hot, add the steaks and sear, turning once, until browned on both sides, about 2 minutes on each side for rare, or until done to your liking.

Meanwhile, in a large nonstick sauté pan over medium heat, melt the butter. Crack an egg into a small bowl. When the butter begins to foam, carefully slide the egg into the pan. Working quickly, repeat with the remaining eggs. Reduce the heat to low and cook until the whites are firm and the yolks have begun to thicken, about 3 minutes (cover the pan if you like firmer yolks). Baste the eggs with a little of the butter, then season with salt and pepper.

Transfer the steaks to warmed individual plates and place the eggs alongside. Divide the caramelized onions among the plates and serve right away.

3 heads garlic, unpeeled and cloves separated

½ cup (4 fl oz/125 ml) chicken broth

10 tablespoons (5 fl oz/ 160 ml) olive oil

6 large red onions, thinly sliced

Salt and ground pepper

4 tablespoons (2 oz/ 60 g) firmly packed light brown sugar

2 tablespoons balsamic vinegar

Cayenne pepper

6 New York strip steaks, each about ½ lb (250 g) and 1 inch (2.5 cm) thick, trimmed of excess fat

Coarse sea salt and ground coarse pepper

2½ tablespoons unsalted butter

6 eggs

MAKES 6 SERVINGS

HUEVOS RANCHEROS

Flavorful and substantial, this midmorning meal for ranch hands has become a favorite brunch dish well beyond Mexico's borders. This version sticks closely to the classic formula: a lightly fried corn tortilla topped with refried beans, diced avocado, and a pair of fried eggs.

4 large, thick corn tortillas, preferably stale

1½ cups (12 fl oz/375 ml) Fresh Tomato Salsa (page 393)

¼ cup (2 fl oz/60 ml) canola oil, or as needed

8 eggs

Sea salt and ground pepper

1 cup (8 oz/250 g) canned refried pinto beans, heated

⅔ cup (5 fl oz/160 ml) *crema*, crème fraîche, or sour cream

⅓ cup (1½ oz/45 g) crumbled *queso añejo* or shredded Monterey Jack cheese

1 tablespoon coarsely chopped fresh cilantro (fresh coriander)

1 avocado, halved, pitted, peeled, and cut into ½-inch (12-mm) cubes, optional

MAKES 4 SERVINGS

Preheat the oven to 200°F (95°C).

If the tortillas are fresh, spread them out on a work surface and let them dry out for 5 minutes. Meanwhile, in a wide saucepan over low heat, warm the salsa. In a large, nonstick frying pan over medium-high heat, warm the ¼ cup oil. One at a time, fry the tortillas, turning once, until softened, about 5 seconds per side. Using tongs, transfer to paper towels to drain, then keep warm in the oven.

Reduce the heat to medium-low and wait for the oil to cool down a bit. Crack an egg into a small bowl and carefully slide the egg into the pan. Working quickly, repeat with 3 more eggs. Fry the eggs slowly until the whites are firm and the yolks have begun to thicken, about 3 minutes (if you like firmer yolks, cover the frying pan). Season with salt and pepper. Transfer the eggs to a roasting pan and keep warm in the oven. Add oil to the frying pan if necessary, and fry the remaining 4 eggs.

Remove the tortillas from the oven. Using tongs, quickly dip the tortillas, one at a time, in the warm salsa and place on warmed plates. Spread one-fourth of the refried beans evenly on each tortilla, and top with 2 fried eggs. Spoon some of the salsa over the edges of each tortilla and the egg whites, leaving the yolks uncovered. Spoon a little *crema* over the salsa, then sprinkle with the cheese and cilantro. Garnish with the avocado (if using) and serve right away.

Tortilla size

You can use 8 small tortillas instead of 4 large. Divide the toppings evenly among them and top each with a single fried egg.

About *crema*

Mexican crema is a rich, thick, lightly soured cream similar in flavor and consistency to crème fraîche and thinner than sour cream.

43

BAKED EGGS PIPÉRADE

Individual servings

If you prefer, divide the pipérade among 6 ramekins and break an egg into each ramekin. Arrange the ramekins on a baking sheet before placing in the oven.

Baked eggs and tomatoes

You can also substitute your favorite hearty tomato sauce for the pipérade. For a selection of tomato sauce recipes, see pages 377–79.

Here, the Basque dish *pipérade*, a mélange of sautéed peppers and tomatoes, forms nests in which eggs are baked. For the full complement of authentic flavors, add some finely diced serrano ham to the pepper mixture before you pour it into the baking dish.

In a large, heavy saucepan over medium-high heat, warm the oil. Add the onion and celery and sauté until slightly softened, about 3 minutes. Add all the bell peppers and sauté until softened, about 5 minutes. Add the garlic and continue cooking until fragrant, about 1 minute longer. Stir in the tomatoes, increase the heat to high, and bring to a boil. Boil rapidly until the liquid given off by the tomatoes reduces and the mixture is slightly thickened, 5–7 minutes. Season well with salt and pepper, then pour into a 2-qt (2-l) baking dish and spread evenly over the bottom.

Preheat the oven to 350°F (190°C).

Using the back of a large spoon, make 6 evenly spaced indentations in the pepper mixture. One at a time, break the eggs into a small bowl or ramekin and slip them into the indentions, being careful not to break the yolks. Sprinkle lightly with salt and pepper.

Bake until the whites and the yolks of the eggs are set but not tough and the pepper mixture is bubbling, 10–15 minutes. Serve right away on warmed plates.

2 tablespoons olive oil

1 yellow onion, finely chopped

1 celery stalk, finely chopped

1 large red bell pepper (capsicum), seeded and finely diced

1 large yellow bell pepper (capsicum), finely diced

1 large green bell pepper (capsicum), finely diced

2 cloves garlic, minced

2 tomatoes, peeled, seeded, and chopped

Salt and ground pepper

6 eggs

MAKES 6 SERVINGS

SCRAMBLED EGGS WITH SMOKED SALMON

Pop the bubbly

If your brunch is a celebration, Champagne goes nicely with this dish. Try a brut rosé, also known as pink Champagne, which gets its color from the skins of the red grapes from which it is made.

The classic combination of smoked salmon and cream cheese is even better when combined with perfectly cooked scrambled eggs. The secret to creamy scrambled eggs is to not overcook them. Stop scrambling the moment they are just set and are still moist.

In a bowl, whisk the eggs just until blended. Add the salmon and stir to mix. Season lightly with salt and pepper.

In a large, heavy frying pan over medium heat, melt the butter. When the butter begins to foam, pour in the egg mixture and cook, stirring gently, until the eggs start to set, about 2 minutes. Sprinkle the cheese evenly over the eggs and continue cooking and stirring until the eggs are scrambled to a soft consistency, 1–2 minutes longer. Taste and adjust the seasoning.

Transfer to a warmed platter, sprinkle with the parsley, and serve right away.

8 eggs

3–4 oz (90–125 g) thinly sliced smoked salmon, coarsely chopped

Salt and ground pepper

2 tablespoons unsalted butter

¼ lb (125 g) herbed cream cheese such as Boursin, broken into small chunks

2 tablespoons chopped fresh flat-leaf (Italian) parsley or chives

MAKES 4 SERVINGS

DENVER SCRAMBLE

The diner-style combination of bell peppers, ham, and cheese may be best known as an omelet, but the casual nature of its contents makes it equally well-suited to a scramble. If you like, top it with Fresh Tomato Sauce (page 378). Garnish with chopped parsley, if desired.

2 tablespoons
unsalted butter

½ yellow onion, diced

½ *each* green and red bell
pepper (capsicum), diced

6 oz (185 g) smoked ham
or Canadian bacon, diced

8 eggs, lightly beaten

Salt and ground pepper

½ cup (2 oz/60 g) shredded
Cheddar cheese

MAKES 4 SERVINGS

In a nonstick frying pan over medium-low heat, melt the butter. Add the onion and bell peppers and sauté, stirring frequently, until the vegetables are tender-crisp, 2–3 minutes. Add the ham and sauté for 1 minute longer to heat through.

Add the eggs to the pan, season with salt and pepper, and continue to cook over medium-low heat, stirring and scraping frequently, until the eggs begin to form soft, moist curds, 2–3 minutes. Stir in the cheese and continue stirring and scraping until the eggs are done to your liking.

Spoon onto warmed individual plates and serve right away.

Omelet style

If you prefer your Denver-style eggs in omelet form, sauté the onion, bell pepper, and ham according to the recipe and set aside. Prepare the eggs according to the instructions for a folded omelet on page 39, top with the sautéed filling, sprinkle with the Cheddar, and fold to serve.

SMOKED TROUT OMELET

This flat, cream-enriched omelet was inspired by an after-theater supper for novelist Arnold Bennett in 1929, then living in London's Savoy Hotel. This recipe, which is simpler than the Savoy's current luxurious version, makes an elegant brunch.

½ lb (250 g) smoked
trout fillet, cut in half

1 sprig fresh flat-leaf
(Italian) parsley

3 peppercorns

1 bay leaf

2 cups (16 fl oz/500 ml) milk

1 cup (4 oz/125 g) coarsely
grated Gruyère cheese

Salt and ground pepper

4 eggs

2 tablespoons
unsalted butter

4 tablespoons (2 fl oz/60 ml)
heavy (double) cream

Coarsely snipped fresh
chives for garnish

MAKES 2 SERVINGS

In a nonreactive saucepan over medium heat, warm the fish, parsley, peppercorns, bay leaf, and milk until small bubbles appear around the pan edge. Reduce the heat to low and simmer until the fish flakes when a knife is inserted into the thickest part, 3–5 minutes. Transfer the fish to a plate to cool; discard the milk mixture.

Preheat the broiler (grill). Remove the skin from the fish. Use a fork to break the flesh into rough flakes, discarding any bones, and place it in a small bowl. Stir in the cheese and season with pepper.

In a bowl, whisk together the eggs and a pinch of salt. Set two 7-inch (18-cm) broiler-proof omelet pans over medium heat. Melt 1 tablespoon butter in each. Tilt the pans to distribute the butter evenly on the bottoms of the pans. Pour half of the eggs into each pan. As the eggs begin to set along the edges, use a spatula to push the edges toward the center, tilting the pan to let the uncooked egg flow to the edges, until the bottom is set but the top is still liquid, about 1 minute. Top each omelet with half of the fish. Pour 2 tablespoons cream over each fish portion. Broil (grill) until the omelets are bubbling and flecked with brown, about 6 minutes.

Remove from the broiler, garnish with the chives, and serve.

Smoked fish

Salt-curing and smoking fish is one of the oldest forms of food preservation. It remains popular in the modern era because of the flavor, and the shelf life the process imparts to the fish.

POTATO, BACON, AND LEEK OMELETS

A sprinkling of grated Gruyère cheese complements the hearty bacon, potato, and leek mixture that fills these rustic, robust omelets. They're as good for a late-night meal as a Sunday brunch. Accompany with crusty bread spread with salted butter.

In a heavy frying pan over medium-high heat, fry the bacon until crisp, about 5 minutes. Transfer to paper towels to drain, then place in a small bowl. Add 1½ teaspoons pepper and toss to coat the bacon evenly. Set aside.

Pour off all but 1 tablespoon bacon fat from the pan and add the 1 tablespoon butter. Place over medium heat until the butter melts and is hot. Add the potatoes and cook, stirring, until slightly softened, about 3 minutes. Add the leeks and ¼ teaspoon salt and cook, stirring, until the leeks begin to soften, about 2 minutes longer. Cover, reduce the heat to low, and cook, stirring occasionally, until the potatoes are just tender, 8–10 minutes longer. Remove from the heat and season with salt. Set aside.

In a bowl, whisk together the eggs and ½ teaspoon salt. Place an 8- or 9-inch (20- or 23-cm) nonstick omelet pan or frying pan over high heat and add 1 teaspoon of the butter. As the butter melts, swirl the pan so the butter covers the bottom and part of the sides. When the butter is hot, add one-fourth of the egg mixture. As the eggs begin to set along the edges, use a spatula to push the edges toward the center, tilting the pan to let the uncooked egg flow to the edges. When the eggs have just set, after about 2 minutes, place one-fourth of the potato mixture on half of the omelet, and top with one-fourth each of the bacon and cheese. Using the spatula, fold the uncovered half of the omelet over the filling.

Slide the omelet onto a warmed plate, sprinkle with one-fourth of the chives, and serve. (The omelets are quickly made, so it is best to serve each one as it is cooked.) Repeat to make 3 additional omelets, using the remaining ingredients.

6–8 slices thick-cut bacon, cut into ½-inch (12-mm) pieces

Salt and ground coarse pepper

1 tablespoon plus 4 teaspoons unsalted butter

¾ lb (375 g) new potatoes, peeled and cut into ½-inch (12-mm) dice

1 cup (4 oz/125 g) chopped leeks, white part only

8 eggs

½ cup (2 oz/60 g) shredded Gruyère cheese

3 tablespoons snipped fresh chives or chopped fresh flat-leaf (Italian) parsley, or a mixture

MAKES 4 SERVINGS

ASPARAGUS AND POTATO FRITTATA

An Italian frittata is made by combining various ingredients with eggs, cooking the mixture on the stove top, and then finishing it in the oven. Some recipes call for longer time on the stove top and a quicker finish under the broiler. Feel free to experiment.

¾ lb (375 g) thin asparagus, tough ends removed

3–4 tablespoons olive oil

2 large green (spring) onions, including tender green tops, chopped

6–8 small red potatoes, unpeeled, cut into slices ⅛ inch (3 mm) thick

Salt and ground pepper

½ teaspoon chopped fresh tarragon

2 tablespoons snipped fresh chives

3 tablespoons unsalted butter

11 eggs

⅓ cup (1½ oz/45 g) grated Parmesan cheese

About ½ cup (2 oz/60 g) shredded Swiss cheese

MAKES 8–10 SERVINGS

Place the asparagus on a steamer rack over boiling water, cover, and steam until tender, about 2 minutes. Remove from the steamer and cut into 1-inch (2.5-cm) lengths. Set aside.

In a large sauté pan over medium heat, warm 3 tablespoons oil. Add the onions and sauté until soft and translucent, about 4 minutes. Add the potatoes, 1 teaspoon salt, the tarragon, and a few grinds of pepper and then sauté until the potatoes glisten, about 3 minutes, adding the remaining 1 tablespoon oil if needed to prevent sticking. Cover and cook until the potatoes are nearly tender, 6–8 minutes. Uncover, raise the heat to high, and cook, stirring constantly, until the potatoes are browned, 7–8 minutes. Stir in the chives and asparagus and remove from the heat.

Preheat the oven to 375°F (190°C).

In a large cast iron frying pan or ovenproof sauté pan over medium-high heat, melt the butter. Meanwhile, in a bowl, whisk the eggs until blended. Stir in the Parmesan cheese and season with a pinch of salt and a few grinds of pepper. Pour the eggs into the hot pan. Stir gently in the center and, as the eggs begin to set along the edges, use a spatula to push the edges toward the center, tilting the pan to let the uncooked egg flow to the edges. Cook until thickened but still moist, 3–4 minutes. Spread the onion-potato mixture evenly over the eggs.

Sprinkle the Swiss cheese on top, transfer to the oven, and bake the eggs until they have set and the cheese has melted, 10–15 minutes.

Remove from the oven and let stand for a few minutes, then cut into wedges and serve.

Frittata variations

You can mix into a frittata almost anything you would use as filling in a folded omelet or a quiche. Try thinly sliced zucchini (courgette); ham and sharp white Cheddar; or diced red bell pepper (capsicum), yellow onion, and sausage. Brown any meats and parboil or sauté any vegetables before combining with the eggs.

47

QUICHE LORRAINE

Quiche variations

Like an omelet or frittata, quiche is endlessly adaptable. Replace the bacon with 1 cup of your favorite cooked vegetables and top with 1 cup shredded cheese of your choice.

Traditionally offered as a first course, quiche is now more commonly served as a main course at brunch or lunchtime. The iconic quiche Lorraine contains bacon and onions. You can also sprinkle 1 cup (4 oz/155 g) shredded Gruyère cheese on top of the custard before baking.

In a heavy frying pan over medium heat, fry the bacon until crisp, about 8 minutes. Transfer to paper towels to drain. Cut the bacon crosswise into 1-inch (2.5 cm) pieces. Scatter evenly over the bottom of the pie shell. Set aside.

Preheat the oven to 350°F (180°C). In a large bowl, whisk together the eggs, ½ teaspoon salt, ⅛ teaspoon pepper, and nutmeg. Add the cream and milk and whisk until well blended. Pour the mixture through a medium-mesh sieve into a measuring pitcher. Slowly pour the mixture over the bacon in the pie shell. Dot the top with the butter pieces.

Bake the quiche until the top is lightly browned and the filling is just barely set when you give the dish a gentle shake, 40–45 minutes.

Let the quiche cool on a wire rack for 5 minutes, then cut into wedges and serve.

4 slices thick-cut lean bacon

Pie Pastry for a single-crust pie (page 447) made without sugar, partially blind baked (page 518)

3 eggs

Salt and ground pepper

Pinch of freshly grated nutmeg

¾ cup (6 fl oz/180 ml) heavy (double) cream

¾ cup (6 fl oz/180 ml) milk

1 tablespoon unsalted butter, cut into ¼-inch (6-mm) pieces

MAKES 8 SERVINGS

CLASSIC CHEESE SOUFFLÉ

Seasoning soufflés

This savory soufflé can be easily varied with the addition of herbs. Snipped fresh chives, for instance, would add both color and flavor.

A soufflé is easier to make than its dramatic, lofty profile suggests. For the maximum volume, the egg whites must be beaten to soft (not stiff) peaks and then evenly folded into the soufflé base. For tips on beating egg whites and folding, see page 443.

Preheat the oven to 375°F (190°C). Butter a 1-qt (1-l) soufflé dish with 1 tablespoon of the butter and dust evenly with 2 tablespoons of the Parmesan cheese. Set aside.

In a heavy saucepan over low heat, melt the remaining 2 tablespoons butter. Using a wooden spoon, stir in the flour and continue to stir until the mixture bubbles, about 3 minutes. Slowly whisk in the hot milk, raise the heat to medium, and continue to cook, stirring constantly, until the flour-milk mixture thickens, is smooth, and begins to boil. Reduce the heat to medium-low and simmer gently, stirring constantly, until very thick, 3–4 minutes. Remove from the heat. Stir in the Gruyère and the remaining 2 tablespoons Parmesan cheese until melted.

In a small bowl, lightly beat the egg yolks. Beat 3 tablespoons of the hot milk-cheese mixture into the yolks, then gradually beat the yolk mixture into the milk-cheese mixture. Season lightly with salt and pepper and the nutmeg. Set aside.

In a large bowl, using an electric mixer on medium-high

3 tablespoons unsalted butter

4 tablespoons (1 oz/30 g) grated Parmesan cheese

2 tablespoons all-purpose (plain) flour

1 cup (8 fl oz/250 ml) milk, heated

1 cup (4 oz/125 g) shredded Gruyère cheese

4 eggs, separated, at room temperature

Salt and ground white pepper

Pinch of freshly grated nutmeg

MAKES 4 SERVINGS

speed, beat the egg whites until soft peaks form. Fold one-fourth of the whites into the cheese sauce to lighten it, then fold in the remaining whites in 3 equal batches, mixing just until combined. Spoon into the prepared dish.

Bake until well risen and golden brown and a wooden skewer inserted into the center comes out moist, about 25 minutes. Serve right away.

Another cheese soufflé

You can make this savory soufflé with extra-sharp Cheddar cheese in place of the Gruyère and a pinch of cayenne instead of the nutmeg.

BUTTERMILK PANCAKES

You can flavor these pancakes a number of ways. Stir a handful of chopped nuts, blueberries, shredded coconut, grated cheese, or crumbled cooked bacon into the batter. Top the pancakes with maple syrup, confectioners' (icing) sugar, or fruit syrups and sauces like those on page 37.

2 eggs

2 cups (10 oz/315 g) all-purpose (plain) flour

2 tablespoons granulated sugar

2 teaspoons baking powder

1 teaspoon baking soda (bicarbonate of soda)

1 teaspoon salt

2 cups (16 fl oz/500 ml) buttermilk

4 tablespoons (2 oz/60 g) unsalted butter, melted

½ teaspoon pure almond extract

1–2 tablespoons canola oil

MAKES TWELVE 6-INCH (15-CM) PANCAKES

Preheat the oven to 200°F (95°C).

In a bowl, beat the eggs until frothy. Add the flour, sugar, baking powder, baking soda, salt, buttermilk, butter, and almond extract. Continue to beat just until the mixture is smooth; do not overbeat.

Heat a large, heavy frying pan or griddle over high heat until a few drops of water flicked onto the surface skitter across it. Lightly grease the pan with 1 tablespoon of the oil. Pour about ⅓ cup (3 fl oz/80 ml) of the batter onto the hot pan. Cook until the batter is set, the surface is covered with tiny bubbles, the bottom is browned, and the edges look dry, about 2 minutes. Flip the pancake over and continue to cook until the second side is golden brown, about 2 minutes longer. Keep warm in the oven while you repeat with the remaining batter, adding more oil to the pan as needed.

When all the pancakes are cooked, serve right away.

Pancake variations

For sourdough pancakes, replace ½ cup (2½ oz/75 g) of the flour with ½ cup (4 fl oz / 125 ml) sourdough starter (page 406), reduce the baking powder to 1 tsp, and reduce the salt to ¼ tsp. For cornmeal pancakes, replace ½ cup of the flour with ½ cup (2½ oz/ 75 g) cornmeal.

CLASSIC WAFFLES

Keeping waffles warm

Set a wire rack on a rimmed baking sheet and place in a 200°F (95°C) oven. Transfer finished waffles or pancakes to the rack, leaving the oven door slightly ajar, while you finish cooking the batter.

Waffle batter is easy to make, requiring ingredients you probably have in your pantry, and can take all the same mix-ins as the Buttermilk Pancakes on page 49. The only special equipment needed is a waffle iron. Be sure to read the manufacturer's instructions for use and cleanup.

Before you start, preheat a waffle iron according to the manufacturer's instructions.

In a large bowl, whisk the eggs until evenly mixed and frothy. Add the buttermilk to a large glass measuring pitcher and then add the oil. Pour the buttermilk-oil mixture into the bowl with the eggs and whisk until blended.

Add the flour, sugar, baking powder, cinnamon (if using), baking soda, and salt and mix just until any large lumps disappear (small lumps are fine). Transfer the batter to the glass measuring pitcher, which will make pouring the batter onto the waffle iron easier.

When the waffle iron is hot, pour enough batter for 1 waffle evenly over the grid, easing it toward, but not into, the corners and edges with a wooden spoon or silicone spatula. Close the waffle iron and cook until it opens easily or according to the manufacturer's instructions, usually about 4 minutes. The waffle will be golden brown when ready. Keep warm while you repeat with the remaining batter.

When all the waffles are cooked, serve right away.

2 eggs

1¾ cups (14 fl oz/430 ml) buttermilk

¼ cup (2 fl oz/60 ml) canola oil

1½ cups (7½ oz/235 g) all-purpose (plain) flour

1 tablespoon sugar

2 teaspoons baking powder

½ teaspoon ground cinnamon, optional

¼ teaspoon baking soda (bicarbonate of soda)

⅛ teaspoon fine sea salt

MAKES 4 SERVINGS

SWEET CREPES

Filling crepes

Lay 1 crepe flat, add filling in a narrow line down the center, and fold both sides over it. Or, leave room at each end of the filling; fold over the ends, then fold in the sides to form a package. Turn the folded crepe over, and dust with confectioners' (icing) sugar or drizzle with syrup or sauce.

Crepes are thin, unleavened pancakes that are either layered or folded around a variety of sweet or savory mixtures. These crepes can be topped with chocolate-hazelnut (filbert) spread such as Nutella, jam or fruit sauce, or Citrus Curd (page 452).

To make the crepe batter, in a blender, combine ½ cup (4 fl oz/125 ml) water, the milk, eggs, flour, sugar, and vanilla and process until free of lumps and very smooth. Transfer to a bowl or measuring pitcher, cover, and refrigerate for at least 1 hour or up to 1 day.

Using a pastry brush dipped in the melted butter, lightly butter the entire surface of a 9-inch (23-cm) crepe pan or nonstick frying pan and place over medium heat. Fill a ¼-cup (2–fl oz/60-ml) ladle with batter to just below the lip. Holding the pan at an angle above the burner, pour the batter into the pan close to one edge, then swirl the pan so the batter covers the entire bottom of the pan. Work quickly, because the batter will start to cook on contact with the hot pan. Cook, shaking the pan occasionally, until small bubbles appear on the top, the bottom is lightly browned, and the batter looks set, about 1 minute. Using a thin-bladed spatula, lift the edge

½ cup (4 fl oz/125 ml) milk

2 eggs

1 cup (5 oz/155 g) all-purpose (plain) flour

2 teaspoons sugar

1 teaspoon pure vanilla extract

Melted unsalted butter for cooking

MAKES 4 SERVINGS

of the crepe, carefully grasp it, and quickly flip the crepe over. Cook until the second side is lightly browned and set, about 10 seconds longer.

Transfer the finished crepe to a plate. Repeat with the remaining batter, stacking the crepes, separated by squares of waxed paper, until they are ready to be filled and served.

Savory crepes

To make savory crepes, omit the sugar and vanilla extract and add a pinch of salt. Fill savory crepes with vegetables, cheese, or meat-based mixtures.

CRISP CORN FRITTERS

These crisp thyme-laced fritters are delicious as part of a brunch main course, paired with slices of baked ham and Cheddar cheese and drizzled with maple syrup. They can also be sprinkled with coarse salt and served in place of bread alongside a scramble or frittata.

8 ears corn

1 or 2 jalapeño chiles, seeded and minced

1–2 tablespoons chopped fresh thyme, or 1 teaspoon dried thyme

1 teaspoon ground black pepper

¼ teaspoon red pepper flakes

4 eggs

1½ cups (12 fl oz/375 ml) milk

1½ cups (7½ oz/235 g) all-purpose (plain) flour

1 teaspoon baking powder

¼ teaspoon salt

About ¼ cup (2 fl oz/60 ml) corn oil

MAKES 3–4 DOZEN 3-INCH (7.5-CM) FRITTERS

Preheat the oven to 200°F (95°C). Line a rimmed baking sheet with paper towels.

Working with 1 ear of corn at a time, hold the ear by its pointed end, steadying the stalk end in the bottom of a shallow bowl. Using a sharp knife, cut down along the ear to strip off the kernels, giving the ear a quarter turn after each cut. Then run the dull side of the knife blade along the ear, scraping out all of the pulp and milk. Stir in the chiles, thyme, black pepper, and red pepper flakes, mixing well.

In another bowl, whisk the eggs until frothy. Whisk in the milk, flour, baking powder, and salt until well blended. Stir the egg mixture into the corn mixture.

Heat a large, heavy frying pan or griddle over high heat until a few drops of water flicked onto the surface skitter across it. Add about 1 teaspoon of the oil to the pan and, working in batches, drop the batter by tablespoons onto the hot surface. Fry, turning once, until golden brown, about 1 minute on each side. Transfer to the prepared baking sheet and keep warm in the oven. Repeat until all the batter is cooked, adding oil to the pan as needed.

When all the fritters are cooked, serve right away.

Add a Latin accent

Corn lends itself to many types of savory or spicy toppings. If desired, top the fritters with fresh tomato salsa and sour cream.

51

CINNAMON FRENCH TOAST

Pure maple syrup

True maple syrup is made from the boiled sap of the sugar maple tree. The caramel-colored, maple-flavored corn syrup sold as "pancake syrup" has no relation to the real thing.

Topped with maple syrup or sautéed fruit, such as Sautéed Bananas with Nuts (page 37) or dusted with confectioners' (icing) sugar, French toast is a timeless breakfast favorite. It can also be made with thickly sliced egg bread. Bacon or sausage links make an excellent accompaniment.

Preheat the oven to 200°F (95°C).

In a bowl, whisk together the eggs, milk, and cinnamon until lightly frothy. Pour into a large, shallow glass or ceramic dish and add enough bread slices to fit comfortably. Soak the slices, turning once, for a few seconds total. Carefully transfer the slices to a plate and repeat until all the slices are soaked.

In a large, heavy frying pan or griddle over medium-low heat, warm 1½ teaspoons each butter and oil. When hot, add enough bread slices to fit comfortably in a single layer and cook until golden brown on the bottoms, about 2 minutes. Turn and cook until golden brown on the second sides, about 2 minutes longer. Transfer to a rimmed baking sheet and keep warm in the oven. Repeat with the remaining soaked bread, adding more butter and oil in equal amounts to the pan as needed.

Just before serving, lightly sprinkle each slice with cinnamon.

4 eggs

1 cup (8 fl oz/250 ml) milk

1 teaspoon ground cinnamon, plus more for serving

8 slices good-quality day-old white bread, each about ½ inch (12 mm) thick

1 tablespoon unsalted butter, or as needed

1 tablespoon canola oil, or as needed

MAKES 4 SERVINGS

FRENCH TOAST SANDWICHES WITH BANANAS

Stuffed French toast

Another approach is to slice the bread double-thick, and then run a knife into the center from one edge, creating a pocket that you can stuff with the filling. Then soak and brown the bread as directed.

Slipping a mixture of bananas and walnuts between slices of egg-soaked bread, sandwich style, results in French toast with a surprise filling. Try other favorite nuts in place of walnuts, if you like. Accompany with jam or maple syrup, along with bacon, ham, or sausage.

In a bowl, whisk together the eggs and milk until lightly frothy. Pour into a shallow glass or ceramic dish and set aside.

Evenly distribute the banana slices over half the bread slices, leaving a ¼-inch (6-mm) border uncovered all around. Sprinkle evenly with the nuts and nutmeg, then top with the remaining bread slices and press down gently to seal.

Place 2 sandwiches in the egg mixture. Soak, carefully turning once to saturate both sides, for several seconds total. Remove from the bowl and repeat with the remaining 2 sandwiches.

In a large frying pan or griddle over medium heat, melt 2 tablespoons of the butter. Add the sandwiches and fry until the undersides are golden brown, about 2 minutes. Cut the remaining 2 tablespoons butter into several pieces and add to the pan, distributing them evenly, and then flip the sandwiches with a spatula. Fry until the second sides are browned, about 2 minutes longer. (If working in batches, add one-fourth of the butter with each sandwich.)

Place on warmed individual plates. Using a fine-mesh sieve, lightly dust the tops with confectioners' sugar. Serve hot.

6 eggs

¼ cup (2 fl oz/60 ml) milk

4 ripe bananas, thinly sliced

8 slices egg bread, each about ½ inch (12 mm) thick

¼ cup (1 oz/30 g) coarsely chopped walnuts

⅛ teaspoon freshly grated nutmeg

4 tablespoons (2 oz/60 g) unsalted butter

Confectioners' (icing) sugar for dusting

MAKES 4 SERVINGS

CITRUS SEGMENTS IN VANILLA BEAN SYRUP

Try flavoring this light, aromatic syrup with 2 cinnamon sticks or 2 fresh mint sprigs instead of the vanilla bean. This dish looks especially pretty made with pink or Ruby Red grapefruits. Intensely colored blood oranges are a good substitute for navel oranges.

⅔ cup (5 oz/155 g) sugar

1 vanilla bean, split lengthwise

4 large navel oranges

2 large grapefruits

MAKES 6 SERVINGS

In a small saucepan, stir together 1⅓ cups (11 fl oz/340 ml) water and the sugar, then add the vanilla bean. Place over medium heat and bring to a simmer, stirring frequently to dissolve the sugar. Remove from the heat and let cool completely. Transfer the syrup to a bowl; discard the vanilla bean or save it for another use.

To section the oranges, working with 1 fruit at a time, and using a small, sharp knife, cut off a thin slice from both the stem and the blossom end to reveal the flesh. Then stand the fruit upright and, following its contour, slice off the peel, pith, and membrane in thick strips. Holding the fruit over the bowl of syrup in order to catch the juice, cut along the membrane on either side of each fruit segment, letting the segments drop into the bowl with the syrup.

To section the grapefruits, follow the instructions for oranges, then remove any seeds from the segments (loosen the seeds with the tip of the knife). Cut each segment in half to approximate the size of the orange segments.

Gently toss the segments in the syrup until well coated. Cover and refrigerate until well chilled, about 1 hour.

Serve in small chilled bowls.

Citrus not required

If you're not a fan of citrus, this treatment also works well with chunks of fresh pineapple or slices of firm, ripe peaches or nectarines.

53

VERY BERRY SMOOTHIES

The secret to a thick, frosty smoothie is to use well-chilled—nearly frozen—fruits and juice. This smoothie is rich in flavor and loaded with vitamins. For an even more healthful version, substitute nonfat yogurt for the low-fat yogurt and omit the honey.

1 pt (8 oz/250 g) strawberries

1 pt (8 oz/250 g) blueberries

2 cups (8 oz/250 g) frozen raspberries, partially thawed

1½ cups (12 oz/375 g) low-fat plain yogurt, chilled

½ cup (4 fl oz/125 ml) cranberry juice, chilled

1–2 tablespoons honey

MAKES ABOUT 6 CUPS (48 FL OZ/1.5 L); 4 SERVINGS

Set aside 4 perfect strawberries for garnish, then stem the remaining berries. Working in batches, in a blender, combine the stemmed strawberries, the blueberries, raspberries, yogurt, cranberry juice, and 1 tablespoon honey. Blend at high speed until smooth, about 3 minutes. Taste and adjust with more honey, if needed.

Pour into chilled tall glasses and garnish with the reserved strawberries. Serve right away.

Breakfast vs. dessert

Although cold ingredients make for the best smoothies, avoid substituting frozen yogurt for the plain yogurt, unless you plan to serve it for dessert.

SAUTÉED APPLES, ONIONS, AND CANADIAN BACON

This simple combination of sweet and savory ingredients is an excellent quick dish to serve hungry guests. You can garnish the dish with pieces of thinly sliced raw apple for a crisp contrast of flavor and texture. Serve with buttered Russian-Style Black Bread (page 411).

In a large, heavy sauté pan over medium-high heat, melt the butter with the oil. When the foam subsides, add the bacon and cook, turning once, until lightly browned and crisp, 5–8 minutes. Using tongs or a slotted spoon, transfer to paper towels to drain; set aside.

Reduce the heat to medium, add the onions to the fat remaining in the pan, and sauté until soft and translucent, about 8 minutes. Add the apple rings and cover the pan. Reduce the heat to low and cook, shaking the pan gently now and again, until the apples are nearly soft but retain their shape, about 6 minutes. Return the bacon to the pan, cover, and cook until the bacon is hot, about 4 minutes. Season generously with pepper.

Transfer to a warmed platter and serve right away.

1 teaspoon unsalted butter

1 tablespoon olive oil

1½ lb (750 g) Canadian bacon, thinly sliced

4 large yellow onions, sliced

4 large Macoun, Jonathan, or other tart, red apples, cored and cut crosswise into rings ½ inch (12 mm) thick

Ground pepper

MAKES 8 SERVINGS

MAPLE POLENTA

Polenta is usually eaten as a savory side dish, but this recipe illustrates how good it can be as a hot breakfast cereal. The finished dish can be topped with a dab of butter, drizzled with milk or cream, and garnished with toasted pine nuts or raisins.

In a saucepan over high heat, combine the milk and salt and bring to a boil. Stirring continuously with a wooden spoon to prevent lumps from forming, pour in the polenta in a thin, steady stream. Reduce the heat to low and cook, stirring frequently, until the polenta is very thick and pulls away from the sides of the pan, 20–30 minutes.

Stir in the maple syrup, transfer to warmed individual bowls, and serve right away.

5 cups (40 fl oz/1.25 l) low-fat milk

½ teaspoon salt

1 cup (5 oz/155 g) polenta

6 tablespoons (3 fl oz/90 ml) maple syrup

MAKES 4–6 SERVINGS

APPLE-CINNAMON OATMEAL

Adding shredded apple and a dash of cinnamon complements the wonderfully earthy flavor of the oatmeal. Seek out good stone-ground oats and follow the package directions for the precise proportion of water to oats and the cooking time.

Salt

1 cup (3 oz/90 g) coarsely ground whole-grain oatmeal

2 large, crisp, sweet apples

1 teaspoon ground cinnamon

About ¼ cup (3 oz/90 g) honey

MAKES 4 SERVINGS

In a saucepan over high heat, bring 3–4 cups (24–32 fl oz/ 750 ml–1 l) water (see note, above) to a rolling boil and add ½ teaspoon salt. Stirring continuously to prevent lumps from forming, stir in the oatmeal.

Reduce the heat to low, cover, and cook until the oatmeal is thick and creamy, following the package directions.

Meanwhile, halve and core the apples. When the oatmeal is ready, remove from the heat and uncover. Using the large holes of a box grater-shredder, shred the apples directly into the pan. Add the cinnamon and stir well.

Spoon the oatmeal into warmed individual bowls and drizzle evenly with the honey. Serve right away.

About cinnamon

Common cinnamon, also called cassia cinnamon, is sold in sticks or already ground. To grind your own, break or crush the sticks into pieces, then grind in a spice grinder.

SWISS BIRCHER MUESLI

A cold grain and fruit cereal, muesli was formulated at the alpine sanatorium of Swiss physician Maximilian Bircher-Benner. Traditionally, the oats are soaked overnight in water. Here, they are toasted first, then soaked in yogurt. Vary the fruits and nuts to your liking.

¾ cup (2 oz/60 g) old-fashioned rolled oats

½ cup (2 oz/60 g) coarsely chopped walnuts

¾ cup (6 oz/185 g) nonfat or low-fat plain yogurt

½ cup (4 fl oz/125 ml) nonfat (skim) milk, plus more for serving

½ cup (3 oz/90 g) coarsely chopped dried apricots

2 crisp, sweet apples

¾ cup (4½ oz/140 g) seedless grapes, halved

Honey for serving

MAKES 4–6 SERVINGS

The night before you plan to serve the muesli, begin preparing the oats: Preheat the oven to 325°F (165°C). Spread the oats on a baking sheet and toast in the oven until golden brown, 15–20 minutes. Remove from the oven, transfer to a bowl, and let cool. Spread the nuts on the baking sheet and toast until lightly browned and fragrant, 8–10 minutes. Remove from the oven, let cool, and set aside overnight.

Add the yogurt and the ½ cup milk to the cooled oats and stir well. Stir in the dried apricots, then cover with plastic wrap and refrigerate overnight.

The next morning, halve and core the apples. Using the large holes of a box grater-shredder, shred the apples directly into the bowl. Add the grapes and nuts and stir well, being careful not to crush the grapes.

Transfer to individual bowls. Pass the honey and additional milk at the table.

Added nutrients

Any of the grain cereals here, as well as the smoothies on page 53, can be made even more nutritious by the addition of a little ground flaxseed or wheat germ.

HASH BROWN POTATOES

Water and starch

In these basic hash browns, the only binding agent is the natural starch in the potatoes, so keep their soak brief. Also, the more water you squeeze out of the raw potatoes, the crispier your hash browns will be.

Hash browns are welcome on nearly any breakfast table. If you like, season them with herbs, spices, or other ingredients that complement your menu. For example, use ground cumin and fresh chiles for a Mexican flavor, or fresh basil and garlic for a Mediterranean accent.

Have ready a large bowl of cool water. Using the small holes of a grater-shredder, shred each potato (peeling is optional), and transfer to the water to prevent it from turning brown. When all of the potatoes are shredded, let stand in the water for 5 minutes to remove excess starch. Drain the potatoes, transfer to a clean kitchen towel, and squeeze out the excess water. Place the potatoes in a bowl, add ½ teaspoon salt and a pinch of pepper, and mix well.

In a large, nonstick frying pan (or 2 smaller pans) over medium-high heat, melt the butter with the oil. Divide the potato mixture into 4 equal portions, and place each portion in a free-form spoonful in the pan(s). Flatten each potato mound with a spatula, then cover the pan and cook until browned on the bottom, 4–6 minutes. Turn each mound over, flatten again, and cook until browned and crisp on the second side, 4–6 minutes longer.

Serve right away.

1 lb (500 g) baking potatoes

Salt and ground pepper

2 tablespoons unsalted butter

1 tablespoon olive oil

MAKES 4 SERVINGS

SMOKED SALMON HASH

Hot and cold smoking

Hot-smoked salmon, which is fully cooked during the smoking process, is the best choice for this dish. It is firmer and flakier than cold-smoked salmon, such as lox, which is smoked at a lower temperature and is cured but still raw.

This surprisingly delicate hash features smoked salmon, which is available in cans and in vacuum-packed pouches in most supermarkets. The recipe also works well with regular canned salmon. Garnish the finished dish with a dollop of sour cream, if desired.

In a saucepan, combine the potatoes with lightly salted cold water to cover and bring to a boil over high heat. Reduce the heat to medium and simmer, uncovered, until just tender enough to pierce with a fork, 5–7 minutes.

Meanwhile, in a nonstick frying pan over medium heat, melt the butter. Add the onion and bell pepper and sauté until tender-crisp, 4–5 minutes. Set aside.

Drain the diced potatoes and place in a bowl. Add the onion and bell pepper to the bowl with the potatoes; set the frying pan aside and do not wash it.

Pick over the salmon to remove any errant bones, then flake into ½-inch (12-mm) pieces. Add to the bowl the salmon, half-and-half, lemon zest, chopped dill, chives, and parsley. Toss to mix well, taking care not to mash the potato pieces. Season with salt and pepper and toss again.

Return the frying pan to medium heat and add 2 tablespoons of the oil. When the oil is hot, add the hash mixture, pressing it down with a spatula to form an even, compact cake.

1¼ lb (625 g) white or red potatoes, unpeeled, cut into ½-inch (12-mm) dice

2 tablespoons unsalted butter

½ red onion, cut into ½-inch (12-mm) dice

1 green bell pepper (capsicum), cut into ½-inch (12-mm) squares

14 oz (440 g) smoked salmon (see note, left), well drained

⅓ cup (3 fl oz/80 ml) half-and-half (half cream)

2 tablespoons grated lemon zest

2 tablespoons finely

chopped fresh dill,
plus sprigs for garnish

2 tablespoons finely
snipped fresh chives

1 tablespoon finely
chopped fresh flat-leaf
(Italian) parsley

Salt and ground pepper

4 tablespoons (2 fl oz/
60 ml) canola oil

MAKES 4 SERVINGS

Reduce the heat to medium-low and cook, shaking the pan occasionally, until the hash cake is crusty on the bottom, about 15 minutes. If the cake does not move freely, use the spatula to loosen the edges.

Invert a large, heatproof plate over the pan. Then, holding the pan and plate firmly together, invert them. Lift off the pan.

Heat the remaining 2 tablespoons oil in the same pan and slide the hash cake, browned side up, into the pan. Cook until the second side is crusty, about 10 minutes.

Unmold the hash onto the same plate, then cut into wedges and serve hot, garnished with dill sprigs.

About hash

The word "hash" is used for a multitude of preparations that combine chopped meat, poultry, or fish with potatoes or other root vegetables and onions. It's easy to vary and is a great way to use up dinner leftovers.

ROAST BEEF HASH

The combination of marjoram and rosemary lends an herbal note to this classic breakfast dish. While it bakes unattended in the oven, you are free to visit with your guests. If you like, top each portion with a fried or poached egg (see page 38).

3 tablespoons
unsalted butter

3 large yellow onions,
chopped

3 large russet potatoes,
peeled and chopped

2–3 tablespoons canola
oil, if needed

2½ lb (1.25 kg) cooked
roast beef, cut into
large cubes (about
5 heaping cups)

¼ cup (⅓ oz/10 g)
chopped fresh flat-leaf
(Italian) parsley, plus
more for garnish

1 tablespoon chopped
fresh rosemary leaves

1 tablespoon chopped
fresh marjoram leaves

Salt and ground pepper

1 cup (8 fl oz/250 ml) milk

MAKES 6 SERVINGS

Preheat the oven to 375°F (190°C).

In a heavy, ovenproof frying pan (preferably cast iron) over medium heat, melt the butter. When the foam subsides, add the onions and sauté until they begin to soften, about 3 minutes. Add the potatoes (and the oil if needed to prevent sticking) and fry, turning often with a spatula, until browned, about 8 minutes. Add the roast beef and fry, stirring often, until lightly browned, 3–4 minutes. Add the ¼ cup (⅓ oz/10 g) parsley, rosemary, and marjoram and season with salt and pepper. Mix well, then taste and adjust the seasoning. Pour in the milk and bring to a boil.

Transfer the pan to the oven and bake, uncovered, until the potatoes are browned and tender, about 30 minutes.

Garnish with parsley and serve hot, directly from the pan, or transfer to a warmed serving dish.

Home fries

The beginning of this dish is another reliable breakfast side dish: home fries. Omit the beef, cook the potatoes and onions in the pan until the potatoes are well browned, season with the herbs and with salt and pepper, and serve hot.

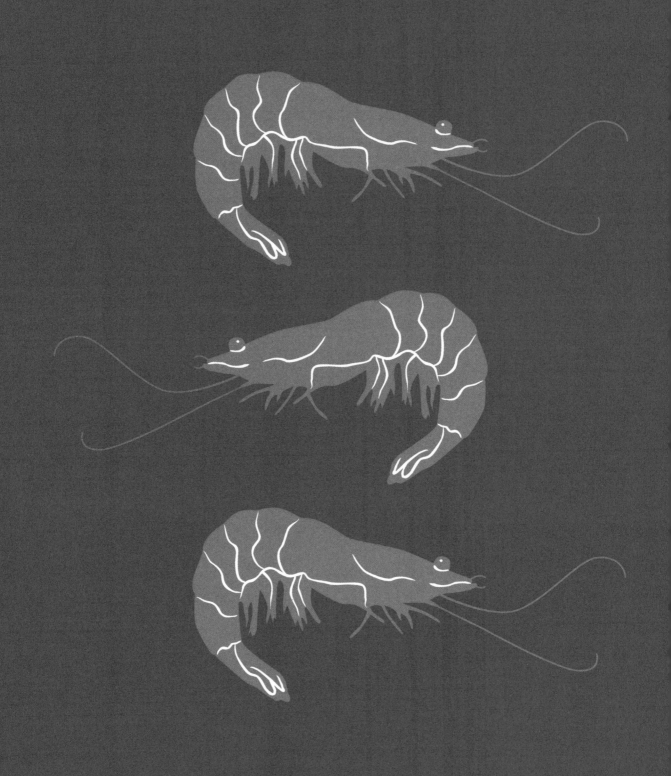

Appetizers & FIRST COURSES

Appetizers & First Courses

Whether cheese-filled bite-size tartlets passed on a tray or a citrus-drenched ceviche served at the table, the first foods to come out of the kitchen at a dinner party or other special event create a sense of anticipation for what will follow. They can also set a tone or establish a theme for a get-together. The best dishes are those that not only taste delicious but are also visually enticing.

60

Mouth teasers
Elegant restaurants serve a complimentary amuse-bouche (amuse the mouth) to guests soon after they are seated. These little bites of highly intriguing foods are intended to stimulate the appetite for what will follow. At your next dinner party, follow this tradition and serve one small, perfect hors d'oeuvre to each guest before the first course.

Plan around a theme
The terms defined at right can serve as a planning tool. Use any one of them as a jumping-off point to create a menu for a cocktail party or a meal of shared small plates.

Feeding a crowd
When feeding a large party, crudités, olives, nuts, charcuterie, cheeses, dips and spreads, crackers, and bread sticks are always crowd-pleasers and require comparatively little effort to assemble.

Mix it up
If you're serving crudités, include half a dozen vegetables of different sizes and colors. For a varied tray of deviled eggs (page 62), use two or three different fillings.

Appetizer Glossary

Different cultures and cuisines use various terms for foods traditionally served before or at the beginning of a meal. Some categories are broad and overlapping, and others define more specific kinds of dishes.

ANTIPASTI Foods served "before the meal" in Italian cuisine, antipasti typically include cured olives, marinated vegetables such as roasted peppers (capsicums) (page 333), cheese-filled rice balls called *supplì* (page 85), rustic salads like the bread salad Panzanella (page 65), bruschetta or crostini (page 61), cured meats, and thinly sliced raw beef Carpaccio (page 90).

ANTOJITOS Literally "little whims," this term for Mexican snacks covers a wide variety of foods, including deep-fried filled tortillas such as the well known folded tacos or rolled *taquitos*, the plump meatballs known as *albóndigas* (page 89), citrus-marinated seafood ceviche (page 91), and deep-fried, cheese-stuffed chiles (page 76), as well as Guacamole (page 392) and various salsas (page 392–94) with crisp tortilla chips.

CANAPÉS Meaning "seats" or "bases," this French term refers to any bite-size foods in which a savory topping or filling rests on a piece of toasted bread or crisp pastry. Other base ideas include rounds cut from tortillas or puff pastry, pressed into miniature muffin tins, and baked until crisp; slices of cucumber, radish, or boiled potato (perhaps cut into a decorative shape with a knife or cookie cutter); or small potato or risotto pancakes.

CHARCUTERIE A French term that broadly covers all kinds of cured meats, including hams and sausages, regardless of their country of origin. Charcuterie is generally cut into thin slices, arrayed on a plate or platter, and accompanied with bread, butter or olive oil, and sometimes pickles or other condiments.

CRUDITÉS Taking its name from the Latin root for "raw," this French approach to finger foods consists of an array of whole or sliced vegetables served raw or lightly blanched or steamed, accompanied with one or more dips. The vegetables are often creatively trimmed: think of radish roses or young carrots halved lengthwise, green tops intact. The dips are sometimes served in small bowls placed on the platter next to the vegetables.

HORS D'OEUVRES Literally "outside the work," this French category of party foods includes everything from simple crudités to crispy croquettes, pâtés and terrines to savory tarts, clever canapés to Gougères (page 64).

MEZE Popular in eastern Mediterranean countries, including Greece and Turkey, this assortment of foods typically includes olives, stuffed grape leaves (page 70), Hummus (page 69), the garlicky yogurt salad or dip Tzatziki (page 68), the roasted eggplant purée Baba Ghanoush (page 69), cubes of feta cheese, small grilled kebabs (page 87), and warm pita bread or crispy pita chips (below) as an accompaniment.

SMALL PLATES A contemporary restaurant term used for foods served in small portions and meant to be shared.

TAPAS Appetizers served in bars and restaurants all over Spain, and now popular worldwide, tapas may be hot or cold. The word *tapa* literally means "lid." Tapas began as simple rounds of bread placed on top of sherry glasses by bartenders, reportedly to keep flies from sneaking into the glasses. These days, tapas range from the very simple, such as a bowl of olives or some marinated mushrooms (page 73), to dishes like Spanish Potato Tortilla (page 74) and spicy pork kebabs (page 88).

ZAKUSKI Meaning "little bites" in Russian, this spread of flavorful foods traditionally adds up to a generous meal in its own right and is often served with iced vodka. Must-have dishes include the little pancakes known as blini (page 86), topped with some form of cured fish or caviar; perhaps potato pancakes (page 364) with similar toppings; smoked or pickled fish; cold cuts; and assorted baked or steamed dumplings.

Appetizer Techniques

When it comes to making appetizers and first courses, knowing a few basic techniques will take you far. Mastering these will enable you to prepare dishes that will please any crowd.

MAKING BRUSCHETTA AND CROSTINI Both of these Italian terms refer to toasted bread served with various toppings and spreads. (See page 63 for several options.) The difference between the two is a matter of size and style. At its most basic, bruschetta refers to a thick slice of coarse country bread that is grilled and then dressed. Crostini, "little toasts," are the more delicate cousins. The French call similar toasts *croûtes* (a term also used for bases or containers made of puff pastry).

For bruschetta, start with good, crusty bread, cut it into thick slices on a slight diagonal, and grill the slices over hot coals until grill marks appear, turning to toast both sides. (Alternatively, toast them under a broiler/grill.) Rub the still-warm slices with raw garlic, brush with olive oil, and season with salt. (For Spain's tomato-rubbed take on bruschetta, see page 65.)

For crostini, slice a baguette or similar bread into slices about ½ inch (12 mm) thick. Lightly brush both sides of the slices with olive oil. Arrange in a single layer on a baking sheet and toast in a preheated 350°F (180°C) oven until lightly browned on both sides, about 25 minutes. Let cool slightly, then rub the top of each slice with a garlic clove.

Bruschetta is often served already topped, arranged on a platter. Crostini may be served the same way, or in a basket or bowl alongside spreads.

MAKING PITA CHIPS Crispy wedges of pita make ideal scoops for dips and spreads. To prepare them, preheat the oven to 375°F (190°C). Separating it along the outside seam, split each pita bread into 2 rounds. Cut each round into 6–8 wedges. Spread the wedges on a baking sheet, drizzle lightly but evenly with extra-virgin olive oil, and sprinkle with salt; if you like, dust the chips very lightly with cayenne pepper or sweet or hot paprika. Bake, turning occasionally, until crisp, 10–12 minutes.

Utensils and receptacles
When serving assorted hors d'oeuvres, be sure to set out a tool or bowl as needed for each item. For example, provide a knife for each cheese, a spoon for each dip, and little saucers for olive pits or toothpicks.

Estimating quantities
When planning and making hors d'oeuvres, the quantity will depend not just on the number of guests, but also on the timeframe and whether a meal will follow. Plan on at least five bite-size pieces per guest per hour. If no meal will be served, include some relatively filling appetizers, like satay or meatballs (pages 87–90).

Circulate new dishes
To boost interest, schedule new dishes to be brought out one or two at a time throughout a cocktail party.

Fresh is best
Use plates for hors d'oeuvres and replenish them frequently, or have extras arranged on plates ready to be swapped out. They look tidier and more appealing than a single large platter.

Don't forget the drinks
Well-chosen beverages are inseparable companions for appetizers and first courses. When you plan your menu, consider the drinks customarily served with the dishes you offer: for example, sherry or sangria with Spanish-style tapas, or Champagne with an array of French-inspired hors d'oeuvres.

61

WORKING WITH FILO Filo (sometimes spelled phyllo) is tissue-thin pastry sheets that are typically wrapped around savory or sweet fillings. Rolled or folded into a variety of shapes, these little pastry packages bake to flaky, golden crispness. Filo can also be layered with a filling in a baking dish and cut into squares or diamonds after baking.

Sold in the refrigerated or freezer cases of most supermarkets, the delicate dough requires special handling for the best results. If frozen, thaw according to the package instructions. Let the filo dough stand in its packaging for 2 hours at room temperature before unfolding and using. The sheets dry out quickly when exposed to the air, so have everything you will need for the recipe—ingredients and tools—ready before you unfold them. When working with filo, always keep the sheets you are not immediately using covered with a sheet of plastic wrap topped with a lightly dampened kitchen towel to prevent them from drying out. Brushing each filo layer with butter ensures it will become crisp as it bakes. Follow individual recipe directions for how many filo sheets to use and how to shape or layer them.

WORKING WITH PUFF PASTRY Made by rolling out a simple dough of flour, salt, water, and butter, and then layering it with butter, folding it around the butter, chilling it, rolling it out, and repeating the process several times, puff pastry consists of scores of ultrathin layers of dough and butter that literally puff up in the oven, turning light, crisp, and golden. Making puff pastry dough from scratch takes more time and patience than skill (see the recipe on page 450). However, commercial puff pastry dough can be found packaged and frozen in well-stocked markets. Look for a good-quality product made with butter, and check the sell-by and use-by dates before purchase.

Keep store-bought puff pastry carefully wrapped in the freezer until you are ready to use it. Following the package instructions, thaw the dough in the refrigerator, keeping it cold until you are ready to roll it out and shape it as directed in individual recipes.

DEEP-FRYING From croquettes (page 84) to tempura (page 78), golden oysters (page 77) to crispy polenta sticks (page 76), some of the most popular bite-size hors d'oeuvres are deep-fried, giving them irresistible golden color and crunchy texture. For successful deep-frying, use a thermometer to be sure the oil is heated to the temperature indicated in the recipe. If the oil is too cool, the food will absorb it and be greasy; if too hot, the food may burn. Also, fry just a few pieces of food at a time. A crowded pan can cause foods to brown unevenly and the oil temperature to drop dramatically.

GRILLING KEBABS The skewered foods known as kebabs are often served in larger portions as main dishes, but smaller skewers of bite-size meats, poultry, seafood, or vegetables make excellent hors d'oeuvres or first courses. See pages 87 and 88 for a few recipes, or try scaling down the recipe on page 250, cutting the pieces smaller and threading them onto smaller skewers.

If using wooden or bamboo skewers, be sure to soak them in cold water to cover for at least 20 minutes before assembling the kebabs. This prevents the skewers from burning and breaking apart when they are on the grill. Wait until the grill is sufficiently hot—if using charcoal, the coals should be covered with white ash—before you begin grilling. Follow the suggested cooking times in individual recipes, keeping in mind that the kind of food you are grilling and the size of the pieces can affect the timing.

BRUSCHETTA TOPPINGS

Follow the instructions for making bruschetta, page 61, then proceed as directed below. Smaller portions of these toppings can be used on crostini or other canapé bases.

Cheese and Fruit

When making the bruschetta, omit the garlic, olive oil, and salt. Spread 1 teaspoon Gorgonzola cheese on each grilled bread slice and top with diced nectarine that has been tossed in fresh lemon juice. Or, combine Brie with thin pear slices, Camembert with thin apple slices, or goat cheese with dried apricots or crushed pistachios.

Chile-Tomato Relish

Finely chop about 1¼ lb (625 g) tomatoes, place in a fine-mesh sieve set over a bowl, and let drain for 1 hour. Discard the juice from the bowl, or reserve for another use. In a bowl, combine the tomatoes; ½ cup (3 oz/90 g) minced yellow onion; 4 Anaheim chiles, seeded and minced; 5 tablespoons (2½ oz/75 g) tomato paste; 2 tablespoons extra-virgin olive oil; 3 tablespoons chopped fresh flat-leaf (Italian) parsley; and ½–1 teaspoon red pepper flakes. Stir to combine. Season with salt and ground pepper. Spoon onto grilled bread slices and garnish with chopped fresh flat-leaf (Italian) parsley.

Eggplant Caviar

Prick 1 large eggplant (aubergine) with a fork and roast in a preheated 350°F (180°C) oven until very soft, 30–40 minutes. Let cool, then peel, discard any large seed pockets, and coarsely chop the flesh. In a blender, combine 2 tomatoes, peeled, seeded, and chopped; ½ yellow onion, chopped; 2 cloves garlic, chopped; and 1 tablespoon olive oil. Process until smooth. Add the eggplant, a small handful of pitted Kalamata olives, and ¼ cup (⅓ oz/10 g) fresh cilantro (fresh coriander) leaves and process until smooth. Season with fresh lemon juice, salt, and ground pepper. Spoon onto grilled bread slices and garnish with chopped fresh cilantro.

Sweet-and-Sour Chicken Livers

In a frying pan over medium heat, warm 1 tablespoon olive oil. Add ⅓ cup (2 oz/60 g) finely chopped pancetta and sauté until browned, about 5 minutes. Add ¼ cup (1½ oz/45 g) finely chopped yellow onion and 1 teaspoon chopped fresh sage and sauté until the onion is tender and golden, about 10 minutes. Add 2 tablespoons white wine and simmer to evaporate. Transfer to a cutting board and mince. In the same pan over low heat, warm 2 tablespoons olive oil. Add ½ lb (250 g) trimmed chicken livers and cook, turning once, until firm but still pink inside, 5–6 minutes. Season with salt and ground pepper and let cool. Coarsely chop and add to the pancetta mixture. Add 1 clove garlic, minced; 1 tablespoon rinsed capers; and 1 tablespoon balsamic vinegar. Season with salt and pepper and stir to combine. Spread onto grilled bread slices and garnish with additional chopped fresh sage.

Tomatoes and Basil

Top grilled bread slices generously with tomatoes that have been sliced into rounds or cut into thin wedges or large dice. Sprinkle with salt and ground pepper, then with torn fresh basil leaves. Using a vegetable peeler, shave Parmesan over the top.

SEE ALSO:

- **Ceviche,** *page 91*
- **Hummus,** *page 69*
- **Tapenade,** *page 388*
- **Tuna Tartare,** *page 91*

OLIVE GLOSSARY

Gaeta
Small, mild-tasting black olives from Italy, either brine cured or dry cured in salt and then coated with olive oil.

Kalamata
Almond-shaped, purplish black, sharp-tasting Greek olives, brine cured and then packed in oil or vinegar.

Lucque
Large green olives common to southern France; originally from Italy, with a sweet, meaty flavor.

Manzanilla
Oval, small to medium olives common to Spain and California, brine cured either when green or fully ripened to black. Green Manzanillas are the variety commonly found pitted and stuffed with pimientos.

Moroccan
Refers to green or black olives marinated with Moroccan seasonings, such as lemon, garlic, cayenne pepper, cinnamon, and allspice.

Niçoise
Tiny black olives from the Mediterranean coast of Provence, cured in brine, and then packed in olive oil. They have a meaty texture and subtly briny flavor.

Picholine
Medium-sized, torpedo-shaped mild green olives; smooth textured and salty.

Sicilian
Large, green, tart, and meaty olives sometimes flavored with red pepper or fennel. A cured black variety is also available.

GOUGÈRES

Made from *pâte à choux,* the same dough that is used for cream puffs, these savory cheese pastries are a specialty of France's Burgundy region. If you like, add 1 tablespoon fresh thyme leaves and 1 teaspoon chopped fresh rosemary to the batter with the cheese.

Bake in advance

These savory pastries freeze well. Bake as directed, let cool completely, and freeze in a single layer. Transfer to a zippered plastic bag and freeze for up to 4 weeks; thaw at room temperature for about 1 hour, then place on a baking sheet in a preheated 350°F (180°C) oven to crisp for about 10 minutes.

Preheat the oven to 375°F (190°C). Line 2 rimmed baking sheets with parchment (baking) paper.

In a heavy saucepan over high heat, combine the 2 cups milk, butter, and salt and bring to a boil. Add the flour all at once, reduce the heat to low, and stir until the mixture forms a ball and pulls cleanly away from the sides of the pan, about 5 minutes. Remove from the heat.

Using an electric mixer on medium speed, add the eggs, one at a time and beating after each addition until thoroughly incorporated, until the paste is very shiny, about 5 minutes. Fold in three-fourths of the cheese.

Using a spoon, scoop out rounds 2–3 inches (5–7.5 cm) in diameter onto the baking sheets, spacing them about 2 inches (5 cm) apart. Brush the rounds with the 2 tablespoons milk and sprinkle evenly with the remaining cheese.

Bake the dough rounds until well puffed and golden brown, 30–35 minutes. Let cool on the pan on wire racks. Serve warm or at room temperature.

2 cups (16 fl oz/500 ml) plus 2 tablespoons milk

½ cup (4 oz/125 g) unsalted butter

2 teaspoons salt

2 cups (10 oz/315 g) all-purpose (plain) flour

8 eggs

½ lb (250 g) Emmentaler, Gruyère, or other Swiss-type cheese, finely shredded

MAKES ABOUT 48 PUFFS

64

CRISP CHEESE CRACKERS

Topped with chives and sea salt, these crisp crackers are perfect with wine or cocktails before a casual dinner. The dough can be made the night before and refrigerated. Keep an eye on them as they bake: if the edges brown too much, the crackers will taste bitter.

Perfect rounds

Refrigerating the dough allows it to rest and the flavors to meld. It also makes the log easier to slice into neat rounds for baking.

In a food processor, combine the Comté and Parmesan cheeses, the butter, flour, and cayenne. Process until well combined and crumbly, 40–60 seconds. Transfer the mixture to a sheet of plastic wrap and shape into a log about 2 inches (5 cm) in diameter and 6–7 inches (15–18 cm) long. Roll up the log in the plastic wrap, patting it to form a smooth, even shape. Refrigerate for at least 1 hour or up to overnight.

Preheat the oven to 350°F (180°C). Unwrap the dough and slice into rounds about ¼ inch (6 mm) thick. Arrange on 2 ungreased rimmed baking sheets, preferably nonstick, spacing them about 2 inches (5 cm) apart. Sprinkle the rounds evenly with chives and top each with a pinch of salt.

Bake the crackers, 1 sheet at a time, until light golden brown, 10–15 minutes, rotating the pan front to back halfway through the baking time. For crispier crackers, bake for up to 3 minutes longer, watching carefully to avoid overbrowning. Serve right away.

2 cups (8 oz/250 g) shredded Comté or Gruyère cheese

½ cup (2 oz/60 g) grated Parmesan cheese

6 tablespoons (3 oz/90 g) unsalted butter

1 cup (5 oz/155 g) all-purpose (plain) flour

Pinch of cayenne pepper

2–3 tablespoons chopped fresh chives

Coarse sea salt

MAKES 24–28 CRACKERS

GRILLED BREAD WITH TOMATO AND OLIVE OIL

Similar to Italy's bruschetta (see page 61), this tomato-rubbed grilled bread is a Spanish staple. Serve it plain or topped with Manchego cheese, ham, and slivered olives. Serrano ham offers the most traditional flavor, but Italian prosciutto or French Bayonne ham can be substituted.

2 cloves garlic

Coarse sea salt
and ground pepper

¼ cup (2 fl oz/60 ml)
extra-virgin olive oil

12 slices coarse country
bread, each about
¾ inch (2 cm) thick

3 very ripe tomatoes,
halved crosswise

MAKES 6 SERVINGS

Prepare a charcoal or gas grill for direct-heat cooking over medium heat (see page 18).

In a mortar, combine the garlic and a big pinch of salt. Mash together with a pestle to form a paste. Mix in the oil.

Place the bread slices on the grill rack 4–5 inches (10–13 cm) from the fire and grill, turning once, until golden brown, 30–60 seconds on each side. Transfer the bread to a platter.

Cupping a tomato half, cut side down, in your palm, rub it over the tops of 2 pieces of the grilled bread, squeezing slightly to leave a smear of pulp, seeds, and juice on the surface. Repeat with the remaining tomato halves and bread. Drizzle the oil-garlic mixture evenly over the bread slices and sprinkle with pepper. Serve right away.

**Manchego
of La Mancha**

*Manchego cheese
is made in the
La Mancha region
of central Spain,
from the milk of the
region's Manchega
sheep. Aged for three
months or longer
in natural caves, it
is firm, white, and
slightly salty, with
a trademark inedible
rind bearing
cross-hatching.*

PANZANELLA

The success of this popular Italian salad depends in part on the type of bread you use. It must have a dense, coarse texture, rather than a cottony one. Full-flavored sun-ripened tomatoes are equally important to a good result. This salad is best served the same day you make it.

½ lb (250 g) 2- to 3-day-old
coarse country bread

1 English (hothouse)
cucumber

6 tomatoes, peeled,
seeded, coarsely diced

1 red onion, thinly sliced

2 tablespoons
rinsed capers

½ cup (½ oz/15 g) fresh
basil leaves, torn into
small pieces

2 tablespoons red
wine vinegar

¼ cup (2 fl oz/60 ml)
balsamic vinegar

¼ cup (2 fl oz/60 ml)
extra-virgin olive oil

Salt and ground pepper

MAKES 6 SERVINGS

Cut the bread into slices 1 inch (2.5 cm) thick. Place in a shallow bowl in a single layer and sprinkle evenly with ½ cup (4 fl oz/125 ml) water. Let stand for 1 minute. Carefully squeeze the water from the bread. Tear the bread into rough 1-inch (2.5-cm) chunks, and place them on paper towels. Let stand for 10 minutes to absorb excess moisture.

Peel the cucumber, halve lengthwise, scoop out any errant seeds, and dice. In a bowl, combine the cucumber, tomatoes, onion, capers, and basil. Add the bread and toss carefully to avoid breaking up the bread too much.

In a small bowl, whisk together the red wine vinegar, balsamic vinegar, and oil. Season with salt and pepper. Drizzle over the bread-tomato mixture and toss gently to mix. Cover and refrigerate for 1 hour.

Transfer to individual bowls and serve right away.

**Cherry tomato
bread salad**

*For another tasty,
summery tomato
salad, toss cherry
tomato halves
and diced fresh
mozzarella in the
same oil-and-vinegar
dressing, along with
a few torn fresh basil
leaves. Serve at room
temperature.*

MUSHROOM SPREAD

This earthy spread can be made with any variety of mushrooms. Serve it alongside crackers or crostini (see page 61), or spread it on the crostini, top each with a pinch of finely chopped fresh flat-leaf (Italian) parsley or a sliver of sun-dried tomato, and pass on a platter.

In a large, heavy frying pan over medium-high heat, warm 2 tablespoons of the oil. Add the mushrooms and cook, stirring often, until lightly browned, about 10 minutes. Add the garlic, parsley, thyme, rosemary, 1 teaspoon salt, and a few grinds of pepper. Cook, stirring, for 2 minutes longer.

Transfer the mushroom mixture to a food processor. Process until very finely chopped. With the processor running, add the remaining 3 tablespoons oil in a thin, steady stream, processing until the mixture is smooth and spreadable. Transfer to a bowl and stir in the sun-dried tomatoes. Season with salt and pepper.

Serve right away. Or, store in a covered container in the refrigerator for up to 1 day, then bring the spread to room temperature before serving.

5 tablespoons (3 fl oz/80 ml) extra-virgin olive oil

¾ lb (375 g) mixed fresh white, cremini, and stemmed shiitake mushrooms, chopped

2 cloves garlic, minced

2 tablespoons finely chopped fresh flat-leaf (Italian) parsley

2 teaspoons fresh thyme leaves

½ teaspoon minced fresh rosemary

Salt and ground pepper

¼ cup (1¼ oz/37 g) oil-packed sun-dried tomatoes, finely chopped

MAKES 6–8 SERVINGS

To spread or not to spread

Letting guests help themselves to the spread allows them to determine the ratio of spread to bread. When you top the crostini, you have control over how far it goes, and you can present the toasts with a pretty garnish.

Fava bean purée

In a food processor, combine 1½ cups (10 oz/315 g) peeled, cooked fresh fava (broad) beans, 1 tbsp chopped fresh mint, 1 tbsp olive oil, and the juice of ½ lemon. Pulse until a thick paste forms. Season with salt and pepper. Serve on crostini and top with pecorino shavings.

WHITE BEAN PURÉE WITH ROSEMARY

Dried beans are delicious kitchen staples, especially if the beans are heirlooms—old-fashioned varieties being revived by small growers. Flavored with rosemary, this purée is equally welcome spread on crostini or served as a side dish with grilled lamb or sausages.

Drain the beans, put them in a saucepan, and add 6 cups (48 fl oz/1.5 l) water, the onion, the celery, and the bay leaf. Bring to a simmer over medium-high heat, cover, and reduce the heat to maintain a bare simmer. Cook until the beans are tender, about 1 hour. Remove from the heat and let cool in the liquid.

In a large frying pan over medium heat, warm the oil. Add the garlic and rosemary and sauté until the garlic is fragrant, about 1 minute. Using a slotted spoon, lift the beans out of the liquid and add them to the frying pan, reserving the liquid. Season the beans with salt and pepper and stir well. Cook gently for 5 minutes to blend the flavors.

Working in batches, transfer the contents of the frying pan to a food processor and process until smooth, adding the reserved bean-cooking liquid as needed to achieve a spreadable consistency. Taste the purée and adjust the seasoning before serving.

2 cups (12 oz/375 g) dried large white beans, sorted and soaked (see page 301)

½ yellow onion

1 celery stalk, cut into thirds

1 bay leaf

⅓ cup (3 fl oz/80 ml) extra-virgin olive oil

3 cloves garlic, minced

1 teaspoon minced fresh rosemary

Salt and ground pepper

MAKES 8–10 SERVINGS

Make and reheat

You can make the purée at right up to 2 hours in advance and reheat it gently in a saucepan, adding additional bean-cooking liquid as needed to thin.

BLUE CHEESE AND SPICED WALNUT SPREAD

Choose a favorite blue here, such as Gorgonzola, Roquefort, or Maytag. This rich spread is best made a day in advance, so the flavors have time to mature. Accompany with an assortment of your favorite purchased plain, whole-grain, or sesame crackers.

¾ teaspoon ground cumin

⅛ teaspoon
cayenne pepper

Coarse sea salt

1 tablespoon canola oil

1 cup (4 oz/125 g) walnuts

3 tablespoons sugar

1 lb (500 g) blue cheese,
crumbled, at room
temperature

5 oz (155 g) cream cheese,
at room temperature

4 tablespoons (2 oz/60 g)
unsalted butter, at room
temperature

2 tablespoons
brandy, optional

MAKES 10–12 SERVINGS

Line a rimmed baking sheet with aluminum foil.

In a small bowl, stir together the cumin, cayenne, and ½ teaspoon salt. In a heavy saucepan over medium heat, warm the oil. Add the walnuts and sauté, stirring constantly, until lightly browned, about 4 minutes. Add the sugar and stir until it melts and turns amber, about 3 minutes. Add the cumin mixture and toss to coat. Turn out onto the prepared baking sheet and let cool for about 30 minutes.

Meanwhile, in a food processor, combine three-fourths of the blue cheese, the cream cheese, and the butter and process until smooth. Mix in the brandy (if using). Transfer to a bowl. When the nuts are cool, chop coarsely. Add the nuts and the remaining blue cheese to the bowl and stir until blended.

Spoon the cheese mixture into a serving bowl. For the best flavor, cover and refrigerate overnight, then bring to room temperature before serving.

Stir constantly

When sautéing the nuts in the oil, stir them constantly to prevent the nuts from burning. Once the sugar is added, continue to stir to ensure even melting and caramelizing.

SALT COD PURÉE

This classic Provençal dish made from salt cod is called *brandade de morue.* The word *brandade* means "something that is stirred." Here, a food processor is used to make the purée, without any sacrifice in taste. Serve with grilled or toasted slices of coarse country bread.

1½ lb (750 g) salt cod fillet

2 cloves garlic,
mashed to a paste

Salt and ground pepper

1½–3 cups (12–24 fl oz/
375–750 ml) olive oil

1¼ cups (10 fl oz/
310 ml) milk

Juice of 1 lemon

Freshly grated nutmeg

MAKES 6–8 SERVINGS

Place the fish in a bowl with water to cover. Cover and refrigerate for 24–48 hours (see note, right), changing the water at least 4 times.

Drain the cod and place in a large saucepan. Add water to cover generously, cover the pan, and bring to a simmer over low heat. Simmer until the cod is just tender when flaked, about 10 minutes. Drain the cod, let cool briefly, then remove all traces of skin. Flake the cod, discarding any errant bones, and place in a food processor. Add the garlic and a pinch of salt and pulse twice just to combine.

In a separate small saucepan over low heat, warm 1½ cups (12 fl oz/375 ml) of the oil and the milk. With the processor running, add the warm olive oil and the milk, alternating, a little at a time. Slowly add as much of the remaining oil as needed to achieve a pale, thick, smooth mixture. Add the lemon juice and season with nutmeg and pepper. Serve the purée right away.

**Working
with salt cod**

Cod preserved in salt must be rehydrated before cooking. Soaking it in water also draws out the salt, with thicker pieces requiring a longer soak and more frequent change of water. Do not allow the salt cod to boil, or it will become tough.

CREAMY TOMATO-PEPPER DIP

More easy dips

For a simple dip or spread, stir mixed chopped fresh herbs and grated lemon zest into mayonnaise, top cream cheese with your favorite chutney, or stir chopped sun-dried tomatoes and black olives into ricotta.

This purée of roasted red pepper, tomato paste, cream, and sour cream makes an ideal dip for Crisp Polenta Sticks (page 76), boiled shrimp, or other finger foods. You can also use it as a sauce, drizzled anywhere the rich flavors of pepper and tomato would be welcome.

Follow the directions on page 333 to roast, peel, seed, and de-rib the pepper. Roughly chop the flesh.

In a blender, combine the roasted pepper pieces, sour cream, and tomato paste and process until a smooth paste forms. Transfer to a bowl and add the cream, vinegar, and cayenne. Whisk until the cream thickens slightly. Season with salt and black pepper.

Cover and refrigerate until serving to blend the flavors.

1 large red bell pepper (capsicum)

2 tablespoons sour cream

1 tablespoon tomato paste

½ cup (4 fl oz/125 ml) heavy (double) cream

1 teaspoon balsamic vinegar

Pinch of cayenne pepper

Salt and ground black pepper

MAKES ABOUT 1 CUP (8 FL OZ/250 ML)

TZATZIKI

Greek-style yogurt

Yogurt labeled "Greek" or "Greek-style" is increasingly available in markets. It is much thicker than standard plain yogurt and does not require draining.

This tangy dip is popular in Greece, home to some of the best yogurt in the world. Serve the dip with wedges of pita bread on its own or with an assortment of other dips. It is also good tucked into a pita round with Chicken Souvlaki (page 87).

If you are not using Greek yogurt, line a sieve with cheese-cloth (muslin) and place over a bowl. Spoon the yogurt into the sieve and refrigerate for 4 hours to drain. (If using Greek yogurt, proceed with the recipe.)

Meanwhile, prepare the cucumber. Peel, halve lengthwise, and scoop out any errant seeds. Using the large holes of a grater-shredder, grate enough cucumber to measure 1 cup (4 oz/125 g). Spread out the cucumber on paper towels, salt lightly, and let drain for 15 minutes.

In a bowl, combine the yogurt, cucumber, garlic, mint, dill, and oil. Add the lemon juice to taste. Stir to mix well, then season with salt.

Transfer to a bowl and serve right away.

2 cups (1 lb/500 g) plain whole-milk yogurt, preferably Greek yogurt

1 English (hothouse) cucumber

Salt

4 cloves garlic, minced

1 tablespoon chopped fresh mint

1 tablespoon chopped fresh dill

1 tablespoon extra-virgin olive oil

2–3 teaspoons lemon juice

MAKES ABOUT 2 CUPS (16 FL OZ/500 ML)

HUMMUS

Tahini, a paste ground from toasted sesame seeds, is a staple of the Middle Eastern kitchen. Here, it is used to make a garlicky chickpea purée flavored with cumin. For a spicier dip, add a pinch of cayenne pepper. Serve with warm pita wedges or crusty bread.

1⅓ cups (9 oz/280 g) dried chickpeas (garbanzo beans), sorted and soaked (see page 301)

½ cup (4 fl oz/125 ml) lemon juice, or as needed

½ cup (5 oz/155 g) tahini

4 tablespoons (2 fl oz/ 60 ml) extra-virgin olive oil

5 cloves garlic, minced

¼ teaspoon ground cumin

Salt

2 teaspoons chopped fresh flat-leaf (Italian) parsley

Large pinch of paprika

MAKES ABOUT 3 CUPS (24 FL OZ/750 ML)

Drain the chickpeas and put them in a saucepan with water to cover by 2 inches (5 cm). Bring to a boil over high heat, reduce the heat to low, and simmer, uncovered, until the skins crack and the chickpeas are very tender, about 1 hour. Remove from the heat and drain, reserving the liquid.

In a food processor or blender, combine the chickpeas, ½ cup (4 fl oz/125 ml) lemon juice, the tahini, 3 tablespoons of the oil, the garlic, cumin, and ¾ teaspoon salt. Process until a soft, creamy paste forms. Taste and adjust the seasoning with salt and lemon juice, if needed.

Transfer the purée to a serving bowl and spread with the back of a spoon to form a shallow well. Drizzle with the remaining 1 tablespoon oil. Sprinkle with the parsley and paprika and serve.

The meze platter

Hummus is a standard feature of any meze platter, along with Baba Ghanoush (below), Dolmas (page 70), and creamy Tzatziki (opposite). If you like, garnish the hummus with pine nuts or diced tomatoes.

BABA GHANOUSH

This creamy dip is made with fire-roasted eggplant, tahini, lemon juice, and plenty of minced garlic. If you opt to cook the eggplant entirely in the oven, it won't have the same smoky flavor, but the dip will still be delicious. Serve with warmed pita wedges or crackers.

1 large eggplant (aubergine)

¼ cup (2½ oz/75 g) tahini, or as needed

3 cloves garlic, minced

¼ cup (2 fl oz/60 ml) lemon juice, or as needed

Large pinch of ground cumin

Salt

1 tablespoon extra-virgin olive oil

1 tablespoon chopped fresh flat-leaf (Italian) parsley

MAKES ABOUT 2 CUPS (16 FL OZ/500 ML)

Prepare a charcoal or gas grill for direct-heat cooking over medium heat (see page 18). Preheat the oven to 375°F (190°C).

Prick the eggplant with a fork in several places and place on the grill rack 4–5 inches (10–13 cm) from the fire. Cook, turning frequently, until the skin blackens and blisters and the flesh just begins to feel soft, 10–15 minutes. Transfer to a rimmed baking sheet and bake in the oven until very soft, 15–20 minutes. (Alternatively, omit the grilling step: bake the eggplant on a rimmed baking sheet in a preheated 350°F/ 180°C oven until soft, 30–40 minutes.)

Let the eggplant cool slightly, and peel off and discard the skin. Discard any large seed pockets, then place the eggplant flesh in a bowl. Using a fork, mash the eggplant to a paste. Add the tahini, garlic, ¼ cup (2 fl oz/60 ml) lemon juice, and cumin and mix well. Season with salt, then taste and adjust with more lemon juice and/or tahini, if needed.

Transfer the mixture to a serving bowl. Drizzle the olive oil over the top, sprinkle with the parsley, and serve.

The perfect olive

An ideal companion for both Hummus (above) and Baba Ghanoush (left) is a handful of brine-cured black olives, such as Kalamata, which can be served alongside the dip or chopped and strewn on top as a garnish. For a guide to olives, see page 63.

APPETIZERS & FIRST COURSES

DOLMAS

Dolmas look impressive on the table, but they are not difficult to make: just a mixture of seasoned rice and currants rolled in grape leaves and then braised until tender. Serve with Tzatziki (page 68) for dipping, or as part of a large meze platter.

Rinse the grape leaves in cold running water. Have ready a bowl filled with ice water. Bring a large saucepan three-fourths full of water to a boil. Add the grape leaves, a few at a time, and blanch for 1 minute. Using a slotted spoon, transfer to the ice water to cool. When all of the leaves have been blanched, drain and cut off the stems. Set aside.

In a large frying pan over medium heat, warm ¼ cup (2 fl oz/ 60 ml) of the oil. Add the yellow onion and cook, stirring occasionally, until soft, about 7 minutes. Add the rice, green onions, and pine nuts and stir until the green onions soften, about 3 minutes. Add the currants, parsley, mint, dill, ¾ teaspoon salt, ¼ teaspoon pepper, and 1 cup (8 fl oz/250 ml) water. Cover and cook over low heat until the water is absorbed and the rice is cooked, about 15 minutes.

Line the bottom of a heavy 4-qt (4-l) saucepan with a few grape leaves. Sprinkle with a pinch of salt. To shape the rolled grape leaves, place a leaf, smooth side down, on a work surface. Put a heaping spoonful of the rice mixture near the base of the leaf at the stem end. Fold the stem end and then the sides over the filling and roll the leaf up toward the point, forming a bundle. Place, seam side down, in the prepared saucepan. Continue stuffing the grape leaves and adding them to the pan, packing them close together. When the bottom is completely covered, drizzle the layer with some of the remaining ¼ cup oil and some of the lemon juice.

Continue stuffing and layering the stuffed grape leaves, drizzling each layer with some of the remaining oil and lemon juice, until all the filling is used. Add another 1 cup water, and then cover the top layer with a few leaves. Invert a small heatproof plate, smaller than the circumference of the pan, directly on top of the stuffed leaves.

Cover the saucepan and bring to a boil over high heat. Reduce the heat to low, cover, and simmer until most of the liquid has been absorbed, about 1½ hours. Check the liquid in the bottom of the pan occasionally and add water as needed so the pan doesn't dry out. Remove from the heat and let the stuffed leaves stand in the pan to cool for about 2 hours.

Transfer to a platter. Serve warm or at room temperature.

Grape leaves

Beautiful and edible, grape leaves are an elegant choice for encasing a variety of fillings. Leaves sold in jars have been brined, so be sure to rinse them well before using. If you can find young, fresh leaves, use them, blanching them first to soften.

Pairing wine with hors d'oeuvres

Trying to pair specific wines with specific appetizers is not practical when you are serving an array of different choices. Instead, offer a sparkling wine or crisp, unoaked, dry white wine. High in acid, these wines will either complement or add contrast to a wide variety of different dips, spreads, and hot and cold hors d'oeuvres.

1 jar (1 lb/500 g, about 6 dozen) grape leaves (see note, left)

½ cup (4 fl oz/120 ml) extra-virgin olive oil

1 large yellow onion, minced

1 cup (7 oz/220 g) long-grain white rice

12 green (spring) onions, including tender green tops, thinly sliced

⅓ cup (2 oz/60 g) pine nuts

⅓ cup (2 oz/60 g) dried currants

¼ cup (⅓ oz/10 g) chopped fresh flat-leaf (Italian) parsley

3 tablespoons chopped fresh mint

3 tablespoons chopped fresh dill

Salt and ground pepper

½ cup (4 fl oz/125 ml) lemon juice

MAKES ABOUT 60 DOLMAS

ROASTED FIGS WITH GOAT CHEESE AND PANCETTA

Choose figs that are very soft, a sign that their sugar content has developed. Black Mission figs are among the most readily available. Their sweetness, combined with the tartness of the cheese and the saltiness of the pancetta, delivers a bouquet of intense and satisfying flavors.

**12 soft, ripe
Black Mission figs**

**¼ lb (125 g) fresh
goat cheese**

**1 teaspoon minced
fresh rosemary, plus
sprigs for garnish**

Ground pepper

**¼ lb (125 g) pancetta
or bacon, thinly sliced**

MAKES 4 SERVINGS

Preheat the oven to 400°F (200°C).

Cut a slit in each fig from the stem end to the base, slicing about three-fourths of the way through the fruit. Set aside.

In a bowl, combine the cheese, minced rosemary, and a few grinds of pepper. Stir until blended. Cut the pancetta into pieces 4 inches (10 cm) long, or just long enough to wrap around a fig once it is filled, plus a 1-inch (2.5-cm) overlap.

Put a spoonful of the cheese mixture inside each fig, wrap the fig with a length of pancetta, and fasten in place with a toothpick. Place the figs on a rimmed baking sheet. Roast until the pancetta is browned, the figs are shiny, and the cheese is nearly melted, 10–15 minutes. If the cheese is nearly melted but the pancetta has not yet browned, place the figs under a hot broiler (grill) for a minute or two.

Transfer to a warmed platter or individual plates. Garnish with rosemary sprigs and serve warm.

**Roast before
serving**

*The stuffed figs
may be completely
assembled, covered,
and refrigerated
several hours in
advance. Bring to
room temperature,
then roast just
before serving.*

71

ARTICHOKES WRAPPED IN PROSCIUTTO

Artichokes are the immature, thick-petaled flowers of an edible thistle. Baby artichokes, however, do not contain the fuzzy center choke, so they can be eaten whole. For this simple hors d'oeuvre, they are blanched, lightly dressed, then wrapped in prosciutto.

**1 lb (500 g) baby
artichokes, trimmed
(see note, right)**

**3 cups (24 fl oz/750 ml)
Chicken Stock (page 23),
broth or water**

**2 teaspoons white
wine vinegar**

Salt and ground pepper

3 tablespoons olive oil

**2 green (spring) onions,
white part only, finely
chopped**

**¼ lb (125 g) prosciutto,
sliced paper-thin**

MAKES 4 SERVINGS

In a saucepan over medium heat, bring the stock to a boil. Drain the artichokes, add them to the broth, and return to a boil. Reduce the heat to low and simmer until tender when pierced with a knife, about 7 minutes.

Meanwhile, in a shallow bowl, combine the vinegar and a pinch of salt. Stir to dissolve. Add pepper to taste. Whisk in the oil until emulsified. Stir in the green onions.

Drain the artichokes, add them to the bowl, and toss to coat well. When cool, wrap each artichoke in a short strip of prosciutto and secure with a toothpick. Arrange on a platter or individual plates, and serve.

**Trimming
baby artichokes**

*Baby artichokes
require less trimming
than large ones. Add
the juice of 1 lemon
to a large bowl of
water. One at a time,
cut off the prickly
tops of each artichoke,
then snap off the
tough outer leaves.
Trim away the dark
green, fibrous layer
at the base. Drop
the artichoke into the
lemon water after
trimming.*

CHERRY TOMATOES FILLED WITH GOAT CHEESE

Red pepper roulades

For a different presentation, spread the filling on the inside of thick strips of roasted red bell peppers (capsicums) (see page 333). Roll into a cylinder, and refrigerate until firm, about 2 hours.

Come summertime, local farmers' markets are stocked with sweet cherry tomatoes, perfect for stuffing. Here, minced tarragon or chervil can be used in place of the basil, and halved plum (Roma) tomatoes (pulp removed) can replace the cherry tomatoes.

Cut the top off each cherry tomato. Using a small spoon, scoop out the pulp to make a hollow yet sturdy shell. Invert on a wire rack over a tray to drain off any excess juice.

In a bowl, combine the cheese and basil and mix with a fork until well blended. Season with salt and pepper.

Using the spoon, fill each tomato with about 1 teaspoon of the cheese mixture. Arrange the filled tomatoes on a large platter and serve right away.

24 cherry tomatoes, a mixture of red and yellow

¼ lb (125 g) fresh goat cheese

¼ cup (⅓ oz/10 g) minced fresh basil

Salt and ground pepper

MAKES 4 SERVINGS

MEDITERRANEAN VEGETABLE TERRINE

Baking dishes

Also known as casserole dishes, and typically made of glass, porcelain, or glazed earthenware, baking dishes are pretty enough to go straight from the oven to the table. They are available in a variety of shapes and sizes.

Think of this large, flat baked omelet as an elegant variation on the classic Provençal ratatouille. If serving the terrine as a first course, cut generous slices. For an hors d'oeuvre, cut the slices into bite-size cubes. This would also make a nice brunch dish.

In a nonstick frying pan over medium heat, warm the oil. Add the onion and cook, stirring, until beginning to color, about 3 minutes. Add the bell peppers and cook, stirring, for 5 minutes. Add the eggplant and cook, stirring, until the peppers and eggplant have softened, about 5 minutes longer. Add the zucchini, tomatoes, and thyme and season with salt and pepper. Stir well, cover, and cook, stirring occasionally, until all the vegetables are tender, about 30 minutes.

Preheat the oven to 350°F (180°C). Oil an 8-by-12-inch (20-by-30-cm) baking dish.

In a bowl, beat the eggs with a fork until blended, then season with salt and pepper.

When the vegetables are ready, stir in the garlic and basil and then the eggs. Mix thoroughly and remove from the heat. Pour the mixture into the prepared baking dish. Cover with aluminum foil and prick the foil all over with a knife.

Bake until set, about 45 minutes. Remove from the oven and let cool completely in the dish. Refrigerate for 6 hours before serving to blend the flavors.

Cut the terrine into slices or cubes (see note, above), and serve right away.

3 tablespoons olive oil

1 white onion, quartered and thinly sliced

1¼ lb (625 g) red and green bell peppers (capsicums), cut into small squares

1 eggplant (aubergine), about ¾ lb (375 g), diced

¾ lb (375 g) zucchini (courgettes), diced

½ lb (250 g) plum (Roma) tomatoes, peeled, seeded, and diced

1 teaspoon fresh thyme leaves

Salt and ground pepper

6 eggs

1 clove garlic, minced

2 tablespoons chopped fresh basil

MAKES 8 SERVINGS

ROASTED PEPPERS WITH ANCHOVIES AND OLIVES

This colorful dish pairs well with the grilled bread on page 65. If you like, garnish the roasted peppers with ¼ cup (2 oz/60 g) rinsed capers. The peppers can be roasted up to 3 days in advance, covered, and refrigerated. Bring to room temperature before continuing.

4 *each* large red and yellow bell peppers (capsicums), roasted and peeled (see page 333)

2 tablespoons extra-virgin olive oil

1 tablespoon balsamic vinegar

Salt and ground pepper

6 anchovy fillets

⅓ cup (2 oz/60 g) Kalamata or Niçoise olives

2 tablespoons minced fresh flat-leaf (Italian) parsley

1 clove garlic, chopped

MAKES 8 SERVINGS

Cut the peppers lengthwise into strips 1 inch (2.5 cm) wide. In a bowl, combine the pepper strips, oil, and vinegar and stir together. Season with salt and pepper. Set aside.

Place the anchovy fillets in a bowl, add cold water just to cover, and let soak for 10 minutes. Remove from the water and pat dry with paper towels.

Arrange the peppers on a platter with the anchovies and olives, or divide among individual plates. Combine the parsley and garlic on a cutting board and chop together finely. Sprinkle over the peppers and serve.

Anchovy fillets

Assertive and salty, tiny anchovies pack a wallop. They are generally filleted, cured, packed in oil, and sold in small cans. If you can find them in jars, they will cost more but offer better flavor and texture.

73

MUSHROOMS WITH GARLIC AND SAFFRON

In the fall and again in the spring, Spain's markets are flooded with wild mushrooms, which are commonly simmered with garlic and seasonings and served as tapas. Here, small cultivated mushrooms are used with excellent results, but use a wild variety if available in your market.

1 cup (8 fl oz/250 ml) *each* dry white wine and white wine vinegar

¼ cup (2 fl oz/60 ml) extra-virgin olive oil

12 cloves garlic, sliced

4 bay leaves

¼ teaspoon red pepper flakes

Large pinch of saffron

Salt and ground black pepper

2½ lb (1.25 kg) fresh small button mushrooms

1 tablespoon minced fresh flat-leaf (Italian) parsley

MAKES 6 SERVINGS

In a saucepan, combine the wine, vinegar, oil, garlic, bay leaves, red pepper flakes, saffron, 2 teaspoons salt, and 1 teaspoon black pepper. Place over high heat and bring to a boil. Reduce the heat to medium-low, cover, and simmer until the liquid thickens slightly and forms a flavorful stock, about 30 minutes. Pour through a fine-mesh sieve placed over a bowl, pressing against the solids with a wooden spoon to extract as much liquid as possible. Return the liquid to the saucepan. Discard the solids.

Add the mushrooms to the saucepan with enough water to almost cover them. Bring to a boil over high heat, reduce the heat to medium-low, and simmer, stirring occasionally, until the mushrooms are tender, about 3 minutes. Using a slotted spoon, transfer the mushrooms to a bowl. Boil the cooking liquid until reduced to ½ cup (4 fl oz/125 ml), 5–10 minutes. Pour the hot liquid over the mushrooms, mix well, and let cool completely. Cover and refrigerate overnight.

Bring the mushrooms and their liquid to room temperature and serve, garnished with the parsley.

Cleaning mushrooms

To clean mushrooms, lightly brush them with a damp kitchen towel or a mushroom brush. Do not rinse them with water, which can make them soggy and dilute their flavor.

SPANISH POTATO TORTILLA

Red pepper tortilla

For a more flavorful tortilla, add to the beaten eggs 2–4 oz (60–125 g) serrano ham, diced, and 1 red bell pepper (capsicum), roasted and peeled (see page 333), then cut into slivers.

Similar to an Italian frittata, the traditional Spanish tortilla *española* is mostly potato bound together with egg and cooked in a frying pan. One of the most popular items on any tapas menu, it is served at room temperature, cut into wedges.

In a large frying pan over low heat, warm the ½ cup oil. Add half of the potato slices and cook, turning occasionally, until tender but not browned, 15–20 minutes. Transfer to a plate and season with salt and pepper. Repeat with the remaining potato slices. Leave the oil in the pan.

Raise the heat to medium and add more oil if needed. Add the onions and cook, stirring occasionally and adding more oil to the pan if they begin to scorch, until soft and golden, about 15 minutes. Remove from the heat.

In a large bowl, whisk the eggs until blended. Stir in the onions and potatoes, and season with salt and pepper.

Warm the oil remaining in the pan over low heat. Pour in the egg mixture and let cook until the bottom is golden, 8–10 minutes. Invert the *tortilla* onto a plate, then slide it back into the pan, browned side up. Cook until the second side is set, about 4 minutes, then slide onto a serving plate.

Let cool to room temperature. Cut into wedges to serve.

½ cup (4 fl oz/125 ml) olive oil, plus more as needed

2 lb (1 kg) potatoes, peeled and sliced ¼ inch (6 mm) thick

Salt and ground pepper

2 yellow onions, thinly sliced

6 eggs

MAKES 6 SERVINGS

CRISP POTATOES WITH ALLIOLI

Patatas bravas

A spicy sauce turns these into "brave potatoes." In a frying pan over low heat, stir 1 tbsp olive oil with 1 tbsp flour and 1 tsp paprika for 3 minutes. Stir in 1 cup (8 fl oz/ 250 ml) beef broth, 2 tbsp red wine vinegar, and a pinch of red pepper flakes and simmer for 10 minutes. Add ¼ cup (2 fl oz/60 ml) tomato sauce and season with salt and pepper. Toss the potatoes in the sauce.

Allioli is the Catalan equivalent of Provençal aioli, or garlic mayonnaise. Drizzled over these hot, crisp potatoes, it melts into them, creating a rich, creamy sauce. The *allioli* is also delicious stirred into a puréed soup, used as a dip, or served with grilled fish.

Position a rack in the upper third of the oven and preheat to 375°F (190°C).

Halve the potatoes crosswise and place in a baking dish large enough to hold them in a single layer. Drizzle with the oil and sprinkle with salt and pepper. Toss to coat evenly. Bake until golden, tender, and crispy, 45–55 minutes.

Meanwhile, make the *allioli*. In a small bowl, combine the olive oil and corn oil. In another bowl, whisk together the egg yolk and 1 tablespoon of the combined oils until an emulsion forms. Drop by drop, add the remaining oil mixture to the egg emulsion, whisking constantly. Always make sure the emulsion is set before adding more oil. Whisk in the garlic and vinegar and season with salt and pepper. Whisking constantly, add 1–2 tablespoons warm water, or as needed to create a smooth, thick consistency.

Transfer the potatoes to a serving platter and pour half of the *allioli* over the top. (Cover and refrigerate the remaining *allioli* and reserve for another use.) Serve right away.

3 lb (1.5 kg) small red potatoes, unpeeled

1 tablespoon olive oil

Salt and ground pepper

FOR THE ALLIOLI

½ cup (4 fl oz/125 ml) olive oil

½ cup (4 fl oz/125 ml) corn oil

1 egg yolk

4 cloves garlic, minced

2 tablespoons white wine vinegar

Coarse sea salt and ground pepper

MAKES 6 SERVINGS

NEW POTATOES WITH TAPENADE

The mild, earthy flavor of boiled potatoes is an ideal backdrop for tapenade, the popular Provençal spread of black olives and anchovies. It is also good on crusty bread or toast, or served as a condiment with cold roasted meats or poultry.

2 lb (1 kg) new potatoes

Fine sea salt

Tapenade (page 388)

MAKES 8 SERVINGS

Place the potatoes in a small, deep, heavy saucepan with a tight-fitting lid. Add ⅔ cup (5 fl oz/160 ml) water and 1 teaspoon salt, cover the pan, and place over medium heat. Cook for 20 minutes without touching the pan. At this point, the potatoes should be cooked and all the water evaporated. To test for doneness, insert the tip of a knife into the center of a potato; it should slide in easily but the potato should not fall apart. Let cool to room temperature.

When ready to serve, cut the potatoes into thin slices and spread each slice with some of the tapenade. Arrange the topped potatoes on a platter and serve.

New potatoes

Freshly harvested immature potatoes, usually round and with white or red skin, are known as new potatoes. But not all small potatoes should be called new. True young, new potatoes are usually in markets in late spring and early summer, and have paper-thin skin and a short shelf life.

HOMEMADE POTATO CHIPS

Paper-thin and a rich golden brown, these homemade chips will spoil you for their store-bought cousins. Whether you use ivory-fleshed russets or yellow-fleshed Yukon golds, the chips will boast a full potato flavor, while frying them twice ensures extra crispness.

2 lb (1 kg) large russet or Yukon gold potatoes

Corn or peanut oil for deep-frying

Kosher or fine sea salt for sprinkling

MAKES 4–6 SERVINGS

Using a mandoline or a food processor fitted with the slicing blade, slice the unpeeled potatoes into thin rounds. Transfer to a bowl of water to prevent discoloring.

In a wok or a deep, heavy frying pan, pour oil to a depth of 2 inches (5 cm) and heat to 325°F (165°C) on a deep-frying thermometer. Spread paper towels in 4 large rimmed baking sheets. Place a colander on a paper towel–lined tray. Have ready a sieve for adding the potatoes to the hot oil, and a wire skimmer for retrieving them.

Drain the potatoes and blot them well to prevent splattering. Working in batches to avoid crowding, transfer the potatoes to the sieve and very carefully slide them into the hot oil. Fry, turning occasionally, until they start to crisp around the edges and are just beginning to turn golden, about 3 minutes. Using the skimmer, carefully transfer the fried potatoes to the colander, then turn them out onto a prepared baking sheet. Repeat with the remaining potatoes. Let stand for at least 15 minutes or up to 6 hours.

Line the baking sheets with a layer of fresh paper towels, bring the oil back to temperature, and repeat the process, frying all the potatoes a second time until crisp and medium brown, 1–2 minutes.

Sprinkle with salt and serve warm or at room temperature.

A more elegant chip

To dress up these basic potato chips, sprinkle them with truffle salt, smoked paprika, ground pepper, or any other seasoning you like.

DEEP-FRIED STUFFED CHILES

Pepper roasting

In addition to the basic method of roasting and peeling peppers described on page 333, they can be blackened over a hot charcoal grill or in hot oil, as described here. Each process results in a slightly different flavor.

Stuffed with cream cheese, dredged in flour, egg, and Parmesan, and lightly fried, these chiles are a delectable treat. Although jalapeño and wax chiles are normally quite fiery, these are soaked for 24 hours to temper their heat without diminishing their flavor.

The day before serving, heat the oil in a small frying pan over high heat until very hot. Have ready a large bowl filled with cold water. Add the chiles, a few at a time, to the hot oil and fry until well blistered, about 3 seconds on each side. Using a slotted spoon, transfer the chiles to the water. Let the cooking oil cool, then reserve in a covered container overnight.

With the chiles still in the water, peel off the skins, using a knife if necessary. Make a lengthwise slit in each chile. Carefully remove and discard the seeds and ribs, leaving the stem intact. Discard the water.

In a bowl, stir together 1 cup (8 fl oz/250 ml) water, the vinegar, and ½ teaspoon salt. Add the chiles, cover, and let soak at room temperature for about 24 hours.

The next day, drain the chiles, rinse under cold running water, and pat dry. Carefully stuff each chile with an equal amount of the cream cheese. Place the flour, egg, and Parmesan cheese in separate small, shallow bowls. Dip each stuffed chile in the flour, then in the egg, and finally in the Parmesan, coating evenly each time.

In a small frying pan over medium heat, warm the reserved oil. When the oil is hot, add the chiles, a few at a time, and fry until lightly golden, about 2 minutes on each side. Using a slotted spoon or tongs, transfer to paper towels to drain.

Serve warm with salsa on the side.

2 cups (16 fl oz/500 ml) corn or other vegetable oil

12 jalapeño chiles

½ cup (4 fl oz/125 ml) distilled white vinegar

Salt

3 oz (90 g) cream cheese

⅓ cup (2 oz/60 g) all-purpose (plain) flour

1 egg, lightly beaten

½ cup (2 oz/60 g) grated Parmesan cheese

Fresh Tomato Salsa (page 393)

MAKES 12 STUFFED CHILES; 4 SERVINGS

CRISP POLENTA STICKS

Buying polenta

For the best flavor and texture, choose imported Italian polenta or domestic stone-ground cornmeal in a fine grind. Stone-ground cornmeal has more fiber and nutrients than the more commonly available degerminated grain.

One of the best things about polenta is its versatility. Here, finger-size sticks of polenta are coated with flour and fried until crisp and golden. A delicious alternative to French fries, serve these with Creamy Tomato-Pepper Dip (page 68).

Butter a 9-by-5-inch (23-by-13-cm) loaf pan. In a saucepan over high heat, bring 3 cups (24 fl oz/750 ml) water to a boil. Add ½ teaspoon salt, reduce the heat to medium, and slowly add the polenta, whisking constantly. Continue to whisk until the mixture thickens, about 2 minutes. Then continue to simmer, stirring occasionally with a wooden spoon, until the polenta pulls away from the sides of the pan and the spoon stands upright, unaided, 20–25 minutes. Add the cheese, butter, and rosemary and stir to mix well. Remove from the heat, season with salt and pepper, and pour into the prepared pan. Smooth the top with a rubber spatula, cover, and refrigerate until set, about 2 hours.

Coarse sea salt and ground pepper

½ cup (3 oz/90 g) plus 2 tablespoons polenta

3 tablespoons grated Parmesan cheese

1 tablespoon unsalted butter, at room temperature

1 teaspoon chopped fresh rosemary

1½ cups (7½ oz/235 g) all-purpose (plain) flour

Olive oil and canola oil for deep-frying

MAKES 6–8 SERVINGS

Run a knife around the edges of the polenta to loosen it from the pan sides. Invert the pan to unmold the polenta. Cut into slices ½ inch (12 mm) thick. Cut the slices into sticks 3 inches (7.5 cm) long by ½ inch (12 mm) wide. You should have about 30 sticks.

Preheat the oven to 200°F (95°C). Line a rimmed baking sheet with paper towels. Place the flour in a bowl. Pour equal parts olive oil and canola oil to a depth of 1 inch (2.5 cm) into a large, deep frying pan or a wide saucepan and heat to 375°F (190°C) on a deep-frying thermometer.

Working in batches, lightly dust the polenta sticks with flour and add to the hot oil. Fry, turning as needed to cook evenly, until the sticks are golden on all sides, 1–2 minutes. Using a slotted spoon or tongs, transfer to the prepared baking sheet. Sprinkle with salt and keep warm in the oven until all the sticks are cooked, then serve right away.

Oil for frying

Olive oil imparts a distinctive flavor to foods cooked in it, but it has a relatively low smoke point. This recipe bolsters the olive oil with canola oil, which can be heated to higher temperatures before it starts to smoke.

FRIED OYSTERS

This dish is at its best when the oysters are shucked just before cooking, so they are as moist as possible. For the best results, buy them in the shell and shuck them yourself (see page 203). Set out a bowl of Tartar Sauce (page 386) for topping the oysters.

24 oysters, freshly shucked (see note, above)

Peanut or canola oil for deep-frying

3 eggs

3 tablespoons heavy (double) cream or milk

About 1 cup (5 oz/155 g) all-purpose (plain) flour

Salt and ground pepper

1 cup (4 oz/125 g) fine cracker crumbs, or as needed

MAKES 4–6 SERVINGS

Line a baking sheet with parchment (baking) or waxed paper. Pour oil to a depth of 2 inches (5 cm) into a large, heavy sauté pan or cast iron frying pan and heat to 375°F (190°C) on a deep-frying thermometer. Preheat the oven to 200°F (95°C).

Meanwhile, in a small bowl, whisk together the eggs and cream. Spread the flour on a plate and season lightly with salt and pepper. Spread the cracker crumbs on another plate. Dip each oyster in the flour, then in the egg mixture, and finally in the cracker crumbs, coating evenly each time. Set aside on the prepared baking sheet until all are ready to fry.

Working in batches to avoid crowding, slip the oysters into the hot oil and fry until golden, 1–2 minutes. Using a slotted spoon or wire skimmer, carefully transfer to paper towels to drain briefly. Sprinkle with salt and keep warm in the oven until all the oysters are cooked.

Arrange the fried oysters on a warmed platter or individual plates and serve right away.

Pour a cava

The toasty crunch and the sprinkle of salt on these delectable oysters make them well suited to sparkling wine, which doesn't have to be complex or expensive. A dry Spanish cava will complement the deep-fried flavor of the shellfish as well as the creaminess of the tartar sauce.

SEAFOOD TEMPURA

Made with only water, egg yolk, and flour, lacy tempura batter coats fresh scallops and shrimp in this crisp and surprisingly light classic Japanese preparation. Accompany the tempura with lemon wedges for spritzing the seafood and soy sauce for drizzling or dipping.

Make shallow parallel cuts along the inside curve of each shrimp so they won't curl during cooking. Slice each scallop in half horizontally to form 2 rounds. Set the shellfish aside.

Pour ¾ cup (6 fl oz/180 ml) very cold water into a bowl. Add the egg yolk and whisk with a fork. Quickly whisk in the flour and a pinch of salt. Be careful not to overbeat the batter. A few small lumps are fine.

Pour oil to a depth of at least 2 inches (5 cm) into a deep, heavy saucepan and heat to 350°F (180°C) on a deep-frying thermometer. Spread flour for dusting in a shallow bowl. When the oil is ready, working in batches to avoid crowding, lightly flour the shrimp and scallops, dip them into the batter, and then carefully slip them into the oil. Cook, turning once, until lightly golden, 2 minutes total for the scallops and 3 minutes total for the shrimp. Using a wire skimmer, transfer to paper towels to drain briefly, then keep warm until all the seafood is cooked.

Arrange the fried shrimp and scallops on a warmed platter and serve right away.

12 large shrimp (prawns), peeled and deveined (see page 202)

12 sea scallops

1 egg yolk

¾ cup (4 oz/125 g) all-purpose (plain) flour, plus more for dusting

Salt

Peanut or canola oil for deep-frying

MAKES 6–8 SERVINGS

Vegetable tempura

If you like, substitute vegetables for some of the shellfish, or double the batter and do a combination of the two. Try snow peas (mangetouts), broccoli florets, or wide, thin slices of carrot, cut on the diagonal.

QUICK POT STICKERS

Store-bought wrappers simplify making pot stickers at home. Look for round wrappers labeled either for pot stickers or for *gyoza,* the Japanese equivalent of these dumplings. Uncooked pot stickers can be frozen for up to 1 month; do not thaw before cooking.

To make the filling, in a bowl, combine the shrimp, pork, green onions, cabbage, garlic, ginger, soy sauce, sherry, and a pinch of pepper. Mix well.

For each pot sticker, transfer a wrapper to a work surface. Put 1 rounded teaspoon filling in the center. Fold the wrapper in half and press together firmly to form a fully sealed edge ½ inch (12 mm) wide. Using your thumb and forefinger, form 3 evenly spaced pleats along the edge. Flatten the bottom slightly so the pot sticker stands upright, then place the pot sticker, seam side up, on a floured baking sheet and cover with a lightly dampened kitchen towel. Repeat until all of the filling has been used.

Preheat the oven to 200°F (95°C). In a wok or frying pan over medium-high heat, warm 1 tablespoon of the oil. When hot, arrange 12 pot stickers in the pan, seam side up. Fry uncovered for about 5 minutes. As the pot stickers in the center brown, move them to the edges and move the less browned ones

½ lb (250 g) shrimp (prawns), peeled and deveined (see page 202), finely chopped

½ lb (250 g) ground (minced) pork or turkey

2 green (spring) onions, including tender green tops, finely chopped

1 cup (3 oz/90 g) finely chopped napa cabbage

2 cloves garlic, minced

1 teaspoon finely chopped fresh ginger

2 tablespoons soy sauce

1 tablespoon dry sherry

Soy dipping sauce

In a bowl, combine ½ cup (4 fl oz/125 ml) soy sauce, 5 tbsp (2½ fl oz/75 ml) rice vinegar, 2 tsp minced fresh ginger, and 2 tsp Asian sesame oil and mix well.

Ground pepper

**1 package (10 oz/315 g)
pot sticker wrappers
(48 wrappers)**

**4 tablespoons (2 fl oz/
60 ml) peanut or corn oil**

**1 cup (8 fl oz/250 ml)
chicken broth**

**MAKES ABOUT
48 POT STICKERS**

into the center, so all cook evenly. Add ¼ cup (2 fl oz/60 ml) of the broth, cover, reduce the heat to low, and cook for 10 minutes longer. Uncover and cook until all the liquid evaporates, 2–3 minutes longer.

Transfer the pot stickers to a heatproof platter and keep warm in the oven. Repeat with the remaining pot stickers, oil, and broth, then serve right away.

Dry sherry

Widely available Spanish sherry is often used in Chinese-style recipes to replace harder-to-find Chinese rice wine. Look for "fino" on the label to ensure a dry wine.

RICE PAPER ROLLS WITH CHINESE BROCCOLI

These refreshing vegetarian rolls make a great warm-weather hors d'oeuvre. Accompany with a bowl of Peanut Sauce (page 391) for dipping. If Chinese broccoli is not available in your market, you can substitute either broccoli rabe or broccoli florets.

**½ lb (250 g) dried rice
vermicelli noodles**

3 tablespoons peanut oil

1 clove garlic, minced

**½ teaspoon Asian
sesame oil**

**½ lb (250 g) Chinese
broccoli (see note, above),
trimmed and coarsely
chopped**

**1 carrot, peeled and
coarsely grated**

**½ cup (1 oz/30 g)
bean sprouts**

**24 rice paper rounds,
6 inches (15 cm) in diameter**

**Fresh mint and cilantro
(fresh coriander) leaves**

**Butter (Boston)
lettuce leaves**

**MAKES 24 ROLLS;
8 SERVINGS**

Soak the noodles in hot water to cover for 15 minutes. Drain the noodles and cut into 2-inch (5-cm) lengths. Set aside.

In a wok or large frying pan over medium heat, warm the peanut oil. Add the garlic and cook, stirring, until lightly golden, about 2 minutes. Add the sesame oil, broccoli, and carrot and toss and stir until softened, 4–5 minutes. Add the noodles and toss and stir until the noodles are hot, 2–3 minutes. Add the bean sprouts, toss to mix and soften, then remove from the heat and set aside to cool completely.

Fill a small bowl with water. Working with 1 rice paper round at a time, place the round on a work surface and brush with a little water. Let stand for a minute or two until pliable. Place a heaping tablespoon of the filling in the center, spreading it into a small rectangle. Top with a few mint and cilantro leaves. Fold the rice paper up over the short ends, then fold in one side and roll lengthwise into a tight cylinder. Repeat to fill and roll 24 pieces in all.

Line a platter with the lettuce leaves. Arrange the rolls, seam side down, on top and serve right away.

Rice paper rounds

The thin, round wrappers used for making wontons and pot stickers are made from wheat flour, and the dumplings must be cooked once they are shaped. Translucent rice paper wrappers, in contrast, are made from rice flour and don't require cooking, but they must be moistened with water before using to make them pliable.

79

FETA AND SPINACH PACKETS

Shape shifting

Filo packets can be fashioned into a variety of shapes. Cut the filo sheets crosswise, rather than lengthwise. Place the filling at one end of the rectangle and fold in the long sides, then roll into a cigar shape. Or, put the filling in the center, roll the filo lengthwise around it, then tie the long ends into a knot.

Common all over Greece, stuffed filo packets make a memorable meze. These *tiropites*—triangle-shaped packets—can be assembled up to 3 days in advance, covered, and refrigerated. Bake as directed just before serving. Pair the pastries with a glass of iced ouzo.

Heat a large frying pan over medium-high heat. Rinse the spinach thoroughly under cold water, add to the pan while wet, and cook until wilted, about 1 minute. Drain well on paper towels, then squeeze out as much of the remaining liquid as possible. Place in a large bowl and add the feta, kefalotiri, eggs, mint, and nutmeg. Stir well to combine. Season with salt and pepper.

Preheat the oven to 375°F (190°C). Lightly butter a rimmed baking sheet and set aside.

Cut the stack of filo sheets lengthwise into thirds, to create strips about 3 inches (7.5 cm) wide. Keep the filo covered with a sheet of plastic wrap topped with a lightly dampened kitchen towel to prevent it from drying out. Remove 1 strip from a stack, place it on a work surface, and brush lightly with melted butter. Place another strip on top and brush lightly with butter. Place a heaping teaspoon of the filling about 1 inch (2.5 cm) from the bottom of the buttered stacked strips. Fold the uncovered end over the filling on the diagonal to form a triangular shape. Bring the bottom of the triangle up against the straight edge. Continue folding in this manner until the top of the strip is reached, forming a triangular pastry. Place on the prepared baking sheet and brush lightly with butter. Repeat with the remaining filo strips and filling.

Bake until crisp and golden, about 15 minutes. Serve warm or at room temperature.

1½ lb (750 g) spinach, tough stems removed and coarsely chopped

1½ cups (7½ oz/235 g) crumbled feta cheese

½ cup (2 oz/60 g) grated kefalotiri, Parmesan, or pecorino cheese

4 eggs, lightly beaten

2 tablespoons chopped fresh mint

½ teaspoon freshly grated nutmeg

Salt and ground pepper

½ lb (250 g) filo sheets (20 sheets), thawed according to package instructions if frozen

½ cup (4 oz/125 g) unsalted butter, melted and cooled

MAKES 30 PASTRIES; 6 SERVINGS

CURRIED VEGETABLES IN FILO PACKETS

Curry powder

In the United States, curry powder can be found in most markets. But in South Asia, many home cooks roast and grind spices, and blend their own curry powders, varying the formula based on regional tradition as well as the type of dish they are planning to cook.

Curry powder gives the mixed vegetable filling for these crispy filo packets a distinctly sweet and spicy flavor and an intense color. For an attractive presentation, cut the packets in half on a slight diagonal and arrange on a platter to serve.

In a large nonstick frying pan, melt 1½ tablespoons of the butter over medium heat. Add the zucchini, carrot, shallots, mushrooms, and chives and sauté until the vegetables are golden, about 3 minutes. Add the curry powder, season with salt, and sauté for 2 minutes. Add 3 tablespoons water to the pan and then stir in the cabbage. Cover and cook over low heat, stirring often, until all the vegetables are tender, about 20 minutes.

While the vegetables are cooking, preheat the oven to 425°F (220°C). Melt the remaining 1½ tablespoons butter and let it cool. With a pastry brush, lightly brush a nonstick rimmed baking sheet with some of the melted butter.

3 tablespoons unsalted butter

1 zucchini (courgette), finely chopped

1 carrot, peeled and finely chopped

2 shallots, finely chopped

3 oz (90 g) fresh button mushrooms, finely chopped

2 tablespoons finely chopped fresh chives

2 teaspoons
curry powder

Salt

2½ cups (8 oz/250 g)
finely chopped tender
heart of green cabbage

Grated zest of ½ lemon

4 filo sheets, thawed
according to package
instructions if frozen

MAKES 16 PACKETS;
8 SERVINGS

When the vegetables are cooked, transfer them to a bowl and let them cool slightly. Stir in the lemon zest. Cut the stack of filo sheets into quarters. Keep the filo covered with a sheet of plastic wrap topped with a lightly dampened kitchen towel to prevent it from drying out. Place 1 quarter sheet on a work surface and brush the edges with a little of the melted butter, covering a border about 1½ inches (4 cm) wide. Place a large spoonful of the vegetable mixture in the center and spread it into a small rectangle. Fold the sides of the pastry inward, then fold in the top and bottom edges, forming a rectangle. Place the packet, seam side down, on the prepared baking sheet. Repeat with the remaining filo and filling.

Bake until crisp and golden, 12–15 minutes. Serve warm.

Curry types

Commercially made curry powder can typically be found in two basic types: standard and Madras. The latter tends to be a little spicier, so choose the type that best suits your taste.

GORGONZOLA, APPLE, AND PECAN FILO ROLLS

The rich combination of toasted nuts, creamy cheese, and crisp fruit encased in layers of buttered filo makes this an especially good appetizer for a holiday meal. If you like, use walnuts in place of the pecans, Roquefort in place of the Gorgonzola, and pears in place of the apples.

Make it simple

This same cheese mixture can be used as a filling for filo triangles. Or, it can be layered between filo sheets in a baking pan, then scored into squares and baked until golden brown.

½ cup (4 oz/125 g) unsalted
butter, melted and cooled

1 cup (4 oz/125 g) peeled,
cored, and finely chopped
Golden Delicious or other
firm cooking apple

¼ lb (125 g) Gorgonzola
cheese, crumbled

2 tablespoons all-purpose
(plain) flour

12 filo sheets, thawed
according to package
instructions if frozen

1 cup (4 oz/125 g) pecans,
toasted (see page 17) and
finely chopped

Ground pepper

MAKES 24 PIECES;
8–12 SERVINGS

Preheat the oven to 350°F (180°C). With a pastry brush, lightly brush a nonstick rimmed baking sheet with a thin layer of the melted butter.

In a bowl, combine the apple, cheese, and flour and toss to mix well. Keep the filo covered with a sheet of plastic wrap topped with a lightly dampened kitchen towel to prevent it from drying out.

Lay a large sheet of waxed paper on a work surface. Place a filo sheet on top and brush with some of the melted butter. Top with a second filo sheet, brush with butter, and continue until you have a stack of 6 buttered sheets.

Sprinkle the buttered filo evenly with half of the pecans, then scatter half of the apple-cheese mixture over the nuts, distributing it as evenly as possible. Sprinkle with pepper. Starting from a long side, carefully roll up the filo layers as tightly as possible, and slide the roll onto the prepared baking sheet. Repeat with the remaining ingredients to make a second roll. Using a sharp, thin-bladed knife, cut about three-fourths of the way through the rolls at 1-inch (2.5-cm) intervals (this will make the rolls easier to cut and serve after they are baked).

Bake until golden, about 25 minutes. Let cool completely on the pan on a wire rack. Carefully slide the rolls onto a cutting board and finish cutting into pieces.

Arrange the pieces on a platter and serve.

81

SPICY POTATO FRITTERS

The batter for these simple fritters is flavored with garam masala, an Indian spice blend found in Indian markets and in the spice section of many supermarkets. You can also make your own: see the recipe at left. Serve the fritters with Green Chile–Cilantro Chutney (page 389).

In a bowl, combine the chickpea flour, broth, 1 tablespoon peanut oil, garam masala, turmeric, and baking powder. Stir until well mixed. Stir in the green onions, chile, and cilantro. The batter should be thick. Season with salt and pepper.

Preheat the oven to 250°F (120°C). Line a rimmed baking sheet with paper towels. Pour oil to a depth of 1 inch (2.5 cm) into a large, deep frying pan and heat to 350°F (180°C) on a deep-frying thermometer. Meanwhile, peel and thinly slice the sweet potato and the russet potato.

Working in batches to avoid crowding, dip the potato slices into the batter to coat evenly, allowing the excess to drip off, and then slip them into the hot oil. Fry, turning once, until golden brown on both sides, 3–5 minutes on each side. Using a slotted spoon, transfer to the prepared baking sheet and keep warm in the oven until all are cooked. Serve right away.

1 cup (5½ oz/170 g) chickpea (garbanzo bean) flour

1 cup (8 fl oz/250 ml) vegetable broth or water

1 tablespoon peanut oil, plus oil for frying

1 tablespoon garam masala

½ teaspoon *each* ground turmeric and baking powder

2 green (spring) onions, including tender green tops, minced

1 serrano chile, minced

2 tablespoons minced fresh cilantro (fresh coriander)

Salt and ground pepper

1 *each* sweet potato and russet potato

MAKES 8 SERVINGS

Homemade garam masala

In a dry frying pan over medium heat, combine 1 cinnamon stick, 4 whole cloves, seeds from 5 cardamom pods, and 1 tbsp each cumin seeds, coriander seeds, and peppercorns. Toast, shaking occasionally, until fragrant and slightly darkened, about 5 minutes. Let cool, then grind in a spice mill to a fine powder. Store in a tightly sealed jar in a cool cupboard for up to 6 months.

82

GREEN OLIVE AND MANCHEGO PUFFS

Chorizo is combined with green olives and Manchego cheese in these bold fritters. The batter, minus the egg whites, can be prepared 1 day in advance, covered, and refrigerated. Bring to room temperature 30 minutes before serving, whip the whites, and proceed with the recipe.

Sift the flour into a bowl. Add the red pepper flakes and stir well. Make a well in the center. Separate the eggs, placing the yolks in a small bowl and the whites in a medium bowl. Beat the yolks with a fork just until blended and pour into the well in the flour. Add the beer, olive oil, ½ teaspoon salt, and a pinch of black pepper. Using a spoon, mix just until thoroughly combined. Do not overmix or the batter will get stringy. Cover and let stand at room temperature for 1 hour.

Preheat the oven to 200°F (95°C). Line a rimmed baking sheet with paper towels. Pour peanut oil to a depth of 2 inches (5 cm) into a deep, heavy frying pan and heat to 375°F (190°C) on a deep-frying thermometer.

1 cup (5 oz/155 g) all-purpose (plain) flour

¼ teaspoon red pepper flakes

3 eggs

¾ cup (6 fl oz/180 ml) beer, at room temperature

2 tablespoons olive oil

Salt and ground black pepper

Peanut or corn oil for deep-frying

Chorizo sausage

Spaniards use many different kinds of sausages in their cooking. The most popular variety, chorizo, is produced in many guises, according to how it will be used and regional tradition. The most common chorizo is made of chopped pork heavily spiced with cumin, garlic, and paprika, which gives the sausage its deep red color.

10 oz (315 g) chorizo
sausages, casings removed

½ cup (2 oz/60 g) grated
Manchego cheese

⅓ cup (2 oz/60 g) Spanish
brine-cured green olives,
pitted and chopped

3 tablespoons
chopped fresh flat-leaf
(Italian) parsley

**MAKES ABOUT 30 PUFFS;
6 SERVINGS**

While the oil is heating, place the chorizo in a frying pan over medium heat and break it up with a wooden spoon. Cook, stirring occasionally, until heated through, 3–4 minutes. At the same time, using an electric mixer, beat the egg whites on medium-high speed until stiff peaks form.

Fold the egg whites, chorizo, cheese, olives, and parsley into the batter. Working in batches to avoid crowding, drop the batter by heaping tablespoons into the hot oil. Fry, turning occasionally, until golden on all sides, 2–3 minutes. Using a slotted spoon, transfer to the prepared baking sheet and keep warm in the oven until all are cooked, then serve right away.

**Spanish-themed
tapas party**

*For a cocktail party,
pair these puffs with
the Spanish Potato
Tortilla (page 74)
and Red Pepper
Roulades (page 72),
and pour a Spanish
Albariño into small,
rustic tumblers.*

VEGETABLE SAMOSAS

Filled with lightly curried potatoes, peas, carrots, and onion, these Indian-style turnovers come together quickly if you use frozen puff pastry. If you prefer to make your own, see the recipe on page 450. Serve the samosas with Green Chile–Cilantro Chutney (page 389).

2 large russet potatoes,
peeled and cut into 2-inch
(5-cm) pieces

1 teaspoon curry powder

6 tablespoons (3 fl oz/
90 ml) canola oil

½ cup (2 oz/60 g)
chopped yellow onion

1 carrot, peeled and
coarsely grated

½ cup (2½ oz/75 g)
shelled peas

3 tablespoons minced fresh
cilantro (fresh coriander)

Salt and ground pepper

1 egg

1–1¼ lb (550–625 g) puff
pastry dough, thawed
if frozen

2 teaspoons caraway seeds

**MAKES ABOUT 24 SAMOSAS;
12 SERVINGS**

In a saucepan, combine the potato pieces with water to cover and bring to a boil over high heat. Cook until very tender, 20–25 minutes. Drain and transfer to a bowl. Using a fork, mash well, mixing in the curry powder and 3 tablespoons of the oil at the same time. Set aside.

In a sauté pan over medium heat, warm the remaining 3 tablespoons oil. Add the onion and sauté until softened, 3–4 minutes. Add the carrot and sauté until the carrot has softened, 3–4 minutes longer. Stir the onion and carrot into the potato mixture.

Bring a small saucepan three-fourths full of water to a boil, add the peas, and blanch for 1 minute. Drain and add to the potato mixture along with the cilantro. Mix well and season with salt and pepper. Set aside to cool.

Beat the egg with 1 tablespoon water to make an egg wash. On a work surface, roll out the puff pastry into a very thin sheet. Using a scalloped biscuit cutter 3 inches (7.5 cm) in diameter, cut out rounds. Place about 1 teaspoon of the potato mixture in the center of each round. Brush the edges of the rounds with the egg wash, fold in half, and press the edges together to seal.

Line a rimmed baking sheet with parchment (baking) paper, and place the filled pastries on it, spacing them about 2 inches apart. Brush the pastries with the remaining egg wash, and sprinkle the tops with the caraway seeds. Cover and chill for 30 minutes. While the pastries are chilling, preheat the oven to 400°F (200°C).

Bake until the samosas are golden brown and crisp, 15–18 minutes. Serve hot.

Make and freeze

*Prepare the samosas
as directed, but do
not bake. Spread on
a baking sheet and
freeze, then transfer
to zippered plastic
bags and store in
the freezer for up to
3 months. To bake,
transfer to a rimmed
baking sheet lined
with parchment
(baking) paper, brush
with the egg wash,
and sprinkle with
the caraway seeds.
Increase the baking
time by 3 minutes.*

83

CHICKEN AND HAM CROQUETTES

Serrano ham

Paper-thin slices of serrano ham, served alone or arranged in neat bundles alongside other foods, are another tapas bar mainstay. The ham is also used as an ingredient in dishes: paired with Manchego cheese atop grilled bread, wrapped around shrimp (prawns) and panfried, or used to flavor a simple vegetable stew.

This dish originated in a less prosperous time in Europe, when meat was a luxury. In Spain, as elsewhere, the leftovers from Sunday's dinner would find their way into Monday's dinner. Today, these fried morsels are on the menu of nearly every tapas bar in the country.

In a small, heavy saucepan over low heat, combine the 3 tablespoons oil and the flour. Cook, stirring constantly, until the flour has absorbed all the oil, 2–3 minutes. Add the milk and broth, little by little, stirring constantly and using a whisk to smooth out any lumps. When all of the liquid has been added, cook the sauce, stirring often, until smooth and thick, 10–15 minutes. Remove from the heat, stir in the chicken, ham, and nutmeg, and season with salt and pepper.

Pour the mixture into a baking pan and let cool to room temperature. Cover with plastic wrap and refrigerate overnight; the mixture will congeal into a thick paste.

Put the bread crumbs in a shallow bowl. In a second bowl, lightly beat the eggs. Using a spoon and your hands, form the chilled paste into short logs about 2 inches (5 cm) long and 1 inch (2.5 cm) in diameter. Roll them in the bread crumbs, then in the egg, and then again in the bread crumbs, making sure each croquette is thoroughly coated.

Preheat the oven to 200°F (95°C). Line a rimmed baking sheet with paper towels. Pour oil to a depth of 1 inch (2.5 cm) into a large, deep frying pan and heat to 375°F (190°C) on a deep-frying thermometer. Working in batches to avoid crowding, add the croquettes, a few at a time, and fry, turning once, until golden brown, about 3 minutes. Using a slotted spoon, transfer to the prepared baking sheet and keep warm in the oven until all are cooked, then serve right away.

3 tablespoons olive oil, plus more for deep-frying

3 tablespoons all-purpose (plain) flour

1½ cups (12 fl oz/ 375 ml) milk

1½ cups (12 fl oz/375 ml) chicken broth

⅓ cup (2 oz/60 g) finely chopped cooked chicken meat

⅓ cup (2 oz/60 g) finely chopped serrano or other salt-cured ham

Pinch of freshly grated nutmeg

Salt and ground pepper

1 cup (4 oz/125 g) fine dried bread crumbs

2 eggs

MAKES 4–5 SERVINGS

BITE-SIZE RICE CROQUETTES

Beyond hors d'oeuvres

These croquettes also make a tasty side dish. Serve with a wedge of frittata, slices of prosciutto, and a glass of dry red wine.

Crispy on the outside and creamy on the inside, these crisp rice croquettes laced with black olive paste are a specialty of northern Italy. You can make them up to 3 days in advance, store them, well covered, in the refrigerator, and then deep-fry them just before serving.

In a saucepan over medium heat, warm the olive oil. Add the onion and sauté until softened, about 5 minutes. Add the rice and sauté until the grains are evenly coated with the oil and translucent, about 2 minutes longer.

In a saucepan over medium heat, combine the broth and milk and bring just to a simmer. Add the broth mixture and half of the olive paste to the rice and season with salt and pepper. Bring to a simmer, reduce the heat to low, cover, and cook until all the liquid has been absorbed and the rice is tender, about 20 minutes. Stir in the remaining olive paste and the cheese. Remove from the heat and let cool completely.

2 tablespoons olive oil

½ small yellow onion, minced

1 cup (7 oz/220 g) Arborio rice

1¼ cups (10 fl oz/310 ml) chicken broth

1¼ cups (10 fl oz/ 310 ml) milk

⅔ cup (5 oz/155 g) black olive paste (see note, right)

Salt and ground pepper

¼ cup (1 oz/30 g) grated Parmesan cheese

1 cup (5 oz/155 g) all-purpose (plain) flour

4 eggs

4 cups (1 lb/500 g) fine dried bread crumbs

Canola oil and olive oil for deep-frying

MAKES 60 CROQUETTES; 12 SERVINGS

Using a scant tablespoon of the rice mixture for each croquette, form the mixture into balls about 1 inch (2.5 cm) in diameter. Place the flour in a shallow bowl. In another bowl, whisk together the eggs and ½ cup (4 fl oz/125 ml) water. Place the bread crumbs in a third shallow bowl. Roll the rice balls in the flour, then in the egg, and finally in the bread crumbs, coating evenly each time. As the balls are coated, place on a rimmed baking sheet.

Preheat the oven to 200°F (95°C). Line a rimmed baking sheet with paper towels and top with a wire rack. Pour equal parts canola oil and olive oil to a depth of 1 inch (2.5 cm) into a deep, heavy frying pan and heat to 375°F (190°C) on a deep-frying thermometer. Working in batches to avoid crowding, add the rice balls to the hot oil and fry, turning occasionally, until golden on all sides, 1–1½ minutes. Using a slotted spoon, transfer to the prepared baking sheet and keep warm in the oven until all are cooked, then serve right away.

Black olive paste

Olive paste is simply crushed olives, in this case, black olives, moistened with olive oil and sometimes seasoned with salt and herbs. It is sold in both tubes and jars. You may not need to add any salt to the rice mixture, depending on how salty your olive paste is.

SUPPLI WITH FONTINA AND PORCINI

Rice croquettes concealing molten cheese are a traditional Roman treat and a great way to use up leftover risotto. Here, a filling of creamy Fontina and flavorful porcini mushrooms is tucked into a cylinder of risotto, which is then rolled in bread crumbs and fried until lightly golden.

1 oz (30 g) dried porcini mushrooms, soaked in hot water to cover for 30 minutes

2 cups (16 fl oz/500 ml) hot water

2 cups (10 oz/315 g) Classic Risotto (page 307), at room temperature

2 eggs, lightly beaten

¾ cup (3 oz/90 g) fine dried bread crumbs

3 oz (90 g) Fontina or Gouda cheese, cut into 12 narrow strips

Canola oil for deep-frying

MAKES 12 CROQUETTES; 6 SERVINGS

Using a slotted spoon, remove the mushrooms from the soaking water. Chop the mushrooms and place in a small saucepan. Line a sieve with cheesecloth (muslin) and pour the soaking water through the sieve into the saucepan. Place over medium-high heat, bring to a boil, and boil until all the liquid evaporates, about 8 minutes. Set aside.

Place the cooked risotto in a bowl. Mix in the eggs. Place the bread crumbs on a plate. Scoop up about 3 tablespoons of the risotto mixture and drop it onto the bread crumbs. Make an indentation in the center of the risotto mound, and stuff 1 cheese strip and 1 teaspoon of the mushrooms into it. Gently mold the risotto around the filling, forming a cylinder. Roll in the bread crumbs to coat, and transfer to a sheet of waxed paper. Repeat to make 12 croquettes. Cover and refrigerate for at least 1 hour or up to 24 hours.

Preheat the oven to 250°F (120°C). Line a rimmed baking sheet with paper towels. Pour oil to a depth of 2 inches (5 cm) into a large, deep frying pan or a saucepan and heat until it reads 350°F (180°C) on a deep-frying thermometer. Working in batches to avoid crowding, add the croquettes to the hot oil and fry, turning occasionally, until golden brown on all sides, about 3 minutes. Using a slotted spoon, transfer to the prepared baking sheet and keep warm in the oven until all are cooked, then serve right away.

Risotto cakes

Mix together 2 cups (10 oz/315 g) Classic Risotto (page 307) and 1 egg, lightly beaten. In a frying pan over medium heat, melt 1 tbsp unsalted butter. Drop large spoonfuls of the mixture into the pan, press flat with a spatula, and fry until golden on both sides, adding more butter as needed to prevent sticking. Top with grated Parmesan cheese, cover, and cook for 1 minute longer. Serve hot.

BLINI WITH CAVIAR

Caspian caviar

Because of restrictions on the Caspian Sea sturgeon harvest, iconic beluga, osetra, and sevruga caviar are now either rarely available or of uneven quality. Happily, farmed caviar from Europe and America is so good you may not miss the traditional Caspian harvest.

These small, quickly prepared pancakes are the classic vehicle for caviar, but are also popular paired with smoked salmon. Whichever accompaniment you choose, place it atop a little crème fraîche or sour cream. If you like, garnish with a sprinkling of snipped fresh dill or chives.

In a food processor or blender, combine the flour, milk, eggs, and melted butter and process until well mixed. Pass the batter through a fine-mesh sieve into a bowl.

To cook the blini, in a large, nonstick frying pan over medium heat, melt 2 tablespoons butter. Using a small ladle, drop small amounts of the batter onto the pan, forming rounds about 2 inches (5 cm) in diameter. When bubbles form on the top and the edges look dry, after about 1 minute, use a spatula to turn the blini over. Continue cooking until the undersides are golden brown, about 1 minute more. Transfer the blini to a platter. Cook the remaining batter the same way, adding butter to the pan as needed.

Serve the blini warm or at room temperature, spread with a little crème fraîche and topped with caviar.

¾ cup (4 oz/125 g) all-purpose (plain) flour

1 cup (8 fl oz/250 ml) milk

2 eggs

4 tablespoons (2 oz/60 g) unsalted butter, melted and cooled, plus 2–3 tablespoons for cooking

Crème fraîche

About 4 oz (125 g) caviar (see note, left)

MAKES 48 BLINI; 10–12 SERVINGS

CORN CAKES WITH SMOKED SALMON

Getting ahead

The batter for the corn cakes can be prepared up to a few hours before cooking, covered, and refrigerated. Sauté the cakes right before serving time.

This dish is the perfect starter for a midsummer dinner or brunch party, when sweet corn is at the peak of its season. The dish can also be served as an hors d'oeuvre, passed hot on trays at a cocktail party. In the latter case, cut the salmon into small pieces for easier eating.

Place the corn kernels in a food processor. Using on-off pulses, process just until a coarse purée forms. Transfer to a bowl and whisk in the cornmeal and flour until smooth.

In another bowl, whisk together the milk, melted butter, and eggs until blended. Add to the corn mixture and mix lightly. Stir in ½ teaspoon salt and ¼ teaspoon pepper.

Preheat the oven to 200°F (95°C).

Warm a large nonstick frying pan over medium heat. When hot, brush with the oil. Using about 2 tablespoons batter for each cake, ladle the batter onto the hot surface and spread to form cakes about 3 inches (7.5 cm) in diameter. The batter should sizzle when it hits the pan. Cook until golden on the first side, about 3 minutes. Turn and cook until the second side is golden and the center is set, about 2 minutes longer. Transfer to a plate and keep warm in the oven. Repeat to cook the remaining batter.

To serve, place 2 corn cakes on each of 4 warmed individual plates. Top each with 2 slices of smoked salmon, a dollop of crème fraiche, and a sprinkling of chives. Serve right away.

1¾ cups (10 oz/325 g) fresh corn kernels (from about 2 ears)

⅓ cup (2 oz/60 g) *each* fine yellow cornmeal and all-purpose (plain) flour

½ cup (4 fl oz/125 ml) milk

¼ cup (2 oz/60 g) unsalted butter, melted

2 eggs

Salt and ground pepper

¼ cup (2 oz/60 ml) canola oil

16 small slices smoked salmon

1 cup (8 fl oz/250 ml) crème fraîche

¼ cup (⅓ oz/10 g) snipped fresh chives

MAKES 4 SERVINGS

CHICKEN SOUVLAKI

This grilled chicken is terrific eaten straight from the skewer or stuffed into pita with Tzatziki (page 68). A broiler (grill) can be used, but you will be giving up the wonderful smoky charcoal flavor. Garnish with parsley leaves, if desired, and lemon wedges for squeezing.

Go fish

This recipe can also be made with 1 lb (500 g) firm-fleshed fish fillets such as tuna or swordfish, cut into 1-inch (2.5-cm) chunks.

3 tablespoons olive oil

2 tablespoons dry white wine

1 tablespoon fresh lemon juice

¼ cup (1½ oz/45 g) minced yellow onion

1 clove garlic, minced

2 bay leaves, chopped

1 teaspoon dried oregano

Salt and ground pepper

1 lb (500 g) skinless, boneless chicken, cut into 1-inch (2.5-cm) pieces

MAKES 6 SERVINGS

In a bowl, stir together the oil, wine, lemon juice, onion, garlic, bay leaves, oregano, a big pinch of salt, and several grinds of pepper. Add the chicken pieces and turn to coat evenly. Cover and marinate in the refrigerator for at least 1 hour or up to overnight.

Prepare a charcoal or gas grill for direct-heat cooking over medium heat (see page 18).

At the same time, soak 6 bamboo skewers in water to cover.

Remove the chicken pieces from the marinade, discarding the marinade. Drain the skewers and thread the chicken pieces onto them, dividing the pieces evenly among them. Place on the grill rack 4–5 inches (10–13 cm) from the fire and grill, turning once, until the chicken is opaque throughout, 3–4 minutes on each side. Season with salt and pepper.

Transfer to a warmed platter and serve right away.

CHICKEN SATAY

Satay can be made with either chicken thigh pieces, as here, or with strips of boneless pork loin. Serve the satay with Peanut Sauce (page 391) for dipping, and accompany with thinly sliced cucumber and red onion, tossed in rice vinegar sweetened with a pinch of sugar.

Coconut cream

This recipe calls for coconut cream, the rich layer of fat that rises to the top of canned coconut milk. Do not shake the can before opening. Spoon off the layer of cream to use in the marinade. The remaining milk can then be stirred and reserved for another use, such as the accompanying peanut sauce.

2 *each* shallots and garlic cloves, halved

1 red serrano chile, halved

2 tablespoons finely chopped lemongrass, center white part only

1 tablespoon ground coriander

2 teaspoons sugar

1 teaspoon ground cumin

Salt

2 tablespoons unsweetened coconut cream (see note, right)

8 boneless, skinless chicken thighs, about 1½ lb (750 g) total weight, cut into 1-inch (2.5-cm) pieces

MAKES 6 SERVINGS

In a blender, combine the shallots, garlic, chile, and lemongrass. Process until finely chopped. Add the coriander, sugar, cumin, 1 teaspoon salt, and about 2 tablespoons water, or just enough to facilitate blending. Process until a smooth paste forms. Pour into a bowl, add the coconut cream, and mix thoroughly. Add the chicken, turn to coat evenly, cover, and refrigerate for at least 4 hours or up to overnight.

Prepare a charcoal or gas grill for direct-heat cooking over medium heat (see page 18).

At the same time, soak 6 bamboo skewers in water to cover.

Remove the chicken pieces from the marinade and discard the marinade. Drain the skewers and thread the chicken pieces onto them, dividing the pieces evenly among them. Place on the grill rack about 2 inches (5 cm) from the fire and grill, turning once, until the chicken is opaque throughout and has charred edges, 8–10 minutes. Serve right away.

SPICY KEBABS WITH MOORISH FLAVORS

Make it a meal

These flavorful pork kebabs are hearty enough to serve as a main course for 3 or 4 people. After grilling, remove the meat from the skewers and pair it with grilled vegetables and saffron rice.

The Moors invaded Spain in the eighth century and remained for half a century. Of Berber and Arab descent, they left their influence on every aspect of Spanish life, including the kitchen. This recipe shows their legacy in its heavy use of spices. Lamb can be substituted for the pork.

In a mortar, combine the garlic with ¼ teaspoon salt. Mash together with a pestle to form a paste. In a small, dry frying pan over high heat, combine the coriander seeds, paprika, cumin seeds, thyme, and red pepper flakes. Heat, shaking the pan occasionally, until hot and fragrant, about 30 seconds. Transfer to a spice grinder and grind to a fine powder.

In a bowl, stir together the garlic paste, ground spices, ¾ teaspoon salt, several grinds of black pepper, oil, lemon juice, and parsley. Add the pork cubes and turn to coat well. Cover and let stand at cool room temperature for 1 hour, stirring occasionally.

Prepare a charcoal or gas grill for direct-heat cooking over medium heat (see page 18). Meanwhile, soak 12 bamboo skewers in water to cover.

Remove the pork cubes from the marinade, reserving the marinade, and drain the skewers. Thread the pork cubes onto the skewers, dividing them evenly among them. In a small saucepan, bring the reserved marinade to a boil over high heat and boil for about 3 minutes. Remove from the heat.

Place the kebabs on the grill rack 4–5 inches (10–13 cm) from the fire and grill, basting occasionally with the reserved marinade and turning every 2–3 minutes, until nicely browned on both sides but still juicy, 10–15 minutes.

Transfer to a warmed platter and garnish with the lemon wedges. Serve right away.

2 cloves garlic, thinly sliced

Salt and ground black pepper

1 teaspoon coriander seeds

1 teaspoon paprika

¾ teaspoon cumin seeds

½ teaspoon dried thyme

¼ teaspoon red pepper flakes

3 tablespoons olive oil

1 tablespoon fresh lemon juice

1 tablespoon chopped fresh flat-leaf (Italian) parsley

1 lb (500 g) lean pork, cut into ¾–1-inch (2–2.5-cm) cubes

6 lemon wedges

MAKES 6 SERVINGS

FIVE-SPICE PORK MEATBALLS

Five-spice powder

Used primarily in Vietnamese and southern Chinese cooking, five-spice powder often includes more than five spices. Most blends begin with star anise, cloves, Sichuan peppercorns, and either ginger or cardamom.

Five-spice powder and chopped peanuts, mint, and cilantro impart an exotic flavor to these pork meatballs. The recipe also works well with lamb or beef. For a simple dipping sauce, mix soy sauce with a squeeze of lemon, or try the soy dipping sauce on page 78.

In a food processor, combine the pork, peanuts, mint, cilantro, egg whites, five-spice powder, and a pinch of salt. Process to a medium-fine texture.

To shape the meatballs, dampen your hands with water, scoop up about 1 tablespoon of the pork mixture, and roll between your palms into a ball.

In a large nonstick frying pan over medium heat, warm 2 tablespoons of the oil. Add half of the meatballs to the pan. Cook, occasionally moving the pan in a smooth, circular motion so the balls cook on all sides without breaking, until

1¼ lb (625 g) boneless pork loin, cut into ¾-inch (2-cm) dice

½ cup (3 oz/90 g) raw peanuts

Leaves from 6 fresh mint sprigs, chopped

Leaves from 6 fresh cilantro (fresh coriander) sprigs, chopped

2 egg whites

2 teaspoons
five-spice powder

Salt

4 tablespoons (2 fl oz/
60 ml) peanut or canola oil

MAKES 6–8 SERVINGS

golden brown, about 10 minutes. Transfer the meatballs
to a serving platter. Add the remaining 2 tablespoons oil to
the pan, cook the remaining meatballs in the same manner,
and transfer to the platter.

Serve hot, warm, or at room temperature.

Asian tacos

*These meatballs
are also delicious
wrapped in crisp
lettuce leaves with
additional herb
sprigs and eaten
like a taco.*

MINIATURE MEATBALLS IN TOMATO SAUCE

Called *albóndigas* all over Spain, these tiny meatballs are among the most common tapas
served both at bars and in homes. They are also added to soups or formed into larger balls
and served as a main course. Beef or lamb can be used in place of the pork or veal.

¾ lb (375 g) ground
(minced) pork

¾ lb (375 g) ground
(minced) veal

1 cup (4 oz/125 g) fine
dried bread crumbs

4 cloves garlic, minced

2 tablespoons
chopped fresh flat-leaf
(Italian) parsley

1½ teaspoons
ground coriander

½ teaspoon ground cumin

Pinch of cayenne pepper

Salt and ground
black pepper

FOR THE SAUCE

3 tablespoons olive oil

1 yellow onion, minced

2 cloves garlic, minced

3 cups (18 oz/560 g) peeled,
seeded, and chopped
tomatoes (fresh or canned)

1 cup (8 fl oz/250 ml)
dry white wine

Salt and ground pepper

MAKES 6 SERVINGS

Preheat the oven to 350°F (180°C). To make the meatballs, in
a bowl, combine the pork, veal, bread crumbs, garlic, parsley,
coriander, cumin, cayenne, ¾ teaspoon salt, and ½ teaspoon
black pepper. Mix well.

To shape the meatballs, dampen your hands with water and
roll the mixture between your palms, forming about 30 balls,
each about 1 inch (2.5 cm) in diameter. As the balls are formed,
place them on an ungreased baking sheet.

Bake until almost firm to the touch, 10–12 minutes. Remove
from the oven and set aside.

While the meatballs are baking, begin making the sauce.
In a frying pan over medium heat, warm the oil. Add the
onion and garlic and cook, stirring occasionally, until soft,
5–7 minutes. Add the tomatoes and wine and simmer slowly
until thickened, about 15 minutes.

Add the meatballs and ½ teaspoon each salt and black pepper
and continue to simmer slowly until the sauce thickens and
the meatballs are cooked through, about 10 minutes.

Transfer the meatballs and sauce to a bowl and serve hot,
warm, or at room temperature.

**Tapas bar
customs**

*In tapas bars in
Spain, these plump,
flavorful meatballs
are usually served
in a cazuelita (small
terra-cotta dish), and
customers pair them
with a glass of fino
sherry. A piece of
crusty bread is handy
for soaking up the
extra sauce.*

89

BEEF MEATBALLS WITH PARMESAN

Uniform meatballs

To ensure your meatballs are all the same size, use an ice cream scoop to scoop the meat mixture, releasing the scoops onto a rimmed baking sheet lined with parchment (baking) or waxed paper. Then dampen your hands with water and roll each scoop between your palms to form it into a round ball.

One of the reasons why Italian meatballs are generally so flavorful is the addition of Parmesan cheese to the mix. You can serve these beef meatballs with cocktail picks for spearing, or thread them onto tiny skewers. Accompany with Creamy Tomato-Pepper Dip (page 68).

Put the beef into a bowl and season with a little salt and plenty of pepper. Add the nutmeg, cheese, and parsley and knead the ingredients together with your hands until thoroughly mixed.

To shape the meatballs, dampen your hands with water, scoop up a walnut-size nugget of the mixture, and roll between your palms into a ball.

In a large, nonstick frying pan over medium heat, warm 2 tablespoons of the oil. Add half of the meatballs to the pan. Cook, occasionally moving the pan in a smooth, circular motion so that the balls cook on all sides without breaking, until golden brown, about 5 minutes. Transfer the meatballs to a serving platter. Add the remaining 2 tablespoons oil to the pan, cook the remaining meatballs in the same manner, and transfer to the platter.

Serve hot, warm, or at room temperature.

1½ lb (750 g) lean ground (minced) beef

Salt and ground pepper

4 pinches of freshly grated nutmeg

½ cup (2 oz/60 g) grated Parmesan cheese

¼ cup (⅓ oz/10 g) finely chopped fresh flat-leaf (Italian) parsley

4 tablespoons (2 fl oz/ 60 ml) extra-virgin olive oil

MAKES 6–8 SERVINGS

CARPACCIO

Carpaccio as a salad course

Divide the beef slices among 6 plates, and drizzle with extra-virgin olive oil. Toss 6–8 oz (185–250 g) arugula (rocket) and 3 apples or pears, cored and thinly sliced, in a dressing of olive oil whisked with a squeeze of lemon juice and salt and pepper to taste. Mound on top of the beef slices.

Raw top-of-the-line beef is sliced to near-translucent thinness for this dish, which originated at Harry's Bar in Venice, Italy, and is said to have been named for the fifteenth-century painter Vittore Carpaccio. If you like, add a little anchovy paste to the sauce.

Place the meat in a zippered plastic bag and place the bag in the freezer for 1 hour. (Partially freezing the meat will make it easier to cut it into thin slices.)

Meanwhile, prepare the sauce. In a blender or food processor, combine the egg yolk and mustard and process briefly to blend. Add a pinch of salt and let rest for 1 minute. With the motor running, slowly pour the oil into the yolk mixture in a thin, steady stream. The mixture will be quite thick. Add the cream, Worcestershire sauce, and brandy and process just until combined. Transfer to a bowl, cover, and refrigerate.

Remove the plastic bag from the freezer. Remove the meat from the bag and place it on a cutting board. Cut the bag along the bottom and one side and open it flat on the board. Snip off the string on the meat, then cut the meat into slices ⅛ inch (3 mm) thick. Place the slices in pairs, side-by-side, on half of the plastic bag, then fold the other half of the bag over the meat. Using a rolling pin, gently roll over the meat to flatten the slices. They will quickly become translucent.

Arrange the slices on a platter and drizzle the sauce over them in a zigzag pattern. Serve at room temperature.

1¼ lb (625 g) beef sirloin fillet, about 2½ inches (6 cm) thick, trimmed of all fat, rolled, and tied

FOR THE SAUCE

1 egg yolk

2 teaspoons Dijon mustard

Salt

¾ cup (6 fl oz/180 ml) peanut oil or canola oil

2 tablespoons heavy (double) cream

1 tablespoon Worcestershire sauce

1 teaspoon Cognac or other brandy

MAKES 6 SERVINGS

TUNA TARTARE

The quality of the fish you use is never more important than when you are serving it raw, as in this dish. Buy sashimi-quality tuna, preferably bigeye or yellowfin, store it carefully, and serve it immediately after preparing the tartare. Serve with toasted baguette slices.

¼ red onion

1 jalapeño chile, seeded

2 green (spring) onions, including tender green tops

2 teaspoons grated lemon zest

¼ cup (2 fl oz/60 ml) olive oil

3 tablespoons Asian sesame oil

Salt and ground pepper

1 lb (500 g) sashimi-quality tuna fillet (see note, above)

4 lemon wedges

MAKES 4 SERVINGS

Finely mince the red onion, chile, and green onions.

In a bowl, combine the red onion, chile, green onions, lemon zest, olive oil, and sesame oil. Season with salt and pepper.

Cut the tuna into ¼-inch (6-mm) dice, season with salt and pepper, and add to the bowl with the vegetables. Toss very gently to combine.

Mound the tuna mixture on individual plates. Serve right away with lemon wedges.

Tiny tartare

To serve tartare as an hors d'oeuvre, spoon tiny mounds onto thin slices of baguette, boiled potato, or radish, or into cucumber cups, spears of Belgian endive (chicory/ witloof), or hollowed-out cherry tomatoes.

CEVICHE

For this classic Latin American starter, small chunks of fish are tossed in lime juice, which flavors the fish and also "cooks" it, thanks to the citric acid. This version includes creamy avocado for contrast. For a little heat, add a small serrano chile, seeded and minced.

1¼ lb (625 g) halibut or flounder fillets

Juice of 5 or 6 limes

2 tomatoes, peeled, seeded, and diced

1 small red bell pepper (capsicum), diced

1 green (spring) onion, including tender green tops, chopped

⅓ cup (½ oz/15 g) finely chopped fresh cilantro (fresh coriander)

Salt and ground pepper

1 avocado, diced

10 black olives, pitted

1 teaspoon dried oregano

MAKES 6 SERVINGS

Cut the fish fillets into 1-inch (2.5-cm) dice and place in a bowl. Pour the lime juice over the fish, making sure all the pieces are covered. Cover and refrigerate for 3–4 hours.

Drain the fish cubes, pat dry on paper towels, and transfer to a bowl. Add the tomatoes, bell pepper, green onion, and cilantro and season with salt and pepper. Stir to blend, cover, and refrigerate for at least 2 hours or up to 12 hours.

At serving time, stir the avocado, olives, and oregano into the fish mixture. Serve chilled.

Shellfish ceviche

You can substitute shellfish, such as halved sea scallops or diced shrimp (prawns), for the fish fillets. Or, make a combination ceviche with all three.

ONION AND OLIVE TART

Serving tarts

A large, wide offset spatula is handy for sliding the tart free of the pan bottom. If it doesn't want to budge, place the tart, still on the base, on the serving plate.

This custard-based tart includes the robust flavors of caramelized onions and tapenade, both of them layered on the pastry shell, and is finished off with creamy, nutty Gruyère. Cut into slender wedges for hors d'oeuvres or more generous portions for a first course or brunch.

In a large frying pan over medium heat, melt the butter with the oil. Add the onions and sauté until very soft, about 20 minutes. Sprinkle with the flour, season with salt and pepper, and continue to cook, stirring, for 2 minutes. Add the thyme, stir briefly, and then let cool for 10 minutes.

Meanwhile, in a small bowl, whisk together the cream and eggs. Season with salt and pepper.

Preheat the oven to 425°F (220°C). Roll out the chilled dough and press it into a 9½-inch (24-cm) tart pan with a removable bottom, trimming off any excess dough (see page 448). Line the pastry shell with aluminum foil and fill with pie weights. Bake until set, about 8 minutes. Remove from the oven and remove the weights and foil. Let cool for 10 minutes. Reduce the oven temperature to 350°F (180°C).

Spread a thin layer of the tapenade in the pastry shell. Top with the onions. Slowly pour in the cream mixture, and sprinkle with the cheese. Bake until the custard is set, about 25 minutes. Let cool on a rack for about 10 minutes, then remove the pan sides and carefully slide the tart off the pan bottom onto a serving plate. Serve warm.

3 tablespoons unsalted butter

1 tablespoon olive oil

3 large yellow onions, cut into slices ¼ inch (6 mm) thick

2 tablespoons all-purpose (plain) flour

Salt and ground pepper

2 teaspoons chopped fresh thyme

1 cup (8 fl oz/250 ml) heavy (double) cream

2 eggs

Tart Pastry (page 448), made without sugar

Tapenade (page 388)

½ cup (2 oz/60 g) shredded Gruyère or Emmentaler cheese

MAKES 8 SERVINGS

PROVENÇAL TOMATO TART

Only the best will do

This tart is all about the tomatoes, so make sure to use only the ripest and most flavorful specimens you can find. To change both the look and the taste, try mixing in heirloom varieties such as Green Zebra or Cherokee Purple.

Bright red slices of ripe tomato arranged on a layer of herbed goat cheese in a rosemary-scented crust combine to create a memorable tart. The tomatoes are also joined by two other staples of Provençal cooking: olive oil and fresh basil.

To make the pastry, in a food processor, combine the flour, cheese, rosemary, ½ teaspoon salt, and ¼ teaspoon pepper and process for about 30 seconds. Scatter the butter over the top and pulse about 10 times, or until the mixture resembles coarse meal. Sprinkle the ice water over the top and pulse about 7 more times. The dough will still appear rather loose, but should hold together when pressed between your fingers. Shape the dough into a disk ¾ inch (2 cm) thick, wrap tightly in plastic wrap, and then refrigerate for at least 30 minutes or up to overnight to firm.

Preheat the oven to 425°F (220°C). Roll out the chilled dough and press it into a 9½-inch (24-cm) tart pan with a removable bottom, trimming off any excess dough (see page 448). Prick the pastry evenly over the bottom with a fork. Line the pastry

FOR THE PASTRY

1½ cups (7 ½ oz/235 g) all-purpose (plain) flour

2 tablespoons grated Parmesan cheese

1 tablespoon fresh rosemary leaves

Salt and ground pepper

½ cup (4 oz/125 g) cold unsalted butter, cut into 8 pieces

3 tablespoons ice water

¼ lb (125 g) fresh
goat cheese

3 tablespoons chopped
fresh basil

Coarse sea salt and
ground pepper

4 tomatoes, cut into slices
¼ inch (6 mm) thick

Extra-virgin olive oil
for drizzling

MAKES 6 SERVINGS

shell with aluminum foil and fill with pie weights. Bake until set, about 8 minutes. Remove the pie weights and foil, return the pastry to the oven, and continue to bake until tender and golden, 8–12 minutes longer. Transfer to a wire rack and let cool to room temperature.

To make the filling, in the food processor, combine the cheese, 2 tablespoons of the chopped basil, and ¼ teaspoon pepper and process until smooth, about 30 seconds. Spread the cheese mixture evenly over the cooled crust. Beginning at the outer edge of the crust, arrange the tomato slices in slightly overlapping concentric circles. Drizzle lightly with the oil and sprinkle with salt, pepper, and the remaining 1 tablespoon chopped basil. Serve right away.

BITE-SIZE BLUE CHEESE TARTLETS

The robust flavor of spinach or Swiss chard—combined with egg, cream, and Emmentaler cheese—is more than a match for the tang of the blue cheese at the bottom of these tiny pastries. Pine nuts add a mellow richness to balance the assertive flavor of the cheese.

3 oz (90 g) spinach or
Swiss chard, stemmed

1 egg

⅔ cup (5 fl oz/160 ml)
heavy (double) cream

¾ cup (3 oz/90 g) shredded
Emmentaler cheese

¼ teaspoon freshly
grated nutmeg

Salt and ground pepper

½ lb (250 g) puff pastry
dough, thawed if frozen

3 oz (90 g) Roquefort
cheese, crumbled

2 tablespoons pine nuts

MAKES 18 TARTLETS;
6 SERVINGS

Preheat the oven to 425°F (220°C).

Fill a large saucepan three-fourths full of water and bring to a boil over high heat. Plunge the spinach into the boiling water and cook for 30 seconds. Immediately drain in a colander and rinse throughly with running cold water. Press against the greens with the back of a spoon to force out as much water as possible. Set aside.

In a bowl, combine the egg, cream, Emmentaler cheese, and nutmeg and season with salt and pepper. Beat with a fork until completely blended. Coarsely chop the spinach, add it to the bowl, and stir well.

Have ready miniature muffin tins with 18 cups. On a lightly floured work surface, roll out the dough into a thin sheet. With a fluted round cutter about 1½ inches (4 cm) in diameter, cut out 18 rounds. Gently press a round into each muffin cup. Divide the Roquefort cheese evenly among the lined cups. Then, add the egg mixture, dividing evenly among the cups. Top each cup with a few pine nuts.

Bake until the filling sets and the pastry is golden, about 15 minutes. Serve warm.

The tartlet
pan approach

You can use this recipe with tartlet pans and Tart Pastry (page 448). Divide the pastry dough and ingredients evenly among the pans, and arrange them on a large rimmed baking sheet before placing in the oven.

93

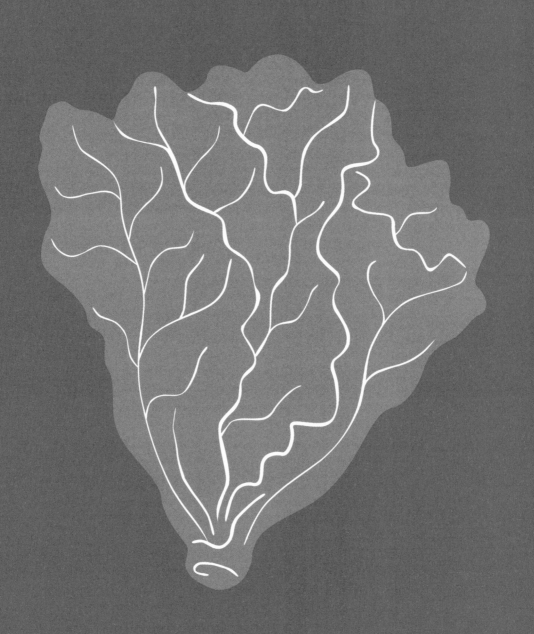

Salads

Salads

A salad is any mix of ingredients combined with a dressing, typically served at room temperature but also chilled and even hot. This versatility means the possibilities are nearly endless. Salads incorporate a dizzying array of foods, flavors, and textures and appear as side dishes or main courses throughout the day. In this chapter, you'll find recipes for dozens of classic salads and directions for creating myriad variations.

Salad Types

For many people, the word *salad* invokes lettuce, but salads are diverse. They can be loosely grouped into categories based on their primary ingredients and the ways in which they are prepared and presented.

GREEN SALADS This broad category is defined by a predominance of lettuces and other salad leaves. A green salad can be a simple combination of lightly dressed greens or it may include other ingredients. Dressings vary from effortless vinaigrettes to complex, creamy mixtures.

TOSSED SALADS These salads typically feature a range of ingredients that have been torn, shredded, sliced, or chopped and then tossed together with a dressing. The chopped salad is a subcategory, made by chopping greens and vegetables along with meat, poultry, or seafood into small, fairly uniform pieces that offer a variety of flavors, colors, and textures with every forkful.

COMPOSED SALADS Here, ingredients are artfully arranged on a platter to make an eye-catching presentation, with the best-known example the Niçoise (page 111). Composed salads highlight the quality, beauty, and variety of their components. Some are eaten as served, and others are presented arranged and then tossed by diners before eating.

SLAWS The word *coleslaw* comes from the Dutch *koolsla*, which means cabbage salad, and is used for the popular American shredded-cabbage picnic dish typically dressed with buttermilk or mayonnaise. The word *slaw* alone is used for any salad in which the vegetables are cut into long, thin shreds.

LEGUME SALADS Hearty pantry staples, beans and lentils are the foundation for many robust salads. Whether made with home-cooked dried legumes or with drained canned beans, these salads benefit from advance preparation, which allows time for the legumes to absorb the flavors of the dressing.

GRAIN SALADS White, brown, or wild rice; nutty bulgur; al dente pasta; and more—grains are a favorite base for salads, absorbing dressings and mixing well with other ingredients. In general, grain salads are not prepared too far in advance, because the grains can turn soggy from the dressing.

POTATO SALADS Nearly everyone has a favorite in this surprisingly diverse group of salads. German potato salads typically feature still-warm potatoes tossed with a bacon-infused oil-and-vinegar dressing. American potato salads employ mayonnaise and chopped vegetables, such as celery and peppers (capsicums), and often also include chopped hard-boiled egg.

SEE ALSO: For additional legume and grain salads, see chapter 11.

Shopping for greens
A salad is often only as good as the greens. Always look for the freshest, best-quality salad leaves available: crisp and bright, with no signs of wilting or discoloration. Apply the same diligence to selecting the other ingredients for the salad.

Washing and drying greens
Separate leaves before washing. Wash the leaves thoroughly but gently, swishing them in a bowl of cold water and then lifting them out. (For spinach, which tends to be sandy, rinse and repeat.) Dry thoroughly, using a salad spinner or patting the leaves between clean kitchen towels, to avoid watering down dressings.

Get it crisp
For the crunchiest salad, after washing the greens, arrange them in a single layer on a clean kitchen towel or paper towels. Gently roll up and refrigerate for at least 1 hour.

Breaking things down
Bite-size pieces of lettuce make eating a salad easy and pleasurable. For a casual tossed salad, tear the clean leaves directly into the salad bowl. For neat shreds, stack leaves on a cutting surface and cut to the desired width.

SALAD DRESSINGS

Although many of the recipes in this chapter include their own dressings, salads have an inherently mix-and-match nature. It's good to have several dressings in your repertoire such as those listed below.

Blue Cheese Dressing
In a small bowl, whisk together ¼ cup (2 fl oz/60 ml) red wine vinegar; 1 teaspoon Worcestershire sauce; ½ teaspoon Dijon mustard; 1 clove garlic, crushed and minced; ¼ teaspoon salt; and ½ teaspoon ground pepper. Using a fork, mash in 1 oz (30 g) Roquefort cheese to make a paste. While whisking, slowly drizzle in ⅓ cup (3 fl oz/ 80 ml) extra-virgin olive oil to form a thick dressing. Makes about 1 cup (8 fl oz/250 ml).

Goat Cheese, Shallot, and Parsley Dressing
In a blender, combine 1 shallot, chopped; 2 tablespoons chopped fresh flat-leaf (Italian) parsley; and 2 teaspoons white wine vinegar and process until puréed. Add ¼ cup (2 fl oz/60 ml) mayonnaise, 2 oz (60 g) fresh goat cheese, and 3 tablespoons milk and process until smooth and creamy. Add more milk, if necessary, to thin to the desired consistency. Season with salt and ground pepper. Makes about 1 cup (8 fl oz/250 ml).

Honey Mustard Dressing
In a small bowl, combine ⅔ cup (5 oz/155 g) low-fat plain yogurt, ¼ cup (3 oz/90 g) honey, 2 tablespoons Dijon mustard, 2 tablespoons water, ½ teaspoon salt, and a pinch of ground pepper. Using a fork or a whisk, stir until well blended and smooth. Makes about 1¼ cups (10 fl oz/310 ml).

Lemon, Mustard, and Yogurt Dressing
In a small bowl, stir together 1 tablespoon Dijon mustard and 1 tablespoon fresh lemon juice until blended, and season with salt and ground pepper. Stir in ⅔ cup (5 oz/ 155 g) plain yogurt until thoroughly incorporated, then vigorously stir in 2 tablespoons extra-virgin olive oil. Finally, stir in 1 tablespoon minced fresh flat-leaf (Italian) parsley. Cover and chill for 30 minutes before serving. Makes about 1 cup (8 fl oz/250 ml).

Lemon-Tarragon Vinaigrette
In a small bowl, whisk together 6 tablespoons (3 fl oz/90 ml) fresh lemon juice, 4 teaspoons minced fresh tarragon, 4 teaspoons Dijon mustard, and 3 cloves garlic, minced. Gradually whisk in ½ cup (4 fl oz/125 ml) extra-virgin olive oil, and season with salt and ground pepper. Let stand for about 30 minutes before serving. Makes about ¾ cup (6 fl oz/185 ml).

Sesame-Miso Vinaigrette
In a food processor, combine 1 clove garlic, chopped; 2 tablespoons chopped red onion; 1 teaspoon grated fresh ginger; 1½ tablespoons white miso; 3 tablespoons rice vinegar; 1 tablespoon honey; 5 tablespoons (3 fl oz/80 ml) canola oil; 2 tablespoons Asian sesame oil; and a pinch of cayenne pepper. Pulse until smooth. Makes about 1 cup (8 fl oz/250 ml).

Green Goddess Dressing
In a blender, combine 1 cup (8 oz/250 g) plain yogurt; 1 cup (1½ oz/45 g) loosely packed watercress leaves; 2 tablespoons chopped fresh dill; 1 green (spring) onion, including tender green tops, thinly sliced; ½ teaspoon sugar; ½ teaspoon salt; and a dash of hot pepper sauce. Process until smooth. Pour into a container with a tight-fitting lid and refrigerate for several hours or up to overnight to thicken and mellow. Shake or stir well before serving. Makes about 1 cup (8 fl oz/250 ml).

Test your flavors
To make sure your dressing is properly seasoned, taste it on a lettuce leaf. That way you'll know how the flavors will work together.

When to dress
Prolonged contact with a dressing will wilt and soften salad leaves and other tender ingredients. Unless you're making a salad in which you intend for the ingredients to absorb the dressing, toss salads with their dressings just moments before serving.

Dress with caution
Add dressing to a salad a little at a time, then toss and observe. You can always add more dressing and toss again; it's much harder to correct for too much dressing.

Perfect presentation
To make your salads picture-perfect, reserve a small portion of one or more key ingredients, such as sliced fruit and nuts. Once the rest of the ingredients have been tossed together and dressed, place the reserved ingredients on top.

Vinaigrette Variations
In addition to the dressings at left and throughout this chapter, you'll find an assortment of versatile vinaigrettes on page 374.

98

SALAD COMPONENTS

For the most intriguing salads, include elements from at least two or three categories, aiming for a complementary mix of colors, textures, flavors, sizes, and shapes.

Herbs

Often appearing in dressings, fresh herbs, either sprigs, whole leaves, or chopped, can also be tossed with greens. A small amount of parsley, tarragon, chives, or basil adds bright, aromatic flavor, especially to simple salads.

Proteins

Adding protein can turn a simple salad into a satisfying meal. Salads are an excellent platform for prepared or leftover meats, poultry, or seafood, whether sliced, chopped, or shredded by hand. Cold cuts can also be used, especially in chopped salads, as can wedges or slices of hard-boiled egg.

Legumes

A wide variety of beans provides earthy, rich flavor and robust texture to salads. The most popular types are chickpeas (garbanzo beans), fava (broad) beans, white beans (such as cannellini, Great Northern, or navy beans), and kidney beans. Whether home-cooked dried beans, or drained and rinsed canned ones, beans often benefit from marinating in the dressing before serving.

Cheeses

The addition of cheese to a salad contributes not only flavor and texture but also calcium and protein. Prep cheeses depending on their

Greens Glossary

Nowadays, supermarkets, natural food stores, and farmers' markets alike provide a wide variety of greens choices on which to build a flavorful salad. Some of the most popular options are listed below.

CRISP LEAVES

CABBAGE Tightly packed spherical heads of red or green cabbage are typically shredded and sometimes wilted for salads, the latter making the sturdy, crisp, somewhat pungent leaves more tender and mild.

ICEBERG LETTUCE Crisp, thick, pale-green leaves good for adding crunch to salads and sandwiches. The sturdy leaves can serve as cups for finely chopped vegetable salads or meat, poultry, or seafood salads. Chilled iceberg heads are also sometimes cut into thick wedges and served with a dressing spooned on top. Also known as crisp-head lettuce, head lettuce, or cabbage lettuce.

NAPA CABBAGE A mild cabbage with heavily crinkled, pale green leaves on crisp white ribs. Napa, sometimes spelled nappa and sometimes called Chinese cabbage or celery cabbage, is popular in Asian-inspired salads.

RADICCHIO Leaves in round or elongated, small or medium heads, with a deep ruby red color and pleasantly bitter flavor. Also sometimes called red chicory. Chioggia (round) and Treviso (elongated) are popular varieties.

ROMAINE Elongated, crisp, sturdy leaves that form a compact head. Juicy and sweet, deeply ribbed and veined romaine leaves, also called cos leaves, hold up well to firm garnishes and strongly flavored dressings, making them the traditional choice for Caesar Salad (page 100). The milder, more tender inner leaves are sometimes sold as hearts of romaine.

SPINACH Baby leaves, which have the mildest and most delicate flavor, are the best choice for use raw in salads. They are often sold prewashed and packaged in plastic bags.

DELICATE LEAVES

BIBB LETTUCE Very tender, pale green leaves loosely gathered into a small, rosettelike head; also known as limestone.

BUTTER LETTUCE Similar to Bibb but larger, loose head with soft, light green leaves with a "buttery" texture; also called Boston or butterhead.

GREEN-LEAF OR RED-LEAF LETTUCE Mildly flavored, large, ruffled leaves in an open, loose head, both types are popular all-purpose salad greens. Red-leaf lettuce has a deep red blush along its outer edges.

LOLLO ROSSO An Italian lettuce variety similar to red-leaf lettuce, this mild-flavored, tender-leaved head has distinctively ruffled, purplish red edges.

MÂCHE Also called field salad, corn salad, or lamb's lettuce, mâche has a delicate, slightly nutty flavor. Its oval leaves grow in diminutive bunches that are typically served intact.

MESCLUN From the Provençal word for *mix*, mesclun is a mixture of young, tender greens, traditionally the first greens and herbs of spring, hence its other name, spring mix. The mixture can vary greatly, but usually includes a range of colors and textures.

OAKLEAF LETTUCE Tender and mild, the notched green leaves, which resemble oak leaves, are sometimes fringed in red. The name is also occasionally applied to red-leaf lettuces.

BITTER OR PEPPERY LEAVES

ARUGULA Also called rocket (and known as *rugula* or *rucola* in Italian and *roquette* in French), these dark green, deeply notched leaves resemble small, elongated oak leaves. Nutty, tangy, and slightly peppery, arugula is usually at its best in its immature form, often sold prewashed and packaged as baby arugula. Larger leaves are more pungent and have a less delicate texture.

BELGIAN ENDIVE Elongated leaves packed in a small, cylindrical head have a pleasingly mild, bitter flavor and a crisp, slightly juicy texture. Also known as endive, French endive, and witloof, most Belgian endive is ivory with pale yellow tips; red-tipped varieties add pretty color to salads.

CURLY ENDIVE Narrow, frilly leaves on long stems are formed into a loose, bushy head; also known as chicory, curly chicory, or chicory endive. The pale yellow leaves at the center are the mildest.

DANDELION GREENS Popular in Europe, young, tender, spear-shaped dandelion leaves—a market variety of the plant that differs from what you find in your lawn—add a distinctively bitter note to salads.

ESCAROLE A loose head of broad, ruffled green leaves, escarole has a slightly bitter flavor similar to that of Belgian endive and curly endive, to which it is related. Also called Batavian endive and *scarola* in Italian, it is popular in wilted salads, standing up well to hot, robust dressings

FRISÉE Term adopted from the French for young, curly, lacy endive loosely gathered in a head with tender, pale green outer leaves and a heart of smaller, pale yellow to white leaves.

MIZUNA Native to Japan but now grown in the West, this type of mustard green boasts long, feathery leaves with a moderately pungent flavor reminiscent of cabbage. Also known as spider mustard, mizuna is often included in mesclun mixes, but is also sold on its own in some farmers' markets and Asian produce markets.

MUSTARD GREENS When picked young and tender, these elongated, curly, medium to dark greens of a variety of mustard plant have a spicy flavor and a robust texture suitable for salads. They are often wilted with a hot dressing.

WATERCRESS Small, round, dark green leaves on short, delicate stems, watercress has a crisp, juicy texture and refreshingly peppery flavor that can turn harsh with age. Look in farmers' markets for other cress varieties, such land cress, upland cress, and curly cress.

consistency and the type of salad you're making: thinly slice, shred, or chop firm cheeses like Cheddar, mozzarella, or provolone; crumble drier varieties such as blue or feta; or grate hard cheeses like Parmesan. Fresh goat cheese is another popular addition: drizzle thick rounds with olive oil, warm in the oven, and place atop dressed greens.

Fruits
In a category of their own, fruit salads appear as side dishes or desserts at any meal of the day. But fruit—apple slices, pear wedges, citrus sections, grapes—can also enhance green salads. And don't overlook dried fruits such as raisins, pitted dates, or dried cherries or cranberries.

Nuts and Seeds
Rich, earthy, and crunchy, nuts and seeds make delightful salad toppings. Consider such nuts as almonds, hazelnuts (filberts), peanuts, pecans, pine nuts, and walnuts. Seeds such as poppy seeds or sesame seeds are typically stirred into dressings. For maximum flavor and texture, toast nuts and seeds (see page 17) before adding them to a salad.

Croutons
Sliced or cubed, tossed with butter or olive oil and seasonings, and then toasted in the oven or on the stove top until crisp and golden, day-old bread becomes croutons, one of the most popular components of basic green salads. Like nuts and seeds, croutons offer textural contrast to leafy salads.

CAESAR SALAD

Anchovy authenticity

Also in dispute is whether anchovy was part of the original Caesar salad. This version includes anchovies and adds capers, but you can choose to omit either or both.

The origin of this famous salad is hotly debated. Most stories credit chef Caesar Cardini, who divided his time between San Diego and Tijuana, with its creation in the Mexican city in 1924. It has since become a ubiquitous menu item in United States restaurants.

In a frying pan over medium-high heat, combine the oil and garlic and fry the garlic until browned, about 4 minutes. Remove the garlic and discard. Add the bread cubes and fry over high heat, stirring, until browned, about 5 minutes. Transfer to paper towels to drain.

Separate the lettuce into leaves. Keep the small lettuce leaves whole and coarsely tear the remainder. Put the lettuce in a large salad bowl. In a medium bowl, mash the anchovies with a fork. Add the capers and bread cubes and toss to mix.

Bring a small saucepan filled with water to a boil and gently slip in the egg, still it its shell. Remove the pan from the heat and let stand for 1 minute. Remove the egg from the pan, immerse it in cold water, and break it into a small bowl. Add the lemon juice, Worcestershire sauce, and mustard. Stir vigorously until well blended.

Add the anchovy mixture to the bowl with the lettuce. Pour the dressing over the salad, scatter the Parmesan over the top, toss gently, and serve right away.

Ingredients

⅓ cup (3 fl oz/80 ml) extra-virgin olive oil

4 cloves garlic, sliced lengthwise

4 thick slices coarse country bread, crusts removed and cut into ¾-inch (2-cm) cubes

1 head romaine (cos) lettuce

4 anchovy fillets in olive oil, drained

2 tablespoons rinsed capers

1 egg

1 tablespoon fresh lemon juice

1 tablespoon Worcestershire sauce

1 teaspoon coarse-grain mustard

Small handful shaved Parmesan cheese

MAKES 4 SERVINGS

Warming eggs

The process of warming eggs still in their shell thickens them slightly for use in salad dressings, but it does not kill any bacteria that may be present. See page 37 for more information on working with raw or undercooked eggs.

WARM SPINACH WITH BACON AND POTATOES

Salad potatoes

The best potatoes for tossed salads, where it's important that they retain their shape when cooked and diced, are small boiling potatoes with waxy flesh. You can also use fingerlings for this recipe or, for a vibrant shock of color, small purple potatoes.

This salad can be a light main meal for two, accompanied by crusty bread. Drizzling the bacon fat over the spinach warms it without wilting it. For a salad with an assertive peppery flavor, you can substitute arugula (rocket) for the spinach.

In a saucepan, combine the potatoes and eggs with water to cover. Place over medium-high heat, bring to a simmer, and adjust the heat to maintain a gentle simmer. Using a slotted spoon, remove the eggs after 8 minutes and run under cold water until cool. Add salt to the water and continue cooking the potatoes until easily pierced with a knife, 5–10 minutes longer. Drain and let cool, peel if desired, and slice ¼ inch (6 mm) thick. Peel the eggs and quarter lengthwise.

In a bowl, combine the spinach, red onion, and potato slices.

Ingredients

½ lb (250 g) red boiling potatoes (about 4 small potatoes), unpeeled

2 eggs

Salt and ground pepper

½ lb (250 g) baby spinach leaves, tough stems removed

½ red onion, thinly sliced

4 slices thick-cut bacon, cut into pieces ½ inch (12 mm) wide

1 tablespoon sherry vinegar or red wine vinegar

MAKES 4 SERVINGS

In a frying pan over medium heat, fry the bacon until it begins to crisp and has rendered much of its fat, about 5 minutes. Pour the bacon and fat over the spinach and toss well. Add the vinegar, season with salt and pepper, and toss again. Taste and adjust the seasoning.

Divide among individual bowls. Arrange the egg wedges around the edge and serve right away.

FRISÉE SALAD WITH BACON AND POACHED EGGS

In this classic French salad, frisée, which is a fine-leaved curly chicory, is combined with strips of bacon, called *lardons,* and topped with a poached egg. You can substitute any crisp mild lettuce greens for the frisée, if you wish.

2 thick slices coarse country bread, cut into 1-inch (2.5-cm) cubes

1½ tablespoons extra-virgin olive oil

Salt and ground pepper

¾ lb (375 g) thick-cut bacon, cut crosswise into ½-inch (12-mm) strips

2 shallots, finely chopped

5 tablespoons (2½ fl oz/ 75 ml) red wine vinegar

1 teaspoon white wine vinegar

4 eggs

2 small heads frisée, leaves torn into 3-inch (7.5-cm) pieces

MAKES 4 SERVINGS

Preheat the oven to 350°F (180°C). Spread the bread cubes on a rimmed baking sheet, sprinkle with the oil, and season with salt and pepper. Toast in the oven, turning once or twice, until golden, about 15 minutes. Set aside.

In a frying pan over medium-high heat, fry the bacon until crisp, 4–5 minutes. Add the shallots and sauté until softened, about 1 minute. Add the red wine vinegar, reduce the heat to medium, and simmer until slightly thickened, about 1 minute longer. Season with salt and pepper. Set the bacon aside and keep warm.

Half fill a large sauté pan with water, add the white wine vinegar and 1 teaspoon salt, and bring to a boil over high heat; reduce the heat to maintain a bare simmer. Break 1 egg into a small cup and slide it carefully into the water. Working quickly, repeat with the remaining eggs. Carefully spoon the simmering water over the eggs until the whites are set and the yolks look glazed but are still soft, 3–4 minutes. Using a slotted spoon, transfer the eggs to a plate and set aside.

In a large bowl, combine the croutons and frisée. Pour the warm dressing with the bacon pieces over the top and toss to coat. Divide among 4 shallow bowls. Place a poached egg on top of each serving and serve right away.

Making lardons

Lardons are typically pieces of fat cut from the belly of a pig, but you can substitute slices of thick-cut bacon cut crosswise into ½-inch pieces. French cooks use lardons to brown meats for stews and braises and to lard meats and poultry for roasting. Or, they cook lardons until crisp for adding to green salads and other dishes.

101

BUTTER LETTUCE WITH GORGONZOLA AND WALNUTS

Gorgonzola dolcelatte is the sweeter version of Italy's renowned cheese. If you cannot find it, select another mild blue cheese. In the fall, 6 figs, quartered, make a nice substitute for the grapes. In winter, serve the salad with 2 small pears cut into wedges.

Preheat the oven to 350°F (180°C).

In a bowl, whisk together the walnut and olive oils and balsamic and sherry vinegars. Season with salt and pepper. Set the vinaigrette aside.

Spread the walnuts on a baking sheet and place in the oven. Toast, stirring once or twice, until lightly browned, 8–10 minutes. Transfer to a small bowl, add 3 tablespoons of the vinaigrette, toss lightly, and let stand for 15 minutes.

Place the lettuce in a large bowl, tearing the leaves into bite-size pieces as needed. Add the marinated walnuts and drizzle with the remaining vinaigrette. Toss well. Divide among individual plates. Top with the grapes, and then with the cheese, dividing the ingredients evenly. Serve right away.

7 tablespoons (3½ fl oz/105 ml) walnut oil

2 tablespoons *each* olive oil and balsamic vinegar

1 tablespoon sherry vinegar

Salt and ground pepper

1 cup (4 oz/125 g) walnut halves

2 heads butter lettuce, leaves separated

1 cup (6 oz/185 g) red or black seedless grapes, halved

½–⅔ lb (250–315 g) Gorgonzola dolcelatte cheese, crumbled, at room temperature

MAKES 6 SERVINGS

GREEK SALAD

In Greece, this familiar salad often includes crisp green tomatoes, which are surprisingly sweet, along with cucumbers, bell peppers (capsicums), olives, and pungent feta cheese tossed with a tart red wine vinaigrette. Some cooks add romaine lettuce to the mix.

Cut the tomatoes into 1- to 1½-inch (2.5- to 4-cm) pieces. Cut the onion into 1-inch (2.5 cm) dice, and cut the bell pepper and cucumber into 1-inch (2.5-cm) pieces.

In a large bowl, toss together the tomato, onion, bell pepper, and cucumber pieces. Drizzle the olive oil and vinegar over the top, season with salt and pepper, and add the oregano. Toss well and let stand at room temperature for about 30 minutes to blend the flavors.

Crumble the feta cheese and add it to the bowl with the vegetables. Add the olives, toss well, and serve right away.

1¼ lb (625 g) small, ripe tomatoes

1 *each* small red onion, red bell pepper (capsicum), and English (hothouse) cucumber

5 tablespoons (2½ fl oz/75 ml) extra-virgin olive oil

3 tablespoons red wine vinegar

Salt and ground pepper

1 teaspoon dried oregano

¾ lb (375 g) feta cheese

¾ cup (4 oz/125 g) Kalamata olives

MAKES 6 SERVINGS

COBB SALAD

The popular Cobb salad, which originated at the Brown Derby restaurant in Hollywood, has something for everyone: eggs, bacon, turkey, blue cheese, tomato, and avocado, all neatly arranged on a bed of dressed greens. It is substantial enough to work as a main course.

3 hard-boiled eggs, peeled (see page 38)

8 slices bacon

1 head romaine (cos) lettuce

2 tablespoons *each* minced fresh flat-leaf (Italian) parsley and chives

2 cups (4 oz/125 g) chopped, stemmed watercress

4 cups (1½ lb/750 g) diced cooked turkey or chicken

2 avocados, diced

2 tomatoes, chopped

¼ lb (125 g) Roquefort cheese, crumbled

Blue Cheese Dressing (page 97)

MAKES 4–6 SERVINGS

Cut the hard-boiled eggs into ½-inch (12-mm) dice. Set aside.

In a frying pan over medium heat, fry the bacon until crisp, 5–8 minutes. Transfer to paper towels to drain. When cool, crumble and set aside.

Tear the romaine into bite-size pieces and arrange in a bed on a platter or in shallow bowls. Mix together the parsley and chives. Neatly arrange the eggs, bacon, mixed herbs, watercress, turkey, avocados, tomatoes, and cheese on the romaine, in rows or in a checkerboard pattern, covering the lettuce almost completely.

Pour a little of the dressing over the salad. Pass the remaining dressing at the table.

Milder blues

This salad is traditionally made with Roquefort cheese, which is among the more pungent, tangier blues. For a milder flavor, try Danish or Maytag blue.

103

WATERCRESS, PEAR, AND GOAT CHEESE SALAD

This easy salad combines peppery, sweet, and tangy flavors for a well-rounded dish. If you prefer, substitute a mixture of young, tender salad greens for the watercress. You can also choose a bold blue cheese to replace the goat cheese.

3 firm but ripe Bartlett (Williams') pears

Juice of ½ lemon

2 or 3 bunches watercress, long stems removed (about 8 cups/8 oz/250 g)

½ cup (2 oz/60 g) dried cherries

Sherry Vinaigrette (page 374)

Salt and ground pepper

6 oz (185 g) semifirm aged goat cheese, cut into small pieces

MAKES 6 SERVINGS

Peel, halve, and core the pears, then cut each pear half into 4 wedges. As the pears are cut, place them in a large bowl and sprinkle with the lemon juice. Add the watercress and cherries to the bowl with the pears.

Drizzle a few tablespoons of the vinaigrette over the watercress mixture, then toss to coat evenly. Season to taste with salt and pepper and add more vinaigrette, if desired.

Divide the salad among individual plates, top with the goat cheese, and serve right away.

Seasoning greens

When making salads, don't forget to season your greens with salt and pepper. Like any other ingredients, greens benefit from the savory accent of the spices.

SALADS

MIXED GREENS WITH PROSCIUTTO AND FIGS

Tender fennel

*The inner layers
of a fennel bulb are
the most tender.
Depending on the
size and maturity
of the bulb, you
may want to discard
the thick outer layer
and use only the
tender center.*

A trio of taste sensations—slightly bitter greens, salty prosciutto, and sweet pear vinaigrette—comes together in this easy salad. The dressing combines pear nectar and rice vinegar, both of which can be found in most supermarkets.

In a small bowl, stir together the pear nectar and vinegar. Season with salt and pepper and set aside.

Cut off the stems, feathery tops, and any bruised outer stalks from the fennel bulb. Reserve the tops. Cut the fennel bulb in half lengthwise, then cut away and discard the core. Slice crosswise paper-thin.

In a bowl, combine the mesclun and arugula. Add half of the dressing and toss well. Divide the greens among individual plates. Top the greens with the fennel, prosciutto, and figs, and drizzle with the remaining dressing.

Using a vegetable peeler, cut the cheese into thin shavings and place atop the salads. Season the salads with pepper and serve right away.

⅔ cup (5 fl oz/160 ml) pear nectar

¼ cup (2 fl oz/60 ml) seasoned rice vinegar

Salt and ground pepper

1 fennel bulb

5 oz (155 g) mesclun salad greens

1 cup (1 oz/30 g) arugula (rocket) leaves, torn into pieces

2 oz (60 g) thinly sliced prosciutto, julienned

4 figs, quartered through stem end

1 oz (30 g) piece Parmesan cheese

MAKES 4 SERVINGS

APPLE AND CHICORY SALAD

About chicory

The word chicory
*is commonly used
to mean curly endive,
but it actually
encompasses a
family of pleasantly
bitter greens,
including Belgian
endive (chicory/
witloof), escarole
(Batavian endive),
radicchio, and frisée.
They are often
combined with fruit
and nuts in salads.*

Quick and easy to prepare, this perfect autumn salad of diced apples and chicory can be enriched with cubed Swiss cheese and/or a thick slice of ham, cut into small pieces. You can also use 1 cup (8 oz/250 g) mayonnaise in place of the sour cream dressing.

Fill a large bowl with water and add the lemon juice. Core the apples, but do not peel them. Cut the apples into 1-inch (2.5-cm) dice, dropping the pieces into the lemon water to prevent them from discoloring.

Thinly slice the celery stalks crosswise and place in a salad bowl. Tear the curly endive into bite-size pieces, adding to the bowl with the celery. Drain the apples well, then add to the bowl and toss to combine.

In a small bowl, stir together the sour cream, yogurt, and horseradish and season with salt and pepper to make a dressing. Pour the dressing over the salad, add the walnuts, toss well, and serve right away.

1 tablespoon fresh lemon juice

3 red apples

3 celery stalks

1 small heart of curly endive (chicory)

⅔ cup (5 fl oz/160 ml) sour cream

2 tablespoons plain yogurt

1 tablespoon freshly grated horseradish

Salt and ground pepper

6 walnut halves, coarsely chopped

MAKES 4 SERVINGS

CHOPPED CHICKEN SALAD

This versatile main-course salad can accommodate other items in your refrigerator. For example, in place of the fennel or radishes, use cucumber, zucchini (courgette), or cauliflower. Omit the chicken to make a vegetarian salad or a side dish.

4 skinless, boneless chicken breast halves

6 cups (48 fl oz/1.5 l) Chicken Stock (page 23), or as needed

1 lb (500 g) hearts of romaine (cos) lettuce

½ small fennel bulb

24 small fresh mushrooms

20 radishes

4 small carrots

1 small head radicchio

1 small red onion

Lemon-Tarragon Vinaigrette (page 97)

MAKES 4 SERVINGS

In a small saucepan over medium heat, combine the chicken breasts and stock as needed to cover. Bring to a simmer, adjust the heat to keep the stock just below a simmer, and cook, uncovered, until the chicken is just opaque throughout, about 10 minutes. Transfer the chicken to a cutting board; reserve the stock for another use. When the chicken is cool, cut into small, neat dice.

Chop the lettuce, fennel, mushrooms, radishes, carrots, radicchio, and onion into pieces approximately the same size as the chicken, combining in a large bowl.

In another bowl, combine the chicken and the dressing and stir to coat, then pour over the vegetables. Toss well. Taste and adjust the seasoning and serve right away.

Repurpose the stock

Use the leftover chicken stock from this recipe for a soup the following day, adding orzo or another small pasta shape; rice; egg noodles; or store-bought tortellini for substance.

105

CUCUMBER SALAD WITH CILANTRO AND CHILES

With its hints of both Southwestern and Asian flavors, this salad makes a good partner for roasted or grilled meats, poultry, or fish. It can also be tossed with mixed greens and cooked shrimp (prawns) and served as a main-course salad.

2 cucumbers

1 cup (1½ oz/45 g) coarsely chopped fresh cilantro (fresh coriander)

2 small dried red chiles

Salt

¼ cup (2 fl oz/60 ml) unseasoned rice vinegar

2 tablespoons canola oil

MAKES 4 SERVINGS

Peel the cucumbers, halve them lengthwise, and scoop out the seeds. Cut the cucumbers into thin slices.

In a bowl, combine the sliced cucumbers and cilantro, then crumble in the dried chiles, removing the seeds if you prefer. Sprinkle with ½ teaspoon salt and add the vinegar and oil. Toss gently but thoroughly to coat well.

Let the salad stand for 30 minutes to blend the flavors. Serve at room temperature.

Leave the peel

If you can find English (hothouse) cucumbers, which have thin green skins without a trace of bitterness, there is no need to peel them. Their green color will add to the salad's visual appeal.

BABY GREENS WITH SAUTÉED MUSHROOMS

Mixing oils

The mushrooms here are sautéed in canola oil rather than the expected olive oil. The latter could muddle the flavor of the hazelnut oil in the dressing.

Serve this salad of sautéed mixed mushrooms on baby greens as a robust and earthy start to a cool-weather meal. Essentially any combination of fresh mushroom varieties can be used, including cremini, porcini, morel, chanterelle, shiitake, and oyster.

In a small saucepan over high heat, combine ¼ cup (1 oz/30 g) of the shallots, the vinegar, and the broth. Bring to a boil and boil until reduced to ¾ cup (6 fl oz/180 ml), about 3 minutes. Season with salt and pepper and set aside.

In a bowl, toss together the salad greens, herb leaves, and hazelnut oil. Season with salt and pepper and set aside.

Cleaning morels

Unlike other varieties of mushrooms, which should be brushed clean with a damp towel, morels have intricately grooved caps that trap sand and other particles. To clean morels, immerse them briefly in water and agitate to dislodge any debris.

Brush the mushrooms clean, trim as needed (discard stems from shiitakes, if using), and then quarter them. In a nonstick sauté pan over medium heat, warm the canola oil. Add the remaining shallots and sauté until softened, about 1 minute. Add the heartier mushrooms, such as cremini and porcini, and sauté until browned, about 5 minutes. Add the more delicate mushrooms, such as morels, chanterelles, and shiitakes. Season all the mushrooms with salt and pepper and sauté just until tender, about 3 minutes longer. If using oyster mushrooms, add them during the last minute or two of cooking. Pour in the shallot-vinegar mixture and stir to dislodge any browned bits from the pan bottom.

Divide the dressed greens among individual plates. Top with the warm mushrooms and their juices, dividing evenly. Serve right away.

3 large shallots, chopped

3 tablespoons sherry vinegar

¾ cup (6 fl oz/180 ml) chicken broth

Salt and ground pepper

5 oz (155 g) assorted baby salad greens

¾ cup (¾ oz/20 g) assorted fresh herb leaves such as tarragon, chive, basil, and parsley, in any combination

2 teaspoons hazelnut (filbert) oil

1 lb (500 g) assorted fresh mushrooms (see note, above)

2 tablespoons canola oil

MAKES 4 SERVINGS

FAVA BEAN AND PECORINO SALAD

Pecorino cheeses

The term pecorino encompasses a number of Italian sheep's milk cheeses—including pecorino romano and pecorino sardo, probably the best known—each with variations in the manner and duration of aging, the rind, and ultimately the flavor. Generally, the paler the rind, the younger the pecorino.

Tender spring fava beans are especially prized in Italy, where they are often eaten raw with young pecorino cheese. Here, this pleasing pairing is turned into a delicate salad with the addition of leaf lettuce, green onion, olive oil, and lemon juice.

Shell the fava beans. Have ready a bowl of ice water. Bring a pot three-fourths full of water to a boil. Add the favas and boil for 2 minutes. Drain, transfer to the ice water to stop the cooking, then drain again. Peel each bean by pinching open the end opposite the end that connected the bean to the pod; the bean will slip easily from its skin.

In a bowl, mix together the beans, oil to taste, and green onion. Season with salt, pepper, and lemon juice. Tear the lettuce into bite-size pieces and add to the bowl. Toss gently. Using a vegetable peeler, shave thin slices of the cheese directly into the bowl. Toss gently. Taste and adjust the seasoning. Transfer to a platter and serve right away.

4 lb (2 kg) fava (broad) beans

2½–3 tablespoons extra-virgin olive oil

2 tablespoons minced green (spring) onion, including tender green tops

Salt and ground pepper

Fresh lemon juice

12 leaves red or green leaf lettuce

2 oz (60 g) young pecorino cheese (see note, opposite)

MAKES 4 SERVINGS

ARUGULA WITH GRILLED TUNA AND WHITE BEANS

This main-course arugula salad, dressed with a lemon-garlic vinaigrette and topped with slices of perfectly seared tuna, is the ideal luncheon centerpiece for summertime guests. The fish can be cooked in a broiler (grill), if you prefer, using the same timing.

1 fennel bulb

3 cans (15 oz/470 g each) cannellini beans, rinsed, drained, and patted dry

6 plum (Roma) tomatoes, seeded and cut into ½-inch (12-mm) dice

1 cup (4 oz/125 g) chopped sweet red onion

15 brine-cured black olives such as Kalamata, pitted and slivered

6 tablespoons (3 fl oz/ 90 ml) fresh lemon juice

2 teaspoons finely chopped garlic

1½ teaspoons dried thyme

Salt and ground pepper

¾ cup (6 fl oz/180 ml) olive oil

1½ lb (750 g) tuna fillet, about ¾ inch (2 cm) thick

2 teaspoons soy sauce

½ lb (250 g) arugula (rocket), tough stems removed

2 teaspoons grated lemon zest

MAKES 6 SERVINGS

Cut off the stems, feathery tops, and any bruised outer stalks from the fennel bulb. Quarter lengthwise, cut away the tough core portion, and dice. Place in a large bowl. Add the beans, tomatoes, onion, and olives and mix well.

In a small bowl, whisk together 4 tablespoons (2 fl oz/60 ml) of the lemon juice, the garlic, thyme, 1 teaspoon salt, and ¼ teaspoon pepper. Whisk in the oil to form a dressing. Remove and reserve ¼ cup (2 fl oz/60 ml). Add the remaining dressing to the bean mixture, toss well, cover, and refrigerate for at least 2 hours or up to 4 hours.

About 45 minutes before you plan to serve, remove the bean mixture from the refrigerator. Place the tuna in a shallow glass dish. Stir the soy sauce into the reserved dressing, and pour over the tuna. Cover the dish and let stand at cool room temperature.

Prepare a charcoal or gas grill for direct-heat cooking over medium-high heat (see page 18).

Remove the tuna from the marinade, discarding the marinade. Place the tuna on the grill rack 4–5 inches (10–13 cm) from the fire. Cook, turning once, until seared on the outside but still pink at the center, 1½–2 minutes on each side, or until done to your liking. Remove the fish from the grill rack and sprinkle lightly with salt and pepper. Cut into slices about ¼ inch (6 mm) thick.

Meanwhile, reserve one-third of the arugula. Roughly chop the remaining arugula, add to the bean mixture, and mix well. Taste and adjust the seasoning.

To serve, divide the reserved arugula evenly among individual plates, arranging it on one side. Mound the bean mixture in the center of the plates, dividing it evenly, and place the tuna on top. Drizzle the remaining 2 tablespoons lemon juice over the tuna, then sprinkle with the lemon zest. Serve right away.

Salad for dinner

The difference between a side salad and a main-course salad is usually the amount of protein included. A salad that incorporates a significant portion of fish, shellfish, chicken, or meat is generally substantial enough to serve as a main course.

107

SALADS

CELERY ROOT WITH BLOOD ORANGES

Celery root

Also called celeriac, celery root is a member of the celery family, but it is the root of a different plant than what we know as common celery. The flavors of celery and celery root are similar, though celery root has an earthier character and denser texture than celery stalks.

Blood oranges and celery root are both available during the cool months of the year, making this salad an ideal first course for a holiday meal. You can use regular oranges and fennel in their place. If you use fennel, chop the bulbs coarsely.

In a small bowl, whisk together the vinegar, ⅛ teaspoon salt, and a few grinds of pepper. Add the mustard and honey and whisk until blended. Add the oil, a little at a time, whisking until blended. Taste and adjust the seasoning. Pour half of the vinaigrette into a medium bowl.

Using a sharp knife, carefully peel the celery root and shred on the medium holes of a grater-shredder. Add to the vinaigrette in the bowl and toss to coat. (This step can be done up to 1 hour in advance of serving.)

If necessary, tear the greens into bite-size pieces. Place in a large bowl. Add the remaining vinaigrette and toss to coat.

Divide the lettuce among 6 individual plates, arranging it in a ring on each plate. Divide the celery root evenly among the plates, mounding it in the center. Arrange the orange segments on the greens and serve right away.

1 tablespoon raspberry or mild white wine vinegar

Salt and ground pepper

2 teaspoons Dijon mustard

2 teaspoons honey

⅓ cup (3 fl oz/80 ml) extra-virgin olive oil

1 celery root (celeriac), about 1 lb (500 g)

8–10 oz (250–315 g) mixed salad greens

3 blood oranges, sectioned (see page 543)

MAKES 6 SERVINGS

WATERCRESS AND BEET SALAD WITH FETA

Beet stains

These days, beets are available in a variety of colors. Traditional red beets are highly pigmented and can color other foods in the dish, as well as your hands and countertops, so handle them carefully.

In Mediterranean countries, salads made with beets are dressed simply with olive oil and vinegar, or, as here, sprinkled with feta cheese. If you buy beets with the greens intact, trim the greens off, boil just until tender, and use in place of the watercress.

If the greens are still attached to the beets, cut them off, leaving about 1 inch (2.5 cm) of the stem intact. Do not pierce the beet skins, or the color will bleed as they are boiled. In a saucepan, combine the beets with water to cover and bring to a boil over high heat. Cover partially, reduce the heat to low, and simmer until tender, 30–40 minutes for large beets or 15–20 minutes for small beets. Drain, place in a bowl of cold water to cool, then peel and slice or cut into quarters. Place the beets in a bowl.

To make a vinaigrette, in a small bowl, whisk together the oil, vinegar, garlic, half of the mint, and the allspice. Season with salt and pepper.

Place the onion slices in a small bowl and dress with a few tablespoons of the vinaigrette. Let stand for 15 minutes.

Add ¼ cup (2 fl oz/60 ml) of the vinaigrette to the beets and toss well. Add the onion and toss to mix. In a separate bowl, toss the watercress with the remaining vinaigrette and arrange on a platter. Neatly arrange the beets and onion on top of the greens. Sprinkle with the cheese and the remaining mint. Serve right away.

4 large or 8 small beets

½ cup (4 fl oz/125 ml) extra-virgin olive oil

3 tablespoons red wine vinegar

1 clove garlic, minced

½ cup (¾ oz/20 g) chopped fresh mint

½ teaspoon ground allspice

Salt and ground pepper

1 red onion, thinly sliced

6–7 cups (6–7 oz/185–220 g) young, tender watercress sprigs (about 4 bunches) or baby spinach leaves

1 cup (5 oz/155 g) crumbled feta cheese

MAKES 4 SERVINGS

ZUCCHINI AND MINT SALAD

What could be simpler or more refreshing than thinly sliced zucchini lightly dressed in lemon juice and tossed with mint? It is important to use very young, tender zucchini for this salad, which works well alongside everything from omelets to grilled fish.

8 baby zucchini (courgettes), about ¾ lb (375 g) total weight

2 tablespoons fresh lemon juice

1 tablespoon finely chopped fresh mint leaves

Salt

Cayenne pepper

¼ cup (2 fl oz/60 ml) extra-virgin olive oil

MAKES 4 SERVINGS

Fill a large bowl three-fourths full with water and ice cubes, immerse the zucchini in the water, and refrigerate for 2 hours to crisp.

Drain the zucchini and dry well. Cut crosswise into paper-thin rounds. Arrange the slices on a platter.

In a small bowl, stir together the lemon juice and mint. Season with salt and cayenne. Vigorously stir in the oil until emulsified to make a dressing.

Pour the dressing over the zucchini and serve right away.

Extra-crunchy zucchini

This recipe calls for refrigerating the baby zucchini in a bowl of ice water for a couple of hours. This cold bath makes them particularly crisp and therefore easier to slice thinly.

TOMATO, CUCUMBER, AND ONION SALAD

Set out a platter of sliced tomatoes, red onion, and cucumber, drizzled with a feta-spiked-oregano vinaigrette, and watch how quickly it disappears. For a lighter but still flavorful salad, omit the cheese from the dressing.

2 cucumbers

4 beefsteak or assorted heirloom tomatoes

½ large red onion

Salt and ground pepper

1 cup (8 fl oz/250 ml) olive oil

2 tablespoons dried oregano

1 tablespoon finely minced garlic

½ cup (2½ oz/75 g) crumbled feta cheese

¼ cup (2 fl oz/60 ml) red wine vinegar, or as needed

MAKES 6 SERVINGS

Peel the cucumbers, halve the cucumbers lengthwise, and scrape out the seeds. Slice thinly crosswise and spread in a single layer on a platter, reserving a small handful of slices. Thinly slice the tomatoes and arrange in rows, slightly overlapping the slices, on top of the cucumber. Cut the onion into paper-thin slices and scatter over the tomatoes, then scatter the reserved cucumber slices on top. Sprinkle lightly with salt and pepper.

To make the vinaigrette, in a blender or food processor, combine the oil, oregano, garlic, cheese, ¼ cup vinegar, and a few grinds of pepper. Pulse briefly to blend. Taste and adjust the seasoning, adding a bit more vinegar if you like.

Spoon the vinaigrette over the sliced vegetables on the platter and serve right away.

Chop and toss

These same ingredients make a colorful chopped salad. Dice the cucumbers and tomatoes, cut the onion into slivers, and toss the vegetables with the vinaigrette.

SALADS

TOMATO AND FRESH MOZZARELLA SALAD

Fresh mozzarella cheese

Unlike the somewhat rubbery cheese that is grated and melted on most pizzas, fresh mozzarella is whiter and has a creamier consistency. It is generally sold in small plastic tubs, packed in water. Drain the cheese well before using.

An Italian classic, called a *caprese,* this salad is quick to prepare and delicious, but only if you choose top-quality ingredients: vine-ripened tomatoes and the freshest mozzarella. If you like, scatter a few capers, chopped anchovy fillets, or black olives over the top.

Tear the basil leaves into large pieces. Slice the tomatoes and mozzarella and arrange on a serving dish in neat, slightly overlapping rows or rings, alternating the tomatoes and mozzarella. Sprinkle with salt and pepper.

Scatter the basil over the top. Drizzle the oil in a thin stream over the salad and serve.

Leaves from 1 bunch fresh basil

4 tomatoes

¾ lb (375 g) fresh mozzarella cheese

Salt and ground pepper

¼ cup (2 fl oz/60 ml) extra-virgin olive oil

MAKES 4 SERVINGS

ROASTED ASPARAGUS AND ARUGULA SALAD

Roast ahead

The roasted asparagus can be roasted up to 4 hours in advance. Return the spears to the oven for a few minutes just to warm through, then proceed with the recipe.

For this elegant salad, lightly dressed arugula and red onion are arranged atop a bed of roasted asparagus. Start with the freshest possible asparagus and peel the stalks to yield beautiful, bright green spears that cook evenly from top to bottom.

Preheat the oven to 450°F (230°C). To prepare the asparagus, snap off the tough, woody ends of the spears and then trim the ends neatly. Using a vegetable peeler, peel the bottom 2 inches (5 cm) or so of each spear to remove the fibrous exterior. Place the asparagus in a baking dish, drizzle with 2 tablespoons of the oil, and turn gently to coat. Spread in a single layer, season with salt and pepper, and roast until tender and slightly wrinkled, about 15 minutes. Remove from the oven and let cool slightly.

In a large bowl, using a fork, whisk together the lemon zest and juice, Cognac, Tapenade, and remaining 2 tablespoons oil. Add the onion and arugula and toss gently to coat.

Arrange the warm roasted asparagus in a neat layer on a platter and mound the onion and arugula mixture over the top. Serve right away.

2 lb (1 kg) medium-thick asparagus

4 tablespoons (2 fl oz/ 60 ml) extra-virgin olive oil

Fine sea salt and ground pepper

Finely grated zest of 1 lemon

1 teaspoon fresh lemon juice

1 teaspoon Cognac or brandy

2 tablespoons Tapenade (page 388)

½ small red onion, sliced paper-thin

3 cups (3 oz/90 g) baby arugula (rocket) leaves

MAKES 6 SERVINGS

NIÇOISE SALAD

This timeless Provençal salad is the perfect summertime main course. Although the ingredients can be tossed together, they are traditionally arranged—like with like, in a tidy pattern—on a platter or on individual plates to show off the elements to their best effect.

2 boiling potatoes, about ¾ lb (375 g) total weight, unpeeled

½ lb (250 g) green beans

4 tomatoes, about ¾ lb (375 g) total weight, cut into wedges

1 can (7 oz/220 g) tuna in olive oil, drained and flaked

¼ lb (125 g) black olives, preferably Niçoise

2 tablespoons rinsed capers

1 tablespoon Dijon mustard

2 tablespoons white wine vinegar

Salt

⅓ cup (3 fl oz/80 ml) extra-virgin olive oil

1 tablespoon finely chopped fresh oregano

MAKES 4 SERVINGS

In a saucepan, combine the potatoes with enough salted water to cover and bring to a boil over high heat. Reduce the heat to medium and cook until tender when pierced with a knife, 15–20 minutes. Drain and peel the potatoes while still hot. Let cool, then cut into 1-inch (2.5-cm) cubes. Place on a platter in a neat row or mound.

Meanwhile, fill another saucepan three-fourths full with salted water and bring to a boil. Add the green beans and boil just until tender, about 5 minutes. Drain, place under cold running water to stop the cooking, and drain again. Add to the platter, lined up neatly.

Add the tomato wedges, tuna, and olives to the platter, again arranging in rows or tidy mounds. Sprinkle the rinsed capers over the top of the composed salad.

To make a vinaigrette, in a small bowl, stir together the mustard, vinegar, and salt to taste until well blended. Vigorously stir in the oil until emulsified.

Drizzle the vinaigrette over the salad, then sprinkle the oregano on top. Serve right away.

MEDITERRANEAN SALAD PLATTER

A vegetarian feast

This salad makes a great vegetarian meal for 4; omit the anchovies or feta cheese if you wish. To round out the meal, offer crusty bread and peppery olive oil.

Mediterranean vegetables, cheese, a trio of olive types, and anchovies come together in this easy-to-assemble outdoor-party salad. The vegetables can be grilled a day in advance. When it is time to serve the salad, arrange everything on a platter and drizzle with the dressing.

Prepare a charcoal or gas grill for direct-heat cooking over medium heat (see page 18).

Brush the zucchini and bell peppers with the 2 tablespoons oil. Place the zucchini on the grill rack 4–5 inches (10–13 cm) from the fire and grill until lightly golden on the first side, 4–5 minutes. Turn and cook until lightly golden on the second side, about 3 minutes longer. Set aside.

Meanwhile, place the bell peppers on the grill rack and grill, turning, until the skins are evenly blackened and blistered, about 10 minutes total. Transfer to a plate, cover with aluminum foil, and let stand for 10 minutes, then peel away the skins. Cut the peppers in half lengthwise, remove the seeds and ribs, then slice lengthwise into narrow strips.

To serve, neatly arrange the zucchini, bell peppers, tomatoes, and onions on a platter. Top with the feta cheese, olives, capers, and anchovies (if using).

To make the dressing, in a bowl, whisk the remaining ½ cup (4 fl oz/125 ml) oil, the vinegar, and ½ teaspoon each salt and pepper until blended. Drizzle over the salad and serve.

4 zucchini (courgettes), trimmed and thinly sliced lengthwise

3 red bell peppers (capsicums)

2 tablespoons plus ½ cup (4 fl oz/125 ml) extra-virgin olive oil

4 large tomatoes, sliced

2 large red onions, thinly sliced

6 oz (185 g) feta cheese, crumbled

½ cup (2½ oz/75 g) Mediterranean-style oil-packed black olives

½ cup (2½ oz/75 g) Kalamata olives or other brine-cured black olives

½ cup (2½ oz/75 g) Mediterranean-style green olives

2 tablespoons rinsed capers

6 anchovy fillets in olive oil, drained, optional

⅓ cup (3 fl oz/80 ml) balsamic vinegar

Salt and ground pepper

MAKES 6–8 SERVINGS

MIDDLE-EASTERN PITA BREAD SALAD

Bread salads have long been a staple throughout the Mediterranean. This particular version, called *fattoush* in its native Syria, combines cucumbers, tomatoes, onions, bell pepper, and herbs. It's an excellent way to use up leftover pita bread.

2 pita rounds, 8 inches (20 cm) in diameter, 3–4 days old

1 English (hothouse) cucumber

Salt and ground pepper

3 tomatoes, about 1¼ lb (625 g) total weight

6 green (spring) onions, including tender green tops

1 green bell pepper (capsicum)

⅓ cup (½ oz/15 g) coarsely chopped fresh mint

¼ cup (⅓ oz/10 g) coarsely chopped fresh flat-leaf (Italian) parsley

¼ cup (⅓ oz/10 g) coarsely chopped fresh cilantro (fresh coriander)

2 large cloves garlic, minced

¼ cup (2 fl oz/60 ml) fresh lemon juice

⅓ cup (3 fl oz/80 ml) extra-virgin olive oil

MAKES 6 SERVINGS

Preheat the oven to 375°F (190°C). Split each pita by separating it along the outside seam, then tear the rounds into 1-inch (2.5-cm) pieces. Spread the pieces on a rimmed baking sheet. Bake until lightly golden and dry, 10–15 minutes. Transfer to a bowl and let cool.

Meanwhile, peel and halve the cucumber lengthwise, scrape out any errant seeds, and cut into small dice. Spread the diced cucumber on paper towels in a single layer, salt lightly, and let drain for 15 minutes. Transfer the cucumber to a colander, place under cold running water for a few seconds, and spread on clean paper towels.

Seed and dice the tomatoes, cut the green onions crosswise into ¼-inch (6-mm) pieces, and seed and dice the bell pepper. Add the vegetables and all the herbs to the pita. Season with salt and pepper and toss well.

In a small bowl, whisk together the garlic, lemon juice and oil. Season with salt and pepper. Drizzle over the salad and toss well. Transfer to a platter and serve right away.

Make it your own

Bread salads are easy to vary. Brined Mediterranean-style black olives are a nice addition, as is crumbled feta cheese. You can also alter the proportions of the vegetables or herbs to suit your personal taste.

113

GARDEN BEANS IN TOMATO VINAIGRETTE

Bean freshness

Before cooking, sample your shell beans (beans that must be shelled before eating) for maturity. Bite into 2 or 3 beans. If your teeth meet resistance, the beans have begun to dry and they will require longer cooking than those that are less firm to the bite.

114

The more colors and types of beans you incorporate into this salad, the better. Seek out yellow wax beans, Blue Lake beans, romano beans, black-eyed peas, pale green limas, mottled cranberry beans, and regional or heirloom varieties at farmers' markets.

Place the snap beans on a steamer rack over gently boiling water, cover, and steam until tender but still bright colored, about 10 minutes. Remove from the steamer and rinse with cold running water to stop the cooking and to retain the color. Set aside.

Working in batches, place each variety of shell bean on the steamer rack over gently boiling water, cover, and steam until the beans are tender and have lost all hint of crunchiness. The cooking time will depend on the size and maturity of the beans: some may cook in only 10 minutes, and others may take 30 minutes or longer. Remove from the steamer and rinse with cold running water to stop the cooking. Set aside.

To make the vinaigrette, combine the tomato, shallots, garlic, oil, vinegar, tarragon, 1 teaspoon pepper, and ½ teaspoon salt in a large bowl and mix until well blended. Add the snap beans and the shell beans and turn in the dressing until well coated. Cover and refrigerate for at least 3 hours or preferably overnight. Serve chilled or at room temperature.

1 lb (500 g) assorted young, tender snap beans, trimmed

2 lb (1 kg) assorted fresh shell beans, shelled

FOR THE VINAIGRETTE

1 large, very ripe tomato, peeled, seeded, and minced

2 shallots, minced

1 clove garlic, minced

½ cup (4 fl oz/125 ml) olive oil

⅓ cup (3 fl oz/80 ml) red wine vinegar

2 tablespoons minced fresh tarragon

Salt and ground pepper

MAKES 4–6 SERVINGS

LENTIL SALAD WITH FETA AND MINT

About French lentils

Puy lentils, slate-green legumes with a robust, earthy character, come from the volcanic area of Le Puy in central France. High in protein and low in carbohydrates, the small lentils keep their shape and color when cooked, making them desirable for use in salads.

Tossed with red onion, bell pepper, and feta in a light vinaigrette, lentils make a lovely salad. You can also make this recipe with other beans such as navy beans, black beans, or chickpeas (garbanzo beans). Fresh goat cheese can also be substituted for the feta.

In a saucepan, combine the lentils with water to cover by 2 inches (5 cm) and bring to a boil over high heat. Reduce the heat to medium-low and simmer, uncovered, until the lentils are tender, 15–20 minutes. Drain immediately and set aside in a large bowl.

To make a vinaigrette, in a small bowl, whisk together the oil, the 6 tablespoons vinegar, the garlic, and cumin. Season with salt and pepper. Add the vinaigrette to the warm lentils and toss to coat evenly. Add the onion and bell pepper and toss gently. Let stand for 20 minutes at room temperature to blend the flavors.

Taste and adjust the seasoning with salt, pepper, and vinegar, if necessary.

1 cup (7 oz/220 g) green lentils, preferably Puy

6 tablespoons (3 fl oz/90 ml) extra-virgin olive oil

6 tablespoons (3 fl oz/90 ml) red wine vinegar, or as needed

2 cloves garlic, minced

½ teaspoon ground cumin

Salt and ground pepper

1 small red onion, diced

1 red bell pepper (capsicum), seeded and finely diced

¼ cup (⅓ oz/10 g) chopped fresh mint, plus sprigs for garnish

6 oz (185 g) feta cheese, crumbled

MAKES 6 SERVINGS

Add the chopped mint to the salad and toss to mix well. Transfer the salad to a platter or divide among individual plates. Sprinkle with the cheese, garnish with the mint sprigs, and serve right away.

Keeping herbs

At many farmers' markets you can find herbs with roots still attached. Immersed in a glass of water, they will keep fresh for weeks.

CORN AND TOMATO SALAD

Ideal picnic fare, this salad, made with vine-ripened tomatoes and garden-fresh corn, is a summertime classic. For a more refined dish, peel the tomatoes. You can make the salad up to 6 hours in advance and refrigerate it; bring to room temperature before serving.

6 ears fresh sweet corn

½ cup (4 fl oz/125 ml) olive oil

1 cup (5 oz/155 g) minced red onion

2 teaspoons chili powder

1 teaspoon ground cumin

1 red bell pepper (capsicum), cut into ¼-inch (6-mm) dice

1 green bell pepper (capsicum), cut into ¼-inch (6 mm) dice

1–1½ cups (6–9 oz/ 185–280 g) seeded and diced tomatoes

¼ cup (⅓ oz/10 g) chopped fresh cilantro (fresh coriander)

3 tablespoons sherry vinegar

Salt and ground pepper

MAKES 6 SERVINGS

Working with 1 ear of corn at a time, hold the ear by its pointed end, steadying the stalk end in the bottom of a shallow bowl. Using a sharp knife, cut down along the ear to strip off the kernels, giving the ear a quarter turn after each cut. You should have about 3 cups (18 oz/560 g) kernels.

Bring a saucepan three-fourths full of salted water to a boil. Add the corn kernels and boil for 1–2 minutes. Drain and immerse in cold water to stop the cooking. Drain again, patting dry with paper towels.

In a small sauté pan over medium heat, warm ¼ cup (2 fl oz/60 ml) of the oil. Add the onion and sauté until softened, about 2 minutes. Add the chili powder and cumin and sauté for 1 minute longer. Remove from the heat and let cool.

In a bowl, combine the corn, bell peppers, tomatoes, and cooled onions and toss to mix. Add the cilantro, the remaining ¼ cup oil, and the vinegar and toss well. Season with salt and pepper, toss again, and serve right away.

Garden mates

Corn and tomatoes are both height-of-summer crops, ready for harvest at the same time, which is why they so often appear together in salads and other types of dishes.

115

WARM RED CABBAGE AND APPLE SLAW

Apple color

The green-skinned apples in this salad provide a nice color contrast with the red cabbage and onion, but red apples will do, too. Just make sure they are crisp and tart.

Chopped rather than shredded and served warm rather than chilled, this striking salad is an appealing twist on traditional coleslaw. To dress it, top with crumbled blue, feta, or fresh goat cheese. A few sprigs of flat-leaf (Italian) parsley make an attractive contrasting garnish.

Cut away the core from the cabbage half. Cut the cabbage into ½-by-2-inch (12-mm-by-5-cm) pieces. Set aside.

In a large frying pan over medium heat, warm the olive oil. Add the onion and sauté, stirring occasionally, until hot, about 2 minutes. Add the cabbage, apples, caraway seeds, and vinegar and stir well. Continue to cook uncovered, stirring occasionally, until the cabbage softens, about 4 minutes. Season with salt and pepper.

Transfer to a platter and serve right away.

½ **head red cabbage**

5 **tablespoons (3 fl oz/ 80 ml) extra-virgin olive oil**

1 **large red onion, cut into 8 wedges**

2 **tart green apples such as pippin or Granny Smith, each cut into 8 wedges and cored**

1 **teaspoon caraway seeds**

3 **tablespoons balsamic vinegar**

Salt and ground pepper

MAKES 6 SERVINGS

TANGY COLESLAW

Shredding cabbage

To shred cabbage uniformly without a food processor, trim off and discard the outer leaves, cut the head into quarters, and cut out the core. Turn each quarter onto a flat side and use a large knife to cut the leaves crosswise into very thin shreds.

Red cabbage gives this classic slaw a bright look. You can substitute green cabbage and use red bell pepper in place of the green pepper. For a crunchy, flavorful garnish, sprinkle crumbled fried bacon over the salad just before serving.

In a large bowl, combine the cabbage, carrot, bell pepper, and onion. Toss to mix.

In a small saucepan over medium-high heat, stir together the vinegar, sugar, celery seeds, and mustard. Bring to a boil, stirring frequently, and then continue to boil, stirring occasionally, until thick, about 15 minutes. Remove from the heat and whisk in ¼ cup (2 fl oz/60 ml) water. Immediately pour over the cabbage mixture. Toss well, cover, and refrigerate for 6–8 hours.

Just before serving, remove the coleslaw from the refrigerator and drain off and discard the liquid. (There will be quite a lot of liquid.) Transfer the coleslaw to a serving bowl, sprinkle with the parsley, and serve.

1 **small head red cabbage, about 1 lb (500 g), cored and shredded**

1 **large carrot, peeled and grated**

½ **green bell pepper (capsicum), minced**

1 **small white onion, finely chopped**

1 **cup (8 fl oz/250 ml) cider vinegar**

⅔ **cup (5 oz/155 g) sugar**

½ **teaspoon celery seeds**

½ **teaspoon dry mustard**

1 **tablespoon chopped fresh flat-leaf (Italian) parsley**

MAKES 6 SERVINGS

JICAMA SLAW WITH CHILE-LIME DRESSING

Because it is so crisp and juicy, jicama can take a spicy, citrusy dressing like the one here. Jicama and citrus are a common marriage. All across Mexico, roadside stands sell slices of cold, peeled jicama garnished with a drizzle of fresh lime juice and a dusting of chili powder.

1 jicama, about 1½ lb (750 g)

¾ lb (375 g) carrots

1 cup (1 oz/30 g) loosely packed fresh cilantro (fresh coriander) leaves

1 jalapeño chile

¼ cup (2 fl oz/60 ml) fresh lime juice

¼ cup (2 oz/60 g) sour cream

¼ cup (2 fl oz/60 ml) mayonnaise

Fine sea salt

½ teaspoon chili powder

8–10 pale, inner leaves from 1 large head romaine (cos) lettuce, optional

MAKES 8–10 SERVINGS

With a vegetable peeler, peel the jicama and the carrots. Using the largest holes of a grater-shredder, shred both vegetables. Set aside.

Finely chop the cilantro leaves. Halve, seed, if desired, and mince the chile.

In a large bowl, whisk together the lime juice, sour cream, mayonnaise, 1 teaspoon salt, the chili powder, cilantro, and chile. Add the jicama and carrot and toss to mix. Cover the salad and refrigerate for at least 1 hour or up to 3 hours to allow the flavors to blend.

Just before serving, remove the salad from the refrigerator and toss again to distribute the dressing. Scoop some salad into each lettuce leaf (if using) and serve.

Versatile jicama

A member of the legume family, jicama can be eaten raw, as in this slaw, or it can be steamed, fried, roasted, or boiled. Its crunchy texture makes it a good choice for crudité platters or as a substitute for water chestnuts in stir-fries.

117

SHAVED FENNEL AND MUSHROOM SALAD

This flavorful salad is made from just four ingredients, but it has a big impact on the plate. If you enjoy the flavor of celery, use it in place of the fennel for a surprisingly delicious variation. Make sure the mushrooms are very fresh and tightly closed, with no gills exposed.

2 fennel bulbs with fronds attached

¾ lb (12 oz/375 g) cremini mushrooms

¼ cup (2 fl oz/60 ml) fresh lemon juice

5 tablespoons (3 fl oz/ 80 ml) extra-virgin olive oil

Salt and ground pepper

MAKES 4 SERVINGS

Trim the fennel bulbs, setting the fronds aside. Using a mandoline or very sharp knife, cut the fennel lengthwise into very thin slices. Cut the mushrooms in the same manner.

Put the sliced fennel and mushrooms in a bowl. Add the lemon juice, oil, ½ teaspoon salt, and 1 teaspoon pepper and toss to mix well.

Transfer the salad to a platter. Mince the fennel fronds and sprinkle over the salad. Serve right away.

Using a mandoline

Mandolines are handy tools for prepping vegetables, offering precision and regularity. Look for a mandoline with a hand guard that keeps your fingers clear of the cutting edge as you move the ingredient back and forth across the extremely sharp cutting blade.

SPICY CHINESE CHICKEN AND RICE SALAD

Long-grain rice

Any rice with grains three to five times longer than they are wide is labeled long grain. When cooked, the rice grains are fluffy and separate, rather than sticky, making them ideal for salads and pilafs. Basmati and jasmine are among the finest varieties.

Dressed with an Asian-inspired vinaigrette and topped with slices of soy-glazed chicken, this rice salad makes a lovely light meal. For a different presentation, chop the chicken into cubes and toss the cubes with the rice, green onion, and dressing.

Preheat the oven to 425°F (220°C). In a small bowl, whisk together 2 tablespoons of the soy sauce, 2 tablespoons of the sesame oil, and the molasses.

Place the chicken, breast side up, in a small roasting pan and roast for 15 minutes. Reduce the oven temperature to 375°F (190°C). Brush the chicken generously with some of the soy mixture and continue roasting, brushing with more of the mixture every 10 minutes, until the skin of the chicken is crisp and shiny, about 1 hour. To test for doneness, insert an instant-read thermometer into the thickest part of the thigh away from bone; it should register 175°F (80°C). Remove from the oven and let cool, then bone the chicken and cut the meat and crisp skin into long, thin slices. Set aside.

Meanwhile, in a heavy saucepan, combine the broth and ½ teaspoon salt and bring to a boil over high heat. Add the rice, reduce the heat to low, cover, and cook, without stirring, for 20 minutes. Uncover and check to see if the rice is tender. If not, re-cover and cook for a few minutes longer. Remove from the heat, transfer to a bowl, and let cool.

To make the dressing, in another bowl, whisk together the peanut oil, vinegar, the remaining 4 tablespoons (2 fl oz/60 ml) soy sauce, the remaining 2 tablespoons sesame oil, the garlic, ginger, chile, and sugar. Season with salt and pepper.

In a large bowl, mix together the cooled rice and the dressing. Transfer to a platter, top with the chicken, sprinkle with the green onion, and serve.

6 tablespoons (3 fl oz/ 90 ml) soy sauce

4 tablespoons (2 fl oz/ 60 ml) Asian sesame oil

2 tablespoons unsulfured light molasses

1 chicken, about 3½ lb (1.75 kg)

1½ cups (12 fl oz/375 ml) chicken broth

Salt and ground pepper

¾ cup (5 oz/155 g) long-grain white rice

3 tablespoons peanut oil

¼ cup (2 fl oz/60 ml) rice vinegar

1 clove garlic, minced

1 tablespoon peeled, minced fresh ginger

½ jalapeño chile, seeded and minced

1 teaspoon sugar

1 green (spring) onion, including tender green tops, sliced on the diagonal

MAKES 6 SERVINGS

ARTICHOKE AND ORZO SALAD

Metals for artichokes

Use only stainless-steel knives and cookware when preparing artichokes, since carbon steel, aluminum, and cast iron will discolor the vegetable.

This simple pasta salad combines baby artichokes with diced red pepper, herbs, and orzo, a tiny rice-shaped pasta. The dish takes well to additions, including cooked shrimp (prawns) or scallops or neatly cut vegetables. You can also add or substitute long-grain white rice.

Have ready a large bowl of water to which you have added 2 tablespoons of the lemon juice. Trim each artichoke (page 332) and cut into halves or quarters, depending on size, to create pieces about ½ inch (12 mm) thick. As each artichoke is cut, drop the pieces into the bowl of lemon water.

In a saucepan, combine 2½ qt (2.5 l) water and the remaining lemon juice and bring to a boil over high heat. Drain the artichokes and add them and the orzo to the boiling water.

½ cup (4 fl oz/125 ml) fresh lemon juice

14–16 baby artichokes, about 1 lb (500 g) total weight

½ lb (250 g) orzo or other rice-shaped pasta

2 tablespoons olive oil

¼ cup (1½ oz/45 g) roasted
red bell pepper (capsicum),
peeled and diced
(see page 333)

2 tablespoons Dijon mustard

2 tablespoons white
wine vinegar

2 tablespoons chopped
fresh tarragon or flat-leaf
(Italian) parsley, or
½ teaspoon dried tarragon

Salt and ground pepper

MAKES 4 SERVINGS

Boil until the orzo is al dente and the artichokes are tender,
8–10 minutes. Drain and transfer to a large bowl. Add the oil
and toss to coat evenly. Let cool.

In a small bowl, combine the roasted bell pepper, mustard,
vinegar, and tarragon and stir to combine. Add to the orzo
mixture and toss to mix well. Season with salt and pepper
and serve right away.

**Substituting
artichoke hearts**

*In a pinch, you
can use prepared
artichoke hearts in
this salad. Look for
frozen or water-
packed artichoke
hearts, not the
marinated hearts
in jars, which would
conflict with the
flavorings here.*

FUSILLI SALAD WITH SWEET PEPPERS

The wide array of sweet peppers available in markets makes this Italian-inspired pasta salad
an especially colorful offering. The ingredients, except for the basil, can be assembled a few
hours in advance and refrigerated. Fontina can be used in place of the mozzarella.

Pasta for salads

*Generally, the best
pasta for salads
are short shapes,
especially twists and
corkscrews, that can
get tangled with the
other ingredients,
keeping everything
evenly distributed
once it is tossed.*

3 red, orange, or
yellow sweet peppers
(capsicums), or a mixture,
roasted and peeled
(see page 333)

1 clove garlic

2 anchovy fillets in
olive oil, drained

1 lb (500 g) dried fusilli

6 tablespoons (3 fl oz/
90 ml) extra-virgin olive oil

2 tablespoons
rinsed capers

10 oz (300 g) fresh
mozzarella cheese, diced

12 fresh basil leaves,
torn into small pieces

Salt and ground pepper

MAKES 6 SERVINGS

Cut the peppers lengthwise into strips about ⅜ inch (1 cm)
wide. Set aside.

Place the garlic and anchovies in a small bowl. With a fork,
mash them together to form a smooth paste. Set aside.

In a large pot, bring 5 qt (5 l) salted water to a boil. Add the
fusilli and cook until al dente, about 8 minutes.

Drain the pasta and place in a bowl. Add the oil, anchovy-
garlic paste, and capers and toss well. Let the pasta cool
to room temperature.

Add the peppers, cheese, and basil. Season with salt
and pepper and toss to combine. Serve right away.

GERMAN POTATO SALAD

Add bacon

If you prefer bacon in your potato salad, cut 4 slices thick-cut bacon into 1-inch (2.5-cm) pieces, fry until crisp, drain on paper towels, and crumble coarsely. Add the bacon to the warm dressing with the vinegar.

In this version of German-style potato salad, olive oil replaces the traditional bacon drippings in the dressing, resulting in a lighter dish. Serve the warm salad for a wintertime weekend lunch alongside deli-style sandwiches or baked ham.

Bring a large saucepan three-fourths full of salted water to a boil over high heat. Add the potatoes and cook until tender but slightly resistant when pierced with a knife, 25–30 minutes. Drain and let cool slightly, then peel and cut into slices 1 inch (2.5 cm) thick. Place in a serving bowl.

In a frying pan over medium heat, warm the oil. Add the onion and sauté until lightly browned, about 5 minutes. Stir in the flour, sugar, ½ teaspoon salt, ¼ teaspoon pepper, and ½ cup (4 fl oz/125 ml) water. Continue to cook until the mixture begins to thicken, 3–5 minutes. Add the vinegar and two-thirds of the parsley and cook for 1 minute longer to make a dressing. Taste and adjust the seasoning.

Pour the warm dressing over the potatoes and mix gently to coat the ingredients evenly. Garnish with the remaining parsley and serve right away.

2 lb (1 kg) red or white potatoes, unpeeled

6 tablespoons (3 fl oz/ 90 ml) olive oil

1 yellow onion, thinly sliced

2 teaspoons all-purpose (plain) flour

1 tablespoon sugar

Salt and ground pepper

¼ cup (2 fl oz/60 ml) cider vinegar

6 tablespoons (½ oz/15 g) finely chopped fresh flat-leaf (Italian) parsley

MAKES 4–6 SERVINGS

CREAMY POTATO SALAD

Celery seeds

Tiny, crescent-shaped dried celery seeds have a strong celery flavor. They are harvested from a close relative of celery that is cultivated only for its seeds, and are used whole in potato salad, coleslaw, and pickling mixtures as well as ground in spice and herb mixtures.

Creamy, chunky, and punctuated with diced bell pepper and celery, this old-fashioned potato salad is sure to please a picnic crowd. At the market, choose potatoes about 2 inches (5 cm) in diameter. Keeping the size uniform will ensure they cook evenly.

In a large saucepan, combine the potatoes, ½ teaspoon salt, and water to cover by 1 inch (2.5 cm). Bring to a boil over high heat, reduce the heat to medium, and boil gently, uncovered, until the potatoes are tender when pierced with a knife, 20–25 minutes. Drain and set aside until cool enough to handle, 15–20 minutes.

In a small bowl, whisk together the olive oil, vinegar, and mustard, and set aside.

Cut the potatoes into large bite-size chunks and place in a large bowl. Sprinkle with the vinegar-oil mixture and stir gently to mix. Set aside for 15 minutes.

In a bowl, combine the celery, bell pepper, mayonnaise, sour cream, celery seeds, and ¼ teaspoon salt and mix well. Spoon the mixture over the potatoes and mix gently until evenly coated. Taste and adjust the seasoning. Cover and refrigerate until well chilled, about 1 hour. Serve chilled.

15 small red potatoes, about 2 lb (1 kg) total weight

Salt

2 tablespoons olive oil

1 tablespoon cider vinegar

1 tablespoon Dijon mustard

2 celery stalks, diced

½ small red bell pepper (capsicum), diced

½ cup (4 oz/125 g) mayonnaise

¼ cup (2 oz/60 g) sour cream

½ teaspoon celery seeds

MAKES 8 SERVINGS

ROASTED RED POTATO SALAD

Be sure to dress the potatoes while they are hot so they will absorb the aromatic flavors of the shallots, tarragon, sherry vinegar, and mustard. This salad tastes wonderful after the flavors have melded in the refrigerator overnight, but it is also delicious served right away.

3 lb (1.5 kg) red potatoes, unpeeled

About ⅔ cup (5 oz/155 g) coarse sea salt

2 tablespoons dry white wine

2 tablespoons plus ¾ cup (6 fl oz/180 ml) extra-virgin olive oil

3 tablespoons sherry wine vinegar

4 shallots, coarsely chopped

3 tablespoons fresh tarragon leaves

2 tablespoons Dijon mustard

Ground pepper

3 green (spring) onions, including tender green tops, chopped

½ bunch fresh flat-leaf (Italian) parsley, chopped

MAKES 8 SERVINGS

Preheat the oven to 400°F (200°C). Place the potatoes in a baking pan large enough to hold them in a single layer and pour the salt over them, covering them generously. Roast the potatoes until tender but firm when pierced with a knife, 50–60 minutes.

Remove the pan from the oven and, using pot holders, rub off the excess salt from the potatoes. Cut the potatoes into thin slices. (If they are still very hot, hold with a pot holder or paper towel as you slice.) Transfer to a bowl. Immediately drizzle the wine, the 2 tablespoons oil, and 1 tablespoon of the vinegar over the hot potatoes. Toss gently and set aside.

In a food processor, combine the shallots and tarragon and pulse to chop finely. Add to the potatoes and toss gently.

In a small bowl, whisk together the ¾ cup (6 fl oz/180 ml) oil, the remaining 2 tablespoons vinegar, and the mustard. Season with pepper. Pour the dressing over the potatoes and turn gently to coat. Cover and refrigerate for at least 1 hour or up to 2 days.

Remove the potato salad from the refrigerator. Add the green onions and parsley and toss gently. Taste and adjust the seasoning. If desired, let the salad stand for about 1 hour before serving to blend the flavors.

Substituting dried tarragon

If you can't find fresh tarragon, chop 1 tbsp dried tarragon with 3 tbsp of the parsley leaves to release the aromatic oils of the dried herb.

121

Soups & STEWS

Soups & Stews

Soups and stews are popular around the world, from the gazpacho of Spain and the minestrone of Italy to the lamb stew of Ireland and the clam chowder of New England. Part of their appeal is their own distinctive flavors and styles, whether creamy or clear, casual or elegant, brimming with seafood or thick with vegetables. But they are also appreciated for the homey warmth they bring to the dining table.

Soup Types

Seasonality
You can make all of the soups in this chapter at any time, but cooking with fresh, seasonal ingredients is the best way to guarantee great flavor.

Precise preparation
Soups are generally forgiving, but taking the time to slice or chop ingredients uniformly contributes to a better result. Potatoes or carrots of the same size and shape, for example, cook in the same amount of time.

Seasoning to taste
Seasoning is a matter of personal preference. Learn to taste soups as you cook, especially nearing the end, and adjust the seasoning to your liking.

Thinning and thickening
If a soup is too thick, thin it by stirring in stock (for a clear soup or stew) or milk (for a cream soup, bisque, or chowder), a little at a time, until it reaches the desired consistency. If it is too thin, thicken it by simmering it a while longer to reduce it. Or, stir in a little mashed potato, cooked rice, or bread crumbs, matching the thickener to the type of soup.

The soups in this chapter include five basic types: clear soups, chowders, puréed soups, cream soups, and bisques. Stews, typically more substantial than soups, are in a category of their own.

CLEAR SOUPS The defining element of clear soups is the use of a clear liquid—stock, broth, or water—as the base. Other ingredients and toppings determine whether the soup is light or hearty. For example, a simple chicken-vegetable soup would make a good light first course, but a bread-and-cheese-topped French onion soup can be a hearty meal in itself.

CHOWDERS Typically creamy because of the addition of milk or cream, chowders are often chunky mixtures, usually containing potatoes, onions, and bacon. They can be made from seafood, such as clams; poultry, such as chicken; or vegetables, such as corn.

PURÉED SOUPS Vegetables, one or a mixture, form the base of puréed soups. Carrots, leeks, tomatoes, potatoes—even dried beans—are cooked in stock or broth and then puréed until smooth. Or, only part of the solids are puréed to create an interesting contrast in textures.

CREAM SOUPS A roux—a mixture of flour and butter—which is both a thickener and a flavor enhancer, is often the first step in making a cream soup. The base is usually a puréed vegetable, stock is the typical liquid, and heavy (double) cream or milk is added to give the soup a silky texture.

BISQUES The term bisque was originally applied only to a smooth, cream-based seafood soup, but now it is routinely used to describe any thick, smooth, cream-enriched soup. Cooked rice is a common thickener.

STEWS A stew is made by simmering bite-size chunks of meat, seafood, or vegetables in liquid. More substantial and thicker than most soups, stews are commonly served as main courses. They are typically economical, as they usually call for ingredients that require long cooking for tenderness, such as root vegetables and tougher, leaner cuts of meat. They sometimes include, or are served with, dried beans, potatoes, or grains, such as pasta or rice. Most stews benefit from being refrigerated overnight before serving, which allows the flavors to deepen.

CHILIS This spicy stew of beef and chiles is formally known as *chili con carne*, literally "peppers with meat." However, chili takes a surprising number of forms. Although considered a sacrilege by some cooks, many versions include pinto or black beans, and in other cases the meat is stewed with tomatoes. There are even "vegetarian chilis," where the beans become the focus.

GARNISHING SOUPS AND STEWS

Garnishes contribute color, texture, and flavor to a soup or stew. Use the suggestions below as a starting point for adding finishing touches that are both delicious and eye-catching.

BACON

Puréed soups, cream soups, bisques, chowders
Brown extra when cooking it for a soup base, then crumble it over individual servings.

BREAD CRUMBS

Puréed soups, cream soups, bisques, chowders
Sprinkle Toasted Bread Crumbs (page 30) or Herbed Bread Crumbs (page 30) directly onto individual servings.

CAYENNE PEPPER

Cream soups and bisques
Sprinkle sparingly over individual portions to lend color and contrasting spiciness to rich soups.

CHEESE

Clear soups, puréed soups, stews
Sprinkle grated Parmesan or aged pecorino, or crumbled feta, queso fresco, or blue cheese directly over individual servings.

CROUTONS

Clear soups, puréed soups, cream soups
Toss bread cubes with olive oil, salt, and pepper, and bake in a 350°F (180°C) oven until golden. Float on individual servings.

FRESH HERBS

All soup types and stews
Strip leafy herb leaves from stems and chop coarsely or snip fresh chives into small pieces. Sprinkle onto individual servings. Use the same herb that flavors the soup or stew, or choose one with a complementary flavor and color.

GREEN (SPRING) ONIONS

All soup types and stews
Sprinkle chopped green (spring) onions onto individual servings for additional color and flavor.

GREMOLATA

Clear, meat- or poultry-based soups and stews
Sprinkle a small amount onto individual servings to brighten the flavor and cut the richness (see page 278)

GUACAMOLE

Chilis or Mexican-style stews
Spoon onto individual servings (see page 392).

NUTS

Vegetable-based puréed soups, cream soups
Toast almonds, hazelnuts (filberts) or pecans (see page 17), chop, and sprinkle over individual servings. Soups featuring winter squash or sweet potato are especially good with nuts.

OLIVE OIL

Puréed soups, cream soups, bisques, chowders
Drizzle extra-virgin olive oil in a zigzag or spiral pattern onto individual servings.

PESTO

Clear soups, puréed soups, cream soups
Spoon homemade Pesto or any of the variations (see page 387) onto individual servings. For best results, choose a pesto that features an herb used in the soup base.

ROASTED BELL PEPPERS (CAPSICUMS)

Puréed soups, cream soups, bisques, chowders
See page 333 for roasting instructions. Cut into narrow strips and scatter on individual servings.

ROUILLE

Seafood-based stews
Spread Rouille (page 389) onto toasted bread slices and serve them alongside or float them on top of individual portions.

SALSAS OR RELISHES

Chile-spiced or Mexican-style puréed soups or stews
Spoon Fresh Tomato Salsa (page 393), Avocado-Tomatillo Salsa (page 392) or Red Pepper–Corn Relish (page 395) onto individual servings.

TORTILLA STRIPS

Chile-spiced or Mexican-style clear or puréed soups
Cut corn tortillas into narrow strips, drizzle with olive oil, and bake in a 350°F (180°C) oven until golden. Float strips on individual servings.

SOUR CREAM, PLAIN YOGURT, CRÈME FRAÎCHE

Puréed soups, spicy stews
Spoon a dollop onto individual servings. Or thin with a little milk and drizzle in a spiral pattern from a spoon.

VEGETABLE PIECES

Vegetable-based puréed soups, cream soups
Top vegetable-based soups with small pieces of the primary vegetable used to make the soup. For example, asparagus tips for an asparagus-based soup; broccoli florets for a creamy broccoli purée.

CHILLED CUCUMBER SOUP

**Serving
cold soups**

*To keep cold soups at
their optimal serving
temperature at the
table, ladle them into
chilled bowls or
thick-walled glasses.
Chill the vessels in
the refrigerator for
at least 10 minutes
before you fill them.*

This light and refreshing cucumber soup makes a good first course to a summertime meal. Shredded carrot or finely diced tomato can be substituted for the diced radish and green onion, or chopped fresh dill can replace the green onion.

Peel the cucumbers, halve them lengthwise, and scrape out the seeds. Dice enough cucumber to measure ⅓ cup (2 oz/60 g). Set aside.

Chop the remaining cucumber and place in a blender or food processor with the onion, buttermilk, and yogurt. Process until smooth. Season with salt and pepper. Cover and refrigerate until cold, about 30 minutes.

To serve, divide the soup among chilled bowls and garnish with the reserved cucumber, the radish, and the green onion tops. Serve right away.

2 lb (1 kg) cucumbers

⅓ cup (1½ oz/45 g) chopped yellow onion

1 cup (8 fl oz/250 ml) low-fat buttermilk

½ cup (4 oz/125 g) plain yogurt

Salt and ground pepper

⅓ cup (1½ oz/45 g) diced radish

¼ cup (¾ oz/20 g) finely chopped green (spring) onion tops

MAKES 4 SERVINGS

CHILLED BEET BORSCHT WITH VODKA

Buried treasures

*Here, instead of
sprinkling the
cucumber and green
onion garnishes on
top, they are put in
the bottom of each
bowl and the soup is
ladled over them.
That way diners will
only discover these
buried treats with a
scoop of their spoon.*

Beet soups, served hot or cold, are popular throughout eastern Europe. This version gains extra spark from the addition of a little vodka. Of course, you can opt to omit the vodka. Accompany the borscht with pumpernickel bread and butter.

In a large saucepan, combine the stock, beets, and bay leaf. Bring to a boil over medium heat, reduce the heat to low, cover, and simmer gently for about 30 minutes. Remove from the heat, stir in the orange juice, and let cool to room temperature. Discard the bay leaf, cover the soup, and refrigerate until well chilled, at least 3 hours or up to 3 days.

Peel and halve the cucumber, then scrape out the seeds. Dice the cucumber flesh, place in a small bowl, cover, and refrigerate. Trim the green onions and slice thinly, including the tender green tops. Place the green onions in another small bowl, cover, and refrigerate.

Shortly before serving, remove the soup from the refrigerator and spoon off any solidified fat from its surface. Put 1½ cups (12 fl oz/375 ml) of the sour cream into a bowl. Stir in the vodka and a ladleful of the chilled beet broth until thoroughly blended, then stir the sour cream mixture back into the soup. Season with salt and pepper.

Distribute the chilled cucumber and green onions evenly among the chilled bowls. Ladle in the soup and garnish with dollops of the remaining ½ cup (4 fl oz/125 ml) sour cream and a sprinkle of dill. Serve right away.

6 cups (48 fl oz/1.5 l) Vegetable Stock (page 26)

2 lb (1 kg) beets, peeled and coarsely shredded

1 bay leaf

½ cup (4 fl oz/125 ml) fresh orange juice

1 cucumber

2 green (spring) onions

2 cups (16 fl oz/500 ml) sour cream

⅓ cup (3 fl oz/80 ml) vodka

Salt and ground pepper

2 tablespoons finely chopped fresh dill

MAKES 6–8 SERVINGS

GAZPACHO

When the weather is hot and the tomato season is at its peak, make a huge batch of this popular cold tomato soup. Garnish with the croutons while they are still warm for an interesting contrast of temperatures and textures.

6–8 large tomatoes, peeled and seeded

4 cloves garlic

1 small sweet yellow or red onion, chopped

6 tablespoons (3 fl oz/ 90 ml) red wine vinegar, or more if needed

2 regular or 1 English (hothouse) cucumber, peeled, halved, seeded, and diced

½ cup (4 fl oz/125 ml) plus 2 tablespoons extra-virgin olive oil

Salt and ground pepper

3 or 4 slices French bread, about 1-inch (2.5 cm) thick, crusts removed and cut into 1-inch cubes

1 small green bell pepper (capsicum), seeded and finely diced

¼ cup (1¼ oz/37 g) finely minced red onion

MAKES 6 SERVINGS

In a blender, process half of the tomatoes until puréed and transfer to a large bowl.

With the blender running, drop in 3 of the garlic cloves to chop them. Stop the machine, add the chopped onion, and then process until puréed, adding a little of the vinegar if needed for a smooth consistency. Add the onion mixture to the bowl holding the tomato purée. Add the cucumber and a little of the vinegar to the blender and pulse until coarsely chopped. Add to the bowl.

Coarsely chop the remaining tomatoes and add to the bowl. Whisk in the ½ cup oil and the remaining vinegar, and season with salt and pepper. Cover and refrigerate until well chilled, about 2 hours.

Just before serving, in a large frying pan over medium heat, warm the 2 tablespoons oil. Crush the remaining garlic clove, add to the pan, and cook for a minute or two to release its fragrance. Remove and discard the garlic. Add the bread cubes and stir and toss until golden brown, about 5 minutes. Transfer to paper towels to drain.

Taste the soup and adjust the seasoning with salt, pepper, and vinegar. Ladle into chilled bowls and garnish each serving with the bell pepper and minced red onion. Float the croutons on top and serve right away.

Gazpacho with seafood

For a more substantial soup, add 1 lb (500 g) cooked, peeled shrimp (prawns) or chunks of crabmeat. Round out the meal with a crisp green salad and crusty bread with fruity olive oil for dipping.

VEGETABLE SOUP WITH BASIL AND GARLIC

Warming soup bowls

Serving hot soups and stews in warmed bowls is a welcome touch. About 15 minutes before the soup is ready, slip the bowls into a 200°F (95°C) oven.

Pistou vs. pesto

In the summertime in southern France, no vegetable soup is complete without a dollop of pistou, a fragrant purée of fresh herbs, garlic, and cheese. Unlike its Italian cousin, Genoese pesto, pistou contains no pine nuts, which makes it lighter.

128

Called *soupe au pistou,* this mélange of spring vegetables and pasta in a fragrant broth is a classic of Provence. If you like, drizzle each serving with extra-virgin olive oil and top with a little grated Parmesan cheese to complement the flavors.

Sort, soak, and simmer the beans according to the method on page 301, simmering them until they are tender but not falling apart. Season with salt during the last 15 minutes of cooking. Remove from the heat, drain, and set aside.

In a large saucepan over medium heat, warm the oil. Add the onions and sauté until translucent and tender, 8–10 minutes. Add the carrots and celery and sauté until slightly softened, about 5 minutes. Add the tomatoes and stock, reduce the heat to low, and simmer, uncovered, for 10 minutes.

Dice the potatoes, add them to the soup, and simmer for 15 minutes. Meanwhile, cut the green beans into 1-inch (2.5 cm) lengths; halve the zucchini lengthwise and slice them crosswise; coarsely chop the Swiss chard.

Add the green beans, zucchini, Swiss chard, pasta, and cooked cannellini beans to the pan, and simmer until all the vegetables are tender and the pasta is al dente, about 10 minutes longer. Season with salt and pepper.

Remove from the heat and stir in the Pistou. Ladle into warmed bowls and serve right away.

½ cup (3½ oz/105 g) dried cannellini beans

Salt and ground pepper

3 tablespoons olive oil

4 yellow onions, diced

6 carrots, peeled and sliced

4 celery stalks, diced

1 lb (500 g) tomatoes, peeled, seeded, and diced

8 cups (64 fl oz/2 l) Vegetable Stock (page 26)

6 red potatoes, unpeeled

½ lb (250 g) green beans

4 zucchini (courgettes)

1 bunch Swiss chard, stems removed

¼ lb (125 g) dried macaroni

1 cup (8 fl oz/250 ml) Pistou (page 387)

MAKES 6–8 SERVINGS

CLASSIC MINESTRONE

Brimming with vegetables, pasta, and beans, minestrone is Italy's best-known soup. Diced potato can replace the pasta and coarsely chopped broccoli or cauliflower can stand in for the cabbage if you want variety. Offer a green salad and crusty bread for a complete meal.

Sort and soak the beans according to the method on page 301. Drain the beans and return to the pan. Add water to cover by 1 inch, bring to a gentle boil over high heat, then reduce the heat and simmer until the beans are tender and most of the liquid is absorbed, 1–1½ hours.

Meanwhile, finely chop the onion and mince the garlic. Peel and chop the carrot, trim and chop the zucchini, and thinly slice the cabbage.

About 30 minutes before the beans are ready, in a saucepan over medium heat, warm the oil. Add the onion and garlic and sauté until translucent, 2–3 minutes. Add the stock and tomatoes, coarsely breaking up the tomatoes with a wooden

½ cup (3½ oz/105 g) dried cannellini beans

1 yellow onion

1 clove garlic

1 large carrot

1 zucchini (courgette)

¼ savoy cabbage

2 tablespoons olive oil

5 cups (40 fl oz/1.25 l) Vegetable Stock (page 26)

1 can (14½ oz/455 g) plum (Roma) tomatoes, with juice

1½ teaspoons *each* dried basil and oregano

1½ teaspoons sugar

1 bay leaf

⅓ cup (1½ oz/45 g) dried small pasta

2 tablespoons balsamic vinegar

Salt and ground pepper

2 tablespoons coarsely chopped fresh flat-leaf (Italian) parsley

⅔ cup (2½ oz/75 g) grated Parmesan cheese

MAKES 6–8 SERVINGS

spoon. Add the carrot, zucchini, cabbage, basil, oregano, sugar, and bay leaf, cover partially, and simmer until the vegetables are tender-crisp, about 20 minutes. Add the pasta to the pan, stir gently, and simmer, uncovered, until the pasta is al dente, 8–10 minutes.

Drain the cannellini beans, add to the pot along with the vinegar, and season with salt and pepper. Remove and discard the bay leaf.

Ladle into warmed bowls. Garnish with the parsley and Parmesan and serve right away.

Small pasta shapes

Elbow macaroni is commonly called for in minestrone recipes, but you can also use orzo, stelline, tubettini, or other tiny pasta shapes. Or, tempt kids into eating their vegetables by using alphabet pasta for the soup.

LENTIL SOUP WITH SPINACH AND CARROTS

This recipe calls for green lentils, but brown or red can also be used. True green lentils— particularly the small French lentils labeled Puy—retain their shape the best. The soup can be prepared the day before and reheated; wilt and add the spinach just before serving.

1 large yellow onion

1 large or 2 small carrots

2 tablespoons olive oil

1 teaspoon ground cumin

2 cups (14 oz/440 g) green lentils

5–6 cups (40–48 fl oz/ 1.25–1.5 l) Vegetable Stock (page 26)

2 cups (4 oz/125 g) spinach leaves, stems removed

Salt and ground pepper

Plain yogurt or crème fraîche

MAKES 6 SERVINGS

Chop the onion, and peel and chop the carrots.

In a saucepan over medium heat, warm the oil. Add the onion and sauté until translucent, about 8 minutes. Then, add the cumin, carrots, lentils, and stock. (The amount of liquid will vary depending on the age of the lentils; older, drier lentils will require the larger amount.) Reduce the heat to low, cover, and simmer until the lentils are tender; begin testing for doneness after 20 minutes.

Meanwhile, rinse the spinach thoroughly, coarsely chop it, and then add it, still wet, to a large sauté pan over medium heat. Cook, turning occasionally, until just wilted, about 2 minutes. Transfer to a sieve and drain well, pressing out the excess liquid.

Stir the wilted spinach into the soup. Season with salt and pepper. Ladle into warmed bowls, top each serving with a dollop of yogurt, and serve right away.

Vegetarian soups

Using vegetable stock for any meatless soup keeps it vegetarian, but if you prefer the rich flavor of chicken stock, feel free to substitute it here.

CHICKEN NOODLE SOUP

Starch options

You can use fresh pasta instead of dried. Or, instead of pasta, add ¼ cup (2 oz/60 g) rice to the soup 15 minutes before it is done.

On a cold night, hot soup is the ultimate comfort food—especially when it's a nourishing bowl of chicken, vegetables, and egg noodles. Precede it with a salad of escarole (Batavian endive) and sliced apple and follow with a favorite bakery cookie or two.

In a saucepan over medium heat, combine the chicken and 8 cups (64 fl oz/2 l) water. Bring to a simmer, skimming off any foam that forms on the surface. Add the onion, parsley, and bay leaf, reduce the heat to maintain a gentle simmer, and cook, uncovered, for 20 minutes. Add the carrot and celery and continue to simmer, uncovered, until the broth is flavorful, about 40 minutes longer.

Using tongs or a slotted spoon, remove and discard the onion, parsley, and bay leaves. Transfer the chicken to a cutting board to cool slightly.

Skim off any fat from the surface of the broth. Raise the heat to high and bring to a boil. Add the noodles and reduce the heat to maintain a gentle boil, and cook until the noodles are al dente, 8–10 minutes.

Meanwhile, cut off and discard the wing tips, skin and bone the chicken, and cut the chicken meat into large bite-size pieces. When the noodles are done, reduce the heat to a simmer, return the meat to the broth, and heat through. Season with salt and pepper.

Ladle into warmed bowls and serve right away.

8 chicken wings, each cut at the joints into 3 pieces

1 yellow onion stuck with 1 whole clove

4 fresh parsley sprigs

1 bay leaf

2 small carrots, peeled and diced

2 small celery stalks, diced

¼ lb (125 g) dried egg noodles

Salt and ground pepper

MAKES 4 SERVINGS

MATZO BALL SOUP

Substituting canned broth

If you use canned broth for this soup, use only 6 cups (48 fl oz/1.5 l) and don't reduce it. Even low-sodium canned broth can become too salty when reduced.

Matzo ball soup is not just for Passover. It is also ideal during the chilly days of winter, when a substantial soup is craved by nearly everyone. Look for matzo meal and jars of rendered chicken fat in the Jewish food sections of most supermarkets or in Jewish delicatessens.

In a saucepan over high heat, bring the stock to a boil. Boil, uncovered, until it has reduced to about 6 cups (48 fl oz/1.5 l), about 30 minutes.

In a large bowl, whisk together the eggs and ⅓ cup (3 fl oz/ 80 ml) water. Add the chicken fat and stir to combine, then stir in ½ teaspoon salt and ¼ teaspoon pepper. Pour in the matzo meal in a slow, steady stream while stirring constantly with a spoon. Do not overbeat. Cover and chill for 30 minutes.

Line 2 large rimmed baking sheets with parchment (baking) paper. Using wet hands and a soup spoon, gently form the chilled matzo mixture into balls about 1½ inches (4 cm) in diameter. Place on the prepared baking sheets, cover, and refrigerate for at least 30 minutes or up to 3 hours.

Bring 2 large saucepans three-fourths full of salted water to a boil over high heat. Add the matzo balls, cover, and return

10–12 cups (2½–3 qt/ 2.5–3 l) Brown Chicken Stock (page 24)

4 eggs

3 tablespoons rendered chicken fat or canola oil

Salt and ground pepper

1¼ cups (7 oz/220 g) matzo meal

1 cup (5 oz/155 g) diced carrots

2 cups (12 oz/375 g) diced cooked chicken

1 cup (5 oz/155 g) shelled peas

¼ cup (⅓ oz/10 g) chopped fresh flat-leaf (Italian) parsley

MAKES 6 SERVINGS

to a boil. Immediately reduce the heat and simmer until the balls are doubled in size and cooked through, 30–40 minutes. Using a slotted spoon, transfer to a large plate and set aside.

Season the stock with salt and pepper, bring to a boil, then reduce to a simmer. Add the carrots and cook for 5 minutes. Add the matzo balls, chicken, and peas. Simmer until all the ingredients are heated through, 8–10 minutes.

Ladle into warmed bowls, dividing the matzo balls evenly. Sprinkle with the parsley and serve right away.

CHICKEN, TORTILLA, AND LIME SOUP

This Yucatecan soup, called *sopa de lima* in its native Mexico, nicely balances the tartness of lime with the heat of chiles. Although it's not authentic, 1 cup (6 oz/185 g) fresh corn kernels can be added to the soup with the tomatoes.

4 qt (16 cups/4 l) Chicken Stock (page 23)

Canola oil for deep-frying

3 corn tortillas, cut into narrow strips

1¼ lb (625 g) boneless, skinless chicken breasts

3 tablespoons olive oil

1 large yellow onion, chopped

2 tablespoons minced garlic

2–3 teaspoons finely minced jalapeño chile, with or without seeds

1½ cups (9 oz/280 g) peeled, seeded, and diced tomatoes

6 tablespoons (¼ oz/7 g) chopped fresh cilantro (fresh coriander)

6 tablespoons (3 fl oz/ 90 ml) fresh lime juice

Salt and ground pepper

MAKES 6 SERVINGS

In a large saucepan over high heat, bring 3½ qt (3.5 l) of the stock to a boil. Reduce the heat slightly and boil gently until reduced to about 7 cups (56 fl oz/1.75 l), about 30 minutes.

Meanwhile, pour the oil to a depth of 2 inches (5 cm) into a deep sauté pan or a saucepan and heat to 375°F (190°C) on a deep-frying thermometer. Working in batches, drop in the tortilla strips and fry until golden and crisp, about 2 minutes. Using a slotted spoon, transfer to paper towels to drain.

In a saucepan, combine the chicken breasts and the remaining 2 cups (16 fl oz/500 ml) stock, bring to a simmer over medium heat, and cook gently until the chicken is opaque throughout, about 8 minutes. Transfer the chicken to a cutting board and cut into bite-size pieces. Set aside. Reserve the stock for another use.

In a large saucepan over medium heat, warm the olive oil. Add the onion and sauté, stirring occasionally, until translucent and tender, about 10 minutes. Add the garlic and the chile to taste and cook for 1–2 minutes to soften. Add the reduced stock, raise the heat to high, and bring to a boil. Reduce the heat to low, add the chicken, tomatoes, cilantro, and lime juice. Season with 1½ teaspoons salt and ½ teaspoon pepper and simmer until the chicken is heated through, about 5 minutes. Taste and adjust the seasoning.

Ladle the soup into warmed bowls and garnish with the tortilla strips. Serve right away.

Latin-style garnishes

In Mexico, soups are often served with an array of fresh garnishes for diners to add as they like. For this soup, you can set out lime quarters for anyone who enjoys extra tartness and some diced avocado to help offset the spiciness of the broth.

Keeping it clear

For this soup, the chicken is not cooked directly in the soup base because the soup would become cloudy. A nice clear stock showcases the colorful ingredients that make this soup so special.

TURKEY-VEGETABLE SOUP WITH RICE

Chicken-rice soup

Turn this soup into a chicken-rice soup by substituting diced cooked chicken meat for the turkey and chicken broth for the turkey stock. Use a rotisserie chicken and good-quality broth from your local market, add crusty bread and a green salad, and you will have dinner on the table in less than an hour.

Here is a great way to make use of the leftovers from a roast turkey: use the carcass to make the stock, and add the leftover meat to the soup, along with rice, mushrooms, broccoli, and aromatic vegetables. Top each bowl with parsley and Parmesan.

In a large saucepan over medium heat, warm 2 tablespoons of the oil. Add the onion, carrot, and celery and sauté, stirring often, until the onion is tender and translucent, about 10 minutes. Add the rice and stock and bring to a boil. Reduce the heat to low and simmer until the rice is tender, about 15 minutes.

Meanwhile, in a sauté pan over medium-high heat, warm the remaining 3 tablespoons oil. Add the mushrooms and sauté, stirring often, until tender, 8–10 minutes. Set aside.

Bring a saucepan three-fourths full of lightly salted water to a boil, add the broccoli florets, and cook until tender but not falling apart, about 5 minutes. Drain, immerse in cold water to halt the cooking, and drain again.

Add the turkey, sautéed mushrooms, cooked broccoli, and thyme to the rice and stock and continue to simmer until all the ingredients are heated through, about 10 minutes. Season with salt and pepper.

Ladle into warmed bowls, sprinkle with the parsley and cheese, and serve right away.

5 tablespoons (2½ fl oz/ 75 ml) olive oil

1½ cups (6 oz/185 g) chopped yellow onion

⅔ cup (3 oz/90 g) *each* diced carrot and celery

½ cup (2½ oz/75 g) diced celery

⅔ cup (4½ oz/140 g) long-grain white rice

8 cups (2 l) Turkey Stock (page 25)

2 cups (6 oz/185 g) sliced fresh mushrooms

2 cups (4 oz/125 g) broccoli florets

2 cups (12 oz/375 g) diced cooked turkey

2 teaspoons fresh thyme leaves

Salt and ground pepper

¼ cup (⅓ oz/10 g) chopped fresh flat-leaf (Italian) parsley

¼ cup (1 oz/30 g) grated Parmesan cheese

MAKES 6–8 SERVINGS

STRACCIATELLA ALLA FIORENTINA

Stracciatella means "little rag" in Italian, a fanciful description of the shreds that form when egg and Parmesan cheese are stirred into simmering stock to make this favorite Roman soup. The deep green strips of spinach add a Florentine touch.

6 cups (48 fl oz/1.5 l) Chicken Stock (page 23)

4 eggs

¼ cup (1 oz/30 g) grated Parmesan cheese

1 cup (2 oz/60 g) packed finely shredded spinach leaves

MAKES 4–6 SERVINGS

In a saucepan, bring the stock to a boil over high heat. Meanwhile, in a bowl, lightly beat the eggs and then stir in the cheese until blended.

Reduce the stock to a brisk simmer. While stirring the stock constantly and steadily, drizzle in the egg mixture to form long strands. Stir in the spinach and simmer for 2–3 minutes. Ladle into warmed bowls and serve right away.

Egg drop soup

Omit the cheese and spinach and stir in a splash of soy sauce mixed with cornstarch (cornflour). Stir in a drop or two of rice vinegar and you have Chinese egg drop soup.

FRENCH ONION SOUP GRATINÉE

The secret to a good onion soup is to cook the onions slowly, so that their natural sugars can caramelize. For a more complex flavor, sauté some thinly sliced leek with the onions, and sprinkle grated Parmesan cheese onto the toasts before topping them with the Gruyère.

½ cup (4 oz/125 g) unsalted butter

4 large yellow onions, thinly sliced

Salt and ground pepper

5 cups (40 fl oz/1.25 l) Brown Chicken Stock (page 24) or Brown Beef Stock (page 22)

2 bay leaves

½ lb (250 g) Gruyère cheese, shredded

4–6 slices French bread, ½ inch (12 mm) thick, toasted golden brown

MAKES 4–6 SERVINGS

In a large saucepan, melt the butter over low heat. Add the onions, season with salt, and stir to coat well with the butter. Cover and cook, stirring occasionally, until very tender but not yet browned, 20–30 minutes.

Uncover, raise the heat slightly, and cook, stirring frequently, until the onions turn a deep caramel brown, about 1 hour. Take care not to let them burn.

Add the stock and bay leaves, raise the heat to medium, and bring to a boil. Reduce the heat to low, cover, and simmer for about 30 minutes longer to blend the flavors.

Preheat the broiler (grill).

Discard the bay leaves. Taste the soup and adjust the seasoning with salt and pepper. Place heavy, flameproof serving crocks or bowls on a rimmed baking sheet. Ladle the soup into the crocks, sprinkle a little of the cheese into each bowl, then top with the bread slices. Sprinkle evenly with the remaining cheese. Broil (grill) until the cheese is bubbly and golden, 2–3 minutes. Serve right away.

A custom vessel

This iconic soup, famous throughout the world, boasts a special crock manufactured just for the purpose of serving it. It is made from porcelain, which holds heat well and stands up to the high heat needed to melt the cap of cheese that gilds the top.

MEATBALL SOUP

Browned meatballs

You can sauté the meatballs in a little olive oil until golden before adding them to the hot stock to finish cooking. Sautéing them first gives them a firmer texture, darker color, and richer flavor.

Meatballs in a tomato-infused broth will warm you up on cold nights. For a heartier soup, add 2 cups (10 oz/315 g) cooked small pasta or white rice and 3 cups (21 oz/655 g) chopped wilted escarole or chicory to the finished soup and heat through.

In a bowl, combine the meat, bread crumbs, grated onion, egg, garlic, cinnamon, cumin, and half of the parsley. Mix well, then season with salt and pepper. (If desired, cook a small amount of the mixture in oil until cooked through and taste for seasonings, adjusting the remaining meatball mixture accordingly.) Line a large rimmed baking sheet with parchment (baking) paper. Form the meat into marble-size balls, and place on the prepared baking sheet. Cover and refrigerate until ready to cook.

In a large saucepan over medium heat, warm the oil. Add the chopped onion and sauté, stirring occasionally, until translucent, about 10 minutes. Raise the heat to high, add the stock and tomato purée, and bring to a boil. Reduce the heat to low and simmer for 10 minutes.

Add the meatballs to the soup and simmer until cooked through, about 20 minutes. Taste and adjust the seasoning.

Ladle into warmed bowls and garnish with the remaining parsley. Serve right away.

½ lb (250 g) ground (minced) beef, veal, or lamb

½ cup (2 oz/60 g) dried bread crumbs

¼ cup (1½ oz/45 g) grated yellow onion, plus 1½ cups (6 oz/185 g) chopped

1 egg, lightly beaten

1 clove garlic, finely minced

½ teaspoon *each* ground cinnamon and cumin

½ cup (¾ oz/20 g) chopped fresh flat-leaf (Italian) parsley

Salt and ground pepper

2 tablespoons olive oil

8 cups (64 fl oz/2 l) Beef Stock (page 22)

2–3 cups (16–24 fl oz/ 500–750 ml) tomato purée

MAKES 6 SERVINGS

BEEF BARLEY SOUP

Tomato products

Shelved near other tomato products in stores, tomato purée is simply a concentrate of puréed tomato flesh, generally without seasoning or other ingredients. Do not substitute tomato sauce or paste for tomato purée in recipes, as you might not achieve the right flavor balance.

This is a hearty soup of beef, vegetables, and barley in a rich tomatoey beef broth. A garnish of sour cream and chopped dill lends the soup a Russian flavor. Serve with warm homemade Rye Bread (page 410) for a complete meal.

Place the shanks in a saucepan and add water to cover generously. Bring to a boil over high heat, skimming often to remove any foam that forms on the surface. Add the carrots, celery, and about two-thirds of the onions, reduce the heat to low, and cook, uncovered, for about 1 hour. Add the tomato purée and the barley, cover partially, and continue to cook over low heat until the barley is tender, about 1 hour longer.

While the soup is cooking, in a large sauté pan over medium heat, melt the butter. Add the remaining onions and sauté, stirring occasionally, until pale gold, 10–12 minutes. Raise the heat to high, add the mushrooms, and sauté, stirring often, until softened, 6–8 minutes. Add the garlic, reduce the heat to medium, and sauté until soft but not brown, about

3 lb (1.5 kg) meaty beef or veal shanks

6 carrots, peeled and chopped

4 celery stalks, chopped

3 large yellow onions, chopped

1 cup (8 fl oz/250 ml) tomato purée

1 cup (7½ oz/235 g) pearl barley

6 tablespoons (3 oz/90 g) unsalted butter

1 lb (500 g) fresh cremini mushrooms, brushed clean and sliced

½ teaspoon minced garlic

Salt and ground pepper

4 tablespoons (⅓ oz/10 g) chopped fresh dill

¼ cup (⅓ oz/10 g) chopped fresh flat-leaf (Italian) parsley

6 tablespoons (3 fl oz/ 90 ml) sour cream

MAKES 6 SERVINGS

3 minutes longer. Season with salt, pepper, and 2 tablespoons of the dill. Set aside.

Remove the shanks from the pan and, when cool enough to handle, remove the meat from the bones and chop it. You should have about 1⅓ cups (8 oz/250 g).

Add the mushroom mixture and chopped beef to the soup and stir to heat through. Season with salt and pepper.

Ladle into warmed bowls and sprinkle with the remaining 2 tablespoons dill and the parsley. Top each serving with a dollop of sour cream and serve right away.

Pearl barley

Barley is a versatile and sustaining grain with a nutty flavor and chewy texture. Widely available pearl barley is whole-grain barley that has been hulled and polished to a pearl-like shape and sheen.

NEW ENGLAND CLAM CHOWDER

Salt pork is traditionally used in clam chowder, but smoky bacon gives it a more refined character. If you like, add 2 cups (12 oz/ 375 g) fresh corn kernels when you add the clams. You can also use lobster, fish, or whole bay scallops.

5 lb (2.5 kg) littleneck or cherrystone clams (48–60 clams), well scrubbed

About 2 cups (16 fl oz/ 500 ml) dry white wine or water

About 3 cups (24 fl oz/ 750 ml) bottled clam juice

2 tablespoons olive oil

6 oz (185 g) bacon, cut into small pieces

2 yellow onions, chopped

6–8 small red potatoes, unpeeled, cubed

1½ cups (12 fl oz/375 ml) heavy (double) cream

Ground black pepper

Pinch of cayenne pepper, optional

2 tablespoons unsalted butter, optional

2 tablespoons chopped fresh flat-leaf (Italian) parsley or chives

MAKES 6 SERVINGS

In a large, wide, heavy saucepan over high heat, combine the clams and wine, cover, and cook until the clams open, about 5 minutes. Using a slotted spoon, transfer the clams to a bowl, discarding any that did not open. Strain the cooking liquid through a sieve lined with damp cheesecloth (muslin) placed over a large bowl. Remove the clams from their shells and chop coarsely, capturing and straining any of the juices. Measure the cooking liquid and add enough clam juice to measure 5 cups (40 fl oz/1.25 l) total. Set aside.

In a saucepan over medium-low heat, warm the oil. Add the bacon and onions and cook, stirring occasionally, until softened, about 10 minutes. Raise the heat to high, add the reserved liquid, and bring to a boil. Add the potatoes, reduce the heat to low, and cook, uncovered, until the potatoes are almost completely cooked through but still slightly firm, 10–15 minutes. Add the clams and simmer until heated through, about 4 minutes. Add the cream and season with the black pepper and the cayenne (if using). Then swirl in the butter (if using).

Ladle the chowder into warmed bowls, garnish with the parsley, and serve right away.

135

Dueling chowders

Bacon or salt pork, potatoes, and fresh clams are constants in the clam chowders of the U.S. eastern seaboard. But Manhattan-style chowder includes tomatoes in its clear broth, and New England chowder calls for adding milk or cream to its soup base. Of course, cooks in both camps declare their chowder is superior.

ROASTED ASPARAGUS AND SHRIMP CHOWDER

Roasting the asparagus and the shrimp imparts an intense flavor to this colorful, chunky soup. Reserve the feathery tops from the fennel bulb for garnishing the bowls. Or, sauté additional asparagus tips in butter and float them on top of the soup.

Snapping asparagus

To trim asparagus spears, grasp each spear with both hands near the cut end and bend it; it will snap naturally at the point at which the stalk turns fibrous. Do not discard too much of the stalk, as it is usually a little sweeter than the tip.

Preheat the oven to 425°F (220°C).

Place the asparagus and the shrimp on a rimmed baking sheet and drizzle with 1 tablespoon of the oil. Toss to coat well, then spread out the shrimp in a single layer. Roast until the shrimp turn pink and are opaque, about 5 minutes. Transfer the shrimp to a plate. Turn the asparagus over and continue to roast until just tender, about 8 minutes longer. Remove from the oven and, when cool enough to handle, cut into 1-inch (2.5-cm) lengths.

Meanwhile, cut off the stems, feathery fronds, and any bruised outer stalks from the fennel bulb. Chop the fronds and reserve for garnish. Cut away and discard the core, then chop the bulb; set aside.

Heat a large saucepan over medium heat. Add the remaining 1 tablespoon oil to the pan and swirl to coat the bottom. Add the chopped fennel bulb, leek, bell pepper, and herbes de Provence and sauté until the vegetables are just beginning to soften, about 4 minutes. Add the stock and potato and bring to a simmer. Cook, uncovered, until the fennel is tender, about 15 minutes.

Pour in the half-and-half and bring the soup back to a simmer. Add the shrimp and asparagus and stir until heated through. Season with salt and pepper.

Ladle into warmed bowls and garnish each serving with the fennel fronds. Serve right away.

10 large asparagus spears, tough ends removed

20 large shrimp (prawns), about 1 lb (500 g) total weight, peeled and deveined (see page 202)

2 tablespoons olive oil

1 small fennel bulb

1 leek, including 2 inches (5 cm) of pale green, chopped

1 small red bell pepper (capsicum), seeded and chopped

1 teaspoon herbes de Provence

3 cups (24 fl oz/750 ml) Vegetable Stock (page 26)

1 russet potato, unpeeled, cut into ½-inch (12-mm) dice

1 cup (8 fl oz/250 ml) half-and-half (half cream)

Salt and ground pepper

MAKES 6 SERVINGS

CORN CHOWDER WITH RED PEPPER CREAM

Using the kernels from both yellow and white ears of corn makes this summer chowder particularly attractive. The red pepper cream garnish adds color and spice without overwhelming the natural sweetness of the corn.

FOR THE RED PEPPER CREAM

2 large red bell peppers (capsicums)

2 tablespoons fresh oregano leaves

1 tablespoon cayenne pepper

1 tablespoon olive oil

Salt

2 tablespoons heavy (double) cream

FOR THE CHOWDER

2 slices bacon, chopped

¼ cup (1½ oz/45 g) finely diced celery

1 small yellow onion, finely diced

2 cups (16 fl oz/500 ml) chicken broth

4 or 5 red potatoes, about ¾ lb (375 g) total weight, unpeeled, diced

2 tablespoons fresh thyme leaves

1 bay leaf

Salt and ground pepper

2 cups (16 fl oz/500 ml) milk, heated

Kernels from 6 ears fresh corn, preferably a mixture of white and yellow

MAKES 6–8 SERVINGS

To make the red pepper cream, roast, peel, and coarsely chop the peppers (see page 333). Add the pepper pieces to a blender along with the oregano, cayenne, oil, and ½ teaspoon salt. With the blender running, drizzle in the cream and process until smooth. Transfer to a bowl and set aside.

To make the chowder, in a heavy saucepan over medium-low heat, fry the bacon, stirring occasionally, until the fat is rendered and the bacon is crisp, about 5 minutes. Using a slotted spoon, transfer the crisp bits to a plate and reserve for another use. Raise the heat to medium-high, add the celery and onion to the fat in the pan, and sauté until nearly translucent, 5–6 minutes.

Raise the heat to high, pour in the broth, bring to a boil, and stir to dislodge any browned bits from the pan bottom. Add the potatoes, thyme, bay leaf, salt, and pepper and return to a boil. Then cover, reduce the heat to low, and cook until the potatoes are just tender, 10–15 minutes. Add the milk and simmer for 5 minutes. Add the corn and simmer just until the corn is tender, 3–4 minutes.

Ladle into warmed bowls and top each serving with a spoonful of the red pepper cream. Serve right away.

Adding bacon

The first step in making the chowder is to sauté the celery and onions in freshly rendered bacon fat. If you like, you can stir the cooked bacon pieces into the finished soup, or you can sprinkle a few bits on top of the pepper cream as an additional garnish.

POTATO-LEEK SOUP

Puréeing soups

If you purée all of a soup, you will end up with a thick, creamy, smooth soup. If you purée only a portion of a soup, you will create a soup with a pleasing contrast of chunky ingredients in a smooth base. Or, if you enjoy rustic soups, you can skip the puréeing step.

Slowly cooked leeks add a natural sweetness to this soup, while starchy potatoes gives it wonderful body without the addition of flour or another thickener. Don't be tempted to use boiling, or waxy, potatoes here or the soup will lack the correct texture.

In a large, heavy saucepan, melt 3 tablespoons of the butter over medium-high heat. Add 4 cups (12 oz/375 g) of the leeks and the white parts of the green onions and sauté until the leeks are just wilted, about 4 minutes. Add the potatoes and stir to coat with the butter.

Add the stock and bring to a boil. Reduce the heat to medium-low, cover, and simmer until the potatoes are very tender, about 25 minutes. Remove from the heat.

Ladle out 3 cups (24 fl oz/750 ml) of the soup (both solids and liquid) and purée in batches in a blender until smooth. Return the purée to the pot and season with salt and pepper.

In a small, heavy frying pan, melt the remaining 1 tablespoon butter over medium-low heat. Add the remaining leeks and 2 tablespoons of the green onion tops (reserve the remainder for another use) and sauté until the leeks are wilted, about 4 minutes. Season with salt and pepper.

Ladle into warmed bowls, sprinkle with the sautéed leeks and green onions and serve right away.

4 tablespoons (2 oz/60 g) unsalted butter

3 large leeks, white and pale green parts, halved lengthwise and thinly sliced

3 green (spring) onions, tender green tops and white part chopped separately

3 russet potatoes, about 1½ lb (750 g) total weight, peeled and diced

5 cups (40 fl oz/1.25 l) Chicken Stock (page 23)

Salt and ground pepper

MAKES 4–6 SERVINGS

SPICY TOMATO SOUP

About hot-pepper sauce

Though recipes vary, hot-pepper sauces begin with hot red chile peppers, vinegar, and salt. Tabasco is the best-known version; its iconic label is printed in Chinese, Dutch, French, and several other languages in more than 100 countries.

A pinch of cayenne pepper or a dash of Tabasco or other hot-pepper sauce adds a pleasant touch of fire to this puréed tomato soup. A garnish of cool, tangy yogurt counteracts the heat. You can substitute flat-leaf (Italian) parsley or snipped fresh chives for the dill.

In a saucepan over medium-high heat, warm the oil. Add the onion and carrot and sauté until softened, about 5 minutes. Add the garlic and ¼ teaspoon cayenne pepper and sauté until the garlic has softened, about 30 seconds. Add the tomatoes and broth and bring to a boil. Reduce the heat and simmer, uncovered, until the flavors are blended, at least 20 minutes or up to 45 minutes. (The longer the mixture cooks, the smoother it will become.) Remove from the heat and let cool slightly.

Working in batches, transfer the soup to a blender or food processor and process until smooth. Return to the saucepan over medium-high heat and season with salt and pepper. Heat to serving temperature.

Ladle into warmed bowls and top with a dollop of yogurt and a sprinkle of dill. Dust with cayenne and serve right away.

2 tablespoons olive oil

1 yellow onion, minced

1 carrot, peeled and grated

4 cloves garlic, chopped

Cayenne pepper

3 lb (1.5 kg) tomatoes, peeled, seeded, and chopped

1⅓ cups (11 fl oz/340 ml) chicken broth

Salt and ground pepper

½ cup (4 oz/125 g) plain yogurt

¼ cup (oz/10 g) minced fresh dill

MAKES 4–6 SERVINGS

CARROT AND MINT SOUP

You can make this soup up to a day in advance through the step of puréeing the vegetables; combine the purée and the cooking liquid, cover, and refrigerate. Any leftover soup can be covered and stored in the refrigerator for 1 day.

**2 tablespoons
unsalted butter**

2 yellow onions, chopped

**10–12 carrots, peeled
and sliced (about 4 cups/
1 lb/500 g)**

**4 cups (32 fl oz/1 l)
Chicken Stock (page 23)**

**3 large fresh mint sprigs,
plus 2 tablespoons
chopped for garnish**

2 cups (16 fl oz/500 ml) milk

**1 cup (8 fl oz/250 ml)
heavy (double) cream**

Salt and ground pepper

**¼ cup (2 fl oz/60 ml)
sour cream**

MAKES 6–8 SERVINGS

In a large saucepan over medium heat, melt the butter. Add the onions and sauté until translucent, 2–3 minutes. Add the carrots, stock, and mint sprigs. Reduce the heat to low, cover, and simmer until the carrots are tender, 25–30 minutes. Remove and discard the mint.

Set a colander over a bowl and pour the contents of the pan into the colander. Reserve the cooking liquid. Transfer the vegetables to a food processor and process until smooth. Return the purée and the reserved liquid to the pan, place over medium-low heat, and stir in the milk and cream. Season with salt and pepper and heat to serving temperature. Do not allow the soup to boil.

Ladle the soup into warmed bowls. Top with sour cream and a sprinkle of chopped mint. Serve right away.

Cooking with dairy

When preparing soups that contain dairy products, take care that you don't allow the soup to boil. High heat can cause milk, yogurt, and other dairy products to curdle and separate, creating an unappealing texture than can't be remedied. Cream, with its high fat content, doesn't curdle as readily and can be cooked over higher heat.

FRESH PEA SOUP WITH CHIVE BLOSSOM CREAM

English peas come into season at the same time chives are putting forth their delicate onion-flavored blossoms, and farmers' market vendors often sell chives with their blossoms intact. For a festive brunch, serve the soup with poppy-seed rolls and a selection of fresh fruits.

7 fresh chive blossoms

**1 cup (8 fl oz/250 ml)
heavy (double) cream**

**3 cups (24 fl oz/750 ml)
Chicken Stock (page 23)**

**2 lb (1 kg) English peas,
shelled, or 2 cup frozen
petite peas, thawed**

Salt and ground pepper

MAKES 4 SERVINGS

In a small saucepan over medium-high heat, combine 3 of the chive blossoms and the cream. Bring to a boil, reduce the heat to low, and simmer until the cream thickens and is reduced by nearly half, 4–5 minutes. Remove from the heat and let stand for 30 minutes to allow the flavors to develop.

In a saucepan over medium-high heat, combine the stock, peas, 1 teaspoon salt, and ½ teaspoon pepper. Bring to a boil, reduce the heat to low, and simmer until the peas are soft, 10–20 minutes. Let cool slightly.

Working in batches, purée the soup base in a blender or food processor. Return to the saucepan, place over medium heat, and heat to serving temperature.

Meanwhile, remove the whole chive blossoms from the cream and discard. Reheat the cream over medium heat. Divide the soup among warmed individual bowls. Garnish with a spoonful of the cream and the remaining chive blossoms. Serve right away.

Mint cream garnish

Whisk together ¼ cup (2 fl oz/60 ml) sour cream or crème fraîche, 1 tbsp finely chopped fresh mint, and 1 tbsp finely chopped green (spring) onion. Use in place of the chive blossom cream.

BLACK BEAN SOUP

Covering beans while cooking

Partially covering beans when they are cooking helps them cook evenly and prevents the liquid from evaporating too quickly before the beans are done. Check the level of the liquid occasionally as the beans cook to make sure they remain immersed in liquid.

A shot of dry sherry and a garnish of paper-thin lemon slices are classic additions to Spanish black bean soup. But black bean soup is versatile. Here, ground cumin and cinnamon and a garnish of guacamole give it a Latin American accent.

Sort and soak the beans according to the method on page 301. Drain the beans and return to the saucepan. Add 8 cups (64 fl oz/2 l) water and the ham bone and bring to a boil over high heat. Cover partially, reduce the heat to low, and simmer while you prepare the other ingredients.

In a large sauté pan over medium heat, warm the oil. Add the onions and sauté, stirring occasionally, until tender and translucent, about 10 minutes. Add the garlic, cumin, cinnamon, and cloves and cook for about 2 minutes longer. Add the onion mixture to the beans and simmer until very tender, 1–1½ hours.

Remove the soup from the heat, and remove and discard the ham bone. Let the soup cool slightly, then, working in batches, purée the soup in a blender. Return the soup to a clean saucepan and season with the vinegar and with salt and pepper. Reheat over medium heat, stirring often to prevent scorching. Thin with water if the soup is too thick, then taste and adjust the seasoning.

Ladle into warmed bowls, top each serving with a spoonful of the guacamole, and serve right away.

3 cups (21 oz/655 g) dried black beans

1 ham bone or ham hock

2 tablespoons olive oil

2 yellow onions, chopped

4 cloves garlic, minced

1 tablespoon ground cumin

½ teaspoon ground cinnamon

¼ teaspoon ground cloves

1–2 tablespoons sherry vinegar

Salt and ground pepper

Guacamole (page 392)

MAKES 8 SERVINGS

HEARTY SPLIT-PEA SOUP

Split peas

Available both pale green and yellow, split peas are a variety of field peas grown specifically for drying. The skins are removed during the dehydrating process, which causes the peas to split in half. A nutritional plus: dried peas contain about triple the protein found in fresh peas.

Chopped spinach and crumbled, crisply cooked bacon bring robust flavor and texture to this satisfying split-pea soup. If you like, garnish with a dollop of sour cream before sprinkling on the crumbled bacon. Accompany with warm slices of Irish Soda Bread (page 431).

Pick over the split peas and discard any misshapen peas or stones. Rinse the split peas and drain.

In a saucepan over medium heat, melt the butter. Add the onion and sauté, stirring occasionally, until tender and translucent, about 10 minutes. Add the split peas, carrots, bay leaf, and 6 cups stock. Raise the heat to high and bring to a boil. Cover, reduce the heat to low, and simmer until the peas are very soft, about 45 minutes. If the mixture becomes too thick, thin with additional stock.

Meanwhile, if using the bacon, in a frying pan over medium heat, fry the bacon until crisp, about 5 minutes. Transfer to paper towels to drain. When cool, crumble.

When the soup is ready, discard the bay leaf. Add the spinach and simmer until it wilts, about 3 minutes. Remove from the heat and let cool slightly.

2 cups (14 oz/440 g) split peas

2 tablespoons unsalted butter

1 large yellow onion, chopped

2 carrots, peeled and chopped

1 bay leaf

6 cups (48 fl oz/1.5 l) Chicken Stock (page 23) or water, or as needed

3 slices bacon, optional

½ lb (250 g) spinach, tough stems removed and finely chopped

Salt and ground pepper

MAKES 4–6 SERVINGS

Working in batches, purée the soup base in a blender or food processor. Return to a clean saucepan and add stock as needed to thin to desired consistency. Place over medium-high heat and reheat to serving temperature. Season with salt and pepper.

Ladle into warmed bowls and sprinkle with the crumbled bacon (if using). Serve right away.

WHITE BEAN SOUP WITH ROSEMARY AND PARMESAN

This thick, hearty soup makes a satisfying main course. Similar soups are popular in Italy, especially Tuscany, where the locals are nicknamed *mangiafagioli,* or "bean eaters." White kidney beans or cannellini beans can be substituted for the small white beans.

1½ cups (10½ oz/330 g) dried small white (navy) beans

3 tablespoons olive oil

1 yellow onion, finely chopped

1 carrot, peeled and finely chopped

1 celery stalk, finely chopped

2 cloves garlic, minced

1 teaspoon minced fresh rosemary

7 cups (56 fl oz/1.75 l) Chicken Stock (page 23) or Vegetable Stock (page 26)

Salt and ground pepper

½ cup (2 oz/60 g) grated Parmesan cheese

1 tablespoon chopped fresh flat-leaf (Italian) parsley

MAKES 6 SERVINGS

Sort and soak the beans according to the method on page 301. Drain and set aside.

In a large saucepan over medium heat, warm the oil. Add the onion, carrot, and celery and sauté, stirring occasionally, until the vegetables are soft, about 10 minutes. Add the garlic and rosemary and continue to sauté for another 3 minutes. Add the drained beans and the stock and bring to a boil. Reduce the heat to low and simmer gently, uncovered, until the beans are tender, 1–1½ hours.

Remove from the heat and let cool slightly.

In a blender or food processor, process one-third of the bean mixture until smooth. Return the purée to the soup and reheat gently. Season with salt and pepper.

Ladle the soup into warmed bowls and garnish with the cheese and parsley. Serve right away.

Buying dried beans

For the best flavor and texture, look for dried beans in bulk bins labeled "new crop," indicating they have been harvested within the past year. Or, lacking labels, shop at a store that has good turnover.

141

CREAMY MUSHROOM SOUP

Italian style

For an Italian-style mushroom soup, omit the sherry and cream. Add 2 tbsp tomato paste to the sautéed onions, and garnish the soup with croutons and freshly grated Parmesan cheese.

Serve this soup in the fall, when mushrooms are in abundance. Although fresh wild mushrooms such as chanterelles or porcini make for a particularly earthy and interesting soup, you can also use cultivated white mushrooms, cremini, portobellos, or a combination.

Rinse the dried porcini and place in a bowl. Add 1 cup (8 fl oz/ 250 ml) hot water and let stand for about 1 hour. Lift out the porcini, squeezing over the bowl to remove as much liquid as possible, and chop. Strain the liquid through a sieve lined with damp cheesecloth (muslin) into a bowl and set aside.

In a heavy saucepan over low heat, melt 2 tablespoons of the butter. Add the onions and sauté, stirring occasionally, until translucent, about 10 minutes. Remove from the heat.

In a large sauté pan over medium heat, melt the remaining 4 tablespoons (2 oz/60 g) butter. Add the fresh mushrooms to the pan and cook, stirring occasionally, until they give off their juices and soften, 10–15 minutes. Measure out 1 cup (8 fl oz/250 ml) of the mushrooms; keep warm.

Add the remaining sautéed mushrooms, the porcini, and the strained liquid to the sautéed onions and return the pan to medium-high heat. Add the stock and bring to a boil. Reduce the heat and simmer, uncovered, until the stock is flavorful, about 20 minutes. Remove from the heat and let cool slightly.

Working in batches, and using a slotted spoon, transfer the mushrooms and onions to a blender or food processor. Add a little of the cooking liquid and purée until smooth. Transfer to a clean saucepan. Thin with as much of the remaining liquid as needed. Add the sherry and cream and season with salt, pepper, and nutmeg. Reheat gently over low heat.

Ladle into warmed bowls and garnish with the reserved mushrooms, dividing them evenly. Sprinkle with the parsley and serve right away.

1 oz (30 g) dried porcini mushrooms

6 tablespoons (3 oz/90 g) unsalted butter

2 yellow onions, chopped

2 lb (1 kg) fresh mushrooms (see note, above), thinly sliced

5 cups (40 fl oz/1.25 l) Chicken Stock (page 23)

¼ cup (2 fl oz/60 ml) dry sherry or Madeira

1 cup (8 fl oz/250 ml) heavy (double) cream

Salt and ground pepper

Fresh grated nutmeg

3 tablespoons chopped fresh flat-leaf (Italian) parsley

MAKES 6 SERVINGS

ROASTED BUTTERNUT SQUASH SOUP

Sage-nutmeg cream

For an elegant garnish, whip about ¾ cup (6 fl oz/180 ml) heavy (double) cream until stiff, and fold in chopped fresh sage and ground nutmeg to taste. Place a dollop on each bowl just before serving.

Roasting the squash before simmering it in liquid deepens the flavor of its flesh and produces a richer, tastier result than if you cooked the squash completely by simmering. The roasting step also makes it easier to peel and seed the squash, a boon for busy cooks.

Preheat the oven to 400°F (200°C).

Prick each squash with the tip of a knife so it won't explode when it bakes. Place the whole squashes on a rimmed baking sheet and roast until they feel somewhat soft to the touch and a knife penetrates the skin easily, about 1 hour. Remove from the oven and let stand until cool enough to handle.

Halve each squash lengthwise and remove and discard the seeds and fibers with a large spoon. Scoop the pulp into a bowl.

2 large butternut squashes, about 2 lb (1 kg) each

6 tablespoons (3 oz/90 g) unsalted butter

2 yellow onions, chopped

8 fresh sage leaves, chopped

6 cups (48 fl oz/1.5 l) Chicken Stock (page 23) or Vegetable Stock (page 26)

Salt and ground pepper

Pinch of ground nutmeg

⅓ cup (2 oz/60 g) hazelnuts (filberts), toasted (see page 17) and chopped

MAKES 6 SERVINGS

In a saucepan over low heat, melt the butter. Add the onions and half of the sage and sauté until the onions are translucent, 8–10 minutes. Add the stock and squash pulp, raise the heat to high, and bring to a boil. Reduce the heat to low and simmer for a few minutes to combine the flavors. Remove from the heat and let cool slightly.

Working in batches, carefully purée the soup in a blender or food processor. Transfer to a clean saucepan. Reheat gently over low heat. Season with salt, pepper, and nutmeg.

Ladle the soup into bowls and garnish with the hazelnuts and the remaining sage. Serve right away.

CRAB BISQUE

This rich and creamy soup is ideal for a special-occasion gathering. The secret to a silky textured soup is long-grain rice, which is cooked and puréed with the other ingredients. Dress it up with chopped fresh chives or parsley, and pour a glass of Champagne for each guest.

2 tablespoons unsalted butter

¼ cup (1 oz/30 g) chopped shallots

½ cup (4 fl oz/125 ml) dry white wine

3 cups (24 fl oz/750 ml) Fish Stock (page 26) or bottled clam juice

3 tablespoons long-grain white rice

1 tablespoon tomato paste

¾ lb (375 g) cooked crabmeat, picked over for shell fragments

1 cup (8 fl oz/250 ml) heavy (double) cream

Kosher salt

⅛ teaspoon cayenne pepper, plus more for garnish, optional

¼ cup (2 fl oz/60 ml) dry sherry or Madeira, optional

MAKES 4–6 SERVINGS

In a large saucepan over medium-low heat, melt the butter. Add the shallots and sauté until softened, about 5 minutes. Raise the heat to medium, stir in the wine, and bring to a boil. Add the stock, rice, and tomato paste and return to a boil. Reduce the heat to low, cover, and simmer until the rice is soft, 20–25 minutes.

Set aside a few nice pieces of crabmeat for garnish. Uncover the pan and add the remaining crabmeat to the soup base. Remove from the heat and let cool slightly.

Working in batches, ladle the soup into a blender and process to a smooth purée. Stop the blender occasionally to scrape down the sides. Transfer to a clean saucepan.

Place the pan over very low heat. Slowly whisk in the cream, ½ teaspoon salt, and the ⅛ teaspoon cayenne pepper until blended. Add the sherry (if using) and whisk slowly to blend. Reheat the soup gently, stirring every now and again, until it is heated through, about 5 minutes. Do not allow to boil. Taste and adjust the seasoning.

Ladle into warmed bowls, garnish with the reserved crabmeat, and sprinkle with a small amount of cayenne pepper, if desired. Serve right away.

Bisque variations
You can also use this recipe as the base for lobster bisque by using cooked lobster meat in place of the crabmeat. For a deeper, richer flavor in either the crab or lobster version, substitute Beef Stock (page 22) for 1 cup of the Fish Stock.

143

GUMBO

Serve this traditional New Orleans stew on a bed of steamed white rice, garnished with parsley. Don't skimp on cooking the roux: it is essential that it turn a dark nut brown for the proper color and flavor. Pass Tabasco or another hot-pepper sauce at the table.

About filé powder

Also known as gumbo filé, this olive green powder, sold in the spice aisle, is made from dried, pulverized leaves of the sassafras plant and is prized by Cajun cooks for its thickening ability. The word filé comes from the French verb filer, *meaning "to spin threads," and true to its name, it can get stringy if cooked too long. Add it just a few minutes before serving.*

Cajun spice rub

In a small bowl, combine 1 tsp sea salt, 1 tsp ground pepper, ½ tsp cayenne pepper, 1 tbsp sweet paprika, 1 tsp fennel seeds, toasted and ground, and 1 tsp dried thyme. Use in gumbo or as a rub for panfried catfish.

In a large, heavy saucepan over medium heat, warm 2 tablespoons of the oil. Add the okra and sauté until golden brown and softened, 12–15 minutes. Using a slotted spoon, transfer to a bowl and set aside.

Add 2 tablespoons of the oil to the pan and heat over medium-high heat. Add the chicken and sauté until lightly browned on all sides, 3–5 minutes. Using a slotted spoon, transfer to a separate bowl and set aside.

Add the remaining 6 tablespoons (3 fl oz/90 ml) oil to the pan and heat for 2 minutes. Add the flour and stir with a wooden spoon to combine, making a roux. Cook the roux, stirring constantly, until dark brown, about 4 minutes. Reduce the heat to medium, add the onion and bell peppers, and cook, stirring occasionally, until softened, 8–10 minutes. Add the garlic and cook for 1 minute longer.

Add the cooked okra, tomatoes and juice, stock, bay leaves, and spice rub, and season with salt and pepper. Bring to a boil, then reduce the heat to low and simmer, uncovered, until slightly thickened, about 20 minutes. Add the browned chicken and cook until the chicken is cooked through, about 10 minutes longer.

Add the sausage and shrimp and cook until the sausage is heated through and the shrimp are evenly pink and opaque throughout, about 3 minutes. Add the filé powder and cook for 1 minute longer to thicken slightly. Discard the bay leaves. Taste and adjust the seasoning, then serve right away in warmed individual bowls.

10 tablespoons (5 fl oz/ 160 ml) canola oil

½ lb (250 g) okra, cut crosswise into ½-inch (12-mm) slices

2 lb (1 kg) skinless, boneless chicken thighs, cut into 2-inch (5-cm) pieces

6 tablespoons (2 oz/60 g) all-purpose (plain) flour

1 large yellow onion, chopped

1 *each* red and green bell pepper (capsicum), diced

3 cloves garlic, minced

1 can (14½ oz/455 g) diced tomatoes, with juice

5 cups (40 fl oz/1.25 l) Chicken Stock (page 23)

2 bay leaves

Cajun Spice Rub (see note, opposite)

Salt and ground pepper

½ lb (250 g) andouille sausage, thickly sliced

1 lb (500 g) large shrimp (prawns), peeled and deveined (see page 202)

1 teaspoon filé powder (see note, opposite)

MAKES 6 SERVINGS

SEAFOOD STEW

Be sure to use good country-style Italian or French bread for making this delightful Mediterranean main course, which combines fish, shrimp, and mussels in a tomato base. You'll want extra bread to soak up the flavorful broth after you've enjoyed the seafood.

2 fennel bulbs, 1½–2 lb (750 g–1 kg) total weight

3 tablespoons extra-virgin olive oil, plus more for brushing

3 cloves garlic, chopped

1 lb (500 g) plum (Roma) tomatoes, peeled, seeded, and chopped

2 bay leaves

2 cups (16 fl oz/500 ml) bottled clam juice

1 cup (8 fl oz/250 ml) dry white wine

1 tablespoon fresh lemon juice

Salt

Pinch of red pepper flakes

12–14 mussels in the shell, well scrubbed and debearded

2 lb (1 kg) white fish fillets (see note, right), in any combination, cut into 2-inch (5-cm) pieces

½ lb (250 g) small shrimp (prawns), peeled with the tail segments intact and deveined (see page 202)

4 slices coarse country bread, each about ½ inch (12 mm) thick

Coarsely chopped fresh flat-leaf (Italian) parsley for garnish

MAKES 4 SERVINGS

Cut off the stems, feathery tops, and any bruised outer stalks from the fennel bulbs. Cut the bulbs lengthwise into quarters, then cut away and discard the hard core portions, keeping the quarters intact. Set aside.

Preheat the oven to 325°F (165°C).

In a large saucepan over medium-low heat, warm the 3 tablespoons oil. Add the garlic and sauté until it begins to color, 1–2 minutes. Add the tomatoes, fennel, and bay leaves and cook, uncovered, until the tomatoes start to release their juices, 8–10 minutes. Stir in 4 cups (32 fl oz/ 1 l) water, the clam juice, wine, lemon juice, 2 teaspoons salt, and red pepper flakes. Cover partially, reduce the heat to low, and cook until the fennel is almost tender, 20–25 minutes.

Meanwhile, discard any mussels that do not close to the touch; set aside. When the fennel is almost tender, add the fish pieces, cover, and simmer gently over low heat for 10 minutes. Add the mussels and shrimp and continue to simmer until the fish is opaque throughout when pierced with a knife, the shrimp are pink, and the mussels are open, another 5–6 minutes. Discard any mussels that are still closed. Taste and adjust the seasoning.

Meanwhile, brush each bread slice with oil and arrange on a baking sheet. Warm in the oven for a few minutes.

To serve, divide the bread among 4 deep, warmed soup bowls. Ladle the stew on top and garnish with the parsley. Serve right away.

Fish types

Vary the fish in this soup according to what looks best at your fish market. Good choices include sea bass, halibut, red snapper, and sole. Avoid oily or strong-flavored fish, such as mackerel, tuna, and salmon.

FISH CURRY

Enriched with coconut milk and flavored with lemongrass, this dish is a cross between an Indian and a Southeast Asian yellow curry. The base for the curry can be made a few hours ahead and the fish added and cooked just before serving. Accompany with steamed rice.

Substitute for lemongrass

If you can't find fresh lemongrass, add 1 tsp grated lemon zest and increase the lemon juice to 3 tbsp.

In a large saucepan or wide sauté pan over medium heat, warm the oil. Add the onions and sauté, stirring, until translucent, about 10 minutes. Add the ginger, garlic, lime zest, lemongrass, coriander, cayenne, and turmeric and sauté until fragrant and translucent, 3–4 minutes longer.

Add the coconut milk and lemon juice, bring to a boil, and immediately reduce the heat to a simmer. Simmer, uncovered, for 3 minutes.

Meanwhile, cut the fish into 2-inch (5-cm) cubes, removing any errant bones. Add the fish cubes to the pan and cook until the fish is opaque throughout when pierced with a knife, 5–8 minutes. Season with salt.

Transfer to a warmed serving dish. Garnish with the mint and basil and serve right away.

3 tablespoons olive oil

2 yellow onions, chopped

1 tablespoon grated fresh ginger

2 teaspoons minced garlic

1 teaspoon grated lime zest

1 lemongrass stalk, center white part only, minced

2 tablespoons ground coriander

½ teaspoon cayenne pepper

1 teaspoon ground turmeric

1½ cups (12 fl oz/375 ml) coconut milk

1 tablespoon fresh lemon juice

1½ lb (750 g) firm white fish fillets such as snapper or sea bass

Salt

2 tablespoons *each* minced fresh mint and basil

MAKES 4 SERVINGS

Make it a meal

Add 2 cups (16 fl oz/ 500 ml) chicken broth with the coconut milk and about 1½ cups each green bean pieces (8 oz/250 g), thinly sliced green cabbage (5 oz/155 g), bell pepper pieces (capsicums, 6 oz/ 185 g), and diced zucchini (courgettes), before adding the fish to the pot.

CHICKEN STEW WITH DUMPLINGS

This stew evokes classic comfort food. With its chunks of chicken, diced vegetables, and pearl onions in a lightly thickened creamy base, it's perfect for cold-weather dining. Use a gentle hand when making the dumpling dough to ensure the dumplings will be light and delicate.

Light cream

Also called light whipping cream, light cream contains less butterfat than heavy cream, but more than half-and- half (half cream). Look for it in the dairy section of the supermarket.

In a heavy-bottomed pot, combine the chicken, celery, onion, 1 teaspoon salt, and water to cover. Bring to a boil, reduce the heat to medium-low, cover, and simmer until the chicken is barely cooked, 20–25 minutes. Using tongs, transfer the chicken to a plate; set aside.

Strain the liquid through a fine-mesh sieve into a clean container. Let cool, then cover and refrigerate until a layer of fat solidifies on top. Meanwhile, skin and debone the chicken breasts. Shred the meat and cover and refrigerate.

4–5 lb (2–2½ kg) skin-on, bone-in chicken breast halves

1 celery stalk with leaves

1 yellow onion, sliced

Salt and ground pepper

4 white boiling potatoes, peeled and cut into bite-sized pieces

4 carrots, peeled
and sliced

3 tablespoons
unsalted butter

⅓ cup (2 oz/60 g) all-
purpose (plain) flour

1½ cups (12 fl oz/375 ml)
light (single) cream

1 lb (500 g) pearl onions,
peeled (see note, opposite)

Old-Fashioned
Dumplings (below),
steamed on a plate

MAKES 8 SERVINGS

Skim the fat from the surface of the stock and reserve. Bring the stock to a boil. Add the potatoes and carrots and boil for 15 minutes. Drain off the stock into a clean container; set the stock and vegetables aside separately.

In a saucepan over medium heat, melt the butter with 3 tablespoons of the reserved chicken fat. Add the flour and stir with a wooden spoon to combine, making a roux. Cook the roux, stirring constantly, for 2–3 minutes; do not brown. Stirring constantly, slowly add 2½ cups (20 fl oz/625 ml) of the reserved stock and the cream, continuing to stir until smooth and thickened, about 2 minutes. Stir in ¼ teaspoon pepper, then pour the sauce over the potatoes and carrots. Add the reserved chicken and the pearl onions and bring to a gentle simmer. Cover and simmer until the chicken is cooked through and the vegetables are tender, 20–30 minutes.

Begin steaming the dumplings about 20 minutes before the stew is ready. To serve, spoon the stew into warmed bowls and slide the dumplings on top.

OLD-FASHIONED DUMPLINGS

Light and airy dumplings turn stew into a hearty one-pot meal. You can cook the dumplings directly on top of a stew or steam them separately and then add them. Steaming is best when the stew ingredients are too delicate for the low boil required to cook the dumplings.

2 cups (10 oz/315 g)
all-purpose (plain) flour

2 teaspoons baking powder

¼ teaspoon baking soda
(bicarbonate of soda)

½ teaspoon salt

1 egg, lightly beaten

¾ cup (6 fl oz/180 ml) milk

MAKES ABOUT
16 DUMPLINGS

In a bowl, sift together the flour, baking powder, baking soda, and salt. Add the egg and milk and mix with a fork until the flour is absorbed and a soft dough has formed.

To cook the dumplings on top of the stew, bring the stew to a boil. Dip a large metal spoon in cold water, then use it to scoop out a spoonful of the dough and drop it gently on top of the stew, letting it rest on the solid ingredients. (If there is too much liquid for the dumplings to rest on solid ingredients, remove as much liquid as necessary and return it to the stew before serving.) Repeat with the remaining dough, arranging the dumplings in a single layer. Cover and cook over medium heat until a toothpick inserted into the center of a dumpling comes out clean, about 12 minutes. Serve right away.

To steam the dumplings on a plate, butter a heatproof plate and place on a rack in a steamer pan filled with water to a depth of about 1 inch (2.5 cm). Bring the water to a boil over high heat. Following the directions above, drop the dumplings onto the plate. Cover and steam until until a toothpick inserted into the center of a dumpling comes out clean, about 20 minutes. To serve, slide the dumplings onto the prepared stew.

**Dumpling
variations**

For crunchy corn bread dumplings, substitute 1 cup (5 oz/155 g) fine-grind cornmeal for an equal amount of the flour. For tangy buttermilk dumplings, substitute ¾ cup (6 fl oz/180 ml) buttermilk for an equal amount of the milk.

CHICKPEA AND POTATO STEW

Using canned chickpeas

To save time, substitute 1 can (15 oz/470 g) chickpeas, drained and well rinsed, for the dried chickpeas. Decrease the stock to 3 cups (24 fl oz/ 750 ml) and proceed with the recipe.

Wonderfully seasoned but not too spicy, this Indian-inspired vegetarian stew of chickpeas, potatoes, and tomato is a good source of protein, fiber, and vitamin E. Serve it with steamed white rice, a dollop of plain yogurt, and warm naan or pita bread.

Pick over the chickpeas and discard any damaged beans or impurities, then rinse. Place in a bowl with water to cover generously. Let soak for 3 hours. Drain.

In a saucepan over high heat, bring the stock to a boil. Add the chickpeas, reduce the heat to medium, and simmer, uncovered, until almost tender, about 1½ hours. Add the potatoes, tomatoes, garam masala, ginger, and turmeric and continue to cook until the chickpeas and potatoes are tender, about 30 minutes longer.

Remove from the heat and let cool slightly. Transfer half of the stock and vegetables to a blender or food processor and process until smooth. Return to the saucepan and season the stew with salt and pepper. Reheat to serving temperature.

Ladle the stew into warmed bowls, sprinkle with the cilantro, and serve right away.

¾ cup (5 oz/155 g) dried chickpeas (garbanzo beans)

5 cups (40 fl oz/1.25 l) Vegetable Stock (page 26)

1 lb (500 g) russet potatoes, peeled and diced

1 lb (500 g) tomatoes, peeled, seeded, and diced

2 teaspoons garam masala

½ teaspoon ground ginger

½ teaspoon ground turmeric

Salt and ground pepper

3 tablespoons chopped fresh cilantro (fresh coriander)

MAKES 6 SERVINGS

IRISH LAMB STEW

Boiling potatoes

Boiling potatoes or waxy potatoes are low in starch. Use them for potato salads or other recipes, such as this stew, where you want them to hold their shape and are not relying on their starch to thicken the dish.

This layered stew of lamb and vegetables cooks slowly for a couple of hours, to yield especially tender results. Offer thick slices of Oat Flour Bread (page 431) or a batch of Buttermilk Biscuits (page 436) alongside. For additional color, garnish each serving with minced fresh parsley.

In a 4-qt (4-l) heavy-bottomed stew pot, combine the lamb with water to cover by 1 inch. Bring to a boil over high heat and boil for 5 minutes. Using a slotted spoon, transfer the lamb to a plate. Pour the broth into a bowl and set aside.

Layer half of the potato slices in the bottom of the same pot. Cover with half of the onion slices and then top with all the turnip slices. Distribute the lamb evenly over the turnips and top with the thyme, parsley, 1 teaspoon salt, and ¼ teaspoon pepper. Top with the remaining onions and finally the remaining potatoes. Strain the broth through a fine-mesh sieve over the potatoes.

Bring to a low boil over high heat. Reduce the heat to medium-low, cover, and simmer gently until the lamb is tender when pierced with a fork, about 2 hours.

Spoon into warmed bowls, discarding the thyme and parsley sprigs, and serve right away.

2 lb (1 kg) boneless lamb shoulder, cut into 1-inch (2.5-cm) cubes

4 white boiling potatoes, peeled and cut into slices ½ inch (12 mm) thick

2 yellow onions, halved and cut into slices ½ inch (12 mm) thick

1 large turnip, peeled and cut into slices ¼ inch (6 mm) thick

2 fresh thyme sprigs

3 fresh flat-leaf (Italian) parsley sprigs

Salt and ground pepper

MAKES 4–6 SERVINGS

HEARTY BEEF STEW

The cinnamon, allspice, and cloves that flavor this hearty stew are also common background flavors in big, bold red wines, making for a perfect winter pairing. Serve the stew with buttered egg noodles or on top of creamy polenta, spooning some of the stew juices over either one.

4 cloves garlic, crushed

3 fresh flat-leaf (Italian) parsley sprigs, plus 2 tablespoons chopped for garnish

3 fresh thyme sprigs

2 orange zest strips, each 3 inches (7.5 cm) long

12 peppercorns

12 whole cloves

2 allspice berries

1 cinnamon stick

1 bottle (24 fl oz/750 ml) dry red wine

½ cup (4 fl oz/125 ml) olive oil

2 yellow onions, coarsely chopped

2½ lb (1.25 kg) boneless stewing beef (see note, right), cut into 2-inch (5-cm) cubes

2 cups (12 oz/375 g) peeled, seeded, and chopped tomatoes (fresh or canned)

¾ lb (375 g) carrots, peeled and cut into 2-inch (5-cm) lengths

⅔ cup (3½ oz/105 g) brine-cured black olives, pitted if desired

Salt and ground pepper

MAKES 4 SERVINGS

Combine the garlic, parsley sprigs, thyme, orange zest, peppercorns, cloves, allspice, and cinnamon stick on a square of cheesecloth (muslin). Bring the corners together and tie securely with kitchen string.

Pour the wine and ¼ cup (2 fl oz/60 ml) of the oil into a deep, nonreactive dish and add the onions, spice bag, and beef. Stir to coat the beef evenly, cover, and refrigerate for 24 hours.

Preheat the oven to 300°F (150°C).

Remove the meat from the marinade and pat dry. Reserve the marinade. In a heavy sauté pan over high heat, warm 2 tablespoons of the oil. Brown half of the meat on all sides, 5–10 minutes. Transfer the browned meat to a Dutch oven or other heavy, ovenproof pot. Add the remaining 2 tablespoons oil to the pan, brown the remaining meat, and add to the pot. Add the reserved marinade, including the cheesecloth bag; the tomatoes; and water just to cover. Cover, bring to a boil over high heat, transfer to the oven, and cook until the meat is meltingly tender, 3–4 hours.

Meanwhile, bring a saucepan three-fourths full of salted water to a boil. Add the carrots and cook until tender when pierced with a knife, about 10 minutes. Drain and set aside.

When the beef is tender, remove the pot from the oven and discard the cheesecloth bag. Using a large spoon, skim off the excess fat from the surface. Add the carrots and olives and place over medium heat until heated through. Season with salt and pepper.

Spoon into warmed bowls, sprinkle with the chopped parsley, and serve right away.

Beef for stewing

If you don't see stewing beef at the butcher shop, ask for chuck, round, or brisket. These cuts tend to be tougher and leaner than cuts you would grill or roast, which means they benefit from long, slow cooking in a covered pot. They also tend to be less expensive than the more tender cuts, making them particularly budget friendly.

BEEF CHILI WITH BLACK BEANS

On a cold and blustery weekend when friends have gathered to watch the big game, offer
them bowls of this pleasantly spicy chili along with plenty of ice-cold beer and warm corn
bread. Add shredded cheese, a dollop of sour cream, and fresh cilantro just before serving.

Pour enough of the oil into a large, heavy, deep-sided pot
to film the bottom and place over medium heat. Working
in batches, and adding more oil as needed, add the meat
to the hot oil in a single layer and cook, turning often, until
browned on all sides, 3–5 minutes. As each batch is ready,
transfer to a plate.

Add more oil to the pot to film the bottom and warm over
medium heat. Add the carrots, two-thirds of the onions, and
the garlic and cook, stirring, until softened, about 2 minutes.
Return the browned meat to the pot, sprinkle with the flour,
and cook, stirring vigorously, for 1 minute. Add the chili
powder, cumin, oregano, 1½ teaspoons salt, red pepper flakes,
tomatoes, 5 cups (40 fl oz/1.25 l) stock, and the chipotle chiles.
Bring to a simmer, reduce the heat to low, cover, and cook
for about 30 minutes. Uncover and continue to cook, stirring
occasionally, until the meat is fork tender, 1½–2 hours longer.
If the chili becomes too thick during simmering, thin with
as much of the remaining 1 cup (8 fl oz/250 ml) stock as
needed. Taste and adjust the seasoning. Remove the chiles
and discard them.

Rinse the beans, drain, and pat dry. In a large, heavy frying
pan over medium-high heat, warm 2 teaspoons of the oil.
Add the remaining onion and cook, stirring often, until
softened, about 3 minutes. Add the beans and cook, stirring,
until hot, 2–3 minutes longer.

Divide the beans among warmed shallow bowls and ladle
the chili over them. Garnish with the cheese, a dollop of sour
cream, and a sprinkle of cilantro and serve right away.

3–4 tablespoons canola oil

3 lb (1.5 kg) lean beef stew
meat (see note, page 149),
trimmed and cut into
¾-inch (2-cm) cubes

2 carrots, peeled and
finely diced

3 yellow onions, chopped

4 teaspoons chopped garlic

3 tablespoons all-purpose
(plain) flour

¼ cup (2 oz/60 g)
chili powder

3½ teaspoons
ground cumin

2¼ teaspoons
dried oregano

Salt

¼ teaspoon red
pepper flakes

2 cans (28 oz/875 g *each*)
plum (Roma) tomatoes,
drained and chopped

5–6 cups (40-48 fl oz/
1.25-1.5 l) Beef Stock
(page 22)

2 chipotle chiles

2 cans (15 oz/470 g *each*)
black beans

1 cup (4 oz/125 g) shredded
Monterey Jack cheese

1 cup (8 fl oz/250 ml)
sour cream

2 tablespoons chopped
fresh cilantro (fresh
coriander)

MAKES 6 SERVINGS

VEGETARIAN CHILI WITH CORNMEAL DUMPLINGS

Thick with kidney beans and topped with hearty dumplings, this meatless chili is a substantial meal. If you like, garnish it with a dollop of sour cream or plain low-fat yogurt in place of the cheese. The chopped fresh cilantro on top lends freshness to the dish.

2 green bell peppers
(capsicums), halved
and seeded

1 large sweet onion

2 teaspoons olive oil

2 cans (19 oz/590 g each)
red kidney beans,
with liquid

2 cups (12 oz/375 g) canned
tomato chunks in purée,
with juice

1 tablespoon chili powder

3–5 dashes hot-pepper
sauce such as Tabasco

Salt and ground pepper

Old-Fashioned Dumplings
(page 147), made with
cornmeal

1 cup (4 oz/125 g) shredded
Monterey jack cheese

2 tablespoons chopped
fresh cilantro (fresh
coriander)

MAKES 6 SERVINGS

Cut the bell peppers lengthwise into strips ½ inch (12 mm) wide. Cut the onion in half and then into slices ½ inch (12 mm) thick. In a heavy-bottomed saucepan over medium-high heat, warm the oil. Add the bell peppers and onion and sauté, stirring, until the onion is translucent, about 5 minutes. Add the kidney beans and their liquid, tomatoes with juice, chili powder, and hot-pepper sauce. Mix until well blended and bring to a simmer. Reduce the heat to medium-low, cover, and simmer gently for 20 minutes to blend the flavors. Season with salt and pepper.

Add the cornmeal dumplings to the top of the stew, cover, and cook as directed.

Spoon the stew and dumplings into warmed bowls, sprinkle with the cheese and cilantro, and serve right away.

Seeding bell peppers

To seed and derib a bell pepper, cut the pepper in half lengthwise. Using your hands or a paring knife, remove the stem. Trim away the seeds and the white membranes, or ribs. For stubborn seeds, quickly rinse them away under running cold water.

151

Pasta & NOODLES

Pasta & Noodles

From traditional Italian pasta-and-sauce combinations to flavorful Asian noodle stir-fries to classic American mac and cheese, pasta is at the heart of many of the world's most popular dishes. Here you'll find all you need to know about putting this staple to use, whether you're tossing dishes together quickly from store-bought pastas or creating your own silken pappardelle and saucing it like a pro.

Pasta Techniques

154

Fresh pasta or dried?
Despite the general championing of fresh foods, fresh pasta is not better than dried pasta. Each type has its uses. Dried pasta is typically served with tomato- or oil-based sauces, while more tender fresh pasta works best with sauces that feature butter, cream, or cheese.

Selecting dried pasta
The finest manufactured dried pastas begin with semolina flour ground from durum wheat, the hardest variety grown. This gives the pasta shapes a desirable firmness and elasticity. Look for the words semolina *and* durum *on the package.*

Buying dried egg noodles
When shopping for dried egg noodles, check to make sure that eggs are, in fact, among the ingredients. Some products are imitation egg noodles colored to look like the real thing.

Storing fresh pasta
Whether homemade or purchased at a high-end supermarket or Italian deli, fresh pasta should be used as soon as possible. If necessary, store it in an airtight container in the refrigerator for up to 2 days.

Most fresh pasta is made from only two or three simple ingredients: flour, eggs, and sometimes salt. Follow the basic techniques given below for both handmade and machine-made fresh pasta to achieve the perfect balance of tenderness and chewiness that aficionados prize. The cooking and saucing guidelines will lead you to expertly prepared dishes.

MAKING FRESH EGG PASTA Hand method: Adhering to the proportions in the recipe you are using, heap the flour on a work surface and make a well in the center. Break the eggs into the well. With a fork, lightly beat the eggs; then, in a circular motion, gradually incorporate flour from the sides of the well until all the ingredients are combined. With the palm and heel of your hand, knead the dough by pushing it down and away, folding it back toward you, and rotating it a quarter turn. If rolling out the dough by hand, repeat these strokes until the dough is smooth and elastic, 5–10 minutes. If rolling out the dough by machine, repeat these strokes until the dough is smooth and no longer sticky, 2–3 minutes. (You will continue kneading with the pasta machine.) If the dough sticks or seems too soft, sprinkle it lightly with flour. Shape into a ball, cover with an overturned bowl, and let rest for 30 minutes.

Food processor method: Combine the flour and eggs in a food processor and pulse briefly to combine. Then, using long pulses, process just until the dough forms a ball that rides on the blade, about 1 minute. Knead, shape into a ball, and let rest as directed above.

ROLLING OUT FRESH PASTA Hand method: Cut the dough into easy-to-manage portions, and keep covered until needed. Dust a work surface and a rolling pin with flour. Flatten a dough portion, then roll out to the desired thinness. To test, lift the dough with one hand. If making ribbons such as fettuccine, your hand should be clearly visible through the dough; if making filled pastas, the dough should be nearly translucent. Lay the pasta sheet on a floured kitchen towel and let stand for about 10 minutes before cutting. The pasta should be neither dry nor sticky.

Machine method: Adjust the rollers of a hand-cranked pasta machine to the widest setting and dust lightly. Cut the dough into smaller portions (usually 4 portions if making 1 lb/500 g dough), and keep covered until needed. Flatten a portion into a thick disk and crank it through the rollers. Fold the dough into thirds like a letter, dust one side with flour, and crank it through the rollers again. Repeat 8–10 times, lightly dusting one side with flour and folding into thirds each time, until supple, satiny, and smooth. Now, reset the rollers one notch narrower and pass the dough through the rollers. Repeat, setting the rollers one notch narrow each time until the dough is the desired thinness, usually the second-to-last setting for ribbons such as fettuccine and the last setting for filled pastas. If the sheet gets unwieldy before it is the desired thinness, cut it in half and continue rolling.

CUTTING FRESH PASTA There are two basic ways to cut fresh pasta into ribbons: by hand with a knife, or by attaching the cutting blades to a hand-cranked or electric pasta machine.

Hand method: Roll up the pasta sheet into a cylinder and flatten it slightly. Using a sharp knife, cut across the roll into slices ⅜ inch (1 cm) wide for tagliatelle or fettuccine, 1¼ inches (3 cm) for pappardelle, a scant ⅛ inch (2 mm) for taglierini, and 4 inches (10 cm) for lasagne. Unfurl the narrow slices, form a few strips at a time into nests about 2 inches (2.5 cm) wide, and place on a floured kitchen towel. Place lasagne strips on a floured towel.

Machine method: Fit the machine with the cutting attachment for the desired width of noodles. Cut a length of rolled-out dough into a manageable length and guide it through the cutters with one hand while cranking the machine with the other hand. Form into nests as described above.

FILLING FRESH PASTA Pasta shapes such as tortellini and various forms of ravioli can be filled and shaped many ways. Common to all of them, however, is the need to seal the filling securely within the pasta so the shapes don't come apart during cooking.

For one method, dot a long pasta sheet at regular intervals with spoonfuls of filling. Then, with a pastry brush or fingertip, lightly brush water or sometimes beaten egg along the edges of the sheet and on the exposed pasta between the mounds of filling. Cover with a second sheet of pasta and press down around each mound and along the edges to seal the sheets together. Finally, using a knife or pastry cutting wheel, cut between the mounds to make individual filled pastas.

Another method calls for cutting pasta sheets into uniform pieces and filling them one at a time. Depending on the recipe, cut circles, squares, or other shapes using a cutting wheel or knife. Place a spoonful of filling in the center of each piece, brush the edges with water or egg, fold the pasta over the filling, and press the edges together, sealing and shaping the pasta as directed in individual recipes.

COOKING PASTA Whether fresh or dried, filled or plain, start with enough boiling salted water for the pasta to circulate freely. For 1 lb (500 g) fresh pasta, which typically serves 4–6 people, 5 qt (5 l) water are sufficient. For 1–1¼ lb (500–625 g) dried pasta, which will also serve 4–6 people, use 5–6 qt (5–6 l). Cook pasta until al dente, the Italian term for tender but still chewy. Fresh pasta generally cooks to the al dente stage in 1–3 minutes and dried pasta in 3–15 minutes, depending on the thickness and shape. Always check the suggested cooking time on the package, even when a time range is given in a recipe. To test for doneness, remove a piece of pasta from the water, let cool briefly, and then taste. If the pasta is too hard or tastes of flour, continue cooking it, checking it often to prevent it from becoming mushy. For recipes that involve cooking the pasta further with the sauce on the stove top or in the oven, drain the pasta when it is still slightly underdone.

SAUCING PASTA Before draining the cooked pasta, scoop out about 1 cup (8 fl oz/250 ml) of the cooking water. Drain the pasta in a colander (or lift the pasta insert) and quickly combine it, still damp, with your sauce, stirring gently to mix well. If the sauce seems too thick when combined with the pasta, add some of the reserved pasta water, a spoonful at a time, to thin it.

Drying fresh pasta
Freshly made and cut pasta can also be left at room temperature until completely dry, then stored in an airtight container in the refrigerator or at cool room temperature for up to a week, or in the freezer for up to 3 months.

Storing dried pasta
Because it is virtually free of moisture, manufactured dried pasta keeps well for up to 1 year if stored in an airtight container at room temperature.

Storing filled pasta
Filled pasta can be stored in an airtight container in the refrigerator for 1 to 7 days, depending on how perishable its filling is.

155

Storing cooked pasta
Once cooked, any pasta will keep in the refrigerator for up to 12 hours. Longer than that, its flavor can begin to sour.

Healthy pasta
A common misconception is that pasta is fattening. In fact, a healthy diet draws the majority of its calories from complex carbohydrates such as those found in pasta. Relatively low in calories and very low in fat and sodium, pasta is also a good source of dietary fiber, which may help prevent heart disease, intestinal disorders, and some cancers.

Less healthy pasta
Although pasta alone is a healthy food, it becomes less so when combined with sauces rich in cheese, cream, or red meat. For the healthiest dishes, dress pasta lightly in good-quality olive oil and toss it with vegetables and poultry.

Asian Noodles

Eaten as often as rice in many eastern countries, Asian-style noodles can be made from a wide variety of grains. Today, noodles of all colors, flavors, and textures have become popular on dinner tables, appearing in dishes from soups to stir-fries to dumplings.

ASIAN NOODLE TYPES Asian noodles are made from a number of different main ingredients, wheat and rice being the most common. Traditionally, wheat noodles were enjoyed in cool, northern countries, and rice noodles were the staple of warmer, southern regions of the continent. Other types of noodles are made from mung beans or even sweet potatoes, yielding unique flavors and textures. All types of Asian noodles come in a wide range of shapes and sizes, rivaling the diversity of their western counterparts. The recipes that follow focus on the two most popular and easy-to-find types in the United States, wheat noodles and rice noodles.

Chinese-style wheat noodles are delicious stir-fried with meat or poultry and a highly flavored sauce, such as in the recipe on page 171 featuring ground pork and a spicy peanut sauce. The noodles are first cooked until still slightly toothsome, drained well, and then mixed with the remaining ingredients. Wheat noodles are also delicious in salads and soups (see note at left).

Delicate rice noodles, also called rice vermicelli, are also popular and accessible noodles for the home cook. These translucent noodles appear in dishes from or inspired by Southeast Asia, such as in Vietnamese Grilled Chicken with Rice Noodles (page 170) and Pad Thai (page 170). The noodles are soaked or cooked briefly in boiling water prior to incorporating them into the dish. Rice noodles also work well for soup (see note at left).

COOKING ASIAN NOODLES Regardless of the type, and unless it's a soup, Asian noodles are usually precooked before using in a recipe. To cook, follow the directions on the package, or follow the guidelines below.

To cook fresh wheat noodles: Bring a large pot of water to a boil over high heat. When the water comes to a rapid boil, add the noodles all at once and stir gently to prevent sticking. If the noodles are to be cooked further, drain them when they are tender but still slightly chewy, 2–3 minutes. If the noodles will not be cooked further, drain them when the texture is to your liking, usually up to 1 minute more.

To cook dried rice noodles: There are two main ways to cook rice vermicelli. Place them in a heatproof bowl with hot water to cover and let stand until plumped and softened, about 15 minutes. Alternatively, bring a large pot of water to a boil over high heat. Add the noodles to the rapidly boiling water and cook until just tender, about 1 minute. Drain the noodles well before using.

ABOUT DUMPLINGS As with Italian tortellini and ravioli, Asian noodles can also take the form of wrappings, surrounding a number of delicious fillings. Translucent rice or wheat wrappers can enclose meat, seafood, or vegetables, for recipes such as Rice Paper Rolls with Chinese Broccoli (page 79) or shrimp and pork-filled pot stickers (page 78) for delicious starters, snacks, or side dishes. Rice paper rounds, and wonton or pot sticker wrappers can be found in Asian markets and in many well-stocked grocery stores. Rice paper wrappers need little special care until they are soaked in water to make them pliable, after which they should be used right away. But like all fresh pasta, wonton wrappers will dry out, so keep them in their packaging until you're ready to use them and, if possible, keep the extra wrappers covered with a plastic wrap and a damp kitchen towel as you are working.

Chilled Wheat Noodles
In hot months, chilled noodles provide a refreshing option served with simple garnishes and dipping sauces. Noodles can also be floated in chilled broths, or tossed in salads with a spicy Asian-style salad dressing, such as the one on page 118. To chill wheat noodles, rinse the cooked, drained noodles in cool running water until no longer warm to the touch, then drain well. Toss with the desired dressing and ingredients and refrigerated until well chilled.

Rice Noodle Soup
Soak 6 oz (185 g) dried rice vermicelli in hot water to cover for 15 minutes. Meanwhile, in a large saucepan over medium heat, combine 6 cups (48 fl oz/ 1.5 l) Chicken Stock (page 23), 3 thinly sliced shallots, 2 tbsp minced fresh ginger, and 1 tsp Chinese five-spice powder and bring to a boil. Drain the noodles, add them to the stock, and heat for about 5 seconds. Garnish bowls with thinly sliced green (spring) onions and serve with Asian fish sauce and lime juice for diners to add to taste.

PASTA TYPES AND PAIRINGS

No firm rules apply to pairing pastas and sauces, but the following descriptions will provide some guidance.

RIBBON PASTAS

Fettuccine *Long, wide ribbons*
Pappardelle *Very wide ribbons*
Tagliatelle *Ribbons slightly wider than fettuccine*
Ribbons of fresh pasta are more tender and absorbent and have a more delicate flavor than dried versions. They call for sauces that will coat but not overpower them. Fresh or dried ribbon pastas are well suited to thick, creamy sauces, hence such classic pairings as fettuccine with Alfredo Sauce (page 381) or Bolognese Sauce (page 380). Simple toppings like Butter and Sage Sauce (page 380) and Marinara Sauce (page 379) also work well.

STRAND PASTAS

Bucatini/perciatelli *Slender, narrow tubes, like "pierced" spaghetti*
Capellini/capelli d'angelo *Fine strands of "little hair" or "angel hair"*
Fedelini *Strands thinner than spaghetti*
Linguine *"Little tongues;" narrow ribbons like flattened spaghetti*
Spaghetti *Thin, cylindrical strands, from spago, for "string"*
Spaghettini *Thinner spaghetti, similar to vermicelli*
Vermicelli *"Little worms;" narrow ribbons like spaghettini*
Strand pastas, like the ribbons above, work well with smooth sauces that can coat the strands evenly, such as tomato- or cream-based sauces. But unlike fresh ribbons, dried strands also work well with oil-based sauces, whether Pesto (page 387) or a simple mixture of oil and crushed garlic. Heartier strands also hold up to chunky sauces or ingredients, such as the time-honored Spaghetti and Meatballs (page 163). For delicate strands like vermicelli and capellini, stay with light, smooth, simple sauces.

TUBE PASTAS

Cavatappi *Corkscrew-shaped tubes*
Macaroni *Short tubes usually curved like elbows*
Mostaccioli *Narrow tubes resembling straight "moustaches"*
Penne *Narrow tubes with angled ends like "quill pens"*
Rigatoni *Ridged bite-size tubes*
Ziti *Short or long hollow tubes*
Tube-shaped pastas pair well with thick sauces, from tomato-based mixtures to meat sauces to rich cheese sauces. Tubes are also good for olive oil–based sauces, since their rough or ribbed textures help the sauce cling. Because they trap sauces well in their openings and are bite-size, tubes are also often used in baked pasta dishes, such as macaroni and cheese (page 176) or the penne with vegetables on page 166.

SHAPED PASTAS

Cavatelli *Narrow football shapes, tapered at the ends*
Conchiglie *"Shells;" small, medium, or large*
Farfalle *"Butterflies;" also called bow ties for their shape*
Fusilli *Corkscrew "fuses"*
Gemelli *"Twins;" bite-size twisted strands*
Orecciette *"Little ears;" small, concave circular shapes*
Radiatore *Ridged, bite-size shapes resembling "radiators"*
Rotelle *Many-spoked wheels, similar to ruote*
Ruote *Bite-size shapes resembling "wagon wheels"*
Short pasta shapes can be matched with essentially any type of sauce, but work especially well with thick sauces, such as Gemelli with Four Cheeses (page 168). Most shapes also toss well with chunky ingredients, with the chunks lodging in the twists and hollows of the pasta. This makes them ideal for pasta salads and other tossed pasta dishes.

BAKING PASTAS

Cannelloni *Short or long hollow tubes*
Lasagne *Wide, flat ribbons for layering and baking*
Manicotti *"Muffs;" large tubes for stuffing and baking*
Large tubes and extra-wide ribbons are made to be stuffed or layered with sauces (whether tomato sauce or béchamel, page 174), cheeses (such as ricotta), and other ingredients (ranging from meats to vegetables), then baked until bubbling hot. Thicker than other pastas, they remain pleasantly al dente even after baking.

FILLED PASTAS

Agnolotti *Bite-size crescents*
Ravioli *Classic stuffed squares or rounds*
Tortellini/tortelloni *"Little pies;" small stuffed rings*
Filled pastas can be paired with just butter or olive oil and Parmesan or tossed with a tomato-, oil-, or cream-based sauce. When choosing a sauce, consider the filling. The flavors should complement one another, and the sauce should not overpower the filling.

DUMPLINGS

Gnocchi *Short, flat, bite sized dumplings made from riced cooked potatoes*
Dumplings can stand up to smooth, tomato based sauces (pages 377–80) and pestos (page 387). They also pair well with creamy sauces.

ASIAN NOODLES

Mein *Thin strands of Chinese wheat-and-egg noodles*
Rice vermicelli *Thin strands made from rice flour*
Asian noodles are used in stir-fries (like those on page 170), salads, or soups (left).

FRESH EGG PASTA

A feel for pasta

The proportions given for the pasta ingredients are approximate, and will vary with the size of the eggs, how you measure the flour, the absorbency of the flour, and how dry or humid the weather is. Your eyes and your hands are the best judges of how the pasta is proceeding, so note the visual and tactile cues in the recipe.

158

Egg-and-flour pasta is surprisingly easy to make at home. Whether you make it by hand or machine, you can have fresh pasta ready to cook in less than an hour. If you opt to use a food processor, you will save time and the result will be just as good.

Hand method Mound the flour on a work surface and make a well in the center. Carefully break the eggs into the well. Using a fork, lightly beat the eggs. Working in a circular motion, gradually incorporate the flour from the walls of the well into the eggs. When the dough becomes too stiff to beat with the fork, continue with the palm of your hand until as much flour as possible is incorporated. Using the palm and heel of your hand, knead the dough, pushing it down and away, folding it back toward you, and rotating it a quarter turn. If you plan to roll out the dough by hand, repeat these strokes until the dough is smooth and elastic, 5–10 minutes. If you plan to roll out the dough by machine, repeat the strokes until the dough is smooth and no longer sticky, 2–3 minutes.

Food processor method Combine the flour and eggs in a food processor. Pulse briefly to combine the ingredients. Then process using long pulses just until the dough forms a ball around the blade, about 1 minute. Turn the dough out onto a work surface and knead with the palm of your hand as described above.

Cover the dough and let it rest for 30 minutes. Roll out and cut the dough according to the method on page 154 and the instructions in individual recipes.

2 cups (10 oz/315 g) all-purpose (plain) flour

3 eggs

MAKES ABOUT 1 LB (500 G) DOUGH

FRESH SPINACH PASTA

More flavored pastas

Here are three additional ways to flavor Fresh Egg Pasta dough. Incorporate each ingredient when beating the eggs: For tomato pasta, add 2 tbsp tomato paste. For black pepper pasta, add 1 tbsp very finely ground black pepper. For red pepper pasta, add 1 tbsp good-quality paprika.

Fresh spinach not only turns egg pasta dough a beautiful grass green, but also imparts a subtle flavor that pairs well with robust sauces. The finished dough is softer than plain egg pasta and has a creamier, more delicate texture when cooked.

Place the spinach, with the rinsing water still clinging to the leaves, in a large frying pan with a tight-fitting lid. Cover and cook over medium heat until the spinach wilts, 2–3 minutes. Drain in a sieve under cold running water. When cool, squeeze until thoroughly dry.

Place the spinach in a food processor with 1 of the eggs. Process to a smooth purée, stopping once or twice to scrape down the sides of the work bowl.

Make the pasta dough as directed for Fresh Egg Pasta (above), putting the spinach mixture and the remaining egg, lightly beaten, into the well of flour (or adding the remaining flour and egg to the food processor), and then gradually working in the flour to make a dough. Cover the dough and let it rest for 30 minutes. Roll out and cut the dough according to the method on page 154 or the instructions in individual recipes.

1 lb (500 g) spinach, thick stems removed

2 eggs

About 3 cups (15 oz/470 g) unbleached all-purpose (plain) flour

Semolina flour for dusting

MAKES ABOUT 1½ LB (750 G) DOUGH

FRESH BASIL PAPPARDELLE

Mixing fresh basil into pasta dough results in attractively flecked noodles with a subtle herb flavor. If pecorino (sheep's milk cheese) is difficult to find, Parmesan may be substituted. For an even more colorful presentation, scatter a few extra herb leaves over the finished dish.

2 cups (10 oz/300 g) all-purpose (plain) flour

1½ cups (12 oz/45 g) fresh basil leaves, well dried after washing

¼ cup (1 oz/30 g) grated pecorino cheese such as pecorino romano or pecorino sardo, plus more for garnish

3 whole eggs plus 1 egg yolk

6 tablespoons (3 fl oz/ 90 ml) extra-virgin olive oil

Ground pepper

Combine the flour, basil, and the ¼ cup pecorino in a blender or food processor. Process until the basil is pulverized and thoroughly mixed with the flour and cheese.

If using a blender, turn the mixture out onto a board. If using a food processor, leave it in the work bowl. Make the pappardelle (by hand or in the processor) using the flour-cheese mixture, whole eggs, and egg yolk and following the directions for Fresh Egg Pasta (opposite page).

Bring a large pot three-fourths full of salted water to a boil. Add the pappardelle and boil until they rise to the surface, about 2 minutes.

Drain the pasta and arrange on a warmed platter. Pour the oil over the top and season with pepper. Toss well, sprinkle with pecorino, and serve right away.

MAKES 6 SERVINGS

Herbed fresh pasta

Change the flavor of the pasta by changing the herbs used. Substitute an equal amount of fresh flat-leaf (Italian) parsley or two-thirds the amount of fresh thyme or rosemary leaves.

159

PASTA PRIMAVERA

Primavera is Italian for "spring," evoking the multitude of vegetables that adorn this dish. The vegetables are first cooked in a small amount of cream, and the drained hot pasta is added to the resulting sauce to ensure the ribbons are coated evenly.

3 tablespoons unsalted butter

½ cup (2½ oz/75 g) asparagus tips, cut on the diagonal

½ cup (2½ oz/75 g) small, tender green beans

½ cup (2½ oz/75 g) small shelled peas

½ cup (2½ oz/75 g) sliced yellow crookneck squash

¾ cup (6 fl oz/180 ml) heavy (double) cream

Salt and ground pepper

1 lb (500 g) dried fettuccine

Grated Parmesan cheese for garnish

In a large sauté pan over medium heat, melt the butter. Add the asparagus, green beans, peas, and squash and sauté, stirring, until tender-crisp, about 5 minutes.

Add the cream and season to taste with salt and pepper. Boil briskly, stirring, for 1–2 minutes to reduce slightly. Remove from the heat and cover to keep warm.

Meanwhile, bring a large pot three-fourths full of salted water to a boil. Add the pasta, stir well, and cook until al dente, 8–10 minutes.

Drain the pasta and return to the warm pot. Add the sauce and toss well. Divide among warmed plates and garnish with the cheese. Serve right away.

MAKES 4–6 SERVINGS

Dried versus fresh pasta

You can typically substitute dried pasta for fresh, and vice versa, in recipes that feature cream sauces. But it's a good idea to use less dried pasta than you would fresh, as it will increase in mass after it is rehydrated. For a recipe calling for 1 lb (500 g) fresh pasta, use ¾ lb (375 g) dried.

FETTUCCINE WITH SHRIMP AND SNOW PEAS

Substituting broccoli

Broccoli, with its assertive flavor and hearty texture, is a good substitute for the snow peas here. Use about ½ lb (250 g) broccoli florets, cook them for 3 minutes, then add the shrimp to the pan and proceed with the recipe.

For this bright and healthful sauce, shrimp and snow peas are combined in a lightly thickened mixture of clam and lemon juices. When shopping for shrimp, remember that the larger ones may look impressive, but the smaller ones generally taste better and cost less.

Bring a large pot three-fourths full of salted water to a boil.

Meanwhile, snap the stem end from each snow pea, pulling it down along the pea to remove any strings; set the snow peas aside. In a large bowl, toss the shrimp with the cornstarch and set aside.

Add the pasta to the boiling water, stir well, and cook until al dente, 8–10 minutes.

While the pasta is cooking, in a large nonstick frying pan over medium-high heat, warm the oil. When hot but not smoking, add the snow peas and the shrimp and stir and toss briskly until the peas are bright green and tender-crisp and the shrimp have started to turn pink, about 2 minutes. Transfer the shrimp and peas to a plate and set aside.

Return the pan to medium-high heat. Add the clam juice, lemon juice, and lemon zest and boil for about 1 minute. Return the shrimp and peas to the pan, add the parsley, and boil just until the liquid thickens slightly, about 1 minute. Season with salt and pepper.

Drain the pasta and return to the warm pot. Add the sauce to the pot and toss well. Divide among warmed plates and serve right away.

2 cups (8 oz/250 g) snow peas (mangetouts)

1 lb (500 g) shrimp (prawns), peeled and deveined (see page 202)

1 tablespoon cornstarch (cornflour)

1 lb (500 g) dried fettuccine

1 tablespoon olive oil

⅔ cup (5 fl oz/150 ml) bottled clam juice or chicken broth

¼ cup (2 fl oz/60 ml) fresh lemon juice

2 teaspoons finely grated lemon zest

½ cup (¾ oz/20 g) chopped fresh flat-leaf (Italian) parsley

Salt and ground pepper

MAKES 4 SERVINGS

FETTUCCINE WITH ARTICHOKES AND PROSCIUTTO

Substituting asparagus

If you don't like artichokes or don't have time to trim them, you can substitute pencil-thin asparagus in this recipe. Snap off the woody ends, then slice on the diagonal into 1-inch (2.5-cm) lengths.

Fettuccine and cream sauce are a match made in heaven. This sauce incorporates thinly sliced artichokes and minced prosciutto. If your market has tender baby artichokes for sale, use about sixteen of them and trim according to the method on page 332.

In a large sauté pan over medium heat, warm the oil. Add the onion and sauté until softened, about 5 minutes.

Meanwhile, drain the artichokes, cut each in half lengthwise, remove and discard the choke, then slice each one thinly lengthwise. Add the artichokes to the onion along with ½ cup (4 fl oz/125 ml) of the broth. Season with salt and pepper. Bring to a simmer over medium-high heat, cover, and adjust the heat to maintain a gentle simmer. Cook gently until the artichokes are tender, about 15 minutes. Uncover and add the remaining ½ cup broth and the cream. Return to a simmer and simmer, uncovered, until the mixture thickens slightly. Stir in the prosciutto and parsley. Taste and adjust the seasoning. Remove the pan from the heat.

2 tablespoons olive oil

½ yellow onion, chopped

Juice of 1 lemon

4 artichokes, trimmed (see page 332)

1 cup (8 fl oz/250 ml) chicken broth

Salt and ground pepper

1 cup (8 fl oz/250 ml) heavy (double) cream

2 oz (60 g) prosciutto, minced

2 tablespoons minced fresh flat-leaf (Italian) parsley

1 lb (500 g) fresh fettuccine

MAKES 4–6 SERVINGS

Bring a large pot three-fourths full of salted water to a boil. Meanwhile, reheat the sauce gently over low heat. Add the pasta to the boiling water, stir well, and boil until al dente, about 2 minutes. Drain the pasta, reserving about 1 cup (8 fl oz/250 ml) of the cooking water. Return the pasta to the warm pot. Add the sauce and toss well, adding the reserved water as needed to thin the sauce. Divide among warmed plates and serve right away.

TAGLIATELLE WITH SMOKED CHICKEN

The natural sweetness of the mixed vegetables in this colorful pasta dish contrasts nicely with the smokiness of the chicken and the tanginess of goat cheese. A generous amount of chopped basil sprinkled on at the end contributes a strong note of freshness.

¼ cup (2 fl oz/60 ml) extra-virgin olive oil

1 small red onion, halved and sliced

½ red bell pepper (capsicum), sliced

10 slender asparagus stalks, tough ends removed and cut on the diagonal into 2-inch (5-cm) lengths

1 *each* small zucchini (courgette) and yellow squash, julienned

½ cup (4 fl oz/125 ml) dry white wine

2 cloves garlic, minced

4 tablespoons (2 oz/60 g) unsalted butter

3 oz (90 g) fresh goat cheese, cut into pieces

1 lb (500 g) fresh tagliatelle, or ¾ lb (375 g) dried tagliatelle

3 plum (Roma) tomatoes, seeded and chopped

6 oz (185 g) boneless smoked chicken, cut into thin strips

Salt and ground pepper

½ cup (¾ oz/20 g) chopped fresh basil

MAKES 4–6 SERVINGS

In a large, nonstick frying pan over medium-high heat, warm the oil. Add the onion and bell pepper and sauté until just softened, 1–2 minutes. Stir in the asparagus, zucchini, and yellow squash and add ¼ cup (2 fl oz/60 ml) water. Cover the pan and cook, stirring occasionally, until all the vegetables are just tender and the water has almost evaporated, about 3 minutes. Remove from the heat.

Meanwhile, in a small saucepan over high heat, combine the wine and garlic. Bring to a boil, reduce the heat to medium, and boil gently, stirring occasionally, until the wine is reduced by one-third, about 3 minutes. Add the butter and goat cheese and stir to melt. Remove from the heat.

Bring a large pot three-fourths full of salted water to a boil. Add the pasta, stir well, and cook until al dente, about 2 minutes for fresh pasta or 8–10 minutes for dried. Drain and return to the warm pot. Just before the pasta is ready, add the tomatoes and chicken to the vegetables, then stir in the wine-garlic mixture. Season with salt and pepper and reheat to serving temperature.

Add the sauce to the pasta and toss well. Divide among warmed plates, garnish with the basil, and serve right away.

Smoked chicken

Fully cooked smoked chicken breast can be found in the deli or meat section of well-stocked grocery stores or at quality butcher shops. It keeps well, making it a great ingredient to keep on hand for quick dishes.

161

LINGUINE WITH FRESH CLAM SAUCE

Saucing dried pasta

Don't be tempted to use fresh pasta for this dish. The large amount of liquid in the sauce will make it soggy. Olive oil–based sauces and pestos also work well with dried pastas, because the sauces readily coat the pastas' lightly textured surface without being absorbed.

Parsley, garlic, and red pepper flakes give this clam sauce its fresh, lively character. Varieties of small clams appropriate for this recipe include littleneck, cherrystone, butter, and Manila. Accompany the pasta with thick slices of crusty bread for soaking up any extra sauce.

Discard any clams that do not close to the touch, then scrub the clams well. In a large pot, combine the wine and ½ cup (4 fl oz/125 ml) water. Bring to a simmer, add the clams, cover, and cook, shaking the pot once or twice, just until the clams open, about 3 minutes. Using a slotted spoon, transfer the clams to a bowl, discarding any that did not open. Line a fine-mesh sieve with a triple thickness of cheesecloth (muslin), and pour the cooking liquid through the sieve into a pitcher or bowl. Set the clams and strained liquid aside.

In a large sauté pan over medium heat, warm the oil. Add the onion and sauté until soft, about 10 minutes. Add the garlic, parsley, and red pepper flakes and sauté for 1 minute to release the fragrance of the garlic. Remove from the heat.

Bring a large pot three-fourths full of salted water to a boil. Add the pasta, stir well, and cook until al dente, 8–10 minutes. Just before the pasta is done, add the strained clam liquid to the sauté pan and reheat over medium heat. Season with salt. Reduce the heat to low, add the clams, and reheat gently.

Drain the pasta and return to the warm pot. Add the sauce and toss well. Divide among warmed plates and serve right away. Set out a large bowl for the discarded clam shells.

4 dozen small clams, about 2 lb (1 kg) (see note, above)

½ cup (4 fl oz/125 ml) dry white wine

¼ cup (2 fl oz/60 ml) olive oil

1 small yellow onion, minced

4 cloves garlic, minced

¼ cup (⅓ oz/10 g) minced fresh flat-leaf (Italian) parsley

¼ teaspoon red pepper flakes

1 lb (500 g) dried linguine

Salt

MAKES 4–6 SERVINGS

BUCATINI ALL'AMATRICIANA

Bucatini with anchovy sauce

In a large frying pan over medium heat, warm ¼ cup (2 fl oz/ 60 ml) olive oil. Stir in 4 cloves garlic, minced, and 2 tbsp chopped fresh flat-leaf (Italian) parsley and cook for 1 minute. Remove from the heat, add 8 anchovy fillets in olive oil, and mash with a wooden spoon. Season with salt and pepper and toss with the hot pasta.

This dish takes its name from Amatrice, a town in Abruzzo. The sauce traditionally calls for tomatoes, onion, and *guanciale* (cured pork cheek), but pancetta is a good substitute. It is typically tossed with bucatini, a thick spaghetti-like noodle with a hole through the middle.

In a large sauté pan over medium heat, warm the oil and pancetta, stirring occasionally, until the pancetta renders some of its fat, about 3 minutes. Add the onion and sauté until softened, about 8 minutes. Add the tomatoes and red pepper flakes and bring to a simmer. Adjust the heat to maintain a simmer and cook, uncovered, stirring occasionally, for 20 minutes, adding a little water if the sauce becomes too thick. Season with salt. Remove from the heat.

Bring a large pot three-fourths full of salted water to a boil. Add the pasta, stir well, and cook until al dente, 10–12 minutes. Meanwhile, reheat the sauce gently over low heat.

Drain the pasta and return to the warm pot. Add the sauce and half of the cheese and toss well. Divide the pasta among warmed individual plates, garnish with the remaining cheese, and serve right away.

2 tablespoons olive oil

⅓ lb (155 g) pancetta, diced

1 yellow onion, thinly sliced

2 cups (12 oz/375 g) peeled, seeded, and chopped plum (Roma) tomatoes

¼ teaspoon red pepper flakes

Salt

1 lb (500 g) dried bucatini or spaghetti

½ cup (2 oz/60 g) grated pecorino cheese

MAKES 4–6 SERVINGS

SPAGHETTI AND MEATBALLS

Fragrant oregano and fennel seeds make these meatballs particularly tasty. If pressed for time, substitute a large jar (26–28 fl oz/810–875 ml) of store-bought sauce for homemade. Coordinate the assembly of this dish so the meatballs and pasta are done at the same time.

FOR THE MEATBALLS

½ lb (250 g) ground (minced) veal

½ lb (250 g) ground (minced) pork

2 eggs, lightly beaten

½ small yellow onion, minced

½ cup (2 oz/60 g) fine dried bread crumbs

¼ cup (1 oz/30 g) grated Parmesan cheese

1 tablespoon minced fresh flat-leaf (Italian) parsley

2 teaspoons minced fresh oregano

½ teaspoon fennel seeds, lightly crushed in a mortar

Salt and ground pepper

FOR THE TOMATO SAUCE

¼ cup (2 fl oz/60 ml) olive oil

4 cloves garlic, minced

1 tablespoon minced fresh flat-leaf (Italian) parsley

Pinch of red pepper flakes, optional

1 can (28 oz/875 g) plum (Roma) tomatoes, finely chopped, with juice

Salt

1 lb (500 g) dried spaghetti

1 cup (4 oz/125 g) grated Parmesan cheese

MAKES 4–6 SERVINGS

To make the meatballs, in a large bowl, combine the ground meats, eggs, onion, bread crumbs, cheese, parsley, oregano, fennel seeds, 1½ teaspoons salt, and several grinds of pepper. Mix gently with your hands until blended. Shape the mixture into 24 meatballs, working gently and dipping your hands in cold water to prevent sticking. Put the meatballs in a single layer on a large plate and refrigerate.

To make the tomato sauce, in a large sauté pan over medium heat, warm the oil. Add the garlic, parsley, and red pepper flakes (if using) and sauté for 1 minute. Add the tomatoes and simmer, uncovered, until the flavors are blended, about 15 minutes. Pass the sauce through a food mill or purée in a food processor, then return to the pan. Season with salt. Bring to a simmer over medium heat.

Add the meatballs to the sauce, cover, and adjust the heat so the sauce simmers gently. Cook the meatballs, turning them once about halfway through cooking, until cooked through, about 15 minutes.

Meanwhile, bring a large pot three-fourths full of salted water to a boil. Add the pasta, stir well, and cook until al dente, 10–12 minutes. Drain and return to the warm pot. Add the meatballs and sauce and toss gently. Divide among warmed plates. Top each serving with a little of the cheese and serve right away. Pass the remaining cheese at the table.

Chicken meatballs

Combine 1 lb (500 g) ground (minced) chicken; ⅓ yellow onion, minced; 2 oz (60 g) prosciutto, minced; ¼ cup (1½ oz/45 g) toasted pine nuts; 1 clove garlic, minced; 2 tsp each chopped fresh oregano, basil, and rosemary; 1 egg; and ⅓ cup (1½ oz/ 45 g) fine dried bread crumbs. Mix gently until blended, form into balls, and proceed with the recipe.

163

SPAGHETTI ALLA CARBONARA

Egg safety

This recipe uses eggs that are not fully cooked. If you have health and safety concerns, you should avoid this dish and any recipe that uses partially cooked eggs (see page 37).

For this simple sauce, a favorite of Romans, the steaming hot pasta partially cooks the egg yolks. There are many theories as to its origin, but many say it was a popular dish of Italian charcoal makers *(carbonari),* which gave the popular dish its name.

In a large bowl, whisk together the eggs, cheese, parsley, ½ teaspoon salt, and 1 teaspoon pepper.

Bring a large pot three-fourths full of salted water to a boil. Add the pasta, stir well, and cook until al dente, 10–12 minutes.

Meanwhile, combine the oil, butter, pancetta, and garlic in a sauté pan over medium heat and cook, stirring occasionally, until the pancetta renders some of its fat, about 3 minutes; do not let it become crisp. Keep warm over low heat.

When the pasta is done, using tongs, transfer it to the bowl with the egg mixture. Toss immediately to coat with the egg. Add the contents of the sauté pan and continue tossing until the egg coats the pasta evenly in a creamy sauce. Add a little of the pasta cooking water if needed to thin the sauce. Divide among warmed plates and serve right away.

4 eggs

¾ cup (3 oz/90 g) grated Parmesan cheese

2 tablespoons minced fresh flat-leaf (Italian) parsley

Salt and coarsely cracked pepper

1 lb (500 g) dried spaghetti

1 tablespoon olive oil

1 tablespoon unsalted butter

¼ lb (125 g) pancetta, coarsely chopped

2 cloves garlic, minced

MAKES 4–6 SERVINGS

ANGEL HAIR WITH SPRING VEGETABLES

Blanching raw vegetables

Vegetables boiled momentarily retain their brilliant colors but become slightly softer to the tooth. Immediately immerse blanched vegetables in ice water to stop the cooking, then drain well.

The best seasonal vegetables—baby carrots, fava beans, sugar snap peas, and yellow pear tomatoes—star in this light and beautiful pasta dish, flavored with basil. Angel hair pasta, also known as capellini, is very thin and cooks quickly, so be careful not to overcook it.

Have ready a bowl of ice water. Bring a saucepan three-fourths full of water to a boil. Add the favas and boil for 2 minutes. Drain, transfer to the ice water to stop the cooking, then drain again. To peel each bean, pinch open the end opposite the end that connected the bean to the pod; the bean will slip easily from its skin. Set aside.

Refill the bowl with ice water. Refill the saucepan three-fourths full with lightly salted water and bring to a boil. Add the carrots, boil for 2 minutes, and remove with a slotted spoon. Immerse immediately in the ice water, then remove and set aside. Repeat to cook the asparagus, boiling for 1 minute, and the snap peas, boiling for 30 seconds.

In a sauté pan over medium heat, warm 3 tablespoons of the oil. Add the onion and sauté until golden brown, 5–7 minutes. Add the stock and bring to a boil. Boil until reduced by half, 10–15 minutes. Add the carrots, asparagus, snap peas, and favas. Heat until the vegetables are warmed through and just tender, 3–4 minutes. Season with salt and pepper.

2 lb (1 kg) fava (broad) beans, shelled

1 bunch baby carrots (about 6 oz/185 g), peeled and halved lengthwise

½ lb (250 g) asparagus, tough ends removed, cut into 2-inch (5-cm) lengths

½ lb (250 g) sugar snap peas, trimmed

6 tablespoons (3 fl oz/90 ml) olive oil

1 yellow onion, chopped

3 cups (24 fl oz/750 ml) Vegetable Stock (page 26)

Salt and ground pepper

1 lb (500 g) angel hair pasta

1 cup (6 oz/185 g) yellow pear tomatoes, halved lengthwise

½ cup (½ oz/15 g) fresh basil leaves, shredded

2 oz (60 g) Parmesan cheese, grated or shaved with a vegetable peeler

MAKES 4–6 SERVINGS

Meanwhile, bring a large pot three-fourths full of salted water to a boil. Add the pasta, stir well, and cook until al dente, 3–4 minutes. Drain and return to the warm pot. Toss with the remaining 3 tablespoons oil. Keep warm.

When the vegetable mixture is ready, add it to the pasta and toss to combine. Divide among warmed plates. Scatter the tomatoes and basil on top, sprinkle with the cheese, and serve right away.

RIGATONI WITH TOMATOES AND EGGPLANT

A light and chunky tomato sauce and cubes of sautéed eggplant are a perfect match for rigatoni. Chopped herbs add color and flavor, while ricotta salata brings richness and contrast. Serve this dish as a main course with a robust Chianti or Sangiovese.

1 eggplant (aubergine), about 1 lb (500 g), peeled and cut into 1-inch (2.5-cm) pieces

Salt and ground pepper

6 tablespoons (3 fl oz/ 90 ml) extra-virgin olive oil, or as needed

6–8 green (spring) onions, including tender green tops, chopped

1½ tablespoons finely minced garlic

½–1 teaspoon red pepper flakes

½ cup (4 fl oz/125 ml) dry white wine

1½ cups (9 oz/280 g) peeled, seeded, and chopped plum (Roma) tomatoes (fresh or canned)

3 tablespoons chopped fresh mint, basil, marjoram, or flat-leaf (Italian) parsley

1 lb (500 g) rigatoni or penne

½ cup (2 oz/60 g) crumbled ricotta salata cheese

MAKES 4–6 SERVINGS

Place the eggplant pieces in a colander and sprinkle lightly but evenly with salt. Let stand for 30 minutes. Rinse and pat dry with paper towels. Set aside.

In a large sauté pan over medium heat, warm 2 tablespoons of the oil. Add the green onions and sauté until softened, about 3 minutes. Add the garlic and red pepper flakes and sauté for 1 minute. Add the wine and cook until almost evaporated, about 3 minutes. Add the tomatoes and simmer, crushing with a wooden spoon, until the sauce thickens slightly, about 5 minutes. Season with salt and pepper. Stir in 2 tablespoons of the mint and keep warm.

Bring a large pot three-fourths full of salted water to a boil. Add the pasta, stir well, and cook until al dente, 10–12 minutes.

Meanwhile, in another sauté pan over high heat, warm the remaining 4 tablespoons (2 fl oz/60 ml) olive oil. Add the eggplant pieces and sauté until golden, about 8 minutes, adding more oil as needed to prevent scorching. Add the eggplant to the tomato sauce and simmer for a few minutes to heat the eggplant through.

Drain the pasta and return to the warm pot. Add the sauce and toss well. Divide among warmed plates, sprinkle with the cheese and the remaining mint, and serve right away.

Ricotta salata

In its most familiar guise, ricotta is a snow white, soft fresh cheese. To make ricotta salata, the fresh cheese is salted, pressed, and aged to produce a crumbly texture and a pleasantly salty flavor, similar to feta, which can be substituted.

165

PENNE WITH WHITE BEANS AND ARUGULA

Choosing dried pasta

Not all dried pastas are created equal. For the best texture, look for pastas that are made from 100 percent durum wheat (or semolina). Often this means choosing varieties imported from Italy, where manufacturers use time-honored traditions to create their products.

Prepare this surprisingly hearty vegetarian pasta dish for a quick and satisfying lunch or casual supper. If you like, chop ½ lb (250 g) smoked chicken or cooked sausage, add it to the pan with the pasta, and cook just until warmed through.

Bring a large pot three-fourths full of salted water to a boil over high heat. Add the penne, stir well, and cook until al dente, 10–12 minutes.

Meanwhile, in a large nonstick frying pan over medium heat, warm the oil. Add the onion and red pepper flakes and sauté until the onion is tender, about 5 minutes. Add the garlic and the beans with their liquid and cook, stirring constantly, until the beans are heated through, about 2 minutes. Add the arugula and continue to cook, stirring, until wilted and heated through, about 1 minute.

Drain the pasta and return it to the warm pot. Add the bean-arugula mixture to the pot and toss well. Sprinkle with the cheese and season with salt and pepper. Divide among warmed plates and serve right away.

¾ lb (375 g) dried penne or farfalle

1 tablespoon olive oil

½ red onion, chopped

½ teaspoon red pepper flakes

3 large cloves garlic, chopped

1 can (15 oz/470 g) cannellini beans, undrained

2 oz (60 g) arugula (rocket) leaves, torn

5 tablespoons (1½ oz/45 g) grated pecorino cheese

Salt and ground pepper

MAKES 4–6 SERVINGS

PENNE WITH ASPARAGUS AND ANCHOVIES

Penne with prosciutto

For a different salty pairing here, use prosciutto instead of anchovies. Mince about 2 oz (60 g) prosciutto and warm it in the olive oil in place of the anchovies.

Each spring, Italians anxiously await the appearance of the first asparagus in the markets and on the hillsides where the plants grow wild. This easy pasta dish plays the distinctive taste of asparagus against the sharp, briny flavor of anchovies.

Bring a large pot three-fourths full of salted water to a boil.

Meanwhile, break off the tough end of each asparagus spear by bending it gently until it snaps. Cut the tender tops on the diagonal into 1-inch (2.5-cm) pieces.

Add the pasta to the boiling water and cook until almost al dente, 8–10 minutes. About 3 minutes before the pasta is ready, add the asparagus to the boiling water.

In a large frying pan, warm the oil over low heat. Add the anchovies and, with the back of a wooden spoon, mash them into the oil for about 1 minute. Drain the penne and asparagus and transfer to the frying pan with the anchovies. Finish cooking over medium heat, stirring often, for about 2 minutes. Season with salt and pepper.

Divide among warmed plates and serve right away.

3 lb (1.5 kg) asparagus

1 lb (500 g) dried penne

6 tablespoons (3 fl oz/ 90 ml) extra-virgin olive oil

6 anchovy fillets in oil

Salt and ground pepper

MAKES 4–6 SERVINGS

FARFALLE WITH PEAS AND PROSCIUTTO

Made with dried bow-tie pasta and frozen peas, this light dish is simple enough for a weeknight supper but also special enough to serve to guests. If you prefer a sharper flavor, substitute pecorino cheese for the Parmesan.

2 tablespoons olive oil

1 large yellow onion, halved and thinly sliced

1 package (10 oz/315 g) frozen petite peas

Salt and ground pepper

1 lb (500 g) dried farfalle

2 oz (60 g) prosciutto, minced

2 tablespoons minced fresh flat-leaf (Italian) parsley

2 tablespoons unsalted butter

¾ cup (3 oz/90 g) grated Parmesan cheese

MAKES 4–6 SERVINGS

In a large sauté pan over medium heat, warm the oil. Add the onion and sauté until soft and beginning to caramelize, about 15 minutes. Add the peas and ½ cup (4 fl oz/125 ml) water, and season with salt and pepper. Bring to a simmer and cook, uncovered, stirring often, until the peas have thawed, 3–5 minutes. Remove from the heat.

Meanwhile, bring a large pot three-fourths full of salted water to a boil. Add the pasta, stir well, and cook until al dente, 10–12 minutes.

If the pea mixture has cooled, reheat gently over low heat. Stir in the prosciutto and parsley.

Drain the pasta and return to the warm pot. Add the butter and toss until it melts. Add the pea mixture and toss again. Divide among warmed plates, sprinkle with the cheese, and serve right away.

Market-day pasta

In the spring and early summer, when fresh peas are available in your local farmers' market, you can substitute 2 cups (10 oz/315 g) small shelled fresh peas for the frozen peas here. Add them to the onion with the water as directed, cover, and simmer until done, about 5 minutes.

167

CAVATAPPI WITH SAUSAGE AND TOMATO

The wide grooves of corkscrew-shaped cavatappi trap the bits of sausage in this creamy sauce; fusilli will work equally well. If you can't find sausage flavored with fennel, add ½ teaspoon lightly crushed fennel seeds when you add the sausage to the pan.

1 tablespoon olive oil

¾ lb (375 g) hot Italian sausages with fennel seeds, casings removed

1 lb (500 g) plum (Roma) tomatoes, peeled, seeded, and chopped

2 tablespoons minced fresh flat-leaf (Italian) parsley

½ cup (4 fl oz/125 ml) heavy (double) cream

Salt and ground pepper

1 lb (500 g) dried cavatappi or fusilli

1 cup (4 oz/125 g) grated Parmesan cheese

MAKES 4–6 SERVINGS

In a large sauté pan over medium-low heat, warm the oil. Add the sausages and cook slowly, breaking them up with a wooden spatula or fork, until they lose their raw color, about 5 minutes; do not allow to brown.

Stir the tomatoes and parsley into the sausage. Raise the heat to medium and cook, uncovered, until the tomatoes have softened, 5–10 minutes. Stir in the cream and simmer briefly until the cream thickens slightly, about 3 minutes. Season with salt and pepper, then remove from the heat.

Meanwhile, bring a large pot three-fourths full of salted water to a boil. Add the pasta, stir well, and cook until al dente, 10–12 minutes.

Drain the pasta and return to the warm pot. Add the sauce and toss well. Divide among warmed plates and serve right away. Pass the cheese at the table.

Flat-leaf parsley

Long relegated to garnish status, parsley is an underused seasoning. It adds vibrant color and bright flavor to almost any savory dish, lending a fresh counterpoint to flavors that might otherwise taste muddled. Flat-leaf (Italian) parsley offers a more complex, faintly peppery flavor to recipes than its curly-leaf cousin.

GEMELLI WITH FOUR CHEESES

Twin twists

Gemelli ("twins" in Italian) look like two intertwined strands of pasta. Like other short dried pastas, they are delicious paired with tomato sauces, chunky vegetable sauces, or cream-based sauces, as shown here. Choose fusilli, macaroni, or penne if gemelli are unavailable.

Parmesan is an essential ingredient for this irresistibly rich pasta dish, but there are many substitutions for the other three cheeses. Try Camembert or Brie for the Fontina; Roquefort or Stilton for the Gorgonzola; and mozzarella for the Gruyère.

Bring a large pot three-fourths full of salted water to a boil.

Meanwhile, in a saucepan over low heat, combine the Fontina, Gorgonzola, and Gruyère cheeses, and the cream. Cook gently, stirring often, until the cheeses have almost completely melted, about 5 minutes. Keep warm.

Meanwhile, add the pasta to the boiling water and cook until al dente, 10–12 minutes.

Drain the pasta and return to the warm pot. Add the sauce, season with salt and pepper, and toss well. Divide among warmed plates, sprinkle the Parmesan cheese over the top, and serve right away.

2 oz (60 g) Fontina cheese, cut into julienne

2 oz (60 g) Gorgonzola cheese, crumbled

2 oz (60 g) Gruyère cheese, cut into julienne

½ cup (4 fl oz/120 ml) heavy (double) cream

1¼ lb (625 g) dried gemelli

Salt and ground pepper

½ cup (2 oz/60 g) grated Parmesan cheese

MAKES 6 SERVINGS

ORECCHIETTE WITH BROCCOLI RABE

Adding sausage

For a heartier version of this dish, add ½ lb (250 g) sweet Italian sausages. Remove the sausages from their casings and brown them, breaking them up into bits. Add the browned sausage with the broccoli rabe to the pan holding the garlic.

This dish is enjoyed throughout Puglia, the "heel" of Italy's boot, where it is drizzled with the region's superb olive oil. Broccoli rabe resembles broccoli but has thinner stems, smaller florets, more leaves, and a sharper flavor. You can substitute kale or collard or mustard greens.

In a large sauté pan over medium heat, warm the oil. Add the garlic and red pepper flakes and sauté until the garlic colors lightly, 1–2 minutes. Set aside.

Have ready a bowl of ice water. Bring a large pot three-fourths full of salted water to a boil. Add the broccoli rabe and cook until just tender, 2–4 minutes. Using tongs, transfer it to the ice water to stop the cooking. Leave the pot of water boiling. Drain the broccoli rabe well and squeeze gently to remove any excess moisture. Cut into 2-inch (5-cm) lengths.

Add the pasta to the boiling water, stir well, and cook until al dente, 10–12 minutes. Meanwhile, add the broccoli rabe to the pan holding the garlic. Return to medium heat, season generously with salt, and cook, stirring occasionally, until the broccoli is hot throughout, 3–5 minutes.

Drain the pasta and return to the warm pot. Add the sauce and toss well. Divide among warmed plates and serve right away. Pass the cheese at the table.

⅓ cup (3 fl oz/80 ml) extra-virgin olive oil

8 cloves garlic, thinly sliced

¼ teaspoon red pepper flakes

1½ lb (750 g) broccoli rabe, stems thicker than a pencil removed (about 2 lb/1 kg before trimming)

1 lb (500 g) dried orecchiette

Salt

1 cup (4 oz/125 g) grated pecorino cheese

MAKES 4–6 SERVINGS

POTATO GNOCCHI

Made from a mixture of flour, egg, and potato, and cut into small pillow-shaped pieces, gnocchi are light and delicate. Don't try to make them with boiling potatoes: they will not have the proper starch and moisture content and thus will lack the correct texture.

5 russet potatoes, about 2½ lb (1.25 kg) total weight

2 eggs

Salt and ground pepper

About 2 cups (10 oz/315 g) unbleached all-purpose (plain) flour

½ cup (4 oz/125 g) unsalted butter

½ cup (2 oz/60 g) grated Parmesan cheese

MAKES 6–8 SERVINGS

Preheat the oven to 350°F (180°C). Using a fork, pierce each potato once or twice about ¼ inch (6 mm) deep. Then, place the potatoes directly on the oven rack and bake until very tender when pierced with a knife, about 1½ hours. Remove from the oven and set aside to cool.

When the potatoes are just cool enough to handle, cut in half lengthwise and scoop out the flesh. Force the flesh through a ricer or food mill onto a large, rimmed baking sheet. Spread into an even layer and let cool completely.

In a small bowl, lightly beat the eggs with 1 teaspoon salt. When the potatoes are cool, drizzle evenly with the egg, then sprinkle evenly with 1 cup (5 oz/155 g) of the flour. Use a bench scraper to gently lift and fold the mixture until a coarse, raggedy dough forms.

Sprinkle ¼ cup (1½ oz/45 g) of the remaining flour on a work surface. Spread the potato mixture on the floured surface and sprinkle with another ¼ cup flour. Using the bench scraper and then your hands, lift and fold the mixture, lightly pressing it as you work, until the flour is incorporated into the potato mixture. Work in only as much of the remaining flour as needed for a smooth dough. Form the dough into a ball, dust it with flour, and cover with a bowl.

Dust 2 large rimmed baking sheets with flour. Scrape the work surface clean, then dust it with flour. Cut the dough into 8 equal portions; place all but one back under the bowl.

On the floured work surface, shape the dough into a cylinder then, with flattened hands, roll it back and forth, gradually shifting your hands to the ends, to form a log about ½ inch (12 mm) in diameter.

Cut the log into ¾-inch (2-cm) pieces. Place in a single layer, not touching, on the prepared baking sheets. Repeat with the remaining dough portions. Cover the gnocchi with aluminum foil and refrigerate for at least 1 hour or up to overnight.

Bring a large pot three-fourths full of salted water to a boil. Have ready a colander set over a bowl. Add half the gnocchi to the water and stir to prevent sticking. Cook until they rise to the surface and are cooked through, about 3 minutes. Using the slotted spoon, transfer to the colander to drain, then cook and drain the remaining gnocchi.

Transfer the cooked gnocchi to a shallow serving bowl, toss well with the butter, sprinkle with the cheese, and season with pepper. Serve right away.

Saucing gnocchi

Gnocchi are as versatile as any pasta, pairing well with a variety of sauces. For example, substitute them for the pasta in Bucatini all'Amatriciana (page 162). Or, toss them with just enough Pesto (page 387) to coat lightly.

Gnocchi gratin

Prepare a batch of White Sauce (page 382) and grate ¼ lb (125 g) Parmesan. Place half the cooked gnocchi in a buttered baking dish, top with half of the sauce and half of the cheese, then repeat. Cut 1 tbsp unsalted butter into bits and dot the top. Sprinkle the top with 1 tbsp fine dried bread crumbs. Bake at 400°F (200°C) until bubbling and browned, about 30 minutes.

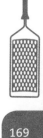

PAD THAI

Rice noodles

Rice vermicelli, so named because they resemble the Italian-style "little worm" pasta with the same name, are brittle, creamy white noodles made from rice flour and water. Also called rice sticks, they are popular ingredients in Southeast Asian cuisine.

This classic Thai dish features shrimp, bean sprouts, green onion, and peanuts tossed with well-seasoned noodles. It is typically made with a narrow, dried flat noodle, but any dried rice noodle will do. Here, the more readily available rice vermicelli is used.

Place the noodles in a bowl with hot water to cover. Let stand for 15 minutes. Drain and spread on a baking sheet to dry.

Meanwhile, in a wok or large frying pan over high heat, warm 1 tablespoon of the oil, swirling to coat the bottom and sides. When very hot but not quite smoking, add the shrimp. Stir and toss until pink and firm, about 1 minute. Add the garlic and stir and toss until fragrant, about 30 seconds longer. Transfer to a bowl and set aside.

Add another 1 tablespoon oil to the pan over medium-high heat, again swirling to coat. When hot, add the eggs and stir until soft curds form, about 1 minute. Add to the shrimp.

Add the remaining 2 tablespoons oil to the pan, again swirling to coat. Add the noodles, distributing them evenly in the pan so they cook evenly. Cook for 2–3 minutes. Using a spatula, flip them, and again spread evenly. Cook, stirring occasionally, until just tender, 2–3 minutes longer.

Push the noodles to the side of the pan and add the sugar and fish sauce to the pan. When the sugar dissolves, using tongs or 2 large forks, toss the noodles with the sauce. Add half each of the bean sprouts and peanuts and all the reserved shrimp and eggs; stir and toss. Turn out onto a warmed platter. Garnish with the remaining bean sprouts and peanuts and with the pepper flakes, green onion, and lime slices. Serve right away.

6 oz (185 g) dried rice vermicelli

4 tablespoons (2 fl oz/60 ml) peanut or corn oil

⅓ lb (155 g) shrimp (prawns), peeled and deveined (see page 202), then cut into 1-inch (2.5-cm) pieces

3 cloves garlic, coarsely chopped

2 eggs, lightly beaten

1 tablespoon sugar

2 tablespoons fish sauce

1 cup (2 oz/60 g) bean sprouts

2 tablespoons coarsely chopped roasted peanuts

½ teaspoon red pepper flakes, or to taste

1 green (spring) onion, including tender green tops, coarsely chopped

2 limes, thinly sliced

MAKES 4 SERVINGS

VIETNAMESE GRILLED CHICKEN WITH RICE NOODLES

About galangal

Resembling its relative fresh ginger, galangal has pink shoots, cream-colored fibrous flesh, and pale yellow skin with thin, dark stripes. It is used throughout Southeast Asia to lend a hot, peppery flavor to dishes. Look for it in Asian markets, or substitute ginger, black pepper, and a bay leaf to mimic the flavor.

Here, dried, thin rice noodles serve as a neutral base for chicken that has been marinated in a richly seasoned coconut milk mixture and then grilled. The fish sauce–based dipping sauce, a classic of Vietnamese cuisine, brightens the flavors of the dish.

Place the chicken pieces in a large, shallow bowl. In a mortar, combine the garlic, shallots, cilantro stems, galangal, 1 teaspoon salt, and ¼ teaspoon pepper and grind with a pestle to form a paste, adding 1 tablespoon water if needed to ease grinding. Transfer the paste to a bowl and stir in the coconut milk, fish sauce, rice wine, soy sauce, and oil. Pour the marinade over the chicken pieces, turning to coat evenly. Cover and refrigerate for at least 2 hours or up to overnight.

Prepare a charcoal or gas grill for indirect-heat cooking over medium-high heat (see page 18).

1 chicken, about 3½ lb (1.75 kg), quartered

4 cloves garlic, chopped

2 shallots, chopped

1 tablespoon chopped fresh cilantro (fresh coriander) stems

1 tablespoon peeled and minced fresh galangal (see note, left)

Salt and ground pepper

⅓ cup (3 fl oz/80 ml) coconut milk

2 tablespoons fish sauce

2 tablespoons Chinese rice wine

1 tablespoon *each* dark soy sauce and peanut oil

½ lb (250 g) dried rice vermicelli

Nuoc Cham (page 390)

1 fresh red chile, seeded and thinly sliced

¼ cup (1 oz/30 g) very finely julienned carrots

4 or 5 fresh cilantro (fresh coriander) sprigs

MAKES 6–8 SERVINGS

Remove the chicken from the marinade, discarding the marinade, and place on the grill rack directly over the fire. Grill, turning until browned on both sides, 5–7 minutes total. Using tongs, move the chicken away from the direct heat. Cover and continue to cook, turning once, until an instant-read thermometer inserted into the thickest part of the thigh away from the bone registers 175°F (80°C) on an instant-read thermometer, 15–20 minutes. While the chicken is cooking, soak the rice vermicelli in hot water to cover.

Just before the chicken is ready, bring a saucepan three-fourths full of water to a boil. Drain the rice vermicelli, add to the boiling water, and cook until just tender, about 1 minute. Drain, place in a bowl, and toss with ¼ cup (2 fl oz/60 ml) of the Nuoc Cham.

Spread the noodles on a warmed platter and arrange the chicken pieces on top. Garnish with the chile, carrots, and cilantro sprigs. Serve right away with the remaining Nuoc Cham for dipping.

Using cilantro stems

Cilantro, a leafy, bright green herb also known as fresh coriander or Chinese parsley, is found in kitchens all over Asia with the exception of Japan. The leaves and seeds are both widely used. In some regions and recipes, so are the stems, which can be ground with shallots and seasonings to form a flavorful paste.

SPICY PEANUT NOODLES WITH PORK

This version of a typical Chinese dish features egg noodles, ground pork, and a balanced blend of sweet hoisin sauce, smooth peanut butter, salty soy sauce, and fiery chile. Minced green onions add a welcome color contrast. You can also serve the noodles as a first course for six.

1 cup (8 fl oz/250 ml) chicken broth

¼ cup (2 fl oz/60 ml) hoisin sauce

2 tablespoons soy sauce

1 tablespoon peanut oil

¾ lb (375 g) ground (minced) pork

Pinch of red pepper flakes

1 cup (3 oz/90 g) minced green (spring) onions, including tender green tops

1 tablespoon minced garlic

1 tablespoon grated fresh ginger

2 tablespoons creamy peanut butter

1 lb (500 g) thin fresh Chinese egg noodles

1 teaspoon hot chile oil

MAKES 4 SERVINGS

In a small bowl, stir together the broth, hoisin sauce, and soy sauce; set aside. Place a frying pan over medium heat and add the peanut oil. When it shimmers, add the ground pork and red pepper flakes and cook, stirring frequently, until the meat is crumbly and the color changes from pink to gray, about 10 minutes. Add ½ cup (1½ oz/45 g) of the green onions, the garlic, and ginger and mix well. Add the broth mixture and peanut butter and stir to combine. Cook until the peanut butter is melted and the sauce is slightly thickened, about 5 minutes. Remove from the heat. Taste and adjust the seasoning with more hoisin, soy, red pepper flakes, or ginger as needed to create a flavorful sauce.

Bring a large pot three-fourths full of water to a boil. Add the noodles, stir gently, and cook until tender but still slightly chewy, 2–3 minutes. Meanwhile, reheat the sauce over medium-low heat.

Drain the noodles and add to the pan with the sauce; toss to combine. Add the remaining ½ cup green onions and the chile oil and toss to distribute evenly.

Divide the noodle mixture evenly among warmed individual plates and serve right away.

Fresh Chinese egg noodles

Varying from fine to thick, these pale yellow noodles are made from a dough of wheat flour, water, and eggs. For this recipe, choose noodles that are about ⅛ inch (3 mm) thick. Dried Chinese egg noodles will also work here.

EASY MUSHROOM RAVIOLI IN BROTH

Serving filled pastas

You can pair filled pastas with any sauce that enhances the flavors of the filling, then sprinkle with your choice of cheese. Or, boil and serve them in your favorite broth, either plain or sprinkled with herbs before serving. Use the same herbs you used in the filling.

Filled with a mixture of mushrooms and goat cheese, these ravioli are served in a flavorful broth along with asparagus tips and chives. Here, gyoza wrappers, fresh dough rounds used for making Asian dumplings, take the place of Italian pasta, speeding the assembly of the dish.

In a nonstick frying pan over medium heat, warm the oil. Add the shallots to the pan and sauté until softened, about 3 minutes. Add the shiitakes and sauté for about 2 minutes. Stir in the oyster mushrooms and thyme and season with salt and pepper. Sauté until the mushrooms are golden, about 3 minutes longer. Transfer to a bowl and stir in the cheese and 2 tablespoons of the chives. Let cool.

Spread out the gyoza wrappers on a work surface, and divide the mushroom mixture evenly among them, positioning a mound in the center of each wrapper. Moisten the edges of each wrapper with water and fold in half. Pinch the edges together firmly to seal.

In a large, shallow saucepan, bring the stock to a simmer over medium heat. Add half of the ravioli and asparagus to the stock and cook, uncovered, turning the ravioli once, until they are just tender, about 1½ minutes. Using a slotted spoon, divide the ravioli and asparagus among warmed soup bowls. Repeat with the remaining ravioli and asparagus.

Ladle the stock over the ravioli, garnish with the remaining chives, and serve right away.

1 tablespoon olive oil

¼ cup (1 oz/30 g) chopped shallots

¼ lb (125 g) fresh shiitake mushrooms, stems discarded, and chopped

¼ lb (125 g) fresh oyster mushrooms, chopped

¾ teaspoon dried thyme

Salt and ground pepper

3 tablespoons basil-flavored fresh goat cheese

4 tablespoons (⅓ oz/10 g) snipped fresh chives

16 gyoza wrappers

4 cups (32 fl oz/1 l) Vegetable Stock (page 26)

16 asparagus tips

MAKES 2–4 SERVINGS

CHICKEN RAVIOLI WITH PARMESAN

Changing shapes

There are no strict rules about what fillings can be folded into which shapes. Form squares, as in the chicken ravioli (right), or tortellini (opposite). Or, use a 2-inch (5-cm) round cookie cutter to cut out fresh pasta. Place 1 tsp filling in the center and top with another round. Or use ½ tsp filling and fold the round in half to form a half-moon.

These traditional square ravioli contain a mild mixture of chicken, carrot, and onion, flavored with Marsala and bound together with egg and Parmesan. They are lightly dressed with olive oil and chopped herbs, but you could also toss them with your favorite tomato or cream sauce.

In a frying pan, melt 2 tablespoons of the butter over low heat. Add the celery, carrot, and onion and sauté, stirring often, until the onion is translucent, about 3 minutes. Add the chicken, raise the heat to medium-low, and sauté, stirring often, until the chicken is golden, about 10 minutes. Add the Marsala, return the heat to low, cover the pan, and cook until the liquid is absorbed, about 5 minutes.

Remove the pan from the heat, turn out the contents onto a cutting board, let cool slightly, and chop very finely. Transfer to a bowl and add the egg yolks and half of the cheese. Mix thoroughly and season with salt and pepper. Set aside.

Roll out the pasta dough into a very thin sheet as directed on page 154. Cut into strips 2½ inches (6 cm) wide and 12 inches (30 cm) long. On half of the strips, place small mounds of the filling at 2½-inch (6-cm) intervals. With cold water, moisten

8 tablespoons (4 oz/125 g) unsalted butter

1 celery stalk, finely chopped

1 carrot, peeled and finely chopped

1 small yellow onion, finely chopped

10 oz (315 g) skinless, boneless chicken breast, cut into 1-inch (2.5-cm) pieces

¼ cup (2 fl oz/60 ml) dry Marsala wine

2 egg yolks

¾ cup (3 oz/90 g) grated Parmesan cheese

Salt and ground pepper

¾ lb (375 g) Fresh Egg Pasta dough (page 158)

MAKES 6 SERVINGS

the edges of the strips and in between the mounds. Cover the filled strips with the remaining strips, pressing all around each filling mound to seal. Using a pastry wheel with a fluted edge, cut the strips into squares. Set the squares aside on a lightly floured work surface.

Bring a large pot three-fourths full of salted water to a boil. In a small saucepan, melt the remaining 6 tablespoons (3 oz/90 g) butter over low heat. Keep warm.

Add the ravioli to the boiling water and cook at a gentle boil until they rise to the surface, about 2 minutes. Drain well, return the ravioli to the pan, drizzle with the melted butter, and toss gently. Divide among warmed plates, sprinkle with the remaining cheese, and serve hot.

Crimped edges

To create an old-fashioned crimped edge, use a knife to cut the ravioli instead of a pastry wheel, then press around the edges with the tines of a fork to crimp and seal.

TORTELLINI STUFFED WITH POTATO AND HERBS

Folded into triangles and then shaped into rings, tortellini are more fancifully shaped than ravioli, but they are still simple to make. These have a filling of potato and ricotta mixed with rosemary, oregano, and marjoram. Tortelloni are the same shape as tortellini, just larger.

8 tablespoons (4 fl oz/125 ml) extra-virgin olive oil

1 small yellow onion, finely chopped

3 russet or Yukon gold potatoes, peeled and cut crosswise into slices 1 inch (2.5 cm) thick

1 tablespoon chopped fresh rosemary

1 tablespoon chopped fresh oregano

1 tablespoon chopped fresh marjoram

¾ cup (6 oz/180 g) ricotta cheese

2 egg yolks

Salt and ground pepper

¾ lb (375 g) Fresh Egg Pasta dough (page 158)

2 tablespoons chopped fresh flat-leaf (Italian) parsley

MAKES 6 SERVINGS

In a large frying pan over low heat, warm 2 tablespoons of the oil. Add the onion and sauté until translucent, about 3 minutes. Add the potatoes, raise the heat to medium, and sauté, stirring often, until the potatoes are tender, about 15 minutes. Add the rosemary, oregano, and marjoram and stir for 1 minute. Remove from the heat and let cool.

In a large bowl, combine the cheese and the potato mixture, mashing with a fork to blend. Add the egg yolks and season with salt and pepper. Stir until smooth, then set aside.

Roll out the pasta dough into a very thin sheet as directed on page 154. Cut into 2-inch (5-cm) squares. Place about ½ teaspoon of the filling in the center of each square. (For tortelloni, cut larger squares and use a little more filling.) Lightly brush dough around the filling with water. Fold one corner of the dough over the filling to form a triangle, pressing to eliminate any air and to seal. Bring the 2 opposite points of the triangle together and pinch to seal. Curl the remaining point backward slightly.

Bring a large pot three-fourths full of salted water to a boil. Add the tortellini and cook at a gentle boil until they rise to the surface, about 2 minutes. Drain in a colander and arrange on a warmed platter.

Sprinkle with the parsley and the remaining 6 tablespoons (3 fl oz/90 ml) oil. Serve right away.

Keeping it sealed

Form filled pastas as soon as possible after rolling out the dough. If the fresh pasta dough dries out, it will be more difficult to seal. To ensure that the shapes stay sealed when you cook them, boil them gently.

Tortellini soup

Whisk together 3 eggs with ½ cup (2 oz/60 g) grated Parmesan. Slowly whisk the mixture into 8 cups (2 l) simmering Chicken Stock (page 23). Add 60 cooked tortellini and sprinkle with chopped fresh parsley. Makes 4 servings.

173

SPINACH LASAGNE WITH MEAT SAUCE

This elegant lasagne features a dozen layers of delicate spinach noodles, rich meat sauce, and creamy béchamel. It can also be made with Fresh Egg Pasta (page 158). Serve it with a dry red wine and a good loaf of crusty bread.

To make a béchamel sauce, in a saucepan over medium heat, melt the butter. Add the flour and whisk to blend. Cook, whisking constantly, for 1 minute. Gradually whisk in the milk and bring to a simmer, while whisking constantly. Add the thyme and bay leaf, and season with nutmeg, salt, and pepper. Reduce the heat to low and cook gently, whisking often, until the sauce thickly coats the back of a wooden spoon, about 30 minutes. Press the béchamel through a coarse-mesh sieve into a bowl; let cool.

Preheat the oven to 400°F (200°C). Roll out the pasta dough into thin sheets as directed on page 154. Fill a large bowl three-fourths full of ice water and add the oil. Bring a large pot three-fourths full of salted water to a boil. Cook the pasta sheets, two at a time, for 10 seconds only. Transfer to the ice water, then lay flat on a lint-free kitchen towel and pat dry.

Pour a thin layer of the béchamel into a 9-by-13-inch (23-by-33-cm) baking dish. Top with a layer of the pasta, cutting the pasta sheets as needed to fit. Spread 3 tablespoons béchamel thinly and evenly over the pasta, then spread about ⅓ cup (3 fl oz/80 ml) of the Bolognese sauce over the béchamel. Sprinkle with 1 tablespoon of the cheese. Repeat the layers of pasta, béchamel, Bolognese sauce, and cheese until you have used up all of the sauces, reserving ⅓ cup (3 fl oz/80 ml) of the béchamel for the top of the casserole. You should have enough to make 9–12 layers of pasta and sauce. Finish with a layer of pasta topped with the reserved béchamel and about 2 tablespoons cheese.

Bake, uncovered, until bubbling, 25–30 minutes. If desired, place under a preheated broiler (grill) briefly (make sure your baking dish is flameproof) to brown the surface. Let cool for 15 minutes, then cut into squares to serve.

Make ahead tips

Lasagne can be assembled and then covered tightly and refrigerated for up to 24 hours before baking. It also freezes well after it is baked. When baking refrigerated lasagne or reheating frozen lasagne, you'll need to cook it longer to heat it through. Once it has been in the oven for an hour, check it every 15 minutes.

Eggplant lasagne

Combine the spinach pasta with layers of eggplant (sliced, oiled, and baked at 400°F/200°C until golden), Marinara Sauce (page 379), 2 cups (1 lb/500 g) ricotta cheese, 2½ cups (10 oz/ 315 g) crumbled fresh goat cheese, and 1 cup (4 oz/125 g) grated Parmesan cheese. Bake at 375°F/190°C for 45–55 minutes.

4 tablespoons (2 oz/60 g) unsalted butter

¼ cup (1½ oz/45 g) all-purpose (plain) flour

3 cups (24 fl oz/750 ml) milk

4 fresh thyme sprigs

1 bay leaf

Freshly grated nutmeg

Salt and ground pepper

Fresh Spinach Pasta (page 158)

1 tablespoon olive oil

Bolognese Sauce (page 380), or 3 cups (24 fl oz/750 ml) purchased meat sauce

1 cup (4 oz/125 g) grated Parmesan cheese

MAKES 6–8 SERVINGS

CHICKEN LASAGNE WITH THREE CHEESES

This simple chicken lasagne has a bit of a kick, thanks to the cayenne pepper in the tomato sauce. Substitute fresh pasta for the dried, if you prefer. You can also substitute ground (minced) beef or pork for the chicken. Or, you can skip the meat for a vegetarian version.

½ lb (250 g) dried
lasagne noodles

2 tablespoons olive oil

1 lb (500 g) ground
(minced) chicken or
finely chopped skinned
thigh meat

1 large yellow onion,
finely chopped

1 red bell pepper
(capsicum), finely chopped

3 cloves garlic, minced

½ teaspoon cayenne
pepper, optional

3 lb (1.5 kg) tomatoes,
peeled, seeded,
and chopped

2 tablespoons chopped
fresh basil

Salt and ground pepper

2 cups (1 lb/500 g)
part-skim ricotta cheese

½ cup (2 oz/60 g) grated
Parmesan or pecorino
cheese

1 egg

½ cup (¾ oz/20 g)
chopped fresh flat-leaf
(Italian) parsley

½ lb (250 g) mozzarella
cheese, shredded

MAKES 4–6 SERVINGS

Bring a large pot three-fourths full of salted water to a boil. Add the lasagne noodles, stir well, and cook until almost al dente, about 8 minutes. Drain and rinse in cool water, then lay flat on a kitchen towel.

Preheat the oven to 350°F (180°C). Oil a 7-by-11-inch (18-by-28-cm) baking dish.

In a frying pan over medium-high heat, warm the oil. Add the chicken and cook, stirring occasionally, until browned, about 6 minutes. Add the onion and bell pepper and sauté until softened, about 2 minutes. Stir in the garlic and cayenne pepper (if using) and sauté until the garlic is softened, about 20 seconds. Add the tomatoes and basil, stir well, and bring to a boil. Reduce the heat to low and simmer until thickened, about 20 minutes. Season with salt and pepper. Remove the pan from the heat.

In a bowl, combine the ricotta, Parmesan, and egg and mix well. Stir in the parsley.

Line the bottom of the prepared baking dish with about one-fourth of the lasagne noodles, arranging them in a single layer and cutting as needed to fit. Spread with one-third of the ricotta mixture, sprinkle with one-third of the mozzarella, and then spoon on one-fourth of the sauce. Repeat the layering two more times, using up all of the ricotta mixture and the mozzarella. Top with the remaining noodles and finally the remaining sauce.

Cover with aluminum foil and bake until heated through and the sauce is bubbling, about 45 minutes. Let the lasagne stand on a wire rack for 10 minutes, then uncover and cut into squares to serve.

Browning the lasagne

If you prefer your lasagna with a crunchier, browned top, save some of the mozzarella to sprinkle on last. When the lasagna is baked through, uncover and leave in the oven for about 10 minutes longer to brown the cheese.

No-boil noodles

Nowadays, an increasing number of lasagne noodles labeled as "no boil" are stocked in supermarkets. In reality, all dried lasagne noodles are no-boil. If your lasagne has enough liquid, as with this tomato sauce, and is cooked covered, you can skip boiling the noodles if you like; they'll cook through as the lasagne bakes.

BAKED MACARONI AND CHEESE

Bake and serve

This dish can be assembled and then refrigerated, tightly covered, for up to 24 hours before baking. If baked directly from the refrigerator, you may need to add as much as 30 minutes to the cooking time. Once the dish has baked for about 30 minutes, start checking it every 10 minutes.

For this family favorite, sharp Cheddar cheese is melted into a thick white sauce then combined with macaroni in a baking dish. It is then topped with bread crumbs, which transform into a crunchy topping in the oven and create the perfect contrast to the creamy pasta below.

Make the sauce as directed, then remove from the heat and stir in the nutmeg and ⅛ teaspoon white pepper. Add three-fourths of the cheese and stir to melt. Taste and adjust the seasoning. Cover with plastic wrap, pressing it onto the surface to prevent a skin from forming.

Preheat the oven to 400°F (200°C). Butter a 9-by-13-inch (23-by-33-cm) baking dish. Bring a large pot three-fourths full of salted water to a boil. Add the pasta, stir well, and cook until slightly undercooked, 6–8 minutes.

Drain the pasta and return to the warm pot. Add the cheese sauce and stir to coat, then transfer to the prepared baking dish. Sprinkle evenly with the remaining cheese, and then with the bread crumbs.

Bake until bubbling around the edges and nicely browned, about 30 minutes. (If the top is browning too fast, cover loosely with aluminum foil and continue to bake.)

Let stand on a wire rack for 5 minutes before serving.

White Sauce (page 382)

⅛ teaspoon freshly grated nutmeg

Salt and ground white pepper

½ lb (250 g) sharp Cheddar or Gruyère cheese, shredded (about 2 cups)

1 lb (500 g) dried elbow macaroni or small shells (conchiglie)

2 tablespoons fine dried bread crumbs

MAKES 6 SERVINGS

MANICOTTI WITH CHICKEN AND SPINACH

Prepping the spinach

Thoroughly rinse 12 oz (375 g) fresh spinach and add, with the rinsing water still clinging to it, to a saucepan. Add 1 tbsp water, place over medium heat, cover, and cook, stirring occasionally, until wilted and tender, 4–5 minutes. Drain in a colander, pressing with a wooden spoon to release as much water as possible. Let cool slightly, then chop.

These manicotti shells, stuffed with a mixture of chicken and spinach, are a bit more healthful than the average baked pasta, thanks to the use of cottage cheese instead of the more traditional ricotta. You can substitute regular or part-skim ricotta, if you prefer.

In a frying pan over medium heat, warm the oil. Add the chicken and onion and cook, breaking up the meat with a spatula or fork, until the meat is opaque, about 10 minutes. Transfer to a large bowl and let cool for 10 minutes.

Add the spinach, cottage cheese, thyme, egg, Parmesan, ½ teaspoon salt, and ¼ teaspoon pepper to the bowl with the chicken and stir to combine.

Preheat the oven to 325°F (165°C). Spread ½ cup (4 fl oz/125 ml) of the marinara sauce over the bottom of a 9-by-13-inch (23-by-33-cm) baking dish.

Bring a large pot three-fourths full of salted water to a boil. Add the manicotti tubes, stir well, and cook until slightly undercooked, about 8 minutes. Drain, rinse under cold running water, and drain again.

Using a small spoon, stuff each tube with about ⅓ cup (3 oz/90 g) of the filling. Arrange in a single layer in the baking

1 tablespoon olive oil

½ lb (250 g) ground (minced) white chicken or turkey meat

½ cup (2½ oz/75 g) yellow onion, finely chopped

1 cup (7 oz/220 g) cooked, drained, and chopped spinach (see note, left)

1½ cups (12 oz/375 g) nonfat small-curd cottage cheese

1 teaspoon dried thyme or basil

1 egg

¼ cup (1 oz/30 g) grated Parmesan cheese

Salt and ground pepper

2½ cups (20 fl oz/625 ml)
Marinara Sauce (page 379)

8 dried manicotti tubes

MAKES 4 SERVINGS

dish and spoon the remaining sauce over the top. Cover with aluminum foil and bake until the sauce is bubbling and the filling is heated through, about 40 minutes.

Transfer to a wire rack, uncover, and let stand for 5 minutes to cool slightly before serving.

BAKED PENNE WITH SQUASH AND TOMATOES

Not all baked pasta dishes are dense and cheesy. Here, eggplant, zucchini, and tomatoes are tossed with penne, sprinkled lightly with Parmesan, and baked. You can assemble the dish several hours ahead of time, cover and refrigerate, and then bake just before serving.

6 Asian eggplants
(slender aubergines)

4 zucchini (courgettes)

2 tablespoons olive oil

1½ cups (9 oz/280 g)
peeled, seeded, and
chopped fresh tomatoes

¼ cup (2 oz/60 g)
well-drained and
chopped oil-packed
sun-dried tomatoes

Salt and ground pepper

¾ lb (375 g) dried penne

⅓ cup (1½ oz/45 g) grated
Parmesan cheese

MAKES 4 SERVINGS

Preheat the oven to 325°F (165°C). Lightly coat a 3-qt (3-l) baking dish with olive oil. Bring a large pot three-fourths full of salted water to a boil.

Meanwhile, trim the eggplants and zucchini and cut crosswise into rounds ½ inch (12 mm) thick. In a large, nonstick frying pan over medium-low heat, warm the oil. Add the eggplants and zucchini and cook, stirring occasionally, until softened, about 10 minutes. Add the fresh and sun-dried tomatoes and simmer, uncovered, until the tomatoes are very soft, about 5 minutes. Season with salt and pepper. Remove from the heat and set aside.

Add the penne to the boiling water, stir well, and cook until slightly undercooked, 8–10 minutes.

Drain the pasta, rinse under cold running water, and transfer to the prepared baking dish. Spoon the vegetable mixture over the top and stir gently to mix. Sprinkle the top evenly with the cheese.

Cover with aluminum foil and bake until heated through, about 20 minutes. Uncover and continue to bake until the cheese has melted and browned slightly, about 10 minutes longer. Serve right away.

Family-style pasta

For a casual meal, serve the pasta directly from the baking dish. Choose a pretty baking dish that will look nice on the table. Insulate the table from the hot dish with a trivet or thick, folded kitchen towel. Set out a large spoon or spatula for serving.

177

Sandwiches & PIZZAS

Sandwiches & Pizzas

Bread has long been the staff of life, sustaining people since ancient times. Over the centuries, it has also become the foundation for myriad handheld foods around the globe, with ingredients layered or pressed between, folded or rolled inside, or baked on top. This chapter reveals a variety of bread-based dishes, from sandwiches to pizzas, burgers to filled pitas, even burritos and quesadillas. The meal possibilities are endless.

Sandwich Breads

Homemade bread
From crusty loaves to pizza crusts, freshly baked bread is welcome on nearly any table. In addition to the pizza dough recipes on pages 32–33, see chapter 14 for an assortment of yeast-raised breads.

Toasting sandwich bread
Some sandwiches benefit from toasting the bread before assembly. Toasting adds extra crunch and deeper flavor; delays moist fillings from turning the bread soggy; and provides a coarser surface that helps to anchor the filling in place.

Condiments
Ketchup, mustard, mayonnaise, and other condiments and spreads provide both flavor and moisture to sandwiches. Keep a variety on hand, including such international options as salsas (pages 392–94) and Guacamole (page 392), Tapenade (page 388), chutneys (pages 397–98), and Hummus (page 69).

Garnishes
Stock up on an assortment of garnishes to add variety to sandwiches. For example, sliced pickles, pickled onions, roasted peppers (capsicums), or pickled pepperoncini add a spark of color, flavor, and texture to a sandwich, whether they are part of the filling or served alongside.

The type and character of a sandwich are largely determined by the bread. Ham and cheese, for instance, are a classic combination slipped between slices of rye, but they take on a new dimension when melted between two tortillas or folded into a calzone.

SLICED BREADS Sliced loaf-style bread is the most common foundation for sandwiches. Look for robust sourdough or rustic country loaves; rich egg breads; healthful whole-wheat (wholemeal) or multigrain loaves; sweet and spicy cinnamon-raisin bread; country-style potato or buttermilk bread; sour, seed-studded rye loaves; and breads flavored with herbs, onion, garlic, olives, nuts, or cheese, with each type suggesting a wide range of possible fillings. Use slices plain or toasted for a variation in texture. Add cheese and cook in a frying pan or on a griddle, or open-faced under the broiler (grill), to make a "melt." Or, press griddled sandwiches under a weight or in an electric sandwich press to make crusty Italian-style panini.

BUNS AND ROLLS This category offers incredible variety, including sturdy round hamburger buns and slender hot dog buns; long, crusty Italian-style rolls (for sandwiches known variously as submarines, hoagies, heroes, or grinders); rich, flaky crescent-shaped croissants; chewy doughnut-shaped bagels; and many other shapes and sizes in a wealth of flavors. Buns and rolls offer the opportunity to mix and match the unexpected, such as serving a burger in a chewy onion roll, or stuffing tuna salad into a croissant.

PITA During baking, these round or oval Middle Eastern flatbreads develop interior pockets. Whether cut crosswise into half-moon pockets, or split along an edge for a large round pocket, pita is ideal for stuffing with anything from eastern Mediterranean fillings, such as a mix of hummus and falafel, to more familiar Western fillings, such as sliced roast beef, tomato, and red onion. Both white flour and whole-wheat (wholemeal) flour varieties are available.

PIZZA DOUGH Pizzas and their close cousins, turnover-shaped calzone, are essentially sandwiches in which the bread bakes at the same time as its topping or filling. Once you have mastered the basic technique of pizza making described on pages 194–97, see the chart at right for more ideas. In Rome's bakeries, pizza dough is also formed into dimpled 6-foot lengths, brushed with oil, and baked, then cut into rectangles for making sandwiches.

TORTILLAS The most common form of bread in Mexico, these thin disks are made from corn flour, known as *masa harina*, or wheat flour. Either type can be used to make a quesadilla, Mexico's version of the grilled cheese sandwich. In the United States, flour tortillas are also rolled around cold or hot sandwich fillings to make so-called wraps.

PIZZA COMBINATIONS

Making your own pizza is a fun and creative pursuit, allowing you to mix and match sauces and toppings as you like. Below are some ideas to get you started. Bake each pizza in a 450°F (230°C) oven for about 10 minutes. For additional details and more recipes, turn to pages 194–97.

BASIC PIZZA DOUGH (PAGE 32)

Arugula and Onion Pizza
Following the directions on page 33, form the dough into a 12-inch (30 cm) round. Spread the dough with a thin layer of Marinara Sauce (page 379). Top with shredded mozzarella cheese and paper-thin yellow onion slices. Bake until the crust is golden brown. Strew with arugula (rocket) leaves and grind pepper over the top. Drizzle the finished pizza with olive oil.

Shrimp and Pesto Pizza
Following the directions on page 33, form the dough into a 12-inch (30 cm) round. Spread the dough with a thin layer of Pesto (page 387). Top with shredded Fontina cheese, grilled shrimp (prawns), diced roasted red bell pepper (capsicum; page 333), and crumbled fresh goat cheese. Bake until the crust is golden brown.

White Pizza
Following the directions on page 33, form the dough into a 12-inch (30 cm) round. Spread the dough with a thin layer of extra-virgin olive oil. Top with ricotta cheese mixed with chopped fresh herbs. Sprinkle with grated Parmesan cheese. Bake until the crust is golden brown. Sprinkle the finished pizza with coarse salt and freshly ground pepper.

CORNMEAL PIZZA DOUGH (PAGE 33)

Barbecue Chicken Pizza
Following the directions on page 33, form the dough into a 12-inch (30 cm) round. Spread the dough with a thin layer of Basic Barbecue Sauce (page 376). Top with shredded cooked chicken, corn kernels, chopped red onion, and shredded smoked mozzarella. Bake until the crust is golden brown.

Pepperoni Pizza
Following the directions on page 33, form the dough into a 12-inch (30 cm) round. Spread the dough with a thin layer of Marinara Sauce (page 379). Top with thinly sliced pepperoni, shredded mozzarella cheese, and grated Parmesan cheese. Bake until the crust is golden brown.

Spicy Steak Pizza
Following the directions on page 33, form the dough into a 12-inch (30 cm) round. Spread the dough with a thin layer of Arrabbiata Sauce (page 379). Top with thinly sliced cooked steak, pickled jalapeño chile slices, crumbled cotija cheese, and shredded Monterey jack. Bake until the crust is golden brown. Sprinkle with chopped fresh cilantro (fresh coriander).

WHOLE-WHEAT PIZZA DOUGH (PAGE

Grilled Vegetable Pizza
Following the directions on page 33, form the a 12-inch (30 cm) round. Spread the dough with of tomato purée. Top with grilled eggplant (auber roasted red bell pepper (capsicum) slices (page 33 shredded mozzarella cheese. Bake until the crust is g brown. Sprinkle with chopped fresh basil.

Salad-Topped Pizza
Following the directions on page 33, form the dough into a 12-inch (30 cm) round. Spread the dough with a thin layer of olive oil. Sprinkle with red pepper flakes and top with shavings of Parmesan cheese. Bake until the crust is golden brown. Top with vinaigrette-dressed mixed baby greens.

Three Cheese Pizza
Following the directions on page 33, form the dough into a 12-inch (30 cm) round. Spread the dough with a thin layer of Marinara Sauce (page 379). Top with equal parts shredded fresh mozzarella, smoked mozzarella, and fontina cheese. Bake until the crust is golden brown.

POTATO PIZZA DOUGH (PAGE 33)

Chicken Pesto Pizza
Following the directions on page 33, form the dough into a 12-inch (30 cm) round. Spread the dough with a thin layer of Pesto (page 387). Top with shredded cooked chicken breast and grated Parmesan cheese. Bake until the crust is golden brown. Top with slivered fresh basil.

Lamb Sausage Pizza
Following the directions on page 33, form the dough into a 12-inch (30 cm) round. Spread the dough with a thin layer of Tapenade (page 388). Top with thin slices of grilled lamb or other sausage, crumbled feta cheese, sliced sun-dried tomatoes, and mozzarella cheese, and sprinkle with dried or chopped fresh oregano. Bake until the crust is golden brown.

Smoked Salmon Pizza
Following the directions on page 33, form the dough into a 12-inch (30 cm) round. Brush the dough with a thin layer of olive oil and bake until golden brown. Cool and spread with cream cheese. Top with thinly sliced smoked salmon and red onion, then sprinkle with capers and drizzle with lemon juice.

SEE ALSO:
- **Basic Cheese Pizza**, *page 194*
- **Pizza Margherita**, *page 194*
- **Pancetta, Goat Cheese, and Olive Pizza**, *page 195*
- **Prosciutto and Egg Pizza**, *page 196*
- **Fresh Herb Pizza**, *page 196*
- **Onion, Walnut, and Goat Cheese Pizza**, *page 197*
- **Potato, Onion and Rosemary Pizza**, *page 197*

ASPARAGUS AND CHEESE WRAP

wrap approach

*ng its cue from
Middle Eastern–
le aram sandwich,
wrap rolls fillings
a tortilla or other
thin flatbread. You
can use any fillings
you like, but include a
soft, moist ingredient,
such as Hummus
(page 69) or a fresh
cheese, to act as the
"glue" that will keep
the sandwich from
unrolling.*

For this recipe, use wild or cultivated asparagus no larger than a pencil. Teleme is a mild-flavored, soft cow's milk cheese coated in rice flour. If you're not able to find it, use Fontina or Brie. Tarragon or flat-leaf (Italian) parsley can be substituted for the chervil.

Place the asparagus on a steamer insert in a saucepan over boiling water. Cover and steam until barely tender, 2–4 minutes. Transfer to a plate.

In a frying pan over medium heat, warm the oil. When it is hot, lay 1 tortilla in the pan. Place 2 or 3 cheese slices down the center and cook until the edges of the tortilla begin to curl and the cheese begins to melt, 2–3 minutes. Place 2 asparagus spears down the center, on top of the cheese, and sprinkle with about 2 teaspoons of the chervil. Using tongs, transfer the topped tortilla to a plate. Roll up the tortilla to form a cylinder, and transfer to a warmed platter or individual plate, seam side down. Keep warm. Repeat until all the tortillas are filled, adding more oil to the pan if needed. Serve right away.

**12 thin asparagus,
tough ends removed**

**1 teaspoon canola oil,
or as needed**

**6 flour tortillas, each
about 8 inches (20 cm)
in diameter**

**3 oz (90 g) Teleme cheese,
thinly sliced**

**¼ cup (⅓ oz/10 g)
chopped fresh chervil**

MAKES 6 SERVINGS

MEDITERRANEAN EGG SALAD SANDWICH

**Sun-dried vs.
fresh tomatoes**

*In summer, when
ripe tomatoes are
abundant, omit the
sun-dried tomatoes
from the egg salad
and add a fresh slice
of tomato to each
sandwich instead.*

Nearly everyone loves an egg salad sandwich, especially with a bowl of hot soup. This one is made more interesting with the addition of sun-dried tomatoes and olives. Plain white toast is traditional, but whole-wheat (wholemeal) or coarse country bread is a flavorful alternative.

Bring a large saucepan three-fourths full of lightly salted water to a boil over high heat. Carefully slip the eggs into the water and cover the pan. Reduce the heat to medium and cook for 7–8 minutes. Do not overcook. Drain the eggs, then immerse in cold water. When cool enough to handle, peel the eggs and chop coarsely.

In a bowl, combine the chopped eggs, sun-dried tomatoes, olives, and just enough mayonnaise to bind the ingredients. Season with salt and pepper.

Spread the egg salad on 6 slices of toast, dividing it evenly. Top with a lettuce leaf, close the sandwich with a second slice of toast, and serve.

12 eggs

**¼ cup (1¼ oz/40 g)
chopped, drained oil-packed
sun-dried tomatoes**

**¼ cup (1¼ oz/40 g) chopped,
pitted Kalamata olives**

**¾–1 cup (6–8 fl oz/
180–250 ml) mayonnaise**

Salt and ground pepper

**12 slices white, whole-
wheat (wholemeal), or
coarse country bread,
toasted**

**6 large leaves butter
or romaine (cos) lettuce**

MAKES 6 SERVINGS

GRILLED VEGETABLE SANDWICH

These easy-to-assemble sandwiches are great for entertaining. The eggplants, onions, red peppers, and basil mayonnaise can be prepared up to 2 days in advance, leaving you with only the task of layering the ingredients in split baguettes before serving.

¼ cup (2 fl oz/60 ml) olive oil

2 tablespoons fresh thyme leaves

2 tablespoons fresh rosemary leaves

Salt and ground pepper

2 globe eggplants (aubergines) or 4 Asian eggplants (slender aubergines), thinly sliced

2 large red onions, thinly sliced

3 large red bell peppers (capsicums)

FOR THE BASIL MAYONNAISE

2 cloves garlic

1 tablespoon olive oil

¼ cup (⅓ oz/10 g) minced fresh basil

½ teaspoon chopped fresh thyme

¾ cup (6 fl oz/180 ml) mayonnaise

2 baguettes, each cut crosswise into thirds and then split lengthwise

6–12 leaves red or green leaf lettuce

MAKES 6 SERVINGS

In a large bowl or shallow dish, stir together the oil, thyme, rosemary, ¼ teaspoon salt, and ½ teaspoon pepper. Add the eggplants, onions, and bell peppers and turn to coat well. Let stand at room temperature for 30 minutes.

Meanwhile, prepare a charcoal or gas grill for direct-heat cooking over medium-high heat (see page 18).

To make the mayonnaise, in a blender or food processor, combine the garlic, oil, basil, and thyme and process until smooth. Add the mayonnaise and process just until blended. Transfer to a bowl, cover, and refrigerate.

Remove the eggplants, onions, and peppers from the marinade, discarding the marinade. Place on the grill rack (or place the eggplant and onion slices in 1 or more grill baskets and place on the grill rack). Cook the eggplant slices until a golden crust forms on the first sides, 7–8 minutes. Turn and cook on the second sides until a golden crust forms and the interiors are cooked through, 6–7 minutes longer. Cook the onion slices until lightly browned on the first sides, 4–5 minutes. Turn and cook until lightly browned on the second sides and the interiors are tender, 3–4 minutes longer. Cook the peppers, turning as necessary, until the skins are evenly blackened and blistered, 4–5 minutes on each side.

Remove the eggplants and onions and set aside. Place the peppers on a plate, cover with aluminum foil, and let stand for 10 minutes, then peel away the skins. Cut the peppers in half lengthwise and remove the stem, seeds, and ribs. Cut the halves in half lengthwise.

Spread the cut sides of the baguette sections evenly with the mayonnaise. Top the bottom halves with the eggplants, onions, bell peppers, and lettuce leaves, dividing evenly. Close the sandwiches with the baguette tops and serve.

Pairing by season

This recipe shows off the summer harvest, with the primary ingredients—eggplant, peppers, and basil—at their peak in the height of the season. Look to the seasonal harvest to create vegetable sandwiches at other times of the year. For example, in the spring, try asparagus and spring onions. In the fall, pair portobello mushrooms and arugula (rocket).

183

ITALIAN SAUSAGE SANDWICHES

About sweet peppers

Sweet peppers, or capsicums, have none of the spicy heat of their chile relatives. Green bell peppers are immature red bells and generally have a sharper flavor than the fully matured red, yellow, and orange bell peppers. The shape of a sweet pepper—heart shaped, bell shaped, long and narrow—does not affect its flavor.

This hearty sandwich combines grilled peppers and sausages. Make it during summer and autumn when markets are ablaze with different colors and varieties of sweet peppers. Serve with a tossed green salad for a satisfying lunch or dinner.

Cut each sausage in half lengthwise. In a large frying pan over medium heat, fry the sausages, turning once, until crisp and cooked through, 4–5 minutes on each side. Remove from the heat, cover, and keep warm.

In a second frying pan over medium-high heat, warm the oil. Add the onions and cook, turning them often, until limp and lightly browned, 7–8 minutes. Using a slotted spoon, transfer to a bowl and keep warm.

While the onions are cooking, stem and seed all the peppers. Cut the long, green peppers into thin rings and the red bell peppers lengthwise into strips ¼ inch (6 mm) wide. Add the peppers to the pan and cook over medium-high heat until softened and browned on the edges, about 10 minutes. Add the vinegar and deglaze the pan, stirring to dislodge any browned bits from the pan bottom, 1–2 minutes longer.

To assemble the sandwiches, lightly spread the cut sides of the rolls with the mustard. Divide the onions, peppers, and sausage halves evenly among the bottom halves. Close the sandwiches with the roll tops and serve right away.

6 hot or sweet Italian sausages, about 1½ lb (750 g) total weight

2 tablespoons olive oil

2 large red onions, thinly sliced

4 long, green Italian sweet peppers (capsicums)

3 red bell peppers (capsicums)

2 tablespoons balsamic vinegar

4 sourdough or other sandwich rolls, split and toasted

2 tablespoons Dijon mustard

MAKES 4 SERVINGS

FRIED OYSTER BLTS

Po' boy sandwiches

You can use fried oysters to create another classic sandwich, the famed po'boy of New Orleans. Split and lightly toast 4 soft French rolls and spread with a thin layer of Tartar Sauce (page 386). Top the bottom half of each roll with 6 fried oysters, shredded iceberg lettuce, and sliced tomatoes, then set the roll tops in place. Pass hot sauce at the table.

Adding cheese, turkey, and avocado are common ways to reinvent a traditional BLT. This version takes a more radical approach, tucking in a few fried oysters. Prepare all of the other ingredients before frying the oysters, then assemble while the oysters are still hot.

Spread each slice of toast with the mayonnaise. Top 6 slices with the lettuce, bacon, and tomatoes, dividing them evenly. Set aside while you fry the oysters.

Pour oil to a depth of at least 1½ inches (4 cm) into a deep-sided frying pan and warm over high heat until it reaches 375°F (190°C) on a deep-frying thermometer. Meanwhile, in a bowl, combine the flour, ½ teaspoon salt, and ¼ teaspoon pepper. Coat the oysters with the seasoned flour, shake off the excess, and set aside on a plate.

When the oil is hot, add the coated oysters and fry until crisp and golden, turning once with tongs, about 1½ minutes. Drain briefly on paper towels.

Top each sandwich with 4 hot oysters. Close the sandwiches with the remaining toast slices and serve right away.

12 slices sourdough bread, toasted and cooled slightly

⅓ cup (3 fl oz/80 ml) mayonnaise

1 small head lettuce, leaves separated

½ lb (250 g) thick-cut sliced bacon, cooked until crisp

2 large tomatoes, sliced

Canola oil

1 cup all-purpose (plain) flour

Salt and ground pepper

24 shucked oysters

MAKES 6 SERVINGS

LAMB, FETA, AND CUCUMBER PITA

For added color, flavor, and texture, tuck a few tomato slices, some lettuce leaves, or several pitted Kalamata olives into this Middle Eastern–style sandwich. If you don't want to fire up the grill, cook the lamb in a preheated broiler (grill), using the same timing.

6 oz (185 g) feta cheese

2 tablespoons olive oil

2 tablespoons fresh lemon juice

Salt and ground pepper

1 cucumber, peeled, halved lengthwise, seeded, and cut into ½-inch (12-mm) dice

2 small red onions, cut into ¼-inch (6-mm) dice

1 tablespoon minced fresh mint

1 tablespoon minced fresh flat-leaf (Italian) parsley

1 tablespoon chopped fresh dill

1 piece boneless leg of lamb, 1½–2 lb (750 g–1 kg), butterflied (see page 261)

6 pita breads, cut crosswise into halves

MAKES 6 SERVINGS

Prepare a charcoal or gas grill for direct-heat cooking over medium heat (see page 18).

Crumble the cheese into a bowl and add 1 tablespoon of the oil and the lemon juice. Season with salt and pepper. Using a fork, mash together to mix thoroughly. Stir in the cucumber, onions, mint, parsley, and dill. Set aside.

Brush the lamb with the remaining 1 tablespoon oil. Place on the grill rack and grill, turning once, until golden brown on both sides and an instant-read thermometer inserted into the thickest portion registers 130°–135°F (54°–57°C) for medium-rare, about 15 minutes on each side. Alternatively, cut into the thickest part with a knife; the meat should be slightly pink at the center. Transfer the lamb to a cutting board, cover loosely with aluminum foil, and let rest for about 10 minutes.

Meanwhile, warm the pita halves on the grill.

Slice the lamb across the grain on the diagonal. Season with salt and pepper. Evenly distribute the lamb and feta-cucumber salad among the pita halves. Place 2 halves on each plate and serve right away.

Seeding a cucumber

Using a large knife, cut the cucumber in half lengthwise. Run a teaspoon lengthwise down the center of each half to scoop out the watery, bitter seeds and pulpy matter. Even if your cucumbers are labeled "seedless," there are typically some errant seeds that should be removed.

BAGUETTES WITH CHICKEN AND TAPENADE

On-site assembly

If you are serving these at a picnic or other outing, pack the components separately and assemble the sandwiches just before serving.

Leftover roast chicken and Tapenade (page 388) are put to good use in these sandwiches, but both can be purchased if you are pressed for time. They are layered with goat cheese, tomato slices, and basil on a garlic-rubbed baguette, to yield hearty sandwiches for a quick meal.

Place the baguette on a work surface and cut crosswise on the diagonal into 4 equal pieces. Split each piece horizontally. Arrange the split baguette lengths, cut sides up, on a work surface. Brush the cut surfaces with the oil.

Place a grill pan over medium heat. When hot, place the bread, cut sides down, on the pan and grill until lightly browned, about 1 minute. Remove from the pan and rub the cut surfaces with the cut sides of the garlic clove.

Spread the 4 bottom halves of the bread generously with the goat cheese, dividing it evenly. Spread a thin layer of the tapenade over the cheese. Place the chicken over the tapenade, and top with the tomato slices and several basil leaves. Grind pepper over the top. Close the sandwiches with the baguette tops and serve right away.

1 baguette

3 tablespoons olive oil

1 large clove garlic, halved

¼ lb (125 g) fresh goat cheese

About ¼ cup (2 oz/60 g) tapenade

1 roasted chicken, about 3½ lb (1.75 kg), at room temperature, skin removed and meat sliced

2 or 3 plum (Roma) tomatoes, sliced

Leaves from 1 small bunch fresh basil

Ground pepper

MAKES 4 SERVINGS

HERO SANDWICHES

Make it your own

A good ratio for a typical hero is about ½ lb (250 g) sliced meat to about ¼ lb (125 g) sliced cheese. For the meats, try turkey, hot coppa, pepperoni, soppressata, or Black Forest ham. For the cheese, try sharp Cheddar, pepper Jack, Swiss, or smoked mozzarella.

Whether you call it a submarine, a grinder, a hoagie, or a hero, this Italian-American sandwich, layered with salami, mortadella, and provolone, is an undisputed classic. Make a batch of these hearty sandwiches to take on a picnic or pack into lunch boxes for the whole family.

Arrange the split rolls, cut sides up, on a work surface. Sprinkle the bread evenly with the oil, and then with the vinegar, oregano, and finally the Parmesan.

Layer the bottom halves of the rolls with the salami, mortadella, and provolone, dividing them evenly. Top each layered half with 2 tomato slices and one-fourth of the lettuce. Close the sandwiches with the roll tops and serve, or wrap tightly in plastic wrap and refrigerate until serving.

4 crusty French rolls, split

3 tablespoons olive oil

1 tablespoon red wine vinegar

1 teaspoon dried oregano

2 tablespoons grated Parmesan cheese

¼ lb (125 g) *each* thinly sliced Genoa salami and mortadella

¼ lb (125 g) thinly sliced provolone cheese

1 large, firm tomato, cut into 8 slices

⅓ head iceberg lettuce, finely shredded

MAKES 4 SERVINGS

TURKEY MELTS

Here, alfalfa sprouts, tomato, onion, and turkey are layered on bread, topped with Muenster cheese, and broiled for a delicious open-faced sandwich. For a more indulgent version, replace the sprouts with sliced avocado and slip a little crisply fried bacon under the turkey.

4 slices whole-wheat (wholemeal) or coarse country bread, toasted

2–3 tablespoons mayonnaise

1 large tomato, sliced

1 red onion, thinly sliced

8 large slices cooked turkey

8 thin slices Muenster or Monterey Jack cheese

MAKES 4 SERVINGS

Preheat the broiler (grill).

Spread 1 side of each toast slice with the mayonnaise. Place the slices, mayonnaise side up, on a rimmed baking sheet. Top with the tomato, onion, and turkey slices, dividing them evenly. Top each sandwich with 2 cheese slices.

Broil (grill) the sandwiches until heated through and the cheese melts and begins to brown, about 5 minutes. Transfer to individual plates and serve right away.

Simple roast turkey breast

To roast your own turkey for the melt, coat 1 skinless, boneless breast half with olive oil, then season with salt and pepper. Place in an oiled baking pan and roast at 325°F (165°C) until done (see page 235), about 1 hour. Use right away, or refrigerate for up to 2 days.

FONTINA AND PROSCIUTTO PANINI

For this luxe take on the grilled cheese sandwich, fontina and prosciutto are layered between slices of crusty bread, then cooked in a hot frying pan until golden. Look for authentic Italian Fontina Val d'Aosta, which has a creamy, nutty flavor and melts beautifully.

8 large slices coarse country bread, each about ½ inch (12 mm) thick

5–6 oz (155–185 g) fontina cheese, sliced

4 thin slices prosciutto, about 2 oz (60 g) total weight

2 teaspoons chopped fresh rosemary, or 1½ teaspoons dried rosemary

Olive oil

MAKES 4 SERVINGS

Place 4 of the bread slices on a work surface. Divide the cheese evenly among them, top the cheese with a slice of prosciutto, and then sprinkle evenly with the rosemary. Cover with the remaining bread slices.

In a large, heavy frying pan, pour in enough oil to film the bottom and place over medium-high heat. When the oil is hot, add as many sandwiches as will fit comfortably in the pan and cook, pressing down often with a metal spatula, until golden brown on the bottoms, 2–3 minutes. Turn over the sandwiches and add more oil to the pan if necessary to prevent scorching. Cook, again pressing down on the sandwiches often, until golden brown on the second sides, about 2 minutes longer. Transfer to a plate and repeat with the remaining sandwiches, adding more oil as needed.

Cut the sandwiches on the diagonal and serve right away.

Panini al fresco

When the weather is nice, cook these sandwiches on an outdoor grill. Before grilling, press down gently but firmly on each sandwich to help seal it, and brush both outer sides of each sandwich with the olive oil.

PHILLY-STYLE CHEESE STEAKS

Steak types

Hanger steak, cut from the underside of the steer, has the perfect beefy flavor and pleasingly chewy texture for this sandwich. Skirt steak or flank steak have similar qualities and either would be a good substitute here.

Philadelphians pride themselves on their cheese steak, a thinly sliced, panfried beefsteak topped with lots of melted cheese, sautéed onions, and juices in a long, crusty bun. Here, that classic sandwich moves to the outdoor grill with delicious results.

In a shallow bowl, stir together the oil, vinegar, oregano, garlic, and ½ teaspoon each salt and pepper. Add the steak, turn to coat evenly, cover, and marinate at room temperature for 30 minutes or in the refrigerator for up to 4 hours.

Prepare a charcoal or gas grill for direct grilling over high heat. Oil the grill rack. Add the onion slices to the marinade and turn to coat both sides.

Remove the meat and onions from the marinade, and discard the marinade. Place the meat and onions on the grill rack and grill, turning once, for 6–8 minutes total for medium-rare steak. Remove the steak from the grill and let rest while the onions continue to cook until golden on both sides and tender, 10–14 minutes total. Just before removing the onions from the grill, toast the rolls, cut sides down, on the grill.

Slice the meat against the grain and heap onto the roll bottoms. Top with the cheese and onions, and close the sandwiches with the roll tops. Let stand for 1 minute, then cut each sandwich in half and serve.

¼ cup (2 fl oz/60 ml) olive oil

3 tablespoons red wine vinegar

2 tablespoons minced fresh oregano

2 large cloves garlic, minced

Salt and ground pepper

1½ lb (750 g) hanger, skirt, or flank steak

2 Vidalia or other sweet onions, thickly sliced crosswise

6 long, crusty sandwich rolls, split

1½ cups (6 oz/185 g) shredded Cheddar cheese

MAKES 6 SERVINGS

BLUE CHEESE BURGERS

Shaping patties

To ensure an evenly cooked burger, make a circular indentation in the center of the patty so it is slightly thinner in the middle than at the edges. During cooking, the meat will even out into a uniform, flat patty.

As long as the patty is well seasoned and perfectly cooked, a hamburger can be made with nearly any type of bread and any topping. Here, the burger sits on a bed of watercress atop garlic toast and is served open-faced, with crumbled Stilton cheese strewn on top.

Place the beef in a bowl and season with salt and pepper. Stir in the onion, mixing well. Divide into 4 equal portions, and shape each portion into a patty about ½ inch (12 mm) thick.

In a large frying pan over high heat, warm the oil. When the oil is very hot, add the patties (in batches, if necessary) and reduce the heat to medium. Cook the patties until browned on the undersides, about 2 minutes. Turn the patties and crumble the blue cheese on top, dividing it evenly, then smashing it lightly. Cook on the second sides until done to your liking, 1–1½ minutes longer for medium-rare. Transfer to a plate and keep warm.

Add the bread to the frying pan (in batches, if necessary) and cook, turning once, until lightly toasted, 1–2 minutes on each side. Remove from the pan and rub one side of each slice with the cut side of a halved garlic clove. Divide the toasts among individual plates, garlic-rubbed side up.

1 lb (500 g) ground (minced) beef chuck

Salt and ground pepper

¼ cup (¾ oz/30 g) finely minced green (spring) onion, including tender green tops

1 tablespoon olive oil

¼ lb (125 g) Stilton, Gorgonzola, or Roquefort cheese, at room temperature

4 slices coarse country bread, about ⅓ inch (9 mm) thick

2 cloves garlic, halved

2 cups (2 oz/60 g)
watercress leaves,
plus more for garnish

Top each toasted bread slice with one-fourth of the watercress, then place the patties on top and pour any accumulated juices over the top. Garnish with additional watercress and serve right away.

MAKES 4 SERVINGS

TURKEY BURGERS WITH PEPPER-CORN RELISH

Seasoned with cumin, lime, and cayenne, these tasty turkey burgers are lower in fat than traditional beef burgers. The relish, which combines fresh corn, red pepper (capsicum), onion, lime juice, and cilantro (fresh coriander), adds both flavor and color.

1 lb (500 g) ground
(minced) turkey or chicken

2 teaspoons ground cumin

1½ teaspoons grated
lime zest

1½ teaspoons fresh
lime juice

⅛ teaspoon
cayenne pepper

Salt

1 tablespoon canola oil

8 thick slices pepper
Jack cheese

4 French rolls or good-
quality hamburger buns,
split and toasted

Red Pepper–Corn Relish
(page 395)

MAKES 4 SERVINGS

In a bowl, combine the turkey, cumin, lime zest and juice, cayenne, and ¾ teaspoon salt and mix well. Divide into 4 equal portions and shape each portion into a patty ½ inch (12 mm) thick. Cover and refrigerate for at least 30 minutes or up to 5 hours to firm.

In a large heavy frying pan over medium heat, warm the oil. Add the patties and cook, turning once, until cooked throughout, about 4 minutes on each side. Top each patty with 2 slices of the cheese and cook until the cheese melts, about 1 minute longer.

Place the rolls on individual plates. Transfer the burgers to the bottom halves and top each burger with a spoonful of the relish. Close with the roll tops and serve right away. Pass the extra relish at the table.

About cumin

A cousin of parsley and coriander, cumin is one of the most widely used spices around the world, found in kitchens from Latin America, South Asia, and western China to the Middle East and North Africa. The long, ridged seeds have a strong flavor that is more earthy than spicy.

189

TUNA BURGERS WITH WASABI MAYONNAISE

Using powdered wasabi

If you cannot find wasabi (Japanese horseradish) in a tube, buy powdered wasabi and mix 2 tbsp of it with 1 tbsp tepid water to form a thick paste.

Asian flavors give this elegant tuna burger a bright flavor. Look for the thinly sliced sweet pink pickled ginger sometimes served with sushi, rather than the red, salty ginger. It can be found in the refrigerated section of Japanese stores and well-stocked supermarkets.

Using a vegetable peeler, remove and discard the outer peel of the cucumber, then continue shaving lengthwise into thin ribbons. Set aside.

In a bowl, combine the tuna, green onions, fresh ginger, and egg white and mix well. Season with salt and pepper. Using your hands, shape the tuna mixture into 4 patties, each 4 inches (10 cm) in diameter and set aside on a plate.

In a small bowl, whisk together the mayonnaise, pickled ginger, and wasabi. Spread the mayonnaise mixture on the bottom halves of the buns.

In a large nonstick frying pan over medium-high heat, warm the oil. When it is hot, add the patties and cook until golden on the first sides, about 2 minutes. Turn the patties and continue to cook until golden on the second sides and medium-rare in the center, about 2 minutes longer.

Transfer the burgers to the bun bottoms. Top each burger with a few of the cucumber ribbons and sprinkle with some of the sprouts. Close with the bun tops and serve right away.

1 small English (hothouse) cucumber

1 lb (500 g) ahi tuna fillet, chopped

3 green (spring) onions, including tender green tops, chopped

2 tablespoons peeled and minced fresh ginger

1 extra-large egg white

Salt and ground pepper

3 tablespoons mayonnaise

3 tablespoons chopped pickled ginger (see note, above)

1½ teaspoons prepared wasabi (see note, left)

4 sesame buns, split and toasted

1 tablespoon canola oil

1 package (3½ oz/105 g) daikon sprouts

MAKES 4 SERVINGS

FALAFEL BURGERS WITH TAHINI MAYONNAISE

The traditional approach

Traditional falafel are about the size of slightly flattened golf balls and are often served in pita, with lettuce, cucumber or tomato, and tzatziki (page 68) or tahini. Use them in place of the grilled lamb on page 185, pairing them with the feta–cucumber mixture.

In the Middle East, falafel are street food—but arguably some of the most nutritious and flavorful street food in the world. Here, the chickpea mixture is formed into patties and served like a beef burger on a roll with all the trimmings.

Bring a large pot of lightly salted water to a boil. Add the chickpeas and cook until slightly softened but still very firm in the center, about 10 minutes. Drain and cool slightly.

In a food processor, combine the chickpeas with the onion, garlic, and parsley and process until coarsely puréed. Transfer the mixture to a bowl and stir in the baking powder, cumin, ¾ teaspoon salt, and the red pepper flakes. Cover and refrigerate until cold, about 30 minutes.

Pour the canola oil to a depth of 1 inch (2.5 cm) into a deep saucepan and heat to 375°F (190°C) on a deep-frying thermometer, or until a tiny nugget of the falafel mixture

1½ cups dried chickpeas (garbanzo beans)

1 yellow onion, chopped

2 cloves garlic, chopped

1 cup packed fresh flat-leaf (Italian) parsley leaves

1 teaspoon baking powder

1 teaspoon ground cumin

Salt

½ teaspoon red pepper flakes

Canola oil for deep-frying

6 crusty round rolls, split

Tahini Mayonnaise
(page 386)

1 large tomato,
cut into 6 slices

1 large red onion,
thinly sliced

6 large romaine (cos)
lettuce leaves, roughly
chopped

MAKES 6 SERVINGS

dropped into the oil sizzles on contact. Meanwhile, using your hands, form the falafel mixture into 6 patties, each about ½ inch (12 mm) thick.

Working in batches, slip the patties into the hot oil and fry, turning once, until golden on both sides, about 6 minutes total. Using tongs or a slotted spoon, transfer to paper towels and keep warm while you fry the remaining patties.

Place the rolls on individual plates. Put 1 falafel patty on the bottom half of each roll, top with a spoonful of the mayonnaise, and then with the tomato, onion, and lettuce, dividing them evenly. Close with the roll tops and serve right away.

About tahini

Tahini paste, made from ground sesame seeds, has a rich creamy flavor and concentrated sesame taste. It is a typical ingredient in Middle Eastern recipes and can be found near the peanut butter in natural-foods stores.

CHILE VERDE PORK BURRITOS

These burritos enfold cubes of braised pork and slices of avocado in warm tortillas. Accompany them with bowls of sour cream, chopped green (spring) onions, fresh cilantro (fresh coriander) leaves, lime wedges, and Guacamole (page 392) for diners to add as desired.

2 tablespoons olive oil

2 lb (1 kg) boneless pork
shoulder, trimmed of
excess fat and cut into
1-inch (2.5-cm) cubes

2 yellow onions,
finely chopped

3 large green bell
peppers (capsicums), cut
into ½-inch (12-mm) dice

1 or 2 jalapeño chiles,
seeded and minced

5 cloves garlic, minced

1½ tablespoons
ground cumin

4 lb (2 kg) tomatillos,
husked, rinsed, chopped,
and drained

1 cup (1⅓ oz/40 g)
chopped fresh cilantro
(fresh coriander)

6 large flour tortillas

1 avocado, halved, pitted,
peeled, and thinly sliced

MAKES 6 SERVINGS

In a Dutch oven over medium-high heat, warm the oil. Working in batches if necessary to avoid crowding, add the pork cubes in a single layer and turn to brown on all sides, 10–12 minutes. Transfer to a plate and set aside.

Reduce the heat to medium, add the onions, bell peppers, and chiles, and sauté, stirring occasionally, until the onions are very soft, about 10 minutes. Add the garlic and cumin and continue to sauté, stirring, for 1 minute. Add the tomatillos, cilantro, and 1 cup (8 fl oz/250 ml) water. Return the pork to the pot and bring to a boil. Reduce the heat to low, cover, and simmer until the pork is very tender and the mixture is thick, 1½–2 hours.

Preheat the oven to 300°F (150°C). Wrap the tortillas in aluminum foil and bake until heated through, 12–15 minutes.

Place the tortillas on individual plates, divide the filling among the warm tortillas, and top with the avocado slices. Fold in two sides, roll to enclose, and then serve right away. Or, accompany with condiments (see note, above) and let diners garnish and fold their own burritos.

Working with tomatillos

Resembling small green tomatoes, tomatillos are surrounded by a papery husk that must be removed before the fruits can be used. They must also be rinsed well under running cold water to wash away the sticky substance that lightly coats the skin.

191

QUESADILLAS WITH TOMATOES AND CORN SALSA

Cheese and chile quesadillas

For a variation on this quesadilla, roast and peel an Anaheim or poblano chile (see page 333), then dice it. Sprinkle the cheese on the tortilla in the pan, then scatter some of the chile and some chopped fresh cilantro (fresh coriander) over the top. Fold and cook as directed.

For the most colorful—and tasty—presentation, use as many different varieties of heirloom tomatoes as you can find for making these quesadillas. A salsa of grilled sweet corn spiked with chiles and cilantro makes the perfect finishing touch.

Coarsely chop the tomatoes, place in a bowl, add 1 teaspoon salt and ½ teaspoon pepper and stir to combine. Set aside.

In a frying pan over medium-high heat, warm the oil. When it is hot, place 1 tortilla in the pan and cook until the edges begin to curl slightly, 1–2 minutes. Sprinkle a thin layer of cheese on half of the tortilla. Using a spatula, fold the other half over the cheese and press on the top. Cook until the underside is golden brown and the cheese has begun to melt, about 30 seconds, then turn and cook until the second side is golden brown, about 30 seconds longer. Remove from the pan and keep warm. Repeat with the remaining cheese and tortillas.

Lift the top of each quesadilla and spoon several tablespoons of the tomatoes and the corn salsa inside. Cut into 6 wedges and serve right away.

2 lb (1 kg) tomatoes, preferably assorted heirloom varieties

Salt and ground pepper

1 tablespoon canola oil

8 flour tortillas, each about 10 inches (25 cm) in diameter

½ lb (250 g) Monterey Jack, shredded

Grilled Corn and Avocado Salsa (page 394)

MAKES 8 QUESADILLAS; 4 SERVINGS

SHRIMP QUESADILLAS

Flat or folded

Quesadillas can be made two basic ways: place the filling on half of the tortilla and fold it over, or cover the whole tortilla with filling and then top with a second tortilla. The choice of method is up to the cook.

Loaded with a mixture of shrimp, two cheeses, and green onions, and served with Avocado-Tomatillo Salsa, these flavor-packed quesadillas make a satisfying meal. You can also make them with cooked crabmeat, scallops, or a combination of all three shellfish.

In a frying pan over medium-high heat, bring the clam juice to a boil. Add the shrimp and reduce the heat to low, cover, and simmer until the shrimp curl and are almost firm, about 1 minute. Using a slotted spoon, transfer the shrimp to a cutting board and chop coarsely.

In a bowl, combine the shrimp, both cheeses, and the green onions. Stir to combine. Distribute the mixture evenly among 3 of the tortillas. Top with the remaining tortillas.

Place a large frying pan over medium heat. When the pan is hot, carefully slide 1 quesadilla into the pan and cook, pressing on the top with a spatula, until the cheese melts and binds the filling, 2–3 minutes. Turn the quesadilla and cook on the second side until golden brown, 1–2 minutes longer. Remove from the pan and keep warm. Repeat with the remaining quesadillas.

Cut each quesadilla into 6 wedges, place 3 wedges on each plate, and serve right away. Pass the salsa at the table.

½ cup (4 fl oz/125 ml) bottled clam juice

1 lb (500 g) shrimp (prawns), peeled and deveined (see page 202)

1 cup (4 oz/125 g) coarsely shredded Monterey Jack cheese

1 cup (4 oz/125 g) coarsely shredded fresh mozzarella cheese

4 green (spring) onions, including 2 inches (5 cm) of the tender green tops, thinly sliced

6 flour tortillas, each about 10 inches (25 cm) in diameter

Avocado-Tomatillo Salsa (page 392)

MAKES 3 QUESADILLAS; 6 SERVINGS

FENNEL SAUSAGE CALZONE

A calzone is a pizza crust that is folded over filling ingredients and sealed before baking. This version features spicy pork sausage, which mellows when it is cooked in red wine. Substitute any hot or sweet sausage or Spanish or Mexican chorizo if you prefer.

3 tablespoons (2 fl oz/ 60 ml) extra-virgin olive oil

3 cloves garlic, chopped

¾ lb (375 g) hot or sweet Italian sausage, cut into slices ½-inch (12-mm) thick

1 tablespoon fennel seeds

2 tablespoons red wine vinegar

½ cup (4 fl oz/120 ml) good-quality red wine

Whole-Wheat Pizza Dough (page 32), risen once but not rolled out

MAKES 4 CALZONE

If using a pizza stone or tiles, place in the oven, then preheat the oven to 450°F (230°C).

In a frying pan over medium heat, warm the oil. Add the garlic and sausage and sauté until the garlic begins to turn golden, about 5 minutes. Add the fennel seeds and vinegar and cook until the vinegar evaporates, about 2 minutes. Add the wine, cover partially, and cook until it evaporates, about 10 minutes. Remove from the heat and let cool slightly.

Divide the pizza dough into 4 equal portions. On a lightly floured work surface, shape each portion into a circle about 6 inches (15 cm) in diameter. Arrange one-fourth of the sausage mixture on one-half of each circle, leaving a ½-inch (12-mm) border uncovered. Brush the edges of the circles with a little water and fold the empty halves over the filling. Pinch the edges to seal.

Transfer the calzone to a baker's peel or baking sheet and then to the oven. Bake for 10 minutes. Reduce the oven temperature to 400°F (200°C) and continue to bake until the crust is golden, about 10 minutes. Serve right away.

Wine for cooking

When choosing wine for cooking, always select a bottle that is good enough to drink. An inferior wine will adversely affect the flavor of a dish. You can choose a wine for cooking that is less expensive than the one you will be serving but is made from the same or a similar grape variety.

193

BASIC CHEESE PIZZA

Cheese pizza variations

For a pleasant change, use a thin layer of Pesto (page 387) or Tapenade (page 388) in place of the tomato sauce. For a slightly nuttier flavor, use Fontina cheese instead of the mozzarella.

Assembling pizzas to everyone's liking is a fun activity for family dinners or parties. This recipe yields one 9- to 12-inch (23- to 30-cm) pizza, spread with sauce and cheese, and ready for your choice of toppings. Multiply the ingredients as needed.

If using a pizza stone or tiles, place in the oven, then preheat the oven to 450°F (230°C).

In a nonstick frying pan over medium-high heat, warm the tomatoes until they begin to boil. Reduce the heat to low and simmer until the tomatoes are the consistency of tomato paste, 30–40 minutes. Remove from the heat, season with salt and pepper, and let cool.

Spread the tomato sauce over the surface of the prepared dough to within ½ inch (12 mm) of the edge. Sprinkle evenly with the cheese. Scatter with additional toppings, if desired.

Transfer the pizza to the oven and bake for 10 minutes. Reduce the oven temperature to 400°F (200°C) and continue to bake until the crust is golden, about 10 minutes. Remove from the oven, cut into wedges, and serve right away.

2 cups (12 oz/375 g) peeled, seeded, and chopped tomatoes (fresh or canned)

Salt and ground pepper

Basic Pizza Dough (page 32)

¼ lb (125 g) fresh mozzarella cheese, shredded

MAKES 1 PIZZA

PIZZA MARGHERITA

Pizza from Naples

In Italy, pizza is made with a respect for tradition. Neapolitan-style pizza is widely regarded as the standard bearer, so much so that it has been given special governmental status to protect its integrity. Pizza Margherita, with its topping of tomato, mozzarella, basil, and olive oil, is one of only three government-assigned versions of Neapolitan pizza.

A well-known and widely traveled pizza, this simple combination was the inspiration of nineteenth-century Neapolitan pizza maker Raffaele Esposito, who created it to honor Italy's Queen Margherita. Perhaps not coincidentally, it features the colors of the Italian flag.

If using a pizza stone or tiles, place in the oven, then preheat the oven to 450°F (230°C).

In a bowl, combine the tomatoes, garlic, and basil. Spread the tomato mixture evenly over the dough, drizzle with oil, and season with salt and pepper. Distribute the mozzarella cheese evenly over the tomatoes and sprinkle with the Parmesan (if using).

Transfer the pizza to the oven and bake for 10 minutes. Reduce the oven temperature to 400°F (200°C) and continue to bake until the crust is golden. Remove from the oven, cut into wedges, and serve right away.

2½ lb (1.25 kg) tomatoes, peeled, seeded and coarsely chopped

2 cloves garlic, minced

6–8 fresh basil leaves, cut into thin strips

Basic Pizza Dough (page 32), rolled thin

Olive oil for drizzling

Salt and ground pepper

6 oz (185 g) fresh mozzarella cheese, thinly sliced

2 tablespoons grated Parmesan cheese, optional

MAKES 1 PIZZA

PANCETTA, GOAT CHEESE, AND OLIVE PIZZA

This sophisticated pizza is cracker thin, sauce free, and topped with two kinds of cheese, tomato wedges, black olives, crispy pancetta, basil, and oregano. To get the crust just right, divide the dough in half and roll each half into extra-thin rounds.

Basic Pizza Dough
(page 32), divided in half
and rolled extra thin

12–16 thin pancetta slices

6–8 plum (Roma) tomatoes,
halved, seeded, and cut
into wedges

2 teaspoons
balsamic vinegar

2 generous pinches
of red pepper flakes

6 oz (185 g) fresh,
creamy goat cheese

30 Kalamata olives,
pitted and sliced

1 teaspoon dried basil

1 teaspoon dried oregano

1 cup (4 oz/125 g) shredded
Fontina cheese

About ¼ cup (2 fl oz/60 ml)
extra-virgin olive oil

¼ cup (⅓ oz/10 g) shredded
fresh basil leaves

MAKES 2 PIZZAS

If using a pizza stone or tiles, place in the oven, then preheat the oven to 450°F (230°C).

Fold over the outer ½-inch (12-mm) edge of each dough round to make a rim. Prick the dough all over with a fork.

In a large frying pan over medium-low heat, fry the pancetta slices, turning occasionally, until crisp, 5–6 minutes. Transfer to paper towels to drain. When cool, crumble the pancetta and set aside. In a bowl, toss together the tomatoes, vinegar, and red pepper flakes.

Transfer the pizza crusts to the oven and bake for 5 minutes to crisp slightly, then remove from the oven. Spread each crust with half of the goat cheese, then top each with half of the tomato mixture. Sprinkle with half each of the olives, pancetta, dried basil, oregano, and Fontina cheese. Drizzle evenly with the oil.

Return the topped pizzas to the oven and bake until the cheese melts and the crusts are crisp, 5–8 minutes. Remove the baked pizzas from the oven and sprinkle each pizza with 2 tablespoons of the fresh basil. Cut into wedges and serve right away.

The right goat cheese

For this recipe, look for disks or logs of fresh goat cheese. Also called chèvre, the cheese is pure white, has a pleasantly tangy flavor, and a moist, soft texture. Avoid aged, semifirm cheeses or any cheeses coated or layered with ash.

Pizza tools

Using a pizza stone or ceramic baking tiles helps you to achieve crisp crusts. The stone absorbs heat as your oven preheats, mimicking the radiant heat of a pizzeria oven. A baker's peel, also known as a pizza peel, is a thin-edged metal or wooden paddle that simplifies moving pizzas to and from the oven. If you don't have a baker's peel, use a rimless baking sheet.

PROSCIUTTO AND EGG PIZZA

This thin pizza is topped with prosciutto, fontina, and chopped tomatoes. Four eggs, cracked onto the top, bake to perfection in the oven. A cornmeal crust adds additional flavor and texture, making this an excellent main course for a brunch, lunch, or casual dinner.

If using a pizza stone or tiles, place in the oven, then preheat the oven to 450°F (230°C).

Cover the dough with the prosciutto and Fontina. Transfer the pizza to the oven and bake for 10 minutes.

Remove the pizza from the oven and break the eggs over it, spacing them evenly around the pizza. Scatter the tomatoes over the entire pizza and season with salt and pepper. Drizzle the oil over the top.

Return to the oven, reduce the temperature to 400°F (200°C), and bake until the crust is golden and the egg whites are set, about 10 minutes. Cut into wedges and serve right away.

Cornmeal Pizza Dough (page 33), rolled thin

¼ lb (120 g) prosciutto, thinly sliced

¼ lb (120 g) Fontina cheese, thinly sliced

4 eggs

4 large plum (Roma) tomatoes, peeled and chopped (fresh or canned)

Salt and ground pepper

3 tablespoons (2 fl oz/ 60 ml) extra-virgin olive oil

MAKES 1 PIZZA

FRESH HERB PIZZA

Here, a thick potato-rosemary crust is topped simply with herbs, onion, and garlic. Serve it as an appetizer, or accompany it with sliced sun-ripened tomatoes and a green salad for a meal. If you substitute dried herbs, cut the quantities in half.

If using a pizza stone or tiles, place in the oven, then preheat the oven to 450°F (230°C).

Place the dough on a lightly floured board and knead in 2 tablespoons of the oil and the rosemary, 1–2 minutes. Shape the dough for a thick, soft pizza as directed on page 33. Transfer to a baker's peel or baking sheet, cover with a kitchen towel, and let rise again until the dough is almost doubled, about 20 minutes.

Sprinkle the risen crust evenly with the marjoram, chives, basil, onion, and garlic. Drizzle the remaining 2 tablespoons oil over the top. Season with salt and pepper.

Transfer the pizza to the oven and bake for 10 minutes. Reduce the oven temperature to 400°F (200°C) and bake until the crust is golden, about 10 minutes. Cut the pizza into wedges and serve right away.

Potato Pizza Dough (page 33), risen but not rolled out

4 tablespoons (2 fl oz/ 60 ml) extra-virgin olive oil

1 tablespoon minced fresh rosemary

1 tablespoon minced fresh marjoram

1 tablespoon minced fresh chives

1 tablespoon minced fresh basil

1 tablespoon chopped yellow onion

1 teaspoon minced garlic

Salt and ground pepper

MAKES 1 PIZZA

ONION, WALNUT, AND GOAT CHEESE PIZZA

The onions that top this pizza are cooked with sugar and vinegar until they are almost caramelized, resulting in a sweet-tart flavor perfectly suited to the creamy goat cheese that covers the dough. If you prefer, divide the dough and shape into 4 individual pizzas.

4 large yellow onions, thinly sliced

1 tablespoon unsalted butter

3 tablespoons extra-virgin olive oil

1 tablespoon sugar

3 tablespoons red wine vinegar

Salt

Potato Pizza Dough (page 33)

6 oz (185 g) fresh goat cheese, crumbled

½ cup (2 oz/60 g) chopped walnuts

MAKES 1 PIZZA

If using a pizza stone or tiles, place in the oven, then preheat the oven to 450°F (230°C).

In a frying pan over low heat, combine the onions, butter, and 2 tablespoons of the oil. Cover and cook, stirring often, until the onions are very soft, about 30 minutes, adding a little water occasionally if needed to prevent sticking. Add the sugar and vinegar and continue to cook until the vinegar evaporates, about 3 minutes. Season with salt.

Cover the pizza dough with the cheese. Scatter the walnuts over the top and then the onions.

Transfer the pizza to the oven and bake for 10 minutes. Reduce the oven temperature to 400°F (200°C) and continue to bake until the crust is golden, about 10 minutes. Drizzle the remaining 1 tablespoon oil over the top, cut into wedges, and serve right away.

Cutting pizza

Position a large chef's knife at the 12 o'clock position and bring it down through the center to cut through the crust, pressing firmly on the top of the blade with your other hand. Make another cut perpendicular to the first to cut the pizza into quarters. Continue cutting in the same manner to create the classic pie-shaped wedges.

197

POTATO, ONION, AND ROSEMARY PIZZA

In this robust specialty of the pizzeria La Baia in Milan, a whole-wheat (wholemeal) pizza crust is topped with slices of potato and onion, then sprinkled with rosemary. A slice of crisp bacon crumbled and scattered over the onions would be a delicious addition.

2 boiling potatoes

Whole-Wheat Pizza Dough (page 32)

1 yellow onion, sliced paper-thin

2 tablespoons fresh rosemary, chopped if desired

4 tablespoons (2 fl oz/ 60 ml) extra-virgin olive oil

Salt and ground pepper

MAKES 1 PIZZA

Boil the potatoes in salted water to cover until tender, about 30 minutes. While the potatoes are cooking, if using a pizza stone or tiles, place in the oven, then preheat the oven to 450°F (230°C).

Drain the potatoes and let cool slightly. When the potatoes are just cool enough to handle, peel them and thinly slice. Arrange the potato slices evenly over the pizza dough. Top with the onion slices and sprinkle with the rosemary. Drizzle with 3 tablespoons of the oil. Season with salt and pepper.

Transfer the pizza to the oven and bake for 10 minutes. Reduce the temperature to 400°F (200°C) and continue to bake until the crust is golden, about 10 minutes. Drizzle the remaining 1 tablespoon oil over the top, cut into wedges, and serve right away.

Pizza wheel

A pizza wheel, which features a rolling blade at the end of an angled handle, is a versatile tool. It can be used not only for cutting pizza, but also for cutting pastry and pasta.

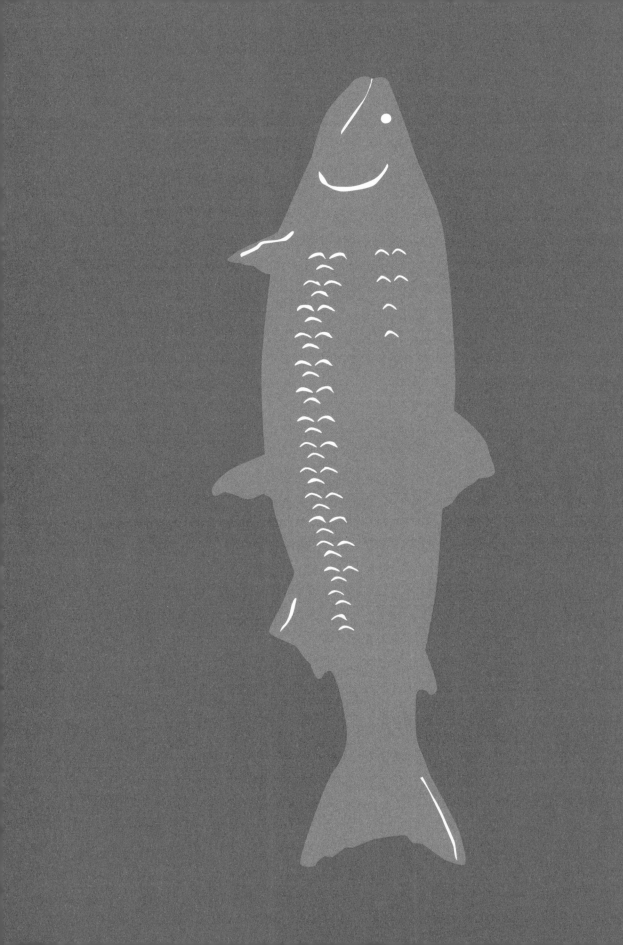

Fish & SHELLFISH

Fish & Shellfish

Cooks everywhere prize freshness and delicacy in fish and shellfish, and your aim should always be to safeguard and enhance those qualities from store to table. The recipes that follow offer a sampling of the myriad ways in which cuisines around the world celebrate the bounty from both rivers and oceans. You'll also find essential shopping, prep, and cooking information to help you achieve a perfect dish every time.

Fish Types

An amazing variety of fish are eaten around the world, leading to diverse means of categorization based on such traits as size, shape, and origin. For culinary purposes, though, fish are typically classified by texture, flavor, and fat content, which determine the optimal ways to prepare them. Fish in the same category can generally be substituted for one another in recipes.

LEAN AND MILD-FLAVORED FISH Most fish you prepare will be of this type. Common examples include bass, catfish, cod, flounder, red snapper, skate, sole, tilapia, and trout. Because of their mild flavor and soft, flaky texture, they should be cooked with liquid or some fat to keep them moist. Suitable cooking methods include poaching, steaming, and sautéing. Thicker fillets, such as those from cod or whitefish, can also be grilled or roasted.

RICH AND FULL-FLAVORED FISH These typically have a high oil content and a deep color and flavor. Both salmon and tuna fall into this category, as do sardines and mackerel. They take well to bold flavors and can withstand harsher, drier cooking methods, such as roasting, broiling, and grilling.

THICK AND MEATY FISH Size factors into this category, which consists of fish that are too large to be cooked whole. They can be rich and full flavored, such as tuna, or lean and mild, like halibut and swordfish. These fish are often sliced crosswise into thick steaks, making them ideal for grilling, broiling, and roasting.

Fish Facts

All fish are high in protein and most are low in fat. Fatty fish, such as salmon, are high in omega-3 fatty acids, which can lower the risk of cardiovascular disease. For these reasons, nutritionists advise eating fish at least twice a week. But you must be cautious about which fish you are eating.

ENDANGERED STATUS Some of the most popular eating fish are endangered due to overfishing or pollution. Online resources such as the Monterey Bay Aquarium's Seafood Watch post up-to-date lists. Substitute another fish with similar qualities, or consult your fishmonger about sustainable alternatives.

TOXINS Some fish species have a high mercury content. Among them are swordfish, shark, king mackerel, tuna, and tilefish. Doctors routinely warn pregnant women against consuming these fish. Nursing mothers and young children are advised to avoid them as well. Farmed salmon can be high in other toxins; select wild salmon when possible.

A sense of smell
A fish market should smell like the sea, and the fish and shellfish should be chilled, preferably on a bed of ice. Avoid shops with a strong fishy odor.

Appearance matters
Fish fillets should glisten and shine. Pass up those with dull colors and dry surfaces. Purchase only whole fish with clear—not cloudy—eyes and scales that are intact. Bivalves such as clams and mussels should have tightly closed shells, or shells that close when touched. Live crabs and lobsters should be active.

Establishing origin
Fresh fish is ideal, but some types are frozen so they can be shipped long distances. Ask if the seafood you are buying is fresh or frozen, wild or farmed, and where it comes from.

Accept substitutes
Many recipes have more than one option for the type of fish or shellfish that can be used. If the exact type you are looking for is not available, ask for a substitute. Or, purchase the freshest catch of the day and build your menu around it.

Shellfish Types and Techniques

Shellfish fall into two categories: crustaceans and mollusks. Crustaceans have legs or fins and delicate bodies protected by tough external skeletons; crabs, lobsters, and shrimp (prawns) are the most familiar types. Mollusks include bivalves and cephalopods. Bivalves, such as clams, mussels, oysters, and scallops, live within a hinged, two-part shell. Cephalopods, the most common being the squid, have quill-like shells inside their bodies.

Buy the freshest live shellfish you can find and use it as soon as possible. If buying precooked (nonfrozen) shellfish, eat it within 2 days of purchase. Always cook and eat thawed frozen shellfish the day you buy it.

CRABS In the United States, the popularity of crab is determined by local availability: Atlantic and Gulf coast blue crabs, southern Florida stone crabs, the Dungeness along the Pacific coast, and Alaskan king and snow crab.

Store live crabs in the refrigerator, wrapped in newspaper in an open paper bag, and cook them the day you purchase them.

To cook crabs: Bring a large pot of water to a full boil. Drop the crabs in headfirst, taking care to avoid any splashing. When the water returns to a boil, reduce the heat to maintain a gentle simmer. Cook for 6 to 10 minutes depending on size, with blue crabs usually done in about 6 minutes and Dungeness crabs in 8 to 10 minutes.

To clean and crack cooked crabs: Pull off and discard the eyes and mouth parts. Pull off the top shell and reserve it. Remove and discard the gills, the white feather-shaped pieces on each side of the body above the legs. Pull out and discard the firm, crooked white intestine along the center of the back. Turn the crab on its back and pull off the small triangular "breastplate" at the top. Spoon out the white and yellow "butter" in the body, reserving if desired. Break the body in half to reveal the meat. Use a mallet or lobster cracker to crack the shells of the claws and legs in several places. Serve the cracked crab or, if using the crabmeat in a recipe, use your fingers or a lobster pick to remove all the meat from the claws, legs, and body.

LOBSTERS Two broad categories of lobster exist: widely familiar large-clawed lobsters, particularly orange and black American or Maine lobsters; and spiny lobsters, also known as rock lobsters or langoustes, which lack large claws and are actually sea-dwelling crayfish.

When buying live lobster, choose active specimens. Store them in the refrigerator, wrapped in newspaper in an open paper bag, and cook within 24 hours of purchase.

To cook lobsters: Bring a large pot of water to a full boil. Drop the lobsters in headfirst, taking care to avoid any splashing. Once the water returns to a boil, reduce the heat to maintain a gentle simmer. Cook for 8 minutes for the first pound plus 2 minutes for each additional pound.

To halve and clean lobsters: If starting with a live lobster, plunge it into boiling water for about 1 minute until limp, then rinse under running cold water to halt the cooking.

Cut through the head, between the eyes, and hold the lobster by its tail over a sink or bowl to drain any liquid. Place the lobster on a cutting surface. Insert the tip of a large knife into the point where the tail and body sections meet and cut through the tail. Turn the lobster around and cut from the center through the head, splitting the lobster in half. Remove and discard the sand sac near the head and the dark intestinal vein that runs under the body. Remove and reserve, if needed, the greenish tomalley (the liver) and any

RUBS AND MARINADES

Coating the flesh of the fish with a seasoning paste, dry rub, or marinade is an ideal way to add flavor to quick-cooking fish. Here are some to try. Follow the instructions below, or cook the fish for about 10 minutes per 1 inch (2.5 cm) of thickness.

Dill and Lemon Zest
Stir together 2 tbsp chopped fresh dill, 2 tsp mild paprika, 1 tbsp grated lemon zest, 1 tsp salt, 1 tsp ground black pepper, and ¼ tsp cayenne pepper. Rub 2 lb (1 kg) meaty or firm fish fillets with olive oil and the marinade; grill or broil (grill) until opaque.

Indian Ginger Masala
In a blender, combine a 2-inch (5-cm) piece fresh ginger, chopped; 6 cloves garlic, minced; 2 jalapeño chiles, seeded and chopped; and 1 large yellow onion, coarsely chopped. Process until smooth. Add 1 tsp ground turmeric and ¼ cup (2 fl oz/60 ml) fresh lemon juice; blend well. Stir in ¼ cup (2 fl oz/60 ml) olive oil. Season with salt. Combine four 6-oz (185-g) meaty or firm fish fillets and the marinade and let stand for 1 hour; grill or broil (grill) until opaque.

Thai Spice
In a blender, combine 6 large cloves garlic, halved; a 1-inch (2.5-cm) piece fresh ginger, chopped; 3 tbsp chopped fresh cilantro (fresh coriander) stems; and ¾ tsp *each* salt and cracked peppercorns. Process to a smooth paste. Stir in 1½ tbsp light soy sauce. Spread inside 2 whole fish, 1½ lb (750 g) each; wrap in banana leaves or aluminum foil and grill until the flesh is opaque, about 15 minutes.

PREPPING FISH

Even if you haven't caught your own fish, you may still have some cleaning to do.

Skin-on fish
Fish fillets are often sold with the skin intact. Skin can hold a fillet together during cooking and shield the meat from the intense heat of a grill. The cooked skin of some fish (particularly salmon) is considered a delicacy in its own right.

Skinning fillets
If you prefer to remove the skin before cooking the fillets, lay the fillet, skin side down, on a cutting board, with the tail end of the fillet nearest you. Holding the edge of the skin at the tail end securely, position a fillet knife or other long-bladed thin knife at a slight upward angle between the skin and the flesh. Using a slight sawing motion, gently work the blade forward along the skin until the fillet meat is separated.

Removing pin bones
Fish fillets often contain small bones known as pin bones. To remove them before cooking, lay the fillet skin(ned) side down and run a fingertip along the center to locate the tips of the bones. Using fish tweezers or needle-nose pliers, pull them out one by one, gripping the tip of each bone and pulling diagonally in the direction the bone is pointing. You can also cut out the flesh containing the pin bones with a sharp knife.

coral-colored roe (the eggs). (If the recipe calls for halved and cleaned lobsters, proceed with the recipe's instructions at this point.) Remove the meat from the tail and body, then carefully crack the claws with a lobster cracker or mallet. Pull away the shell pieces and remove the claw meat in a single piece.

If you prefer to keep the tail meat whole, before cutting the body in half twist and pull the tail to detach it. Break off the end flaps. Carefully cut through the thin underside of the shell and pry it open to reveal the meat.

SHRIMP Raw shrimp (prawns) come in a wide range of shell colors and patterns, but all turn orange-pink and opaque white when cooked. Shrimp are classified by size according to number per pound (500 g): miniature (100), also called cocktail or bay shrimp; medium (25–30); large (16–20); and jumbo (10–15). Large shrimp and jumbo shrimp are also sometimes labeled as prawns in the United States.

Look for plump, firm, fresh-smelling shrimp in the shell; the freshest will still have their heads. Frozen shrimp are usually better quality than frozen and thawed. Store fresh shrimp in their original wrapping in the coldest part of the refrigerator. If refrigerating overnight, put the package in a zippered plastic bag and store on top of ice cubes in a baking dish, or place on top of frozen ice packs. Thaw frozen shrimp in the refrigerator, or in a heavy-duty zippered plastic bag submerged in cold water.

To peel shrimp: Working with one shrimp at a time, pull off the small "legs" on the underside. Starting with the section of shell closest to the head, gently pull it up and lift it away. Leave the tail shell intact or remove it according to your preference or recipe. To remove it, hold the meat firmly and pull the shell to detach the tail.

To devein shrimp: Use a small, sharp paring knife to make a shallow cut down the center of the outer curve of the shrimp, then gently lift out the vein, scraping if necessary.

To butterfly shrimp: Large shrimp may be butterflied for stuffing, cooking, or a more dynamic presentation. After shelling and deveining, cut through the shrimp on the outside curve without slicing all the way through, so it can be opened flat.

CLAMS Two types of clams exist: hard shelled and soft shelled. Despite the name, soft-shelled clams have quite firm shells, though thin and brittle. East Coast steamers and geoducks are two well-known varieties. Littlenecks and Manila clams are hard shelled. Soft-shelled clams may be slightly open; hard-shelled varieties are usually tightly closed.

When preparing live clams for cooking, discard any hard-shelled clams with shells that do not close when touched, indicating they are no longer alive. Soft-shelled clams have a small neck that protrudes from the shell. The clam is alive if the neck retracts into the shell when tapped, though the shell will not close as tightly as the shell of a hard-shelled clam. Refrigerate both types wrapped in paper or placed in a bowl and covered with a cloth.

To clean clams: Foraged clams tend to be sandy and must be soaked in seawater or salted water (1½ tablespoons salt per qt/l) for 3 hours before using. If using commercially raised clams, you need only rinse them under running cold water and scrub them with a soft-bristled brush.

MUSSELS The slightly pointed oval shells range from blue-green to yellowish brown to inky black. Most mussels sold today are cultivated, and the two most widely available species are the Atlantic blue or common mussel, which has an almost black shell 2–3 inches (5–7.5 cm) long; and the larger Pacific green-lipped or New Zealand mussel, 3–4 inches (7.5–10 cm) long.

When preparing live mussels for cooking, discard any with shells that do not close when touched, indicating they are no longer alive. Refrigerate wrapped in paper or placed in a bowl and covered with a cloth.

To clean mussels: Using a stiff-bristled brush, scrub the shells well under running cold water. Most cultivated mussels have little or no beard, the threadlike tuft near the shell's hinge the mussel uses to attach itself to pilings or rocks. If a beard is visible, grasp it with your fingertips and pull firmly downward to remove it. Never remove the beard more than an hour before cooking, as doing so kills the mussel.

OYSTERS Live oysters in the shell should be tightly closed when purchased. Take them straight home from the fishmonger's, or transport in an ice chest, and shuck and eat raw or cook as soon as possible. Refrigerate rounded side down and covered with a damp towel.

Shucked oysters for preparations such as stews are sold in jars in the meat and fish departments of many supermarkets; use within 24 hours.

To shuck oysters: Use an oyster knife, which has a thick handle and a wide, dull stainless-steel blade that will not transfer any metallic flavor. With a folded cloth or oven mitt, grasp the oyster in your nondominant hand, positioning the shell so its rounded edge points out toward the space between your thumb and fingers and the hinge points toward you. Holding the knife in your dominant hand, insert its tip into the dark, rounded spot at the oyster's hinge. Twist the knife sharply to break the hinge. Once the shell opens, slip the knife carefully up along the inside surface of the top shell, severing the adductor muscle that grips it. Take care not to cut the oyster itself or to spill its liquor. Lift off and discard the top shell. Carefully cut the muscle under the oyster to loosen it from the bottom shell. Remove any small particles of shell.

SCALLOPS The two most popular scallops are the large sea scallop, which is 1–2 inches (2.5–5 cm) in diameter and is preferred for sautéing and grilling, and the small bay scallop, which is about ½ inch (12 mm) in diameter and is good in soups and sauces. The best sea scallops are labeled "diver" (collected by hand) or "day boat" (caught and brought to shore within 24 hours), and "dry pack" (kept on ice in cloth bags) or "chemical free." Always purchase sea scallops that are not sitting in liquid, as some are soaked in phosphates to keep them plump. Sea scallops should be creamy white or pale coral, not bright white, and bay scallops should be pale orange or pale pink. When buying bay scallops, make sure you are getting the real thing: unprincipled merchants sometimes trim sea scallops and label them bay scallops.

To trim scallops: A hard piece of connective tissue is typically found on one side of a scallop meat. Before cooking, pull or cut it off.

SQUID Harvested from spring to early fall on the northern Pacific Coast, and from winter to spring on the southern Pacific Coast, squid—also known by the Italian *calamari*—is sold either whole or already cleaned; cleaned squid often do not include the tentacles but are convenient to use. Squid must be cooked either very quickly or they must be slowly stewed or braised.

To clean squid: First cut off the tentacles just above the eyes. Squeeze the hard, round "beak" from the base of the tentacles. With one hand holding the tail end of the body flat on a cutting board, scrape the side of a chef's knife along the body with the other hand, pressing hard to remove the innards. Still holding down the tail end, pull out the long quill protruding from the body. Rinse the squid well inside and out under running cold water. The mottled gray skin covering the body can be left intact or peeled away. If a recipe calls for rings, slice the body crosswise.

JUDGING DONENESS

For the best results, remove seafood from the refrigerator 30 minutes before cooking. Follow the cooking times and cues in your recipe, as well as these guidelines, being careful not to overcook.

Fish
Most fish is done when the flesh is barely opaque throughout and still moist and it separates into large flakes with a fork. Common kitchen wisdom holds that any fish should be cooked for a total of 10 minutes per 1 inch (2.5 cm) of thickness at its thickest point. However, as moistness and texture vary widely from species to species, it is wise to start checking for doneness after 8 minutes.

Tuna and salmon
These meaty fish are often eaten medium-rare to rare. They are done when opaque on the outside and still slightly raw in the center, according to preference.

Shrimp
Fully cooked shrimp will be pink on the outside and opaque in the center. Check the head end or cut off a head if necessary.

Mollusks
Clams and mussels are generally done the moment their shells have opened. Discard any that remain closed after cooking. Oysters are often eaten raw but are also quickly grilled or fried.

Scallops
Tender, delicate scallops require only brief cooking. The interior is typically cooked until just opaque or sometimes until still slightly translucent at the center.

SEAFOOD PREPARATIONS

PREPARATION	FISH FILLETS	WHOLE FISH
Grilling *Cooking over a hot fire or under a preheated broiler (grill).*	Best for rich and full-flavored fish such as salmon and tuna, and thick and meaty fish like halibut and swordfish. Brush lightly with olive oil or butter, season, and broil or grill 8–10 minutes per 1 inch (2.5 cm) of thickness at the thickest point (less for fish served rare such as salmon or tuna).	Grilling is suitable for striped bass, snapper, trout, small salmon, and other varieties that can fit on your grill. Slash the flesh in several places to help heat penetrate. To prevent sticking, brush the outside of the fish with oil; wrap the fish in banana leaves, grape leaves, or aluminum foil; or place in a hinged wire grill basket.
Pan-Frying/Sautéing/Stir-frying *Cooking in a moderate amount of fat (pan-frying) or small amount of fat (sautéing and stir-frying) in a hot frying pan or wok until fully cooked.*	Suitable for all lean and mild fish fillets, as well as thick and meaty fish. Heat a pan well, add oil or butter, swirl to coat the cooking surface, and add the seasoned fish; take care not to turn too often.	Not generally suitable.
Deep-Frying *Cooking in a pan of hot deep fat, often with a coating of bread crumbs or batter.*	Deep-frying is ideal for lean and mild fish such as catfish or cod and firm white-fleshed fish such as snapper. For even, nongreasy cooking, heat oil to 350°–375°F (180°–190°C), depending on the recipe, before coating large chunks of fish fillet with batter or bread crumbs.	Fish ranging from tiny smelt to medium snapper and catfish can be floured or battered and deep-fried. For the larger specimens, make a series of deep cuts in a checkerboard pattern in the flesh on both sides of the fish, down to the bone. Coat as desired and fry until golden brown in oil preheated to 350°– 375°F (180°–190°C).
Roasting/Baking *Cooking in the dry heat of the oven, uncovered (roasting) or covered, sometimes accompanied with a small amount of liquid and/or other ingredients.*	Roasting is suitable for most types of fish, though delicate ones can be protected from the heat with a flavorful crust. Baking is suitable for any fillets or steaks. Use a shallow baking pan and pour dry white wine, water, or other cooking liquid into the pan to a depth of ⅛ inch (3 mm).	Excellent for such whole fish as snapper, salmon, bluefish, sardines, pompano, and whitefish. Filling the body cavity with a stuffing helps keep the fish moist and flavorful.
Poaching/Stewing/Braising *Cooking in liquid on the stove top, either gently with seasonings (poaching), in chunks in a large amount of liquid (stewing), or in large pieces with a small amount of liquid (braising).*	Best for mild, tender fish such as snapper or halibut, as well as for meaty, rich-tasting fish such as salmon.	Whole small to medium fish, whether mild such as snapper or trout or rich-tasting such as salmon, benefit from the gentle, moist heat of poaching.
Steaming *Cooking on the stove top over simmering liquid, often seasoned to produce fragrant steam.*	Best for mild, tender fish such as snapper or sole, as well as for meaty, rich-tasting fish such as salmon. You can enclose any type of fish in parchment and oven-steam (see page 223).	Best for mild, tender fish such as snapper or sole, as well as for meaty, rich-tasting fish such as salmon.

204

BIVALVES	SHRIMP (PRAWNS)	LOBSTER
Larger mollusks and oysters can be grilled on a special seafood rack designed to prevent them from falling into the fire. Spread the cleaned shellfish on the rack, cover, and cook for a few minutes, just until their shells open. Serve with melted butter or another sauce for dipping.	Large and jumbo shrimp can be peeled and deveined before cooking, though some cooks prefer to leave the shells on to retain moisture. Skewer each shrimp through the head and tail ends to make them easier to turn and to guard against them falling through the rack. Cook just until they turn pink and opaque.	Excellent cooked on a grill or in a broiler. Split whole lobsters in half and clean before cooking (see page 201). Brush the meat with butter or oil and seasoning, then cook with the shell toward the heat to guard against drying out the meat. Then turn the meat briefly to brown.
Steamed clams and mussels can be removed from their shells and added to stir-fry dishes. Add them to the pan at the end and leave over the heat just long enough to warm them through.	Shelled small or medium shrimp can be quickly sautéed in a little hot oil or butter over medium-high heat just until cooked through.	Lobster meat can be removed from the shell, cut into bite-size pieces, seasoned, and stir-fried or sautéed with other ingredients in fat or oil just until it turns snowy white.
Whole shucked oysters are good candidates for deep-frying. Coat with seasoned flour, bread crumbs, or cornmeal and cook in oil or fat preheated to 350°–375°F (180°–190°C).	Shrimp of all sizes can be cooked by dipping in batter or coating in bread crumbs and shallow frying or deep-frying.	Chunks of lobster meat are excellent cooked tempura style: dipped in a light batter and quickly fried. (See Seafood Tempura, page 78, for a batter recipe and frying details.)
Mollusks can be spread in an even layer in a heavy-duty roasting pan, along with seasonings and a little wine, covered, and cooked in a 500°F (260°C) oven. Larger clams, mussels, and oysters can be pried open, filled with a moist stuffing, and baked in a 350°F (180°C) oven until the stuffing is hot and browned.	Arrange shelled or shell-on shrimp in a single layer in a baking dish, along with any herbs or accompaniments, and bake in a 400°F (200°C) oven just until they turn pink and opaque. Larger shrimp can be stuffed before baking.	Arrange halved and cleaned lobsters (see page 201) in a baking dish, cover with a moist sauce and a buttery bread crumb topping, and bake in a 425°F (220°C) oven until the bread crumbs have turned deep golden brown.
All kinds of mollusks can be simmered gently in flavorful liquid. Cook briefly, just until their shells have opened; if adding them to a stew with mixed seafood, do so toward the end of cooking to avoid overcooking the shellfish.	Although they require only brief cooking, shrimp of all sizes gain both flavor and moisture from well-seasoned poaching, stewing, or braising liquid. If combining them with other seafood in a stew or braise, add them toward the end of cooking to avoid overcooking them.	Whole lobsters are traditionally boiled rather than poached or braised (see page 201). Chunks of cooked (or slightly undercooked) lobster meat can be incorporated into stews.
The most traditional way to cook clams and mussels. Bring a small quantity of seasoned liquid to a boil in a large pot, add the scrubbed mollusks, and cook in the fragrant steam just until the shells open.	Excellent for medium to jumbo shrimp in the shell.	Live lobsters can be cooked in a steamer basket or tray above boiling water, though boiling them is considered a more humane cooking method.

205

BROILED TUNA WITH PEPPERCORNS

Sautéed tuna

If you prefer, you can sauté the tuna steaks in olive oil in a hot frying pan, rather than broil them. Cook them for 3–4 minutes on each side.

Tuna is a meaty fish, with a texture reminiscent of steak. This recipe is a variation on the classic beef dish Steak au Poivre (page 268). It is simplicity itself and may become your favorite way to serve this prime fish. The redder the tuna, the better and moister the result will be.

Preheat the broiler (grill).

In a small bowl, mix together the butter and lemon juice and zest until thoroughly combined. Season with salt. Set aside.

Pour the oil onto a plate. Place 2 tablespoons cracked pepper on another plate. Dip each tuna steak in the oil, coating both sides, and then press cracked pepper onto both sides. Sprinkle with salt.

Place the steaks on a broiler pan and broil (grill), turning once, until cooked to desired degree of doneness, 2–3 minutes on each side for medium-rare.

Serve right away. Pass the lemon butter at the table.

4 tablespoons (2 oz/60 g) unsalted butter, at room temperature

2 tablespoons fresh lemon juice

2 teaspoons grated lemon zest

Salt and cracked pepper

3 tablespoons olive oil

4 tuna steaks, each 6–8 oz (185–250 g) and 1½ inches (4 cm) thick

MAKES 4 SERVINGS

ROASTED RED SNAPPER AND CORN

On dredging

Dredging, or coating, fish fillets in flour keeps them moist and promotes good color and crispness. Dredge the fillets just before searing or the flour coating will become gummy.

Rice flour forms a thin crust on these snapper fillets, which are first dredged in rice flour and seared on the stove top, and then roasted on a bed of basil-seasoned corn with thin lime slices. The characteristic red snapper flavor marries well with the mild acidity of the lime juice.

Preheat the oven to 450°F (230°C). Lightly oil 2 baking dishes large enough to hold the fillets in a single layer.

In a bowl, stir together the onion, corn, chives, and half of the basil. Season with a pinch of coriander, salt, and pepper. Mix well and add 2 tablespoons of the oil and the lime juice. Toss lightly. Divide the mixture evenly between the prepared baking dishes, and scatter the lime slices over the top.

In a shallow bowl, stir together the rice flour and ½ teaspoon *each* coriander, salt, and pepper. Pat the fillets dry, then dredge in the seasoned flour, tapping off any excess.

Rice flour

Ground from white rice, this flour is used to create a light, crisp texture in recipes. Look for rice flour in the Asian foods section of the supermarket or in an Asian market.

In a large nonstick frying pan over high heat, warm the remaining 1 tablespoon oil. In batches, add the fillets and cook, turning once, until lightly browned on both sides, about 2 minutes on each side. Transfer the fillets, skin sides up, to the baking dishes on top of the corn mixture; leave a bit of space around each fillet. Repeat with the remaining fillets, adding more oil to the pan if needed to prevent sticking.

Roast until the vegetables are tender and the fillets are opaque throughout when pierced with a knife, about 20 minutes.

Remove from the oven and garnish with the remaining basil. Serve right away.

1 yellow onion, chopped

3 cups (18 oz/560 g) corn kernels (from 3–4 ears corn)

3 tablespoons snipped fresh chives

10 large fresh basil leaves, finely shredded

Ground coriander

Salt and ground pepper

3 tablespoons olive oil, or as needed

2 tablespoons fresh lime juice, plus 1 lime, thinly sliced

⅔ cup (2½ oz/75 g) rice flour

6 red snapper fillets with skin intact, about 6 oz (185 g) each

MAKES 6 SERVINGS

MISO-GLAZED SEA BASS

Sea bass marinated in a ginger-flecked marinade of miso, mirin, and sake broils to a shimmery, subtly sweet glaze. You can use the same method with any firm-fleshed white fish fillets, such as halibut, swordfish, or cod, or even with richer-tasting fish, particularly salmon and tuna.

½ cup (4 oz/125 g) white miso

¼ cup (2 fl oz/60 ml) mirin

¼ cup (2 fl oz/60 ml) sake

3 tablespoons sugar

1 teaspoon finely grated fresh ginger

6 sea bass fillets, each about 6 oz (185 g) and ¾–1 inch (2–2.5 cm) thick, skinned

1 teaspoon grated lemon zest

MAKES 6 SERVINGS

In a shallow baking dish, whisk together the miso, mirin, sake, sugar, and ginger until smooth. Add the fish and turn to coat evenly. Cover and refrigerate for at least 2 hours or up to overnight.

Preheat the broiler (grill).

Remove the fish from the marinade, reserving the marinade. Place the fillets on a broiler pan and broil (grill) until browned with crusty edges, about 4 minutes. Turn, brush with the reserved marinade, and grill until browned on the second side, 3–4 minutes.

Transfer to a warmed platter or individual plates, sprinkle with the lemon zest, and serve right away.

Miso and mirin

The fermented soybean paste called miso, a staple of Japanese cooking that comes in a variety of types, is used in salad dressings; as a base for soups; and, as here, to flavor marinades. Mirin, like sake, is a Japanese rice wine, but it is quite sweet and used for cooking only. Look for miso and mirin near the soy sauce and sake in your supermarket.

FISH ROASTED WITH OLIVES AND BASIL

For this simple yet sophisticated dish, fish fillets are placed in a baking dish with wine, olive oil, garlic, basil, and black olives and baked to flaky perfection. Use a firm white fish such as snapper, halibut, rock cod, flounder, sea bass, or swordfish.

4 firm white fish fillets, each 6–7 oz (185–220 g), skinned (see note, above)

Kosher salt and ground pepper

4 tablespoons (2 fl oz/ 60 ml) extra-virgin olive oil

⅓ cup (3 fl oz/80 ml) dry white wine

1½ tablespoons finely minced garlic

5 tablespoons (⅓ oz/10 g) fresh basil leaves, shredded

½ cup (2½ oz/75 g) Mediterranean-style green and/or black olives, pitted if desired

¼ cup (1 oz/30 g) pine nuts, toasted (see page 17)

MAKES 4 SERVINGS

Preheat the oven to 400°F (200°C).

Sprinkle the fillets with salt and pepper, then arrange in a single layer in a baking dish. In a small bowl, stir together 3 tablespoons of the oil and the wine. Pour over the fillets, top with half each of the garlic and the basil, and then scatter the olives around the fish. Cover with aluminum foil.

Bake until the fish is opaque throughout when pierced with a knife, 10–15 minutes. The timing will depend on the thickness of the fillets. Using a slotted spatula, transfer the fillets to warmed individual plates.

Pour the pan juices and olives into a small sauté pan, add the pine nuts, and place over medium heat. Swirl in the remaining 1 tablespoon oil and the remaining garlic and basil. When warm and fragrant, spoon over the fish. Serve right away.

Wine suggestion

The bright fruit and moderately rich texture of a French Chardonnay pair nicely with this Mediterranean dish. Use the same wine for roasting the fish.

SAFFRON-SCENTED HALIBUT AND VEGETABLES

208

About halibut

Halibut is a large flatfish from the cold waters of the Atlantic and Pacific. Because of its size, it can be cut into large, meaty fillets, rather than the delicate fillets typical of its cousins sole and flounder. Its firm, white flesh is extremely versatile.

Saffron seasons all the elements of this healthful and colorful dish, from the bed of shallot-laced spinach to the oven-roasted halibut to the topping of sautéed zucchini and tomato. Serve this dish with plenty of coarse country bread to soak up the fragrant juices on the plate.

In a small bowl, whisk together the lemon juice, olive oil, and saffron. Season the fish fillets with salt and pepper. Place the fillets in a shallow dish in a single layer. Pour the oil mixture over the fish and turn to coat. Cover and marinate in the refrigerator for 1–2 hours.

Preheat the oven to 450°F (230°C).

Pour 1 tablespoon canola oil into a roasting pan large enough to hold the fillets in a single layer and tilt the pan to film the bottom evenly, adding more oil if necessary. Place the pan in the oven until hot, about 5 minutes. Sprinkle a little salt on the bottom of the hot pan. Lift the fish fillets from the marinade, reserving the marinade, and place them, skinned sides down, on the hot pan. Roast until opaque throughout when pierced with a knife, 7–10 minutes.

Meanwhile, prepare the vegetables. In a large sauté pan over medium-high heat, warm 3 tablespoons olive oil. Add the shallots and sauté until they begin to soften, 2–3 minutes. Add the saffron and continue to cook until the shallots are soft, about 4 minutes longer. Transfer about 1 tablespoon of the shallots to a small dish and set aside.

Raise the heat under the sauté pan to high. Working in 3 batches, add the spinach to the shallots remaining in the pan. Sauté, tossing constantly, until the spinach is wilted but still bright, 4–5 minutes. Using a slotted spoon, transfer to a plate, season with salt and pepper, and keep warm.

Return the sauté pan to medium heat and add the reserved shallots. Add the zucchini and cook, stirring occasionally, until they begin to soften, 2–3 minutes, adding additional olive oil to the pan if needed to prevent sticking. Add the tomatoes and cook, stirring, until the tomatoes begin to soften, 3–4 minutes. Add the reserved marinade, raise the heat to high, and cook until the sauce is slightly thickened and the vegetables are just tender, 5–7 minutes longer. Season with salt, pepper, and the lemon juice.

Mound a portion of the spinach in the center of each individual plate. Top each mound with a fish fillet, and spoon the zucchini mixture over the fish. Dust the fish and the plate with the parsley. Divide the lemon wedges among the plates and serve right away.

Juice of 1 lemon

3 tablespoons olive oil

Pinch of saffron threads

6 halibut fillets, each 6–7 oz (185–220 g) and about ¾ inch (2 cm) thick, skinned

Coarse salt and ground pepper

1–2 tablespoons canola oil

FOR THE VEGETABLES

3–4 tablespoons olive oil

3 large shallots, diced

⅛ teaspoon saffron threads

1 lb (500 g) spinach, tough stems removed

Coarse salt and ground pepper

3 or 4 small zucchini (courgettes) diced

2 large tomatoes, peeled, seeded, and diced

Juice of 1 lemon

½ bunch fresh flat-leaf (Italian) parsley, minced

1 lemon, cut into wedges

MAKES 6 SERVINGS

MAPLE-GLAZED SALMON WITH SWEET POTATOES

In this recipe, a whole salmon fillet is basted with maple syrup—boiled until it's thick enough to coat the fish—then roasted on top of spiced sweet potato slices. The maple syrup begins to give a caramelized edge to the potatoes just as the salmon is done.

4 orange-fleshed sweet potatoes, about 2 lb (1 kg) total weight, peeled and thinly sliced on the diagonal

2 tablespoons unsalted butter, melted

Salt and ground pepper

Pinch of ground cinnamon

⅓ cup (3 fl oz/80 ml) pure maple syrup

2 tablespoons Worcestershire sauce

1 whole salmon fillet, about 1⅔ lb (815 g), skinned

Snipped fresh chives for garnish

MAKES 6 SERVINGS

Preheat the oven to 400°F (200°C).

In a bowl, toss the sweet potatoes with the melted butter, ½ teaspoon salt, a few grinds of pepper, and cinnamon to coat evenly. Arrange in a single layer on a large rimmed baking sheet. Place in the oven and roast until the potatoes begin to brown on the bottom, about 20 minutes.

Meanwhile, in a small saucepan, stir together the maple syrup and Worcestershire sauce. Place over medium heat and bring to a boil. Reduce the heat to low and cook until the mixture is thickened and reduced by half, about 5 minutes. Remove from the heat and set aside.

Sprinkle the salmon fillet with salt and pepper.

Remove the sweet potatoes from the oven. Raise the oven temperature to 450°F (230°C). Carefully turn over the sweet potatoes and place the salmon fillet on top of them. Brush half of the maple mixture evenly on the salmon fillet. Place in the oven and roast for 10 minutes. Remove from the oven and baste the salmon with the remaining maple mixture. Return to the oven and roast until the salmon is opaque throughout when pierced with a knife, 5–10 minutes longer.

To serve, divide the salmon into serving portions and arrange on warmed individual plates with the sweet potatoes. If you like, spoon some of the pan juices onto each plate. Sprinkle with chives and serve right away.

Know the source

A good fish market will clearly identify its products, where they came from, and whether they are fresh or frozen and wild or farmed. Ask questions; if the answers are vague, shop elsewhere.

209

PAN-SEARED SALMON WITH GREENS

A tangle of pea shoots and watercress dressed with a lemon vinaigrette makes a colorful and flavorful bed for pan-seared salmon. If you can't find pea shoots, substitute baby arugula (rocket) or spinach. The salmon can also be seared on a grill over a hot fire.

In a large bowl, whisk together the oil, one-third of the lemon juice, the sugar, shallots, and ½ teaspoon each salt and pepper to make a dressing. Add the watercress leaves and pea shoots to the dressing and turn gently to coat evenly. Divide the greens evenly among 8 individual plates.

To prepare the salmon, sprinkle 1½ teaspoons salt in a wide, heavy frying pan and place over medium-high heat until nearly smoking. Add the salmon fillets and sear for 2 minutes on the undersides. Turn and sear for 1 minute on the second sides. Sprinkle with 1 teaspoon pepper. Reduce the heat to low and pour in the wine and 2 tablespoons of the lemon juice. Cover and cook until the juices are nearly absorbed and the fish is half cooked, about 3 minutes. Uncover and add 2 more tablespoons of the lemon juice and 3 tablespoons water. Re-cover and cook just until the fish is opaque throughout when pierced with a knife, about 3 minutes longer. Most of the pan juices will have been absorbed.

Place a fillet on each mound of greens. Raise the heat to high, add the remaining lemon juice and 1 tablespoon water, and deglaze the pan, stirring to dislodge any browned bits from the pan bottom. Spoon the pan juices evenly over the fish and serve right away.

⅔ cup (5 fl oz/160 ml) extra-virgin olive oil

1 cup (8 fl oz/250 ml) fresh lemon juice

¼ teaspoon sugar

3 shallots, minced

Salt and ground pepper

5 cups (5 oz/155 g) watercress leaves

5 cups (5 oz/155 g) pea shoots

8 salmon fillets, each about 5 oz (155 g) and ½ inch (12 mm) thick, skinned

½ cup (4 fl oz/125 ml) dry white wine

MAKES 8 SERVINGS

Using Meyer lemons

You can use Meyer lemons for this recipe, which are sweeter and more floral than the more common Eureka or Lisbon lemon. If using Meyer lemon juice, omit the sugar.

210

SAUTÉED SOLE WITH LEMON AND BUTTER

This lemon and butter treatment is the simplest, fastest, and arguably most popular way to prepare fillet of sole. If you like, add 2 tablespoons rinsed capers with the lemon juice. To round out the meal, serve with roasted potatoes and sautéed spinach.

Spread the flour on a plate and season with salt and pepper. Dip the fish fillets into the seasoned flour to coat completely, tapping off any excess.

In a large frying pan over medium-high heat, warm the clarified butter. When hot, working in batches, add the sole fillets and sauté quickly, turning once, until golden brown on both sides, about 2 minutes on each side. Using a slotted spatula, transfer the fish to warmed individual plates.

Return the pan to medium-high heat, stir the lemon juice into the pan juices, and then stir in the 2 tablespoons butter until melted and incorporated. Spoon the sauce over the fish, top with the parsley, and serve right away.

½ cup (2½ oz/75 g) all-purpose (plain) flour

Salt and ground pepper

1½ lb (750 g) sole fillets, skinned

6 tablespoons (3 oz/90 g) Clarified Butter (page 28)

2 tablespoons fresh lemon juice

2 tablespoons unsalted butter

Finely chopped fresh flat-leaf (Italian) parsley

MAKES 4 SERVINGS

Sole amandine

For sole amandine, stir 1 cup (4 oz/125 g) slivered blanched almonds into the pan juices with the 2 tbsp butter and fry until the almonds are golden and the sauce is bubbly. Spoon over the fish and serve with lemon wedges.

GINGER–SESAME MONKFISH

This lovely monkfish dish is layered with flavor. First it is treated to a gingery rub, then it's rolled in sesame seeds, sautéed, and finally drizzled with a flavorful sauce. Serve the fish accompanied by steamed white rice or crispy rice noodles (see note, right).

2 lb (1 kg) monkfish
fillet, skinned

½ cup (1½ oz/45 g)
sesame seeds

½ cup (2½ oz/75 g)
minced fresh ginger

1 cup (8 oz/250 g)
granulated sugar

Coarse salt

½ teaspoon cayenne pepper

1 cup (8 fl oz/250 ml)
rice vinegar

½ cup (4 fl oz/125 ml)
fresh lime juice

¼ cup (2 fl oz/60 g)
Asian fish sauce

¼ cup (2 oz/60 g)
tomato paste

½ cup (3½ oz/105 g) firmly
packed dark brown sugar

3 tablespoons grated
lemon zest

2 tablespoons canola oil

Fresh cilantro (fresh
coriander) sprigs for garnish

MAKES 4 SERVINGS

Cut the monkfish on the diagonal into 4 equal pieces.

Spread the sesame seeds on a plate. In a small bowl, stir together the ginger, ½ cup (125 g) of the granulated sugar, 4 teaspoons salt, and the cayenne. Coat the fish pieces evenly on all sides with the ginger mixture, then roll the fish in the sesame seeds, pressing lightly so the seeds adhere to the fish well. Set aside.

In a small saucepan, whisk together the vinegar, lime juice, fish sauce, tomato paste, the remaining granulated sugar, the brown sugar, lemon zest, and ½ teaspoon salt. Set aside.

In a large frying pan over medium heat, warm the oil. Add the fish and cook, turning once, until browned on both sides, about 3 minutes total. Watch the fish carefully, because the sugar in the rub will color the fish quickly. Reduce the heat and cook the fish until opaque throughout when pierced with a knife, about 4 minutes.

While the fish is cooking, place the pan holding the vinegar mixture over low heat and warm the sauce to serving temperature, stirring occasionally.

Transfer the fish to warmed individual plates. Drizzle each portion with the warm sauce and garnish with the cilantro sprigs. Serve right away.

Crispy rice noodles

Put 2 oz (60 g) dried rice vermicelli in a paper bag and break them up a little. Heat canola oil 4 inches (10 cm) deep to 350°F (180°C). Working in 4 batches, fry the noodles until they puff up and turn opaque, about 30 seconds. Drain on paper towels.

211

POACHED WHOLE SALMON

About fish poachers

A fish poacher is a deep, elongated metal pan, with an oval shape roughly the same as that of a whole fish. Its narrow capacity ensures the fish can be kept submerged without a lot of extra liquid. A deep roasting pan can also be used with fine results.

A whole fish makes a spectacular hot or cold dish for a dinner party or an elegant buffet. Here, a salmon is poached in a flavorful bouillon, then skinned before serving. Accompany with Hollandaise Sauce (page 385) or mayonnaise laced with finely chopped fresh herbs.

Select a fish poacher or roasting pan longer than the salmon. (If necessary, cut off the head of the fish.) Add the wine, onions, carrots, thyme, celery, half of the parsley sprigs, the peppercorns, bay leaves, 3 tablespoons sea salt, and 3 qt (3 l) water to the pan and place over medium-high heat. Bring just to a boil, reduce the heat to medium, and simmer, uncovered, for 20–30 minutes to make a full-flavored bouillon. Reduce the heat so the liquid simmers gently.

Measure the fish as its thickest point, then determine the poaching time by figuring 10 minutes for each 1 inch (2.5 cm) of thickness. Cut a piece of cheesecloth (muslin) about 24 inches (60 cm) long. Lay the fish in the middle of the cheesecloth and, holding the two ends, lower the salmon into the simmering liquid; lay the cheesecloth ends on top. Add hot water to cover the fish if needed.

Cover and gently simmer for the determined time. To test for doneness, insert a knife into the thickest part; the flesh near the bone should be opaque. Turn off the heat and let the fish rest in the liquid for about 5 minutes.

With the aid of the cheesecloth, carefully lift out the fish and place on a warmed platter, slipping the cheesecloth free. Carefully peel off the skin from the top side of the salmon and discard. Gently turn the salmon over and peel the skin from the opposite side. Using a long, thin knife, loosen the flesh from the bone to make it easier to serve. Garnish with the lemon and cucumber slices and the remaining parsley sprigs and serve. Alternatively, let cool to room temperature, then garnish and serve.

3 cups (24 fl oz/750 ml) dry white wine

3 yellow onions, sliced

3 carrots, peeled and sliced

6 fresh thyme sprigs

3 celery stalks, sliced

1 large bunch fresh parsley

¼ teaspoon peppercorns

3 bay leaves

Sea salt

1 whole salmon, 6 lb (3 kg), scaled and cleaned

1 lemon, sliced

½ cucumber, sliced paper-thin

MAKES 8 SERVINGS

GRILLED WHOLE TROUT IN GRAPE LEAVES

Two plates apiece

Peeling away the grape leaves can be a messy job if they have burned slightly, as they may crumble. Provide two sets of plates for each dinner: one on which to peel away the leaves and another on which to place the ready-to-eat fish.

Wrapping fish in grape leaves for grilling protects the fish from the direct heat of the fire and infuses the flesh with a hint of the leaves' flavor. Here, trout are served in their leaf packets, hot from the grill, accompanied by a mayonnaise-based lemon-basil sauce.

Prepare a charcoal or gas grill for direct-heat cooking over medium-high heat (see page 18).

To make the sauce, in a bowl, stir together the mayonnaise, lemon juice, oil, basil, ¼ teaspoon salt, and ½ teaspoon pepper. Taste and adjust the seasoning. Cover and refrigerate the sauce until serving.

Rub the cavities and the skin of the trout with the lemon halves, squeezing a little juice on them as you do. Sprinkle

FOR THE LEMON-BASIL SAUCE

1 cup (8 fl oz/250 ml) mayonnaise

¼ cup (2 fl oz/60 ml) fresh lemon juice

1 tablespoon olive oil

8 fresh basil leaves, chopped

Salt and ground pepper

4 whole trout, about
10 oz (315 g) each, cleaned

2 lemons, halved,
plus 4 slices for garnish
(optional)

Salt and ground pepper

8 long fresh thyme sprigs

16–24 large brine-packed
jarred grape leaves,
well rinsed

Olive oil for brushing

MAKES 4 SERVINGS

inside and out with the salt and pepper, then tuck 2 thyme sprigs inside each cavity. Lay 1 grape leaf, smooth side down, on a work surface and place 1 fish on top. Wrap the leaf around the fish. Repeat with more leaves until the fish is snugly wrapped in 2 layers of leaves. Repeat with the remaining trout and leaves, fastening the leaves in place with toothpicks or wooden skewers. Brush the packets on both sides with oil.

Place the wrapped trout, seam side down, on the grill rack. Grill until the grape leaves are slightly browned on the first side, about 5 minutes. Turn and cook until browned on the second side, 4–5 minutes longer. Remove some of the grape leaves from 1 trout and test the flesh with a knife; it should be just opaque near the bone.

To serve, place the trout on 4 individual plates and let diners unwrap their own fish (see note, left). Garnish each plate with a lemon slice. Pass the sauce at the table.

Fresh grape leaves

If you have access to fresh grape leaves, you can use them in this recipe. Blanch the leaves in boiling water for about a minute before using.

ROAST WHOLE FISH WITH ALMOND STUFFING

This whole roasted fish, with an almond and bread crumb stuffing, makes a memorable main course, perfect for a special occasion. You can substitute fresh fennel for the celery; if you do, use fresh tarragon or dill rather than marjoram.

2 tablespoons
unsalted butter

½ yellow onion, diced

1 celery stalk, diced

2 cups (4 oz/125 g) fresh
bread crumbs

¼ cup (⅓ oz/10 g) chopped
fresh flat-leaf (Italian)
parsley, plus more for
garnish, optional

1 tablespoon chopped
fresh marjoram

2 teaspoons grated
lemon zest

½ cup (2½ oz/75 g)
chopped almonds,
toasted (page 17)

Salt and ground pepper

1 sea bass or snapper,
4–5 lb (2–2.5 kg), cleaned

½ cup (4 fl oz/125 ml)
melted unsalted butter

MAKES 4 SERVINGS

Preheat the oven to 425°F (220°C). Oil a baking dish large enough to hold the fish flat.

In a frying pan over medium heat, melt the butter. Add the onion and sauté until softened, about 5 minutes. Then, add the celery and sauté, stirring, for 3 minutes. Remove from the heat. Add the bread crumbs, parsley, marjoram, lemon zest, and almonds. Season with salt and pepper. Stuff the mixture snugly into the fish cavity and skewer closed. Place the fish in the prepared baking dish.

Bake the fish, basting occasionally with the melted butter, for 8–10 minutes per inch (2.5 cm) of thickness or about 40 minutes total cooking time. Test the flesh with a knife; it should just be opaque near the bone.

Carefully transfer to a warmed platter, garnish with additional parsley (if using), and serve right away.

About snapper

A family of tender, firm, lean, mild fish from the warm waters of the Atlantic, snappers are versatile, suitable for sautéing and steaming, roasting and frying, and also good in stews and chowders. Red and yellowtail snapper are the most popular varieties.

FISH TACOS

Fresh fish cooked quickly and folded into tortillas is a popular dish in fishing villages all over Mexico. Since the flavors are so simple, be sure to use the freshest fish you can find. The same goes for the tortillas: if possible, make your own or buy them freshly made from a local shop.

Season both sides of each fish fillet with salt and a generous amount of pepper. Spread the flour on a plate and dip the fish into it to coat evenly, tapping off any excess.

In a large frying pan over medium-high heat, warm the oil. When it is hot but not quite smoking, add the fish fillets and fry, turning once, until golden on both sides and opaque throughout when pierced with a knife, about 4 minutes total. Transfer to paper towels to drain.

While the fillets are still hot, shred them with a fork. Put the salsa in a bowl and stir in the fish.

To assemble the tacos, spoon some fish on each tortilla, add some cabbage, and fold to enclose loosely. Serve right away with the limes on the side.

1½ lb (750 g) red snapper or other firm white-fleshed fish fillets, skinned

Sea salt and ground pepper

¾ cup (4 oz/125 g) all-purpose (plain) flour

¼ cup (2 oz/60 ml) corn oil

Fresh Tomato Salsa (page 393)

10 small corn tortillas, warmed

1 cup (3 oz/90 g) chopped cabbage

2 limes, quartered

MAKES 10 TACOS

Get it hot

Be sure your frying pan is hot before adding fish fillets. Because fillets cook quickly, a cool pan will extend cooking time and compromise the texture of the final dish.

FRIED COD WITH GREEK GARLIC SAUCE

Skordalia, a full-flavored Greek garlic sauce or dip, is traditionally thickened with bread if you are poor, potatoes if you have a bit of money, and nuts if you are wealthy. It can accompany roasted beets, crispy pita chips (see page 61), or this golden, crispy, batter-dipped cod.

To make the sauce, place the bread in a bowl and pour 4 cups (32 fl oz/1 l) water over it. Immediately remove the bread from the water and squeeze it to remove the excess moisture. Discard the water.

In a food processor or blender, process the walnuts almost to a paste. Add the soaked bread, vinegar, oil, mayonnaise, and garlic and process to form a smooth paste. Season with salt and pepper. Set aside.

In a bowl, whisk together 1¼ cups (6½ oz/200 g) of the flour, the baking powder, ¼ teaspoon each salt and pepper, and 1¼ cups (10 fl oz/310 ml) of the beer. The batter should be the consistency of pourable pancake batter. Add more beer or some water, if necessary, to achieve the proper consistency.

Preheat the oven to 200°F (95°C). Pour the oil to a depth of 2 inches (5 cm) into a deep, heavy saucepan and heat to 375°F (190°C) on a deep-frying thermometer. Meanwhile, place the remaining 1 cup (5 oz/160 g) flour in a shallow bowl. Dip the fish into the flour to coat it completely, tapping off any excess, then dip the flour-coated fish into the batter.

FOR THE GARLIC SAUCE

6 oz (185 g) coarse country bread, crusts removed

½ cup (2 oz/60 g) walnuts

2 tablespoons white wine vinegar

½ cup (4 fl oz/125 ml) olive oil

3 tablespoons mayonnaise

3 large cloves garlic, minced

Salt and ground pepper

2¼ cups (11½ oz/360 g) all-purpose (plain) flour

1 teaspoon baking powder

Salt and ground pepper

1½ cups (12 fl oz/375 ml) beer, at room temperature

Deep-frying savvy

For perfectly crisp, golden fish, use a deep-frying thermometer and make sure the temperature stays between 350°F (180°C) and 375°F (190°C). If the oil is cooler than that, the fish pieces will absorb the oil; if the oil is hotter, the batter will cook before the fish does.

214

Canola or peanut oil
for deep-frying

2 lb (1 kg) rock cod or
halibut fillets, skinned
and cut into 1½-inch
(4-cm) pieces

Lemon wedges for garnish

MAKES 6 SERVINGS

Working in batches, add the battered fish to the oil and fry until golden and crispy, 1–2 minutes. Using a slotted spoon, transfer to paper towels to drain. Keep the fish warm in the oven until all the fish is cooked.

Transfer the fish to a warmed platter and garnish with lemon wedges. Pass the sauce at the table and serve right away.

English-style fish and chips

Enjoy this dish as they do in Britain: Use cod instead of rock cod, omit the sauce, and accompany the fish with malt vinegar. Serve with French Fries (page 367).

SWORDFISH AND SUGAR SNAP STIR-FRY

Swordfish is a firm, meaty fish that lends itself well to stir-frying. For this dish, it is combined with sugar snap peas and carrots in a lime sauce. You can also use halibut here, and snow peas (mangetouts) can be substituted for the sugar snap peas.

⅓ cup (3 fl oz/80 ml)
fresh lime juice

1 clove garlic, minced

1 tablespoon finely
chopped fresh cilantro
(fresh coriander)

Dash of Chile Oil (page 27)

2 teaspoons prepared
lemon or lime marmalade

Salt

1 egg white

1 tablespoon sake

2 teaspoons soy sauce

1 tablespoon cornstarch
(cornflour)

1 lb (500 g) swordfish
fillets, each about ¾ inch
(2 cm) thick

4 tablespoons (2 fl oz/
60 ml) peanut or canola oil

2 green (spring) onions,
including tender green
tops, finely chopped

1 teaspoon minced
fresh ginger

¼ lb (125 g) sugar
snap peas

2 small carrots, peeled and
cut into thin strips 2 inches
(5 cm) long and ¼ inch
(6 mm) wide

MAKES 2 OR 3 SERVINGS

In a small bowl, combine the lime juice, garlic, cilantro, chili oil, marmalade, and ¼ teaspoon salt in a small bowl and stir well to make a sauce. Set aside.

In another bowl, stir together the egg white, sake, soy sauce, and cornstarch until blended to make a marinade.

Skin the swordfish and then cut it into ¾-inch (2-cm) pieces. Add the swordfish pieces to the bowl with the marinade and toss gently to coat. Set aside.

In a wok or frying pan over high heat, warm 2 tablespoons of the oil, swirling to coat the bottom and sides of the pan. When the oil is hot but not quite smoking, add the green onions, ginger, sugar snap peas, and carrots and cook, stirring and tossing, until the vegetables are tender-crisp, 2–3 minutes. Transfer to a dish.

Add the remaining 2 tablespoons oil to the pan over high heat, again swirling to coat the pan. When the oil is hot but not quite smoking, add the swordfish and stir and toss gently until firm and opaque throughout when pierced with a knife, 2–3 minutes. Return the vegetables to the pan and stir and toss gently once or twice, cooking for about 30 seconds.

Quickly stir the reserved sauce and add it to the pan. Stir and toss to combine and heat through, about 1 minute longer. Taste and adjust the seasoning, then transfer to a warmed platter and serve right away.

Stir-frying savvy

When stir-frying, have all your ingredients prepped and near the stove before you begin, as the cooking goes quickly. Be sure to distribute the fish evenly in the pan so it comes into maximum contact with the heat and cooks evenly.

215

BAKED SHRIMP WITH FRESH HERBS

**Shrimp
vs. prawns**

*What cooks in the
United States call
shrimp are often
called prawns
elsewhere in the
English-speaking
world. In the United
States, the term
prawn is applied
only to extra-large
shrimp. But true
prawns are actually
either a type of
freshwater shrimp
or certain miniature
members of the
lobster family.*

True shrimp lovers prefer them cooked simply, so their delicate flavor can be enjoyed. Here butterflied shrimp are sprinkled with herbs and shallots and drizzled with olive oil, then baked briefly until pink. Serve them with lemon wedges and crusty bread for sopping up the juices.

Oil a large, shallow baking dish with some of the oil. Arrange the shrimp in the dish in a single layer, tails upward. In a small bowl, stir together the thyme, parsley, and shallots and sprinkle over the shrimp. Season with salt and pepper. Drizzle with the remaining olive oil. Cover with plastic wrap and let marinate at cool room temperature for 30 minutes or in the refrigerator for up to several hours. If refrigerated, bring to room temperature before baking.

Preheat the oven to 400°F (200°C). Bake until the shrimp turn pink and the juices are bubbly, about 8 minutes.

Transfer to warmed individual plates and spoon the juices from the baking dish over the top. Serve right away.

3 tablespoons olive oil

2 lb (1 kg) large shrimp (prawns), peeled with the tail segments intact and deveined, then butterflied (see page 202)

1 tablespoon chopped fresh thyme or marjoram

2 tablespoons chopped fresh flat-leaf (Italian) parsley

2 shallots or cloves garlic, finely chopped

Salt and ground pepper

MAKES 4 SERVINGS

SIZZLING GARLIC SHRIMP WITH SHERRY

Pimentón

*Pimentón is a
Spanish paprika
made from peppers
(capsicums) dried
by smoking over
wood. It comes in
hot (picante), sweet
(dulce), and bitter-
sweet (agridulce)
varieties. Look
for pimentón at
specialty-foods
stores and Spanish
food purveyors.*

These succulent shrimp are tossed in a hot frying pan with olive oil and red pepper flakes, lightly glazed with sherry, then sprinkled with fresh parsley. Serve them piping hot in a *cazuela*, a traditional terra-cotta baking dish, with lots of crusty bread and a glass of good sherry.

In a large frying pan over medium-high heat, warm the oil. Add the garlic and red pepper flakes and cook, stirring, for 15 seconds. Add the shrimp and *pimentón* (if using) and cook, stirring, until the shrimp curl and turn pink, about 3 minutes.

Add the sherry to the pan and cook until the sherry is reduced by half, about 1 minute. Season with salt and pepper.

Transfer the shrimp and the juices to a serving dish and garnish with the parsley. Serve right away.

3 tablespoons extra-virgin olive oil

6 cloves garlic, thinly sliced

Pinch of red pepper flakes

1¼ lb (625 g) shrimp (prawns), peeled and deveined (see page 202)

½ teaspoon *pimentón*, optional

⅓ cup (3 fl oz/80 ml) dry sherry

Salt and ground pepper

1½ teaspoons chopped fresh flat-leaf (Italian) parsley

MAKES 6 SERVINGS

STUFFED SHRIMP WITH LEMON AND PARMESAN

This Italian-inspired bread crumb stuffing for jumbo shrimp can be embellished by adding 3 tablespoons thinly sliced oil-packed sun-dried tomatoes or sautéed sliced mushrooms or fennel. Accompany with leafy greens dressed with Lemon-Shallot Vinaigrette (page 374).

6 tablespoons (3 fl oz/ 90 ml) olive oil

¼ cup (1½ oz/45 g) minced yellow onion

3 cloves garlic, chopped

¾ cup (1½ oz/45 g) fresh bread crumbs

¼ cup (2 oz/60 g) rinsed capers

⅓ cup (1½ oz/45 g) grated Parmesan cheese

1½ teaspoons grated lemon zest

1½ tablespoons chopped fresh flat-leaf (Italian) parsley

1 egg, lightly beaten

Salt and ground pepper

⅓ cup (3 fl oz/80 ml) extra-virgin olive oil

3 tablespoons fresh lemon juice

½ teaspoon chopped fresh oregano

½ teaspoon chopped fresh thyme

18 jumbo shrimp (prawns), peeled and deveined with the tail segments intact (see page 202)

Lemon wedges for garnish

MAKES 6 SERVINGS

In a frying pan over medium heat, warm 4 tablespoons (2 fl oz/60 ml) of the olive oil. Add the onion to the pan and sauté, stirring, until soft, about 7 minutes. Add the garlic and sauté for 2 minutes. Reduce the heat to low, add the bread crumbs, and stir for 30 seconds. Transfer to a bowl. Add the capers, cheese, 1 teaspoon of the lemon zest, 1 tablespoon of the parsley, and the egg. Mix well and season with salt and pepper.

To make the dressing, in a bowl, whisk together the extra-virgin olive oil, lemon juice, the remaining ½ teaspoon lemon zest, the oregano, thyme, and the remaining ½ tablespoon parsley. Season with salt and pepper. Set aside.

Starting at the tail end, cut a pocket along the inside edge of each shrimp, stopping just short of the head end. Press as much filling as possible into the pocket of each shrimp. Cover and refrigerate until ready to cook.

Preheat the broiler (grill). Oil a broiler pan.

Brush the shrimp evenly with the remaining 2 tablespoons olive oil. Arrange in a single layer on the prepared pan. Broil (grill), turning once, until the shrimp is pink and firm to the touch, 2–2½ minutes on each side.

Transfer to a warmed platter and drizzle with the dressing. Garnish with the lemon wedges and serve right away.

Head-on shrimp

If you find shrimp with their heads still on, buy them. Even if you don't eat the heads, which some consider a delicacy, they contribute flavor to a dish. If desired, cut or pull off the heads just before serving.

TANDOORI SHRIMP

About skewers

Bamboo skewers are inexpensive, come in a variety of lengths, and, unlike metal, cool quickly when they are removed from the grill. Soaking the skewers in water before loading them lessens their tendency to burn.

You don't need a special oven to make tasty tandoori-style dishes. It's the seasoning that counts. Here, shrimp are marinated in yogurt and Indian spices, then skewered and cooked on a hot grill. You can also cook them in a preheated broiler (grill).

In a food processor or blender, combine the garlic, ginger, lemon juice, cumin, salt, turmeric, chiles, yogurt, and paprika. Process until well blended. Transfer to a bowl, add the shrimp, and toss to coat evenly. Cover and refrigerate for about 1 hour.

Prepare a charcoal or gas grill for direct-heat cooking over medium-high heat (see page 18). At the same time, soak 12 bamboo skewers in water to cover.

Drain the skewers, then remove the shrimp from the marinade. Holding 2 skewers parallel to each other, and holding the shrimp flat, thread 4 or 5 shrimp onto the pair of skewers, piercing near the head of each shrimp with 1 skewer and near the tail with the other. (Parallel skewers make turning the shrimp on the grill easier.) Repeat with the remaining shrimp and skewers.

Place the threaded skewers on the oiled grill rack and grill for 2–3 minutes. Turn the shrimp and grill until they turn pink and are opaque, 2–3 minutes longer.

Transfer the skewers to a warmed platter or individual plates. Garnish with lemon wedges and serve right away.

2 cloves garlic, chopped

2-inch (5-cm) piece fresh ginger, chopped

3 tablespoons fresh lemon or lime juice

1 tablespoon ground cumin

½ teaspoon salt

¼ teaspoon ground turmeric

2 jalapeño chiles, seeded, if desired, and chopped

1 cup (8 oz/250 g) nonfat plain yogurt

1 tablespoon paprika

1½ lb (750 g) large shrimp (prawns), peeled and deveined (see page 202)

Lemon or lime wedges for garnish

MAKES 6 SERVINGS

GRILLED SHRIMP AND SAUSAGE WITH RED RICE

Salting shrimp

To improve the texture and flavor of shrimp that have been frozen, combine them in a bowl with enough salt to coat evenly and let stand for 1 minute. Rinse, repeat, then rinse again and pat dry before using.

This robust dish combines grilled shrimp and sausages with rice and green onions, all tossed together in a savory red pepper purée. The shrimp are first treated to a tangy marinade of apricot preserves thinned on the stove top with olive oil, lemon juice, and mustard.

In a saucepan over medium heat, combine the apricot preserves, oil, lemon juice, and mustard. Bring to a boil, then immediately pour into a bowl and let cool. Add the shrimp, cover, and refrigerate for 3 hours. Remove the shrimp from the refrigerator 20 minutes before grilling.

In a saucepan over medium-high heat, combine the rice and 2⅔ cups (21 fl oz/660 ml) water and bring to a boil. Reduce the heat to low, cover, and cook until the water is absorbed and the rice is tender, about 18 minutes. Keep warm.

Meanwhile, in a large saucepan over medium-low heat, melt the butter. Add the white parts of the green onions and sauté until softened, about 2 minutes. Stir in the bell peppers, chili powder, ½ teaspoon salt, and the broth. Cover and cook until the peppers are soft, 3–4 minutes. Transfer to a blender and process until smooth. Return to the pan; set aside.

½ cup (6 oz/185 g) apricot preserves

2 tablespoons olive oil

2 teaspoons fresh lemon juice

2 teaspoons Dijon mustard

16 large shrimp (prawns), peeled and deveined (see page 202)

1⅓ cups (10 oz/315 g) long-grain white rice

2 tablespoons unsalted butter

4 green (spring) onions, white parts and tender green tops chopped separately

2 large red bell peppers (capsicums), roasted and peeled (see page 333), then chopped

2 teaspoons chili powder

Salt

¼ cup (2 fl oz/60 ml) chicken broth

½ cup (4 fl oz/125 ml) dry white wine

4 sweet Italian sausages, about ¾ lb (375 g) total weight

1 tablespoon chopped fresh flat-leaf (Italian) parsley

MAKES 4 SERVINGS

Prepare a charcoal or gas grill for direct-heat cooking over medium-high heat (see page 18). At the same time, soak 3 or 4 bamboo skewers in water to cover.

In a frying pan over high heat, bring the wine to a boil. Reduce the heat to medium, add the sausages in a single layer, and cook, turning once, for 4 minutes total. Transfer to the oiled grill rack. Cover the grill and open the vents halfway. Cook, turning once, until cooked through, about 5 minutes total. Remove from the grill.

Meanwhile, remove the shrimp from the marinade and discard the marinade. Skewer the shrimp, passing a skewer through each shrimp twice, once near the head and once near the tail. Place the skewers on the grill rack and grill, uncovered, turning once, until they turn pink and are opaque, 3–4 minutes on each side.

Slide the shrimp from the skewers. Slice the sausages, add to the red pepper purée, and place over medium-low heat. Stir in the rice, shrimp, and green onion tops until evenly warmed through. Transfer to a warmed serving bowl, sprinkle with the parsley, and serve right away.

GRILLED COCONUT-LIME SHRIMP

These shrimp are marinated in rum, honey, lime, and coconut, and then skewered with lime slices and onion wedges and grilled until the outside is golden and crisp. If too much of the coconut and lime zest stays behind in the marinade, spoon it over the skewers before grilling.

½ cup (2 oz/60 g) unsweetened flaked dried coconut

½ cup (4 fl oz/125 ml) milk

¼ cup (2 fl oz/60 ml) golden rum

1 tablespoon honey

Zest and juice of 2 limes

24 extra-large shrimp (prawns), peeled and deveined (see page 202)

1 red onion, cut into ¾-inch (2-cm) wedges

2 tablespoons olive oil

½ teaspoon chopped fresh tarragon

Steamed white rice for serving

MAKES 4 SERVINGS

In a food processor, combine the coconut, milk, rum, and honey. Process until the coconut is finely chopped but not puréed. Transfer to a large bowl, then stir in the lime zest, lime juice, and the shrimp and mix well. Cover and let marinate in the refrigerator for 45 minutes. Remove from the refrigerator 20 minutes before grilling.

Meanwhile, in a bowl, stir together the onion, olive oil, and tarragon. Cover and set aside.

Prepare a charcoal or gas grill for direct-heat cooking over medium-high heat (see page 18). At the same time, soak 6–8 bamboo skewers in water to cover

Remove the shrimp from the marinade, allowing as much marinade as possible to cling to the shrimp. Pass a skewer through each shrimp twice, once near the head and once near the tail. Alternate the shrimp with the onion wedges.

Place the skewers on the oiled grill rack and grill, turning once, until the shrimp are crisp on the outside and opaque throughout, 4–5 minutes on each side.

Remove the shrimp and onion from the skewers and arrange on a warmed platter. Serve right away with the steamed rice.

Dress it up

For a more formal presentation, butterfly the shrimp (see page 202) before marinating. Grill the shrimp in a lightly oiled hinged grill basket to prevent them from slipping through the grill rack into the fire.

SESAME-CRUSTED SCALLOPS

Sesame products

As a garnish or a coating, sesame seeds add rich, nutty flavor to foods. They are also pressed into two types of oil. The light-colored oil, from raw seeds, has a subtle flavor, popular for dressings. The darker oil, from toasted seeds, has a potent flavor and is used sparingly in Asian dishes. Sesame products spoil easily; store them in the refrigerator.

Sea scallops develop a lightly crisped, tasty exterior when they are dredged in flour and egg, coated in sesame seeds, and cooked in a little butter. You can also use peeled large shrimp (prawns), or a combination of the two. Serve with braised Asian greens.

Place the flour in a bowl. In another bowl, whisk the eggs. In a third bowl, stir together the sesame seeds, 1 teaspoon salt, and ¼ teaspoon pepper.

Working with a few at a time, dip the scallops into the flour to coat evenly, tapping off any excess. Dip the scallops into the egg, and then finally into the sesame seeds, turning to coat the scallops completely.

In a large frying pan over medium heat, melt the butter. Add the scallops and cook, turning once, until golden on both sides and just opaque in the center, 3–4 minutes total, depending on the thickness of the scallops.

Transfer to a warmed platter and serve right away.

½ cup (2½ oz/75 g) all-purpose (plain) flour

3 eggs

2 cups (8 oz/250 g) sesame seeds

Kosher salt and ground pepper

1½ lb (750 g) sea scallops

3 tablespoons unsalted butter

MAKES 4–6 SERVINGS

SAUTÉED SCALLOPS AND FENNEL

Contrasting textures

For scallops with a more delicate texture, poach them gently for 2–3 minutes in the wine after the ginger is added, transfer them to a plate, and then reduce the wine. The softness of the shellfish will create a textural counterpoint to the crispness of the fennel.

Sea scallops have an inherently succulent, sweet nature. Here, that quality is enhanced by the orange, shallots, and ginger that flavor both the scallops and the sautéed fennel. Serve over saffron-scented rice sprinkled with clippings of the delicate fennel fronds.

Cut off the stems and feathery tops and any bruised outer stalks from the fennel bulbs. Coarsely chop enough of the feathery fronds to yield ¼ cup (⅓ oz/10 g) and set aside. Core the fennel bulbs and thinly slice crosswise or lengthwise.

In a frying pan over medium heat, melt 1 tablespoon of the butter. Add the sliced fennel bulb and sauté, turning often and gradually adding the broth, until the fennel is tender and most of the broth is absorbed, about 10 minutes. Remove from the heat and set aside.

In a large frying pan over high heat, melt 1 tablespoon of the butter. Add the scallops and cook, turning once, until pale gold on both sides, but still quite soft, 2–3 minutes total. Transfer the scallops to a plate.

In the same pan over medium heat, melt 1 tablespoon of the butter. Add the shallots and sauté until softened, about 5 minutes. Add the orange zest, ginger, and wine and cook until the liquid is reduced by half, 5–8 minutes. Return the fennel and scallops to the pan and warm through quickly. Stir in the remaining 1 tablespoon butter, if desired.

Transfer to a warmed serving dish and sprinkle with the chopped fennel fronds. Serve right away.

2 fennel bulbs

3–4 tablespoons unsalted butter

1 cup (8 fl oz/250 ml) fish or chicken broth

2 lb (1 kg) sea scallops

2 shallots, minced

1 tablespoon grated orange zest

1 teaspoon grated fresh ginger

1 cup (8 fl oz/250 ml) dry white wine or vermouth

MAKES 6 SERVINGS

SCALLOPS WITH APPLE-ONION MARMALADE

Pan-seared scallops on a savory mixture of apples and onions, topped with crumbled bacon, is guaranteed to impress dinner guests. And yet they're simple to prepare. Buy the largest sea scallops available. You can make the marmalade up to 3 days in advance.

FOR THE MARMALADE

¼ cup (2 fl oz/60 ml) olive oil

2 large Vidalia or other sweet onions, cut into thin wedges

2 large Golden Delicious apples, peeled, halved, cored, and cut into thin wedges

½ teaspoon cumin seeds

2 teaspoons cider vinegar, or more to taste

Salt and ground pepper

6 slices thick-cut lean bacon

18 large sea scallops, about 1½ lb (750 g) total weight, patted dry

Salt and ground pepper

1 cup (8 fl oz/250 ml) apple cider

MAKES 4–6 SERVINGS

To make the marmalade, in a large nonreactive frying pan over medium heat, warm the oil. Add the onions and cook, stirring often, until softened, about 15 minutes. Stir in the apples and cumin seeds. Cook, stirring, until the onions are golden and the apples soften, about 30 minutes longer. Add the vinegar, ¾ teaspoon salt, and a few grinds of pepper, stir well, and remove from the heat. You should have about 3 cups (scant 2 lb/1 kg).

In another large frying pan over medium-high heat, fry the bacon until crisp, 3–5 minutes. Transfer to paper towels to drain. Discard all but about 1 tablespoon (a light coating) of the drippings from the pan.

Sprinkle the scallops lightly with salt and pepper. Return the frying pan to medium-high heat. When the pan is hot, add the scallops, a few at a time, and cook, turning once, until lightly browned on both sides, about 1 minute on each side. Transfer to a plate and keep warm while you cook the remaining scallops. When all the scallops are cooked, add the apple cider to the pan and boil until reduced by half, about 5 minutes. Pour any juices that have collected on the scallop plate into the frying pan and heat through. Remove from the heat and keep warm.

Meanwhile, reheat the marmalade over medium-low heat until heated through. Spread about ½ cup (5 oz/155 g) of the marmalade on each individual plate. Top the marmalade on each plate with 3 scallops, then drizzle with about 1 tablespoon of the pan sauce. Crumble the bacon over the scallops, dividing it evenly. Serve right away.

Nonreactive pans

When cooking with acidic ingredients, such as lemon juice, vinegar, and wine, avoid pans made from materials that will react with the acid, such as cast iron, unlined copper, or nonanodized aluminum. Instead, use pans made from such materials as enameled cast iron, stainless steel, or tempered glass. Otherwise, the dish may suffer from an off taste or color.

SCALLOPS AND ASPARAGUS WITH ORANGE DRESSING

Caramelizing scallops

Pan searing— cooking quickly in a frying pan over high heat—gives scallops a pleasing browned exterior that caramelizes the natural juices, accenting the sweetness of the meat.

For this dish, sea scallops are halved and sautéed briefly in olive oil, then tossed with asparagus in a sprightly dressing of orange, ginger, and sesame oil. Serve as a first course for 6 or accompany with steamed jasmine rice for a full meal.

To make the dressing, in a bowl, whisk together the orange zest and juice, ginger, vinegar, sesame oil, and 4 tablespoons (2 fl oz/60 ml) of the olive oil. Season with salt and pepper.

Bring a saucepan three-fourths full of salted water to a boil. Meanwhile, trim off the tough ends of the asparagus and then cut on the diagonal into 1½-inch (4-cm) lengths. When the water is boiling, add the asparagus and cook until tender-crisp, about 5 minutes. Drain and set aside.

In a frying pan over high heat, warm 1 tablespoon of the olive oil. Add half of the scallops and sauté, stirring occasionally, until almost firm to the touch, 2–3 minutes. Season with salt and pepper. Transfer to a plate. Cook the remaining scallops the same way, using the remaining 1 tablespoon olive oil.

Return the first batch of scallops to the pan, along with the dressing and asparagus. Warm gently, stirring occasionally, for 1 minute. Transfer to a warmed platter and garnish with the sesame seeds. Serve right away.

1 teaspoon grated orange zest

Juice of ½ orange

½ teaspoon grated fresh ginger

3 tablespoons balsamic vinegar

½ teaspoon Asian sesame oil

6 tablespoons (3 fl oz/ 90 ml) olive oil

Salt and ground pepper

1 lb (500 g) asparagus

1½ lb (750 g) sea scallops, cut horizontally into slices ½ inch (12 mm) thick

1 tablespoon sesame seeds, toasted (see page 17)

MAKES 4–6 SERVINGS

BROILED OYSTERS WITH HERBED BREAD CRUMBS

The flavor of an oyster

Water-filtering oysters take on the flavor of their environment, so they are often named after their place of origin. In general, colder waters yield a firmer texture and sharper, saltier flavor, and warmer waters create a milder, softer oyster.

This is a popular dish wherever fresh oysters are available. The topping can be varied with the addition of 3 tablespoons chopped wilted spinach, green (spring) onion, fennel bulb, or fresh mushrooms. Serve the oysters piping hot, accompanied with lemon wedges.

Shuck the oysters (see page 203), reserving their liquor in a bowl. Place the oysters in their bottom shells on a baking sheet. Cover the oysters and the bowl of liquor separately and refrigerate.

Preheat the oven to 450°F (230°C).

In a frying pan over medium heat, melt 4 tablespoons (2 oz/ 60 g) of the butter. Add the shallots and sauté, stirring, until soft, about 8 minutes. Add the garlic and continue to sauté for 1 minute. Add the bread crumbs, parsley, chives, oregano, and thyme and sauté, stirring occasionally, until the bread crumbs are lightly golden, about 10 minutes. Add the reserved oyster liquor, the clam juice, and 2 teaspoons of the lemon juice and mix well. Remove from the heat. Season with salt and pepper and more lemon juice, if needed. The mixture should be slightly moist.

36 oysters in the shell, well scrubbed

6 tablespoons (3 oz/90 g) unsalted butter

4 large shallots, minced

1 clove garlic, minced

2½ cups (5 oz/155 g) fresh bread crumbs

2 tablespoons chopped fresh flat-leaf (Italian) parsley

1 tablespoon chopped fresh chives

½ teaspoon chopped fresh oregano

**½ teaspoon chopped
fresh thyme**

**2 tablespoons bottled
clam juice**

**2–3 teaspoons fresh
lemon juice**

Salt and ground pepper

MAKES 6 SERVINGS

Spoon the topping onto the oysters, dividing it evenly. In a small saucepan or frying pan, melt the remaining 2 tablespoons butter. Drizzle the butter evenly over the topping. Bake the oysters until very hot, about 6 minutes. Remove from the oven.

Preheat the broiler (grill). When it's hot, broil (grill) the oysters until the topping is a light golden brown and crisp, 1–2 minutes. Serve right away.

PARCHMENT-BAKED OYSTERS

Cooking seafood in parchment pouches traps the juices, which steams the ingredients and creates a natural sauce. Cut open the packets before serving, or place them on individual plates for guests to snip open at the table. Be careful, as the escaping steam will be hot.

**½ small red onion, cut
into ¼-in (6-mm) dice**

**1 red bell pepper
(capsicum), roasted and
peeled (see page 333),
then diced**

**10 large radishes,
thinly sliced**

**¼ cup (⅓ oz/10 g) finely
chopped fresh chives**

**¼ cup (⅓ oz/10 g)
chopped fresh flat-leaf
(Italian) parsley**

Salt and ground pepper

**1 teaspoon fresh
orange juice**

**½ teaspoon grated
orange zest**

**¼ teaspoon saffron
threads, steeped in
1 teaspoon hot water**

**4 tablespoons (2 oz/60 g)
unsalted butter, at
room temperature, plus
2 tablespoons, melted**

**24 oysters, freshly
shucked (see page 203)**

MAKES 4 SERVINGS

Preheat the broiler (grill).

In a small bowl, combine the onion with water to cover. Let stand for 5 minutes, then drain. Add the bell pepper, radishes, chives, and parsley to the bowl with the onion. Season with salt and pepper and mix well. Set aside.

In another small bowl, mash together the orange juice and zest, saffron and water, and the room-temperature butter. Season with salt and pepper.

Preheat the oven to 400°F (200°C). Cut out 6 heart shapes from parchment (baking) paper, each 12 inches (30 cm) long and 12 inches (30 cm) wide at its widest point. Brush the hearts on one side with the melted butter. Place 4 oysters on the right half of each heart. Top the oysters with equal amounts of the vegetable mixture. Season with salt and pepper. Dot each portion equally with the saffron-orange butter. Fold the other half of each heart over the filling, and crease the edges together securely so the juices will not escape. Wrap each packet in aluminum foil and place on rimmed baking sheets.

Bake until the packets have puffed noticeably, 6–10 minutes. Remove from the oven and cut open the top of each packet (see note, above). Serve right away.

**Steamed fish
in parchment**

Using this same buttered parchment method, place 1 sole or snapper fillet on each heart. Season with salt and pepper, strew with thinly sliced fennel and carrot, and sprinkle with chopped fresh herbs and 1 tsp dry white wine. Seal and bake until puffed and browned, about 9 minutes.

223

SPANISH CLAMS WITH TOMATOES AND HERBS

Clam juice

Bottled clam juice, the strained liquid of shucked clams, has a refreshing briny flavor. A good substitute for fish stock, it is often used as a cooking liquid in seafood dishes. Look for it near the seafood counter at the supermarket or on a shelf at the fishmonger's.

Spanish cooks have long paired briny yet sweet fresh clams with tart tomatoes. To add a smoky-spicy flavor, cook 1 ounce (30 g) fully cooked Spanish-style chorizo, cut into small dice, with the onion. Mussels can be substituted for the clams.

In a frying pan over medium heat, warm 2 tablespoons of the oil. Add the onion and sauté, stirring, until the onion begins to turn golden, 12–15 minutes. Add the tomatoes and tomato paste to the pan and sauté, stirring occasionally, until the mixture is thickened, 5–6 minutes. Add the wine and cook until reduced by half, about 5 minutes. Add the clam juice, raise the heat to high, and cook until thickened, about 5 minutes. Remove from the heat and let cool slightly. Transfer to a blender and process until smooth. Season with salt and pepper. Set aside.

In a frying pan large enough to hold the clams in a single layer, warm the remaining 2 tablespoons oil over high heat. Add the garlic, parsley, and clams. Cover and cook, shaking the pan occasionally, until the clams open, 3–5 minutes. Discard any that failed to open.

Using a slotted spoon, transfer the clams to a plate and keep warm. Add the reserved tomato mixture to the pan over high heat, bring to a boil, and boil until reduced by one-fourth. Return the clams to the pan and mix well.

Transfer to a warmed platter and serve right away.

4 tablespoons (2 fl oz/ 60 ml) olive oil

1 yellow onion, chopped

¾ cup (4½ oz/140 g) peeled, seeded, and chopped tomatoes

1 tablespoon tomato paste

½ cup (4 fl oz/125 ml) dry white wine

1 cup (8 fl oz/250 ml) bottled clam juice

Salt and ground pepper

1 large clove garlic, minced

2 tablespoons chopped fresh flat-leaf (Italian) parsley

2 lb (1 kg) clams, well scrubbed

MAKES 4–6 SERVINGS

STEAMED CLAMS WITH WHITE WINE AND GARLIC

Sopping up the sauce

When serving steamed mollusks, or any dish with a flavorful broth or abundant sauce, offer slices of crusty French or Italian bread for soaking up every last delicious drop.

Here, clams are steamed in white wine, garlic, and parsley, a classic French preparation. If desired, accompany the mollusks with hot fettuccine or linguine tossed in some of the cooking juices. You can substitute mussels for the clams; they will cook a minute or two faster.

In a saucepan over medium-high heat, combine the wine, garlic, shallot, bay leaf, and half of the minced parsley. Bring to a simmer and cook for 1 minute. Add the clams, cover tightly, and cook, shaking the pan occasionally, until the clams open, 3–5 minutes.

Uncover and discard any clams that failed to open. Cut the butter into small pieces, add to the pan, and toss lightly. Using a slotted spoon, transfer the clams to a large bowl, discarding the bay leaf. Pour the pan juices over them and top with the remaining parsley. Serve right away.

1 cup (8 fl oz/250 ml) dry white wine

1 clove garlic, minced

1 large shallot, minced

1 bay leaf

2 heaping tablespoons minced fresh flat-leaf (Italian) parsley

2 lb (1 kg) littleneck clams, well scrubbed

1½ tablespoons unsalted butter

MAKES 4–6 SERVINGS

KETTLE-SEARED GARLIC-PEPPER MUSSELS

This Vietnamese-style dish infuses fresh mussels with intense flavors of garlic, pepper, and fish sauce. A cast-iron pot, the ideal cooking vessel, gets very hot, cooking the mussels quickly and heightening the flavors of the seasonings. You can also use a wok or Dutch oven.

2 tablespoons canola oil

6 cloves garlic, chopped

2 shallots, thinly sliced

½ teaspoon coarse sea salt

2 lb (1 kg) mussels, scrubbed and debearded

2 tablespoons *each* sugar and Asian fish sauce

Coarsely ground pepper

1 red jalapeño chile, seeded and finely diced

Fresh cilantro (fresh coriander) sprigs for garnish

MAKES 4–6 SERVINGS

Warm a 3-qt (3-l) cast-iron kettle over medium-high heat. When hot, add the oil, garlic, shallots, and salt and sauté until golden brown, about 1 minute. Raise the heat to high, add the mussels, and toss to coat with the oil. Add the sugar, fish sauce, and 1 teaspoon pepper and stir to combine.

Reduce the heat to medium-high, cover, and cook until the mussels open, 3–5 minutes. Discard any that failed to open. The sauce should be the consistency of a light syrup. If the sauce is too thin, using a slotted spoon, transfer the mussels to a plate. Raise the heat to high and cook the sauce, stirring frequently, until reduced, 3–5 minutes. Return the mussels to the kettle and toss to coat.

Garnish the mussels with the chile and cilantro sprigs and serve right away.

Serving mussels

For a more formal supper, set out a small seafood fork at each place setting. At a more casual meal, your guests can also use an empty mussel shell as a pair of pincers to pick the meats from the shells. Show diners this trick at the table. Set out a large bowl for the empty shells.

225

MUSSELS WITH FETA AND TOMATOES

This Greek meze combines mussels with a robust mixture of chopped tomatoes, white wine, oregano, and feta cheese. The dish can also be made with other shellfish, such as clams, shrimp (prawns), or scallops. Accompany it with the tomato-rubbed grilled bread on page 65.

2 tablespoons olive oil

1 yellow onion, minced

2 cups (12 oz/375 g) peeled, seeded, and chopped tomatoes

1 cup (8 fl oz/250 ml) dry white wine

¼ teaspoon dried oregano

Pinch of red pepper flakes

1 teaspoon wine vinegar

2 lb (1 kg) mussels, well scrubbed and debearded

6 oz (185 g) feta cheese

Salt and ground pepper

1 tablespoon coarsely chopped fresh flat-leaf (Italian) parsley

MAKES 4–6 SERVINGS

In a large frying pan over medium heat, warm the oil. Add the onion and cook, stirring occasionally, until soft, about 7 minutes. Raise the heat to high and add the tomatoes, wine, oregano, red pepper flakes, and vinegar. Stir well and bring to a boil. Reduce the heat to low and simmer uncovered, stirring occasionally, until thick, 20–30 minutes.

Add the mussels and cook until they open, 3–5 minutes. Using tongs, transfer the mussels to a bowl, discarding any that failed to open. Remove the pan from the heat.

When the mussels are just cool enough to handle, remove the meats and return them to the pan; discard the shells. Crumble the cheese into the pan and return to medium heat. Simmer until the mussels are heated through and the cheese is softened, about 30 seconds. Season with salt and pepper and scatter the parsley over the top.

Transfer to a warmed platter and serve right away.

Seafood with cheese

Feta and shellfish (particularly mussels or shrimp) are a popular combination all over Greece. The tangy cheese complements the briny seafood. Here, the sweetness of onion and tomatoes helps bring the elements into balance.

LOBSTER AND FAVA BEAN SALAD

**Storing
live lobsters**

*Store live lobsters
in the refrigerator
surrounded by
damp newspaper
or seaweed (ask
for the latter from
the fishmonger)
in an open bag, so
they can breathe.*

Fresh fava beans and chunks of lobster meat are tossed with romaine and an orange-garlic vinaigrette for this simple yet special salad. You can also substitute 1 pound (500 g) asparagus or green bean pieces for the favas, simmered in water until tender-crisp, about 5 minutes.

Follow the instructions on page 201 for cooking and cleaning the lobsters. Cut the tail and claw meat into ½-inch (12-mm) dice, reserving the body meat for another use, and place in a large salad bowl. Set aside.

Shell the fava beans. Have ready a bowl of ice water. Bring a saucepan three-fourths full of water to a boil. Add the favas and boil for 2 minutes. Drain, transfer to the ice water to stop the cooking, then drain again. To peel each bean, pinch open the end opposite the end that connected the bean to the pod; the bean will slip easily from its skin.

Add the fava beans to the salad bowl. Cut or tear the lettuce into bite-size pieces and add to the bowl.

In a bowl, whisk together the orange juice, vinegar, orange zest, oil, garlic, and parsley. Season with salt and pepper.

Add the dressing to the salad and toss well. Serve right away.

2 lobsters, about
1¼ lb (625 g) each

4 lb (2 kg) fava (broad) beans

1 head romaine
(cos) lettuce

¼ cup (2 fl oz/60 ml)
fresh orange juice

1 tablespoon
balsamic vinegar

½ teaspoon finely
grated orange zest

½ cup (4 fl oz/125 ml)
extra-virgin olive oil

1 clove garlic, minced

2 tablespoons
chopped fresh flat-leaf
(Italian) parsley

Salt and ground pepper

MAKES 6 SERVINGS

ROAST LOBSTER WITH COGNAC–HERB BUTTER

Flambéing safety

*When using a gas
stove, always pour
alcohol into the pan
well away from the
heat. The flame can
follow the alcohol
into the bottle and
cause it to burst.
Keep your hair,
sleeves, and face
away from the
pan as you ignite
the alcohol.*

Lobster doesn't have to be reserved for special occasions—a simple preparation can make any meal feel like a celebration. Here halved lobsters are roasted in the oven and then served with an impressive butter-and-Cognac dipping sauce.

Preheat the oven to 425°F (220°C). Line 2 rimmed baking sheets with aluminum foil. Arrange the lobster halves, split sides up, on the prepared sheets. Squeeze half of the lemon wedges over the lobsters and drizzle with the 1 tablespoon Cognac. Sprinkle with the tarragon, then brush with the melted butter.

Roast the lobsters until the claw and tail meat is opaque, 14–16 minutes. Transfer the lobsters to warmed large individual plates and cover to keep warm.

Pour the ¼ cup Cognac into the still-hot baking sheets and deglaze them, stirring to dislodge any browned bits from the pan bottoms, then pour the liquid from both pans into a small frying pan. Place over high heat. Using a long match, carefully ignite the Cognac, then gently tilt the pan back and forth until the flames subside and only a few tablespoons of

4 lobsters, halved and
cleaned (see page 201)

2 lemons, cut into wedges

¼ cup (2 fl oz/60 ml) plus
1 tablespoon Cognac

Leaves from 3 or 4 fresh
tarragon sprigs, minced

2 tablespoons unsalted
butter, melted, plus
6 tablespoons (3 oz/90 g)

Ground pepper

About ⅓ cup (⅓ oz/10 g)
minced mixed fresh herbs

MAKES 4 SERVINGS

liquid remain. Working quickly, whisk the 6 tablespoons butter, 1 tablespoon at a time, into the pan juices until the mixture becomes a creamy sauce. Season with pepper and the mixed herbs, reserving 1 tablespoon of the herbs for garnish. Taste and adjust the seasoning.

Spoon the butter sauce into 4 small ramekins and set a ramekin on each plate alongside the lobster. Scatter the reserved herbs over the lobsters. Pass the rest of the lemon wedges at the table.

GRILLED LOBSTER WITH CITRUS BUTTER

If you are using a charcoal grill, dousing the embers with water gives these grilled lobsters a pleasantly smoky flavor. If you like, garnish with citrus wedges and sprigs of flat-leaf (Italian) parsley. Provide lobster crackers or nutcrackers for cracking the heavy claws.

6 live lobsters, 1½ lb (750 g) each

½ cup (4 oz/125 g) plus 2 tablespoons unsalted butter, at room temperature

¼ teaspoon grated lemon zest

¼ teaspoon grated lime zest

¼ teaspoon grated orange zest

2 tablespoons chopped fresh flat-leaf (Italian) parsley

½ teaspoon dried herbes de Provence

Salt and ground pepper

MAKES 6 SERVINGS

Bring a large pot of water to a full boil. Working with two at a time, drop the lobsters in headfirst, taking care to avoid any splashing. Once the water returns to a boil, reduce the heat to maintain a gentle simmer. Boil until the shells turn red, about 4 minutes. Using tongs, remove the lobsters and place under cold running water to halt the cooking.

Prepare a charcoal or gas grill for direct-heat cooking over medium-high heat (see page 18).

To ready each lobster for the grill, halve and clean it as directed on page 201.

In a small saucepan over medium heat, melt the butter. Stir in the lemon, lime, and orange zests, the parsley, and herbes de Provence, and season with salt and pepper. Remove from the heat and keep warm.

Place the lobsters on the grill rack, cut sides up. Cover the grill and cook for 2 minutes. If you are using a charcoal grill, pour ½ cup (4 fl oz/125 ml) water over the coals to create smoke and continue to cook, covered, for 2 minutes. Remove the cover and drizzle the lobsters with half of the citrus butter. Re-cover and cook until the meat is almost firm to the touch, about 2 minutes.

Transfer the lobsters, cut sides up, to a platter and drizzle with the remaining citrus butter. Serve right away.

227

CRACKED DUNGENESS CRAB WITH TWO SAUCES

**Keeping
the leftovers**

*Freshly cooked
crabmeat will keep
in the refrigerator
for up to 2 days. If
the cooked crabmeat
has been frozen and
thawed, eat it on
the day you buy it.
Frozen crab will keep
in the freezer for
4 months; thaw it
in the refrigerator
before using.*

Here, sweet Dungeness crab is served with a pair of flavorful dipping sauces. To save time, buy freshly cooked and cracked crabs at your local fishmonger. Blue or stone crabs can be used if Dungeness crabs are unavailable; adjust the cooking time as necessary.

To make the tangerine butter, in a small saucepan over medium heat, melt the butter. Stir in the tangerine zest and juice, and the mustard and season with salt and pepper. Immediately remove from the heat and let stand for 1 hour before serving to blend the flavors.

To make the vinaigrette, in a small bowl, whisk together the lemon juice, garlic, and oil, and season with salt and pepper. Stir in the dill and green onions until well mixed. Set aside.

Bring a large pot of water to a full boil. Carefully add the crabs to the boiling water. When the water returns to a boil, reduce the heat to maintain a gentle simmer. Simmer until just cooked through, 8–10 minutes. Follow the instructions on page 201 to crack and clean the crabs.

When ready to serve, reheat the tangerine butter over medium heat, whisking constantly. Pour into a small bowl. Arrange the crab on a platter. Serve right away with the tangerine butter and dill vinaigrette.

FOR THE TANGERINE BUTTER

¾ cup (6 oz/185 g) unsalted butter

½ teaspoon grated tangerine zest

3 tablespoons fresh tangerine juice

1 tablespoon Dijon mustard

Salt and ground pepper

FOR THE DILL VINAIGRETTE

¼ cup (2 fl oz/60 ml) fresh lemon juice

1 clove garlic, minced

½ cup (4 fl oz/125 ml) extra-virgin olive oil

Salt and ground pepper

2 tablespoons chopped fresh dill

2 green (spring) onions, including tender green tops, thinly sliced

Salt

3 live Dungeness crabs, 2–2½ lb (1–1.25 kg) each

MAKES 6 SERVINGS

228

CRAB CAKES WITH AVOCADO SALSA

Jalapeño and cayenne season these plump crab cakes, which are paired with a lively avocado-tomatillo salsa. Only a small amount of bread crumbs is mixed into the crab cake mixture, so don't skip the chilling time or the cakes will fall apart when you cook them.

2 lb (1 kg) cooked lump crabmeat

½ cup (1½ oz/45 g) minced green (spring) onions, including tender green tops

½ cup (4 oz/125 g) minced red bell pepper (capsicum)

½ cup (4 fl oz/125 ml) mayonnaise

3 egg yolks, lightly beaten

1 tablespoon minced jalapeño chile, or to taste

½ teaspoon cayenne pepper

Salt and ground black pepper

2 cups (4 oz/120 g) fresh bread crumbs

⅓ cup (3 fl oz/80 ml) canola oil

Avocado-Tomatillo Salsa (page 392)

MAKES 4–8 SERVINGS

Pick over the crabmeat for shell fragments, then break the meat into large flakes. In a bowl, combine the flaked crabmeat, green onions, bell pepper, mayonnaise, egg yolks, jalapeño chile, and cayenne pepper. Season with salt and black pepper and mix well. Add ½ cup (1 oz/30 g) of the bread crumbs and mix again.

In a small sauté pan, fry about 1 tablespoon of the mixture in a little oil, then taste and adjust the seasoning. Place the remaining 1½ cups (3 oz/90 g) crumbs on a plate. Line a rimmed baking sheet with plastic wrap.

Form the crab mixture into 8 cakes, each ½ inch (12 mm) thick. Coat evenly with the bread crumbs, then place on the lined baking sheet. Cover with plastic wrap and refrigerate until firm, at least 3 hours or up to 6 hours.

Just before serving, in a large sauté pan over medium-high heat, warm the oil. Working in batches, add the crab cakes and sauté, turning once, until golden brown on both sides, about 4 minutes on each side. Transfer to paper towels to drain briefly and keep warm until all the cakes are cooked.

Serve right away on warmed individual plates. Pass the salsa in a bowl at the table.

Serving crab cakes

The crab cakes can be topped with Garlic Mayonnaise or Tartar Sauce (page 386) in place of the salsa. For an elegant presentation, serve them atop mixed greens dressed with Vinaigrette (page 374).

229

SOFT-SHELL CRABS WITH CHILE SAUCE

About soft-shell crabs

Soft-shell crabs, immature crabs that have shed their hard shell, have a short season. Look for them in stores from the spring to early autumn and cook them right away. They are meant to be eaten whole, soft shell and all.

In this signature Singaporean dish, soft-shell crabs are sautéed, then bathed in a rich, sweet, tangy red chile sauce. To speed preparation, ask the fishmonger to clean the crabs. Accompany with steamed rice or chunks of French bread to sop up the sauce.

To make the sauce, in a blender, combine the garlic, chiles, ginger, and just enough water to facilitate blending. Process until a smooth paste forms.

Warm a wok or large frying pan over medium heat. Add the oil, stir in the paste mixture, and cook until fragrant and creamy, about 1 minute. Stir in the tomato paste, Sriracha sauce, soy sauce, sugar, and broth. Quickly restir the cornstarch mixture, add to the pan, and cook, stirring constantly, until the sauce thickens, about 30 seconds. Add the lime juice, then crack the egg into the wok and cook, without stirring, until it begins to set, about 2 minutes. Fold the egg into the sauce; do not overmix. Specks of egg should be visible throughout the sauce. Remove from the heat, cover, and keep warm.

To clean each crab, place it on its back and twist or cut off the small, triangular apron-shaped shell flap. Turn the crab, lift up the shell, and, using your fingers or kitchen scissors, remove and discard any gray gills. Using the scissors, cut off the eyes and mouth. Scoop out the soft matter just inside this cut and discard. Rinse the crabs and pat dry.

Dust the crabs with the cornstarch, tapping off any excess. In a large frying pan over medium-high heat, warm the oil. Add the crabs and fry, turning once, until browned and crisp, about 3 minutes on each side. Season with salt and pepper.

Reheat the sauce gently over low heat, add the crabs, and turn to coat evenly. Transfer to a warmed platter, garnish with the green onions and cilantro, and serve right away.

FOR THE CHILE SAUCE

4 cloves garlic, chopped

4 red jalapeño chiles, halved and seeded

1½-inch (4-cm) piece fresh ginger, coarsely chopped

2 tablespoons peanut or corn oil

¼ cup (2 oz/60 g) tomato paste or ketchup

1 tablespoon Sriracha sauce or sweet chile sauce

1 tablespoon soy sauce

1 tablespoon firmly packed brown sugar

1 cup (8 fl oz/250 ml) chicken broth

1 tablespoon cornstarch (cornflour) mixed with 3 tablespoons water

1 tablespoon fresh lime juice

1 extra-large egg

6 soft-shell crabs, about ¼ lb (125 g) each

¼ cup (1 oz/30 g) cornstarch (cornflour)

3 tablespoons peanut or corn oil

Salt and ground pepper

2 green (spring) onions, including tender green tops, chopped

6 fresh cilantro (fresh coriander) sprigs

MAKES 2 OR 3 SERVINGS

PAELLA

Although originally from Valencia, paella has spread all around Spain's coastline and inland, with every region boasting its own version. Here is a fairly traditional recipe that combines chicken, chorizo, shrimp, and clams with saffron-and-tomato-infused rice.

1½ tablespoons finely minced garlic

1½ tablespoons dried oregano

Salt and coarsely ground pepper

3 tablespoons red wine vinegar

5 tablespoons (2½ fl oz/ 75 ml) extra-virgin olive oil

4 small bone-in, skin-on chicken thighs

4 small bone-in, skin-on chicken breast halves

½ teaspoon saffron threads

¼ cup (2 fl oz/60 ml) dry white wine

6 oz (185 g) chorizo sausages

6 tablespoons (3 fl oz/ 90 ml) olive oil

2 yellow onions, chopped

2–3 cups (12–18 oz/ 375–560 g) peeled, seeded, and chopped tomatoes

1 tablespoon minced garlic

1½ cups (10½ oz/330 g) short-grain white rice

4 cups (32 fl oz/1 l) Chicken Stock (page 23), or as needed

16 shrimp (prawns), peeled and deveined (see page 202)

1 cup (5 oz/155 g) shelled peas, blanched in boiling water for 1 minute and drained

24 clams, scrubbed

MAKES 4 SERVINGS

In a small bowl, stir together the garlic, oregano, 1 teaspoon salt, and 2 teaspoons pepper. Stir in the vinegar to form a paste, then stir in the extra-virgin olive oil. Rub the mixture on the chicken pieces and place in a shallow dish or bowl. Cover and refrigerate overnight.

Crumble the saffron into a small saucepan, add the wine, and bring to a simmer. Remove from the heat and let steep for 10 minutes.

In a frying pan over medium-high heat, sauté the sausages until golden brown, about 5 minutes. Cut into 1-inch (2.5-cm) chunks and set aside.

In a large, deep frying pan over medium-high heat, warm 3–4 tablespoons of the olive oil. Add the marinated chicken pieces and brown on all sides, about 10 minutes. Using tongs, transfer to a plate. Wipe out the pan. Add the remaining 2–3 tablespoons olive oil and place over medium heat. Add the onions and sauté until soft, about 10 minutes. Add the tomatoes and garlic and cook, stirring occasionally, until blended, about 5 minutes. Add the rice and stir until opaque, about 3 minutes. Raise the heat to high, add stock as needed to cover, and the saffron and wine. Bring to a boil, reduce the heat to low, and simmer, uncovered, until the rice is half cooked, about 10 minutes. Return the chicken to the pan and cook until most of the liquid has been absorbed, the chicken is cooked through, and the rice is tender, about 10 minutes longer. Stir in the shrimp, sausages, and peas during the final 5–8 minutes of cooking; the shrimp will be pink when ready.

Meanwhile, in a wide saucepan, pour water to a depth of 1 inch (2.5 cm). Add the clams, cover, and place over medium-high heat. Cook, shaking the pan occasionally, until the clams open, 3–5 minutes. Discard any that fail to open. Stir the clams and their pan juices into the paella.

Let stand for 10 minutes before serving.

Make it your own

Paella is infinitely variable. If you wish, mussels can be used here in place of the clams, and crayfish, squid, or monkfish would be a nice addition to the other ingredients.

Poultry

Poultry

From everyday dinners to festive occasions, poultry plays the lead in so many meals that it is often easy to take it for granted. But as the wealth of information and the wide range of recipes on the following pages illustrate, with only a little effort and imagination, chicken, turkey, and duck can play a starring role in any menu. Poultry dishes are often healthful choices, making them suitable for any day of the week.

Poultry Basics

The skin game
About one-third of the fat on any bird is in the skin. To remove the skin, grasp it firmly and pull, working from the thickest part of the meat toward the thinnest part. Use a paring knife to trim any excess as needed.

Pounding breast meat
To pound boneless breasts to uniform thickness, place a breast half between two sheets of plastic wrap. Using a flat meat pounder or small, heavy frying pan, and working from the center outward, pound lightly. A few glancing blows should do it.

On basting
Basting prevents meat from drying out, adds flavor, and promotes even browning. Use a brush, long-handled spoon, or bulb baster.

Storing poultry
Store fresh poultry in the coldest part of the refrigerator for up to 48 hours or in the freezer for up to 6 months. Thaw in the refrigerator, never at room temperature, allowing 3 to 4 hours per pound (500 g). It can also be thawed in a bowl of cool water (never warm), though this leads to a loss of juices and thus drier meat.

Cooking and serving poultry—whether a quick weeknight sauté or a roasted bird for the holidays—can be both simple and rewarding. Here are some tips and techniques to ensure your time in the kitchen goes smoothly.

BUYING POULTRY   Look for plump, evenly colored birds or parts with no signs of wrinkling or drying. Always check the sell-by date, which is calculated for industrial refrigeration cases. Some butcher shops, supermarkets, and natural-foods stores offer poultry labeled "free range" and/or "organic," which many shoppers favor over mass-produced chickens. A free-range bird has been raised in uncrowded conditions and allowed access to the outdoors. Organic poultry has enjoyed free-range conditions and has been fed a diet of organically grown feed.

In the past, whole chickens were classified by weight. Although it is more common to see just "chicken" on the label these days, you sometimes still see the following classifications in butcher shops and some cookbooks. A broiler-fryer weighs 2¾ to 4½ pounds (1.4 to 2.2 kg) and is small enough to cook through when broiled (grilled) or fried. A roasters is a 5 to 7 pound (2.5 to 3.5 kg) hen and is ideal for roasting due to its succulent flesh.

Turkeys that weigh more than 10 pounds (5 kg) will deliver the best taste; if you want a smaller option, a turkey breast or a capon is a better choice. Plan on ¾ pound (375 g) uncooked weight per person, increasing the amount if you want turkey meat for leftovers.

Ducks are usually sold frozen. When purchased, they should be solidly frozen, with no signs of thawing. If fresh ducks are available, look for smooth skin without discoloration. Duck breast is considered the finest part and often is sold separately. Whole duck legs (drumstick and thigh combination) can also be purchased separately.

PREPPING WHOLE BIRDS   If you are starting with a frozen bird, thaw it in the refrigerator (see note, left). Before roasting, remove the fresh or thawed bird from the refrigerator. Remove the package of giblets from the body or neck cavity, reserving the giblets or discarding them. Pat the bird dry, inside and out. Cut off any excess fat. Pluck any feathers missed in processing, using tweezers or needle-nose pliers if needed. Leave the bird on a baking sheet so it comes to room temperature: allow 30 minutes for most chickens or ducks, and up to 2 hours (but no longer) for a turkey.

STUFFING AND SEASONING   If stuffing a whole bird or bone-in breast, do so just before roasting. Start with freshly made, room-temperature stuffing and pack the cavities only three-fourths full, allowing room for expansion. If you are not stuffing the bird, sprinkle the cavities with salt and ground pepper and fill with aromatics such as lemon quarters, herb sprigs, or onion halves.

Whole birds and skin-on poultry parts can also be flavored under the skin with mixtures of fat and seasonings, such as compound butters (see page 246) or olive oil and herbs. Carefully ease your fingers between the skin and meat, taking care not to tear the skin. Then, rub the seasoning mixture evenly between them and pat the skin back into place.

TRUSSING Securing the legs and wings during roasting gives a bird a more uniform, compact appearance and ensures more even cooking.

To partially truss the bird: Tie a piece of kitchen string (also called butcher's twine) around the ends of the drumsticks to hold them in place; bend the wing tips backward and tuck them behind the shoulder areas.

To fully truss the bird: Tuck the wing tips behind the shoulder areas. Cut a long piece of kitchen string (five times the bird's length) and lay it across the work surface. Lay the bird breast side up, with the tail over the center point of the string. Lift the two ends of the string up, crisscrossing them above the tail and between the legs. Loop around the legs, crossing again beneath them and coming back together to the top. Tuck the tail into the cavity, pull the string to bring the legs together, and tie snugly. Bring the ends of the strings up toward the wings. Turn the bird breast side down, bringing each string end over a wing to meet in the back. Tuck the neck skin under the string and knot securely. Snip the loose ends of the string.

CUTTING UP A RAW CHICKEN When cutting up a chicken, you can use a heavy chef's knife, but a pair of poultry shears will make certain steps easier.

To cut a chicken into serving pieces: Cut the chicken into 2 wings, 2 breasts, 2 drumsticks, 2 thighs, and 1 back. (The back has little meat on it; freeze for making stock.) Place the chicken breast up, with drumsticks toward you. Pull one of the thighs away from the body, then make an incision to reveal the hip joint. Cut down through the joint to remove the entire leg (thigh and drumstick); repeat on the opposite side. On each leg, cut through the joint between the thigh and drumstick to separate them. Pull each wing away from the body, then make an incision to reveal the shoulder joint. Cut through the joint. Turn the chicken over. Cut along one side of the backbone, from the body cavity to the neck cavity. Repeat on the other side and remove the back. Slit the thin membrane covering the breastbone along its center. Bend the breast upward at the center to pop out the breastbone, then pull or cut it free and discard. Cut the breast lengthwise into halves.

To butterfly a chicken: Using poultry shears, cut down each side of the backbone and remove the backbone; freeze the backbone for making stock. Open up the chicken like a book and place it skin up. With the heel of your palm, press hard on the breastbone to break it and flatten the chicken.

CARVING Before carving any roasted bird, tent it with aluminum foil and let it rest at room temperature for at least 10 minutes to allow the juices to redistribute throughout the flesh. If the bird is trussed, snip the string at the knot and discard it.

Lay the bird breast up. Using a long, sharp knife, and a meat fork to hold the bird steady (don't insert the tines into the flesh), cut through the skin between the thigh and breast. Pull the leg away to locate the thigh joint, then cut through the joint. If desired, cut through the joint between the drumstick and thigh. Cut through the skin between the wing and breast and pull the wing away to locate the shoulder joint. Cut through the joint. To carve the breast, just above the thigh and wing joints, make a deep horizontal cut though the meat toward the bone, creating a base cut. Starting near the breastbone, carve long thin slices vertically, cutting downward toward the base cut.

JUDGING DONENESS

All poultry should be cooked to a minimum temperature of 165°F (74°C) to kill food-borne bacteria such as salmonella. Be careful not to overcook poultry or the meat will be dry. To test for doneness of whole birds, use a thermometer for absolute certainty. For small boneless and bone-in pieces, use your senses of touch and/or sight.

Whole birds
Insert an instant-read thermometer into the thickest part of a thigh, not touching any bones. It should register 170°F (77°C) for a chicken or duck, 180°F (82°C) for a turkey.

Stuffing
When baked in the cavity of a whole bird, stuffing should register 165°F (74°C) on an instant-read thermometer inserted into its center through the neck opening.

Boneless cuts
Press on the center with a fingertip. The meat should feel firm and spring back.

Bone-in cuts
Make an incision near the bone. The meat should appear opaque, with no sign of pink, and the juices should run clear.

POULTRY SAFETY

Poultry should never stand at room temperature for more than 2 hours. After handling raw poultry, thoroughly wash your hands and any surfaces and tools that came into contact with it. Always cook poultry until it tests done as described above.

BRINED ROASTED CHICKEN WITH WINE JUS

Using the giblets

The small package in the body cavity of most whole birds contains the giblets: the heart, gizzard, and liver. The heart and gizzard can be used to make gravy, stock, or soup. The liver, considered a delicacy by some, can be cooked separately. Giblets also make a nice addition to bread stuffings.

Brining in a bag

Poultry can be brined in a heavy-duty, 2-gallon (8-l) zippered plastic bag. Place the whole bird in the bag and add the brine. Press out the air from the bag and seal. Make sure the bird is completely submerged in the brine. Place in a large bowl for support.

Soaking poultry in brine before roasting adds moisture and enhances taste. Despite the saltiness of the brine, the result is not an overly salty bird, but rather increased juiciness and a fuller flavor. This brined and roasted chicken is served with a simple white-wine pan sauce.

In a bowl large enough to hold the chicken, add the salt to 1 qt (1 l) hot water and stir to dissolve. Add 3 qt (3 l) cold water and stir to mix. Submerge the chicken in the brine. Cover and refrigerate for at least 1 hour or preferably for 4 hours.

Preheat the oven to 400°F (200°C). Remove the chicken from the brine and pat dry thoroughly. Rub the outside with the butter, and season inside and out with pepper. Place the herb sprigs in the cavity.

Place the chicken on its side on a V-shaped rack in a roasting pan. Roast for 30 minutes. Turn the chicken on its other side and roast for 30 minutes longer. Turn the chicken on its back and place the onion, carrot, and celery in the cavity. Roast until an instant-read thermometer inserted into the thickest part of a thigh away from bone registers 170°F (77°C), about 45 minutes longer.

Remove from the oven. Insert a wooden spoon into the body cavity and tilt the chicken so the juices in the cavity flow into the pan. Transfer the chicken to a warmed platter. Tent with aluminum foil and let rest for 10 minutes.

Meanwhile, make the wine jus. Strain the pan juices into a bowl. Skim off any visible fat from the surface, then pour the juices back into the pan. Set the pan over 2 burners at medium-high heat. Add the wine and boil until reduced by half, about 1 minute. Add the broth and boil until the liquid is reduced to ½ cup (4 fl oz/125 ml), about 6 minutes. Remove from the heat and whisk in the butter. Season with salt and pepper. Pour the jus into a warmed sauceboat.

Carve the chicken and serve hot with the wine jus.

1 cup (8 oz/250 g) kosher salt or ½ cup (4 oz/125 g) iodized or plain table salt

1 roasting chicken, 6½ lb (3.25 kg), giblets removed

2 tablespoons unsalted butter, at room temperature

Ground pepper

4 fresh thyme sprigs

4 fresh rosemary sprigs

1 small yellow onion, coarsely chopped

1 small carrot, coarsely chopped

1 small celery stalk, coarsely chopped

FOR THE WINE JUS

½ cup (4 fl oz/125 ml) crisp, dry white wine

1 cup (8 fl oz/250 ml) chicken broth

1 tablespoon cold unsalted butter

Salt and ground pepper

MAKES 6–8 SERVINGS

ROSEMARY CHICKEN WITH POTATOES

On kitchen string

When trussing, be sure to use kitchen string, also called butcher's twine. Made from uncolored linen, it won't char or impart flavor or color to the poultry.

Here, potatoes roasted in the pan alongside a chicken absorb both the flavorful juices of the bird and the flavor of rosemary and thyme. If you like, add large chunks of carrot and small whole cipollini onions to the pan along with the potatoes.

Preheat the oven to 350°F (180°C).

Trim any visible fat from the chicken and pat it dry. Rub the chicken inside and out with the cut sides of the lemon halves. Place 2 of the rosemary sprigs along with the lemon halves in the body cavity. Truss the chicken (see page 235) and tuck 1 rosemary sprig under each wing. Place the chicken on its side in a roasting pan and surround with the potatoes.

1 chicken, about 3½ lb (1.75 kg), giblets removed

1 lemon, halved

6 fresh rosemary sprigs

4 russet potatoes, peeled and cut into 3-inch (7.5-cm) cubes

3 tablespoons
unsalted butter

3 tablespoons olive oil

2 teaspoons
dried rosemary

1 teaspoon dried thyme

½ cup (4 fl oz/125 ml)
chicken broth

Salt and ground pepper

MAKES 4 SERVINGS

In a small pan, melt the butter and stir in the oil. Brush the butter mixture evenly over the chicken and potatoes and then sprinkle with the dried rosemary and thyme.

Place the chicken in the oven and roast for 30 minutes. Turn the bird so it rests on its opposite side. Add the broth to the pan and baste the chicken with the pan juices. Roast for another 30 minutes. Turn the chicken breast side up, baste with the pan juices, and season with salt and pepper. Roast until an instant-read thermometer inserted into the thickest part of a thigh away from the bone registers 170°F (77°C), 20–30 minutes longer.

Transfer the chicken to a warmed platter and surround with the potatoes. Garnish with the remaining rosemary sprigs. Tent with aluminum foil and let rest for 10 minutes before carving. Serve the pan juices in a warmed bowl on the side.

Keeping food safe

To prevent cross-contamination and the transfer of odors, reserve separate cutting boards for different tasks. Mark each board on one edge, using a permanent marker in a color that corresponds to use: red for poultry, meats, and seafood; green for produce; and blue for dessert-related tasks.

GARLIC-ROASTED CHICKEN

Don't be alarmed by the large amount of garlic in this recipe, a version of a classic French braised dish. As the garlic roasts and enhances the flavor of the chicken, it turns mild and creamy, perfect for spreading on good crusty bread at the dinner table.

237

Simple roast chicken

To make a basic roast chicken, follow the recipe at left but omit the garlic. Instead of olive oil, rub the bird with 2 tbsp room-temperature butter before seasoning. Roast breast side up on an oiled rack in a roasting pan until the bird tests done.

4 fresh thyme sprigs

2 bay leaves

4 fresh rosemary sprigs

6 fresh sage leaves

1 chicken, 3–4 lb (1.5–2 kg), giblets removed

1 lemon, halved

Salt and freshly
ground pepper

½ cup (4 fl oz/125 ml)
olive oil

40 unpeeled cloves garlic

Chicken broth, if needed

MAKES 4 SERVINGS

Preheat the oven to 350°F (180°C).

Tie together half of the thyme sprigs, bay leaves, rosemary sprigs, and sage leaves with kitchen string. Repeat with the remaining herbs to make an identical bundle. Trim any visible fat from the chicken and pat it dry. Rub inside and out with the cut sides of the lemon halves. Sprinkle inside and out with salt and pepper. Place 1 herb bouquet inside the chicken along with the spent lemon halves.

In a Dutch oven over medium heat, warm the oil. Add the garlic cloves and sauté until they release their fragrance, about 3 minutes. Add the chicken, turn it in the scented oil, and position breast side up. Add the second herb bouquet to the pot and cover tightly. Place in the oven and cook until an instant-read thermometer inserted into the thickest part of a thigh away from the bone registers 170°F (77°C), 1–1½ hours.

Remove the chicken from the oven and transfer to a cutting board. Using a slotted spoon, transfer the garlic cloves to a small bowl and keep warm; discard the herb bouquets. Tent the chicken with aluminum foil and let rest for 10 minutes.

Carve the chicken and arrange on a warmed platter. Add a little broth to the pan juices if they seem scant, reheat, and season with salt and pepper. Drizzle the juices over the chicken. Serve right away with the garlic cloves on the side.

HERB-BASTED BROILED CHICKENS

Using leftovers

Leftover chicken is great to have on hand for quick meals during the week. Remove the meat from the bones and pack it in an airtight container. Store it in the refrigerator for up to 3 days.

The term *spring chicken* refers to small, young birds that are most often available in specialty markets. Here, they are rubbed with an herbed butter beneath their skin, and then broiled. Ready in less than half an hour, they make an easy main course for a weeknight supper.

Preheat the broiler (grill). Pat dry the chickens.

In a bowl, stir together the butter, parsley, chives, and tarragon until well mixed. Season with salt and pepper. Gently loosen the skin covering each breast half. Spread 1 tablespoon of the butter-herb mixture over the breast meat of each chicken half, then pat the skin back into place.

Melt the remaining butter-herb mixture. Brush some of it on both sides of the chicken halves and place the chicken, skin side down, on a rimmed baking sheet. Broil about 3 inches (7.5 cm) from the heat source for about 15 minutes.

Turn the chicken skin side up and brush with the remaining melted butter mixture and the pan juices. Broil until golden brown on the outside and an instant-read thermometer inserted into the thickest part of a thigh away from the bone registers 170°F (77°C), about 12 minutes longer.

Season with salt and pepper. Divide among warmed individual plates and serve right away.

2 young chickens, about 2 lb (1 kg) each, halved lengthwise, excess fat trimmed

½ cup (4 oz/125 g) unsalted butter, at room temperature

½ cup (¾ oz/20 g) chopped fresh flat-leaf (Italian) parsley

¼ cup (⅓ oz/10 g) chopped fresh chives

1 teaspoon dried tarragon

Salt and ground pepper

MAKES 4 SERVINGS

BACON-WRAPPED CORNISH HENS

About Cornish hens

Cornish hens are miniature hybrid chickens that usually weigh about 1½ lb (750 g) but can weigh as much as 2 lb (1 kg) or more. They are typically, though not always, a crossbreed of two types of poultry and are mostly white meat. Their small size makes them ideal for serving one or two people.

Because they are small, Cornish hens can dry easily out during cooking. But a couple of slices of blanched bacon tied around each bird will keep these grilled hens moist and succulent. Most supermarkets stock frozen Cornish hens and will order fresh ones for you on request.

Prepare a charcoal or gas grill for indirect-heat cooking over medium-high heat (page 18).

Bring a large saucepan two-thirds full of water to a boil over high heat. Add the bacon and blanch for 3 minutes. Drain, then rinse the bacon with cold water and pat dry. Set aside.

Pat the hens dry and sprinkle inside and out with salt and pepper. Tuck a few herb sprigs into each body cavity. Crisscross 2 slices of bacon across the breast of each hen. Using kitchen string, tie the bacon securely to the birds.

Place the hens, breast side up, on the oiled grill rack. Cover the grill and open the vents halfway. Cook for 30 minutes, then turn breast side down. Continue cooking in the covered grill until the birds are well browned and an instant-read thermometer inserted into the thickest part of a thigh registers 170°F (77°C), 20–25 minutes longer.

To serve, snip the strings and arrange the birds on a warmed platter or individual plates, with the bacon alongside.

8 slices thick-cut bacon

4 Cornish hens, about 1½ lb (750 g) each

Salt and ground pepper

4–8 fresh parsley sprigs

4–8 fresh thyme sprigs

MAKES 4 SERVINGS

CITRUS-MARINATED CORNISH HENS

This elegant dish of butterflied Cornish hens—marinated in citrus juice and jalapeño chile and then roasted until the skin nicely browned—is ideal for a festive lunch or dinner. Get a head start on the preparations and marinate the hens overnight.

4 Cornish hens, about
1½ lb (750 g) each,
butterflied (see page 235)

2 teaspoons finely
grated lemon zest

½ cup (4 fl oz/125 ml)
fresh lemon or lime juice

½ cup (4 fl oz/125 ml)
fresh orange juice

2 cloves garlic, minced

2 tablespoons minced
shallots or green (spring)
onions, white part only

2 jalapeño chiles,
seeded and minced

Salt

Canola oil for pan

10 fresh thyme or
rosemary sprigs,
plus more for garnish

MAKES 4 SERVINGS

Put the hens in a zippered heavy plastic bag and set aside.

To make the marinade, in a small bowl, stir together the lemon zest, lemon juice, orange juice, garlic, shallots, chiles, and ½ teaspoon salt. Reserve ¼ cup (2 fl oz/ 60 ml) of the marinade. Pour the remaining marinade into the plastic bag with the hens. Press the air from the bag and seal. Set in a bowl and refrigerate for at least 2 hours or up to overnight.

Preheat the oven to 425°F (220°C). Oil a roasting pan.

Remove the hens from the marinade and pat them dry. Discard the marinade. Place 5 of the herb sprigs in the prepared pan and put the hens, breast sides up, on top in a single layer, laying them flat. Tuck the remaining 5 herb sprigs around the hens.

Roast for 15 minutes. Brush the hens with some of the reserved marinade, then reduce the heat to 325°F (165°C). Roast for another 15 minutes and brush again with the marinade. Continue roasting until the skin is well browned and the juices run clear when a thigh joint is pierced, about 15 minutes longer.

Transfer the hens to a warmed platter or individual plates and spoon the pan juices over the top. Garnish with herb sprigs and serve right away.

**An alternative
to Cornish hens**

You can substitute poussins, young chickens that weigh 1 to 1½ lb (500 to 750 g), for the Cornish hens here. Their flavor is sometimes a little milder than that of the hens.

**Butterfly for
crisp skin**

A butterflied bird, that is, one that has been split down the backbone and flattened, cooks more quickly than an intact bird. Because more of its skin is exposed to the hot oven air, you end up with a particularly crisp finish.

FRIED CHICKEN WITH HERBS

An updated version of a traditional Sunday favorite, this chicken is marinated in buttermilk, then breaded, browned in oil, and finally baked to a crispy finish in a hot oven, rather than frying it in oil from start to finish. Accompany with mashed potatoes and corn on the cob.

Place the chicken pieces in a bowl with 1 cup (8 fl oz/250 ml) of the buttermilk. Cover and refrigerate for at least 1 hour or up to 18 hours.

Preheat the oven to 400°F (200°C).

In a shallow bowl, beat the egg with a fork until blended, then beat in the remaining ½ cup (4 fl oz/125 ml) buttermilk. On a plate, mix together the flour, bread crumbs, garlic, basil, marjoram, paprika, 1 teaspoon salt, and ½ teaspoon pepper.

Using tongs, lift the chicken pieces one at a time from the buttermilk, and dip first into the flour mixture, coating evenly, and then into the egg mixture. Dip each piece again into the flour mixture and set aside on a rimmed baking sheet. When all the chicken pieces are coated, refrigerate them for 15 minutes.

Pour oil to a depth of 1 inch (2.5 cm) into a large, deep frying pan and heat to 350°F (180°C) on a deep-frying thermometer, or until the corner of a piece of chicken dipped into the hot oil sizzles immediately upon contact. Working in batches to avoid crowding, fry the chicken pieces, turning as needed, until well browned on all sides, about 10 minutes total for each batch. As soon as the pieces are browned, transfer them to a clean rimmed baking sheet.

When all of the pieces are browned, place in the oven and bake until opaque throughout and the juices run clear when an incision is made near the bone, 20–30 minutes. The timing will depend on the pieces; breasts will take the shorter time, thighs and drumsticks the longer. As soon as the quicker-cooking pieces are done, transfer them to a plate.

Arrange all the pieces on a platter and serve warm or at room temperature, garnished with the parsley.

1 chicken, 3½–4 lb (1.75–2 kg), cut into serving pieces (page 235)

1½ cups (12 fl oz/375 ml) buttermilk

1 egg

¾ cup (4 oz/125 g) all-purpose (plain) flour

¾ cup (3 oz/90 g) fine dried bread crumbs

2 cloves garlic, minced

1 tablespoon *each* finely chopped fresh basil and marjoram

1 teaspoon paprika

Salt and ground pepper

Canola oil for frying

2 tablespoons chopped fresh flat-leaf (Italian) parsley

MAKES 4 SERVINGS

"BARBECUED" CHICKEN

Grilled chicken coated with a tangy, tomato-based sauce is a summertime favorite. In this version, the chicken is rubbed with a mild ancho chile paste, grilled, and basted with barbecue sauce. Serve with corn on the cob, your favorite potato salad, and baked beans.

In a small heatproof bowl, combine the ancho chile and boiling water. When the chile has softened, about 20 minutes, drain, reserving ¼ cup (2 fl oz/60 ml) of the liquid.

In a food processor or blender, combine the softened ancho, the reserved liquid, and the oil. Process until a thick, smooth

1 ancho chile, seeded and cut into pieces

1 cup (8 fl oz/250 ml) boiling water

1 tablespoon olive oil

2 chickens, about
3½ lb (1.75 kg) each,
cut into serving
pieces (see page 235)

Basic Barbecue Sauce
(page 376), heated

MAKES 6 SERVINGS

paste forms. Rub the chicken with the paste, cover, and refrigerate for at least 2 hours or up to 24 hours. Remove from the refrigerator 30 minutes before grilling.

Prepare a charcoal or gas grill for direct-heat cooking over medium heat (see page 18).

Place the drumsticks and thighs on the oiled grill rack. Cover the grill and open the vents halfway. Cook, turning once, until browned, about 7 minutes on each side. Move to the cooler outer edges of the rack and place the breasts and wings in the center. Cover and cook until browned, about 8 minutes. Turn over all the pieces and continue to cook until the juices run clear when a thigh is pierced near the bone, about 8 minutes longer.

Transfer ½ cup (4 fl oz/120 ml) of the heated barbecue sauce to a small serving bowl. Brush the chicken with half of the reserved barbecue sauce. Turn over the chicken and brush with the remaining sauce. Continue to grill uncovered, turning once, until crisp, about 2 minutes on each side.

Transfer to a platter and serve warm. Pass the remaining sauce at the table.

Mild or hot

Ancho chiles—dried poblano peppers— have a sweet, earthy flavor with just a touch of heat, making for a mild marinade. For more bite, add ½ teaspoon or more cayenne pepper to the marinade and marinate the chicken overnight.

241

JAMAICAN-STYLE JERK CHICKEN

Jerk is a traditional Jamaican style of cooking that begins with rubbing meat or poultry with a pastelike marinade of chile, lime juice, herbs, and spices. The meat is then grilled slowly so the marinade forms a coating that seals in the juices. It's a great dish for spicy food lovers.

8–10 jalapeño chiles,
halved and seeded

¼ cup (2 fl oz/60 ml)
fresh lime juice

¼ cup (⅓ oz/10 g) chopped
fresh rosemary, plus sprigs
for garnish

2 tablespoons fresh
thyme leaves

2 tablespoons
mustard seeds

2 tablespoons
Dijon mustard

½ yellow onion,
cut into chunks

2 large cloves garlic

Salt

4–5 lb (2–2.5 kg)
chicken pieces

MAKES 4–6 SERVINGS

To make the marinade, in a blender or food processor, combine the chiles, lime juice, chopped rosemary, thyme, mustard seeds, Dijon mustard, onion, garlic, and 1 teaspoon salt. Process to a thick, smooth paste. Scrape into a small bowl, cover, and refrigerate for about 2 hours or up to 2 days.

Pat the chicken pieces dry. Rub with the marinade, coating them completely, and place them in a single layer in 1 or 2 shallow baking dishes. Cover with plastic wrap and refrigerate for at least 2 hours or up to 24 hours.

Prepare a charcoal or gas grill for indirect-heat cooking over medium heat (see page 18).

Place the chicken, skin side down, on the oiled grill rack. Cover the grill and open the vents slightly less than halfway. Cook slowly, turning the chicken every 15 minutes, until opaque throughout and the juices run clear when a thigh joint is pierced, about 45 minutes.

To serve, transfer to a warmed platter or individual plates, garnish with the rosemary sprigs, and serve right away.

Scotch bonnet chiles

For an even spicier, more authentic jerk, substitute 2–3 Scotch bonnet chiles for the jalapeños. Typically 1 to 1½ inches (2.5 to 4 cm) long and yellow or orange, the Scotch bonnet is one of the hottest chiles on the planet, but in addition to the fire, it has a wonderful citrusy-floral flavor.

COQ AU VIN

Coq au vin (literally "cock with wine") is a rustic Burgundian dish of chicken simmered in red wine with mushrooms and pearl onions. Pinot Noir would be the authentic choice, but you can use any good-quality dry red wine. Pour the same wine varietal at the table.

Soaking up the sauce

Like all braised dishes, coq au vin yields a generous quantity of sauce. If you like, serve with an accompaniment that will absorb the savory cooking liquid, such as egg noodles or boiled potatoes.

Trim any visible fat from the chicken quarters and pat them dry. Spread the flour on a plate and season with salt, pepper, and nutmeg. Dip the chicken pieces in the seasoned flour, coating evenly and shaking off the excess. Set aside.

In a large frying pan over high heat, warm 2 tablespoons each of the butter and oil. Working in batches to avoid crowding, add the chicken pieces and brown on all sides, about 15 minutes per batch. As the pieces are browned, transfer them to a Dutch oven or other heavy pot. When all the pieces have been browned, pour the brandy over them and ignite with a long match. Let the flames die out, then add the wine, garlic, thyme, and bay leaf. Bring to a boil over medium-high heat, cover, reduce the heat to low, and cook gently until opaque throughout when pierced with a knife, about 45 minutes.

Meanwhile, in a large frying pan over high heat, warm 2 tablespoons of the butter and the remaining 2 tablespoons oil. Add the mushrooms and sauté until golden, 6–8 minutes. Transfer to a plate and rinse out the pan.

Bring a saucepan three-fourths full of water to a boil. Add the pearl onions and boil for 2–3 minutes. Drain, then cut off the root ends and slip off the skins. Cut a shallow cross in the root ends. Return the onions to the saucepan, add water just to cover, and bring to a boil. Reduce the heat to low, cover partially, and cook until the onions are tender but firm, 10–15 minutes. Drain well.

Return the frying pan to high heat and melt the remaining 2 tablespoons butter. Add the onions and sugar and sauté until the onions are lightly caramelized, 4–5 minutes. Remove from the heat.

About 10 minutes before the chicken is done, add the mushrooms and onions to the pan and continue cooking as directed. Taste and adjust the seasoning.

Transfer the chicken and onions to a warmed platter, sprinkle with the parsley, and serve right away.

1 chicken, 4–5 lb (2–2.5 kg), cut into serving pieces (page 235)

½ cup (2½ oz/75 g) all-purpose (plain) flour

Salt and ground pepper

Freshly grated nutmeg

6 tablespoons (3 oz/90 g) unsalted butter

4 tablespoons (2 fl oz/ 60 ml) olive oil

3 tablespoons brandy, warmed

2 cups (16 fl oz/500 ml) dry red wine

2 cloves garlic

2 fresh thyme sprigs

1 bay leaf

24 fresh cremini or white button mushrooms, stem ends trimmed

16 pearl onions

2 teaspoons sugar

3–4 tablespoons chopped fresh flat-leaf (Italian) parsley

MAKES 4 SERVINGS

BAKED CHICKEN WITH ARTICHOKES

This family-style dish features a whole chicken that is cut into serving pieces and baked with shallots and baby artichokes in a tangy broth until the skin is crisp and golden brown. You can buy a whole chicken and cut it up yourself, or you can buy it already cut into serving pieces.

10 baby artichokes, about 1 lb (500 g) total weight, trimmed (see page 332) and halved lengthwise

6 tablespoons (3 fl oz/ 90 ml) fresh lemon juice

1 chicken, 3½–4 lb (1.75–2 kg), cut into serving pieces (see page 235)

1 tablespoon unsalted butter

1 tablespoon olive oil

8 fresh sage leaves

2 large shallots, chopped

¼ cup (2 fl oz/60 ml) dry white wine or water

Salt and ground pepper

1 lemon

MAKES 4 SERVINGS

Preheat the oven to 425°F (220°C).

Bring a large saucepan half full of water to a boil over high heat. Add the artichokes and 3 tablespoons of the lemon juice, reduce the heat to medium-high, and cook, uncovered, until the artichokes are almost tender when pierced with a small knife, 5–6 minutes. Drain and set aside.

Trim any excess fat from the chicken pieces. Cut each breast half crosswise into 2 pieces. Cut off the wing tips and discard.

In a large sauté pan over medium-high heat, melt the butter with the oil. Working in batches to avoid crowding, add the chicken pieces and sauté, turning once, until lightly browned on both sides, 4–5 minutes on each side. Using tongs, transfer to a baking pan, skin side down. Tuck 4 of the sage leaves under the chicken.

Reduce the heat under the sauté pan to medium-low and add the shallots. Sauté gently until translucent, 2–3 minutes. Pour in the wine and deglaze the pan, stirring to dislodge any browned bits from the pan bottom. Bring to a boil and pour over the chicken. Sprinkle with 1½ tablespoons of the lemon juice. Season with salt and pepper.

Bake for 20 minutes, basting several times with the pan juices. Turn the chicken skin side up, add the artichoke halves, and continue to bake, basting occasionally, until the chicken and artichokes are tender and the juices run clear when a thigh is pierced, 20–30 minutes longer.

Using tongs or a slotted spoon, transfer the chicken and artichokes to a warmed serving dish. If necessary, place the pan over high heat to thicken the juices. Add the remaining 1½ tablespoons lemon juice and season with salt and pepper. Pour the juices over the chicken. Holding the lemon over the serving dish, grate the zest directly onto the chicken pieces. Garnish with the remaining sage leaves and serve right away.

Using sage

A favorite of Italian cooks, soft, gray-green sage leaves are sweet and aromatic. Used fresh or dried, they deliver a distinctive woodsy aroma and mildly peppery flavor that nicely complement poultry. Sage is also wonderful paired with pork and sweet vegetables, such as sweet potatoes or winter squash.

243

CHICKEN WITH SAGE AND PROSCIUTTO

**With onion
and apple**

*For a different flavor
using the same
technique, substitute
1 thin yellow onion
slice for each slice
of prosciutto, and
2 or 3 thin tart
apple slices for
each sage leaf.*

This is an easy recipe to double for a large crowd. The scent of sage permeates the chicken hot from the oven. Any leftovers are delicious served cold the next day, when the distinctive flavor of the prosciutto predominates. Serve with Oven-Baked Brown Rice (page 302).

Preheat the oven to 400°F (200°C)

Pat the chicken pieces thoroughly dry. Trim the excess fat from the prosciutto, then cut each slice to the dimensions of one of the chicken pieces.

Carefully slide your fingers under the skin on each chicken piece, separating it from the meat but leaving it attached on one side. Place a slice of prosciutto directly on the meat and top it with a sage leaf. Carefully pull the skin back in place, and press gently with your palm to secure it.

Arrange the chicken pieces in 1 or 2 shallow baking dishes or in a roasting pan large enough to hold the pieces in a single layer. Brush the skin with the olive oil, and season generously with salt and pepper.

Roast until the chicken skin is crisp and deep golden brown and the juices run clear when a thigh is pierced at the thickest part, about 55 minutes. Remove from the oven and let rest for 10 minutes before serving.

Transfer the chicken pieces to a warmed platter and garnish with sage sprigs. Serve right away.

**3 chickens, 3½–4 lb
(1.75–2 kg) each, cut into
serving pieces (page 235)**

18 thin slices prosciutto

**18 fresh sage leaves,
plus sprigs for garnish**

1½–2 tablespoons olive oil

**Coarse sea salt and
ground pepper**

MAKES 10–12 SERVINGS

CHICKEN WITH LEMON-GARLIC SAUCE

Fruity wines

*A wine described
as fruity means that
when you taste it,
the flavor of fruit is
the most pronounced
perception. These
wines are not
necessarily sweet,
but their fruitiness
outweighs any oak
flavors or spicy
characteristics. For
whites, try a dry
Riesling or Chenin
Blanc. For reds, Pinot
Noir and Gamay are
good choices.*

These chicken breasts make a refreshing dinner on a hot summer's night. In addition to the lemony pan sauce, the chicken is topped with a mixture of lemon zest, parsley, and garlic, reminiscent of the *gremolata* that traditionally tops Milan's famed Osso Buco (page 278).

Spread the flour on a plate, then lightly coat both sides of each chicken breast with the flour, shaking off the excess. Finely chop 2 or 3 garlic cloves and set aside. Mince 1 or 2 additional cloves. In a small bowl, stir together the minced garlic, parsley, and lemon zest.

In a frying pan over high heat, warm the oil. Add the chicken to the pan and sauté, turning once, until lightly browned, about 2 minutes on each side. Transfer to a platter, season with salt and pepper, and set aside.

Pour off all but 2 tablespoons of the fat from the pan. Add the finely chopped garlic to the pan and sauté over high heat until softened, about 20 seconds. Add the broth, lemon juice, and white wine, bring to a boil, and deglaze the pan, stirring to dislodge any browned bits from the pan bottom. Boil until slightly reduced, about 3 minutes.

**2 tablespoons all-purpose
(plain) flour**

**4 skinless, boneless
chicken breast halves,
about ½ lb (250 g) each**

3–5 cloves garlic

**⅓ cup (½ oz/15 g)
chopped fresh flat-leaf
(Italian) parsley**

**1 tablespoon finely
chopped lemon zest**

2 tablespoons olive oil

Salt and ground pepper

**¾ cup (6 fl oz/180 ml)
chicken broth**

½ cup (4 fl oz/125 ml) fresh lemon juice

½ cup (4 fl oz/125 ml) fruity white wine (see note, left)

MAKES 4 SERVINGS

Return the chicken to the pan and reduce the heat to medium. Cook until the chicken is opaque throughout and the juices run clear when pierced in the thickest part, about 10 minutes. Using tongs, transfer to a warmed platter.

Raise the heat to high and boil the pan sauce until reduced to about ¼ cup (2 fl oz/60 ml), about 5 minutes. Pour evenly over the chicken and sprinkle the parsley-garlic mixture evenly over the top. Serve right away.

GRILLED TARRAGON–MUSTARD CHICKEN

A tangy tarragon-mustard marinade flavors these grilled whole chicken breasts. Cooking the whole breast helps to keep it juicy and makes for an attractive presentation. Carve the meat from the bone in thick slices on the diagonal, so that each slice has a grill-marked edge.

⅓ cup (3 fl oz/80 ml) dry white wine

2–3 tablespoons tarragon-flavored mustard

2 tablespoons extra-virgin olive oil

2 cloves garlic, minced

3 teaspoons finely chopped fresh tarragon

1 teaspoon sugar

Salt and ground pepper

2 whole chicken breasts, about 1 lb (500 g) each, skinned

MAKES 4 SERVINGS

In a small bowl, whisk together the wine, mustard, oil, garlic, 2 teaspoons of the tarragon, the sugar, and ¼ teaspoon each salt and pepper. Scoop out and reserve ¼ cup (2 fl oz/60 ml) of the mustard mixture. Place the chicken in a shallow baking dish. Pour the remaining mustard mixture evenly over the chicken, cover, and refrigerate, turning the chicken occasionally, for at least 1 hour or up to 4 hours. Remove from the refrigerator 20 minutes before grilling.

Prepare a charcoal or gas grill for indirect-heat cooking over medium heat (see page 18). Remove the chicken from the marinade and discard the marinade.

Place the chicken on the oiled grill rack directly over the fire. Grill, turning once, until seared on both sides with grill marks, about 2 minutes on each side.

Move the chicken pieces, skin side up, so they are not directly over the fire. Cover the grill, open the vents halfway, and cook, turning once or twice and basting occasionally with the reserved marinade, until the chicken is opaque throughout and the juices run clear when pierced in the thickest part, about 20 minutes.

Transfer to a warmed platter and let rest for 5 minutes. Carve into slices, and sprinkle with the remaining 1 teaspoon tarragon. Serve right away.

About chicken breasts

When purchasing chicken breasts, be wary of the labeling, which can be confusing. A whole breast consists of two lobes connected in the middle by the breastbone. A breast half is only one of the lobes. Many stores label boneless breast halves "breasts."

245

GRILLED CHICKEN TERIYAKI

Dress it up

For a pretty look, garnish the platter with 2 green (spring) onions, thinly sliced on the diagonal, and a sprinkling of both black and white sesame seeds.

Chicken takes on a beautiful mahogany finish when brushed with this Japanese-style glaze. The saltiness imparted by the soy sauce complements the smoky flavor from the fire. Using both mirin, a sweet rice cooking wine, and dry sake adds depth to the sauce.

Prepare a charcoal or gas grill for direct-heat cooking over medium-high heat (see page 18).

In a small saucepan over high heat, combine the soy sauce, mirin, sake, ginger, garlic, and brown sugar. Stir well and bring to a boil. Boil for 1 minute, then remove from the heat, pour into a shallow bowl, and let cool completely.

One at a time, place the chicken breasts between 2 sheets of plastic wrap and flatten with a meat pounder or small, heavy frying pan until an even ½ inch (12 mm) thick. Cover and refrigerate until needed.

About 15 minutes before the fire is ready, scoop out and reserve about ½ cup (4 fl oz/125 ml) of the soy mixture to use for basting. Then, place the chicken breasts in the remaining cooled soy mixture, coating evenly.

When the grill is ready, remove the chicken breasts from the soy mixture and place on the oiled grill rack. Discard any soy mixture remaining in the bowl. Grill, turning once and brushing with some of the reserved soy mixture, until the chicken feels firm and springs back to the touch, about 4 minutes on each side.

Transfer the chicken to a warmed platter, brush with the remaining reserved soy mixture, and serve right away.

½ cup (4 fl oz/125 ml) soy sauce

¼ cup (2 fl oz/60 ml) mirin

¼ cup (2 fl oz/60 ml) dry sake or dry sherry

1 tablespoon chopped fresh ginger

2 cloves garlic, minced

1 teaspoon firmly packed brown sugar

4 skinless, boneless chicken breast halves, about ½ lb (250 g) each

MAKES 4 SERVINGS

246

GRILLED CHICKEN WITH BLACK OLIVE BUTTER

More flavoring options

Rubbing a compound butter under the skin is an easy way to flavor chicken. To vary the taste, replace the olives in the recipe with Pesto (page 387), sun-dried tomato pesto, or whole-grain mustard.

Here's an unusual way to prepare and serve chicken breasts. Start with boneless breasts with the skin intact, rub black olive butter under the skin, then roll and tie each breast, forming logs. Once grilled, the logs are thickly sliced with a ring of crispy, flavorful skin around the outside.

In a small bowl, using a fork or wooden spoon, beat together the butter, olives, parsley, and lemon juice until blended. Season with pepper. Transfer half of the butter mixture to a sheet of plastic wrap and shape it into a log about 3 inches (7.5 cm) long and 1 inch (2.5 cm) in diameter. Wrap tightly and refrigerate until firm, at least 1 hour. Set the remaining butter mixture aside.

Prepare a charcoal or gas grill for indirect-heat cooking over medium heat (see page 18).

Working with 1 chicken breast at a time, gently slide your fingertips under the skin to loosen it. Divide the butter mixture into 3 equal portions and, using your fingertips, slip a portion

FOR THE BLACK OLIVE BUTTER

½ cup (4 oz/125 g) unsalted butter, at room temperature

¼ cup (1¼ oz/37 g) chopped black olives

2 tablespoons chopped fresh flat-leaf (Italian) parsley or tarragon

1 tablespoon fresh lemon juice

Ground pepper

3 boneless whole chicken breasts with skin intact, 10–12 oz (315–375 g) each

4 teaspoons olive oil

Salt and ground pepper

MAKES 6 SERVINGS

under the skin of each breast, distributing it evenly. Starting from a long side, roll up each breast into a cylinder and tie with kitchen string in 2 or 3 places to secure. Rub the breasts with the olive oil, and sprinkle with salt and pepper.

Place the chicken rolls on the oiled grill rack, cover, open the vents halfway, and grill for 20 minutes. Turn the chicken and continue to cook until browned on the outside and opaque throughout, or an instant-read thermometer inserted into a log registers 170°F (77°C), about 20 minutes longer.

Transfer to a cutting board and let rest for 5 minutes. Snip the strings and cut each breast crosswise into slices ½ inch (12 mm) thick. Divide evenly among warmed plates. Cut the butter log into 6 slices and place a slice on each serving. Serve right away.

European-style butter

European-style butter has a dense texture and buttery flavor, thanks to its high butterfat content. Use it in any recipe, but it's especially welcome in recipes in which butter is a featured ingredient.

247

CHICKEN-FONTINA ROULADES

Like the previous recipe, these breasts are rolled, cooked, and sliced into rounds. For this dish, skinless breasts are flattened, then rolled around a filling of cheese and herbs and baked along with mushrooms. If you have leftovers, serve them cold with a little Pesto (page 387).

About fontina

Fontina is a rich, mild-flavored, nutty cow's milk cheese with a pleasing firmness and good melting properties. For the best flavor, look for cheese from the northern Italian region of Val d'Aosta, in the Alps near the border with France and Switzerland.

4 skinless, boneless chicken breast halves, about ½ lb (250 g) each

8 thin slices fontina cheese

1 tablespoon green peppercorns, crushed

1 clove garlic, chopped

¼ cup (2 fl oz/60 ml) olive oil

3 tablespoons chopped fresh flat-leaf (Italian) parsley

2 tablespoons chopped fresh basil, or 1 tablespoon dried basil

Salt and ground pepper

16 fresh button mushrooms

½ cup (4 fl oz/125 ml) chicken broth, heated

MAKES 4 SERVINGS

Preheat the oven to 350°F (180°C).

One at a time, place the chicken breasts between 2 sheets of plastic wrap and flatten with a meat pounder or small, heavy frying pan until an even ¼ inch (6 mm) thick. Place 2 cheese slices on each breast.

In a bowl, stir together the green peppercorns, garlic, oil, 2 tablespoons of the parsley, the basil, and a pinch each of salt and pepper. Place 1 tablespoon of the parsley mixture on each cheese slice. Starting from a long side, roll up each breast and secure with 2 toothpicks. Arrange the rolled breasts, seam side down, in a baking dish. Surround the rolls with the mushrooms and spoon the remaining herb mixture over the chicken and mushrooms.

Bake for 15 minutes. Pour the hot broth into the dish and baste the chicken and mushrooms. Continue baking, basting frequently with the pan juices, until the chicken is tender and opaque throughout, or an instant-read thermometer inserted into a log registers 170°F (77°C), 20–25 minutes.

Transfer to a cutting board and let rest for 5 minutes. Cut each rolled breast into thick slices and arrange on warmed individual plates. Divide the mushrooms among the plates, and sprinkle the chicken and mushrooms with the remaining 1 tablespoon parsley. Serve right away.

CHERRY-STUFFED CHICKEN BREASTS

Pressing matters

Use 2 large glass baking dishes of the same size (for example, 9 by 13 inches/23 by 33 cm) or 4 large pie dishes for pressing the chicken.

Pressing the meat during and after cooking intensifies the sweet-tart nature of these roasted chicken breasts, which are slit and stuffed with dried cherries, then marinated in a savory mixture. The pretty red centers are revealed when the breasts are sliced and plated.

One at a time, place the chicken breasts on a cutting board. Holding the meat firmly in place, use a small, sharp knife to cut a horizontal slit through one side, creating a deep pocket.

Spoon one-eighth of the dried cherries into each pocket. Press on each breast with your hand to flatten the meat and seal the edges. Arrange in a single layer in a shallow baking dish.

In a small bowl, stir together the shallots, lemon juice, oil, lemon zest, summer savory, thyme, and ½ teaspoon each salt and pepper. Spoon the marinade over the chicken breasts. Cover and refrigerate for at least 2 hours or up to 24 hours.

Preheat the broiler (grill). Transfer the chicken to a broiler pan, reserving the marinade. Broil (grill) until browned on top, 4–5 minutes. Meanwhile, pour the reserved marinade into a small saucepan over high heat. Bring to a boil, then remove from the heat.

Remove the chicken from the broiler. Set the oven at 375°F (190°C). Arrange the chicken in a single layer in a shallow baking dish. Pour the marinade over the meat, and set another baking dish on top of the meat (see note, left). Roast until the juices run clear when the meat is pierced at the thickest point, or until the chicken feels firms and springs back to the touch, 15–20 minutes.

Remove from the oven and set heavy cans or bricks in the top (empty) baking dish. Let rest for at least 20 minutes or up to 30 minutes before serving.

Transfer the chicken to a cutting board, and slice against the grain, revealing the cherry stuffing. Arrange on a warmed platter. Spoon the dish juices over the top.

8 skinless, boneless chicken breast halves, ½ lb (250 g) each

1 cup (4 oz/125 g) pitted dried sweet cherries

2 large shallots, minced

¼ cup (2 fl oz/60 ml) fresh lemon juice

3 tablespoons olive oil

Grated zest of ½ lemon

½ teaspoon dried summer savory

½ teaspoon dried thyme

Coarse sea salt and ground pepper

MAKES 8 SERVINGS

BUFFALO WINGS

Meatier wings

Instead of whole wings, whose bony tips burn easily on a grill, consider using only the largest, meatiest section of the wings. These are often labeled drumettes.

Spicy chicken wings, served hot or cold, are a perfect finger food—equally welcome at a football party, a picnic, or the dinner table. Make them spicier by upping the quantity of pepper sauce. Serve with blue cheese dipping sauce (see note, right) and celery sticks.

In a bowl, stir together the vinegar, oil, Worcestershire sauce, Tabasco sauce, chili powder, red pepper flakes, and 1 teaspoon each salt and pepper. Reserve ¼ cup (2 fl oz/60 ml) of the marinade. Put the chicken wings in a large zippered plastic bag and pour in the remaining marinade. Press out the air from the bag and seal. Massage the bag gently to distribute the marinade. Set in a large bowl and

1 cup (8 fl oz/250 ml) cider vinegar

2 tablespoons *each* canola oil and Worcestershire sauce

1 tablespoon Tabasco sauce

2 tablespoons chili powder

1 teaspoon red pepper flakes

Salt and ground pepper

4 lb (2 kg) chicken wings

MAKES 4–6 SERVINGS

refrigerate for 2–3 hours, turning and massaging the bag occasionally.

Prepare a charcoal or gas grill for direct-heat cooking over medium heat (see page 18), or preheat the broiler (grill). Remove the wings from the marinade and pat dry. Arrange the wings on the oiled grill rack or on a broiler pan. Grill or broil, brushing with the reserved marinade and turning frequently, until opaque throughout when pierced, about 25–30 minutes. Serve hot or at room temperature.

CHICKEN POTPIE

Chicken potpie is one of the all-time great comfort foods. For this version, chicken, carrots, peas, corn, and shallots are combined in a thickened sauce of chicken broth, white wine, and half-and-half, then topped with pie pastry and baked to perfection.

1 cup (4 oz/125 g) sliced carrots

1 cup (5 oz/155 g) shelled fresh peas or thawed frozen peas

1 cup (6 oz/185 g) corn kernels (from 2–3 ears)

2 tablespoons unsalted butter

4 skinless, boneless chicken thighs, about 1¼ lb (625 g) total weight, cut into bite-size pieces

2 tablespoons minced shallot

¼ cup (1½ oz/45 g) all-purpose (plain) flour

1½ cups (12 fl oz/375 ml) chicken broth

½ cup (4 fl oz/125 ml) dry white wine

½ cup (4 fl oz/125 ml) half-and-half (half cream)

1 tablespoon chopped fresh flat-leaf (Italian) parsley

Salt and ground pepper

1 egg yolk

Pie Pastry (page 447), rolled out into a 9-inch (23-cm) round

MAKES 4–6 SERVINGS

Preheat the oven to 400°F (200°C). Bring a saucepan three-fourths full of salted water to a boil. Using a pasta insert or large sieve, immerse the carrots and peas in the water and boil until tender-crisp, 3–5 minutes. Lift out, drain, and transfer to a bowl. Repeat to cook the corn in the same pan of water, boiling it for just 1 minute. Set aside.

In a large frying pan over medium-high heat, melt the butter. Add the chicken and cook, stirring occasionally, until browned on all sides, about 8 minutes. Add the shallot and cook, stirring, until softened, about 2 minutes.

Sprinkle in the flour and stir well. Stir in the broth, wine, half-and-half, and parsley and bring to a simmer. Cover, reduce the heat to low, and simmer for 10 minutes.

Stir in the carrots, peas, and corn. Season with salt and pepper. Transfer to a 9-inch (23-cm) deep-dish pie dish.

Beat the egg yolk with 1 teaspoon water. Brush some of the egg yolk mixture in a 1-inch (2.5-cm) border around the edge of the pastry round. Place the round, egg side down, over the filling, and press the dough to the rim of the dish. Trim off any overhanging dough and brush the top surface lightly with the remaining egg yolk mixture. Cut 2 or 3 slits in the center of the top with the tip of a knife.

Place the pie dish on a rimmed baking sheet. Bake until the crust is golden brown, about 30 minutes, then let stand for 10 minutes before serving. Serve hot.

CHICKEN AND EGGPLANT KEBABS

Herb smoke

For extra flavor, plunge branches of oregano or rosemary into ice water to cover while you soak the skewers. Drain the herbs and toss them directly onto the hot coals of a charcoal grill to generate billows of herb-scented smoke.

For these tasty kebabs, cubes of chicken are threaded onto skewers with pieces of eggplant, bell pepper, and onion and then brushed with seasonings characteristic of the Greek kitchen. Serve on a bed of Perfect Pilaf (page 302) and accompany with lemon wedges.

Cut the chicken breasts into 1½-inch (4-cm) cubes. Next, cut the eggplant (aubergine) crosswise into slices. Then, cut the bell pepper (capsicum) into 1-inch (2.5 cm) squares. Finally, halve the onion, separate it into layers, and cut the layers into 1½-inch (4-cm) squares.

In a large bowl, stir together the lemon juice, wine, oil, garlic, oregano, lemon zest, and a large pinch each of salt and pepper. Stir in the chicken, eggplant, bell pepper, and onion. Cover and refrigerate for 1 hour.

Prepare a charcoal or gas grill for indirect-heat cooking over medium-high heat (see page 18). At the same time, soak 8 bamboo skewers in water to cover.

When the grill is ready, drain the skewers and thread the chicken, eggplant, bell pepper, and onion pieces onto them, alternating the pieces and dividing them equally. Place on the oiled grill rack directly over the fire. Grill, turning the skewers once or twice, until the chicken is browned, about 5 minutes total. Move the skewers so they are not directly over the fire. Cover the grill, open the vents halfway, and cook, turning the skewers occasionally, until the chicken is opaque throughout and the vegetables are tender, 10–15 minutes longer.

Transfer to a warmed platter and serve right away.

1½ lb (750 g) skinless, boneless chicken breasts or thighs

1 Asian eggplant (slender aubergine)

1 red bell pepper (capsicum)

1 yellow onion

½ cup (4 fl oz/125 ml) fresh lemon juice

¼ cup (2 fl oz/60 ml) dry white wine

2 tablespoons olive oil

2 cloves garlic, minced

2 tablespoons chopped fresh oregano

Grated zest of ½ lemon

Salt and ground pepper

MAKES 4 SERVINGS

CHICKEN STIR-FRY WITH WALNUTS

Rice vinegar types

Widely used in China, Japan, and the Koreas, rice vinegar is made from fermented rice and comes in a variety of styles, depending on the country. Japanese rice vinegar may be found either plain or seasoned (with sake, sugar, and salt) and is used in the recipe at right. Chinese cooks use red, white, and black varieties.

Stir-frying is one of the best ways to put together a quick dish. This one features chicken breasts, walnut pieces, and green onion in a ginger-garlic-mirin sauce. Steam a pot of jasmine rice while the chicken is marinating, and it will be ready to serve when the stir-fry is done.

Cut the chicken into thin strips 1 inch (2.5 cm) long and ¼ inch (6 mm) wide. In a bowl, stir together the soy sauce, mirin, vinegar, ginger, and garlic. Add the chicken and stir to mix well. Let stand at room temperature for at least 15 minutes or refrigerate for up to 1 hour.

Place a wok or large, heavy frying pan over high heat. When the pan is hot, add the oil and swirl to coat the bottom and sides of the pan. Add the walnuts and toss and stir until the nuts begin to deepen in color, about 1 minute. Using a slotted spoon, transfer to a small plate.

Add the green onions to the oil remaining in the pan and toss and stir just until their color brightens, about 30 seconds.

1 lb (500 g) skinless, boneless chicken breasts

¼ cup (2 fl oz/60 ml) soy sauce

2 tablespoons mirin or sweet sherry

2 tablespoons seasoned rice vinegar

1 tablespoon minced fresh ginger

2 cloves garlic, minced

2 tablespoons canola oil

½ cup (2 oz/60 g)
walnut pieces

5 green (spring) onions,
including tender green
tops, cut on the diagonal
into 1½-inch (4-cm) lengths

1 cup (8 fl oz/250 ml)
chicken broth

2 tablespoons cornstarch
(cornflour) dissolved in
1 tablespoon water

MAKES 4 SERVINGS

Using the slotted spoon, transfer to another small plate.
Leave the pan over high heat.

Remove the chicken from the marinade, reserving the
marinade, and add the chicken to the pan. Toss and stir
until opaque throughout, 1–2 minutes.

Add the broth and the reserved marinade and bring to a boil.
Quickly stir the cornstarch mixture and add to the pan along
with the reserved green onions. Cook, stirring, until the liquid
has thickened, about 1 minute. Transfer to a warmed serving
dish. Garnish with the reserved walnuts and serve.

Storing walnuts

*If you enjoy walnuts
and like to have
them on hand, store
the nuts in the
refrigerator or
freezer to prevent
their oils from
turning rancid.*

CHICKEN FAJITAS

Chicken fajitas are both easy and delicious. All you do is sauté chicken with vegetables and
bold seasonings, and then serve with warm tortillas and condiments. You can even use leftover
chicken—stir it in with the cooked vegetables and heat through before serving.

8–12 flour tortillas,
6–8 inches (15–20 cm)
in diameter

2 tablespoons canola oil

1 lb (500 g) skinless,
boneless chicken breasts

1 yellow onion, halved
and sliced

½ red bell pepper
(capsicum), sliced

½ green bell pepper
(capsicum), sliced

1 jalapeño or Anaheim
chile, seeded and
finely chopped

2 teaspoons chopped
fresh oregano

½ teaspoon ground cumin

2 cloves garlic, minced

2 tablespoons plus ¾ cup
(6 fl oz/ 180 ml) Fresh
Tomato Salsa (page 393)

2 plum (Roma) tomatoes,
seeded and chopped

Salt and ground pepper

Guacamole (page 392)

MAKES 4 SERVINGS

Preheat the oven to 350°F (180°C). Wrap the tortillas in
aluminum foil and place in the oven until warmed through,
about 10 minutes.

Meanwhile, in a frying pan over medium-high heat, warm
the oil. Cut the chicken into narrow, thin strips, add to the
pan, and sauté until opaque and firm, about 4 minutes. Using
a slotted spoon, transfer the chicken to a plate and set aside.

Add the onion and red and green bell peppers to the oil
remaining in the pan and sauté over medium-high heat
until softened, about 4 minutes. Stir in the chile, oregano,
cumin, and garlic and sauté until the garlic is softened,
about 20 seconds. Stir in the 2 tablespoons salsa and ½ cup
(4 fl oz/125 ml) water and bring to a boil. Add the tomatoes
and season with salt and pepper. Cook, uncovered, until the
liquid evaporates, about 5 minutes. Return the chicken to
the pan, mix well, and heat to serving temperature. Transfer
to a warmed platter.

To serve, remove the tortillas from the oven and place
the remaining ¾ cup salsa in a small bowl. Set the chicken,
tortillas, guacamole, and salsa on the table and let diners
assemble their own fajitas.

Fajita variations

*You can substitute
peeled and deveined
shrimp (see page 202)
in this recipe: cook
the shrimp just until
opaque throughout,
2–3 minutes. For
vegetarian fajitas,
substitute cubes of
firm tofu and sauté
until browned and
heated through,
about 8 minutes. For
Grilled Steak Fajitas,
see page 276.*

HERB-RUBBED ROASTED TURKEY

Stuffing tips

If you plan to stuff the turkey (see the recipes on pages 31–32), make the stuffing just before using it and let cool to room temperature. Next, stuff the bird loosely to allow for expansion. Then, when checking the bird for doneness, get a read on the stuffing, too. It should register 165°F (74°C) on an instant-read thermometer. Finally, expect a stuffed turkey to take 30 to 45 minutes longer to cook than an unstuffed one.

252

This traditional roasted turkey, the star of the Thanksgiving table, is rubbed with olive oil and herbs, then drizzled and basted with butter. Once removed from the oven, the pan juices form the basis for a tasty mushroom gravy. Be sure to serve with mashed potatoes (see page 335).

Position a rack in the lower third of the oven and preheat the oven to 325°F (165°C).

In a small bowl, stir together the chopped herbs, 4 teaspoons salt, and 1 tablespoon pepper. Pat the turkey dry and place on a rack in a roasting pan. Slip the herb sprigs into the body cavity. Brush the outside of the bird with the oil and then rub the herb mixture all over the turkey. Tie the legs together. Tuck the wing tips under the body. Drizzle the butter evenly over the turkey.

Roast the turkey for 45 minutes, then baste with the pan juices. Continue roasting, basting every 20 minutes, until an instant-read thermometer inserted into the thickest part of a thigh away from the bone registers 180°F (82°C), about 2½ hours longer. Transfer to a platter, tent with aluminum foil and let rest for 15 minutes. Pour the pan juices into a measuring pitcher; skim off and discard the fat.

To make the gravy, pour the stock into the roasting pan and place on the stove top over high heat. Bring the stock to a boil and deglaze the pan, stirring to dislodge any browned bits from the pan bottom. Remove from the heat. In a large frying pan over medium-high heat, melt the butter. Add the shallots and stir to coat. Add the mushrooms and thyme and sauté until the mushrooms soften, about 5 minutes. Add the flour and cook, stirring frequently, for 1 minute. Add the stock and the pan juices and bring to a boil, stirring constantly. Add the cream and boil, stirring occasionally, until the gravy thickens slightly, about 3 minutes. Season with salt and pepper. Stir in the parsley. Pour into a warmed sauceboat.

Carve the turkey at the table. Serve with the gravy.

¼ cup (⅓ oz/10 g) chopped fresh flat-leaf (Italian) parsley

3 tablespoons chopped fresh rosemary, plus 2 or 3 sprigs

3 tablespoons chopped fresh thyme, plus 2 or 3 sprigs

Salt and ground pepper

1 turkey, 14–16 lb (7–8 kg), neck and giblets removed

2 tablespoons olive oil

4 tablespoons (2 oz/60 g) unsalted butter, melted

FOR THE GRAVY

3¼ cups (26 fl oz/810 ml) Turkey Stock (page 25)

½ cup (4 oz/125 g) unsalted butter

6 large shallots, chopped

2 lb (1 kg) fresh white mushrooms, sliced

1 tablespoon chopped fresh thyme

⅓ cup (2 oz/60 g) all-purpose (plain) flour

1 cup (8 fl oz/250 ml) heavy (double) cream

Salt and ground pepper

1 cup (1½ oz/45 g) chopped fresh flat-leaf (Italian) parsley

MAKES 8–10 SERVINGS

CIDER-GLAZED TURKEY WITH CIDER GRAVY

Apples and poultry are a time-tested classic, lending a hint of sweetness to savory roast birds. Here, a turkey is brushed with an apple cider glaze during cooking, and then served with an apple brandy-infused pan gravy, with shallots and thyme to round out the autumnal flavors.

3 cups (24 fl oz/750 ml) apple cider

¾ cup (6 oz/185 g) unsalted butter, at room temperature

2 tablespoons chopped fresh thyme

1 turkey, 14–16 lb (7–8 kg), neck and giblets removed

Salt and ground pepper

FOR THE GRAVY

6 tablespoons unsalted butter

3 oz (90 g) shallots, sliced

2 tablespoons chopped fresh thyme

6 tablespoons (2 oz/60 g) all-purpose (plain) flour

About 4½ cups (36 fl oz/ 1.1 l) Turkey Stock (page 25)

3 tablespoons applejack, Calvados, or brandy

Salt and ground pepper

MAKES 8–10 SERVINGS

In a saucepan over high heat, bring the cider to a boil. Cook until it is reduced to 1 cup (8 fl oz/250 ml), about 30 minutes. Set aside ½ cup (4 fl oz/125 ml) of the reduced cider. Mix the butter and thyme into the remaining reduced cider and refrigerate until cold.

Position a rack in the lower third of the oven and preheat the oven to 325°F (165°C).

Pat the turkey dry and place on a rack in a roasting pan. Spread the cider butter inside and over the outside of the turkey. Sprinkle with salt and pepper. Tie the legs together. Tuck the wing tips under the body. Roast for 45 minutes, then baste the turkey with the pan juices. Continue roasting, basting every 20 minutes, until an instant-read thermometer inserted into the thickest part of a thigh away from the bone registers 180°F (82°C), about 2½ hours longer. Transfer the turkey to a platter, tent with aluminum foil, and let rest for 15 minutes. Pour the pan juices into a measuring pitcher; skim off and discard the fat.

To make the gravy, in a saucepan over medium-high heat, melt the butter. Add the shallots and thyme and sauté until the shallots are golden brown, about 8 minutes. Add the flour and cook, stirring frequently, until browned, about 5 minutes. Add enough stock to the pan juices to measure 5 cups (40 fl oz/1.25 l). Gradually whisk the stock mixture into the flour mixture, then bring to a boil, whisking frequently. Mix in the reserved cider mixture and boil until thickened, about 10 minutes. Mix in the applejack and return to a boil. Season with salt and pepper. Pour into a warmed sauceboat.

Carve the turkey at the table. Serve with the gravy.

Don't skimp on resting

Letting the bird stand before carving allows the juices to redistribute throughout the meat and is a key to a juicy bird. Carving right away can lead to flavorful juices left on the carving board and dry meat.

253

GRILL-ROASTED TURKEY

Cooking a turkey on a grill leaves the oven available for side dishes and dinner rolls. The turkey comes out juicy, with a smoky flavor and dark brown skin. To grill-roast a chicken (5–6 lb/2.5–3 kg), halve the ingredients and cook for about 1½ hours.

Prepare a charcoal or gas grill for indirect-heat cooking over medium heat (see page 18).

Pat the turkey dry and rub with the oil and rosemary. Sprinkle inside and out with salt and pepper. Place the lemon quarters and herb sprigs in the cavity; truss the bird (page 235). Toss half of the wood chips on the fire, or for a gas grill, wrap them in aluminum foil, poke holes in the bottom of the packet, and place on a heat element. Place the turkey, breast side up, on the grill rack. Cover the grill and cook for 1 hour.

In a small bowl, stir together the butter and lemon juice. Add the remaining wood chips to the grill. Brush the turkey with half of the butter mixture; cover and cook for 45 minutes longer. Brush with the remaining butter mixture, then cook, covered, until an instant-read thermometer inserted in the thickest part of a thigh away from the bone registers 180°F (82°C), 30–45 minutes longer. Total cooking time is about 2½ hours. Tent the turkey with aluminum foil and let rest for 15 minutes before carving.

1 turkey, 10–12 lb (5–6 kg), neck and giblets removed

2 tablespoons olive oil

2 tablespoons chopped fresh rosemary

Salt and ground pepper

2 lemons, quartered

Large handful of fresh sage sprigs

2 large handfuls hickory chips, soaked in water to cover for 1 hour

½ cup (4 oz/125 g) unsalted butter, melted

2 tablespoons fresh lemon juice

MAKES 6–8 SERVINGS

GRILLED GARLIC-RUBBED TURKEY BREAST

Turkey breasts are perfect for grilling. A breast will need to cook for at least 1½ hours, so charcoal users will need to add preheated coals to the fire after the first 45 minutes. Serve with Fresh and Dried Fruit Relish (page 396).

Pat the turkey breast dry, then rub the garlic and ½ teaspoon each salt and pepper into the skin. Cover and refrigerate for at least 6 hours or up to overnight. Remove from the refrigerator for 45 minutes before grilling.

In a small saucepan over medium-high heat, melt the butter. Add the wine and ½ cup (4 fl oz/125 ml) water and bring to a boil. Remove from the heat.

Prepare a charcoal or gas grill for indirect-heat cooking over medium heat (see page 18).

Place the breast, skin side up, on the grill rack over a drip pan. Cover the grill and open the vents halfway. Grill, basting occasionally with the butter-wine mixture, until an instant-read thermometer inserted into the thickest part away from the bone registers 165°F (74°C), about 1½ hours.

Transfer the breast to a cutting board, tent with aluminum foil, and let rest for 10 minutes. Slice the breast against the grain and arrange on a warmed platter. Serve right away.

1 bone-in whole turkey breast, about 5 lb (2.5 kg)

1 clove garlic, crushed

Salt and ground pepper

¼ cup (2 oz/60 g) unsalted butter

½ cup (4 fl oz/125 ml) dry white wine

MAKES 6–8 SERVINGS

Take off the chill

To ensure that poultry cooks evenly, remove whole birds and large cuts such as turkey breasts from the refrigerator at least 30 minutes before cooking. Larger birds such as whole turkeys will benefit from standing at room temperature for up to 2 hours, but no longer.

TURKEY TENDERLOINS WITH CURRIED APRICOT GLAZE

Apricot-glazed turkey tenderloins are a festive alternative to a roasted bird and a good choice for any special-occasion dinner for four. Accompany the sliced tenderloins with wild rice tossed with cooked corn kernels and green (spring) onions.

¼ cup (2½ oz/75 g) apricot preserves

2 tablespoons white wine vinegar

2½ teaspoons Dijon mustard

2½ teaspoons curry powder

1 teaspoon minced garlic

Canola oil

3 turkey tenderloins, ½ lb (250 g) each

Salt and ground pepper

1½ tablespoons dried cranberries or dried tart cherries

MAKES 4 SERVINGS

In a small bowl, stir together the apricot preserves, vinegar, mustard, curry, and garlic. Set aside.

Preheat the broiler (grill).

Warm an extra-large frying pan over medium heat. Add 1 or 2 tablespoons oil to the pan and swirl to coat the pan bottom evenly. Pat the turkey tenderloins dry, season with salt and pepper, and add them to the pan. Cook until the turkey is browned on the first side, about 5 minutes. Turn the turkey, cover, and cook until just barely opaque throughout, about 5 minutes longer. Remove from the heat.

Arrange the tenderloins on a rimmed baking sheet. Spoon 1 tablespoon of the apricot mixture over each tenderloin. Broil (grill) for 2 minutes. Remove from the oven

Mix the cranberries into the remaining apricot mixture and spoon over the turkey, dividing it evenly. Continue to broil until the tenderloins are well glazed, about 2 minutes longer.

Transfer the tenderloins to a carving board and let rest for 5 minutes. Slice the tenderloins on the diagonal against the grain and divide among warmed individual plates, fanning the slices. Serve right away.

Substituting breast cutlets

If turkey tenderloins are unavailable, use two 3-oz (90-g) boneless turkey breast cutlets per serving. Sauté over medium heat for 2 minutes, then turn and cook for 1 minute longer. Reduce the total broiling time to 2 minutes.

255

ROASTED DUCKS WITH CRANBERRY GLAZE

Releasing duck fat

Ducks have a generous amount of fat under the skin, which is hard to render completely during roasting. Piercing the skin in several places allows the fat to melt more readily, dripping into the roasting pan, from which it is easily removed with a bulb baster.

Duck is a treat many people have only in restaurants, believing it requires a special skill to prepare at home. That's a shame, because duck is rich and full flavored and is no more difficult to cook than other poultry. Here, two ducks are roasted with a simple cranberry glaze.

Pat the ducks completely dry. Sprinkle each duck inside and out with the lemon juice, salt, and pepper.

Pierce each onion quarter with 1 whole clove. Stuff each duck cavity with 2 onion quarters, 2 orange quarters, and 1 bay leaf. Cross the ends of the drumsticks and tie securely together with kitchen string. Using a knife tip, pierce the skin of both ducks at about 1-inch (2.5-cm) intervals.

Preheat the oven to 350°F (180°C).

To make the glaze, in a saucepan over medium heat, combine the cranberry sauce, lemon zest, lemon juice, ground cloves, and ½ teaspoon salt. Heat, stirring, until the cranberry sauce is melted, about 5 minutes.

Brush the ducks with a thin layer of the glaze, then arrange, breast sides up, on a rack in a large roasting pan.

Roast the ducks, basting them every 30 minutes with the glaze. As excess fat accumulates in the pan, use a bulb baster to remove it. After 1 hour of cooking, carefully turn the ducks breast sides down and roast for 1 hour. Then, turn the ducks breasts up again and continue to roast until the skin is crisp and an instant-read thermometer inserted into the thickest part of a thigh registers 170°F (77°C), about 30 minutes longer. The total roasting time is about 2½ hours.

Transfer the ducks to a large cutting board and let rest for 10 minutes. Cut into quarters and arrange on a warmed platter. Serve right away, passing the relish at the table.

2 ducks, 4½–5½ lb (2.25–2.75 kg) each, thawed in the refrigerator if frozen

2 tablespoons fresh lemon juice

Salt and ground pepper

1 yellow onion, quartered

4 whole cloves

1 orange, quartered

2 bay leaves

FOR THE GLAZE

1 can (1 lb/500 g) jellied cranberry sauce

1 teaspoon grated lemon zest

2 tablespoons fresh lemon juice

¼ teaspoon ground cloves

Salt

Cranberry Relish (page 396)

MAKES 4–6 SERVINGS

ORANGE-GRILLED DUCK BREASTS

Ducks and fruit

The meaty flesh of duck is complemented by nearly any type of fruit, including oranges, cherries, apricots, and other stone fruits. The fruits' balance of sweet and tart flavors nicely offsets the richness of the meat.

The easiest cut of duck to grill is a bone-in breast, because it isn't as fatty as other parts of the bird. This orange-infused duck breast makes an elegant meal for two. Serve with puréed parsnips or celery root (celeriac) and a green vegetable such as green beans or asparagus.

In a bowl, whisk together the orange juice, vermouth, marmalade, thyme, and 1 teaspoon salt. Using a knife, score the duck skin with several crisscross diagonal cuts about ¼ inch (6 mm) deep. Do not cut into the meat. Lay the breast halves flat in a shallow baking dish. Pour the marinade over the duck and turn to coat both sides. Cover and refrigerate, turning occasionally, for at least 1 hour or up to 8 hours.

Prepare a charcoal or gas grill for direct-heat cooking over medium-high heat (see page 18).

1 cup (8 fl oz/250 ml) fresh orange juice

½ cup (4 fl oz/125 ml) dry white vermouth

¼ cup (2½ oz/75 g) orange marmalade

1 tablespoon minced fresh thyme, or 1 teaspoon dried thyme

Salt

2 boneless duck breast halves, about 7 oz (220 g) each

MAKES 2 SERVINGS

Remove the duck from the marinade, reserving the marinade, and pat the duck very dry. Place the duck on the oiled grill rack. Grill, turning often and brushing 3 or 4 times with the reserved marinade, until the skin is well browned and the meat is still pink in the center, 8–10 minutes total for medium-rare. (For medium to well done meat, grill for another 5–7 minutes.) Stop brushing the duck with the marinade 5 minutes before the duck is done.

Transfer the duck to a board and let rest for 5 minutes before carving. Cut the meat against the grain into thin slices and arrange on warmed individual plates. Serve right away.

On duck breasts

Most of the duck breasts you will find are frozen. Look for Muscovy duck breasts at the butcher shop for the best flavor and texture.

BRAISED DUCK THIGHS WITH PLUM SAUCE

Prune plums, also known as Italian or French plums, are a seasonal specialty of late summer and early autumn. Their intense sweetness pairs well with the robust flavor of duck. Serve with Potato Gnocchi (page 169) and sautéed chard, or with rice pilaf and steamed broccoli.

Salt and ground pepper

4 skinless duck thighs

¼ cup (2 fl oz/60 ml) brandy

8 prune plums, halved and pitted

1 teaspoon sugar

4–5 tablespoons (2–2½ fl oz/60–75 ml) chicken broth

MAKES 4 SERVINGS

Sprinkle 1 teaspoon salt in a nonstick frying pan just large enough to hold the 4 duck thighs in a single layer. Place the pan over high heat. When the pan is hot, add the duck and sprinkle with 1 teaspoon pepper. Sear, turning once, until browned on both sides, 1–2 minutes on each side. Add the brandy and half the plums. Reduce the heat to medium-high and deglaze the pan, stirring to dislodge any browned bits from the pan bottom, 1–2 minutes.

In a small bowl, dissolve the sugar in 4 tablespoons of the broth and add to the pan. Reduce the heat to low and cover tightly. Cook for 7–8 minutes. If the pan has dried out, add another 1 tablespoon broth. Turn the duck thighs, re-cover the pan, and continue to cook until cooked through and tender, 7–8 minutes longer. Transfer the duck to a plate.

Skim off any fat from the frying pan. There should be about 2 tablespoons juices remaining. Return the pan to medium-low heat and return the duck and any accumulated juices from the plate to the pan along with the remaining plums. Cook, turning the duck once, until the added plums are heated through, 2–3 minutes.

Transfer the duck thighs to warmed individual plates and spoon the sauce and plums over the top. Serve right away.

Shopping for plums

Prune plums are smallish, oblong fruits with deep purple skin covering amber flesh. If you are not able to find them, substitute any round variety with the same coloring. Cut them into quarters instead of into halves.

Meat

Meat

Beef, veal, lamb, pork, and a variety of sausages—meat is a big category. And for many people, a meal without meat is incomplete. The preparations run the gamut, too, from basic grilled fajitas or broiled pork chops to an elegant rib roast, a rustic yet sophisticated beef bourguignon, or a glazed holiday ham. But once you know the cuts and some basic techniques, you'll discover it's surprisingly easy to create impressive fare.

Meat Basics

Refrigerating meat
As soon as you return home from the market, put any meat purchases in the coldest part of the refrigerator. Use uncooked whole cuts of beef, lamb, or pork, or leftover cooked meat, within 3 to 4 days; use uncooked veal or ground meat within 1 to 2 days.

Freezing meat
You can freeze meat for up to 2 weeks in its retail package. For longer freezing of up to 6 months, wrap securely in freezer-grade plastic wrap, heavy-duty aluminum foil, or freezer paper; label and date the package.

Defrosting meat
Thaw frozen meat in the refrigerator, allowing 4 to 7 hours per pound (500 g) for large cuts, 3 to 5 hours per pound for smaller cuts. Or, defrost in a microwave oven, removing any foil or other metallic wrapping and following manufacturer's directions.

Precooking warm-up
Remove steaks, chops, or other small meat cuts from the refrigerator 20 to 30 minutes before cooking; set out roasts and other large cuts for up to 1 hour. This will help the meat to cook more quickly and evenly.

From selecting a cut at the market, to cooking it to the perfect stage of doneness, to carving it with aplomb, the following guidelines will help you maximize the results whenever meat is on the menu.

BEEF Not only is beef an excellent source of protein, iron, phosphorous, zinc, and B vitamins, but today's cuts are much leaner than the same cuts were just a few decades ago. Whatever cut you seek, in most cases, select a piece in which the lean portions appear bright cherry red. Vacuum-packed beef and the interior of ground beef are the exceptions, with a darker, purplish red the standard. A good butcher can help you select the right cut for what you are cooking and can lead you through the labyrinth of terminology, grades, and private labels (the latter typically indicating a prized breed or a proprietary claim by the market).

In the United States, all beef is inspected by a government agency, but grading is voluntary. Of the eight grades, the top three are prime, choice, and select. Generally, the greater the amount of marbling, or flecks of fat in the interior of the meat, the higher the grade—prime being the highest—because marbling makes the meat tender, juicy, and more flavorful. Age and color are also considered in grading. Aged beef has been hung in carefully controlled cold storage for 10 days to six weeks, during which time excess blood drains away and natural enzymes partially soften the meat fibers, enhancing tenderness and flavor. Ungraded meat is available, but to ensure you are purchasing quality, buy only meat marked prime, choice, or select. Keep in mind, however, that prime beef is rarely available except at topnotch butcher shops or fine restaurants.

To tie a roast: A large, boneless roast, such as a rib-eye or a round (rump) roast, is usually rolled into a compact cylindrical shape and tied for more even cooking. To do this, first roll the roast into as uniform and compact a cylindrical shape as possible, folding any flaps or narrower portions of the cut underneath the thickest part. Then, securely tie a length of kitchen string around the center of the roll. Continue tying pieces of string at intervals of about 1 inch (2.5 cm) along the length of the roast, parallel to the first string. Before carving the cooked roast, carefully snip off the strings.

VEAL Most of the veal sold is the meat of 3- to 5-month-old male calves that have been primarily fed a grain diet. A smaller part of the market is made up of milk-fed calves no more than 3 months old. Veal is prized for its pale color, mild flavor, and leanness. Since the animals are immature, all veal cuts are tender. Their leanness, however, calls for careful cooking to prevent drying out. Meat from milk-fed calves is fine grained and creamy pink; slightly darker rosy meat comes from grain-fed animals. Any visible fat should be a pure milky white color.

260

When large veal cuts are roasted or grilled, they are often rubbed first with oil or butter to keep the flesh moist in the dry heat of the oven. Veal and other lean meats can also be topped with strips of pork fat or bacon, a process called barding, which bastes the veal as it cooks.

LAMB Mild and tender lamb, the meat of a young sheep, is a far cry from the strong, gamy flesh of adult sheep, or mutton. To qualify for labeling as lamb, the meat must come from an animal less than 12 months old. Most lamb found in the market is between 5 and 7 months old. Lamb raised in the United States tends to be milder than meat imported from Australia and New Zealand. Look for lamb graded prime or choice, with a fresh smell and firm, pinkish red meat with pure white fat. Any cut bones should appear moist, red, and porous. Darker meat or dry, whiter bones could indicate mutton.

To butterfly a leg of lamb: Leg of lamb is the most prized cut for roasting. Boning and butterflying it—that is, removing the bones and then cutting it so it lies flat and is of nearly uniform thickness—makes it possible to cook the leg more evenly and quickly. A good butcher will be able to do the job for you, but you might also like to try doing it yourself, using a sharp, sturdy, thin-bladed knife. First, chill the leg of lamb in the refrigerator for 3 hours to firm up the meat. Gripping the surrounding white skin with a cloth or paper towel, tear away the outer membrane. With the knife, carefully trim away excess fat, cutting parallel to the surface. Locate the pelvic bone in the wide rounded end, perpendicular to the length. With the pelvic bone end closest to you, gradually cut around the bone until its ball-and-socket joint is exposed; cut through the joint ligaments and pull out the pelvic bone. Next, grasp the shank bone at the top of the leg and cut through the ligaments surrounding the bone. Then, keeping the knife blade against the bone, carefully cut the meat away from the bone; when you reach the joint between the shank bone and the leg bone, cut through the ligaments and remove the shank bone. Cut down through the center of the meat to the leg bone; cut around the joint at one end and ease the bone out of the meat, holding the free joint and cutting and scraping down the bone's length to free it. Finally, with the knife blade parallel to the work surface, cut into the thickest parts of the leg meat from the center outward toward the edge to open it out in a flap, taking care not to cut completely through. You should have one large, flat piece of meat of nearly uniform thickness.

PORK Look to pork for an inexpensive, lean, flavorful, and remarkably versatile meat. Today's pork has been bred, raised, and butchered to be increasingly leaner, so it benefits from quick cooking to avoid dryness. High modern standards of hygiene also make it possible to cook pork to a point of juicy, rosy pinkness, rather than to the state of gray well doneness insisted on in the past. Seek out a reliable source for buying pork. The meat should be pale pink and fine textured, the fat pure and white, and any bones slightly reddish, and it should smell clean and fresh.

To stuff and/or tie pork cuts: Moist stuffings help to keep today's leaner meat from drying out. Thin pork cutlets can be rolled or wrapped around a filling. To stuff a thick pork chop, place the chop on a work surface; insert the blade of a small, sharp knife into the middle of the meat on the side opposite the bone; swivel the blade to form a pocket; and then add a stuffing and close the opening with toothpicks. To stuff a whole pork tenderloin, slit it lengthwise halfway through; from the center cut, slit outward halfway through each half again to open it up into a wide piece of uniform thickness, similar to butterflying a leg of lamb (above). Then add the stuffing, roll up the tenderloin, and tie it using the same method employed for a boneless beef roast (above).

JUDGING DONENESS

The temperature ranges listed below serve as a guide to achieving the desired degree of doneness.

To test, insert an instant-read thermometer into the thickest part not touching bone. Keep in mind that meats should be allowed to rest after cooking so that the juices can fully redistribute; the temperature will rise 5°–10°F (3°–6°C) during resting. (Note that these may differ from governmental food safety guidelines.)

BEEF AND LAMB

Rare	120°–125°F (49°–52°C)
Medium-rare	125°–130°F (52°–54°C)
Medium	135°–140°F (57°–60°C)
Medium-well	140°–150°F (60°–65°C)
Well	150°F (65°C)

VEAL

Medium-rare	125°–130°F (52°–54°C)
Medium	135°–140°F (57°–60°C)
Medium-well	140°–150°F (60°–65°C)

PORK

Medium	135°–140°F (57°–60°C)
Medium-well	140°–150°F (60°–65°C)
Well	150°F (65°C)

Testing steaks and chops

You can also check the doneness of steaks and chops by pressing the thickest part with your fingertip. If it feels very soft and yielding, it is rare; slightly firmer indicates medium-rare to medium; and firm indicates well done. For a more exact test, insert an instant-read thermometer horizontally into the steak, away from the bone, and consult the guidelines above.

261

MEAT CUTS

A basic understanding of where different meat cuts come from on each animal will help you navigate the many choices available in the butcher's case, from tender beef fillets, to an elegant rack of lamb, to a succulent pork shoulder.

Beef and Veal

Butchers in the United States divide the beef steer into eight primary sections, as shown below. In general, muscles that get little exercise, such as from the rib, short loin, and sirloin, are more tender and can be cooked relatively quickly using dry-heat methods. Cuts from more exercised parts of the steer, such as the chuck, brisket, and round, are generally better when cooked more slowly with moist heat. Veal (not shown) tends to be more tender overall than beef. Still, the relative tenderness and corresponding cooking method for each cut is similar to those of beef.

Lamb

Lamb sold in the United States is divided into six primary sections, shown at right. The rib and loin, the less exercised parts of the animal, yield the most tender cuts. The leg and shoulder are tougher, but become moist and flavorful when slow-roasted or braised, which break down the tough muscle fibers and connective tissue in the meat.

Pork

Many U.S. butchers divide the pig into five primal sections, illustrated below right. Some also divide the loin into two parts: the sirloin and center loin. The cuts range from the small, lean tenderloin and single-serving chops to the large, moist ham from the leg. Like with beef and lamb, the less exercised parts tend to be the most tender.

Beef Cuts

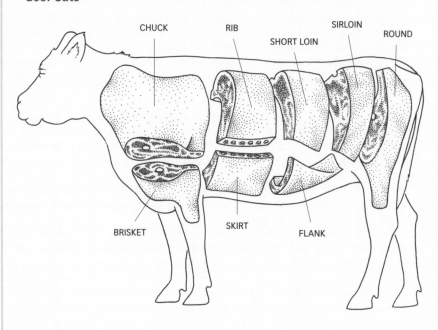

Cuts for Sautéing
Small thin cuts, from any animal or section, are generally suitable for cooking on the stove top. Tender cuts, such as steaks, chops, and cutlets, are favorites for searing in a frying pan, cooking to perfect doneness in just minutes. For stir-fries, take care to select cuts that will do best with quick cooking in the wok, such as beef sirloin and pork tenderloin.

Cuts for Grilling
As with sautéing, small, thin cuts from the less-exercised parts of the animal are generally suitable for direct-heat cooking on the grill, from pork and lamb chops, to any of the many varieties of beef steaks. Larger, less tender cuts are also suitable for the grill when slowly cooked over indirect-heat for longer periods of time to develop a tender texture.

Lamb Cuts

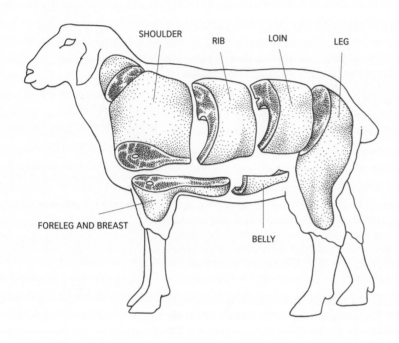

SHOULDER
RIB
LOIN
LEG
FORELEG AND BREAST
BELLY

Pork Cuts

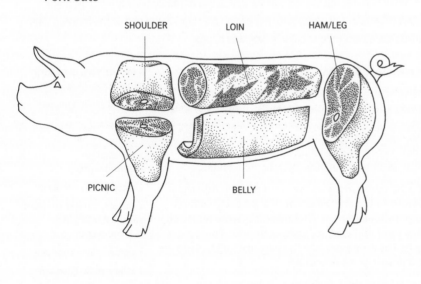

SHOULDER
LOIN
HAM/LEG
PICNIC
BELLY

Cuts for Roasting

Roasting is a versatile technique, suitable for many cuts of meat. It works particularly well for larger cuts, but smaller, thinner cuts also gain an appealing browned crust and juicy interior when roasted. For quick, high temperature roasting, choose tender cuts from the least exercised parts of the animal. For slow, lower temperature roasting, less tender cuts can also be roasted to juicy perfection.

Cuts for Braising and Stewing

Braising and stewing have remarkable tenderizing capabilities, making them the methods of choice for tough meat cuts. Beef chuck and lamb or pork shoulder are the ideal cuts for braises and stews, and cubed stewing beef or lamb typically comes from these parts. Other leg, flank, or belly cuts also benefit from braising, emerging tender, moist, and flavorful from the oven.

GRILLED BOURBON-MARINATED CHUCK ROAST

Marinade safety

When using a marinade for basting, do one of two things to prevent cross-contamination from the raw meat: either stop basting 5 minutes before the meat finishes cooking, or boil the marinade for 2 minutes before basting with it. Both methods will kill any bacteria present in the marinade.

Marinating a chuck roast in bourbon, olive oil, and mustard yields a flavorful result. Although the meat marinates for a full day, once it is on the grill, it is ready to eat in about an hour. Serve the carved meat with roasted vegetables and mashed potatoes.

In a bowl, whisk together the whiskey, oil, vinegar, mustard, 1 teaspoon salt, and ½ teaspoon pepper. Reserve ¼ cup (2 fl oz/ 60 ml) of the marinade. Place the beef in a large zippered plastic bag and pour in the remaining marinade. Press out the air from the bag and seal. Massage the bag gently to distribute the marinade evenly. Set in a large bowl and refrigerate, turning and massaging the bag occasionally, for at least 1 day, or up to 3 days.

Prepare a charcoal or gas grill for indirect-heat cooking over medium heat (page 18).

Remove the meat from the marinade and pat dry thoroughly. Discard the marinade. Place the meat on the oiled grill rack, cover the grill, and open the vents halfway. Cook, brushing with the reserved marinade and turning, until the roast is well browned and an instant-read thermometer inserted into the thickest part registers 125°–130°F (52°–54°C) for medium-rare, about 45 minutes.

Transfer the roast to a carving board, tent with aluminum foil, and let rest for 10 minutes. Carve crosswise into thin slices and arrange on a warmed platter or individual plates.

⅔ cup (5 fl oz/160 ml) **bourbon whiskey**

⅓ cup (3 fl oz/80 ml) **olive oil**

⅓ cup (3 fl oz/80 ml) **cider vinegar**

1 tablespoon Dijon mustard

Salt and ground pepper

1 boneless beef chuck roast, 3–3½ lb (1.5–1.75 kg)

MAKES 6–8 SERVINGS

CLASSIC POT ROAST

Slow-cooker method

Place the browned roast and broth mixture in the slow cooker, cover, and cook for 8 hours on low. Strain and skim the liquids; cook for 1 hour longer with the vegetables, adding the peas during the last 15 minutes of cooking.

This recipe is a twist on a comfort-food classic. It starts in a traditional way, with aromatic vegetables slow cooked in a savory liquid. But as you are nearing the end of the braising time, fresh vegetables are added to lend color, flavor, and appeal.

Preheat the oven to 325°F (165°C).

In a large bowl, stir together 3 tablespoons of the flour, 1 teaspoon salt, and ½ teaspoon pepper. Turn the roast in the seasoned flour, shaking off any excess. In a large Dutch oven over medium-high heat, melt the butter with the oil. Add the roast and cook, turning occasionally, until browned on all sides, about 10 minutes. Transfer the roast to a plate.

Pour off all but 2 tablespoons of the fat in the pot. Add the chopped carrots, onion, and celery and sauté over medium-high heat until softened, about 5 minutes. Stir in the remaining 2 tablespoons flour and cook for about 1 minute. Pour in the stock, bring to a boil, and deglaze the pan, stirring to dislodge any browned bits on the pan bottom.

Add the roast back to the Dutch oven, cover, and bake, turning the roast occasionally, until the meat is very tender,

5 tablespoons (2 oz/60 g) all-purpose (plain) flour

Salt and ground pepper

1 beef chuck roast, 3–4 lb (1.5-2 kg)

2 tablespoons unsalted butter

2 tablespoons canola oil

4 carrots, 2 finely chopped and 2 cut into 1-inch (2.5-cm) pieces

1 yellow onion, chopped

1 celery stalk, chopped

3 cups (24 fl oz/750 ml) Beef Stock (page 22)

3 Yukon gold potatoes, about 1 lb (500 g) total weight, peeled and quartered

1 cup (6 oz/185 g) frozen pearl onions

½ cup (3 oz/90 g) frozen peas

MAKES 6–8 SERVINGS

about 3 hours. Remove the pot from the oven and transfer the roast to a platter.

Strain the cooking liquid through a fine-mesh sieve into a heatproof bowl; discard the solids. Skim any fat from the surface of the cooking liquid. Return the roast and liquid to the pot and stir in the potatoes, carrot pieces, and pearl onions. Cover and bake for 30 minutes. Uncover and stir in the peas. Re-cover and bake until all the vegetables are tender, about 15 minutes longer.

Transfer the roast to a cutting board, tent with aluminum foil, and let rest for about 10 minutes. To serve, cut the roast against the grain into slices and divide among warmed individual shallow bowls. Using a large spoon, divide the vegetables and cooking liquid among the plates. Season with salt and pepper and serve right away.

The best pot roast

Many believe that chuck roast, a muscular shoulder section of the steer, makes the best pot roast. Not actually roasted at all but braised in a savory cooking liquid, the beef becomes meltingly tender and juicy after long, slow cooking in a covered pot.

GRILLED RIB ROAST

Cooking this old-fashioned rib roast on an outdoor grill infuses it with smoky flavors that are hard to achieve in an oven. For accompaniments, place russet potatoes on the grill rack around the roast for the last hour or so and oil-brushed onion wedges for the last 20 minutes.

Coarse sea salt and ground pepper

3 tablespoons minced fresh thyme, or 2 teaspoons dried thyme

2 large cloves garlic, minced

Grated zest of 1 lemon or lime

1 beef rib roast, 6–7 lb (3–3.5 kg), trimmed of excess fat

2 tablespoons olive oil

MAKES 6–8 SERVINGS

Prepare a charcoal or gas grill for indirect-heat cooking over low heat (page 18).

In a small bowl, stir together 4 teaspoons salt, 1½ teaspoons pepper, the thyme, garlic, and lemon zest.

Pat the roast dry. Rub with the oil, then rub the salt mixture over the surface of the meat.

Place the roast, rib side down, on the oiled grill rack, cover the grill, and open the vents halfway. Cook for 45 minutes. If using a charcoal grill, replenish the fire with hot coals. Turn the roast rib side up and cook until an instant-read thermometer inserted into the thickest part away from the bone registers 125°–130°F (52°–54°C) for medium-rare, about 15 minutes longer.

Transfer the roast to a cutting board, tent with aluminum foil, and let rest for 15 minutes. To serve, snip any strings, then carve the meat against the grain into thick slices and arrange on a warmed platter or individual plates.

Ask for quality

For the best-quality rib roast, ask the butcher for the "first cut." This roast comes from the loin end of the steer and has the biggest eye, or meaty portion.

MEAT

RIB-EYE ROAST WITH MUSTARD AND GINGER

Trimming the fat

When preparing roasts, it is a good idea to trim the excess fat from the surface of the meat. As you trim, be sure to leave an even fat layer, ¼ to ½ inch (6 to 12 mm) thick, which will flavor and moisturize the meat as it cooks.

This easy-to-make rib-eye roast has a Far Eastern accent, thanks to a seasoning paste of garlic, ginger, lemon juice, and mustard. For added flavor, slivers of garlic are inserted into the meat. If you prefer, use an 8-pound (4-kg) standing rib roast in place of the boneless rib eye.

Using the tip of a sharp knife, make several slits 1 inch (2.5 cm) deep at regular intervals over the entire surface of the meat. Insert one-third of the garlic slivers into the meat slits. Place the remaining garlic and the ginger in a blender or food processor. Process to a paste, adding some of the lemon juice as needed to moisten the ginger. Add the mustard, the remaining lemon juice, and 1 teaspoon pepper and process to mix well. Alternatively, combine the ingredients in a mortar and pound them to a paste with a pestle.

Coat the roast with the mustard mixture, place in a roasting pan (on a rack, if you like), cover, and let stand at room temperature for about 2 hours, but no longer.

Preheat the oven to 350°F (180°C). Roast the beef, calculating the timing as follows: for medium-rare, about 14 minutes per pound until a meat thermometer registers 125°–130°F (52°–54°C); for medium, about 15 minutes per pound or until a thermometer registers 135°–140°F (57°–60°C).

Transfer the roast to a cutting board, tent with aluminum foil, and let rest for 10 minutes. To serve, snip the strings, then carve the meat against the grain into thick slices and arrange on a warmed platter or individual plates.

1 boneless rib-eye roast, about 4 lb (2 kg), rolled and tied (see page 260)

6 cloves garlic, cut into slivers

½ cup (4 fl oz/125 g) sliced fresh ginger

½ cup (4 fl oz/125 ml) fresh lemon juice

1 cup (8 oz/250 g) Dijon mustard

Ground pepper

MAKES 8 SERVINGS

ROAST PRIME RIB OF BEEF

Carving a rib roast

Using the carving fork, position the roast on the carving board so that the bones stand upright. Cut the rib bones away from the large meaty section, called the eye. Lay the roast, top side up, on the board and cut against the grain into slices ¼ to ½ inch (6 to 12 mm) thick. If desired, cut between the ribs to separate them into large "chops."

A prime rib roast is an excellent choice for a special occasion. It is important to choose the beef with care, so seek out a source that carries high-quality, dry-aged beef. Allow the roast to sit at room temperature for up to 1 hour before cooking.

Position a rack in the lower third of the oven and preheat to 500°F (260°C). Place the roast rib side down (fat side up) in a roasting pan without a rack. Sprinkle with pepper, if you like. If you wish to salt the roast, do so toward the end of roasting.

Roast for 15 minutes. Reduce the heat to 325°F (165°C) and continue roasting. After 1¼ hours, start testing for doneness by inserting an instant-read thermometer into the thickest part of the meat away from the bone; it should register 125°–130°F (52°–54°C) for medium-rare. It should reach this point 2–2½ hours after you turned down the heat.

Transfer the roast to a warmed platter, tent with aluminum foil, and let rest for 15 minutes. Meanwhile, skim off any visible fat from the surface of the pan juices, and set the pan over medium heat. Add ½ cup (4 fl oz/125 ml) water and deglaze the pan, stirring to dislodge any browned bits from

1 prime rib roast with 3–4 ribs, 7–8 lb (3.5–4 kg) trimmed weight

Salt and ground pepper

MAKES 8–10 SERVINGS

the pan bottom. Bring the juices to a boil and season with salt and pepper. Add water as needed for desired consistency and taste. Pour into a warmed bowl.

To serve, carve the roast (see note, opposite) and arrange on a warmed platter or individual plates. Pass the pan juices at the table.

Pan juices

Called jus in French, serving the pan juices along with a roast is a long-standing tradition. Be sure to degrease the juices well before serving.

HERB-CRUSTED BEEF MEDALLIONS

A rich-tasting but low-fat version of a restaurant-style dish, these beef medallions are coated with a crumb mixture made from herbs and *panko* (coarse dried Japanese bread crumbs), seared, and served with a wine and shallot sauce. Serve with oven-roasted potato wedges.

2 large shallots, chopped

1 cup (8 fl oz/250 ml) Zinfandel or other full-bodied red wine

2 cups (16 fl oz/500 ml) beef broth

2 tablespoons plus ½ cup (2 oz/60 g) *panko* or other coarse dried bread crumbs

1 teaspoon unsalted butter

3 tablespoons chopped fresh flat-leaf (Italian) parsley

1 tablespoon chopped fresh thyme

1 tablespoon chopped fresh sage

1 egg white

Canola oil

4 filets mignons, trimmed, each 5 oz (155 g) and 1¼ inches (3 cm) thick

Salt and ground pepper

MAKES 4 SERVINGS

In a heavy saucepan over medium heat, combine the shallots and wine. Bring to a boil and boil until the liquid has evaporated, about 20 minutes. Add the broth and boil until reduced to ¾ cup (6 fl oz/180 ml), about 20 minutes longer. Remove from the heat and pour into a blender or food processor. Add the 2 tablespoons bread crumbs and the butter and purée to form a smooth sauce.

About 10 minutes before the sauce is ready, in a small bowl, stir together the remaining ½ cup bread crumbs, the parsley, thyme, sage, and egg white.

Coat a large frying pan with a thin layer of oil and heat over medium-high heat. Season the filets mignons with salt and pepper and add to the pan. Sear the meat, turning once, about 2 minutes on each side. Remove from the pan and press the herb mixture onto one side of each beef medallion.

Again, coat the pan with oil and return to medium-high heat. Return the medallions to the pan, crumb sides down, and cook until the crumbs are golden and the meat is medium-rare, about 2 minutes.

Remove from the heat. Ladle the puréed sauce onto warmed individual plates, dividing it evenly. Place the beef medallions, crumb sides up, on the sauce. Serve right away.

Mise en place

This French term, literally "putting in place," describes the practice of having all your ingredients cut and measured and any necessary tools gathered before you begin to cook. This is especially important for quick-cooking recipes, because it means you won't have to dash around the kitchen looking for an ingredient or tool when you should be tending what is on the stove.

267

STEAK AU POIVRE

Fats for sautéing

Some recipes use both butter and oil when sautéing for a sound reason. The butter provides flavor but can burn quickly at even moderate temperatures. The oil can withstand higher heat without burning. If you combine the two, you can cook at a higher temperature and still have a buttery flavor.

Pepper and steak have a natural affinity, and this classic recipe consisting of beef fillets crusted with cracked black peppercorns never goes out of style. Serve the meat with garlic-flavored Mashed Potatoes (page 335) or French Fries (page 367).

Spread the cracked peppercorns on a plate. Press the fillet slices into the peppercorns, turning to coat both sides, then push the peppercorns into the meat. Let stand at room temperature for 30 minutes.

Sprinkle the fillets on both sides with salt. In a large, heavy sauté pan over high heat, melt the butter with the oil. When the foam subsides, add the fillets. Sear, turning once, for 3 minutes on each side for rare. Transfer to a warmed platter and keep warm.

Pour off the excess fat from the pan and place over high heat. Pour in the Cognac and deglaze the pan, stirring to dislodge any browned bits from the pan bottom. Add the broth, mustard (if using), and cream and cook until reduced by half, about 5 minutes.

Pour the pan sauce over the fillets and serve right away.

5 tablespoons coarsely cracked peppercorns

4 slices beef fillet, each about ½ lb (250 g) and about 1½ inches (4 cm) thick

Salt

¼ cup (2 oz/60 g) unsalted butter

1 tablespoon olive oil

½ cup (4 fl oz/125 ml) Cognac or Armagnac

½ cup (4 fl oz/125 ml) beef broth

2 tablespoons Dijon mustard, optional

1 cup (8 fl oz/250 ml) heavy (double) cream

MAKES 4 SERVINGS

BROILED STEAK WITH BALSAMIC VINEGAR

Grilling vs. broiling

You can typically use your broiler (grill) or a charcoal or gas grill interchangeably for recipes that call for direct-heat cooking. The timing will be about the same. If using a broiler, make sure you fully preheat it, which takes about 15 minutes, and you turn on your kitchen fan when the meat is cooking.

This recipe is so simple and tasty: affordable sirloin steak is marinated in a honey and balsamic vinegar mixture, then broiled or grilled for a few minutes, sliced, and served. Flank steak can stand in for sirloin steak, if you like, and will provide a slightly chewier texture.

Place the steak in a shallow glass dish just large enough to hold it. In a small bowl, stir together the vinegar, oil, honey, and 1 tablespoon pepper. Pour over the steak. Let stand at room temperature for 1–2 hours.

Preheat a broiler (grill), or prepare a charcoal or gas grill for direct-heat cooking over high heat (page 18).

Lightly sprinkle the steak on both sides with salt. Place the steak on a broiler pan or on the oiled grill rack. Broil or grill, turning once, for 3–4 minutes on each side for medium-rare, or until done to your liking.

Transfer to a cutting board and let rest for 5 minutes. Slice against the grain and serve right away.

1 sirloin steak, 1½ lb (750 g)

⅓ cup (3 fl oz/80 ml) balsamic vinegar

2 tablespoons olive oil

2 tablespoons honey

Salt and ground pepper

MAKES 4 SERVINGS

GRILLED PORTERHOUSE STEAK WITH ROUILLE

Arguably, the best steaks for grilling are cut from the short loin: porterhouse, T-bone, club, and shell or New York strip steaks. Here, a thick, marbled porterhouse is paired with a traditional French red pepper–based sauce. You could also use two smaller T-bones.

1 porterhouse steak,
2½–3 lb (1.25–1.5 kg) and
about 2 inches (5 cm) thick

1 clove garlic, minced

1 teaspoon anchovy paste

2 teaspoons olive oil

Ground pepper

Rouille (page 389)

MAKES 6 SERVINGS

Trim the fat from the edges of the steak, leaving a layer about ¼ inch (6 mm) thick, then slash the layer of fat at 1-inch (2.5-cm) intervals.

In a small bowl, using the back of a spoon, mash together the garlic, anchovy paste, oil, and pepper until smooth. Rub into both sides of the steak. Cover and let stand at room temperature for 1 hour.

Prepare a charcoal or gas grill for direct-heat cooking over high heat (page 18).

Place the steak on the oiled grill rack and sear, turning once, until nicely browned, about 1 minute on each side. Grill over medium-high heat (move the steak to a cooler area or raise the grill rack), turning once, until done to your liking, 16–20 minutes total for medium-rare.

Transfer to a cutting board, tent with aluminum foil, and let rest for 5 minutes. To serve, cut the meat from the bone, then slice the meat against the grain and arrange on a warmed platter. Pass the sauce at the table.

Scoring steaks

Steaks can curl when cooked over high heat. To prevent this, cut 2 or 3 shallow, evenly spaced slashes into the layer of fat that surrounds each steak. The steaks will cook more evenly and make a nicer presentation.

269

LATIN-STYLE GRILLED STEAK

A cumin-scented onion and citrus marinade accents the beefiness of this pleasantly chewy steak. In addition to the Guacamole, serve with black beans, tortillas, and roasted potatoes topped with sour cream, chiles, and tomatoes.

1 flank steak, about 2 lb
(1 kg), or 4 rib-eye steaks,
about ½ lb (250 g) each

1 yellow onion

2 cloves garlic,
finely minced

2 teaspoons ground cumin

½ cup (4 fl oz/125 ml)
fresh lemon juice

Salt and ground pepper

Olive oil for brushing

Guacamole (page 392)

MAKES 4 SERVINGS

Put the steak(s) in a shallow dish. Coarsely chop the yellow onion. In a blender or food processor, combine the onion, garlic, cumin, lemon juice, and 2 teaspoons pepper. Pulse a few times to chop. Pour over the steak(s), cover, and let stand at room temperature for 1 hour.

Prepare a charcoal or gas grill for direct-heat cooking over high heat (page 18), or preheat a broiler (grill).

Remove the steak(s) from the marinade. Brush lightly with oil and sprinkle with salt. Place on the oiled grill rack or on a broiler pan. Grill or broil, turning once, for about 4 minutes on each side for medium-rare.

If using flank steak, transfer to a cutting board, let rest for 5 minutes, and then slice against the grain on the diagonal, arrange on a warmed platter, and garnish with some of the salsa. If using rib-eye steaks, divide among individual plates and garnish. Pass the remaining salsa at the table.

The name game

The same steak is often called by a different name depending on where you live. For example, a strip steak can be labeled a New York, Kansas City, or Delmonico steak. London broil is flank steak in some shops and top sirloin in others. When in doubt, ask your butcher to help you locate the steak you seek.

CHILIED FLANK STEAK

A versatile option

Flank steak is one of the most adaptable and least expensive cuts of beef, making it a good choice for everyday meals. Marinated, quickly cooked, and cut against the grain, it is the perfect meat for a backyard barbecue. Because it is lean, it is also a good candidate for stir-fries.

Flank steak, a flavorful, lean, moderately tender cut, benefits from a long stint in a marinade. Scoring the steak helps keep it from shrinking too much as it cooks. Top round (often sold as London broil) or skirt steak can be substituted for the flank steak.

Using a sharp knife, score the flank steak in a diamond pattern on both sides, cutting about ⅛ inch (3 mm) deep.

In a bowl, whisk together the vegetable juice cocktail, soy sauce, oil, brown sugar, garlic, chili powder, and cumin. Pour half of the marinade into a shallow dish. Place the steak in the dish and pour the remaining marinade over the top. Cover and refrigerate for 24 hours. Remove from the refrigerator 30 minutes before grilling.

Prepare a charcoal or gas grill for direct-heat cooking over high heat (page 18).

Remove the steak from the marinade and set aside. Pour the marinade into a small saucepan and bring to a boil over medium heat. Boil for 2 minutes, remove from the heat, and strain through a fine-mesh sieve into a bowl. Cover and keep warm until serving.

Place the steak on the oiled grill rack. Cook the flank steak, turning once, until done to your liking, about 4 minutes on each side for medium-rare.

Transfer the steak to a cutting board and let rest for 5 minutes. To serve, carve the steak against the grain on the diagonal into slices about ¼ inch (6 mm) thick. Arrange on a warmed platter or individual plates. Pass the reserved marinade at the table as a sauce.

1 flank steak, about 1½ lb (750 g)

⅓ cup (3 fl oz/80 ml) regular or spicy vegetable juice cocktail such as V-8

⅓ cup (3 fl oz/80 ml) soy sauce

¼ cup (2 fl oz/60 ml) safflower oil

⅓ cup (2½ oz/75 g) firmly packed dark brown sugar

2 cloves garlic, minced

1 tablespoon chili powder

⅛ teaspoon ground cumin

MAKES 4 SERVINGS

ROASTED TOP ROUND STEAK AND TOMATOES

Going against the grain

The main thing to remember when carving or slicing meats is to cut them against the grain, or opposite the direction of the muscle fibers. This cutting process enhances tenderness and makes a prettier presentation.

Here, round steak is tenderized in a marinade of tomato juice, then roasted on a bed of basil-scented onions and ripe tomatoes. Buy the first cut of the top round, if possible, as it is the most tender. Use the longer marinating time if you have purchased a less tender cut.

Place the steak in a large zippered plastic bag or a shallow glass dish. Add the tomato juice, the 1 tablespoon basil, 1 teaspoon pepper, and two-thirds of the minced garlic cloves. Slice one of the onions and add it as well. Press out the air from the bag and seal, or cover the dish. Refrigerate, turning occasionally, for at least 12 hours or up to 24 hours.

Preheat the oven to 400°F (200°C).

Remove the steak from the marinade, pat dry, and season with salt and pepper. Discard the marinade.

In a Dutch oven over high heat, warm the 1 tablespoon oil. Add the meat and sear on both sides until browned, about 4 minutes on each side. Remove from the heat.

1 top round steak, first cut, 3–3½ lb (1.5–1.75 kg) and 1½ inches (4 cm) thick

2 cups (16 fl oz/500 ml) tomato juice

1 tablespoon plus 2 teaspoons dried basil

Coarse sea salt and ground pepper

6 cloves garlic, minced

2 yellow onions

1 tablespoon olive oil,
plus more as needed

3 large tomatoes,
seeded and chopped

½ bunch fresh flat-leaf
(Italian) parsley, chopped,
plus more for garnish

2 pinches of sugar

MAKES 8 SERVINGS

Chop the remaining onion. Pour enough oil into a saucepan to film the bottom and place over medium heat. Add the onion and the remaining garlic and sauté until the onion begins to soften, about 2 minutes. Add the tomatoes, the remaining 2 teaspoons basil, the parsley, and the sugar and season with salt and pepper. Taste and add more sugar if needed. Stir well and cook until the tomatoes begin to release their juices, 2–3 minutes. Remove from the heat. Spoon the tomato mixture around the steak.

Roast the steak, uncovered, until the meat is browned on top, about 25 minutes. Cover and continue to roast until the meat is tender, 25–30 minutes longer.

Transfer the steak to a cutting board and let rest for 5 minutes. To serve, cut against the grain into thick slices and arrange the slices on a warmed platter. Spoon the tomato mixture alongside the slices and garnish the platter with parsley.

**Working with
top round beef**

*Top round steak, cut
from a well exercised
part of the steer, is
usually considered
too tough for dry-heat
cooking methods such
as roasting. But a
long marinating time
in an acidic mixture
helps tenderize the
meat while infusing
it with flavor.*

GRILLED STEAK WITH BLACK PEPPER SAUCE

The traditional French sauce for these grilled steaks can be made as much as 1 day in advance, up to the point where the butter is added. Freshly grated nutmeg can be substituted for the mace in the sauce, if desired. Accompany the steaks with Homemade Potato Chips (page 75).

1 yellow onion,
finely chopped

1 carrot, peeled
and finely chopped

2 cloves garlic, minced

½ cup (4 fl oz/125 ml)
red wine vinegar

½ cup (4 fl oz/125 ml)
beef broth

1 cup (8 fl oz/250 ml)
dry red wine

¼ teaspoon ground mace

1 teaspoon chopped
fresh thyme

Salt and ground pepper

4 rib-eye or New York
strip steaks, about
½ lb (250 g) each

Olive oil for brushing

6 tablespoons (3 oz/90 g)
unsalted butter

Chopped fresh flat-leaf
(Italian) parsley for garnish

MAKES 4 SERVINGS

In a saucepan over high heat, combine the onion, carrot, garlic, and vinegar, bring to a boil, and boil until the liquid is reduced by half, 3–4 minutes. Add the broth, wine, mace, and thyme, return to a boil, and boil again until reduced by half. Add 1 tablespoon pepper, season with salt, and set aside.

Prepare a charcoal or gas grill for direct-heat cooking over high heat (page 18), or preheat the broiler (grill). Brush the steaks with oil and sprinkle lightly on both sides with salt and pepper. Place the steaks on the oiled grill rack or on a broiler pan. Grill or broil, turning once, for 3–4 minutes on each side for medium-rare, or until cooked to your liking. Transfer to a platter and let rest for 5 minutes.

Meanwhile, return the sauce to high heat, bring to a boil, reduce the heat to low, and swirl in the butter, 1 tablespoon at a time. Spoon the sauce over the steaks, top with the parsley, and serve right away.

**Evenly cooked
steaks**

*For even cooking,
note the order in
which you place the
steaks on the grill
and turn them
accordingly. On a
round grill, arrange
the steaks in a
clockwise pattern
starting at 12 o'clock.
On a rectangular
grill, put the steaks
in a left-to-right
pattern, just like you
are reading a book.*

BRAISED BEEF BRISKET

Brisket types

Brisket is usually sold parsed into two different cuts: flat cut and point cut. The flat cut is the leaner of the two. The point cut includes the deckle, a lusciously marbled piece of meat much prized by brisket aficionados.

Brisket is one of the best cuts of beef to use for braising because the meat is marbled with fat and remains tender and moist during long, slow cooking. Don't worry about the absence of liquid in this recipe; the meat and onions give off considerable juice.

Pat the brisket dry and rub on both sides with the paprika, ½ teaspoon salt, and 1 teaspoon pepper.

In a large, heavy frying pan over high heat, melt 2 tablespoons of the oil. Add the brisket and brown on both sides, about 15 minutes total. Set aside.

In a large Dutch oven over medium heat, melt the remaining 2 tablespoons oil. Add the onions and cook, stirring, until soft and golden, 15–20 minutes. Place the brisket on top of the onions and cover the pot. Reduce the heat to low and simmer for 1½ hours.

Uncover the pot, add the tomato purée, re-cover, and continue to simmer until the meat is tender, about 1 hour longer. If using, add the carrots and mushrooms during the last 30 minutes of cooking.

Transfer the meat to a platter, tent with aluminum foil, and let rest for about 10 minutes. If you have added the carrots and mushrooms, transfer them with a slotted spoon to a warmed serving bowl or the platter. Taste the pan juices, adjust the seasoning, and pour into a warmed bowl. Slice the brisket against the grain. Serve right away with the vegetables, if using, and the pan juices.

1 beef brisket, 3–4 lb (1.5–2 kg)

2 teaspoons sweet Hungarian paprika

Salt and ground pepper

4 tablespoons canola oil

4 large yellow onions, chopped

2 cups (16 fl oz/500 ml) canned tomato purée

8 large carrots, peeled and cut into 3-inch (7.5-cm) lengths, optional

1 lb (500 g) white or cremini mushrooms, cut into quarters if large, optional

MAKES 6 SERVINGS

KANSAS CITY–STYLE BARBECUED BRISKET

Barbecue styles

The sauce served with barbecued meats in the United States differs according to region. For example, in North Carolina, the sauce is vinegar based; in South Carolina, it is mustard based; and in Kansas City, only a sweet, thick tomato-based sauce will do.

Brisket of beef, another flavorful, none-too-tender cut, is a perfect choice for slow roasting in a covered grill. Here it is prepared Kansas City style, with plenty of spices and a classic tomato-based barbecue sauce, then shredded for serving as is or on fluffy sandwich buns.

Prepare a charcoal or gas grill for indirect-heat cooking over low heat (page 18).

In a small cup or bowl, stir together the paprika, 1½ teaspoons salt, ½ teaspoon black pepper, and the cayenne pepper. Pat the brisket dry and rub the entire surface with the oil, then rub the paprika mixture over the meat.

Sprinkle half of the wood chips on the fire, or for a gas grill, wrap them in aluminum foil, poke holes in the bottom of the packet, and place on the lava rocks. Place the brisket on the oiled grill rack. Cover the grill and open the vents slightly less than halfway, or enough to maintain slow, steady heat. Cook for 1 hour. Turn the brisket, add the remaining wood chips to the grill, and replenish the coals if using a charcoal grill. Cook for 1 hour longer. Brush the meat lightly with the

2 teaspoons sweet Hungarian paprika

Salt and ground black pepper

½ teaspoon cayenne pepper

1 beef brisket, 4–5 lb (2–2.5 kg), trimmed of excess fat

2 tablespoons olive oil

3 handfuls hickory chips, soaked in water to cover for 1 hour

6 cups (48 fl oz/1.5 l) Basic Barbecue Sauce (page 376)

MAKES 8 SERVINGS

barbecue sauce, then turn the brisket and cook, repeating 2 or 3 times, until the brisket is well browned and has formed a crust on the outside, about 3½ hours total. Add fresh ignited coals to the charcoal fire every hour or so.

Transfer the meat to a cutting board, tent with aluminum foil, and let rest for 10 minutes. To serve, carve into thin slices against the grain, allowing it to crumble, and/or pull the meat apart with 2 forks. Arrange on a warmed platter and spoon some of the barbecue sauce over the top. Pass the remaining sauce at the table.

True barbecue

Although many people use the terms interchangeably, barbecuing and grilling are not the same. Barbecuing means smoking foods on an outdoor grill over low, indirect heat for a long time.

KOREAN GRILLED SHORT RIBS

Most short ribs are braised or roasted, but Korean cooks have an ingenious method for tenderizing the meat before grilling it to a crusty turn. They rub cross-cut ribs with sugar to soften the flesh and then marinate them in a rich sesame, soy, and ginger paste.

4 lb (2 kg) flanken-style beef short ribs

⅓ cup (3 oz/90 g) sugar

½ cup (2 oz/60 g) sesame seeds

¼ cup (2 fl oz/60 ml) Asian sesame oil

½ cup (4 fl oz/125 ml) plus 2 tablespoons soy sauce

3 cloves garlic, minced

2 teaspoons red pepper flakes

1 tablespoon grated fresh ginger

3 tablespoons all-purpose (plain) flour

MAKES 4 OR 5 SERVINGS

Make deep cuts through the meat on the ribs at regular intervals. Rub the sugar into the meat and let stand at room temperature for 30 minutes.

In a small, dry frying pan over medium-low heat, toast the sesame seeds, stirring, until golden, about 3 minutes. Pour onto a plate to cool, then pulverize using a mortar and pestle.

In a bowl, stir together the ground sesame seeds, sesame oil, soy sauce, garlic, red pepper flakes, ginger, and flour. Coat the ribs with the mixture and let stand for about 1 hour.

Prepare a charcoal or gas grill for direct-heat cooking over high heat (page 18), or preheat the broiler (grill). Place the ribs on the oiled grill rack or the broiler pan. Grill or broil, turning once, until well browned on the outside but still somewhat rare in the center, about 5 minutes on each side. Serve right away.

Flanken-style short ribs

This recipe uses flanken-style, or cross-cut short ribs. They are thinner and more tender than traditional American or English beef ribs and cook more quickly on the grill.

BEEF BOURGUIGNON

Troubleshooting browning

Browning meat before adding the liquid is a critical first step in many braised recipes. But crowding meat into a pan will cause it to steam rather than brown. If you can't fit all the meat in a single, generously spaced layer, brown it in batches, transferring each batch to a plate as it is ready.

This classic dish is the perfect illustration of how to take a handful of rustic ingredients—tough beef chuck, humble brown mushrooms, and ordinary vegetables—and turn them into a rich, tender braise fit for entertaining. Serve with steamed potatoes to soak up the delicious sauce.

In a frying pan over medium heat, sauté the salt pork until the fat is rendered, 8–10 minutes. Using a slotted spoon, transfer the pork to paper towels to drain; set aside.

Add enough oil to the fat in the pan to measure ¼ cup (2 fl oz/ 60 ml). Add the shallots, yellow onions, carrots, and garlic. Sauté until the vegetables begin to soften, about 10 minutes. Using a slotted spoon, transfer the vegetables to a Dutch oven. Set the frying pan aside.

Spread the flour on a plate and season with salt, pepper, and nutmeg. Coat the beef cubes with the flour mixture, shaking off the excess. Add oil as needed to the fat remaining in the frying pan and place over high heat. Working in batches if necessary to avoid crowding, add the beef cubes and brown well on all sides, about 15 minutes. Using the slotted spoon, transfer the beef to the Dutch oven. Add the Cognac and a little of the broth to the frying pan and deglaze, stirring to dislodge any browned bits from the pan bottom. Add to the beef along with the thyme, all but ½ cup (4 fl oz/125 ml) of the remaining broth, the wine, and the bay leaf. Bring to a boil, reduce the heat to low, cover, and simmer on the stove top or in an oven preheated to 325°F (165°C) until the beef is tender, about 3 hours.

In a frying pan over medium heat, melt 2 tablespoons of the butter. Add the pearl onions in a single layer, then sprinkle with the sugar. Cook, stirring, until tender and golden, 8–10 minutes; add only enough of the ½ cup reserved broth to prevent scorching. Transfer to a bowl and set aside.

In the same pan over medium heat, melt the remaining 3 tablespoons butter. Add the mushrooms and sauté until browned, about 5 minutes; set aside.

Add the pearl onions and mushrooms to the beef during the last 30 minutes of cooking. Just before serving, remove and discard the thyme and bay leaf and taste and adjust the seasoning. Transfer to a warmed serving dish, sprinkle with the salt pork and parsley, and serve right away.

½ lb (250 g) salt pork, cut into ¼-inch (6-mm) dice

Olive oil as needed

8 shallots, minced

2 yellow onions, finely diced

2 carrots, peeled and finely diced

2 cloves garlic, minced

About 2 cups (10 oz/315 g) all-purpose (plain) flour

Salt, ground pepper, and freshly grated nutmeg

3 lb (1.5 kg) well-marbled beef chuck, cut into 2-inch (5-cm) cubes

¼ cup (2 fl oz/60 ml) Cognac

2 cups (16 fl oz//500 ml) beef broth

2 fresh thyme sprigs

3 cups (24 fl oz/750 ml) dry red wine

1 bay leaf

5 tablespoons (2½ oz/75 g) unsalted butter

18–24 pearl onions, peeled (see page 333)

2 tablespoons sugar

1 lb (500 g) white or cremini mushrooms, stemmed

Chopped fresh flat-leaf (Italian) parsley for garnish

MAKES 6 SERVINGS

TOMATO-GLAZED MEAT LOAF

This is a basic, old-fashioned, crowd-pleasing meat loaf, complete with tomato sauce on top. If you like, skip the tomato sauce and top the loaf with a few slices of bacon. If there are leftovers, make meat loaf sandwiches with a little chili sauce spread on the bread.

Canola oil for pan

3 slices bread

Tomato juice

2 lb (1 kg) ground (minced) beef chuck

2 eggs

1 large yellow onion, finely chopped

1 tablespoon herbes de Provence

¼ cup (⅓ oz/10 g) chopped fresh flat-leaf (Italian) parsley

Salt and ground pepper

1 cup (8 fl oz/250 ml) All-Purpose Tomato Sauce (page 377) or chili sauce

MAKES 4 SERVINGS

Preheat the oven to 350°F (180°C). Oil a baking pan.

In a shallow bowl, soak the bread in tomato juice just to cover, then remove and squeeze very dry.

In a bowl, combine the ground meat, soaked bread, eggs, onion, herbs, and parsley and season with salt and pepper. Mix well with your hands. Form the meat mixture into an oval loaf about 1 inch (2.5 cm) thick, and place in the prepared pan. Spread the tomato sauce over the top.

Bake until the meat is no longer pink in the center when tested with a knife, about 1¼ hours. Let rest for 15 minutes, then slice and serve hot.

Chili sauce

Not to be confused with Asian-made chile sauces, this American-style sauce is a mild ketchuplike blend of tomatoes, chili powder, onions, green bell peppers (capsicums), vinegar, sugar, and spices. Look for chili sauce near the condiments in the supermarket.

GINGER BEEF AND ASPARAGUS STIR-FRY

Fast, easy, and economical, this Asian-inspired dish calls for a large amount of oil for cooking the beef to prevent sticking. But almost all the oil is then poured off, so the finished dish is not oily at all. Salting the ginger softens it and speeds up cooking time. Serve with steamed rice.

1 lb (500 g) flank steak

1 tablespoon *each* soy sauce, Asian sesame oil, and cornstarch (cornflour)

¼ lb (125 g) fresh ginger, cut into matchstick strips

Salt

1 cup (8 fl oz/250 ml) peanut oil

1 lb (500 g) asparagus, cut into 1-inch lengths

1 clove garlic, minced

3 tablespoons dry sherry

1 teaspoon sugar

MAKES 4 SERVINGS

Cut the steak against the grain into slices about 2½ inches (6 cm) long and ⅛ inch (3 mm) thick. Place in a bowl and add the soy sauce, sesame oil, and cornstarch. Mix well and let stand at room temperature for about 30 minutes. In another bowl, toss the ginger strips with 1 teaspoon salt. Let stand until the ginger softens, about 20 minutes. Rinse and pat dry.

Place a wok or large, heavy frying pan over high heat. When hot, add the peanut oil and swirl to coat the pan. When the peanut oil is almost smoking, add the beef and toss and stir until the beef changes color, 1–2 minutes. Transfer to a plate.

Pour off all but 3 tablespoons of the oil and return the pan to high heat. Add the asparagus and 3 tablespoons water and stir-fry until the asparagus is almost cooked, about 2 minutes. Add the ginger, garlic, sherry, sugar, and beef. Toss and stir until the beef is heated through, 1–2 minutes.

Transfer to a warmed platter and serve right away.

Hot wok, cold oil

For the best results when stir-frying, Chinese chefs follow the adage "hot wok, cold oil." In other words, get your wok as hot as possible before adding the cold oil; get the oil searing hot before adding the other ingredients.

GRILLED STEAK FAJITAS

Slicing skirt steak

The grain on a skirt steak will vary slightly down its length. To ensure tenderness, you may need to change the angle of your knife as you progress to ensure you are cutting in the opposite direction of the meat fibers.

Fajitas are typically made from skirt steak, but flank steak can also be used. Tuck the grilled meat into flour tortillas that have been wrapped in aluminum foil and warmed on the grill. Offer Fresh Tomato Salsa (page 393), Guacamole (page 392), and sour cream as accompaniments.

In a small bowl, whisk together the tequila, lime juice, 2 tablespoons oil, garlic, ½ teaspoon salt, and red pepper flakes. Reserve ¼ cup (2 fl oz/60 ml) of the marinade. Place the meat in a shallow bowl large enough for it to lie flat. Pour the remaining marinade over the steak and turn to coat both sides. Cover and refrigerate, turning the meat occasionally, for at least 3 hours, or all day if you wish.

Prepare a charcoal or gas grill for direct-heat cooking over high heat (page 18), or preheat the broiler (grill).

Remove the steak from the marinade and pat very dry. Discard the marinade.

Brush the onion slices and bell pepper rings with oil and sprinkle with salt. Place on the oiled grill rack or on a broiler pan. Grill or broil for 3 minutes, then brush with oil, turn, and grill until lightly browned, about 3 minutes longer. Transfer to a warmed platter, separating the onion slices into rings; set aside while you cook the meat.

Place the steak on the grill rack or on a broiler pan. Grill or broil, turning and brushing with the reserved marinade twice, after 2 minutes of cooking, until done to your liking, about 9 minutes for medium-rare.

Transfer the steak to a cutting board and let rest for 5 minutes. To serve, cut the steak on the diagonal against the grain into thin slices. Mound the steak slices on the platter with the onions and peppers. Serve with the tortillas and pass the cilantro.

⅓ cup (3 fl oz/80 ml) tequila

¼ cup (2 fl oz/60 ml) fresh lime juice

2 tablespoons olive oil, plus more for brushing

2 cloves garlic, minced

Salt

½ teaspoon red pepper flakes

2 lb (1 kg) skirt steak or flank steak

2 red or yellow onions, sliced ½ inch (12 mm) thick

3 red or green bell peppers (capsicums), seeded and sliced into rings

12 or more flour tortillas, 6–8 inches (15–20 cm) in diameter, warmed

Chopped fresh cilantro (fresh coriander) for garnish

MAKES 6 SERVINGS

SHREDDED BEEF TACOS

Beef cooked for several hours with bold flavorings becomes pleasantly spicy and so tender that it can be shredded with a fork. To serve, mound the beef on warmed tortillas, top with Avocado-Tomatillo Salsa, and accompany with Black Beans and Rice with Corn Salsa (page 317).

1 tri-tip or boneless chuck roast, 2 lb (1 kg)

Salt and ground pepper

4 ancho chiles

2 yellow onions, halved

4 cloves garlic, crushed

1 tablespoon fresh oregano leaves

12 corn tortillas, about 6 inches (15 cm) in diameter, warmed

Avocado-Tomatillo Salsa (page 392)

MAKES 4–6 SERVINGS

Preheat the oven to 325°F (165°C).

Rub the roast with 1 teaspoon each salt and pepper. Place in a Dutch oven and crumble the ancho chiles over the top. Add the onion halves, garlic, and oregano. Cover, place in the oven, and cook until the meat is juicy and easily shreds with a fork, about 5 hours.

Remove the pot from the oven and discard the onions. Using a fork, shred the beef in the pot, blending it with the juices. Keep warm until ready to serve, or let cool and refrigerate until ready to serve, then reheat over low heat. Serve the beef warm in the tortillas. Top with the salsa.

Ovenproof cookware

Not all pots and pans are made to go into the oven. Be sure to read the instructions that come with your cookware to determine if they are ovenproof. For example, if they have plastic handles, they should not be used in the oven.

HERB-RUBBED VEAL ROAST

This lean cut of veal is kept moist by an herb rub that forms a flavorful golden brown crust as the meat roasts. When the veal is sliced, you will see where the tarragon and garlic have worked their way under the surface of the meat and mingled with the veal's natural juices.

1 boneless veal loin roast, 4–5 lb (2–2.5 kg)

4 cloves garlic, minced

1 tablespoon minced fresh tarragon

Salt

1 teaspoon lemon pepper spice blend

1 tablespoon olive oil, or as needed

MAKES 8–10 SERVINGS

With a thin, sharp knife, trim all but ¼–½ inch (6–12 mm) of fat from the exterior of the meat. Use the tip of the knife to cut through the fat layer in 4 or 5 places across the top of the meat, making slits about ⅛ inch (3 mm) wide and ½ inch (12 mm) deep. Put the meat on a plate.

In a small bowl, combine the garlic, tarragon, 2 teaspoons salt, and the lemon pepper. Stir in enough oil to form a thick paste. Spread the paste evenly over the meat, pressing it into the slits on top. Let the roast stand at room temperature for 30–60 minutes to absorb the flavors.

Preheat the oven to 350°F (180°C). Place a rack in a roasting pan just large enough to accommodate it, and put the veal on the rack. Roast until an instant-read thermometer inserted into the center of the roast registers 125°–130°F (52°–54°C) for medium-rare or 135°–140°F (57°–60°C) for medium, 1½–2 hours. Begin checking for doneness every 15 minutes after the first hour.

Transfer the roast to a cutting board, tent with aluminum foil, and let it rest for 15 minutes. Cut the meat across the grain into slices ¼–½ inch (6–12 mm) thick. Serve on warmed individual plates with the pan juices spooned over the top.

Shopping for veal

The most tender and white veal is from a milk-fed calf. Grass-fed veal is also delicious but has a slightly stronger flavor and redder color. Veal is popular in Italian cookery. If you're having trouble finding it in your regular meat market, try a butcher shop in an Italian neighborhood.

VEAL CHOPS WITH PROSCIUTTO AND CHEESE

Sandwiching thin chops

If you cannot find large, thick veal chops, sandwich thin cutlets together with the filling, dip in seasoned flour, then beaten egg, then bread crumbs. Sauté in olive oil and top with the sauce.

This stuffed veal chop recipe comes from Val d'Aosta, a mountainous area of northern Italy known for its Fontina cheese and rustic cuisine. The chops can be stuffed and refrigerated for up to 8 hours before cooking; the tomato sauce can also be made ahead of time.

Cut a horizontal pocket in each veal chop as for a pork chop (see page 261). Carefully insert 1 prosciutto slice, 1 cheese slice, and 2 sage leaves into each pocket.

Preheat the broiler (grill).

Brush the chops with oil and sprinkle on both sides with salt and pepper. Arrange on a broiler pan and broil, turning once, for about 5 minutes on each side for medium, or until done to your liking. Meanwhile, in a saucepan, warm the tomato sauce over medium-high heat.

Transfer the veal chops to warmed individual plates, spoon the hot tomato sauce over the top, and serve right away.

6 bone-in veal chops, each about 1 inch (2.5 cm) thick

6 thin slices prosciutto

6 thin slices Fontina cheese

12 fresh sage leaves

Olive oil for brushing

Salt and ground pepper

2 cups (16 fl oz/500 ml) All-Purpose Tomato Sauce (page 377)

MAKES 6 SERVINGS

OSSO BUCO, MILAN STYLE

Gremolata

In a bowl, mix together 5 tbsp (⅓ oz/10 g) chopped fresh Italian (flat-leaf) parsley; 2 tbsp grated lemon zest; and 2 tsp finely minced garlic. Always sprinkle it onto food at the end of cooking. If the gremolata is added too early, the heat will dissipate its fresh flavors.

Osso buco means "bone with a hole," a good description of a veal shank. In this classic dish from Milan, the shanks are braised with aromatic vegetables, wine, and stock, then topped with *gremolata*, a mixture of parsley, grated lemon zest, and minced garlic, just before serving.

Put the flour in a shallow bowl and season generously with salt and pepper. Coat the shanks with the seasoned flour, shaking off the excess.

In a large, heavy frying pan over high heat, warm ¼ cup (2 fl oz/60 ml) of the oil. Add as many veal shanks as will fit without crowding and brown on all sides, 15–20 minutes. Transfer to a platter and add the remaining ¼ cup oil to the pan. Brown the remaining shanks. Transfer the shanks to the platter and set aside.

In a Dutch oven over medium heat, melt the butter. Add the onions, carrots, and celery and cook, stirring occasionally, until tender, about 15 minutes. Place the veal shanks on top of the vegetables and add the wine and tomatoes. Pour in enough stock to cover. Bring to a boil, reduce the heat to low, cover, and simmer until the veal is very tender, 1–1¼ hours. The meat should be almost falling off the bones. Season the vegetable sauce with salt and pepper.

Sprinkle the gremolata over the shanks, re-cover, and cook for 5 minutes longer just to warm the mixture. Serve right away with the vegetable sauce.

1½ cups (7½ oz/235 g) all-purpose (plain) flour

Salt and ground pepper

6 meaty veal shanks, each about 1½ lb (750 g), cut crosswise in half by the butcher

½ cup (4 fl oz/125 ml) olive oil, or as needed

½ cup (4 oz/125 g) unsalted butter

3 large onions, chopped

1½ cups (8 oz/250 g) *each* diced carrots and celery

1 cup (8 fl oz/250 ml) dry white wine

4 cups (1½ lb/750 g) diced plum (Roma) tomatoes

About 4 cups (32 fl oz/1 l) Beef Stock (page 22)

Gremolata (see note, left)

MAKES 6 SERVINGS

VEAL PARMESAN

Despite its name, this classic veal dish is from the Italian south. Parmesan cheese does come from northern Italy, but the topping of mozzarella and tomato speaks of Naples. If you like, sauté eggplant slices and lay them atop the sautéed veal, then cover with the mozzarella.

1½ lb (750 g) veal scallops, about ½ inch (12 mm) thick

¾ cup (4 oz/125 g) all-purpose (plain) flour

Salt and ground pepper

½ cup (2 oz/60 g) grated Parmesan cheese

¼ cup (2 fl oz/60 ml) extra-virgin olive oil

8–12 thin slices fresh mozzarella

1 cup (8 fl oz/250 ml) All-Purpose Tomato Sauce (page 377)

MAKES 4 SERVINGS

One at time, place the veal scallops between 2 sheets of plastic wrap and flatten with a meat pounder until an even ¼ inch (6 mm) thick. Put the flour in a shallow bowl and season with salt and pepper and a few tablespoons of the Parmesan. Coat the veal with the seasoned flour, shaking off any excess.

In a large frying pan over medium-high heat, warm the oil. Working in batches if necessary to avoid crowding, add the veal and brown lightly on the first sides, about 2 minutes. Turn the veal, brown on the second sides for 1 minute, and top with the mozzarella slices. Reduce the heat to low, cover, and cook until the cheese softens, about 2 minutes.

Meanwhile, in a saucepan, warm the tomato sauce over medium-high heat.

Divide the veal among warmed individual plates and spoon the sauce evenly over the top. Sprinkle with the remaining Parmesan and serve.

Veal scallops

Also known as scaloppine in Italian and escalopes in French, scallops are slices of boneless veal pounded to an even thickness to tenderize them and enable quick cooking. Scallops can be breaded or simply floured, and are usually sautéed.

279

VEAL PICCATA

This is the most basic of veal scallop recipes: coated with flour, browned in a frying pan, and dressed with a quick lemon-caper pan sauce. The veal should be cut from the leg and pounded gently. The sauce is made by deglazing the pan with a little broth and lemon juice.

1½ lb (750 g) veal scallops, about ½ inch (12 mm) thick

¾ cup (4 oz/125 g) all-purpose (plain) flour

Salt and ground pepper

4 tablespoons (2 oz/60 g) unsalted butter

1½ teaspoons extra-virgin olive oil

1 cup (8 fl oz/250 ml) beef broth

3 tablespoons fresh lemon juice

¼ cup (2½ oz/75 g) rinsed capers

2 tablespoons chopped fresh flat-leaf (Italian) parsley

MAKES 4 SERVINGS

One at time, place the veal scallops between 2 sheets of plastic wrap and flatten with a meat pounder until an even ¼ inch (6 mm) thick. Put the flour in a shallow bowl and season with salt and pepper. Coat the veal with the seasoned flour, shaking off any excess.

In a large frying pan over high heat, melt 2 tablespoons of the butter with the oil. Working in batches if necessary to avoid crowding, add the veal and cook, turning once, until golden on both sides, 2–3 minutes on each side. Transfer to a warmed platter and keep warm.

Pour off the excess fat from the pan and return to high heat. Pour in the broth, bring to a boil, and deglaze the pan, stirring to dislodge any browned bits from the pan bottom. Boil until the broth is reduced by half. Add the lemon juice and capers, then stir in the remaining 2 tablespoons butter. Pour the sauce over the veal. Sprinkle with the parsley and serve right away.

Milanese-style veal scallops

For a Milanese-style dish, dip the veal in seasoned flour, then beaten egg, then bread crumbs. Sauté the coated veal in olive oil until golden. Omit the lemon juice and capers.

HERBED RACK OF LAMB

Depending on the rest of your menu, one rack of lamb will serve two or three people. For a neater presentation, ask your butcher to french the ribs. For easy accompaniments, cook eggplant slices, onion wedges, and red pepper halves on the grill with the lamb.

Prepare a charcoal or gas grill for direct-heat cooking over medium-high heat (page 18).

Trim the excess fat from the rack of lamb. Make a small slit between each rib and insert a sliver of garlic. Coat the meat lightly with olive oil, then rub it with the dry rub. If the ribs are frenched (see note, above), cover the exposed rib tips with a strip of aluminum foil so they won't burn.

Place the lamb on the oiled grill rack and grill, turning several times, until an instant-read thermometer inserted in the center of the rack away from the bone registers 125°–130°F (52°–54°C) for medium-rare, 20–25 minutes.

Transfer to a cutting board and let rest for 5 minutes. Cut the ribs into individual chops to serve.

Dry rub for lamb or pork

Combine 2 tsp dried rosemary; 2 large cloves garlic, minced; 1½ tsp salt; 1 tsp ground pepper; and the grated zest of 1 lemon or lime.

1 rack of lamb, about 2 lb (1 kg), with 8 ribs

1 clove garlic, cut into slivers

Olive oil for coating

2 tablespoons dry rub (see note, left)

MAKES 2 OR 3 SERVINGS

GRILLED FILLET OF LAMB AND VEGETABLES

For this simple dish, lamb fillets are marinated and then grilled with vegetables and topped with an herb vinaigrette. Serve with rice and a green salad and pour a light red wine at the table. Any leftovers can be tucked into warmed pita bread with crumbled feta the next day.

In a large bowl, whisk together the oil, rosemary, and a pinch each of salt and pepper. Reserve half of the mixture. Add the lamb fillets to the bowl and turn to coat evenly. Set aside at room temperature for 1 hour.

When the lamb has marinated for 1 hour, put the bell peppers and onion slices on a plate and brush them generously with the reserved marinade.

Prepare a charcoal or gas grill for direct-heat cooking over medium-high heat (page 18).

To make the vinaigrette, in a bowl, whisk together the olive oil, vinegar, and mixed fresh herbs. Season with salt and pepper. Set aside.

Place the lamb fillets on the oiled grill rack. Grill, turning the lamb every 5 minutes, until an instant-read thermometer inserted into the thickest part of a fillet registers 125°–130°F (52°–54°C) for medium-rare, 15–20 minutes. When the lamb has been on the grill for 5 minutes, place the onion slices on the grill and cook until soft on one side, 5–7 minutes. Carefully turn the onions and, at the same time, place the bell peppers, skin side down, on the grill rack. Continue

About lamb fillets

Similar to a tenderloin of pork or beef, a lamb fillet is the long eye of meat attached to the rib bones of a rack of lamb. Some butchers carry fillets already removed from the racks, and others stock only lamb racks. If only the latter is available, you can easily cut the meat from the rack yourself, or ask the butcher to do it for you.

¼ cup (2 fl oz/60 ml) olive oil

1 tablespoon minced fresh rosemary

Salt and ground pepper

3 racks of lamb, 1½–2 lb (750 g–1 kg) each, boned and trimmed of excess fat

2 red and 2 yellow bell peppers (capsicums), quartered lengthwise and seeded

3 large red onions, cut into slices ¾ inch (2 cm) thick

FOR THE VINAIGRETTE

¼ cup (2 fl oz/60 ml) olive oil

1 tablespoon red wine vinegar

2 teaspoons mixed minced fresh herbs such as rosemary, oregano, mint, chives, and/or thyme

Salt and ground pepper

MAKES 6 SERVINGS

to cook the onions and peppers, turning the peppers once, until soft, 5–10 minutes longer.

When the lamb is ready, transfer to a cutting board, tent with aluminum foil, and let rest for 10 minutes. Slice across the grain and transfer the lamb and the vegetables to a warmed platter. Quickly whisk the vinaigrette and drizzle evenly over the top. Serve right away.

STUFFED LEG OF LAMB

This Provençal-inspired recipe is stuffed with a bold mixture of sun-dried tomatoes, olives, and minced fresh herbs. Natural partners include steamed spinach and creamy mashed potatoes flavored with roasted garlic. Have your butcher bone the leg of lamb for stuffing.

3 cloves garlic, minced

¼ cup (2 oz/60 g) well-drained, oil-packed sun-dried tomatoes, thinly sliced

2 tablespoons chopped, pitted brine-cured black olives

5 tablespoons (½ oz/15 g) chopped fresh flat-leaf (Italian) parsley

1½ teaspoons minced fresh rosemary

½ teaspoon minced fresh sage

1 cup (4 oz/125 g) dried Herbed Bread Crumbs (page 30)

4 tablespoons (2 oz/60 g) unsalted butter, melted

Salt and ground pepper

1 boneless leg of lamb, 5–6 lb (2.5–3 kg), trimmed of excess fat and butterflied (see page 261)

1 tablespoon olive oil

Fresh rosemary and/or thyme sprigs for garnish

MAKES 8–10 SERVINGS

In a bowl, combine the garlic, sun-dried tomatoes, olives, parsley, minced rosemary, sage, bread crumbs, melted butter, and a pinch each of salt and pepper. Mix well.

Lay the lamb flat on a work surface, with the outside surface of the meat facing down. Season with salt and pepper. Spread the crumb mixture evenly over the lamb. Roll up the lamb into a bundle resembling its original shape, completely enclosing the stuffing. Using kitchen string, tie the roast crosswise on 2 sides like a package. Sprinkle the outside lightly with salt and pepper.

Position an oven rack in the lower third of the oven and preheat to 450°F (230°C).

In a large frying pan over medium heat, warm the oil. Add the lamb and brown on all sides, about 10 minutes. Transfer the lamb to a rack in a roasting pan.

Roast for 30 minutes. Turn the lamb over and reduce the heat to 325°F (165°C). Continue to roast until an instant-read thermometer inserted into the thickest part registers 125°–130°F (52°–54°C) for medium-rare, about 40 minutes.

Transfer to a cutting board, tent with aluminum foil, and let rest for 15 minutes. To serve, snip the strings, cut the lamb against the grain into thin slices, and arrange on a warmed platter. Garnish with the herb sprigs.

Matching lamb with wine

Choose a wine with good acidity to stand up to the tomatoes in this dish. Ideally, it also boasts an herbal quality to echo the fresh herbs in the recipe. Try a domestic Syrah or a wine from the southern Rhône region of France to find both qualities.

GRILLED BUTTERFLIED LEG OF LAMB

**Butterflied
leg of lamb**

*A butterflied leg of
lamb is an uneven
piece of meat, which
can be a good thing
if your guests all like
their lamb cooked to
different degrees of
doneness. If you are
a novice when it
comes to boning and
butterflying a lamb
leg, ask the butcher
to do it for you.*

This butterflied leg of lamb is bathed in a simple marinade, grilled, and then served with a mint-laced mustard sauce. It can instead be accompanied with mint jelly, any fruit chutney (pages 397–98), or Tzatziki (page 68). If you like, garnish the platter with mint sprigs.

In a bowl, whisk together the oil and garlic and season with salt and pepper. Put the lamb in a shallow glass dish and rub the oil mixture over the entire surface. Let the lamb marinate at room temperature for 1 hour, or cover and refrigerate for up to overnight.

Prepare a charcoal or gas grill for direct-heat cooking over medium-high heat (page 18), or preheat the broiler (grill).

To make the mint mustard, in a small bowl, stir together the mint, mayonnaise, mustard, garlic, and lemon juice. Set aside.

Place the lamb on the oiled grill rack or on a broiler (grill) pan. Grill or broil, turning once, until an instant-read thermometer inserted into the thickest part registers 125°–130°F (52°–54°C), about 12 minutes on each side.

Transfer to a cutting board, tent with aluminum foil, and let rest for 10 minutes. To serve, cut against the grain into thin slices and arrange on a warmed platter. Pass the mint mustard at the table.

¼ cup (2 fl oz/60 ml) olive oil

3 cloves garlic, minced

Salt and ground pepper

1 bone-in leg of lamb, 5–6 lb (2.5–3 kg), trimmed of excess fat, boned, and butterflied (see page 261)

FOR THE MINT MUSTARD

6 tablespoons (⅓ oz/10 g) minced fresh mint

3 tablespoons mayonnaise

¾ cup (6 oz/185 g) Dijon mustard

1 clove garlic, minced

1 teaspoon fresh lemon juice

MAKES 8–10 SERVINGS

FAST MUSTARD LAMB CHOPS

**Working with
lamb chops**

*When working with
lamb, trim off as
much of the external
fat as possible, as it
can taste and smell
unpleasant when
charred. For the best
taste, serve lamb
chops while they are
still hot, after just a
brief resting period.*

This recipe is for the person who loves good food but has little time to cook. The succulent, tender loin lamb chops roast in only 10 minutes. Serve them with quick-cooking couscous laced with toasted pine nuts and snipped fresh chives or chopped fresh mint.

Preheat the oven to 500°F (260°C). Lightly rub a shallow roasting pan with oil.

Rub both sides of each chop with pepper and place in the prepared roasting pan. Slather about 1 teaspoon mustard on one side of each chop, and let the lamb come to room temperature, 10–15 minutes.

Roast the chops, mustard sides up, until they are browned on top, about 5 minutes. Turn the chops and spread about 1 teaspoon mustard on the second sides. Continue to roast until the meat is pink when cut in the center, about 5 minutes longer (depending on thickness), or until done to your liking.

Let rest for 5 minutes. Divide the chops among warmed individual plates, placing 2 chops on each plate. Sprinkle with the parsley and serve right away.

Canola oil for pan

8 loin lamb chops, each 4–5 oz (125–155 g) and 1–1¼ inches (2.5–3 cm) thick, trimmed of fat and edges scored

Ground pepper

5–6 tablespoons whole-grain Dijon mustard, or as needed

Chopped fresh flat-leaf (Italian) parsley for garnish

MAKES 4 SERVINGS

LAMB CHOPS WITH CORIANDER-ORANGE BUTTER

Simply cooked lamb chops are classic French bistro fare. Here, they are served topped with a slice of coriander-orange butter. Oven-roasted vegetables and a glass of Pinot Noir or Cabernet Sauvignon are the ideal accompaniments.

FOR THE CORIANDER-
ORANGE BUTTER

6 tablespoons (3 oz/90 g) unsalted butter, at room temperature

3 tablespoons minced fresh cilantro (fresh coriander)

½ teaspoon ground coriander

¾ teaspoon grated orange zest

Salt and ground pepper

12 lamb chops, about 3 lb (1.5 kg) total weight and each about 1 inch (2.5 cm) thick, trimmed of excess fat

2 tablespoons olive oil

Salt and ground pepper

MAKES 6 SERVINGS

To make the butter, in a small bowl, using a fork or a wooden spoon, beat together the butter, cilantro, ground coriander, and orange zest until well blended. Season with salt and pepper. Cover and refrigerate for 15 minutes. Transfer the butter mixture to a sheet of plastic wrap and shape it into a log about 3 inches (7.5 cm) long and 1 inch (2.5 cm) in diameter. Wrap the butter tightly. Refrigerate until firm, about 30 minutes.

Preheat the broiler (grill).

Brush the lamb chops on both sides with the oil and season with salt and pepper. Broil (grill), turning once, until browned on the outside and pink in the center when cut into with a small knife, about 5 minutes on each side.

Let rest for 5 minutes. Transfer the lamb chops to warmed individual plates. Cut the butter into slices ¼ inch (6 mm) thick, and place 1 slice on top of each chop. Serve right away.

Chop types

Lamb chops come either from the loin section or the rib section of the animal. Loin chops have the signature T-shaped bone of the loin and are the more costly of the two. On rib chops, the bone runs along the outer edge of one side of the meat. Rib chops have more fat than loin chops, which means rib chops boast a bit more flavor.

SPICED LAMB MEATBALLS IN TOMATO SAUCE

Seasoning to taste

To check the meatballs for seasoning, you can fry a small nugget of the raw meatball mixture until fully cooked. Let cool slightly, then taste and adjust the seasoning as needed in the rest of the mixture.

For this Moroccan-inspired dish, flavor-packed lamb meatballs are browned in the oven and then cooked through in a tomato sauce infused with saffron and cilantro. Serve with steamed couscous and a hearty red wine. For a richer, milder flavor, use ground pork for the meatballs.

Preheat the oven to 450°F (230°C). Oil a rimmed baking sheet.

To make the meatballs, in a bowl, combine the lamb, half of the onion, half of the garlic, the parsley, half of the cilantro, the cumin, paprika, ginger, bread crumbs, 1 teaspoon salt, and ½ teaspoon pepper. Form into balls about 1 inch (2.5 cm) in diameter. Put the meatballs on the prepared baking sheet.

Bake until browned, about 10 minutes. Remove from the oven and set aside.

In a blender or food processor, combine the tomatoes; the remaining onion, garlic, and cilantro; and red pepper flakes and process until smooth. Season with salt and pepper. Pour the tomato sauce into a large frying pan, bring to a simmer over medium-low heat, and cook, uncovered, until the sauce thickens, about 30 minutes.

Add the meatballs to the sauce and continue to simmer gently, uncovered, until the meatballs are no longer pink in the center, 10–15 minutes.

Transfer the meatballs and the sauce to a large warmed bowl. Serve right away.

Olive oil for pan

1 lb (500 g) ground (minced) lamb

1 cup (5 oz/155 g) finely chopped yellow onion

4 cloves garlic, minced

¼ cup (⅓ oz/10 g) minced fresh flat-leaf (Italian) parsley

½ cup (⅔ oz/20 g) chopped fresh cilantro (fresh coriander)

1 teaspoon *each* ground cumin and paprika

¾ teaspoon ground ginger

¼ cup (2 oz/60 g) dried bread crumbs

Salt and ground pepper

3 cups (18 oz/560 g) peeled, seeded, and chopped tomatoes

¼ teaspoon red pepper flakes

MAKES 6 SERVINGS

SWEET-AND-SPICY LAMB CURRY

Using lamb shoulder

Although not as tender as other cuts of lamb, the shoulder develops a depth of flavor and succulence when cooked for a long period of time over low heat, which also softens its connective tissue. Don't skip the browning step, which adds richness and color to the dish.

Aromatic and hearty, this curry features lamb stewed with bold, aromatic flavorings and sweet fruit. It is served on a mound of basmati rice and can be garnished with toasted coconut, toasted almonds or peanuts, dried currants, or chopped green (spring) onions.

Trim the lamb of excess fat and cut into 1-inch (2.5 cm) pieces. In a bowl, toss the lamb pieces with the flour to coat evenly, shaking off the excess.

In a Dutch oven over medium-high heat, warm the oil. Working in batches if necessary to avoid crowding, add the lamb and brown on all sides, about 10 minutes for each batch. Transfer the lamb to a plate. Add the celery, onions, and chile, reduce the heat to medium, and sauté for about 10 minutes. Add the garlic and sauté for 2 minutes. Return the lamb to the pot and add the broth, curry powder, and

2–2½ lb (1–1.25 kg) lamb shoulder or leg

3 tablespoons *each* all-purpose (plain) flour and canola oil

1 celery stalk, chopped

2 yellow onions, chopped

1 jalapeño chile, minced

4 cloves garlic, minced

2 cups (16 fl oz/500 ml) chicken broth

3 tablespoons curry powder

1½ tablespoons grated fresh ginger

½ cup (3 oz/90 g) golden raisins (sultanas)

1 cup (7 oz/220 g) basmati rice

Salt and ground pepper

2 tart green apples, peeled and cut into small dice

¼ cup (2 fl oz/60 ml) coconut milk

MAKES 6 SERVINGS

ginger and stir well. Cover, reduce the heat to low, and simmer until the meat is tender, 1½–2 hours.

About 25 minutes before the curry is done, soak the raisins in very hot water; set aside. In a heavy saucepan over high heat, bring 2½ cups (20 fl oz/625 ml) water to a boil. Rinse and drain the rice. Add ½ teaspoon salt and the rice to the pan, reduce the heat to low, cover, and cook for 20 minutes, covered. After 20 minutes, uncover the rice; the water should be absorbed and the rice should be tender. If the rice is not ready, re-cover and cook for 2–3 minutes longer. Remove from the heat, fluff the grains with a fork, and keep warm.

Meanwhile, drain the raisins and add them to the curry along with the apples and coconut milk. Simmer, uncovered, over low heat until the sauce thickens, about 15 minutes. Season with salt and pepper.

Mound the rice on a serving platter. Make a well in the center and spoon the curried lamb into the well. Serve right away.

BRAISED LAMB SHANKS WITH PRESERVED LEMON

Called a *tagine,* after the cooking vessel in which it is braised, this robust Moroccan stew is flavored with salt-cured lemons. You can substitute 2 tablespoons grated lemon zest for the preserved version, although the taste will not be the same. Serve with couscous or rice pilaf.

4 lamb shanks, each about ½ lb (250 g)

Salt and ground pepper

3 tablespoons olive oil

2 yellow onions, diced

3 cloves garlic, minced

½ teaspoon saffron threads, crushed

1 teaspoon ground cumin

2 teaspoons paprika

1 cup (8 fl oz/250 ml) beef broth or water

Peel of 2 preserved lemons (page 29), cut into strips

⅔ cup (4 oz/125 g) brine-cured black olives

¼ cup (2 fl oz/60 ml) fresh lemon juice, or to taste

¼ cup (⅓ oz/10 g) *each* chopped fresh cilantro (fresh coriander) and flat-leaf (Italian) parsley

MAKES 4 SERVINGS

Sprinkle the lamb shanks with salt and pepper. In a *tagine* or Dutch oven over high heat, warm the oil. Add the lamb shanks and brown well on all sides, 8–10 minutes.

Add the onions, garlic, saffron, cumin, paprika, and broth to the pot. Reduce the heat to low, cover, and simmer until the lamb shanks are tender, about 1½ hours. Check the liquid level periodically and add more water if needed to keep the lamb halfway covered at all times.

When the shanks are ready, add the lemon peel strips, olives, lemon juice, cilantro, and parsley. Re-cover and simmer for 15 minutes longer.

Transfer the shanks to warmed individual plates and spoon the pan juices, lemon peel, and olives over the top. Serve right away. Set out small bowls for collecting the olive pits.

About tagines

This traditional cooking vessel consists of a shallow circular pan and a conical lid that fits over it. As the food cooks, steam rises and condenses on the lid's angled walls, then drips back down onto the slowly cooking stew. A tagine is typically made of glazed earthenware. You can also use a Dutch oven or other large, heavy pot with a lid in its place.

BAKED HAM WITH MAPLE-PINEAPPLE GLAZE

**About
country ham**

*Country ham refers
to the hind leg of
the pig, which is
traditionally dry
cured or brined,
then smoked and
aged for months
to develop its
distinctive flavor.
Some are sugar
cured, meaning the
brine includes sugar.
The traditional
country hams of the
United States must
be repeatedly soaked
and then cooked
before eating.*

An old-fashioned country ham glazed a rich mahogany color makes a memorable meal. The flavors are a pleasant mix of sweet and salty. Buy the best ham you can afford, preferably one that has been dry cured with salt and sugar and then lightly smoked, such as a Virginia ham.

Rinse the ham well in several changes of cold water. Place the ham in a very large bowl, add water to cover the meat completely, and refrigerate overnight.

Remove the ham from the water and discard the water. Pat the ham dry. Place in a roasting pan. Using a sharp knife, remove the skin and slice off enough fat so that a layer only ½ inch (12 mm) thick remains. Score the fat layer in a diamond pattern. Stick a clove in the center of each diamond.

Preheat the oven to 325°F (165°C).

In a small saucepan, combine the pineapple juice, maple syrup, and brown sugar. Cook over medium heat, stirring, until the sugar dissolves, about 1 minute. Brush the surface of the ham with some of the glaze.

Bake the ham, basting every 30 minutes with the remaining glaze, until golden brown and a thick glaze has formed on the surface, 2–2½ hours.

Transfer the ham to a cutting board, tent with aluminum foil, and let rest for about 15 minutes. To serve, slice the meat against the grain and arrange on a warmed serving platter or individual plates.

½ partially boned country-style cured ham, 6–7 lb (3–3.5 kg)

About 30 whole cloves

½ cup (4 fl oz/125 ml) pineapple juice

3 tablespoons pure maple syrup

3 tablespoons firmly packed light brown sugar

MAKES 12–14 SERVINGS

ROAST PORK LOIN WITH TARRAGON CREAM

Enriching sauces

*Enriching, or
finishing, a sauce
with cream adds
a bit more fat, but
it gives the sauce
a luscious, velvety
quality. Always use
heavy (double) cream
for this step. Its high
fat content keeps it
from curdling at high
temperatures.*

The slight sweetness delivered by the cream in this sauce complements the sweetness of the pork loin, a characteristic intensified by roasting. The mustard in the sauce offers just the right balance of tartness. Accompany the pork loin with sautéed apples and roasted potatoes.

Preheat the oven to 400°F (200°C).

With the tip of a sharp knife, cut slits ¾ inch (2 cm) deep all over the pork loin. Insert the garlic slivers into the slits. Sprinkle the meat generously with salt and pepper and place in a roasting pan.

Roast until an instant-read thermometer inserted into the thickest part of the loin away from the bone registers 135°–140°F (57°–60°C) for medium, about 55 minutes.

Transfer to a cutting board, tent with aluminum foil, and let rest while you make the sauce.

In a sauté pan over low heat, melt the butter. Add the shallot and sauté slowly until soft, about 5 minutes. Add the broth and let cook until almost totally evaporated, about 5 minutes.

1 bone-in pork loin, 3–4 lb (1.5–2 kg)

3 large cloves garlic, slivered

Salt and ground pepper

4 tablespoons (2 oz/60 g) unsalted butter

3 tablespoons minced shallot

½ cup (4 fl oz/125 ml) chicken broth

2–3 tablespoons Dijon mustard

1 cup (8 fl oz/250 ml)
heavy (double) cream

2–3 tablespoons chopped
fresh tarragon

MAKES 6 SERVINGS

Whisk in 2 tablespoons of the mustard and the cream and simmer until the sauce is slightly thickened, about 5 minutes. Stir in 2 tablespoons of the tarragon and season with salt and pepper. Taste and adjust the seasoning with more mustard or tarragon. Remove from the heat and keep warm.

To serve, carve the pork roast into single chops with the bone and arrange on a warmed platter or individual plates. Spoon the sauce over the chops.

PORK LOIN WITH MADEIRA MARINADE

A boneless pork loin marinated in wine, oil, and spices and cooked on the grill is an elegant centerpiece for a special-occasion meal. As is true of most pork dishes, this loin goes well with a side dish based on apples, such as Applesauce (page 399) or grilled apples (right).

1 boneless pork loin,
3½–4 lb (1.75–2 kg)

1½ cups (12 fl oz/375 ml)
Madeira wine

¼ cup (2 fl oz/60 ml)
olive oil

¼ cup (2 fl oz/60 ml) red
or white wine vinegar

1 teaspoon ground allspice

½ teaspoon ground cloves

Salt and ground pepper

MAKES 8 SERVINGS

Trim the pork of excess fat, then tie the meat (see page 261).

In a small bowl, whisk together the wine, oil, vinegar, allspice, cloves, 1 teaspoon salt, and ½ teaspoon pepper. Place the pork in a large zippered plastic bag and pour in the wine mixture. Press the air from the bag and seal. Massage the bag gently to distribute the marinade evenly. Set in a large bowl and refrigerate, turning and massaging the bag occasionally, for at least 6 hours or for up to 2 days.

Prepare a charcoal or gas grill for indirect-heat cooking over medium heat (page 18). Remove the pork from the marinade and pat dry. Discard the marinade.

Place the pork loin on the grill rack, cover the grill, and open the vents halfway. Cook for 45 minutes. Turn the loin and replenish the coals if using a charcoal grill. Continue to cook, turning once more, until an instant-read thermometer inserted into the thickest part registers 135°–140°F (57°–60°C) for medium, 40–50 minutes longer.

Transfer the pork to a cutting board, tent with aluminum foil, and let rest for 10 minutes. To serve, snip the strings, cut the meat against the grain into slices about ¼ inch (6 mm) thick, and arrange on a warmed platter.

Grilled apples

Halve, peel, and core Golden Delicious apples. Brush with melted butter and place on the grill, cut side down. Grill, turning every 10 minutes, until tender but not mushy, about 30 minutes total.

287

CHIPOTLE-MARINATED PORK TENDERLOIN

Using dried
chipotles

*If you can't find
canned chipotle
chiles, reconstitute
3 dried chipotles
in very hot water
until softened,
10–15 minutes.
Drain, stem, and
seed the chiles before
puréeing with the
glaze ingredients.*

A sweet-and-hot glaze gives this pork a full, delicious flavor. Be sure not to overcook the pork, or it will be tough and dry. Serve the sliced tenderloin with Black Bean and Bell Pepper Salad (page 318) and warmed corn tortillas.

Cut the tenderloin in half crosswise. Set aside. In a blender, combine the chiles, lime juice, honey, garlic, soy sauce, and cumin. Process until smooth. Stir in the cilantro. Transfer half of the mixture to a shallow bowl. Reserve the other half. Add the pork to the bowl and turn to coat. Cover and refrigerate for 4–6 hours.

Prepare a charcoal or gas grill for direct-heat cooking over medium-high heat (page 18), or preheat a griddle over medium-high heat and oil the surface.

Remove the pork from the marinade and discard the marinade. Place on the oiled grill rack or on the griddle. Cook until seared on the first side, about 4 minutes. Turn the pork and spoon the reserved chile mixture evenly on top of the pieces. Tent with aluminum foil. Continue to cook until the pork is just firm to the touch and pale pink when cut into at the thickest part, about 4 minutes longer.

Transfer to a cutting board, tent with aluminum foil, and let rest for 10 minutes. To serve, slice against the grain and arrange on warmed individual plates.

1 pork tenderloin, about 1¼ lb (625 g), trimmed

3 canned chipotle chiles in adobo sauce, seeded

2 tablespoons fresh lime juice

3 tablespoons honey

2 large cloves garlic

1 tablespoon soy sauce

2 teaspoons ground cumin

¼ cup (⅓ oz/10 g) chopped fresh cilantro (fresh coriander)

Olive oil for griddle, optional

MAKES 4 SERVINGS

ORANGE-GINGER PORK TENDERLOINS

Silver skin

*To remove the tough
white membrane,
called silver skin,
running the length
of the tenderloin,
position the knife
where the silver skin
meets the flesh and
cut the skin away,
using your fingers to
pull it in the direction
of the cut. Continue
to remove the silver
skin in sections,
taking care not to
cut into the meat.*

Marinated in soy sauce and sesame oil, then glazed with orange, molasses, and ginger, these are succulent and flavorful tenderloins. Serve with sesame-flecked coleslaw and green beans for a warm-weather meal. If you have any leftovers, make them into pita sandwiches.

Pat the tenderloin dry. Place in a zippered plastic bag or a shallow dish. In a small bowl, stir together the orange juice concentrate, soy sauce, sherry, sesame oil, ginger, garlic, thyme, and a pinch of salt. Pour over the pork and press the air from the bag and seal, or cover the dish. Refrigerate for at least 6 hours or up to overnight, turning the meat occasionally. Bring to room temperature before cooking.

Prepare a charcoal or gas grill for direct-heat cooking over medium-high heat (page 18).

To make the glaze, in a small bowl, stir together the orange juice concentrate, molasses, ginger, thyme, and ¼ teaspoon pepper. Set aside.

Remove the tenderloin from the marinade and discard the marinade. Place on the oiled grill rack and cook, turning frequently, for 10 minutes. Then brush generously with some of the glaze and continue grilling, basting frequently, until

2 pork tenderloins, about 1 lb (500 g) each, trimmed

½ cup (4 fl oz/125 ml) thawed frozen orange juice concentrate

4 teaspoons soy sauce

1 tablespoon dry sherry

1 teaspoon Asian sesame oil

2 teaspoons grated fresh ginger

1 teaspoon minced garlic

1 teaspoon dried thyme

Salt

FOR THE GLAZE

¼ cup (2 fl oz/60 ml) thawed frozen orange juice concentrate

2 tablespoons unsulfured light molasses

2 teaspoons grated fresh ginger

¼ teaspoon dried thyme

Ground pepper

MAKES 6 SERVINGS

an instant-read thermometer inserted into the thickest part of the tenderloin registers 135°–140°F (57°–60°C) for medium, about 10 minutes longer.

Transfer to a cutting board, tent with aluminum foil, and let rest for 10 minutes. To serve, cut the tenderloins crosswise on a sharp diagonal into slices ¼ inch (6 mm) thick. Arrange the slices, overlapping them, on a warmed platter, season lightly with salt, and brush with any remaining glaze.

On dried herbs

When using dried herbs in recipes, crush them in your hand first to release their aromatic oils. This will increase the flavor dried herbs impart to recipes.

PORK MEDALLIONS WITH LEMON AND ROSEMARY

Pork medallions are slices of tenderloin pounded thin. They cook quickly and make a simple but impressive main course. In this recipe, they are lightly breaded, sautéed until golden, and then topped with a lemon-garlic-rosemary pan sauce.

1 pork tenderloin, about 1½ lb (750 g), trimmed

½ cup (2½ oz/75 g) all-purpose (plain) flour

Salt and ground pepper

About 4 tablespoons (2 fl oz/60 ml) olive oil

4 cloves garlic, minced

½ teaspoon minced fresh rosemary

½ cup (4 fl oz/125 ml) dry white wine

2 cups (16 fl oz/500 ml) chicken broth

¼ cup (2 oz/60 g) rinsed capers, optional

1–2 tablespoons fresh lemon juice

Lemon wedges for garnish

MAKES 6 SERVINGS

Cut the tenderloin crosswise into slices ½ inch (12 mm) thick. One at a time, place each slice between 2 sheets of plastic wrap and flatten with a meat pounder until an even ¼ inch (6 mm) thick.

Put the flour on a plate and season with salt and pepper. In a large frying pan over medium-high heat, warm 2 tablespoons of the oil. Coat the pork with the seasoned flour, shaking off the excess. Working in batches to avoid crowding, add the pork to the pan in a single layer and sauté, turning once, until golden brown on both sides, 2–4 minutes for each batch, adding the remaining olive oil if needed. Transfer to a platter and keep warm.

Reduce the heat to low, add the garlic and rosemary to the pan, and sauté for 30–60 seconds. Raise the heat to high, add the wine, and deglaze the pan, scraping up any browned bits from the pan bottom. Boil the wine until reduced by half, about 1 minute. Add the broth and boil until reduced by half, about 5 minutes. Stir in the capers, if using. Season with the lemon juice, salt, and pepper.

Pour the sauce over the pork and garnish with the lemon wedges. Serve right away.

Matching wine with tart foods

Serve this dish with a crisp white wine, such as Sauvignon Blanc or Pinot Grigio. Both wines are pleasantly acidic and won't be overwhelmed by the tart capers and lemon juice.

PORK CHOPS WITH APPLES

Judging pan sizes

Here is how to make sure meat will fit in a pan before you begin cooking, without getting any pans dirty. Line the pan with parchment (baking) paper and then put the raw meat into it. This eliminates the need to wash the pan if it is the wrong size. When browning or sautéing, there should be at least 1 inch (2.5 cm) of space around each piece of meat to ensure even cooking.

These pork chops are marinated in cider with garlic and thyme, then pan seared and roasted on slices of apples and onions. Cider tenderizes the meat, and the thyme, garlic, and onion add flavor. Serve with Mashed Potatoes (page 335) and steamed green vegetables.

Place the chops in a large zippered plastic bag or shallow dish. Add the cider, olive oil, onion, thyme, garlic, and peppercorns to the bag or dish. Press out the air and seal the bag securely, or cover the dish with plastic wrap. Refrigerate, turning occasionally, for at least 4 hours or up to 24 hours.

Preheat the oven to 400°F (200°C).

Remove the chops from the marinade, pat dry, and season with salt and pepper. Discard the marinade. Peel, core, and slice the fresh apples. In a large frying pan over high heat, melt the butter with the olive oil. When the foam subsides, add the chops and sear, turning once, until browned on both sides, about 2 minutes on each side. Meanwhile, scatter the fresh and dried apples and onion slices in a baking dish large enough to hold the chops in a single layer. Set the browned chops on top of the apples and onion slices, pour the cider around the chops, and cover the dish.

Bake for 10 minutes, then reduce the heat to 350°F (180°C). Continue to cook the chops until nearly tender, 15–20 minutes longer. Uncover and baste with the Calvados. Re-cover and continue to cook the chops until pale pink when cut into at the center, about 10 minutes longer.

Serve the pork chops, apples, and onions directly from the baking dish. Pass the applesauce at the table.

6 loin pork chops, each 7–8 oz (220–250 g) and 1 inch (2.5 cm) thick, trimmed of fat and edges scored

FOR THE MARINADE

⅔ cup (5 fl oz/160 ml) apple cider

1 teaspoon olive oil

1 small yellow onion, sliced

1 tablespoon fresh thyme leaves

2 cloves garlic, minced

1 teaspoon peppercorns

Salt and ground pepper

2 tart green apples

1 tablespoon unsalted butter

1 tablespoon olive oil, or as needed

1 generous cup (3 oz/90 g) dried apples

1 yellow onion, sliced

¼ cup (2 fl oz/60 ml) apple cider

¼ cup (2 fl oz/60 ml) Calvados or other dry apple brandy

Applesauce (page 399)

MAKES 6 SERVINGS

PORK CHOPS WITH SHALLOT–TOMATO RELISH

Perfect for nights when you don't feel like cooking, these quickly seared pork chops are easier to prepare than a sandwich. At the same time, their colorful relish of roasted shallots, tomatoes, and rosemary makes them pretty enough for a dinner party.

Roasted Shallot–Tomato Relish (page 395)

Olive oil

4 boneless pork loin chops, 6 oz (185 g) each, trimmed of fat

Salt and ground pepper

MAKES 4 SERVINGS

If the relish has been made ahead and refrigerated, bring it to room temperature before serving.

Pour enough oil into a large frying pan to film the bottom and heat over medium-high heat. Season the pork chops on both sides with salt and pepper. Add the chops to the pan and cook on the first sides until well seared, about 4 minutes. Turn and continue to cook until pale pink when cut into at the center, about 3 minutes longer.

Transfer the pork chops to a warmed platter and top with the relish, dividing evenly. Serve hot.

Simple herbed pork chops

Coat 6 center-cut pork chops in the dry rub on page 280 and let stand at room temperature for 30 mintues. Preheat the broiler (grill). Place the chops on a broiler pan and broil (grill), turning once, until golden on the outside and pale pink inside, about 20 minutes.

BRAISED PORK CHOPS WITH CARAWAY CABBAGE

A bed of sautéed shredded cabbage and sliced onion develops a delectable flavor when a pair of pork chops is cooked on top of it. Accompany this satisfying dinner for two with your favorite mustard, Russian-Style Black Bread (page 411), and cold beer.

1 teaspoon olive oil

2 pork loin chops, about ½ lb (250 g) each

Salt, ground pepper, and paprika

1 tablespoon unsalted butter, or as needed

1 small yellow onion, thinly sliced

½ head green cabbage, thinly sliced

¼ teaspoon caraway seeds

MAKES 2 SERVINGS

In a large frying pan over medium heat, warm the oil. Season the pork chops on both sides with salt, pepper, and paprika. When the oil is hot, add the chops and cook, turning once, until browned on both sides, about 1 minute on each side. Transfer to a plate.

Pour off any oil in the frying pan, let the pan cool for about 1 minute, and then add the butter. Return the pan to medium-low heat. When the butter melts, add the onion and sauté until softened, about 5 minutes; do not allow to brown. Add the cabbage and caraway seeds, season with salt and pepper, and stir to mix with the onion. Cover and cook until the cabbage is almost tender, about 10 minutes, lowering the heat and/or adding a little more butter if necessary to prevent the vegetables from browning.

Lay the pork chops on top of the cabbage, cover, and cook over medium-low heat until the chops are pale pink and juicy when cut into at the center, about 10 minutes.

Transfer the cabbage and pork to warmed individual plates and serve right away.

Using leftover cabbage

Unused raw cabbage will keep for at least 1 week in the refrigerator. Shred it for coleslaw or steam wedges and dress them with butter, salt, and paprika.

FOIL-WRAPPED STUFFED PORK CHOPS

Self-contained sides

For a complete meal in each packet, cut the foil into a larger piece and include such vegetables as disks of corn on the cob, wedges of bell pepper (capsicum), and tomato halves.

When the sealed packets are unfolded at the table, each guest is greeted with an aromatic prelude to the herb-infused chops. Include a bowl for diners to discard the wrappers. Serve the chops with lots of crusty bread for dipping into the juices.

Preheat the oven to 350°F (180°C).

To make the stuffing, place the bread in a bowl and pour in 1 cup of the milk. Let stand until the bread is very soft and has absorbed the milk, about 15 minutes. This timing will depend on the kind of bread and how dry it is. If necessary, add up to 1 cup more milk. Squeeze the bread dry and place in a clean bowl. Discard the milk. Add the onion, parsley, sage and thyme to the bowl with the bread and mix well. Season with salt and pepper.

Open with caution

These foil packets are full of steam and flavorful juices when they come out of the oven, so warn diners to be careful to avoid burns when opening the packets.

Using a small, sharp knife, cut a horizontal slit 1 inch (2.5 cm) long into the side of each pork chop. Working inward from the slit, cut almost to the opposite side of the chop; be careful not to cut through the chop completely. Spoon an equal amount of the stuffing into each chop. They will be quite full.

Sprinkle ½ teaspoon salt onto the bottom of a wide, heavy frying pan and place over medium-high heat. When the pan is hot, add the pork chops and sear, turning once, until nicely browned on both sides, about 2 minutes on each side. Remove from the heat.

Cut 4 pieces of aluminum foil each large enough to wrap and seal a pork chop completely. Place a chop on each piece of foil, sprinkle with pepper, and then fold in the ends of the foil, overlapping them. Bring the foil sides together and fold over to make a tight seal. Place the sealed packets on a rimmed baking sheet.

Bake for 45–50 minutes. To test for doneness, open 1 foil packet and check that the stuffing is cooked through and the pork is pale pink when cut into at the center. Do not overcook or the pork will be dry.

To serve, place the packets on 4 individual plates and let diners open them at the table.

FOR THE STUFFING

2½ cups (5 oz/155 g) cubed day-old bread (1-inch/2.5-cm cubes), preferably coarse country bread

1–2 cups (8–16 fl oz/ 250–500 ml) milk

3 tablespoons minced yellow onion

2 tablespoons chopped fresh flat-leaf parsley

1 tablespoon minced fresh sage

2 teaspoons minced fresh thyme

Salt and ground pepper

4 large pork loin chops, each about 10 oz (315 g) and 1½ inches (4 cm) thick

Salt and ground pepper

MAKES 4 SERVINGS

292

TANGY GRILLED SPARERIBS

These pork spareribs are baked in foil until tender, then finished off on the grill. When the ribs are on the grill, watch them closely, turning them to ensure even browning and checking often to keep them from burning. If using a charcoal grill, use mesquite charcoal if possible.

6 lb (3 kg) pork spareribs in 2 racks, trimmed of excess fat

Salt and ground pepper

Spicy Barbecue Sauce (page 377)

MAKES 6 SERVINGS

Preheat the oven to 350°F (180°C).

Arrange the ribs in a single layer on a rimmed baking sheet. Season on both sides with salt and pepper and cover with aluminum foil. Bake until tender when pierced, 1¼–1½ hours.

Prepare a charcoal or gas grill for direct-heat cooking over medium heat (page 18).

Set aside half of the sauce for serving. Place the ribs on the oiled grill rack and brush them with barbecue sauce. Cover the grill partially and cook the ribs until browned on the first sides, 5–10 minutes. Turn the ribs over, baste with additional sauce, cover partially, and cook until the second sides are golden brown, 5–10 minutes.

Remove the ribs from the grill, cut into serving portions, and serve right away with the reserved sauce.

Milder ribs

This barbecue sauce has a bit of a kick, thanks to the hot-pepper sauce in the ingredients. For a milder sauce, substitute either of the recipes on page 376.

PORK RAGOUT WITH POLENTA

For pork stews and ragouts, use shoulder, blade-end loin, or boneless country-style ribs, which become tender with long, gentle cooking. For this classic dish, the pork is browned and then simmered until tender with onions and carrots in red wine and broth.

2½ lb (1.25 kg) boneless pork (see note, right)

1–2 tablespoons olive oil

1 large onion, sliced

4 cloves garlic, chopped

¼ cup (2 fl oz/60 ml) balsamic vinegar

Salt

2 carrots, diced

1 bay leaf

1½–2 cups (12–16 fl oz/ 375–500 ml) dry red wine

¾–1 cup (6–8 fl oz/ 180–250 ml) chicken broth

Soft Polenta (page 300)

½ cup (2½ oz/75 g) oil-packed sun-dried tomatoes, chopped

MAKES 6 SERVINGS

Cut the pork into 1½-inch (4-cm) cubes, trimming off any excess fat. In a large frying pan over medium-high heat, warm 1 tablespoon of the oil. Working in batches if necessary to avoid crowding, add the pork and cook until evenly browned, about 6 minutes. Transfer to a heavy saucepan.

If the frying pan is dry, add the remaining 1 tablespoon oil, then place over medium heat. Add the onion and sauté, stirring often, until translucent, about 5 minutes, adding the garlic during the last 30 seconds. Add the vinegar and stir to dislodge any browned bits from the pan bottom. Pour the liquid over the pork and season with salt. Add the carrots, bay leaf, and enough wine and broth almost to cover. Bring to a boil, reduce the heat to low, cover, and simmer until the meat is tender, about 1½ hours. About 30 minutes before the pork is done, begin cooking the polenta.

About 15 minutes before the pork is done, stir the tomatoes into the cooking liquid.

Taste and adjust the seasoning. To serve, spoon the polenta onto warmed individual plates and top with the ragout.

Pork cuts for braising

The best cuts of pork for ragouts, stews, and braises come from the much-used muscles of the shoulder, leg, and side of the animal. These parts of the pig get more exercise and therefore develop more collagen and connective tissue, both of which become soft and succulent when cooked slowly in moist heat.

CASSOULET MADE EASY

Regional
wine pairing

To play up the regional connection at a dinner party, serve the cassoulet with a wine from the Languedoc-Roussillon area of France. Widely available and very affordable, these wines boast appealing spicy-herbal-earthy qualities that pair nicely with the rustic dish.

Authentic cassoulet is a multiday affair using special ingredients that typify the pantry of southwestern France. This modified version of the traditional bean and meat dish uses more familiar, accessible ingredients to create a delicious, comforting main course in its own right.

Sort and soak the beans according to the method on page 301. Drain the beans and place in a saucepan with the onion and water to cover by 2 inches (5 cm). Simmer, uncovered, until tender, 40–50 minutes. Drain, reserving the liquid.

Preheat the oven to 350°F (180°C). In a large, heavy, shallow ovenproof frying pan over low heat, fry the bacon until crisp, 5–7 minutes. Using a slotted spoon, transfer the bacon to a plate. Reserve the drippings in the pan.

Season the lamb and pork with salt and pepper and place in the pan. Roast, basting occasionally with the bacon drippings, until just tender, about 1¼ hours. Let cool and cut into 1-inch (2.5-cm) cubes. Leave the oven set at 350°F.

Meanwhile, prick the sausages all over with a fork. Place in a saucepan, add water to cover generously, and simmer over low heat until almost cooked, 12–15 minutes. Let cool and cut on the diagonal into slices ½ inch (12 mm) thick.

Place one-third of the beans on the bottom of the pan in which the meats were cooked (or in a large baking dish). Sprinkle with half of the bacon, garlic, meat, and sausage slices and season with salt and pepper. Assemble a bouquet garni: Combine the parsley stems, thyme, and bay leaf on a square of cheesecloth (muslin). Bring the corners together and tie securely with kitchen string. Add to the pan. Repeat the layers, using half of the remaining beans and all of the remaining bacon, garlic, lamb, pork, and sausage. Top with the remaining beans.

In a bowl, stir together the tomato paste, allspice, 1 teaspoon salt, and 2 cups (16 fl oz/500 ml) of the bean liquid; pour into the pan. (The liquid should reach just below the level of the beans; add more liquid as needed.) Bake for 1 hour. Top with the bread crumbs and continue to bake until golden, about 1 hour longer. Discard the bouquet garni and serve.

2¼ cups (1 lb/500 g) dried Great Northern or flageolet beans

1 yellow onion, stuck with 6 whole cloves

¾ lb (375 g) thick-cut sliced bacon, cut into ¼-inch (6-mm) dice

2 lb (1 kg) lamb cut from leg, in a single piece

2 lb (l kg) boneless pork loin, in a single piece

Salt and ground pepper

1 lb (500 g) Toulouse or other high-quality pork-and-garlic sausages

8 cloves garlic, minced

6 fresh parsley stems

½ teaspoon fresh or dried thyme leaves

1 bay leaf

2 tablespoons tomato paste

¾ teaspoon ground allspice

1 cup (4 oz/125 g) fine dried bread crumbs

MAKES 10–12 SERVINGS

SAUSAGES WITH SAUERKRAUT RELISH

For these mustard-glazed grilled sausages, you can use any type of fresh sausage you like, including pork, beef, chicken, or turkey, or a variety. Whichever type you choose, check to make sure they are cooked through before plating them with the sauerkraut relish.

3 cups (1–1¼ lb/500–625 g) sauerkraut

¼ cup (⅓ oz/10 g) minced fresh flat-leaf (Italian) parsley

6 tablespoons (3 fl oz/ 90 ml) cider vinegar

3 tablespoons olive oil

4 teaspoons sugar

Ground pepper

½ cup (4 oz/125 g) Dijon mustard

¼ cup (3 oz/90 g) honey

2 lb (1 kg) fresh sausages (see note, above), 1–1¼ inches (2.5–3 cm) in diameter

MAKES 4–6 SERVINGS

To make the sauerkraut relish, put the sauerkraut in a colander and rinse under cold running water. Drain well, then squeeze to remove the excess water. In a large bowl, combine the sauerkraut, parsley, 4 tablespoons of the vinegar, the oil, sugar, and ¼ teaspoon pepper, stirring to combine. Cover tightly and refrigerate for at least 2 hours or up to 3 days.

Prepare a charcoal or gas grill for direct-heat cooking over medium-high heat (page 18), or preheat the broiler (grill).

In a small bowl, whisk together the mustard, honey, and 2 tablespoons vinegar; set aside.

Arrange the sausages on the oiled grill rack or on a broiler pan. Grill or broil, turning often, until well browned and fully cooked, 15–18 minutes. During the last 6–8 minutes of grilling, brush 2 or 3 times with the mustard mixture.

Spread the sauerkraut relish on individual plates and arrange the sausages on top. Serve right away.

About sauerkraut

Purchase sauerkraut in bulk from a delicatessen or in a clear plastic bag from a supermarket, so you can see what you are getting. It should be moist, but not soupy. Avoid sauerkraut packed in cans. Like other fermented foods, sauerkraut has a long shelf life. Refrigerated in its own juices in a covered nonmetal container, it will last for 1 month or longer.

295

ITALIAN SAUSAGES WITH PEPERONATA

Peperonata is a popular Italian dish in which strips of red bell pepper are simmered with tomato and herbs until tender and flavorful. Here, it is topped with slices of browned Italian sausage. The dish can also be served on a bed of Soft Polenta (see page 300).

2 tablespoons olive oil

1 yellow onion, thinly sliced

2 cloves garlic, minced

1⅓ cups (4 oz/125 g) grated plum (Roma) tomato

3 red bell peppers (capsicum), cut lengthwise into narrow strips

10 fresh basil leaves, torn into small pieces

Salt and ground pepper

2 Italian pork, turkey, or chicken sausages, 4–6 oz (125–185 g) each

MAKES 2 SERVINGS

In a frying pan over medium-low heat, warm 1 tablespoon of the oil. Add the onion and garlic and sauté until softened, about 5 minutes. Add the tomato and sauté for 5 minutes. Add the bell peppers and basil, season with salt and pepper, and stir well. Add 2 tablespoons water, cover, and simmer until the bell peppers are tender, 25–30 minutes, adding a little water if the mixture looks too dry. Transfer to a bowl.

Add the remaining 1 tablespoon oil to a clean frying pan over medium heat. Prick the sausages in 3 or 4 places with a knife, add to the pan, and cook, turning as needed, until browned on all sides and cooked through, about 10 minutes. Transfer to a cutting board. Pour off any fat from the frying pan, add the pepper mixture, and reheat gently.

Cut the sausages on the diagonal into slices ½ inch (12 mm) thick. Divide the pepper mixture between individual plates, top with the sausage slices, and serve right away.

Incorporating fennel flavor

For an authentic Italian taste, look for a sausage seasoned with fennel seeds. If you can't find one, add a pinch of fennel seeds to the peperonata.

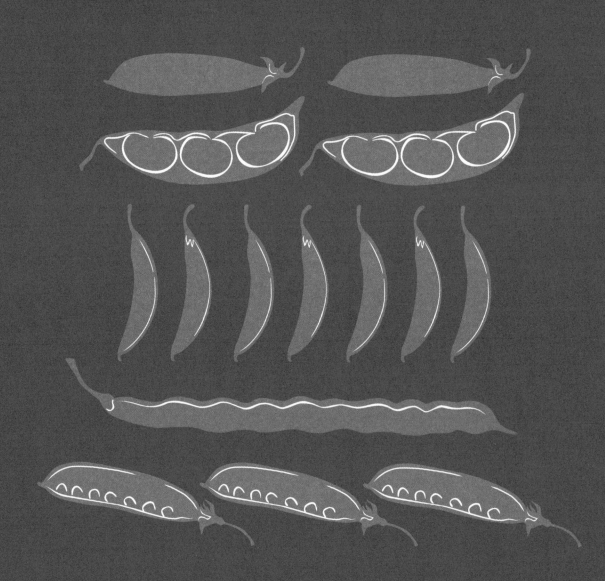

Rice, grains & BEANS

Rice, Grains & Beans

Time honored, practical, and budget friendly, rice, grains, and beans are also among the most healthful of all foods. They are typically important sources of low-fat, nutrient-dense calories and are rich in the fiber, vitamins, and minerals essential to a sound diet. As the recipes in this chapter demonstrate, these popular pantry staples are also remarkably versatile, turning up in countless guises on dining tables around the world.

Selecting grains
Most supermarkets carry a relatively good assortment of grains. Look in the specialty and/or ethnic foods sections for less common varieties. For a full array of grains, visit a large natural-foods store.

The whole truth
Whole grains contain every edible part of the grain and are considered the most healthful choice, rich in nutrients and fiber. Be aware that packages can be deceiving. Read labels carefully, and look for logos for institutions that verify product claims, such as the Whole Grains Council or the Food and Drug Administration.

Storing polished grains
Grains that have been hulled and degermed, a process referred to as polishing, generally keep well in an airtight container at cool room temperature for up to 1 year.

Storing whole grains
Whole and cracked grains include the germ (or embryo), which is rich in oil. For this reason, they can turn rancid relatively quickly. Buy in small quantities, no more than you will use in a few months, and store in an airtight container in the refrigerator for up to 6 months.

Grains Glossary

A wide world of grains awaits the adventurous cook, from tried-and-true staples like rice and cornmeal to lesser-known varieties such as bulgur and *farro* to tiny pastas that are commonly treated like grains.

ARBORIO RICE This northern Italian variety of short-grain rice has a high surface-starch content. When the rice is simmered and constantly stirred, the starch dissolves into a creamy sauce that complements the chewy rice, making Arborio the variety most commonly used for risotto. (See risotto details on page 300 and recipes on pages 307–09.) Other starchy, short- or medium-grain rices include the Spanish Bomba and Calasparra and the Italian Carnaroli and Vialone Nano.

BARLEY One of the earliest grains cultivated, barley has sustained humankind for as long as ten millennia. In addition to its use in soups and the making of Scotch whiskey, barley's nutty flavor and chewy texture lend themselves to many delicious preparations, including risotto-style dishes (like that on page 310), stews, and salads. Barley is primarily available in two types, hulled (the least processed) and pearled. The latter term refers to the most commonly used form, in which the grains are hulled and then polished to a pearl-like shape and sheen.

BASMATI RICE A highly aromatic, long-grain variety, basmati rice is grown primarily in India, Iran, and the United States. It has a sweet, nutlike taste and perfume and a light fluffy consistency, all of which make it ideal for pilafs (pages 302–04). You can buy white or brown basmati rice. American-grown basmati rice is sometimes labeled "Texmati," after its state of origin.

BROWN RICE The term is used to refer to rice that has not been processed by milling or polishing, leaving its nutrient- and fiber-rich hull intact, a definition that makes both black and red rice, specialties of Asia, technically brown rice, as well. Brown rice takes longer to cook than its comparable white rice variety and has a chewier texture and a nutlike taste.

BULGUR Made from wheat that has been steamed, dried, and cracked, nutty-tasting bulgur is most commonly found in Middle Eastern and Balkan cooking, used much like other cuisines use rice. Bulgur comes in different grinds, from fine to coarse. Tabbouleh (page 311), a salad that also includes parsley, onion, tomatoes, and lemon juice, is the best-known dish based on the bulgur.

CORNMEAL Ground from yellow, white, or blue corn, cornmeal is available in fine, medium, and coarse grinds, any one of which can be used in recipes requiring cornmeal, unless otherwise specified. There is no difference between yellow and white cornmeal in terms of taste and usage, but yellow cornmeal has more vitamin A. Blue cornmeal is considered a specialty food and produces pleasingly nutty, full-flavored baked goods. Stone-ground cornmeal is preferred by many home cooks because it contains the germ of the corn, giving it a fuller, slightly nutty flavor and more nutrients. Literally ground between millstones, rather than cut by modern industrialized equipment, stone-ground cornmeal is softer, moister, and more perishable. Other cornmeal, labeled "enriched degerminated," contains only the starchy endosperm and has a longer shelf life. In addition to its use in tortillas and corn bread, cornmeal is used to make the popular and versatile Italian dish called polenta (see page 300 for details), puddinglike spoon bread (page 316), and other side dishes. *See also* Grits; Polenta.

FARRO An ancient wild variety of wheat that originated and was first cultivated in the Near East, *farro* is now primarily grown in Italy, and can be found in Italian delicatessens, well-stocked supermarkets, and natural-foods stores. The uncooked grains look like elongated, tan-colored barley. When cooked, the grain has a nutty flavor and chewy texture, making it well suited for use in salads (such as the one on page 312), pilafs, risottos, and soups.

GRITS Related to cornmeal, grits are made by grinding dried yellow or white hominy (hulled dried corn kernels) into a coarse meal. Cooked to a thick porridge, grits, a favorite throughout the American South, are served as a side dish (page 314) at breakfast, lunch, or dinner. The grain is available in three forms: regular coarse-ground, slow-cooking grits; finer quick-cooking grits; and precooked and dried instant grits.

POLENTA In Italy, polenta may be either yellow or white, made from either coarsely ground or finely ground cornmeal, but the classic version is made from coarsely and evenly ground yellow corn. Polenta is available in instant form, but it lacks the flavor and texture of classic polenta. *See also* Cornmeal.

QUINOA Native to the Andes, this highly nutritious grain looks like sesame seeds and has a mild taste and light texture perfect for pilafs, salads, and other preparations. Quinoa has a bitter-tasting natural residue and must be rinsed well before cooking.

RICE The seeds of a grass first domesticated in Asia thousands of years ago, rice varieties generally fall into three main types, described by their size and shape: short, medium, and long grain. (Types of rice labeled "medium grain" in the United States are called short grain elsewhere; the term is used only in the United States.) Short- or medium-grain varieties are generally starchier and stick together when cooked; long-grain rice yields separate, fluffy grains. Most rice is sold in the so-called polished form commonly known as white rice; the hulls have first been removed and then the brown coating of grain milled away, leaving just the white, starchy interior. For descriptions of individual varieties of rice, see left and below.

WILD RICE Although its shape resembles that of extra-long-grain rice, wild rice is in fact the seed of a marsh grass native to the northern Great Lakes of the United States. Kernels of the wild grass have long been harvested from boats by Native Americans of the region, though today, wild rice is also cultivated elsewhere in the Midwest, in Canada, and in California and harvested by machine. It is dark brown, almost black, and has a pronounced nutty flavor and chewy texture that stand up well to other robust ingredients. Although wild rice can be substituted for white or brown rice in many recipes, keep in mind that its texture is firmer and it takes longer to cook.

On rice cookers
Also called a rice steamer, this countertop electric appliance takes the guesswork out of cooking rice: it turns itself off when it senses a slight rise in interior temperature that indicates the rice is done cooking. Cookers are fitted with an insert in which the rice steams, and most come with a small measuring vessel and a spatula for serving the rice. Rice cookers come in all volumes to accommodate households of all sizes.

Grainlike pastas
Both couscous and orzo are popular ingredients that look and cook like grains, but they are actually forms of pasta. Couscous is sold in regular or instant (quick-cooking) forms, and as standard tiny grains or larger almost barley-size grains sometimes called Israeli couscous. Orzo's slender, seed-like shape resembles a large, slightly flattened kernel of rice. It can be used to make pilafs, in salads, or added to soups much like you would add rice.

Planning for leftovers
Rice is relatively quick and simple to cook, but leftover rice can also be easily stored and reheated. Refrigerate in an airtight container for no more than 5 days. Use leftover rice in fried rice dishes; reheat in a microwave oven on the high setting for a minute or two; or place in a saucepan, add a spoonful or two of water per 1 cup (5 oz/155 g) of cooked rice, cover, and warm over low heat until heated through.

Techniques for Cooking Grains

Highly adaptable, steamed rice, risotto, and creamy polenta are like building blocks. With the three techniques below, the recipes in the following pages, and your imagination, you can create dozens of new dishes to grace your table.

COOKING RICE The basic method for cooking rice involves simmering the rice gently in liquid, usually water. To cook most rice varieties, combine 2 parts water, 1 part rice, and a small amount of salt, if desired, in a heavy saucepan with a tight-fitting lid. Bring the water and rice to a boil over high heat, reduce the heat to low, cover the pan, and cook until the rice is tender and all the water has been absorbed. Remove the pan from the heat and let stand, covered, for 5 to 10 minutes longer. Then use a fork to "fluff" the rice—gently comb its tines through the grains to separate them—before serving.

Note that rice is sometimes rinsed before cooking to remove excess surface starch. The starch binds the grains together, which is desirable for dishes such as risotto but not for other preparations, such as pilaf, where the grains are meant to be fluffy and separate. To rinse rice, put it in a large pot or bowl and add cold water. Gently swish the rice with your fingers, then drain away the starch-clouded water by pouring the rice into a fine-mesh sieve. Repeat the process until the rinsing water is clear.

MAKING RISOTTO Risotto is a classic Italian dish with a creamy consistency, the result of adding the liquid gradually and of constantly stirring naturally starchy rice. When making a risotto recipe (such as those on pages 307–10), follow the instructions carefully to achieve the best results.

First, bring the liquid for the risotto to a gentle simmer in a saucepan, then adjust the heat to keep the liquid hot as you cook. In a large, heavy saucepan, warm the oil and/or butter over medium heat, add the chopped onion or other vegetables, and sauté until softened. Add the rice and stir until the grains are coated with fat and translucent with a white dot in the center, about 2 minutes. If wine is called for, add it and cook, stirring, until completely absorbed. Next, add a ladleful of the hot stock and cook, stirring frequently, until it is almost completely absorbed. Continue adding stock, a ladleful at a time, cooking and stirring after each addition, until the liquid has been nearly absorbed. After 20–25 minutes of cooking, taste the rice: when done, the grains will be tender but still slightly firm at the center and the rice will look creamy. (If it's not quite done, continue cooking, adding more warm stock or hot water as needed.) Proceed as directed in the recipe and serve the risotto right away or let cool and refrigerate for making risotto pancakes or *supplì* (page 85).

MAKING POLENTA For classic, soft polenta, in a heavy saucepan over high heat, bring 5 parts water to a boil and add a large pinch of salt. Add 1 part polenta in a thin, steady stream while stirring constantly with a whisk. Reduce the heat to low and simmer, stirring in one direction with a wooden spoon, until the polenta is thick and creamy and begins to pull away from the sides of the pan, 20–45 minutes for slow-cooking polenta, 5–10 minutes for quick-cooking polenta. (Check the package instructions for suggested cooking time.) Remove the pan from the heat and stir in butter, grated Parmesan, or other additions, if desired. Serve right away.

For firm polenta, pour the hot polenta into a buttered rimmed baking sheet or baking pan and spread in an even layer. Cover the pan and refrigerate until the polenta is firm enough to cut into shapes, at least 2 hours. Panfry or grill the polenta shapes as desired. (See Fried Polenta at left and consult the index for other dishes throughout the book.)

Bean Basics

Preparing dried beans requires both planning and time, but it demands little hands-on work. Canned beans are usually fine in a pinch when you don't have time to cook dried beans. Fresh shell beans are some of the stars of summer, and are simmered relatively briefly to bring out their best flavors.

SORTING BEANS Beans and other legumes used to be dried and processed somewhat carelessly, leading to misshapen specimens or debris in the package. Today's commercial products are generally clean, although you should still check. Some recipes instruct you to "sort" or "pick over" the beans, which means to discard any imperfect beans, small stones, and other foreign matter. Then rinse thoroughly in a colander under running cold water.

SOAKING BEANS Dried beans are typically soaked before cooking to rehydrate them and to allow quicker, more even cooking. Use the long-soak or quick-soak method depending on your schedule.

For the long-soak method: Put the beans in a large bowl and add cold water to cover by 2 inches (5 cm) or more. Soak the beans at room temperature until visibly swelled and rehydrated, about 4 hours, or for up to overnight if it better suits your schedule.

For the quick-soak method: Put the beans in a large pot and add cold water to cover by about 2 inches (5 cm). Bring to a boil over high heat. Adjust the heat so the beans simmer for 2 minutes. Remove from the heat, cover, and let cool in the liquid for at least 1 hour.

SIMMERING BEANS To cook soaked dried beans, drain and then put them in a wide pot with fresh cold water to cover by about 2 inches (5 cm). Add other ingredients as called for in the recipe, avoiding acidic ingredients such as tomatoes, which will toughen the beans. Bring the liquid to a boil over high heat, skim off any foam that rises to the top, and reduce the heat to low. Partially cover the pot and simmer the beans until tender (soft but not mushy). Check the liquid level every 30 minutes or so, adding as necessary to keep the beans covered.

COOKING TIMES FOR BEANS AND LEGUMES

The instructions below are based on 1 cup (7 oz/220 g) dried legumes, measured before soaking (see above), yielding 2½ to 3 cups (20 oz/625 g) when cooked. Lentils and dried peas do not require soaking. Unsoaked beans will take about 30 minutes longer to cook.

5–10 minutes	Young fresh fava (broad) beans
10–15 minutes	Dried red or yellow lentils
15–25 minutes	Fresh cranberry (borlotti) beans
20–30 minutes	Dried green or brown lentils; fresh lima beans and mature fava (broad) beans
30–60 minutes	Dried adzuki beans, black beans, black-eyed peas, mung beans, split peas
1–1½ hours	Dried cannellini, cranberry (borlotti) beans, flageolets, Great Northerns, kidney beans, lima beans, pink beans, pinto beans
1½–2 hours	Dried chickpeas (garbanzo beans), navy beans

Cannellini Beans with Roasted Tomatoes

Cut 1¼ lb (625 g) plum (Roma) tomatoes into ½-inch (12-mm) wedges. Place in a baking dish, drizzle with olive oil, and roast in a preheated 400°F (200°C) oven for about 25 minutes. Meanwhile, rinse 1⅔ cups (12 oz/375 g) canned cannellini beans. Add the beans, 1 tbsp finely chopped fresh flat-leaf (Italian) parsley leaves, ½ tsp herbes de Provence, ½ tsp chopped orange zest, and 1 tbsp rinsed capers to the tomatoes, stir, and return to the oven until warmed through, about 10 minutes. Serve with grilled or roasted fish or poultry.

Warm Chickpeas and Spinach

On a rimmed baking sheet, toss together 3½ cups (24 oz/750 g) rinsed canned chickpeas (garbanzo beans); 2 tomatoes, thinly sliced; 2 tbsp olive oil; salt; and ground pepper. Broil (grill) until lightly browned. Toss while warm with 3 to 4 handfuls baby spinach and a sprinkling of lemon juice. Sprinkle with additional pepper, if desired. Serve with sautéed fish or poultry or as a vegetarian main dish.

Quick Bean and Corn Salad

In a large bowl, combine 2 cups cooked dried beans of your choice; 2 cups (12 oz/370 g) corn kernels; ¼ red onion, finely chopped; ¼ cup (⅓ oz/10 g) minced fresh cilantro (fresh coriander); ¼ tsp ground cumin; and 2 tsp extra-virgin olive oil. Season with salt, ground pepper, and fresh lime juice. Mix well and let stand at room temperature for about 15 minutes to blend the flavors. Serve as part of a picnic or as a side dish for a backyard barbecue.

PERFECT PILAF

Mint pilaf

To complement lamb dishes, make this flavorful pilaf variation: Follow the recipe for Perfect Pilaf, replacing the Chicken Stock with Beef Stock (page 22) or broth. After fluffing the rice, stir in 1 cup (1½ oz/ 45 g) chopped fresh mint. Omit the parsley.

This simple, aromatic baked pilaf is highly adaptable. For example, you can sauté a large handful of sliced mushrooms or diced bell peppers (capsicums) and stir them into the finished dish. Or, add 1 cup (6 oz/185 g) cooked cubed chicken meat with the stock.

Preheat the oven to 350°F (180°C). Lightly butter a shallow 2-qt (2-l) baking dish.

Rinse the rice well and drain. Set aside.

In a frying pan over medium heat, melt the butter. Add the onion and sauté until it has softened, about 2 minutes. Stir in the rice and sauté until the grains are translucent at the edges, 1–2 minutes. Transfer to the prepared baking dish, add the hot stock, and stir to mix. Season with salt and pepper.

Cover and bake until all the liquid is absorbed, 25–30 minutes. Remove the pilaf from the oven and let stand, covered, for 10 minutes. Uncover, fluff with a fork, garnish with the parsley (if using) and serve right away.

1½ cups (10½ oz/330 g) long-grain white rice

2 tablespoons unsalted butter or canola oil

½ cup (2 oz/60 g) chopped yellow onion, or 1 shallot, chopped

3 cups (24 fl oz/750 ml) Chicken Stock (page 23) or water, heated

Salt and ground pepper

1 tablespoon chopped fresh flat-leaf (Italian) parsley and/or chives, optional

MAKES 4–6 SERVINGS

OVEN-BAKED BROWN RICE

Moisture control

If you have baked the dish in advance, slip a double thickness of paper towels under the lid to absorb the condensation as the dish cools, then refrigerate. Bring to room temperature before reheating in a 325°F (165°C) oven for about 30 minutes.

Baking this rich, creamy rice dish, reminiscent of a risotto, makes it especially easy to prepare because it requires no attention once it is in the oven. To approximate a risotto even more closely, stir in a handful of grated Parmesan cheese and a dollop of butter just before serving.

Preheat the oven to 400°F (200°C). Line a rimmed baking sheet with aluminum foil.

Sprinkle the tomato pieces with salt and spread them on the prepared baking sheet. Roast until the edges of the tomato skins are browned but not burned, 10–12 minutes. Remove from the oven and set aside. Reduce the oven temperature to 375°F (190°C).

Meanwhile, in a Dutch oven or a large, heavy ovenproof saucepan with a lid, melt the butter with the oil over medium heat. Add the onion and sauté until soft and translucent, about 5 minutes. Add the rice and thyme and season with salt and pepper. Continue to cook, stirring constantly, until the rice is shiny, about 3 minutes.

Stir in the tomatoes and the hot stock, cover, and bring to a boil. Cover, transfer to the oven, and cook until all the liquid is absorbed, 40–45 minutes.

Remove from the oven and fluff the rice with a fork. Transfer to a warmed serving bowl and serve right away.

8 plum (Roma) tomatoes, seeded and coarsely chopped

Coarse sea salt and ground pepper

1 teaspoon unsalted butter

2 tablespoons olive oil

1 yellow onion, chopped

2 cups (14 oz/440 g) short-grain brown rice

1 tablespoon fresh thyme leaves

4¼ cups (34 fl oz/1 l) Chicken Stock (page 23) or broth, heated

MAKES 8 SERVINGS

WILD RICE AND DRIED CRANBERRY PILAF

Here, pine nuts, dried cranberries, golden raisins, wild rice, and long-grain rice are combined to yield an intriguing mix of fruitiness and nuttiness. Dried cranberries, also known as craisins, lend a pleasing tartness. This is a delicious addition to a menu featuring turkey or ham.

9 cups (72 fl oz/2.25 l) Vegetable Stock (page 26) or equal parts stock and water

1⅓ cups (8 oz/250 g) wild rice, well rinsed

4 tablespoons (2 oz/60 g) unsalted butter

3 large yellow onions, chopped

¾ teaspoon ground cardamom

1 teaspoon ground allspice

2 bay leaves

1 cup (4 oz/125 g) dried cranberries

1 cup (6 oz/185 g) golden raisins (sultanas)

2 teaspoons grated orange zest

Salt and ground pepper

1½ cups (10½ oz/330 g) long-grain white rice, rinsed, if desired (see page 300)

½ cup (2½ oz/75 g) pine nuts, toasted (see page 17)

½ cup (¾ oz/20 g) chopped fresh flat-leaf (Italian) parsley

MAKES 8–10 SERVINGS

In a saucepan over high heat, bring 6 cups (48 fl oz/1.5 l) of the stock to a boil. Add the wild rice and return to a boil. Reduce the heat to medium and simmer uncovered, stirring occasionally, until the wild rice is tender but still slightly firm to the bite, about 40 minutes.

Meanwhile, in a large, heavy saucepan over medium-high heat, melt the butter. Add the onions and sauté, stirring occasionally, until tender, about 12 minutes. Add the cardamom and allspice and stir for about 20 seconds until aromatic. Add the remaining 3 cups (24 fl oz/750 ml) stock, the bay leaves, cranberries, raisins, and orange zest and season with salt and pepper. Bring to a boil. Add the white rice, reduce the heat to low, cover, and cook until the liquid is absorbed and the rice is tender, about 20 minutes.

When the wild rice is ready, drain well. Remove and discard the bay leaves from the white rice. Gently mix the wild rice into the white rice. Stir in the pine nuts and parsley. Taste and adjust the seasoning. Transfer to a warmed serving dish and serve right away.

An exotic spice

Highly aromatic, cardamom is often used to season baked goods, fruit dishes, and Indian-style curries. It is sold in small round pods or as whole or ground black seeds. If you have only pods on hand, remove the seeds from the pods before grinding.

On rinsing rice

Many cooks rinse rice before using it to remove excess starch that can create a gummy texture. The practice is optional, but if you prize rice dishes with fluffy, separate grains, it's a good idea to rinse.

303

BASMATI WITH DRIED FRUITS AND NUTS

Optimizing crunch

In cooking, nuts are valued as much for their crunchiness as their flavor. Toasting them enhances both qualities. In contrast, untoasted nuts can sometimes taste pasty. See page 17 for toasting techniques for a variety of nuts.

Dried fruits, spices, and nuts are ideal companions for sweet, nutty, basmati rice. Although brown basmati rice is available, use white basmati for this dish to show off the other colorful ingredients. Almonds, pine nuts, walnuts, cashews, or pistachios can replace the pecans.

In a saucepan over medium heat, melt the butter. Add the onion and sauté, stirring, until soft, 8–10 minutes.

Meanwhile, rinse the rice well and drain. When the onion is ready, add the rice, 3¼ cups (26 fl oz/810 ml) water, the cinnamon, allspice, cherries, apples, apricots, ¾ teaspoon salt, and a few grinds of pepper to the saucepan. Bring to a boil, reduce the heat to low, cover, and cook, without uncovering the pan, for 20 minutes. After 20 minutes, uncover and check to see if the rice is tender and the water is absorbed. If not, re-cover and cook for a few minutes longer until the rice is done.

Add the pecans and toss gently to combine. Transfer to a warmed dish and serve right away.

¼ cup (2 oz/60 g) unsalted butter

1 small yellow onion, minced

1½ cups (10½ oz/330 g) basmati rice

¼ teaspoon *each* ground cinnamon and allspice

¼ cup (1½ oz/45 g) pitted dried sweet cherries

¼ cup (1 oz/30 g) dried apples, coarsely chopped

½ cup (2 oz/60 g) dried apricots, coarsely chopped

Salt and ground pepper

½ cup (2 oz/60 g) pecans, toasted (see page 17) and coarsely chopped

MAKES 6 SERVINGS

RICE WITH SPRING VEGETABLES

Fennel and dill

Members of the same botanical family, dill and fennel share differences as well as similarities. Fennel looks like a giant dill plant, and the fine, feathery tops can be chopped and used like an herb. But fennel has an anise flavor and is mainly grown for the bulb rather than the fronds.

This light and pretty salad of long-grain rice with sugar snap peas, asparagus, fennel, and dill works as either a side dish or a first course. If any of the vegetables are unavailable in the market, you can substitute green beans, zucchini (courgettes), broccoli, or even shelled peas.

In a heavy saucepan, combine the stock and ½ teaspoon salt and bring to a boil. Slowly add the rice, reduce the heat to low, cover, and cook, without stirring, for 20 minutes; do not remove the cover. After 20 minutes, uncover and check to see if the rice is tender and the water is absorbed. If not, re-cover and cook for a few minutes longer until the rice is done. Remove from the heat, fluff the grains with a fork, and transfer to a bowl to cool.

Bring a saucepan three-fourths full of salted water to a boil. Add the fennel and peas and boil just until tender-crisp, about 2 minutes. Using a slotted spoon, transfer the vegetables to a bowl and let cool. Add the asparagus to the same water and boil until tender-crisp, 3–4 minutes. Drain and let cool with the other vegetables.

2½ cups (20 fl oz/625 ml) Vegetable Stock (page 26) or water

Salt and ground pepper

1 cup (7 oz/220 g) long-grain white rice, well rinsed

1 large fennel bulb, cut lengthwise into slices ¼ inch (6 mm) thick

½ lb (250 g) sugar snap peas or snow peas (mangetouts)

½ lb (250 g) asparagus, cut into 1-inch (2.5-cm) lengths

3–4 tablespoons
fresh lemon juice

3–4 tablespoons
chopped fresh dill

1 clove garlic, minced

½ cup (4 fl oz/125 ml)
extra-virgin olive oil

MAKES 6–8 SERVINGS

In a large bowl, whisk together the lemon juice, dill, garlic, and oil and season with salt and pepper. Add the cooled rice and vegetables and toss together to coat evenly.

Spoon the salad onto a large platter or into a bowl and serve at room temperature.

TOFU-VEGETABLE FRIED RICE

Fried rice is also a highly adaptable dish and a great way to use up leftover rice. This version features bite-size bits of broccoli, carrot, zucchini, napa cabbage, tofu, and a little scrambled egg. Alter the ingredients list as you like, including omitting the eggs for a vegan version.

6 tablespoons (3 fl oz/
90 ml) peanut or canola oil

2 eggs, lightly beaten

½ lb (250 g) firm tofu, cut
into ½-inch (12-mm) cubes

1 tablespoon
balsamic vinegar

1 leek, including light green
tops, finely chopped

1 cup (2 oz/60 g)
broccoli florets

1 carrot, cut into 1-inch
(2.5-cm) pieces

1 zucchini (courgette),
finely chopped

2 cups (6 oz/185 g) finely
chopped napa cabbage

1 teaspoon dry sherry

4 cups (1¼ lb/625 g)
cooked white rice, cold

¼ cup (2 fl oz/60 ml)
vegetable broth

2 tablespoons soy sauce

½ cup (2 oz/60 g) canned
water chestnuts, rinsed,
well drained, and sliced

2 tablespoons thinly
sliced green (spring)
onions, including tender
green tops

MAKES 6–8 SERVINGS

In a wok or frying pan over medium heat, warm 1 tablespoon of the oil, swirling to coat the bottom and sides of the pan. When the oil is hot, add the eggs and stir until soft curds form, about 1 minute. Transfer to a bowl and set aside.

Return the frying pan to medium-high heat. Add another 1 tablespoon oil and again swirl to coat the pan. When the oil is hot but not smoking, add the tofu and stir and toss until it begins to brown, 4–5 minutes. Add the vinegar and cook, stirring once, for 30 seconds. Add to the bowl with the eggs.

Return the frying pan to medium-high heat. Add another 1 tablespoon oil and again swirl to coat the pan. When hot but not smoking, add the leek and stir and toss until slightly softened, 2–3 minutes. Add another 1 tablespoon oil to the pan and again swirl to coat. When hot, add the broccoli, carrot, zucchini, and cabbage to the leek and stir and toss the vegetables every 15–20 seconds until they just begin to soften, 2–3 minutes. Add the sherry and stir and toss for 1 minute longer. Add to the bowl with the eggs and tofu.

Add the remaining 2 tablespoons oil to the pan over medium-high heat, again swirling to coat the pan. When hot, break up any clumps in the rice and add to the pan. Stir and toss until lightly browned, about 5 minutes. Add the broth, soy sauce, water chestnuts, and green onions and stir to combine. Add the tofu, vegetables, and eggs and stir and toss until the eggs are in small pieces and the mixture is heated through, about 1 minute longer. Taste and adjust the seasoning. Transfer to a warmed platter and serve right away.

Tofu types
and uses

Tofu comes in ivory-colored blocks in various textures, including silken, soft, medium, firm, and extra firm. It has a mild flavor and can be used in a variety of preparations, from soups to stews to stir-fries. For the latter, choose firm tofu, which has a nice balance of firmness and tenderness.

CHILE FRIED RICE WITH CRAB

Thai fried rice, a cousin of the better-known Chinese fried rice, is made with generous amounts of garlic, shallots, chiles, and Thai basil. The latter can be found in Asian markets, or you can use regular basil. A sprinkling of fish sauce gives this dish an authentic flavor.

Heat a wok or large frying pan over medium-high heat. Add 1 tablespoon of the oil and swirl to coat the bottom and sides. Add the shallots and cook, stirring, until golden brown, about 1 minute. Using a slotted spoon, transfer the shallots to paper towels to drain.

Return the pan to medium-high heat, add the remaining 1 tablespoon oil, and swirl to coat the pan. Add the garlic and salt and cook until the garlic is golden brown, about 1 minute. Raise the heat to high, break up any clumps in the rice, and add to the pan. Stir and toss until the grains are separated, about 2 minutes. Add 1 tablespoon fish sauce, the soy sauce, and sugar and stir and toss until the grains are evenly seasoned, about 30 seconds. Taste and add more fish sauce, if desired.

Push the rice up the sides of the pan to make a well in the center. Crack the eggs into the well, beat lightly, and cook, without stirring, until set, about 30 seconds. Gently fold the eggs into the rice until specks of cooked egg appear throughout the grains. Add the green onions, chiles, basil, and crabmeat and toss to mix thoroughly.

Transfer to a warmed platter, top with the reserved shallots, and serve right away.

2 tablespoons peanut oil

2 shallots, finely chopped

3 cloves garlic, finely chopped

½ teaspoon salt

4 cups (20 oz/625 g) cooked long-grain rice, cold

1–2 tablespoons Thai fish sauce

1 tablespoon soy sauce

½ teaspoon sugar

2 eggs

3 green (spring) onions, including 1 inch (2.5 cm) tender green tops, chopped

2 red serrano chiles, finely chopped

½ cup (½ oz/15 g) fresh Thai basil leaves or sweet basil leaves

¼ lb (125 g) cooked crabmeat, picked over for shell fragments and flaked

MAKES 4–6 SERVINGS

WILD RICE AND BLUE CHEESE SKILLET SOUFFLÉ

This easy-to-make soufflé differs from a traditional soufflé in that it uses beaten whole eggs rather than whipped egg whites, and it is cooked on the stove top in a frying pan rather than in the oven in a straight-sided soufflé dish. Serve it with a salad for brunch, lunch, or dinner.

In a small saucepan, combine the wild rice, boiling water, and ½ teaspoon salt. Bring to a boil over high heat, reduce the heat to medium-low, cover, and cook, without stirring, until the rice is tender, about 40 minutes. Check the pan from time to time and add a little water if the pan is dry but the rice is not yet tender. Remove from the heat, fluff the grains with a fork, and let cool completely.

In a bowl, using a fork, mash together the milk and blue cheese. Add the eggs and cooled rice; mix well. Set aside.

Preheat the broiler (grill).

¼ cup (1½ oz/45 g) wild rice, well rinsed

1 cup (8 fl oz/250 ml) boiling water

Salt and ground pepper

2 tablespoons milk or cream

3 oz (90 g) blue cheese such as Maytag, Roquefort, or Gorgonzola, crumbled

6 eggs, lightly beaten

3 tablespoons olive oil

1 yellow onion, chopped

2 cloves garlic, minced

¾ lb (375 g) spinach, tough stems removed and coarsely chopped

6 tablespoons (1½ oz/45 g) grated Parmesan cheese

MAKES 4–6 SERVINGS

In a 9-inch (23-cm) nonstick flameproof frying pan over medium heat, warm the oil. Add the onion and garlic and sauté until soft, 8–10 minutes. Add the spinach, season with salt and pepper, and stir until the spinach begins to wilt, about 2 minutes.

Add the egg mixture to the pan holding the spinach and stir together. Cook over medium heat, without stirring, until the eggs are set at the bottom, 2–3 minutes.

Sprinkle the surface with the Parmesan cheese. Slip under the broiler and broil until puffed and golden, 2–3 minutes. Serve right away, directly from the pan.

Leftover blue

Serve extra blue cheese, in lieu of dessert, along with a glass of Port. A classic paring, the sweet, acidic wine contrasts beautifully with the salty, pungent cheese.

CLASSIC RISOTTO

Delicious on its own, risotto can be easily varied. To make a main-course risotto, first brown or sauté your choice of meats and vegetables in the pan; remove them to a plate before proceeding with the onions and rice, then stir them back in at the end.

7 cups (56 fl oz/1.7 l) Chicken Stock (page 23)

2 tablespoons unsalted butter

1 yellow onion, chopped

2½ cups (17½ oz/545 g) Arborio rice

⅔ cup (5 fl oz/160 ml) dry white wine

½ cups (2 oz/60 g) grated Parmesan cheese

Salt and ground pepper

MAKES 6 SERVINGS

Pour the stock into a saucepan and bring to a gentle simmer. Adjust the heat to keep the stock hot.

In a large, heavy saucepan over low heat, melt the butter. Add the onion and sauté until starting to turn translucent, about 8 minutes. Add the rice and stir until the grains are coated with the butter and translucent with a white dot in the center, about 2 minutes. Add the wine and stir until absorbed, about 2 minutes.

Add a ladleful of the hot stock, adjust the heat under the rice to maintain a gentle simmer, and cook, stirring constantly, until the liquid is absorbed. Continue adding the stock, a ladleful at a time, cooking and stirring after each addition, until the liquid is nearly absorbed. After 20–25 minutes, the grains will be tender but still slightly firm at the center and the rice will look creamy. (You may not need all of the liquid. Or, if you need more, add hot water.)

Add the cheese, season with salt and pepper, and mix well. Spoon into warmed shallow bowls and serve right away.

307

Risotto rice

Arborio rice, harvested in Italy's Po Valley, is the best-known rice for making risotto. But if you are in an Italian market or other specialty store, you can often find other wonderful rice varieties to try, such as Carnaroli, Vialone Nano, and Baldo, to name a few.

LOBSTER RISOTTO

Champagne and sparkling wine

To be labeled as true Champagne, sparkling wine must be made in the Champagne region of France. Sparkling wines made by the same process in other regions or countries typically include the phrase méthode champenoise somewhere on the label.

Risotto made with lobster is a celebration in itself. If you buy cooked lobsters and have them cleaned and cracked, ask the fishmonger to give you the shells. Cook the shells in a tablespoon or two of olive oil, add 6 cups (48 fl oz/1.5 l) water, and then proceed with the recipe.

Cook, halve, and clean the lobsters according to the method on page 201, reserving 6 cups (48 fl oz/1.5 l) of the cooking liquid and the shells. Cut the body, tail, and claw meat into large dice and set aside. Add the shells to the reserved cooking liquid and reduce over high heat to 3 cups (24 fl oz/ 750 ml), about 15 minutes. Strain through a fine-mesh sieve lined with cheesecloth (muslin) into a saucepan; add the Champagne and bring to a simmer. Adjust the heat to keep the liquid hot as you cook.

In a large, heavy saucepan over medium heat, melt the butter. Add the onion and sauté until translucent, about 8 minutes. Add the rice and cook, stirring, until the grains are coated with the butter and translucent with a white dot in the center, about 2 minutes. Add a ladleful of the hot liquid, adjust the heat under the rice to maintain a gentle simmer, and cook, stirring constantly, until the liquid is absorbed. Continue adding the liquid, a ladleful at a time, cooking and stirring after each addition, until the liquid is nearly absorbed. After 20–25 minutes, the grains will be tender but still slightly firm at the center and the rice will look creamy. (You may not need all of the liquid. Or, if you need more, add hot water.) With the final ladleful of liquid, stir in the lobster meat, chives, parsley, ½ teaspoon of the lemon juice, and the cream. Season with salt, pepper, and more lemon juice.

Spoon into warmed shallow bowls and serve right away.

2 live lobsters, about 1¼ lb (625 g) each

3 cups (24 fl oz/750 ml) Champagne or dry sparkling wine

3 tablespoons unsalted butter

1 large yellow onion, minced

1½ cups (10½ oz/330 g) Arborio rice

¼ cup (⅓ oz/10 g) snipped fresh chives

2 tablespoons chopped fresh flat-leaf (Italian) parsley

½–1 teaspoon fresh lemon juice

½ cup (4 fl oz/125 ml) heavy (double) cream

Salt and ground pepper

MAKES 6 SERVINGS

PORCINI AND SAUSAGE RISOTTO

Using dried porcini

Dried porcini mushrooms are worth seeking out. Fresh porcini are hard to find and often prohibitively expensive, but the dried version is widely available, packed with flavor, and only a small amount is needed to impart a woodsy essence.

This main-course risotto calls for spicy Italian sausages. If you prefer a milder dish, you can substitute sweet sausages. You can also omit the sausage for a vegetarian main course or for serving as a side dish. The porcini mushrooms and their soaking liquid provide plenty of flavor.

In a heatproof bowl, combine the porcini mushrooms with the hot water and let soak for 30 minutes. Using a slotted spoon, remove the mushrooms from the soaking water, chop, and set aside. Line a fine-mesh sieve with cheesecloth (muslin) and pour the soaking water through it into a saucepan.

Add the stock to the saucepan and bring to a simmer. Adjust the heat to keep the liquid hot.

In a large, heavy saucepan over medium heat, warm the oil. Add the onion and sauté until it begins to soften, about 5 minutes. Add the sausage meat, increase the heat to high, and cook, breaking up the meat with a fork, just until it is no longer pink, about 6 minutes. Add the button mushrooms

1½ oz (45 g) dried porcini mushrooms

3 cups (24 fl oz/750 ml) very hot water

3½ cups (28 fl oz/875 ml) Chicken Stock (page 23)

1 tablespoon olive oil

1 large yellow onion, chopped

½ lb (250 g) fresh spicy Italian sausages, casings removed

¾ lb (375 g) button
mushrooms, sliced

1½ teaspoons finely
chopped fresh rosemary

2½ cups (17½ oz/545 g)
Arborio rice

¾ cup (6 fl oz/180 ml)
dry white wine

1 bay leaf

⅓ cup (3 fl oz/80 ml)
half-and-half (half cream),
optional

½ cup (2 oz/60 g) grated
Parmesan cheese

Salt and ground pepper

MAKES 6 SERVINGS

and rosemary and cook, stirring, until the mushrooms
begin to soften, about 5 minutes.

Reduce the heat to medium, add the porcini mushrooms and
the rice to the pan, and stir until the grains are coated with
the oil and translucent with a white dot in the center, about
2 minutes. Add the wine and bay leaf and stir until absorbed,
about 2 minutes. Add a ladleful of the hot stock, adjust the
heat under the rice to maintain a gentle simmer, and cook,
stirring constantly, until the liquid is absorbed. Continue
adding the stock, a ladleful at a time, cooking and stirring
after each addition, until the liquid is nearly absorbed. After
20–25 minutes, the grains will be tender but still slightly firm
at the center and the rice will look creamy. (You may not
need all of the liquid. Or, if you need more, add hot water.)

Remove and discard the bay leaf. Add the half-and-half (if
using) and cheese and season with salt and pepper. Mix well.
Spoon into warmed shallow bowls and serve right away.

Dried mushrooms

*Dried mushrooms
can be substituted
for fresh ones in
most cooked dishes,
although they may
take longer to become
tender. Their intense
flavor also helps
reinforce the flavor
of fresh mushrooms
when used together.*

SAFFRON RISOTTO WITH SCALLOPS

Treat yourself to a creamy seafood risotto with the heady fragrance of saffron. Although an
expensive spice, it takes only a few threads of saffron to color and flavor a dish. If you prefer,
you can use lump crabmeat or chopped shrimp in place of the scallops.

3 cups (24 fl oz/750 ml)
bottled clam juice

About ½ teaspoon
saffron threads

1 lb (500 g) bay scallops
or sea scallops

2 tablespoons olive oil

Salt and ground pepper

6 green (spring) onions,
white and tender green
parts, minced

2 cloves garlic, minced

2 cups (10½ oz/330 g)
Arborio rice

¾ cup (6 fl oz/180 ml)
dry white wine

2 tablespoons
unsalted butter

2 tablespoons minced fresh
flat-leaf (Italian) parsley

MAKES 6 SERVINGS

In a small saucepan over medium heat, combine the clam
juice, 3 cups (24 fl oz/750 ml) water, and the saffron. Bring
to a simmer. Adjust the heat to keep the liquid hot.

If using sea scallops, cut them into ½-inch (12-mm) pieces. In
a saucepan wide enough to hold the scallops in a single layer,
heat 1 tablespoon of the oil over high heat until very hot.
Add the scallops, season with salt and pepper, and sauté just
until lightly browned, less than 1 minute. Transfer to a plate.

Return the saucepan to medium heat and add the remaining
1 tablespoon oil. Add the green onions and garlic and sauté
until the onions are softened, about 1 minute. Add the rice
and stir until the grains are coated with the oil and translucent
with a white dot in the center, about 2 minutes. Add the wine
and stir until absorbed, about 2 minutes. Add a ladleful of
the hot liquid, adjust the heat under the rice to maintain a
gentle simmer, and cook, stirring constantly, until the liquid
is absorbed. Continue adding the liquid, a ladleful at a time,
cooking and stirring after each addition, until the liquid is
nearly absorbed. After 20–25 minutes, the grains will be tender
but still slightly firm at the center and will look creamy.
(You may not need all of the liquid. Or, if you need more,
add hot water.) With the final ladleful of liquid, stir in the
reserved scallops and the butter and parsley. Season with
salt and pepper.

Spoon into warmed shallow bowls and serve right away.

**Adjusting
the saffron**

*If you taste the clam
juice mixture and feel
the saffron flavor
isn't strong enough,
you can add a few
more threads. Be
careful, however:
saffron can impart
a medicinal taste
if overused.*

BARLEY RISOTTO WITH GREEK LAMB RAGOUT

Barley "risotto"

When cooked using the same method as for risotto, that is, slowly incorporating small amounts of stock into cooking grains, barley becomes as creamy and satisfying as the Italian specialty. Barley is also considered a whole grain, making it a healthful choice for any meal.

310

Lamb and barley are time-honored companions. Here, a ragout of lamb, tomatoes, and olives is served on creamy cooked barley risotto and garnished with feta cheese and fresh basil. If you like, substitute boneless chicken breast for the lamb and chicken stock for the beef.

To make the risotto, pour the stock into a saucepan, add the oregano sprig, and bring to a boil. Remove from the heat.

In a large, heavy saucepan over medium-low heat, warm the oil with the garlic for 1–2 minutes. Add the barley and stir until the grains glisten with the oil, about 30 seconds longer. Stir in 4½ cups (36 fl oz/1.1 l) of the stock and adjust the heat to maintain a brisk simmer. Cook the barley, stirring frequently, for 10 minutes. Stir in the remaining 2 cups (16 fl oz/500 ml) stock, discard the oregano sprig, and continue to simmer, stirring frequently, until the barley is tender and creamy, about 15 minutes longer.

Meanwhile, make the lamb ragout. Season the lamb chunks with salt and pepper. In a frying pan over high heat, warm the oil. Add the lamb and sauté, stirring constantly, just until they lose their pink color, 4–5 minutes. Transfer to a plate and set aside. Return the pan to medium heat, add the onions, and sauté until soft, about 5 minutes. Return the lamb to the pan and stir in the tomatoes, oregano, sugar, and olives. Cook, stirring frequently, until the lamb is tender and the tomatoes are reduced to a thick sauce, about 15 minutes. Taste and adjust the seasoning with salt and pepper.

Divide the barley risotto among warmed individual bowls. Spoon the lamb ragout over the risotto, top with the cheese and basil, and serve right away.

FOR THE BARLEY RISOTTO

6½ cups (52 fl oz/1.6 l) Beef Stock (page 22)

1 large fresh oregano sprig

3 tablespoons extra-virgin olive oil

3 cloves garlic, minced

2¼ cups (15 oz/470 g) pearl barley

FOR THE LAMB RAGOUT

2¼ lb (1.1 kg) well-trimmed boneless lamb loin, cut into ½–¾ inch (12-mm–2-cm) chunks

Salt and ground pepper

⅓ cup (3 fl oz/80 ml) extra-virgin olive oil

2 yellow onions, coarsely chopped

1½ lb (750 g) tomatoes, coarsely chopped

1½ tablespoons dried oregano

1½ teaspoons sugar

1 cup (5 oz/155 g) pitted Kalamata olives, halved

6 oz (185 g) feta cheese, crumbled

6 tablespoons (½ oz/15 g) finely shredded fresh basil leaves

MAKES 6 SERVINGS

SAFFRON ORZO WITH SHRIMP AND VEGETABLES

This colorful one-pot meal looks fancy but is quick and easy to make. Bright green vegetables join pink shrimp in orzo that has been simmered with aromatics. You could substitute boneless chicken chunks for the shrimp, or leave out the shrimp and serve as a side.

2 teaspoons olive oil

½ yellow onion, chopped

2 cloves garlic, minced

1 teaspoon saffron threads

1⅓ cups (9½ oz/295 g) orzo

2¼ cups (18 fl oz/560 ml) Chicken Stock (page 23)

½ lb (250 g) shrimp (prawns)

½ lb (250 g) *each* asparagus and sugar snap peas

Salt and ground pepper

MAKES 4 SERVINGS

In a large saucepan over medium-high heat, warm the oil. Add the onion, garlic, and saffron and sauté until the onion is soft, about 5 minutes. Stir in the orzo, then pour in the stock. Bring to a boil, cover, reduce the heat to low, and simmer, until the orzo is just tender, about 8 minutes.

Meanwhile, peel and devein the shrimp (see page 202) and cut crosswise into thirds. Trim the sugar snap peas and asparagus, and cut the asparagus into 1-inch (2.5-cm) pieces

Add the asparagus and peas to the orzo and simmer until partially cooked, about 3 minutes. Add the shrimp and cook until just pink and opaque throughout, about 3 minutes. Season with salt and pepper.

Transfer to warmed shallow bowls and serve right away.

Not a true grain

Resembling rice in shape and texture, orzo is actually a slender, seed-shaped pasta. The name means "barley" in Italian, and can be used in the same way as the grain: in soups, salads, and risotto-like dishes.

TABBOULEH

In this version of the popular Middle Eastern grain salad, olive oil and lemon juice are poured over the bulgur, then the remaining ingredients are layered on top. Make it at least 1 day before serving so the bulgur has time to soften and the flavors can fully develop.

4 large, ripe tomatoes

1 English (hothouse) cucumber

¾ cup (4½ oz/140 g) fine bulgur

1 cup (8 fl oz/250 ml) fresh lemon juice, or as needed

½ cup (4 fl oz/125 ml) extra-virgin olive oil

5 cloves garlic, minced

8 green (spring) onions, including tender green tops, chopped

1 cup (1½ oz/45 g) chopped fresh flat-leaf (Italian) parsley

⅓ cup (½ oz/15 g) chopped fresh mint

Salt and ground pepper

MAKES 6 SERVINGS

Cut the tomatoes in half, scoop out the seeds, and cut into small dice. Peel the cucumber, then cut in half lengthwise. Scoop out the seeds with a small spoon, then cut into small dice. Set both aside separately.

Place the bulgur in the bottom of a large bowl. In a small bowl, whisk together the lemon juice, oil, and garlic and drizzle evenly over the bulgur.

In the following order, layer the green onions, parsley, mint, tomatoes, and cucumber on top of the bulgur. Season the top layer with 1½ teaspoons salt and ¼ teaspoon pepper and cover the bowl with plastic wrap. Refrigerate for at least 24 hours or up to 48 hours before serving.

Remove the tabbouleh from the refrigerator and let stand at room temperature for 30 minutes. Toss the ingredients together, then taste and season with about 1 teaspoon salt and more lemon juice, if needed, and serve.

Mistaken identity

Do not confuse bulgur with cracked wheat. They look alike, but bulgur is steamed and dried before it is cracked and cracked wheat is not. The latter must be boiled to soften it before use.

RICE, GRAINS & BEANS

FARRO SALAD WITH CHERRY TOMATOES

Farro, an ancient form of wheat, is cultivated primarily in nothern Italy. The light brown grains have a full, nutty flavor that is delicious in soups and salads. Here, *farro* is tossed with cherry tomatoes, green onions, basil, and ricotta salata, making the perfect summer side dish.

In a large saucepan, combine the *farro* and 2 qt (2 l) water and let stand for 1 hour. Place the pan over medium-high heat, bring to a boil, and add 1 teaspoon salt. Reduce the heat to medium or medium-low, so the *farro* simmers steadily, and cook, uncovered, until tender yet still slightly firm and chewy, about 25 minutes.

While the *farro* cooks, stem the tomatoes and slice them in half. Thinly slice the green onions, including the tender green tops. Set aside.

When the *farro* is ready, remove from the heat and drain well in a sieve.

In a serving bowl, whisk together the oil and lemon juice and season with salt and pepper. Add the *farro* and toss well. Gently stir in the tomatoes, green onions, cheese, and basil until all the ingredients are evenly distributed. Serve at room temperature.

1 cup (6 oz/185 g) *farro*

Sea salt and ground pepper

1 cup (6 oz/185 g) cherry tomatoes

2 green (spring) onions

2 tablespoons extra-virgin olive oil

1 tablespoon fresh lemon juice

½ cup (2 oz/60 g) crumbled ricotta salata cheese

¼ cup (⅓ oz/10 g) shredded fresh basil

MAKES 4 SERVINGS

312

COUSCOUS WITH WINTER VEGETABLES

Oven roasting brings out the full flavor of winter squashes and root vegetables, which pair beautifully with nutty-tasting couscous. You can substitute any earthy vegetables you like, such as potatoes or beets, as long as everything is cut into bite-size chunks for even roasting.

Preheat the oven to 425°F (220°C). Oil a large roasting pan.

As you prepare each of the following vegetables, add it to the pan: Scrape out the seeds from the squash, then, using a vegetable peeler, peel away the skin. Cut the flesh into 1-inch (2.5 cm) cubes. Peel the onions and cut each into 8 wedges. Peel the rutabagas and cut into 1-inch (2.5-cm) chunks or cubes. Peel the parsnips and carrots, halve lengthwise, and then cut crosswise into 1-inch (2.5 cm) pieces. Add the garlic, sage, oil, 1 teaspoon salt, and ½ teaspoon pepper to the vegetables. Toss to combine and coat the vegetables evenly.

Bake, stirring occasionally, until all of the vegetables are lightly browned and tender when pierced with the tip of a knife, 45–55 minutes.

When the vegetables are nearly done, prepare the couscous. In a saucepan, bring the stock to a boil over high heat. Stir in the couscous, cover, and remove from the heat. Let stand for 5 minutes. Fluff with a fork and season with salt and pepper.

To serve, mound the couscous on a warmed platter. Spoon the roasted vegetables on top and serve right away.

½ small butternut squash, about ¾ lb (375 g)

2 yellow onions

2 rutabagas (swedes) or turnips, or 1 each

2 parsnips

2 carrots

10 large cloves garlic

¼ cup (⅓ oz/10 g) chopped fresh sage

3 tablespoons olive oil

Salt and ground pepper

2¼ cups (18 fl oz/560 ml) Vegetable Stock (page 26)

1⅓ cups (6½ oz/200 g) quick-cooking couscous

MAKES 4 SERVINGS

BAKED SEMOLINA GNOCCHI

While the bite-size Potato Gnocchi on page 169 are treated like pasta, these gnocchi have more in common with polenta. After the semolina mixture is spread in a large pan and left to set, rounds are cut from the sheet, layered in a baking dish, and baked until golden.

4 cups (32 fl oz/1 l) milk

Salt and ground pepper

Pinch of freshly grated nutmeg

1 cup (6 oz/185 g) semolina flour

1 tablespoon unsalted butter, at room temperature, plus ¼ cup (2 oz/60 g) melted

⅔ cup (2½ oz/75 g) grated Parmesan cheese

2 egg yolks, lightly beaten

MAKES 4 SERVINGS

In a deep, heavy saucepan over medium heat, gently warm the milk until small bubbles appear around the edge of the pan; do not allow to boil. Add ½ teaspoon salt, a few grinds of pepper, and the nutmeg. Stirring constantly with a heavy whisk or wooden spoon, slowly pour in the semolina. Reduce the heat to low and continue to cook, stirring constantly, until the mixture is very thick and stiff, 10–12 minutes.

Remove from the heat and add the room temperature butter; stir until fully melted. Stir in half of the cheese until combined. Add the egg yolks and stir vigorously until well blended and smooth.

Wet a 10-by-15-inch (25-by-38-cm) baking pan with cold water. Using a wet spatula or spoon, spread the semolina mixture evenly in the pan. It should be about ¼ inch (6 mm) thick. Let cool completely until set, 40–50 minutes.

Preheat the oven to 425°F (220°C). Generously butter a round 10-inch (25-cm) baking dish or a 9-by-11-inch (23-by-28-cm) rectangular or oval baking dish.

Using a round cutter 1½–2 inches (4–5 cm) in diameter, cut out rounds of the firm semolina. Place in a single layer in the prepared baking dish, overlapping them slightly. Gather up the scraps, cut out additional rounds, and add to the dish. Drizzle the melted butter evenly over the rounds. Sprinkle the remaining cheese evenly over the top.

Bake until the top is golden brown, about 15 minutes. Serve right away. (The gnocchi can be made ahead and refrigerated: reheat in a 425°F/220°C oven, covered, for 15 minutes.)

About semolina

Semolina is milled from durum wheat, an especially hard, high-protein wheat, that is best known as the flour used for making high-quality dried pasta. But it is also the basis of this gnocchi and is used for making cakes and puddings, among other dishes.

313

CHEESE-HERB GRITS

Grits cakes

Use only 1¼ cups (10 fl oz/310 ml) stock in the recipe to yield a thicker texture. Pour the fully cooked grits into an oiled loaf pan, let cool, cover, and chill until set. Turn out of the pan and cut into slices, then sauté or grill as you like.

For this recipe, a great accompaniment to hearty main courses, grits are combined with tangy goat cheese and brightened with fresh chives and basil. For a different spin, substitute grated Parmesan for the goat cheese and 1 tablespoon dried herbes de Provence for the fresh herbs.

In a saucepan over medium heat, warm the oil. Add the onion and sauté until soft, about 5 minutes. Stir in the grits and then whisk in the stock. Season with salt and pepper. Simmer uncovered, whisking occasionally, until the grits are thick and translucent, about 10 minutes.

Whisk in the buttermilk and cook until incorporated, about 2 minutes longer. Stir in the cheese, chives, and basil until incorporated. Taste and adjust the seasoning. Transfer to a warmed serving dish and serve right away.

2 teaspoons corn oil

½ small yellow onion, chopped

¾ cup (4½ oz/140 g) quick-cooking hominy grits

2 cups (16 fl oz/500 ml) Chicken Stock (page 23)

Salt and ground pepper

¼ cup (2 fl oz/60 ml) buttermilk

2 tablespoons fresh goat cheese

2 tablespoons *each* chopped fresh chives and basil

MAKES 4 SERVINGS

CREAMY POLENTA WITH MUSHROOMS

Topping polenta

Creamy polenta makes a terrific base for any number of toppings, from Bolognese Sauce (page 380) to Peperonata (page 295). To cut back on the richness of the dish, omit the mascarpone.

This extra-creamy polenta is enriched with mascarpone cheese, then topped with sautéed mushrooms and freshly grated Parmesan. The combination of earthy mushrooms and slightly sweet polenta makes an excellent companion for a steak or roast and a full-bodied red wine.

To make the sauce, in a small bowl, combine the porcini mushrooms with the hot water and let soak for 30 minutes. Using a slotted spoon, remove the mushrooms from the soaking liquid and chop finely. Line a fine-mesh sieve with cheesecloth (muslin) and pour the soaking water through it into a bowl. Set the mushrooms and liquid aside separately.

In a large frying pan over medium heat, warm 2 tablespoons of the oil. Add the onion and sauté, stirring occasionally, until tender, 8–10 minutes. Remove from the pan and set aside. Return the pan to high heat and warm the remaining 2 tablespoons oil with the butter. Add the fresh mushrooms and sauté until softened, about 8 minutes. Return the onion to the pan and stir in the garlic and thyme. Sauté until fragrant, about 1 minute. Stir in the porcini mushrooms and the soaking liquid and cook, stirring, for 2 minutes to blend the flavors. Season with salt and pepper. Remove from the heat and keep warm.

To make the polenta, in a heavy saucepan over high heat, bring the water to a boil and add a large pinch of salt. Add the polenta in a thin, steady stream while stirring constantly

FOR THE MUSHROOM SAUCE

1 oz (30 g) dried porcini mushrooms

About ⅓ cup (3 fl oz/80 ml) hot water

4 tablespoons (2 fl oz/60 ml) olive oil

1 yellow onion, chopped

3 tablespoons unsalted butter

1 lb (500 g) assorted fresh mushrooms such as cremini, portobello, chanterelle, or white button, in any combination, sliced ¼ inch (6 mm) thick

1 tablespoon *each* minced garlic and fresh thyme

Salt and ground pepper

FOR THE POLENTA

4 cups (32 fl oz/1 l) water

Salt

1 cup (5 oz/155 g) polenta

3–4 tablespoons
unsalted butter

½ cup (4 oz/125 g)
mascarpone cheese

⅓ cup (1½ oz/45 g) grated
Parmesan cheese

MAKES 4 SERVINGS

with a whisk to prevent lumps. Reduce the heat to low and simmer the polenta, stirring in one direction with a wooden spoon, until it is thick and creamy and begins to pull away from the sides of the pan, about 30 minutes. Season to taste with salt and stir in the butter and mascarpone cheese.

To serve, reheat the mushrooms. Spoon the polenta onto a warmed platter or individual plates. Top with the mushrooms and sprinkle with the Parmesan cheese. Serve right away.

**Cooking
mushrooms**

When mushrooms are sautéed, they will give off a great deal of liquid and cook down quite a bit. Some mushrooms will shrink to less than half their original size.

BAKED POLENTA WITH ROASTED VEGETABLES

Polenta made with garlic and thyme is poured into a loaf pan to cool, then cut into large slices and finished off in a hot oven alongside a pan of roasting vegetables. You can prepare the polenta up to 2 days in advance, if desired, then cut it into slices and proceed with the recipe.

2¾ cups (22 fl oz/680 ml)
Chicken Stock (page 23)

1 cup (5 oz/155 g) polenta

1 tablespoon plus
4 teaspoons minced garlic

4 teaspoons fresh lemon
or regular thyme leaves

Salt and ground pepper

¼ cup (2 fl oz/60 ml)
balsamic vinegar

2 tablespoons minced oil-
packed sun-dried tomatoes

5 Asian eggplants (slender
aubergines), halved
lengthwise and cut into
1-inch (2.5-cm) pieces

3 zucchini (courgettes),
cut into slices 1 inch
(2.5 cm) thick

8 small red potatoes,
unpeeled, quartered

1 large red bell pepper
(capsicum), cut into 1-inch
(2.5-cm) pieces

Olive oil for pans

2 red onions, each cut
into eighths

MAKES 6 SERVINGS

Line an 8½-by-4½-inch (21.5-by-11.5-cm) loaf pan with plastic wrap, letting the wrap hang over the sides.

In a saucepan over medium heat, whisk together 2½ cups (20 fl oz/ 625 ml) of the stock, the polenta, 1 tablespoon of the garlic, and 2 teaspoons of the thyme. Continue to whisk until the cornmeal is thick and smooth, about 12 minutes. Season liberally with salt and pepper. Pour the cornmeal into the prepared pan, spreading it evenly and smoothing the top. Let cool, cover, and refrigerate until firm, at least 5 hours.

Preheat the oven to 400°F (200°C).

In a large bowl, combine the remaining ¼ cup (2 fl oz/60 ml) stock, the vinegar, sun-dried tomatoes, and the remaining 4 teaspoons garlic and 2 teaspoons thyme leaves. Add the eggplants, zucchini, potatoes, and bell pepper. Toss well and let stand for 20 minutes.

Coat 3 rimmed baking sheets with olive oil. Turn out the polenta onto a cutting board, and cut into 12 equal slices. Place the polenta slices in a single layer on 1 prepared baking sheet. Arrange the marinated vegetables and onions on the other 2 prepared baking sheets. Season with salt and pepper.

Place all 3 baking sheets in the oven and roast for 15 minutes. Turn over the vegetables and polenta and continue to roast until the polenta is browned and the vegetables are tender, about 10 minutes longer for the vegetables and 15 minutes longer for the polenta.

Transfer the vegetables to warmed individual plates. Add 2 polenta slices to each plate. Serve right away.

**Firm polenta
variations**

In addition to the loaf pan method here and the baking sheet method on page 300, you can also cool polenta in a pie pan. Slice into wedges and brown them in the oven or in a lightly oiled frying pan. Serve alongside meat or top with pesto, tomato sauce, or meat sauce.

PARMESAN CORNMEAL SPOON BREAD

Working with egg whites

If you're not familiar with the techniques for separating eggs, whipping egg whites to soft peaks, and folding delicate mixtures together, see pages 442–43 for instructions.

Spoon bread is a cross between a soufflé and a quick bread. It puffs up when hot and deflates slightly as it cools. Here, it is flavored with Parmesan, garlic, and red pepper and baked in individual soufflé dishes. It can also be made in a 1-quart (1-l) soufflé dish; bake for 45 minutes.

Preheat the oven to 375°F (190°C). Lightly butter eight ½-cup (4–fl oz/125-ml) soufflé dishes.

In a frying pan over medium-low heat, melt the butter. Add the onion and bell pepper and sauté until the onion is soft, about 5 minutes. Add the garlic and cook for 1 minute. Remove from the heat and set aside to cool.

In a large saucepan over medium heat, bring the milk just to a boil. Meanwhile, pour 1¾ cups (14 fl oz/430 ml) water into a bowl and stir in the cornmeal until smooth. When the milk comes to a boil, add the cornmeal mixture and cook, stirring, until thick, about 5 minutes. Stir in the cheese, ¾ teaspoon salt, and the cayenne pepper. Remove from the heat and let cool for 15 minutes.

Meanwhile, in a large bowl, whisk the egg yolks. Gradually stir the cooled cornmeal mixture and the cooled onion mixture into the yolks.

In a separate bowl, combine the egg whites and a pinch of salt and whisk or beat with an electric mixer until soft peaks form. Using a rubber spatula, fold the egg whites into the cornmeal-onion mixture just until blended. Spoon the mixture into the prepared dishes.

Bake until the tops are slightly puffed and browned, about 30 minutes. Serve right away.

1 tablespoon unsalted butter

½ cup (2½ oz/75 g) finely chopped yellow onion

¼ cup (1½ oz/45 g) minced red bell pepper (capsicum)

1 clove garlic, crushed

1 cup (8 fl oz/250 ml) milk

¾ cup (4 oz/125 g) yellow cornmeal

⅔ cup (2½ oz/75 g) grated Parmesan cheese

Salt

⅛ teaspoon cayenne pepper

3 eggs, separated

MAKES 8 SERVINGS

RED BEANS AND RICE, SOUTHERN STYLE

Choosing tomato sauce

Among the canned tomato products in the supermarket is "tomato sauce," an all-purpose tomato reduction (perhaps most familiar atop meat loaf) that may include any number of ingredients, including corn syrup. When shopping, be sure to check the label, or make your own according to the recipe on page 377.

The combination of rice and beans has long been a staple in the southern United States. For this dish, red beans are cooked with a ham hock, then combined with onion, garlic, tomato sauce, and bell peppers, simmered until thick, and then served on a bed of rice.

Sort and soak the beans (page 301).

Drain the beans and place in a saucepan with the ham hock and water to cover by 2 inches (5 cm). Bring to a boil, reduce the heat to low, and simmer, uncovered, until the beans are tender, 1–1½ hours.

In a frying pan over medium heat, warm the oil. Add the onion, garlic, and half of the bell peppers and sauté until soft, about 10 minutes. Add to the beans along with the parsley, tomato sauce, and hot-pepper sauce and season with salt and pepper. Simmer until thick, about 2 hours. Remove the ham hock (reserve the meat for another use).

1¼ cups (9 oz/280 g) dried pinto beans

1 ham hock, ½ lb (250 g)

2 tablespoons olive oil

1 yellow onion, chopped

3 cloves garlic, minced

2 small red bell peppers (capsicums), cut into ¼-inch (6-mm) dice

¼ cup (⅓ oz/10 g) chopped fresh flat-leaf (Italian) parsley

2 cups (16 fl oz/500 ml) tomato sauce

2–3 teaspoons hot-pepper sauce such as Tabasco

Salt and ground pepper

1 cup (7 oz/220 g) basmati rice

MAKES 6 SERVINGS

About 30 minutes before the beans are ready, rinse the rice well and drain. In a heavy saucepan, combine 2 cups (16 fl oz/ 500 ml) water and ½ teaspoon salt and bring to a boil. Slowly add the rice, cover, reduce the heat to low and cook, without removing the cover, for 20 minutes. Check to see if the rice is tender and the water is absorbed. If not, re-cover and cook for a few minutes longer.

To serve, spoon the rice into warmed individual bowls. Top with the beans and garnish with the remaining bell peppers.

BLACK BEANS AND RICE WITH CORN SALSA

In this flavorful, high-contrast rendition of rice and beans, white rice is topped with black beans that have been simmered with red onion and then combined with a mixture of garlic, herbs, spices, and a little brown sugar. A bright corn salsa tops the beans.

2 cups (14 oz/440 g) dried black beans

1 *each* large yellow onion and green bell pepper (capsicum), chopped

2 cups (12 oz/375 g) corn kernels (from about 3 ears)

2 jalapeño chiles, seeded and minced

2 tablespoons fresh lime juice

½ cup (2½ oz/75 g) finely chopped red onion

1 cup (1⅓ oz/45 g) chopped fresh cilantro (fresh coriander)

Salt and ground pepper

¼ cup (2 fl oz/60 ml) olive oil

6 cloves garlic, minced

⅓ cup (½ oz/15 g) chopped fresh flat-leaf (Italian) parsley

1 tablespoon *each* firmly packed dark brown sugar and ground cumin

1½ teaspoons dried oregano

1 cup (7 oz/220 g) basmati rice

¾ cup (6 fl oz/180 ml) dry white wine

MAKES 6 SERVINGS

Sort and soak the beans (page 301).

Drain the beans and place in a saucepan with the yellow onion, bell pepper, and water to cover by 2 inches (5 cm). Bring to a boil over high heat. Reduce the heat to medium-low and simmer, uncovered, until the beans are tender, 30–60 minutes. Remove from the heat and set the beans aside in their cooking liquid.

Meanwhile, to make the salsa, bring a saucepan three-fourths full of water to a boil. Add the corn kernels and boil for 30 seconds. Drain, place in a bowl, and let cool. Stir in the chiles, lime juice, red onion, and one-third of the cilantro and season with salt and pepper. Set aside.

In a large frying pan over medium-low heat, warm the oil. Add the garlic, parsley, the remaining cilantro, the brown sugar, cumin, oregano, 1½ teaspoons salt, and a few grinds of pepper. Sauté, stirring occasionally, until the garlic is golden, about 10 minutes.

Rinse and drain the rice. In a heavy saucepan, combine 2 cups (16 fl oz/500 ml) water and ½ teaspoon salt and bring to a boil. Add the rice, stir once, then cover, reduce the heat to low, and cook for 20 minutes. Uncover and check to see if the rice is tender and the water is absorbed. If not, re-cover and cook for a few minutes longer.

Meanwhile, add the wine to the garlic mixture and simmer over high heat until the wine is reduced by one-fourth, about 5 minutes. Reduce the heat to medium, add the beans and their cooking liquid, and simmer, uncovered, until the liquid has evaporated, about 15 minutes.

To serve, spoon the rice into warmed individual bowls. Top with the beans and then the corn salsa.

Good and good for you

In addition to their wonderful flavor and texture, black beans are an extremely healthful food. They are high in protein and other nutrients, are an excellent source of cholesterol-lowering fiber, and are loaded with antioxidants.

BLACK BEAN AND BELL PEPPER SALAD

Using canned beans

To simplify this dish and speed up the process, you can use canned beans instead of cooking dried beans. Buy good-quality beans and drain and rinse them well before tossing with the other ingredients.

This striking dish, perfect for summer entertaining, is a colorful mix of black beans, yellow corn kernels, and finely diced red onion and red, yellow, and green bell pepper. It can be made several hours ahead of time and slipped into the refrigerator until serving time.

Sort and soak the beans (page 301).

Drain the beans and place in a saucepan with water to cover by 2 inches (5 cm). Bring to a boil over high heat. Reduce the heat to medium-low and simmer, uncovered, until the beans are tender, 30–60 minutes. Drain and let cool.

Bring a saucepan three-fourths full of water to a boil. Add a pinch of salt and the corn kernels and cook for 1 minute. Drain and let cool.

Cut the bell peppers and the onion into ¼-inch (6-mm) dice.

In a large bowl, combine the bell peppers, onion, corn kernels, garlic, and parsley and toss to combine. Add the oil and 4 tablespoons (2 fl oz/60 ml) vinegar to the bowl, season with salt and pepper, and toss again. Add the beans, toss well, taste and adjust the seasoning as needed with salt, pepper, and vinegar. Toss again and serve.

1 cup (7 oz/220 g) dried black beans

Salt and ground pepper

Kernels from 1 ear corn

½ red bell pepper (capsicum)

1 *each* green and yellow bell pepper (capsicum)

1 small red onion

1 clove garlic, minced

3 tablespoons chopped fresh flat-leaf (Italian) parsley

½ cup (4 fl oz/125 ml) olive oil

4–5 tablespoons (2–2½ fl oz/60–75 ml) red wine vinegar

MAKES 6–8 SERVINGS

BOSTON BAKED BEANS

About salt pork

Salt pork, which is similar to slab bacon in appearance, is usually made from pork belly or pork side. As the name implies, salt pork is salt cured and not smoked like most of the bacon in the United States. If you cannot find salt pork, bacon can be substituted.

Centuries ago in what is now the United States, the Indians baked beans in underground pits with local maple syrup and bear fat. The Pilgrims made their own version, using molasses and salt pork. This modern take is less sweet than those of the past and cooks more quickly.

Sort and soak the beans (page 301).

Drain the beans and place in a saucepan with water to cover by 2 inches (5 cm). Bring to a boil, reduce the heat to low, and simmer, uncovered, until the beans are almost tender, 25–35 minutes. Drain, reserving the liquid.

Preheat the oven to 300°F (150°C).

Fill a saucepan three-fourths with water and bring to a boil. Using a sharp knife, cut a diamond pattern ¼ inch (6 mm) deep in the top of the salt pork. Add to the boiling water and boil for 1 minute, then drain.

Spoon the beans into a 2-qt (2-l) baking dish. Top with the salt pork and onion slices. In a saucepan, combine the molasses, brown sugar, mustard, 1½ teaspoons salt,

3 cups (21 oz/660 g) dried navy beans

¼ lb (125 g) salt pork

4 thin yellow onion slices

⅓ cup (4 oz/125 g) unsulfured light molasses

½ cup (3 ½ oz/105 g) firmly packed dark brown sugar

2 teaspoons dry mustard

Salt and ground pepper

MAKES 10–12 SERVINGS

½ teaspoon pepper, and 1 cup (8 fl oz/250 ml) of the bean cooking liquid. Heat, stirring, to dissolve the sugar. Pour evenly over the beans and add just enough additional bean cooking liquid to cover the beans.

Cover the dish and bake for 4 hours. Uncover, scoop up the pork so it rests on top of the beans, and continue to bake, uncovered, until the beans are cooked through and caramel colored and the salt pork is golden, 1½–2 hours longer.

Serve directly from the dish. If you like, slice the salt pork and serve alongside.

On molasses

Widely available in jars, molasses is a by-product of sugar refinement. It is used as a sweetener and can be found in both light and dark forms. Processed without sulfur, molasses tends to have a milder flavor.

MIXED BAKED BEANS WITH PANCETTA

This flavorful pot of white beans, red kidney beans, and chickpeas mixed with pancetta, tomatoes, onions, garlic, and herbs seems custom-made for serving alongside grilled sausages or other casual fare. You can also serve them on their own for a cold-weather supper.

White bean types

Navy beans are small, sturdy, oval white beans that hold their shape well. Other white beans, including Great Northerns and the larger cannellini (also known as white kidney beans), can generally be substituted for them.

319

1 cup (7 oz/220 g) dried red kidney beans

1 cup (7 oz/220 g) dried navy beans

1 cup (7 oz/220 g) dried chickpeas (garbanzo beans)

2 cups (16 fl oz/500 ml) Chicken Stock (page 23)

1 tablespoon olive oil

¼ lb (125 g) pancetta, chopped

2 yellow onions, sliced

3 cloves garlic, minced

1 teaspoon dried thyme

1 teaspoon dried sage

3-inch (7.5-cm) orange zest strip pierced with 4 whole cloves

1 can (14½ oz/455 g) chopped tomatoes, with juice

Salt and ground pepper

1 cup (2 oz/60 g) fresh bread crumbs tossed with 2 tablespoons melted unsalted butter

MAKES 6–8 SERVINGS

Sort and soak the beans (page 301).

Drain the beans and place in a saucepan. Add the stock and then hot water to cover by 1 inch (2.5 cm). Bring to a boil, reduce the heat to low, cover, and simmer gently until the beans are tender, about 1½ hours; the timing will depend on the size and age of the beans.

Preheat the oven to 350°F (180°C).

In a large sauté pan over medium heat, warm the oil. Add the pancetta and sauté until lightly cooked, about 5 minutes. Using a slotted spoon, transfer to a small bowl. Add the onions, garlic, thyme, and sage to the same pan, cover, and cook over medium-low heat until soft, 6–7 minutes. Uncover and stir in the beans and their liquid, the pancetta, clove-studded orange zest, and tomatoes with juice. Season with 1–2 teaspoons salt and several grinds of pepper. Raise the heat to medium-high and bring to a boil.

Transfer the bean mixture to a deep baking dish. Top evenly with the buttered bread crumbs. Bake until the top is browned, about 30 minutes.

Serve right away, directly from the baking dish.

MEXICAN POT BEANS

About epazote

Epazote is easily grown from seed, but the herb is generally only sold dried, which robs it of its strong, distinctive flavor, reminiscent of anise but more pungent. It is a favorite seasoning of cooks in central and southern Mexico and is also believed to reduce the gastric effects of beans.

Frijoles de olla, a staple of Mexican cuisine, are traditionally simmered in a clay pot, although modern Mexican cooks often use a pressure cooker to cut the cooking time. An *epazote* sprig is a classic addition to the pot, but easier-to-locate fresh cilantro is a suitable substitute.

Sort and soak the beans (page 301).

Drain the beans and place in a large saucepan. Add the onion, lard, and 2½ qt (2.5 l) water and bring to a boil over high heat. Cover, reduce the heat to medium, and simmer gently until the beans are tender, 1½–2 hours. Make sure the beans are always well covered with water, adding more hot water as needed to keep them submerged.

When the beans are tender, add the epazote, 2 teaspoons salt, and the chiles. Simmer, uncovered, for 20 minutes longer. Discard the onion, epazote, and chiles, and taste and adjust the seasoning, then serve.

2 cups (14 oz/440 g) dried black, pinto, or pink beans

⅓ yellow onion

3 tablespoons lard or bacon drippings

1 sprig fresh epazote or cilantro (fresh coriander)

Salt

2 serrano chiles

MAKES 8 SERVINGS

TORTILLAS IN BEAN PURÉE

Mexican beans

Nearly all Mexican bean dishes start with frijoles de olla, as is the case with the tortilla dish at right. Black beans are common in the southern part of the country, and pinto beans are favored in the northern regions and throughout central Mexico.

Among the simplest of tortilla preparations, this delicious dish, known as *enfrijoladas rellenas de queso,* makes a high-protein luncheon main course. If you like, fill the tortillas with scrambled eggs as well. Serve the tortillas with a green salad and a choice of beer or fresh fruit drink.

In a blender, purée the beans until they are the consistency of a sauce, adding a little water if needed.

In a frying pan over medium heat, warm the 2 tablespoons oil. Add the white onion and sauté until browned, about 2 minutes. Add the puréed beans, reduce the heat to low, and cook uncovered, stirring often, for 2 minutes. Discard the onion. Season the purée with salt, cover, and keep warm over low heat while you fry the tortillas.

In another frying pan over high heat, pour in oil to a depth of ½ inch (12 mm). One at a time, fry the tortillas quickly, turning once, until softened, about 5 seconds on each side. Using tongs, transfer to paper towels to drain briefly, then dip in the hot bean purée, fold it in half, and transfer to warmed individual plates, placing 2 tortillas on each plate.

Spoon additional bean purée over the tortillas, then top with the sour cream and cheese. Garnish with the red onion rings and serve right away. Pass the salsa at the table.

2 cups (14 oz/440 g) Mexican Pot Beans (above) made with dried black beans

2 tablespoons canola oil, plus more for frying

¼ white onion

Salt

12 corn tortillas, each about 6 inches (15 cm) in diameter

½ cup (4 fl oz/125 ml) sour cream

¾ cup (4 oz/125 g) crumbled queso fresco or feta cheese

1 red onion, thinly sliced and separated into rings

Green Salsa (page 393)

MAKES 6 SERVINGS

REFRIED PINTO BEANS

These twice-cooked beans make a regular appearance in any Mexican meal. For a dish with more bite, don't seed the chiles. To serve, top the beans with sour cream, sliced avocado, and salsa, or serve all three as accompaniments alongside and let diners garnish their own.

1½ cups (10½ oz/330 g) dried pinto beans

¼ cup (2 oz/60 g) canola oil

1 yellow onion, minced

2 serrano or jalapeño chiles, seeded and minced

4 cloves garlic, minced

1 teaspoon dried oregano

½ teaspoon ground cumin

1 tomato, diced

Salt and ground pepper

MAKES 6 SERVINGS

Sort and soak the beans (page 301).

Drain the beans and place in a saucepan with water to cover by 2 inches (5 cm). Bring to a boil, reduce the heat to low, and simmer, uncovered, until the beans are tender, 1–1½ hours.

Drain the beans, reserving the liquid separately.

In a large nonstick frying pan over low heat, warm the oil. Add the onion, chiles, garlic, oregano, and cumin and sauté until the onion is very soft, about 15 minutes.

Add the tomato and beans. With the pan still on the heat, mash the beans with a potato masher or wooden spoon until creamy, adding some of the reserved bean cooking liquid if necessary to achieve the desired consistency. Season the beans with salt and pepper.

Transfer to a warmed serving dish and serve right away.

Serrano and jalapeño

Not all chiles are interchangeable. Serranos and jalapeños are similar in shape and flavor, with the serrano typically the smaller but hotter of the two. Like bell peppers, chiles are green when immature and red when ripe, with the ripe chiles being milder in flavor.

321

LENTILS WITH SHALLOTS AND PROSCIUTTO

Here, earthy lentils, aromatic vegetables, tangy wine vinegar, and salty prosciutto combine to make an easy side dish with complex flavors. A versatile recipe, it can be served as an accompaniment to roasted or sautéed meats, poultry, or fish.

¾ cup (5 oz/155 g) brown lentils, rinsed

1 tablespoon olive oil

¾ cup (4 oz/125 g) finely chopped celery

¼ cup (½ oz/45 g) finely chopped shallots

2 tablespoons red wine vinegar

¼ cup (2 oz/60 g) finely diced prosciutto

Salt and ground pepper

MAKES 4 SERVINGS

In a deep saucepan over medium-high heat, combine the lentils and 3 cups (24 fl oz/750 ml) water. Bring just to a boil, then reduce the heat to low, cover, and simmer until tender, about 35 minutes. Drain the lentils in a colander, reserving ¼ cup (2 fl oz/ 60 ml) of the cooking liquid. Transfer the lentils to a bowl.

In a frying pan, warm the oil over medium-high heat. Add the celery and shallots to the pan and sauté until golden, about 8 minutes. Add the contents of the pan to the lentils. Add the vinegar and reserved cooking liquid to the pan, bring to a boil, and cook until the liquid is reduced by half, about 3 minutes. Add the hot liquid to the lentils with the prosciutto and stir well. Season with salt and pepper.

Serve right away.

About lentils

Small and flat, lentils can be green, brown, yellow, red, pink, or mottled. Mild flavored and quick to cook, they are extremely versatile, working equally well in soups, salads, side dishes, and main courses.

LENTILS WITH BACON AND WALNUTS

Sherry vinegar

Like the wine of the same name, sherry vinegar varies in flavor according to the grape used in making it. Sherry vinegar is typically matured in oak barrels, and the rich, mellow, complex character that results not only flatters salads and cold vegetables, but also soups, stews, and other hot dishes.

Tossed with toasted walnuts, green onions, and diced bacon in a walnut vinaigrette, these warm lentils are an ideal side dish for the cool months of the year. Accompany with a few leaves of arugula (rocket) for color. The dish can also be served at room temperature.

Pick over and discard any damaged lentils or stones. Rinse the lentils. Drain and place in a saucepan with water to cover by 2 inches (5 cm). Bring to a boil, reduce the heat to low, and simmer, uncovered, until the lentils are tender, 20–30 minutes. Drain immediately and set aside.

Meanwhile, preheat the oven to 350°F (180°C).

In a small bowl, whisk together the vinegar, mustard, olive oil, and 2 tablespoons of the walnut oil and season with salt and pepper to make a vinaigrette. Set aside.

In another small bowl, toss together the walnuts and the remaining 1 tablespoon walnut oil and season with salt and pepper. Spread the nuts on a rimmed baking sheet and toast until fragrant and beginning to color, 5–8 minutes. Remove from the oven, let cool slightly, and chop coarsely. Set aside.

In a large frying pan over medium heat, fry the bacon until lightly golden, about 8 minutes. Remove from the heat and immediately add the lentils, vinaigrette, walnuts, and green onions to the bacon and drippings. Toss to mix well. Season with salt and pepper.

Transfer to a platter, sprinkle with the parsley, and serve.

1½ cups (10½ oz/330 g) dried green lentils

¼ cup (2 fl oz/60 ml) sherry vinegar or red wine vinegar

1 tablespoon Dijon mustard

¼ cup (2 fl oz/60 ml) olive oil

3 tablespoons walnut oil

Salt and ground pepper

1 cup (4 oz/125 g) walnuts

¼ lb (125 g) thin-cut sliced bacon or pancetta, cut into ½-inch (12-mm) dice

½ cup (1½ oz/45 g) thinly sliced green (spring) onions, including tender green tops

2 tablespoons chopped fresh flat-leaf (Italian) parsley

MAKES 6 SERVINGS

SPICED RICE, RED LENTILS, AND SMOKED FISH

Working with lentils

Lentils have a skin that's thinner than other legumes, and are also smaller and less dense. As a result, lentils don't require the lengthy soaking and cooking time of most dried beans. For best results, bring lentils slowly to a full boil, then boil briefly before reducing the heat for simmering.

Known as *kedgeree,* this traditional English breakfast dish originated in India. It is typically made with smoked haddock or *finnan haddie,* but flaked poached fresh cod or snapper fillets can also be used. Serve the dish for brunch or dinner, accompanied with lemon wedges.

Rinse the rice well and drain. In a heavy saucepan, bring 1½ cups (12 fl oz/375 ml) water and ½ teaspoon salt to a boil. Slowly add the rice, reduce the heat to low, cover, and cook, without stirring, for 20 minutes.

After 20 minutes, uncover and check to see if the rice is tender. If not, re-cover and cook for a few minutes longer. Fluff the grains with a fork and let cool.

Meanwhile, pick over and discard any damaged lentils and stones. Rinse the lentils and place in a saucepan with water to cover by 2 inches (5 cm). Bring to a boil, reduce the heat to low, and simmer, uncovered, until the lentils are tender, about 15 minutes. Drain and let cool.

¾ cup (5 oz/155 g) basmati rice

Salt

¾ cup (5 oz/155 g) dried red lentils

2 tablespoons olive oil

1 yellow onion, minced

1 lb (500 g) smoked fish fillets, flaked

3 hard-boiled eggs, chopped

¾ cup (6 fl oz/180 ml) heavy (double) cream

1 teaspoon *each* grated fresh ginger and curry powder

¼ teaspoon freshly grated nutmeg

2 tablespoons chopped fresh flat-leaf (Italian) parsley

1 tablespoon fresh lemon juice

Cayenne pepper

2 tablespoons chopped green (spring) onions, including tender green tops

MAKES 6 SERVINGS

In a frying pan over medium heat, warm the oil. Add the yellow onion and sauté until soft, about 10 minutes. Transfer to a large bowl and add the rice, lentils, fish, eggs, cream, ginger, curry powder, nutmeg, parsley, and lemon juice and season with salt and cayenne pepper. Mix well and transfer to a double boiler or heatproof bowl placed over (not touching) simmering water. Heat to serving temperature.

Transfer to a warmed serving dish. Garnish with the green onions and serve right away.

Take care with cayenne

Because different blends vary in heat, always begin with a very small amount of cayenne and add more to taste in small increments.

BLACK-EYED PEAS WITH YOGURT AND GINGER

This East Indian–inspired black-eyed pea dish is thickened with a little yogurt, flavored with ginger, cumin, and cardamom, and garnished with cilantro. Serve it as a vegetarian main course with steamed basmati rice. Or, serve it alongside roasted chicken, meat, or fish.

1½ cups (10½ oz/330 g) dried black-eyed peas

¼ cup (2 fl oz/60 ml) olive oil

2 yellow onions, minced

¼ cup (1 oz/30 g) minced fresh ginger

6 cloves garlic, minced

1 teaspoon ground coriander

¾ teaspoon ground cumin

¼ teaspoon ground cardamom

2 tomatoes, chopped

½ cup (4 oz/125 g) plain yogurt

¼ teaspoon cayenne pepper

Salt

¼ cup (⅓ oz/10 g) chopped fresh cilantro (fresh coriander)

MAKES 6 SERVINGS

Sort and soak the beans (page 301).

Drain the peas and place in a saucepan with water to cover by 2 inches (5 cm). Bring to a boil, reduce the heat to low, and simmer, uncovered, until almost tender, about 35 minutes. Drain the peas, reserving the liquid. Set aside.

In a large frying pan over low heat, warm the oil. Add the onions and sauté until soft, about 10 minutes. Add the ginger, garlic, coriander, cumin, and cardamom and cook, stirring, for 2 minutes. Add the tomatoes, cover the pan, and cook for 2 minutes longer. Uncover and raise the heat to medium. Add 1 tablespoon of the yogurt and stir until fully incorporated into the sauce. Continue in the same manner with the remaining yogurt, adding 1 tablespoon at a time.

Add the peas, ½ cup (4 fl oz/125 ml) of the reserved cooking liquid, and the cayenne pepper and season with salt. Cover the pan and simmer over medium heat for 15 minutes. Uncover and continue to cook, stirring occasionally, until the liquid is very thick, 3–5 minutes.

Transfer the pea mixture to a warmed platter, garnish with the cilantro, and serve right away.

About black-eyed peas

Also called cowpeas or black-eyed beans, black-eyed peas are kidney shaped and have a black spot with a yellow center on one side. Native to Africa, they are widely grown in Asia and are also popular in the American South, where they are traditionally eaten for good luck on New Year's Day.

CHICKPEA SALAD WITH FRESH MINT

Mint for cooking

Of all the herbs in the world, mint is perhaps the one most accurately described as refreshing. There are many varieties of mint, including chocolate, but the most common is spearmint.

Earthy and satisfying, chickpeas are enjoyed on all sides of the Mediterranean, appearing in salads, stews, and soups from Cannes to Crete. To save time, you can use rinsed and drained canned chickpeas, though the flavor and texture won't be as good.

Sort and soak the beans (page 301).

Drain the beans and place in a saucepan with water to cover by 3 inches (7.5 cm). Add the yellow onion and thyme sprig and bring to a simmer over medium heat. Cook, uncovered, until the chickpeas are tender but not falling apart, about 1¼ hours. Add 1½ teaspoons salt to the pan during the last 10 minutes of cooking.

Drain the chickpeas and discard the onion and thyme sprig. Transfer the chickpeas to a bowl of cold water, let stand for a minute of two, then drain well. (At this point, the chickpeas can be covered and refrigerated for up to 2 days before proceeding with the recipe.)

In a small bowl, whisk together the oil, vinegar, garlic, and cumin and season with salt and pepper. Add the chickpeas and toss together to coat evenly. Add the red onion and toss gently. Let the salad stand at room temperature for about 20 minutes to blend the flavors.

Taste the salad and adjust the seasoning with more salt, pepper, and vinegar, if necessary. Add the chopped mint and toss to combine. Transfer the salad to a platter or individual plates and serve right away.

1¾ cups (12 oz/375 g) dried chickpeas (garbanzo beans)

½ small yellow onion

1 sprig fresh thyme

Salt and ground pepper

5 tablespoons (3 fl oz/80 ml) extra-virgin olive oil

5 tablespoons (3 fl oz/80 ml) red wine vinegar, or as needed

3 or 4 cloves garlic, minced

1 teaspoon ground cumin

1 small red onion, diced

¼ cup (¼ oz/7 g) chopped fresh mint

MAKES 6–8 SERVINGS

CHICKPEAS STEWED WITH CHORIZO

Party fare

You can make this recipe up to 2 days in advance and store it, tightly covered, in the refrigerator, making it ideal for entertaining. Reheat over medium heat before serving.

The use of clove and cinnamon in a savory dish is reminiscent of the cooking of North Africa, just a stone's throw from the southern tip of Spain, where this recipe originated. The dish is commonly found on the tapas table, especially in the winter months.

Sort and soak the beans (page 301).

Drain the beans and place in a saucepan with the cloves, cinnamon, bay leaf, thyme, and water to cover by 2 inches (5 cm). Bring to a boil over high heat, reduce the heat to low, and simmer, uncovered, until the skins just begin to crack and the chickpeas are tender, 45–60 minutes. Remove from the heat and set aside in the liquid.

In a large frying pan over medium heat, warm the oil. Add the onion, garlic, and chorizo and cook, stirring, until the onion is soft, about 10 minutes. Add the chickpeas and their liquid and simmer slowly uncovered, stirring occasionally, until the liquid is almost evaporated, about 40 minutes. Season with salt and pepper.

2 cups (14 oz/440 g) dried chickpeas (garbanzo beans)

¼ teaspoon ground cloves

¼ teaspoon ground cinnamon

1 bay leaf

Large pinch of dried thyme

¼ cup (2 fl oz/60 ml) extra-virgin olive oil

1 yellow onion, finely chopped

4 cloves garlic, finely chopped

3 chorizo sausages, about ¾ lb (375 g) total weight, pricked with a fork

Salt and ground pepper

1½ teaspoons chopped fresh flat-leaf (Italian) parsley

MAKES 8 SERVINGS

Transfer the chorizo to a cutting board. Cut on the diagonal into slices ¼ inch (6 mm) thick. Return the chorizo slices to the pan and heat through for 1 minute.

Transfer to a warmed serving dish. Garnish with the parsley and serve right away.

Chorizo styles

For this recipe, use the smoked Spanish-style chorizo that is packed in casings rather than the loose, fresh Mexican-style chorizo.

CHICKPEAS WITH ZUCCHINI AND TOMATOES

This colorful dish combines chickpeas with sweet onion, zucchini, red bell pepper, cherry tomatoes, and herbs. For a quicker version of the recipe, you can use 1 can (20 oz/625 g) drained chickpeas in place of the dried. Add them to the simmering broth with the tomatoes.

1 cup (7 oz/220 g) dried chickpeas (garbanzo beans)

2 tablespoons olive oil

2 cloves garlic, minced

1 large sweet onion, cut into wedges ½ inch (12 mm) thick

2 zucchini (courgettes), trimmed and cut into slices ½ inch (12 mm) thick

1 red bell pepper (capsicum), cut lengthwise into strips ½ inch (12 mm) wide

1 lb (500 g) cherry tomatoes

½ cup (4 fl oz/125 ml) dry red wine

1½ cups (12 oz/375 g) canned tomato chunks in purée, with juice

½ teaspoon dried oregano

½ teaspoon dried basil

Salt and ground pepper

MAKES 4 SERVINGS

Sort and soak the beans (page 301).

Drain the beans and place in a saucepan with water to cover by 2 inches (5 cm). Bring to a boil over high heat, reduce the heat to low, and simmer, uncovered, until the skins just begin to crack and the chickpeas are almost tender, about 40 minutes. Remove from the heat and set aside.

In a large soup pot over medium heat, warm the oil. Add the garlic, onion, and zucchini and sauté until the onion is translucent, about 10 minutes. Add the bell pepper, cherry tomatoes, wine, canned tomatoes and juice, oregano, and basil. Drain the chickpeas and add them to the pot. Stir well and bring to a simmer. Reduce the heat to medium-low, cover, and simmer gently until the liquid is slightly thickened and the beans and vegetables are tender, about 25 minutes. Season with salt and pepper.

Spoon into warmed shallow bowls and serve right away.

Sweet onions

Mild and juicy, sweet onions are named for their place of origin, since their sweetness is dependent on the soil and climate. The best known are from Vidalia, Georgia, Walla Walla, Washington, and Maui, Hawaii.

325

WARM SHRIMP AND WHITE BEAN SALAD

Pick your beans

You can use any type of large dried white bean here, including the slightly flattened gigande of Greece, the buttery white emergo, the Italian corona, or even dried lima beans. Smaller white beans will work, too, such as cannellini or navy.

Bright pink shrimp look beautiful next to plump white beans. The duo is tossed with red onion and parsley, creating a substantial starter or side dish that can also be served in larger portions as a main course. Use dried beans that are less than a year old, or they will not cook evenly.

Sort and soak the beans (page 301).

Drain the soaked beans and place in a saucepan with 6 cups (48 fl oz/1.5 l) water. Add the yellow onion and rosemary and bring to a simmer over medium heat. Cover partially, adjust the heat to maintain a gentle simmer, and cook until the beans are tender, about 1½ hours. Remove from the heat and discard the onion and rosemary sprig (leave any detached leaves). Season the beans generously with salt and pepper. Keep the beans warm while you cook the shrimp.

Bring a large pot three-fourths full of salted water to a boil. Add the shrimp and cook just until they turn pink and opaque, about 1 minute; do not overcook. Drain and transfer to a large, shallow serving bowl.

Drain the warm beans and add to the shrimp. Add the oil, red onion, parsley, garlic, and vinegar and toss well. Taste and adjust the seasoning. Serve right away.

1 rounded cup (8 oz/250 g) dried large white beans (see note, left)

½ yellow onion

1 fresh rosemary sprig

Salt and ground pepper

18 large shrimp (prawns), peeled, deveined, and butterflied (see page 202)

⅓ cup (3 fl oz/80 ml) extra-virgin olive oil

⅓ cup (2 oz/60 g) minced red onion

¼ cup (⅓ oz/10 g) minced fresh flat-leaf (Italian) parsley

2 cloves garlic, minced

1 tablespoon red wine vinegar

MAKES 6 SERVINGS

FLAGEOLET BEANS WITH CREAM

Substituting lentils

This dish can also be made with green Puy lentils. Lentils don't require soaking, so you can skip that step and instead just simmer the lentils with the vegetables and seasonings until tender, about 30 minutes.

Flageolets are small, pale green or white kidney-shaped beans. Here, they are simmered with onion, celery, cloves, and herbs. The cooked beans are then combined with a warm mustard-cream sauce flavored with tarragon. Serve them alongside grilled lamb, chicken, or fish.

Sort and soak the beans (page 301).

Drain the beans and place in a saucepan with water to cover by 1 inch (2.5 cm). Place the thyme and parsley sprigs and the bay leaf between the celery pieces and tie securely with kitchen string to form a bouquet garni. Add to the pan along with the clove-studded onion and ½ teaspoon salt. Bring the beans to a boil over medium-high heat, reduce the heat to low, cover partially, and simmer gently until the beans are tender, 30–45 minutes.

Remove and discard the herb bouquet and onion. Let cool for 10 minutes, then drain the beans and return them to the pan. In a small bowl, stir together the sour cream and 1½ teaspoons of the mustard. Stir in ½ cup of the heavy cream and then 1 teaspoon of the tarragon. Add the cream mixture to the beans, stir gently to blend, and place over

1½ cups (10½ oz/330 g) dried flageolet beans

2 fresh thyme sprigs

2 fresh parsley sprigs

1 bay leaf

1 celery stalk, cut crosswise into 4 equal pieces

1 small white sweet onion, stuck with 2 whole cloves

Salt and ground pepper

1 tablespoon sour cream

1½–2 teaspoons Dijon mustard

½–¾ cup (4–6 fl oz/ 125–180 ml) heavy (double) cream

2 teaspoons chopped fresh tarragon, or as needed

MAKES 6 SERVINGS

medium-low heat. Warm gently to serving temperature. Season with salt, pepper, and more mustard, cream, or tarragon, if needed. Do not stir too much or the beans will become mushy.

Transfer to a warmed serving dish or warmed individual plates. Sprinkle evenly with any remaining tarragon and serve right away.

Salting beans

Salt added too early to simmering beans can affect their texture. To avoid hard beans, follow the seasoning cues in the recipes.

CRANBERRY BEANS WITH BROCCOLI RABE

Red and white–spotted cranberry beans appear at farmers' markets in summer, as does broccoli rabe. The latter is at its peak flavor when you can see a bit of yellow in the buds. The pleasantly bitter taste provides an appealing counterpoint to the beans and pancetta.

1½–2 lb (750 g–1 kg) fresh cranberry (borlotti) beans or other shell beans

Salt and ground pepper

1 bay leaf

2 sprigs fresh thyme

¼ lb (125 g) pancetta, thinly sliced and cut into 1-inch (2.5-cm) pieces

1 lb (500 g) broccoli rabe

⅓ cup (3 fl oz/80 ml) extra-virgin olive oil

2 cloves garlic, minced

3–4 tablespoons red wine vinegar

MAKES 4 SERVINGS

Shell the beans; you should have about 1 cup (6 oz/185 g). Place them in a saucepan with water to cover by 2 inches (5 cm). Add ½ teaspoon salt, the bay leaf, and the thyme and bring to a boil over high heat. Reduce the heat to medium and cook, uncovered, until tender, 15–25 minutes.

In a frying pan over medium-high heat, cook the pancetta until the fat is translucent, 3–4 minutes. Transfer to a bowl with any rendered fat.

Remove any tough stems from the broccoli rabe and discard. Chop the tender portions; you should have about 2 cups (6 oz/185 g). When the beans are almost done, in the frying pan over medium-high heat, warm the oil. Add the garlic and sauté until translucent, 2–3 minutes. Add the broccoli rabe and sprinkle with ¼ teaspoon salt and ½ teaspoon pepper. Cook, stirring often, until the greens brighten in color and are tender to the bite, 4–5 minutes. Remove from the heat and cover to keep warm. Set aside.

Drain the beans and place in a warmed serving bowl. Add the broccoli rabe and the pancetta with its rendered fat to the bowl. Add 3 tablespoons of the vinegar and toss to mix well. Taste the dish and adjust the vinegar, salt, and pepper as needed. Serve right away.

Testing beans for freshness

To determine the maturity of any fresh shell beans (beans that are eaten fresh from the pod), bite through a raw bean: the more resistance it has, the older the bean. Fresher beans cook more quickly than older ones.

327

MIXED-BEAN SALAD WITH BALSAMIC DRESSING

Heirloom beans

Most dried beans can be substituted for one another in recipes. There are many varieties of heirloom beans currently being cultivated by enterprising growers. Seek out these beautiful, flavorful beans at farmers' markets, in specialty-food stores, and in mail order catalogs.

Bursting with colors and flavors, this nutritious salad is made from a medley of black beans, black-eyed peas, adzuki beans, and green beans. Accompany with slices of toasted or grilled bread rubbed with garlic and drizzled with olive oil.

Keeping the varieties separate, sort and soak the dried beans according to the method on page 301.

Drain the beans and place in separate saucepans with water to cover by 2 inches (5 cm). Bring to a boil, reduce the heat to low, and simmer, uncovered, until the beans are tender, about 1 hour for the black beans, 45 minutes for the black-eyed peas, and 30 minutes for the adzuki beans. Drain and combine in a large bowl.

Meanwhile, in a small bowl, whisk together the vinegar, mustard, and oil and season with salt and pepper. Add to the warm beans, toss well, and let cool.

Bring a saucepan three-fourths full of water to a boil. Add salt to taste and the green beans and boil until tender, 4–5 minutes. Drain and let cool.

Add the green beans, onion, and parsley to the cooled mixed beans. Toss well and serve at room temperature, or cover and refrigerate and serve chilled.

½ cup (3½ oz/105 g) *each* **dried black beans, black-eyed peas, and adzuki beans**

¼ cup (2 fl oz/60 ml) balsamic vinegar

2 teaspoons Dijon mustard

½ cup (4 fl oz/125 ml) extra-virgin olive oil

Salt and ground pepper

½ lb (250 g) green beans, cut into 1-inch (2.5-cm) lengths

1 small red onion, chopped

3 tablespoons chopped fresh flat-leaf (Italian) parsley

MAKES 6 SERVINGS

SUMMER SUCCOTASH

Beans and pork

Pairing beans with a highly flavored pork product, such as bacon, ham, or salt pork, is a common technique in many cuisines. The saltiness and richness of the meat enhance the mild beans without overwhelming their natural flavors.

When lima beans and sweet corn are both in season, succotash appears on New England dinner tables. If fresh limas are not available, you can use soaked dried beans: drain, then simmer in water to cover by 2 inches (5 cm) until tender, adding the bacon after 45 minutes.

Bring a kettle of water to a boil. In a saucepan, combine the bacon and lima beans and add boiling water to cover generously. Place over medium heat and cook until the lima beans are almost tender, 15–20 minutes. Add the corn and green beans, season with salt, and cook until the green beans are tender, 7–10 minutes. Drain and let cool.

In a sauté pan over medium heat, melt the butter. Add the boiled cooled vegetables and cook for 2 minutes.

In a glass measuring cup, combine the milk and cream. Add ¼ cup (2 fl oz/60 ml) of the milk-cream mixture and the sugar to the pan with the vegetables and season with salt and pepper. Simmer over medium-high heat, stirring occasionally, until most of the liquid is gone. Continue to add the milk-cream mixture, ¼ cup at a time, and cook until it is almost gone before adding more liquid.

When all the liquid has been absorbed, transfer to a warmed serving dish and serve right away.

¼ lb (125 g) thick-cut sliced bacon, finely diced

1½ cups (8 oz/250 g) shelled fresh lima beans

2 cups (12 oz/375 g) corn kernels (from about 3 ears)

½ lb (250 g) green beans, cut into 1-inch (2.5-cm) lengths

Salt and ground pepper

2 tablespoons unsalted butter

½ cup (4 fl oz/125 ml) *each* **milk and heavy (double) cream**

Pinch of sugar

MAKES 6 SERVINGS

FAVA BEANS WITH PANCETTA AND CARROT

Fava beans grow inside thick pods. Shell them as you would peas by snapping off the stem and pulling away the tough string on the side of the pod. Then pop each pod open by pressing your thumbnails along its seam. This dish is a lovely accompaniment to herbed veal or lamb chops.

2¼ lb (1.1 kg) fava (broad) beans, shelled

2 thin slices pancetta, chopped

1 large carrot, peeled and thinly sliced

1½ teaspoons minced lemon zest

1 teaspoon chopped fresh sage

Salt and ground pepper

MAKES 4 SERVINGS

Have ready a bowl of ice water. Bring a pot three-fourths full of water to a boil. Add the favas and boil for 2 minutes. Drain, transfer to the ice water to stop the cooking, then drain again. To peel each bean, pinch open the end opposite the end that connected the bean to the pod; the bean will slip easily from its skin. Set the beans aside.

In a heavy frying pan over medium heat, sauté the pancetta until crisp, about 3 minutes. Add the carrot and sauté until tender, about 5 minutes.

Stir in the fava beans, lemon zest, and sage, mixing well. Season with salt and pepper. Transfer to a warmed serving dish and serve right away.

About pancetta

Deriving its name from the Italian word for belly, pancetta is a baconlike product made by rubbing a slab of pork belly with a mixture of spices and then curing it for at least 2 months. Unlike bacon, pancetta is not smoked. Ask for it at the deli counter.

LEMONY FAVA BEANS WITH PARMESAN

Young fava beans, which are at their peak in the springtime, make a light and refreshing side dish tossed with a garlic-lemon dressing and shaved Parmesan cheese. For added color and flavor, throw in a few strips of prosciutto or poached shrimp (prawns).

4 lb (2 kg) fava (broad) beans, shelled

3 tablespoons extra-virgin olive oil

2 tablespoons fresh lemon juice

1 clove garlic, minced

1 tablespoon chopped fresh flat-leaf (Italian) parsley

½ teaspoon grated lemon zest

Salt and ground pepper

Wedge of Parmesan cheese, about 3 oz (90 g)

6 lemon wedges

MAKES 6 SERVINGS

Have ready a bowl of ice water. Bring a pot three-fourths full of water to a boil. Add the favas and boil for 2 minutes. Drain, transfer to the ice water to stop the cooking, then drain again. To peel each bean, pinch open the end opposite the end that connected the bean to the pod; the bean will slip easily from its skin.

In a bowl, whisk together the oil, lemon juice, garlic, parsley, and lemon zest. Season with salt and pepper. Add the skinned fava beans and toss together. Using a vegetable peeler, cut the Parmesan into thin shavings directly over the bowl. Toss the mixture gently.

Transfer to a platter and garnish with the lemon wedges. Serve at room temperature.

Peel in advance

Peeling a batch of fava beans can seem like a daunting task, but the process is simple and the results are well worth the time. You can peel them a day in advance, then cover and refrigerate them until needed.

Vegetables

Vegetables

Nowadays, with the increasing quality and diversity of fresh produce, the idea of vegetables as something to be endured is thankfully in the past. The plain boiled vegetables of yesteryear are gone, too. Today, a whole new philosophy puts fresh vegetables cooked in imaginative ways in a prominent place on the table, where they add color, flavor, and essential nutrients to every meal.

Preparing Vegetables

Peeling root vegetables
Removing tough or discolored skin is often the first step in preparing root vegetables, such as carrots and turnips, and preparing tubers, such as potatoes and sweet potatoes. For removing thinner peels, use a good-quality swivel-bladed vegetable peeler that feels comfortable in your hand. Tougher peels, such as those on turnips or celery root (celeriac), are more easily removed with a sharp paring knife.

Cleaning mushrooms
Submerging fresh mushrooms in water can make them soggy and dilute their flavor. Instead, brush them or wipe them clean with a damp cloth. (Morels are the exception to the rule; see note, opposite.) Trim the dried ends of tender stems, or remove tough stems completely.

Handling chiles
The spiciness of chiles comes from volatile oils that can cause painful burning on contact with sensitive areas, so avoid touching your eyes or lips when handling chiles. Once you have finished, thoroughly wash your hands and tools (knife, cutting board). If you have cuts on your hands, wear kitchen gloves when working with chiles.

Most vegetables require little preparation apart from rinsing, drying, and basic trimming. But those that follow require a little know-how.

ARTICHOKES All artichokes require trimming before cooking. Use only stainless-steel knives and cookware with artichokes; other metals will discolor them. Fill a bowl with cold water and add some lemon juice. As each artichoke is trimmed, drop it into the lemon water to prevent browning.

To trim artichokes: Working with 1 artichoke at a time, and starting at the base, pull off and discard the tough outer leaves. Trim off the base of the stem and then, using a paring knife, peel the stem. Or, cut off the stem flush with the bottom and discard. Using a serrated knife or kitchen scissors, slice off the top 1 to 2 inches (2.5 to 5 cm) of the remaining leaves to remove the spiny tips. If trimming a baby artichoke, remove leaves as directed until you reach the pale green center, cut off the stem flush with the base, and then cut off about ½ inch (12 mm) from the top to remove the spiny tips.

To remove the choke: Depending on the recipe, you can halve or quarter each artichoke lengthwise and scrape out the choke from each half with the edge of a spoon or a small, sharp knife. Or, after trimming (above), gently spread open the leaves and dig out the choke with a spoon. Most baby artichokes will not have developed a choke.

ASPARAGUS Most asparagus spears require only removal of the tough end of the stalk. Hold a spear near the center and at the cut end. Bend the cut end until it breaks; it will snap off where the tough portion begins. For thick spears, use a vegetable peeler to remove some of the fibrous outer skin to within about 1 inch (2.5 cm) of the tips.

CORN Although sweet corn is often eaten straight from the cob, many recipes call for cutting off the cooked or raw kernels, or for removing the pulp and juice.

To cut off the kernels: Hold an ear of corn upright, stem end down, on a work surface or in a shallow bowl. Using a sharp knife, cut straight down between the kernels and cob, being careful not to cut into the fibrous cob and giving the ear a quarter turn after each cut.

To remove the pulp and juice: Hold an ear of corn, stem end down, in a shallow bowl. Using a sharp, heavy knife, make a lengthwise cut down the center of each row of kernels. Holding the dull side of the knife at an angle to the cob, carefully scrape downward along the kernels to release the pulp and juice.

EGGPLANT After eggplants (aubergines) are cut, they are often salted before they are cooked to draw out some of the bitterness in larger specimens and also some of the excess moisture, which makes eggplant easier to brown. Cut the eggplant as directed in individual recipes and put the pieces in a colander set in the sink or over a bowl, sprinkling them with salt as you go. Let drain for about 30 minutes or as directed in individual recipes, then thoroughly pat dry. Do not rinse off the salt or the eggplant will reabsorb moisture.

LEEKS Because they grow partly underground, these mild members of the onion family usually have grit lodged between their layers, requiring diligent cleaning. Trim off the roots and tough, dark green tops. If the outer layer is wilted or discolored, slit and peel it away. If using the leek whole, halve the leek lengthwise, stopping just short of the opposite side and leaving the root end intact, then rinse well under cold running water, fanning the layers to rinse between them. If a recipe calls for sliced leeks, slice the leek crosswise, then rinse the slices thoroughly in a colander.

PEARL AND BOILING ONIONS To peel these miniature dried onions, bring a saucepan three-fourths full of water to a boil over high heat. Add the onions and boil for 1 minute, counting from when the water returns to a boil. Drain in a colander, then rinse under running cold water until cool. With a sharp paring knife, trim the root and stem ends of each onion. Pinch the onion to remove the skin. Many cooks then cut a shallow X in the root end to reduce cooking time, ensure even cooking, and retain the onion's shape.

PEPPERS AND CHILES Both mild bell peppers (capsicums) and spicier chiles can be roasted to facilitate peeling and to develop their flavor. For bell peppers, remove their stems, seeds, and ribs with a paring knife after the peppers are halved or quartered. Remove the stems of chiles. Their seeds and ribs, or membranes, are a source of heat; remove them according to your taste.

Roasting peppers and chiles: Using tongs or a long fork, hold the pepper or chile over the flame of a gas burner, turning it until the skin is evenly blistered and blackened. Alternatively, place the pepper or chile, skin-side up if needed, on a baking sheet and broil (grill), turning as needed and watching carefully to prevent burning, until evenly blistered and blackened. Transfer to a paper bag until cool. Peel, rub, or cut away the charred skin.

SHELL BEANS AND PEAS Shell beans, such as lima beans, cranberry (borlotti) beans, and fava (broad) beans, and peas must be removed from their pods before cooking. To do this, hold each pod above a bowl, split it open with your thumbs, then slide a thumb along the inside to dislodge the beans or peas, letting them drop into the bowl. For more on shell beans, turn to page 301.

SNAP AND POD BEANS Eaten whole, these fresh beans—called green, string, or snap beans depending on where you shop; slender French-style haricots verts; and yellow wax beans—require only simple preparation. Just remove any stems or brown-tipped ends, snapping them by hand in the direction of the seam on each bean and then pulling along the seam to remove any strings.

TOMATOES Some recipes call for peeled and/or seeded tomatoes, usually when the tomatoes are to be chopped for a sauce.

To peel tomatoes: First, cut out the stem and then, with a small, sharp knife, cut a shallow X in the blossom end. Plunge the tomato into a pot of boiling water just until its skin begins to wrinkle, 10–30 seconds, depending on ripeness. Remove with a slotted spoon or wire skimmer and transfer to a bowl of ice water to cool. When cool enough to handle, use your fingertips and, if necessary, the knife to peel away the skin, starting at the X.

To seed tomatoes: Cut in half crosswise. Holding each half in turn over a sink or bowl, lightly squeeze and shake to dislodge the seeds, using a fingertip if necessary to help ease them out .

MUSHROOM TYPES

For culinary purposes, mushrooms are divided into two groups: cultivated and wild mushrooms. Today, many previously wild varieties are also cultivated, but they are still often referred to as wild to distinguish them from more common varieties.

Button or White
The cultivated all-purpose mushrooms sold in grocery stores. "Button" refers to young, tender specimens with closed caps.

Chanterelle
Golden, trumpet-shaped wild mushrooms with tender texture and unique flavor.

Cremini
Similar to white mushrooms, but light brown and with a firmer texture and fuller flavor. Also known as brown or baby portobello.

Morel
Wild mushrooms with elongated, spongelike caps and hollow stems, prized for their intense, musky flavor.

Oyster
Cream to pale gray with a fan shape, these have a subtle shellfish flavor.

Porcini
Also known as *cèpes,* porcini are firm, plump wild mushrooms with a sweet smell and full, earthy flavor.

Portobello
Mature cremini mushrooms, these have wide, dark brown caps with a rich, smoky flavor and meaty texture.

Shiitake
A widely cultivated Japanese variety with smooth, plump, meaty-tasting dark brown caps. The tough stems must be discarded.

(See page 16 for cutting techniques.)

VEGETABLES BY SEASON

For the best-tasting vegetable dishes, aim to use produce grown locally and in season, rather than transported from around the globe. Farmers' markets are good sources. Here is a list of vegetables and their seasons. Keep in mind that availability varies with location and climate.

Spring

Shoots and Stalks Artichokes and asparagus

Leaves Arugula (rocket), baby spinach, kale, and lettuces

Cabbage Family Broccoli rabe and cabbages

Roots and Tubers Daikon, new potatoes, radishes, and turnips

Mushrooms Button, morel, oyster, porcini, portobello, and shiitake

Peas, Beans, and Seeds Peas, fava (broad) beans, and green beans

Bulbs Baby leeks, green garlic, green (spring) onions, and Vidalia onions

Summer

Leaves Arugula, romaine (cos) lettuce, and spinach

Vegetable Fruits Bell peppers (capsicums), chiles, eggplants (aubergines), summer squashes, tomatillos, tomatoes, and zucchini (courgettes)

Roots and Tubers Carrots, and potatoes

Peas, Beans, and Seeds Corn, peas, green beans, haricots verts, wax beans, and shell beans such as cranberry (borlotti) or flageolet

Bulbs Garlic, leeks, onions, and shallots

Vegetable Cooking Techniques

Vegetables can be cooked by a variety of methods. Following are tips for some of the most common. Whichever you use, always start by cutting pieces to a uniform size to ensure even cooking. (See page 16 for cutting techniques.)

BLANCHING Blanching involves briefly submerging vegetables in boiling water, then immediately plunging them into ice water or placing them under running cold water to stop the cooking. It is used to mute strong flavors of ingredients like onions and garlic, and to brighten and set the color of vegetables before they are cooked by other means.

GRILLING A grill is ideal for cooking all kinds of vegetables: tender vegetable-fruits, stalks, root vegetables, winter squashes, and alliums are all good choices. Cut larger or thicker vegetables into thinner, smaller pieces that will cook through before burning on the outside; blanch firmer vegetables until just tender; and skewer vegetables that would otherwise fall through the grill rack. Marinate the vegetables in advance, or brush with oil. Grill, turning 2 or 3 times, until nicely browned and tender-crisp, from as briefly as 4 minutes for thin asparagus to as long as 12 minutes for onion wedges or baby artichokes.

ROASTING Dense autumn and winter vegetables are particularly well suited to roasting in the oven, but roasting also has positive effects on more tender vegetables. Preheat the oven to 400–425°F (200–220°C). Cut the vegetables into wedges or chunks and toss with oil and any seasonings desired. Spread vegetables evenly in a roasting pan, without crowding, and roast until browned and tender, usually 10 to 30 minutes, depending on size and firmness.

SAUTÉING Relatively tender vegetables such as asparagus, bell peppers (capsicums), mushrooms, spinach, and zucchini, cook quickly in a little fat over high heat. Sautéing also sears and caramelizes the exterior and keeps the interior crisp but tender. After heating oil or butter in the pan, add bite-size pieces of vegetable and season with salt and pepper. Keep the pieces moving briskly until golden brown and tender-crisp.

STEAMING Cooking food over boiling water in a covered pan, steaming retains the color, shape, flavor, texture, and nutrients of vegetables. Pour water to a depth of about 1 inch (2.5 cm) into a saucepan. Place a steamer basket or steamer insert inside; the water should come just to its bottom. Cover and bring to a vigorous boil over high heat. Add bite-size vegetable pieces, cover, and steam until tender and bright colored. To test for doneness, lift the lid, opening it away from you to avoid being burned by the steam, and insert the tip of a paring knife into a piece of vegetable. You should be able to pierce it easily, but it should still retain its shape and some firmness.

STIR-FRYING This Asian technique involves rapidly stirring and tossing small pieces of food in an oil-coated pan over high heat. A wok is ideal, as it distributes heat evenly and provides maximum cooking surface, but a large, deep frying pan can be used. Almost any vegetable can be stir-fried as long as it is cut into small, uniform pieces. Add the vegetables (including aromatics like ginger and garlic) to the pan in the order of their cooking time: tougher vegetables like carrots cook the longest and tender vegetables like green (spring) onions cook only briefly. Add fresh herbs or other seasonings and any sauce near the end of cooking and toss briefly over the heat before serving.

CLASSIC SIDE DISHES

As illustrated in Vegetable Cooking Techniques, opposite, one of the best things about vegetables is how simple they are to cook. Here are several easy recipes for traditional favorites. Each recipe makes 4–6 servings.

Boiled Corn on the Cob

Fill a large pot three-fourths full with water. Add about ½ teaspoon sugar per 1 qt (1 l) water. Bring to a boil over high heat. Meanwhile, pull off the husks from 4–6 ears of fresh sweet corn and brush away the silk; cut or break off any long stems. Rinse the ears under running cold water. Add to the boiling water and cook the ears until tender, 4 to 8 minutes, depending on size. Transfer to a platter. Pass butter and salt at the table.

Grilled Corn on the Cob

Prepare a grill for direct-heat cooking over medium heat (see page 18). Pull back the husks from 4–6 ears of corn, but leave them attached; remove and discard the silk, then replace the husks around the ear. Soak the ears in cold water to cover for at least 20 minutes, then drain. Carefully pull back the husks from each ear and evenly spread about 1 tablespoon butter and desired seasonings over the kernels. Replace the husks. Place the corn on the grill rack, cover the grill, and open the vents. Grill the corn until the husks are browned and the kernels are tender, about 15 minutes.

Mashed Potatoes

Fill a large saucepan half full with water. Peel and quarter 4 large russet or Yukon gold potatoes. Add to the pan with 1 teaspoon salt. Bring to a boil over high heat, then reduce the heat and cook, uncovered, until the potatoes are very tender when pierced with a fork, 15 to 20 minutes. Drain thoroughly and then return the potatoes to the dry pan. Shake the pan over medium heat to evaporate any remaining water. Turn off the heat, add ¼ cup (2 fl oz/60 ml) milk or cream, heated, and 2 tablespoons unsalted butter, at room temperature, and mash with a potato masher until fairly smooth. Mash in 1 tablespoon more butter and up to ¼ cup more warmed milk or cream until the potatoes are smooth to your liking. Season with salt and ground pepper.

Roasted Beets

Preheat the oven to 425°F (220°C). Cut 1½ pounds (750 g) small peeled red or yellow beets into 2-inch (5-cm) chunks and add to a baking dish just large enough to hold them. Toss the beets with 1 tablespoon chopped fresh rosemary, 4 teaspoons olive oil, ¼ teaspoon sea salt, and ⅛ teaspoon ground pepper. Roast, turning occasionally, until golden brown and tender when pierced with the tip of a knife, about 1 hour.

Sautéed Zucchini

Trim 1½ lb (750 g) zucchini (courgettes) and cut into bite-size pieces. In a large frying pan over high heat, warm 2 tablespoons olive oil. Add the zucchini and toss to coat with the oil. Sprinkle with ¼ teaspoon sea salt and a pinch of ground pepper and sauté, stirring or tossing frequently, until golden brown, 8 to 10 minutes.

Steamed Broccoli or Cauliflower

Trim 1½ lb (750 g) broccoli or cauliflower and cut into bite-size florets. Pour water into a saucepan to a depth of about 1 inch (2.5 cm). Place a steamer basket or steamer insert in the pan. Arrange the florets in the steamer basket and bring the water to a boil. Cover the pan and cook until the vegetables are tender and bright in color, 4–5 minutes. Toss with ¼ cup (2 fl oz/60 ml) extra-virgin olive oil, 2 tablespoons fresh lemon juice, and salt and pepper to taste.

Autumn

Shoots and Stalks
Artichokes and fennel

Leaves Escarole (Batavian endive), spinach, and Swiss chard

Cabbage Family Broccoli, broccoli rabe, Brussels sprouts, cabbages, and cauliflower

Vegetable Fruits Bell peppers, eggplants, pumpkins, and winter squashes

Roots and Tubers Celery root (celeriac), parsnips, potatoes, rutabagas (swedes), sweet potatoes, and turnips

Mushrooms Button, chanterelle, oyster, porcini, portobello, and shiitake

Bulbs Garlic, leeks, and shallots

Winter

Leaves Escarole (Batavian endive), frisée, kale, radicchio, and Swiss chard

Cabbage Family Broccoli, broccoli rabe, Brussels sprouts, and cabbages

Roots and Tubers Beets, carrots, celery root, Jerusalem artichokes, parsnips, rutabagas, sweet potatoes, turnips, and yams

Mushrooms Button, chanterelle, and portobello

SPINACH WITH GARLIC AND PARMESAN

Wilting spinach

Dishes in which spinach is wilted require full-grown spinach leaves. Baby spinach does not have the same texture or moisture content, and its more delicate flavor doesn't hold up.

This simple dish makes a quick accompaniment for myriad dishes, from soup to steak to roast chicken. Start with spinach that has been well rinsed and thoroughly dried (see page 96). The vegetable releases plenty of its own liquid as it cooks.

In a large frying pan over medium-high heat, warm the oil. Add the garlic and sauté until fragrant, about 1 minute. Add the spinach and sauté for about 1 minute to coat with the oil and garlic. Cover, reduce the heat to medium, and cook until wilted, about 2 minutes longer.

Uncover and raise the heat to high to boil away any excess liquid. Season with salt and pepper.

Spoon into a warmed serving bowl, sprinkle with the cheese, and toss to mix. Serve right away.

1 tablespoon olive oil

2 cloves garlic, minced

2 bunches spinach, about ½ lb (250 g) each

Salt and ground pepper

1 tablespoon grated Parmesan cheese

MAKES 2 SERVINGS

SWISS CHARD WITH FETA AND PINE NUTS

Chard for brunch

For a main-course brunch variation on this dish, see Poached Eggs in Chard Nests (page 40), which offers a different approach to dealing with the thick chard stalks.

For this dish, Swiss chard is wilted with sautéed shallots. Crumbled feta cheese, added at the end, melts slightly and adds a savory-salty counterpoint, and then the finished dish is topped with toasted pine nuts. Add some chopped pancetta to the pan with the shallots, if you like.

Remove the stalks from the Swiss chard and discard or reserve for another use. Tear the chard leaves into 2-inch (5-cm) pieces and set aside.

In a small dry frying pan over medium heat, toast the pine nuts, stirring constantly, until lightly browned, 1–2 minutes. Watch carefully so they do not burn. Transfer to a plate to stop the cooking and set aside.

In the same frying pan over medium-high heat, warm the oil. Add the shallots and sauté until they just begin to brown, 1–2 minutes. Add the chard leaves, stir to coat with the oil, cover, and cook until wilted, about 2 minutes. Uncover and raise the heat to high to boil away any excess liquid.

Add the cheese, re-cover, and cook until the cheese just begins to melt, about 30 seconds longer. If more liquid is released, carefully drain the chard in a sieve, being careful not to drain away any of the cheese.

Transfer to a warmed serving bowl. Season with salt and pepper and top with the pine nuts. Serve right away.

2 bunches Swiss chard, about ½ lb (250 g) each

2 tablespoons pine nuts

2 tablespoons peanut or canola oil

2 shallots, finely chopped

⅓ cup (1½ oz/45 g) crumbled feta cheese

Salt and ground pepper

MAKES 4 SERVINGS

CHARD, SPINACH, AND MUSHROOM GRATIN

This gratin combines sautéed mushrooms and shallot with wilted spinach and chard. The mixture is placed in a baking dish and topped with bread crumbs and Parmesan. The buttery, crunchy bread-crumb topping complements the earthy flavors of the greens and mushrooms.

4 tablespoons (2 oz/60 g) unsalted butter

1 shallot, minced

6 oz (185 g) cremini mushrooms, sliced

1½ teaspoons dry mustard

2 tablespoons red wine vinegar

1 small bunch Swiss chard, about 6 oz (185 g), coarsely chopped

1 bunch spinach, about ¾ lb (375 g), tough stems removed and coarsely chopped

Salt and ground pepper

⅓ cup (1½ oz/45 g) fine dried bread crumbs

3–4 tablespoons grated Parmesan cheese

1 tablespoon olive oil

MAKES 4–6 SERVINGS

Preheat the oven to 325°F (165°C). LIghtly butter a shallow 1-qt (1-l) baking dish.

In a large frying pan over medium heat, melt 2 tablespoons of the butter. Add the shallot and mushrooms and sauté until softened, about 2 minutes. Stir in the mustard and sauté for 10 seconds longer. Stir in ½ cup (4 fl oz/125 ml) water and the vinegar. Add the chard and spinach, a handful at a time, waiting for each handful to wilt before adding the next one. It should take about 30 seconds for each addition to wilt. When all of the greens have been added, season with salt and pepper and remove from the heat.

Transfer to the prepared baking dish. Sprinkle the bread crumbs and cheese evenly over the top, and then drizzle evenly with the oil. Cut the remaining 2 tablespoons butter into small pieces and dot the top.

Bake until heated through and the top is golden brown, 15–20 minutes. Serve right away, directly from the dish.

Chard varieties

The terms chard and Swiss chard are used interchangeably. There are several different types on the market, including varieties with white, red, yellow, or multi-colored stems. Any variety will work for this recipe.

337

RADICCHIO AND PROSCIUTTO BUNDLES

Rustic yet elegant, these baked prosciutto-wrapped radicchio wedges can be served as a starter or a side dish. Three small-to-medium heads Belgian endive (chicory/witloof) can be substituted for the radicchio. Cut each endive head in half lengthwise before wrapping.

2 heads radicchio, about ¾ lb (375 g) each

2 tablespoons olive oil

12 large, thin slices prosciutto

Lemon wedges

MAKES 6 SERVINGS

Preheat the oven to 400°F (200°C). Oil a rimmed baking sheet.

Cut each radicchio head into 6 wedges through the stem end. Brush each wedge lightly with the oil. Wrap each wedge with a slice of prosciutto, then arrange on the prepared baking sheet and turn to coat the prosciutto with the oil.

Bake until the radicchio is tender and the prosciutto begins to crisp, 12–14 minutes. Transfer to a platter and serve right away, accompanied by lemon wedges.

Tapas style

To serve this dish tapas style, divide among small plates. Place 2 radicchio bundles and 1 lemon wedge on each plate and scatter some olives alongside.

ESCAROLE SOUFFLÉ

Hot-water caution

A hot-water bath, or bain-marie, provides moist, even heat for baked delicate egg dishes, such as soufflés and custards. Take care when removing the two containers from the oven; the water will be dangerously hot.

Escarole, a member of the chicory family, is at its peak in fall and winter. Here it's incorporated into a fluffy and flavorful soufflé. Other bitter greens, such as beet greens or curly endive, can be used in its place. The soufflé complements a variety of main dishes.

Preheat the oven to 350°F (180°C). Brush a 1-qt (1-l) soufflé dish with the 1½ tablespoons melted butter. Coat with the cheese, tapping out the excess.

In a sauté pan over medium heat, warm the oil. Add the leeks and sauté until softened, 5–7 minutes. Add the escarole and sauté until tender, 3–4 minutes longer. Remove from the heat and set aside to cool.

In a saucepan over medium heat, melt the 2 tablespoons butter. Add the flour and cook, stirring, until well blended and smooth, 3–4 minutes. Slowly add the broth while whisking constantly. Bring to a boil, reduce the heat to low and cook, stirring, until thickened, 5–6 minutes. Stir in the cayenne pepper and season with salt and black pepper. Set the mixture aside to cool.

In a large bowl, combine the cooled escarole mixture and broth mixture. Add the egg yolks and stir with a large spoon to mix well. In a bowl, using an electric mixer on medium-high speed, beat the egg whites until stiff peaks form. Stir about one-third of the whites into the escarole mixture to lighten it. Then fold in the remaining egg whites just until no white streaks are visible.

Pour the mixture into the prepared soufflé dish and place the dish in a large baking pan. Pour hot water into the baking pan to reach halfway up the sides of the soufflé dish. Bake until the soufflé rises nicely and is lightly browned, about 30 minutes. Serve right away.

1½ tablespoons unsalted butter, melted, plus 2 tablespoons

3 tablespoons grated Parmesan cheese

3 tablespoons extra-virgin olive oil

2 leeks, white part only, halved lengthwise and thinly sliced

2 cups (4 oz/125 g) finely shredded escarole (Batavian endive)

2 tablespoons all-purpose (plain) flour

¾ cup (6 fl oz/180 ml) vegetable broth

¼ teaspoon cayenne pepper

Salt and ground black pepper

3 eggs, separated

MAKES 6 SERVINGS

STIR-FRIED CABBAGE AND RED PEPPER

Julienned carrots

To cut carrots into thin matchsticks for quick cooking, cut the carrots into 2-inch (5-cm) lengths. Cut each carrot piece lengthwise into very thin slices, then stack the slices neatly and cut down through them at intervals equal to the thickness of the slices.

This Asian-style vegetable stir-fry is crunchy and colorful, brightly spiced with chile paste, and makes an excellent side dish for beef or chicken. Stir-fries come together very quickly once you start cooking, so make sure all of your vegetables are chopped as directed and ready to use.

In a small bowl, stir together the chile-garlic paste, soy sauce, sherry, and a pinch each salt and pepper. Set aside.

In a dry wok or large frying pan over medium heat, toast the pine nuts, stirring constantly, until lightly browned, 1–2 minutes. Watch carefully so they do not burn. Transfer to a dish and set aside.

In the same pan over medium-high heat, warm the oil, swirling to coat the bottom and sides of the pan. When the oil is almost smoking, add the leek, carrots, and bell pepper and stir and toss the vegetables together every 15–20 seconds

1 teaspoon Asian chile-garlic paste

2 tablespoons soy sauce

¼ cup (2 fl oz/60 ml) dry sherry

Salt and ground pepper

2 tablespoons pine nuts

3 tablespoons peanut or corn oil

1 leek, including pale green parts, finely chopped

2 carrots, peeled and julienned (see note, left)

½ red bell pepper (capsicum), cut lengthwise into narrow strips

1 head green cabbage, about 1 lb (500 g), cored and finely shredded

MAKES 4–6 SERVINGS

until they are just beginning to soften, about 3 minutes. Add the cabbage and stir and toss every 15–20 seconds until just softened, about 3 minutes longer.

Quickly stir the chile-garlic paste mixture, add it to the pan, and stir to combine. Bring to a boil over high heat and cook for 1 minute longer, stirring once or twice, until the vegetables are well mixed with the other ingredients. Taste and adjust the seasoning.

Stir in the toasted pine nuts, or transfer to a warmed platter and sprinkle with the pine nuts. Serve right away.

RED CABBAGE ROLLS

These rice-filled cabbage rolls are delicious served at room temperature, accompanied by sour cream seasoned with a little minced cilantro. To serve as a main course, place the rolls in a baking dish, top with tomato sauce, and bake in a 375°F (190°C) oven until warmed through.

1 head red cabbage

¼ cup (2 fl oz/60 ml) canola oil

½ cup (2 oz/60 g) chopped yellow onion

2 cloves garlic, minced

1½ cups (12 fl oz/375 ml) vegetable broth

¼ cup (2 fl oz/60 ml) tomato sauce, homemade (page 377) or canned

¾ cup (5 oz/155 g) jasmine or other long-grain white rice

1 teaspoon red pepper flakes, or to taste

¼ cup (⅓ oz/10 g) minced fresh flat-leaf (Italian) parsley

3 tablespoons minced fresh cilantro (fresh coriander)

½ teaspoon ground cumin

¼ teaspoon ground coriander

Salt and ground pepper

MAKES 8 SERVINGS

Remove the tough outer leaves of the cabbage and discard. Cut out the core but leave the head whole.

Have ready a large bowl of ice water. Bring a large pot three-fourths full of water to a boil. Immerse the cabbage in the boiling water and cook until the leaves are pliable and separate easily when gently pulled apart with tongs, 5–7 minutes. Drain and immerse immediately in the ice water to stop the cooking. Drain again and blot dry. Carefully separate and set aside 16 large leaves.

In a saucepan over medium heat, warm the oil. Add the onion and garlic and sauté until lightly golden, 4–5 minutes. Add the broth, tomato sauce, rice, and red pepper flakes and bring to a boil. Cover, reduce the heat to low, and cook, undisturbed, until the rice is tender and the liquid is absorbed, about 20 minutes.

Remove the pan from the heat, add the parsley, cilantro, cumin, and coriander and mix well. Season with salt and pepper and set aside to cool to room temperature.

Trim off the heavy rib from the base of each cabbage leaf, squaring off the end. Place a heaping tablespoon of the filling in the center of the leaf and, starting from the rib end, roll up the leaf, tucking in the sides and forming a cylinder.

If serving at room temperature, place the rolls, seam sides down, on a serving platter. If baking, see note, above.

About red pepper flakes

Red pepper flakes are red chiles that have been dried and then crushed. Store them in an airtight container in a cool cupboard. Suitable substitutes include hot paprika or pure chile powder, such as chipotle or New Mexico.

BRUSSELS SPROUTS WITH GARLIC AND PARMESAN

Buying brussels sprouts

Brussels sprouts are related to cabbage, kale, and broccoli. A cool-season, coastal crop, the tiny heads grow in clusters on long stalks. Buy them on the stalk if you can, or look for heads that are bright green, compact, and look as if they have been recently cut from the stalk.

Brussels sprouts have an appealing nutty flavor and vivid green color that come through in simple preparations like this one. They also stand up well to the large quantity of garlic added to this dish. If you like, cook a little chopped bacon in the pan before adding the garlic.

Trim the ends from the brussels sprouts and cut the sprouts in half lengthwise. Select a frying pan large enough to hold all the sprouts in a single layer, place over low heat, and add the butter and oil. When the butter melts, add the garlic and sauté until softened, about 2 minutes.

Add the brussels sprouts and the broth to a depth of about 1½ inches (4 cm), cover, and simmer, stirring occasionally, until tender-crisp, 5–8 minutes. Season with salt and pepper.

Transfer to a warmed serving bowl and sprinkle the cheese over the top. Serve right away.

1½ lb (750 g) brussels sprouts

2 tablespoons unsalted butter

2 tablespoons olive oil

6 large cloves garlic, minced

¾–1 cup (6–8 fl oz/ 180–250 ml) chicken broth

Salt and ground pepper

¾ cup (3 oz/90 g) grated Parmesan cheese

MAKES 6 SERVINGS

BRUSSELS SPROUTS WITH MUSTARD AND LEMON

Brussels sprouts and nuts

Halve and boil brussels sprouts as at right. Melt several tablespoons of compound butter (see page 246) in a frying pan over medium heat, toss the sprouts in the butter to warm through, then transfer to a serving bowl and sprinkle with toasted nuts.

Mustard and lemon add sparkle and flair to this easy-to-assemble dish. If you're cooking for a crowd, the brussels sprouts can be boiled several hours in advance, cooled, and then covered and refrigerated until you are ready to finish the dish.

Trim the ends from the brussels sprouts and cut the sprouts in half lengthwise. Bring a large saucepan three-fourths full of salted water to a boil. Add the sprouts and boil until tender-crisp, 2–3 minutes. Drain the sprouts well and let cool to room temperature.

In a bowl, stir together the lemon juice and mustard until well blended. Set aside.

Just before serving, heat the oil in a frying pan over medium-high heat. Add the brussels sprouts and stir and toss until their edges just begin to turn golden, 1–2 minutes. At the last moment, add the lemon juice–mustard mixture and stir briskly. Season with salt and pepper.

Transfer to a warmed bowl and serve right away.

1½ lb (750 g) brussels sprouts

3 tablespoons fresh lemon juice

1½ tablespoons whole-grain mustard

3 tablespoons extra-virgin olive oil

Salt and ground pepper

MAKES 6–8 SERVINGS

BROCCOLI WITH CAPERS AND OLIVES

Here is a simple, attractive dish of tender broccoli, lightly dressed and then tossed with capers and olives. It is a great way to use broccoli stalks after the florets have been used for another dish. Serve at room temperature, as the Italians do, with pasta and a loaf of crusty bread.

1 lb (500 g) broccoli stalks

3 tablespoons olive oil

1 tablespoon red wine vinegar

Juice of ½ lemon

Salt and ground pepper

1 tablespoon rinsed capers

½ cup (2½ oz/75 g) pitted black olives, chopped

MAKES 4 SERVINGS

Split each broccoli stalk lengthwise into thin pieces. Cut off and discard any coarse leaves and tough lower stems.

Fill a saucepan with just enough water to cover the broccoli. Bring to a boil over high heat. Add the broccoli and cook, uncovered, just until tender, 4–5 minutes.

Drain and transfer to a serving bowl. Drizzle with the oil and vinegar, spritz with the lemon juice, and toss to coat evenly. Season with salt and pepper.

Add the capers and olives and toss the broccoli gently. Serve at room temperature.

About capers

The small unopened flower buds of a Mediterranean shrub, capers are packed in brine or salt, which gives them a pleasantly pungent flavor and light crunch. Drain and quickly rinse brined capers before using. Thoroughly rinse salted capers before using. Or, if particularly salty, soak in cool water for about 10 minutes.

341

CURRIED POTATOES, CAULIFLOWER, AND PEAS

This pungent and savory vegetable stew is delicious served as a vegetarian main course or as a side to roasted or grilled meats. Look for brown or black mustard seeds in Indian markets and specialty-food stores. Garnish with chopped fresh cilantro (fresh coriander) if desired.

1½ lb (750 g) red new or Yukon gold potatoes

2 teaspoons mustard seeds

2 tablespoons ghee or clarified butter (see note, right)

1 yellow onion, sliced

2 cloves garlic, minced

2 teaspoons minced fresh ginger

1 teaspoon *each* ground cumin and garam masala

½ teaspoon ground turmeric

¼ teaspoon cayenne pepper

2 cups (4 oz/125 g) small cauliflower florets

Salt and ground pepper

1 cup (5 oz/155 g) shelled fresh peas or thawed, frozen petite peas

MAKES 6 SERVINGS

Peel the potatoes and cut into 1-inch (2.5-cm) cubes. Place in a bowl, add water to cover, and set aside.

In a large saucepan over medium heat, add the mustard seeds and cook until they begin to pop, 1–2 minutes. Add the ghee, onion, garlic, and ginger and cook, stirring occasionally, until the onion begins to soften, about 1 minute. Sprinkle in the cumin, garam masala, turmeric, and cayenne and cook, stirring constantly, until fragrant, about 30 seconds.

Drain the potatoes, add the potatoes and cauliflower to the pan, and stir to coat with the spices. Add 1 cup (8 fl oz/250 ml) water, cover, and cook until the potatoes are almost tender, 10–12 minutes. Season with salt and pepper. Add the peas and cook, uncovered, until tender and the liquid is absorbed, about 3 minutes longer.

Transfer the vegetables to a serving dish and serve hot or let cool to room temperature before serving.

Butter in Indian cooking

Ghee is a type of clarified butter used in Indian cooking. There are two kinds, the most common of which is usli ghee, typically referred to simply as ghee. It can be purchased in Indian and other ethnic markets. If you cannot find it, Clarified Butter (page 28) can be substituted.

SAUTÉED ARTICHOKES WITH HERB SAUCE

Wine with artichokes

Artichokes contain cynarin, an acid that enhances the natural sweetness in other foods or beverages that you consume along with them. For example, if you are drinking white wine with artichokes, the wine might taste "off," unless you choose a highly acidic one, such as a dry Chenin Blanc or Sauvignon Blanc.

Artichokes have a flush in the spring and then again in autumn. The autumn vegetables are more open and often are tinged with brown from cold exposure, which does not detract from their flavor. Here, they are cut into wedges and lightly browned in olive oil with a little garlic.

Trim the artichokes according to the method on page 332, cut each artichoke lengthwise into quarters, scoop out the choke, and then cut each quarter lengthwise in half again. When all the artichokes are trimmed, drain and pat dry.

In a heavy saucepan over medium heat, warm the oil. Add the garlic and artichokes and sauté until the artichokes turn lightly golden, 4–5 minutes. Raise the heat to high, add the lemon juice, and stir to dislodge any browned bits from the pan bottom. Add the broth and ½ teaspoon salt to the pan, reduce the heat to low, cover, and simmer until the bases of the artichoke pieces are easily pierced, about 10 minutes.

Stir in the parsley and remove from the heat. Transfer the artichokes to warmed individual plates. Spoon the pan sauce over the top. Serve hot or at room temperature.

6 artichokes

3 tablespoons extra-virgin olive oil

1 clove garlic, minced

⅓ cup (3 fl oz/80 ml) fresh lemon juice

⅓ cup (3 fl oz/80 ml) chicken broth

Salt

2 tablespoons minced fresh flat-leaf (Italian) parsley

MAKES 4 SERVINGS

BAKED STUFFED ARTICHOKES

Keeping it stainless

Use only stainless-steel knives and cookware when preparing artichokes, since carbon steel, aluminum, and cast iron will discolor the vegetable within moments of contact.

For this dish, the artichokes are trimmed, partially cooked, and then filled with a stuffing of mushrooms and bread crumbs and baked. If you like, secure a slice of bacon around the "waist" of each artichoke with a toothpick before baking.

Preheat the oven to 375°F (190°C).

Bring a large saucepan half full of water to a boil. Cut off the stem of each artichoke flush with the base. Stand the artichokes upright in the saucepan and add the lemon juice. When the water comes back to a boil, reduce the heat to medium, cover, and simmer for 15 minutes.

Remove the artichokes and invert to drain. When they are cool enough to handle, gently open the leaves and, using a spoon, scoop out the center choke. Set the artichokes aside.

In a frying pan over medium heat, warm 2 tablespoons of the oil. Add the garlic, shallots, and mushrooms and sauté until soft, about 2 minutes. Add 2 tablespoons of the parsley and the mint and season with salt and pepper. Mix in the bread crumbs and remove from the heat.

Fill each artichoke with an equal amount of the mixture. Place upright in a baking dish and sprinkle with the remaining 1 tablespoon oil. Pour in the warm stock. Bake until the artichokes are tender, about 30 minutes.

Remove from the oven and garnish with the remaining 1 tablespoon parsley. Serve hot or at room temperature.

4 artichokes, trimmed (see page 332)

Juice of 1 lemon

3 tablespoons olive oil

2 cloves garlic, chopped

2 shallots, chopped

½ cup (2 oz/60 g) chopped fresh white mushrooms

3 tablespoons chopped fresh flat-leaf (Italian) parsley

1 tablespoon chopped fresh mint

Salt and ground pepper

⅓ cup (1½ oz/45 g) fine dried bread crumbs

2 cups (16 fl oz/500 ml) Vegetable Stock (page 26), heated

MAKES 4 SERVINGS

ASPARAGUS WITH CHOPPED EGGS

Here, tender asparagus spears are served warm with a shallot vinaigrette and topped with finely chopped hard-boiled egg yolks. If you prefer, poach or fry 4 eggs (see page 38). Divide the asparagus among 4 plates, drizzle with the dressing, and drape an egg over each portion.

1 lb (500 g) asparagus,
peeled if thick
(see note, right)

½ cup (4 fl oz/125 ml)
olive oil

2 tablespoons
chopped shallots

3 tablespoons red
wine vinegar

1½ teaspoons
Dijon mustard

Salt and ground pepper

2 tablespoons
chopped fresh flat-leaf
(Italian) parsley

2 hard-boiled egg yolks

MAKES 4 SERVINGS

Select a frying pan large enough to hold the asparagus in a single layer and fill with water to a depth of about 1½ inches (4 cm). Bring to a boil, then reduce to a simmer. Add the asparagus and cook until tender-crisp, 3–6 minutes; begin testing with the tip of a knife after 3 minutes. Remove from the heat and drain.

In a small bowl, whisk together the oil, shallots, vinegar, and mustard. Season with salt and pepper, and add the parsley.

Arrange the asparagus on a warmed platter and drizzle with the dressing. Finely chop the egg yolks and spread the chopped yolks across the center of the asparagus. Or, using a wooden spoon, force the yolks through a fine-mesh sieve held over the asparagus. Serve right away.

Thickness matters

Asparagus ranges from pencil thin to as thick as ¾ inch (2 cm) in diameter. The stouter the spear is, the longer it will take to cook, and the more likely the skin will be fibrous. If you've bought fat spears, run a vegetable peeler down the length of the spears to within an inch (2.5 cm) or so of the tip.

343

PROSCIUTTO-WRAPPED ASPARAGUS

Prosciutto and Parmesan heighten the flavor of the fresh asparagus in this classic Italian dish. These baked asparagus bundles make an attractive first course. Or, double the portion size and serve two bundles per person with good crusty bread for a light dinner.

12 large asparagus, peeled

4 thin slices prosciutto

2 tablespoons unsalted
butter, cut into small pieces

Ground pepper

½ cup (2 oz/60 g) grated
Parmesan or Fontina cheese

½ teaspoon paprika

MAKES 4 SERVINGS

Preheat the oven to 375°F (190°C). Butter a baking dish just large enough to hold the asparagus in a single layer.

Gather the asparagus together and cut off the tough ends so all the spears are the same length.

Select a frying pan large enough to hold the asparagus in a single layer and fill with water to a depth of about 1½ inches (4 cm). Bring to a boil, then reduce to a simmer. Add the asparagus and cook until tender-crisp, 3–6 minutes; begin testing with the tip of a knife after 3 minutes. Remove from the heat and drain.

Divide the asparagus into 4 bundles of 3 spears each. Wrap 1 prosciutto slice around the center of each bundle. Place the bundles in the prepared baking dish. Dot with the butter, season with pepper, and sprinkle with the cheese. Bake until the cheese begins to brown, about 5 minutes.

Remove the bundles from the oven, dust with the paprika, and serve right away.

Using unsalted butter

Unsalted butter isn't just for baking: it allows you control over the salt content of any dish, which is especially important in a preparation like this one, in which the prosciutto and Parmesan are already supplying a good measure of saltiness.

ASPARAGUS WITH POTATOES AND ALMONDS

About blanched almonds

Blanched almonds are almonds that have had their dark outer skins removed. They are most commonly sold whole, sliced (flaked) lengthwise, or slivered lengthwise (cut into thin strips).

In this quickly assembled side dish, asparagus lengths are tossed with chunks of roasted potatoes and simmered in chicken broth with a little garlic. Chopped mint or basil adds a note of freshness. You can substitute pine nuts for the almonds, if you like.

Preheat the oven to 400°F (200°C).

Place the potatoes in a baking pan, coat them with about 2 tablespoons of the oil, and sprinkle with salt and pepper. Roast until the potatoes are cooked through but firm, 25–35 minutes. Set aside until cool enough to handle.

Select a frying pan large enough to hold the asparagus in a single layer and fill with water to a depth of about 1½ inches (4 cm). Bring the water to a boil, then reduce the heat to maintain a simmer. Add the asparagus and cook until tender-crisp, 3–6 minutes; begin testing with the tip of a knife after 3 minutes. Remove from the heat, drain, and pat dry.

Cut the asparagus into 2-inch (5-cm) lengths. Cut the cooled potatoes into quarters. In a very large frying pan over medium heat, warm the remaining 4 tablespoons (2 fl oz/60 ml) oil. Add the potatoes and heat through, turning occasionally. Add the asparagus, broth, and garlic and simmer for a few minutes to heat through. Season with salt and pepper, then add the almonds and mint and stir gently to mix. Transfer to a warmed serving bowl and serve right away.

24 small red potatoes, about 3 lb (1.5 kg) total weight

6 tablespoons (3 fl oz/ 90 ml) olive oil

Salt and ground pepper

2 lb (1 kg) asparagus, tough ends removed and peeled if thick

1 cup (8 fl oz/250 ml) chicken broth

2 cloves garlic, minced

½ cup (2 oz/60 g) sliced (flaked) or slivered blanched almonds, toasted (see page 17)

½ cup (¾ oz/20 g) chopped fresh mint or basil

MAKES 6 SERVINGS

SAUTÉ OF GARDEN VEGETABLES

French-style beans

In French, haricots verts means literally "green beans." Since French green beans are short and very thin, the same term is popularly used in English for some varieties of slender green beans.

For this dish, carrots and celery are julienned to mimic the size and shape of young green beans. All the vegetables are blanched so they are tender and bright, then lightly sautéed. Look for slender Blue Lake beans or for beans labeled "haricots verts."

Keeping them separate, cut the carrots and celery stalks into strips 2 inches (5 cm) long and ¼ inch (6 mm) thick and wide. If the beans are more than 2 inches (5 cm) long, cut them to match the carrots and celery.

Bring a saucepan three-fourths full of water to a boil. Add the carrots and boil for 1 minute. Using a slotted spoon, scoop out the carrots, drain, and set aside. Add the celery to the boiling water and boil for 30 seconds, then scoop them out, drain, and set aside. Add the green beans and boil for 2 minutes, then drain and set aside.

In a frying pan over medium heat, melt the butter with the oil. Add the onion and sauté, stirring, until soft, 3–5 minutes. Add the carrots, celery, and green beans and continue to sauté until the vegetables are tender but not too soft, about 3 minutes. Add ½ teaspoon salt, a few grinds of pepper, and the parsley and mix well.

Transfer to a warmed serving dish and serve right away.

4 carrots, peeled

4 celery stalks

¾ lb (375 g) slender green beans

1 tablespoon unsalted butter

1 tablespoon extra-virgin olive oil

1 red onion, thinly sliced

Salt and ground pepper

1 tablespoon finely chopped fresh flat-leaf (Italian) parsley

MAKES 6 SERVINGS

GREEN BEANS WITH GARLIC AND BASIL

Stir-frying blanched green beans in olive oil gives them a rich green color, and mixing them with garlic and fresh basil brings out their inherent sweetness. For the best results, look for tender, medium beans. Serve with grilled, roasted, or braised meat or fish.

1½ lb (750 g) tender green beans, trimmed

2 tablespoons olive oil

1 clove garlic, minced

2 tablespoons finely chopped fresh basil

Salt and ground pepper

MAKES 4–6 SERVINGS

Bring a large saucepan three-fourths full of water to a boil. Add the beans and boil until barely tender and still slightly resistant to the bite, 3–5 minutes. Drain, immerse the beans in cold water to stop the cooking, and drain again.

In a wok or frying pan over medium-high heat, warm the oil, swirling to coat the bottom and sides of the pan. When the oil is almost smoking, add the beans and stir and toss every 15–20 seconds until tender-crisp, about 3 minutes. Add the garlic and basil and stir and toss for 30 seconds longer.

Remove from the heat, season with salt and pepper, and toss to combine. Taste and adjust the seasoning. Transfer to a warmed serving dish and serve right away.

345

GREEN BEANS WITH ONIONS AND BLUE CHEESE

Here is a sophisticated take on traditional green beans. The beans are tossed in a vinaigrette, then topped with caramelized onion wedges and crumbled blue cheese. The beans, onions, and dressing can each be prepared early in the day and assembled at serving time.

2½ lb (1.25 kg) green beans, trimmed

⅔ cup (5 fl oz/160 ml) olive oil

3 tablespoons plus 2 teaspoons sherry vinegar

2 tablespoons chopped fresh thyme

2 teaspoons soy sauce

1 teaspoon sugar

Salt and ground pepper

3 large red onions, cut through the stem end into wedges ½ inch (12 mm) thick

1 cup (5 oz/155 g) crumbled blue cheese or fresh goat cheese

MAKES 8–10 SERVINGS

Preheat the broiler (grill). Oil a rimmed baking sheet.

Bring a large pot three-fourths full of salted water to a boil over high heat. Add the beans and boil until tender-crisp, about 5 minutes. Drain, rinse with cold water to stop the cooking, and drain again.

To make a vinaigrette, in a small bowl, whisk together the oil, vinegar, thyme, soy sauce, and sugar until well blended and season with salt and pepper.

Arrange the onion wedges on the prepared baking sheet. Brush with some of the vinaigrette. Broil (grill) the onions, without turning, until deep brown, 8–12 minutes.

Place the beans in a large bowl. Add the remaining vinaigrette and toss to coat. Divide the beans evenly among individual plates. Top with the onions. Drizzle with any remaining vinaigrette, sprinkle with the cheese, and serve.

SESAME SNOW PEAS AND PEPPERS

Peas in the pod

Unlike so-called English or garden peas, which are shelled before they are cooked and eaten, snow peas (mangetouts) are nearly flat, bright green pods that are eaten whole. You can use them interchangeably with their plumper relative, the sugar snap pea.

Quick and multihued, this dish of stir-fried snow peas and sliced red and yellow bell peppers is the perfect choice when a simple accompaniment is all you need. Sesame seeds lend texture and nuttiness to the mix. Accompany the dish with steamed white rice.

In a dry wok or frying pan over medium heat, toast the sesame seeds, stirring constantly, until lightly browned, about 1 minute. Watch carefully so they do not burn. Transfer to a dish and set aside.

Add the oil to the pan over high heat, swirling to coat the pan. When the oil is almost smoking, add the bell peppers and stir-fry until they begin to soften, 2–3 minutes. Add the snow peas and stir-fry for 1 minute.

Quickly stir the sauce and add to the pan. Stir and toss until the vegetables are mixed with the other ingredients, about 1 minute. Taste and adjust the seasoning.

Transfer to a warmed platter, drizzle with the sesame oil, and sprinkle with the sesame seeds. Serve right away.

1 tablespoon sesame seeds

2 tablespoons peanut or corn oil

1 red bell pepper (capsicum), thinly sliced

1 yellow bell pepper (capsicum), thinly sliced

¼ lb (125 g) snow peas (mangetouts), trimmed

All-Purpose Stir-fry Sauce (page 375)

½ teaspoon Asian sesame oil

MAKES 2 OR 3 SERVINGS

MINTED GREEN PEAS

Hearts of lettuce

A lettuce heart is the inner part of a head of lettuce, with the looser outer leaves of the head removed. For this dish, choose young, small heads and strip them yourself, or buy the hearts, often sold already bagged.

This is a thoroughly satisfying vegetable dish—especially when made with the best peas and hearts of lettuce at the market—unadorned except for butter to enhance the fresh flavors. The dish goes especially well with simple lamb preparations.

Pour the broth into a frying pan and bring it to a boil over medium heat. Meanwhile, tie together the parsley sprigs, bay leaf, and mint sprig with kitchen string to make a bouquet garni. Add the bouquet garni, sugar, peas, and lettuce hearts to the boiling broth. Simmer, uncovered, until the peas are almost tender, about 5 minutes.

Pour off all but ¼ cup (2 fl oz/60 ml) of the broth and discard or reserve for another use. Add the butter to the vegetables and season with salt and pepper. Cook over medium heat, stirring, for 2 minutes. Remove from the heat and discard the bouquet garni. Cut the lettuce hearts in half.

To serve, divide the peas among warmed individual plates, add ½ lettuce heart to each plate, and sprinkle with the chopped mint. Serve right away.

1 cup (8 fl oz/250 ml) vegetable broth

2 fresh flat-leaf (Italian) parsley sprigs

1 bay leaf

1 fresh mint sprig, plus 1 tablespoon finely chopped

½ teaspoon sugar

2 cups (10 oz/315 g) shelled fresh peas or thawed, frozen petite peas

2 hearts butter (Boston) lettuce

2 tablespoons unsalted butter

Salt and ground pepper

MAKES 4 SERVINGS

BAKED TOMATOES AND ZUCCHINI

Sautéed red onions form an aromatic base for this pretty, Mediterranean-inspired dish. For the best-looking presentation, look for tomatoes and zucchini that are similar in diameter, to ensure uniform slices for arranging in neat rows on top of the onions.

2 tablespoons olive oil

1 red onion, sliced

Salt and ground pepper

¾ lb (375 g) plum (Roma) tomatoes, sliced

2 small zucchini (courgettes), sliced

1 tablespoon minced fresh basil

1 tablespoon minced fresh marjoram

¼ cup (2 fl oz/60 ml) chicken broth or water

MAKES 4 SERVINGS

Preheat the oven to 350°F (180°C). Lightly oil a shallow 2-qt (2-l) baking dish.

In a frying pan over medium heat, warm the oil. Add the onion and sauté slowly until very soft and beginning to brown, about 10 minutes. Transfer the onion to the prepared baking dish, spreading it evenly over the bottom. Season with salt and pepper.

Arrange the tomato and zucchini slices over the onion in slightly overlapping, alternating rows. Sprinkle with the basil and marjoram and season with salt and pepper. Pour the broth evenly over the vegetables. Cover with aluminum foil and bake until the vegetables are bubbling and tender, about 40 minutes.

Serve right away, directly from the baking dish.

Adding Parmesan

If you have used a flameproof baking dish, sprinkle the baked vegetables with ¼ cup (1 oz/30 g) grated Parmesan cheese, preheat the broiler (grill), and broil the vegetables until golden brown on top.

BAKED TOMATOES WITH GARLIC AND PARSLEY

For this Provençal-inspired dish, it's important to start with ripe, flavorful tomatoes. The key to success is to drain the moisture from the tomato halves before topping them with the bread crumbs; this will ensure that the tops become crusty and the sides don't split during baking.

6 large ripe but firm tomatoes

Salt and ground pepper

6 tablespoons (3 fl oz/ 90 ml) olive oil

½ cup (2 oz/60 g) fine dried bread crumbs

3 cloves garlic, minced

½ cup (¾ oz/20 g) chopped fresh flat-leaf (Italian) parsley

MAKES 6 SERVINGS

Cut the tomatoes in half crosswise. Sprinkle the cut sides with salt and drain, cut sides down, in a colander for about 10 minutes. Pat dry.

Preheat the oven to 400°F (200°C). Lighty oil a baking dish large enough to hold the tomato halves in a single layer.

In a sauté pan over medium-high heat, warm 2 tablespoons of the oil. Add half of the tomato halves, cut sides down, and cook until golden, 3–5 minutes. Transfer the browned tomatoes to the prepared dish, cut sides up. Repeat with the remaining tomato halves and 2 additional tablespoons olive oil. Sprinkle the tomatoes with salt and pepper.

In a small bowl, stir together the bread crumbs, garlic, and half of the chopped parsley. Spread the mixture on top of the tomatoes, dividing it evenly. Drizzle evenly with the remaining 2 tablespoons oil.

Bake until the tomatoes are puffed and juicy, 10–15 minutes. Transfer the tomatoes to a warmed platter and sprinkle with the remaining parsley. Serve right away.

Moisture and salt

Salt is often used to season and to draw moisture out of foods, including fully curing salt cod, salt pork, and other foods. In this dish, it ensures that vegetables with a high moisture content will cook without stewing or steaming in their own juices, which would lead to sogginess.

TOMATO AND POTATO GRATIN

Basil during and after

Popular basil is often used two ways in the same dish, as here. Cooked into the dish, it infuses the other ingredients with its flavor. Then more basil is sprinkled on the finished dish to reinforce the herb's bright, fresh character.

This zesty, layered dish makes a wonderful accompaniment to lamb chops (pages 282–83) or Roast Prime Rib of Beef (page 266). You can also serve it as a vegetarian main course with a mixed-green salad. If the bell pepper is long, cut it in half crosswise before cutting into strips.

Preheat the oven to 400°F (200°C). Oil a 9-by-13-inch (23-by-33-cm) gratin dish with 2-inch (5-cm) sides.

In a frying pan over medium heat, warm 2 tablespoons of the oil. Add the onion and sauté until soft, about 5 minutes. Add the bell pepper and sauté for 3 minutes. Add the tomatoes and sauté for 3 minutes. Raise the heat to high and cook, stirring occasionally, until the moisture exuded by the tomatoes evaporates, 1–2 minutes. Add the garlic and cook for 1 minute longer. Add the red pepper flakes (if using) and 2 tablespoons of the basil and season with salt and pepper. Taste and adjust the seasoning.

Spread half of the potatoes on the bottom of the prepared dish. Arrange half of the vegetable mixture on top, and sprinkle with half of the cheese. Repeat the layers. Drizzle the remaining 1 tablespoon oil evenly over the top. Cover tightly with aluminum foil.

Place the covered dish on a rimmed baking sheet. Bake for 30 minutes, then remove the foil and continue to bake until the potatoes are tender when tested with the top of a small knife and the top is browned, 15 minutes longer. Sprinkle with the remaining 2 tablespoons basil and serve.

3 tablespoons olive oil

1 yellow onion, sliced

1 red bell pepper (capsicum), cut lengthwise into narrow strips

2 tomatoes, peeled, seeded, and chopped

2 cloves garlic, minced

¼ teaspoon red pepper flakes, optional

4 tablespoons (⅓ oz/10 g) chopped fresh basil

Salt and ground black pepper

4 large russet potatoes, about 2 lb (1 kg) total weight, peeled and cut into slices ¼ inch (6 mm) thick

1 cup (4 oz/125 g) shredded Gruyère cheese

MAKES 4–6 SERVINGS

OVEN-FRIED GREEN TOMATOES

The art of breading

When you "bread" a food, that is, coat it alternately with a wet and dry coating, use one hand to dip the food into the wet ingredient and the other hand to dip it into the dry mixture. This will help ensure evenly breaded foods, crisp coatings, and little mess.

If you have a vegetable garden, pick your tomatoes in early summer, when they are full size but still green, with just a tinge of pink. Otherwise, green tomatoes are available seasonally in farmers' markets and some produce stores.

Preheat the oven to 350°F (180°C). Spread the bread crumbs in a small pan and toast in the oven until lightly browned, about 8 minutes. Transfer to a shallow dish and let cool.

Reduce the oven temperature to 325°F (165°C). Pour enough oil into a rimmed baking sheet to film the bottom.

Add the Parmesan cheese, cornmeal, parsley, and thyme to the cooled bread crumbs and stir to mix. Season with salt and pepper. In another shallow dish, beat the eggs until blended. Place the flour in a third dish.

One at a time, dip the tomato slices into the flour, lightly dusting both sides. Then dip into the eggs and immediately into the crumb mixture, coating both sides well. Place slightly apart on the prepared baking sheet.

¼ cup (1 oz/30 g) fine dried bread crumbs

Olive oil for pan

¼ cup (1 oz/30 g) grated Parmesan cheese

¼ cup (1½ oz/45 g) yellow cornmeal

1 tablespoon minced fresh flat-leaf (Italian) parsley

2 teaspoons fresh thyme leaves

Salt and ground pepper

3 eggs

½ cup (2½ oz/75 g) all-purpose (plain) flour

1 lb (500 g) unripe green tomatoes, cut into slices ½ inch (12 mm) thick

1 cup (8 oz/250 g) part-skim ricotta cheese

1 teaspoon grated lemon zest

MAKES 6 SERVINGS

Bake until golden brown on top, about 15 minutes. Turn the slices and continue baking until golden brown on the second side, about 10 minutes longer.

Meanwhile, place the ricotta in a bowl and, using an electric mixer, whip until light and smooth. Mix in the lemon zest and season lightly with salt and pepper.

Transfer the tomatoes to a warmed platter, and top each slice with a dollop of the ricotta cream. Serve warm.

CREAMY CHILI-LIME CORN

Here, corn is seasoned in Tex-Mex style, with lime, cumin, and chili powder, but it can also be flavored to fit other cuisines. For example, for an Indian-inspired dish, use curry powder, lemon zest, and cilantro in place of the chili powder, lime, and chives.

3–4 ears fresh corn

Olive oil for cooking

1 *each* large shallot and clove garlic, chopped

1 teaspoon *each* ground cumin and chili powder

1 cup (8 fl oz/250 ml) nonfat milk

2 tablespoons fresh goat cheese

1½ teaspoons minced lime zest

¼ cup (⅓ oz/10 g) snipped fresh chives

Salt and ground pepper

MAKES 4 SERVINGS

Following the instructions on page 332, cut the kernels from the ears of corn; you need about 3 cups (18 oz/560 g) kernels.

Pour enough oil into a large nonstick frying pan to film the bottom and sides and warm over medium heat. Add the corn kernels, shallot, garlic, cumin, and chili powder and sauté until the corn starts to soften, about 4 minutes.

Stir in the milk and cheese and simmer, uncovered, until the liquid thickens, about 4 minutes. Mix in the lime zest and chives and season with salt and pepper.

Transfer to a warmed serving bowl and serve right away.

Mexican beer

When serving Mexican or Tex-Mex foods, the latter a blend of the kitchens of the American Southwest and Mexico, it makes sense to pair them with a good Mexican beer. Cold, crisp beer both complements the flavors and tamps the characteristic heat.

349

CORN AND RED PEPPER PUDDING

Corn varieties

Interest in corn has been on the rise in recent years, with more varieties filling farmers' markets and supermarket bins in summer. Look for white (actually pale yellow) and bicolor (yellow and white) options and more supersweet types. Experiment to find your favorite.

You can make this colorful corn dish year-round, using frozen corn in winter, and serve it alongside roasted meat or poultry. But it is an especially delightful summer recipe that pairs perfectly with meat, fish, or poultry fresh off the grill.

Preheat the oven to 350°F (180°C). Butter a 1½-qt (1.5-l) soufflé dish.

In a large bowl, beat the eggs until light and frothy. Stir in the corn, green onion, and bell pepper.

In a small bowl, stir together the flour, a large pinch of cayenne pepper, and a pinch of salt. Add to the corn mixture, stirring to blend. Stir in the butter and half-and-half and mix well. Pour into the prepared dish and place the dish in a baking pan. Pour hot water into the baking pan to reach about one-fourth of the way up the sides of the dish.

Bake the pudding until the top is golden and a knife inserted in the center comes out clean, about 40 minutes. Let rest for 5 minutes before serving.

3 eggs

2 cups (12 oz/375 g) corn kernels (from 3–4 ears)

2 tablespoons chopped green (spring) onion, including tender green tops

½ cup (2½ oz/75 g) chopped red bell pepper (capsicum)

5 tablespoons (2 oz/60 g) all-purpose (plain) flour

Salt and cayenne pepper

4 tablespoons (2 oz/60 g) unsalted butter, melted

1 cup (8 fl oz/250 ml) half-and-half (half cream)

MAKES 4 SERVINGS

RICOTTA-STUFFED POBLANO CHILES

Heartier stuffing

For a heartier version, add 1 cup (6 oz/185 g) cooked shrimp (prawns) or shredded cooked chicken to the ricotta mixture. Add 5–10 minutes to the baking time.

Here, roasted and peeled chiles are stuffed with a mixture of ricotta, sun-dried tomatoes, oregano, and pine nuts, quickly heated through, and then topped with chopped tomatoes and herbs. The roasting and stuffing can be done ahead of time, then warmed as directed to serve.

Preheat the broiler (grill). Place the chiles on a broiler pan and broil (grill), turning as needed, until the skins are evenly blistered and blackened. Transfer to a paper bag and let stand for 10 minutes, then peel away the skins. Cut a lengthwise slit down one side of each chile, leaving the stem intact. Carefully remove the seeds. Set aside.

In a bowl combine the pine nuts, sun-dried tomatoes, cheese, oregano, and ½ teaspoon each salt and pepper. Mix well. Divide the cheese mixture evenly among the chiles, carefully spooning it into each chile through the slit. Pinch the edges of the slits together to close.

In a frying pan over medium heat, warm the oil. Place the chiles in the pan and gently press down with the back of a wooden spoon or a spatula. Cook just until the cheese begins to soften, 1–2 minutes. Turn, gently press again, and cook until heated through, about 1 minute longer.

Transfer to a warmed platter and spoon the chopped fresh tomatoes over the tops. Serve right away.

4 poblano chiles

¼ cup (1¼ oz/37 g) pine nuts, toasted (see page 17)

12 drained, oil-packed sun-dried tomatoes, minced

1 cup (8 oz/250 g) ricotta cheese

¼ cup (⅓ oz/10 g) finely chopped fresh oregano

Salt and ground pepper

1 teaspoon canola oil

3 tomatoes, peeled, seeded, and finely chopped

MAKES 4 SERVINGS

RICE-STUFFED ANAHEIM CHILES

For this hearty main course, mild Anaheim chiles are stuffed with a rice, tomato, and Cheddar cheese filling and baked until the cheese melts. If you prefer a slightly spicier dish, use poblano chiles and sprinkle a little chili powder on top before serving.

8 Anaheim chiles

3 tablespoons olive oil

1 red onion, minced

3 cloves garlic, minced

1¼ cups (10 fl oz/310 ml) vegetable broth

½ cup (3 ½ oz/105 g) medium-grain white rice

2 plum (Roma) tomatoes, peeled, seeded, and chopped

2 tablespoons minced fresh cilantro (fresh coriander)

½ cup (2 oz/60 g) shredded Cheddar cheese

Salt and ground pepper

Guacamole (page 392)

MAKES 4 SERVINGS

Preheat the broiler (grill). Place the chiles on a broiler pan and broil (grill), turning as needed, until the skins are evenly blistered and blackened. Transfer to a paper bag and let stand for 10 minutes, then peel away the skins. Cut a lengthwise slit down one side of each chile, leaving the stem intact. Carefully remove the seeds. Set aside.

Preheat the oven to 375°F (190°C). Lightly oil a baking sheet.

In a frying pan over medium heat, warm the oil. Add the onion and garlic and sauté until softened, about 3 minutes. Raise the heat to medium-high, pour in the broth, and stir to dislodge any browned bits from the pan bottom. Add the rice, reduce the heat to low, and simmer until the liquid is absorbed, 10–15 minutes. Stir in the tomatoes, cilantro, and cheese and season with salt and pepper.

Divide the rice mixture evenly among the chiles, carefully spooning it through the slits. Place on the prepared baking sheet, slit sides up, and cover with aluminum foil. Bake until the cheese is melted, about 20 minutes.

Transfer the chiles to warmed individual plates, placing 2 chiles on each plate. Pass the Guacamole at the table.

Anaheim chiles

The Anaheim, which is also know as the long green chile, is relatively mild and has a thick skin that peels away easily when it is roasted. Usually about 6 inches (15 cm) long, it is the traditional chile for chiles rellenos and is also available in cans usually labeled "green chiles."

351

RED BELL PEPPERS STUFFED WITH POLENTA

Bell pepper halves stuffed with polenta and topped with Gruyère cheese are delicious and visually striking and can be prepared in advance. Offer the peppers as an accompaniment to rustic meat or poultry dishes, or serve them as a antipasto.

2 large red bell peppers (capsicums), halved lengthwise and seeded

Soft Polenta (page 300)

2 tablespoons olive oil

2 large tomatoes, thinly sliced

1 teaspoon dried oregano

Salt and ground pepper

1 cup (8 fl oz/250 ml) vegetable broth

1 cup (4 oz/125 g) shredded Gruyère cheese

MAKES 4 SERVINGS

Preheat the oven to 375°F (190°C).

Place the peppers, cut sides up, in a baking dish. Fill each pepper with one-fourth of the polenta. Drizzle the oil into the dish. Spread the tomatoes around the peppers and sprinkle with the oregano, salt, and pepper. Add half of the broth.

Bake until the peppers are tender, about 40 minutes. During baking, stir and mash the tomatoes with the back of a spoon and baste the peppers with the tomato-broth mixture several times. After the first 20 minutes of baking, pour the remaining broth into the dish.

When the peppers are tender, sprinkle the cheese evenly over the tops and bake until the cheese is melted, about 5 minutes. Transfer the peppers to a warmed platter or individual plates and spoon the sauce from the baking dish over the top. Serve right away.

Stabilizing the peppers

If you're having trouble keeping the halved peppers upright, cut a thin slice from the underside of each pepper, creating a flat spot for the pepper half to rest.

BAKED RATATOUILLE

Ratatouille with chickpeas

To vary this dish, drain and rinse 1 can (15 oz/470 g) chickpeas (garbanzo beans) and stir them into the vegetables before baking. Sprinkle grated Parmesan cheese over the top for the last 20 minutes of baking time.

Traditional ratatouille is made on the stove top, with the vegetables sautéed separately and then simmered together to blend the flavors. Baking the mélange instead simplifies the preparation. Serve it hot or cold, by itself or with roasted or grilled meat or poultry.

Preheat the oven to 400°F (200°C). Oil a roasting pan.

As you prepare each of the following vegetables, add it to the pan: Trim the eggplant and cut into 1-inch (2.5-cm) cubes. Trim the zucchini and cut into rounds ½ inch (12 mm) thick. Halve the bell peppers lengthwise, remove the stem and seeds, and cut lengthwise into narrow strips. Depending on the size of the mushrooms, cut them into halves or quarters. Thinly slice the onion.

In a small bowl, combine ¼ cup (2 fl oz/60 ml) water, the tomato paste, vinegar, oil, garlic, thyme, 1 teaspoon salt, and ½ teaspoon pepper and stir until blended and smooth. Add to the pan, then stir and toss to coat the vegetables evenly.

Bake until the vegetables begin to soften, about 30 minutes, stirring once after 15 minutes of baking. Reduce the heat to 325°F (165°C), cover the pan, and continue to bake until the vegetables are soft and tender but not mushy, about 30 minutes longer, stirring every 10 minutes.

Remove from the oven, uncover, and let stand for 10 minutes. Stir in the basil and serve warm, at room temperature, or cold.

1 large eggplant (aubergine)

2 zucchini (courgettes)

2 red or green bell peppers (capsicums), or 1 each

½ lb (250 g) white mushrooms

1 yellow onion

⅓ cup (3 fl oz/90 g) tomato paste

⅓ cup (3 fl oz/80 ml) red wine vinegar

2 tablespoons olive oil

2 cloves garlic, minced

1 tablespoon fresh thyme leaves

Salt and ground pepper

½ cup (¾ oz/20 g) chopped fresh basil

MAKES 6 SERVINGS

EGGPLANT PARMESAN

Eggplant varieties

Fresh eggplants (aubergines) come in a variety of shapes, sizes, and colors (purple, lavender, and white, as well as green and white striped). For this dish, which calls for rolling long slices around a filling, you can substitute twice the number of Asian (slender) eggplants, which are shaped like cucumbers, for the globe eggplants.

Here, roasted eggplant slices are layered with fresh tomato sauce, two cheeses, and herbs, and then baked until bubbly. Deep red, late-harvest tomatoes yield the best sauce. If using large eggplants, select the hardest ones you can find, as they will have the fewest seeds.

To make the sauce, in a large saucepan over medium heat, warm 2 tablespoons of the oil. Add the garlic and sauté for 2 minutes. Add the tomatoes and marjoram, raise the heat to high, and bring to a boil. Reduce the heat to a simmer and cook, uncovered, until thickened to a sauce, 30–40 minutes. Season with salt.

Preheat the oven to 450°F (230°C).

Place the eggplant slices in a single layer on a rimmed baking sheet. Drizzle with 2 tablespoons of the oil and sprinkle with ½ teaspoon salt. Turn and drizzle with the remaining 2 tablespoons oil. Top with the thyme and place in the oven. Cook until lightly browned, about 10 minutes. Turn and cook until lightly browned on the second side, 5–6 minutes longer. Place under a preheated broiler (grill) and broil (grill) until

6 tablespoons (3 fl oz/ 90 ml) extra-virgin olive oil

2 cloves garlic, chopped

3 lb (1.5 kg) fully ripened tomatoes, peeled and coarsely chopped

1 tablespoon chopped fresh marjoram or oregano

Salt

4 or 5 small or 2 medium-large eggplants (aubergines), cut into crosswise slices ½ inch (12 mm) thick

2–3 tablespoons
fresh thyme leaves

6 oz (185 g) mozzarella
cheese, shredded

¼ cup (⅓ oz/10 g)
chopped fresh oregano

¼ cup (1 oz/30 g) grated
Parmesan cheese

1½ tablespoons unsalted
butter, cut into small pieces

MAKES 4–6 SERVINGS

a lightly golden crust forms, 2–3 minutes. Turn and broil on the second side until golden, 2–3 minutes longer. Reduce the oven temperature to 400°F (200°C).

Arrange one-third of the eggplant slices in a shallow 2-qt (2-l) baking dish. Top with one-third of the sauce, half of the mozzarella and oregano, and one-third of the Parmesan. Repeat the layers, then add a third layer of eggplant, sauce, and Parmesan. Dot evenly with the butter.

Bake for 15 minutes. Remove from the oven and carefully tip the dish, pressing on the surface with a spoon or spatula. If there seems to be too much juice, spoon off the excess. Return to the oven and cook until the top is lightly browned and bubbling, 15–20 minutes longer. Let stand, loosely covered, for 10 minutes before serving.

Global eggplant

Native to Africa and Asia, closely associated with Mediterranean cooking, and also integral to Chinese, South Asian, Southeast Asian, and Middle Eastern cuisines, eggplant is a lead player on the global food stage. In many places, it stands in for meat.

BAKED EGGPLANT ROLLS

These tender eggplant rolls have a bright red, savory stuffing of bell pepper, pecorino cheese, and bread crumbs. The rolls are drizzled with oil and vinegar, baked until tender, and then sprinkled with a little more pecorino before serving. Allow 2 rolls per person.

**The stars
of the garden**

Eggplants (aubergines), zucchini (courgettes), tomatoes, and bell peppers (capsicums) are the foundation of the summer vegetable garden. They ripen together at the peak of the season and are also found, in various combinations, in many classic dishes, such as the ones on these two pages.

353

2 eggplants (aubergines),
about 1 lb (500 g) each

Salt and ground pepper

2 red bell peppers
(capsicums), roasted and
peeled (see page 333),
then finely chopped

¼ cup (1 oz/30 g) fine
fresh bread crumbs,
lightly toasted

¾ cup (3 oz/90 g)
grated pecorino cheese

1 tablespoon pine nuts

4 tablespoons (2 fl oz/
60 ml) extra-virgin olive oil

2 cloves garlic, minced

About 16 fresh basil leaves,
torn into small pieces

White wine vinegar for
sprinkling

1 tablespoon minced fresh
flat-leaf (Italian) parsley

MAKES 4 SERVINGS

Trim the eggplants, then cut lengthwise into slices ⅓ inch (9 mm) thick. Choose the 8 longest slices and arrange them on a rack over a rimmed baking sheet. Sprinkle the slices with 1½ teaspoons salt and let stand for 2 hours. Pat dry.

Bring a large pot three-fourths full of salted water to a boil. Add the eggplant slices and cook until supple enough to roll, 5–6 minutes. Transfer to a towel to drain.

In a bowl, stir together the bell peppers, bread crumbs, ¼ cup (1 oz/30 g) of the pecorino, the pine nuts, and 1 tablespoon of the oil. In a small frying pan over medium-low heat, warm 1 tablespoon of the oil. Add the garlic, sauté for 1 minute, and add to the pepper mixture. Season with salt and pepper.

Preheat the oven to 375°F (190°C). Oil a baking dish large enough to accommodate the eggplant rolls in a single layer.

Arrange the eggplant slices on a work surface. Divide the stuffing evenly among them, spreading it in a thin layer over the slices. Scatter the basil over the stuffing. Roll up each slice and place, seam sides down, in the prepared baking dish. Drizzle with the remaining 2 tablespoons oil, and sprinkle lightly with vinegar.

Bake until the eggplant is completely tender when pierced with a knife, about 1 hour.

Remove the eggplant from the oven and sprinkle evenly with the remaining ½ cup (2 oz/60 g) pecorino cheese and the parsley. Serve right away.

SUMMER SQUASH "PASTA" WITH MINT PESTO

Squash al dente

Be careful not to overcook the squashes. If they remain on the heat too long, they will release too much of their moisture.

This multicolored "pasta" is actually long ribbons of zucchini and yellow squash, tossed with mint pesto and Asiago cheese. For vibrant color, the squashes are left unpeeled, so some of the colored skin is included on many of the ribbons

To make the pesto, in a blender or food processor, combine the mint, broth, 2 tablespoons of the cheese, the garlic, and the oil. Process until smooth. Set aside.

Using a mandoline or a vegetable peeler, cut the yellow squashes and zucchini into long, narrow ribbons.

Pour enough oil into a large nonstick frying pan to film the bottom and heat over medium heat. Add the shallots and sauté until softened, about 3 minutes. Add the squashes and thyme and season generously with salt and pepper. Sauté until the squashes are just tender, about 8 minutes longer.

Stir in the mint pesto and heat for 1 minute. Remove from the heat and stir in the remaining 1 tablespoon cheese.

Transfer to a warmed serving dish and sprinkle with additional cheese. Serve right away.

1 cup (1½ oz/45 g) firmly packed fresh mint leaves

⅓ cup (3 fl oz/80 ml) vegetable broth

3 tablespoons grated Asiago cheese, plus more for garnish

2 cloves garlic, chopped

2 teaspoons olive oil, plus more for cooking

3 *each* yellow summer squashes and zucchini (courgettes), about 1½ lb (750 g) total weight

¼ cup (1 oz/30 g) chopped shallots

1½ teaspoons dried thyme

Salt and ground pepper

MAKES 4–6 SERVINGS

ZUCCHINI FRITTERS

About canola oil

Pressed from rapeseed, a mustard relative, canola oil is an increasingly popular choice for general cooking. It originated in Canada: the name comes from the phrase "Canada oil, low acid." It is low in saturated fats, high in monounsaturated fats, and has a high smoke point.

These tasty zucchini fritters make a wonderful side dish or party appetizer. Serve them with Roasted Shallot–Tomato Relish (page 395), Garlic Mayonnaise (page 386), Tahini Mayonnaise (page 386), or Green Salsa (page 393).

Using the large holes of a grater-shredder or a food processor fitted with the shredding blade, shred the zucchini. Place in a colander set over a bowl and sprinkle with ½ teaspoon salt to draw out the moisture. Let stand for 1 hour.

Remove the zucchini from the colander and pat dry. In a bowl, lightly beat the egg. Sift the flour over the egg and stir to mix well. Stir the zucchini into the egg mixture. Season with pepper and mix well.

Pour oil to a depth of 1 inch (2.5 cm) into a deep, heavy saucepan and heat until it reads 375°F (190°C) on a deep-frying thermometer. Working in small batches to avoid crowding, drop the zucchini mixture by tablespoons into the hot oil and fry, turning once, until golden brown on both sides, 1–2 minutes total. Using a slotted spoon, transfer to paper towels to drain.

Transfer to a warmed platter and serve right away.

6 small zucchini (courgettes), 1¼ lb (625 g) total weight, trimmed

Salt and ground pepper

1 egg

⅔ cup (3 oz/90 g) all-purpose (plain) flour

Canola oil for deep-frying

MAKES ABOUT 24 FRITTERS; SERVES 6

GRILLED STUFFED ACORN SQUASH

For this substantial side dish, acorn squashes are complemented by a savory bread and dried cranberry stuffing. Shielding the cut sides of the squash with aluminum foil on the grill prevents the flesh from drying out. This dish would be a crowd-pleaser for an Indian summer soirée.

4 tablespoons (2 oz/60 g) unsalted butter

½ cup (2½ oz/75 g) finely chopped yellow onion

½ cup (2½ oz/75 g) finely chopped celery

2 cups (4 oz/125 g) fresh white bread crumbs (see note, right)

½ cup (3 oz/90 g) dried cranberries

¼ cup (1 oz/30 g) chopped walnuts

1 teaspoon dried sage

Salt and ground pepper

2 acorn squashes

MAKES 4 SERVINGS

Prepare a charcoal or gas grill for indirect-heat cooking over medium-high heat (page 18).

In a frying pan over medium heat, melt the butter. Add the onion and celery and sauté until softened, about 5 minutes. Scrape into a large bowl and add the bread crumbs, dried cranberries, walnuts, sage, ½ teaspoon salt, and ¼ teaspoon pepper. Sprinkle 3 tablespoons water over the top. Stir and toss with a fork to combine. Set aside.

Cut out four 6-inch (15-cm) squares of aluminum foil; set aside. Using a large, sharp knife, cut each squash in half through the stem end. Using a spoon, scrape out the seeds and any fibers and discard. Season the cut sides of the squash generously with salt and pepper. Divide the bread crumb mixture evenly among the squash cavities, pressing it down lightly. Cover each squash with a square of aluminum foil, folding it down over the sides.

Place the stuffed squashes, foil-wrapped side up, on the grill rack, cover the grill, and open the vents halfway. Cook for 45 minutes. Remove the foil and continue cooking in the covered grill until the squash is tender when pierced with the tip of a knife and the stuffing is lightly browned, about 15 minutes longer.

Transfer to a warmed platter and serve right away.

Making fresh bread crumbs

Start with a good-quality rustic loaf with a firm, coarse-textured "crumb," or interior. Cut away the crust, crumble the bread by hand into a blender or food processor, and process until fine crumbs form.

355

GARLICKY BABY SQUASH

Garlic marinade

In a bowl, combine ½ cup (4 fl oz/125 ml) extra-virgin olive oil; 2 tbsp white wine vinegar; 3 cloves garlic, crushed; 2 tsp each minced fresh thyme and rosemary; and ½ tsp each salt and ground pepper.

A mixture of colorful baby summer squashes, imbued with the flavor and aroma of garlic and fresh herbs, makes an impressive first course. Use a combination of squash varieties, such as green or gold zucchini (courgettes), crookneck, or pattypan, or use all zucchini.

Trim the ends of the squashes but leave whole. Place on a steamer rack over boiling water, cover the steamer, and steam until tender when pierced with the tip of a knife, 2–3 minutes. Transfer to a plate.

Add the squashes to the marinade and turn to coat. Cover and let stand at room temperature for 6–8 hours.

To serve, divide the lettuce leaves among 4 individual plates. Using a slotted spoon, remove the squashes from the marinade and arrange on the lettuce. Garnish with the red pepper. Serve at room temperature.

16 baby squashes (see note, above)

Garlic marinade (see note, left)

4–8 butter (Boston) or red lettuce leaves

¼ cup (1½ oz/45 g) thinly sliced red bell pepper (capsicum)

MAKES 4 SERVINGS

356

CREAMY BUTTERNUT SQUASH WITH FRUIT CHUTNEY

Store-bought chutney

Chutney is a popular condiment that originated in India and takes many forms. The fruit used may be raw or cooked with numerous other additions and flavorings. Most supermarkets have a wide selection of chutneys, so if you are pressed for time, you can substitute a purchased chutney in this recipe.

The butternut, one of early autumn's most flavorful squashes, adapts to both sweet and savory preparations. Here, it is roasted whole, then the flesh is mixed with butter and pressed into a perfect round on each plate. It pairs well with the sweet-tart fruit chutney.

Preheat the oven to 350°F (180°C).

Using a sharp knife, puncture the squash in 4 or 5 places; place on a rimmed baking sheet. Bake until the squash is thoroughly tender and can be easily pierced to the center with the knife, 2–2½ hours.

Remove from the oven and let cool for 10 minutes. Using a large, sharp knife and steadying the squash with a hand well protected by an oven mitt, cut the squash in half lengthwise. Using a large spoon, scoop out and discard the seeds and fibers. Then scoop out the hot flesh and put it in a warmed bowl. Add the butter and ¼ teaspoon salt and stir until the butter has melted and the squash is creamy.

Butter the inside of a round pastry cutter 4 inches (10 cm) in diameter and 1½ inches (4 cm) deep. Place on a warmed individual plate. Fill it to the brim with the hot squash, then lift the cutter straight up, leaving a tidy round of squash. Make 3 more molds on 3 additional plates.

Place 2 tablespoons chutney on top of each squash round and serve. Pass the remaining chutney at the table.

1 butternut squash, about 3 lb (1.5 kg)

2 tablespoons unsalted butter

Salt

Dried Fruit Chutney (page 397)

MAKES 4 SERVINGS

MINTED PEARL ONIONS

These luscious little onions are an elegant addition to any special-occasion table. Cook in the liquid early in the day, and then just before serving, boil to reduce the liquid to a glaze and add the mint. You can replace the mint with 2 tablespoons chopped fresh thyme.

3 lb (1.5 kg) white pearl or boiling onions, unpeeled

4 tablespoons (2 oz/60 g) unsalted butter

1 cup (8 fl oz/125 ml) dry sherry

½ cup (4 fl oz/125 ml) beef broth

2 teaspoons honey

Salt and ground pepper

¼ cup (⅓ oz/10 g) chopped fresh mint

MAKES 8–10 SERVINGS

Bring a saucepan three-fourths full of water to a boil over high heat. Add the onions and boil for 1 minute, counting from when the water returns to a boil. Drain in a colander, then rinse under running cold water, tossing repeatedly, until cool. With a sharp paring knife, trim the root and stem ends of each onion. Pinch the onion to remove the skin.

In a large, heavy frying pan over medium-high heat, melt the butter. When hot, add the onions, sherry, broth, and honey. Season with salt and pepper and bring to a boil. Reduce the heat to low, cover, and simmer gently, stirring occasionally, until the onions are tender, about 45 minutes.

Uncover the frying pan, raise the heat to high, and boil until the liquid evaporates and the onions are lightly glazed, about 5 minutes. Sprinkle the onions with the chopped mint. Taste and adjust the seasoning.

Transfer to a warmed serving dish and serve right away.

Boiling onions and pearl onions

Pearl onions are small, dried onions that are no more than 1 inch (2.5 cm) in diameter, available in white and red varieties. Boiling onions are white and slightly larger than pearl onions.

357

ROASTED SHALLOTS WITH SHERRY GLAZE

This dish offers a delicious twist on a holiday classic. Shallots, rather than pearl onions, are roasted with olive oil and sage, then drizzled with a sherry reduction. Shallots are available in many sizes, but larger ones are easier to peel. If they are quite large, halve them lengthwise.

2 lb (1 kg) shallots, peeled (see note, right)

2 tablespoons olive oil

2 teaspoons dried sage

Salt and ground pepper

¾ cup (6 fl oz/180 ml) sweet sherry

MAKES 4–6 SERVINGS

Preheat the oven to 400°F (200°C).

In a 10-inch (25-cm) pie dish or baking dish, combine the shallots, oil, 1 teaspoon of the sage, ½ teaspoon salt, and a few grinds of pepper. Toss to mix well. Place the shallots in the oven and roast, stirring once or twice, until the shallots are tender and golden, about 45 minutes.

About 5 minutes before the shallots are done, pour the sherry into a small frying pan and bring to a boil over medium-high heat. Boil gently until reduced by half, about 5 minutes.

Remove the shallots from the oven, sprinkle the remaining 1 teaspoon sage over the sizzling shallots, and pour the reduced sherry on top. Season with salt and pepper and toss to coat. Transfer to a serving dish and serve right away.

Peeling shallots

To peel the shallots quickly, blanch them in boiling water for 5 minutes, drain, and rinse with cold water. The skins will come right off.

BAKED BEETS WITH ORANGE VINAIGRETTE

The beet goes on

Grandma might be surprised to see this hardy root vegetable showing up on chic menus after years as an unglamorous kitchen staple. Sometimes called beetroot, beets have a sweet, earthy flavor and tender texture and are now available in many shapes (round, oval, cylindrical) and colors (red, orange, gold, purple, pink, and white striped).

358

Vividly colored and requiring only limited active time by the cook, these baked beets and beet greens are served at room temperature. The smaller the beets, the better the dish will be. If fresh tarragon isn't available, substitute fresh flat-leaf (Italian) parsley or chives.

Preheat the oven to 350°F (180°C).

Cut off the greens from the beets, leaving about ½ inch (12 mm) of the stems intact. Discard any tough, damaged outer beet leaves. Rinse both the beets and greens well. Chop the greens coarsely.

Place the whole beets and the greens in a baking dish. Add ½ cup (4 fl oz/125 ml) water, cover the dish, and place in the oven. Bake until the beets are tender, 40–50 minutes, depending on the size. Remove from the oven and set the beets aside to cool.

Trim off the stem and root ends of the beets, then slip off the skins. Slice the beets into thin rounds and place in the center of a platter. Using a slotted spoon, transfer the greens to the platter, arranging them around the beets.

In a bowl, whisk together the oil, vinegar, orange juice, and 2 tablespoons of the tarragon. Season with salt and pepper.

Pour the dressing evenly over the beets and greens. Garnish with the remaining 1 tablespoon tarragon and serve.

12 small, young beets with greens attached

½ cup (4 fl oz/125 ml) olive oil

¼ cup (2 fl oz/60 ml) red wine vinegar

¼ cup (2 fl oz/60 ml) fresh orange juice

3 tablespoons chopped fresh tarragon

Salt and ground pepper

MAKES 4 SERVINGS

BEETS WITH ONION AND CREAM

The skinny on cream

Cream is labeled according to the amount of milk fat it contains, with heavy (double) cream containing the most and half-and-half (half cream) the least. In between are light whipping cream and light cream.

Baked beets have a more intense taste and texture than boiled beets. For this traditional dish, the beets are baked in foil until tender, then peeled and sliced. The slices are arranged artfully in a baking dish, and topped with a rich mixture of chopped onions and cream.

Preheat the oven to 450°F (230°C).

Trim the greens from the beets (reserve for another use), leaving about ½ inch (12 mm) of the stems intact. Rinse the beets well but do not peel. Pat dry and wrap together in aluminum foil, sealing tightly. Using a knife, make a small slit in the top of the packet for steam to escape and place the wrapped beets in a baking pan.

Bake until the beets are tender when pierced, 45–60 minutes, depending on the size and age of the beets. Remove from the oven and open the package partway to let the beets cool a little. Reduce the oven temperature to 375°F (190°C).

When cool enough to handle, trim and peel the beets, then cut them crosswise into slices about ⅛ inch (3 mm) thick. Arrange the sliced beets, layered in straight rows or in concentric circles, in a baking dish.

6 beets, about 3 lb (1.5 kg) total weight

2 tablespoons unsalted butter

1 white sweet onion, finely chopped

1 cup (8 fl oz/250 ml) heavy (double) cream

Salt and ground pepper

2 tablespoons chopped fresh flat-leaf (Italian) parsley

MAKES 4 SERVINGS

In a frying pan over medium-low heat, melt the butter. Add the onion and sauté gently until translucent, 6–7 minutes. Add 2–3 tablespoons water, cover, and steam over low heat until the onion is tender, 8–10 minutes. Watch carefully so that the onion does not burn or brown. When the moisture has evaporated, add the cream and season with salt and pepper. Raise the heat to medium, bring the cream to a boil, and cook for 1 minute. Remove from the heat and pour the cream mixture evenly over the beets. Bake, uncovered, until the sauce is bubbly, 10–15 minutes.

Sprinkle with parsley and serve right away.

In the pink

To avoid beet-red stains on your hands and cutting boards when working with red or pink beets, you may want to work on waxed paper and wear gloves.

GRILLED FENNEL AND ENDIVE WITH OLIVE VINAIGRETTE

Olive vinaigrette is a good match for strongly flavored vegetables, such as grilled fennel and Belgian endive. But you can also serve the vegetables plain, drizzled with just a little lemon juice. For a pretty presentation, garnish the platter with the feathery tops of the fennel bulbs.

FOR THE OLIVE VINAIGRETTE

½ cup (2½ oz/75 g) oil-cured black olives, pitted

½ cup (4 fl oz/125 ml) extra-virgin olive oil

1 clove garlic, minced

Salt and ground pepper

2 tablespoons white or red wine vinegar

3 large fennel bulbs

6 heads Belgian endive (chicory/witloof)

¼ cup (2 fl oz/60 ml) extra-virgin olive oil

Salt and ground pepper

MAKES 6 SERVINGS

Prepare a charcoal or gas grill for indirect-heat cooking over medium-high heat (see page 18).

To make the vinaigrette, rinse the olives briefly in cold water. Drain and pat dry. Chop finely and combine in a small bowl with the oil, garlic, ¼ teaspoon salt, and ¼ teaspoon pepper. Whisk briskly until smooth and blended, then whisk in the vinegar. Set aside.

Cut off the stems, feathery tops, and any bruised outer stalks from the fennel bulbs. Cut each bulb in half lengthwise. Cut each endive in half lengthwise.

In a large bowl, gently toss the fennel and endive halves with the oil and season with salt and pepper.

Place the fennel on the grill rack, cover the grill, and open the vents halfway. Cook for 15 minutes, then turn the fennel and place the endives on the rack. Re-cover and continue to cook, turning the vegetables again after 10 minutes, until they are lightly browned and tender when pierced with the tip of a knife, 10–15 minutes longer.

Transfer the vegetables to a platter and spoon some of the vinaigrette over them. Serve hot, warm, or at room temperature. Pass the remaining vinaigrette at the table.

Quickly pitting olives

To remove olive pits without a pitter, spread the olives on a clean work surface and gently roll over them with a rolling pin. Most of the pits will roll out of the split olives, and you can quickly pull out any stubborn pits with your fingers.

359

JERUSALEM ARTICHOKES WITH BACON

**Roasting
garlic cloves**

*To roast cloves rather
than a head of garlic,
break the head into
cloves and put the
unpeeled cloves in
a small baking dish.
Drizzle with olive
oil and sprinkle with
salt and pepper.
Bake in a preheated
400°F (200°C) oven
until tender, about
25 minutes. When
cool enough to
handle, peel off the
papery skins.*

Jerusalem artichokes have a nutty, potatolike flavor and they readily absorb other flavors. For this dish, they are thinly sliced and sautéed in bacon drippings with minced onion and roasted garlic, and then tossed with the bacon and dressed with a balsamic vinegar pan sauce.

Using a vegetable peeler or paring knife, peel the Jerusalem artichokes. Then, using a mandoline or sharp knife, cut into paper-thin slices. Set aside.

In a frying pan over medium heat, cook the bacon, turning as needed, until crisp, about 5 minutes. Using a slotted spoon, transfer to paper towels to drain.

Pour off all but 1 teaspoon of the bacon fat from the frying pan. Add the oil and return to medium heat. When the oil is hot, add the Jerusalem artichokes, onion, roasted garlic, and ½ teaspoon pepper and sauté, stirring often, until the onion is translucent and the Jerusalem artichokes are tender to the bite but not soft, 4–5 minutes.

Transfer the contents of the frying pan to a serving bowl, then return the pan to medium heat. Pour in the vinegar and 1 teaspoon water and stir to dislodge any browned bits from the pan bottom. Pour the pan sauce over the vegetables, add the bacon, and toss gently to mix. Serve right away.

1 lb (500 g) Jerusalem artichokes

2 or 3 slices bacon, about 2 oz (60 g) total weight, finely diced

1 tablespoon extra-virgin olive oil

3 tablespoons minced yellow onion

3 cloves roasted garlic, halved (see note, left)

Ground pepper

2 tablespoons balsamic vinegar

MAKES 4 SERVINGS

MARSALA-GLAZED CARROTS AND HAZELNUTS

About Marsala

*Marsala, an Italian
fortified wine similar
to port or sherry,
is made in several
styles defined by
color, sweetness, and
aging. For this recipe,
use a dry Marsala.
If you are unsure
about making a good
choice, ask your wine
merchant for a
recommendation.*

Here, lengths of carrot are simmered until tender, then tossed with hazelnuts and a glaze of butter, shallots, and Marsala. The glaze is a good match for the sweetness of the carrots, and the crunchy hazelnuts provide the right contrast of flavor and texture.

Cut the carrots in half crosswise, then cut the thicker portions in half lengthwise. In a sauté pan over medium-high heat, combine the carrot pieces, 1 cup (8 fl oz/250 ml) water, 1 tablespoon of the butter, and ½ teaspoon salt. Bring to a boil, reduce the heat to low, cover, and simmer gently until the carrots are tender when pierced with the tip of a knife, 10–15 minutes, adding a few spoonfuls water if needed to prevent sticking. Drain and set aside.

In the same pan over medium-low heat, melt the remaining 2 tablespoons butter. Add the shallots and sauté gently, stirring, until translucent, 4–5 minutes. Add the Marsala and sugar and simmer, stirring, until the sugar dissolves. Continue to simmer, stirring occasionally, until thickened to a syrup, 4–5 minutes. Return the carrots to the pan, add the hazelnuts, and stir gently to coat.

Transfer to a warmed serving dish and serve right away.

1 lb (500 g) carrots, peeled

3 tablespoons unsalted butter

Salt

2 shallots, minced

½ cup (4 fl oz/125 ml) dry Marsala

⅓ cup (3 oz/90 g) sugar

½ cup (2½ oz/75 g) hazelnuts (filberts), toasted (see page 17) and coarsely chopped

MAKES 4 SERVINGS

ROASTED CARROTS, PARSNIPS, AND GARLIC

Add a splash of color to any holiday meal with carrots and parsnips, a perfect partnership of flavor and texture. In this oven-roasted dish, the root vegetables cook along with whole garlic cloves, thyme, and butter until tender and caramelized.

1 lb (500 g) parsnips

1 lb (500 g) carrots

12 cloves garlic, peeled but left whole

1 tablespoon fresh thyme leaves, or 1 teaspoon dried thyme

Salt and ground pepper

4 tablespoons (2 oz/60 g) unsalted butter, cut into small pieces

MAKES 6–8 SERVINGS

Preheat the oven to 350°F (180°C).

Peel the parsnips and carrots and cut on the diagonal into slices ½ inch (12 mm) thick.

In a 10-inch (25-cm) pie dish or baking dish, combine the parsnips, carrots, and garlic. If using fresh thyme, add half of it at this time; if using dried thyme, add all of it. Season with salt and pepper and toss to mix. Dot with the butter.

Bake, stirring occasionally, until the vegetables are tender and lightly browned, about 55 minutes.

Taste and adjust the seasoning, then add the remaining fresh thyme leaves, if using.

Transfer to a warmed serving dish and serve right away.

361

Stripping fresh thyme leaves

Thyme leaves grow in slightly upward clusters around thin, woody stems. To strip the leaves, hold the tip of a stem with one hand and draw the fingertips of your other hand downward along the stem. Or, add whole stems to a dish like this. The leaves will fall off during cooking; remove the bare stems before serving.

CELERY ROOT AND POTATO PURÉE

At a special dinner, replace your regular mashed potatoes with this distinctive side dish. Pass the cooked root vegetables through a ricer or food mill into a saucepan and mix with butter and cream. The celery root lends a subtle edge of sweetness and lightness to the potatoes.

4 large russet potatoes

2 celery roots (celeriacs), peeled and diced

1½–2 cups (12–16 fl oz/ 375–500 ml) chicken broth

3 tablespoons unsalted butter, or as needed

½ cup (4 fl oz/125 ml) heavy (double) cream, or as needed

Salt and ground pepper

Freshly grated nutmeg

MAKES 6–8 SERVINGS

Preheat the oven to 400°F (200°C).

Pierce the potatoes in several places with fork tines and place them directly on the oven rack or on a rimmed baking sheet on the oven rack. Bake until very tender, about 1 hour.

While the potatoes are baking, in a saucepan, combine the celery roots with enough broth to cover. Place over low heat and cook, uncovered, until very tender, about 25 minutes. Drain and pass through a ricer or food mill placed over a large, heavy saucepan.

When the potatoes are ready, remove them from the oven and set aside to cool slightly. When cool enough to handle, cut in half, scoop out the pulp, discarding the skins, and pass through the ricer or food mill placed over the saucepan holding the celery root. Place the saucepan over medium heat and stir in the 3 tablespoons butter and ½ cup cream. Heat to serving temperature, stirring often to prevent scorching. If necessary, add more butter and cream or broth to achieve a thick, smooth consistency.

Season with salt, pepper, and a little nutmeg. Spoon into a warmed serving dish and serve right away.

Ricing and mashing

Overprocessing potatoes can cause them to become gluey, so never use a food processor. If you don't have a ricer or food mill, both excellent hand tools, use an old-fashioned potato masher here.

SCALLOPED POTATOES

Cover and bake

Covering a baking dish traps the steam and moisture in, allowing the contents to cook through without drying out or browning too quickly. Once it's cooked through, the cover can be removed for a short period to brown the top.

In this classic comfort dish, layers of potato and onion slices are baked in a creamy milk-based sauce, with the onions providing a sweet undertone. For maximum creaminess, use baking potatoes, such as russet, which take on a softer texture during cooking.

Preheat the oven to 350°F (180°C). Brush a 9-by-13-inch (23-by-33-cm) baking dish with 1 tablespoon of the melted butter and set aside.

In a small bowl, stir together the garlic, flour, 1½ teaspoons salt, and ⅛ teaspoon pepper.

Arrange one-third of the sliced potatoes in the bottom of the prepared dish and top with half of the onion slices. Sprinkle half of the flour mixture evenly over the onion and dot with 1 tablespoon of the butter pieces. Top with half of the remaining potato slices and all of the onion slices. Sprinkle the remaining flour mixture over the top, and dot again with 1 tablespoon of the butter pieces. Layer with the remaining potato slices on top, and dot with the remaining 1 tablespoon butter pieces. Pour the milk evenly over the top. Brush the remaining melted butter on a piece of aluminum foil and cover the dish, buttered side down.

Place the dish on a rimmed baking sheet. Bake for 50 minutes. Remove the foil and continue baking until the top is golden brown and the potatoes are tender, about 45 minutes longer.

Sprinkle with the parsley and serve right away.

1½ tablespoons unsalted butter, melted, plus 3 tablespoons unsalted butter, cut into small pieces

1 clove garlic, minced

3 tablespoons all-purpose (plain) flour

Salt and ground pepper

3 lb (1.5 kg) russet potatoes, peeled and sliced ¼ inch (6 mm) thick

1 small yellow onion, thinly sliced

3 cups (24 fl oz/750 ml) milk

2 tablespoons finely chopped fresh flat-leaf (Italian) parsley

MAKES 6–8 SERVINGS

POTATOES DAUPHINOIS

The gratin dish

The term gratin *is used for both a dish with a browned crust and for the vessel in which the food is baked. The vessel, which is designed to go from the oven to the table, is shallow, usually glazed ceramic, and typically oval, often with a handle at each end. The shape produces a large surface area, which means a bigger expanse for the crisp crust.*

There are many versions of this rustic, cheese-laced, layered potato dish, which originates in the Dauphiné region of France. If you want a richer dish, substitute Crème Fraîche (page 384 or purchased) or heavy (double) cream for the half-and-half.

Preheat the oven to 350°F (180°C). Brush a 9-inch (23-cm) gratin dish with 2-inch (5-cm) sides with the melted butter.

Layer half of the sliced potatoes in the prepared dish. Sprinkle evenly with all of the garlic and half of the cheese. Pour ½ cup (4 fl oz/125 ml) of the half-and-half evenly over the top. Sprinkle lightly with salt and pepper. Layer the remaining potatoes on top, and then top with the remaining cheese. Again, sprinkle lightly with salt and pepper. Pour the remaining ½ cup half-and-half evenly over the top.

Place the dish on a rimmed baking sheet. Bake until the top is golden brown and the potatoes are tender when tested with the tip of a knife, about 1 hour. Serve right away.

1 tablespoon unsalted butter, melted

2 lb (1 kg) russet potatoes, peeled and cut into slices ¼ inch (6 mm) thick

2 cloves garlic, minced

1 cup (4 oz/125 g) shredded Gruyère cheese

1 cup (8 fl oz/250 ml) half-and-half (half cream)

Salt and ground pepper

MAKES 4 SERVINGS

362

SWEET AND WHITE POTATO GRATIN

This contemporary version of scalloped potatoes combines orange-fleshed sweet potatoes and white-fleshed russet potatoes to create an interesting contrast, visually and texturally. A perfect dish for a large gathering, the baking dish can go from the oven to the table.

1½ lb (750 g) russet potatoes, peeled and thinly sliced

1 lb (500 g) sweet potatoes, peeled and thinly sliced

1½ cups (6 oz/185 g) coarsely shredded Fontina cheese

¼ lb (125 g) fresh goat cheese, crumbled

¼ cup (1 oz/30 g) grated Parmesan cheese

2 teaspoons fresh thyme leaves

Salt and ground pepper

2 tablespoons all-purpose (plain) flour

1 cup (8 fl oz/250 ml) heavy (double) cream

1 cup (8 fl oz/250 ml) chicken broth

4 tablespoons (2 oz/60 g) unsalted butter

2 cups (4 oz/125 g) fresh white bread crumbs (see note, page 355)

MAKES 8 SERVINGS

Preheat an oven to 350°F (180°C). Lightly butter a 9-by-13-by-2-inch (23-by-33-by-5-cm) baking dish.

Arrange half of the potato and sweet potato slices, slightly overlapping, in the prepared baking dish, alternating the white and sweet potatoes randomly.

In a bowl, combine the Fontina, goat, and Parmesan cheeses; the thyme; 1 teaspoon salt; and a few grinds of pepper. Stir to blend. Sprinkle half of the cheese mixture over the potatoes. Sprinkle evenly with the flour. Arrange the remaining potato and sweet potato slices on top, again slightly overlapping and alternating randomly. Sprinkle evenly with the remaining cheese mixture. Pour the cream and broth evenly over the potatoes. Cover loosely with aluminum foil.

Bake until the potatoes are tender, about 1 hour.

Meanwhile, in a sauté pan over low heat, melt the butter. Add the bread crumbs and toss to coat. Remove from the heat.

Remove the potatoes from the oven and uncover. Sprinkle the buttered crumbs evenly over the surface. Return to the oven, uncovered, and bake until the top is crisped and brown, about 25 minutes longer.

Let stand for 20 minutes before serving.

Potato oxidation

To keep peeled potatoes from turning brown, drop them into to a bowl of cold water as you work. When all of them are cut, drain well and pat dry before using.

363

POTATO LATKES

These potato-and-onion pancakes are a traditional part of the Hanukkah menu, but they are equally delicious as a side dish or appetizer in nearly any setting. You can peel the potatoes before shaping the latkes, if you like, but leaving the skin on imparts extra texture and flavor.

364

Have ready a large bowl filled with ice water. Grate the potatoes on the large holes of a grater-shredder or in batches in a food processor fitted with the shredding blade. Transfer to the ice water. Refrigerate for 2–3 hours, changing the water twice. Grate the onions in the same manner and set aside.

Drain the potatoes in a sieve, pressing out as much water as possible. In a large bowl, combine the potatoes and onions and mix well. In a small bowl, beat the eggs until blended. In another small bowl, stir together the flour and baking soda. Stir the eggs and the flour mixture into the potatoes along with 1 tablespoon salt and 2 teaspoons pepper.

Pour oil to a depth of ¼ inch (6 mm) into a large, deep frying pan and place over high heat. When the oil is hot enough to make a drop of water sizzle on contact, spoon mounds of batter about 2½ inches (6 cm) in diameter into the hot oil, being careful not to crowd the pan. Flatten the tops slightly with a spatula and fry until the undersides are golden brown and crisp, about 4 minutes. Gently turn the cakes and cook the second sides until brown, another 4 minutes longer. Using a slotted metal spatula, transfer to paper towels to drain. Keep warm until all the cakes are ready. Arrange on a warmed platter and serve right away. Pass the applesauce, if using, at the table.

6 russet or Yukon gold potatoes, about 2½–3 lb (1.25–1.5 kg) total weight, cut into 2-inch (5-cm) pieces

2 yellow onions, quartered

2 extra-large eggs

½ cup (2½ oz/75 g) all-purpose (plain) flour

½ teaspoon baking soda (bicarbonate of soda)

Salt and ground pepper

Corn oil for deep-frying

Applesauce (page 399) for serving, optional

MAKES 8 SERVINGS

ROSEMARY ROASTED RED POTATOES

For this aromatic side dish, halved new potatoes are parboiled and then roasted with rosemary and garlic until slightly crisp on the outside and tender in the center. If you have good-quality coarse sea salt, use it for this dish. Substitute thyme and/or chives for the rosemary, if you like.

2–2½ lb (1–1.25 kg) red potatoes, 1½–2 inches (4–5 cm) in diameter, cut in half crosswise

¼ cup (2 fl oz/60 ml) olive oil

4–5 cloves garlic, halved

1 tablespoon chopped fresh rosemary

Salt and ground pepper

2 tablespoons chopped fresh flat-leaf (Italian) parsley

MAKES 6–8 SERVINGS

Preheat the oven to 375°F (190°C).

Bring a large pot three-fourths full of salted water to a boil. Add the potatoes, return the water to a boil, reduce the heat slightly, cover partially, and cook for 5 minutes. Drain well.

Arrange the potatoes in a baking dish, preferably in a single layer. Drizzle the oil over the top, then turn the potatoes to coat. Scatter the garlic over the potatoes. Sprinkle on the rosemary and a little salt and pepper.

Bake, turning the potatoes several times, until tender and golden, 20–25 minutes.

Transfer the potatoes to a serving dish, sprinkle with the parsley, and serve right away.

Oven companions

Roasted potatoes are a good companion for meat, both on the table and in the oven. Roast them alongside the meat, keeping in mind that their cooking time will depend on the temperature used for the meat.

365

MIXED POTATO SAUTÉ

This recipe for crisp sautéed potatoes calls for Yukon gold, fingerling, and small red potatoes, yielding an interesting and delicious mix of colors and textures. Green (spring) onions flavor the potatoes as they cook, and bright-tasting parsley is added at the end.

6 small Yukon gold potatoes

6 fingerling potatoes

6 small red potatoes

10 green (spring) onions, including tender green tops, cut into ½-inch (12-mm) lengths

2 teaspoons chopped fresh thyme

5 tablespoons (2½ oz/75 g) unsalted butter

¼ cup (2 fl oz/60 ml) canola oil, or as needed

Salt and ground pepper

¼ cup (⅓ oz/10 g) chopped flat-leaf (Italian) parsley

MAKES 6 SERVINGS

Have ready a large bowl of cold water. Peel the Yukon gold potatoes, cut them into slices ⅛ inch (3 mm) thick, and immediately drop them into the water. Cut but do not peel the remaining potatoes the same thickness and add to the water. Drain and pat dry just before cooking.

In a bowl, toss the green onions with the thyme. In a large, heavy cast iron frying pan over high heat, melt the butter with the ¼ cup oil. Add the potato slices in layers, alternately with the green onion mixture, season with salt and pepper, and let cook, undisturbed, until an even brown crust forms on the bottom, 8–10 minutes. Using a metal spatula, turn the potatoes, shaking the pan to redistribute the potatoes. If necessary, add more oil and adjust the heat to prevent burning. Continue cooking until the potatoes are browned on the bottom, about 5 minutes.

Reduce the heat to medium-low, cover, and cook until the potatoes are almost tender, about 10 minutes. Uncover, raise the heat to medium-high, and carefully turn often until the potatoes are cooked through, about 5 minutes longer.

Season with salt and pepper, transfer to a warmed platter, and sprinkle with the parsley. Serve right away.

Getting it crisp

As is typical, these potatoes are added to cold water as they are sliced, to prevent them from turning brown. The water also draws out some of the starch, which here leads to a crispier result.

BAKED SWEET POTATOES WITH CRÈME FRAÎCHE

Sweet potatoes and yams

A relative of the Irish potato, sweet potatoes are large tubers with either yellow-brown skin and yellow flesh or dark reddish or purplish skin and orange flesh. The latter are often mistakenly called yams in the United States, although they are a different species from the true yam.

Simple to assemble and bake, this colorful dish includes pale orange sweet potatoes, bright white crème fraîche, and chopped green onions. For best results, start with sweet potatoes as similar in size and shape as possible, so they'll be done at the same time.

Preheat the oven to 400°F (200°C).

Rub the sweet potatoes all over with the oil and place on a rimmed baking sheet. Bake for 30 minutes. Prick the skin in a few places with a fork, and continue baking until the potatoes are tender when pierced with the tip of a knife, about 30 minutes longer.

Remove from the oven, and working carefully to avoid burning your hands, cut off both ends of each sweet potato, then peel, if desired. Cut crosswise into slices 1½ inches (4 cm) thick. Arrange a few slices on each individual plate, or spoon the potatoes into a serving bowl. Top with the crème fraîche and green onion. Serve right away.

2 sweet potatoes, ½–¾ lb (250–375 g) each, unpeeled

2 teaspoons vegetable oil

¼ cup (2 fl oz/60 ml) Crème Fraîche (page 384 or purchased), or sour cream

1 tablespoon finely chopped green (spring) onion, including the tender green tops

MAKES 4–6 SERVINGS

SWEET POTATOES ANNA

Using clarified butter

Clarified butter is butter from which the milk solids and water have been removed, leaving behind a pure, clear, golden liquid that can be used in high-temperature preparations like this one with little risk of burning.

Pommes Anna, an elegant dish of molded potato layers, was reportedly created at the time of the Second Empire for a stylish French woman named Anna Deslions. Here is a creative modern version that uses sweet potatoes instead of regular potatoes.

Preheat the oven to 400°F (200°C). Butter a 9-inch (23-cm) straight-sided, nonstick cake pan or ovenproof frying pan.

Starting at the center of the pan and forming concentric circles, cover the bottom with a layer of sweet potato slices, overlapping the slices. Drizzle with some of the butter and sprinkle with salt and pepper. Continue layering until all the potatoes have been used.

Butter one side of a piece of aluminum foil and cover the pan. Place a heavy lid (smaller than the pan) on top to weigh down the potato layers. Bake for 40 minutes. Remove the lid and foil and continue to bake until golden and tender when pierced with the tip of a knife, about 20 minutes longer; do not overcook. Let cool for 10 minutes.

Using a narrow spatula, loosen the potatoes from the pan bottom. Invert a platter over the pan and, holding the platter and pan firmly, invert them together. Lift off the pan. Pour off any excess butter from the platter.

Garnish with the parsley, cut into wedges, and serve.

2½ lb (1.25 kg) sweet potatoes, peeled and sliced ⅛ inch (3 mm) thick

1½ cups (¾ lb/375 g) Clarified Butter (page 28)

Salt and ground pepper

2 tablespoons finely chopped fresh flat-leaf (Italian) parsley

MAKES 8 SERVINGS

RUM-GLAZED SWEET POTATOES

Rum adds a slightly exotic touch to this traditional holiday dish. You can make it on the stove top or in the oven, depending on which method fits best with the other dishes you are cooking. If you like, you can use ½ teaspoon pumpkin pie spice in place of the assorted spices.

4 orange-fleshed sweet potatoes, about ½ lb (250 g) each, unpeeled

¾ cup (6 oz/185 g) firmly packed dark brown sugar

6 tablespoons (3 fl oz/ 90 ml) light rum

4 tablespoons (2 oz/60 g) unsalted butter

⅛ teaspoon ground cinnamon

⅛ teaspoon ground allspice

⅛ teaspoon freshly grated nutmeg

⅛ teaspoon ground ginger

MAKES 6–8 SERVINGS

Bring a large pot three-fourths full of water to a boil. Add the sweet potatoes and simmer until tender but slightly resistant when pierced with a fork, 35–45 minutes. Drain and let cool. Peel the sweet potatoes and slice off the ends. Cut crosswise into slices about 2 inches (5 cm) thick.

Preheat the oven to 400°F (200°C). Butter a 9-inch (23-cm) baking dish. Arrange the sweet potato slices, with a cut side down, in the prepared dish.

To make the glaze, in a saucepan over medium heat, combine the brown sugar, rum, butter, cinnamon, allspice, nutmeg, and ginger. Simmer, stirring, until the sugar dissolves and the syrup is slightly thickened, about 3 minutes. Pour the glaze evenly over the sweet potatoes. Bake, basting about every 5 minutes, until a glaze forms on top, about 15 minutes. Serve directly from the dish.

Rum styles

Distilled from sugarcane and traditionally aged in wooden barrels, rum can be labeled in a variety of ways, with light rum and dark rum the two most common classifications. Light rum, also known as silver or white rum, has a sweet, mild flavor. Dark rum, sometimes called black rum, is usually aged longer and has a more robust flavor.

FRENCH FRIES

The secret to perfect French fries is to cook them twice: once at a lower temperature to cook the potatoes through, then again at a higher temperature to crisp and brown them. Serve these with ketchup, homemade mayonnaise (page 386) or malt vinegar.

4 large russet potatoes, about 2½ lg (1.25 kg) total weight

Peanut or canola oil for deep-frying

Salt and ground pepper

MAKES 6 SERVINGS

In a large heavy pot, pour the oil to a depth of 2 inches (5 cm). Clip a deep-frying thermometer onto the side and warm over medium-high heat until the thermometer registers 325°F (165°C).

Meanwhile, line 2 rimmed baking sheets with a couple layers of paper towels. Peel the potatoes and cut each lengthwise into slices ⅓ inch (9 mm) thick. Cut the slices lengthwise into sticks ⅓ inch (9 mm) thick. Spread the potato sticks on one of the lined baking sheets and cover with another layer of paper towels to soak up the moisture.

Working in 4 batches, fry the potatoes until just tender but not brown, about 3 minutes. Using a large skimmer, transfer the potatoes to the second lined baking sheet to drain. Between batches, let the oil return to 325°F.

When all the potatoes have been fried once, turn up the heat under the pot and warm the oil until it reaches 375°F (190°C). In 4 batches, fry the potatoes in the same manner until deep golden brown and crisp, 3–4 minutes per batch. Transfer to a freshly lined baking sheet and season with salt and pepper. Serve right away.

Potatoes for frying

To achieve the desired texture–fluffy on the inside and crisp on the outside–always use starchy potatoes for frying. Easy-to-find russets, also known as Burbank or Idaho potatoes, are the perfect choice.

ROASTED SWEET POTATO FRIES

Oven fries

You can use this same recipe to roast regular potatoes, a healthy and simple alternative to deep-frying. Leave out the cumin, if you like, or substitute a dusting of chili powder or cayenne pepper for spicy fries.

Once your family samples these crisp, sweet potato fries dusted with nutty, aromatic cumin, they will request them often. You can cook them alongside any roasting meat or poultry, adjusting their cooking time according to the temperature of the oven.

Preheat the oven to 425°F (220°C).

Line 2 or 3 rimmed baking sheets with aluminum foil. Spread the oil on the pan bottoms, dividing it evenly.

Peel the sweet potatoes. Using a sharp knife, cut the sweet potatoes lengthwise into julienne strips about ¼ inch (6 mm) thick and wide. As the sticks are cut, immediately roll them in the oil on the baking sheets to prevent them from turning black. When all the sweet potato strips have been coated, spread them out in a single layer.

Sprinkle each pan of sweet potatoes with about ½ teaspoon cumin and a little salt.

Roast until crisp on the outside and tender on the inside, 25–30 minutes. Transfer the cooked sweet potatoes to paper towels to drain briefly.

Sprinkle with salt, pepper, and 1–1½ teaspoons cumin. Transfer to a warmed platter and serve right away.

About ½ cup (4 fl oz/125 ml) canola oil

6–8 large orange-fleshed sweet potatoes

1½–2 teaspoons ground cumin

Coarse sea salt and ground pepper

MAKES 6–8 SERVINGS

368

NIÇOISE MUSHROOMS

Using anchovies

Salt-cured anchovies are usually found in cans in Italian shops or specialty-food stores. Use what you need, then cover the remaining anchovies with fresh coarse salt and store in the refrigerator.

Here, the earthy character of mushrooms is heightened by the floral scent of the herbs and the piquancy of the anchovies. Prepare the mushrooms to accompany roasted meat, cooking them in the oven alongside the meat and adjusting the timing as needed.

Preheat the oven to 400°F (200°C). Spread the oil on the bottom of a baking dish large enough to hold the mushrooms in a single layer.

Place the anchovies in a single layer in a small shallow bowl. Add milk nearly to cover and let stand for 5–10 minutes. Drain off the milk and discard. Pat the anchovies dry, removing any tiny bones in the process.

On a cutting board, chop together the anchovies, garlic, rosemary, thyme, and lavender until the mixture is evenly minced but not reduced to a paste.

Place the mushrooms in the prepared baking dish and toss to coat evenly with the oil. Sprinkle the anchovy mixture over the mushrooms. Season with salt and pepper.

Roast until tender, 15–17 minutes, depending on the size. Transfer to a warmed serving dish and serve right away.

2 tablespoons olive oil

4 salt-cured anchovies, halved and filleted

About 2 tablespoons milk

2 large cloves garlic, chopped

½ teaspoon dried rosemary

½ teaspoon dried thyme

½ teaspoon dried lavender

1½ lb (750 g) small to medium button mushrooms, stemmed

Coarse sea salt and ground pepper

MAKES 6–8 SERVINGS

CHANTERELLES WITH CHESTNUTS AND PEARL ONIONS

Here is a sumptuous side dish to accompany roast poultry, for the holidays or otherwise: sautéed mushrooms tossed with chestnuts, tender pearl onions, and thyme. Peeling chestnuts is a painstaking task. To save time, purchase vacuum-packed whole peeled chestnuts.

1 lb (500 g) chestnuts
(see note, above)

1 lb (500 g) pearl
or cipollini onions

2 lb (1 kg) chanterelle
or cremini mushrooms

½ cup (4 oz/125 g)
unsalted butter

2 tablespoons chopped
fresh thyme

½ cup (4 fl oz/125 ml)
chicken broth, or as needed

Salt and ground pepper

MAKES 12 SERVINGS

Using a small, sharp knife, cut an X in the rounded side of each chestnut. In a small saucepan over high heat, bring 2 cups (16 fl oz/500 ml) water to a boil. Add the chestnuts. Reduce the heat to low, cover, and simmer until the nuts are tender, about 30 minutes. Drain the chestnuts and, while they are still hot, remove both the hard outer shell and the thin, brown inner skin.

Using a small, sharp, knife, carefully trim away the roots from the onions without cutting into the ends. Cut a shallow cross into the stem end of each onion to prevent it from telescoping during cooking. In a saucepan over high heat, combine the onions with water to cover and bring to a boil. Reduce the heat to medium and simmer, uncovered, until barely tender, 8–10 minutes. Drain, let cool slightly, and then slip off the peels. Set aside.

Preheat the oven to 350°F (180°C).

If the mushrooms are small, leave them whole; if they are large, slice them thickly. In a large sauté pan over high heat, melt half of the butter. Add half of the mushrooms and sauté until softened, 3–5 minutes. Transfer to a bowl. Repeat with the remaining butter and mushrooms and add to the bowl.

Add the cooked chestnuts and onions and the chopped thyme to the mushrooms. Pour in enough broth to moisten the mixture and season with salt and pepper. Transfer to a baking dish. Bake until heated through, about 15 minutes. Serve right away.

About chanterelles

The most common chanterelles are golden and trumpet shaped and have a subtle apricot taste. Other members of the chanterelle family include white, red, and yellow foot chanterelles and the black trumpet mushroom. At the market, select chanterelles with firm, fleshy caps and no sign of dampness.

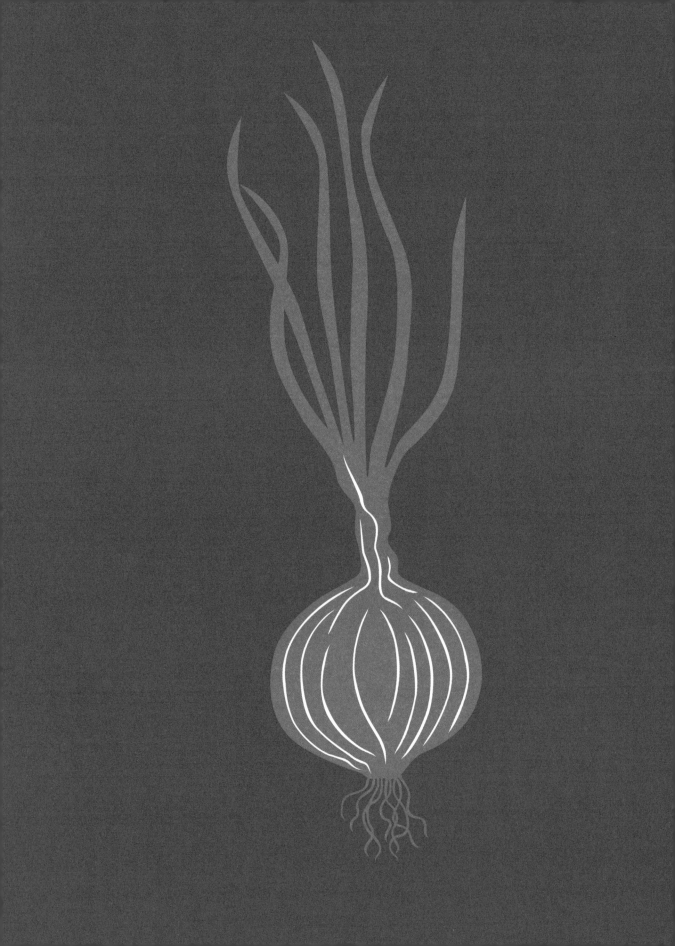

Sauces, salsas & CONDIMENTS

Sauces, Salsas & Condiments

The sauce, salsa, or condiment that accompanies a preparation or joins the main ingredients in a recipe can make the difference between a humdrum dish and one that wins raves from everyone at the table. At their best, these culinary essentials contribute vivid flavor, color, texture, and moisture. And as the recipes on the following pages illustrate, they are also typically easy to make, delivering a big payoff for minimal effort.

Degreasing pan drippings

Before turning pan drippings into a pan sauce or gravy, let the drippings stand for about 5 minutes to allow the fat to rise to the top. Then, use a large metal spoon to skim the fat from the surface. Reserve some or all of the fat for making a roux if you are preparing gravy (right), or discard the fat.

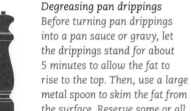

372

Using a degreasing cup

If there is a large quantity of drippings, such as when cooking a large roast, pour them into a fat separator, a measuring cup with a long spout that pours from the bottom of the container. Let the drippings stand for a few minutes so the fat rises, then pour the juices into a clean measuring cup, leaving the fat behind.

Mounting a sauce with butter

In some recipes, pan sauces are quickly enriched and thickened by whisking in butter, a process called "mounting." Start with cold butter and cut it into small cubes. Remove the pan sauce from the heat and add 1 or 2 cubes of butter at a time, whisking constantly until fully incorporated before adding more. The sauce will gain rich flavor and an attractive sheen.

Sauce Basics

Sauces should seamlessly complement the dish they accompany, neither overwhelming the other ingredients nor being overshadowed by them. They can be rich, like Hollandaise Sauce (page 385), or light and fresh tasting, like Applesauce (page 399). They can be complex and slow simmered, like Italian Bolognese Sauce (page 380), or lightning quick to prepare, like Vinaigrette (page 374). In this chapter, you'll not only find representatives of the classic French tradition, but also popular sauces from all over the globe

ESSENTIAL TECHNIQUES The goal in making most sauces is to thicken a flavorful liquid so that it coats the main ingredients in a pleasing way. If a sauce is too thin, it will run off onto the plate and the dish will not benefit from its flavor. Conversely, if the sauce is too thick, it will be neither pleasing to the eye nor tempting to the palate. Several techniques are used to infuse liquids with flavor and to thicken them to the desired consistency.

MIXING VINAIGRETTES As its name implies, a vinaigrette—from the French *sauce vinaigrette*, meaning "little vinegar sauce"—is one of the simplest sauces to make. First, be sure to use a bowl big enough to allow you to whisk vigorously. Start with good-quality vinegar or fresh citrus juice, then add seasonings such as minced herbs. Slowly drizzle in the oil—extra-virgin olive oil and buttery hazelnut and walnut oils are good choices—whisking constantly until the mixture emulsifies, becoming partially opaque and thickened. Adding a small amount of finely minced shallot or a teaspoon of mustard to the vinegar will help the dressing to thicken. Finally, season with salt and pepper. It's best to whisk the vinaigrette again just before using; most dressings separate on standing.

DEGLAZING TO MAKE PAN SAUCES When fish, poultry, or meat is sautéed or roasted in a pan, caramelizing takes place. As the item sizzles in the pan, often with butter or oil, a coating or glaze of crisp, flavorful bits forms on the pan bottom. To transfer this flavor to a pan sauce, first the main ingredient is removed and any excess fat is spooned off from the juices that remain. Then, a liquid—usually wine, often mixed with broth and sometimes water or fruit juice—is added to the sizzling pan. *Deglazing*, the term most commonly used to describe this process, involves simmering or boiling the liquid while stirring continuously with a wooden spoon or spatula to soften and dissolve the coating and distribute it throughout the liquid.

After the bits and coating have been deglazed, the liquid is allowed to boil until it has reduced—that is, evaporated and concentrated—as directed in the recipe. Then, additions, such as crème fraîche, sour cream, or heavy cream, are stirred in and the sauce is further reduced to the desired consistency. Finally, a little butter is often whisked in for body and the sauce is seasoned.

MAKING GRAVY The drippings from roasted or panfried meats or poultry can also be transformed into traditional gravies by thickening them with a roux, a paste formed by briefly cooking flour in fat. To do this, pour off the pan drippings into a fat separator, let the fat rise to the surface, and then pour off and reserve the juices. Or, pour the drippings into a glass measuring pitcher, let stand for a few minutes until the fat settles on the top, and spoon off and reserve the fat. Next, following the recipe you are using, place the pan over medium heat on the stove top, using two burners for a large roasting pan, and heat a measured amount of the reserved fat in the pan (adding butter if you are short of fat). Sprinkle in an equal amount of flour and use a flat whisk to mix together the fat and flour until smooth, letting the mixture bubble until the raw flour smell is gone, about 1 minute. Then, deglaze the pan (see left), using wine, broth, or another liquid. Add the reserved juices and additional liquid, usually broth (about 1 cup/8 fl oz/250 ml liquid for each 1½ tablespoons fat and flour) and continue cooking over medium-low heat, whisking often, until the roux has thickened the liquid to the consistency of heavy (double) cream (it should coat the back of a wooden spoon), about 2 minutes. Finally, adjust the seasoning to taste.

EMULSIFYING When creating an emulsion, two liquids that tend to remain separate, such as oil and water, are coaxed into forming one thickened, opaque liquid with the help of an emulsifier such as egg yolk or mustard. Mustard is an easy emulsifier to use, and it commonly turns up in oil-and-vinegar emulsions like vinaigrettes. These tenuous emulsions usually separate after a few minutes but can quickly be whisked back into a creamy state.

Hot emulsions such as hollandaise are the trickiest to make. Do not use eggs that have been frozen or pasteurized, as they can separate and are less likely to create a successful emulsion. Making a hollandaise calls for three steps: First, melt the butter in a small saucepan over low heat and transfer it to a heatproof pitcher. Next, in another small saucepan, continuously whisk egg yolks with water and salt over low heat until the mixture begins to steam lightly and thickens to the consistency of a thin yogurt, about 2 minutes. Finally, whisk in the melted butter a little at a time while moving the pan on and off the heat to keep the mixture lukewarm, until all the butter has been added and the sauce is smooth.

PLATING SAUCES For the most attractive presentation of thick, creamy sauces accompanying meats, poultry, seafood, or vegetables, spoon a little sauce onto a plate and tip the plate to spread the sauce into a thin, even layer (or use the back of a spoon). Pan sauces are usually drizzled in part on the plate under the featured ingredient, and then more sauce is spooned on top. Salsas and relishes look best in a neat mound or, if they are more liquid, in a small bowl or ramekin placed on or alongside the plate.

PASTA SAUCE BASICS Some pasta sauces are based on tomatoes, either puréed or simply chopped and cooked until almost liquefied. Others, mainly from northern Italy, are based on cream, cheese, or butter. And still others are hardly sauces at all in the conventional sense, but rather an amalgamation of dry ingredients—usually vegetables and herbs, such as the basil in pesto—that coats and flavors the pasta. Some sauces are helped by the addition of a small amount of the pasta cooking water. The cooking water, which contains starch and nutrients, thins and extends the sauce and helps the sauce adhere to the pasta. Reserve about ¼ cup (2 fl oz/60 ml) of the water just before draining the pasta, and either add it to the sauce itself, or add it to the bowl of pasta and sauce once they have been combined.

Smooth or chunky gravy
When making gravy, you can choose how refined you want it to be. Serve it as it comes straight from the pan in which you made it (see left) for rustic results that include browned bits left from roasting. For a finer gravy, pour it through a fine-mesh sieve to remove any undissolved pan drippings.

Icing away egg emulsion problems
One of the main problems cooks encounter when making hollandaise and other egg-emulsified sauces is the ingredients getting too hot, which can cause the egg yolks to curdle. To prevent this from happening, keep a couple of ice cubes in a bowl close at hand. If the yolk mixture begins to look even slightly grainy, remove the pan from the heat and vigorously whisk in an ice cube until it melts and the mixture is smooth again. Do the same thing if the sauce begins to curdle when you're whisking in the melted butter.

Storing sauces, salsas, and condiments
Most sauces are highly perishable. Salsas will quickly discolor, and hot emulsions solidify when cooled and cannot be rewarmed without breaking. Tomato-based pasta sauces can be refrigerated for up to 5 days, but any sauce that contains eggs or cream should not be kept for more than 2 days.

373

VINAIGRETTE

It's science

The salt is added before the oil because it dissolves more easily in vinegar alone. Mustard adds flavor and helps emulsify (bind) the oil and vinegar.

Mixing tips

A whisk is not the only option when making a vinaigrette. You can also use a fork or a handheld mixer, or vigorously shake the ingredients in a tightly covered jar or bottle.

Blender vinaigrette

For a smoother, thicker vinaigrette, put the vinegar, salt, and mustard (if using) in a blender. Process to combine. With the blender running, gradually add the oil in a thin, steady stream through the hole in the lid. Season with pepper. The mustard will ensure a thick emulsion.

Oil, vinegar, salt, and pepper—that's all you need for a traditional vinaigrette. When properly mixed, the ingredients emulsify to form a vibrant and versatile sauce. By varying the ingredients, you can create a wealth of useful, simple, flavorful sauces.

In a bowl, whisk together the vinegar and ¼ teaspoon salt until the salt begins to dissolve. If using the mustard, whisk it into the vinegar-salt mixture. Gradually add the oil while whisking rapidly. Continue whisking until the ingredients have emulsified and thickened. Whisk in ⅛ teaspoon pepper.

Taste and adjust the seasoning. (If using the vinaigrette to dress a green salad, dip a piece of lettuce into the dressing to see how they taste together.)

Use the vinaigrette right away, or cover and store in the refrigerator for up to 5 days. The oil will solidify when chilled but will melt if left at room temperature for about 30 minutes.

For sherry vinaigrette Use sherry vinegar and omit the mustard, if desired. Use on any salad or other dish that calls for a vinaigrette.

For raspberry-walnut vinaigrette Use raspberry vinegar and replace the olive oil with walnut oil. Use to dress a green salad with toasted walnuts.

For lemon-shallot vinaigrette Replace the vinegar with fresh lemon juice. Whisk the finely grated zest of 1 lemon and 1 tablespoon minced shallot into the finished vinaigrette. Use to dress seafood salads.

For orange-tarragon vinaigrette In a small saucepan, cook 1 cup (8 fl oz/250 ml) fresh orange juice over high heat until reduced by half. In a bowl, whisk together the reduced juice, 3 tablespoons balsamic vinegar, ½ teaspoon Dijon mustard, and ¼ teaspoon salt. Gradually whisk in ¼ cup (2 fl oz/60 ml) extra-virgin olive oil. Stir in 2 teaspoons finely chopped fresh tarragon, then taste and adjust the seasoning. Use on chicken, shrimp (prawns), steamed asparagus, or artichokes.

For Roquefort-walnut vinaigrette In a bowl, whisk together 3 tablespoons sherry vinegar and ¼ teaspoon salt. Gradually whisk in ¾ cup (6 fl oz/180 ml) walnut oil. Stir in 3 oz (90 g) Roquefort cheese, crumbled, and ½ shallot, minced. Adjust the seasoning. Use on salads featuring roasted beets.

For Asian vinaigrette Peel 1 large piece fresh ginger. Use the large holes of a grater-shredder to shred ¼ cup (1 oz/30 g) ginger into a small bowl. Squeeze the ginger in your hand over the bowl to extract the juice. You should have about 1 tablespoon ginger juice. (Discard the shredded ginger.) In a bowl, whisk together the ginger juice, 3 tablespoons rice vinegar, and 1 tablespoon soy sauce. Gradually whisk in ⅔ cup (5 fl oz/160 ml) canola oil and 1 tablespoon Asian sesame oil. Adjust the seasoning. Use on mildly bitter greens or napa cabbage slaw.

3 tablespoons vinegar, such as red or white wine, cider, or balsamic

Salt and ground pepper

½ teaspoon Dijon mustard, optional

¾ cup (6 fl oz/180 ml) extra-virgin olive oil

MAKES ABOUT 1 CUP (8 FL OZ/250 ML)

SAUCES, SALSAS & CONDIMENTS

CHICKEN OR TURKEY GRAVY

Make gravy to accompany your roasted bird while it rests. Have your ingredients measured out in advance, so you can get started as soon as the bird is removed from the pan. Sprinkle the flour evenly in the pan and whisk steadily to prevent lumps from forming.

5 tablespoons (2 oz/60 g) all-purpose (plain) flour

¼ cup (2 fl oz/60 ml) dry white wine

About 4 cups (32 fl oz/1 l) Chicken Stock (page 23), heated

Salt and ground pepper

1–2 tablespoons dry sherry, optional

MAKES ABOUT 4 CUPS (32 FL OZ/1 L)

After removing the chicken or turkey from the roasting pan, skim or pour off the fat from the pan drippings, reserving 4–5 tablespoons (2–2½ fl oz/60–75 ml) of the fat. Reserve the pan juices. Place the roasting pan over medium heat on the stove top, and heat the reserved fat. Sprinkle the flour into the pan and whisk the fat and flour together until the mixture bubbles and the raw flour smell is gone, about 1 minute. Add the wine and ¼ cup (2 fl oz/60 ml) water and deglaze the pan, stirring to dislodge any browned bits from the pan bottom. Add the reserved juices and 3½ cups (28 fl oz/875 ml) of the stock and continue cooking over medium-low heat, whisking often, until smooth and thickened enough to coat the back of a wooden spoon, about 2 minutes. Add the remaining stock as needed to achieve the desired consistency.

Season with salt and pepper. Transfer the gravy to a warmed sauceboat, pouring it through a fine-mesh sieve, if desired. Stir in the sherry, if using. Serve right away.

Herbed gravy

For a more aromatic gravy, add about 4 tsp chopped fresh sage (or whatever herb you used to season the chicken or turkey) at the same time as the stock.

375

ALL-PURPOSE STIR-FRY SAUCE

Here is a great sauce to have around for last-minute stir-fry dishes. Added near the end of cooking, it works with any meat, seafood, or vegetable. This amount is sufficient to season about 1 pound (500 g) of ingredients, but you can make the sauce in larger quantities.

3 tablespoons soy sauce

1 teaspoon finely chopped fresh ginger

1 small clove garlic, minced

1 green (spring) onion, including tender green tops, finely chopped

½ teaspoon Chile Oil (page 27)

MAKES ABOUT ¼ CUP (2 FL OZ/60 ML)

In a small bowl, combine the soy sauce, ginger, garlic, green onion, and chile oil and stir well.

This sauce will keep in a jar with a tight-fitting lid in the refrigerator for up to 1 week. If you make it in advance, add the green onion just before using.

Storing chile oil

Vibrantly red, chile oil's color and heat are derived from steeping hot red chiles in vegetable oil. Store it at room temperature in a cool, dry cupboard for up to 4 months.

BASIC BARBECUE SAUCE

Applying barbecue sauce

When grilling, apply barbecue sauce to food only during the last 10 minutes of cooking—5 minutes on each side—to prevent the sugar in the sauce from burning and forming undesirable charred bits on the surface of the food.

Reminiscent of what you might find in a restaurant specializing in Kansas City–style barbecue, this all-purpose, tomato-based sauce is a touch hot and a touch sweet and wonderful on pork ribs, beef brisket (page 272), or chicken. It is also a good table sauce.

In a saucepan over medium-low heat, melt the butter. Add the onion and cook, stirring, until softened, about 5 minutes.

Stir the ketchup, ½ cup (4 fl oz/125 ml) water, the Worcestershire sauce, steak sauce, vinegar, and brown sugar into the pan. Bring to a boil, reduce the heat to low, cover partially, and simmer until slightly thickened, about 20 minutes.

Use the sauce right away, or let cool, cover, and store in the refrigerator for up to 5 days.

2 tablespoons
unsalted butter

1 yellow onion,
finely chopped

1½ cups (12 fl oz/
375 ml) ketchup

⅓ cup (3 fl oz/80 ml)
Worcestershire sauce

¼ cup (2 fl oz/60 ml)
steak sauce

2 tablespoons cider vinegar

⅓ cup (2½ oz/75 g) firmly
packed dark brown sugar

MAKES ABOUT 3 CUPS
(24 FL OZ/750 ML)

376

RED WINE BARBECUE SAUCE

Dry wine

When applied to wine, the term dry refers to the amount of residual sugar in the wine. The less sugar, the drier the wine. Most red table wines are dry.

You can use this herbal, wine-based mixture as a marinade or a basting sauce for chicken, pork, lamb, or beef. The recipe makes enough for about 4 pounds (2 kg) of meat or poultry. Any extra sauce can be stored in the refrigerator.

In a saucepan over high heat, combine the wine, vinegar, oil, onion, Worcestershire sauce, rosemary, orange zest, red pepper flakes, and ½ teaspoon salt. Bring to a boil, stirring once or twice to combine the ingredients. Reduce the heat to low, cover partially, and simmer until the onion has wilted and the sauce has reduced slightly, about 15 minutes.

Use the sauce right away, or let cool, cover, and store in the refrigerator for up to 4 days.

1½ cups (12 fl oz/375 ml)
dry red wine

½ cup (4 fl oz/125 ml)
red wine vinegar

⅓ cup (3 fl oz/80 ml)
olive oil

1 yellow onion,
finely chopped

2 tablespoons
Worcestershire sauce

2 tablespoons chopped
fresh rosemary or thyme,
or 2 teaspoons dried
rosemary or thyme

2 teaspoons grated
orange zest

Pinch of red pepper flakes

Salt

MAKES ABOUT 2 CUPS
(16 FL OZ/500 ML)

SPICY BARBECUE SAUCE

This bold sauce is decidedly spicy, thanks to a generous dose of Tabasco sauce added to the base. If you like your food even hotter, substitute a habanero hot sauce for the relatively tame Tabasco. Use this sauce with grilled chicken, fried chicken wings, barbecued ribs, or pulled pork.

1 tablespoon olive oil

1 small yellow onion, finely chopped

1 cup (8 fl oz/250 ml) canned tomato purée

3 tablespoons Dijon mustard

¼ cup (2 fl oz/60 ml) fresh lemon juice

¼ cup (2 oz/60 g) firmly packed light brown sugar

2 tablespoons Worcestershire sauce

2 tablespoons Tabasco sauce

¼ teaspoon *each* ground allspice and ginger

Salt and ground pepper

MAKES ABOUT 2 CUPS (16 FL OZ/500 ML)

In a saucepan over medium heat, warm the oil. Add the onion and sauté until golden, about 10 minutes.

Add the tomato purée, mustard, lemon juice, brown sugar, Worcestershire sauce, Tabasco sauce, allspice, ginger, and ¼ cup (2 fl oz/60 ml) water to the pan and season with salt and pepper. Bring the sauce to a boil, reduce the heat to low, and simmer gently, uncovered, until reduced and thickened, 5–10 minutes.

Use the sauce right away, or let cool, cover, and store in the refrigerator for up to 1 week.

Storing barbecue sauce

The high acid and sugar content of many types of barbecue sauce discourage bacterial growth, so the sauce keeps well. Be sure to cool it completely before refrigerating.

377

ALL-PURPOSE TOMATO SAUCE

Rather than buying canned tomato sauce, which often contains a lot of salt and can conceal unnecessary additives, make this quick-to-assemble homemade version. For the best results, buy Italian-style plum tomatoes, packed in tomato purée.

2 cans (28 oz/875 g each) plum (Roma) tomatoes

About 1 cup (8 fl oz/250 ml) canned tomato purée

3 tablespoons unsalted butter or olive oil

Salt and ground pepper

MAKES ABOUT 6 CUPS (48 FL OZ/1.5 L)

Process the tomatoes with some of their juices in a blender or food processor until finely chopped. Transfer the tomatoes to a saucepan, place over low heat, and stir in the tomato purée. (If you prefer a thick sauce that coats food well, add up to ½ cup/4 fl oz/250 ml additional purée.) Cook, stirring often, until the sauce thickens slightly, about 10 minutes. Stir in the butter and season with salt and pepper.

Use the sauce right away, or let cool, cover, and store in the refrigerator for up to 1 week.

Freezing tomato sauce

Cooked tomato-based sauces are good candidates for freezing. Let cool to room temperature and transfer to airtight containers. Leave 1 inch head room to allow for expansion during freezing. Or, pack the sauce in zippered plastic freezer bags.

FRESH TOMATO SAUCE

Heirloom tomato sauce

In the summertime, when multicolored heirloom tomatoes arrive in farmers' markets, select an assortment of colors and shapes and use them in place of the plum tomatoes in this sauce.

Here, vine-ripened tomatoes and fresh basil are combined to make an uncooked pasta sauce that is ideal for summertime dining. Add a little of the pasta water when you toss together the sauce and pasta to ensure the sauce coats it well. Top with grated Parmesan cheese.

Peel, seed, and chop the tomatoes. If you are using thin-skinned heirloom tomatoes (see note, left), you can skip the peeling step.

In a large bowl, mix together the tomatoes, basil, garlic, and oil. Season with the salt and pepper and let stand for 30 minutes to allow the flavors to blend before using.

2 lb (1 kg) ripe tomatoes

¼ cup (⅓ oz/10 g) chopped fresh basil

1 clove garlic, minced

¼ cup (2 fl oz/60 ml) extra-virgin olive oil

Salt and ground pepper

MAKES ENOUGH SAUCE FOR 1 LB (500 G) PASTA; 4–6 SERVINGS

TOMATO-BASIL PASTA SAUCE

Taming tomatoes

Get in the habit of tasting tomatoes before cooking with them. If their flavor is a bit acidic, add a pinch or two of sugar with the salt to mellow their edge.

Italian style tomatoes

Italian cooks regularly use canned tomatoes for sauce when fresh tomatoes are not in season. Look for canned tomatoes, preferably San Marzano variety, imported from Italy at well-stocked markets.

It takes only about 30 minutes and little active work to make this pasta sauce. If using fresh tomatoes, make sure they are the ripest you can find. The butter in this recipe is typical of northern Italian cooking. For a southern Italian version, use two tablespoons of olive oil.

In a large frying pan over medium heat, melt the butter. Add the onion and 3–4 tablespoons water, cover, and cook gently, stirring occasionally, until the onion is tender and translucent, about 10 minutes.

Add the tomatoes, cover partially, and cook over low heat until the sauce has a thickened, creamy consistency, about 20 minutes. If the sauce begins to dry out before it becomes creamy, add a few tablespoons water to the pan.

Season with salt, add the basil, and stir well. Remove from the heat, cover, and let stand for a few minutes to allow the basil to release its aroma before using.

5 tablespoons (2½ oz/75 g) unsalted butter

1 small white onion, thinly sliced crosswise

1 lb (500 g) fresh plum (Roma) tomatoes, peeled, seeded, and sliced lengthwise, or 1 can (15 oz/470 g) plum (Roma) tomatoes, drained and chopped

Salt

8 fresh basil leaves, torn into small pieces

MAKES ENOUGH SAUCE FOR 1 LB (500 G) PASTA; 4–6 SERVINGS

MARINARA SAUCE

Marinara sauce starts with olive oil and garlic instead of the butter and sweet vegetables of many Italian sauces. The assertive sauce can stand on its own or pair with equally assertive ingredients, such as browned sausage or sautéed mushrooms.

¼ cup (2 fl oz/60 ml) olive oil

2 cloves garlic, minced

1 can (28 oz/875 g) plum (Roma) tomatoes, drained and chopped

Salt and ground pepper

6 fresh basil leaves, torn into small pieces

MAKES ENOUGH SAUCE FOR 1 LB (500 G) PASTA; 4–6 SERVINGS

In a large frying pan over medium heat, warm the oil. Add the garlic and sauté until lightly golden, about 2 minutes.

Add the tomatoes, 1 teaspoon salt, and ¼ teaspoon pepper to the pan and bring to a simmer. Reduce the heat to low and cook, stirring occasionally, until thickened, about 20 minutes. Remove from the heat and taste and adjust the seasoning.

Use right away, adding the basil leaves after you toss the sauce with pasta.

Arrabbiata sauce

Arrabbiata means "angry" in Italian and refers to the red pepper flakes used to make this traditional sauce. Add ½ tsp red pepper flakes to the pan with the garlic and proceed with the recipe. Taste the sauce after it thickens, adding more red pepper if you like more heat.

379

PUTTANESCA SAUCE

Theories abound about why the sauce is named for *puttane,* women in the world's oldest profession. Some believe that because the sauce it is so quickly made, the ladies of the evening could prepare the piquant olive- and caper-spiked tomato sauce between clients.

¼ cup (2 fl oz/60 ml) olive oil

2 cloves garlic, minced

½ teaspoon red pepper flakes

1 can (28 oz/875 g) plum (Roma) tomatoes, drained and chopped

Salt and ground pepper

6–8 olive oil–packed anchovy fillets, chopped

¼ cup (1½ oz/45 g) chopped pitted Gaeta or Kalamata olives

2 tablespoons rinsed capers

2 tablespoons chopped fresh flat-leaf (Italian) parsley

MAKES ENOUGH SAUCE FOR 1 LB (500 G) PASTA; 4–6 SERVINGS

In a large frying pan over medium heat, warm the oil. Add the garlic and red pepper flakes and sauté until lightly golden, about 2 minutes.

Add the tomatoes, 1 teaspoon salt, and ¼ teaspoon pepper to the pan and bring to a simmer. Reduce the heat to low and cook, stirring occasionally, until thickened, about 20 minutes.

Add the anchovies, olives, capers, and parsley and simmer for about 1 minute longer. Remove from the heat and taste and adjust the seasoning before serving.

Nonreactive pans

The culinary term nonreactive is used to describe cookware materials—stainless steel, enamel, ceramic, glass—that will not react with acidic ingredients, such as tomatoes, citrus juice, or wine, and cause an off flavor or color. Reactive materials include nonanodized aluminum, cast iron, and unlined copper.

BOLOGNESE SAUCE

Soffrito

Most Italian meat sauces begin with a soffrito, a mixture of onion, carrot, and celery sautéed in fat. Similar to a French mirepoix, it helps add complexity, depth, and a faint sweetness to long-simmered sauces.

The secret to making a successful Bolognese sauce is long, slow cooking. Milk adds richness and a creamy texture to the iconic meat sauce. Serve with fresh or dried pasta, on top of Soft Polenta (page 300), or incorporated into a lasagne, such as the one on page 174.

In a large frying pan over medium heat, warm the oil, butter, and pancetta, stirring occasionally, until the pancetta renders some of its fat, about 3 minutes. Add the onion, carrot, and celery and sauté until softened, about 5 minutes. Add the beef, reduce the heat to medium-low, and cook, breaking up the meat with the back of a wooden spoon, just until the meat is no longer pink, 3–5 minutes; do not allow to brown or harden.

Add the wine to the pan, raise the heat to medium, and simmer until the wine evaporates, 2–3 minutes. Add ¾ cup (6 fl oz/180 ml) of the milk and the nutmeg and simmer until the milk is absorbed.

Add the tomatoes and season with salt. Bring to a simmer, cover partially, and adjust the heat to very low. Cook, stirring occasionally, until the sauce is thick, mellow, and tasty, about 4 hours, adding a little water if needed to keep the sauce from sticking. During the final 45 minutes, stir in the remaining ¾ cup (6 fl oz/180 ml) milk in 3 additions, allowing the sauce to absorb the milk before adding more. Taste and adjust the seasoning before serving.

2 tablespoons olive oil

2 tablespoons unsalted butter

2 oz (60 g) pancetta, diced

½ large yellow onion, chopped

1 carrot, peeled and diced

1 large or 2 small celery stalks, diced

¾ lb (375 g) ground (minced) beef

½ cup (4 fl oz/125 ml) dry white wine

1½ cups (12 fl oz/ 360 ml) milk

⅛ teaspoon freshly grated nutmeg

1 can (15 oz/470 g) plum (Roma) tomatoes, finely chopped, with juice

Salt

MAKES ENOUGH SAUCE FOR 1 LB (500 G) PASTA, 4–6 SERVINGS

BUTTER AND SAGE SAUCE

Parmesan cheese

To distinguish true Parmesan cheese from other similarly named cheeses, look for the words Parmigiano-Reggiano stenciled on the rind. Grate it fresh for the best flavor. Grana padano and Asiago are good substitutes.

Although there is no cream, this recipe is a kin of Alfredo Sauce (see right) because of its generous use of butter and cheese. If you're making your own pasta (page 158), stir 1 teaspoon ground pepper into the flour before proceeding. It will play off the aromatic sage in the sauce.

In a large frying pan over medium-low heat, combine the butter, ¼ cup (2 fl oz/60 ml) water, the sage, and ½ teaspoon salt. Cook, stirring with a wooden spoon, just until the butter is melted. Remove the pan from the heat and taste and adjust the seasoning.

Serve the sauce right away, adding the cheese when you toss the pasta with the sauce.

½ cup (4 oz/125 g) unsalted butter

3 or 4 fresh sage leaves, torn into small pieces

Salt

¾ cup (3 oz/90 g) grated Parmesan cheese

MAKES ENOUGH SAUCE FOR 1 LB (500 G) PASTA; 4–6 SERVINGS

ALFREDO SAUCE

Tender, porous fresh fettuccine is the traditional companion to this thick, creamy sauce built from just a trio of ingredients: butter, cream, and Parmesan cheese. When tossed, the pasta ribbons should be lightly, yet evenly, coated with the sauce.

4 tablespoons (2 oz/60 g) unsalted butter

1 cup (8 fl oz/250 ml) heavy (double) cream

Salt

¾ cup (3 oz/90 g) grated Parmesan cheese

MAKES ENOUGH SAUCE FOR 1 LB (500 G) PASTA; 6–8 SERVINGS

Place a large frying pan over medium-low heat and add the butter. When the butter has melted, add the cream and ½ teaspoon salt, heat just until the mixture begins to bubble, and then simmer until slightly thickened, about 5 minutes.

Remove from the heat and add the cooked pasta and Parmesan to the pan, tossing thoroughly to combine. Adjust the thickness of the sauce with some of the pasta cooking water, if needed, then serve right away.

Let it thicken

The thickening step is critical; if the sauce is too thin, it will sit in a pool beneath the pasta, rather than nicely coat the strands.

MUSHROOM CREAM SAUCE

When the cool autumn months arrive, the earthy flavor of mushrooms mixes well with this creamy pasta sauce. Like other cream sauces, this one pairs well with ribbon pastas, especially fresh egg pasta, luxuriously coating the strands.

2 tablespoons unsalted butter

10 oz (315 g) sliced white mushrooms

Kosher salt and ground pepper

1 cup (8 fl oz/250 ml) heavy (double) cream

2 tablespoons chopped fresh flat-leaf (Italian) parsley

MAKES ENOUGH SAUCE FOR 1 LB (500 G) PASTA; 4–6 SERVINGS

In a large frying pan over medium heat, melt the butter. Add the mushrooms, 1 teaspoon salt, and ⅛ teaspoon pepper and sauté until the mushroom juices evaporate and the mushrooms are golden brown, about 10 minutes. Reduce the heat to medium-low, add the cream, and simmer until thickened, about 5 minutes. Stir in the parsley.

Remove from the heat and taste and adjust the seasoning. Adjust the thickness of the sauce with some of the pasta cooking water, if needed, then serve right away.

Heavy cream

Also known as heavy whipping cream and double cream, heavy cream usually contains 36–40 percent milk fat and lends a rich flavor and texture. The high milk fat content also means the cream can be boiled without separating when making a sauce.

WHITE SAUCE

Cooking the roux

Slowly cooking the roux (the flour and butter mixture) is important because it helps the sauce to thicken properly when the milk is added later. Carefully follow the visual and timing cues for this step.

382

Cheese sauces

To make a Cheddar cheese sauce, whisk 2 cups (8 oz/250 g) shredded extra-sharp Cheddar cheese into the finished sauce and whisk over low heat until the cheese has melted and the sauce is smooth. To make a Mornay sauce, whisk in ½ cup (2 oz/60 g) shredded Gruyère cheese and 3 tbsp freshly grated Parmesan cheese.

This rich, versatile sauce, similar to French béchamel, carries the wholesome flavors of fresh butter and milk. On its own, white sauce is often an element in lasagne or other baked dishes. When cheese is added, it becomes a sauce for Baked Macaroni and Cheese (page 176).

In a small saucepan over medium heat, warm the milk until small bubbles appear around the edge of the pan, about 5 minutes. Do not let the milk boil or develop a skin. Remove from the heat and cover to keep warm.

In a heavy saucepan over medium-low heat, melt the butter. Add the flour and stir well until the mixture is pale and ivory, 2–3 minutes. Remove from the heat.

Whisking constantly, drizzle the warm milk into the flour mixture about 2 tablespoons at a time. The sauce will gradually become smooth. After one-fourth of the milk has been added, you can add the rest more quickly. When all of the milk has been added, the sauce should have the consistency of thick cream. Stir in the salt.

Return the pan to medium-low heat and cook, stirring constantly, until bubbles begin to appear around the edge of the pan and the sauce is thick enough to coat the back of the spoon, about 1 minute. Taste the sauce; it should taste creamy with no trace of raw flour flavor. (Do not season further, because the sauce will be combined with other ingredients.) If any lumps are visible, strain the sauce through a fine-mesh sieve into a bowl.

Use the sauce right away, or transfer to a bowl and press a piece of plastic wrap directly onto the surface of the sauce. Let cool, then store in the refrigerator for up to 2 days. To reheat, pour into a heavy saucepan, place over low heat, and stir constantly with a wooden spoon until hot, adding a little hot milk to thin, if necessary.

2 cups (16 fl oz/500 ml) milk

4 tablespoons (2 oz/60 g) unsalted butter

¼ cup (1½ oz/45 g) all-purpose (plain) flour

½ teaspoon kosher salt

MAKES ABOUT 2 CUPS (16 FL OZ/500 ML)

BEURRE BLANC

Using leftover beurre blanc

Leftover sauce can be chilled for up to 1 day and then used like a compound butter (see page 246). Put small pieces of the cold beurre blanc on top of hot food, and it will melt to form a flavorful sauce.

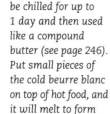

Rich with butter, beurre blanc is similar to Hollandaise Sauce (page 385), but with more punch. It starts with a base of dry white wine, vinegar, and shallot, which helps to hold the pale yellow sauce together and gives it a distinctive flavor. Serve with seafood or vegetables.

In a small saucepan over high heat, combine the wine, vinegar, and shallot and bring to a boil. Cook until the liquid reduces to 2 tablespoons, about 5 minutes. Remove from the heat and let cool for about 30 seconds. Meanwhile, cut the butter into ½-inch (12-mm) cubes.

Return the saucepan to medium-low heat. Add a few butter cubes and whisk until melted and almost completely

1 cup (8 fl oz/250 ml) dry white wine such as Sauvignon Blanc or Pinot Grigio

2 tablespoons white wine vinegar

1 shallot, chopped

1 cup (8 oz/250 g)
cold unsalted butter

Salt and ground
white pepper

Leaves from 2 fresh
tarragon sprigs,
chopped, optional

MAKES ABOUT ⅔ CUP
(5 FL OZ/160 ML)

incorporated. Continue whisking in the butter, a few cubes at a time, until all of it has been added and the sauce is ivory colored and the consistency of thick cream.

Stir in a pinch of salt and ⅛ teaspoon pepper, then taste and adjust the seasoning. If desired, strain the sauce through a fine-mesh sieve into a bowl. Stir in the tarragon (if using).

For orange beurre blanc Use the grated zest of 1 orange in place of the tarragon. Use on grilled or sautéed fish fillets.

For lemon beurre blanc Replace the wine vinegar with lemon juice, and replace the tarragon with the grated zest of 1 lemon. Use on steamed or boiled artichokes or to complement shellfish dishes.

For lime beurre blanc Use the grated zest of 1 lime in place of the tarragon. Use on grilled or sautéed chicken.

For balsamic beurre blanc Replace the wine vinegar with balsamic vinegar, and replace the tarragon with the minced leaves from 1 fresh rosemary sprig. Use on lamb dishes.

Beurre rouge

Make Beurre Blanc as directed, but replace the white wine with dry red wine, preferably one that is not heavily oaked, and the white wine vinegar with red wine vinegar. Spoon over grilled or sautéed veal chops or beef steaks.

MUSTARD CREAM SAUCE

Here is a rich, tangy sauce that complements everything from roast beef or panfried veal chops to sautéed chicken or roast pork loin. It provides a nice accent to vegetables as well. If desired, prepare it a few hours in advance and then reheat over low heat just before serving.

2 tablespoons
unsalted butter

2 tablespoons all-purpose
(plain) flour

1 cup (8 fl oz/250 ml)
chicken broth, heated

5–6 tablespoons (about
3 oz/90 g) Dijon mustard

1 cup (8 fl oz/250 ml)
heavy (double) cream

2 tablespoons
chopped fresh tarragon
or chives, optional

Salt and ground pepper

MAKES ABOUT 2 CUPS
(16 FL OZ/500 ML)

In a heavy saucepan over medium heat, melt the butter. Add the flour and cook, stirring, until the mixture is pale and ivory, 3–4 minutes. Whisking constantly, slowly pour in the broth. Whisk in the mustard, followed by the cream, and simmer, whisking occasionally, until slightly thickened, about 5 minutes.

Stir in the tarragon (if using). Season with salt and pepper and serve right away.

Mustard dregs

Before recycling a just-emptied mustard jar, add 3 or 4 parts oil, 1 part vinegar, and salt and pepper. Screw on the top securely and shake to make a mustard-flavored vinaigrette for salads or vegetables.

HORSERADISH CREAM

Sourcing horseradish

The best time to find fresh horseradish root in the market is in spring around Passover, as the pungent root is part of the holiday's traditional meal.

This is a great sauce for beef, whether cold rare roast beef or a just-cooked steak. In a pinch, you can use 5 tablespoons (3 oz/90 g) prepared horseradish instead of the fresh. If using prepared horseradish, use the smaller amount or even less of the vinegar and a little less salt.

In a blender or food processor, combine the horseradish and 3 tablespoons vinegar and process until smooth. Transfer to a serving bowl.

Stir in the onion, sour cream, heavy cream, 1 teaspoon salt, ½ teaspoon pepper, and dill (if using). Taste and add more vinegar if it is not tangy enough.

Serve cold or warm. To warm, add to a small saucepan and warm over low heat just until heated through.

½ cup (4 oz/125 g) peeled, thinly sliced fresh horseradish

3–4 tablespoons (about 2 fl oz/60 ml) distilled white vinegar

3 tablespoons finely minced white onion

1½ cups (12 fl oz/375 ml) sour cream

½ cup (4 fl oz/125 ml) heavy (double) cream

Salt and ground pepper

3 tablespoons chopped fresh dill or chives, optional

MAKES ABOUT 2 CUPS (16 FL OZ/500 ML)

CRÈME FRAÎCHE

Storing crème fraîche

Homemade crème fraîche will keep in a covered container in the refrigerator for up to 1 week. For the best flavor, however, use it within a day or two of making it.

A traditional soured, cultured cream product, crème fraîche is similar to sour cream. The silken, thick cream is tangy with a hint of nuttiness and adds incomparable flavor to both sweet and savory dishes. Prepared crème fraîche is available, but it is also easy to make at home.

In a small saucepan over medium-low heat, combine the cream and buttermilk and heat to lukewarm. Do not allow the mixture to simmer.

Remove the saucepan from the heat, cover, and let stand at room temperature until thickened, 8–48 hours. The longer the mixture sits, the thicker and tangier it will become. Chill for 3–4 hours before using.

1 cup (8 oz/250 ml) heavy (double) cream, not ultrapasteurized

1 tablespoon buttermilk

MAKES ABOUT 1 CUP (8 FL OZ/250 ML)

HOLLANDAISE SAUCE

This delicate sauce is best known for its role in Eggs Benedict (page 40). It should taste primarily of butter, with only a hint of citrus, so use the best butter you can find. The use of the blender here yields a thicker hollandaise than is typically made by hand.

4 egg yolks

1 tablespoon fresh lemon juice

Salt and ground black pepper

Pinch of cayenne pepper

1 cup (8 oz/250 g) unsalted butter, melted and cooled slightly

MAKES ABOUT 1 CUP (8 FL OZ/250 ML)

In a small, heavy saucepan over very low heat, combine the egg yolks, lemon juice, and 1 tablespoon water. Whisk constantly until the mixture begins to thicken. Continue whisking for 1 minute, but remove the pan from the heat as soon as the mixture thickens. Scrape into a blender, add ⅛ teaspoon salt, 2 pinches of black pepper, and the cayenne pepper, and blend until smooth. Let cool for 1 minute. With the blender running, slowly pour in the melted butter in a thin, steady stream until all of it has been incorporated.

Taste and adjust the seasoning. Serve right away or keep warm until using: pour into a bowl and place over (not touching) hot water in a saucepan.

For Béarnaise sauce In a small nonreactive saucepan over medium heat, combine ¼ cup (1½ oz/45 g) minced shallots, 3 tablespoons white wine vinegar, 2 tablespoons chopped fresh tarragon, and ¼ teaspoon coarsely ground pepper. Bring the mixture to a boil and cook until reduced and syrupy, about 2 minutes. Add the mixture to the blender with the egg yolk mixture instead of the seasonings. Pair the sauce with grilled meats and fish.

For orange hollandaise Stir 1½ teaspoons finely grated orange zest and 1 tablespoon snipped fresh chives into the finished sauce. Pair with grilled or panfried fish.

For tomato-lime hollandaise Use fresh lime juice in place of the lemon juice and stir 2 tablespoons finely diced peeled and seeded tomato into the finished sauce. Pair with grilled meats and fish.

Egg freshness

If you are unsure about the freshness of your eggs, put them in a bowl of cold water. If the eggs sink to the bottom and lie on their sides, they are fresh. If they float or stand on one end, the eggs are past their prime.

385

MAYONNAISE

Mellower mayonnaise

The noticeable flavor of olive oil in this mayonnaise may not be desirable for all uses. For a milder, more versatile mayonnaise, replace the olive oil with canola oil.

Cornichons

Also called gherkins, these tart, crisp pickles are prepared from a close relative of the cucumber— same species but different cultivar— and are no bigger than a little finger. They lend a unique briny flavor to mayonnaise-based sauces and are common companions to charcuterie in France.

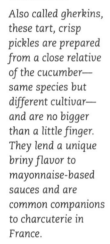

386

Homemade mayonnaise is richer and creamier than its commercial counterpart. This recipe calls for a food processor, but you can also use an electric mixer or a blender. Be careful not to mix the oil into the egg mixture too quickly or the sauce will develop a curdled appearance.

In a food processor, combine the egg yolk, lemon juice, and mustard and season with salt and pepper. Process briefly to combine. With the processor running, add the oil in a thin, steady stream and continue to blend until the mixture has a thick, smooth consistency. Use right away, or cover and refrigerate for up to 2 days.

For garlic mayonnaise (aioli) Stir 1 or 2 cloves garlic, minced, into the finished mayonnaise. Use as a dip for fried foods or raw or cooked vegetables.

For red pepper aioli In a clean food processor bowl, process 3 cloves garlic until puréed. Add 1 roasted red bell pepper (see page 28), chopped, and process until well blended. Add the finished mayonnaise and process just until mixed. Taste and adjust the seasoning. Use to flavor mashed potatoes or potato salad, or serve as a dip.

For pesto mayonnaise Stir 1 tablespoon Pesto (opposite) into the finished mayonnaise. Use as a sandwich spread.

For lemon-herb mayonnaise Stir the grated zest of ½ lemon and 2 teaspoons *each* minced fresh flat-leaf (Italian) parsley, chives, and dill into the finished mayonnaise. Use as a dip or sauce for chilled seafood.

For tahini mayonnaise Stir 1 clove garlic, minced, into the finished mayonnaise. A little at a time, whisk in 2 teaspoons tahini. Then whisk in ½ teaspoon ground cumin and 1 teaspoon warm water. Adjust the seasoning.

For tartar sauce Stir 3 tablespoons finely minced white onion; 2 tablespoons *each* minced fresh chives, flat-leaf (Italian) parsley, and cornichons; and 1 tablespoon *each* coarsely chopped capers, Creole or Dijon mustard, and fresh lemon juice into the finished mayonnaise. Adjust the seasoning. Use as a dip or sauce for fish or shellfish.

1 egg yolk

1 tablespoon
fresh lemon juice

1 teaspoon Dijon mustard

Salt and ground pepper

⅔ cup (5 fl oz/160 ml)
extra-virgin olive oil

**MAKES ABOUT ¾ CUP
(6 FL OZ/180 ML)**

PESTO

Purists make this versatile Italian sauce by hand with a mortar and pestle, which takes time and patience. A food processor makes the process quick and convenient. Among the variations included below is *pistou,* the popular southern French equivalent.

2 cloves garlic

½ cup (2 oz/60 g) grated pecorino romano or Parmesan cheese

¼ cup (1 oz/30 g) pine nuts, toasted (see page 17)

2 cups (2 oz/60 g) packed fresh basil leaves

½ cup (4 fl oz/125 ml) extra-virgin olive oil

Salt and ground pepper

MAKES ABOUT 1 CUP (8 OZ/250 G)

With a food processor running, drop the garlic cloves through the feed tube. Turn off the machine, add the cheese and pine nuts, and pulse briefly. Turn on the processor again and pour the oil in a thin, steady stream through the feed tube, processing until a moderately thick paste forms. As you work, stop the machine occasionally and scrape down the sides of the work bowl with a silicone spatula.

Transfer the pesto to a bowl, stir in ¼ teaspoon salt and ⅛ teaspoon pepper, and then taste the pesto. Add more cheese, salt, or pepper until the flavors are nicely balanced.

Use the pesto right away, or top with a thin layer of oil (to prevent discoloration), cover, and store in the refrigerator for up to 1 week. Before using, bring the pesto to room temperature and stir well.

For pesto with walnuts and pecorino Replace the pine nuts with chopped walnuts and use pecorino romano cheese. Use when you want a sharper-flavored sauce.

For rosemary-walnut pesto Replace the pine nuts with chopped walnuts, and replace the basil with 1¾ cups (1¾ oz/50 g) packed fresh flat-leaf (Italian) parsley leaves and ¼ cup (⅓ oz/10 g) chopped fresh rosemary. Pair with grilled chops and steaks.

For mint pesto Replace the basil with fresh mint leaves. Spread on lamb during the last 10 minutes of roasting or grilling, or use as a zesty condiment.

For arugula pesto Replace the basil with stemmed arugula (rocket) leaves. Use on pasta or grilled shrimp (prawns).

For cilantro pesto With the processor running, drop 2 cloves garlic and 1 jalapeño chile, seeded and chopped, through the feed tube. Stop the machine, add ¼ cup (1 oz/30 g) shelled pumpkin seeds and ½ cup (2 oz/60 g) grated cotija cheese, and pulse briefly. Add 2 cups (2 oz/ 60 g) packed fresh cilantro (fresh coriander) leaves and pulse to chop. Turn on the machine and slowly pour ½ cup (4 fl oz/125 ml) extra-virgin olive oil through the feed tube to form a moderately thick paste. Stir in the grated zest of 1 lime and 1 tablespoon fresh lime juice and season with salt and pepper. Use to accompany roasted pork or grilled chicken.

For pistou Replace the pine nuts with sliced (flaked) natural or blanched almonds and the pecorino romano cheese with finely shredded Gruyère cheese. Use as a condiment for vegetable soup or grilled fish.

The smaller the better

The flavor of fresh basil becomes stronger and more bitter as it matures. For the best-tasting pesto, look for basil bunches with small, young, bright green leaves.

Keep them fresh

Shelled nuts have a relatively short shelf life. Store them in an airtight container at room temperature for up to 2 months, in the refrigerator for up to 6 months, or in the freezer for up to 9 months. Delicate nuts, such as pine nuts and pistachios, should be kept for only about half as long.

387

TAPENADE

388

Olives for tapenade

For the most authentic tapenade, choose the small, brownish black Niçoise olive from Provence. It's nutty flavor adds a nice counterpoint to the other assertive ingredients in the paste. If Niçoise olives are unavailable, brine-cured Greek Kalamatas are a good substitute.

This time-honored paste of olives, capers, anchovies, and garlic hails from Provence, where olive trees and caper bushes abound in the sunny climate. It is a delicious spread for grilled bread or pizza, dip for crudités, or relish for grilled foods. A little tapenade goes a long way.

In a food processor, combine the olives, capers, anchovy, garlic, lemon zest, ½ teaspoon pepper, and 2 tablespoons olive oil. Pulse to form a coarse purée, adding more oil if needed for spreadability.

Transfer the tapenade to a bowl and use right away, or cover and store in the refrigerator for up to 5 days. Bring to room temperature before using.

½ cup (2½ oz/75 g) pitted Niçoise or Kalamata olives

1 tablespoon rinsed capers

2 teaspoons chopped anchovy fillet

1 teaspoon *each* minced garlic and grated lemon zest

Ground pepper

2–3 tablespoons fruity extra-virgin olive oil

MAKES ABOUT ¾ CUP (6 OZ/185 G)

LEMON–HERB SAUCE

Chopping fresh herbs

Fresh herbs are easiest to work with when they are completely dry. After rinsing well, whirl the herbs in a salad spinner to remove every trace of rinsing water.

This simple sauce lies somewhere between a vinaigrette and a pesto. It has olive oil and lemon juice as its base, combined with chopped shallot, capers, anchovies, and lots of fresh parsley and basil. Serve it on or alongside grilled vegetables, or with simple fish preparations.

In a food processor, combine the oil, lemon juice, shallot, capers, anchovies, a few grinds of pepper, and the coarsely chopped parsley. Process until smooth.

Transfer the sauce to a bowl and stir in the finely chopped parsley and the basil. Use right away, or cover and refrigerate for up to 1 day. Bring to room temperature before using.

½ cup (4 fl oz/125 ml) olive oil

¼ cup (2 fl oz/60 ml) lemon juice

1 shallot, chopped

2 teaspoons rinsed capers

2 anchovy fillets in olive oil, coarsely chopped

Ground pepper

½ cup (¾ oz/20 g) coarsely chopped fresh flat-leaf (Italian) parsley plus ½ cup (¾ oz/20 g) finely chopped

¼ cup (⅓ oz/10 g) chopped fresh basil

MAKES ABOUT 1¼ CUPS (10 FL OZ/310 ML)

GREEN CHILE–CILANTRO CHUTNEY

This brightly colored, robust chutney is suitable for dipping or drizzling, it is an excellent accompaniment to Indian-inspired fare, such as Spicy Potato Fritters (page 82) or Vegetable Samosas (page 83), and it lends an exotic note to simple meat or fish dishes.

3 cups (3 oz/90 g) fresh cilantro (fresh coriander) leaves

¼ cup (¼ oz/7 g) fresh mint leaves

1–3 serrano chiles, seeded and coarsely chopped

½-inch (12-mm) piece fresh ginger, coarsely chopped

1 clove garlic

Juice of ½ lime

1 teaspoon sugar

Salt

MAKES ABOUT 1¼ CUPS (10 FL OZ/310 ML)

In a blender or food processor, combine the cilantro, mint, chiles, ginger, garlic, lime juice, ½ cup (4 fl oz/125 ml) water, the sugar, and a pinch or two of salt. Purée until smooth. Add more water if needed to achieve the desired consistency.

Transfer the chutney to a bowl. Taste and adjust the seasoning. Use right away, or set aside at room temperature until serving time.

Chile heat

If you are not sure about the heat level of a chile, add the chile a little at a time. You can always add more. Remember, too, that if you prepare a dish in advance that includes chiles, the chiles will continue to impart more heat to the dish as it sits.

389

ROUILLE

This robust red sauce is made by puréeing a roasted red pepper, potatoes, garlic, and olive oil. It is excellent spooned on top of a classic grilled steak, such as a porterhouse or T-bone, or it can be used as a flavorful dip for vegetables or spread for crostini.

1 cup diced cooked peeled potato

½ cup roasted red bell pepper (capsicum) pieces (page 333)

4 cloves garlic, finely chopped

Salt

½ teaspoon red pepper flakes

½ cup (4 fl oz/125 ml) extra-virgin olive oil

MAKES ABOUT 1 CUP (8 FL OZ/250 ML)

In a food processor, combine the cooked potato, roasted pepper pieces, garlic, 1 teaspoon salt, and the red pepper flakes and process until smooth. With the motor running, slowly pour the olive oil into the blender in a thin, steady stream until incorporated.

Transfer the rouille to a bowl and refrigerate until needed. Bring to room temperature before using.

Using rouille

The classic way to use rouille is as a partner to bouillabaisse or other seafood stews. Thick slices of bread are smeared with the rust-colored sauce and served as part of the traditional meal.

NUOC CHAM

A classic Vietnamese condiment, this sauce is made from pungent fish sauce, sugar, lime juice, and vinegar. It is offered as a partner to myriad Vietnamese dishes, including the noodle dish on page 170, and is a delicious alternative to peanut sauce for the Asian rolls on page 79.

Using a mortar and pestle, grind together the garlic and sugar until a paste forms. (Alternatively, combine the ingredients in a mini food processor and process to a paste.)

Transfer the garlic paste to a bowl and whisk in the fish sauce, rice vinegar, lime juice, and ¼ cup (2 fl oz/60 ml) water. Pour through a fine-mesh sieve into a clean bowl and add the chile, carrot, and daikon.

Use the sauce right away, or set aside at room temperature until serving time.

3 cloves garlic, chopped

1½ tablespoons sugar

3 tablespoons fish sauce

2 tablespoons *each* rice vinegar and fresh lime juice

1 serrano chile, seeded and thinly sliced on the diagonal

1 tablespoon *each* grated carrot and daikon

MAKES ABOUT ⅔ CUP (5 FL OZ/160 ML)

Daikon

Long, cylindrical, white-skinned daikon is a radish of Asian origin. Peppery in flavor, it is thought to aid in the digestion of oily foods. It often appears raw, thinly sliced or grated, in many types of Asian preparations.

390

GINGER-SOY DIPPING SAUCE

This easy, Asian-style dipping sauce balances sour, salty, sweet, and hot flavors. It's great for the pot stickers on page 78 and for noodle dishes. Be sure to choose unseasoned rice vinegar and to adjust the amount of vinegar, sugar, and chile to your personal taste.

In a small bowl, whisk together the vinegar, light and dark soy sauces, 3 tablespoons warm water, sugar, sesame oil, and chile sauce until the sugar dissolves.

Add the ginger, garlic, and chile and whisk well. Let stand for a few minutes to blend the flavors.

Use right away, or cover and refrigerate for up to 2 days. Bring the sauce to room temperature before using.

5 tablespoons (2½ fl oz/ 75 ml) rice vinegar

¼ cup (2 fl oz/60 ml) light soy sauce

2 tablespoons dark soy sauce

1½ tablespoons sugar

1 tablespoon Asian sesame oil

1 teaspoon Sriracha chile sauce

2 tablespoons minced fresh ginger

2 teaspoons minced garlic

2 teaspoons thinly sliced, seeded red jalapeño chile or other fresh red chile

MAKES ABOUT 1¼ CUPS (10 FL OZ/310 ML)

Sriracha sauce

Originating in the southern part of Thailand, this smooth, red-orange, general-purpose chile sauce, a mixture of chiles, tomatoes, vinegar, and garlic, is used sparingly to add zest to salads, noodle soups, and other dishes.

PEANUT SAUCE

Rich, creamy, and packed with the tart, hot, and spicy flavors of Southeast Asia, this sauce is used to accompany grilled skewered meats or chicken. For the best results, use natural peanut butter, stirring it first to incorporate any oil floating on the surface.

½ cup (4 fl oz/125 ml) coconut milk, well shaken

½ cup (5 oz/155 g) smooth peanut butter

1 green (spring) onion, including tender green tops, minced

1 lemongrass stalk, center white part only, minced

2 cloves garlic, minced

Juice of ½ lime

1 tablespoon soy sauce

1 teaspoon *each* curry powder and ground coriander

½ teaspoon ground cumin

1 teaspoon chile paste, or as needed

MAKES ABOUT 1¼ CUPS (10 FL OZ/310 ML)

In a saucepan over medium heat, combine the coconut milk, peanut butter, green onion, lemongrass, garlic, lime juice, soy sauce, curry powder, coriander, and cumin. Cook, stirring constantly, until well blended, about 3 minutes.

Transfer the mixture to a blender or food processor and purée until smooth, thinning the sauce with a teaspoon or two of water if it seems too thick.

Pour the sauce into a bowl and stir in the 1 teaspoon chile paste. Taste and add more chile paste if desired. Use right away, or cover and refrigerate for up to 1 day. Bring the sauce to room temperature before serving.

Coconut milk

Coconut milk, made by soaking grated coconut in water, is sold in cans in Asian and Latin markets and well-stocked supermarkets. Do not confuse coconut milk with the product labeled "cream of coconut," which is sweetened coconut cream primarily used for desserts and tropical drinks.

RAITA

A *raita* is a yogurt-based Indian salad used to temper the spicy dishes typical of the cuisine. Outside of India, *raita* is usually considered a sauce or condiment. The yogurt cools the heat of the chiles, while the garlic, cumin, and cilantro complement the flavors in Indian-style dishes.

½ cup (2½ oz/75 g) peeled, seeded, and minced cucumber

Salt and ground pepper

2 cloves garlic, minced

1 cup (8 oz/250 g) low-fat plain yogurt

2 tablespoons fresh lemon juice

½ teaspoon ground cumin

2 tablespoons minced fresh cilantro (fresh coriander)

MAKES 1½ CUPS (12 FL OZ/375 ML)

Place the minced cucumber in a sieve, toss with 1 teaspoon salt, place over a bowl, and let drain for 30 minutes. Pat the cucumber dry.

In a mortar, combine the garlic and ½ teaspoon salt and grind together with a pestle until a paste forms. (Alternatively, combine the ingredients on a cutting board and mash together with a knife to form a paste.)

In a bowl, combine the cucumber, garlic paste, yogurt, lemon juice, cumin, cilantro, and ⅛ teaspoon pepper and stir to mix. Taste and adjust the seasoning. Use right away, or cover and refrigerate for up to 2 days.

Seeding cucumbers

Using a large knife, cut the cucumber in half lengthwise. Using a melon baller or small spoon, scoop out the seeds and surrounding pulpy matter from end to end.

GUACAMOLE

Pitting and peeling avocados

Cut into the avocado lengthwise until the knife meets the pit, then rotate the fruit on the blade until cut all the way around. Rotate the halves in opposite directions to separate them. Lift out the avocado pit with the tip of a spoon, then ease the spoon between the flesh and peel to scoop out the flesh.

Perhaps Mexico's best-known table condiment, guacamole marries the creamy, buttery taste of perfectly ripe avocados with onion, garlic, tomato, and serrano chiles. Lime juice delivers a bright flavor and prevents the avocado from turning brown.

In a bowl, using a fork, mash 4 tablespoons (1½ oz/45 g) of the onion, the chiles, and the garlic to form a coarse paste. Add the avocado flesh and mash until well blended. Stir in all but 2 tablespoons of the tomato and all of the cilantro and lime juice. Season with salt. Let stand for a few minutes to allow the flavorings to blend.

Transfer the mixture to a serving bowl, sprinkle evenly with the remaining 2 tablespoons each onion and tomato, and serve right away.

6 tablespoons (2 oz/60 g) finely chopped white onion

2 serrano chiles, seeded and finely chopped

1 clove garlic, minced

2 ripe Hass avocados, halved, pitted, and peeled (see note, left)

1 large, ripe tomato, finely chopped

¼ cup (¼ oz/7 g) lightly packed fresh cilantro (fresh coriander) leaves, finely chopped

1 tablespoon fresh lime juice

Salt

MAKES ABOUT 2½ CUPS (1¼ LB/625 G)

AVOCADO-TOMATILLO SALSA

Removing tomatillo husks

Tomatillos must be husked before use. Hold each tomatillo under warm running water and use your fingers to peel away the brown papery husk and rub away the sticky, resinous substance coating the skin.

This is the spicier, all-green cousin of guacamole (above). Here, mild avocados, cilantro, and onion are combined with tomatillos and chiles, with an extra measure of lime juice to tamp down the heat. Serve with Shredded Beef Tacos (page 277) or as an alternative to guacamole.

Bring a saucepan three-fourths full of water to a boil. Add the tomatillos and parboil until softened, about 5 minutes. Drain and let cool.

Mince the tomatillos and place in a bowl. Add the chiles, cilantro, onion, garlic, and ½ teaspoon salt and stir to combine. Add the avocado flesh and, using a fork, mash into the tomatillo mixture, maintaining a slightly chunky consistency. Stir in the lime juice. Let stand for a few minutes to blend the flavors.

Transfer the salsa to a serving bowl and serve right away.

10 tomatillos, husks removed (see note, left)

2 serrano chiles, seeded and minced

2 tablespoons *each* minced fresh cilantro (fresh coriander) and yellow onion

1 clove garlic, minced

Salt

2 ripe Hass avocados, halved, pitted, and peeled (see note, above left)

Juice of 2 limes

MAKES ABOUT 3½ CUPS (24 FL OZ/750 ML)

GREEN SALSA

This versatile condiment complements everything from tacos and enchiladas to grilled meats, chicken, and fish. It is made from tomatillos, called *tomates verdes,* or "green tomatoes," in Spanish, which are the same size, shape, and texture as tomatoes but are green and tangy.

Salt

2 cloves garlic

4 serrano chiles

1 lb (500 g) tomatillos, husks removed (see note, opposite)

½ cup (½ oz/15 g) loosely packed fresh cilantro (fresh coriander) leaves

¼ cup (1¼ oz/40 g) finely chopped red onion

MAKES ABOUT 2 CUPS (16 FL OZ/500 ML)

In a large saucepan over high heat, combine 3 cups (24 fl oz/750 ml) water and 1 teaspoon salt and bring to a boil. Add the garlic, chiles, and tomatillos and cook, uncovered, stirring occasionally, until the tomatillos are soft, 8–10 minutes. Drain, reserving ½ cup (4 fl oz/125 ml) of the cooking liquid.

When cool enough to handle, stem the chiles and tomatillos. If a milder sauce is desired, seed the chiles.

In a food processor or a blender, combine the garlic, chiles, tomatillos, the reserved cooking liquid, cilantro, and 1½ teaspoons salt and process until fairly smooth. Transfer to a bowl and stir in the onion.

Let cool to room temperature before serving. Or, let cool, cover, and store in the refrigerator for up to 1 week. Bring to room temperature before serving.

About tomatillos

Although tomatillos look like green tomatoes and, like them, are in the nightshade family, they are actually a much closer relative of the cape gooseberry, a marble-size berry native to South America. Tomatillos are at their best from August through November. Choose firm, unblemished fruits with lightly clinging husks.

393

FRESH TOMATO SALSA

Once you make this bright-flavored uncooked salsa, you will pass up its bottled counterparts on supermarket shelves. Serve it as a dip for chips and as a table condiment for grilled meat, chicken, or seafood. For a milder version, use fewer chiles.

3 tomatoes

½ red onion

2–4 serrano chiles, seeded and finely chopped

1 tablespoon finely chopped fresh cilantro (fresh coriander)

2 teaspoons fresh lime juice

Salt

MAKES ABOUT 1½ CUPS (12 FL OZ/375 ML)

Finely chop the tomatoes and onion into equal pieces. Seed and mince the chiles.

In a large bowl, stir together the tomatoes, onion, chiles, cilantro, lime juice, and 2 teaspoons salt. Let the salsa stand for 1 hour to blend the flavors.

Serve the salsa right away or cover and store in the refrigerator for up to 3 days.

Cherry tomato salsa

For a colorful, contemporary take on this salsa, use cherry tomatoes in a mix of colors, cutting them in half before tossing with the other ingredients. If desired, add halved grape tomatoes as well, also in a mix of colors.

ROASTED-TOMATO SALSA

Molcajete and tejolote

The three-legged molcajete and its accompanying tejolote, or pounder, both made from coarse-textured lava rock, are the mortar and pestle of Mexico, ideal for making salsas and other pounded and ground concoctions. Look for them in a Mexican market or through Web sites featuring specialty cookware.

A popular condiment throughout most of Mexico, this salsa gets much of its deep flavor from roasting the chiles and tomatoes. If you can, use a *molcajete*—a mortar made from lava rock—to give the salsa a traditional rustic texture and flavor.

Warm a dry, heavy frying pan or griddle over medium heat. Place the chiles and tomatoes on the pan and roast, turning occasionally, until they are well charred on all sides and slightly softened, 5–8 minutes, depending on their size. Remove from the heat and, when cool enough to handle, stem the chiles and tomatoes.

In a blender or food processor, combine the roasted tomatoes and chiles, the garlic, and 1 teaspoon salt. Process until chopped into small chunks; do not purée.

Transfer the salsa to a bowl and serve right away or cover and store in the refrigerator for up to 1 week.

5 serrano chiles

2 ripe tomatoes

1 clove garlic

Salt

MAKES ABOUT 1½ CUPS (12 FL OZ/375 ML)

GRILLED CORN AND AVOCADO SALSA

Choosing fresh corn

Choose corn with bright green husks. Feel the kernels through the husks (at the market, if you tear back the husk to peek at the corn, you are shortening its shelf life) and select ears with kernels in tightly packed rows and moist, pale yellow silk peeking out of the top.

A salsa of grilled sweet corn and diced avocado spiked with chiles provides the perfect finishing touch to simple dishes like the quesadillas on page 192. You can also serve the salsa as a dip or a condiment with grilled meat, fish, or poultry.

Prepare a charcoal or gas grill for direct-heat cooking over medium-high heat (see page 18).

Brush the corn ears with the oil and place on the grill rack directly over the heat. Cook, turning often, until tender and lightly bronzed, 8–10 minutes. Let cool.

In a bowl, combine the avocado, onion, cilantro, chiles, garlic, lime juice, chili powder, and ½ teaspoon each salt and pepper. Cut off the kernels from the corncobs and add to the avocado mixture. Stir to mix well, then serve right away.

4 ears corn, white or yellow or a mixture, husks removed

1 tablespoon canola or other light vegetable oil

1 large, ripe avocado, cut into ½-inch (12-mm) dice

½ cup (3 oz/90 g) minced red onion

¼ cup (⅓ oz/10 g) chopped fresh cilantro (fresh coriander)

1 or 2 serrano chiles, seeded and minced

2 cloves garlic, minced

2 tablespoons fresh lime juice

½ teaspoon chili powder

Salt and ground pepper

MAKES ABOUT 3½ CUPS (1½ LB/750 G)

RED PEPPER–CORN RELISH

This piquant relish adds both flavor and color to anything you might top with it. Corn kernels, bell pepper, onion, and garlic are sautéed briefly, then seasoned and tossed with lime juice and cilantro. It is particularly tasty spooned on top of a burger (pages 188–89).

1 teaspoon olive oil

1 cup (6 oz/185 g) corn kernels (from about 2 ears)

1 red bell pepper (capsicum), chopped

6 tablespoons (2 oz/60 g) finely chopped red onion

1¼ teaspoons minced garlic

Salt and ground pepper

1½ tablespoons fresh lime juice

1½ tablespoons chopped fresh cilantro (fresh coriander)

MAKES ABOUT 1¾ CUPS (10 OZ/315 G)

In a large frying pan over medium heat, warm the oil. Add the corn kernels and bell pepper and cook, stirring constantly, until the vegetables are softened, about 5 minutes. Add the onion and garlic and cook, stirring, until the onion is softened, about 3 minutes. Stir in ⅛ teaspoon each salt and pepper. Remove from the heat.

Transfer the relish to a bowl and stir in the lime juice and cilantro. Taste and adjust the seasoning, cover, and let stand at room temperature for at least 1 hour before serving. Or, cover and refrigerate for up to 5 hours, then bring to room temperature before serving.

Cutting kernels from corncobs

Holding the corn ear by its pointed end, steady the stalk end in the bottom of a shallow bowl or on a cutting board. Then, using a sharp knife, cut down along the ear between the kernels and the cob to strip the kernels off, giving the ear a quarter turn after each cut. Don't cut too deeply. You want to leave the fibrous bases of the kernels behind on the cob.

395

ROASTED SHALLOT–TOMATO RELISH

Roasted shallots and chopped fresh rosemary heighten the flavor and aroma of this simple tomato relish. Serve this versatile condiment with everything from grilled chicken or steak to the pork chops on page 291 or Zucchini Fritters (page 354).

6 large shallots, halved

Salt and ground pepper

Olive oil for drizzling

4 plum (Roma) tomatoes, seeded and chopped

¼ cup (⅓ oz/10 g) chopped fresh flat-leaf (Italian) parsley

1 tablespoon balsamic vinegar

1 tablespoon honey

2 teaspoons minced fresh rosemary

¼ teaspoon cayenne pepper

MAKES ABOUT 2¼ CUPS (14 OZ/440 G)

Preheat the oven to 400°F (200°C).

Place the shallots in a small baking dish, season with salt and pepper, and drizzle lightly with olive oil. Roast the shallots for 15 minutes. Turn over the shallots and continue to roast until soft, about 10 minutes longer. Remove from the oven, let cool, and chop coarsely.

In a bowl, combine the chopped shallots, tomatoes, parsley, vinegar, honey, rosemary, and cayenne. Season with salt and pepper. Use right away, or cover and refrigerate for up to 3 days. Bring to room temperature before serving.

Have it on hand

The flavor of this relish is best if made 2 or 3 days before serving. You might even make a double batch and keep the second one on hand for a quick dinner later in the week.

SAUCES, SALSAS & CONDIMENTS

FRESH AND DRIED FRUIT RELISH

Fresh pineapple

Many supermarkets now stock fresh pineapple sliced or cubed and packed in juice. Look for the plastic containers in the produce department.

This unique fruit relish mixes tangy citrus, sweet pineapple, tart and chewy dried cranberries, tart-sweet cherry tomatoes, and pleasingly spicy chile. Serve it alongside Grilled Turkey Breast (page 254) or grilled or panfried pork chops.

Using a small, sharp knife, cut off a thin slice from both the stem and the blossom end of the orange to reveal the flesh. Then stand the fruit upright and, following its contour, slice off the peel, pith, and membrane in thick strips. Cut the orange crosswise into slices ¼ inch (6 mm) thick, and then cut each slice into sections. Transfer the pieces to a bowl and stir in the cranberries. Add the pineapple, tomatoes, chile, lime juice, and chives. Stir to mix well, then cover, and refrigerate for 1 hour.

Drain the salsa and transfer to a serving bowl. Add the cilantro to the salsa and toss to mix. Serve right away.

1 large navel orange

1 cup (4 oz/125 g) dried cranberries

1¼ cups (8 oz/250 g) diced fresh pineapple

12 cherry tomatoes, halved

1 small jalapeño chile, seeded and finely chopped

1 tablespoon fresh lime juice

1 teaspoon chopped fresh chives

1 tablespoon chopped fresh cilantro (fresh coriander)

MAKES ABOUT 3 CUPS (18 OZ/560 G)

CRANBERRY RELISH

Golden raisins

Also called sultanas, golden raisins are seedless grapes that have been treated with a solution to preserve their color and are dried in a dehydrator. Look for plump, moist raisins in a store that has good turnover.

Cranberries are harvested during the autumn months, which means you can often find fresh ones in the market around Thanksgiving time. This sweet-tart condiment is the perfect companion to the holiday turkey, or roast pork or game birds.

In a large frying pan, combine the sugar and ½ cup (4 fl oz/ 125 ml) water over medium-low heat. Cook, stirring, until the mixture turns a golden amber, 5–10 minutes.

Add the cranberries, raisins, and lemon zest to the pan and cook, stirring to break up any sugar lumps, until the cranberries pop and the mixture is thick, about 10 minutes. Remove the pan from the heat, stir in the vinegar, and season lightly with pepper.

Transfer the relish to a bowl and serve warm, or let cool and serve at room temperature.

1 cup (8 oz/250 g) sugar

3 cups (12 oz/375 g) fresh or frozen cranberries

½ cup (3 oz/90 g) golden raisins (sultanas)

2 teaspoons grated or finely chopped lemon zest

1 tablespoon aged red wine vinegar or fruit-flavored vinegar

Ground pepper

MAKES ABOUT 3½ CUPS (1¾ LB/875 G)

DRIED-FRUIT CHUTNEY

The use of dried fruits in this spicy chutney means you can make it any time of the year. It's the perfect partner for roasted or grilled meats. Store any extra chutney in a tightly sealed container in the refrigerator for up to 3 weeks.

½ lb (250 g) dried
peaches, chopped

½ lb (250 g) dried
apricots, chopped

½ lb (250 g) dried
Calimyrna figs, stemmed
and chopped

2 cups (16 fl oz/500 ml)
cider vinegar

½ lb (250 g) pitted
dates, chopped

½ lb (250 g) pitted
prunes, chopped

1 large yellow
onion, chopped

1 cup (8 oz/250 g) sugar

1½ teaspoons Madras
curry powder

1 teaspoon ground ginger

¼ teaspoon red
pepper flakes

Salt

MAKES ABOUT 3½ PT
(56 FL OZ/1.75 L)

In a bowl, combine the peaches, apricots, and figs. Pour in hot water to cover and let stand for 30 minutes. Drain, reserving 1¼ cups (10 fl oz/310 ml) of the soaking water.

In a large saucepan over high heat, combine the soaked fruits, the reserved soaking water, the vinegar, dates, prunes, onion, sugar, curry powder, ginger, red pepper flakes, and ¼ teaspoon salt. Bring to a boil, stirring until the sugar dissolves. Reduce the heat and simmer, stirring frequently, until the chutney is thick and the dried fruits are tender, about 10 minutes.

Serve warm or at room temperature.

Choosing dried fruit

Look for recently dried fruits, either packaged or in bulk, which have a softer texture than older dried fruits. Health food stores and farmers' markets often have a more rapid turnover of stock, making them good places to shop for dried fruits.

397

FRESH-FRUIT CHUTNEY

Using chutney

Chutney can be used as a condiment for baked ham or grilled or panfried chicken or pork chops; as an accompaniment to Indian dishes; or as an unexpected sandwich spread. It can also be mixed with cream cheese and served as a dip.

This chunky mixed-fruit chutney, made from late-season stone fruits and grapes, captures the essence of summer. Its full fruit flavor complements a variety of dishes. Although the recipe yields a large amount, the chutney keeps well in the refrigerator for up to 2 months.

Pit, peel, and coarsely chop the peaches and plums.

In a large saucepan, combine the peaches, plums, grapes, onions, brown sugar, currants, ginger, garlic, cayenne pepper, and vinegar. Arrange the cinnamon sticks, peppercorns, and cloves on a square of cheesecloth (muslin). Bring the corners together and tie securely with kitchen string. Add the bundle of spices to the saucepan.

Bring the mixture to a boil over high heat, stirring often. Reduce the heat to low and simmer uncovered, stirring occasionally, until the mixture develops a somewhat loose, jamlike consistency, 50–60 minutes. When the chutney begins to thicken, during the last 10–15 minutes of cooking, stir often with a wooden spoon to prevent burning.

Remove the chutney from the heat, stir in the butter, and season with salt. Let cool to room temperature and discard the spice bundle. Serve right away, or cover and store in the refrigerator until ready to serve.

1½ lb (750 g) peaches

½ lb (250 g) plums

½ lb (250 g) seedless grapes

2 yellow onions, chopped

1¾ cups (13 oz/410 g) firmly packed brown sugar

1 cup (6 oz/185 g) dried currants or raisins

¼ cup (1¼ oz/37 g) peeled, finely chopped fresh ginger

4 cloves garlic, minced

1 teaspoon cayenne pepper

1½ cups (12 fl oz/375 ml) cider vinegar

3 cinnamon sticks

1 tablespoon peppercorns

1 tablespoon whole cloves

2 tablespoons unsalted butter

Salt

MAKES ABOUT 2½ PT (40 FL OZ/1.2 L)

TANGY MANGO RELISH

Relishes, pickles, chutneys, and salads add breadth and sparkle to many Southeast Asian dishes. Called *kerabu,* this Malaysian chile-spiked relish of cubed mango is substantial enough also to be served as a side dish. It is just the right tonic for spicy-hot dishes.

1 large firm mango

2 red jalapeño chiles, seeded

3 tablespoons distilled white vinegar

4 teaspoons sugar

Salt

1 tablespoon fresh lime juice

1 tablespoon coarsely chopped fresh mint

1 tablespoon coarsely chopped fresh cilantro (fresh coriander)

MAKES 8 SERVINGS

Hold the mango on a narrow side, with the stem end toward you. With a large knife, cut down about ¾ inch (2 cm) to one side of the stem, just grazing the side of the pit. You should have 1 large mango half. Repeat on the other side of the stem, leaving the pit behind. Carefully score the flesh of each half in a crosshatch pattern, cutting down to, but not through, the skin. Press against the skin with your thumbs, forcing the mango cubes upward. Cut across the bottom of the cubes to free them. Set aside.

In a food processor or blender, combine the chiles and ¼ cup (2 fl oz/60 ml) water and process until coarsely puréed, leaving small bits of chile in the mixture. Transfer to a small saucepan and add the vinegar, sugar, and ½ teaspoon salt. Cook over medium heat, stirring occasionally, until the sugar dissolves, about 3 minutes. Remove from the heat, transfer to a bowl, and let cool completely.

Add the mango cubes, lime juice, mint, and cilantro and stir gently to combine. Cover and let stand at room temperature for about 20 minutes to blend the flavors before serving.

About mangoes

Choose mangoes that emit a full aroma at their stem end, give slightly to gentle pressure, and have perfectly smooth skin. Depending on the variety, they can range in color from all green to all red, or blushed of every shade of yellow and orange in between.

APPLESAUCE

When you see how easy it is to make homemade applesauce, you'll never settle for store-bought again. It can be stored in the refrigerator for up to 1 week or the freezer for up to 6 months. Serve it with roasted pork, or with Potato Latkes (page 364).

8–10 large apples, 2–3 lb (2–2.5 kg) total weight, quartered and cored

1½ cups (12 fl oz/375 ml) apple cider or water

½ teaspoon ground cinnamon

¾–1 cup (6–8 oz/ 185–250 g) sugar

Fresh lemon juice

MAKES 8 SERVINGS

Peel the apples. (If you are using a food mill to pureé the apples, you can leave the peels on.) In a deep saucepan over low heat, combine the apples and cider. Cook, stirring once or twice, until the apples are very tender, 20–30 minutes.

Drain the apples, reserving the liquid. Pass the apples through a food mill placed over a bowl. Mix in the cinnamon, the ¾ cup (6 oz/185 g) sugar, a small amount of lemon juice, and ⅓–½ cup (3–4 fl oz/80–125 ml) of the cooking liquid, or as needed to achieve a good consistency. (Alternatively, in a food processor, combine the apples and the remaining ingredients, using the smaller amounts to start, and process to a good consistency.) Taste and add more sugar and lemon juice as needed.

Serve right away at room temperature.

Apples for applesauce

For the most satisfying applesauce, use sweet, flavorful apples, such as Rome, Baldwin, or Macintosh. If you like a sharper-flavored applesauce, use Granny Smith, Braeburn, or other tart apples.

Yeast BREADS

Yeast Breads

Baking your own bread is surprisingly easy to do, as the instructions here and the recipes that follow demonstrate. With a handful of no-frills equipment and some quickly acquired know-how, you'll be able to produce loaves in far greater variety than nearly any single bakery can, and you'll gain the satisfaction of both delicious homemade bread and a kitchen filled with wonderful aromas.

Yeast Bread Basics

Second and third risings
Most yeast-leavened bread doughs rise just once, but some recipes call for second or even third risings, which help develop finer texture and even more flavor. When repeated risings are called for, do not shape the dough into its final form until it has risen at least once.

Tapping for doneness
Most loaves are baked until they are well risen and lightly browned and sound hollow when tapped on the bottom. Take the bread from the oven, but do not turn the oven off. Protecting your hand with an oven mitt, invert the loaf onto it and then knock on the bottom of it with bare knuckles. If it does not sound hollow, return the loaf to the oven, checking again after 5 to 7 minutes.

Storing bread
Store bread at room temperature, on a cupboard shelf or in a bread box or drawer. Fresh-baked bread usually lasts only 1 or 2 days before it begins to go stale (perfect for bread crumbs, stuffing, or French toast). Bread also freezes well enclosed in a zippered plastic bag. Thaw at room temperature, still in the bag, before serving.

Most bread recipes have in common three ingredients: flour, yeast, and water. No matter what additional ingredients are used, understanding these basic ingredients will make your bread making more pleasurable and will give you the confidence to try a wide range of variations.

FLOUR Wheat contains a protein known as gluten that, when combined with water, becomes elastic. When dough is kneaded, gluten forms a web that traps the gas released by yeast, causing bread to rise and, during baking, develop a fine, honeycombed "crumb," or texture. Different wheat varieties have varying gluten contents. Bread (strong) flour, milled from hard wheat, has the most, between 10 and 13 percent. All-purpose (plain) flour, a combination of hard wheat and soft wheat, has between 9 and 12 percent. Because of its higher gluten content, bread flour produces loaves that rise high and have an airy texture. When possible, use unbleached bread flour. Bleaching, a chemical process used to whiten flour, inhibits good gluten formation; unbleached flour is whitened through an aging process that does not affect gluten.

YEAST When combined with flour and liquid, yeast feeds on the starch present in flour and releases gas that causes bread to rise. The most common forms of yeast available today are active dry yeast, ideal for breads that gain flavor and texture from slower rising, and quick-rise yeast, which cuts the rising time of bread roughly in half, making bread making more convenient. Use both of these yeasts before the expiration date printed on the package. Fresh cake yeast is sold in foil-wrapped packets and is preferred by some bakers, but the following recipes call only for dry yeast for its convenience and shelf stability. Some recipes call for a sourdough "starter" (page 406), an old-fashioned fermented paste of yeast, water, and flour that produces a distinctively tangy taste in loaves made with it.

LIQUIDS Most bread recipes call for water. Tap water is generally fine, although some bakers think bottled or filtered water makes better-tasting bread. If your tap water tastes heavily of chemicals, you might want to consider these other options.

Other liquids can contribute richness and flavor to bread. Using milk yields bread with a soft, delicate texture. Buttermilk adds tang, and beer delivers heartiness and additional yeastiness. Any liquid should be warmed to about 110°F (43°C) to promote the yeast's activity. Liquid that is too hot will kill the yeast, and liquid that is too cool will slow its leavening action. When starting out as a bread maker, use an instant-read thermometer to measure the temperature of the liquid. Once you become accustomed to the process, gauging the temperature is possible by allowing a drop or two of the liquid to fall onto your wrist. It should feel warm, not hot.

FATS Butter, oil, eggs, and other fats incorporated into the dough yield richer, more tender, more flavorful breads. Some breads are rubbed with oil or softened butter before baking to encourage browning.

FLAVORINGS Salt strengthens gluten, controls yeast, and enhances the flavor of other ingredients. Sugar not only sweetens dough but also supplies energy to help yeast grow and caramelizes for a browner crust. All kinds of other flavorings—from cocoa to nuts, herbs to spices—can contribute still more distinction to individual bread doughs.

Bread-Making Techniques

Too many home bakers believe that yeast-leavened breads require special expertise. The process actually consists of just a few simple steps that, once you've done them a few times, will become second nature.

PROOFING Quick-rise yeast does not require proofing, but some recipes still call for it to give the yeast a head start. Sprinkle the yeast into warm liquid, following the guidelines in the recipe. Some recipes call for a little sugar or honey to help feed the yeast. Let the mixture stand until bubbling and foamy, 5 to 10 minutes. If the yeast does not bubble, start over with fresh yeast.

MIXING AND KNEADING Bread doughs can be mixed and kneaded by hand or by machine.

To mix and knead by hand, combine the ingredients as directed in the recipe, stirring the dough in a bowl with a wooden spoon until it forms a rough mass. Using a plastic pastry scraper, scrape the dough onto a floured work surface. Using the heel of one hand, push the dough away from you, and then pull it back with your fingertips, folding it in half toward you. Rotate the dough a quarter turn and repeat. Continue this push-pull motion until the dough feels smooth and elastic (or as described in individual recipes), usually about 10 minutes. Form the dough into a ball by tucking the sides of the dough underneath and lightly pinching them together, then let rise as instructed in the recipe, usually in an oiled or buttered bowl covered with plastic wrap.

To mix and knead by stand mixer, combine the ingredients as directed in the recipe in the bowl of a stand mixer fitted with the dough hook. Turn the mixer on low speed and mix, adding flour as instructed, until the dough comes cleanly away from the sides of the bowl and is no longer sticky (or as described in individual recipes), usually 5 to 7 minutes. Remove the bowl from the mixer and use your hand or a spatula to ease the dough onto a floured work surface. Knead briefly on the surface if directed in the recipe, then form into a ball by tucking the sides of the dough underneath and lightly pinching them together. Let rise as instructed in the recipe, usually in an oiled or buttered bowl covered with plastic wrap.

PUNCHING DOWN AND DIVIDING DOUGH After the dough has risen, usually until doubled in bulk, it must be punched down to release gases that have built up during rising. To punch down the dough, using your fist, simply press down on the dough, either in the bowl or on the work surface, until it has lost most of its air.

If the recipe calls for dividing the dough into smaller portions, use a bench scraper (also called a dough scraper) or a sharp knife to cut it. Cover the dough portions you aren't using immediately with a dampened kitchen towel so the dough doesn't dry out.

FLOURS AND GRAINS

Most breads are made from some form of wheat flour. But many other grains provide flours that, in combination with wheat, yield breads with varied flavors, textures, and colors.

All-Purpose (Plain) Flour
Blend of high- and low-gluten flours. Can be used in place of bread (strong) flour, with slightly denser and more cakelike results.

Bread (Strong) Flour
Flour milled from the endosperm of hard wheat, producing a particularly high-gluten product.

Whole-Wheat (Wholemeal) Flour
Milled from whole wheat kernels. Richer in flavor and texture than white flour but does not rise as easily.

403

High-Gluten Flour
Made from hard wheat that has been milled to intensify its protein and thus its gluten; generally used in combination with low-gluten flours.

Bran
The outer coating of whole grains such as wheat and oats. Provides rich flavor, texture, and fiber.

Rye Flour
Available in light (a white flour with the bran and germ sifted out), medium (the most common), and dark varieties (with a higher proportion of bran), the recipes in this chapter use medium rye flour. It provides rich, sour flavor. Low in gluten, rye flour yields a dense texture and is usually combined with wheat flour.

OLD-FASHIONED WHITE BREAD

Unbleached flour

Unbleached flour has not been chemically treated, so it appears ivory colored rather than stark white. It also contains more protein and has a more "wheaty" flavor than bleached flour.

This genuine home-style loaf has excellent flavor and texture. Keep it on hand for sandwiches, toast, croutons, or bread crumbs. It also freezes well. Don't substitute all-purpose flour for the bread flour here, as it won't develop enough gluten during kneading, resulting in poor texture.

In a large bowl or the bowl of a stand mixer, combine 4 cups (1¼ lb/625 g) of the flour, the salt, and yeast. In a saucepan over low heat, combine the water, milk, and butter. Heat briefly, stirring often, until lukewarm (110°F/43°C). Slowly stir the water-milk mixture into the flour mixture, incorporating enough of the remaining flour to make a soft dough that holds its shape well.

Knead by hand or with a stand mixer (see page 403), adding flour as necessary: Knead by hand until smooth and elastic, about 10 minutes; knead by stand mixer with the dough hook on low speed until the dough is sticky and pulls cleanly from the bowl sides, 6–7 minutes.

Form the dough into a compact ball and place in a clean, oiled bowl, turning the dough to coat all sides. Cover the bowl with oiled plastic wrap and let the dough rise until doubled, 45–60 minutes.

Oil two 8½-by-4½-inch (21.5-by-11.5-cm) loaf pans. Turn out the dough onto a lightly floured work surface and press flat. Cut in half and form each half into a ball. Using a rolling pin, roll out each ball into a 12-by-7-inch (30-by-18-cm) rectangle. Starting from a short side, roll up the dough like a jelly roll. Pinch the seams and ends to seal and place in the prepared pans, seam sides down. Cover loosely with oiled plastic wrap, and let rise in a warm place until doubled, 30–45 minutes.

Preheat the oven to 400°F (200°C).

Brush the loaves with the egg yolk mixture. Bake until golden brown and the loaves sound hollow when tapped on the bottoms, 30–40 minutes. Turn the loaves out onto wire racks to cool completely.

5–6 cups (25–30 oz/ 780–940 g) unbleached bread (strong) flour

2 teaspoons salt

1 package (2¼ teaspoons) quick-rise yeast

1 cup (8 fl oz/250 ml) water

1 cup (8 fl oz/250 ml) milk

3 tablespoons unsalted butter

Canola oil for bowl and pans

1 egg yolk beaten with 1 teaspoon water

MAKES TWO 1¼-LB (625-G) LOAVES

404

HONEY AND BRAN LOAF

Unlike typical high-fiber loaves, which can be dense and heavy, this bread has a light texture and a delicate, nutty flavor. Serve it alongside a green salad for dinner, or spread with Maple-Cranberry Butter (page 37) or Honey Butter (page 433) for a satisfying snack.

1 package (2¼ teaspoons) quick-rise yeast

2½ cups (20 fl oz/ 625 ml) lukewarm water (110°F/43°C)

3 cups (15 oz/470 g) whole-wheat (wholemeal) flour

2–2½ cups (10–12½ oz/ 315–390 g) unbleached bread (strong) flour

2 cups (5 oz/155 g) wheat bran

¼ cup (3 oz/90 g) honey

1 tablespoon canola oil

1½ teaspoons salt

1 egg yolk beaten with 1 teaspoon water

MAKES TWO 23-OZ (720-G) LOAVES

In a small bowl, dissolve the yeast in ½ cup (4 fl oz/125 ml) of the lukewarm water and let stand until bubbles start to rise, about 5 minutes. In a large bowl or the bowl of a stand mixer, combine the whole wheat flour, 1 cup (5 oz/155 g) of the bread flour, and the bran. Stir in the remaining 2 cups (16 fl oz/500 ml) lukewarm water, the honey, oil, salt, and yeast mixture. Gradually stir in enough of the remaining bread flour to make a soft dough that holds its shape.

Knead by hand or with a stand mixer (see page 403), adding flour as needed: Knead by hand until smooth and elastic, about 10 minutes; knead by stand mixer with the dough hook on low speed until the dough pulls cleanly from the bowl sides and is no longer sticky, 6–7 minutes.

Form the dough into a compact ball and place in a clean, oiled bowl, turning the dough to coat all sides. Cover the bowl with oiled plastic wrap and let the dough rise in a warm place until doubled, 45–60 minutes.

Oil two 8½-by-4½-inch (21.5-by-11.5-cm) loaf pans. Turn out the dough onto a lightly floured work surface and press flat. Cut in half and form each half into a ball. Using a rolling pin, roll out each half into a 12-by-7-inch (30-by-18-cm) rectangle. Starting at a short side, roll up tightly and pinch the seams to seal. Place in the prepared pans, seam sides down. Cover with a clean kitchen towel and let rise in a warm place until doubled, 45–60 minutes.

Preheat the oven to 375°F (190°C).

Brush the loaves with the egg yolk mixture. Bake until well browned and a thin wooden skewer inserted into the center of each loaf comes out clean, 30–35 minutes. Turn the loaves out onto wire racks to cool completely.

Reviving bread

To refresh a slightly stale loaf of bread, sprinkle it with water, wrap it in aluminum foil, and bake it at 350°F (180°C) until it is warm and soft, usually about 10 minutes. It will be good for one more use.

405

WALNUT BREAD

Charlotte mold

Named for a classic baked French dessert, a charlotte mold is a round metal baking pan with slightly flared sides. If you don't have one, use a 1-qt (1-l) porcelain soufflé dish or other round, ovenproof mold for this recipe.

Scented with walnut oil and studded with chopped walnuts, this easy-to-make batter bread is delicious served in thin slices alongside a selection of artisanal cheeses. The dark molasses delivers a robust sweetness, and the walnut oil imparts a welcome richness.

In a large bowl, combine the whole-wheat flour, 1 cup (5 oz/ 155 g) of the bread flour, the salt, and the yeast. In a small bowl, stir together the warm water, egg, molasses, and oil. Stir the water mixture into the flour mixture. Using an electric mixer on medium speed, beat until smooth, about 2 minutes. Gradually beat in enough of the remaining bread flour to form a batter that almost holds its shape. (If it is too stiff, stir in a little warm water.) Cover the bowl with oiled plastic wrap and let the dough rise in a warm place until doubled, 45–60 minutes.

Oil a 1-qt (1-l) tinned-steel charlotte mold. Uncover the bowl and stir the batter to deflate. Stir in the walnuts. Spoon the batter into the prepared mold and smooth the top with a rubber spatula. Scatter walnuts evenly over the top (if using). Cover the mold with a clean kitchen towel and let the dough rise until doubled, 30–45 minutes.

Preheat the oven to 375°F (190°C).

Bake until the loaf is golden brown, 30–40 minutes. Turn the loaf out onto a wire rack to cool completely.

1 cup (5 oz/155 g) whole-wheat (wholemeal) flour

1¾–2 cups (9–10 oz/ 280–315 g) unbleached bread (strong) flour

½ teaspoon salt

1½ teaspoons quick-rise yeast

1 cup (8 fl oz/250 ml) warm water (115°F/46°C)

1 egg, at room temperature

1 tablespoon unsulfured dark molasses

2 tablespoons walnut oil

2 tablespoons chopped walnuts, plus more for sprinkling, optional

MAKES ONE 1¼-LB (625-G) LOAF

SOURDOUGH STARTER

About starters

Starters are typically kept for long periods of time and can even be passed from one generation to the next. Atmospheric conditions contribute to the starter's flavor, which is why sourdough loaves made from starters originating in a particular region (notably San Francisco) have a distinctive flavor.

A reliable method for initiating the fermentation process for a good starter is to mix commercial yeast with flour and water. Properly prepared, the mixture should bubble up and develop a good sour aroma. If your starter develops a foul odor or turns pinkish, discard it.

In a glass or earthenware bowl, combine the yeast and ½ cup (4 fl oz/125 ml) of the lukewarm water and let stand until bubbles start to rise, about 5 minutes. Stir in the 2½ cups flour and the remaining 2 cups (16 fl oz/500 ml) lukewarm water and mix well. Pour into a 4-qt (4-l) or larger ceramic or glass crock and cover with cheesecloth (muslin). Let stand for 4 days in a warm place (70°–75°F/21°–24°C). The mixture will bubble and ferment, increasing 4–6 times in volume and then sinking to its original size.

Transfer the starter to a tightly covered glass container and store in the refrigerator.

Feed the starter every 10 days by stirring in ½ cup (2½ oz/ 75 g) flour and ½ cup lukewarm water. Each time the starter is used, reserve at least 1 cup (8 fl oz/250 ml) of the original mixture and replace the amount taken with equal amounts of flour and lukewarm water. Bring to room temperature and stir gently before using.

1 package (2¼ teaspoons) active dry yeast

2½ cups (20 fl oz/625 ml) lukewarm water (110°F/ 43°C), plus lukewarm water as needed for feeding starter

2½ cups (12½ oz/390 g) unbleached bread (strong) flour, plus flour as needed for feeding starter

MAKES ABOUT 4 CUPS (32 FL OZ/1 L)

SAN FRANCISCO–STYLE SOURDOUGH BREAD

The dough for these loaves must rise slowly to develop the characteristic porous crumb, crisp crust, and wonderful sour tang. In San Francisco, famous for its truly sour sourdough, the bread can be found next to steaming bowls of cioppino or platters of cracked Dungeness crab.

1 package (2¼ teaspoons) active dry yeast

1 cup (8 fl oz/250 ml) lukewarm water (110°F/43°C)

2 cups (16 fl oz/500 ml) Sourdough Starter (opposite page), at room temperature

2 teaspoons salt

4–4½ cups (20–22½ oz/ 625–700 g) unbleached bread (strong) flour

Canola oil for bowl

Cornmeal for pan

MAKES TWO 1-LB (500-G) LOAVES

In a large bowl or the bowl of a stand mixer, dissolve the yeast in the lukewarm water and let stand until bubbles start to rise, about 5 minutes. Stir in the Sourdough Starter, salt, and 2½ cups (12½ oz/390 g) of the flour. Gradually stir in enough of the remaining flour to make a soft dough that holds its shape.

Knead by hand or with a stand mixer (see page 403), adding flour as necessary: Knead by hand until smooth and elastic, about 10 minutes; knead by stand mixer with the dough hook on low speed until the dough is no longer sticky and pulls cleanly from the bowl sides, 5–6 minutes.

Form the dough into a compact ball and place in a clean, oiled bowl, turning the ball to coat all sides. Cover the bowl with oiled plastic wrap and let rise in a warm place until tripled in volume, 2–3 hours.

Sprinkle a rimmed baking sheet with cornmeal. Turn out the dough onto a lightly floured work surface and press flat. Knead twice and cut in half. Form each half into a ball, stretching the sides down and under. Flatten each ball into a round loaf 8 inches (20 cm) in diameter. Place on the prepared baking sheet, cover with a clean kitchen towel, and let rise until doubled, about 1 hour.

Preheat the oven to 450°F (230°C).

Bring a kettle filled with water to a boil, and pour into a shallow pan. Carefully place the pan on the floor of the preheated oven. Holding a sharp knife at a 45-degree angle to the loaf, slash a shallow, diagonal grid pattern on top of each loaf. Bake for 15 minutes, then reduce the oven temperature to 350°F (180°C). Continue to bake until the loaves are well browned and sound hollow when tapped on the bottoms, 20–25 minutes longer. Transfer the loaves to a wire rack to cool completely before serving.

Olive sourdough

To give this bread a distinctive olive flavor, stir in ½ cup (3 oz/90 g) Tapenade (page 388) with the starter and proceed with the recipe.

Slashing bread dough

Cutting slits in the top of yeast dough allows carbon dioxide and steam that builds up during baking to be released more evenly, helping to ensure that the bread develops a more uniform shape. The slashes also increase the surface area of the crust.

HEARTY COUNTRY-STYLE BREAD

Three risings give this free-form loaf an airy texture, and lightly spraying the walls and floor of the oven with water helps to ensure a crisp crust. Sprinkling the loaf with flour before baking lends a pleasingly rustic look after baking. This is a versatile bread, perfect for everyday use.

A substitute for high-gluten flour

High-gluten flour is available by mail order through specialty baking suppliers. If you can't locate it, use additional bread (strong) flour in this recipe. The bread will not be quite as chewy, but it will still be delicious.

In a large bowl or the bowl of a stand mixer, combine 1 cup (5 oz/155 g) of the bread flour, the high-gluten flour, salt, and the yeast. Add the lukewarm water and stir well. Gradually stir in enough of the remaining flour to make a soft dough that holds its shape.

Knead by hand or with a stand mixer (see page 403), adding flour as necessary: Knead by hand until smooth and elastic, about 10 minutes; knead by stand mixer with the dough hook on low speed until the dough is no longer sticky and pulls cleanly from the bowl sides, 5–6 minutes. Form the dough into a compact ball and place in a clean, oiled bowl, turning to coat all sides. Cover the bowl with oiled plastic wrap and let the dough rise in a warm place until it has doubled in volume, 45–60 minutes.

Turn out the dough onto a lightly floured work surface and press flat. Knead for 1 minute, form into a ball, and return to the oiled bowl, again turning to coat all sides. Cover and let rise until doubled, 30–45 minutes.

Turn out the dough onto a lightly floured surface and press flat. Form into a ball, stretching the sides down and under, then form into a plump oval. Sprinkle a rimmed baking sheet with cornmeal, place the loaf on it, and cover with a clean kitchen towel. Let rise until doubled, about 30 minutes.

Preheat the oven to 400°F (200°C).

Uncover the loaf and sprinkle with bread flour. Using a sharp knife, make 3 parallel diagonal cuts, each ½ inch (12 mm) deep, across the top. Using a spray bottle, spritz the oven sides and floor with water. Bake until the bread is browned and crusty and sounds hollow when tapped on the bottom, 30–35 minutes. Transfer to a wire rack to cool completely.

2¾–3¼ cups (14–16½ oz/ 440–515 g) unbleached bread (strong) flour

¾ cup (4 oz/125 g) high-gluten flour

1 tablespoon salt

1 package (2¼ teaspoons) quick-rise yeast

2 cups (16 fl oz/500 ml) lukewarm water (110°F/43°C)

Canola oil for bowl

Cornmeal for pan

MAKES ONE 1½-LB (750-G) OVAL LOAF

POTATO BREAD

This delicious bread supplements the flour with mashed potatoes, whose natural starch contributes to a pleasingly mild flavor and open-crumbed texture. Remember to save the potato cooking water. The natural sugar into the water helps feed the yeast during proofing.

2 small starchy potatoes, about ½ lb (250 g) total weight, peeled and quartered

1 package (2¼ teaspoons) quick-rise yeast

3½–4 cups (17½–20 oz/ 545–625 g) unbleached bread (strong) flour

1 tablespoon corn oil

1½ teaspoons salt

MAKES ONE 22-OZ (685-G) LOAF

In a saucepan, combine the potatoes with water to cover. Bring to a boil and cook until tender, 20–25 minutes. Using a slotted spoon, transfer the potatoes to a large bowl and reserve the water in the pan. Mash the potatoes until smooth; let cool. Pour ½ cup (4 fl oz/125 ml) of the potato water into another large bowl and let cool to lukewarm (110°F/43°C). Stir in the yeast and then 3 tablespoons of the flour. Let stand until bubbles start to rise, about 15 minutes.

Reheat ½ cup of the remaining potato water to lukewarm and add to the bowl with the yeast mixture along with the oil, salt, mashed potatoes, and 3 cups (15 oz/470 g) of the flour. Stir well. Gradually stir in enough of the remaining flour to a make a soft dough.

Knead by hand or with a stand mixer (see page 403), adding flour as necessary: Knead by hand until smooth and elastic, about 10 minutes; knead by stand mixer with the dough hook on low speed until the dough is no longer sticky and pulls cleanly from the bowl sides, 5–6 minutes. Form the dough into a compact ball and place in a clean, oiled bowl, turning to coat all sides. Cover the bowl with oiled plastic wrap and let the dough rise in a warm place until doubled, 1–1½ hours.

Oil a rimmed baking sheet and dust with flour. Turn out the dough onto a lightly floured work surface, press flat, and knead lightly for 2 minutes. Form into a ball and stretch the sides down and under (page 403). Flatten the dough into a round 10 inches (25 cm) in diameter and place on the prepared baking sheet. Cover with a clean kitchen towel and let rise until doubled, 30–40 minutes. Preheat the oven to 425°F (220°C).

Bake for 15 minutes, then reduce the heat to 375°F (190°C). Continue to bake until the loaf is browned and sounds hollow when tapped on the bottom, 35–40 minutes. Transfer to a wire rack to cool completely.

Starchy potatoes

Sometimes dubbed baking potatoes, these starchy tubers, have a high proportion of starch to water, which means they end up dry and lightly textured after cooking. Look for russet, Idaho, or Burbank potatoes in the market.

RYE BREAD

Cornmeal-lined pans

Baking bread on a layer of cornmeal helps prevent the loaves from sticking to the pan, which could hinder the rising process during baking. If you don't have cornmeal on hand, line the baking sheet with parchment (baking) paper before adding the dough.

Wonderful for making a variety of deli-style sandwiches, this robust, dark bread is also good spread with cream cheese and topped with lox, dill, and red onion for a weekend brunch. The addition of caraway seeds offers a delicious change of pace for morning toast.

In a large bowl or the bowl of a stand mixer, combine the rye flour, ¾ cup (4 oz/125 g) of the bread flour, and the whole-wheat flour. Add the salt, caraway seeds, and yeast and mix well. In another bowl, stir together the warm water, oil, and molasses. Pour the liquid mixture into the flour mixture, then stir to make a soft dough.

Knead by hand or with a stand mixer (see page 403), adding flour as necessary: Knead by hand until smooth and elastic, about 15 minutes; knead by stand mixer with the dough hook on low speed until the dough is no longer sticky and pulls cleanly from the bowl sides, about 10 minutes. The dough will be heavy. Form the dough into a compact ball and place in a clean, oiled bowl, turning to coat all sides. Cover with greased plastic wrap and let rise in a warm place until doubled, 1–1½ hours.

Turn out the dough onto a lightly floured work surface and press it out flat. Cut in half and form each half into a ball, stretching the sides down and under. Let rest for 5 minutes. Flatten each ball slightly and roll into a tapered log about 10 inches (25 cm) long. Sprinkle a rimmed baking sheet with cornmeal and place the loaves on it. Cover with a clean kitchen towel and let rise until doubled, 20–30 minutes.

Preheat the oven to 375°F (190°C).

Brush the loaves with the egg yolk mixture. Bake until they are browned and sound hollow when tapped on the bottoms, 25–30 minutes. Transfer to wire racks to cool completely.

2½ cups (7½ oz/235 g) medium rye flour

1–1½ cups (5–7½ oz/ 155–235 g) unbleached bread (strong) flour

1 cup (5 oz/155 g) whole-wheat (wholemeal) flour

2 teaspoons salt

2 teaspoons caraway seeds

1 package (2¼ teaspoons) quick-rise yeast

1½ cups (12 fl oz/375 ml) warm water (115°F/46°C)

1 tablespoon canola oil

⅓ cup (3½ oz/105 g) unsulfured dark molasses

Cornmeal for pan

1 egg yolk beaten with 1 teaspoon water

MAKES TWO 18-OZ (560-G) LOAVES

RUSSIAN-STYLE BLACK BREAD

This bread gets its deep brown, nearly black color from cocoa powder and dark molasses. Hearty and slightly sweet, it is studded with caraway and fennel seeds. Use it for breakfast toast or for sandwiches, particularly pastrami or Reuben.

2¼ cups (6½ oz/200 g) rye flour

2¾–3¼ cups (14–16½ oz/ 440–515 g) unbleached bread (strong) flour

¾ cup (2 oz/60 g) wheat bran

2 tablespoons unsweetened cocoa powder

1½ teaspoons caraway seeds, crushed

1 teaspoon fennel seeds, crushed

1 teaspoon salt

1 teaspoon sugar

1 package (2¼ teaspoons) quick-rise yeast

1 tablespoon red wine vinegar

3 tablespoons unsulfured dark molasses

4 tablespoons (2 oz/60 g) unsalted butter

1 teaspoon cornstarch (cornflour) dissolved in ½ cup (4 fl oz/125 ml) water

MAKES TWO 1-LB (500-G) LOAVES

In a bowl, whisk together the rye flour and 2¾ cups (14 oz/ 440 g) of the bread flour. In another bowl, combine the bran, cocoa powder, caraway seeds, fennel seeds, salt, and sugar. Mix well, then add the yeast and mix again. Stir in 1 cup (4 oz/125 g) of the flour mixture.

In a saucepan over low heat, combine 1½ cups (12 fl oz/375 ml) water, the vinegar, molasses, and butter. Heat to lukewarm (110°F/43°C); the butter does not need to be entirely melted. Stir into the bran mixture. Add ½ cup (2 oz/60 g) of the flour mixture and beat until smooth. Gradually stir in the remaining flour mixture to make a stiff dough.

Knead by hand or with a stand mixer (see page 403), adding flour as necessary: Knead by hand until smooth and elastic, about 15 minutes; knead by stand mixer with the dough hook on low speed until the dough is springy and pulls cleanly from the bowl sides, about 10 minutes. The dough will be heavy and slightly sticky. Form the dough into a compact ball and place in a clean, buttered bowl, turning to coat all sides. Cover the bowl with buttered plastic wrap and let the dough rise in a warm place until doubled, 45–60 minutes.

Butter two 8-inch (20-cm) round cake pans. Turn out the dough onto a floured work surface and press flat. Knead for 1 minute. Cut in half and form each half into a 6-inch (15-cm) round, stretching the sides down and under. Place in the prepared pans. Cover with a clean kitchen towel and let rise until doubled, 40–45 minutes.

Preheat the oven to 350°F (180°C).

Bake the loaves for 45 minutes. Put the cornstarch mixture in a saucepan over medium heat and cook, stirring, until it boils, turns clear, and thickens, about 1 minute. Remove the loaves from the oven, then remove from the pans. Brush with the cornstarch mixture and return to the oven, placing the loaves directly on the oven rack. Bake until the glaze sets and the loaves are browned and sound hollow when tapped on the bottoms, about 3 minutes longer. Transfer the loaves to wire racks to cool.

The flavor of rye bread

Caraway seeds have a strong, pungent taste that is closely identified with rye bread. Almost always used whole, they are found in many other breads throughout northern and central Europe and are also added to meat and poultry dishes.

411

FRENCH BAGUETTES

Baguette pans

Made from heavy-duty metal, baguette pans have 2 or more curved loaf cradles, with each cradle measuring about 2⅜ inches (6 cm) across. The center ridge is perforated to allow for good heat circulation, which contributes to even baking and a crisp crust. Look for baguette pans in cookware stores.

Testing kneaded dough

A good test to determine if you have kneaded the bread long enough is to insert your fingertips into the dough. If the indentation springs back, the dough is well kneaded. The dough should also have a shiny look to its surface.

The dough for these traditional loaves can be quite soft. If you do not have a stand mixer, stir together the ingredients as directed, then lift and turn the dough with a bench scraper, adding flour as needed, until the dough is firm enough to be kneaded by hand.

In the bowl of a stand mixer, combine 4 cups (20 oz/625 g) of the flour, the salt, yeast, and lukewarm water. Knead with the dough hook on low speed until the dough is elastic and pulls cleanly from the bowl sides, about 10 minutes. The dough will be very soft. Turn out onto a lightly floured surface and knead for 1 minute. Form a compact ball and place in a clean, lightly oiled bowl. Dust the dough lightly with flour, cover with oiled plastic wrap, and let rise in a warm place until doubled, 45–60 minutes.

Turn out the dough onto a lightly floured work surface. Press flat, knead for a few seconds, and return to the bowl. Cover the dough with oiled plastic wrap and let rise again until doubled, 20–30 minutes.

Line each of 2 double baguette pans (4 molds total), each 18 inches (45 cm) long and 6 inches (15 cm) wide, with a clean kitchen towel and sprinkle the towel with flour, rubbing it into the fabric. Turn out the dough onto a lightly floured work surface and press flat. Cut into 4 equal pieces, knead into balls, and let rest for 5 minutes. Press each ball flat and fold into thirds. Using your palms, roll each into a rope 16 inches (40 cm) long with tapered ends. Place in the towel-lined pans. Cover with a clean kitchen towel and let rise until doubled, about 20 minutes.

Preheat the oven to 450°F (230°C).

Bring a kettle filled with water to a boil, and pour into a shallow pan. Carefully place the pan on the floor of the preheated oven. Pull the pans out from under the dough-filled towels. Oil the pans and sprinkle with cornmeal. One at a time, flip the loaves into the pans, underside up. Brush with the egg white mixture. Using a sharp knife, make 3 parallel diagonal cuts, each ¼ inch (6 mm) deep, on each loaf. Using a spray bottle, spritz the oven sides and floor with water. Bake until the loaves are browned and crusty, 20–25 minutes. Turn the baguettes out onto wire racks to cool. Serve warm or at room temperature.

5–5½ cups (25–27½ oz/ 780–855 g) unbleached bread (strong) flour

2 teaspoons salt

1 package (2¼ teaspoons) quick-rise yeast

2 cups (16 fl oz/500 ml) lukewarm water (110°F/43°C)

Canola oil for bowl and pans

Cornmeal for pans

1 egg white beaten with a pinch of salt

MAKES FOUR ½-LB (250-G) BAGUETTES

CHALLAH

Challah is the traditional Jewish egg bread served on the Sabbath. Although it can be shaped in many different ways, such as rolls and knots, a braided loaf is the most common. Here, the addition of fragrant saffron turns the finished bread a deep gold.

About 5 cups (25 oz/780 g) all-purpose (plain) flour

¼ cup (2 oz/60 g) sugar

1 tablespoon active dry yeast

1 teaspoon salt

⅛ teaspoon powdered saffron

1¼ cups (10 fl oz/315 ml) lukewarm water (110°F/43°C)

6 tablespoons (3 oz/90 g) unsalted butter, at room temperature

3 eggs

1 tablespoon milk

1 tablespoon sesame seeds

MAKES 1 LARGE LOAF

In a large bowl or the bowl of a stand mixer fitted with the dough hook, combine 1½ cups (7½ oz/235 g) of the flour, the sugar, yeast, salt, and saffron. Add the lukewarm water and beat by hand with a wooden spoon or on medium-high speed until well mixed. Beat in the butter and 2 of the eggs. Then beat in about 3 cups (15 oz/470 g) more flour to make a dough that is semisoft but no longer sticky.

Transfer the dough to a floured work surface and knead, adding more flour as needed to prevent sticking, until smooth and elastic, about 5 minutes. Form the dough into a ball and place in a clean, buttered bowl, turning to coat all sides. Cover the bowl with a clean kitchen towel and let rise in a warm place until doubled, about 1½ hours.

Turn out the dough onto a lightly floured work surface. Press flat and knead until smooth, about 3 minutes. Cut into 3 equal pieces. Cover with a clean kitchen towel to prevent drying. One at time, using your palms, roll the pieces into a rope 20 inches (50 cm) long. Butter a rimmed baking sheet. Arrange the ropes side by side, then braid them. Transfer the braid to the baking sheet, tucking the ends under. Cover with the kitchen towel and let the loaf rise in a warm place until doubled, about 1 hour.

Preheat the oven to 350°F (180°C).

In a small bowl, beat the remaining egg with the milk until blended. Brush evenly over the braid. Sprinkle with the sesame seeds. Bake until the bread is golden brown and sounds hollow when tapped on the bottom, about 55 minutes. Transfer to a wire rack to cool completely.

Challah variations

If desired, you can top the shaped dough with poppy seeds in place of the sesame seeds or use a mixture of the two seeds. Or, leave the bread unseeded for a more versatile loaf.

FOCACCIA

This flat Italian-style bread is delectable served warm from the oven accompanied by cheese, fruit, and a glass of wine. Or, split the foccaccia horizontally for making sandwiches. For the best flavor and texture, eat the focaccia the day it is baked.

In a large bowl or the bowl of a stand mixer, dissolve the yeast in the lukewarm water. Stir in the oil and the salt. Slowly stir in 3 cups (15 oz/470 g) of the flour to make a soft dough.

Knead by hand or with a stand mixer (see page 403), adding flour as necessary: Knead by hand until smooth and elastic, about 10 minutes; knead by stand mixer with the dough hook on low speed until the dough is no longer sticky and pulls cleanly from the bowl sides, 6–7 minutes. Form the dough into a ball and place in a clean, oiled bowl, turning to coat all sides. Cover the bowl with oiled plastic wrap and let rise in a warm place until doubled in volume, 45–60 minutes.

Oil an 11-by-17-inch (28-by-43-cm) heavy rimmed baking sheet. Turn out the dough onto a lightly floured work surface and knead lightly. Place on the prepared baking sheet and let rest for 5 minutes. Using your fingers, stretch out the dough so that it evenly covers the pan bottom. Cover with a clean kitchen towel and let rise until puffy, about 30 minutes.

Preheat the oven to 400°F (200°C). Using your fingertips, make a pattern of dimples at 2-inch (5-cm) intervals over the entire surface of the dough. Brush the surface with oil and lightly sprinkle with sea salt.

Bake until golden brown, 15–20 minutes. Serve warm.

1 package (2¼ teaspoons) quick-rise yeast

1¼ cups (10 fl oz/310 ml) lukewarm water (110°F/43°C)

2 tablespoons olive oil, plus more for brushing

2 teaspoons table salt

3–3½ cups (15–17½ oz/ 470–545 g) unbleached bread (strong) flour

Coarse sea salt for sprinkling

MAKES ONE 1-LB (500-G) FLAT BREAD

Focaccia toppings

You can easily vary focaccia by adding different toppings before baking. Try one of the following: ½ lb (250 g) yellow onions, thinly sliced and sautéed; ¾ cup (4 oz/125 g) pitted black or green olives; 2 tbsp chopped mixed fresh herbs; or 3–4 oz (90–125 g) Gorgonzola cheese, crumbled.

SESAME BREAD STICKS

Bread sticks are long, thin strips of bread dough baked until crisp all the way through. Shaped by hand, they are appealingly uneven when baked and will keep in an airtight container for up to 3 days. Serve these crunchy bread sticks with salad, soup, or a glass of wine.

In a large bowl or the bowl of a stand mixer, combine 2 cups (10 oz/315 g) of the flour, the salt, and the yeast. Stir in the lukewarm water. Gradually stir in enough of the remaining flour to make a soft dough.

Knead by hand or with a stand mixer (see page 403), adding flour as necessary: knead by hand until smooth and elastic, about 10 minutes; knead by stand mixer with a dough hook on low speed until the dough is no longer sticky and pulls from the bowl sides, 6–7 minutes. Form the dough into a compact ball and place in a clean, oiled bowl, turning to coat all sides. Cover with oiled plastic wrap and let the dough rise in a warm place until doubled, 45–60 minutes.

Turn out the dough onto a lightly floured work surface and press flat. Let rest for 5 minutes. Oil 2 rimmed baking sheets.

3–3½ cups (15–17½ oz/ 470–545 g) unbleached bread (strong) flour

2 teaspoons salt

1 package (2¼ teaspoons) quick-rise yeast

1 cup (8 fl oz/250 ml) lukewarm water (110°F/43°C)

Olive oil for bowl and pans

Bread stick variations

Change the flavor of these bread sticks by using cheese, herbs, or spices in place of the sesame seeds. Try ½ cup (2 oz/60 g) freshly grated Parmesan cheese, 2 tbsp dried thyme, 2 tbsp fennel seeds, or 1 tsp each coarse sea salt and coarsely ground black pepper.

1 egg yolk beaten with
2 teaspoons water and
½ teaspoon salt

1 cup (3 oz/90 g)
sesame seeds

**MAKES TWENTY 14-INCH
(35-CM) BREADSTICKS**

Using a rolling pin, roll out the dough into a 10-by-12-inch
(25-by-30-cm) rectangle about ½ inch (12 mm) thick. Using
a sharp knife, cut lengthwise into 20 strips each ½ inch
(12 mm) wide. Cover the dough pieces with a dampened
kitchen towel. Using your hands, roll out each strip to form
a rope 14 inches (35 cm) long. Place on the prepared pans
about 1 inch (2.5 cm) apart. Cover with a clean kitchen towel
and let rest for 20 minutes.

Preheat the oven to 300°F (150°C).

Bake the bread sticks, switching the pans between the
oven racks and rotating them front to back halfway through
baking, until lightly golden, about 25 minutes. Remove from
the oven and transfer to a work surface. Brush with the egg
yolk mixture on all sides, and then sprinkle with sesame
seeds. Return the bread sticks to the baking sheets. Continue
to bake until deep gold and crisp, 14–17 minutes longer.
Transfer to wire racks to cool completely.

**Italian
bread sticks**

*Bread sticks are
called grissini in
Italian. Serve them
as they would in that
country by wrapping
strips of thinly sliced
prosciutto around the
tops of each bread
stick and arrange on
an appetizer platter.*

BUTTERMILK DINNER ROLLS

These all-purpose dinner rolls, which are both mildly sweet and slightly tangy, complement
nearly any meal. They can be shaped two ways, in a casual pull-apart cluster in a cake pan and
in more refined knots on a sheet pan (see opposite).

Scant 1½ packages
(3½ teaspoons) active
dry yeast

⅓ cup (3 fl oz/80 ml)
lukewarm water
(110°F/43°C)

Pinch of sugar

1 cup (8 fl oz/250 ml)
buttermilk, heated to
tepid (90°F/32°C)

¼ cup (3 oz/90 g) honey
or (2 oz/60 g) sugar

½ cup (4 oz/125 g)
unsalted butter, melted

2 eggs, lightly beaten

1 teaspoon salt

4½–5 cups (22½–25 oz/
705–780 g) unbleached
all-purpose (plain) flour,
plus extra as needed

Canola oil for bowl
and pans

MAKES 36 ROLLS

In a small bowl, sprinkle the yeast over the lukewarm water,
stir in the sugar, and let stand until foamy, about 5 minutes.

In a large bowl or the bowl of a stand mixer, combine the
buttermilk, honey, butter, eggs, salt, and 1 cup (5 oz/ 155 g) of
the flour. Using a wooden spoon or the paddle attachment on
medium-low speed, mix until creamy. Add the yeast mixture
and 1 cup of the flour and beat for 1 minute. Gradually beat
in enough flour to make a soft dough.

Knead by hand or with a stand mixer with the dough hook
(see page 403) on low speed until the dough is smooth and
springy but still very soft, about 1 minute. Form the dough
into a ball and place in a clean, oiled bowl, turning to coat
all sides. Cover the bowl with oiled plastic wrap and let the
dough rise in a warm place until doubled, about 1½ hours.

Oil two 8-inch (20-cm) round cake pans. Turn out the dough
onto a lightly floured work surface and press flat. Cut the
dough in half. Using your palms, roll each half into a rope
18 inches (45 cm) long. Cut each rope into eighteen 1-inch
(2.5-cm) pieces. Cover with a clean kitchen towel. One at
a time, form each piece into a ball. Divide the balls evenly
between the prepared pans, arranging them so they are just
touching. Cover loosely with plastic wrap and let rise until
puffy, 30–45 minutes. Preheat the oven to 375°F (190°C).

Bake the rolls until light golden brown, 18–23 minutes.
Let cool briefly in the pans on wire racks. Serve warm.

Knot-shaped rolls

*To make slightly
larger knot-shaped
rolls, after the first
rise, divide the dough
into 24 equal pieces.
Roll each piece into
a 7 inch (18 cm) rope
and tie each loosely
into a knot, leaving
2 long ends. Cover
with a towel and
let rise until puffy,
30–45 minutes.
Arrange the rolls
1½ inches (4 cm)
apart on an oiled
baking sheet and
bake until golden,
12–14 minutes.*

POPPY SEED ROLLS

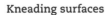

Kneading surfaces

Many bakers prefer kneading on a wood surface; it holds in warmth and creates a hospitable environment for the living yeast.

The crisp exterior of these elegant bread rolls contrasts nicely with their delicate crumb. Serve them any time of the day: with butter and jam for breakfast; split and layered with sliced meats and cheeses for lunch; or as an accompaniment to a first-course salad for dinner.

In a large bowl or the bowl of a stand mixer, combine 1 cup (5 oz/155 g) of the flour, the salt, and the yeast. Using a wooden spoon or the paddle attachment of the mixer on medium speed, beat in the warm water and butter until smooth. Add 1 cup (5 oz/155 g) of the remaining flour and continue beating until smooth. Gradually beat in enough of the remaining flour to make a soft dough.

Knead by hand or with a stand mixer (see page 403), adding flour as necessary: Knead by hand until smooth and elastic, about 10 minutes; knead by stand mixer with the dough hook until the dough is not sticky and pulls cleanly from the bowl sides, 6–7 minutes. Form the dough into a compact ball and place in a clean, buttered bowl, turning to coat all sides. Cover the bowl with buttered plastic wrap and let the dough rise in a warm place until doubled in volume, 45–60 minutes.

Turn out the dough onto a lightly floured work surface and press flat. Form into a ball and let rest for 5 minutes. Cut the dough in half. Using your palms, roll each half into a log 9 inches (23 cm) long. Cut each log crosswise into 9 equal pieces. Cover with a clean kitchen towel to prevent drying. One at a time, form each piece into a ball. Sprinkle 2 rimmed baking sheets with the cornmeal, and place the rolls on them, spacing them well apart. Cover with a clean kitchen towel and let rise until doubled, about 35 minutes. Meanwhile, preheat the oven to 425°F (220°C).

Brush the rolls with the egg white mixture and sprinkle with the poppy seeds. Using a spray bottle, spritz the oven sides and floor with water. Bake the rolls, switching the pans between the oven racks and rotating them front to back halfway through baking, until golden brown, 15–20 minutes. Transfer the rolls to wire racks to cool completely.

4½–5 cups (22½–25 oz/ 700–780 g) unbleached bread (strong) flour

2 teaspoons salt

1 package (2¼ teaspoons) quick-rise yeast

1½ cups (12 fl oz/375 ml) warm water (115°F/46°C)

4 tablespoons (2 oz/60 g) unsalted butter, at room temperature

Cornmeal for sprinkling

1 egg white beaten with 2 teaspoons water

Poppy seeds for sprinkling

MAKES 18 ROLLS

BAGELS

Chewy on the outside and soft on the inside, the distinctive texture of authentic bagels comes from the two-step process of first boiling and then baking them. Serve them simply with butter or cream cheese, or with a platter of lox and the trimmings for an easy brunch dish.

1 package (2¼ teaspoons) quick-rise yeast

2½–3 cups (12½–15 oz/ 390–470 g) unbleached bread (strong) flour

1 cup (8 fl oz/250 ml) milk, heated to lukewarm (110°F/43°C)

¼ cup (2 fl oz/60 ml) corn oil

1 teaspoon salt

1 egg, separated

1 tablespoon sugar

Poppy seeds, sesame seeds, or coarse sea salt for sprinkling

MAKES 16 BAGELS

In a large bowl or the bowl of a stand mixer, combine the yeast and ½ cup (2½ oz/75 g) of the flour. Stir in the lukewarm milk and let stand until frothy, about 10 minutes. Using a wooden spoon, beat in the oil, table salt, egg yolk, and sugar. Gradually beat in enough of the remaining flour to make a stiff but workable dough.

Knead by hand or with a stand mixer (see page 403), adding flour as necessary: Knead by hand until smooth and elastic, about 10 minutes; knead by stand mixer with the dough hook on low speed until the dough is no longer sticky and pulls cleanly from the bowl sides, 6–7 minutes. Form the dough into a compact ball and place in a clean, oiled bowl, turning to coat all sides. Cover with oiled plastic wrap and let the dough rise in a warm place until doubled, 45–60 minutes.

Turn out the dough onto a lightly floured work surface and press flat. Using your palms, roll into a log about 8 inches (20 cm) long. Cut into 16 equal pieces. Cover with a clean kitchen towel to prevent drying. One at a time, form each piece into a ball, then flatten it into a disk 2½ inches (6 cm) in diameter. For each disk, using the handle of a wooden spoon, make a hole through the center, then gently widen the hole to 1 inch (2.5 cm) in diameter. Leave the disks on the work surface, cover with a clean kitchen towel, and let rise until doubled, about 20 minutes.

Preheat the oven to 375°F (190°C). Oil a rimmed baking sheet.

In a pot, bring 3 qt (3 l) water to a boil. Reduce the heat to low. Slip 3 bagels at a time into the simmering water. Poach, turning once, for 3 minutes on each side. Using a slotted spoon, transfer to the prepared baking sheet; reform the holes if necessary.

Lightly beat the egg white and brush over the bagels. Sprinkle the bagels with the seeds. Bake until golden brown, about 30 minutes. Transfer to wire racks to cool completely.

Cream cheese spread

For a flavorful spread for homemade bagels, mix together 1 lb (500 g) whipped cream cheese, 2 tbsp chopped fresh dill, 3 tbsp chopped rinsed capers, 2 tbsp fresh lemon juice, and salt and ground pepper to taste.

Slicing bagels

Bagels can be tricky to slice, so take care to avoid cutting your fingers. Place the bagel flat on a cutting board. Using a serrated knife, begin cutting in the middle of one side of the roll, using a sawing motion. When you reach the center, stop cutting and turn the bagel clockwise. Continue to cut the next section. Repeat all the way around the bagel until it is completely split.

417

CHEDDAR CHEESE BUNS

These onion-topped cheese buns are the perfect addition to a brunch buffet or a surprising addition to a basket of sweet muffins or breads. You can also split them, spread the cut sides with mustard, and fill with slices of country ham.

In a small saucepan over medium heat, gently warm the milk until small bubbles appear around the edge of the pan. Remove from the heat, add the ⅓ cup (3 oz/90 g) sugar, the 4 tablespoons butter, and the salt; stir to dissolve the sugar. Let cool to lukewarm (110°F/43°C).

Meanwhile, in a small bowl, sprinkle the yeast over the lukewarm water, stir in the 1 teaspoon sugar, and let stand until foamy, about 5 minutes. Transfer the yeast mixture to a large bowl and add the lukewarm milk mixture, egg, and cheese. Using a wooden spoon, beat until smooth. Add 3 cups (15 oz/470 g) of the flour and beat until well mixed. Continue adding the flour, about ½ cup (2½ oz/75 g) at a time and beating well after each addition, until the dough is smooth and comes away from the bowl sides, 10–12 minutes. (The dough can also be made with a stand mixer fitted with a dough hook; it will take 6–8 minutes.)

Turn out the dough onto a floured work surface, cover with the bowl, and let rest for 5 minutes. Then knead the dough until it is smooth and elastic and holds the imprint of a finger when poked, 7–9 minutes. Form the dough into a ball and place in a clean, buttered bowl, turning to coat all sides. Cover the bowl with a damp kitchen towel and let the dough rise in a warm place until doubled, about 1 hour.

Grease 3 baking sheets with the shortening. Using your hands, pinch off a tennis ball–size piece of dough, shape into a ball, and place on a prepared sheet. Repeat until all the dough is shaped, spacing the balls about 2 inches (5 cm) apart. Flatten each bun with your fingers, brush the tops with the melted butter, and sprinkle about 1 teaspoon onion over each bun. Cover with a damp kitchen towel and let rise until doubled, 30–40 minutes.

Preheat the oven to 375°F (190°C).

Bake until the tops are browned and the bottoms sound hollow when tapped, 25–30 minutes. Remove from the oven and serve warm.

1½ cups (12 fl oz/ 375 ml) milk

⅓ cup (3 oz/90 g) plus 1 teaspoon sugar

4 tablespoons (2 oz/60 g) unsalted butter, plus about 3 tablespoons, melted

1 tablespoon salt

2 packages (2¼ teaspoons each) active dry yeast

½ cup (4 fl oz/125 ml) lukewarm water (110°F/43°C)

1 egg, lightly beaten

1½ cups (6 oz/185 g) shredded sharp Cheddar cheese

About 6 cups (1 lb 14 oz/ 940 g) all-purpose (plain) flour

Solid vegetable shortening (vegetable lard) or nonstick cooking spray for baking sheets

1 yellow onion, finely chopped

MAKES ABOUT 30 BUNS

418

HOT CROSS BUNS

An Easter tradition, these are yeast rolls studded with dried fruits. Their name comes from the practice of marking each bun in the shape of a cross, signifying the holiday. Here, the buns are slashed with an X to evoke the traditional symbol, then brushed with a shiny, sweet glaze.

1 package (2¼ teaspoons) active dry yeast

3½–4 cups (17½–20 oz/ 545–625 g) unbleached bread (strong) flour

1¼ cups (10 fl oz/310 ml) milk heated to lukewarm (110°F/43°C)

1 teaspoon salt

3 tablespoons firmly packed light brown sugar

½ teaspoon ground nutmeg

½ teaspoon ground cinnamon

¼ teaspoon ground cloves

¼ teaspoon ground allspice

2 eggs, at room temperature

3 tablespoons unsalted butter, at room temperature, cut into small pieces

½ cup (3 oz/90 g) dried currants

½ cup (3 oz/90 g) golden raisins (sultanas)

¼ cup (2 fl oz/60 ml) milk and ½ cup (4 oz/125 g) granulated sugar, heated together until bubbling

MAKES 18 BUNS

In a small bowl, whisk the yeast and ½ cup (2½ oz/75 g) of the flour into the lukewarm milk and let stand until bubbles start to rise, about 10 minutes. In a large bowl or the bowl of a stand mixer, combine 3 cups (15 oz/470 g) of the flour, the salt, brown sugar, nutmeg, cinnamon, cloves, and allspice. Stir in the yeast mixture. Beat in the eggs, one at a time, and then beat in the butter.

Knead by hand or with a stand mixer (see page 403), adding flour as necessary: Knead by hand until smooth and elastic, about 10 minutes; knead by stand mixer with the dough hook on low speed until no longer sticky and pulls cleanly from the bowl sides, 6–7 minutes. The dough will be soft.

Form the dough into a ball and place in a clean, buttered bowl, turning to coat all sides. Cover with buttered plastic wrap and let rise in a warm place until doubled, 1½–2 hours.

Turn out the dough onto a lightly floured work surface and press flat. Scatter the currants and raisins over the dough. Fold in half, then knead to distribute the fruits. Dust lightly with flour and let rest for 10 minutes.

Butter and flour a rimmed baking sheet, tapping out the excess flour. On the work surface, using your palms, roll the dough into a log 9 inches (23 cm) long. Cut the log crosswise into 18 equal pieces. Knead each piece into a ball. Arrange the dough balls on the prepared baking sheet, spacing them well apart. Cover with a clean kitchen towel and let rise until doubled in volume, about 40 minutes.

Preheat the oven to 400°F (200°C).

Bring a kettle filled with water to a boil, and pour into a shallow pan. Carefully place the pan on the floor of the preheated oven Using a sharp knife, slash a cross ½ inch (12 mm) deep on each bun. Bake the buns until golden brown, 15–20 minutes. Transfer to wire racks and immediately brush with the sugar syrup. Serve slightly warm.

About allspice

Allspice tastes like a mixture of cinnamon, nutmeg, and cloves, but it is actually a single spice, the berry of an evergreen tree. For the best flavor, buy whole allspice berries and grind them at home in a spice grinder or in a mortar with a pestle.

Kneading with a food processor

Many food processors include a plastic kneading blade. If you wish to use a food processor for kneading, follow the manufacturer's instructions. Take care not to overknead the bread, which can happen more easily with a machine than by hand. An over-kneaded dough will suddenly turn gooey and inelastic.

419

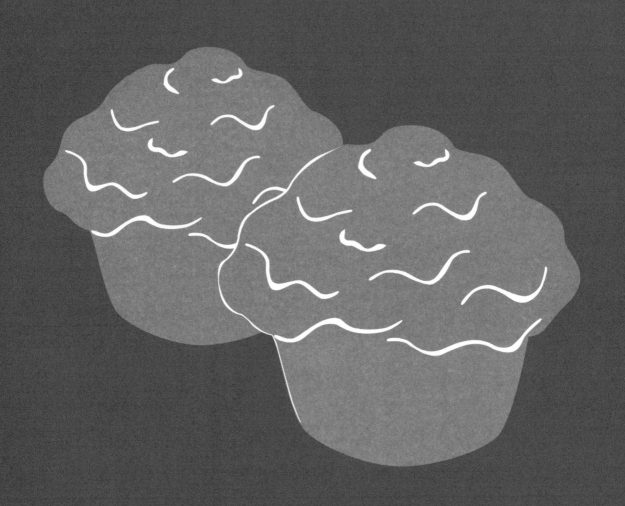

Muffins
& QUICK BREADS

Muffins & Quick Breads

Fresh-baked breads are within every home baker's grasp thanks to recipes in which quickly mixed batters or doughs are leavened by baking powder or baking soda (bicarbonate of soda). In less than half an hour for muffins, biscuits, or scones, and no more than an hour for quick bread loaves, you can serve hot-from-the-oven sweet or savory treats to complement breakfast, brunch, lunch, teatime, or dinner.

Quick Bread Types

Greasing pans
To prevent quick breads from sticking, grease the sides and bottoms of pans with butter or oil. If oil is used in the batter or dough, use the same oil for greasing the pan. Nonstick cooking spray is another good choice for evenly coating muffin cups and other baking pans. Lightly greasing even nonstick pans guarantees that breads release effortlessly. If you are baking an especially dense batter, you may need to grease the pan, line it with parchment (baking) paper, and then grease the paper.

Greasing and flouring pans
Some recipes call for both greasing and flouring a pan. First, coat the pan lightly with oil or butter. Then add a small amount of flour and shake and tilt the pan to distribute it evenly, tapping out the excess.

Using paper liners
Paper liners for standard or miniature muffin cups are ideal for muffins that will be served at room temperature. They can be hard to remove from hot muffins without pulling away the crumb. They also speed cleanup and help keep stored muffins moist.

Depending on how they are flavored, mixed, shaped, and baked, quick breads are delightfully varied, ranging from small muffins and large coffee cakes served for breakfast or brunch to tender teatime scones to flaky, buttery biscuits to savory loaves for the dinner table.

MUFFINS Straddling the line between cake and bread, a muffin can be as healthful as the oat bran–laced, raisin-studded gems on page 426, or as decadent as the savory buttermilk-bacon version on page 427. The modern muffin is usually made from a batter leavened with baking powder or baking soda (bicarbonate of soda) and is baked in distinctive multiwelled pans with cup-shaped compartments.

SCONES Originally from Scotland, these quick breads are made from lightly kneaded dough enriched with butter and heavy (double) cream. Traditionally, scones were unleavened, featured oat flour and sometimes dried currants, and were shaped into large, flat cakes, scored into wedges, and cooked on a hot griddle. Modern scones are usually made from wheat flour and baked in the oven. They can be flavored with a variety of fruits or spices and are formed into rounds or other shapes, such as the heart-shaped scones on page 429.

BISCUITS These small, raised quick breads are usually unsweetened and served piping hot or warm. Biscuits, which are most readily associated with the cooking of the American South, are generally made from white flour, butter, a leavening agent, and milk or buttermilk. The most desirable qualities for most biscuits are tenderness, flakiness, and a rich yet delicate flavor. They should be served straight from the oven, split, and spread with butter, preserves, or honey. They are also delicious bases for miniature baked ham or roast turkey sandwiches.

QUICK BREAD LOAVES The batters for quick bread loaves and muffins are basically interchangeable, with the pan in which they are baked defining the outcome. Freshly baked loaves, such as the crowd-pleasing banana-nut bread on page 434, are usually allowed to cool in their pan briefly, and then are turned out onto wire racks to cool so their crusts will remain lightly crisp. Traditional loaf pans are not the only option for baking these breads. Shallow square or round pans or decoratively shaped pans are also good choices.

COFFEE AND TEA CAKES Some quick breads seem more like cakes than breads, and are popular candidates for serving with morning coffee or afternoon tea. These range from pecan-studded Cinnamon Streusel Coffee Cake (page 438) to fruity Blueberry Crumb Cake (page 438) to pleasantly spiced Lemon-Clove Tea Cake (page 439).

Quick Bread Basics

LEAVENING Most quick breads rise because they contain baking powder or baking soda (bicarbonate of soda), chemical leavening agents that react with liquids and heat to release carbon dioxide gas, which gives batters a lift.

Baking powder is a mixture of an acid and an alkaline, or base, that is activated when exposed to moisture or heat. It also typically includes cornstarch (cornflour), which absorbs moisture to keep the powder dry, preventing a reaction until liquid is added. Nearly all baking powder sold today is "double acting," which means that it contains two acids that react at two different times: cream of tartar, which dissolves quickly, releasing some gas as soon as it comes in contact with liquid, and either sodium aluminum sulfate or anhydrous monocalcium phosphate, which dissolves more slowly and reacts later, when the batter or dough is exposed to the heat of the oven.

Baking soda is an alkaline, or base, that releases carbon dioxide gas only when it comes into contact with acidic ingredients such as sour cream, yogurt, buttermilk, or citrus juice. When a recipe calls for baking soda alone, rather than baking soda and baking powder, an acidic ingredient must also be present. Also, because baking soda is single, rather than double, acting, wet and dry ingredients should be mixed separately for recipes leavened by it alone. Then, as soon as the two mixtures are combined, the quick bread should go directly into its pan and straight into a preheated oven.

BAKING AND COOLING Unless otherwise specified, always bake quick breads on the middle rack of the oven. If baking more than one pan at a time, allow at least 2 inches (5 cm) between the pans so heat can circulate freely. If you are doubling a muffin recipe and using two pans, arrange them side by side rather than on separate racks. Avoid opening the oven until near the end of baking, or the temperature will drop, causing the item to rise unevenly.

Always check breads 5 to 10 minutes before the end of the specified baking time to make sure the tops are not browning too fast. Muffins are done when golden brown around the edges and springy to the touch. Most quick bread loaves are ready when they look well risen, their tops are browned, they have begun to pull away from the pan sides, and they have a characteristic crack down the center. Coffee cakes are generally done when the top or topping is golden brown. To check the interior of a muffin, quick bread, or coffee cake for doneness, insert a wooden toothpick into the center; it should come out clean.

Most muffins and quick breads are cooled in their pans on wire racks for 5 minutes or more. This allows some of the heat to dissipate, which helps to set a tender texture. They are then unmolded and cooled upright on the racks.

Many loaves and coffee cakes are easiest to slice when cooled to room temperature, which allows their textures to set properly. If sliced too soon after baking, they will be too crumbly. For this reason, some cooled quick loaf breads are wrapped in plastic wrap and refrigerated or left at room temperature overnight before serving.

STORING Once they are completely cooled, most muffins, coffee cakes, and quick bread loaves are good keepers. Muffins can be kept in plastic bags for up to 1 week at room temperature. If they contain cheese or other ingredients that can spoil easily, store them in the refrigerator. Most coffee cakes and quick breads can be wrapped and stored in the refrigerator for up to 4 days.

Muffins and quick bread slices, and whole quick breads and coffee cakes can be frozen for up to 3 months in doubled zippered plastic bags. Be sure to label and date the baked goods before freezing.

Toppings
Muffins and quick breads are easily enhanced with simple flourishes. A sweet crumble or streusel topping adds an attractive, flavorful, crunchy crust to such recipes as Cinnamon Streusel Coffee Cake (page 438) or to a batch of spice-laced muffins.

Fillings
Other treats can be hidden inside a muffin or quick bread before baking: spoon half of the batter into the muffin cups or loaf pan, add jam, cream cheese, chopped chocolate, or chunks of ripe summer fruit, and cover with the remaining batter.

423

Glazes
A thin coating of glaze or a flavored sugar syrup can be spooned or drizzled on top after baking. If you are using a thin syrup on a relatively dense loaf hot from the oven, poke holes over its surface with the tines of a fork or a thin skewer, then drizzle the syrup over it.

Reheating quick breads
To reheat quick breads and coffee cakes, warm the unwrapped item on a baking sheet in a preheated 300°F (150°C) oven until heated through, 10 to 20 minutes. Muffins, slices of quick-bread loaves, and wedges of coffee cake need only 5 to 8 minutes.

Flours for muffins and quick breads
For a guide to some of the most common flours used for making muffins and other quick breads, see page 403.

BLUEBERRY MUFFINS

Fiber-rich muffins

For a heartier muffin filled with healthful fiber, reduce the flour to 1½ cups (7½ oz/235 g) and add ½ cup (1½ oz/ 45 g) toasted wheat germ to the dry ingredients.

These muffins are sweet, buttery, and delicately spiced, with a cakelike texture. Fresh blueberries are the best choice here, but frozen berries can be used. Stir them into the batter without thawing them first, or their dark juice will turn the muffins purple.

Preheat the oven to 400°F (200°C). Butter 16 standard muffin cups; fill any unused cups one-third full with water.

In a bowl, stir together the flour, sugar, baking powder, baking soda, salt, and cinnamon. Set aside. In another bowl, whisk together the milk, melted butter, and eggs until smooth. Add the flour mixture to the milk mixture and stir just until blended. Add the blueberries and stir just until they are evenly incorporated.

Spoon the batter into the prepared muffin cups, filling them about three-fourths full. Bake until a toothpick inserted into the center of a muffin comes out clean, 15–20 minutes. Let cool in the pans on wire racks for 3–5 minutes, then remove. Serve warm or at room temperature.

2 cups (10 oz/315 g)
all-purpose (plain) flour

⅔ cup (5 oz/155 g) sugar

2½ teaspoons
baking powder

¼ teaspoon baking soda
(bicarbonate of soda)

½ teaspoon salt

1 teaspoon ground
cinnamon

1 cup (8 fl oz/250 ml) milk

½ cup (4 oz/125 g)
unsalted butter, melted

2 eggs

1 cup (4 oz/125 g)
blueberries

MAKES 16 MUFFINS

POPPY SEED MUFFINS

Glaze for muffins

*Stir together
1 cup (4 oz/125 g) confectioners' (icing) sugar, sifted; 2 tbsp fresh lemon or orange juice; and 2 tsp grated lemon or orange zest, adding more citrus juice if needed to achieve a good consistency.*

Poppy seeds have a mild yet unique flavor that is both earthy and a little peppery. Mixed into the batter, they provide a subtle textural contrast to the cakelike texture of the muffins. The light spiciness of the seeds is nicely complemented by a sweet lemon glaze.

Preheat the oven to 400°F (200°C). Butter 12 standard muffin cups; fill any unused cups one-third full with water.

In a bowl, stir together the flour, poppy seeds, sugar, baking powder, and salt. Set aside. In another bowl, whisk together the milk, egg, and melted butter until smooth. Add the milk mixture to the flour mixture and stir just until blended.

Spoon the batter into the prepared muffin cups, filling them about two-thirds full. Bake until a toothpick inserted into the center of a muffin comes out clean, 15–18 minutes. Let cool in the pan on a wire rack for 3–5 minutes, drizzling the hot muffins with the glaze, if using. Then remove from the pan. Serve warm or at room temperature.

2 cups (10 oz/315 g)
all-purpose (plain) flour

⅓ cup (1½ oz/45 g)
poppy seeds

⅓ cup (3 oz/90 g) sugar

1 tablespoon baking powder

½ teaspoon salt

1 cup (8 fl oz/250 ml) milk

1 egg

4 tablespoons (2 oz/60 g)
unsalted butter, melted

Lemon glaze, optional
(see note, left)

MAKES 12 MUFFINS

STRAWBERRY-ORANGE MUFFINS

These pretty muffins are laced with strawberry slices and orange zest. They also have a dab of strawberry jam hidden in the center. Sour cream in the batter makes them moist and tangy. Slice the berries thinly, then pat them dry to keep their juices from coloring the batter.

2¼ cups (11½ oz/360 g) all-purpose (plain) flour

2 teaspoons baking powder

1 teaspoon baking soda (bicarbonate of soda)

½ teaspoon salt

¾ cup (6 oz/185 g) sugar

½ cup (4 fl oz/125 ml) *each* milk and sour cream

⅓ cup (3 fl oz/80 ml) canola oil

1 egg

1 tablespoon grated orange zest

1 cup (6 oz/185 g) thinly sliced strawberries

About ⅓ cup (4 oz/125 g) strawberry jam

MAKES 16 MUFFINS

Preheat the oven to 400°F (200°C). Oil 16 standard muffin cups; fill any unused cups one-third full with water.

In a bowl, stir together the flour, baking powder, baking soda, and salt. Set aside. In another bowl, whisk together the sugar, milk, sour cream, oil, egg, and orange zest until smooth; stir in the strawberries. Add the milk mixture to the flour mixture and stir just until blended.

Place a spoonful of batter in each prepared muffin cup. Add a scant teaspoon of strawberry jam to each cup, then spoon the remaining batter on top, filling each cup about two-thirds full. Bake until a toothpick inserted into the center of a muffin comes out clean, 15–18 minutes. Let cool in the pans on wire racks for 3–5 minutes, then remove. Serve warm or at room temperature.

Fruit jam fillings

Change the flavor of these muffins by replacing the strawberry jam with another fruit jam. Raspberry, blackberry, peach, and apricot are all excellent choices. You can also use orange marmalade, which will offer tangy bits of rind in every bite.

BANANA-WALNUT MUFFINS

These intensely flavored muffins get their taste from very ripe bananas (you'll need 2 or 3 fruits) and chopped walnuts. Using walnut oil in place of a flavorless oil reinforces the nut flavor. The muffins don't rise as high as some others, resulting in a pleasantly dense crumb.

2–3 large ripe bananas

1½ cups (7½ oz/235 g) all-purpose (plain) flour

¾ cup (6 oz/185 g) sugar

¾ cup (3 oz/90 g) walnuts, coarsely chopped

1½ teaspoons baking soda (bicarbonate of soda)

¼ teaspoon salt

½ cup (4 fl oz/125 ml) walnut oil

1 egg

3 tablespoons buttermilk

MAKES 10 MUFFINS

Preheat the oven to 375°F (190°C). Oil 10 standard muffin cups; fill any unused cups one-third full with water. Mash the bananas with a fork; you'll need 1¼ cups (10 oz/315 g).

In a bowl, stir together the flour, sugar, chopped walnuts, baking soda, and salt. In another bowl, whisk together the walnut oil, egg, mashed bananas, and buttermilk until blended. Add the banana mixture to the flour mixture and stir just until blended.

Spoon the batter into the muffin cups, filling them level with the rim of the cup. Bake until a toothpick inserted into the center of a muffin comes out clean, 20–25 minutes. Let cool in the pan on wire racks for 3–5 minutes, then remove. Serve warm or at room temperature.

Walnut oil types

For this recipe, do not use toasted walnut oil, as it is not the same as plain walnut oil. Store it in the refrigerator to prevent the highly perishable oil from becoming rancid. If you cannot find walnut oil, you can substitute canola oil in this recipe.

OAT BRAN MUFFINS

Evenly baked muffins

Filling empty muffin cups with water prevents the pan from buckling and the cups from smoking in the heat of the oven and helps the batter-filled cups to bake more evenly.

Oat bran muffins are lighter and more cakelike than wheat bran muffins. This recipe takes well to all kinds of additions, especially chopped dried fruits such as raisins, apricots, pears, or prunes; add up to 1½ cups (9 oz/275 g) of any one fruit or a combination.

Preheat the oven to 425°F (220°C). Oil 16 standard muffin cups; fill any unused cups one-third full with water.

In a bowl, stir together the oat bran, flour, brown sugar, baking powder, cinnamon, and salt. Set aside. In another bowl, whisk together the milk, eggs, and oil. Add the milk mixture to the flour mixture and stir just until blended.

Spoon the batter into the prepared muffin cups, filling each cup about two-thirds full. Bake until a toothpick inserted into the center of a muffin comes out clean, 15–18 minutes. Let cool in the pans on wire racks for 3–5 minutes, then remove. Serve warm or at room temperature.

2 cups (6 oz/185 g) oat bran

1 cup (5 oz/155 g) all-purpose (plain) flour

½ cup (3½ oz/105 g) firmly packed light brown sugar

4 teaspoons baking powder

1 teaspoon ground cinnamon

½ teaspoon salt

1¼ cups (10 fl oz/ 310 ml) milk

2 eggs

⅓ cup (3 fl oz/80 ml) canola oil

MAKES 16 MUFFINS

SPICE MUFFINS

Filling muffin cups with batter

Pay attention to the recipe cues indicating how much batter to put in each muffin cup. If the cups are too full, the batter can overflow the sides into the oven. If they contain too little batter, you will end up with homely flat-topped muffins.

The addition of heavy cream gives these muffins a fine, moist texture and a delicate crumb, making them a superb accompaniment to your morning coffee or afternoon tea. You can add ¼ cup (1½ oz/45 g) dark or golden raisins (sultanas) or currants with the liquids, if you like.

Preheat the oven to 400°F (200°C). Butter 12 standard muffin cups; fill any unused cups one-third full with water.

In a bowl, stir together the flour, sugar, baking powder, salt, nutmeg, cinnamon, cloves, and allspice. Set aside. In another bowl, whisk together the egg, cream, milk, and melted butter. Add the egg mixture to the flour mixture and stir just until blended.

Spoon the batter into the prepared muffin cups, filling them about two-thirds full. Bake until a toothpick inserted into the center of a muffin comes out clean, about 20 minutes. Let cool in the pan on a wire rack for 3–5 minutes, then remove. Serve warm or at room temperature.

2 cups (10 oz/315 g) all-purpose (plain) flour

⅔ cup (5 oz/155 g) sugar

1 tablespoon baking powder

½ teaspoon salt

1 teaspoon *each* ground nutmeg and cinnamon

½ teaspoon *each* ground cloves and allspice

1 egg

1 cup (8 fl oz/250 ml) heavy (double) cream

½ cup (4 fl oz/125 ml) milk

⅓ cup (3 oz/90 g) unsalted butter, melted

MAKES 12 MUFFINS

CHILE-CORN MUFFINS

Moist and rich, these savory muffins are perfection when warm from the oven and spread with butter. Serve them alongside huevos rancheros for brunch or bowls of hearty chili for lunch. Roasted, peeled, and diced green chiles are readily available in cans.

¾ cup (4 oz/125 g) *each* all-purpose (plain) flour and yellow or white cornmeal

2 teaspoons baking powder

½ teaspoon baking soda (bicarbonate of soda)

½ teaspoon salt

1½ teaspoons chili powder

¾ cup (6 oz/180 g) sour cream

2 eggs

4 tablespoons (2 oz/60 g) unsalted butter, melted

¼ cup (2 oz/60 g) diced roasted green chiles

½ cup (2 oz/60 g) finely shredded Cheddar cheese

MAKES 12 MUFFINS

Preheat the oven to 400°F (200°C). Butter 12 standard muffin cups; fill any unused cups one-third full with water.

In a bowl, stir together the flour, cornmeal, baking powder, baking soda, salt, and chili powder. Set aside. In another bowl, whisk together the sour cream, eggs, and melted butter until smooth. Stir in the chiles and cheese. Add the sour cream mixture to the flour mixture and stir just until the batter is blended.

Spoon the batter into the prepared muffin cups, filling them about two-thirds full. Bake until a toothpick inserted into the center of a muffin comes out clean, about 15 minutes. Let cool in the pan on a wire rack for 3–5 minutes, then remove. Serve warm or at room temperature.

Muffin pans

Standard muffin pans have 6 or 12 cups, each with a capacity of 6 to 7 tbsp (3–3½ fl oz/ 90–105 ml). Muffin pans with jumbo cups or miniature (gem) cups are also available. Although aluminum and steel are common materials, cast iron tins with stick resistant surfaces are ideal.

427

BUTTERMILK-BACON MUFFINS

Apples and bacon are always a wonderful combination, including in these great-tasting muffins. Serve them for breakfast with fried or scrambled eggs or with a bowl of hot cereal, or surprise guests at a brunch party by tucking them into a basket of sweet muffins.

6 slices thick-cut bacon

1 small Golden Delicious apple

2 cups (10 oz/315 g) all-purpose (plain) flour

2 tablespoons sugar

2 teaspoons baking powder

½ teaspoon *each* baking soda (bicarbonate of soda) and salt

1 cup (8 fl oz/250 ml) buttermilk

⅓ cup (3 fl oz/80 ml) corn oil

1 egg

MAKES 12 MUFFINS

Preheat the oven to 400°F (200°C). Oil 12 standard muffin cups; fill any unused cups one-third full with water.

In a frying pan over high heat, fry the bacon until crisp, about 5 minutes. Transfer to paper towels to drain and cool. Crumble the bacon and set aside. Peel, core, and finely chop the apple and set aside.

In a bowl, stir together the flour, sugar, baking powder, baking soda, and salt. Set aside. In another bowl, whisk together the buttermilk, oil, and egg until smooth. Add the buttermilk mixture, apple, and bacon to the flour mixture and stir just until the batter is blended.

Spoon the batter into the prepared muffin cups, filling them about three-fourths full. Bake until a toothpick inserted into the center of a muffin comes out clean, about 20 minutes. Let cool in the pan on a wire rack for 3–5 minutes, then remove. Serve warm or at room temperature.

Better bacon

Look for thick-cut, apple wood–smoked bacon for this recipe. Smoking bacon over apple wood imparts pleasing sweet nuances to the meat that complement the chopped apple in the muffins.

POPOVERS

Popover pan

Resembling a muffin tin, a popover pan has deeper, narrower cups set in a sturdy metal frame that prevents the cups from touching one another. This unique construction helps the oven heat circulate evenly around the miniature breads, promoting even puffing.

Light, puffy, and hollow, popovers need to be baked just before serving, so have the ingredients measured and ready for quick assembly. For bigger popovers to accompany roast beef for a holiday dinner, use a jumbo muffin tin; the cooking time will be about the same.

Butter a 12-cup popover pan or butter the cups of a 12-cup standard muffin pan.

In a large bowl, whisk together the eggs and salt until blended. Stir in the milk and butter, and then beat in the flour just until blended. Do not overbeat.

Fill each prepared cup about half full and place in the cold oven. Set the oven temperature to 425°F (220°C) and bake for 20 minutes. Reduce the oven temperature to 375°F (190°C) and continue to bake until the popovers are golden, 10–15 minutes longer. They should be crisp on the outside.

Quickly pierce each popover with a thin metal skewer or the tip of a small knife to release the steam. Leave in the oven for a couple of minutes longer for further crisping, then remove and serve right away.

2 eggs

¼ teaspoon salt

1 cup (8 fl oz/250 ml) milk

2 tablespoons unsalted butter, melted and cooled

1 cup (5 oz/155 g) all-purpose (plain) flour

MAKES 12 POPOVERS

CURRANT SCONES

More scone flavors

It is easy to vary the flavor of these scones. For lemon-ginger scones, omit the currants and add ⅓ cup (2 oz/60 g) diced crystallized ginger and 2 tsp grated lemon zest. For cranberry-orange scones, omit the currants and add ½ cup (2 oz/60 g) chopped dried cranberries and 2 tsp finely grated orange zest.

In the past, these small Scottish cakes were always cooked on a griddle. Delicious for breakfast or afternoon tea, scones are at their best warm from the oven, split and spread with butter. Or, for a more traditional presentation, serve them with Citrus Curd (page 452).

Preheat the oven to 375°F (190°C). Butter and flour a baking sheet and tap out the excess flour.

In a bowl, sift together the flour, baking powder, salt, and sugar. Scatter the butter over the top. Using your fingertips, rub the butter into the flour mixture until the mixture resembles fine meal. Stir in the currants. Make a well in the center of the flour mixture and pour in the milk. Using a rubber spatula, quickly mix together to form a soft dough. Do not overmix.

Turn out the dough onto a lightly floured work surface and cut in half. Place each half on the prepared baking sheet. Lightly form each half into a round about ½ inch (12 mm) thick. Brush the tops with the egg yolk mixture. Using a sharp knife, score each round into 10 equal wedges, cutting about halfway through.

Bake until the scones are well risen and golden brown, 15–17 minutes. Let cool slightly on the pan on a wire rack, then cut apart. Serve warm.

2 cups (10 oz/315 g) all-purpose (plain) flour

1 teaspoon baking powder

¼ teaspoon salt

⅓ cup (3 oz/90 g) sugar

4 tablespoons (2 oz/60 g) cold unsalted butter, cut into 8 pieces

½ cup (3 oz/90 g) dried currants

½ cup (4 fl oz/125 ml) milk

1 egg yolk beaten with 1 teaspoon water

MAKES 20 SCONES

CHERRIES AND CREAM SCONES

Laced with tart dried cherries and rich cream and butter, these indulgent, heart-shaped scones are great for a Valentine's Day breakfast or afternoon tea. You can also cut them into rounds or squares for other occasions. They are best enjoyed on the day they are baked.

**2 cups (10 oz/315 g) plus
2 tablespoons all-purpose
(plain) flour**

**⅓ cup (3 oz/90 g) plus
2 tablespoons sugar**

1 tablespoon baking powder

½ teaspoon salt

**6 tablespoons (3 oz/90 g)
cold unsalted butter, cut
into 12 pieces**

**⅔ cup (3 oz/90 g) dried
pitted sour cherries**

**1 cup (8 fl oz/250 ml)
heavy (double) cream**

MAKES ABOUT 12 SCONES

Preheat the oven to 400°F (200°C).

In a large bowl, combine the 2 cups flour, the ⅓ cup sugar, the baking powder, and the salt. Scatter the butter over the top of the flour mixture. Using your fingertips or a pastry blender, work in the butter until the mixture resembles coarse crumbs. Using a fork, stir in the cherries and then the cream to form a soft dough. Let stand for 2 minutes.

Transfer the dough to a lightly floured surface. Sprinkle the dough with the 2 tablespoons flour. Gently press out the dough into a round ½ inch (12 mm) thick. Lightly flour a heart-shaped cookie cutter 3 inches (7.5 cm) in diameter and cut out as many scones as possible. Transfer the scones to ungreased baking sheets, spacing them 2 inches (5 cm) apart. Gather together the scraps, press out into a round ½ inch thick, and cut out as many additional scones as possible. Add to the baking sheets. Sprinkle the scones evenly with the 2 tablespoons sugar.

Bake until golden brown, about 15 minutes. Serve right away or transfer to a wire rack to cool.

Fresh leavening

To ensure all your quick breads keep on rising, replace baking powder or baking soda (bicarbonate of soda) that has been open in your pantry for more than 6 months.

429

BUTTERMILK CORN BREAD

Corn bread is wonderful served warm with butter for spreading. For herbed corn bread, add 1 teaspoon *each* dried sage and marjoram. You can also use this to make the red pepper stuffing at left. For a more traditional take on corn bread stuffing, see the recipe on page 31.

Preheat the oven to 400°F (200°C). Butter an 11-by-7-inch (28-by-18-cm) baking dish.

In a large bowl, stir together the cornmeal, flour, sugar, baking powder, salt, baking soda, and pepper. Scatter the butter over the top. Using your fingertips, rub the butter into the flour mixture until the mixture resembles coarse meal. In a bowl, whisk together the buttermilk and eggs until blended. Add to the cornmeal mixture and stir with a wooden spoon until thoroughly combined.

Transfer the batter to the prepared dish. Bake until the corn bread is golden brown on top and a toothpick inserted into the center comes out clean, about 30 minutes. Let cool in the pan on a wire rack. Cut the bread into squares and serve warm or at room temperature.

2 cups (10 oz/315 g) yellow cornmeal

1 cup (5 oz/155 g) all-purpose (plain) flour

⅓ cup (3 oz/90 g) sugar

1 tablespoon baking powder

¾ teaspoon salt

½ teaspoon baking soda (bicarbonate of soda)

1 teaspoon ground pepper

½ cup (4 oz/125 g) cold unsalted butter, cut into 12 to 16 pieces

1½ cups (12 fl oz/375 ml) buttermilk

3 eggs

MAKES 8–10 SERVINGS

Red pepper–corn bread stuffing

Cut the cornbread into small cubes and toast in a 375°F (190°C) oven. In a frying pan, sauté 2 red bell peppers (capsicums), diced; 2 onions, chopped; 3 celery stalks, chopped; and 2 tsp each dried sage and marjoram in 4 tbsp (2 oz/60 g) unsalted butter until tender. Add to the bread cubes along with 2 eggs, beaten. Season with salt and pepper. Bake as directed for the stuffings on pages 31–32.

430

IRISH SODA BREAD

This rustic round loaf, best eaten warm from the oven, is the traditional bread of Ireland. The dough will begin to rise as soon as you mix in the yogurt, so you will need to work quickly to get the loaf into the oven as soon as possible after mixing.

Place a large baking sheet in the oven and preheat the oven to 425°F (220°C).

In a large bowl, stir together the flour, oats, wheat bran, baking soda, and salt. Cut the butter into 8 pieces. Scatter the pieces over the top. Using your fingertips, rub the butter into the flour mixture until the mixture resembles coarse meal. Add the yogurt and quickly stir to blend the ingredients as evenly as possible, forming a rough ball.

Turn out the dough onto a lightly floured work surface and knead gently for about 30 seconds, dusting the dough with just enough flour to avoid sticking. The dough should feel quite soft to the touch.

Lightly dust a clean work surface with flour and set the ball of dough on it. Flatten the ball slightly into a 7-inch (18-cm) dome and sprinkle it with flour, spreading it lightly over the surface with your fingertips.

2¼ cups (11½ oz/360 g) unbleached bread (strong) flour

½ cup (1½ oz/45 g) old-fashioned rolled oats

¼ cup (½ oz/15 g) wheat bran

1½ teaspoons baking soda (bicarbonate of soda)

1 teaspoon salt

4 tablespoons (2 oz/60 g) cold unsalted butter

1½ cups (12 oz/375 g) low-fat plain yogurt

MAKES ONE ROUND LOAF

Bread for later

Since soda bread is best when fresh, consider making two small loaves instead of one large one. Reduce the baking time for the smaller loaves to 25 minutes, let cool, and freeze one loaf for later use. Or, bake a single large loaf, cut it in half, and freeze half.

Using a sharp knife, cut a shallow X from one side of the loaf to the other.

Remove the baking sheet from the oven. Using a large metal spatula, transfer the loaf to the preheated baking sheet. Bake until well risen, brown, and crusty and the loaf sounds hollow when tapped on the bottom, 30–35 minutes. Transfer the loaf to a wire rack to cool slightly, then serve warm.

Storing baking soda

Store your box of baking soda in a cool, dry place, as it tends to absorb moisture from the air.

OAT FLOUR BREAD

Oat flour is made by grinding whole oats to a powder. Here, it imparts the subtle taste of oatmeal and a sturdy, chewy character to a tasty breakfast bread. The loaf is crumbly when warm, so let it cool completely before slicing. It is also delicious toasted.

1 cup (5 oz/155 g) all-purpose (plain) flour

1 cup (5 oz/155 g) oat flour

¼ cup (2 oz/60 g) firmly packed light or dark brown sugar

2 teaspoons baking powder

½ teaspoon baking soda (bicarbonate of soda)

½ teaspoon salt

1 cup (8 fl oz/250 ml) buttermilk

1 egg

¼ cup (2 fl oz/60 ml) olive oil

¼ cup (1½ oz/45 g) raisins, optional

¼ cup (1 oz/30 g) chopped walnuts or almonds, optional

MAKES 1 MEDIUM LOAF

Preheat the oven to 375°F (190°C). Oil and flour an 8½-by-4½-inch (21.5-by-11.5-cm) loaf pan.

In a bowl, stir together the flours, brown sugar, baking powder, baking soda, and salt. Set aside. In another bowl, whisk together the buttermilk, egg, and oil until smooth. Stir in the raisins and nuts (if using). Add the buttermilk mixture to the flour mixture and stir just until blended.

Pour and scrape the batter into the prepared pan and spread evenly. Bake until a toothpick inserted into the center of the loaf comes out clean, about 50 minutes. Let cool in the pan on a wire rack for 10 minutes, then turn out onto the rack and let cool completely before serving.

Baking soda and buttermilk

Recipes calling for buttermilk are usually leavened all or in part by baking soda. Because baking soda is an alkaline, it reacts with the acids in the buttermilk, creating carbon dioxide bubbles that expand in the oven to create a light, airy crumb.

431

WHOLE WHEAT–WALNUT BREAD

Preventing overbrowning

When baking bread, check its progress 5 to 10 minutes before the end of the specified baking time to make sure the top isn't browning too fast. If it is, cover the bread loosely with aluminum foil and continue to bake until it tests done.

Dark and dense, this egg-free quick bread boasts a wheaty flavor and the crunch of toasted walnuts. Serve it with everything from hearty soups and stews to main-course salads to a plate of fruit and cheese. Easy to make, it is also a first-rate candidate for morning toast.

Preheat the oven to 350°F (180°C). Oil and flour a 9-by-5-inch (23-by-13-cm) loaf pan and tap out the excess flour.

In a bowl, stir together the flours, baking powder, baking soda, and salt. Set aside. In another bowl, whisk together the buttermilk, oil, and molasses until smooth. Stir in the walnuts. Add the buttermilk mixture to the flour mixture and stir just until blended.

Pour and scrape the batter into the prepared loaf pan and spread evenly. Bake until a toothpick inserted into the center of the loaf comes out clean, about 55 minutes. Let cool in the pan on a wire rack for 10 minutes, then turn out onto the rack to cool completely.

1½ cups (7½ oz/235 g) whole-wheat (wholemeal) flour

1 cup (5 oz/155 g) all-purpose (plain) flour

1 teaspoon *each* baking powder and baking soda (bicarbonate of soda)

½ teaspoon salt

1½ cups (12 fl oz/375 ml) buttermilk

⅓ cup (3 fl oz/80 ml) canola oil

⅓ cup (4 oz/125 g) unsulfured light molasses

1 cup (4 oz/125 g) chopped walnuts, toasted (page 17)

MAKES 1 LARGE LOAF

432

HERBED CHEESE AND BEER BREAD

Beer types

The bread will take on the flavor and character of whatever beer or ale you use. Choose your favorite, or try a different type each time you bake the recipe. Pilsner, pale ale, amber ale, or porter are good choices and will lend a wide variety of flavors to the loaf.

Even though no packaged yeast is called for in this recipe, the loaf has a wonderful yeasty flavor and aroma from the addition of the beer. With no milk or eggs, this is also an easy loaf to make. Serve it with a wide variety of soups and salads, or slice it thinly and use for sandwiches.

Preheat the oven to 375°F (190°C). Butter and flour a 9-by-5-inch (23-by-13-cm) loaf pan and tap out the excess flour.

In a bowl, stir together the flour, sugar, baking powder, baking soda, salt, and sage. Stir in the beer and cheese until the batter is completely blended.

Pour and scrape the batter into the prepared loaf pan and spread evenly. Bake until a toothpick inserted into the center of the loaf comes out clean, about 50 minutes. Let cool in the pan on a wire rack for 10 minutes, then turn out onto the rack to cool completely.

Unsalted butter for pan

2½ cups (12½ oz/390 g) all-purpose (plain) flour

2 tablespoons sugar

1 tablespoon baking powder

1½ teaspoons baking soda (bicarbonate of soda)

1 teaspoon salt

1 tablespoon chopped fresh sage

1½ cups (12 fl oz/375 ml) beer or ale, freshly opened

1 cup (4 oz/125 g) finely shredded Cheddar cheese

MAKES 1 LARGE LOAF

HONEY-NUT BREAD

Dense, moist, and golden, this lightly sweetened loaf is the perfect accompaniment to fruit-based breakfast dishes. The bread is even better the day after it is baked, making it a good loaf to have on hand for the holidays. For a round loaf, bake the batter in a springform pan.

1 cup (8 fl oz/250 ml) milk

1 cup (12 oz/375 g) honey

½ cup (4 oz/125 g) sugar

2½ cups (12½ oz/390 g) all-purpose (plain) flour

1 teaspoon baking soda (bicarbonate of soda)

1 teaspoon salt

¼ cup (2 oz/60 g) unsalted butter, melted

2 egg yolks

½ cup (2 oz/60 g) chopped walnuts

MAKES 1 LARGE LOAF

Preheat the oven to 325°F (165°C). Butter and flour a 9-by-5-inch (23-by-13-cm) loaf pan or a 7-inch (18-cm) springform pan and tap out the excess flour.

In a saucepan over medium heat, bring the milk to a simmer. Add the honey and sugar and stir until the sugar dissolves. Set aside to cool to lukewarm.

Meanwhile, in a bowl, stir together the flour, baking soda, and salt. Set aside. Add the melted butter and egg yolks to the cooled honey mixture and whisk until blended. Add the butter-honey mixture to the flour mixture and beat until thoroughly blended. Stir in the walnuts.

Pour and scrape the batter into the prepared pan and spread evenly. Bake until a toothpick inserted into the center of the loaf comes out clean, about 65 minutes. Let cool in the pan on a wire rack for 15 minutes, then turn out onto the rack (or release the pan sides) to cool completely.

Honey butter

This easy topping nicely complements the bread: In a bowl, beat together ½ cup (6 oz/185 g) honey, ½ cup (4 oz/125 g) room-temperature unsalted butter, and a large pinch of salt until light and fluffy.

433

PISTACHIO-OLIVE BREAD

Pistachios, black olives, and olive oil give this bread flecks of color and an enticing flavor and aroma. Greek olives are pungent and salty, so a few go a long way. Other cured olives can be used in their place (see page 63 for a guide to olive types).

1½ cups (7½ oz/235 g) all-purpose (plain) flour

1 tablespoon sugar

2½ teaspoons baking powder

½ teaspoon salt

¾ cup (6 fl oz/180 ml) milk

¼ cup (2 fl oz/60 ml) olive oil

2 eggs

⅓ cup (1½ oz/45 g) chopped pistachios

3 tablespoons chopped pitted Greek olives

MAKES 1 MEDIUM LOAF

Preheat the oven to 350°F (180°C). Oil and flour an 8½-by-4½-inch (21.5-by-11.5-cm) loaf pan and tap out the excess flour.

In a bowl, stir together the flour, sugar, baking powder, and salt. Set aside. In another bowl, whisk together the milk, oil, and eggs until smooth. Stir in the pistachios and olives. Add the milk mixture to the flour mixture and stir just until blended; do not overmix.

Pour and scrape the batter into the prepared loaf pan and spread evenly. Bake until a toothpick inserted into the center of the loaf comes out clean, about 50 minutes. Let cool in the pan on a wire rack for 10 minutes, then turn out onto the rack to cool completely.

Loaf pans

Also known as a bread pan, a standard loaf pan measures 9 by 5 by 3 inches (23 by 13 by 7.5 cm). A smaller pan, 8½ by 4½ by 2½ inches (21.5 by 11.5 by 6 cm), is also useful, as shown here. Metal loaf pans produce loaves with evenly browned crusts; glass ones tend to encourage fast browning, sometimes at the expense of the interior of the loaf.

WHOLE WHEAT BANANA-NUT BREAD

Freezing bananas for baking

If bananas are ripening quicker than they can be consumed, you can peel them, then wrap in plastic wrap and freeze for using at a later date. Frozen bananas keep for up to 3 months.

A slice or two of this dark, rich, sweet bread is good for breakfast, toasted and spread with softened cream cheese. This recipe makes two loaves; freeze one to enjoy later. For a firmer bread with a lighter crumb, substitute all-purpose (plain) flour for half of the whole wheat flour.

Preheat the oven to 350°F (180°C). Butter and flour two 8½-by-4½-inch (21.5-by-11.5-cm) loaf pans and tap out the excess.

In a bowl, stir together the flour, baking soda, and salt. Set aside. In another bowl, beat together the butter and sugar until blended (an electric mixer is useful for this step). Beat in the banana, then beat in the eggs until completely mixed. Don't worry if the mixture looks lumpy and curdled. Stir in the nuts. Add the flour mixture to the banana mixture and stir just until blended.

Pour and scrape the batter into the prepared loaf pans and spread evenly. Bake until a toothpick inserted into the center of the loaves comes out clean, about 1 hour. Let the loaves cool in the pans on a wire rack for 10 minutes, then turn out onto the racks to cool completely.

2½ cups (12½ oz/390 g) whole-wheat (wholemeal) flour

2 teaspoons baking soda (bicarbonate of soda)

1 teaspoon salt

1 cup (8 oz/250 g) unsalted butter, at room temperature

2 cups (1 lb/500 g) sugar

2 cups (1 lb/500 g) mashed ripe bananas (4 large fruits)

4 eggs

1 cup (4 oz/125 g) chopped walnuts or pecans

MAKES 2 MEDIUM LOAVES

OATMEAL-RAISIN BREAD

Buying rolled oats

Look for rolled oats, hulled and steamed whole-grain oats that have been pressed into flakes, in bulk bins of natural-foods stores or in the cereal aisle of the supermarket. Packaged rolled oats are typically labeled "old fashioned."

Golden, cakelike, and spicy, this bread is popular with adults and kids alike. Children, especially, enjoy it slathered with peanut butter and jelly. Other dried fruits, such as cranberries or sour cherries, can be substituted for the raisins.

In a bowl, stir together the buttermilk and oatmeal. Let stand for 30 minutes.

Preheat the oven to 350°F (180°C). Butter and flour an 8½-by-4½-inch (21.5-by-11.5-cm) loaf pan and tap out the excess.

In another bowl, stir together the flour, cinnamon, ginger, baking soda, baking powder, and salt. Set aside. Add the sugar, melted butter, eggs, and raisins to the oatmeal mixture and beat until blended (an electric mixer is useful for this step). Add the flour mixture to the oatmeal mixture and beat just until blended.

Pour and scrape the batter into the prepared loaf pan and spread evenly. Bake until a toothpick inserted into the center of the loaf comes out clean, about 1 hour. Let the bread cool in the pan on a wire rack for 10 minutes, then turn out onto the rack to cool completely.

1¼ cups (10 fl oz/310 ml) buttermilk

½ cup (1½ oz/45 g) old-fashioned rolled oats

1½ cups (7½ oz/235 g) all-purpose (plain) flour

1 teaspoon *each* ground cinnamon and ginger

1 teaspoon *each* baking soda (bicarbonate of soda) and baking powder

½ teaspoon salt

½ cup (4 oz/125 g) sugar

½ cup (4 oz/125 g) unsalted butter, melted

2 eggs

½ cup (3 oz/90 g) raisins

MAKES 1 MEDIUM LOAF

FIG AND ANISE QUICK BREAD

For a memorable finish to a company dinner, offer a plate of assorted farmstead cheeses, such as a fresh goat's milk cheese, a bloomy rind cheese, an aged hard cheese, and a pungent blue, with thin wedges of this aromatic round loaf. A glass of Port is a perfect accompaniment.

1 cup (5 oz/155 g) all-purpose (plain) flour

1 cup (5 oz/155 g) whole-wheat (wholemeal) flour

3 tablespoons firmly packed light or dark brown sugar

1½ teaspoons baking powder

1 teaspoon aniseed, lightly crushed in a mortar, plus more for sprinkling

½ teaspoon baking soda (bicarbonate of soda)

½ teaspoon salt

4 tablespoons (2 oz/60 g) unsalted butter, cut into 8 pieces, at room temperature

1 cup (6 oz/185 g) coarsely chopped dried figs

¾ cup (6 fl oz/180 ml) buttermilk, plus more for brushing

1 egg

MAKES 1 ROUND LOAF

Preheat the oven to 375°F (190°C). Butter a 9-inch (23-cm) round cake pan.

In a large bowl, stir together the flours, brown sugar, baking powder, 1 teaspoon aniseed, baking soda, and salt. Scatter the butter over the top. Using your fingertips, rub the butter into the flour mixture until the mixture resembles coarse meal. Stir in the figs.

In a small bowl, whisk together the ¾ cup buttermilk and the egg until blended. Make a well in the center of the flour mixture and pour the buttermilk mixture into the well. Stir the liquid ingredients into the dry ingredients just until blended and a soft dough forms.

Transfer the dough to a well-floured work surface and knead until smooth, about 20 turns. Form the dough into a ball. Place in the prepared pan and flatten to 1½ inches (4 cm) thick. Cut a large cross ⅓ inch (9 mm) deep into the dough. Brush with buttermilk and sprinkle with aniseed.

Bake until the bread is light brown and sounds hollow when tapped on the bottom, about 40 minutes. Turn out onto a wire rack and then turn right side up to cool. Serve warm or at room temperature, cut into thin wedges.

Aniseed

A popular addition to European-style baked goods, aniseeds are the seeds of the anise plant, a member of the parsley family. Used whole and ground, they impart a taste that is distinctly licorice.

435

CHOCOLATE-NUT QUICK BREAD

Grating instead of chopping

To make quick work of chopping small amounts of chocolate, run the chocolate chunk over the large holes of a grater-shredder instead of chopping it with a knife.

Richly flavored with chocolate, cinnamon, and nuts, this loaf doesn't rise especially high, but it has a sophisticated flavor and a lovely, moist texture. Cut it into generous slices and serve with Chocolate Whipped Cream (page 454) for an elegant dessert appropriate for any occasion.

Preheat the oven to 375°F (190°C). Butter and flour an 8½-by-4½-inch (21.5-by-11.5-cm) loaf pan and tap out the excess flour.

Place the egg whites and about half of the sugar in a bowl. Using an electric mixer on high speed, beat until stiff and shiny but not dry. Set aside.

Rinse the mixer beaters. In another bowl, combine the egg yolks and the remaining sugar and beat on high speed until thick and pale, 3–5 minutes. Beat in the melted butter and vanilla until incorporated.

In a large bowl, sift together the sifted flour and cinnamon. Stir the flour mixture into the yolk mixture, mixing until completely incorporated. Stir in half of the beaten egg whites to lighten the mixture. Then gently fold in the remaining egg whites just until combined. Fold in the chocolate and nuts just to distribute them evenly in the batter.

Pour and scrape the batter into the prepared pan. Smooth the top of the batter with a rubber spatula, mounding the batter slightly higher along the center. Bake until a toothpick inserted into the center of the loaf comes out clean and dry, 45–50 minutes. Let cool in the pan on a wire rack for 15 minutes, then turn out onto the rack to cool completely.

5 eggs, separated, at room temperature

¾ cup (6 oz/185 g) sugar

4 tablespoons (2 oz/60 g) unsalted butter, melted and cooled slightly

1 teaspoon pure vanilla extract

1 cup (4 oz/125 g) sifted all-purpose (plain) flour

¼ teaspoon ground cinnamon

3 oz (90 g) unsweetened chocolate, finely chopped

1 cup (4 oz/125 g) ground pecans, almonds, or toasted hazelnuts (filberts) (page 17)

MAKES 1 MEDIUM LOAF

BUTTERMILK BISCUITS

More biscuit shapes

Round is the classic shape for biscuits, but you can also pat out the dough into a rectangle and cut out squares. And that way, you'll have no scraps to reroll. You can also make drop biscuits by dropping the dough by tablespoons onto the pan.

Like other quick breads, biscuits are leavened with baking powder or soda instead of yeast, making them easy and quick to bake. Some insist that vegetable shortening (vegetable lard) makes a flakier biscuit than butter. If you like, replace half or all of the butter with shortening.

Preheat the oven to 425°F (220°C).

In a bowl, stir together the flour, baking powder, salt, and baking soda. Scatter the butter over the top. Using a pastry blender or 2 knives, cut in the butter until the mixture forms large crumbs the size of small peas. Add the buttermilk and stir with a fork just until the ingredients are moistened. Do not overwork the dough.

Turn the dough out onto a lightly floured work surface and knead gently and briefly just until it clings together. Pat the dough into a round about ¾ inch (2 cm) thick.

Lightly flour a 3-inch (7.5-cm) round biscuit cutter or cookie cutter and cut out as many biscuits as possible from the dough round. Transfer the biscuits to an ungreased baking

2 cups (10 oz/315 g) all-purpose (plain) flour

2 teaspoons baking powder

½ teaspoon salt

½ teaspoon baking soda (bicarbonate of soda)

6 tablespoons (3 oz/90 g) cold unsalted butter, cut into 12 pieces

¾ cup (6 fl oz/180 ml) buttermilk

MAKES ABOUT 10 BISCUITS

sheet, spacing them 1 inch (2.5 cm) apart. Gather together the dough scraps, press them out into a round ¾ inch (2 cm) thick, and cut out as many additional biscuits as possible. Add the new biscuits to the baking sheet.

Bake until light golden brown, 15–18 minutes. Let cool slightly on the pan on a wire rack, then serve warm.

CHIVE CREAM BISCUITS

For an extra burst of chive flavor, stir minced fresh chives into softened butter for spreading on the warm biscuits at the table. Or, for a bolder flavor, substitute ¼ cup (¾ oz/20 g) minced green (spring) onion, including the tender green tops, for the chives.

2 cups (10 oz/315 g) all-purpose (plain) flour

¼ cup (⅓ oz/10 g) minced fresh chives

1 tablespoon baking powder

½ teaspoon salt

1 teaspoon ground pepper, plus more for sprinkling

About 1⅓ cups (11 fl oz/340 ml) heavy (double) cream

2 tablespoons unsalted butter, melted

MAKES ABOUT 12 BISCUITS

Position a rack in the upper third of the oven and preheat the oven to 425°F (220°C).

In a large bowl, stir together the flour, chives, baking powder, salt, and pepper. Gradually stir in enough of the cream to form a dough that comes together into a ball.

Transfer the dough to a floured work surface and knead gently, adding flour as needed to prevent sticking, until smooth, about 10 turns. Roll out the dough ½ inch (12 mm) thick. Using a round biscuit cutter 2½ inches (6 cm) in diameter, cut out as many biscuits as possible. Transfer the biscuits to an ungreased baking sheet, spacing them 1 inch (2.5 cm) apart. Gather together the scraps, roll out ½ inch (12 mm) thick, and cut out as many additional biscuits as possible. Add to the baking sheet. Brush the biscuits with the melted butter and sprinkle with pepper.

Bake until light brown, about 15 minutes. Remove the biscuits from the oven and serve hot, or let cool on the pan on a wire rack and serve warm.

Cutting biscuits

When stamping out biscuits, do not twist the cutter. Lift straight up to prevent the sides of the dough from pinching together or twisting, which can inhibit rising or result in misshapen or tough biscuits.

437

CINNAMON STREUSEL COFFEE CAKE

A homemade coffee cake elevates any morning meal to a special occasion. This classic version is excellent with the day's first mug of coffee, as a midmorning snack, or cut into squares for a brunch buffet table. Substitute other nuts for the pecans, if you like.

Preheat the oven to 375°F (190°C). Butter an 8-inch (20-cm) square baking pan.

In a bowl, stir together the flour, 1 cup (8 oz/250 g) of the sugar, and the baking powder. Scatter the butter over the top. Using a pastry blender or 2 knives, cut in the butter until the mixture resembles coarse crumbs. Add the egg, milk, and vanilla and stir just until combined. Pour and scrape the batter into the prepared pan.

In another bowl, stir together the remaining ¼ cup (2 oz/60 g) sugar, the cinnamon, and the pecans. Sprinkle the pecan mixture evenly over the surface of the batter. Using a table knife, cut gently down through the batter at even intervals of about 2 inches (5 cm) to ease a little of the topping under the surface of the batter.

Bake until well risen and golden and a toothpick inserted into the center comes out clean, 25–30 minutes. Let cool in the pan on a wire rack for 15 minutes. Cut into squares and serve warm directly from the pan.

1¾ cups (9 oz/280 g) all-purpose (plain) flour

1¼ cups (10 oz/310 g) sugar

2 teaspoons baking powder

4 tablespoons (2 oz/60 g) unsalted butter, cut into 8 pieces

1 egg, lightly beaten

¾ cup (6 fl oz/180 ml) milk

1 teaspoon pure vanilla extract

2 teaspoons ground cinnamon

½ cup (2 oz/60 g) coarsely chopped pecans

MAKES ONE 8-INCH (20-CM) SQUARE CAKE; SERVES 8–12

438

BLUEBERRY CRUMB CAKE

Plump blueberries top this cinnamon and lemon–scented cake, which tastes best the day it is baked. It is a welcome addition on nearly any brunch table, but you can also serve it for dessert topped with vanilla-flavored Whipped Cream (page 454).

Preheat the oven to 350°F (180°C). Butter and flour a 9-by-13-inch (23-by-33-cm) pan and tap out the excess.

In a food processor, combine 2 cups (6 oz/185 g) of the flour and the brown sugar and pulse to mix. Add the butter and process until crumbly, about 20 seconds. Transfer to a bowl; measure out ¾ cup (6 oz/185 g) and reserve for the topping.

Add the egg to the remaining crumb mixture and mix well. In a small bowl, stir together the remaining ½ cup (1½ oz/45 g) flour, the baking powder, cinnamon, and lemon zest. Stir the flour mixture into the crumb mixture in 3 batches, alternating with the milk in 2 batches, beginning and ending with the flour mixture. Pour the batter into the prepared pan.

In a bowl, toss the reserved crumb mixture with the blueberries, and then scatter the mixture evenly over the batter. Bake until browned on top and a toothpick inserted into the center comes out clean, 30–40 minutes. Let cool in the pan on a wire rack for at least 20 minutes before serving.

2½ cups (7½ oz/230 g) sifted cake (soft-wheat) flour

2 cups (14 oz/440 g) firmly packed light brown sugar

½ cup (4 oz/125 g) cold unsalted butter, cut into 8 pieces

1 egg, beaten

2 teaspoons baking powder

1 teaspoon ground cinnamon

Grated zest of 1 lemon

1 cup (8 fl oz/250 ml) milk

1½ cups (6 oz/185 g) blueberries

MAKES 8–10 SERVINGS

LEMON-CLOVE TEA CAKE

Offer this dense lemon loaf cake with hot tea or coffee, or pack it into a box lunch for a loved one. It is best enjoyed the day it is made. If you bake it in advance, wrap it in aluminum foil and keep it at room temperature for up to 8 hours.

1½ cups (6 oz/185 g) cake (soft-wheat) flour

1 teaspoon baking powder

¼ teaspoon salt

¼ teaspoon ground cloves

¾ cup (6 oz/185 g) unsalted butter, at room temperature

¾ cup (6 oz/185 g) granulated sugar

3 eggs, at room temperature

1 tablespoon grated lemon zest

½ cup (2 oz/60 g) confectioners' (icing) sugar

3 tablespoons fresh lemon juice

MAKES 1 MEDIUM LOAF

Preheat the oven to 350°F (180°C). Butter and flour an 8½-by-4½-by-2½-inch (21-by-11-by-6-cm) loaf pan and tap out the excess flour.

In a bowl, sift together the flour, baking powder, salt, and cloves. Set aside. In another bowl, using an electric mixer on medium-high speed, beat the butter until light. Gradually add the granulated sugar, beating until fluffy and ivory colored, about 2 minutes.

In a small bowl, whisk together the eggs and lemon zest until blended. Using the mixer on medium speed, gradually beat the egg mixture into the butter mixture. On low speed, add the flour mixture and beat just until combined. Pour and scrape the batter into the prepared pan and smooth the top.

Bake until a toothpick inserted into the center comes out clean, about 1 hour. Let cool in the pan on a wire rack for 5 minutes, then turn out onto the rack and turn right side up.

In a small bowl, whisk together the confectioners' sugar and lemon juice until blended and smooth. Brush the mixture over the top and sides of the hot cake. Let the cake cool completely before serving.

About cloves

The word clove *derives from the French* clou, *which means "nail," reflecting the shape of the spice. The dried buds of a tropical evergreen, cloves have a strong, sweet, peppery flavor, so that only a small amount is typically needed in a recipe.*

439

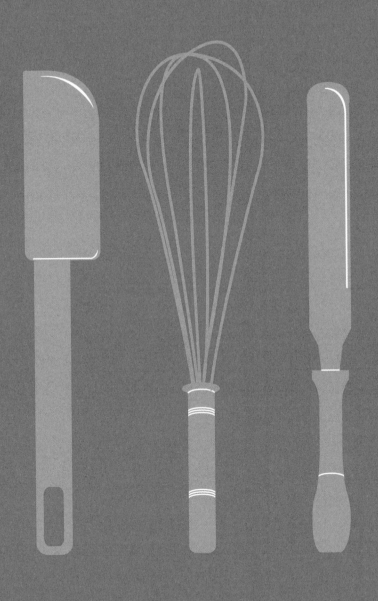

Dessert BASICS

Dessert Basics

When people delight in a dessert, they often mention specific features: crisp, golden pastry; a smooth, rich chocolaty filling, a light-as-air meringue topping; a mellow, rich caramel sauce; a sparkling fruit glaze. Such outstanding elements are what make the difference between an ordinary dessert and an extraordinary one. This chapter provides you with all you will need to know to make memorable desserts at home.

442

Plan for dessert
During the weekend, think about desserts you may want to prepare in the week ahead, planning ones that complement the meal they follow: a simple fruit dessert after a rich supper, or a pan of brownies after a casual weeknight dinner. If possible, prepare desserts on the weekend, making double batches of items that freeze well, such as pound cake or butter cookies. Or, complete the time-consuming part of a recipe, such as making the pastry dough for a tart.

Dress it up
Several easy additions can turn simple desserts into elegant treats. Put a small scoop of vanilla, caramel, or chocolate ice cream on a plate with nearly any dessert. Or, add a small or large dollop of Whipped Cream (page 454), which takes only minutes to make.

Top it off
Pair fresh fruits like raspberries with plain desserts such as pound cake, or drizzle berries with a fruit liqueur. Spoon good-quality store-bought chocolate, butterscotch, or caramel sauce over cake or ice cream.

Dessert Techniques

Dessert recipes routinely involve such tasks as sifting dry ingredients, whipping egg whites, and caramelizing sugar. These guidelines for some of the most commonly used dessert-making techniques will help you achieve good results every time.

SIFTING DRY INGREDIENTS Sifting dry ingredients such as flour, cocoa powder, or confectioners' (icing) sugar aerates them, eliminates any lumps, and, when mixing more than one item, blends them uniformly. To sift, rest a fine-mesh sieve or sifter inside a large bowl. As you measure the dry ingredients to be sifted, add them to the sieve or sifter. If using a sieve, lift its handle with one hand and gently tap its edge with the other to pass the ingredients through the mesh into the bowl. If using a sifter, squeeze or crank its handle to pass the ingredients through.

Note that some recipes call for measuring flour or other dry ingredients *after* sifting. The distinction is important because sifting increases volume, which means volume measurements will be off if you don't sift when directed.

SEPARATING EGGS Cold eggs are easier to separate than room-temperature eggs, so it's best to separate eggs that are just out of the refrigerator. Have ready three clean, small bowls. Crack the side of the egg sharply on a flat surface. Hold the cracked egg over the first bowl and, with the fingertips of both hands near the crack, carefully pull the shell apart, keeping the yolk cupped in one shell half as you let the white begin dropping into the bowl below. Gently transfer the yolk back and forth between the shell halves, letting the rest of the white fall into the bowl and taking care to avoid cutting the yolk on a shell edge. Drop the yolk into the second bowl. Keeping egg whites free of any yolk is essential if you plan to whip them. Even a trace of yolk (or other fat) will prevent whites from foaming and forming peaks, so look closely at the white to make sure no speck of yolk is present. If the white has separated cleanly, transfer it to the third bowl.

Repeat the steps outlined above to separate the remaining eggs called for in your recipe. Transfer the white of each egg to the third bowl only if it is free of any yolk. If any yolk does get into the first bowl, discard the white or use it for another purpose, such as scrambled eggs, and wash the bowl thoroughly before continuing to separate.

WHIPPING EGG WHITES Whipping incorporates air into egg whites, producing a fluffy foam that lightens some cakes, soufflés, mousses, and other desserts and, when sugar is incorporated, becomes sweet meringue. Room-temperature egg whites can be whipped to higher peaks, so separate the eggs when they are still cold, as described above, but leave the whites at room temperature for 30 minutes before whipping.

To whip egg whites, fit a stand mixer with the whip attachment or fit a handheld mixer with its whip attachment, if your mixer has one, or the twin beaters. Put the egg whites in a clean bowl. At this point, some recipes call for adding a pinch of cream of tartar, which helps stabilize the tiny air bubbles. Beat at medium speed until foamy, about 1 minute.

If the recipe calls for whites whipped to the soft-peak stage, increase the speed to medium-high and continue beating until they look opaque but still moist, 2 to 3 minutes. Then, stop the mixer and lift out the whip: the whites should form peaks that droop slightly. If stiff peaks are called for, continue beating until the whites look glossy, 1 to 2 minutes more, then stop again and lift out the whip: the peaks should stand up straight and firm.

If the egg whites begin to separate and appear grainy, you have beaten them too long. The only solution is to start again with fresh whites.

WHIPPING CREAM Whipped cream lightens and enriches many dessert mixtures and is a popular garnish. For the best results, start with everything well chilled: the cream, the bowl, and the whip attachment or beaters. Pour the cream into the bowl and add any sweeteners or flavorings if specified in the recipe. (Some recipes call for adding these additions after the soft-peak stage is reached.) Fit a stand mixer with the whip attachment or a handheld mixer with its whip attachment, if your mixer has one, or the twin beaters. For soft to medium peaks (typically for serving on top of or alongside a dessert), beat on medium speed until the cream begins to thicken, then increase the speed to medium-high and beat just until slightly bent peaks form when you stop the mixer and lift out the whip, 3 to 4 minutes. For stiff peaks (typically for folding into a heavier mixture), which stand straight, continue beating for 1 to 2 minutes longer.

CREAMING BUTTER Creaming—essentially beating—softened, but not melted, butter until it is soft and smooth makes it easier to blend it into batters. It also incorporates air, which gives a lift to baked goods. To cream butter, fit a stand mixer with the paddle attachment or fit a handheld mixer with twin beaters. Put cool room-temperature butter in a bowl and beat on medium speed until light and fluffy, about 2 minutes. Its color will change from pale yellow to ivory, and it will have the consistency of stiffly whipped cream. (Traditional recipes may tell you to cream butter by hand using a sturdy wooden spoon. This is not difficult to do, but it takes several minutes longer.)

Sometimes sugar or other ingredients are creamed along with the butter or are added after the butter is creamed. When sugar is included, make sure it is fully dissolved—the mixture should not feel gritty when rubbed between fingertips—before you stop beating.

CUTTING IN Recipes for everything from flaky pastry dough to biscuit-type cobbler toppings call for cutting cold butter into a flour mixture. To cut in the butter, first cut it into cubes or slices. If making the dough by hand, cut the butter into the flour using a pastry blender, two table knives, or fingertips. Usually the mixture is ready when it resembles large, coarse crumbs, with pea-sized pieces of butter. If using a food processor, pulse the cold butter into the flour using short bursts until the same consistency is reached.

FOLDING When a recipe calls for mixing two preparations of different densities—for example, light whipped egg whites and a heavy mixture of melted chocolate and butter—recipes often call for folding, which involves combining the two without deflating the lighter of the two. This is done by a gentle, yet thorough, mixing motion.

SEASONAL THINKING

Here is a guide to using the best of the season whenever you make dessert.

Spring
Celebrate warm weather's return and the start of the growing season by show-casing early spring produce, such as ripe strawberries in Strawberries Romanoff (page 552), or by featuring tropical fruits, as in Caramelized Pineapple (page 545).

Summer
Summer brings juicy stone fruits, ripe berries, and fresh melons. Use them to make easy-to-assemble desserts such as Nectarine-Blackberry Cobbler (page 560). Beat the heat with frozen desserts like Mint–Chocolate Chip Ice Cream (page 605) or Ruby Red Grapefruit Sorbet (page 613).

Autumn
As the weather cools, warm up desserts with pie spices, and enjoy the harvest's bounty by preparing desserts with apples, cranberries, pears, and pumpkin. Choices include Cinnamon-Baked Apples (page 545) to Favorite Pumpkin Pie (page 525) and Pear and Dried Cranberry Bread Pudding (page 583).

Winter
During the holidays, indulge in chocolate in its many guises, from Dark Chocolate Pudding (page 584) to Cognac Truffles (page 576). Bake with year-round staples to make desserts like Maple-Pecan Pie (page 526). Citrus and tropical fruits help desserts like Lemon Meringue Pie (page 523) or Mango Mousse (page 586) brighten cold, dark days.

443

DESSERT PANS AND DISHES

Whether you need the perfect pan for a pie, tart, or custard, or an attractive container for serving an iced dessert, having a wide range of pans and dishes within arm's reach will help you achieve success.

Baking Pans and Dishes

These come in many shapes and sizes and are usually made of heavy-gauge aluminum or tempered glass. It's useful to have on hand 8-inch (20-cm) and 9-inch (23-cm) square baking pans, a 9-by-13-inch (23-by-33-cm) pan, and two loaf pans.

Baking Sheets

These large, rectangular metal pans either have a shallow rim on four sides or a low-flared rim on one or two ends. It's handy to have at least two baking sheets, so you can fill one while the other one is in the oven. Heavy baking sheets bake and brown cookies and other items more evenly than thinner sheets.

Bundt Pan

Usually made of heavy cast aluminum, with or without a nonstick coating, this specialized, one-piece tube pan has deeply fluted sides and a hole in the center that distinguish the dense cakes baked in it.

Cake Pans

These round pans are generally 1½ to 2 inches (4 to 5 cm) deep and 8 or 9 inches (20 or 23 cm) in diameter. You will want to have at least two same-size pans on hand for making layer cakes.

To fold, pour or spoon the light mixture on top of the heavy one. With the blade of a rubber spatula, slice down into the center of the ingredients to the bottom of the bowl. Rotate the blade and drag its flat side along the bottom and up the side of the bowl, then pull it up and over the lighter mixture on top, bringing some of the heavier mixture from the bottom with it. Rotate the bowl a quarter turn. Repeat folding until the mixtures are fully incorporated. (Note that some recipes will specify whether or not streaks of the lighter mixture should remain visible after the folding process is completed.)

TEMPERING EGGS If you are incorporating eggs into a hot mixture (usually based on milk or cream), such as when making custards for pastry cream or French-style ice cream, you need to be careful the eggs don't cook on contact and turn the mixture lumpy. That's the purpose of tempering, which gently raises the temperature of the eggs for even blending.

To temper eggs, in a heatproof glass or stainless steel bowl, whisk the eggs or egg yolks with any other ingredients specified in the recipe. While whisking rapidly and constantly to prevent curdling, slowly add a small amount of the hot mixture to the beaten egg mixture. Then, slowly pour the tempered eggs into the rest of the hot mixture, again whisking constantly until thoroughly combined.

CARAMELIZING SUGAR Sugar becomes less purely sweet and develops a more complex color when it is caramelized, turning from light to dark brown as it cooks. Caramelizing sugar is commonly done in two ways: White or brown sugar is sprinkled over food and then heated under a broiler (grill) until it melts and darkens to form a crunchy, sweet crust, such as the topping on Classic Crème Brûlée (page 596). Or, sugar is dissolved in water to make a syrup that is cooked until it turns a caramel brown color and takes on a deeply nutty, almost charred, flavor.

To caramelize a sugar syrup, put the sugar and any other ingredient (usually water and sometimes corn syrup and/or lemon juice) specified in the recipe in a deep, heavy saucepan. If you have a candy thermometer, clip it to the side of the pan, with the tip of the stem immersed in the mixture but not touching the bottom of the pan. Using a wooden spoon, stir the ingredients together; they will look cloudy and grainy. Place the pan over medium heat and stir constantly until the sugar has dissolved completely, with no grains visible, 1 to 2 minutes. Raise the heat to medium-high and continue cooking, without stirring. Do not take your eyes off the mixture, as it can go from perfectly cooked to burned within seconds. As soon as the mixture turns a rich amber, or registers 320° to 360°F (160° to 180°C) on the thermometer, immediately remove the pan from the heat; the color will continue to darken slightly. Do not let it turn dark brown, or it will tasted burned. As soon as possible, use the caramel as directed, as it thickens quickly. If necessary, remelt over low heat.

Caution: Always use caution when caramelizing sugar, as both the caramel and the pan will be very hot, and any burns can be serious. Handle pans and utensils with heavy pot holders, and keep a bowl of ice water next to the stove to cool down the pan bottom quickly if the syrup overheats.

TOASTING NUTS Toasting nuts before using them in some recipes gives them a fuller flavor, crunchier texture, and darker color. A small amount of nuts can be toasted on the stove top, but larger amounts are best toasted in the oven. Spread them in a single layer on a baking sheet and bake in a 325°F (165°C) oven, stirring occasionally to prevent overbrowning, until the nuts are fragrant, colored, and coated in a thin layer of their own oil. Depending on the type and size of the nut, this may take 10 to 20 minutes.

The Dessert Pantry

A pantry, which can be a dedicated closet or one or more kitchen cupboards, is essential for storing the basic nonperishable staples for dessert making: flours, sugars, spices, extracts and other flavorings, dried fruits, nuts, and canned and bottled or jarred foods. Make sure you store these items in a relatively cool, dry, dark space. It should also be a good distance from the stove, as heat can dry out many of these staples, especially spices, robbing them of their flavor and aroma.

Routinely check your pantry to see what dessert-making staples you have on hand. Replace basic ingredients soon after you use them.

CHOCOLATE AND COCOA See page 567.

DRIED FRUITS Store dried fruits in airtight containers at room temperature for up to 1 month, or in the refrigerator for up to 6 months.

EXTRACTS Buy only pure extracts and avoid imitation products whenever possible. Store extracts in a cool, dark cupboard for up to 1 year.

FLOURS AND GRAINS See page 403.

LEAVENING AGENTS See page 423.

NUTS Shelled nuts have a relatively short shelf life. Store them in an airtight container at room temperature for up to 2 months, in the refrigerator for up to 6 months, or in the freezer for up to 9 months. More delicate nuts, such as pistachios and pine nuts, should be kept for only about half as long. Nuts in the shell will keep in a cool, dark place for up to 6 months.

SPICES AND FLAVORINGS The flavor of spices starts to fade after about 6 months. Buy spices in quantities small enough so you are likely to use them up in that time, and replace them if you don't. Ethnic markets and natural-foods stores usually sell spices in bulk. They are typically fresher and less expensive than the prepackaged spices on supermarket shelves. Buy the highest quality you can afford and avoid artificial or imitation products. Store in small, airtight containers or in the original packaging.

SPIRITS Buy good-quality spirits in small bottles. You never need more than a few spoonfuls, and cheaper versions tend to taste harsh or contain artificial ingredients that impart an off flavor. A splash of orange-scented Cointreau or almond-flavored amaretto can turn a simple fruit salad into an elegant dessert, especially when paired with homemade pound cake. Keep spirits tightly closed in their original bottles. They will keep indefinitely, but have the best flavor if used within 6 months.

SWEETENERS Store all types of sugar, honey, and maple syrup in airtight containers. Brown sugar, which is granulated sugar that has been mixed with molasses to add flavor and give it a soft, packable consistency, hardens when exposed to air. If this happens, warm it gently in a low oven or in a microwave until it softens. Confectioners' (icing) sugar is made from granulated sugar that has been milled until very fine and mixed with a small amount of cornstarch (cornflour) to prevent clumping. If lumps form, pass the sugar through a fine-mesh sieve. If honey crystallizes, stand the jar in a saucepan of warm water over low heat or warm in a microwave (make sure the container is microwave safe) until it is a smooth and pourable liquid.

Pie Pans
Round aluminum pie pans are generally 9 to 10 inches (23 to 25 cm) in diameter with sloping 1½-inch (4-cm) sides. Double-crust fruit pies, as well as prebaked crusts for cream pies, bake well in aluminum pans because the metal absorbs heat, helping the pastry brown and crisp. Deep-dish pans for top crust–only pies are 2 to 3 inches (5 to 7.5 cm) deep; many are made of ceramic or porcelain, which conduct heat less effectively than metal to prevent scorching.

Ramekins
These single-serving, ovenproof porcelain dishes, usually 3 to 4 inches (7.5 to 10 cm) in diameter, look like miniature soufflé dishes. They are useful for making individual baked desserts.

Springform Pans
These deep metal cake pans have sides secured by a clamp that, when closed, forms a tight seal with the bottom. When the clamp is released, the sides expand and lift off, making a cake easy to unmold. Although they come in a range of sizes and shapes, a round pan 9 inches (23 cm) in diameter is the most common.

Tart Pans
Available in many sizes and shapes, shallow metal tart pans usually have fluted edges and a removable bottom for easy unmolding.

445

CRUMB CRUST

Picking the right pan

A metal pie pan or glass pie dish conducts heat more effectively than a porcelain or ceramic pie dish, resulting in a firmer crust.

To make the crumbs, use graham crackers, gingersnaps, or biscotti and process them in a food processor or slip them into a heavy-duty plastic bag and crush with a rolling pin. Whatever your choice, be sure it is fresh: the taste of stale crackers and cookies will linger in your pie.

In a bowl, combine the crumbs, sugar, and salt and toss with a fork to mix. Add the butter and stir and toss with the fork until the crumb mixture is evenly moistened and crumbly.

Using your fingers, press and pat the mixture evenly over the bottom and sides of a 9-inch (23-cm) pie pan, taking care not to make the sides too thick.

For a crisper shell, bake the pie shell in a preheated 325°F (165°C) oven for 8 minutes. Let cool completely on a wire rack before filling the shell.

1½ cups (5 oz/165 g) crumbs (see note, above)

2 tablespoons sugar

Pinch of salt

½ cup (4 oz/125 g) unsalted butter, melted

MAKES ONE 9-INCH (23-CM) PIE SHELL

CHOCOLATE CRUMB CRUST

Imperfection is appealing

In a springform pan, the crumb coating will come only halfway up the sides and will be slightly uneven, giving your finished dessert a more rustic look.

The best cookies for making this crust are Famous Chocolate Wafers, available at most supermarkets. Use this for cakes or pies that are served cold, such as Chocolate Cheesecake (page 514), Chocolate Cream Cheese Pie (page 521), and Peanut Butter Chiffon Pie (page 524).

Preheat the oven to 450°F (230°C). Have ready a 9- to 10-inch (23- to 25-cm) metal pie pan, glass pie dish, or springform pan. If using a springform pan, butter the bottom and sides.

Break the cookies into pieces, place in a food processor, and process to fine crumbs. Alternatively, slip the cookies into a heavy-duty plastic bag and crush them with a rolling pin. You will have about 3 cups.

In a bowl, combine the crumbs and sugar and toss with a fork to mix. Add the butter and stir and toss with the fork until the crumb mixture is evenly moistened and crumbly.

Using your fingers, press and pat the mixture evenly over the bottom and sides of the pan. (If using a springform pan, it will reach only about halfway up the sides.)

Bake for 5 minutes, then let cool completely, cover, and refrigerate well before filling.

1 package (7 oz/220 g) chocolate wafer cookies (see note, above)

¼ cup (2 oz/60 g) sugar

⅓ cup (3 oz/90 g) unsalted butter, melted

MAKES ONE 9- OR 10-INCH (23- OR 25-CM) PIE SHELL

PIE PASTRY

To make a tender, flaky crust, follow these three rules: don't overmix the fat and flour, add water just until the dough holds together when pinched, and keep it cold. If you like, you can substitute vegetable shortening (vegetable lard) for the butter, or use equal parts of both.

FOR A SINGLE-CRUST PIE

1½ cups (7½ oz/235 g) all-purpose (plain) flour

1 tablespoon sugar, optional (see note, right)

½ teaspoon salt

½ cup (4 oz/125 g) cold unsalted butter, cut into tablespoon-size pieces

3–4 tablespoons cold water

FOR A DOUBLE-CRUST PIE

2¼ cups (11½ oz/360 g) all-purpose (plain) flour

1½ tablespoons sugar, optional (see note, right)

¾ teaspoon salt

¾ cup (6 oz/180 g) cold unsalted butter, cut into tablespoon-size pieces

6–7 tablespoons (3–3½ fl oz/90–105 ml) cold water

MAKES ENOUGH DOUGH FOR 1 SINGLE- OR DOUBLE-CRUST 9-INCH (23-CM) PIE

Food-processor method: In a food processor, combine the flour, sugar (if using), and salt and pulse a few times to mix. Scatter the butter over the top, then pulse until you have a mix of small, irregular flakes and crumbs and bits of butter the size of peas. Add 2 tablespoons of the water (4 tablespoons for a double-crust pie) and pulse about 5 times. Add 1 more tablespoon water (2 tablespoons for a double-crust pie) and pulse 3 or 4 times. Stop and feel the dough; it should be just damp enough to form a rough mass. If necessary, add more water by teaspoons, pulsing once or twice after each addition. The total mixing time should be less than 1 minute. Do not mix until the dough forms a ball. It should remain a rough, shaggy mass.

Hand method: In a bowl, combine the flour, sugar (if using), and salt and toss with a fork to mix. Scatter the butter over the top. With your fingertips, 2 knives, or a pastry blender, cut the butter into the flour mixture until the mixture forms large, coarse crumbs. Sprinkle in the water 1 tablespoon at a time, stirring and tossing with a fork after each addition until evenly moist. Stop adding water once the dough comes together into a rough, shaggy mass.

Chilling the dough: Remove the dough from the food processor or bowl. With lightly floured hands, gently shape the dough into a smooth disk, or into 2 disks, one slightly larger than the other, if making a double-crust pie. The dough may be rolled out and used right away. Or, for easier rolling, wrap the dough in plastic wrap and refrigerate for at least 1 hour or up to overnight.

To roll out pie pastry: Lightly dust a work surface, the dough, and the rolling pin with flour. Place the dough in the center of the surface. Rolling from the center toward the edges and in all directions, use a rolling pin to roll the dough into a round 2–3 inches (5–7.5 cm) larger than your pie dish or pan. Using a bench scraper or offset spatula, lift and turn the dough several times as you roll to prevent sticking. Dust the surface and the rolling pin with flour as needed.

To transfer the pastry to a pie pan: Carefully roll the dough around the rolling pin, brushing off the excess flour with a pastry brush. Position the rolling pin over a pie pan or dish. Unroll the dough and center it in the dish. Gently press the dough into the bottom and up the sides of the dish, taking care not to pull or stretch it.

Sweetening the deal

Adding a little sugar to pie dough is common for desserts. Minus the sugar, this pastry is suitable for savory pies, such as the Chicken Potpie on page 249.

447

CHOCOLATE-WALNUT PASTRY

Chill before rolling

If you prefer to roll out the dough, shape it into a disk, wrap in plastic wrap, and chill for 1 hour, then roll out on a well floured surface.

This easy-to-assemble cookielike pastry may be pressed into the pan, rather than rolled out. For a quick dessert, fully bake the pie shell (see page 518), then let cool completely, fill with softened ice cream, and return it to the freezer to firm up before serving.

In a bowl, combine the flour, walnuts, cocoa powder, sugar, and salt and toss with a fork to mix. Scatter the butter over the top. With your fingertips, 2 knives, or a pastry blender, cut the butter into the flour mixture until the mixture forms large, coarse crumbs. Add the ¼ cup milk and the vanilla and stir and toss with the fork until the dough comes together into a rough, shaggy mass. If the dough is too dry, add a few drops more milk.

Working with walnut-size pieces of dough, press and pat them evenly over the bottom and sides of a 9-inch (23-cm) pie pan or tart pan with a removable bottom. Fill and bake as directed in individual recipes.

1 cup (5 oz/155 g) all-purpose (plain) flour

½ cup (2 oz/60 g) ground walnuts

⅓ cup (1 oz/30 g) unsweetened cocoa powder

¼ cup (2 oz/60 g) sugar

¼ teaspoon salt

½ cup (4 oz/125 g) cold unsalted butter, cut into tablespoon-size pieces

¼ cup (2 fl oz/60 ml) milk, or as needed

1 teaspoon pure vanilla extract

MAKES ONE 9-INCH (23-CM) PIE OR TART SHELL

TART PASTRY

Rolling out tart pastry

To roll out tart pastry, follow the directions for Pie Pastry on page 447. Use the same method for transferring the pastry to the tart pan, too, lightly pressing the dough into the sides of the pan around its circumference.

Because it has a slightly higher proportion of fat than a basic pie pastry, tart pastry is firm and crumbly, rather than flaky. Use this recipe whenever you want the taste of butter to come through. For savory tarts, omit the sugar.

Food-processor method: In a food processor, combine the flour, sugar, if using, and salt and pulse a few times to mix. Scatter the butter over the top, then pulse until the mixture forms small, irregular flakes and bits of butter the size of peas. Add 1 tablespoon of the water and pulse once or twice. Add the remaining 1 tablespoon water and pulse 3 or 4 times. Stop and feel the dough; it should be just damp enough to form a rough mass. If necessary, add a few more drops of water to achieve the correct consistency, pulsing once or twice after each addition.

Hand method: In a bowl, combine the flour, sugar, if using, and salt and toss with a fork to mix. Scatter the butter over the top. With your fingertips, 2 knives, or a pastry blender, cut the butter into the flour mixture until the mixture forms large, coarse crumbs. Sprinkle 1 tablespoon of the water over the flour mixture, then stir and toss with the fork until evenly moist. Sprinkle the remaining 1 tablespoon water over the flour mixture and again stir and toss until evenly moist.

1¼ cups (6½ oz/200 g) all-purpose (plain) flour

1 tablespoon sugar, optional

¼ teaspoon salt

½ cup (4 oz/125 g) cold unsalted butter, cut into tablespoon-size pieces

2 tablespoons cold water, or as needed

MAKES ONE 9½-INCH (24-CM) TART SHELL

Feel the dough; it should be just damp enough to form a rough mass. If necessary, add a few more drops of water to achieve the correct consistency.

Remove the dough from the food processor or bowl. With lightly floured hands, gently shape the dough into a smooth disk. The dough may be rolled out and used right away. Or, for easier rolling, wrap it in plastic wrap and refrigerate for at least 1 hour or up to overnight.

Controlling the salt

Always use unsalted butter when making pastry, or the overall proportion of salt in the dough will be off.

RICH TART PASTRY

Sweeter and richer than standard tart pastry, this version also has a sandy, cookielike texture similar to shortbread. Like the Chocolate-Walnut Pastry (see left), this dough may be pressed into a tart pan with your fingers—a boon if you don't like to roll out pastry.

1¼ cups (6½ oz/200 g) all-purpose (plain) flour

3 tablespoons sugar

¼ teaspoon salt

10 tablespoons (5 oz/ 155 g) cold unsalted butter, cut into tablespoon-size pieces

1 egg yolk

1½ tablespoons cold water, or as needed

MAKES ONE 9½-INCH (24-CM) TART SHELL

Food-processor method: In a food processor, combine the flour, sugar, and salt and pulse a few times to mix. Scatter the butter over the top, then pulse just until you have a mixture of small, irregular flakes and crumbs and bits of butter the size of peas. In a small bowl, stir together the egg yolk and 1½ tablespoons water. With the processor running, slowly add the egg yolk mixture through the feed tube, stopping the processor when the mixture forms clumps. Stop and feel the dough; it should be just damp enough to form a rough mass. If necessary, add a few more drops of water to achieve the correct consistency, pulsing once or twice after each addition.

Hand method: In a bowl, combine the flour, sugar, and salt and toss with a fork to mix. Scatter the butter over the top. With your fingertips, 2 knives, or a pastry blender, cut the butter into the flour mixture until the mixture forms large, coarse crumbs. In a small bowl, stir together the egg yolk and 1½ teaspoons water. Add the egg mixture to the flour mixture and stir gently with the fork until evenly distributed and the mixture forms clumps. Feel the dough; it should be just damp enough to form a rough mass. If necessary, mix in a few more drops of water to achieve the correct consistency.

Working with walnut-size pieces of dough, press and pat them evenly over the bottom and sides of a 9½-inch (24-cm) tart pan with a removable bottom. (If you prefer to roll out the dough, wrap it in plastic wrap and refrigerate for at least 1 hour or up to overnight, then roll it out on a generously floured work surface.)

A tidy edge

The easiest way to trim away excess dough when you are lining a tart pan is to let it drape over the sides of the pan. Then, roll your rolling pin across the top of the tart pan, cutting off the surplus cleanly at the pan rim.

449

CLASSIC PUFF PASTRY

The simplest of tarts

Cut a piece of puff pastry dough into any shape you like. Leaving a border all the way around the edge, prick the pasty with the tines of a fork, spread on a layer of pastry cream or fruit curd, top with thinly sliced fruit and a sprinkling of sugar, and bake in a preheated 400°F (200°C) until the border puffs up and turns golden.

The key to success with this butter-enriched dough lies in a simple secret: start with cold ingredients and return the dough to the refrigerator often as you work. Puff pastry forms the foundation of many baked treats, both sweet and savory.

In a large bowl, stir together the 3 cups all-purpose flour, the cake flour, and the salt. Scatter the butter pieces over the top. Using a pastry blender or your fingers, work the butter into the flour mixture until the mixture is crumbly.

Make a well in the center of the flour mixture and pour in the 1 cup ice water. Using a wooden spoon, gradually stir the flour mixture into the water until it is fully incorporated and a rough mass holds together. If necessary, add more ice water, 1 tablespoon at a time.

Turn the dough out onto a lightly floured work surface and knead until smooth, 15–20 seconds. The dough should not be sticky. Set aside.

Place the block of butter on a work surface. Using a rolling pin or the heel of your hand, knead or beat the butter to flatten it and warm it until it is smooth and pliable. Sprinkle the butter with the 2 tablespoons flour and gently beat the butter with the rolling pin to press the flour into the butter. Shape the floured butter into a 6-inch (15-cm) square about ¾ inch (2 cm) thick.

On a lightly floured surface, and using a ruler as a guide, roll out the dough into a 12-inch (30-cm) square. Place the butter square at a diagonal in the center of the dough square. Fold over the dough corners to meet in the center, covering the butter completely. Pat the dough packet with your hands to form a compact square. Roll out the dough into a rectangle 24 inches (60 cm) long by 8 inches (20 cm) wide.

With a short side facing you, fold the bottom third of the dough up, then fold the top third of the dough down over it, as if folding a letter. Brush off any excess flour with a pastry brush. Wrap the dough in plastic wrap and refrigerate for 20–30 minutes. Clean the work surface.

Remove the dough from the refrigerator. Lightly flour the work surface. Unwrap the dough and place it on the floured surface with a short side facing you and the folded side to your left. Roll out the dough again into a 24-by-8-inch (60-by-24-cm) rectangle and fold it into thirds, again folding the bottom third up and then the top third down. This is called a *turn*. Repeat to make 4 more turns, wrapping the dough in plastic wrap and refrigerating it for 20–30 minutes between each turn.

After the final turn, wrap the dough in plastic wrap, place in a plastic bag, and refrigerate for at least 4 hours or up to overnight before using.

3 cups (15 oz/470 g) plus 2 tablespoons unbleached all-purpose (plain) flour

1 cup (4 oz/125 g) cake (soft-wheat) flour

1 teaspoon salt

2 tablespoons cold unsalted butter, cut into small pieces, plus 1 lb (500 g) unsalted butter, in a single block

1 cup (8 fl oz/250 ml) ice water, or as needed

MAKES ABOUT 2 LB (1 KG) DOUGH

PRALINE CUPS

Just about any fruit tastes delicious spooned into these crisp, nutty cups. It is best to bake only 2 at a time, so you have time to mold them into shape before they set. The cups will keep for 1 week in a tightly covered container at room temperature.

1 cup (5 oz/155 g) all-purpose (plain) flour

1 cup (4–5 oz/125–155 g) finely chopped almonds or pecans

½ cup (5 oz/155 g) light corn syrup

½ cup (4 oz/125 g) unsalted butter

⅔ cup (5 oz/155 g) firmly packed dark brown sugar

MAKES 12 CUPS

Preheat the oven to 375°F (190°C). Cut aluminum foil into twelve 8-inch (20-cm) squares. Butter each square. Place 2 foil squares on a rimmed baking sheet. Butter the outsides of two ¾-cup (6 fl oz) ramekins (or similarly sized flat-bottomed vessels, such as water glasses) for use as molds.

In a bowl, stir together the flour and nuts. Set aside.

In a small saucepan, combine the corn syrup, butter, and brown sugar. Bring to a slow boil over medium-high heat, stirring gently. Stir in the flour and nuts, then remove from the heat. Drop 2 rounded tablespoons of the mixture onto the center of each prepared foil square on the baking sheet.

Bake for 7 minutes. The mixture on each square should have bubbled and spread out into a round 4–5 inches (10–13 cm) in diameter. Remove from the oven and let cool on the foil squares for 2 minutes. Place 1 of the prepared custard cups in the center of each praline round. Lift up the foil and gently shape the praline to the outside of the mold.

Cool upside down for 3 minutes, then remove the molds. Let the praline cups cool completely before removing the foil. Repeat with the remaining praline mixture, buttering the molds as necessary. If the praline mixture in the saucepan hardens, reheat gently over low heat until softened.

Soften before serving

Once you have added your filling of choice, let the cups sit for about 10 minutes before serving, so they will soften for easier eating.

451

FAST FONDUE

Looking for a quick chocolate fix? This instant yet elegant dessert is the answer. Just heat and mix. All you need to add is fresh or dried fruit, pound cake pieces, or marshmallows for dipping. Use a fondue pot to keep the chocolate warm at the table.

⅔ cup (6½ oz/200 g) dark corn syrup

½ cup (4 fl oz/125 ml) heavy (double) cream

9 oz (280 g) semisweet (plain) chocolate, chopped

Assorted sliced fresh fruits such as apples, peaches, pears, nectarines, or pineapple, or whole strawberries

MAKES 1½ CUPS (12 FL OZ/ 375 ML); SERVES 4

In a saucepan over medium heat, combine the corn syrup and cream and bring to a gentle boil. Remove from the heat. Add the chocolate and stir until the chocolate has melted and the mixture is smooth.

Arrange the fruits on a platter. Pass toothpicks or skewers to spear the fruits for dipping into the warm chocolate.

Flavoring fondue

For more complex flavor, substitute ¼ cup (2½ oz/75 g) orange or apricot marmalade for the corn syrup. To spice things up, stir in 3 tbsp Grand Marnier or brandy once the chocolate mixture is smooth.

PASTRY CREAM

The thick of it

Flour is often used to thicken soups, pan sauces, and gravies, but corn-starch is typically the thickener of choice for sweets. Fillings and glazes thickened with cornstarch have a glossy sheen.

Plain, or vanilla, pastry cream is delicious spread in a baked tart shell and topped with ripe berries, sliced peaches, or other fruit. To make chocolate pastry cream, finely chop 2 oz (60 g) bittersweet or semisweet (plain) chocolate and whisk in with the butter.

In a small, heavy saucepan over medium heat, bring the milk to a simmer. Meanwhile, in a heatproof bowl, whisk together the egg yolks, sugar, cornstarch, and salt until well blended. Slowly add about one-third of the hot milk to the bowl with the yolk-sugar mixture, whisking constantly. Then pour the combined mixture back into the saucepan and cook over medium heat, stirring constantly, until the mixture comes to a boil and thickens slightly, about 3 minutes. Continue cooking, stirring constantly, for 1 minute longer.

Remove from the heat and pour through a fine-mesh sieve placed over a heatproof bowl. Gently stir in the butter until melted, then stir in the vanilla. Cover with plastic wrap, pressing it directly onto the surface to prevent a skin from forming. Poke a few holes in the plastic wrap to hasten cooling. Let cool, then cover tightly and refrigerate until well chilled, at least 2 hours, or up to 3 days.

1 cup (8 fl oz/250 ml) milk

2 egg yolks

¼ cup (2 oz/60 g) sugar

4½ teaspoons cornstarch (cornflour)

Pinch of salt

2 tablespoons unsalted butter

1 teaspoon pure vanilla extract

MAKES ABOUT 1 CUP (8 FL OZ/250 ML)

CITRUS CURD

Spread the love

Like homemade jam, citrus curd makes a great gift. Fill clean jars with hot tap water to warm the glass while you work, then drain the jars and fill them with curd while both are still hot. Seal tightly and let cool to room temperature.

You can use this old-fashioned curd in tarts, with fruit, as a filling for cake layers, or for spreading on scones or muffins. It freezes well, too: put the chilled curd in an airtight container, press plastic wrap directly onto the surface, cover tightly, and freeze for up to 1 month.

In a bowl, using a fork, lightly beat the eggs until blended. Set the eggs aside.

In a heatproof bowl, combine the sugar, orange and lemon juices, butter, orange zest, and cardamom. Set over (but not touching) simmering water in a saucepan and stir gently until the sugar dissolves and the butter melts.

Strain the beaten eggs through a fine-mesh sieve into a pitcher. Gradually add the eggs to the juice-butter mixture, whisking constantly. Cook, stirring constantly with a wooden spoon, until the custard thickens, 10–15 minutes. To test the consistency of the curd, draw your finger across the back of the spoon; it is ready when it leaves a trail that does not fill in immediately.

Remove from the heat and pour into a heatproof bowl. Cover with plastic wrap, pressing it directly onto the surface to prevent a skin from forming. Poke a few holes in the plastic wrap to hasten cooling. Let cool, then cover tightly and refrigerate until set, at least 3 hours, or up to 3 weeks.

3 eggs

1 cup (8 oz/250 g) sugar

6 tablespoons (3 fl oz/90 ml) fresh orange juice

2 tablespoons fresh lemon juice

6 tablespoons (3 oz/90 g) unsalted butter, cut into tablespoon-size pieces

3 tablespoons grated orange zest

¼ teaspoon ground cardamom

MAKES ABOUT 2 CUPS (16 FL OZ/500 ML)

WHITE CHOCOLATE CREAM

This topping, which has the consistency of soft cream cheese, must be made at least 4 hours in advance of using, to allow time for it to set up. Use it to top off a slice of chocolate cake, or spoon it over a bowl of mousse or fresh fruit, to turn a simple dessert into a fancy one.

1 cup (8 fl oz/250 ml) heavy (double) cream

12 oz (375 g) white chocolate, chopped

¼–⅓ cup (2–3 fl oz/60–80 ml) bourbon whiskey

MAKES ABOUT 3 CUPS (24 FL OZ/750 ML)

In a small saucepan over medium heat, gently warm the cream until small bubbles appear around the edge of the pan. Remove from the heat, add the chocolate, and stir gently until it has melted completely and the mixture is smooth. Stir in the whiskey to taste.

Alternatively, place the chocolate in a food processor or blender, pour in the hot cream, and let stand for 15 seconds, then process until smooth. Add the bourbon to taste and process briefly. Transfer to a bowl, passing the mixture through a fine-mesh sieve if there are any visible lumps.

Let cool completely, cover, and chill for at least 4 hours, or until the mixture no longer flows. Cover and refrigerate for up to 1 week or freeze for up to 6 months.

Read the label

When purchasing white chocolate, be sure you buy the real thing. White chocolate contains cocoa butter, but the similar looking white confectionary coating (also known as coating chocolate) contains other vegetable fats in place of the cocoa butter. It costs less and is less fussy to work with, but it also has a less-satisfying flavor and texture.

GINGER OR ORANGE SABAYON CREAM

Flavoring this whipped cream sauce with either ginger or orange produces equally delicious results. Serve it with steamed puddings, gingerbread, poached fruit, and fruit breads. It can be made several hours ahead, and leftover sauce can be covered and refrigerated for up to 2 days.

3 egg yolks

¼ cup (2 oz/60 g) granulated sugar

1 teaspoon grated fresh ginger, or the grated zest of 1 orange plus 1 tablespoon fresh orange juice

1 cup (8 fl oz/250 ml) cold heavy (double) cream

1 tablespoon confectioners' (icing) sugar

MAKES 2½–3 CUPS (20–24 FL OZ/625–750 ML)

Have ready a large bowl of ice mixed with a little water. In a heatproof bowl, combine the egg yolks and granulated sugar. Set over (not touching) barely simmering water in a saucepan and whisk until well blended. Whisk in the ginger, or the orange zest and juice. Using a whisk or a handheld mixer on medium speed, beat until light colored and thickened, 5–6 minutes. Remove the bowl from the heat and nest it in the ice water. Continue whisking the mixture until cold. It will become quite thick. Set aside.

Pour the cream into a chilled bowl. Using the whisk or the mixer on medium-high speed, whip the cream until soft peaks form. Add the confectioners' sugar and continue to whip until stiff peaks form.

Stir the whipped cream into the egg yolk mixture just until blended and smooth. Cover and refrigerate, then stir well just before serving.

Easy on the wrist

For the best result, do not use ultra-pasteurized cream. It has been heated to a high temperature to extend its shelf life, which makes it slightly harder to whip and gives it a subtle cooked taste.

WHIPPED CREAM

The other pastry cream

Don't think of whipped cream only as a topping. Spread it in a fully baked tart shell and crown it with fresh figs, berries, or peaches for a simple dessert.

A dollop of whipped cream contributes a dash of richness to countless desserts. If you need the cream to hold up for a long time, add 1 tablespoon nonfat dry milk with the sugar. It imparts no flavor, but acts as a stabilizer, keeping the peaks from losing their loft.

In a chilled bowl, combine the heavy cream, sugar, and vanilla. Using a whisk, beat until soft peaks form. (Alternatively, using an electric mixer, beat on medium-high speed until soft peaks form.)

If you want to use a pastry (piping) bag to pipe the cream, beat until stiff peaks form.

Use the whipped cream right away, or cover and refrigerate until serving time.

1 cup (8 fl oz/250 ml) cold heavy (double) cream

4 teaspoons sugar

1 teaspoon pure vanilla extract

MAKES ABOUT 2 CUPS (16 FL OZ/500 ML)

CHOCOLATE WHIPPED CREAM

A frosting alternative

Pipe a pretty swirl of this chocolate-flavored cream onto a cupcake in place of frosting.

You can make this chocolaty topping up to 4 hours in advance, though it will not be as light and fluffy as it is when it is freshly made. Be sure to sift both the confectioners' sugar and cocoa powder to remove any lumps before adding them to the cream.

Using a chilled bowl and chilled beaters, whip the cream for a few minutes until it starts to thicken.

Add the sugar and cocoa powder and continue beating until it stands in stiff peaks. Use right away, or spoon it into a fine-mesh sieve placed over a bowl (so any liquid it releases won't dilute the cream), cover with plastic wrap, and refrigerate until ready to use.

After topping the dessert with the cream, serve it right away.

2 cups (16 fl oz/500 ml) cold heavy (double) cream

1 cup (4 oz/125 g) sifted confectioners' (icing) sugar

½ cup (1½ oz/45 g) sifted unsweetened cocoa powder

MAKES ABOUT 4 CUPS (32 FL OZ/1 L)

MERINGUE PIE TOPPING

Quick-dissolving sugar

Superfine (caster) sugar dissolves faster than regular granulated sugar, making it a good choice for meringues. Superfine sugar is also great to have on hand for sweetening cold drinks.

This meringue remains light and tender without shrinking and weeping. It makes enough to cover a 9-inch (23-cm) pie with a thick layer. If you prefer a thin meringue, halve the ingredients. It can also be piped from a pastry (piping) bag to create a decorative pattern.

Preheat the broiler (grill). Arrange the rack so the top of the pie will be about 4 inches (10 cm) from the heat source.

In a large, heatproof bowl, combine the egg whites and sugar. Set the bowl in a pan of simmering water (not touching). Stir gently until the sugar has dissolved and the mixture is warm, 1–2 minutes. Remove the bowl from the pan and add the cream of tartar and salt. Using an electric mixer, beat the egg whites on high speed until stiff peaks form. Using a rubber spatula, distribute the meringue evenly over the pie filling, mounding it slightly toward the center and spreading it to

⅔ cup (5 fl oz/160 ml) egg whites (about 5)

½ cup (3½ oz/105 g) superfine (caster) sugar

½ teaspoon cream of tartar

¼ teaspoon salt

MAKES TOPPING FOR ONE 9-INCH (23-CM) PIE

the edge to seal the crust. Use the back of a spoon to form peaks and swirls in the meringue.

Immediately slip the meringue under the broiler and broil (grill) until the peaks are browned, 1–2 minutes. (Alternatively, use a kitchen torch to brown the peaks.)

BASIC BAKED MERINGUES

Unlike a soft meringue used for topping (see opposite), this meringue uses more sugar and is formed into small or large disks, which are baked until light, dry, and slightly chewy. The meringue can then be used as a base for whipped cream and fresh fruit.

6 egg whites

¼ teaspoon cream of tartar

1 cup (8 oz/250 g) superfine (caster) sugar

MAKES THREE 8-INCH (20-CM) MERINGUES OR EIGHT 4-INCH (10-CM) MERINGUES

Position 2 racks in the lower third of the oven and preheat to 300°F (150°C). Cut sheets of parchment (baking) paper to fit the bottoms of 2 rimmed baking sheets. Depending on whether you are making individual meringues or large layers, draw eight 4-inch (10-cm) or three 8-inch (20-cm) circles on the parchment sheets, making the lines dark enough to show through the sheets. Place the sheets, circle sides down, on the baking sheets.

Place the egg whites in a large bowl. Using an electric mixer, beat on medium speed until blended. Sprinkle in the cream of tartar and continue beating until white and foamy and beginning to thicken. On medium-high speed, gradually add the sugar and continue beating until stiff, shiny peaks form. The whole process should take about 4 minutes.

Spoon the egg whites onto the circles on the prepared baking sheets, spreading to fill the circles and building up the edges slightly. Alternatively, fill a pastry (piping) bag fitted with a large plain tip and pipe the meringue in a tight spiral, starting at the center of each circle, filling each circle completely, and building up the edges slightly.

Bake until firm and dry, about 1 hour. Turn off the oven and open the oven door. When the meringues are completely cool, remove them from the oven and carefully peel off the parchment. The meringues can be used immediately or stored, uncovered, on a rack (so the air can circulate around them) in a dry place (not refrigerated) for several days. If humid weather softens the meringues, dry them in a 150°F (65°C) oven for 10 minutes, then leave them to cool completely in the turned-off oven until ready to serve.

Make it hazelnut

For a nut-laced meringue, finely grind ⅓ cup (2 oz/ 60 g) toasted and skinned hazelnuts (filberts/page 478), in a food processor, then gently fold the ground nuts into the egg whites before forming the disks.

455

Presenting meringues

For individual meringues, spread each meringue with Whipped Cream (opposite, left), top each with sliced fruit or berries, and serve. For a more elegant presentation, make 3 large disks, layer the cream and fruit between them, then top off the stack with more fruit.

CONFECTIONERS' SUGAR ICING

Watch for lumps

Confectioners' sugar is also known as powdered sugar or icing sugar. To keep it free-flowing, always stir the sugar well (or recipes sometimes call for sifting it) to remove any lumps before combining the sugar with a liquid.

This basic white icing is perfect for drizzling on warm cakes, allowing it to run down the sides, or for spreading or piping onto cooled cupcakes or cookies. It can also be flavored in a variety of ways (see the variations that follow).

In a small saucepan over medium heat, stir together the butter and 1 tablespoon water until the butter melts. Remove from the heat; let stand until cool, about 5 minutes.

Add the sugar to the butter mixture and whisk vigorously until completely smooth and thickened, about 1 minute. If you plan to drizzle the icing, use it within 5 minutes or it may become too thick. If it does become too thick, rewarm it over low heat for 2–3 seconds, whisking constantly until it loosens.

For orange icing Use 1 tablespoon undiluted thawed, frozen orange juice concentrate in place of the water.

For brown sugar icing Add ¼ cup (2 oz/60 g) firmly packed brown sugar to the warm butter mixture and stir until the sugar dissolves. Let the mixture cool, then whisk in the confectioners' sugar.

For lime or lemon icing Use 1 tablespoon fresh lime or lemon juice in place of the water and add ½ teaspoon grated lime or lemon zest with the sugar.

4 tablespoons (2 oz/60 g) unsalted butter

½ cup (2 oz/60 g) confectioners' (icing) sugar

MAKES A SCANT ½ CUP (4 FL OZ/125 ML)

CREAM CHEESE FROSTING

The real deal

Substituting fat-free, light, or whipped cream cheese here will compromise the outcome. If you're counting calories, spread the frosting on thinly or eat a smaller piece.

You can use this rich, tangy frosting on a variety of desserts, but it is especially popular on spice-laced treats, such as those based on carrot, pumpkin, or ginger. It's a natural on Carrot Cake (page 498), but you could also try it on Spiced Walnut Cake (page 512).

In a large bowl, using an electric mixer, beat together the cream cheese and butter on medium-high speed until smooth. On low speed, add the sugar and beat until smooth. Beat in the vanilla.

Use immediately, or cover and refrigerate for up to 1 week, then bring back to room temperature before using.

For orange–cream cheese frosting Add 2 tablespoons undiluted thawed, frozen orange juice concentrate and 1½ teaspoons grated orange zest with the vanilla.

For coconut–cream cheese frosting Beat 1½ teaspoons coconut extract and 1 cup (3 oz/90 g) toasted sweetened flaked dried coconut (see note, opposite) into the finished frosting.

1 lb (500 g) cream cheese, at room temperature

6 tablespoons (3 oz/90 g) unsalted butter, at room temperature

1¼ cups (5 oz/155 g) confectioners' (icing) sugar

1½ teaspoons pure vanilla extract

MAKES ABOUT 2¾ CUPS (22 FL OZ/680 ML)

DECORATING ICING

Use this easy-to-make icing to decorate cakes and cutout cookies. Add enough milk to achieve the desired consistency: less milk yields a thick frosting appropriate for piping or spreading; more milk results in a thin glaze perfect for drizzling.

1 cup (4 oz/125 g) confectioners' (icing) sugar

¼ teaspoon pure vanilla extract

4–5 teaspoons milk

Food coloring, optional

MAKES ABOUT ½ CUP (4 FL OZ/125 ML)

Sift the confectioners' sugar into a small bowl. Add the vanilla extract and stir until smooth.

Stir in enough milk to thin the icing to the desired consistency (see note, above). Mix in food coloring (see note, right) and use the icing right away for piping, spreading, or drizzling on baked goods.

Coloring with care

When using food coloring to tint an icing or frosting, add only a drop at a time, then stir to combine. It's easier to add another drop of coloring to darken it further than it is to correct an icing that is too dark.

VANILLA BUTTERCREAM

This is a must-have recipe for any baker's repertoire. The smooth, creamy, full-flavored frosting is used on layer cakes or cupcakes and in rolled cakes. Add a flavoring (see the variations that follow) or food coloring to fit the dessert and the occasion.

⅔ cup (5 oz/155 g) sugar

4 egg yolks, at room temperature

1 tablespoon water

1 cup (8 oz/250 g) unsalted butter, at room temperature, cut into tablespoon-size pieces

1½ teaspoons pure vanilla extract, or 1 vanilla bean, split lengthwise

MAKES ABOUT 2⅓ CUPS (19 FL OZ/580 ML)

457

In a heatproof bowl, whisk together the sugar, egg yolks, and water. Set over (but not touching) simmering water in a saucepan. Whisk constantly until the mixture registers 170°F (77°C) on a candy thermometer, about 4 minutes.

Remove the bowl from over the water. Using an electric mixer on high speed, beat the egg mixture until cool and thick, about 5 minutes. Add the butter, 1 tablespoon at a time, beating until smooth after each addition. Beat in the vanilla extract, if using. Or, if using the vanilla bean, with the tip of a sharp knife, scrape the seeds from the pod into the buttercream, then beat to distribute the seeds evenly. If the buttercream appears broken or lumpy, set the bowl back over simmering water for a few seconds, then beat again until smooth.

To store, cover and refrigerate for up to 2 days. Before using, let stand at room temperature until softened. If necessary, rewarm over a saucepan of simmering water for a few seconds, stirring until smooth.

For coconut buttercream Add 1 teaspoon coconut extract with the vanilla extract. Toast ½ cup (1½ oz/45 g) sweetened flaked dried coconut (see note, right), and stir it into the finished buttercream.

For chocolate buttercream Add 8 oz (250 g) semisweet (plain) chocolate, melted and cooled, with the vanilla.

Worth the investment

Vanilla is produced in tropical countries around the world, from Mexico to Tahiti to Madagascar, and each source boasts the distinctive flavor of its product. Always use the best-quality vanilla you can afford. Tightly capped and stored in a cool, dark place, it keeps indefinitely.

Toasting coconut

To toast flaked dried coconut, spread the desired amount evenly on a baking sheet and bake in a 350°F (180°C) oven, stirring occasionally, until pale gold, about 8 minutes.

SOUR CREAM FUDGE FROSTING

Go nuts

If you like nuts with your chocolate, stir a handful of finely chopped nuts, preferably toasted (page 17), into the frosting. Or, arrange whole nuts or nut halves in a decorative pattern on the top or sides of the frosted cake.

When a cake calls for something ultrarich, creamy, and chocolaty, this is the answer. Sour cream can curdle if exposed to high heat, so be sure to let the butter-cream-chocolate mixture cool until it is just warm enough to melt the sour cream when it is added.

In a heavy saucepan , combine the butter and cream over low heat and heat, stirring frequently, until the butter melts. Add the chocolate and whisk until melted and smooth, about 2 minutes. Remove the mixture from the heat and let cool to lukewarm, about 8 minutes.

Whisk in the sour cream until fully combined, then whisk in the confectioners' sugar. Let stand until thick enough to spread, about 10 minutes.

If the frosting becomes too stiff to spread, rewarm it briefly over low heat and whisk again until smooth.

For mocha frosting Add 1 tablespoon instant espresso powder or regular coffee powder to the butter and cream.

For tangerine-fudge frosting Whisk in 1 tablespoon grated tangerine zest before adding the confectioners' sugar.

4 tablespoons (2 oz/60 g) unsalted butter

¼ cup (2 fl oz/60 ml) heavy (double) cream

10 oz (315 g) bittersweet chocolate, chopped

¾ cup (6 oz/180 g) sour cream

1 cup (4 oz/125 g) confectioners' (icing) sugar

MAKES ABOUT 2⅔ CUPS (21 FL OZ/660 ML)

CHOCOLATE GANACHE

Adding flavor

To flavor the ganache, add a liqueur, such as Grand Marnier, framboise, or amaretto, or an extract, perhaps almond or orange, starting with a tiny amount and adding more as needed to taste.

Made from just two ingredients, ganache is versatile: While still barely warm, it can be poured over cakes to form a smooth glaze. Once cooled, it can be used to fill cookie sandwiches or frost bar cookies, or it can be fashioned into truffles or whipped to fill various pastries.

In a small saucepan over medium heat, gently warm the cream until small bubbles appear around the edge of the pan. Remove from the heat. Stir in the chocolate until it has melted and the mixture is smooth. Do not stir so vigorously that bubbles form. Alternatively, place the chocolate in a food processor or blender, pour in the hot cream, and let stand for 15 seconds, then process until smooth.

Use right away, or let cool, transfer to a tightly covered container, and refrigerate for up to 1 month or freeze for up to 6 months.

1 cup (8 fl oz/250 ml) heavy (double) cream

10 oz (315 g) semisweet (plain) or bittersweet chocolate, chopped

MAKES ABOUT 3 CUPS (24 FL OZ/750 ML)

BITTERSWEET CHOCOLATE GLAZE

The addition of dark corn syrup makes this glaze a bit thicker, shinier, and more deeply flavored than Chocolate Ganache (see left). Light corn syrup may be substituted. The flavor will not be as intense, but the consistency of the glaze will be the same.

6 tablespoons (3 fl oz/90 ml) heavy (double) cream

6 tablespoons (3 oz/90 g) dark corn syrup

8 oz (250 g) bittersweet chocolate, chopped

MAKES ABOUT 1⅓ CUPS (11 FL OZ/330 ML)

In a heavy saucepan over medium heat, combine the cream and corn syrup and bring to a simmer. Reduce the heat to low, add the chocolate, and whisk over the heat until the mixture is smooth, about 1 minute.

Remove from the heat and let stand until lukewarm, about 10 minutes. The glaze should be thick but still pourable.

Chocolate on the outside

Use this glaze when you want a firm chocolate shell on the surface of a cheesecake, such as the Peanut Butter Cheesecake on page 515.

CHOCOLATE COATING

A versatile performer, this scrumptious coating can be applied to biscotti or other cookies in a variety of ways, four of which are detailed here. Be sure to store chocolate-coated cookies in the refrigerator to prevent the chocolate from softening.

8 oz (250 g) semisweet (plain) or bittersweet chocolate, chopped

2 teaspoons vegetable shortening (vegetable lard)

MAKES ABOUT ¾ CUP (6 FL OZ/180 ML)

In a heatproof bowl, combine the chocolate and shortening. Set over (but not touching) simmering water in a saucepan. Heat, stirring occasionally, just until the chocolate and shortening melt and the mixture becomes smooth. Remove from the heat and use right away.

To coat cookie tops (or bottoms) with the chocolate: using a small icing spatula or a table knife, spread the chocolate evenly over the surface. Set the cookies, chocolate sides up, on a baking sheet.

To coat one end of cookies with the chocolate: grasp the cookie with your fingers and dip the opposite end or half in the chocolate. Set on aluminum foil-lined baking sheets.

To drizzle the chocolate decoratively over cookies: dip the tines of a fork (or the tip of a small spoon) in the chocolate and wave the fork back and forth over the cookies.

To create a cookie sandwich: spread a thick layer of the chocolate over the flat side (bottom) of a cookie, stopping just short of the edge. Top with a second cookie, flat side down, and press gently to adhere.

Refrigerate all coated cookies until the chocolate sets.

Fruit loves chocolate

Fruit, such as strawberries or dried apricots, can also be partially dipped in this coating. Refrigerate to firm up the chocolate.

459

HOMEMADE CHOCOLATE SYRUP

Chocolate-mint syrup

To make mint-flavored chocolate syrup, substitute ½ tsp mint extract for the vanilla. Use it to flavor milk or top ice cream.

You'll never have to rely on store-bought chocolate syrup again. Use the syrup hot, or let cool, cover, and chill before serving. Spoon it over ice cream or stir it into a glass of cold milk. The syrup will keep for several weeks in the refrigerator.

In a saucepan over high heat, bring ¾ cup (6 fl oz/180 ml) water to a boil. Reduce the heat to medium-low, add the chocolate, and stir just until the chocolate has melted and the mixture is smooth.

Stir in the sugar and adjust the heat to maintain a bare simmer. Cook the mixture, stirring constantly, until the sugar has completely dissolved and the mixture is smooth and thick, about 5 minutes.

Remove from the heat and stir in the vanilla.

4 oz (125 g) unsweetened chocolate, chopped

1¼ cups (10 oz/310 g) sugar

1 teaspoon pure vanilla extract

MAKES ABOUT 1½ CUPS (12 FL OZ/375 ML)

HOT FUDGE SAUCE

Keep it light

Do not substitute dark corn syrup for the light corn syrup indicated in the recipe. Its more intense flavor will overpower the flavor of the chocolate.

A decadent topping for ice cream, and a classic component of The Ultimate Banana Split (page 618), this sauce can be prepared up to 1 week in advance and stored, tightly covered, in the refrigerator. To use, reheat in a saucepan over low heat, stirring often, until warm and smooth.

In a heavy saucepan over medium-low heat, combine the cream, butter, corn syrup, and sugar. Cook, stirring constantly, until the butter melts and the sugar dissolves, about 3 minutes.

Add the chocolate to the pan and stir until melted and smooth, about 2 minutes.

Remove the sauce from the heat and stir in the vanilla. Let cool slightly before using.

½ cup (4 fl oz/125 ml) heavy (double) cream

½ cup (4 oz/125 g) unsalted butter, cut into pieces

½ cup (4 fl oz/125 ml) light corn syrup

½ cup (2 oz/60 g) confectioners' (icing) sugar

9 oz (280 g) bittersweet chocolate, chopped

1 teaspoon pure vanilla extract

MAKES ABOUT 2½ CUPS (20 FL OZ/625 ML)

BUTTERSCOTCH SAUCE

Spoon this buttery, rich old-fashioned sauce over vanilla ice cream or a slice of gingerbread or pound cake. It can be prepared up to 1 week in advance and stored in a tightly covered container in the refrigerator. Reheat in a heavy saucepan over low heat, stirring often.

1 cup (7 oz/220 g) firmly packed light brown sugar

½ cup (4 fl oz/125 ml) heavy (double) cream

4 tablespoons (2 oz/60 g) unsalted butter, cut into pieces

2 tablespoons dark corn syrup

3 tablespoons Scotch whisky or water

1 teaspoon pure vanilla extract

MAKES ABOUT 1⅓ CUPS (11 FL OZ/340 ML)

In a heavy saucepan over low heat, combine the brown sugar, cream, butter, corn syrup, and whisky and stir with a wooden spoon until the sugar dissolves and the butter melts, about 3 minutes. Raise the heat to medium-high and bring to a boil. Continue to boil, without stirring, until the sauce thinly coats the back of the wooden spoon or a candy thermometer registers 224°F (107°C), about 4 minutes.

Remove the sauce from the heat. Stir in the vanilla and let cool slightly before using.

For orange butterscotch sauce Add 2 teaspoons grated orange zest with the vanilla extract.

For nutty butterscotch sauce Add ⅓ cup (2 oz/60 g) whole pine nuts, pecan or walnut pieces, or crushed macadamia nuts with the vanilla extract.

Substituting honey

If you don't have dark corn syrup in the pantry, you can substitute 2 tbsp honey. The flavor will be slightly different, but the sauce will still be delicious.

461

CARAMEL GLAZE

Ordinary cookies become something special when dressed up with this easy-to-make glaze. Using prepared caramel candies means it's far easier to make than making caramel from scratch. For the best results, start with good-quality caramels.

½ lb (250 g) caramel candies (about 1 cup packed)

MAKES ABOUT ¾ CUP (6 FL OZ/180 ML)

In a small, heavy saucepan over low heat, combine the caramels and ¼ cup (2 fl oz/60 ml) water and stir until the caramels melt and the mixture is smooth. Remove from the heat.

To coat cookie tops with the glaze: using a small icing spatula or a table knife, spread the glaze over the surface. Set the cookies, caramel sides up, on a baking sheet and let stand until cool and set, about 30 minutes.

To drizzle the glaze decoratively over cookies: dip the tines of a fork (or the tip of a spoon) in the caramel and wave the fork back and forth over the cookies. Let stand until cool and set, about 30 minutes.

Caramel vs. butterscotch

Although they are similar, caramel and butterscotch are different. Caramel uses granulated sugar, which is cooked to a deep brown color before mixing it with other ingredients. Butterscotch is simply a mixture of butter and brown sugar.

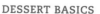

APRICOT GLAZE

Apricots, preserved

Fresh apricots are particularly delicate, which means they don't travel well, plus their season is short. Dried apricots and apricot jam are handy stand-ins for bakers who are looking to add apricot flavor to their desserts.

A coating of warm apricot glaze applied to a just-baked fruit tart makes it glisten. The classic method, in which the jam is strained, makes a perfectly clear glaze, while the food processor version is faster and less wasteful, but not as sparkling.

Classic method: In a small saucepan over medium heat, bring the jam to a boil, stirring frequently. Remove from the heat and strain through a fine-mesh sieve placed over a bowl, pressing on the pulp with the back of a spoon to extract as much liquid as possible. Discard the contents of the sieve, and return the strained jam to the saucepan. Bring to a boil over medium-low heat before using.

Food-processor method: Place the jam in a food processor and process until smooth. Transfer to a small saucepan, place over medium-low heat, and bring to a boil, stirring often. Remove from the heat and use immediately.

1½ cups (15 oz/470 g) apricot jam

MAKES ABOUT 1 CUP (8 FL OZ/250 ML) FOR CLASSIC METHOD, OR 1½ CUPS (12 FL OZ/375 ML) FOR FOOD PROCESSOR METHOD

CURRANT GLAZE

A twist of liqueur

If you like, add 2 tbsp kirsch or other fruit-flavored liqueur to the pan with the jelly and lemon juice.

Currant glaze is darker than apricot glaze and is perfectly clear. It is especially good for brushing on tarts filled with fresh red berries, such as raspberries or strawberries. Use a pastry brush with fine, soft bristles for the best coverage.

In a small, nonreactive saucepan over medium heat, bring the jelly and lemon juice to a boil, stirring often. Remove from the heat and let cool for a minute or two before using.

If the glaze thickens too much upon standing, reheat it gently over low heat to liquefy.

1 cup (10 oz/315 g) red currant jelly

1 tablespoon fresh lemon juice

MAKES ABOUT 1 CUP (8 FL OZ/250 ML)

RASPBERRY SAUCE

Natural pectin

Red currants are high in pectin, a natural jelling agent, which makes them a popular component of jams, jellies, and fruit glazes.

Fresh or frozen raspberries can be used for making this brightly colored sauce. Because the sauce is not cooked, it retains a full raspberry flavor. If you are using frozen raspberries, allow them to thaw before you combine them with the warm currant jelly.

In a small saucepan over medium heat, warm the jelly until it is fully melted, 2–3 minutes.

Place the raspberries in a bowl, stir in the melted jelly, and let cool to room temperature.

Use the sauce right away, or store in a tightly covered container in the refrigerator for up to 3 weeks or in the freezer for up to 2 months.

⅓ cup (3½ oz/105 g) red currant jelly

2 cups (8 oz/250 g) fresh or thawed, frozen raspberries

MAKES 2⅓ CUPS (19 FL OZ/580 ML)

ORANGE MARMALADE–RASPBERRY SAUCE

With just five ingredients and only minutes of prep time, this vibrant red fruit sauce is destined to become a dessert staple in your house. Spoon it over ice creams or granitas, sliced peaches or pears, or Double-Raspberry Soufflés (page 562).

3 cups (12 oz/375 g) fresh or thawed, frozen raspberries

½ cup (5 oz/155 g) orange marmalade

1 tablespoon grated orange zest

2 tablespoons sugar

2 tablespoons orange liqueur (optional)

MAKES ABOUT 1¼ CUPS (10 FL OZ/310 ML)

In a food processor, combine the raspberries and marmalade and process until smooth. Strain the mixture through a fine-mesh sieve placed over a bowl to remove the seeds. It is difficult to remove every seed, so don't worry if a few make their way into the sauce. Stir in the orange zest, sugar, and orange liqueur (if using).

Store the sauce in a tightly covered container in the refrigerator for up to 5 days.

Liqueur levels

With alcohol levels ranging from 50 to 100 proof, liqueurs can overpower the flavor of a sauce. As a general rule, add no more than 2 tbsp liqueur for every 1 cup (8 fl oz/ 250 ml) sauce.

BLUEBERRY SAUCE

The intense color and flavor of blueberries make them a natural for use in sauces and as a garnish. This easy-to-assemble sauce can be served hot, warm, or cold, and on anything from pound cake to custard to pancakes.

¼ cup (2 oz/60 g) sugar

2 tablespoons cornstarch (cornflour)

2 cups (8 oz/250 g) fresh or frozen blueberries

¼ cup (2 fl oz/60 ml) crème de cassis liqueur

¼ cup (2 fl oz/60 ml) fresh orange juice

Juice of 1 lemon, or to taste

MAKES ABOUT 2⅓ CUPS (19 FL OZ/580 ML)

In a small bowl, stir together the sugar and cornstarch.

In a small, nonreactive saucepan over medium heat, combine the blueberries, liqueur, and orange juice. Cook, stirring constantly, until the blueberries begin to release their liquid, 2–3 minutes. Remove from the heat and stir in the cornstarch mixture. Return the pan to low heat and cook, stirring constantly, until the mixture thickens slightly and is no longer cloudy, 3–4 minutes.

Remove the sauce from the heat and stir in the lemon juice. To store, let cool completely, cover tightly, and refrigerate for up to 2 weeks.

Blueberry bloom

Blueberries are in season from May to October. Look for plump berries with a powdery white "bloom" on the skin, which indicates they are fresh. If the season has passed, frozen berries will work fine for this sauce.

VANILLA SUGAR

Cinnamon sugar

For classic cinnamon sugar to dust on cookies or on warm buttered toast, stir together ½ cup (4 oz/125 g) sugar and 1½ tsp ground cinnamon.

This quick preparation will keep for months and can be substituted for the vanilla extract and sugar in almost any recipe. Or, you can sprinkle it over sugar cookies just before you slip them into the oven for baking. It's also good stirred into cups of fresh-brewed coffee.

Cut the vanilla beans into 1½-inch (4-cm) lengths. Place in a blender or food processor and process until coarsely chopped. Add ½ cup (4 oz/125 g) of the sugar and process until the vanilla beans are finely chopped. Add the remaining 1½ cups (12 oz/375 g) sugar and process until thoroughly incorporated.

Sift the sugar through a fine-mesh sieve to remove any large pieces of vanilla bean, then store the sugar in an airtight container at room temperature.

1½ vanilla beans

2 cups (1 lb/500 g) sugar

MAKES 2 CUPS (1 LB/500 G)

CANDIED CITRUS PEEL

464

Calling all citrus

Although orange, lemon, and lime are the most common candidates for candied peels, any citrus will work. For a twist, try the peel of grapefruit or tangerine.

Sweet, tangy strips of candied citrus peel placed on or around a dessert add a bright finishing touch. The candied peel is easy to prepare and can be made in advance. Store it in its own syrup in the refrigerator for up to 5 days.

Using a vegetable peeler, remove the colored part of the peel—the zest—from each fruit in long, wide strips. Leave as much of the bitter white pith on the fruit as you can. Using a small, sharp knife, trim away any pith that remains on the zest, then use a chef's knife to cut the zest into matchsticks.

In a small, nonreactive saucepan, combine the zest strips with water just to cover and place over high heat. As soon as you see large bubbles start to form, remove the pan from the heat and pour the contents into a sieve held over the sink. Hold the sieve under running cold water to cool the strips and help set the color.

In the same pan over medium heat, combine ⅔ cup (5 fl oz/ 160 ml) water, the vinegar, and the sugar. Heat until small bubbles begin to form on the surface of the liquid and stir to dissolve the sugar. Add the citrus strips and continue to simmer until the strips soften and the liquid thickens slightly, about 10 minutes.

If using the candied peel right away, pour into a sieve to drain, discarding the syrup, and spread on a piece of aluminum foil to cool. If not using the peel right away, let the candied peel and syrup cool for several minutes, then transfer to a small bowl, let cool, cover, and refrigerate. Drain well and discard the syrup before using the peel.

2 oranges, lemons, or limes

2 tablespoons cider vinegar

½ cup (4 oz/125 g) sugar

MAKES 2–3 TABLESPOONS

SUGARED FLOWERS

Almost nothing looks prettier atop a cake or cupcake than delicate sugared flowers, and there are many varieties of edible flowers in nature. However, be sure to use flowers that have been grown for consumption and are free of pesticides.

3 tablespoons pasteurized egg whites

3 tablespoons superfine (caster) sugar

20–25 small pesticide-free edible flowers or flower petals such as pansies or rose petals

MAKES 20–25 FLOWERS

Cover a wire rack with parchment (baking) paper. In a small bowl, whisk the eggs whites until foamy, about 1 minute. Put the superfine sugar in another small bowl. Holding 1 flower (or petal) with tweezers, dip a clean paintbrush in the egg white and lightly and evenly coat the flower. For a stiffer flower or petal, paint the underside as well.

Sprinkle the egg white–coated flower lightly and evenly with a little of the sugar, then gently shake any excess sugar back into the bowl. Place the flower or petal, sugar side up (if only one side is sugared), on the prepared rack. Repeat with the remaining flowers or petals, then let stand in a cool, dry place to dry completely, at least 4 hours or up to overnight. (If the weather is hot and humid, dry them in an air-conditioned room.)

Use the flowers right away. Or, arrange them between layers of parchment or waxed paper in an airtight tin, stacking them no more than 4 layers high, and keep in a dry place for up to 2 weeks or in the freezer for up to 3 months.

Picking blossoms

Any edible flowers with small blossoms and simple shapes, such as violets and Peruvian lilies, are good choices for sugaring.

465

NUT CRUNCH

This is an excellent topping for any ice cream or dessert that can use a little crunch. Try it on Fresh Peach or Pumpkin Spice ice creams (pages 606 and 608) or Simple Lemon Custard (page 590). Use your favorite nut or a combination of nuts.

4 tablespoons (2 oz/60 g) unsalted butter

⅔ cup (5 oz/155 g) sugar

½ teaspoon baking soda (bicarbonate of soda)

1 cup (4–5 oz/125–155 g) nuts (see note, left), toasted (page 17) and coarsely chopped

MAKES ABOUT 2 CUPS (8 OZ/250 G)

Generously butter a sheet of aluminum foil about 18 inches (45 cm) long. In a heavy saucepan over medium-low heat, combine the butter, sugar, and ¼ cup (2 fl oz/60 ml) water and cook, stirring, until the sugar dissolves and the butter has melted, about 2 minutes.

Using a pastry brush dipped in water, brush down any sugar crystals that form on the sides of the pan. Raise the heat to medium-high and boil, stirring constantly to prevent burning, until the mixture turns a caramel color, about 8 minutes.

Stir in the baking soda and then the nuts. Immediately turn out the nut mixture onto the buttered foil, separating any large clumps with the back of a spoon. Let cool completely.

Transfer the nut mixture to a work surface and chop coarsely. Use immediately, or transfer to an airtight container and freeze for up to 1 month.

Good and nutty

Many types of nuts work for this recipe. Try almonds, pecans, hazelnuts (filberts), macadamia nuts, walnuts, pecans, or pale green pistachios.

Cookies, BROWNIES & BARS

Cookies, Brownies & Bars

It is hard for anyone to resist a home-baked cookie. Large or small, crisp or chewy, plain or decorated, round, square, or fancifully shaped—cookies are among the easiest treats to mix and shape, whether dropped from a spoon, spread in a pan and cut into bars, or stamped out with a cutter. In this chapter, you'll find basic guidelines for successful cookie making, followed by over two dozen recipes for cookies of all kinds.

Cookie Types and Techniques

Have enough equipment
For most home cookie baking, two large baking sheets and two or three large wire racks for cooling are adequate. If you often bake large batches of cookies, consider buying more.

Difficult dough
Hot, humid weather can make it tricky to roll out cookie dough. One solution is to bake only on cool, dry days. If that isn't an option, chill the dough before rolling and rub the rolling pin and work surface with ample flour. If the dough still softens too much during rolling and rips or tears, refrigerate it for about 20 minutes and rub the rolling pin with a little more flour.

Preventing overbrowning
Sugar-rich cookie doughs brown more than other types of dough. To slow browning so cookies bake thoroughly without getting too dark, use insulated baking sheets or line regular ones with aluminum foil. Check your oven temperature with an oven thermometer and reduce the heat if necessary. Dark-colored baking sheets absorb heat more readily and promote more rapid baking; if you are using them, you may need to lower the oven temperature by 20° to 25°F (10° to 15°C).

Most cookies are easy to make: Just combine flour, a sweetener, butter and/or eggs, and a flavoring to make a batter or dough, form it into small rounds or another shape, and bake until golden. But countless small changes in ingredients, proportions, and techniques can lead to a wide variety of cookies, all of which are typically categorized according to how they are made.

DROP COOKIES   These are probably the easiest cookies to make. You simply mix the batter in a bowl, drop it onto a baking sheet, and bake. Soft, butter-rich batters generally yield tender, chewy cookies. Longer baking times produce crispier results.

To make drop cookies, follow the recipe instructions to beat together the softened butter and sugar until light and fluffy. Beat in the eggs, and then the dry ingredients. Scoop up the batter with a tablespoon and use a second spoon to push it off onto an ungreased baking sheet. Space the cookies as directed in the recipe, because some drop cookies spread more than others.

CUTOUT COOKIES   Shapes for these rolled-out cookies vary widely. Much of the fun of cutouts comes in decorating the cooled baked cookies with colored icings or frostings, sprinkles, and other embellishments.

To make cutouts, use a firm, chilled dough. With a rolling pin, roll out the dough on a floured work surface to a uniform thickness. Then, using a cookie cutter, press down into the dough to cut out a shape. If the dough is sticking to the cutter, dip the edges first in flour. Repeat to cut out as many cookies as possible. Gather the scraps together, reroll, and cut out more cookies.

REFRIGERATOR COOKIES   These old-fashioned treats are made from a fairly firm dough that is chilled and then sliced for baking.

To make refrigerator cookies, mix the dough, place it near the center of a sheet of waxed paper or plastic wrap, and shape into a rough log. Fold one side of the paper or plastic over the dough, and shape the dough into a log in the size specified in the recipe. Roll up the log tightly in the paper and refrigerate until firm. Unwrap, slice into individual cookies, and bake.

COOKIE-PRESS COOKIES   A cookie press, a cylindrical tool outfitted with a plunger mechanism and a variety of decorative plates, is used to shape firm, pliable dough into shapes by extruding it through a plate onto a baking sheet.

To shape cookies with a cookie press, roll the dough into a cylinder with a diameter slightly smaller than that of the press and about the same length and slip the log into the cookie press. Select a design plate, fit it into its holder, and screw it on securely. Then, hold the press upright, grasp its handle, and, applying even pressure, press out the dough to form cookies. Cookie press models vary, so read the manufacturers' instructions carefully for your model.

BISCOTTI The term generally refers to firm, crisp Italian cookies that are baked twice, once in the form of a log and then again after slicing.

To make biscotti, form the smooth, uniform dough into 1 or more logs on a floured work surface, then carefully transfer to a prepared baking sheet. Smooth the surface with floured palms or a large spoon onto the prepared baking sheet in 1 or more rough log shapes, and then shape with floured hands. Make sure the logs are well spaced on the pan and, if the recipe directs, slightly flatten the logs. Bake until lightly browned and firm to the touch. Let cool as directed in individual recipes, then cut crosswise into slices with a sharp, serrated knife. Arrange the slices cut side down on the baking sheets, and bake again until crisp and golden.

BROWNIES AND OTHER BAR COOKIES Simple-to-assemble bar cookies are made from soft, rich batters and baked in straight-sided pans. Once cooled, the sheet of tender, cakelike cookies is cut into bite-size squares or rectangles. Some also feature a flavorful bottom crust.

To make bar cookies without a bottom crust, such as brownies, line the baking pan with a sheet of aluminum foil large enough to cover the bottom and sides, pressing the foil into the pan and folding any excess over the rim, or butter the pan. Prepare and add the batter and bake according to the recipe instructions. Among the most common doneness tests for bar cookies are the following: until the center is springy to the touch; until the top is browned; or until a tester such as a toothpick inserted into the center comes out with a few moist crumbs attached. Let cool completely in the pan on a wire rack. If you have lined the pan with foil, grasp the foil at opposite ends, lift out onto a work surface, peel back the foil, and cut into squares or bars. If you have buttered the pan, cut into squares or bars in the pan.

Decorating Tips, Ideas, and Methods

As the recipes in this chapter demonstrate, you can bring variety and add a personal touch to the cookies you bake by decorating them in simple ways. Here are some of the most common approaches.

FOOD COLORING Add a few drops of food coloring to a cookie dough or its icing. Because it is highly concentrated, be sure to add it sparingly.

SUGARS You can use sugar in various forms to add a decorative or flavorful touch to cookies before they go into the oven or after baking. Look for colored sugar crystals in your market's baking section.

SPRINKLES All kinds of colorful and flavorful sprinkles—rainbow hued, chocolate, or metallic; tiny balls; elongated, confetti shapes—await purchase. Depending on the recipe, some can be added before baking, and others after the cookies come out of the oven or are iced.

GLAZES Ordinary cookies become special when drizzled with an easy-to-make glaze such as Caramel Glaze (page 461).

ICINGS A basic confectioners' (icing) sugar icing gives a finished look to baked treats. Spread Decorating Icing (page 457) on with a small icing spatula, drizzle from a fork, or use a pastry (piping) bag to pipe on decorative patterns.

COATINGS Thicker than icings, coatings can be spread or drizzled onto cookies, or used as a dip or filling. Try Chocolate Coating on page 459.

Rotating baking sheets
If you're baking two sheets of cookies at once, switch the sheets between the racks and rotate them front to back halfway through the baking time to ensure they bake more evenly and at the same rate.

Let baking sheets cool
If you're making multiple batches of cookies, be sure to let the pans cool before placing more cookie dough on them. Otherwise, the hot sheets will cause the cookies to spread too much as they bake in the oven.

Planning ahead
If you are lining baking sheets with parchment (baking) paper, you can save time by preparing each batch of cookies on parchment off the pan and then transferring the loaded parchment to the cooled baking sheet just before the sheet goes into the oven.

Storing cookies
Most baked cookies can be stored at room temperature for about 5 days. Soft cookies with lots of fat, such as chocolate chunk (page 471), will not keep as long as crispier ones, such as biscotti (page 482). Transfer fully cooled cookies to an airtight container.

Storing bars
Cover bars that have not been cut and removed from the pan with aluminum foil and set aside at room temperature for up to a day. For longer storage, transfer cut bars to an airtight container for up to 5 days.

VANILLA BEAN REFRIGERATOR COOKIES

The vanilla is wonderfully aromatic in this recipe, with vanilla-scented sugar both mixed into the batter and sprinkled on the cookies just before they go into the oven. For miniature versions of the cookies, form logs 1 inch (2.5 cm) in diameter.

Logs in different shapes

In this recipe, the dough is formed into a cylinder, but logs can be formed into different shapes. Form the log on waxed paper as directed, but shape it into a square, rectangle, or triangle. Whatever shape you decide on, leave about 1½ inches (4 cm) uncovered on either end of the waxed paper sheet, so you can twist the ends tightly to seal.

In a bowl, sift together the flour, baking powder, and salt. Set aside. In a large bowl, using an electric mixer on high speed, beat the butter until light and fluffy. Add 1 cup (8 oz/250 g) of the Vanilla Sugar and beat until thoroughly incorporated. Add the egg and beat until light and fluffy. On low speed, add the flour mixture and mix just until incorporated.

Form the dough into a rough log, positioning near the center of a sheet of waxed paper. Fold 1 side of the paper over the dough and press to shape it into an even log about 10 inches (25 cm) long. Wrap tightly in the waxed paper and refrigerate until firm, at least 4 hours or up to overnight.

Preheat the oven to 400°F (200°C). Butter 2 baking sheets.

Unwrap the dough and transfer to a cutting board. Carefully cut into slices ¼ inch (6 mm) thick. Transfer the cookies to the prepared baking sheets, spacing them 1 inch (2.5 cm) apart. Sprinkle with the remaining Vanilla Sugar.

Bake the cookies until the edges are browned, about 12 minutes. Transfer the cookies to wire racks to cool completely. Store the cookies in an airtight container at room temperature for up to 5 days.

1¾ cups (7 oz/220 g) sifted all-purpose (plain) flour

1½ teaspoons baking powder

⅛ teaspoon salt

½ cup (4 oz/125 g) unsalted butter, at room temperature

About 1⅓ cups (11 oz/345 g) Vanilla Sugar (page 464)

1 egg

MAKES ABOUT 42 COOKIES

470

CHOCOLATE CRINKLE COOKIES

These cookies decorate themselves in the oven: the coating of confectioners' sugar crackles in the heat to reveal a fudgelike interior. A combination of unsweetened and semisweet chocolate adds an intense chocolate taste, and a touch of coffee adds complexity to the rich, dark flavor.

Confectioners' sugar coating

Confectioners' (icing) sugar has a tendency to form tiny lumps on sitting, so when you are rolling cookies in it to coat them with a light dusting, it is a good idea to sift the sugar before using.

Line 2 large baking sheets with parchment (baking) paper.

Combine the butter and both chopped chocolates in the top pan of a double boiler or a heatproof bowl. Place over (not touching) barely simmering water and heat, stirring occasionally, until smooth. Set aside to cool slightly.

In a bowl, stir together the flour, baking powder, and salt. Set aside. In another bowl, using an electric mixer on medium-high speed, beat together the eggs and granulated sugar until pale yellow, about 2 minutes. Add the chocolate mixture, vanilla, and dissolved coffee (if using) and beat until incorporated. On low speed, slowly add the flour mixture and beat just until incorporated. Cover the dough and refrigerate until firm, about 2 hours.

Preheat the oven to 325°F (165°C).

4 tablespoons (2 oz/60 g) unsalted butter, at room temperature

4 oz (125 g) unsweetened chocolate, chopped

2 oz (60 g) semisweet (plain) chocolate, chopped

2 cups (10 oz/315 g) all-purpose (plain) flour

1 teaspoon baking powder

¼ teaspoon salt

4 large eggs

2 cups (1 lb/500 g) granulated sugar

1 teaspoon pure
vanilla extract

1 teaspoon instant
coffee powder dissolved
in 2 teaspoons water,
optional

½ cup (2 oz/60 g)
confectioners' (icing)
sugar, sifted

MAKES ABOUT 32 COOKIES

Place the confectioners' sugar in a small, shallow bowl. Scoop up about 1 tablespoon dough, roll it into a ball between your palms, and then roll the ball in the sugar. Place it on the prepared baking sheet. Repeat with the remaining dough, spacing the cookies 2½ inches (6 cm) apart.

Bake the cookies, 1 sheet at a time, until the tops are puffed and crinkled and the cookies feel firm when touched gently. Check after 13 minutes; if the cookies are not done, set the timer for 1 minute, continue to bake, and check again. Leave the cookies to cool on the pan for 5 minutes, then transfer to wire racks to cool completely. Store in an airtight container at room temperature for up to 3 days.

CHOCOLATE-CHUNK COOKIES

Chocolate chip cookies are almost universally loved; big chunks of premium chocolate make them extra special. Dress these up by mixing in about 1½ cups (6 oz/185 g) chopped pitted dried sour or sweet cherries or dried cranberries with the chocolate.

1 cup (5 oz/155 g)
all-purpose (plain) flour

¾ teaspoon baking powder

⅛ teaspoon baking soda
(bicarbonate of soda)

⅛ teaspoon salt

½ cup (4 oz/125 g) plus
2 tablespoons unsalted
butter, at room temperature

¾ cup (6 oz/185 g) firmly
packed dark brown sugar

1 teaspoon pure
vanilla extract

1 egg

8 oz (250 g) semisweet
(plain) chocolate, cut into
½-inch (12-mm) pieces
(about 1½ cups)

MAKES ABOUT 24 COOKIES

Preheat the oven to 350°F (180°C).

In a bowl, sift together the flour, baking powder, baking soda, and salt. Set aside. In another bowl, using an electric mixer on high speed, beat together the butter, brown sugar, and vanilla until fluffy, about 4 minutes. Beat in the egg. On low speed, add the flour mixture and mix just until incorporated. Mix in the chocolate.

Drop the batter by slightly rounded tablespoons onto ungreased baking sheets, spacing the mounds 2 inches (5 cm) apart. Bake until golden brown, about 16 minutes. Transfer the cookies to wire racks to cool. Store in an airtight container at room temperature for up to 4 days.

Cooling cookies

Footed metal cooling racks raise cookies above the work surface, allowing air to circulate and preventing moisture from being trapped on the cookie bottoms. Don't skimp on the cooling step, which will help produce the proper texture.

471

CLASSIC SPRITZ COOKIES

**Patience
makes perfect**

*When working with
a cookie press, be
patient. The first
two or three cookies
may not be perfect.
Gather them up and
repack them into the
cookie press with
the remaining dough.*

Decorating cookies is a favorite holiday-season activity. With this basic dough, a cookie press, some food coloring, and embellishments of your choice, you can shape and decorate cookies to enjoy at home and give as gifts. For cookie press and decorating tips, see page 468–69.

Preheat the oven to 400°F (200°C).

In a large bowl, using an electric mixer on medium-high speed, beat together the butter, sugar, egg, and vanilla and almond extracts until smooth and creamy, about 5 minutes. On low speed, slowly add the flour and mix just until incorporated. If desired, add a few drops of food coloring and mix until evenly distributed. If you want more than one color, divide the dough into 2 or more portions, put each portion in a separate bowl, and tint each portion.

Attach the top and the handle to the cookie press. Pack the dough into the tube, fit the design plate of choice into its holder, and screw the tube onto the press. Press out the cookies onto ungreased baking sheets and add any desired embellishments to the cookies.

Bake the cookies until they are set and just starting to color around the edges, 7 to 10 minutes. Let cool on the pans on wire racks for 1 to 2 minutes, then carefully transfer to wire racks to cool completely. Store in an airtight container at room temperature for up to 5 days.

½ cup (4 oz/125 g) unsalted butter, at room temperature

6 tablespoons (3 oz/90 g) sugar

1 egg

½ teaspoon pure vanilla extract

¼ teaspoon pure almond extract

1¼ cups (6½ oz/200 g) all-purpose (plain) flour

Food coloring, optional

Candied fruits, sprinkles, crystal sugars, or other decorations, optional

MAKES ABOUT 36 COOKIES

HOLIDAY CUTOUT COOKIES

Metal is best

*Some cookie cutters
are made of plastic,
but the best cutters
are made of tinned
steel or stainless
steel, which keeps
a sharp cutting edge
better. Be sure to
dry metal cutters
thoroughly before
storing to avoid
rust deposits or
discoloration.*

These classic Christmas cookies can be cut into any shape, sprinkled with colored sugar crystals and dragées before baking, or decorated with Decorating Icing (page 457) after baking. The dough can be made and refrigerated up to 3 days ahead.

In a large bowl, using an electric mixer on medium speed, beat together the butter and sugar until light and fluffy, about 4 minutes. Beat in the egg yolks, one at a time, beating well after each addition. Split the vanilla bean in half lengthwise and, using a small, sharp knife, scrape the seeds into the butter mixture. Mix well.

In a fine-mesh sieve or a sifter, combine the flour, baking powder, and salt. Sift the flour mixture directly onto the butter mixture. On low speed, beat the butter and flour until they are thoroughly incorporated.

Divide the dough into 4 equal portions. Flatten each portion into a disk, wrap the disks separately in plastic wrap, and refrigerate overnight or up to 3 days. Let soften slightly at room temperature before continuing.

Position a rack in the upper third of the oven and preheat to 350°F (180°C). Butter 2 baking sheets.

1 cup (8 oz/250 g) unsalted butter, at room temperature

¾ cup (6 oz/185 g) sugar

3 egg yolks

1 piece vanilla bean, about 2 inches (5 cm) long, or 1 teaspoon pure vanilla extract

2½ cups (12½ oz/390 g) all-purpose (plain) flour

1 teaspoon baking powder

½ teaspoon salt

MAKES 48–60 COOKIES

On a lightly floured work surface, roll out a dough disk ¼ inch (6 mm) thick. Using cookie cutters in any shape desired, cut out as many cookies as possible. Transfer the cutouts to the prepared baking sheets, spacing them about 1 inch (2.5 cm) apart. Repeat with the remaining dough disks. Gather the scraps together, reroll, and cut out more cookies.

Bake the cookies until golden on the edges, about 8 minutes. Transfer to wire racks to cool completely. Store in an airtight container at room temperature for up to 1 week.

DOUBLE-PEANUT PEANUT BUTTER COOKIES

Here, crunchy chopped salted peanuts are mixed into a sweet-and-salty, peanutty dough for the ultimate peanut butter cookies. If you like, you can pipe lines of Chocolate Coating (page 459) into the grooves on top of the cooled cookies. Refrigerate briefly to set the chocolate.

1⅓ cups (7 oz/220 g) all-purpose (plain) flour

½ teaspoon baking powder

½ teaspoon baking soda (bicarbonate of soda)

Large pinch of salt

½ cup (4 oz/125 g) unsalted butter, at room temperature

½ cup (5 oz/155 g) crunchy peanut butter

½ cup (4 oz/125 g) granulated sugar

½ cup (3½ oz/105 g) firmly packed dark brown sugar

1 egg

1 teaspoon pure vanilla extract

¾ cup (4 oz/125 g) salted dry-roasted peanuts, coarsely chopped

MAKES 24 COOKIES

Preheat the oven to 375°F (190°C). Lightly butter 1 large rimmed baking sheet.

In a bowl, stir together the flour, baking powder, baking soda, and salt. Set aside. In a large bowl, using an electric mixer on medium-high speed, beat together the butter, peanut butter, granulated sugar, brown sugar, egg, and vanilla until smooth and creamy, about 4 minutes. On low speed, slowly add the flour mixture and beat just until the flour is incorporated. Stir in the peanuts.

Scoop up about 1 tablespoon dough, roll it into a ball between your palms, and place on a prepared baking sheet. Repeat with the remaining dough, spacing the balls 3 inches (7.5 cm) apart. Flatten each ball by pressing on the top with the back of a fork. (If the dough sticks to the fork, dip the fork into granulated sugar before pressing.) Each cookie should be about ½ inch (12 mm) thick.

Bake the cookies until lightly browned, about 12 minutes. Let cool on the pan on a wire rack for 2 minutes, then transfer to wire racks to cool completely. Store in an airtight container at room temperature for up to 5 days.

Cookie-filled care packages

Most cookies ship well if individually wrapped, or paired back to back, and packed securely. Avoid delicate cookies that break easily, cookies with frostings or fillings that could melt in hot weather, or cookies that require refrigeration. Ship the cookies early in the week to ensure they don't sit in a warehouse over the weekend.

SNICKERDOODLES

A topping of cinnamon sugar distinguishes these classic cookies. The sugar crystals add an appealing crunchy contrast to the cookies' soft interiors. Serve with a tall glass of cold milk for a favorite afternoon snack.

Preheat the oven to 400°F (200°C).

In a small, shallow bowl, stir together the 2 tablespoons sugar and the cinnamon. Set aside. In another bowl, whisk together the flour, cream of tartar, baking soda, and salt. Set the mixture aside.

In a large bowl, using an electric mixer on medium-high speed, beat together the butter, the ¾ cup sugar, the egg, and vanilla until smooth and creamy, about 4 minutes. Reduce the mixer speed to low, slowly add the flour mixture, and beat just until incorporated.

Scoop up about 1 teaspoon dough, roll it into a ball between your palms, roll it in the cinnamon sugar, and place on an ungreased baking sheet. Repeat with the remaining dough, spacing the balls 2 inches (5 cm) apart.

Bake the cookies until they are round, flat, and light golden brown, 8–10 minutes. Let the cookies cool on the pan on a wire rack for 1–2 minutes, then transfer to wire racks to cool completely. Store in an airtight container at room temperature for up to 5 days.

2 tablespoons plus
¾ cup (6 oz/185 g) sugar

2 teaspoons ground
cinnamon

1⅓ cups (5½ oz/170 g)
all-purpose (plain) flour

1 teaspoon cream of tartar

½ teaspoon baking soda
(bicarbonate of soda)

Pinch of salt

½ cup (4 oz/125 g)
unsalted butter,
at room temperature

1 egg

½ teaspoon pure
vanilla extract

MAKES ABOUT 24 COOKIES

CHEWY GINGER COOKIES

A good, gingery ginger cookie is irresistible. These are a bit chewy and full of flavor. You can double the recipe and keep extra logs of the dough in the freezer for up to 1 month. When you want to bake them, thaw partially, slice with a serrated knife, and bake as directed.

In a bowl, sift together the flour, baking soda, ground ginger, cinnamon, salt, and white pepper. Set aside. In a large bowl, using an electric mixer on medium-high speed, beat together the butter and sugar until creamy, about 5 minutes. Add the egg and beat until the mixture is fluffy, about 5 minutes. Then add the molasses and beat until incorporated. On low speed, slowly add the flour mixture to the butter mixture and beat until fully incorporated, 2–3 minutes. Stir in the crystallized ginger and nuts until evenly distributed.

Divide the dough in half. Form half of the dough into a rough log in the center of a sheet of waxed paper. Fold 1 side of the paper over the dough and press to shape it into an even log 1½ inches (4 cm) in diameter. Wrap tightly in the waxed paper. Repeat with the remaining dough. Refrigerate the logs until firm, at least 4 hours or up to 2 days.

2½ cups (12½ oz/390 g)
all-purpose (plain) flour

2½ teaspoons baking soda
(bicarbonate of soda)

1½ tablespoons
ground ginger

½ teaspoon *each* ground
cinnamon and salt

¼ teaspoon ground
white pepper

¾ cup plus 2 tablespoons
(7 oz/220 g) unsalted butter,
at room temperature

1¼ cups (10 oz/315 g) sugar,
plus more for sprinkling

1 extra-large egg

½ cup (scant 6 oz/185 g) unsulfured dark molasses

¼ cup (1½ oz/45 g) minced crystallized ginger

1¼ cups (5 oz/155 g) pecans or (6 oz/185 g) macadamia nuts, toasted (see page 17) and coarsely chopped

MAKES ABOUT 48 COOKIES

Preheat the oven to 325°F (165°C). Line 2 baking sheets with parchment (baking) paper.

Using a sharp knife, cut each log into slices ⅛ inch (3 mm) thick. Arrange the slices on the prepared baking sheets, spacing them about 1 inch (2.5 cm) apart.

Bake the cookies until golden, 8–10 minutes. Transfer to wire racks, sprinkle with sugar, and let cool completely. Store in an airtight container at room temperature for up to 1 week.

GINGERBREAD CUTOUTS

This is the perfect dough for making gingerbread people, but you can cut the cookies into any shape you like. Apply the icing with a pastry bag or knife, let dry, and then, using a tiny brush and food coloring, paint on decorations as desired.

¾ cup (6 oz/185 g) unsalted butter, at room temperature

¾ cup (6 oz/185 g) firmly packed light brown sugar

¼ cup (3 oz/90 g) unsulfured light molasses

2 egg yolks

2⅓ cups (12 oz/375 g) unbleached all-purpose (plain) flour

2 teaspoons ground cinnamon

2 teaspoons ground ginger

1 teaspoon ground allspice

½ teaspoon baking soda (bicarbonate of soda)

¼ teaspoon ground cloves

¼ teaspoon salt

½ cup (4 fl oz/125 ml) Decorating Icing (page 457)

MAKES ABOUT 20 COOKIES

In a bowl, using an electric mixer on medium-high speed, beat together the butter, brown sugar, and molasses until fluffy, about 3 minutes. Beat in the egg yolks one at a time. In a fine-mesh sieve or a sifter, combine the flour, cinnamon, ginger, allspice, baking soda, cloves, and salt. Sift the flour mixture directly onto the butter mixture. With the mixer on low speed, beat until thoroughly incorporated.

Divide the dough into 3 equal portions. Shape each portion into a disk, wrap the disks separately in plastic wrap, and refrigerate overnight.

Position 2 racks in the upper third of the oven and preheat to 375°F (190°C). Butter 2 baking sheets.

Remove 1 dough disk from the refrigerator. On a lightly floured work surface, roll it out ¼ inch (6 mm) thick. Using a figure-shaped or other cookie cutter, cut out as many cookies as possible. Transfer the cutouts to the prepared baking sheets, spacing them about 1 inch (2.5 cm) apart. Repeat with the remaining dough disks. Gather the scraps together, reroll, and cut out more cookies.

Bake the cookies until they begin to turn golden brown on the edges, about 10 minutes. Transfer the cookies to wire racks to cool completely.

Decorate the cooled cookies with the icing as desired. Store the finished cookies in an airtight container at room temperature for up to 1 week.

Softening butter quickly

If you are short on time and want to use butter that is still cold from the refrigerator, thinly slice it and use an electric mixer to beat the butter for a couple of minutes to soften it.

CHRISTMAS SPICE CUTOUTS

Difficult dough

If the chilled dough disks are too firm to roll out easily, let them stand at room temperature for 5 to 10 minutes, depending on the temperature of your kitchen, then try again.

This is a recipe guaranteed to give your house the aroma of the holidays. If you like, sprinkle with Vanilla Sugar or Cinnamon Sugar (page 464) instead of the colored crystal sugars. Or, spread the cookies with Confectioners' Sugar Icing (page 456) after baking and cooling.

In a food processor, pulse the walnuts to grind finely (do not grind to a paste). Add ¼ cup (1½ oz/45 g) of the flour and ¼ cup (2 oz/60 g) of the brown sugar and grind to a powder. Set aside. In a bowl, sift together the remaining 1¾ cups (9 oz/270 g) flour, the spices, and baking soda. Set aside.

In a large bowl, using an electric mixer on medium-high speed, beat together the butter, vanilla, and the remaining ½ cup (4 oz/125 g) brown sugar until light and fluffy, about 5 minutes. Beat in the honey and egg. On low speed, slowly add the flour-spice mixture and the nut mixture and beat just until incorporated.

Gather the dough into a ball, then divide in half. Flatten each half into a disk, wrap the disks separately in plastic wrap, and refrigerate for at least 1 hour or up to overnight.

Preheat the oven to 350°F (180°C). Butter 2 baking sheets.

Flour 1 disk and place between 2 sheets of waxed paper. Roll out the dough ¼ inch (6 mm) thick. Using decoratively shaped cutters, cut out as many cookies as possible. Transfer the cutouts to a prepared baking sheet, spacing them ½ inch (12 mm) apart. Sprinkle with the crystal sugars, if using. Repeat with the remaining disk. Gather the scraps together, reroll, and cut out more cookies.

Bake the cookies until lightly golden, about 10 minutes. Transfer to wire racks to cool completely. Store in an airtight container in the refrigerator for up to 2 weeks.

½ cup (2 oz/60 g) walnuts

2 cups (10 oz/315 g) all-purpose (plain) flour

¾ cup (6 oz/185 g) firmly packed light brown sugar

½ teaspoon ground cloves

½ teaspoon ground ginger

½ teaspoon ground allspice

½ teaspoon ground cinnamon

½ teaspoon baking soda (bicarbonate of soda)

½ cup (4 oz/125 g) unsalted butter, at room temperature

2 teaspoons pure vanilla extract

¼ cup (3 oz/90 g) honey

1 egg

Colored sugar crystals, optional

MAKES ABOUT 36 COOKIES

Reusing baking sheets

If you are using the same baking sheet to make multiple batches of cookies, let the pan cool completely before adding another batch of dough, or the dough will spread too much in the oven. Three baking sheets is ideal, so you can have one in the oven, one cooling off, and one you are topping with dough.

PFEFFERNEUSSE

With its familiar coating of confectioners' sugar, this version of the popular northern European "pepper nut" cookie is a favorite at Christmastime. The bite-size treats are characterized by their heady mix of spices, including the pepper for which they are named.

In a bowl, sift together the flour, salt, pepper, aniseed, cinnamon, baking soda, allspice, nutmeg, and cloves. In a large bowl, using an electric mixer on medium speed, beat together the butter, brown sugar, and molasses until light and fluffy, about 4 minutes. Beat in the egg. On low speed, slowly add the flour mixture and beat until incorporated. Cover and refrigerate for several hours.

Preheat the oven to 350°F (180°C). Butter 2 baking sheets.

2¼ cups (11½ oz/360 g) all-purpose (plain) flour

½ teaspoon salt

½ teaspoon ground pepper

½ teaspoon crushed aniseed

½ teaspoon ground cinnamon

¼ teaspoon baking soda (bicarbonate of soda)

¼ teaspoon ground allspice

¼ teaspoon ground nutmeg

⅛ teaspoon ground cloves

½ cup (4 oz/125 g) unsalted butter, at room temperature

¾ cup (6 oz/185 g) firmly packed light brown sugar

¼ cup (3 oz/90 g) unsulfured light molasses

1 egg

About 2 cups (8 oz/250 g) confectioners' (icing) sugar

MAKES ABOUT 30 COOKIES

Scoop up a spoonful of dough, roll between your palms into a ball about 1½ inches (4 cm) in diameter, and place on a prepared baking sheet. Repeat with the remaining dough, spacing the balls 2 inches (5 cm) apart.

Bake the cookies until golden brown on the bottom and firm to the touch, about 14 minutes. Let cool on the pans on wire racks for about 3 minutes or so. Put the confectioners' sugar in a sturdy paper bag, drop in a few warm cookies, close the top securely, and shake gently to coat the warm cookies with the sugar. Transfer to the wire racks to cool completely. Repeat with the remaining warm cookies. Store in an airtight container at cool room temperature for up to 1 week.

MEXICAN WEDDING COOKIES

These traditional cookies can be baked and coated with confectioners' sugar up to 2 days before serving and stored in an airtight container at room temperature. Uncoated cookies can be kept in an airtight container for up to 1 week; roll in the sugar just before serving.

1 cup (4 oz/125 g) pecans, toasted (page 17)

1 cup (8 oz/250 g) unsalted butter, at room temperature

⅓ cup (3 oz/90 g) granulated sugar

1 teaspoon pure vanilla extract

Grated zest of 2 oranges

¼ cup (2 fl oz/60 ml) orange juice

2 egg yolks

3 cups (15 oz/470 g) all-purpose (plain) flour

About 1 cup (4 oz/125 g) confectioners' (icing) sugar, sifted

MAKES ABOUT 36 COOKIES

In a food processor, pulse the pecans to grind finely (do not grind to a paste). Set aside.

In a large bowl, using an electric mixer on medium speed, beat together the butter and granulated sugar until light and fluffy, 5–8 minutes. Add the vanilla, orange zest and juice, and egg yolks and beat until fully blended. On low speed, beat in the flour, 1 cup at a time, beating well after each addition. Stir in the ground pecans. The dough should be soft and light. Cover the bowl and refrigerate the dough until slightly chilled, about 30 minutes.

Preheat the oven to 350°F (180°C). Line a baking sheet with parchment (baking) paper.

Scoop up about 1 teaspoon dough, roll it into a ball between your palms, and place on the prepared baking sheet. Repeat with the remaining dough, spacing the balls of dough about 1 inch (2.5 cm) apart.

Bake until golden, about 10 minutes. Transfer to wire racks to cool for a few minutes. Put the confectioners' sugar in a bowl. Roll as many warm cookies as you think will be eaten within 2 days in the sugar, coating evenly. Let the coated and uncoated cookies cool completely on wire racks.

Securing parchment paper

To prevent the parchment (baking) paper from sliding around on the cookie sheet, dot the corners of the pan with butter to "glue" the paper down.

BROWN SUGAR–HAZELNUT RUGELACH

This tasty variation on a Jewish favorite combines hazelnuts and brown sugar, instead of the traditional walnuts and granulated sugar. To cut each dough round into 12 even wedges, divide it into quarters, then cut each quarter into 3 equal wedges.

**Natural
cream cheese**

*Many bakers prefer
natural cream cheese
for its taste and
because it does not
contain the stabilizers
or additives present
in most commercial
brands. Look for
natural cream cheese
in natural-foods stores
or cheese shops.*

To make the dough, in a large bowl, using an electric mixer on high speed, beat together the butter and cream cheese until smooth. Mix in the salt. On low speed, add the flour and mix just until a dough forms.

Turn out the dough onto a floured work surface. Using floured hands, form the dough into a log. Cut into 4 equal portions. Flatten each portion into a disk, wrap the disks separately in waxed paper, and refrigerate until firm, at least 2 hours or up to overnight.

Preheat the oven to 350°F (180°C). Spread the hazelnuts on a baking sheet and toast, stirring occasionally, until they deepen in color and the papery skins begin to pull away, about 10 minutes. Let cool, rub off most of the skins (see left), then chop finely. Raise the oven temperature to 375°F (190°C).

Butter 2 baking sheets. Let the dough disks stand at room temperature for about 10 minutes to soften slightly. Meanwhile, make the filling: In a small bowl, stir together the brown sugar, granulated sugar, and cinnamon.

Lightly flour 1 dough disk and place between 2 sheets of waxed paper. Roll out into a round 10 inches (25 cm) in diameter and ⅛ inch (3 mm) thick. Remove the top sheet, brush the dough with 1 tablespoon of the melted butter, and then sprinkle the dough with one-fourth of the sugar mixture. Top evenly with one-fourth of the nuts. Using a rolling pin, gently roll over the filling to help it adhere to the dough. Cut the round into 12 wedges. Starting at the wide end, roll up each wedge. Transfer to a prepared baking sheet, arranging them point side down and 1 inch (2.5 cm) apart. Repeat with the remaining dough disks and filling.

To make the topping, in a bowl, stir together the granulated sugar and cinnamon. Brush the cookies with the egg white–water mixture, then sprinkle with the cinnamon sugar.

Bake until golden brown, about 20 minutes. Transfer to wire racks to cool completely. Store in an airtight container at room temperature for up to 5 days.

**Skinning
hazelnuts**

*Spread the nuts
in a single layer on
a baking sheet and
toast in a preheated
350°F (180°C) oven
until the skins start
to darken and wrinkle,
about 8 minutes.
When cool enough
to handle, wrap the
nuts in a kitchen towel
and rub vigorously
to remove the skins.
It's fine if a few
skin pieces cling
to the nuts.*

FOR THE DOUGH

1 cup (8 oz/250 g) unsalted butter, at room temperature

½ lb (250 g) cream cheese, at room temperature

¼ teaspoon salt

2 cups (10 oz/315 g) all-purpose (plain) flour

FOR THE FILLING

1½ cups (7½ oz/235 g) hazelnuts (filberts)

⅓ cup (2½ oz/75 g) firmly packed light brown sugar

⅓ cup (3 oz/90 g) granulated sugar

2 teaspoons ground cinnamon

4 tablespoons (2 oz/60 g) unsalted butter, melted and cooled

FOR THE TOPPING

¼ cup (2 oz/60 g) granulated sugar

¾ teaspoon ground cinnamon

1 egg white beaten with 1 tablespoon water

MAKES 48 COOKIES

478

HAZELNUT AMARETTI

Ground hazelnuts and almond extract flavor these sophisticated cookies. Pearl sugar, large, white grains of granulated sugar, is used to top the cookies. Look for it in stores specializing in ingredients for dessert making, or substitute coarsely crushed sugar cubes.

1¼ cups (6½ oz/200 g) hazelnuts (filberts)

¾ cup (3 oz/90 g) plus 3 tablespoons confectioners' (icing) sugar

1 teaspoon all-purpose (plain) flour

2 egg whites

⅓ cup (3 oz/90 g) granulated sugar

¾ teaspoon pure almond extract

Pearl sugar for sprinkling (see note, above)

MAKES ABOUT 36 COOKIES

Preheat the oven to 300°F (150°C). Line a baking sheet with parchment (baking) paper.

In a food processor, pulse the hazelnuts to grind finely (do not grind to a paste). Add ¼ cup (1 oz/30 g) of the confectioners' sugar and grind to a powder. Transfer to a bowl and stir in the remaining ½ cup (2 oz/60 g) plus 3 tablespoons confectioners' sugar and the flour. Set aside.

In a bowl, using an electric mixer on medium-high speed, beat the egg whites until soft peaks form. Gradually add the granulated sugar and beat until stiff, shiny peaks form. Fold in the almond extract and the nut mixture. Spoon the batter into a pastry bag fitted with a ½-inch (12-mm) plain tip (page 493). Pipe mounds 1½ inches (4 cm) in diameter onto the prepared pan, spacing them about 1 inch (2.5 cm) apart. Using a wet finger, smooth the top of each mound. Sprinkle the mounds with pearl sugar.

Bake the cookies until just beginning to brown around the edges, about 45 minutes. Turn off the oven, leave the door closed, and let the cookies dry for 30 minutes. Transfer the cookies to wire racks to cool completely. Store in an airtight container at room temperature for up to 1 month.

A gift of goodness

Amaretti make a great host gift in place of the typical bottle of wine or bouquet of flowers. Wrap each cookie in tissue paper, twist the ends, and pack in a decorative cookie tin or box.

479

CRISP OATMEAL COOKIES

Slim and crisp rather than thick and chewy, these oatmeal cookies are in the same class as *tuiles, palmiers,* and biscotti: ideal after-dinner treats with tea or coffee. These crunchy cookies also make an irresistible late-night snack paired with a glass of milk.

1 cup (3 oz/90 g) old-fashioned rolled oats

1 cup (8 oz/250 g) sugar

2 tablespoons plus 2 teaspoons all-purpose (plain) flour

½ teaspoon salt

½ teaspoon baking powder

1 egg

1 teaspoon pure vanilla extract

½ cup (4 oz/125 g) unsalted butter, melted and cooled

MAKES 50–54 COOKIES

In a bowl, stir together the oats, sugar, flour, salt, and baking powder. In another bowl, beat the egg and vanilla until just blended. Add the egg mixture to the oat mixture and mix thoroughly. Add the butter and stir just until combined. Let rest, stirring occasionally, until thickened, 15–20 minutes.

Preheat the oven to 325°F (165°C). Line 2 large baking sheets with parchment (baking) paper.

Drop the batter by teaspoons onto the prepared baking sheets, spacing the mounds 2½ inches (6 cm) apart. Bake one sheet at a time until the cookies are golden, 8–12 minutes. Remove from the oven and slide the parchment with the cookies onto a work surface. Let the cookies cool until firm, about 5 minutes. Peel the cookies off the parchment and transfer to wire racks to cool completely. Store in an airtight container at room temperature for up to 3 days.

Nonstick baking liners

Silicone-coated fiberglass baking mats, widely known by the brand name Silpat, can be used any time a recipe calls for a pan lined with parchment (baking) paper. Reusable and with a nonstick finish that can be easily wiped clean, these liners are perfect for baking thin, delicate cookies.

DOUBLE CHOCOLATE COOKIES

Insulated cookie sheets

Made of two layers of metal with a cushion of air between them, insulated cookie sheets prevent scorching and promote even browning. They are a particularly good choice when baking thin cookies, such as those at right, or delicate cookies, such as meringues.

Other chocolate cookies pale next to these deeply rich, moist treats. If you find the bottoms are burning, slip a second clean, unlined baking sheet under the one holding the cookies to create a double thickness. Or, use insulated cookie sheets to prevent overbaking.

Preheat the oven to 350°F (180°C). Line 2 large baking sheets with aluminum foil, shiny side down, or line them with parchment (baking) paper.

Combine the chocolate and butter in the top pan of a double boiler or a heatproof bowl. Place over (not touching) barely simmering water and heat, stirring occasionally, until melted and smooth. Set aside to cool slightly.

In a small bowl, sift together the flour and baking powder. In another bowl, using an electric mixer on high speed, beat together the eggs, sugar, and vanilla until light and fluffy, 5–7 minutes. Fold in the cooled chocolate mixture, the flour mixture, and finally, the chocolate chips and nuts; do not overmix. Using a tablespoon, drop mounds of the batter about 1½ inches (4 cm) in diameter onto the prepared baking sheets, spacing them about 1½ inches apart.

Bake the cookies, 1 sheet at a time, for 6 minutes. Then turn the sheet front to back and continue baking just until the tops appear dry, 3–4 minutes; they will still be very soft. Let cool completely on the pans on wire racks. Store in an airtight container at room temperature for up to 2 weeks.

8 oz (250 g) bittersweet chocolate, chopped (about 1⅔ cups)

2 tablespoons unsalted butter

3 tablespoons all-purpose (plain) flour

¼ teaspoon baking powder

2 extra-large eggs, at room temperature

⅔ cup (5 oz/155 g) sugar

1 teaspoon pure vanilla extract

1⅔ cups (10 oz/315 g) semisweet (plain) chocolate chips

2 cups (8 oz/250 g) whole macadamia nuts, pecan halves, or walnuts

MAKES ABOUT 36 COOKIES

CHOCOLATE-DIPPED ORANGE COOKIES

Managing hot spots

Small pockets of higher heat, called hot spots, can occur in any oven. To compensate for them and ensure even baking, bake cookies and bars on the middle rack of the oven, one sheet at a time.

These delicate, orange-scented cookies look and taste wonderful partially dipped in melted chocolate. They can also be cut into other shapes and brushed on one side with chocolate. Or, you can omit the chocolate coating and sprinkle the cookies with sugar before baking.

Preheat the oven to 350°F (180°C).

In a food processor, combine the flour, sugar, cornstarch, orange zest, and salt and process briefly until well mixed. Scatter the butter over the top, add the vanilla, and pulse until the mixture resembles fine meal. Then process continuously until moist clumps form.

Turn out onto a sheet of waxed paper and gather the clumps together into a disk. Top with a second sheet of waxed paper. Roll out the dough about ¼ inch (6 mm) thick. Remove the top sheet. Using a 2½–3-inch (6–7.5-cm) cookie cutter, cut out as many cookies as possible. Transfer to an ungreased baking sheet, spacing them about ½ inch (12 mm) apart. Gather the scraps together, reroll, and cut out more cookies.

1½ cups (7½ oz/235 g) all-purpose (plain) flour

½ cup (4 oz/125 g) sugar

¼ cup (1 oz/30 g) cornstarch (cornflour)

1 tablespoon plus 1 teaspoon grated orange zest

¼ teaspoon salt

¾ cup (6 oz/185 g) chilled unsalted butter, cut into pieces

½ teaspoon pure
vanilla extract

4 oz (125 g) semisweet
(plain) or bittersweet
chocolate, chopped

MAKES ABOUT 24 COOKIES

Bake the cookies just until they are beginning to brown, about 15 minutes. Let cool on the pans on wire racks for 5 minutes, then transfer to wire racks to cool completely.

Place the chocolate in the top pan of a double boiler or in a heatproof bowl. Place over (not touching) barely simmering water and heat, stirring occasionally, until melted and smooth. Remove from the heat.

Line a baking sheet with waxed paper. Dip an edge of each cookie into the chocolate, covering the cookie halfway. Arrange in a single layer on the waxed paper and refrigerate until the chocolate sets. Store in an airtight container in the refrigerator for up to 1 week.

HONEY AND ORANGE MADELEINES

These cakelike cookies are baked in a special pan with shell-shaped molds. Sifting the flour before measuring ensures that the cookies will have the appropriate light texture. If you like, sprinkle the madeleines with Vanilla Sugar (page 464) as soon as you turn them out of the pan.

About 3 tablespoons
unsalted butter, melted,
for pan, plus ¾ cup (6 oz/
185 g), melted and cooled
to lukewarm

2 eggs

½ cup (6 oz/185 g) honey

¼ cup (2 oz/60 g) sugar

1½ teaspoons grated
orange zest

⅛ teaspoon ground allspice

½ teaspoon pure
vanilla extract

1 cup (4 oz/125 g) sifted
all-purpose (plain) flour

MAKES 24 COOKIES

Preheat the oven to 400°F (200°C). Generously brush a 12-mold madeleine pan with melted butter and then dust with flour, tapping out the excess.

Combine the eggs, honey, sugar, orange zest, and allspice in the top pan of a double boiler or in a heatproof bowl. Place over (but not touching) simmering water and whisk just until lukewarm. Remove from the heat. Using an electric mixer on high speed, beat the mixture until pale yellow, light, foamy, and tripled in volume, about 10 minutes. Beat in the vanilla. With the mixer on low speed, slowly add the flour and mix the batter until incorporated.

Transfer one-third of the batter to another bowl and gradually fold the ¾ cup lukewarm melted butter into it. Gently fold the butter-enriched mixture into the remaining batter. Then, spoon the batter into the prepared molds, filling each mold almost to the top and using half the batter.

Bake until golden brown and springy to the touch, about 12 minutes, rotating the pan front to back halfway through baking. Immediately turn out the cookies onto a wire rack. Wipe out the pan, brush with melted butter, dust with flour, and repeat with the remaining batter once or twice, depending on the number of molds in your pan. Let the cookies cool completely on the racks. Store in an airtight container at room temperature for up to 3 days.

Madeleine pans

Also called plaques, *madeleine pans typically have 8 or 12 shallow molds and come in tinned steel, metal with a nonstick finish, or pliable silicone. They are indispensable for making these special cookies, but you can also use them for baking corn sticks and other small quick breads. Look for the pans in kitchenware stores or through mail-order sources.*

ALMOND, LEMON, AND ANISE BISCOTTI

Biscotti variations

For orange-pistachio biscotti, omit the aniseed and replace the lemon zest with orange zest and the almonds with pistachios. For chocolate chip–walnut biscotti, omit the aniseed and lemon zest; replace the almonds with coarsely chopped walnuts, and stir in 1 cup (6 oz/ 185 g) semisweet (plain) chocolate chips with the nuts.

Here is twist on a traditional recipe for *mandelbrot,* the Jewish version of biscotti. The aniseed add an appealing flavor, but you can omit them and you will end up with a batch of delectable lemon cookies. The cookies can be made up to 2 weeks in advance of serving.

Preheat the oven to 350°F (180°C).

In a large bowl, whisk together the eggs, sugar, oil, lemon zest, aniseed (if using), baking powder, vanilla, and salt until well blended. Add the flour and almonds and stir until a smooth dough forms.

Turn out the dough onto a lightly floured work surface and knead until smooth, about 10 turns. Divide the dough in half. Form each half into a log 2 inches (5 cm) in diameter. Carefully transfer the logs to an ungreased baking sheet, spacing them well apart, and pat to even the shapes. Sprinkle the tops of the logs with Vanilla Sugar.

Bake until firm to the touch, about 30 minutes (the logs will spread during baking). Remove from the oven and let cool on the baking sheet for 10 minutes. Leave the oven on.

Using a spatula, carefully transfer the logs to a work surface. Using a serrated knife, cut crosswise into slices ½ inch (12 mm) thick. Arrange the slices cut side down on the baking sheet. Return to the oven and bake until brown and crisp, about 20 minutes. Transfer to wire racks to cool completely. Store in an airtight container at room temperature for up to 2 weeks.

2 eggs

¾ cup (6 oz/185 g) sugar, plus more for sprinkling

½ cup (4 fl oz/125 ml) canola oil

1 tablespoon grated lemon zest

2 teaspoons aniseed, crushed, optional

1¼ teaspoons baking powder

1 teaspoon pure vanilla extract

¼ teaspoon salt

2 cups (10 oz/315 g) all-purpose (plain) flour

1 cup (5½ oz/170 g) almonds, coarsely chopped

Vanilla Sugar for sprinkling (page 464)

MAKES ABOUT 36 COOKIES

CARDAMOM PALMIERS

Puff pastry tips

If using purchased pastry, for the best flavor and texture, look for all-butter puff pastry at natural-foods stores or your neighborhood bakery, and thaw according to package directions. To ensure flaky cookies, keep the puff pastry well chilled. If it begins to soften, slip it in the freezer briefly before continuing with the recipe.

A bakeshop favorite, these bite-size cookies are surprisingly easy to make at home. Cinnamon can replace the more exotic-tasting cardamom with equally tasty results. Serve these tender, crisp cookies with that last cup of coffee or tea near evening's end.

In a small bowl, stir together the sugar and cardamom. Sprinkle a work surface with about 1 tablespoon of the cardamom-sugar. Open the sheet of pastry atop the sugar and roll it into a rectangle 9 by 11 inches (23 by 28 cm) and ⅛ inch (3 mm) thick. Cut the pastry rectangle lengthwise into 3 uniform strips each about 3 inches (7.5 cm) wide. Sprinkle each strip evenly with 1 tablespoon of the cardamom-sugar. Working with 1 pastry strip at a time, fold each long side so they meet in the center. Then, fold the pastry strip in half lengthwise so that you have a ¾ inch (2 cm) wide piece of pastry, 4 layers thick; do not compress. Roll the outside in more cardamom-sugar to coat. Repeat with the 2 remaining pastry strips. Refrigerate the folded strips for 30 minutes.

⅓ cup (3 oz/90 g) sugar

½ teaspoon ground cardamom

½ lb (250 g) puff pastry dough, homemade (page 450) or purchased, and thawed if frozen

Unsalted butter for pans

MAKES ABOUT 18 COOKIES

Preheat the oven to 350°F (180°C). Butter 2 baking sheets.

Using a sharp knife, cut the pastries crosswise into slices ½ inch (12 mm) wide. Arrange the slices on the prepared baking sheets, loosening the coil of each cookie slightly and spacing them about 2 inches (5 cm) apart.

Bake the cookies until the bottoms are caramelized, about 20 minutes. Turn the cookies over and bake until the tops are deeply caramelized, about 5 minutes longer. Transfer to wire racks to cool completely. Store in an airtight container at room temperature for up to 5 days.

MINIATURE JELLY THUMBPRINT COOKIES

This is a great recipe to make with kids, who will love pressing a thumb or finger into each cookie to form the indentation. The cookies are delicious served with another kid favorite, hot cocoa. Use your favorite jam, with or without seeds, or several jellies of different flavors.

¾ cup (3 oz/90 g) sliced (flaked) almonds, toasted (page 17)

1 cup (5 oz/155 g) all-purpose (plain) flour

⅛ teaspoon salt

½ cup (4 oz/125 g) unsalted butter, at room temperature

⅓ cup (2½ oz/75 g) firmly packed light brown sugar

¾ teaspoon pure vanilla extract

1 egg yolk

¼ cup (2½ oz/75 g) currant jelly

MAKES ABOUT 42 COOKIES

Preheat the oven to 375°F (190°C).

Finely chop the almonds and set aside. In a small bowl, sift together the flour and salt. Set aside. In a large bowl, using an electric mixer on medium-high speed, beat together the butter, brown sugar, and vanilla until light and fluffy, about 4 minutes. Beat in the egg yolk. On low speed, add the flour mixture and almonds and mix just until incorporated.

Scoop up a small spoonful of dough, roll between your palms into a ball about ¾ inch (2 cm) in diameter, and place on an ungreased baking sheet. Repeat with the remaining dough, spacing the balls 1½ inches (4 cm) apart. Using your index finger, make a depression in the center of each ball.

Bake the cookies for 7 minutes. Remove from the oven and use a small spoon to fill the depressions with the jelly. Return to the oven and continue to bake until the cookies begin to color, about 8 minutes longer. Transfer to wire racks to cool completely. Store in an airtight container at room temperature for up to 5 days.

Kid-friendly hot cocoa

Warm 1⅓ cups (11 fl oz/360 ml) milk in a saucepan over low heat until small bubbles appear around the edge of the pan. Add 1 tsp each unsweetened cocoa powder and sugar and 1 drop of pure vanilla extract to a large mug. Stir well. Slowly pour in the hot milk, stirring until smooth. Top with Whipped Cream (page 454), if desired, and serve right away. Makes 1 serving.

PECAN TUILES

Cookie cups

You can also shape the cookies into edible cups for serving ice cream or sorbet: Lift the warm cookies from the baking sheet and drape them onto overturned small ramekins, molding them gently with your hands. Let cool completely.

These delicate, crisp pecan cookies are named for the old-fashioned French curved roof tiles whose shape they resemble. If the cookies cool too much on the baking sheet and become too brittle to form, return the sheet to the oven briefly to soften them.

Preheat the oven to 350°F (180°C). Butter a large baking sheet.

In a food processor, process the ½ cup pecans and the sugar until finely ground. Transfer to a bowl. Stir in the flour, followed by the butter, egg whites, and vanilla. Working in batches, spoon the batter by heaping teaspoonfuls onto the prepared baking sheet, spacing them at least 3 inches (7.5 cm) apart. Using an icing spatula or a knife, spread each mound into a round 2½ inches (6 cm) in diameter. Sprinkle each round with ½ teaspoon of the chopped pecans.

Bake the cookies until the edges are darkly golden and the centers are lightly golden, about 9 minutes. Working quickly and using a thin, flexible metal spatula, lift each cookie from the sheet and drape it over a rolling pin. Let cool until firm, about 1 minute, then carefully transfer to a wire rack to cool completely. Repeat with the remaining batter and chopped pecans, buttering the baking sheet for each batch. Store in an airtight container in the refrigerator for up to 2 weeks.

½ cup (2 oz/60 g) pecans, plus ⅓ cup (1½ oz/45 g), finely chopped

½ cup (4 oz/125 g) sugar

¼ cup (1¼ oz/37 g) all-purpose (plain) flour

5 tablespoons (2½ oz/75 g) unsalted butter, melted and cooled

2 egg whites, lightly beaten

½ teaspoon pure vanilla extract

MAKES ABOUT 24 COOKIES

ENGLISH TOFFEE SHORTBREAD

Homemade vanilla extract

If you use a lot of vanilla extract, making your own saves money and allows you to control the flavor. Cut a whole vanilla bean in half lengthwise and place both halves in a glass jar with ¾ cup (6 fl oz/180 ml) vodka. Cap tightly and store in a cool, dark place for at least 6 months before using.

Cut these crisp, crumbly, toffee-flecked cookies into rounds or decorative shapes and serve them after an elegant dinner or take them along to a party as a host gift. For extra flavor, you can sprinkle the finshed cookies with Vanilla Sugar (page 464) instead of the unflavored sugar.

Preheat the oven to 350°F (180°C).

In a food processor, combine the flour, brown sugar, cornstarch, and salt and process briefly until well mixed. Scatter the butter over the top, add the vanilla, and, using rapid on-off pulses, process until the mixture resembles fine meal. Add the pecans and process until finely chopped. Add the toffee and process just to incorporate.

Transfer the dough to a large sheet of waxed paper and shape it into a disk. Top with a second sheet of waxed paper. Roll out the dough ¼ inch (6 mm) thick. Using a 3-inch (7.5-cm) round or fluted cutter, cut out as many cookies as possible. Transfer to an ungreased baking sheet, spacing them about 1 inch (2.5 cm) apart. Gather the scraps together, reroll, and cut out more cookies. Sprinkle with granulated sugar.

Bake the cookies until just beginning to color, about 20 minutes. Let cool on the pan on a wire rack for 5 minutes, then transfer to wire racks to cool completely. Store in an airtight container at room temperature for up to 5 days.

1 cup (5 oz/155 g) all-purpose (plain) flour

⅓ cup (2½ oz/75 g) firmly packed light brown sugar

2½ tablespoons cornstarch (cornflour)

⅛ teaspoon salt

½ cup (4 oz/125 g) cold unsalted butter, cut into ½-inch (12-mm) pieces

¾ teaspoon pure vanilla extract

½ cup (2 oz/60 g) pecans

⅓ cup (2 oz/60 g) finely chopped chocolate-covered English toffee candy bar

Granulated sugar

MAKES ABOUT 16 COOKIES

COCONUT MACAROONS

Requiring just four ingredients and a few minutes of baking time, these are perhaps the easiest cookies you can bake, making them a great afternoon activity with kids. For orange macaroons, add the grated zest of 1 orange to the batter.

3½ cups (14 oz/440 g)
sweetened flaked coconut

1 can (14 fl oz/430 ml)
sweetened condensed milk

2 teaspoons pure
almond extract

1 teaspoon pure
vanilla extract

MAKES ABOUT 40 COOKIES

Preheat the oven to 350°F (180°C). Line 2 large rimmed baking sheets with parchment (baking) paper.

In a bowl, combine the coconut, sweetened condensed milk, and almond and vanilla extracts. Using a wooden spoon, stir the ingredients until well mixed.

Drop the mixture by scant tablespoons onto the prepared baking sheets, spacing the mounds about 1 inch (2.5 cm) apart. If necessary, wet your fingers with cool water and gently shape and press each mound to make it neat.

Bake the cookies until lightly browned, 10–15 minutes. Let cool completely on the pans on wire racks. Store in an airtight container at room temperature for up to 3 days.

**Uniform
dough portions**

It's important when shaping cookies that the dough portions be as uniform as possible so the cookies will bake in the same amount of time. For a precise measurement, use a miniature spring-loaded ice cream scoop to form uniform balls.

485

ALMOND FLORENTINES

Arrange these crisp cookies on a pretty plate for serving after a special-occasion dinner. Replace the almonds with walnuts, pecans, pistachios, or another favorite nut, if desired, but be sure to toast the nuts first to bring out their flavors (page 17).

½ cup (4 fl oz/125 ml)
plus 2 tablespoons
heavy (double) cream

½ cup (4 oz/125 g)
granulated sugar

¼ cup (2 oz/60 g) firmly
packed dark brown sugar

2 tablespoons
unsalted butter

1 cup (4 oz/125 g) sliced
(flaked) almonds, toasted
(see page 17)

¼ cup (1½ oz/45 g)
all-purpose (plain) flour

1 tablespoon grated
orange zest

2 teaspoons grated
lemon zest

4½ oz (140 g) semisweet
(plain) chocolate, chopped

½ oz (15 g) unsweetened
chocolate, chopped

MAKES ABOUT 36 COOKIES

Preheat the oven to 350°F (180°C). Line 2 baking sheets with aluminum foil. Lightly butter the foil.

In a heavy saucepan over medium heat, combine the cream, granulated and brown sugars, and butter. Heat, stirring constantly, just until the sugars dissolve and the butter melts. Add the almonds, flour, and orange and lemon zests. Bring to a boil, stirring constantly. Remove from the heat.

Drop the runny batter by teaspoons onto the prepared baking sheets, spacing the cookies at least 2 inches (5 cm) apart. Set the remaining batter aside. Bake the cookies until deep brown, about 8 minutes, rotating the pans front to back halfway through the baking time. Remove from the oven and slide the foil with the cookies onto a work surface. Repeat to bake the remaining batter.

Line 2 baking sheets with fresh foil and arrange the baked cookies, smooth side up, on top. Combine the chocolates in the top pan of a double boiler or heatproof bowl. Place over (not touching) barely simmering water and heat, stirring, until melted and smooth. Remove from the heat.

Using a small icing spatula, spread the chocolate over the flat side of each cookie and return to the baking sheets, chocolate side up. Refrigerate until the chocolate sets. Store in an airtight container in the refrigerator for up to 2 weeks.

Storing cookies

Do not store crisp and cakey cookies together. The crisp cookies will absorb moisture from the softer ones and soften. Store frosted or topped cookies in single layers, separated by waxed or parchment paper to prevent them from sticking together.

COOKIES, BROWNIES & BARS

WHITE CHOCOLATE AND MACADAMIA BLONDIES

**Choosing
your chips**

*To make sure you are
using chips made
with authentic white
chocolate, read the
label. You should see
cocoa butter as a
primary ingredient.
Avoid chips that list
vegetable fat.*

Here, traditional blondies are dressed up with white chocolate and macadamia nuts. Rich and dense, they travel well on outdoor excursions, such as picnics and bicycling trips. If you're feeling indulgent, drizzle them liberally with Caramel Glaze (page 461) as they cool in the pan.

Preheat the oven to 350°F (180°C). Butter an 8-inch (20-cm) square baking pan.

Coarsely shop the macadamia nuts and white chocolate, aiming for similar-size pieces; set aside separately.

In a large bowl, using an electric mixer on high speed, beat together the butter, brown sugar, espresso powder, and vanilla until light and fluffy, about 5 minutes. Beat in the eggs, one at a time, beating well after each addition. Continue to beat on high speed until very fluffy, about 2 minutes. On low speed, add the flour and mix just until incorporated. Fold in the nuts and white chocolate just until blended.

Pour and scrape the batter into the prepared pan and spread the top evenly. Bake until a toothpick inserted into the center comes out clean, about 40 minutes. Let cool completely in the pan on a wire rack.

Cut into 24 bars. Store in an airtight container at room temperature for up to 3 days.

¾ cup (4 oz/125 g)
macadamia nuts

3–4 oz (90–125 g)
white chocolate

½ cup (4 oz/125 g)
**unsalted butter,
at room temperature**

1¼ cups (9 oz/280 g) firmly
packed light brown sugar

2 teaspoons instant
espresso powder

1 teaspoon pure
vanilla extract

2 **eggs**

1 cup (5 oz/155 g)
all-purpose (plain) flour

MAKES 24 BARS

CLASSIC CHOCOLATE BROWNIES

The toothpick test

*If a few moist
crumbs cling to the
toothpick, it is time
to remove the pan
from the oven. If
you're in doubt, run
your fingers over the
toothpick. If it feels
wet, it has moist
batter on it, which
means the brownies
need more time in
the oven.*

A batch of classic brownies is a treat for anyone who likes chocolate. For a variation, add any one or all of the following to the completed batter: ⅔ cup (3 oz/90 g) coarsely chopped walnuts or ½ cup (3 oz/90 g) semisweet (plain) chocolate, milk chocolate, or white chocolate chips.

Preheat the oven to 325°F (165°C). Line an 8-inch (20-cm) square baking pan with aluminum foil, allowing the foil to overhang the sides slightly.

Combine the chocolate and butter in a large heatproof bowl. Place over (not touching) barely simmering water in a saucepan and heat, stirring occasionally, until melted and smooth. Remove from the heat and let cool slightly.

Whisk the sugar, vanilla, and salt into the chocolate mixture. One at a time, whisk in the eggs, mixing well after each addition, then continue to whisk until the mixture is velvety, about 2 minutes. Add the flour and whisk just until blended.

Scrape the batter into the prepared pan and smooth the top. Bake until the top is just springy to the touch and a toothpick inserted into the center comes out with a few moist crumbs attached, about 40 minutes. Let cool in the pan on a rack.

Grasp the foil at opposite ends and lift out the brownie sheet onto a work surface. Cut into 16 squares. Store in an airtight container at room temperature for up to 4 days.

4 oz (125 g) unsweetened
chocolate, chopped

½ cup (4 oz/125 g)
unsalted butter

1¼ cups (10 oz/315 g) **sugar**

1 teaspoon pure
vanilla extract

¼ teaspoon **salt**

3 **eggs**

¾ cup (4 oz/125 g)
all-purpose (plain) flour

MAKES 16 BROWNIES

PECAN PIE BARS

These satisfying bars have all the dark, rich flavor of pecan pie in miniature form, without all the work: You don't need to roll out the crust—you just press it into the pan—and you don't need to prebake it. Plus, the one-bowl filling takes just minutes to mix.

FOR THE CRUST

1⅓ cups (7 oz/220 g)
all-purpose (plain) flour

½ cup (3½ oz/105 g) firmly
packed light brown sugar

½ teaspoon baking powder

½ cup (4 oz/125 g)
unsalted butter, cut into
½-inch (12-mm) pieces,
at room temperature

FOR THE FILLING

¾ cup (7½ oz/245 g)
dark corn syrup

¼ cup (2 oz/60 g) firmly
packed light brown sugar

3 tablespoons
all-purpose flour

2 eggs

1 teaspoon pure
vanilla extract

Large pinch of salt

1 cup (4 oz/125 g)
chopped pecans

MAKES 24 BARS

Preheat the oven to 350°F (180°C). Lightly butter a 9-by-13-inch baking dish.

To make the crust, in a bowl, stir together the flour, sugar, and baking powder. Scatter the butter over the top. Using your fingertips, rub the butter into the flour mixture until fine crumbs form. Transfer the mixture to the prepared baking dish and press evenly and firmly onto the bottom.

To make the filling, in a large bowl, using an electric mixer on medium speed, beat together the corn syrup, sugar, flour, eggs, vanilla, and salt until well combined. Stir in the pecans.

Pour and scrape the filling onto the crust and spread evenly. Bake until the top is a light golden brown, 20–25 minutes. Let cool completely in the dish on a wire rack.

Cut into 24 bars. Store in an airtight container at room temperature for up to 3 days.

Light vs. dark corn syrup

Light corn syrup is flavored with vanilla and salt, with light referring to the fact it is clear, rather than colored. Dark corn syrup, which includes caramel flavor and color, is medium brown and has a more assertive flavor than its light counterpart.

487

CHOCOLATE CHIP AND PECAN BARS

Bringing butter to room temperature

For recipes that call for room-temperature butter, remove the butter from the refrigerator about 1 hour before you plan to use it. If it is a hot day, keep an eye on the butter to make sure it doesn't get too soft. Return oily-looking butter to the refrigerator for a bit to cool and firm up.

Chocolate chips and pecans add texture and contrasting flavor to this big batch of blondies. You can substitute butterscotch chips, or a mixture of butterscotch chips and white chocolate chips, for the chocolate chips, and walnuts for the pecans.

Preheat the oven to 350°F (180°C). Butter a 9-by-13-inch (23-by-33-cm) baking dish or pan.

In a bowl, sift together the flour, baking powder, and salt. Set aside. In a large bowl, using an electric mixer on medium speed, beat together the butter and brown sugar until light and fluffy, 3–5 minutes. Add the eggs, one at a time, beating well after each addition. Stir in the vanilla. On low speed, beat in the flour mixture just until incorporated. Fold in the chocolate chips and pecans.

Pour and scrape the batter into the prepared baking dish, smoothing the surface with the spatula. Bake until the top looks dry, 40–45 minutes. Let cool completely in the dish on a wire rack.

Cut into 24 bars. Store in an airtight container at room temperature for up to 1 week.

2¾ cups (11 oz/345 g) sifted all-purpose (plain) flour

2½ teaspoons baking powder

¼ teaspoon salt

¾ cup (6 oz/185 g) unsalted butter, at room temperature

2⅓ cups (16½ oz/515 g) firmly packed dark brown sugar

3 extra-large eggs

2 teaspoons pure vanilla extract

2 cups (12 oz/375 g) semisweet (plain) chocolate chips

1¼ cups (5 oz/155 g) pecan halves, coarsely chopped

MAKES 24 BARS

LEMON-COCONUT SQUARES

Baked crusts for bar cookies

Partially baking the crust for these lemon squares before adding the filling ensures the crust will not absorb too much moisture, which can make it soggy.

Baked into the crust, toasted coconut adds surprising tropical flavor to every bite of these otherwise traditional lemon squares. To create a stripe pattern on the squares, arrange strips of parchment (baking) paper on top just before dusting with confectioners' (icing) sugar.

Preheat the oven to 350°F (180°C). Line an 8-inch (20-cm) square baking pan with aluminum foil, allowing the foil to overhang the sides slightly. Butter the foil.

To make the crust, in a food processor, combine the flour, sugar, and salt and process briefly until well mixed. Add the butter and coconut and process until the mixture resembles a fine meal. Transfer to the prepared pan and press evenly and firmly onto the bottom. Bake until light brown around the edges, about 25 minutes.

Meanwhile, to make the filling, combine the sugar, eggs, lemon juice and zest, baking powder, and salt in the food processor and process until smooth.

FOR THE CRUST

1 cup (5 oz/155 g) all-purpose (plain) flour

¼ cup (2 oz/60 g) granulated sugar

¼ teaspoon salt

6 tablespoons (3 oz/90 g) cold unsalted butter, cut into ½-inch (12-mm) pieces

¾ cup (2¼ oz/68 g) sweetened flaked coconut, toasted (page 457)

FOR THE FILLING

¾ cup (6 oz/185 g) granulated sugar

2 eggs

3 tablespoons fresh lemon juice

1 tablespoon grated lemon zest

½ teaspoon baking powder

Pinch of salt

Confectioners' (icing) sugar for dusting

MAKES 16 SQUARES

When the crust is ready, pour the filling onto the hot crust. Continue to bake until the filling begins to brown around the edges and is just springy to the touch, about 30 minutes longer. Let cool completely in the pan on a wire rack.

Grasp the foil at opposite ends and lift out the lemon square sheet onto a work surface. Gently peel back the foil sides. Cut the sheet into 16 squares. Using a fine-mesh sieve, dust the tops of the squares with confectioners' sugar, then carefully remove the squares from the foil. Store in an airtight container in the refrigerator for up to 5 days.

FROSTED PUMPKIN BARS

Redolent with holiday spices, these bars will remind you of pumpkin pie without the crust. Instead, a rich and satisfying cream cheese frosting lends appeal. They are a great dish to serve at a Halloween-themed get-together with kids or an autumn potluck.

1 cup (5 oz/155 g) all-purpose (plain) flour

¾ cup (6 oz/185 g) sugar

1 teaspoon *each* baking powder and ground cinnamon

½ teaspoon ground allspice

¼ teaspoon salt

1 cup (8 oz/250 g) pumpkin purée

½ cup (4 fl oz/125 ml) canola oil

2 eggs

Cream Cheese Frosting (page 456)

MAKES 18 BARS

Preheat the oven to 350°F (180°C). Lightly oil a 9-inch (23-cm) square baking pan.

In a large bowl, stir together the flour, sugar, baking powder, cinnamon, allspice, and salt. Add the pumpkin purée, oil, and eggs. Using an electric mixer on medium speed, beat until the mixture is well blended.

Pour and scrape the mixture into the prepared pan and spread evenly. Bake the bars until a toothpick inserted into the center comes out clean, 18–25 minutes. Let cool completely in the pan on a wire rack.

Spread the frosting evenly over the top of the cooled pumpkin sheet, making the layer as thick as you like. (Reserve any remaining frosting for another use.) Cut into 18 bars. Store in an airtight container in the refrigerator for up to 3 days.

Pumpkin purée

Many excellent brands of canned pumpkin purée are in markets nowadays. For this recipe, look for unsweetened, unseasoned pumpkin purée. Avoid cans labeled "pie filling," which include sugar and spices.

489

Cakes &
CHEESECAKES

Cakes & Cheesecakes

A cake is a welcome sight at nearly any get-together—large or small, elegant or casual. Some home bakers are tempted to use a mix, but most cakes, from angel food cake to pound cake, layer cake to cheesecake, pudding cake to cupcakes, are easy to make from scratch once you are armed with some basic knowledge on mixing and baking batters and a cache of reliable recipes, both of which you will find in this chapter.

Cake Basics

Check your oven
Before preparing any cake, check the accuracy of your oven. Use an oven thermometer to gauge the heat, then adjust the dial to compensate for any difference between the temperature you set and the actual temperature inside the oven.

High-altitude cake baking
At high altitudes, lower air pressure causes leavening agents to act more quickly, leading standard recipes to fall flat. Here are a few tips to avoid disappointment: Beat egg whites to the soft-peak stage instead of firm peaks. Use 15 to 25 percent less chemical leavening depending on how high you are above 5,000 feet (1,500 m). Raise the oven temperature by about 20°F (10°C) and shorten the baking time slightly to help batters set more quickly.

Storing cakes
Wrap cooled, unfrosted cakes in plastic wrap, place in an airtight container or under a cake dome, and store at room temperature for up to 2 days. Store frosted cakes the same way if the frosting does not contain cream or butter. If it does, cover the cake loosely with plastic wrap and refrigerate for up to 3 days; bring to room temperature before serving.

Cakes are mixed, shaped, and baked in various ways, but a few basic principles apply to the preparation of nearly every cake. (For processes that also apply to other desserts, such as creaming butter, separating and beating egg whites, and folding mixtures together, see Dessert Basics on pages 442–45.)

MIXING BATTERS Unless otherwise specified in a recipe, all ingredients should be at room temperature before a cake batter is mixed. This is particularly true for butter, which will be easier to blend, and egg whites, which will allow more air to be incorporated.

PREPARING CAKE PANS To help keep the cake from sticking to the pan as it bakes, the pan is usually prepared with butter alone or butter and flour, and sometimes also with parchment (baking) paper. Instructions will vary, depending on the ingredients in the batter and how much the cake will rise. Delicate batters that need to cling to the pan sides may skip this step.

To butter and flour a cake pan, use your fingers, a paper towel, or a piece of waxed paper to smear a thin, even coating of softened butter on the bottom and sides of the pan. Then, add a spoonful of flour to the pan and tilt and turn the pan to distribute the flour evenly over the buttered surface. Over the sink or a trash can, tap out any excess flour.

To line a round cake pan with parchment (baking) paper, cut out a square of parchment (baking) paper 2 inches (5 cm) larger than the diameter of the pan. Fold it into quarters to make a smaller square. Fold the square diagonally in half to make a triangle. Position the point of the triangle in the center of the pan, unfold the paper one fold, and press it into the pan to form a crease where the bottom and side of the pan meet. Remove the creased paper from the pan and use scissors to cut along the crease; then, unfold the paper, which should form a circle that fits the bottom of the pan exactly. Place the circle back in the pan. Butter and flour the parchment, if called for in the recipe.

TESTING CAKES FOR DONENESS Start testing cakes for doneness toward the end of the baking time specified in the recipe. The cake should look well risen, and yellow or white cakes should appear nicely browned. Some cakes will also shrink slightly from the pan sides. Another cue is if the cake springs back when lightly touched in the center. The most common doneness test is to insert a long, thin wooden toothpick or skewer into the center of the cake. If it comes out clean, the cake is ready to come out of the oven. If it comes out wet, bake for another 5 minutes before testing again.

UNMOLDING CAKES Some recipes call for cooling cakes in their pans before unmolding. Others call for unmolding while they are hot and leaving them to cool on wire racks. Still others require partial cooling in their pans and then unmolding to cool further. In all three cases, you can use a simple technique to remove the cake from its pan without causing cracks or other damage.

To unmold a cake that is still hot, carefully place the hot pan on top of large, thick pot holders or folded kitchen towels. Whether the pan is hot or cool, invert a wire rack larger than the pan on top of the pan. Using pot holders or oven mitts to protect your hands from the heat if necessary, firmly grasp the pan and rack together and invert them. Return the rack and pan to the work surface, with the rack underneath the pan. Gently lift off the pan. If the cake does not unmold, invert it again and run a table knife around the sides of the cake to loosen it from the pans sides, then repeat to unmold it onto the rack.

FROSTING AND GLAZING CAKES Rich, thick frostings based on butter or cream and thin, shiny glazes provide the finishing touch that can elevate any cake. An icing spatula is all you need to apply these final flourishes; follow the instructions at right.

To glaze a cake, follow the instructions in the recipe. Or, place the cooled, unmolded cake on a wire rack over a piece of waxed or parchment paper to catch drips. Carefully pour the glaze over the top of the cake and, using an icing spatula, spread it smoothly and uniformly over the top so that it spills over the edges, flowing down to coat the sides. When the glaze sets, use a wide metal spatula to ease the cake onto a plate for serving.

DUSTING A CAKE For an attractive decorative effect, dust a cake with confectioners' (icing) sugar or cocoa powder.

To dust a cake, place the cooled, unmolded cake on a wire rack or on its serving plate. Hold a small, fine-mesh sieve above the cake and put several spoonfuls of either confectioners' (icing) sugar or unsweetened cocoa powder in the sieve. Using a knife, a wooden spoon, or your hand, gently tap the rim of the sieve while slowly moving the sieve to apply an even dusting. For a more decorative effect, use a stencil.

USING A PASTRY BAG You can spoon frosting or whipped cream into a pastry (piping) bag fitted with a pastry tip and pipe decorations on cakes or other desserts. Many different tips can be used, including plain and star tips specially designed for making a variety of decorative shapes. When you pipe, you use one hand to guide the tip and the other to force the mixture from the top of the bag out through the tip.

To fill a pastry bag, start with a frosting or filling mixture that is firm enough to hold its shape, yet soft enough to flow smoothly. Bags with couplers and screw-on tips are the most convenient, allowing you to switch tips quickly, but any 12- to 16-inch (30- to 40-cm) pastry bag will work fine. Insert the tip, then twist the bag just above the tip and push it into the tip to prevent leakage as you fill the bag. Fold the top edge of the bag down about 6 inches (15 cm) to create a cuff, and prop the bag upright inside a tall glass. Use a silicone spatula to fill the bag no more than half full with the frosting. Unfold the cuff, untwist the bag near the tip, and press all the frosting down toward the tip, squeezing out the air. Twist the top of the bag several times to seal it.

To pipe with a pastry bag, grip the filled bag at the twisted part with your dominant hand, and squeeze only with this hand. With your other hand, lightly support the bottom of the bag, just behind the tip, to guide your movements. As you pipe, maintain a small, consistent gap between the tip and the surface onto which you are piping. Hold the bag at a 45-degree angle, or an angle that is comfortable for you. Squeeze with steady pressure for even piping; more force will create larger shapes, less force smaller ones. Twist the bag regularly to keep it smooth and taut over the frosting.

FILLING AND FROSTING A LAYER CAKE

Follow these easy steps for perfect results with a two-layer cake; use the same techniques for cakes with more layers, following recipe directions.

Mark the layers
With a ruler, measure the height of the unfrosted cake. At equally spaced intervals around its perimeter, insert toothpicks horizontally to mark the midpoint.

Cut the layers
Using a long serrated knife and a sawing motion, and with the toothpicks as your guide, cut the cake horizontally into layers as called for in the recipe. Carefully lift off the top layer.

Fill the cake
Transfer the bottom layer to a cake stand or plate. Mound the specified amount of filling or frosting on it and, using a large offset spatula, spread it evenly to the edges. Carefully position the second layer on top of the filling, lining up the cake edges.

Spread a crumb coat
With a clean spatula, spread a thin layer of frosting over the top and sides of the filled cake. This thin coating will adhere the crumbs to the surface, ensuring they don't mar the finished cake.

Complete the frosting
With a clean spatula, mound half the remaining frosting on top and, using broad strokes, spread it over the top evenly. In small batches, evenly apply the remaining frosting to the sides. Finally, go over the top one last time to ensure it is smooth.

POUND CAKE

This dense, buttery cake takes its name from the fact that it was traditionally made with 1 pound (500 g) each butter, flour, sugar, and eggs. Here is a smaller version that is just as wonderfully rich. It can be wrapped and stored at room temperature for up to 2 days.

Preheat the oven to 350°F (180°C). Butter and flour an 8½-by-4½-inch (21-by-11-cm) loaf pan and tap out the excess flour.

In a bowl, whisk together the eggs and vanilla until blended. In a small bowl, sift together the flour, baking powder, and salt. In a large bowl, using an electric mixer on medium-high speed, beat the butter until light. Gradually add the sugar and beat until pale and fluffy, about 2 minutes. Then gradually beat in the egg mixture until well mixed. On low speed, slowly add the flour mixture and beat just until combined. Do not overmix. Pour and scrape the batter into the prepared pan and smooth the top evenly with a rubber spatula.

Bake until the top is deep golden brown and a toothpick inserted into the center comes out clean, about 1 hour and 10 minutes. Let cool in the pan on a wire rack for 10 minutes. Invert onto the rack, turn right side up, and let cool completely before serving.

3 eggs, at room temperature

1½ teaspoons pure vanilla extract

1½ cups (6 oz/185 g) cake (soft-wheat) flour

¾ teaspoon baking powder

¼ teaspoon salt

¾ cup (6 oz/185 g) unsalted butter, at room temperature

¾ cup (6 oz/185 g) sugar

MAKES 1 LOAF CAKE

Flavored pound cakes

For a poppy seed cake, add 2½ tbsp poppy seeds with the dry ingredients. For an almond cake, use only 1 tsp pure vanilla extract and add ½ tsp pure almond extract. For a lemon cake, beat 1½ tsp grated lemon zest with the butter. Then, if desired, mix together ½ cup (1½ oz/45 g) sifted confectioners' (icing) sugar with 1 tbsp fresh lemon juice until smooth and drizzle it over the cooled cake.

494

CHOCOLATE POUND CAKE

For a pretty finish, dust this cake with confectioners' (icing) sugar. Slice and serve plain or topped with Whipped Cream (page 454), ice cream, or sliced strawberries. If you prefer a deeper chocolate flavor, use bittersweet chocolate in place of the semisweet chocolate.

Preheat the oven to 350°F (180°C). Butter a 9-by-5-inch (23-by-13-cm) loaf pan.

In a bowl, sift together the flour, cocoa powder, and salt. Set aside. Place the chocolate in the top pan of a double boiler or in a heatproof bowl. Place over (not touching) barely simmering water and heat, stirring occasionally, until melted and smooth. Remove from the heat.

In a large bowl, using an electric mixer on medium speed, beat together the butter and brown sugar until light and fluffy, about 5 minutes. Add the eggs, one at a time, beating well after each addition. Add the vanilla and the melted chocolate and mix well. Using a rubber spatula, fold the flour mixture into the butter mixture in 3 batches, alternately with the sour cream in 2 batches, beginning and ending with the flour mixture and mixing until incorporated. Pour and scrape the batter into the prepared pan and smooth the top with the spatula. Bake until a toothpick inserted into the center comes out clean, about 1 hour. If the cake is browning too quickly, cover it loosely with aluminum foil. Let cool in the pan on a wire rack for 10 minutes. Invert onto the rack, turn right side up, and let cool completely.

1½ cups (7½ oz/235 g) all-purpose (plain) flour

½ cup (1½ oz/45 g) Dutch-processed cocoa powder

¼ teaspoon salt

2 oz (60 g) semisweet (plain) chocolate

1 cup (8 oz/250 g) unsalted butter, at room temperature

2 cups (14 oz/440 g) firmly packed light brown sugar

3 eggs, at room temperature

1 teaspoon pure vanilla extract

1 cup (8 oz/250 g) sour cream

MAKES 1 LOAF CAKE

Testing butter for softness

To make sure your butter is at room temperature, press on it lightly with a clean fingertip. If it leaves an imprint, the butter is ready to use.

POLENTA–VANILLA BEAN CAKE

Polenta contributes a pleasant texture to this fragrant cake. Any medium-grind yellow cornmeal can be used here. If you like, serve slices of the cake with Whipped Cream (page 454) and lightly sweetened boysenberries, blackberries, or peach slices spooned over the top.

1¼ cups (5 oz/155 g)
cake (soft-wheat) flour

⅔ cup (3½ oz/105 g)
polenta or other
yellow cornmeal

½ teaspoon baking powder

¼ teaspoon salt

¾ cup (6 oz/185 g)
unsalted butter,
at room temperature

1 vanilla bean,
split lengthwise

1 cup (8 oz/250 g) sugar

3 eggs, at room
temperature

MAKES 1 LOAF CAKE

Preheat the oven to 350°F (180°C). Butter and flour an 8½-by-4½-inch (21-by-11-cm) loaf pan and tap out the excess flour.

In a a bowl, stir together the flour, cornmeal, baking powder, and salt. Place the butter in a large bowl. With the tip of a sharp knife, scrape out the seeds from the vanilla bean into the bowl with the butter. Using an electric mixer on medium-high speed, beat the butter until light. Gradually add the sugar and beat until fluffy and ivory colored, about 2 minutes. Add the eggs, one at a time, beating well after each addition. On low speed, slowly add the flour mixture and beat just until combined. Do not overmix. Pour and scrape the batter into the prepared pan and smooth the top with a rubber spatula.

Bake until a toothpick inserted into the center comes out clean, about 1¼ hours. Let cool in the pan on a wire rack for 10 minutes. Invert onto the rack, turn right side up, and let the cake cool completely.

**Buying
vanilla beans**

Choose vanilla beans that are plump and flexible, rather than flat and brittle. Their flavor will be heady and pronounced, translating to a more delicious dessert. It is also easier to scrape the seeds out of softer beans.

495

GINGERBREAD

Do not disturb

Resist the urge to open the oven door during the first 15 minutes of baking any cake. Changes in air pressure or temperature can prevent the cake from rising properly.

Dust this traditional cake with confectioners' sugar before serving. For a decorative effect, cut any shapes you like—leaves, stars, stripes—out of parchment (baking) paper and use them as a stencil before dusting. You could also frost the cake with Cream Cheese Frosting (page 456).

Preheat the oven to 350°F (180°C). Butter and flour an 8-inch (20-cm) square baking pan with 2-inch (5-cm) sides and tap out the excess flour.

In a bowl, sift together the flour, cinnamon, ground ginger, baking powder, baking soda, and salt. In another bowl, using an electric mixer on medium-high speed, beat the butter until light. Add the brown sugar and beat until fluffy, about 3 minutes. Add the egg and molasses and beat until well blended. On low speed, add the flour mixture in 3 batches, alternately with the apple cider in 2 batches, beginning and ending with the flour mixture and mixing until incorporated. Stir in the crystallized ginger. Pour and scrape the batter into the prepared pan and smooth the top with a rubber spatula.

Bake until a toothpick inserted into the center comes out clean, about 35 minutes. Let cool in the pan on a wire rack for 20 minutes. Invert onto the rack and turn right side up. Serve warm or at room temperature.

1½ cups (7½ oz/235 g) all-purpose (plain) flour

1 teaspoon ground cinnamon

¾ teaspoon ground ginger

½ teaspoon *each* baking powder, baking soda (bicarbonate of soda), and salt

½ cup (4 oz/125 g) unsalted butter, at room temperature

½ cup (3½ oz/105 g) firmly packed dark brown sugar

1 egg, at room temperature

½ cup (5½ fl oz/170 ml) unsulfured light molasses

½ cup (4 fl oz/125 ml) apple cider

¼ cup (1½ oz/45 g) chopped crystallized ginger

MAKES ONE 8-INCH (20-CM) SQUARE CAKE

BUTTER CAKE

Peeling parchment

If the parchment paper used to line the pan sticks to the bottom of the cake, dip a pastry brush in warm water and lightly brush the paper. The water should loosen it, making it easier to remove without damaging the cake.

A generous measure of butter in this recipe gives the finished cake a particularly fine-grained, moist texture. Unlike a sponge cake (opposite), which relies on beaten eggs for its loft, these sunny yellow cake layers use a chemical leavener, baking powder, to achieve their height.

Preheat the oven to 350°F (180°C). Butter the bottoms and sides of two 9-inch (23-cm) round cake pans and line the bottoms of the pans with parchment (baking) paper. Butter and flour the paper and tap out the excess flour.

In a bowl, sift together the flour, baking powder, and salt. Set aside. In a large bowl, using an electric mixer on medium speed, cream together the butter and sugar until light, airy, and very pale yellow, about 2 minutes. Add the eggs, one at a time, beating well after each addition Add the vanilla and beat for 1 minute. On low speed, add the flour mixture in 3 batches, alternately with the milk in 2 batches, beginning and ending with the flour mixture and mixing until

2¾ cups (11 oz/345 g) cake (soft-wheat) flour

2 teaspoons baking powder

¼ teaspoon salt

1 cup (8 oz/250 g) unsalted butter, at room temperature

2 cups (1 lb/500 g) sugar

4 eggs, at room temperature

**2 teaspoons pure
vanilla extract**

**1 cup (8 fl oz/250 ml) milk,
at room temperature**

**MAKES TWO 9-INCH (23-CM)
CAKE LAYERS**

incorporated. Divide the batter evenly between the prepared pans and smooth the top with a rubber spatula.

Bake until the tops look set and are lightly browned and a toothpick inserted into the centers comes out dry, about 30 minutes. Let cool in the pans on wire racks for 15 minutes. Invert onto the racks, peel off the parchment, turn right sides up, and let cool completely. Use as directed in individual recipes, or fill and frost as desired.

SPONGE LAYER CAKE

Airy sponge cake layers owe their height to vigorously beaten eggs, which form a network of air bubbles that rise in the heat of the oven. You can fill and frost these delicate cake layers with anything you like, such as Vanilla Buttercream or one of its variations (page 457).

Unsalted butter for pans

**1 cup (4 oz/125 g) cake
(soft-wheat) flour**

Pinch of salt

**6 eggs, separated,
at room temperature**

1 cup (8 oz/250 g) sugar

**1 teaspoon pure
vanilla extract**

**MAKES TWO 9-INCH (23-CM)
CAKE LAYERS**

Preheat the oven to 350°F (180°C). Butter the bottoms and sides of two 9-inch (23-cm) round cake pans and line the bottoms of the pans with parchment (baking) paper. Butter and flour the paper and tap out the excess flour.

In a small bowl, sift together the flour and salt. In a large bowl, using an electric mixer on medium-high speed, beat together the egg yolks and ½ cup (4 oz/125 g) of the sugar until thickened, pale yellow, and the batter falls back on itself like a ribbon when the beater is lifted, about 3 minutes. Beat in the vanilla. Set aside.

In a large bowl, using clean beaters, beat the egg whites on medium-high speed until soft peaks form, 2–3 minutes. On medium speed, beat in the remaining ½ cup sugar, a little at a time. Then continue to beat until stiff peaks form, about 1 minute. Using a rubber spatula, fold the whites into the yolk mixture in 3 batches. Then gently fold in the flour mixture in 4 batches. Divide the batter evenly between the prepared pans and smooth the tops with the spatula.

Bake until the tops feel firm to the touch and are lightly browned and a toothpick inserted into the centers comes out clean, about 20 minutes. Let cool in the pans on wire racks for 15 minutes. Invert onto the racks, peel off the parchment, turn right sides up, and let cool completely before using.

**Chocolate
sponge cake**

For chocolate sponge cake, replace ¼ cup (1 oz/30 g) of the flour with Dutch-processed cocoa powder. If you like, add ½ tsp instant coffee powder to the dry ingredients.

497

CARROT CAKE

Dress it up

This cake is also good flavored with coconut: Spread with Coconut Cream Cheese Frosting (page 456), then press 1 cup (3 oz/ 90 g) toasted sweetened shredded coconut evenly onto the sides of the cake.

One of the most requested cakes for birthdays, this hearty celebratory classic is traditionally spread with a thick layer of cream cheese frosting. It is surprisingly easy to make, requiring no special equipment and less than an hour in the oven.

Preheat the oven to 350°F (180°C). Butter and flour two 9-inch (23-cm) round cake pans and tap out the excess flour.

In a bowl, sift together the flour, baking soda, baking powder, cinnamon, salt, and allspice. In another bowl, whisk together the eggs, oil, granulated and brown sugars, and buttermilk until well blended. Stir the flour mixture into the egg mixture just until combined. Fold in the carrots. Divide the batter evenly between the prepared pans and smooth the tops of the batter with a rubber spatula.

Bake until a toothpick inserted into the centers comes out clean, about 40 minutes. Let cool in the pans on wire racks for 15 minutes. Invert onto the racks, turn right sides up, and let cool completely.

Place 1 cake layer, top side down, on a plate. Spread 1¼ cups (10 fl oz/310 ml) of the frosting over the top. Place the second cake layer, top side down, on top. Spread the remaining frosting decoratively over the top and sides of the cake. Serve right away, or cover with a cake dome and refrigerate for up to 2 days. Bring to room temperature before serving.

Unsalted butter for pans

2 cups (10 oz/315 g) all-purpose (plain) flour

2 teaspoons *each* baking soda (bicarbonate of soda), baking powder, and ground cinnamon

½ teaspoon *each* salt and ground allspice

4 eggs, at room temperature

¾ cup (6 fl oz/180 ml) canola oil

¾ cup (6 oz/185 g) granulated sugar

1 cup (7 oz/220 g) firmly packed light brown sugar

½ cup (4 fl oz/125 ml) buttermilk

3 cups (12 oz/375 g) lightly packed shredded carrots

Cream Cheese Frosting (page 456)

MAKES ONE 9-INCH (23-CM), 2-LAYER CAKE

ITALIAN PLUM CAKE

About Italian prune plums

Also known as sugar plums and French prune plums, these small, late-season, oval plums have purplish blue skin and yellowish flesh. Although they are not particularly juicy, they are quite sweet, and they are an especially good choice for baking because they hold their shape.

Filled with plums doused with orange liqueur, this rustic yet lovely round cake is a great way to end nearly any meal. The plums don't need to be perfectly ripe for this cake, but if they are very firm, put them in a paper bag with an apple for a couple of days and they will ripen nicely.

Preheat the oven to 375°F (190°C). Butter and flour a 9-inch (23-cm) springform pan with 2½-inch (6-cm) sides and tap out the excess flour.

Place the plum halves in a bowl and sprinkle with ¼ cup (2 oz/60 g) of the granulated sugar. Set aside.

In a large bowl, using an electric mixer on high speed, beat together the butter and the remaining 1 cup (8 oz/250 g) granulated sugar until light and fluffy, about 5 minutes. Beat in the egg yolks, one at a time, beating well after each addition. Stir in the orange zest, lemon zest, and vanilla.

1 lb (500 g) Italian prune plums, halved and pitted

1¼ cups (10 oz/310 g) granulated sugar

¾ cup (6 oz/185 g) plus 2 tablespoons unsalted butter, at room temperature

4 eggs, separated, at room temperature

Grated zest of 1 orange

Grated zest of ½ lemon

1 teaspoon pure
vanilla extract

1½ cups (7½ oz/235 g)
all-purpose (plain) flour

½ cup (2 oz/60 g)
cornstarch (cornflour)

2 teaspoons baking powder

2 tablespoons
orange liqueur

1 tablespoon confectioners'
(icing) sugar

**MAKES ONE 9-INCH
(23-CM) CAKE**

In a bowl, sift together the flour, cornstarch, and baking powder. In another bowl, using the electric mixer fitted with clean beaters, beat the egg whites on medium-high speed until stiff peaks form.

Using a silicone spatula, fold the flour mixture and egg whites in into the butter mixture in 3 batches each, starting with the flour mixture and ending with the whites. Do not overmix. Spread half of the batter in the prepared pan.

Bake for 10 minutes. Remove from the oven and arrange the plum halves, cut sides up, on top of the prebaked batter. Sprinkle with the liqueur. Carefully spread the remaining batter evenly over the plums. Return to the oven and bake until lightly browned on top, 50–55 minutes. Let the cake cool in the pan on a wire rack for 5 minutes, then run a knife around the sides of the cake to loosen them from the pan sides. Let cool for 45 minutes longer.

Remove the pan sides and transfer the cake to a serving plate. Using a fine-mesh sieve, dust the top of the cake with the confectioners' sugar. Serve slightly warm.

PEACH UPSIDE-DOWN CAKE

Peaches are a twist on the classic pineapple recipe, but you can easily use pineapple (see note, right) or another type of stone fruit if you prefer. For a modern twist on the old-fashioned presentation, top each slice with a fresh cherry instead of the traditional maraschino.

⅓ cup (3 oz/90 g) unsalted
butter, plus 1 tablespoon,
melted and cooled

¾ cup (6 oz/185 g) firmly
packed dark brown sugar

5 large, ripe peaches,
peeled, halved, and pitted

4 eggs, separated,
at room temperature

1 teaspoon pure
almond extract

1 cup (4 oz/125 g)
all-purpose (plain) flour

1 teaspoon baking powder

¼ teaspoon salt

1 cup (8 oz/250 g)
granulated sugar

**MAKES ONE 9- OR 10-INCH
(23- OR 25-CM) CAKE**

Preheat the oven to 350°F (180°C).

In a 9- or 10-inch (23- or 25-cm) ovenproof frying pan over medium heat, melt the ⅓ cup (3 oz/90 g) butter. Add the brown sugar and cook, stirring, until the sugar dissolves and forms a syrup, 6–7 minutes. Remove from the heat. Snugly pack the peach halves, cut sides up, into the pan. Set aside.

In a bowl, whisk together the egg yolks, the 1 tablespoon melted butter, and the almond extract until blended. In another bowl, sift together the flour, baking powder, and salt.

In a large bowl, using an electric mixer on medium speed, beat the egg whites just until they hold firm peaks. Using a rubber spatula, fold the granulated sugar, about one-fourth at a time, into the egg whites. Then fold in the yolk mixture, again about one-fourth at a time. Finally, fold in the flour mixture in the same manner. Pour the batter over the peaches and spread with the spatula to cover evenly.

Bake until a toothpick inserted into the center comes out clean, about 30 minutes. Let cool in the pan for 10 minutes.

Run a knife around the sides of the cake to loosen the cake from the pan sides and invert the cake onto a large plate. Lift off the frying pan. Carefully replace any peach halves that are dislodged. Serve warm or at room temperature.

**Pineapple
upside-down cake**

Instead of peaches, use 1 pineapple, peeled, cored, and cut into slices ½ inch (12 mm) thick. Arrange 8 pineapple rings, slightly over-lapping them for a snug fit, on top of the butter-sugar mixture and proceed as directed. Reserve any remaining pineapple for another use.

CAKES & CHEESECAKES

SPONGE SHEET CAKE

Chocolate sponge sheet cake

For chocolate cake, reduce the amount of cake flour to ½ cup (2 oz/60 g) and add 2 tbsp Dutch-processed cocoa powder to the dry ingredients.

Sponge cakes, perfect for cake layers, are also the choice for rolled cakes. Here, an all-purpose sponge cake is baked in a large, shallow pan. The batter bakes up light and tender but sturdy, making the finished sheet cake easy to roll with your choice of fillings and frostings.

Preheat the oven to 350°F (180°C). Butter the bottom and sides of a 10-by-15-by-1-inch (25-by-38-by-2.5-cm) rimmed baking sheet and line the bottom with parchment (baking) paper. Butter and flour the paper and tap out the excess flour.

In a small bowl, sift together the flour and salt. Set aside. In a large bowl, using an electric mixer on medium speed, beat together the 5 egg yolks and ⅓ cup (2½ oz/75 g) of the sugar until thickened, pale yellow, and the batter falls back on itself like a ribbon when the beater is lifted, about 3 minutes. Beat in the vanilla. Set aside.

In a large bowl, using clean beaters, beat the egg whites on medium-high speed until they form soft peaks, 2–3 minutes. On medium speed, beat in the remaining ⅓ cup sugar, a little at a time. Then continue to beat until stiff peaks form, about 1 minute. Using a rubber spatula, fold the whites into the yolk mixture in 3 batches. Then gently fold in the flour mixture in 4 batches. Spread the batter evenly in the prepared pan and smooth the top with the spatula.

Bake until the top feels firm and is lightly browned and a toothpick inserted into the center comes out clean, about 14 minutes. Let cool in the pan on a wire rack until cool to the touch, about 25 minutes. Run a knife around the sides of the cake to loosen it from the pan sides. Invert onto a wire rack and peel off the parchment. Using both hands, carefully turn the cake right side up.

Fill and frost the cooled sheet cake as directed in individual recipes. If not using right away, sandwich between 2 sheets of waxed paper dusted with the confectioners' sugar (or with cocoa powder if make a chocolate cake). Roll the cake up lengthwise, tuck the ends of the paper under, and store at room temperature for up to 2 days.

Unsalted butter for the pan

⅔ cup (2½ oz/75 g) cake (soft-wheat) flour

Pinch of salt

4 eggs, separated, plus 1 egg yolk, at room temperature

⅔ cup (5 oz/155 g) granulated sugar

½ teaspoon pure vanilla extract

1 tablespoon confectioners' (icing) sugar if storing the cake

MAKES ONE 10-BY-15-INCH (25-BY-38-CM) SHEET CAKE

RASPBERRY JELLY ROLL

A light sponge sheet cake forms the base for this old-fashioned treat, which is filled with jam and dusted with confectioners' sugar. Make the cake in advance, and you can assemble it quickly just before serving. Dress up slices with lightly sweetened Whipped Cream (page 454).

¼ cup (2 oz/60 g) granulated sugar

2 tablespoons raspberry liqueur

1½ cups (12½ oz/390 g) seedless raspberry jam

Sponge Sheet Cake *(opposite)*, baked and cooled

About 2 tablespoons confectioners' (icing) sugar

MAKES 1 JELLY ROLL

To make the raspberry syrup, in a small saucepan, stir together ¼ cup (2 fl oz/60 ml) water and the granulated sugar over low heat until the sugar dissolves. Stir in the raspberry liqueur and let cool.

In another small saucepan, warm the raspberry jam over low heat, stirring often, just until it melts.

Brush the cake lightly with the raspberry syrup. Then, using an icing spatula, spread the warm jam evenly over the cake.

Roll up the cake lengthwise into an even cylinder. Transfer the roll, seam side down, to a platter. Using a fine-mesh sieve, dust the cake with the confectioners' sugar.

Jelly-roll variations

Jelly rolls are easy to vary: change the flavor of the syrup, match it with a complementary filling, and you have a whole new dessert. For example, you could replace the raspberry liqueur with orange and use orange marmalade as a filling. Or, you could use crème de cassis and seedless blackberry jam.

ALMOND CAKE WITH FRESH CHERRIES

Almond paste gives this cake a bold, nutty flavor that echoes the ground almonds in the batter. Fresh cherries are a classic partner to almond-flavored desserts, heightened here by the cherry-based kirsch in the syrup. Dust the finished cake with confectioners' (icing) sugar.

1¼ cups (10 oz/315 g) plus 2 tablespoons sugar

6 eggs, separated, at room temperature

Grated zest of 1 lemon

1 cup (5 oz/155 g) ground almonds

½ cup (2½ oz/75 g) all-purpose (plain) flour

1 teaspoon baking powder

1 teaspoon pure almond extract

3 tablespoons kirsch

1 tablespoon fresh lemon juice

½ lb (250 g) Bing cherries, pitted and halved

1½ cups (12 fl oz/375 ml) Whipped Cream (page 454)

MAKES ONE 9-INCH (23-CM) CAKE

Preheat the oven to 325°F (165°C). Butter the bottom and sides of a 9-inch (23-cm) springform pan and line the bottom with parchment (baking) paper.

In a large bowl, using an electric mixer on medium speed, beat together the 1¼ cups sugar, the egg yolks, and the lemon zest until thick and pale, about 10 minutes. In a bowl, stir together the ground almonds, flour, and baking powder. Add the almond mixture and almond extract to the egg yolk mixture and stir to blend.

In a bowl, using clean beaters, beat the egg whites on medium-high speed until soft peaks form. Using a silicone spatula, fold the beaten whites into egg yolk mixture. Pour the batter into the prepared pan and gently smooth the top.

Bake until the cake springs back when lightly touched, 60–65 minutes. Place the pan on a wire rack and remove the pan sides. In a small saucepan over medium heat, combine the kirsch, lemon juice, and the remaining 2 tablespoons sugar and heat, stirring, until the sugar is dissolved. Remove from the heat and brush the hot syrup gently and evenly over the hot cake. Let the cake cool completely.

When ready to serve, using a serrated knife, split the cake in half horizontally (page 493). Gently mix the cherries into the whipped cream and spread over the bottom cake layer. Cover with the top cake layer. Serve right away.

Cherry season

Make this cake in the summer, when cherries proliferate at roadside farm stands. Because they have a shorter distance to travel from tree to table, locally grown cherries (and other fruits) can stay on the tree until they're fully ripened, which translates to sweeter, more delicious flavor.

BOSTON CREAM PIE

Despite its name, this dish is nothing like a pie. It begins as a moist, tender-crumbed butter cake with a well cut out of the bottom layer. The well is filled with thick, smooth pastry cream—an unexpected surprise when the cake is cut. A shiny chocolate glaze tops the cake.

Calculating egg parts

If you forget how many eggs you have separated, you can weigh the yolks or the whites. A single large yolk weighs about ¾ oz (20 g), and 1 large egg white weighs about 1 oz (30 g). Divide the total weight by the weight of a single yolk or white to get the correct number.

To make a chocolate glaze, in the top of a double boiler or in a heatproof bowl, combine the chocolate, butter, and corn syrup. Place over (not touching) barely simmering water and heat, stirring occasionally, until melted and smooth. Remove from the heat and let cool until the mixture thickens to a pourable consistency, about 20 minutes.

Place 1 cake layer, top side up, on a serving plate. Using a small knife and beginning ½ inch (12 mm) from the edge, mark a circle ½ inch deep in the cake. Use the knife to cut out the circle, creating an indentation 8 inches (20 cm) in diameter and ½ inch deep and leaving a ½-inch border. Spread the pastry cream in the indentation. Top with the second cake layer. Pour about half of the chocolate glaze over the top of the cake and use an icing spatula to spread it evenly. Spread the remaining chocolate glaze evenly onto the sides of the cake.

Refrigerate the finished cake for 1 hour to firm the glaze, then cover the cake with plastic wrap and refrigerate for up to 2 days before serving; let stand at room temperature for 30 minutes before slicing and serving.

8 oz (250 g) semisweet (plain) chocolate, finely chopped

½ cup (4 oz/125 g) unsalted butter, at room temperature, cut into 8 equal pieces

1 tablespoon light corn syrup

Butter Cake (page 496), baked and cooled

2 cups (16 fl oz/500 ml) Pastry Cream (page 452)

MAKES ONE 9-INCH (23-CM) CAKE

ORANGE LAYER CAKE

This refreshing cake is perfect for any occasion. For a pretty garnish, press thin half slices of orange, curved side up, firmly against the bottom edge of the cake. To add a more intense orange flavor, brush each layer with 2 tablespoons orange liqueur before frosting.

Warming eggs

To bring cold eggs up to room temperature quickly, put the eggs in a bowl of lukewarm water (hot water might cook them) for 30 minutes.

Preheat the oven to 350°F (180°C). Butter and flour two 9-inch (23-cm) round cake pans and tap out the excess flour.

In a small bowl, sift together the flour, baking powder, and baking soda. In another bowl, using an electric mixer on medium-high speed, beat together the butter and sugar until fluffy, about 2 minutes. Beat in the orange zest and vanilla. Add the eggs, one at a time, beating well after each addition. On low speed, add the flour mixture in 3 batches, alternately with the milk and orange juice concentrate in 2 batches, beginning and ending with the flour mixture and mixing until incorporated. Divide the batter evenly between the prepared pans and smooth the tops.

Bake until a toothpick inserted into the centers comes out clean, about 25 minutes. Let cool in the pans on wire racks for 10 minutes. Invert onto the racks, turn right sides up, and let cool completely.

2½ cups (10 oz/315 g) cake (soft-wheat) flour

¾ teaspoon baking powder

¼ teaspoon baking soda (bicarbonate of soda)

¾ cup (6 oz/185 g) unsalted butter, at room temperature

1⅓ cups (11 oz/330 g) sugar

2 teaspoons grated orange zest

1 teaspoon pure vanilla extract

4 eggs, at room temperature

½ cup (4 fl oz/125 ml) milk

¼ cup (2 fl oz/60 ml) thawed, undiluted frozen orange juice concentrate

Orange–Cream Cheese Frosting (page 456)

MAKES ONE 9-INCH (23-CM) CAKE

Place 1 cake layer, top side down, on a serving plate. Using an icing spatula, spread 1¼ cups (10 fl oz/310 ml) of the frosting over the top. Place the second cake layer, top side down, on top of the first, lining up the edges. Spread the remaining frosting over the top and sides of the cake. Serve right away, or cover with a cake dome and refrigerate for up to 1 day. Bring to room temperature before serving.

SOUR CREAM–CHOCOLATE CAKE

This splendid cake is the perfect centerpiece for a birthday or other celebration and can be made a day in advance of the party. The sour cream in both the cake and the frosting lends a slight tanginess that nicely complements the chocolate flavor.

1¼ cups (6½ oz/200 g) all-purpose (plain) flour

½ cup (1½ oz/45 g) unsweetened cocoa powder

½ teaspoon salt

½ teaspoon baking powder

½ teaspoon baking soda (bicarbonate of soda)

¾ cup (6 oz/185 g) unsalted butter, at room temperature

1¼ cups (9 oz/280 g) firmly packed light brown sugar

3 eggs, at room temperature

⅔ cup (5 oz/160 g) sour cream

Sour Cream Fudge Frosting (page 458)

MAKES ONE 9-INCH (23-CM) CAKE

Preheat the oven to 350°F (180°C). Butter the bottoms and sides of two 9-inch (23-cm) round cake pans and line the bottoms with parchment (baking) paper. Butter the paper.

In a small bowl, sift together the flour, cocoa, salt, baking powder, and baking soda. In a large bowl, using an electric mixer on medium-high speed, beat the butter until light, about 4 minutes. Gradually add the brown sugar and beat until fluffy, about 2 minutes. Add the eggs one at a time, beating well after each addition. On low speed, add the flour mixture in 3 batches, alternately with the sour cream in 2 batches, beginning and ending with the flour mixture and mixing until incorporated. The batter will be thick. Divide the batter evenly between the prepared pans and smooth the tops with a rubber spatula.

Bake until a toothpick inserted into the centers comes out clean, about 25 minutes. Let cool in the pans on wire racks for 10 minutes. Invert onto the racks, peel off the parchment, turn right sides up, and let cool completely.

Place 1 cake layer, top side down, on a plate. Using an icing spatula, spread ⅔ cup (5 fl oz/150 ml) of the frosting over the top. Place the second cake layer, top side down, on top, lining up the edges. Spread the remaining frosting decoratively over the top and sides of the cake. Serve right away, or cover and store at room temperature for up to 1 day.

Easy cake decorating

For a special touch and extra flavor and texture, press chopped toasted walnuts, peanuts, or pistachio nuts into the sides of the frosted cake. Or, leave the cake plain and use the back of a spoon to make a scallop pattern in the frosting all over the cake.

503

ANGEL FOOD CAKE

A stabilizing effect

Cream of tartar is used in angel food cakes primarily to stabilize the egg whites, but it also lowers the pH of the batter, resulting in a whiter crumb.

Everything about an angel food cake is light. The whipped egg white batter looks like a soft, fluffy marshmallow and bakes into a creamy, delicately textured, stunningly high-rise cake. Since the batter includes no fat, the cake is also a light addition to any cholesterol-conscious diet.

Position a rack in the lower middle of the oven and preheat to 325°F (165°C).

In a small bowl, sift together the flour and ¾ cup (6 oz/185 g) of the sugar. Set aside. In a large bowl, using an electric mixer on medium speed, beat together the egg whites, cream of tartar, and salt until the mixture is opaque and foamy and the cream of tartar has dissolved, about 1 minute. On medium-high speed, continue to beat until the whites look white and shiny and hold soft peaks, 2–3 minutes. On medium speed, add the remaining 1 cup (8 oz/250 g) sugar, a little at a time. Then continue to beat until stiff peaks form, about 2 minutes. Add the vanilla and almond extracts and beat on medium speed for 1 minute.

1 cup (4 oz/125 g) cake (soft-wheat) flour

1¾ cups (14 oz/435 g) sugar

12 egg whites, at room temperature

1 teaspoon cream of tartar

¼ teaspoon salt

2 teaspoons pure vanilla extract

½ teaspoon pure almond extract

MAKES ONE 10-INCH (25-CM) CAKE

Cooling upside down

Angel food cakes need to be cooled upside down because the egg proteins that give the cake its height firm up as the cake cools. If cooled upright, they might collapse and deflate the cake.

504

On low speed, add one-third of the flour mixture and beat just until well incorporated. Add the remaining flour mixture in 2 batches and beat just until incorporated. The batter will look soft and fluffy.

Using a large rubber spatula, scrape the batter into a 10-inch (25-cm) angel food cake pan or other tube pan, preferably with a removable bottom, then gently smooth the top of the batter with the spatula.

Bake the cake undisturbed for 40 minutes. If the top looks set and is lightly browned, touch it gently. If it feels firm, insert a thin wooden skewer or toothpick near the center of the cake, equidistant from the pan sides and the tube. If it comes out dry, the cake is done. If it comes out wet or with crumbs clinging to it, bake for 5 minutes longer and check again. Repeat this test until the cake is done. It will probably take a total of 50 minutes.

Remove the cake from the oven. If the pan has feet, invert it onto a wire rack, resting the feet on the wires. If the pan does not have feet, invert the pan onto the neck of a full wine bottle. Let cool until the cake and the pan are cool to the touch, about 1 hour.

Run a knife around the sides of the pan and the tube to loosen the cake sides. Invert a large plate over the pan, and invert the plate and pan together. Lift off the pan, then invert the cake onto a wire rack. Let the cake cool completely on the rack before serving. Use a serrated knife and a light sawing motion to cut the cake.

DRIED FRUIT AND NUT CAKE

A fresh take on the traditional fruitcake, this cake is peppered with bits of dried orange peel and crystallized ginger. For the best flavor, buy dried fruits in bulk bins at natural-foods stores, rather than the neon-colored stock found in many supermarkets.

1 cup *each* (6 oz/185 g) chopped dried pears, apricots, and pitted prunes

½ cup *each* (3 oz/90 g) dark raisins and golden raisins (sultanas)

½ cup *each* (2 oz/60 g) pitted dried sour cherries and chopped pitted dates

3 tablespoons finely chopped candied orange peel

2 tablespoons finely chopped crystallized ginger

½ cup (4 fl oz/125 ml) plus 3 tablespoons brandy

1½ cups (12 oz/375 g) unsalted butter, at room temperature

2½ cups (1¼ lb/625 g) sugar

8 eggs, at room temperature

1 tablespoon pure vanilla extract

½ teaspoon salt

3 cups (9 oz/280 g) sifted cake (soft-wheat) flour

2 cups (8–10 oz/250–315 g) walnuts, pecans, hazelnuts (filberts), or almonds, toasted (page 17) and chopped

MAKES ONE 10-INCH (25-CM) CAKE

In a bowl, combine the pears, apricots, prunes, dark and golden raisins, cherries, dates, orange peel, and crystallized ginger. Pour the ½ cup (4 fl oz/ 125 ml) brandy over the top. Let stand for at least 4 hours or up to overnight at room temperature, stirring occasionally.

Preheat the oven to 325°F (165°C). Butter the bottoms and sides of a 10-inch (25-cm) tube pan and line the bottom with parchment (baking) paper. Butter and flour the paper and tap out the excess flour.

In a large bowl, using an electric mixer on medium speed, beat the butter until light and fluffy, about 7 minutes. Add the sugar and continue beating until once again fluffy, about 4 minutes. Beat in the eggs, one at a time, beating well after each addition. Beat in the vanilla and salt. On low speed, slowly add the flour and beat until incorporated. Using a wooden spoon, fold in the nuts and the brandy-fruit mixture until fully incorporated. Spoon the batter into the pan and smooth the top with the back of the spoon.

Bake until a toothpick inserted near the center of the cake comes out clean, about 1 hour and 50 minutes. Transfer the pan to a wire rack. Brush 1 tablespoon of the remaining brandy over the cake. Let cool in the pan for 5 minutes. Invert the cake onto the rack. Carefully lift off the pan and peel off the parchment. Brush the remaining 2 tablespoons brandy over the top and sides. Let cool completely before serving. If not serving right away, wrap the cake in plastic wrap and store at cool room temperature for up to 5 days.

Dried sour cherries

Dried sour cherries have an appealing sweet-tart flavor. Pitted before drying, they resemble raisins or dried cranberries and can be used in the same way. Look for them in well-stocked markets.

505

APPLESAUCE-SPICE BUNDT CAKE

Maple frosting

In a saucepan over medium-high heat, reduce 1 cup (8 fl oz/ 250 ml) pure maple syrup by half, about 15 minutes. Remove from the heat and stir in 4 tbsp (2 oz/ 60 g) unsalted butter, ½ cup (4 fl oz/125 ml) heavy (double) cream, and ½ tsp pure vanilla extract. Beat into 2 cups (8 oz/250 g) sifted confectioners' (icing) sugar until smooth and creamy. Let cool before using.

Applesauce gives this versatile cake a moist texture. For a simple presentation, accompany slices with a dollop of Whipped Cream (page 454) sprinkled with cinnamon. For an autumnal flavor, omit the Brown Sugar Icing and frost the top with Maple Frosting (see note, left).

Preheat the oven to 350°F (180°C). Butter a 10-inch (25-cm) nonstick Bundt pan.

Toast the pecans (page 17) and set aside to cool.

In a bowl, sift together the flour, cinnamon, baking soda, allspice, nutmeg, and salt. In another bowl, using an electric mixer on medium speed, beat together the butter and brown sugar until well blended. Add the eggs, one at a time, beating well after each addition. Beat in the vanilla extract. Whisk in the flour mixture in 3 batches, alternately with the applesauce in 2 batches, beginning and ending with the flour mixture and whisking until incorporated. Stir in the 1 cup pecans. Pour and scrape the batter into the prepared pan.

Bake until a toothpick inserted near the center comes out clean, about 55 minutes. Let cool in the pan on a wire rack for 10 minutes. Invert onto the rack and let cool completely.

Drizzle the icing evenly over the top, allowing it to run slightly over the sides. Sprinkle the 2 tablespoons pecans on top, then let stand until the icing sets, about 1 hour, before serving.

1 cup (4 oz/125 g) plus 2 tablespoons chopped pecans

3⅓ cups (13½ oz/420 g) cake (soft-wheat) flour

1 tablespoon ground cinnamon

1½ teaspoons baking soda (bicarbonate of soda)

1¼ teaspoons *each* ground allspice and ground nutmeg

¼ teaspoon salt

1 cup (8 oz/250 g) unsalted butter, at room temperature

1⅔ cups (12 oz/375 g) firmly packed dark brown sugar

3 eggs

2 teaspoons pure vanilla extract

2 cups (18 oz/560 g) unsweetened applesauce

Brown Sugar Icing (page 456)

MAKES ONE 10-INCH (25-CM) CAKE

ALMOND BUNDT CAKE

Almond paste

Almond paste is a mixture of ground blanched almonds, sugar, and corn syrup. It is similar to marzipan but contains more nuts and is thus coarser, stiffer, and has a stronger almond flavor. Almond paste and marzipan are not interchangeable in recipes.

The almond paste in this deceptively rich cake gives it a bold, straightforward flavor and pleasingly dense texture. Serve thin slices of the cake garnished with chilled orange segments, sliced strawberries, or diced stone fruit, depending on what's best in season.

Preheat the oven to 350°F (180°C). Butter and flour a 9-inch (23-cm) Bundt pan and tap out the excess flour.

In a bowl, sift together the flour, baking powder, and salt. In a large bowl, break up the almond paste with a spoon, then add the granulated sugar and butter. Using an electric mixer on medium-high speed, beat until light and creamy, about 5 minutes. Add the eggs, one at a time, beating well after each addition. Don't worry if the mixture looks curdled. Beat in the vanilla. Using a rubber spatula, gently fold in half of

1 cup (4 oz/125 g) cake (soft-wheat) flour

1 teaspoon baking powder

¼ teaspoon salt

7 oz (220 g) almond paste, at room temperature

1 cup (8 oz/250 g) granulated sugar

1 cup (8 oz/250 g)
unsalted butter,
at room temperature

6 eggs, at room
temperature

1 teaspoon pure
vanilla extract

Confectioners' (icing)
sugar for dusting

**MAKES ONE 9-INCH
(23-CM) CAKE**

the flour mixture until almost fully incorporated. Then fold
in the remaining flour mixture until the batter is smooth.
Scrape the batter into the prepared pan and smooth the top.

Bake until a toothpick inserted into the center comes out
clean, 40–45 minutes. Let cool in the pan on a wire rack
for 10 minutes. Invert onto the rack and let cool completely.
Cover the cake with a clean, slightly dampened kitchen towel
to prevent the exterior of the cake from drying out as it cools.

Using a fine-mesh sieve, liberally dust the top of the cooled
cake with confectioners' sugar just before serving.

If not serving right away, store the cake tightly wrapped
at room temperature for up to 3 days or in the freezer for
up to 1 month. Thaw before serving.

SOUR CREAM–BLUEBERRY CAKE

This is a terrific cake for brunch or afternoon tea. Look for fresh blueberries in markets during
the warm summer months. If using frozen blueberries, do not thaw them first or they will release
too much juice. You can flavor the icing with lime or orange in place of the lemon.

3 cups (15 oz/470 g)
all-purpose (plain) flour

1 tablespoon
baking powder

½ teaspoon salt

6 tablespoons (3 oz/90 g)
unsalted butter, at room
temperature

1⅓ cups (11 oz/345 g) sugar

2 eggs, at room
temperature

2 teaspoons pure
vanilla extract

1 teaspoon grated
lemon zest

¼ cup (2 oz/60 g)
sour cream

¾ cup (6 fl oz/180 ml)
whole milk

2 cups (8 oz/250 g) fresh
or frozen blueberries

Lemon Icing (page 456)

**MAKES ONE 10-INCH
(25-CM) CAKE**

Preheat the oven to 350°F (180°C). Generously butter
a 10-inch (25-cm) Bundt pan.

In a large bowl, sift together the flour, baking powder, and
salt. In another bowl, using an electric mixer on medium-
high speed, beat the butter until light. Add the sugar and beat
until blended. Add the eggs, one at a time, beating well after
each addition. Beat in the vanilla and lemon zest, and then
beat in the sour cream. On low speed, add the flour mixture
into 3 batches, alternately with the milk in 2 batches, beginning
and ending with the flour and mixing until incorporated.
The batter will be very thick.

Spoon half of the batter into the prepared pan. Sprinkle with
1 cup (4 oz/125 g) of the blueberries. Gently press the berries
into the top of the batter. Spoon the remaining batter over
the berries and then sprinkle the remaining berries over the
top, again pressing them gently into the batter.

Bake until a toothpick inserted near the center comes out
clean, about 1 hour. Let cool in the pan on a wire rack for
10 minutes. Invert onto the rack and let cool completely.

Drizzle the icing evenly over the top, allowing it to run
slightly over the sides. Let stand until the icing sets, about
1 hour, before serving.

507

Sour cream
in baking

*Look for sour
cream that contains
neither additives nor
preservatives. Unless
a recipe specifies that
you can use reduced-
fat sour cream, don't
substitute it for
full-fat sour cream.
The butterfat is often
essential to the
success of the recipe.*

CHOCOLATE PUDDING CAKE

Using a double boiler

This two-part pan, which heats mixtures in the top pan over hot or simmering water in the lower pan, creates a gentle heating environment to preserve the integrity of delicate foods. If you don't have a double boiler, you can use a heatproof bowl and a saucepan (see page 566).

This delectable dessert comes out of the oven with a cake layer on the top and a chocolaty saucelike layer on the bottom. It tastes best when served warm from the oven, but it is also good chilled. Serve with vanilla ice cream or Whipped Cream (page 454).

Preheat the oven to 350°F (180°C). Butter a 9-inch (23-cm) square baking pan.

Place the chocolate in the top pan of a double boiler. Place over (not touching) barely simmering water and heat, stirring occasionally, until melted and smooth. Remove from the heat and let cool slightly.

In a bowl, using an electric mixer on high speed, beat the butter with half of the granulated sugar until light and fluffy, 4–5 minutes. Stop the mixer. Sift together the sifted flour, baking powder, and salt onto the butter mixture, then pour in the milk. On low speed, beat until well mixed. Using a rubber spatula, fold in the chocolate and 1 teaspoon of the vanilla. Spread the mixture evenly in the prepared pan.

In the same bowl, stir together the remaining granulated sugar, the brown sugar, and the cocoa powder. Sprinkle evenly over the batter in the pan. Add the remaining 1 teaspoon vanilla to the boiling water and slowly pour the mixture over the batter, disturbing it as little as possible.

Bake until the top is firm to the touch, about 1 hour. Let cool slightly in the pan on a wire rack. To serve, cut the cake into 8 squares, and spoon some of the sauce from the bottom of the pan over each serving.

2 oz (60 g) unsweetened chocolate, chopped

½ cup (4 oz/125 g) unsalted butter, at room temperature

1⅓ cups (11 oz/345 g) granulated sugar

1 cup (4 oz/125 g) sifted all-purpose (plain) flour

1½ teaspoons baking powder

½ teaspoon salt

½ cup (4 fl oz/125 ml) milk

2 teaspoons pure vanilla extract

½ cup (3½ oz/105 g) firmly packed dark brown sugar

3 rounded tablespoons unsweetened cocoa powder

1½ cups (12 fl oz/375 ml) boiling water

MAKES ONE 9-INCH (23-CM) SQUARE CAKE

CHOCOLATE DECADENCE CAKE

Pairing chocolate with wine

Chocolate desserts are challenging partners for most wines because they are both bitter and sweet. For best results, choose a wine that is sweeter than the dessert, such as a ruby Port or late-harvest Zinfandel.

Sinfully rich, this nearly flourless chocolate cake is perfect for a special occasion or anytime you wish to treat your family or friends. An easy raspberry sauce lends pleasing contrasting flavors to the plate. If you like, garnish servings with fresh raspberries.

Preheat the oven to 425°F (220°C). Butter the bottom and sides of an 8-inch (20-cm) springform pan, line the bottom with parchment (baking) paper, and butter the paper.

Place the chocolate in a heatproof bowl. Place over (not touching) barely simmering water and heat, stirring occasionally, until melted and smooth. Remove from the heat and whisk in the butter, sugar, and flour. In a bowl, whisk the egg yolks until blended. Add to the chocolate mixture and whisk until blended.

In a bowl, using an electric mixer on medium-high speed, beat the egg whites until they hold their shape but are not

1 lb (500 g) semisweet chocolate, broken into small pieces

1 cup (8 oz/250 g) unsalted butter, cut into pieces, at room temperature

¼ cup (2 oz/60 g) sugar

1 tablespoon all-purpose (plain) flour

4 eggs, separated, at room temperature

1 package (12 oz/375 g) frozen unsweetened raspberries, thawed

Whipped Cream (page 454)

MAKES ONE 8-INCH (20-CM) CAKE

stiff. Using a rubber spatula, fold them into the chocolate mixture just until combined. Spoon into the prepared pan.

Bake for about 15 minutes. The cake will still be wiggly. Turn off the oven, position the oven door ajar, and let the cake cool in the oven for 1 hour. Then, place in the freezer for at least 2 hours or in the refrigerator for up to 8 hours.

Remove the pan sides and invert the cake onto a plate. Peel off the parchment and invert onto a serving plate. Bring to room temperature before serving.

Just before serving, place the thawed raspberries in a blender and process until smooth. Pour through a fine-mesh sieve into a bowl to remove the seeds.

To serve, cut the cake into narrow wedges, dipping a sharp knife in hot water and wiping dry before each cut. Top each serving with the raspberry sauce and Whipped Cream.

QUEEN OF SHEBA TORTE

Known in French as *Reine de Saba* torte, this rich cake was made popular in the United States by Julia Child in her first cookbook. Traditionally made with ground almonds, you can choose either almonds, walnuts, or pecans to complement the intense chocolate flavor.

All-purpose (plain) flour for pan

8 oz (250 g) bittersweet chocolate, chopped (1⅔ cups)

¾ cup (6 oz/185 g) unsalted butter, at room temperature

¾ cup (6 oz/185 g) sugar

6 extra-large eggs, separated, at room temperature

1½ cups (6 oz/185 g) ground nuts (see note, above)

3 cups (24 fl oz/750 ml) Chocolate Ganache (page 458), warmed

MAKES ONE 10-INCH (25-CM) CAKE

Position a rack in the lower third of the oven and preheat the oven to 350°F (180°C). Butter the bottom and sides of a 10-inch (25-cm) round cake pan or springform pan with 3-inch (7.5-cm) sides and line the bottom with parchment (baking) paper. Butter and flour the paper and tap out the excess flour.

Place the chocolate in the top pan of a double boiler or in a heatproof bowl. Place over (not touching) barely simmering water and heat, stirring occasionally, until melted and smooth. Remove from the heat and let cool slightly.

In a bowl, using an electric mixer on high speed, beat the butter with the sugar until light and fluffy, 8–10 minutes. Add the egg yolks, one at a time, beating well after each addition. Beat in the cooled chocolate and the nuts.

In a large bowl, using clean beaters, beat the egg whites on medium-high speed until they are stiff and glossy but not dry. Using a rubber spatula, gently but thoroughly fold the egg whites into the chocolate mixture. Pour into the prepared pan and smooth the top with the spatula.

Bake the cake until the top puffs and forms a thin crust, about 50 minutes. Be careful not to overbake. Let cool in the pan on a wire rack for 15 minutes. If using a springform pan, remove the pan sides. Invert the cake onto the rack and let cool completely. Peel off the parchment.

Invert the cake onto a serving plate and spread the warm ganache over the top and sides. Let stand until the ganache sets before serving.

Troubleshooting egg whites

Overbeaten egg whites appear grainy and can separate. Be sure to watch closely while beating to prevent this from happening. If you beat the egg whites to this stage, you'll need to discard them and start again with fresh egg whites.

LIGHT-AS-AIR CHOCOLATE CUPCAKES

These cupcakes don't rise very high, but they are rich and heavenly light. If desired, pipe the Chocolate Whipped Cream (page 454) inside each cupcake: using a pastry (piping) bag fitted with a star tip, gently push the tip into the top of a cake and squeeze to release a dab of cream.

Pastry bag alternative

If you don't have a pastry (piping) bag, you can insert the desired decorating tip into a snipped corner of a heavy-duty zippered plastic bag. Fill the bag with the whipped cream or other filling or topping, press out the air, seal closed, and proceed as you would with a pastry bag.

510

Preheat the oven to 350°F (180°C). Line 12 standard muffin cups with paper liners.

Combine the chocolate and butter in a large, heatproof bowl. Place over (not touching) barely simmering water and heat, stirring occasionally, until melted and smooth. Remove from the heat and let cool for 5 minutes. Stir in the whole eggs, sugar, and flour until well blended.

In a bowl, using an electric mixer on high speed, beat the egg whites until stiff, glossy peaks form. Using a rubber spatula, fold the egg whites into the chocolate mixture just until combined. Spoon the batter into the prepared muffin cups, filling them two-thirds full.

Bake until the tops look dry and a toothpick inserted into the center of a cupcake comes out clean, 12–14 minutes. Let cool completely in the pan on a wire rack, then remove.

Top the cupcakes with the whipped cream. Serve right away, or refrigerate for no more than 6 hours.

4 oz (125 g) unsweetened chocolate, chopped

6 tablespoons (3 oz/90 g) unsalted butter, at room temperature

3 extra-large eggs, lightly beaten, at room temperature

½ cup (4 oz/125 g) sugar

2 tablespoons all-purpose (plain) flour

3 extra-large egg whites, at room temperature

Chocolate Whipped Cream (page 454)

MAKES 12 CUPCAKES

CITRUS CUPCAKES WITH LEMON ICING

The grated lemon and orange zest in the batter and the tangy lemon icing on top give these cupcakes a wonderful sweet-tart taste. They are a refreshing twist on the predictable vanilla or chocolate flavors and are crowd-pleasers at a potluck or picnic.

Miniature citrus cupcakes

You can also bake these cupcakes in miniature muffin tins, sometimes called gem pans. Decrease the baking time from 20 to about 12 minutes. You will have 32 cupcakes.

Preheat the oven to 350°F (180°C). Line 10 standard muffin cups with paper liners, filling any unused cups in the pan one-third full with water.

In a bowl, sift together the flour, baking powder, baking soda, and salt. Stir in the sugar. In a small, heavy saucepan over medium heat, combine the butter, milk, and lemon and orange zests and heat until the butter melts. Whisk the hot milk mixture into the flour mixture until well combined. Then whisk in the whole egg and egg yolk until blended. Spoon the batter into the prepared muffin cups, filling them about half full.

Bake until a toothpick inserted into the center of a cupcake comes out clean, about 20 minutes. Immediately invert the cupcakes onto a wire rack, then turn them right sides up and let cool completely.

Spread the icing on the cupcakes and serve.

1⅓ cups (6½ oz/200 g) all-purpose (plain) flour

1¼ teaspoons baking powder

½ teaspoon baking soda (bicarbonate of soda)

¼ teaspoon salt

¾ cup (6 oz/185 g) sugar

¼ cup (2 oz/60 g) unsalted butter

⅔ cup (5 fl oz/160 ml) milk

1½ teaspoons *each* grated lemon zest and orange zest

1 egg, plus 1 egg yolk

1 cup (8 fl oz/250 ml) Lemon Icing (page 456)

MAKES 10 CUPCAKES

RASPBERRY CUPCAKES

Each of these light, frosted cupcakes carries a hidden pocket of sweet raspberry preserves. Kids and adults alike will appreciate the surprise inside. This method also works with other types of preserves, such as strawberry, peach, or plum.

1½ cups (7½ oz/235 g) all-purpose (plain) flour

2 teaspoons baking powder

¼ teaspoon salt

1 cup (8 oz/250 g) sugar

¾ cup (6 fl oz/180 ml) milk

6 tablespoons (3 oz/90 g) unsalted butter, melted and cooled

3 egg whites, at room temperature

1 teaspoon pure vanilla extract

4 tablespoons raspberry preserves

1 cup (8 fl oz/250 ml) Lemon Icing (page 456)

MAKES 11 CUPCAKES

Preheat the oven to 350°F (180°C). Line 11 standard muffin cups with paper liners, filling any unused cups in the pan one-third full with water.

In a bowl, sift together the flour, baking powder, and salt. Stir in the sugar. Add the milk, melted butter, egg whites, and vanilla and whisk until smooth. Spoon an equal amount of the batter into each prepared muffin cup.

Bake until a toothpick inserted into the center of a cupcake comes out clean, about 20 minutes. Immediately invert the cupcakes onto a wire rack, then turn them right sides up and let cool completely.

Using the small end of a melon baller, scoop out a small indentation in the top center of each cupcake. Spoon a heaping teaspoon of preserves into each indentation. Carefully spread the icing over the cupcakes and serve.

Preserves vs. jam

The term preserves *refers to any fruit that has been prepared for long-term storage through the use of sugar to slow spoilage. In common usage, preserves contain chunks of fruit and jams are usually a smooth purée.*

ESPRESSO TIRAMISU

Mascarpone alternative

If you can't find mascarpone cheese, use 1½ lb (750 g) light cream cheese blended with ½ cup (4 fl oz/125 ml) heavy (double) cream and 6 tbsp (3 fl oz/ 90 ml) sour cream.

Tiramisu (literally, "pick me up") is a popular Italian layered dessert that pairs cake with sweetened mascarpone, espresso syrup, and a liqueur. It is traditionally made with ladyfingers, but they are sometimes hard to find. Homemade or purchased pound cake works well, too.

In a bowl, using an electric mixer on medium speed, beat together the mascarpone cheese, 1 cup (4 oz/125 g) of the confectioners' sugar, and the Marsala until well blended. Add the cream and beat until fluffy, about 1 minute. Set aside.

In a small saucepan over high heat, combine ⅔ cup (5 fl oz/ 160 ml) water, the remaining ½ cup (2 oz/60 g) confectioners' sugar, and the espresso powder and bring to a boil, stirring occasionally. Remove from the heat and let the syrup cool.

In a 2½-qt (2.5-l) oval or rectangular glass dish about 11 inches (28 cm) long and 2 inches (5 cm) deep, arrange enough of the cake slices in a single layer to cover the bottom completely, trimming to fit as needed. Brush half of the sugar syrup over the cake slices and then pour in half of the cheese mixture, spreading evenly. Top with enough of the remaining cake slices to cover in a single layer, again trimming to fit. Brush with the remaining syrup. Spread the remaining cheese mixture over the top. Cover with plastic wrap and refrigerate until firm, at least 2 hours or up to 2 days.

Using a fine-mesh sieve, dust the top with cocoa powder just before serving. Use a large spoon to scoop out servings.

3 cups (1½ lb/750 g) mascarpone cheese

1½ cups (6 oz/185 g) confectioners' (icing) sugar

¼ cup (2 fl oz/60 ml) Marsala or light rum

¾ cup (6 fl oz/180 ml) cold heavy (double) cream

5 teaspoons instant espresso powder or regular coffee powder

Pound Cake, homemade (page 494) or purchased, cut crosswise into slices ¼–⅓ inch (6–9 mm) thick

Unsweetened cocoa powder for dusting

MAKES 10–12 SERVINGS

SPICED WALNUT CAKE

Retrieving egg shells

If tiny egg shell fragments fall into the bowl of egg whites or yolks as you separate them, scoop them up with an emptied half shell. They readily cling to it, and it works better than your fingers or a spoon or knife tip.

Studded with walnuts and flavored with warm spices, this light and delicate Greek-style cake is the ideal companion for baked or poached fruits. A little sweetened plain Greek yogurt or Whipped Cream (page 454) would be a nice garnish.

To make the syrup, in a heavy saucepan over medium heat, combine the sugar, honey, and 1 cup (8 fl oz/250 ml) water and bring to a simmer, stirring to dissolve the sugar. Add the cloves, cinnamon stick, and lemon zest and juice, then reduce the heat to medium-low and simmer until slightly thickened, about 10 minutes. Remove the syrup from the heat and let cool.

Preheat the oven to 350°F (180°C). Lightly butter and flour a 9-by-12-by-3-inch (23-by-30-by-7.5-cm) baking pan and tap out the excess flour.

To make the cake, in a bowl, using an electric mixer on high speed, beat together the butter and sugar until light and fluffy, 5–8 minutes. Add the egg yolks, one at a time, beating well after each addition. In another bowl, sift together the flour, baking powder, cinnamon, cloves, and salt. Using a rubber

FOR THE SYRUP

¾ cup (6 oz/185 g) sugar

½ cup (6 oz/185 g) honey

4 whole cloves

1 cinnamon stick

1 lemon zest strip, 2-by-½ inches (5-by-12 mm)

2 tablespoons fresh lemon juice

FOR THE CAKE

½ cup (4 oz/125 g) unsalted butter, at room temperature

½ cup (4 oz/125 g) sugar

8 eggs, separated

½ cup (2½ oz/75 g) all-purpose (plain) flour

2 teaspoons baking powder

2 teaspoons ground cinnamon

¼ teaspoon ground cloves

Pinch of salt

2½ cups (10 oz/315 g) ground walnuts

1 tablespoon grated orange zest

MAKES ONE 9-BY-12-INCH (23-BY-30-CM) CAKE

spatula, gently fold the flour mixture into the butter mixture, then fold in the nuts and orange zest.

In a large bowl, using the electric mixer fitted with clean beaters, beat the egg whites on high speed until stiff peaks form. Stir one-third of the beaten whites into the batter to lighten it, then, using a rubber spatula, gently fold in the remaining whites just until no white streaks remain. Pour and scrape the batter into the prepared pan.

Bake until golden brown and the top springs back when lightly touched, about 45 minutes. Place the pan on a wire rack and immediately pour the syrup evenly over the top. Let cool completely. Cut into squares or diamonds to serve.

CLASSIC CHEESECAKE

This is the classic cheesecake with its signature graham cracker crust. For a colorful presentation, top the cake with your favorite tropical fruits such as sliced mango, papaya, and pineapple. Once topped with fruit, store it in the refrigerator for no more than 4 hours.

FOR THE CRUST

1¾ cups (5½ oz/170 g) graham cracker crumbs

¼ cup (2 oz/60 g) firmly packed light brown sugar

½ cup (4 oz/125 g) unsalted butter, melted and cooled

FOR THE FILLING

2 lb (1 kg) cream cheese, at room temperature

1 cup (8 oz/250 g) granulated sugar

1 cup (8 oz/250 ml) heavy (double) cream

1 teaspoon unflavored gelatin

MAKES ONE 9-INCH (23-CM) CAKE

Preheat the oven to 350°F (180°C). Have ready a 9-inch (23-cm) springform pan with 2½-inch (6-cm) sides.

To make the crust, in a food processor, combine the graham cracker crumbs and brown sugar and process until well mixed. Add the melted butter and process just until the crumbs being to stick together. Press the crumb mixture firmly onto the bottom and 2 inches (5 cm) up the sides of the pan. Bake the crust until set, about 10 minutes. Let cool completely on a wire rack.

To make the filling, in a bowl, using an electric mixer on medium speed, beat the cream cheese with the granulated sugar until well blended. Beat in ½ cup (4 fl oz/125 ml) of the cream until well mixed.

Place 1 tablespoon water in a small saucepan. Sprinkle the gelatin over the top and let stand for 5 minutes to soften. Place the saucepan over low heat and stir just until the gelatin dissolves. Remove from the heat and gradually whisk in the remaining ½ cup cream. Add the gelatin mixture to the cream-cheese mixture and beat on medium-high speed until fluffy, about 1 minute.

Pour and scrape the filling into the cooled crust and smooth the top with a rubber spatula. Cover with aluminum foil and refrigerate for at least overnight or up to 2 days.

To serve, run a knife around the sides of the cake to loosen it from the pan sides, remove the pan sides, and carefully transfer the cake to a serving plate.

Lemon cheesecake

To the crust mixture, add 1 tsp grated lemon zest. To the filling, add 3 tbsp fresh lemon juice and 2 tsp grated lemon zest with the cream cheese and sugar.

513

CHOCOLATE CHEESECAKE

Cheesecakes are perfect party desserts, as they are easy to mix and can be made long before serving. This version blends melted dark chocolate into the base for a rich, chocolaty flavor. If you like, add a pool of Raspberry Sauce (page 462) to each serving.

Cream cheese

Don't be tempted to substitute low-fat or fat-free cream cheese in standard cheesecake recipes. Both the taste and the drier texture will be disappointing. Full-fat cream cheese delivers more moisture and a fuller flavor because of its high fat content.

Preheat the oven to 300°F (150°C). Butter the bottom and sides of an 8-inch (20-cm) springform pan and line the bottom with parchment (baking) paper.

Follow the recipe to make the crumb crust, then press the crumbs firmly onto the bottom of the prepared pan and 2 inches (5 cm) up the sides. Do not bake in advance.

Place the chocolate in the top pan of a double boiler or in a heatproof bowl. Place over (not touching) barely simmering water and heat, stirring occasionally, until melted and smooth. Remove from the heat and let cool slightly.

In a food processor, combine the cream cheese, cream, eggs, sugar, and vanilla and process until very smooth. Add the chocolate and process just to mix, about 10 seconds. Pour into the prepared pan; shake gently to level the top. Wrap the outside of the pan with aluminum foil to make it watertight. Set the pan in a roasting pan and add enough hot water to reach 2 inches (5 cm) up the sides of the springform pan.

Bake for 1½ hours. Then, turn off the oven and leave the cake in the oven for 1 hour with the oven door closed. Transfer the cake to a wire rack and let cool completely. Cover and refrigerate the cake for at least 8 hours or up to overnight.

To serve, run a knife around the sides of the cake to loosen it from the pan sides, remove the pan sides, and carefully transfer the cake to a serving plate. Using a fine-mesh sieve, dust the top with the cocoa powder.

Chocolate Crumb Crust (page 446)

4 oz (125 g) bittersweet chocolate, chopped

2 lb (1 kg) cream cheese, at room temperature

½ cup (4 fl oz/125 ml) heavy (double) cream

4 extra-large eggs, at room temperature

1½ cups (12 oz/375 g) sugar

2 teaspoons pure vanilla extract

Unsweetened cocoa powder for dusting

MAKES ONE 8-INCH (20-CM) CAKE

CRANBERRY-ORANGE CHEESECAKE

With its cranberry-orange flavor profile, this cheesecake is particularly suitable for the fall or winter holidays. Plan ahead, as the cake needs to be refrigerated overnight. If you like, garnish the top with orange slices just before serving.

Preserving appearances

If you are worried about marring the top of the cheesecake when you cover it for chilling, invert a large plate over the top of the pan before wrapping.

In a small saucepan over low heat, combine the cranberries with water to cover and bring to a simmer. Cook until soft and plump, about 4 minutes. Remove from the heat and let cool. Drain off any liquid.

Preheat the oven to 350°F (180°C). Have ready a 10-inch (25-cm) springform pan with 3-inch (7.5-cm) sides.

In a bowl, using a fork, stir together the graham cracker crumbs, melted butter, and ¼ cup (2 oz/60 g) of the sugar. Press the crumbs firmly onto the bottom and 2 inches (5 cm) up the sides of the pan. Bake the crust just until

1 cup (4 oz/125 g) dried cranberries

2 cups (6 oz/185 g) graham cracker crumbs

½ cup (4 oz/125 g) unsalted butter, melted and cooled

1¼ cups (10 oz/310 g) plus 2 tablespoons sugar

2 lb (1 kg) cream cheese, at room temperature

514

½ cup (4 fl oz/125 ml) thawed, undiluted frozen orange juice concentrate

1 tablespoon grated orange zest

2 tablespoons orange liqueur

5 eggs, at room temperature

2 cups (16 oz/500 g) sour cream

MAKES ONE 10-INCH (25-CM) CAKE

golden, about 12 minutes. Let the crust cool completely on a wire rack. Leave the oven on.

In a bowl, using an electric mixer on medium speed, beat together the cream cheese and 1 cup (8 oz/250 g) of the sugar until smooth. Beat in the orange juice concentrate, orange zest, and liqueur until well mixed. Add the eggs, one at a time, beating well after each addition. Fold in the cranberries. Pour the cream cheese mixture into the cooled crust.

Bake the cheesecake until just set when the pan is gently shaken, about 1 hour. Transfer to the wire rack and let cool slightly. Leave the oven on.

In a bowl, stir together the sour cream and the 2 tablespoons sugar. Pour over the cheesecake and spread evenly with a rubber spatula. Bake until the sour cream is set, about 8 minutes. Let cool completely in the pan on the wire rack. Cover and refrigerate overnight.

To serve, run a knife around the sides of the cake to loosen it from the pan sides, remove the pan sides, and carefully transfer the cake to a serving plate.

Cutting dense cakes

A hot knife cuts cleanly through dense cakes. Fill a tall pitcher with very hot water. Before each cut, dip the blade of a long, sharp knife into the water, let it sit for a few seconds, then wipe dry with a clean towel.

515

PEANUT BUTTER CHEESECAKE

This silky cheesecake is a kid-friendly dessert, but it's appropriate for gatherings of any ages. Use regular commercial peanut butter, which includes additives for spreadability. The grainy texture of natural peanut butter will not blend smoothly with the other ingredients.

1 cup (6 oz/185 g) unsalted roasted peanuts

1 cup (3 oz/90 g) graham cracker crumbs

⅓ cup (2½ oz/75 g) firmly packed light brown sugar

¼ cup (2 oz/60 g) unsalted butter, melted and cooled

1 lb (500 g) cream cheese, at room temperature

2 cups (1¼ lb/625 g) chunky peanut butter

2⅓ cups (9 oz/280 g) confectioners' (icing) sugar

1 teaspoon pure vanilla extract

1 cup (8 fl oz/250 ml) heavy (double) cream, chilled

Bittersweet Chocolate Glaze (page 459)

MAKES ONE 9-INCH (23-CM) CAKE

Preheat the oven to 350°F (180°C). Have ready a 9-inch (23-cm) springform pan with 2½-inch (6-cm) sides.

In a food processor, combine the peanuts, graham cracker crumbs, and brown sugar and process until the nuts are finely ground. Add the melted butter and process until the crumbs begin to stick together. Press the crumbs firmly onto the bottom and 2¼ inches (5.5 cm) up the sides of the pan. Bake the crust just until set, about 10 minutes. Let cool completely on a wire rack.

In a bowl, using an electric mixer on medium speed, beat the cream cheese with the peanut butter until smooth. Beat in the confectioners' sugar and vanilla. In another bowl, using clean beaters, beat the cream on medium-high speed until stiff peaks form. Add the whipped cream to the cream cheese mixture and beat on medium speed until well blended. Pour into the cooled crust and smooth the surface with a rubber spatula. Cover and refrigerate overnight.

Heat the glaze to lukewarm and pour over the cake. Re-cover and refrigerate until the set, at least 2 hours or up to 3 days.

To serve, run a knife around the sides of the cake to loosen it from the pan sides, remove the pan sides, and carefully transfer the cake to a serving plate.

Easy application

To prevent the crust mixture from sticking to your hand as you press it into the pan, drape your hand with plastic wrap to form a glove.

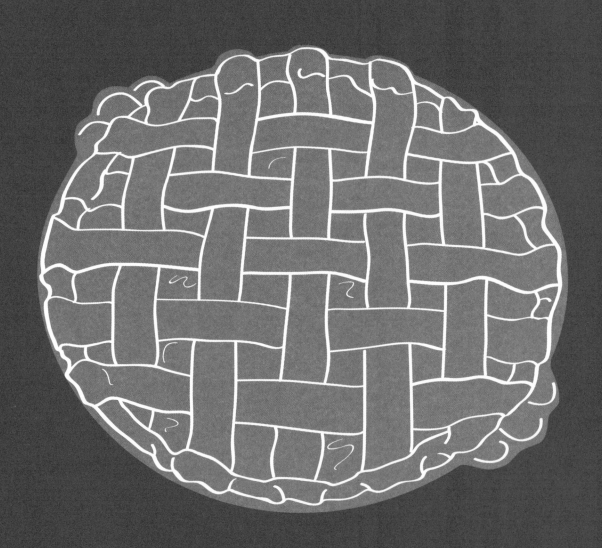

Pies & TARTS

Pies & Tarts

For nearly everyone, a freshly made pie or tart is baking at its best. But too many home cooks shy away from making these crowd-pleasers because they mistakenly believe they require highly specialized skills. With the help of a few simple guidelines, a handful of easy techniques, and a little practice, anyone can turn out such classics as double-crust apple pie, lattice-topped cherry pie, and lemon tart with ease.

Forming a decorative rim
Whether you're making a single- or double-crust pie, it's easy to give it a decorative rim—and, for double-crust pies, seal the two edges together at the same time. Press your thumb down into the rim at regular intervals to flute it. Or, press the tines of a table fork into the pastry, just deep enough to make a distinct impression, all around the rim.

518

Cutting steam vents
Small vents cut into the top of a double-crust pie allow steam to escape during baking, so the crust won't puff up, crack, or turn soggy. To make the vents, use a small, sharp knife and cut 4 or 5 short slits in the center of the top crust.

Blind baking a single crust
To bake a single crust partially or fully, first line the crust with aluminum foil and fill it with pie weights or dried beans. This prevents the pastry from buckling in the heat of the oven. Follow the recipe instructions for baking. Otherwise, bake for 20 minutes at 375°F (190°C), then remove the weights and foil and bake until pale gold, about 5 minutes longer for a partially baked crust; or until deep gold, 8 to 10 minutes longer for a fully baked crust.

Pie and Tart Types

The terms *pie* and *tart* are occasionally used interchangeably, but some clear-cut distinctions can be made. Here are descriptions of the most common types of pies and tarts, including the kinds of fillings they usually feature.

SINGLE-CRUST PIES As the name implies, these have no top crust. The bottom crust, also called a pie shell, can be filled when unbaked, partially baked, or fully baked, depending on the recipe. Unbaked pie shells work well for fillings that require a long baking time. Partially baked shells are used for fillings that are very moist, such as cream fillings or juicy fruit mixtures, but still cook fairly quickly; blind-baking the shells before filling (see left) ensures that the crust and filling finish baking at the same time. Fully baked pie shells hold fillings that need no cooking, such as fresh fruit, fully cooked fillings, or fillings that bake only for a short time.

DOUBLE-CRUST PIES Pies with pastry fully enclosing the filling are called double-crust pies. These work for all sorts of classic oven-baked fruit fillings, such as apple pie (page 527) and cherry pie (page 528).

   To make a double-crust pie: First line the pie pan with the bottom crust and fill as directed in the recipe. Brush the rim with water. Lay the rolled-out top crust over the filling and, with a small, sharp knife, trim the pastry all around so you have an overhang of about ½ inch (12 mm). Press firmly around the rim to seal the two crusts together, then fold the overhang under itself all around to make a high vertical edge. Finally, flute the edge (left) and cut vents (left). Double-crust pies can also be decorated with dough scraps and trimmings cut with a small knife or small pastry cutters into leaves or other shapes, then moistened with water and placed on the top crust in an attractive pattern.

LATTICE-TOPPED PIES A subcategory of double-crust pies, lattice tops are made by weaving pastry strips directly on top of the filling (right). They are a nice way to show off brightly colored fruits, such as berries or peaches.

CRUMB-CRUST PIES These pies (pages 520–22) feature a single crust made from crushed cookies that is pressed by hand into the pan and then briefly baked. Crumb crusts work well for a wide variety of fillings, from light and airy chiffons to cream pies to rich mixtures of cream cheese and fruit.

CLASSIC TARTS These close cousins to single-crust pies have only a bottom crust, which tends to be firmer, richer, and more crumbly than pie pastry. They are usually baked in tart pans with vertical straight or fluted sides.

RUSTIC TARTS AND GALETTES Resembling sweet versions of pizza, these free-form tarts (pages 531–32) are shaped by hand and baked on a baking sheet instead of in a tart pan.

EASY FRUIT FILLINGS FOR PIES

Each of the following recipes makes enough filling for one 9-inch (23-cm) pie.

Apple-pear filling

In a large bowl, combine 3 large apples, peeled, halved, cored, and sliced, and 3 large, firm but ripe pears, peeled, halved, cored, and sliced. Add 2 tablespoons fresh lemon juice and toss to coat the fruit. In a small bowl, stir together ½ cup (3½ oz/105 g) firmly packed light brown sugar, 3 tablespoons all-purpose (plain) flour, ½ teaspoon ground cinnamon, and ¼ teaspoon salt; add to the fruit and toss to combine. Add 3 tablespoons dry or sweet sherry and toss until completely mixed. After filling the pie shell, dot the fruit with 2 tablespoons unsalted butter in small bits.

Apple-spice filling

In a large bowl, combine 6 apples, peeled, halved, cored, and thinly sliced; 1 tablespoon fresh lemon juice; 2 tablespoons unsalted butter, melted; ¼ cup (2 oz/60 g) firmly packed light brown sugar; 1½ teaspoons ground cinnamon; and ⅛ teaspoon freshly grated nutmeg. Toss to mix well.

Apricot-pineapple filling

Peel 1 ripe pineapple, cutting deeply enough to remove all the prickly "eyes"; quarter the fruit lengthwise and cut out and discard the fibrous core from each piece; cut each slice lengthwise in half; then, cut each piece crosswise into slices ¼ inch (6 mm) thick. In a large bowl, stir together ⅔ cup (5 oz/155 g) sugar, 2 tablespoons quick-cooking tapioca, ¼ teaspoon freshly grated nutmeg, and a pinch of salt. Add the pineapple and 3 cups (18 oz/560 g) pitted and quartered apricots. Toss to mix well.

Berry-cherry filling

In a large bowl, stir together 2 tablespoons quick-cooking tapioca, ¾ cup (6 oz/185 g) sugar, and ¼ teaspoon salt. Add 3 cups (12 oz/375 g) pitted sweet or sour cherries and 3 cups (12 oz/375 g) blackberries, raspberries, or boysenberries. After filling the pie shell, dot the fruit with 2 tablespoons unsalted butter in small bits.

Cranberry-apple filling

In a large bowl, stir together 1 cup (8 oz/250 g) sugar, 2 tablespoons all-purpose (plain) flour, and ¼ teaspoon salt. Add 2 cups (8 oz/250 g) fresh or frozen cranberries; ½ cup (3 oz/90 g) raisins; 4 pippin or Granny Smith apples, peeled, halved, cored, and thinly sliced; and the grated zest of 1 orange. Toss to mix well. After filling the pie shell, dot the fruit with 2 tablespoons unsalted butter in small bits.

Peach-raspberry filling

In a large bowl, combine 6 peaches, peeled, halved, pitted, and thinly sliced; ¼ cup (1½ oz/45 g) all-purpose (plain) flour; 3 tablespoons sugar; 1 tablespoon fresh lemon juice; and 1 teaspoon pure vanilla extract. Toss to mix well. When ready to fill the pie, fold in 1 cup (4 oz/125 g) fresh raspberries.

Three-berry filling

In a large bowl, combine 3 cups (12 oz/375 g) blueberries; 1 cup (4 oz/125 g) *each* blackberries and raspberries; ¼ cup (1½ oz/45 g) all-purpose (plain) flour; ¼ cup (2 oz/60 g) granulated sugar; and 1 tablespoon fresh lemon juice. Toss to mix well.

SEE ALSO:
- **Rhubarb-Berry Pie,** *page 528*
- **Sour Cherry Lattice Pie,** *page 528*
- **Fresh Peach Pie,** *page 529*

MAKING A LATTICE-TOP PIECRUST

Giving a fruit pie a lattice top is good way show off a beautiful filling. Weaving the lattice takes a little time, but it is not difficult to do.

Cut the dough strips
Roll out the dough into a 14-by-11-inch (35-by-28-cm) rectangle that is ⅛ inch (3 mm) thick. Trim if necessary to achieve the right dimensions. Using a pizza wheel or paring knife and a ruler as a guide, trim the edges even and cut the rectangle into 16 strips about ¾ inch (2 cm) wide.

Arrange a row of strips
Starting 1 inch (2.5 cm) from the edge of the pie pan, lay 8 dough strips over the filling, spacing them evenly. If any of the strips stick to the work surface, use a thin metal spatula to free them.

Fold back alternating strips
Fold back every other dough strip halfway, laying it onto itself. Lay a vertical strip down the center of the filling and at a slight angle. Return the folded strips to their flat position over the filling.

Weave the remaining strips
Fold back the strips you did not fold back previously. Lay another dough strip just to the left of the center strip, leaving small strips of the filling visible. Return the folded strips to their flat position. Add the remaining dough strips to both sides of the center dough strip in the same manner until all of the strips have been woven into a lattice. Trim the overhanging strips so they are just longer than the pan rim and tuck them under the bottom crust.

CHOCOLATE ANGEL PIE

A good day for pie

Meringues attract moisture and will eventually sweat and shrink, so plan on serving meringue pies the same day they are made.

This crustless "pie" is technically a thick chocolate meringue baked in a pie dish. Garnish it with fresh berries or chocolate curls (see page 566) in place of the chips, if you like. For a pie with a softer texture, refrigerate for 1 hour after topping with the whipped cream.

Preheat the oven to 300°F (150°C). Generously butter and flour a 10-inch (25-cm) pie dish with 2-inch (5-cm) sides and tap out the excess flour

In a large bowl, using an electric mixer on medium speed, beat together the egg whites and cream of tartar until foamy, about 1 minute. On high speed, slowly add the sugar and then continue to beat until stiff, glossy peaks form. With the mixer on low speed, beat in the cocoa powder, mixing only until incorporated.

Pour and scrape the batter into the prepared pie dish. Use a silicone spatula to smooth the top, building the rim slightly higher than the center.

Bake until light brown and no longer sticky, about 1 hour. Let cool completely on a wire rack. The center will sink as it cools.

Just before serving, top with the whipped cream and sprinkle with the chocolate chips.

Unsalted butter and all-purpose (plain) flour for pie dish

4 extra-large egg whites, at room temperature

¼ teaspoon cream of tartar

⅔ cup (5 oz/155 g) sugar

2 tablespoons unsweetened cocoa powder

Whipped Cream (page 454)

Miniature chocolate chips for topping

MAKES ONE 10-INCH (25-CM) PIE

520

BLACK-AND-WHITE FUDGE PIE

Marble rolling surfaces

If you make pies or tarts often, consider investing in a marble pastry board. Its smooth, hard surface stays cool to keep the fat in the dough from melting. On warm days, you can chill the board in the refrigerator before using it.

Here, cream cheese is swirled into a brownielike batter and then baked in a chocolate-walnut pastry crust to yield a rich, dense pie that looks like a contest winner. With its deep, chocolatey flavor, this recipe is guaranteed to appeal to adults and children alike.

Preheat the oven to 375°F (190°C). Press the pastry into a 9-inch (23-cm) pie pan (or roll it out after chilling the dough for 1 hour), then partially blind bake the pie shell (page 518). Let cool completely on a wire rack. Reduce the oven temperature to 325°F (180°C).

To make the chocolate batter, combine the butter and chocolate in the top pan of a double boiler or in a heatproof bowl. Place over (not touching) barely simmering water and heat, stirring occasionally, until melted and smooth. Set aside to cool slightly.

In a bowl, whisk together the eggs until blended. Add the sugar, flour, and salt and whisk until thoroughly mixed. Stir in the melted chocolate and walnuts. Remove ½ cup (4 fl oz/125 ml) of the batter and set aside; spread the remainder in the cooled pie shell.

To make the cream cheese mixture, in a bowl, using a wooden spoon, beat the cream cheese until smooth. Add the sugar,

Chocolate-Walnut Pastry (page 448)

FOR THE CHOCOLATE BATTER
½ cup (4 oz/125 g) unsalted butter

4 oz (125 g) bittersweet chocolate, broken into pieces

2 eggs

⅔ cup (5 oz/155 g) sugar

¼ cup (1½ oz/45 g) all-purpose (plain) flour

¼ teaspoon salt

½ cup (2 oz/60 g) chopped walnuts

FOR THE CREAM
CHEESE MIXTURE

½ lb (250 g) cream cheese,
at room temperature

⅓ cup (3 oz/90 g) sugar

1 egg

1 teaspoon pure
vanilla extract

**MAKES ONE 9-INCH
(23-CM) PIE**

egg, and vanilla and beat until well blended. Spread the
cheese mixture over the chocolate batter in the pie shell
(don't worry about getting it perfectly even) then spoon
the reserved chocolate batter randomly over the top. With
a knife, swirl the batters together to create a marbled effect.

Bake until the filling is set, about 40 minutes. Let cool completely
on a wire rack. Serve the pie at room temperature or cold
from the refrigerator.

CHOCOLATE CREAM CHEESE PIE

This twist on chocolate cheesecake yields a divine combination of chocolate textures and
tastes, marrying the dark chocolate cookie crumb crust, the smooth baked cream cheese
filling, and the ethereal chocolate cream topping. Garnish as you like to suit the occasion.

Chocolate Crumb
Crust (page 446)

⅓ cup (3 fl oz/80 ml)
heavy (double) cream

3 tablespoons instant
coffee granules

4 oz (125 g) semisweet
(plain) chocolate, chopped

1 lb (500 g) cream cheese,
at room temperature

2 extra-large eggs

¾ cup (6 oz/180 g) sugar

1 teaspoon pure
vanilla extract

1½ cups (12 fl oz/375 ml)
Chocolate Whipped Cream
(page 454)

Chocolate-covered
coffee beans or sliced
strawberries for garnish

**MAKES ONE 10-INCH
(25-CM) PIE**

Prepare the crumb crust and press onto the bottom and up
the sides of a 10-inch (25-cm) pie dish. Prebake as directed,
then let cool completely on a wire rack. Reduce the oven
temperature to 325°F (165°C).

In a small saucepan over medium heat, warm the cream
until small bubbles appear around the edge of the pan.
Add the coffee, stir to dissolve, and remove from the heat.

Place the chocolate in the top of a double boiler or in a
heatproof bowl. Place over (not touching) barely simmering
water and heat, stirring occasionally, until melted and
smooth. Remove from the heat and let cool slightly.

In a bowl, using an electric mixer on low speed, beat together
the cream cheese, eggs, sugar, and vanilla until very smooth.
Stir in the coffee mixture, and then the cooled chocolate
until fully incorporated. Pour and scrape into the cooled pie
shell, smoothing the top.

Bake until the top is dry to the touch and slightly firm,
35–45 minutes. Let cool completely on a wire rack. Just before
serving, top with the whipped cream and garnish as desired.

**About glass
pie dishes**

*Glass pie dishes
are good choices for
pies with crumb
crusts because the
crust adheres better
to the sloping sides.
If you are baking
a pastry crust in a
glass pie dish, plan
on baking it up to
15 minutes longer
than in a metal
pan, because glass
is a less efficient
heat conductor
than metal.*

PIES & TARTS

FRESH PINEAPPLE MERINGUE PIE

Fresh pineapple, simmered in maple syrup and folded into a homemade vanilla custard, makes a delicious filling for a single-crust pie. Topped with a billowy meringue filling, it is a show-stopper. This recipe uses only partially cooked eggs; for more information, turn to page 37.

This recipe uses only partially cooked eggs; for more information, turn to page 37.

In a saucepan over medium heat, combine the pineapple and maple syrup and bring to a simmer. Cover and cook gently until the fruit is tender, about 10 minutes. Remove from the heat and let stand for 30 minutes. Transfer to a food processor and pulse to chop the pineapple coarsely. Set aside.

Preheat the oven to 375°F (190°C). Roll out the pastry and use to line a 9-inch (23-cm) pie pan, then partially blind bake (page 518). Let cool completely on a wire rack.

In a heavy saucepan, stir together the sugar, cornstarch, and salt. Add the milk and whisk until smooth. Place over medium heat and cook, stirring constantly, until the mixture boils. Cook for 2 minutes, then remove from the heat and whisk in the egg yolks, being careful not to let them curdle. Return to medium heat and bring to a boil, stirring constantly. Reduce the heat to medium-low and continue to cook, stirring, for 2 minutes more. Add the pineapple mixture to the pan and cook for 1 minute longer. Remove from the heat and stir in the butter and vanilla. Let the mixture cool for 20 minutes, then spread in the cooled pie shell.

Preheat a broiler (grill). Gently spread the meringue topping over the pie filling, completely covering it. Broil (grill) as directed in the topping recipe.

2 cups (12 oz/375 g) cubed fresh pineapple (½-inch/12-mm cubes)

½ cup (4 fl oz/125 ml) pure maple syrup

Pie Pastry for a 9-inch (23-cm) single-crust pie (page 447)

⅓ cup (3 oz/90 g) sugar

5 tablespoons (1½ oz/45 g) cornstarch (cornflour)

¼ teaspoon salt

2½ cups (20 fl oz/ 625 ml) milk

4 egg yolks, lightly beaten

4 tablespoons (2 oz/60 g) unsalted butter, at room temperature

1 teaspoon pure vanilla extract

Meringue Pie Topping (page 454)

MAKES ONE 9-INCH (23-CM) PIE

Pie pan or dish sizes

When making pies, pay close attention to both the dimension and depth of the vessel called for in the recipe. For example, you will come up short if you mistakenly put the filling for a standard pie pan in a deep-dish pie dish.

522

OLD-FASHIONED PEACH ICEBOX PIE

For this satisfying pie, perfect for the height of peach season, a gingersnap crust is filled with cooked peaches flavored with only sugar and lemon. Swirls of plain whipped cream top it off. Except for a few minutes in the oven to crisp the crust, this is a convenient no-bake dessert.

Prepare the crumb crust and press onto the bottom and up the sides of a 9-inch (25-cm) pie dish. Prebake as directed, then let cool completely on a wire rack.

To prepare the filling, peel, halve, and pit the peaches. Cut into slices ¼ inch (6 mm) thick and place in a colander to drain for 10 minutes. Put half of the peach slices in a heavy saucepan and crush well with a pastry blender or potato masher. Stir in the sugar, cornstarch, and lemon juice. Place the pan over medium heat and cook, stirring constantly, until the mixture starts to bubble. Reduce the heat to low and cook, stirring, until the mixture thickens and turns

Crumb Crust (page 446), made with gingersnaps

FOR THE FILLING

2¼ lb (1.1 kg) firm but ripe peaches (about 6)

1 cup (8 oz/250 g) sugar

3 tablespoons cornstarch (cornflour)

3 tablespoons fresh lemon juice

Choosing peaches

Make sure you choose ripe, juicy peaches that give slightly when gently squeezed. If they have been bruised in shipping or handling, they will spoil quickly, so check them carefully before purchase.

FOR THE TOPPING

1 cup (8 fl oz/250 ml) cold heavy (double) cream

1 peach

1–2 gingersnaps, crushed to make crumbs

MAKES ONE 9-INCH (23-CM) PIE

clear, 5–8 minutes. Remove from the heat and let stand until the mixture is cool, about 30 minutes.

Stir the remaining peach slices into the cooled mixture. Pour the filling into the crust, cover, and refrigerate for at least 2 hours or up to overnight.

To make the topping, in a chilled bowl using a whisk or an electric mixer on medium-high speed, whip the cream until firm peaks form. Using a silicone spatula, spread the whipped cream over the pie filling, forming attractive swirls over the surface. Cover and refrigerate for at least 1 hour or up to 3 hours before serving.

When ready to serve, peel, halve, and pit the peach and cut lengthwise into slices ½ inch (12 mm) thick. Arrange the slices in a decorative border over the cream. Finish by sprinkling the cookie crumbs over the top.

LEMON MERINGUE PIE

This popular lemon pie is surprisingly easy to make. Secrets to success include adding the hot lemon filling to the fully baked crust, immediately topping the filling with the meringue, and spreading the meringue so that it touches the crust, concealing the filling completely.

Working with citrus

When a recipes calls for both citrus zest and juice, always grate the zest first. It is always harder to grate the zest on spent citrus halves.

Pie Pastry for a single-crust pie (page 447)

6 tablespoons (1½ oz/45 g) cornstarch (cornflour)

5 egg yolks

1¾ cups (14 oz/440 g) sugar

½ cup (4 fl oz/125 ml) fresh lemon juice

2 teaspoons grated lemon zest

Meringue Pie Topping (page 454)

MAKES ONE 9-INCH (23-CM) PIE

Preheat the oven to 375°F (190°C). Roll out the pastry and use to line a 9-inch (23-cm) pie pan, then fully blind bake (page 518). Let cool completely on a wire rack. Reduce the oven temperature to 350°F (180°C).

In a small bowl, stir together the cornstarch and ½ cup (4 fl oz/125 ml) water and until the cornstarch dissolves. In a saucepan, whisk together the egg yolks, sugar, lemon juice, and 1 cup (8 fl oz/250 ml) water until well blended. Whisk in the cornstarch mixture, place over medium heat, and bring to a boil while whisking constantly, about 8 minutes. Boil until the mixture thickens and looks clear, about 1 minute. Remove from the heat and stir in the lemon zest.

Immediately pour the warm filling into the cooled crust. Using a rubber spatula, spread the meringue evenly over the filling, mounding it toward the center and spreading it out to the edges to seal the crust. Use the back of a spoon to form swirls and peaks on the meringue. Bake until the meringue is lightly browned, 12–17 minutes. Transfer the pie to a wire rack and let cool for 1 hour.

Place in an airtight container and refrigerate until cold, at least 5 hours or up to overnight. Serve cold.

MANGO CHIFFON PIE

About chiffon pie fillings

Chiffon pie fillings are prized for their light, fluffy character. They are typically made by flavoring an egg-yolk base—here with mangoes—and then folding in stiffly beaten whites. The addition of gelatin ensures a stable, velvety texture.

Highly aromatic and refreshing mangoes make this chiffon pie rich and creamy, even though there is no cream in it. Ground ginger lends a subtle spice note that marries well with the tropical fruit. Turn to page 37 for information on working with raw eggs.

Prepare the crust and press onto the bottom and up the sides of a 9-inch (23-cm) pie pan. Prebake as directed, then let cool completely on a wire rack.

Peel the mangoes and slice the flesh off the pit. Place in a food processor and process until smooth. You should have about 1½ cups (12 fl oz/375 ml). Set aside. In a small bowl or cup, sprinkle the gelatin over ¼ cup (2 fl oz/60 ml) water and let stand for a few minutes to soften.

Meanwhile, in a heavy saucepan, whisk together the egg yolks, lemon juice, and ¼ cup (2 oz/60 g) of the sugar. Place over medium heat and cook, whisking constantly, until the mixture is thick, foamy, and very hot, about 4 minutes. Do not allow to boil. Add the softened gelatin and whisk over the heat for about 30 seconds longer. Pour into a bowl and stir in the mango purée and ginger. Cover the bowl and refrigerate, stirring occasionally, until the mixture is the consistency of unbeaten egg whites and mounds slightly when dropped from a spoon, about 1 hour.

In a large bowl, using an electric mixer on medium-high speed, beat together the egg whites and salt until soft peaks form. Slowly add the remaining ¼ cup sugar and continue to beat until stiff peaks form. Gently fold the egg whites into the mango mixture. Pile the filling into the crust and chill for several hours before serving.

Crumb Crust (page 446), made with graham crackers

2 large, ripe mangoes

1 envelope (1 tablespoon) unflavored gelatin

5 eggs, separated

2 tablespoons fresh lemon juice

½ cup (4 oz/125 g) sugar

1 teaspoon ground ginger

¼ teaspoon salt

MAKES ONE 9-INCH (23-CM) PIE

PEANUT BUTTER CHIFFON PIE

About gelatin

Gelatin is an odorless, colorless, tasteless thickener derived from the collagen of animals. Look for unflavored powdered gelatin in small paper envelopes packed in boxes in the baking section of grocery stores. It will keep for up to 3 years in an airtight container in a cool, dry place.

Like all chiffon pies, this peanut version is light and airy. Make the crust with either graham crackers or chocolate wafers, according to your preference. Both flavors are delicious paired with the peanut butter filling. Turn to page 37 for information on cooking with raw eggs.

Prepare the crust and press onto the bottom and up the sides of a 9-inch (23-cm) pie pan. Prebake as directed, then let cool completely on a wire rack.

In a small bowl or cup, sprinkle the gelatin over ¼ cup (2 fl oz/60 ml) water and let stand for a few minutes to soften. Meanwhile, in a saucepan, whisk the egg yolks just until blended. Stir in ¾ cup (6 oz/190 g) of the sugar, the peanut butter, and the milk. Place over medium heat and cook, stirring constantly, until the mixture just reaches a simmer and thickens slightly, about 4 minutes. Do not allow to boil. Remove from the heat, add the softened gelatin, and stir

Crumb Crust (page 446)

1 envelope (1 tablespoon) unflavored gelatin

4 eggs, separated

1 cup (8 oz/250 g) sugar

1 cup (8 oz/250 g) smooth peanut butter

1 cup (8 fl oz/250 ml) milk

½ cup (4 fl oz/125 ml) heavy (double) cream

¼ cup (1 oz/30 g) chopped unsalted roasted peanuts, optional

Whipped Cream (page 454)

MAKES ONE 9-INCH (23-CM) PIE

until completely dissolved. Pour into a bowl, cover, and refrigerate, stirring occasionally, until the mixture mounds slightly when dropped from a spoon, about 1 hour.

In a bowl, using a whisk or an electric mixer on medium-high speed, whip the cream until stiff peaks form. In another bowl, using an electric mixer with clean beaters, beat the egg whites on medium-high speed until soft peaks form. Slowly add the remaining ¼ cup sugar and continue to beat until stiff peaks form. Gently fold the beaten whites and cream into the peanut butter mixture until completely blended. Pile the mixture in the crust and sprinkle with the peanuts, if using. Chill for several hours before serving.

Top slices with large dollops of whipped cream.

FAVORITE PUMPKIN PIE

No Thanksgiving meal is complete without this iconic dessert. Here is a classic no-frills recipe, lightly perfumed with cinnamon and allspice, which will please everybody at the table. Top wedges with large dollops of Whipped Cream (page 454).

Pie Pastry for a single-crust pie (page 447)

2 eggs

1 can (15 oz/470 g) pumpkin purée

1½ cups half-and-half (half cream)

¾ cup (6 oz/185 g) granulated sugar

1 teaspoon ground cinnamon

¾ teaspoon ground allspice

¼ teaspoon salt

MAKES ONE 9-INCH (23-CM) PIE

Preheat the oven to 425°F (220°C).

On a lightly floured work surface, roll out the pastry into a round ⅛ to ¼ inch (3 to 6 mm) thick. Transfer to a 9-inch (23-cm) pie pan and trim and flute the edges to create a decorative rim (page 518). Set aside.

In a large bowl, beat the eggs until blended. Add the pumpkin, half-and-half, sugar, cinnamon, allspice, and salt and stir until well blended and smooth. Carefully pour the filling into the pie shell.

Bake for 15 minutes. Reduce the oven temperature to 350°F (180°C) and continue baking until a knife inserted into the center comes out clean and the pastry is a rich golden brown, 40–50 minutes longer.

Let cool completely on a wire rack.

Managing spills

If the filling bubbles over and drips during baking, the pie pan may be too full, the pie pan may not be deep enough, or the filling may be too moist. Place a sheet of aluminum foil on the rack below the rack the pie is on (or place a foil-lined baking sheet directly under the pie) to catch drips.

MAPLE-PECAN PIE

Sweet crusts

Pastry crusts made with sugar will brown more quickly than those without sugar. A high-sugar crust can scorch if not watched closely. If you are worried about scorching, use a tempered glass pie dish instead of a metal pie pan.

This pie is excellent for serving with afternoon coffee or tea. Pecans are a perfect foil for the unique taste of maple syrup. Although pie pastry will work, the buttery flavor of tart pastry is especially good with this filling. Top each serving with Whipped Cream (page 454).

Preheat the oven to 425°F (220°C). On a lightly floured work surface, roll out the pastry into a round ⅛ inch (3 mm) thick. Transfer to a 9-inch (23-cm) pie pan and trim and flute the edges to create a decorative rim (see page 518). Set aside.

In a large bowl, beat the eggs until blended. Add the maple syrup, corn syrup, sugar, butter, vanilla, and salt; beat until thoroughly combined. Stir in the pecan halves. Carefully pour the filling into the pie shell.

Bake for 15 minutes. Reduce the oven temperature to 350°F (180°C) and continue baking until the filling has puffed and set around the edges but the center is slightly soft, about 25 minutes longer. Let the pie cool on a wire rack. Serve warm or at room temperature.

Tart Pastry (page 448)

3 eggs

1 cup (8 fl oz/250 ml) pure maple syrup

¼ cup (2 fl oz/60 ml) dark corn syrup

¼ cup (2 oz/60 g) sugar

4 tablespoons (2 oz/60 g) unsalted butter, melted

1 teaspoon pure vanilla extract

¼ teaspoon salt

1½ cups (6 oz/185 g) pecan halves

MAKES ONE 9-INCH (23-CM) PIE

CHOCOLATE-HAZELNUT PIE

Choosing a rolling pin

Choose a hardwood rolling pin at least 12 inches (30 cm) long. The length makes it easier to roll out a dough round wide enough to line a pie or tart pan. Dowel-type rolling pins, with or without tapered ends, give the baker the best control.

This is no ordinary hazelnut pie. There is a double dose of chocolate—in the pastry and in the filling—and the texture of the pie is moist and brownielike. Serve with Classic Vanilla Bean Ice Cream (page 604) or Whipped Cream (page 454).

Preheat the oven to 425°F (220°C). Press the pastry into a 9-inch (23-cm) pie pan. Alternatively, chill the dough for 1 hour, roll it out, and use it to line a 9-inch (23-cm) pie pan.

Combine the butter and chocolate in the top pan of a double boiler or in a heatproof bowl. Place over (not touching) barely simmering water and heat, stirring occasionally, until melted and smooth. Remove from the heat.

In a bowl, beat the eggs until blended. Add the corn syrup, sugar, vanilla, and salt and beat until blended. Beat in the chocolate mixture. Coarsely chop the hazelnuts, then stir them into the chocolate mixture. Carefully pour the filling into the pie shell.

Bake for 15 minutes. Reduce the oven temperature to 350°F (180°C) and continue baking until the filling is set around the edges and the center quivers slightly, about 25 minutes longer. Let cool completely on a wire rack.

Chocolate-Walnut Pastry (page 448)

3 tablespoons unsalted butter

2 oz (60 g) unsweetened chocolate, chopped

3 eggs

1 cup (8 fl oz/125 ml) light corn syrup

½ cup (4 oz/125 g) sugar

1 teaspoon pure vanilla extract

¼ teaspoon salt

1½ cups (6 oz/185 g) hazelnuts (filberts), toasted and skinned (page 478)

MAKES ONE 9-INCH (23-CM) PIE

APPLE PIE

This classic pie, which calls for a particularly buttery crust, is made with a mixture of sweet and tart apples for a well-rounded apple flavor. For the tart apples, look for Granny Smith, pippin, or Baldwin. Sweet apples include Golden Delicious and Rome Beauty.

FOR THE PASTRY

2⅔ cups (13½ oz/425 g) all-purpose (plain) flour

2 tablespoons sugar

½ teaspoon salt

½ cup (4 oz/125 g) vegetable shortening (vegetable lard), chilled and diced

½ cup (4 oz/125 g) cold unsalted butter, diced

1 egg

3–4 tablespoons ice water

FOR THE FILLING

7 or 8 large apples, a mixture of sweet and tart, peeled, quartered, cored, and sliced ¼ inch (6 mm) thick

¾ cup (6 oz/185 g) sugar

¼ cup (1½ oz/45 g) all-purpose (plain) flour

½ teaspoon *each* ground cinnamon and freshly grated nutmeg

FOR THE GLAZE

1 tablespoon sugar

¼ teaspoon *each* ground cinnamon and freshly grated nutmeg

1 tablespoon milk

MAKES ONE 9-INCH (23-CM) DOUBLE-CRUST DEEP-DISH PIE

To make the pastry, in a food processor, combine the flour, sugar, and salt and process briefly to mix. Scatter in the shortening and butter and pulse until the mixture resembles coarse meal. In a small bowl, whisk together the egg and 3 tablespoons ice water until blended. With the processor running, gradually add the egg mixture and process until moist clumps form. Add more ice water by teaspoons if the dough is too dry. Form into a ball and divide in half. Flatten each half into a disk. Wrap separately in plastic wrap and refrigerate for at least 1 hour or up to 1 day.

Position a rack in the lower third of the oven and preheat the oven to 400°F (200°C). To make the filling, in a large bowl, combine the sliced apples, sugar, flour, cinnamon, and nutmeg. Toss to mix well.

Place 1 dough disk between sheets of waxed paper and roll out into a round 13 inches (33 cm) in diameter. Transfer the pastry to a pie pan 9 inches (23 cm) in diameter and 2 inches (5 cm) deep, discarding the paper, and gently press into the pan. Trim the overhang to ½ inch (12 mm). Brush the edges lightly with water. Transfer the filling to the pie shell, mounding it slightly in the center. Roll out the second dough disk the same way into a round 12 inches (30 cm) in diameter. Place atop the filling and trim the overhang to 1 inch (2.5 cm). Fold the top crust edge under the bottom crust edge; press and crimp decoratively (page 518). Cut 4 or 5 slits in the top crust for steam vents (page 518).

Place the pie on a baking sheet, and bake for 45 minutes.

Meanwhile, make the glaze. In a small bowl, stir together the sugar, cinnamon, and nutmeg. After the pie has baked for 45 minutes, remove it from the oven, brush the top crust with the milk, then sprinkle evenly with the sugar mixture. Return to the oven and bake until the crust is golden brown and the apples are tender when tested through a vent, about 20 minutes longer; cover the edges with aluminum foil if browning too quickly. Let cool on a wire rack. Serve warm or at room temperature.

Metal pans for double crusts

Double-crust pies turn out better when baked in metal pie pans, preferably aluminum. Metal is an excellent heat conductor and will produce a crispier, more golden crust than will glass or ceramic.

527

Structural support for pies

To prevent top crusts from sagging as fruit fillings cook down, some cooks stand a pie bird, an old-fashioned ceramic device sometimes shaped like a bird, in the center of the filling.

RHUBARB-BERRY PIE

Decorative steam vents

Instead of cutting plain slits for steam vents in the top crust, use small cookie or candy cutters or the tip of a small, sharp knife to cut a pattern of decorative vents. It is easiest to do this before you lay the top crust over the filling.

Raspberries, blackberries, loganberries, and boysenberries would all make excellent partners to the rhubarb in this sweet-tart pie, though you may need to increase the sugar if they are very tart. Serve wedges of the pie with a spoonful of crème fraîche or sour cream.

Preheat the oven to 425°F (220°C). Roll out the pastry for the bottom crust and use to line a 9-inch (23-cm) pie pan. Roll out the pastry for the top crust and set it aside.

In a large bowl, stir together the sugar, cornstarch, and salt. Add the rhubarb and berries and toss to mix well. Taste the fruit and add more sugar if needed. Pile the fruit mixture in the pastry-lined pan and dot with the butter. Cover the fruit with the top crust, trim and flute the edges, and cut 4 or 5 slits in the top crust for steam vents (page 518).

Bake for 20 minutes. Reduce the oven temperature to 350°F (180°C) and continue baking until the juices are bubbling and the crust is golden brown, 30–40 minutes longer. Let cool completely on a wire rack.

Pie Pastry for a double-crust pie (page 447)

1 cup (8 oz/250 g) sugar, or as needed

3 tablespoons (1 oz/30 g) cornstarch (cornflour)

¼ teaspoon salt

1¼ lb (625 g) rhubarb stalks, peeled and sliced into ½-inch (12-mm) pieces, about 4 cups

2 cups (8 oz/250 g) fresh berries (see note, above)

2 tablespoons unsalted butter, cut into bits

MAKES ONE 9-INCH (23-CM) DOUBLE-CRUST PIE

528

SOUR CHERRY LATTICE PIE

Sour cherries

Cherries come in two primary types: sweet and sour (or tart). Sour cherries need to be cooked before eating and are delicious in pies. During their short summer season, look for sour cherries at roadside farm stands or farmers' markets. Other times of the year, look for them in jars.

This iconic recipe is a harbinger of summer, as cherries are in season just as the weather begins to turn hot. Sour cherries are best, but if you can find only sweet cherries, reduce the amount of sugar to ⅓ cup (3 oz/90 g) and increase the lemon juice to taste.

Preheat the oven to 400°F (200°C). Roll out the pastry for the bottom crust and use to line a 9-inch (23-cm) pie pan. Roll out the pastry for the lattice top and set it aside (page 519).

In a large bowl, combine the cherries, sugar, cornstarch, lemon juice, and almond extract and stir until mixed. Taste the cherries and add more sugar if needed. Pour the cherries into the pie shell. Cut the lattice-top pastry into strips ¾ inch (2 cm) wide, weave the lattice top (see page 519 for instructions), and then trim and flute the pie edges (page 518).

Bake the pie for 15 minutes. Reduce the oven temperature to 350°F (180°C) and continue baking until the crust is golden brown and the fruit is tender, 40–45 minutes. Let cool on a wire rack. Serve warm or at room temperature.

Pie Pasty for a double-crust pie (page 447)

5 cups (2 lb/1 kg) pitted sour cherries

½ cup (4 oz/125 g) sugar, or as needed

1½ tablespoons cornstarch (cornflour)

1 tablespoon fresh lemon juice

¼ teaspoon pure almond extract

MAKES ONE 9-INCH (23-CM) LATTICE-TOP PIE

FRESH PEACH PIE

Here is one of the best-tasting pies you'll ever make, with a lattice top to show off the beautiful fresh fruit filling below. It's flavored only minimally to let the fresh peach flavor shine through. Some peach lovers insist the fruits taste even better baked in a pie than they do out of hand.

Pie Pastry for a double-crust pie (page 447)

6 cups (1¼ lb/625 g) peeled and sliced peaches

2 tablespoons fresh lemon juice

¼ cup (1 oz/30 g) all-purpose (plain) flour

⅔ cup (5 oz/155 g) sugar

¼ teaspoon salt

Pinch of grated nutmeg

2 tablespoons unsalted butter, cut into bits

MAKES ONE 9-INCH (23-CM) LATTICE-TOP PIE

Preheat the oven to 425°F (220°C). Roll out the pastry for the bottom crust and use to line a 9-inch (23-cm) pie pan. Roll out the pastry for the lattice top and set it aside (page 519).

Place the peaches in a large bowl. Sprinkle with the lemon juice and toss to coat well; set aside. In a small bowl stir together the flour, sugar, salt, and nutmeg. Add the flour mixture to the bowl with the peaches and toss to mix well. Pile the fruit mixture in the pastry-lined pan and dot with the butter. Cut the remaining pastry into strips ¾ inch (2 cm) wide, weave the lattice top (see page 519 for instructions), and then trim and flute the pie edges (page 518).

Bake the pie for 25 minutes. Reduce the oven temperature to 350°F (180°C) and continue baking until the crust is golden brown and the juices are bubbling, about 25 minutes longer. Let cool on a wire rack. Serve warm or at room temperature.

On lattice tops for fruit pies

Lattice crusts are a traditional favorite for cherry pie, peach pie, and other pies made from stone fruits. The woven crust reveals the fruit underneath, whose juices bubble up through the lattice to enhance the pie's homey appearance.

PEAR AND MINCE PIE

Here is a light version of the traditional wintertime pie. Use firm but ripe baking pears, such as Bosc, Comice, or Anjou. You can also top the pie with a solid crust rather than the lattice crust. If you opt for the solid crust, be sure to cut vents in the top to allow steam to escape.

Pie Pastry for a double-crust pie (page 447)

5 large pears, peeled, cored, and chopped

1¼ cups (10 oz/315 g) prepared mincemeat

¼ cup (2 oz/60 g) firmly packed dark brown sugar

1 tablespoon all-purpose (plain) flour

1 teaspoon *each* ground cinnamon and grated orange zest

½ teaspoon ground allspice

⅛ teaspoon ground cloves

1 egg

1 tablespoon milk

MAKES ONE 9-INCH (23-CM) LATTICE-TOP PIE

Position a rack in the lower third of the oven and preheat the oven to 400°F (200°C).

Roll out the pastry for the bottom crust and use to line a 9-inch (23-cm) pie pan. Roll out the pastry for the lattice top and set it aside (page 519).

In a large bowl, combine the pears, mincemeat, brown sugar, flour, cinnamon, orange zest, allspice, and cloves and stir to mix well. Spoon the pear filling into the pie shell. Cut the remaining pastry into strips ¾ inch (2 cm) wide, weave the lattice top (see page 519 for instructions), and then trim and flute the edges (page 518).

In a small bowl, whisk together the egg and milk until blended. Brush the egg mixture evenly over the lattice top. Bake until the crust is golden brown and the juices are bubbling, about 1 hour. Check periodically and cover the edges with aluminum foil if they are browning too quickly. Let cool on a wire rack. Serve warm or at room temperature.

Overbrowning crusts

If the edges of the crust are browning too quickly, your oven may be too hot or its heat may be unevenly distributed. Shield the edges during the final minutes of baking by covering with strips of aluminum foil, shiny side out.

TARTE TATIN

Choose an ovenproof pan

Be sure to use an ovenproof frying pan (a pan that can withstand high oven heats and does not have a plastic handle) to make this recipe. While the initial cooking starts on the stove top, the majority of it occurs in the oven.

A popular specialty from France, this upside-down caramel-apple tart is named for the two Tatin sisters who originated it in the kitchen of their small hotel in the French countryside. It is made in a frying pan instead of a tart pan and topped with butter-rich puff pastry.

Preheat the oven to 350°F (180°C).

In a 10-inch (25-cm) cast-iron or other heavy ovenproof frying pan over medium-high heat, melt together the butter and sugar, stirring to prevent scorching. Heat until the syrup is a rich caramel color, about 8 minutes.

Reduce the heat to low. Add the apple slices, arranging them in a decorative swirl starting from the outside edge of the pan and placing them rounded sides down, because the tart will be turned upside down when it is served. Simmer, uncovered, until the apples are slightly tender yet still firm, about 10 minutes. Shake the pan occasionally to prevent scorching. Remove from the heat.

Trim the corners of the puff pastry square to form a rough 10-inch (25-cm) circle. Place the pastry over the apples and, using the tip of a knife, push it down between the apples and the edge of the pan. Bake the tart until the pastry is golden and puffed, about 20 minutes. Let cool for 10 minutes.

Run a knife around the sides of the tart to loosen it from the pan sides. Invert a large plate on top of the frying pan and, holding the plate and frying pan firmly together with oven mitts or pot holders, invert them. Lift off the frying pan. Carefully replace any apple slices that have become dislodged. Serve warm or at room temperature.

3 tablespoons unsalted butter

½ cup (4 oz/125 g) sugar

6 Granny Smith or other crisp, tart apples, peeled, quartered, cored, and thickly sliced

10-inch (25-cm) square puff pastry, thawed if frozen

MAKES ONE 10-INCH (25-CM) TART

PEAR TART

Pears for baking

The best pears for baking remain firm and smooth when cooked, such as Bartlett (Williams') and Anjou. Select fruits that are firm but not rock hard, fragrant, and smooth and unblemished, with the stem still attached.

For this beautifully simple tart, pear slices are lined up in slightly overlapping rows on a rectangle of puff pastry, then glazed with warm apricot jam. Although it takes only about 20 minutes to assemble, it looks like it came from a French pâtisserie.

Preheat the oven to 400°F (200°C). Thaw the pastry if frozen.

On a floured work surface, roll out the puff pastry into a 12-by-6-inch (30-by-15-cm) rectangle. Using a pastry wheel, trim off a strip ¼ inch (6 mm) wide from each side. Lightly beat the egg with 1 tablespoon water to make an egg wash. Using a pastry brush dipped in the egg wash, dampen the edges of the rectangle. Then return the strips to the edges, using them to form a rim around the rectangle. Brush the entire pastry with the egg wash. Transfer the pastry to an ungreased baking sheet.

Peel, halve, and core the pears. Cut into lengthwise slices about ⅜ inch (1 cm) thick and immediately roll in the lemon juice to prevent discoloring.

½ lb (250 g) Classic Puff Pastry (page 450) or purchased

1 egg

2 large, firm but ripe Bartlett (Williams') pears

Juice of 1 lemon

1½ tablespoons sugar

¼ cup (2½ oz/75 g) apricot jam

MAKES ONE 11½-BY-5½-INCH (29-BY-14-CM) TART

Sprinkle the pastry with about 1 teaspoon of the sugar. Arrange the pear slices on the pastry, overlapping them in an attractive design. Sprinkle the pears with the remaining sugar, adjusting the amount according to the tartness of the pears. Bake for 15 minutes.

In a small saucepan over medium heat, melt the jam with about 2½ teaspoons water, or enough water to thin the jam to a brushing consistency. Remove from the heat and pass through a fine-mesh sieve placed over a small bowl.

Remove the tart from the oven and lightly brush the tops of the pears with the jam. Continue to bake, glazing the pears about every 10 minutes, until the pears are tender when pierced with the point of a knife and the crust is browned on the edges, 25–35 minutes. The baking time depends on the ripeness of the pears and the thickness of the slices. Transfer to a rack and brush once again with the glaze. Let cool completely before serving.

Fixing dough cracks

If small cracks cannot be repaired by pressing them together with your fingers, the dough is too dry. Cover with a damp kitchen towel and refrigerate for 30 minutes. If the problem persists, discard the dough and start over.

RUSTIC FRESH FRUIT TART

This rustic tart is made from thin, sugared pastry that is baked and then filled with fresh fruit. Fill it with a mix of berries, cherries, melon balls, or whatever is in season. You can bake the pastry ahead of time, then add the fruit just before serving.

Seasonal tarts

In the spring, try a tart topped with strawberries and kiwifruit. In the summer, use peaches, plums, or other stone fruits. In the fall, try figs and late-season stone fruits. In the winter, create a tart of mixed tropical fruits like mango and pineapple.

Pie Pastry for a double-crust pie (page 447)

2 tablespoons sugar, plus more for sprinkling on the fruit, optional

5–6 cups (1¼–1½ lb/ 600–750 g) prepared fresh fruit (see above and right)

Whipped Cream (page 454)

MAKES 1 FREE-FORM TART

Preheat the oven to 425°F (220°C).

Prepare the pastry but form it into a single disk. Roll out the pastry about ⅛ inch (3 mm) thick into any shape you wish. Transfer it to a baking sheet and prick it all over with a fork. Fold up ½ inch (12 mm) of the dough all around the edge to make a low rim. Bake the pastry sheet until golden brown and crisp, 15–20 minutes. Remove from the oven and sprinkle with the sugar. Return the crust to the oven and bake for 1 minute longer. Remove from the oven once again, let cool on the baking sheet for about 3 minutes, then carefully slide it onto a wire rack and let cool completely.

To serve the tart, transfer the cooled pastry sheet to a large platter or board. Top with the prepared fruit, being as casual or as fancy as you like with the arrangement. If the fruit is tart, sprinkle it with sugar.

Pass the whipped cream at the table.

BRANDIED APPLE AND DRIED CHERRY GALETTE

Pleating galettes

To create a nice-looking folded edge for a galette, pleat the dough in sections around the perimeter of the tart. Carefully fold a small section of the pastry up over the filling, folding it into a loose pleat. Continue to fold loosely in small sections all the way around the perimeter of the dough, leaving the filling open in the center.

Easy to assemble, this tart calls for loosely draping the sides of a pastry round over the edges of a filling of brandied apples and dried cherries. It is baked until the pastry is flaky and golden, then dusted with sugar. If dried cherries are not available, substitute dried cranberries.

In a small bowl, combine the cherries and brandy. Cover and let stand until plump, about 30 minutes.

Peel, quarter, and core the apples, then cut into ½-inch (12-mm) wedges. Place in a large bowl, add the cherries and brandy, and toss to coat. In a small bowl, stir together the granulated sugar and flour, then sprinkle over the apples.

Position a rack in the lower third of the oven and preheat to 400°F (200°C). Lightly butter a large baking sheet.

On a lightly floured work surface, roll out the dough into a round 14 inches (35 cm) in diameter. Carefully drape it loosely over the rolling pin and transfer to the prepared baking sheet. Spread the apples on the pastry, mounding them slightly in the center and leaving a 3-inch (7.5-cm) border uncovered all around. Fold the dough edges up to cover the filling partially (left).

Bake for 15 minutes. Reduce the oven temperature to 350°F (180°C) and continue baking until the crust is golden and the apple mixture is bubbly, about 40 minutes longer. Let cool completely on a wire rack. Just before serving, using a fine-mesh sieve, sift confectioners' sugar over the top.

¼ cup (1 oz/30 g) dried pitted cherries

2 tablespoons brandy

3 lb (1.5 kg) Golden Delicious or other baking apples

¼ cup (2 oz/60 g) granulated sugar

2 tablespoons all-purpose (plain) flour

Unsalted butter for pan

Pie Pastry for a single-crust pie (page 447)

Confectioners' (icing) sugar for dusting

MAKES ONE 8-INCH (20-CM) GALETTE

QUINCE TART

Shrinking crusts

If the crust shrinks from the sides of the pan during baking, the dough was stretched too tightly when you put it in the pan. Always loosely drape and press dough into the pan to avoid shrinkage.

Quinces are in the market from October through December, and their fragrant flesh makes an unusual and delicious tart. Uncooked quinces are harsh tasting, but simmering them in sugar syrup transforms them, turning their flavor sweet and delicate and their color a lovely rose.

Preheat the oven to 375°F (190°C). Roll out the pastry and line a 9-inch (23-cm) tart pan as directed in the pastry recipe, then fully blind bake (page 518) the shell. Let the pie shell cool completely on a wire rack.

In a saucepan over medium heat, combine 2½ cups (20 fl oz/ 625 ml) water, the sugar, cinnamon stick, and lemon zest and bring to a boil, stirring until the sugar dissolves. Reduce the heat to low so the syrup simmers gently.

Peel, halve and core each quince—just as you would an apple. Cut each half into 4 wedges. Drop into the simmering sugar syrup, cover partially, and cook until tender but not mushy, about 1 hour. Remove from the heat and let cool completely. Drain the quinces well, reserving the liquid. Pat them dry.

Cut each wedge lengthwise into 2 or 3 slices; set aside. In a small, heavy saucepan, combine the apricot jam with ¼ cup

Tart Pastry (page 448)

1½ cups (12 oz/375 g) sugar

1 cinnamon stick, about 2 inches (5 cm)

1 teaspoon grated lemon zest

3 quinces

½ cup (5 oz/155 g) apricot jam

MAKES ONE 9-INCH (23-CM) TART

(2 fl oz/60 ml) of the reserved quince liquid. Place over high heat and boil until thick and syrupy, which should take several minutes. Pass the syrup through a fine-mesh sieve into a small bowl. Brush a thin coating of the warm glaze over the bottom of the cooled tart shell.

Arrange the quince attractively in the tart shell, overlapping the slices. Carefully brush with the remaining glaze and serve as soon as possible.

BLUE PLUM TART

This rectangular tart showcases halved Italian prune plums flavored with hazelnuts, sugar, and spices. When the tart is still hot from the oven, it is brushed with warm orange marmalade and sprinkled with more hazelnuts. You can also make the tart it in a round tart pan.

Tart Pastry (page 448)

½ cup (2½ oz/75 g) plus 2 tablespoons hazelnuts (filberts), toasted and skinned (see page 478)

½ cup (4 oz/125 g) plus 2 tablespoons sugar

½ teaspoon ground cinnamon

½ teaspoon ground ginger

3 tablespoons unsalted butter, at room temperature

16–20 Italian prune plums, halved and pitted

¾ cup (7½ oz/235 g) orange marmalade

Whipped Cream (page 454) flavored with about 1 teaspoon grated orange zest, optional

MAKES ONE 8-BY-11-INCH (20-BY-28-CM) RECTANGULAR TART

Preheat the oven to 400°F (200°C). Roll out the pastry about 2 inches (5 cm) larger than an 8-by-11-inch (20-by-28-inch) rectangular tart pan and line the pan as directed in the pastry recipe. Place in the freezer while you make the filling.

Finely chop the ½ cup hazelnuts and place in a food processor. Add the ½ cup sugar, cinnamon, ginger, and butter and pulse until a paste forms. Press evenly over the bottom of the pastry-lined tart pan. Top with the plums, cut sides down, covering the pastry completely. Sprinkle the remaining 2 tablespoons sugar over the top.

Bake for 10 minutes. Reduce the oven temperature to 350°F (180°C) and continue baking until the plums are bubbling and the crust is golden, 20–30 minutes longer.

Meanwhile, in a small saucepan over medium heat, melt the orange marmalade. Remove from the heat and pass through a fine-mesh sieve into a small bowl; keep warm. Coarsely chop the remaining 2 tablespoons hazelnuts.

When the tart is done, transfer to a wire rack and brush the marmalade over the plums. Sprinkle with the nuts. Let cool completely. Serve with the cream, if desired.

Tart pans

Tart pans come in many shapes and sizes and have plain or fluted vertical sides. For the most versatility, look for a tart pan with a removable bottom, which allows you to free a tart easily from its pan and place it on a plate for serving.

533

STRAWBERRY AND LEMON CURD TART

Uses for lemon curd

Lemon curd is a versatile kitchen staple. The classic accompaniment to scones, it can also be used as a filling for sandwich cookies, layer cakes, and tarts. Lemon curd can be frozen for up to 1 month.

Sliced strawberries heaped in a crisp crust make a beautiful tart, but a thin layer of lemon curd between the pastry and berries transforms the tart into something special. To lighten the flavor and texture of the lemon curd, fold in 1½ cups (12 fl oz/375ml) whipped cream.

To make the lemon curd, in a heavy saucepan, vigorously whisk together the egg yolks and sugar for 1 minute. Add the lemon juice and zest and whisk for 1 minute longer. Place over low heat and cook, stirring constantly, until slightly thickened. Do not allow it get too hot or the egg yolks will scramble. Remove from the heat, add the butter, and stir until smooth. Let cool, stirring occasionally. There should be about 1 cup (11 oz/345 g). Transfer to an airtight container and chill before assembling the tart.

Preheat the oven to 375°F (190°C). Roll out the pastry and line a 9-inch (23-cm) tart pan as directed in the pastry recipe, then fully blind bake (page 518). Let the tart shell cool completely on a wire rack.

Spread the lemon curd in the cooled tart shell. Stem the strawberries. If they are large, slice each one lengthwise into 2 or 3 pieces. Arrange the strawberries on top of the lemon curd. Warm the glaze until spreadable, then brush the fruit with the warm glaze. Serve the tart as soon as possible.

FOR THE LEMON CURD

5 egg yolks

½ cup (4 oz/125 g) sugar

¼ cup (2 fl oz/60 ml) fresh lemon juice

Grated zest of 2 lemons

6 tablespoons (3 oz/90 g) unsalted butter, cut into tablespoon-size pieces

Tart Pastry (page 448)

4 cups (1 lb/500 g) strawberries

⅓ cup (3 fl oz/80 ml) Currant Glaze (page 462)

MAKES ONE 9-INCH (23-CM) TART

ALMOND-FRUIT TART

Unmolding tarts

To remove a finished tart from the pan, place the pan on a large aluminum can or overturned glass and let the sides fall away. You can transfer the tart still on the pan's removable bottom directly to the serving plate.

A lovely almond crust is the perfect palette for berries or sliced stone fruits. You can use whole raspberries or blackberries or sliced strawberries in place of the blueberries, or nectarines can stand in for the peaches. Always choose the fruit that looks best at the market.

Preheat the oven to 375°F (190°C).

To make the crust, in a food processor, combine the almonds and sugar and process until fairly finely ground. Add the flour to the work bowl and pulse to mix. Scatter the butter over the top and pulse until the mixture resembles coarse meal. Add 2 tablespoons of the liqueur and pulse until the dough comes together into a rough mass, adding the remaining 1 tablespoon liqueur if the mixture is too dry.

Transfer the mixture to a 9-inch (23-cm) round tart pan with a removable bottom. Using your fingers, pat the mixture evenly over the bottom and up the sides of the pan. Fully blind bake the crust (page 518).

Meanwhile, make the filling. In a bowl, combine the almond paste and butter and beat with an electric mixer on low speed until smooth. Add the egg white and beat until thoroughly combined.

FOR THE CRUST

1 heaping cup (6 oz/185 g) almonds

2 tablespoons sugar

1¼ cups (6½ oz/200 g) all-purpose (plain) flour

¾ cup (6 oz/185 g) cold unsalted butter, cut into tablespoon-size pieces

2–3 tablespoons almond liqueur or light corn syrup

FOR THE FILLING

¼ lb (125 g) almond paste, at room temperature

2 tablespoons unsalted butter, at room temperature

1 egg white

2 cups (8 oz/250 g) blueberries, or 4 or 5 small peaches, sliced

¾ cup (7½ oz/235 g) red currant jelly or apple jelly

MAKES ONE 9-INCH (23-CM) TART

When the crust is ready, remove it from the oven and let cool on a wire rack for about 5 minutes. Spread the almond paste mixture evenly over the bottom of the warm crust and then let it cool completely.

Arrange the fruit decoratively over the almond paste layer. In a small saucepan over low heat, warm the jelly until it melts, about 5 minutes. Remove from the heat and let cool slightly. Brush the jelly glaze evenly over the fruit. Let cool completely and serve at room temperature.

ORANGE TART

This stunning tart, which features glazed orange slices arranged atop pastry cream, is deceptively simple to make. Since you are using the whole orange, peel and all, look for organic fruits. Cinnamon and cloves add an exotic note to the tart's bright, fragrant flavors.

Tart Pastry (page 448)

3 oranges, unblemished and preferably seedless

1 cup (8 oz/250 g) sugar

¼ cup (2 fl oz/60 ml) light corn syrup

1 cinnamon stick, about 2 inches (5 cm), broken into pieces

4 whole cloves

½ cup (4 fl oz/125 ml) Pastry Cream (page 452)

½ cup (5 oz/155 g) orange marmalade

1 tablespoon fresh grated orange zest

MAKES ONE 9-INCH (23-CM) TART

Preheat the oven to 375°F (190°C). Roll out the pastry and line a 9-inch (23-cm) tart pan as directed in the pastry recipe, then fully blind bake (page 518). Let the tart shell cool completely on a wire rack.

In a large saucepan, combine the oranges with enough water to cover and bring to a boil over high heat. Reduce the heat to medium and cook until tender when pierced but not mushy, 15–20 minutes. Drain and let cool. Cut the oranges crosswise into slices ⅛–¼ inch (3 mm–6 mm) thick. Discard the end slices; pick out any seeds from the fruit.

In a saucepan, combine the sugar, corn syrup, 1 cup (8 fl oz/ 250 ml) water, the cinnamon stick, and cloves and bring to a boil over high heat, stirring to dissolve the sugar. Boil for 5 minutes. Add the orange slices, reduce the heat to medium, and boil very gently, swirling the pan occasionally, until the syrup is thick and the oranges are tender, about 1 hour. Remove from the heat and let cool completely in the liquid.

Spread the pastry cream evenly over the bottom of the tart shell. Using a slotted spoon, carefully remove the orange slices from the syrup, draining them well and reserving the syrup, and arrange the slices decoratively on the pastry cream, overlapping them slightly.

In a small saucepan, combine ¼ cup (2 fl oz/60 ml) of the reserved syrup and the orange marmalade, bring to a boil over medium-high heat, and boil until thick, about 3 minutes. Strain through a fine-mesh sieve into a small bowl. Stir in the orange zest, then brush the warm glaze over the orange slices. Serve the tart as soon as possible.

Fig and berry tart

You can also top the pastry cream with 1 cup (4 oz/125 g) each blackberries and raspberries and 6 fresh figs, halved lengthwise. Boil ⅓ cup (4 oz/125 g) red currant jelly with 1 tsp fresh lemon juice and spread the glaze over the fruit in place of the marmalade glaze.

535

POACHED PEAR TART

536

This tart of glistening pear halves on whipped cream–cloaked pastry is a perfect dinner party finale. The pears can be poached and stored in the refrigerator, in their poaching liquid, for several days before using. You can also serve the poached pears and cream on their own.

To cook the pears, in a saucepan, combine the wine, sugar, cinnamon stick, and cloves and bring to a boil over high heat. Reduce the heat to medium, cover partially, and simmer for 5 minutes. Peel, halve, and core the pears. Place them in the simmering liquid, adding a little water if necessary to cover completely with liquid. Adjusting the heat as needed, poach the pears gently until tender when pierced with a knife, about 15 minutes. Remove from the heat and let the pears cool in the liquid for at least 2 hours.

Preheat the oven to 375°F (190°C). Press the pastry onto the bottom and up the sides of a 9-inch (23-cm) tart pan as directed in the pastry recipe, then fully blind bake the tart shell (page 518). Let cool completely on a wire rack.

Remove the pears from the poaching liquid and pat them dry. Brush a thin coating of the warm apricot glaze over the bottom of the tart shell. In a bowl, using an electric mixer on medium-high speed, combine the cream, sugar, and dry milk and beat until stiff peaks form. Stir in the vanilla. Spread the whipped cream in an even layer in the tart shell. Then, arrange the pear halves, cut sides down, on top of the cream, positioning them at the edge of the tart with the narrow ends pointing toward the center. Place 1 or 2 pear halves in the middle of the tart to cover the center. Carefully brush the pear halves with the remaining apricot glaze. Serve the tart as soon as possible.

FOR THE PEARS

2 cups (16 fl oz/500 ml) dry red wine

¾ cup (6 oz/185 g) sugar

1 cinnamon stick, about 2 inches (5 cm)

3 whole cloves

5 firm but ripe pears, preferably Bosc

Rich Tart Pastry (page 449)

½ cup (4 fl oz/125 ml) Apricot Glaze (page 462), warm

⅓ cup (3 fl oz/80 ml) heavy (double) cream

2 teaspoons sugar

1 teaspoon nonfat dry milk

1 teaspoon pure vanilla extract, or 2 tablespoons pear brandy

MAKES ONE 9-INCH (23-CM) TART

OLD-FASHIONED LEMON TART

Inspired by a classic Shaker recipe, this is an unusual tart because it uses whole lemon slices, which are simmered in syrup and then arranged on a delicate lemon custard in a pastry shell. The tart is pleasingly sour, with sweet, rich, and fruity elements to temper the lemon flavor.

Preheat the oven to 375°F (190°C). Press the pastry onto the bottom and up the sides of a 9-inch (23-cm) tart pan as directed in the pastry recipe, then fully blind bake the tart shell (page 518). Let cool completely on a wire rack.

Grate the zest from 2 lemons and juice them. Set the juice and zest aside. With a small, sharp knife, peel the remaining 4 lemons, cutting deeply enough to remove all the white pith and expose the flesh all around. Slice crosswise ¼ inch (6 mm) thick. Pick out any seeds.

In a saucepan over low heat, combine 1½ cups (12 oz/375 g) of the sugar and ½ cup (4 fl oz/125 ml) water and stir until the sugar dissolves. Raise the heat to medium-high and clip

Rich Tart Pastry (page 449)

6 lemons

2 cups (1 lb/500 g) sugar

2 eggs

½ cup (4 fl oz/125 ml) heavy (double) cream

Pinch of salt

½ cup (5 oz/155 g) apricot jam

MAKES ONE 9-INCH (23-CM) TART

a candy thermometer onto the side of the pan. Boil the syrup until the thermometer registers 238°F (114°C), 10–15 minutes. Add the lemon slices and return to a simmer. Remove from the heat; set aside for 1 hour.

Preheat the oven to 350°F (180°C). In a bowl, whisk together the reserved lemon juice and zest, the remaining ½ cup (4 oz/125 g) sugar, and the eggs until blended. Stir in the cream and salt. Pour into the tart shell and bake until just set, about 20 minutes. Let cool completely.

Using a slotted spoon, carefully remove the lemon slices from the syrup, draining them well and reserving the syrup, and arrange them on the filling. In a small saucepan, combine ¼ cup (2 fl oz/60 ml) of the cooking syrup and the jam, bring to a boil over medium-high heat, and boil until thick, about 3 minutes. Strain through a fine-mesh sieve into a small bowl. Brush the warm glaze over the lemon slices. Serve the tart as soon as possible.

COCONUT CREAM TART

This tart is a fresh take on coconut cream pie. It uses coconut in three guises: as a flavorful liquid for the custard, as a textural contrast in the filling, and as a crunchy garnish on the top. If desired use a pastry bag fitted with a star tip to pipe the whipped cream onto the finished tart.

Tart Pastry (page 448)

2½ cups (10 oz/315 g) sweetened shredded dried coconut

1 cup (8 fl oz/250 ml) boiling water

½ cup (4 oz/125 g) sugar

1 tablespoon cornstarch (cornflour)

¼ teaspoon salt

1 cup (8 fl oz/250 ml) milk

4 egg yolks

6 tablespoons (3 oz/90 g) unsalted butter, cut into tablespoon-size pieces

1 teaspoon pure vanilla extract

Whipped Cream (page 454) for serving, optional

MAKES ONE 9-INCH (23-CM) TART

Preheat the oven to 375°F (190°C). Roll out the pastry and line a 9-inch (23-cm) tart pan as directed in the pastry recipe, then fully blind bake (page 518). Let cool completely on a wire rack. Reduce the oven temperature to 350°F (180°C).

Place 1½ cups (6 oz/180 g) of the coconut in a heatproof bowl. Pour in the boiling water and let stand for 30 minutes. Pour the mixture into a fine-mesh sieve placed over a bowl and press firmly on the coconut to extract every bit of liquid. Discard the solids in the sieve.

While the coconut is soaking, spread the remaining 1 cup (4 oz/125 g) coconut on a baking sheet and toast in the oven, stirring occasionally, until lightly browned, about 20 minutes. Pour onto a plate and let cool.

In a saucepan, stir together the sugar, cornstarch, and salt. Whisk in the milk and the reserved coconut liquid until combined. Place over medium heat and bring to a boil, stirring constantly. Remove from the heat and whisk in the egg yolks, then return to medium heat and cook, stirring, until thickened, about 3 minutes. Remove from the heat and stir in the butter and then the vanilla until smooth. Stir in three-fourths of the toasted coconut and let cool until lukewarm. Spread the mixture evenly in the tart shell and let cool completely.

To serve, garnish with whipped cream, if desired, and sprinkle with the remaining toasted coconut.

Tempering the sweetness

Some brands of packaged sweetened dried coconut are overly sweet. If desired, you can remove some of the sugar by rinsing the coconut under running cold water, then squeezing it dry, a handful at a time.

BANBURY TART

Crushing crackers

To crush crackers, place them in a zippered plastic bag, press out the air, and seal well. Using a rolling pin, smash the crackers repeatedly until they form fine, even crumbs. Or, pulse the crackers in a mini food processor until fine crumbs form.

Here is a full-size version of the individual raisin tartlets made popular in Banbury, England. This tart calls for a streusel topping, and the dark filling looks and tastes remarkably like mincemeat. It is perfect for afternoon tea with guests, especially during the fall months.

Preheat the oven to 375°F (190°C). Roll out the pastry and line a 9-inch (23-cm) tart pan as directed in the pastry recipe, then partially blind bake (page 518). Let cool completely on a wire rack.

In a heavy saucepan, combine the raisins, 1 cup (8 fl oz/250 ml) water, the sugar, crackers, and lemon zest and bring to a boil over high heat, stirring to dissolve the sugar. Reduce the heat to low and simmer until slightly thickened, about 10 minutes. Remove the pan from the heat and stir in the lemon juice and egg until blended. Set aside.

To make the topping, in a small bowl, stir together the flour, butter, sugar, and salt. Using your fingertips, blend the ingredients until the mixture resembles fine crumbs.

Pour the raisin mixture into the tart shell and sprinkle the crumb mixture evenly over the top. Bake until lightly browned on top, about 35 minutes. Let the tart cool on a wire rack. Serve warm.

Tart Pastry (page 448)

1½ cups (9 oz/280 g) raisins

⅔ cup (5 oz/155 g) sugar

4 soda crackers, finely crushed

2 teaspoons grated lemon zest

2 tablespoons fresh lemon juice

1 egg, lightly beaten

FOR THE TOPPING

½ cup (2½ oz/75 g) all-purpose (plain) flour

3 tablespoons unsalted butter

2 tablespoons sugar

¼ teaspoon salt

MAKES ONE 9-INCH (23-CM) TART

BLACK BOTTOM TART

About dark rum

Typically made in the Caribbean, rum is distilled from the juice of sugarcane. Dark rum has a full, deep flavor and color. In a quality brand, the flavor and color come from aging the liquor in oak barrels for a number of years. Lesser quality rums may include caramel color.

Dark chocolate custard, an airy rum chiffon, and a topping of lightly sweetened whipped cream—this tart is destined to be a crowd-pleaser. You will need to plan ahead, as the filling needs to chill for an hour. This recipe uses raw eggs. For more information turn to page 37.

Preheat the oven to 375°F (190°C). Roll out the pastry and line a 9-inch (23-cm) tart pan as directed in the pastry recipe, then fully blind bake (page 518). Let the shell cool completely on a wire rack.

In a small bowl or cup, sprinkle the gelatin over ¼ cup (2 fl oz/60 ml) water and let stand for a few minutes to soften.

In a heatproof bowl, whisk the egg yolks until blended. In a saucepan over medium heat, warm the milk until small bubbles appear around the edge of the pan. Slowly pour the hot milk into the egg yolks while whisking constantly. Return the mixture to the saucepan off the heat.

In a bowl, stir together the ⅓ cup sugar, the cornstarch, and salt. Add to the milk mixture along with the gelatin mixture

Tart Pastry (page 448)

2 teaspoons unflavored gelatin

2 eggs, separated

1¼ cups (10 fl oz/ 310 ml) milk

2 eggs, separated

⅓ cup (3 oz/90 g) plus 2 tablespoons sugar

1 tablespoon cornstarch (cornflour)

¼ teaspoon salt

1 oz (30 g) unsweetened chocolate, chopped and melted

1 teaspoon pure vanilla extract

¼ cup (2 fl oz/60 ml) dark rum

FOR THE TOPPING

½ cup (4 fl oz/125 ml) heavy (double) cream

2 teaspoons sugar

1 tablespoon grated unsweetened chocolate

MAKES ONE 9-INCH (23-CM) TART

and whisk the custard until blended. Place over medium heat and cook, stirring constantly, until the custard thickens slightly and barely reaches a simmer, about 10 minutes. Do not allow to boil. Remove from the heat. Pour ½ cup (4 fl oz/125 ml) of the custard into a small bowl and stir in the melted chocolate until thoroughly combined. Spread the chocolate mixture in the tart shell and set aside. Stir the vanilla and rum into the remaining custard. Cover and refrigerate, stirring occasionally, until the mixture mounds when dropped from a spoon, about 1 hour.

In a bowl, using a clean whisk or an electric mixer on medium-high speed, beat the egg whites until soft peaks form. Slowly add the 2 tablespoons sugar and continue to beat until stiff peaks form. Fold the egg whites into the chilled rum custard. Spread the lightened custard mixture over the chocolate layer in the tart shell, mounding it slightly.

To make the topping, in a bowl, using a whisk, whip together the cream and sugar until stiff peaks form. Spoon the cream evenly over the custard layer. Sprinkle with the chocolate.

CARAMELIZED WALNUT TART

Only five ingredients go into the filling for this elegant but easy tart. Walnuts are slightly bitter, but heating them in a honey-caramel mixture and then adding cream tempers the bitterness. Serve the tart at dinner's end with small glasses of sweet wine.

Pie Pastry for a single-crust pie made with 2 tablespoons brown sugar (page 447)

1¼ cups (10 oz/315 g) granulated sugar

3 cups (12 oz/375 g) chopped walnuts

¾ cup (6 oz/185 g) unsalted butter, cut into slivers, at room temperature

1 cup (8 fl oz/250 ml) heavy (double) cream

⅓ cup (3 fl oz/90 ml) honey

MAKES ONE 9½- OR 10-INCH (24- OR 25-CM) TART

Preheat the oven to 375°F (190°C). On a lightly floured work surface, roll out the pastry and line a 9½- or 10-inch (24- or 25-cm) tart pan with a removable bottom. Then, partially blind bake (page 518) the tart shell. Let cool completely on a wire rack. Keep the oven on.

To make the filling, in a saucepan, combine the granulated sugar and ½ cup (4 fl oz/125 ml) water and bring to a boil over high heat, stirring until the sugar dissolves. Boil rapidly until the mixture thickens and turns pale brown, 10–15 minutes. Remove from the heat and stir in the nuts and butter and then the cream. Return to low heat and simmer until very thick, 15–20 minutes. Stir in the honey, remove from the heat, and let cool slightly.

Line a baking sheet with aluminum foil. Pour the filling into the pastry shell and place on the baking sheet to catch any spills. Bake until lightly browned, 25–35 minutes. Let cool completely on a wire rack.

Dessert wine pairing

Both tawny port and cream sherry echo the aromas and tastes in this sweet, rich tart of caramel and nuts. Or, try a sweet Madeira, which lends a lemony, refreshing counterpoint to the dessert.

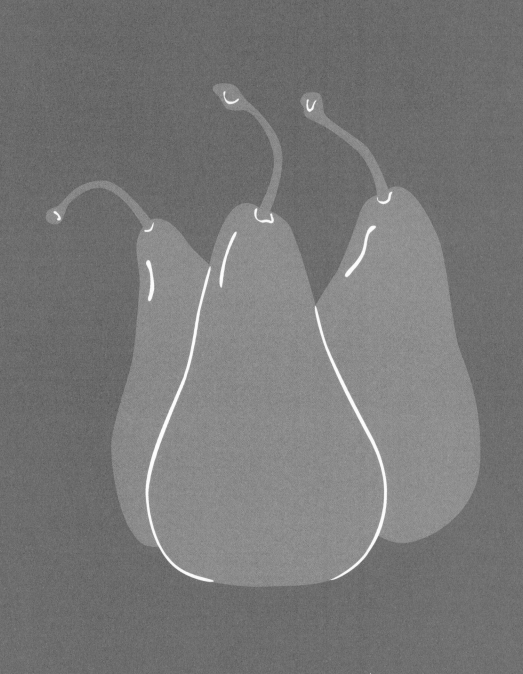

Fruit DESSERTS

Fruit Desserts

Sweet and juicy, fruit is a perfect end to many meals. Most fruit desserts offer the benefit of being easy to make, good examples of the culinary principle that if you start with the finest ingredients—here, in-season produce—and prepare them in ways that highlight their natural qualities, you'll get outstanding results. Use the guidelines on these pages and the recipes that follow to create dozens of memorable fruit desserts.

Essential fruit prep tools
If you enjoy fruit desserts, consider investing in a handful of specialized, inexpensive tools, which make prepping fruit easier: a citrus juicer, a shallow bowl with a deeply fluted, inverted cone at its center against which you push and twist a citrus half to extract juice; a cherry pitter, a hinged utensil that securely grasps an individual cherry and pushes out its pit; and a melon baller, a metal scoop that neatly carves out small spheres of ripe melon.

Preventing discoloration
When cut up and exposed to air, some fruits, especially apples, pears, and bananas, will discolor. Toss them with lemon juice, or keep them in a bowl of water, with or without lemon, until ready to use.

Ripening fruit
It's not always easy to find fruits at their point of ripeness. Pears, bananas, and peaches, for example, are picked before their peak and benefit from sitting at room temperature for a few days. To hasten ripening, put the fruits in a paper bag to trap the ethylene gas they naturally emit, punching several holes in the bag to let the fruit breathe.

Fruit Dessert Types

From recipes that require little more than cutting up and combining fresh fruits to heartwarming baked treats, fruit desserts offer a cornucopia of variety. Here are the main categories into which they are divided.

FRESH FRUIT DESSERTS Fresh fruit salads are easy to assemble: leave small items like berries or grapes whole and cut up larger fruits in a variety that appeals to you. You can serve fresh fruit with a sauce or topping, such as Whipped Cream (page 454), Citrus Curd (page 452), or Hot Fudge Sauce (page 460); you can layer lightly sweetened yogurt with berries and peaches, such as in Fruit and Yogurt Parfaits (page 550), or you can mix sliced fruits with a flavored syrup, as in Navel Oranges with Grand Marnier (page 547). Fruit desserts that are cooked on the stove top or in the oven, then quickly doused with a fruit liqueur or other spirit and ignited are old-fashioned crowdpleasers, as with Bananas Foster and Flambéed Cherries (page 548).

ROASTED, BAKED, AND GRILLED FRUITS The dry heat of an oven or grill intensifies the flavor of fruits while caramelizing some of their natural sugars. That caramelization is what makes roasted, baked, or grilled desserts—made with whole fruits or large pieces—so delicious and attractive. Caramelized Pineapple (page 545) and Roasted Figs with Vanilla Crème Fraîche (page 544) are examples. Sometimes, the hollows in cored or pitted fruit are stuffed before cooking, as in Amaretti-Stuffed Baked Peaches (page 546).

POACHED FRUITS Gently simmering fruits in a sweet liquid coaxes them to delectable tenderness and mingles the flavors of fruit mixtures. Recipes like Summer Fruit Compote (page 544) or Pears Poached in Red Wine (page 546) are not only excellent served on their own but also yield sauces that make wonderful toppings for ice creams, cakes, or plain custards.

CLAFOUTIS AND OTHER BAKED PUDDINGS Surrounded by a rich, thick batter and baked in the oven, fruits can be transformed into satisfying custards that seem the very definition of comfort food. Traditional French-style *clafoutis* (pages 554–55) are prime examples of this preparation. A similar effect can be achieved by adding a bottom crust to a fruit and custard combination, as in Black Plums in Almond Custard (page 554).

COBBLERS, CRISPS, CRUMBLES, AND GRATINS All sorts of other baked fruit desserts are, in fact, close cousins to pies: sweetened fruit mixtures spread in a baking dish and topped with a crust based on some sort of pastry or biscuit dough, batter, mixture of grains, or nuts, butter, and sugar. Their charming names—Apple Crumble (page 559), Strawberry-Rhubarb Brown Betty (page 559), Cranberry-Apple Slump (page 560), and Nectarine-Blackberry Cobbler (page 560)—suggest their many generations of tradition.

Prepping Fruits

Most fruits require little in the way of special preparation before they can be used in cooking. These few easy techniques will be all you need to know to make most fruit dessert recipes.

PEELING Some fruits have inedible skins that are removed easily by hand, including bananas, oranges, and tangerines, or with a vegetable peeler, such as apples or pears. Other fruits, however, require simple tools or techniques to remove their skins.

To peel stone fruit: First, use a paring knife to cut a shallow X on the blossom end (bottom) of each fruit. Using a slotted spoon, lower the fruit, one or two at a time, into a pot of boiling water. Let sit until the skin loosens and wrinkles slightly, 10 to 20 seconds, depending on the ripeness of the fruit, then immediately transfer to a large bowl of ice water to stop the cooking. When the fruit is cool enough to handle, grasp the loose skin at the X with your fingers, aided with a paring knife, if necessary, and pull off the skin in strips.

CORING Apples and pears contain fibrous seed cores that are nearly always removed as part of their preparation.

To core a whole apple: Hold the apple firmly upright on a work surface. Push a sharp-edged, tube-shaped apple corer straight down through the center of the apple. (It may take a little muscle.)

To core an apple that will be cut into pieces: Cut the fruit in half from stem to blossom end. Turn the halves flat side down and cut them in half again to make quarters. Using a paring knife, make an angled incision on each side of the core in the quarter to create a V-shape, releasing the core.

To core a whole pear, leaving the stem end intact: Use a melon baller to scoop out the seeds and tough core from the blossom end (bottom) of the pear.

To core a pear that will be cut into pieces: Cut the pear in half lengthwise. Use a melon baller to scoop the seeds from the center of the wider portion of each pear half. Then, use the edge of the melon baller to scoop out the fibers in a shallow channel from the stem end to where the seeds were lodged.

PITTING The hard pits of stone fruit are generally removed before the fruits are prepared in a recipe.

To pit large stone fruit: Use a paring knife to cut the fruit in half lengthwise, cutting carefully around the pit at the center. Rotate the halves in opposite directions to separate them. Use the tip of the knife to dig gently under the pit and ease it out. You may have to try from a couple of different angles or do a bit of cutting, depending on the ripeness of the fruit and whether you are pitting a clingstone variety in which the flesh is more tightly attached to the pit.

To pit cherries: Use a cherry pitter for whole cherries. If cherry halves are required, follow the same procedure described above for large stone fruit.

SECTIONING Also called "segmenting," this refers to freeing individual wedges of a citrus fruit from their peel, pith, and the membranes that separate them.

To section a citrus fruit: Use a sharp knife to cut a slice from the top and the bottom of the fruit, making each slice thick enough to expose the flesh. Stand the fruit upright and, following the contour of the fruit, cut downward to remove all the peel, white membrane, and pith in a strip from top to bottom. Continue in this fashion, working your way around the fruit. Use a gentle sawing motion to trim away any remaining bits of pith. Holding the peeled fruit over a bowl, carefully make a cut on both sides of each segment to free it from the membrane, letting the segment and juice drop into the bowl below.

FRUITS BY SEASON

Some of the most appealing fruit desserts feature in-season produce, and you'll get the best results—as well as the best prices—if you use locally grown crops.

Fruits don't strictly follow the calendar, and seasonality will vary by region and climate, but below are some general guidelines on finding in-season fruits.

Spring

Berries Strawberries, wild strawberries (*fraises des bois*).

Citrus Fruits Oranges (blood, Valencia).

Tropical Fruits Bananas, mangoes, papayas, passion fruits, pineapples.

Summer

Berries Blackberries, blueberries, boysenberries, gooseberries, loganberries, raspberries, strawberries.

Melons Cantaloupe, honeydew, watermelon.

Tree Fruits Apricots, cherries, figs, nectarines, peaches, plums.

Autumn

Berries Cranberries.

Grapes Ruby, Thompson seedless.

Tree Fruits Apples, figs, kiwifruits, pears, persimmons, pomegranates, quinces.

Winter

Berries Cranberries.

Citrus Fruits Grapefruits, oranges (navel), mandarins (including clementines, tangerines, and tangelos).

Tree Fruits Apples, kiwifruits, pears, quinces.

SUMMER FRUIT COMPOTE

This recipe of mixed fruits in a light syrup makes the best of summer's bounty. If desired, substitute a fruit wine such as blueberry, cherry, or raspberry for ¾ cup (6 fl oz/180 ml) of the water. Serve in glass bowls as is or garnished with Whipped Cream (page 454) or vanilla yogurt.

Cut the larger fruits into smaller, same-size pieces; leave the berries whole. Set aside.

In a saucepan over medium heat, combine the sugar and 1½ cups (12 fl oz/375 ml) water and bring to a boil, stirring to dissolve the sugar. Add the fruits and reduce the heat to medium-low. Simmer gently until the fruits are soft but have not begun to disintegrate, 3–4 minutes. Using a slotted spoon, transfer the fruits to a serving bowl and set aside. Allow the liquid to continue to simmer.

In a small cup, stir together the cornstarch and 2 tablespoons water. Whisk the cornstarch mixture into the simmering liquid. Cook, stirring constantly, until the liquid is clear and has thickened slightly, 2–3 minutes. Remove from the heat and let cool for about 15 minutes.

Pour the partially cooled syrup over the fruit, cover, and chill well before serving.

2 lb (1 kg) mixed summer fruits such as raspberries, blackberries, blueberries, hulled strawberries, cherries, apricots, peaches, or nectarines

¾ cup (5½ oz/170 g) superfine (caster) sugar

1 tablespoon cornstarch (cornflour)

MAKES 6 SERVINGS

Hulling strawberries

To hull strawberries is to remove the stems. Insert the tip of a sharp paring knife near the edge of the stem, at a slight angle, and guide the knife tip around the stem cap, removing both the leaves and any white core directly beneath them. The berry is now ready for cutting as directed in a recipe.

544

ROASTED FIGS WITH VANILLA CRÈME FRAÎCHE

Figs have two short seasons, one in summer and one in autumn, so act quickly when you see them in the market. Here, they are split open, drizzled with vanilla syrup, then roasted. Choose firm but ripe figs, so they will hold their shape in the oven.

In a small saucepan, combine the sugar and 1 cup (8 fl oz/ 250 ml) water and bring to a boil over high heat, stirring until the sugar dissolves. Add the vanilla bean and boil for 3 minutes. Remove from the heat, cover, and let stand at room temperature for 3 hours or up to 24 hours. Remove and discard the vanilla bean.

Preheat the oven to 500°F (260°C).

Starting at the stem end, cut each fig lengthwise into quarters, stopping just short of the bottom so the quarters remain attached. Arrange the figs in a shallow baking dish. Pour about ⅔ cup (5 fl oz/160 ml) of the sugar syrup over and around the figs. (If you wish, reserve the remaining syrup for sweetening iced drinks.) Roast until the figs are tender yet hold their shape, 6–7 minutes. Meanwhile, stir the vanilla extract into the crème fraîche.

Remove the figs from the oven and transfer to a platter. Place a dollop of the crème fraîche in the center of each fig and serve right away.

1¼ cups (10 oz/315 g) sugar

½ vanilla bean, split lengthwise

16 firm but ripe figs

1 tablespoon pure vanilla extract, or as needed

1 cup (8 fl oz/250 ml) crème fraîche

MAKES 8 SERVINGS

Fig types

There are more than 150 recorded varieties of figs, with skin that can be purple, green, yellow, brown, or white. The most widely available are the green-skinned Adriatic; the small, dark purple Black Mission; the gold-skinned Calimyrna; the yellow-green, nearly seedless Kadota; and the amber-hued Smyrna.

CARAMELIZED PINEAPPLE

The juxtaposition of tart-sweet pineapple and a caramelized sour cream crust is irresistible. This is the perfect finale to a brunch meal, as it can be prepared in advance and broiled at the last minute. You can prepare 1½ pounds (750 g) seedless green grapes the same way.

1 large pineapple, peeled, cut into ½-inch (12-mm) thick slices, and cored, if necessary (see note, right)

3 tablespoons kirsch

1½–2 cups (12–16 oz/ 375–500 g) sour cream

⅔ cup (5 oz/155 g) firmly packed light brown sugar

MAKES 6 SERVINGS

Arrange the pineapple slices, slightly overlapping, in a shallow, flameproof baking dish. They should fit snugly. Sprinkle the kirsch evenly over the top. Cover tightly and refrigerate for at least 2 hours or up to 6 hours.

Preheat a broiler (grill).

Just before serving, spread the sour cream over the pineapple. Be sure the edges are completely covered and the layer of sour cream is about 1 inch (2.5 cm) thick. Evenly sprinkle the brown sugar over the sour cream. Immediately slip under the broiler and broil (grill) until the brown sugar bubbles and is caramelized, about 4 minutes. Serve right away.

Peeling and slicing pineapple

Cut off the top and bottom of the fruit. Stand the pineapple upright and cut off the peel in vertical strips. With the tip of the knife, cut out the small, brown round "eyes." Slice the pineapple crosswise, then check the core at the center of each slice. If it is fibrous, cut it out.

545

CINNAMON-BAKED APPLES

Brushing apples with cream and then rolling them in sugar before baking gives them an appealing crisp crust. Among baking apples, Rome Beauty holds its shape well. For the best results, select a baking dish large enough to hold the apples close together without touching.

8 large Rome Beauty apples

1¼ cups (10 oz/315 g) sugar

2 cups (16 fl oz/500 ml) heavy (double) cream

Ground cinnamon for sprinkling

MAKES 8 SERVINGS

Preheat the oven to 300°F (150°C).

Working with 1 apple at a time, use an apple corer to remove the core of the apple. Then, using a paring knife, make a cut just through the skin around the "waist" of each apple.

Place the sugar in a shallow bowl. Pour ⅓ cup (3 fl oz/80 ml) of the cream into another small bowl. Dip a pastry brush into the bowl of cream and paint the surface of an apple, then roll the apple in the sugar to coat completely. Place in the baking dish, stem end up, and sprinkle inside and out with cinnamon. Repeat with the remaining apples. Divide the sugar and cream remaining in the bowls among the apples, spooning them into the hollow cores. Pour ½ cup (4 fl oz/125 ml) water into the bottom of the baking dish.

Bake, basting occasionally with the pan liquid, until tender when pierced with a fork, about 1½ hours.

Serve warm or at room temperature. Pass the remaining cream at the table.

Storing apples

Because apples will continue to ripen at room temperature, refrigerate them in the cold back part of the refrigerator for 1 week or longer. If you plan to use the apples within a few days of purchase, they can be stored at room temperature.

AMARETTI-STUFFED BAKED PEACHES

About Marsala

A fortified wine from Sicily, Marsala is available either dry or sweet. For this recipe, look for sweet Marsala, which can also be served as an after-dinner drink to accompany the peaches.

Amaretti, Italy's classic almond-flavored cookies, are easy to find and make a delicious filling for baked peaches. The peaches can be assembled up to 6 hours in advance and refrigerated until baking time. Serve with peach, almond, or vanilla ice cream.

Preheat the oven to 375°F (190°C). Lightly butter a baking dish in which the halved peaches will fit loosely in a single layer.

Cut each peach in half through the stem end, then remove and discard the pit. Place the peach halves, cut sides up, in the prepared baking dish.

In a food processor, combine the amaretti, ½ cup (2 oz/60 g) of the almonds, the sugar, and ginger. Pulse a few times until crumbled. Add the butter and process just until a paste forms. Mound the almond paste in the centers of the peach halves, dividing it evenly.

Bake, basting the peaches with a little Marsala, until the fruit is tender and golden, about 25 minutes. Transfer to individual plates and garnish with the remaining ¼ cup (1 oz/30 g) almonds. Serve the peaches right away.

6 ripe peaches, peeled (see page 543)

14 amaretti

¾ cup (3 oz/90 g) sliced (flaked) almonds, toasted (see page 17)

¼ cup (2 oz/60 g) sugar

½ teaspoon ground ginger

½ cup (4 oz/125 g) unsalted butter, cut into 8 slices, at room temperature

½ cup (4 fl oz/125 ml) sweet Marsala, white wine, or fresh orange juice

MAKES 6 SERVINGS

546

PEARS POACHED IN RED WINE

About poaching

Poaching, or cooking foods in liquid just below the boiling point, is a gentle method that works well for delicate foods like fruits. As soon as the liquid comes to a boil, reduce the heat as needed to maintain a gentle simmer, with small bubbles slowly breaking on the surface of the liquid.

Prepare this recipe one or two nights before serving. Bosc, Winter Nellis, or Bartlett (Williams') pears are all perfect for poaching. To speed the preparation time, cut the pears in half lengthwise and remove the core, and reduce the poaching time by 10 minutes.

Fill a large bowl three-fourths full of water and add the lemon juice. Peel the pears. Using a corer and starting at the bottom, remove the core from each pear to within about ½ inch (12 mm) of the stem. As each pear is peeled and cored, slip it into the lemon water to cover.

In a large saucepan over high heat, combine the lemon and orange zests, cinnamon stick, star anise, cloves, sugar, wine, and ½ cup (4 fl oz/125 ml) water and bring to a boil. Add the pears, reduce the heat to low, and poach, uncovered, until a skewer penetrates a pear easily, about 35 minutes. Using a slotted spoon, transfer the pears to a bowl; set aside. Let the poaching liquid cool. Strain the liquid through a fine-mesh sieve into the bowl with the pears. Cover and refrigerate at least overnight or up to 2 days.

To serve, bring to room temperature or warm slightly over low heat. Serve in individual bowls with a little of the liquid.

Juice of 1 lemon

6 small, firm yet ripe pears

Grated zest of 1 lemon

Grated zest of 1 orange

1 cinnamon stick

1 star anise

3 whole cloves

1 cup (8 oz/250 g) sugar

3 cups (24 fl oz/750 ml) dry red wine such as Pinot Noir

MAKES 6 SERVINGS

PRUNES AND ORANGES IN ARMAGNAC

This is an adaptation of a famous recipe served in Gascony, a region of southwest France where both prunes and Armagnac—a smooth, aromatic brandy—are made. If Armagnac is unavailable, use a Cognac or other first-rate brandy. If desired, accompany with crisp cookies.

2 navel oranges

3 cups (18 oz/560 g) pitted whole prunes

1 cup (8 fl oz/250 ml) Armagnac

1 cup (8 fl oz/250 ml) fresh orange juice

1 cinnamon stick

2 cups (16 fl oz/500 ml) crème fraîche

MAKES 6–8 SERVINGS

Cut the oranges in half vertically. Cut each half crosswise into slices 1 inch (2.5 cm) thick or into wedges.

In a heavy 1½-qt (1.5-l) saucepan, combine the oranges, prunes, Armagnac, orange juice, ½ cup (4 fl oz/125 ml) water, and cinnamon stick. Place over medium heat, cover, and bring to a boil. Reduce the heat to low and simmer, covered, stirring gently every 10 minutes and adding more water if the pan becomes too dry, until the prunes are very soft and most of the liquid has been absorbed, 35–40 minutes. The liquid that remains should be very thick and syrupy. Remove from the heat and let cool to room temperature; cover and refrigerate until ready to serve.

To serve, discard the cinnamon stick. Spoon the fruit and syrup into individual bowls and top with the crème fraîche.

Substituting candied oranges

High-quality candied oranges can be used in place of the fresh oranges. Use 1 cup (6 oz/185 g), cut into 2-inch (5-cm) pieces, and add them during the last 10 minutes of cooking.

547

NAVEL ORANGES WITH GRAND MARNIER

Refreshing and brightly colored, this dessert offers a complex blend of orange flavors: navel oranges, candied orange peel, and a splash of Grand Marnier. In the wintertime, use red-hued blood oranges. Be sure to remove all of the pith from the oranges before using (see page 543).

4 large navel oranges

½ cup (4 oz/125 g) sugar

2–3 tablespoons Grand Marnier

Candied Citrus Peel (page 464), using oranges

MAKES 6 SERVINGS

Working with 1 orange at a time, and using a sharp knife, cut a thin slice from the top and the bottom to expose the flesh. Stand the fruit upright and, following the contour of the fruit, cut downward to remove all the peel, white membrane, and pith in a wide strip from top to bottom. Repeat, working your way around the fruit. Then cut each orange in half vertically and remove any white membrane on the cut surfaces. Cut the halves crosswise into slices ¼ inch (6 mm) thick. Place in a serving bowl and set aside.

In a small, heavy saucepan over medium-high heat, combine the sugar and 2 tablespoons water. Bring to a boil, without stirring, until bubbles cover the entire surface of the syrup. Boil for 1 minute longer and remove from the heat. Add the Grand Marnier to taste and stir well.

Pour the hot syrup over the orange slices and mix gently until evenly coated. Let cool to room temperature, then cover and refrigerate until cool, about 1 hour.

Garnish with the candied orange peel and serve.

Orange liqueurs

A wide variety of orange liqueurs are on the market. If you don't have or can't find Grand Marnier, you can substitute Cointreau, Curaçao, or Triple Sec.

BANANAS FOSTER

Spotless bananas

For this dessert, look for firm, bright yellow bananas with only a few dark speckles. Save any bananas with lots of brown spots for quick breads and other baked goods. Be sure to peel the fruits just before using, so they won't brown from exposure to the air.

This famous dessert was created by the Brennan family and has been served in their New Orleans restaurants since the 1950s. But you don't need to travel to New Orleans to enjoy it, because it is surprisingly easy to make it at home. Warming the rum makes igniting it easier.

In a chafing dish or frying pan over medium heat, melt the butter with the brown sugar. Add the lemon zest and cook, stirring to blend the butter and sugar thoroughly, for 2 minutes. Stir in the cinnamon. Reduce the heat to low, add the bananas, and cook, spooning the hot sauce over them frequently, until tender, 5–7 minutes; the timing depends on how ripe the bananas are.

Just before serving, divide the ice cream among 4–6 bowls. Pour the liqueur, rum, and lemon juice into a small saucepan and place over medium heat until warm.

Bring the pan holding the bananas, the pan of warmed spirits, and the bowls of ice cream to the table. Pour the liqueur mixture over the bananas and ignite with a long match. When the flames die out, spoon the bananas over the ice cream and serve right away.

6 tablespoons (3 oz/90 g) unsalted butter

½ cup (3½ oz/105 g) firmly packed dark brown sugar

Finely grated zest of 1 lemon

½ teaspoon ground cinnamon

4 bananas, peeled and halved lengthwise

1 pt (16 fl oz/500 ml) vanilla ice cream

¼ cup (2 fl oz/60 ml) banana liqueur

⅓ cup (3 fl oz/80 ml) light or dark rum

2 tablespoons fresh lemon juice

MAKES 4–6 SERVINGS

FLAMBÉED CHERRIES

About flambéing

When liquor is heated and ignited, some or most of the alcohol burns off, leaving behind a subtle flavor. Use a very small saucepan to warm the liquor over low heat until it is hot; do not allow the liquor to boil. When you are ready to flambé, move the liquor away from the stove, and hold a lighted long kitchen match just over the warmed liquor to light the fumes rising from it.

Using both kirsch and orange liqueur in this classic recipe ensures a decidedly adult dish. For a kid-friendly version, you can substitute orange juice for both the liqueurs; in that case, skip the flambéing step and instead pour the warmed fruit over the ice cream.

The night before, in a small saucepan over low heat, combine the dried cherries, ¼ cup (2 fl oz/60 ml) of the kirsch, and the orange juice and bring to a gentle simmer. Cook, uncovered, until the cherries have softened slightly and have begun to absorb the liquid; this will take several minutes. Remove from the heat, let cool, cover tightly, and let stand at room temperature overnight.

The same night, place the cherries, whether fresh or canned, in a bowl and add the liqueur. Cover the bowl and let the fruit stand at room temperature overnight.

At serving time, place the jelly in a large sauté pan over medium heat. Stir until the jelly melts, 2–3 minutes. Add both the dried and fresh or canned cherries and their soaking liquids and the orange zest. Reduce the heat to low; when the mixture begins to simmer, cook for 5 minutes.

¾ cup (3 oz/90 g) pitted dried sour cherries

¾ cup (6 fl oz/180 ml) kirsch

1 cup (8 fl oz/250 ml) fresh orange juice

2 lb (1 kg) dark sweet cherries, pitted, or 2 cans (16 oz/500 g each) pitted dark sweet cherries, drained

½ cup (4 fl oz/125 ml) orange liqueur

1 cup (10 oz/315 g) red currant jelly

1 tablespoon grated
orange zest

1 qt (1 l) vanilla or
cherry ice cream

MAKES 8–10 SERVINGS

Divide the ice cream among individual bowls. Pour the remaining ½ cup (4 fl oz/120 ml) kirsch into a small pan and warm over low heat. Pour the warm kirsch over the cherries and ignite with a long kitchen match. Stir, or slide the pan back and forth over the burner, until the flames die down, then immediately spoon the hot cherries and sauce over the ice cream and serve.

CARAMEL APPLES

Both children and grown-ups find these treats hard to resist, especially at Halloween time. If you wish, you can give the apples as Halloween-themed gifts: once the caramel is set, wrap each apple in orange cellophane, and then tie the with a black licorice whip.

6 small, unwaxed apples

1 cup (4 oz/125 g) sliced
almonds, chopped pecans,
granola, cookie crumbs,
or shredded dried coconut
for coating

1 package (14 oz/440 g)
caramels, unwrapped

MAKES 6 APPLES

Twist off the apple stems. Stick a wooden ice cream stick into the stem end of each apple until it's firmly inserted. Set the apples with sticks aside.

Line a rimmed baking sheet with waxed paper. Divide the nuts, granola, or other ingredients for coating into 6 equal rounds, each about as wide as an apple, on the waxed paper, spacing the rounds well apart.

Combine the caramels and 2 tablespoons water in the top pan of a double boiler or in a heatproof bowl. Place over (not touching) simmering water and heat, stirring often, until melted and smooth, about 10 minutes. Remove from the heat.

Holding an apple by the wooden stick, dip it in the hot caramel, turning the apple to coat and using a spoon as needed to coat the surface fully. Lift the apple, hold it over the pan, and twirl gently so that any excess caramel drips back into the pan. Set the bottom of the apple on a round of nuts (or other coating) on the baking sheet. Tip and turn the apple so the nuts coat the sides. Repeat with the remaining apples. If the caramel gets too firm before you have coated all of the apples, place the pan over the simmering water again until the caramel is soft enough to coat.

Put the tray of apples in the refrigerator until the caramel is set, at least 1 hour, before serving.

Getting sticky

When it comes time to coat the apples with nuts or other coating ingredients, you may need to use your fingers to press the coating to help it stick.

549

CREPES SUZETTE

Flambéing safety

To flambé safely, remove the pan from the heat before adding any liquor. Make sure the overhead fan is off. Keep loose clothing and hair away from the pan, and use a long-handled kitchen match to ignite the hot liquor. Keep a pot lid nearby to cover the pan if the flames don't subside within a minute.

A French bistro classic, these orange-flavored sweet crepes are easy to make at home. If you don't own a crepe pan, you can cook the crepes in a small nonstick frying pan. The first one you make will probably not turn out well enough to use. Snack on it while you make the others.

To make the filling, in a bowl, mix together the butter, confectioners' sugar, 1 tablespoon Grand Marnier, and the orange zest until smooth.

Place 1 crepe, speckled side up, on a work surface. Spread 1½ teaspoons filling on the top half of the crepe. Fold the bottom half over the filling, then fold again to form a triangle. Repeat with the remaining crepes and filling. Use right away, or cover and refrigerate for up to 6 hours.

Pour the orange juice into a large frying pan and set over medium-high heat. Bring to a boil and cook until reduced by about ½ cup (4 fl oz/125 ml). Reduce the heat to medium-low and slide all the folded crepes into the pan. Baste with the orange juice, then simmer gently until the crepes are warm, about 1 minute. Arrange the crepes on a warmed serving platter and sprinkle the sugar over the crepes.

Pour the ⅓ cup (3 fl oz/80 ml) Grand Marnier and the Cognac into a small saucepan and warm gently over low heat. Remove from the heat and carefully ignite with a long match. Pour the flaming liquid over the crepes and serve right away, garnished with zest strips.

½ cup (4 oz/125 g) unsalted butter, at room temperature

⅓ cup (1⅓ oz/40 g) confectioners' (icing) sugar

1 tablespoon plus ⅓ cup (3 fl oz/80 ml) Grand Marnier or other orange liqueur

1½ teaspoons grated orange zest

Sweet Crepes (page 50)

1¾ cups (14 fl oz/430 ml) fresh orange juice

2 tablespoons granulated sugar

2 tablespoons Cognac

Orange zest strips for garnish

MAKES 4 SERVINGS

FRUIT AND YOGURT PARFAITS

A healthful alternative

You can make this dessert more healthful by using nonfat milk, low-fat yogurt, and by substituting low-fat cottage cheese for the ricotta. Prepared this way, and without the liqueur, it also makes a delicious breakfast.

A sweetened and flavored purée of ricotta cheese and yogurt makes a luxurious filling for a fresh-fruit parfait. You'll need to plan ahead, as the ricotta mixture must chill for an hour or two before you assemble the parfaits.

In a small saucepan, sprinkle the gelatin over the milk and let stand for a few minutes to soften.

In a food processor or blender, combine the ricotta, yogurt, vanilla, salt, and 6 tablespoons (3 oz/90 g) of the sugar. Process until the mixture is smooth and well blended. Scrape the mixture into a bowl.

Place the saucepan with the softened gelatin over low heat and stir until the gelatin dissolves, about 2 minutes. Do not allow to boil. Add the gelatin to the cottage cheese mixture and whisk to mix thoroughly. Cover tightly and refrigerate, stirring occasionally, until chilled, 1–2 hours.

Halve and pit the peaches, then slice. In a bowl, combine the peaches, berries, rum, and remaining 2 tablespoons sugar. Toss gently to mix.

1½ teaspoons unflavored gelatin

¼ cup (2 fl oz/60 ml) milk

1 cup (8 oz/250 g) ricotta cheese

⅓ cup (3 oz/90 g) plain yogurt

1½ teaspoons pure vanilla extract

Pinch of salt

8 tablespoons (4 oz/125 g) sugar

3 ripe peaches, peeled (see page 543)

2 cups (8 oz/250 g) mixed berries such as raspberries, blueberries, or sliced strawberries, or a mixture

2 tablespoons light or dark rum or orange liqueur

2 tablespoons finely crushed gingersnaps, optional

MAKES 4 SERVINGS

To assemble the parfaits, in glass dishes or tall, footed glasses, alternate layers of the cheese and fruit mixtures, beginning with the cheese and ending with the fruit. Dust the tops with the gingersnap crumbs, if using. Serve right away or refrigerate for up to 6 hours before serving.

RHUBARB FOOL

A fool is a traditional English dessert, usually made from puréed fruit combined with whipped cream. It is among the simplest types of fruit dessert you can make, and a variety of different fruit purées will work, particularly those with a tart edge, such as raspberries, apricots, or plums.

2½ cups (10 oz/315 g) rhubarb pieces (½-inch/12-mm pieces)

¾ cup (6 oz/185 g) granulated sugar, or more as needed

1½ cups (12 fl oz/375 ml) heavy (double) cream

1½ tablespoons confectioners' (icing) sugar

1 tablespoon raspberry liqueur, optional

MAKES 6 SERVINGS

In a saucepan over low heat, combine the rhubarb, ⅔ cup (5 fl oz/160 ml) water, and the granulated sugar, cover, and cook, stirring occasionally, until the rhubarb is tender and is starting to break down, about 8 minutes.

Transfer the rhubarb and its juices to a food processor and process until smooth. Taste and add more sugar as needed. Transfer to a bowl, cover, and refrigerate for at least 1 hour or for up to 3 days.

In a bowl, using a whisk or an electric mixer on medium-high speed, whip the cream with the confectioners' sugar until soft peaks form. Whisk in the liqueur, if using.

To serve the dessert, divide half of the rhubarb purée evenly among goblets or dessert cups. Layer half of the flavored cream on top. Spoon the remaining rhubarb on top of the cream, then top with the remaining cream. Refrigerate for at least 30 minutes or up to 1 hour before serving.

Rhubarb types

Field rhubarb is available in summer and is a bright cherry red. Its flavor is more pronounced than that of hothouse rhubarb, which is a brilliant pink and is available year-round.

551

BROWN SUGAR BANANAS IN COOKIE CUPS

Lemon zester

This specialized tool boasts a row of 4 to 6 sharp-edged small holes at the end of a short handle. When drawn across the surface of a citrus fruit, it removes thin, even strips of colorful zest, while leaving behind the bitter white pith.

This impressive dessert is a good recipe for entertaining, because much of it can be made ahead. The *tuile* cups can be baked up to 2 weeks in advance, and the cream mixture can be assembled up to 1 hour before serving and refrigerated. Slice the bananas at the last minute.

In a bowl, using an electric mixer on medium-high speed, whip the cream until stiff peaks form. In another bowl, stir together the brown sugar and yogurt. Gently fold the yogurt mixture into the whipped cream.

Using a zester (see note, left), remove the zest from the lemon in long, fine strips. Finely chop enough of the zest to yield 1 teaspoon. Reserve the remaining zest strips. Then squeeze 1 tablespoon juice from the lemon.

Peel and slice the bananas. Place in a bowl and sprinkle with the lemon juice and the chopped zest. Toss gently to mix. Fold the bananas into the cream-yogurt mixture.

Divide the mixture among the cookie cups. Decorate with the zest strips and serve right away.

1 cup (8 fl oz/250 ml) heavy (double) cream

2 tablespoons firmly packed dark brown sugar

1 cup (8 oz/250 g) plain yogurt

1 lemon

4 bananas

8 Pecan Tuiles (page 484), shaped into cups

MAKES 8 SERVINGS

552

STRAWBERRIES ROMANOFF

Topping alternatives

Other good toppings for a bowl of perfectly ripe strawberries include White Chocolate Cream (page 453), Ginger or Orange Sabayon Cream (page 453), or Chocolate Whipped Cream (page 454).

The perfect ending to a summer meal, this eye-catching yet easy dessert requires a little advance planning. Prepare the strawberries at least 2 hours before serving. The macerated berries and the whipped cream are also good spooned between split shortcakes (page 562).

Stem the strawberries and cut in half lengthwise. Place in a bowl and sprinkle with the orange juice, sugar, and liqueur. Cover and refrigerate for at least 2 hours or up to 8 hours.

Just before serving, soften the ice cream on the counter for 15–20 minutes or in a microwave oven for 15–20 seconds. In a bowl, using an electric mixer on medium-high speed, whip the heavy cream until stiff peaks form. Add the softened ice cream and beat until blended.

Divide the strawberries and their juices among individual bowls. Top each serving with a generous amount of the cream and serve right away.

4 cups (1 lb/500 g) strawberries

¼ cup (2 fl oz/60 ml) fresh orange juice

2 tablespoons sugar

2 tablespoons orange liqueur

1 cup (8 fl oz/250 ml) vanilla ice cream

2 cups (16 fl oz/500 ml) heavy (double) cream

MAKES 8 SERVINGS

FRUIT WITH LEMON-SCENTED RICOTTA

You will need very fresh and creamy ricotta for this easy, elegant recipe. Look for it at an Italian deli, cheese store, or at a food store with a well-stocked cheese department. Accompany with berries such as raspberries or sliced strawberries, or 2 or 3 peaches, peeled, pitted, and sliced.

2 cups (1 lb/500 g) ricotta cheese

⅓ cup (3 oz/90 g) sugar

⅓ cup (3 fl oz/80 ml) dark rum

2 tablespoons grated lemon zest, plus finely shredded zest for garnish

2 tablespoons fresh lemon juice

1½–2 cups (280–370 g) fruit of your choice (see note, above)

MAKES 4–6 SERVINGS

In a bowl, using an electric mixer on medium speed, beat together the ricotta, sugar, rum, grated lemon zest, and lemon juice until well blended.

Spoon the ricotta mixture into ramekins or custard cups, cover, and refrigerate until well chilled and the flavors have married, about 24 hours.

Top each ramekin evenly with fruit. Serve right away garnished with shredded lemon zest.

Lemon-ricotta parfaits

To serve the ricotta in a fruit parfait, layer it in tall, narrow, footed glasses with diced fresh fruits of your choice. Garnish with lemon zest or small fresh mint leaves and serve with long spoons.

553

APPLE FRITTERS

Eat these deep-fried treats as soon as they are made. If left to sit, they will turn soggy and unappealing. They are a welcome brunch dessert, especially when drizzled with maple syrup. If you have an open kitchen, invite guests to snatch them off a plate as soon as they are made.

4 Granny Smith or other firm, tart apples, peeled, cored (see page 543), and sliced into rings ½ inch (12 mm) thick

½ cup (3½ oz/105 g) firmly packed light brown sugar

1 cup (5 oz/155 g) all-purpose (plain) flour

1 tablespoon canola oil, plus oil for deep-frying

1 extra-large egg, separated

¾ cup (6 fl oz/180 ml) milk

Confectioners' (icing) sugar for dusting

MAKES 4–6 SERVINGS

In a bowl, toss together the apple rings and brown sugar until evenly coated. Spread on paper towels to dry slightly.

Sift the flour into a large bowl. Make a well in the center, and add the 1 tablespoon oil and the egg yolk to the well. While mixing gently with a fork, drizzle the milk into the well, stirring to form a smooth batter.

In a separate bowl, beat the egg white until it holds firm peaks. Fold the egg white into the batter.

Pour oil to a depth of 1½ inches (4 cm) into a deep frying pan and heat 375°F (190°C) on a deep-frying thermometer. Dip 1 apple ring into the batter, allowing any excess batter to drip back into the bowl, and slip the ring into the hot oil. Repeat with 1 or 2 more rings. Fry on the first sides until golden brown, about 4 minutes. Using a slotted spoon, turn and fry on the second sides until golden brown, 2–3 minutes longer. Using a slotted spoon, transfer to paper towels to drain. Repeat with the remaining apple rings.

Place the warm fritters on a warmed serving platter or on individual plates. Using a fine-mesh sieve, dust with confectioners' sugar and serve right away.

Deep-frying safety

The following tips will help you cook safely whenever you are deep-frying. Make sure the handle of the pot is turned away from the front of the stove. Do not let the oil heat to 400°F (200°C) or beyond, or it could burst into flames. And clean any drips on the outside of the pan, as they can catch fire.

PLUMS IN ALMOND CUSTARD

Halving and pitting a plum

The best way to cut plums in half is to cut completely around the pit, working from the stem end at top to the blossom end at bottom. (Some plums have a natural indentation, which you can trace with your knife.) Then, grasping each half of the plum, twist the halves in opposite directions. Dislodge the pit and discard.

Here, the cinnamon-scented cookielike crust makes an ideal platform for the tartness of the plums. A thin layer of almond-scented custard surrounding each piece of fruit mellows the flavor even more. Any leftovers are a great breakfast for a lucky early riser.

Preheat the oven to 400°F (200°C). In a food processor, combine the butter and sugar and process until fluffy, about 1 minute. Add the flour, cinnamon, salt, and baking powder and process until the mixture is crumbly. Remove about ¼ cup (2 oz/60 g) of the mixture and set aside.

Transfer the remaining crumb mixture to a 9-by-13-inch (23-by-33-cm) baking dish or an 11-inch (28-cm) quiche dish. Pat and press the mixture evenly over the bottom and about 1 inch (2.5 cm) up the sides. Halve the plums lengthwise, discarding their pits. Cut each half in half again to make quarters. Arrange the plum quarters in a single layer on top of the crust. Sprinkle the reserved crumb mixture around the plums. Roast for 20 minutes.

Meanwhile, whisk together the cream, half-and-half, egg, and almond extract. Set aside.

Remove the plums from the oven, pour the egg mixture over them, return to the oven, and roast until a knife inserted into the custard comes out clean, about 25 minutes longer. Let cool completely on a wire rack before serving.

½ cup (4 oz/125 g) unsalted butter, at room temperature

1 cup (8 oz/250 g) sugar

1¼ cups (6½ oz/200 g) all-purpose (plain) flour

½ teaspoon *each* ground cinnamon and salt

¼ teaspoon baking powder

8 or 9 tart, firm, slightly underripe black plums

½ cup (4 fl oz/125 ml) *each* heavy (double) cream and half-and-half (half cream)

1 egg

½ teaspoon pure almond extract

MAKES 6–8 SERVINGS

CHERRY CLAFOUTIS

Keeping things clean

When pitting a large quantity of cherries, slip your hands inside a plastic bag. That way, the cherry juice won't stain the work surface, and the stems and pits are easy to discard.

A clafoutis is a traditional cherry pudding cake from the Limousin region of France. Today, it is also made with other fruits, including apricots, nectarines, pears, and blackberries. The cake puffs in the oven as it bakes, but collapses almost immediately once it is removed.

Preheat the oven to 350°F (180°C). Generously butter a shallow 2-qt (2-l) baking dish.

In a bowl, using an electric mixer on medium speed, beat together the milk, cream, eggs, vanilla, flour, granulated sugar, and salt until frothy, about 5 minutes.

Pour the batter into the prepared baking dish to a depth of about ¼ inch (6 mm) deep. Bake for 2 minutes, then remove from the oven. Cover the surface with the cherries in a single layer, and pour the remaining batter on top. Continue to bake until puffed and brown and a knife inserted into the center comes out clean, 30–35 minutes. Let cool on a wire rack.

Serve warm or at room temperature directly from the dish. Just before serving, using a fine-mesh sieve, dust the top with the confectioners' sugar.

1 cup (8 fl oz/250 ml) milk

¼ cup (2 fl oz/60 ml) heavy (double) cream

3 eggs

1 tablespoon pure vanilla extract

⅔ cup (3 oz/90 g) all-purpose (plain) flour, sifted

¼ cup (2 oz/60 g) granulated sugar

½ teaspoon salt

1–1½ lb (500–750 g) sweet or sour cherries, pitted

1 tablespoon confectioners' (icing) sugar

MAKES 6–8 SERVINGS

PEAR AND HONEY CLAFOUTIS

Choose a good all-purpose pear for this recipe, such as Royal Riviera or Comice, which will hold its shape well in the heat of the oven. Lining the baking pan with aluminum foil make spills or overflows easier to clean up.

3 lb (1.5 kg) ripe pears, peeled, halved cored, and sliced

1 cup (6 oz/185 g) dried pears, cut into 1-inch (2.5-cm) pieces

1 teaspoon grated lime zest

4 eggs, lightly beaten

⅓ cup (2½ oz/75 g) firmly packed dark brown sugar

1 cup (8 fl oz/250 ml) half-and-half (half cream)

2 tablespoons unsalted butter, melted

⅓ cup (3 fl oz/90 ml) honey

MAKES 6–8 SERVINGS

Preheat the oven to 350°F (180°C). Line a large baking pan with aluminum foil. Generously butter a shallow 1½-qt (48–fl oz/1.5-l) baking dish or quiche dish. Place the dish in the prepared baking pan.

Place the ripe and dried pears in a large bowl. Add the lime zest, eggs, brown sugar, half-and-half, and butter and mix gently to coat the pears evenly. Using a spoon, transfer enough of the liquid from the pear mixture to the prepared dish to form a thin layer on the bottom. Using a slotted spoon, transfer the fruit to the dish, arranging it in an even layer. Pour the remaining liquid over the top. Drizzle evenly with the honey.

Bake until the top is puffed and golden brown, 25–30 minutes. Serve warm or at room temperature.

An authentic finale

For a fitting ending to a dinner party that features this French-inspired dessert, serve small glasses of poire Williams, a French fruit brandy, or eau-de-vie, made from Bartlett (Williams') pears, which were first cultivated in England.

PAVLOVA WITH KIWIFRUIT

Both Australia and New Zealand claim credit for this dessert, a light dish created to commemorate a visit by Russian ballerina Anna Pavlova. The baked meringue can be made several days ahead and stored, lightly covered, at room temperature in a dry place.

2 egg whites

1 teaspoon cornstarch (cornflour)

1 cup (8 oz/250 g) sugar

1 teaspoon fresh lemon juice

1 teaspoon pure vanilla extract

6 kiwifruit, about 1 lb (500 g) total weight

Whipped Cream (page 454)

MAKES 6–8 SERVINGS

Position a rack in the lower third of the oven and preheat to 300°F (150°C). Line a baking sheet with parchment (baking) paper. Draw a 9-inch (23-cm) circle on the parchment, then turn the parchment upside down; the circle should be visible.

In a bowl, using an electric mixer on medium speed, beat the egg whites until blended. Sprinkle on the cornstarch and beat until opaque and foamy. On medium-high speed, gradually add the sugar and then continue to beat until stiff, glossy peaks form. Beat in the lemon juice and vanilla. Use a pastry (piping) bag fitted with a large star or plain tip to pipe a tight spiral of meringue to fill the circle completely.

Bake until crisp, about 40 minutes. Turn off the oven and open the oven door. When the meringue is completely cool, transfer to a serving plate.

Peel the kiwifruit and slice them ¼ inch (6 mm) thick. Spread the whipped cream evenly over the meringue. Arrange the kiwifruit slices in an attractive pattern on top. Let stand for 10 minutes before serving.

Vary the fruits

Although kiwifruits are classic in the Pavlova, you can use nearly about any fruit you like. Try strawberries, raspberries, peaches, plums, nectarines, or mangoes.

APPLE CHARLOTTE

Double the apple flavor

If desired, use Calvados in place of the brandy to lend an extra layer of apple flavor to this recipe. A specialty of Normandy, France, Calvados is distilled from the juice of the apples that proliferate in the fertile region.

A charlotte is a molded dessert traditionally baked in a pail-like metal baking pan with fluted sides. If you don't have a charlotte mold, you can use a 1½-qt (1.5-l) soufflé dish. The mold is lined with white bread, which soaks up the delicious juices from the apple filling as it bakes.

Position a rack in the lower third of the oven and preheat to 425°F (220°C).

In a large, heavy sauté pan over medium heat, combine the apples and 2 tablespoons of the melted butter and cook, stirring occasionally, until the apples begin to soften, about 5 minutes. Add the granulated sugar, cinnamon, and lemon zest and stir until well blended. Continue to cook, stirring occasionally, until the apples break down into a very thick purée, about 15 minutes. Remove from the heat and stir in the vanilla. If the apples are very tart, add a bit more sugar. You should have 5–6 cups (40–48 fl oz/1.25–1.5 l) apple purée.

Line the bottom and sides of a 1½-qt (1.5-l) charlotte mold with the bread slices, without overlapping them, trimming them to fit as needed. Pour the remaining melted butter into a shallow bowl. Remove the bread slices from the mold, dip them in the melted butter, and then return them to the mold. Spoon in the apple mixture. Dip the remaining bread in the remaining butter and arrange on top of the apple mixture in a single layer, again trimming as needed.

Bake for 10 minutes. Reduce the oven temperature to 350°F (180°C) and continue baking until golden, about 30 minutes longer. Let cool on a wire rack for 30 minutes. Invert the charlotte onto a serving plate and lift off the mold.

Meanwhile, in a chilled bowl, using chilled beaters, whip together the cream and confectioners' sugar on medium-high speed until soft peaks form. Fold in the 3 tablespoons brandy, if using, then cover and refrigerate until serving.

In a small saucepan over low heat, stir together the jam and ¼ cup (2 fl oz/60 ml) water until the jam melts and a sauce forms. Stir in the ¼ cup (2 fl oz/60 ml) brandy, if using.

To serve, top the warm charlotte with the brandy whipped cream and garnish with the orange zest. Serve the apricot sauce on the side.

12 McIntosh, Empire, or Rome Beauty apples, peeled, cored, and cubed

¾ cup (6 oz/185 g) unsalted butter, melted

¾ cup (6 oz/185 g) granulated sugar, or as needed

½ teaspoon ground cinnamon

1 tablespoon grated lemon zest

1 teaspoon pure vanilla extract

12–15 slices white bread, each about ¼ inch (6 mm) thick, crusts removed

1 cup (8 fl oz/250 ml) heavy (double) cream

¼ cup (1 oz/30 g) confectioners' (icing) sugar, sifted

3 tablespoons plus ¼ cup (2 fl oz/60 ml) brandy, optional

1 cup (10 oz/315 g) apricot jam

Grated orange zest or Candied Citrus Peel (page 464) for garnish

MAKES 6–8 SERVINGS

PEACH OR NECTARINE GRATIN

Several hours in advance, you can assemble the fruit in a baking dish and make the sour cream topping and refrigerate them. Then, just before serving, bring the fruit to room temperature, spoon the topping on the fruit, sprinkle with the sugar, and broil.

4 cups (1½ lb/750 g) peeled, pitted, and sliced ripe peaches or nectarines

1½ teaspoons fresh lemon juice

½ teaspoon pure almond extract

1 cup (8 oz/250 g) sour cream

2 tablespoons milk or half-and-half (half cream)

¼ cup (2 oz/60 g) granulated sugar

½ cup (3½ oz/105 g) firmly packed dark brown sugar, or as needed

MAKES 4 SERVINGS

Preheat a broiler (grill).

Butter a flameproof 9-inch (23-cm) square baking dish. Place the fruit in the dish. Sprinkle evenly with the lemon juice and ¼ teaspoon of the almond extract and toss lightly.

In a bowl, whisk together the sour cream, milk, the remaining ¼ teaspoon almond extract, and the granulated sugar. Spoon evenly over the fruit. Sprinkle the ½ cup (3½ oz/105 g) brown sugar evenly over the sour cream layer, adding more sugar if needed to cover.

Broil (grill) until the sugar melts, 6–8 minutes. Serve right away directly from the dish.

About gratins

Any recipe with the term gratin, gratinée, or au gratin in its name refers to a dish with a browned, crisp crust, which is usually the result of topping the dish with bread crumbs, sugar, ground nuts, grated cheese, or some kind of sauce and then browning in the oven or broiler (grill). The terms are used for both sweet and savory preparations.

557

BERRY GRATIN

You can use any berries you like for this dish, but the combination of bright, flavorful raspberries and plump, sweet blackberries is a showstopper. Plan on preparing the light, frothy sabayon topping at least 4 hours before serving to allow time for it to chill fully.

3 extra-large egg yolks

½ cup (4 oz/125 g) sugar

½ cup (4 fl oz/125 ml) framboise

2 cups (16 fl oz/500 ml) heavy (double) cream

3 cups (12 oz/375 g) raspberries

3 cups (12 oz/375 g) blackberries

MAKES 8 SERVINGS

Combine the egg yolks, 1 tablespoon water, and sugar in a heatproof bowl and place over (not touching) simmering water. Whisk constantly until the mixture is foamy and begins to thicken slightly, 2–3 minutes. Immediately remove from the heat and strain through a fine-mesh sieve into a 2-qt (2-l) metal bowl. (The metal bowl will help to quickly cool down the mixture.) Stir in the framboise, cover, and refrigerate for at least 4 hours or up to overnight.

Preheat the broiler (grill).

In a large chilled bowl, using chilled beaters, whip the cream on medium-high speed until stiff peaks form. Gently fold the cream into the chilled custard just until combined. Scatter the berries over the bottom of a 2-qt (2-l) flameproof baking dish with at least 1-inch (2.5-cm) sides. Place the dish on a baking sheet. Gently pour and spoon the custard evenly over the berries. Broil (grill) until the top is browned and bubbling, 1½–2 minutes. Serve right away directly from the dish.

About framboise

Framboise is a popular French clear brandy, or eau-de-vie (in French, framboise means "raspberry"), made by distilling fermented berries. It should not be confused with raspberry liqueur, which is sweeter and more viscous.

WARM PLUMS WITH ALMOND STREUSEL

**Almond
streusel topping**

*Stir together 6 tbsp
(2 oz/60 g) all-purpose
(plain) flour, 6 tbsp
(3 oz/90 g) firmly
packed light brown
sugar, and ¼ tsp
cinnamon. Add ⅔ cup
(2½ oz/75 g) sliced
(flaked) almonds and
4½ tbsp (2¼ oz/67 g)
cold unsalted butter,
diced. Rub the
mixture between
your fingertips until
small clumps form.*

In this mouthwatering gratin, a sweet almond streusel covers spice-dusted plums. Plums vary in sweetness; after mixing the plums with the spices and sugar, taste to see if additional sugar is needed. Top each serving with a dollop of sour cream sweetened to taste with honey.

Preheat the oven to 375°F (190°C). Generously butter a shallow 2-qt (2-l) baking dish.

Halve the plums and discard the pits. Cut each half into 4 wedges. In a large bowl, stir together the brown sugar, flour, cinnamon, and ginger. Add the plums and toss to coat well. Spread the plum mixture in the prepared baking dish. Pat the streusel evenly over the top of the plums.

Bake until the top has browned, the juices are bubbling, and the plums are tender when pierced with a fork, about 40 minutes. Let cool slightly before serving.

Unsalted butter
for baking dish

2 lb (1 kg) firm, slightly
underripe dark red or
purple plums

5 tablespoons (2½ oz/75 g)
firmly packed light
brown sugar

3 tablespoons all-purpose
(plain) flour

¾ teaspoon ground
cinnamon

¼ teaspoon ground ginger

Almond streusel topping
(see note, left)

MAKES 6 SERVINGS

BLUEBERRY CRISP

Individual crisps

*To make this dessert
into individual
crisps, divide the
blueberry mixture
among 6 small
buttered ramekins.
Top with the oat
mixture and reduce
the baking time by
5–10 minutes.*

Tart blueberries and a slightly crunchy, sweet topping come together in this easy-to-make dessert. For maximum flavor, look for fresh or frozen wild berries or even huckleberries. Serve with vanilla ice cream or Whipped Cream (page 454).

Preheat the oven to 375°F (190°C). Generously butter a shallow 1½-qt (1.5-l) baking dish.

Spread the berries evenly over the bottom of the prepared baking dish and sprinkle evenly with the lemon juice.

In a bowl, using a fork, toss and stir together the brown sugar, flour, cinnamon, butter, and oats until well combined. Sprinkle evenly over the blueberries.

Bake until the top is golden and the blueberries are bubbling, about 30 minutes. Let cool for at least a few minutes on a wire rack. Serve hot or warm.

4 cups (1 lb/500 g) fresh or
thawed, frozen blueberries

1 tablespoon fresh
lemon juice

¾ cup (6 oz/185 g) firmly
packed light brown sugar

½ cup (2½ oz/75 g)
all-purpose (plain) flour

½ teaspoon ground
cinnamon

¼ cup (2 oz/60 g) unsalted
butter, cut into pieces, at
room temperature

¾ cup (2½ oz/75 g)
old-fashioned rolled oats

MAKES 6 SERVINGS

STRAWBERRY-RHUBARB BROWN BETTY

Here, the fruits are sandwiched between two layers of a nutmeg-laced mixture of bread crumbs and brown sugar, with the crumb mixture on the bottom of the baking dish soaking up the juices of the fruits and the mixture on top forming a crisp crust.

2 cups (4 oz/125 g) fine fresh bread crumbs

1 cup (7 oz/220 g) firmly packed light brown sugar

½ teaspoon freshly grated nutmeg

½ cup (4 oz/125 g) unsalted butter, melted

2½ cups (12 oz/375 g) thinly sliced rhubarb

6 cups (1½ lb/750 g) sliced strawberries

MAKES 8 SERVINGS

Preheat the oven to 375°F (190°C). Butter a 2½-qt (2.5-l) shallow baking dish.

In a bowl, using a fork, stir together the bread crumbs and brown sugar. Add the nutmeg and melted butter and stir until all the ingredients are evenly distributed. In another bowl, combine the rhubarb and strawberries and toss to mix. Sprinkle half of the crumb mixture in the bottom of the prepared dish. Spread the fruit mixture evenly over the top, then sprinkle with the remaining crumb mixture.

Bake until the top is golden and the fruit is bubbling, about 45 minutes. Let cool on a wire rack for at least for 15 minutes. Serve warm or at room temperature.

About betties

The old-fashioned brown Betty, which originated in England, was a popular dessert during colonial times in the United States. It uses toasted, sweetened bread crumbs to give baked fruit a nutty flavor and crisp texture.

559

APPLE CRUMBLE

Most apples are harvested in the fall, the best time to make this comforting dessert that takes just minutes to assemble. If desired, you can substitute Anjou pears for the apples and reduce the baking time by 10 to 20 minutes. Or, you can add 1 cup fresh cranberries before baking.

5 large apples, peeled, halved, cored, and thickly sliced

½ cup (4 fl oz/125 ml) apple cider

Juice of ½ lemon

½ teaspoon ground cinnamon

¼ teaspoon ground allspice

¾ cup (6 oz/185 g) sugar

¾ cup (4 oz/125 g) all-purpose (plain) flour

½ cup (4 oz/125 g) unsalted butter, cut into 8 pieces

MAKES 6 SERVINGS

Preheat the oven to 350°F (180°C). Generously butter a 2½-qt (2½-l) baking dish.

Arrange the apple slices in the prepared dish. Pour the apple cider over the apples, and then sprinkle evenly with the lemon juice, cinnamon, and allspice. Toss gently to combine.

In a bowl, stir together the sugar and flour. Scatter the butter pieces over the top. Using your fingertips, 2 knives, or a pastry blender, cut in the butter until the mixture resembles fine crumbs. Sprinkle the crumb mixture evenly over the apples in the baking dish.

Bake until the apples are tender, the juices are bubbling, and the topping is light golden brown, about 1 hour. Serve right away, or let cool on a wire rack and serve warm or at room temperature directly from the baking dish.

Crumbles vs. crisps

For crumbles, fruit is topped with a crumbly pastry mixture, similar to streusel, before baking. Crisps, in contrast, add oats and sometimes nuts to the flavorful topping.

CRANBERRY-APPLE SLUMP

About slumps

Similar to cobblers, slumps are fruit mixtures that are topped with a biscuit-type dough before baking. Cooks differ in their approach to the biscuit topping. Some like to cut biscuits from rolled-out dough and others prefer drop-style biscuits.

The flavors of apples and cranberries complement each other. In this cobblerlike dessert, they are baked with a biscuit topping. The juices from the fruit bubble up through the nooks and crannies and are absorbed by the flaky dough. Accompany servings with vanilla ice cream.

Preheat the oven to 375°F (190°C).

In a large bowl, combine the apples and cranberries. Add the sugar and toss to mix. Scatter the fruit mixture evenly over the bottom of a large ovenproof frying pan. Place over medium heat and cook, uncovered, until the juices are bubbling, about 10 minutes.

Meanwhile, make the biscuit topping. In a bowl, sift together the flour, baking powder, and salt. Scatter the butter over the top. Using a pastry blender or 2 knives, cut the butter into the flour mixture until the mixture is the consistency of coarse meal. Gradually add the milk while stirring with a fork just until the ingredients are moistened and cling together. Do not overmix.

For cut biscuits, turn the dough out onto a lightly floured work surface, knead briefly to bring the dough together, and roll out ¾ inch (2 cm) thick. Using a biscuit cutter or a glass 2 inches (5 cm) in diameter, cut out the biscuits. Place atop the apples and cranberries, arranging them evenly on the surface. For drop biscuits, drop the dough by heaping tablespoons evenly onto the fruits.

Bake until the biscuits are golden and the fruit is bubbling, about 35 minutes. Serve right away, or let cool on a wire rack and serve warm or at room temperature.

1½ lb (750 g) Granny Smith or other firm, tart apples, peeled, halved, cored, and sliced

2 cups (8 oz/250 g) fresh or thawed, frozen cranberries

1 cup (8 oz/250 g) sugar

FOR THE BISCUIT TOPPING

1¼ cups (6½ oz/200 g) all-purpose (plain) flour

2 teaspoons baking powder

½ teaspoon salt

6 tablespoons (3 oz/90 g) unsalted butter, cut into tablespoon-sized pieces, at room temperature

½ cup (4 fl oz/125 ml) milk

Grated zest of 1 orange

MAKES 6 SERVINGS

NECTARINE-BLACKBERRY COBBLER

Local blackberries

In the height of summer, comb your local farm stand for blackberry hybrids, which are perfect for baking into cobblers and other desserts. Depending on where you live, you might find large, purple boysenberries; dark, cone-shaped logan-berries; sweet, firm marionberries; or large, fragrant olallieberries.

For this old-fashioned dish, the tart, distinct flavors of nectarines and blackberries meet under a shortcake crust. To be sure the blackberries are at their sweet best, look for fruits that are completely black with no traces of green or red.

Preheat the oven to 450°F (230°C).

In a bowl, combine the blackberries and nectarines. Gently stir in the lemon juice. In a small bowl, stir together the sugar and flour, then sprinkle over the fruits. Turn the fruits in the sugar mixture, coating them evenly. Set aside.

To make the crust, in a bowl, stir together the flour, baking powder, and salt. Scatter the butter over top. Using a pastry blender or 2 knives, cut the butter into the flour mixture until pea-size pieces form. You might want to finish this step with your fingertips. Using a fork, gradually stir in the milk, mixing just until the dough clings together. Gather the dough into a ball and transfer to a floured work surface. Using your

2 cups (8 oz/250 g) blackberries

3 firm but ripe nectarines, pitted and sliced to make about 2 cups (12 oz/375 g)

1 teaspoon fresh lemon juice

½ cup (4 oz/125 g) sugar

2 tablespoons all-purpose (plain) flour

FOR THE CRUST

1 cup (5 oz/155 g) all-purpose (plain) flour

1¼ teaspoons baking powder

½ teaspoon salt

4 tablespoons (2 oz/60 g) cold unsalted butter, cut into 3 or 4 pieces

¼ cup (2 fl oz/60 ml) milk

MAKES 6 SERVINGS

fingers, pat out the dough into a 9-inch (23-cm) square about ¼ inch (6 mm) thick.

Gently turn the fruits and their juices into an 8-inch (20-cm) square baking pan with 2½-inch (6-cm) sides. Lay the dough across the top and trim away any excess.

Bake for 20 minutes. Reduce the oven temperature to 300°F (150°C) and continue baking until the berries and nectarines are tender but not dissolved, 15–20 minutes longer. To test, lift up a corner of the crust and taste a piece of the fruit. Let cool on a wire rack. Serve warm or at room temperature, scooped from the pan.

THREE-BERRY COBBLER

Traditional desserts in the American South, cobblers conjure up memories of irresistible aromas filling warm, friendly kitchens. This recipe combines blackberries, raspberries, and strawberries under a sweet biscuit crust. If you like, use just one or two types of berries.

FOR THE FILLING

1½ cups (6 oz/185 g) sliced strawberries

1½ cups (6 oz/185 g) raspberries

1½ cups (6 oz/185 g) blackberries

½ cup (4 oz/125 g) sugar

FOR THE BISCUIT TOPPING

⅓ cup (3 oz/90 g) unsalted butter, at room temperature

⅓ cup (3 oz/90 g) sugar, plus more for sprinkling, optional

2 cups (10 oz/315 g) all-purpose (plain) flour

½ teaspoon salt

1 teaspoon baking powder

½ cup (4 fl oz/125 ml) milk

MAKES 6–8 SERVINGS

Preheat the oven to 375°F (190°C). Generously butter a deep 2-qt (2-l) baking dish.

To make the filling, in the prepared dish, combine the strawberries, raspberries, and blackberries. Then, sprinkle the sugar over the berries and toss to mix. Set aside.

To make the topping, in a bowl, combine the butter and sugar. Using a wooden spoon or an electric mixer on medium-high speed, beat until fluffy, about 3 minutes. In another bowl, sift together the flour, salt, and baking powder. Add the flour mixture to the butter mixture in 3 batches, alternately with the milk in 2 batches, beginning and ending with the flour mixture and mixing with a fork just until incorporated. Do not overmix.

Turn the dough out onto a lightly floured work surface and roll out or pat into the shape and size of the baking dish. Lift the dough onto the dish to cover the fruit; it should reach just slightly short of the dish sides. Cut a few slits in the top for steam to escape. Sprinkle with sugar, if desired.

Bake until the top is golden and the berries are bubbling, about 50 minutes. Let cool briefly on a wire rack. Serve hot, warm, or at room temperature.

Perking up berries

To bring out the flavor of lackluster berries, put them in a bowl and sprinkle with a little sugar, 1–2 tbsp for every 2 cups (8 oz/250 g). Let them stand at room temperature for 15 minutes. The sugar draws moisture from the berries to make a sweet, natural syrup.

561

BERRY SHORTCAKES

Making your own

If you don't have superfine sugar on hand, which dissolves more rapidly when whipping cream than granulated sugar does, you can make your own by whirling granulated sugar in a blender for about a minute.

This quintessential American summer dessert can be made with a mixture of berries. Handle the shortcake dough gently, leaving tiny lumps of butter in the mixture. The butter pieces will melt during baking to create air pockets that help form a flaky structure in the shortcakes.

Preheat the oven to 400°F (200°C). Butter a baking sheet.

To make the shortcakes, in a bowl, sift together the flour, granulated sugar, baking powder, and salt. Scatter the butter over the top. Using a pastry blender or 2 knives, cut in the butter until the mixture forms crumbs the size of large peas. Add the milk and stir with a fork just until the dough clings together in a rough mass.

Turn the dough out onto a lightly floured surface and knead gently. Lightly form into a ball, transfer to the prepared baking sheet, and pat into a disk about 7 inches (18 cm) in diameter. Cut into 4 equal wedges. Bake the shortcakes until golden, 12–15 minutes. Let cool on the pan on a wire rack.

Meanwhile, place ½ cup (2 oz/60 g) of the berries in a bowl and mash with a fork. Stir in 4 tablespoons (2 oz/60 g) of the superfine sugar. Add the remaining berries and stir to mix. In a separate bowl, using a whisk or an electric mixer on medium-high speed, whip the cream with the remaining 1 tablespoon sugar and the liqueur until soft peaks form.

Use a fork to split the cooled shortcakes in half horizontally. Place the bottom halves, cut sides up, on individual plates. Spoon the berries and cream onto the bottoms. Replace the top halves and serve.

FOR THE SHORTCAKES

1 cup (5 oz/155 g) all-purpose (plain) flour

2 tablespoons granulated sugar

1 teaspoon baking powder

¼ teaspoon salt

¼ cup (2 oz/60 g) cold unsalted butter, cut into cubes

6 tablespoons (3 fl oz/ 90 ml) milk

3 cups (12 oz/375 g) mixed fresh berries

5 tablespoons (2 oz/60 g) superfine (caster) sugar

½ cup (4 fl oz/125 ml) heavy (double) cream

1 tablespoon orange liqueur

MAKES 4 SERVINGS

DOUBLE-RASPBERRY SOUFFLÉS

Choosing berries

Always select berries with care. Avoid those that are moist, overly soft, or pale colored. Check the carton bottom and pass it up if signs of leaking, dampness, or staining are visible.

Once you have made these individual soufflés, which take longer to bake than they do to assemble, you will forever forget the notion that soufflés are difficult or fussy. When the soufflés come out of the oven, you can dust the tops with confectioners' (icing) sugar.

Preheat the oven to 375°F (190°C). Coat six ⅔-cup (5–fl oz/ 160-ml) soufflé molds with nonstick cooking spray. Then coat the molds with sugar and tap out the excess. Divide the fresh raspberries among the soufflé molds; each mold should have 10–12 raspberries.

Place the thawed raspberries in a blender and process just until smooth. Pass the berries through a fine-mesh sieve placed over a bowl, pressing hard on the solids with the back of a spoon to extract as much juice as possible. Transfer the purée to a small saucepan, add the sugar and lemon juice, and place over medium heat. Bring to a simmer, stirring to dissolve the sugar, and simmer for about 3 minutes.

Nonstick cooking spray for molds

1½ cups (6 oz/185 g) fresh raspberries

1 package (10 oz/315 g) frozen raspberries in syrup, thawed

2½ tablespoons sugar

2 teaspoons fresh lemon juice

4 egg whites

Pinch of cream of tartar

1 tablespoon
orange liqueur

1 teaspoon pure
vanilla extract

MAKES 6 SERVINGS

Meanwhile, in a bowl, using an electric mixer on medium-high speed, beat together the egg whites and cream of tartar until stiff peaks form.

Remove the purée from the heat and stir in the liqueur and vanilla. Immediately pour the hot purée into the egg whites. Continue to beat on medium-high speed just until the purée is incorporated.

Spoon the purée mixture into the soufflé molds, dividing it evenly and filling them to the top. Smooth the tops, then run a thumb completely around the outer edge of the purée mixture to form a shallow indentation alongside the rim. (This will ensure a nice rise in the oven.)

Bake until puffed and golden brown on top, about 12 minutes. Serve right away.

FIG TOASTS

At the height of fig season, use some of the fully ripe fruits to make these elegant toasts. At other times of the year, soak dried figs in very hot water for 30 minutes, then slice and use in place of the fresh ones. A small glass of sweet wine is the ideal partner.

6 tablespoons (3 oz/90 g) mascarpone cheese

1 tablespoon sweet Marsala

1½ teaspoons plus
1 tablespoon sugar

¼ teaspoon ground cinnamon

6 slices coarse country bread, each 5 by 3 inches (13 by 7.5 cm)

Unsalted butter,
at room temperature

6 figs, sliced lengthwise

MAKES 6 SERVINGS

Preheat the broiler (grill).

In a small bowl, stir together the mascarpone, Marsala, and the 1½ teaspoons sugar. In another small bowl, stir together the 1 tablespoon sugar and the cinnamon.

Place the bread slices on a small baking sheet. Broil (grill) until nicely toasted on the top. Remove the bread from the broiler and turn the slices over. Spread each slice with butter, then sprinkle with ½ teaspoon of the cinnamon sugar. Return to the broiler and broil until beginning to brown.

Remove from the broiler. Spread about 1 tablespoon of the mascarpone mixture over each toast. Top with the fig slices, arrange on a platter, and serve right away.

563

Versatile and easy

Not only good for dessert, these simple-to-assemble crostini can also be served at a cocktail party. Pass them on a tray near the end of the event, or arrange them on a platter alongside an array of savory bites for contrast.

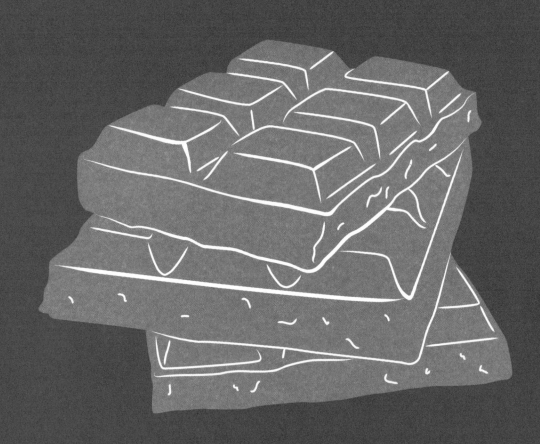

Candies & CONFECTIONS

Candies & Confections

For most people, eating just one piece of homemade candy, whether it's a swirl of minty chocolate, a chewy caramel, a crunchy cluster of nuts, or a dense truffle, is always calories well spent. Happily, many candies aren't difficult to make, either. In this chapter, you'll find all the techniques, details on ingredients, and recipes you'll need to fill your kitchen candy jar with homemade sweets as well as ideas for presenting them as gifts.

Using a candy thermometer
Some candies rely for their final texture on cooking a sugar mixture to a specific, usually high, temperature. A candy thermometer, which has an adjustable clip to secure it to the side of a pan, will ensure that the syrup or other candy mixture you are making reaches the correct temperature. When attaching a thermometer to a pan, always check to make sure its stem is suspended in the syrup or other mixture and isn't touching the pan bottom.

Candy cups and wrappers
When making candies, it's a good idea to have on hand an assortment of individual fluted cups of plain or decorated paper or foil for holding individual candies while they set and for presentation. Sheets of cellophane, plastic wrap, or waxed paper are also useful: cut them into small strips or squares for wrapping individual pieces of candy, particularly sticky ones, for mess-free serving.

Chocolate Techniques

When chopping or grating chocolate, start with bars at cool room temperature or briefly refrigerated, so they will be harder and cut more cleanly. For curls, the chocolate should be at warmer room temperature so it is slightly soft.

CHOPPING   A recipe may call for chopping chocolate for incorporating it into mixtures or for melting it for a sauce or batter.

   To chop chocolate: Place the block of chocolate on a cutting board. With one hand, grasp the handle of a serrated or chef's knife. With your other hand placed midpoint on the back of the blade, cut the chocolate into medium-size pieces, gradually moving the knife across the block. For smaller, more even pieces, move your other hand slightly closer to the front of the blade and rock the knife to chop the chocolate more finely.

CURLING AND SHAVING   Pretty, delicate chocolate curls and larger chocolate shavings are popular and simple dessert decorations. After creating curls or shavings, refrigerate until ready to use.

   To make chocolate curls: Slightly soften a 3- to 4-inch (7.5- to 10-cm) block of chocolate in a microwave oven on medium (50 percent power) for a few seconds (or use a handheld hair dryer on the low setting). Hold the chocolate in one hand and, with the other hand, draw a swivel-bladed vegetable peeler along an edge to create wide, thin, curled chocolate bits.

   To shave chocolate: Place a block of room-temperature chocolate on a work surface. Draw a swivel-bladed vegetable peeler across its surface—cutting from a narrow side for thin shavings or a broader edge for larger shavings.

GRATING   Fine particles of grated chocolate can be used for decoration or for incorporating easily into batters, doughs, or other mixtures.

   To grate chocolate: With one hand, steady a box-style grater-shredder on a work surface or plate. With the other hand, quickly and repeatedly run a block of cool chocolate over the shredding holes. To transfer the grated chocolate to a bowl or plate, scoop it up with a bench scraper or quickly pick up with cool hands. Or, place the grater-shredder on a piece of waxed paper when you grate and transfer the chocolate on the paper.

MELTING   A step in making many chocolate candies, sauces, batters, and other preparations, melting is usually done in a double boiler.

   To melt chocolate: Put small pieces in the top pan of a double boiler or in a heatproof bowl. Pour water to a depth of about 1½ inches (4 cm) in the bottom pan of the double boiler or in a saucepan and heat until barely simmering. Place the pan or bowl on top, making sure it doesn't touch the water. Heat, stirring occasionally, until melted and smooth. Lift out the top pan or bowl and use as directed in the recipe.

Chocolate Types

Possibly the world's most popular flavor, chocolate stars in candies, cookies, and all sorts of other desserts. Several types of chocolate, each with specific properties, are used for cooking. Here is a guide to the most common ones.

BITTERSWEET CHOCOLATE Bittersweet chocolate is a dark chocolate made from chocolate liquor—the pure chocolate paste ground from roasted cocoa beans—enriched with additional cocoa butter and sweetened with sugar. It consists of at least 35 percent chocolate liquor, with sugar making up about 40 percent of its weight. It is commonly sold in bars. In general, European dark chocolates are called bittersweet, while American dark chocolates are called semisweet (plain). For everything but the most specialized candy making, the two can be used interchangeably.

CHOCOLATE CHIPS These droplets of semisweet, milk, or white chocolate are made for easy incorporation into batters or doughs. Although their slightly lower cocoa butter content helps them hold their shape when baked, chocolate chips also melt easily and evenly, eliminating the need to chop.

COCOA POWDER Cocoa powder is made by removing most of the cocoa butter from ground chocolate liquor and then grinding the solids to form an unsweetened fine powder. It contains less fat than other sources of chocolate flavor and it is naturally acidic, reacting with baking soda (bicarbonate of soda) to create carbon dioxide that leavens some baked goods. Dutch-processed cocoa powder, also known as alkalized cocoa, has been specially treated to reduce its acidity. It has a darker color and mellower flavor than nonalkalized cocoa powder, sometimes labeled "natural cocoa powder." It also burns more easily. Do not confuse it with hot chocolate drink mixes.

DARK CHOCOLATE Term used for any sweetened chocolate that does not include milk solids, usually bittersweet or semisweet (plain) chocolate.

MILK CHOCOLATE Primarily used for eating in the form of candy bars, milk chocolate is enriched with powdered milk and contains considerably less chocolate liquor than dark chocolate, with a less intense chocolate flavor.

SEMISWEET CHOCOLATE Another eating or cooking chocolate, semisweet (plain) chocolate is usually, but not always, slightly sweeter than bittersweet chocolate. Sold in bars and drop-shaped chips.

SWEET CHOCOLATE This dark eating or cooking chocolate, sometimes labeled German sweet chocolate, is generally sweeter than semisweet chocolate; but, like semisweet, it contains no milk.

UNSWEETENED CHOCOLATE Also known as baking chocolate or bitter chocolate, unsweetened chocolate consists of pure chocolate liquor ground from roasted cacao beans and then molded into chunky blocks. It provides an intense chocolate flavor in recipes.

WHITE CHOCOLATE Not, strictly speaking, a chocolate, since it contains no cocoa solids, this chocolate-like product is made by combining pure cocoa butter with sugar, powdered milk, and sometimes vanilla. Check labels to make sure that the fat in the product you buy comes exclusively from cocoa butter. Less-expensive products made without cocoa butter are sometimes labeled confectionery coating.

Gift wrapping
Candies are some of the most welcome gifts from your kitchen. Look in shops carrying party supplies and kitchen equipment for decorative items in which to pack your homemade treats, including sturdy gift boxes of cardboard or straw, small baskets, airtight tins or canisters, widemouthed glass jars, or gift bags. Don't forget wrapping paper, ribbons, and small gift cards to complete the presentation.

Storing chocolate
Store chocolate at cool room temperature, unopened in its original wrapper or, after opening, well wrapped in aluminum foil and plastic wrap. Do not keep chocolate, especially milk and white chocolates, near foods with strong odors or flavors. Properly stored, dark chocolate keeps for up to 1 year; milk and white chocolates keep for up to 8 months.

567

CANDY-MAKING CAUTION

Many candy recipes involve working with hot sugar syrups and other molten mixtures. To avoid severe burns, always exercise extreme caution when cooking with sugar, protecting your hands and forearms with heavy oven mitts. And always keep a bowl of ice water next to the stove to cool the bottom of a pan of sugar syrup quickly if it overheats. Never touch hot syrup with your fingers.

CARAMEL-WALNUT SHARDS

Cleaning up hardened caramel

If the caramel hardens and sticks to the bottom and sides of your saucepan, fill the pan three-fourths full of water and bring to a boil. The hardened caramel will soften and can be poured out.

Arrange these elegant, toffeelike candies on a pretty plate for guests to nibble on while sipping coffee or a digestif such as tawny port. For the best flavor, rinse the orange well before grating the zest. Hazelnuts (filberts) or almonds can be substituted for the walnuts.

Butter a small rimmed baking sheet. In a heavy 2½-qt (2½-l) saucepan over low heat, melt the butter. Add the granulated sugar, brown sugar, ¼ cup (2 fl oz/60 ml) water, and molasses and stir until the sugars dissolve, about 5 minutes. Raise the heat to medium and clip a candy thermometer onto the side of the pan. Cook, stirring slowly but constantly, until the thermometer registers 290°F (143°C), about 15 minutes.

Remove from the heat. Stir in the 1 cup coarsely chopped walnuts and the orange zest. Immediately pour the mixture all at once onto the prepared baking sheet; do not scrape the residue from the pan bottom. Let stand for 1 minute to firm slightly. Sprinkle the chocolate evenly over the surface. Let stand for 1 minute to soften. Then, using the back of a metal spoon, spread the chocolate over the candy until melted. Sprinkle with the medium-fine chopped walnuts. Refrigerate, uncovered, until the candy is firm, about 2 hours.

Break the candy into 2-inch (5-cm) pieces. Store in an airtight container in the refrigerator for up to 3 weeks.

1¼ cups (10 oz/315 g) unsalted butter

1 cup (8 oz/250 g) granulated sugar

¼ cup (2 oz/60 g) firmly packed light brown sugar

1 tablespoon unsulfured dark molasses

1 cup (4 oz/125 g) very coarsely chopped walnuts, plus ½ cup (2 oz/60 g) medium-fine chopped walnuts

1 tablespoon grated orange zest

6 oz (185 g) semisweet (plain) chocolate, finely chopped

MAKES ABOUT 1½ LB (750 G)

MIXED-NUT BRITTLE

Heavy cookware

Many recipes specify a heavy pan, referring primarily to its bottom. Look for pans with thick bases, which help in the rapid and even conduction of heat. Thin-bottomed pans will heat unevenly, resulting in scorched food if the cooking is not watched closely.

The addition of mixed nuts to a basic brittle results in a cosmopolitan twist on an old favorite. Of course, you can substitute any of your favorite nuts for those included here, or you can use them in different combinations. Make the brittle on a dry day. Humid weather will turn it sticky.

Generously butter a rimmed baking sheet. In a bowl, stir together all the nuts, the butter, and the salt. Set aside.

In a heavy 2-qt (2-l) saucepan over low heat, combine the sugar and ⅓ cup (3 fl oz/80 ml) water. Stir constantly until the sugar dissolves. Using a pastry brush dipped in water, brush down the sides of the pan to prevent sugar crystals from forming. Raise the heat to high and bring to a rolling boil. Boil, swirling the pan occasionally but not stirring, until the mixture turns a deep amber, about 8 minutes.

Add the nut mixture to the sugar mixture and stir until coated, then immediately pour onto the prepared baking sheet. Using a wooden spoon, spread into a thin sheet, distributing the nuts evenly. Let cool completely.

Break the brittle into irregular pieces. Store in an airtight container at room temperature for up to 1 week.

1¼ cups (about 8 oz/250 g) blanched almonds and hazelnuts (filberts), toasted (see page 17); halved roasted macadamia nuts; cashews; and shelled pistachio nuts, in any combination

1½ tablespoons unsalted butter

¼ teaspoon salt

1 cup (8 oz/250 g) sugar

MAKES ABOUT ¾ LB (375 G)

CHOCOLATE, CHERRY, AND MACADAMIA BARK

If your prefer, chopped toasted walnuts or almonds can be substituted for the macadamia nuts here. Either way, the result is an elegant, easy-to-prepare candy. Pack the bark, between layers of waxed paper, in decorative tins for holiday gifts.

Unsalted butter for the baking sheet

7 oz (220 g) milk chocolate, chopped

1 oz (30 g) unsweetened chocolate, chopped

¾ cup (4 oz/120 g) halved roasted macadamia nuts

¾ cup (4 oz/120 g) pitted dried sour cherries

MAKES ABOUT ¾ LB (375 G)

Butter a baking sheet and line with waxed paper. Combine the chocolates in the top pan of a double boiler or in a heatproof bowl. Place over (not touching) barely simmering water and heat, stirring occasionally, until melted and smooth. Stir ½ cup (2½ oz/75 g) of the macadamias and ½ cup (2½ oz/75 g) of the cherries into the melted chocolate, then pour onto the prepared baking sheet, tilting to spread slightly. Sprinkle with the remaining ¼ cup (1½ oz/45 g) each of the nuts and cherries. Refrigerate the candy, uncovered, until firm, about 1 hour.

Gently peel the candy from the waxed paper. Then, holding the candy with the waxed paper (to prevent fingerprints), break the chocolate into large, irregular pieces. Store in an airtight container in the refrigerator for up to 2 weeks.

About macadamias

These rich nuts originated in Australia, but are now widely grown in Hawaii. Smooth, off-white, and round, macadamia nuts resemble large chickpeas (garbanzo beans). Oil rich, they add crunch and buttery flavor to candies and baked goods.

CARAMEL-NUT POPCORN

This is likely the most luxurious popcorn you will ever eat. To take it a step further, spread the clumps (after baking and cooling) on a baking sheet and drizzle them with Chocolate Coating (page 459). If the chocolate-coated corn is not consumed right away, store it in the refrigerator.

3 qt (3 l) freshly popped corn (about ½ cup/3 oz/ 90 g unpopped)

1 cup (5 oz/155 g) *each* roasted cashews and macadamia nuts

1 cup (5½ oz/170 g) whole almonds

1 cup (7 oz/220 g) firmly packed dark brown sugar

½ cup (4 fl oz/125 ml) light corn syrup

½ cup (4 oz/125 g) unsalted butter

1 tablespoon grated orange zest

½ teaspoon salt

1 teaspoon pure vanilla extract

½ teaspoon baking soda (bicarbonate of soda)

MAKES ABOUT 4 QT (4 L)

Preheat the oven to 250°F (120°C). Butter a large roasting pan. Combine the popped corn and nuts in the pan, mixing well. Place the pan in the oven.

In a large, heavy saucepan over medium heat, combine the brown sugar, corn syrup, butter, orange zest, and salt. Bring to a boil, stirring until the sugar dissolves. Boil for 4 minutes without stirring. Remove from the heat and stir in the vanilla and baking soda. Pour the glaze over the popped corn mixture and stir to coat. Return the pan to the oven and bake, stirring occasionally, until dry, about 1 hour.

Using a metal spatula, free the popcorn from the bottom of the pan. Let cool completely in the pan, then break into clumps. Store in an airtight container at room temperature for up to 1 week.

Beating a bad rap

Corn syrup turns up in all kinds of commercial foods, both savory and sweet, and many health authorities insist consumers are ingesting an unhealthy amount of the sweetener because of its widespread use. But corn syrup is invaluable in candy making, because it controls the tendency of sugar to crystallize when it is heated.

CHOCOLATE, MACADAMIA, AND COCONUT CLUSTERS

Another way to melt

To melt chocolate in a microwave oven, put small pieces in a microwave-safe dish. Heat on medium (50 percent power) for 1 minute. Check to see if the chocolate looks shiny and softened. If not, continue heating, checking every 30 to 40 seconds to prevent scorching. The chocolate will not melt completely in the microwave, but will become smooth and liquid when stirred.

If you like, you can vary the ratio of milk chocolate to bittersweet chocolate, or use only one or the other. If desired, place the individual pieces in paper candy cups, wrap the cups in cellophane, tie with a decorative ribbon, and give as gifts.

Line a baking sheet with parchment paper.

Combine the milk and bittersweet chocolates in the top pan of a double boiler or in a heatproof bowl. Place the pan over (not touching) barely simmering water and heat, stirring constantly, until melted and smooth. Pour off the hot water from the bottom pan and replace it with lukewarm water. Replace the top pan or heatproof bowl. Let the chocolate stand uncovered, stirring frequently, until it cools slightly and begins to thicken, about 10 minutes.

Stir the macadamia nuts and coconut into the chocolate, mixing thoroughly. Using a small spoon, scoop out slightly rounded teaspoons of the mixture and drop onto the prepared sheet, spacing them evenly. Refrigerate uncovered until set, about 2 hours.

Store in an airtight container in the refrigerator for up to 1 month or in the freezer for up to 2 months.

10 oz (315 g) milk chocolate, chopped

3 oz (90 g) bittersweet or semisweet (plain) chocolate, chopped

2 cups (10 oz/315 g) coarsely chopped lightly salted roasted macadamia nuts

1½ cups (6 oz/185 g) sweetened shredded coconut, lightly toasted (page 457)

MAKES ABOUT 48 CANDIES

MAPLE-NUT PRALINES

Grating nutmeg

The flavor of freshly grated nutmeg is unmatched. Whole nutmegs look like unshelled pecans. Grate your nutmeg, if possible, on a specialized nutmeg grater, which has tiny rasps and usually a small compartment for storing a nutmeg or two. Or, grate the nutmeg on the smallest holes of your regular rasp grater.

These are a modern twist on New Orleans–style candies, which are enriched with the New England accent of maple syrup. Stacked on a plate or piled in a decorated canister, they make a wonderful host gift or snack for a buffet table.

Generously oil 2 rimmed baking sheets.

In a saucepan over medium heat, stir together the maple syrup and the 1 cup cream. Clip a candy thermometer onto the side of the pan. Bring to a boil and boil the mixture until the thermometer registers 238°F (114°C), about 15 minutes.

Remove from the heat and let cool to 220°F (104°C), about 5 minutes. Add the butter and stir just until melted and the mixture is creamy, about 1 minute. Stir in the walnuts, pecans, and nutmeg. Immediately, using a tablespoon, scoop up spoonfuls of the mixture and drop onto the prepared baking sheets, spacing them evenly. If the mixture becomes too dry to drop, add 2 tablespoons cream and stir over low heat until melted.

Let the candies cool completely. Store in an airtight container at room temperature for up to 3 weeks.

Canola oil for pans

2 cups (16 fl oz/500 ml) pure maple syrup

1 cup (8 fl oz/250 ml) plus 2 tablespoons, if needed, heavy (double) cream

1 tablespoon unsalted butter

1 cup (4 oz/125 g) walnuts, chopped

1 cup (4 oz/125 g) pecans, chopped

½ teaspoon freshly grated nutmeg

MAKES ABOUT 30 CANDIES

COFFEE TOFFEE BARK

The freshly ground coffee intensifies the flavor of the finished candy, and the toffee lends crunch. Do not substitute instant espresso granules or the result will be disappointing. For the best texture, purchase a good-quality white chocolate made with only cocoa butter.

Unsalted butter for the baking sheet

8 oz (250 g) white chocolate, finely chopped

2 teaspoons freshly ground fine-grind, dark-roast coffee or espresso

½ cup (2½ oz/75 g) chopped plain English toffee bits (not chocolate covered)

⅓ cup (1½ oz/45 g) chopped chocolate-covered English toffee candy bar

MAKES ABOUT ½ LB (250 G)

Butter a baking sheet and line it with waxed paper.

Place the white chocolate in the top pan of a double boiler or in a heatproof bowl. Place over (not touching) hot (not simmering) water and turn off the heat. Let stand, without stirring, until the chocolate begins to melt. Then stir until just melted and smooth. Mix in the coffee and the chopped plain toffee. Pour onto the prepared baking sheet. Using a rubber spatula, spread into an even layer ¼ inch (6 mm) thick. It should form a rectangle approximately 12 by 6 inches (30 by 15 cm). Immediately sprinkle evenly with the chocolate-covered toffee. Refrigerate the candy, uncovered, until firm, about 1 hour.

Gently peel the candy from the waxed paper. Holding the candy with the waxed paper (to prevent fingerprints), break the candy into large, irregular pieces. Store in an airtight container in the refrigerator for up to 2 weeks.

English toffee

A traditional English candy, toffee is made from a sugar syrup that is usually lightly caramelized, then enriched with a generous amount of butter. Toasted almonds are often added for flavor and texture. Look for toffee in candy shops and in specialty-foods stores.

CHOCOLATE MINT SWIRLS

Rich chocolate coupled with refreshing peppermint makes an ideal end-of-the-meal treat. Happily, these go together quickly—and disappear quickly, too. Look for the peppermint oil at cake-decorating shops, candy supply stores, and specialty-foods stores.

¼ cup (2 fl oz/60 ml) plus 2 tablespoons heavy (double) cream

2 tablespoons unsalted butter

6 oz (185 g) semisweet (plain) chocolate, chopped

½ teaspoon peppermint oil

MAKES ABOUT 20 CANDIES

In a small, heavy saucepan over medium heat, combine the cream and butter. Bring to a boil, stirring until the butter melts. Remove from the heat. Add the chocolate and stir until melted and smooth. Mix in the peppermint oil. Refrigerate the mixture, stirring occasionally, until the mixture mounds in a spoon, about 20 minutes.

Fit a pastry (piping) bag with a ½-inch (12-mm) star tip, and spoon the chocolate mixture into the bag (page 493). Pipe the chocolate into about 20 silver or gold foil candy cups each 1 inch (2.5 cm) in diameter. Refrigerate, uncovered, until set, at least 1 hour. Store the candy in an airtight container in the refrigerator for up to 2 weeks. Serve at room temperature.

Powdery chocolate

If your chocolate bar appears powdery, pale, and blotchy, don't worry. This look, called bloom, is the result of storing the chocolate at too warm a temperature or in too humid an environment. The chocolate can still be used; the flavor and texture are only slightly altered.

VANILLA BEAN CARAMELS

Cleaning the thermometer

After you remove a candy thermometer from a hot, syrupy mixture, submerge it in hot water for easy cleaning. Cold water might crack it. Let it soak for a few minutes, then wash with soapy water.

If you're making these caramels to give as gifts, you will need 36 pieces of cellophane, waxed paper, or colored waxed paper (sold at kitchenware shops)—each measuring 4½ by 6 inches (11.5 by 15 cm)—for wrapping them. Set them out on a plate as a treat for departing guests.

Line an 8-inch (20-cm) square baking pan with aluminum foil, covering the bottom and sides. Oil the foil generously.

In a heavy 3-qt (3-l) saucepan over medium heat, combine the brown sugar, granulated sugar, corn syrup, whole milk, condensed milk, cream, butter, vanilla bean, and salt. Cook, stirring constantly, until the sugars dissolve and the mixture comes to a boil. Using a pastry brush dipped in water, brush down the sides of the pan to prevent sugar crystals from forming. Raise the heat to medium-high and clip a candy thermometer onto the side of the pan. Cook, stirring slowly but constantly, until the thermometer registers 240°F (115°C), about 10 minutes.

Remove from the heat. Remove the vanilla bean and discard. Immediately pour the caramel into the prepared baking pan all at once; do not scrape the residue from the pan bottom. Let the caramel cool completely, about 2 hours.

Oil a cutting board. Turn out the caramel onto the board and peel off the foil. Oil a large knife and cut the caramel into strips about 1½ inches (4 cm) wide. Cut the strips crosswise into pieces 1 inch (2.5 cm) long, re-oiling the knife from time to time to prevent sticking. Store in an airtight container at room temperature for up to 2 weeks.

Canola oil for pan, cutting board, and knife

½ cup (3½ oz/105 g) firmly packed light brown sugar

½ cup (4 oz/125 g) granulated sugar

½ cup (4 fl oz/125 ml) light corn syrup

¼ cup (2 fl oz/60 ml) plus 2 tablespoons whole milk

¼ cup (2 fl oz/60 ml) plus 2 tablespoons condensed milk

¼ cup (2 fl oz/60 ml) heavy (double) cream

¼ cup (2 oz/60 g) unsalted butter

1 vanilla bean, split lengthwise

Pinch of salt

MAKES ABOUT 36 CARAMELS

COCOA MERINGUE KISSES

Superfine sugar

Superfine (caster) sugar is ideal for making meringues, because it dissolves more quickly and completely than regular granulated sugar. Look for it in the baking aisle near the regular granulated sugar.

The two secrets to success when making these melt-in-your-mouth, chocolate-flecked morsels are to make them when the weather is dry (humid weather affects their texture) and to use natural, not Dutch-processed, cocoa powder (see page 567).

Position a rack in the upper third (not the highest point) of the oven and preheat the oven to 275°F (135°C). Line a rimmed baking sheet with parchment (baking) paper or with aluminum foil, shiny side down.

In a bowl, using an electric mixer on medium speed, beat together the egg whites and cream of tartar until foamy. With the mixer on medium-high speed, slowly add the sugar and then continue to beat until stiff, glossy peaks form. With the mixer on low speed, beat in the cocoa powder, mixing only until incorporated. Using a rubber spatula, fold in the chopped chocolate just until evenly distributed.

Using a tablespoon, scoop up high mounds about 2 inches (5 cm) in diameter and place them 1 inch (2.5 cm) apart on the prepared baking sheet.

4 extra-large egg whites, at room temperature

Pinch of cream of tartar

1 cup (8 oz/250 g) superfine (caster) sugar

3 tablespoons unsweetened cocoa powder (not Dutch-processed), sifted

1 cup (5 oz/155 g) coarsely chopped bittersweet chocolate

MAKES ABOUT 24 MERINGUES

Bake for 1 hour. The kisses should not color. If they begin to brown, reduce the oven temperature to 250°F (120°C). Turn off the oven but leave the kisses in the oven with the oven door closed for 1 hour longer.

Lift the kisses off the parchment and let cool completely on wire racks. Store the kisses in a covered container at room temperature for up to 1 month.

ALMOND AND SPICE MERINGUES

Serve these bite-sized meringues after a rich meal, when their nicely balanced sweetness and lightness will be appreciated. If you can't find pumpkin pie spice, substitute a mixture of cinnamon, ground ginger, nutmeg, and allspice, or use just one or two of these spices.

3 egg whites, at room temperature

½ cup (4 oz/125 g) sugar

¼ teaspoon pumpkin pie spice

½ cup (2½ oz/75 g) slivered blanched almonds, toasted (see page 17) and finely chopped

MAKES ABOUT 30 MERINGUES

Preheat the oven to 200°F (95°C). Line 2 large baking sheets with waxed paper.

In a large bowl, using an electric mixer on medium-high speed, beat the egg whites until soft peaks form. Gradually add the sugar and continue to beat until stiff, glossy peaks form. Beat in the pumpkin pie spice, mixing only until incorporated. Using a rubber spatula, fold in the almonds just until evenly distributed.

Fit a pastry bag with a ½-inch (12-mm) star tip, and spoon the egg whites into the bag (page 493). Pipe the meringue in mounds 1½ inches (4 cm) in diameter onto the prepared pans, spacing them about 1½ inches apart.

Bake until crisp and dry, about 2 hours. Remove from the oven and, using a narrow-bladed metal spatula, gently loosen the meringues from the paper. Let cool completely on the pans on wire racks. Store in an airtight container at room temperature for up to 5 days.

Humidity and meringues

Meringues are tricky to bake on humid days and may not be crisp after 2 hours in the oven. If that happens, turn off the heat, leave the oven door closed, and let the meringues remain in the oven until dry and crisp, up to 2 hours longer.

573

PISTACHIO AND ALMOND KISSES

Rose water

A popular flavoring in Middle Eastern and South Asian cuisines, rose water lends a sweet, floral fragrance and flavor to candies and confections. Look for this essence, distilled from fresh rose petals, in specialty-foods stores.

The flavors of both pistachios and rose water make these delicate kiss-shaped meringues a good ending to an Indian- or Middle Eastern–inspired meal. If the cookies become soft during storage, place them in a preheated 200°F (95°C) oven for 10 minutes, then let cool until crisp.

Position a rack in the upper third of the oven and preheat to 325°F (165°C). Butter a large baking sheet.

In a small bowl, stir together the pistachios, almonds, and cornstarch. In a large bowl, using an electric mixer on medium-high speed, beat together the egg whites and rose water until soft peaks form. Gradually add the sugar and beat until stiff, glossy peaks form. Using a rubber spatula, gently fold in the nut mixture just until evenly distributed.

Fit a pastry bag with a ½-inch (12-mm) star tip, and spoon the egg whites into the bag (page 493). Pipe the meringue in mounds 2 inches (5 cm) in diameter onto the prepared pans, spacing them about 1½ inches apart.

Bake until golden brown and set, about 15 minutes. Turn off the oven and let the meringues stand in the oven with the oven door closed for 1 hour.

Using a thin-bladed metal spatula, gently transfer the kisses to a wire rack to cool completely. Store in an airtight container at room temperature for up to 5 days.

Unsalted butter for pan

¼ cup (1 oz/30 g) finely chopped pistachio nuts

2 tablespoons ground, toasted almonds

1 tablespoon cornstarch (cornflour)

3 egg whites

¼ teaspoon rose water

¼ cup (2 oz/60 g) sugar

**MAKES ABOUT
25 MERINGUES**

SUGARPLUMS

Grinding your own cinnamon

For the best flavor, buy cinnamon in stick form and grind it yourself: break or crush the stick into small pieces and then grind to a powder in a mortar, a spice grinder, or an electric coffee mill reserved for spices.

These sweet, spiced-infused confections are the perfect addition to a holiday cocktail party. They are easy to put together and can be made weeks before the get-together. If you like, both the dried fruits and the nuts can be varied. Apples, pears, and pecans are excellent alternatives.

Line a small rimmed baking sheet with waxed paper.

In a food processor, combine the dates, walnuts, apricots, figs, pistachios, brandy, apricot jam, cinnamon, and cloves. Pulse until the mixture begins to clump together; do not grind it to a paste.

Put the sugar in a shallow bowl. Using a teaspoon, scoop up a rounded spoonful of the mixture, press together, and roll between your palms into a compact ball. Roll the ball in the sugar, coating evenly. Place on the prepared pan. Repeat with the remaining fruit-and-nut mixture and sugar.

Refrigerate until firm, at least 1 hour. Store in an airtight container in the refrigerator for up to 2 weeks.

½ cup (3 oz/90 g) finely chopped pitted dates

½ cup (2 oz/60 g) finely chopped walnuts

¼ cup (1½ oz/45 g) *each* finely chopped dried apricots and dried figs

¼ cup (1 oz/30 g) finely chopped pistachio nuts

2 tablespoons brandy

1 tablespoon apricot jam

¼ teaspoon ground cinnamon

⅛ teaspoon ground cloves

⅓ cup (3 oz/90 g) sugar

MAKES ABOUT 18 CANDIES

NO-FAIL FUDGE

Despite its simplicity, this recipe makes first-rate fudge. Many fudge recipes require precise cooking temperatures to ensure a creamy consistency. But here, the addition of evaporated milk eliminates the need for such precision and guarantees perfect results every time.

1½ cups (12 oz/375 g) sugar

2 tablespoons unsalted butter

½ teaspoon salt

½ cup (4 fl oz/125 ml) evaporated milk

2 cups (12 oz/375 g) semisweet (plain) or bittersweet chocolate chips

2 teaspoons pure vanilla extract

¾ cup (3 oz/90 g) large walnut pieces, optional

MAKES ABOUT 36 SQUARES

Butter an 8-inch (20-cm) square baking pan.

In a large saucepan over medium heat, combine the sugar, butter, salt, and evaporated milk. Stir constantly until the mixture comes to a boil. Reduce the heat to medium-low and continue to simmer for 5 minutes, again stirring constantly. Remove from the heat and stir in the chocolate chips. Continue to stir the mixture gently until the chocolate melts and the mixture is completely smooth. Stir in the vanilla and add the walnuts, if using.

Pour and scrape into the prepared pan.

Cover and refrigerate until firm, about 2 hours. Cut into pieces about 1¼-inch (3-cm) squares to serve. Store in an airtight container at room temperature for up to 1 week.

Evaporated milk

Sold in small cans and available in most supermarkets, evaporated milk has had about 60 percent of its water removed by heat. The process darkens the color of the milk slightly and gives it a faint caramelized flavor. Do not confuse it with condensed milk, which has been sweetened.

575

CHOCOLATE-DIPPED FRUITS

Fruits dipped in chocolate are elegant and universally appreciated, yet they are exceedingly easy to make. You can use milk or white chocolate, if you prefer. For a pretty presentation, serve the finished fruits in paper or foil candy cups set out on a platter.

8 oz (250 g) semisweet or bittersweet chocolate, chopped

12–16 pieces fresh fruit such as strawberries, peach slices, and seedless orange sections

MAKES 12–16 CONFECTIONS

Line a baking sheet with waxed paper.

Place the chocolate in the top pan of a double boiler or in a heatproof bowl. Place over (not touching) barely simmering water and heat, stirring occasionally, until melted and smooth. Remove from the heat.

Dip each piece of fruit about two-thirds of the way into the chocolate and then set on the prepared pan. Refrigerate until the chocolate is set, about 15 minutes. Serve right away, or keep refrigerated for up to 2 hours before serving.

Chocolate-dipped dried fruits

Dried fruits, such as apricots, oranges, pears, or apples, as well as crystallized ginger slices, are also delicious dipped in chocolate. The same treatment can be used for unsalted nut clusters.

DARK AND WHITE CHOCOLATE TRUFFLES

Seized chocolate

If your melted chocolate suddenly becomes hard and lumpy, it has come in contact with a bit of moisture during melting and stiffened up, a phenomenon known as seizing. To salvage it, remove from the heat and stir in water, a tablespoon at a time, until it becomes smooth. The restored mixture will be fine for icings or fillings, but you'll need to start over for recipes in which the chocolate needs to set, such as candies.

576

These small, irregularly shaped treats hold a surprise: folded into the smooth, dark-chocolate centers are bits of white chocolate and pecans. They can be frozen for up to 4 months, making them the ideal treat to have on hand for unexpected guests.

Place the bittersweet chocolate in the top of a double boiler or in a heatproof bowl. Place over (not touching) barely simmering water and heat, stirring occasionally, until melted and smooth. Add the butter and stir until shiny and smooth. Stir in the rum. Pour into a shallow pan. Cover with plastic wrap and refrigerate until cool but still soft, 1–1½ hours.

Fold in the pecans and white chocolate. Re-cover and refrigerate until firmly set, about 2 hours.

Place the cocoa powder in a shallow bowl. Using a teaspoon, scoop up a 1-inch (2.5-cm) spoonful of the chocolate mixture and, with cool fingers, form the mixture into an irregularly shaped ball. Drop the ball into the cocoa powder and turn to coat it completely. Transfer to a plate. If your fingers are not cool, drop the mixture directly into the cocoa and quickly form it into balls as you coat it.

Store the truffles in a single layer in an airtight container in the refrigerator for up to 2 weeks. Remove 30 minutes before serving. You can also freeze the truffles in a tightly sealed container for up to 4 months. Thaw in the storage container at room temperature.

8 oz (250 g) bittersweet chocolate, chopped

6 tablespoons (3 oz/90 g) unsalted butter, at room temperature

1 tablespoon rum, preferably dark

⅔ cup (2½ oz/75 g) pecans, toasted (see page 17) and finely chopped

3 oz (90 g) white chocolate, finely chopped

⅓ cup (1 oz/30 g) unsweetened cocoa powder

MAKES ABOUT 20 TRUFFLES

COGNAC TRUFFLES

Other spirits

These intensely chocolaty candies can be made with a variety of liquors or liqueurs besides the Cognac listed here. Rum, bourbon, Grand Mariner, or even Champagne are all delicious options.

Here, truffles are piped into mounds with a pastry bag, firmed up in the refrigerator, and then rolled between palms into uniform balls. Using a pastry bag for the first step of forming the truffles is faster and less messy than doing it by hand.

To make the truffles, place the bittersweet and unsweetened chocolates in a heatproof bowl. In a saucepan over medium heat, bring the milk to a boil, then remove from the heat and let cool for 5 minutes. Pour over the chocolate and stir until melted and smooth. Stir in the butter and Cognac. Refrigerate, stirring occasionally, just until firm enough to hold a shape when scooped, 15–20 minutes.

Line a baking sheet with aluminum foil. Fit a pastry (piping) bag with a ½-inch (12-mm) plain tip, and spoon the chocolate mixture into the bag (page 493). Pipe the chocolate in mounds about 1 inch (2.5 cm) in diameter onto the prepared pan. Flatten the peaks with a fingertip and refrigerate, uncovered, until firm, about 2 hours.

To make the coating, combine the bittersweet and unsweetened chocolates in the top of a double boiler or in a heatproof bowl.

FOR THE TRUFFLES

½ lb (250 g) bittersweet chocolate, finely chopped

1 oz (30 g) unsweetened chocolate, finely chopped

½ cup (4 fl oz/125 ml) milk

2 tablespoons unsalted butter, at room temperature

2 tablespoons Cognac, dark rum, or Grand Marnier

FOR THE COATING

6 oz (185 g) bittersweet chocolate, finely chopped

½ oz (15 g) unsweetened chocolate, finely chopped

1 tablespoon canola oil

Unsweetened cocoa powder for dusting

MAKES ABOUT 25 TRUFFLES

Place over (not touching) barely simmering water and heat, stirring occasionally, until melted and smooth. Stir in the oil. Remove from the heat.

Using your hands, quickly roll each mound of chocolate into a ball. Using a fork, dip the balls, one at a time, into the melted chocolate, then return them to the lined baking sheet. Refrigerate until set, about 20 minutes.

Using a fine-mesh sieve, lightly dust the truffles with cocoa powder. Serve right away, or store in a single layer in an airtight container in the refrigerator for up to 3 days.

Decoding cacao percentages

The higher the cacao percentage, the more intense the chocolate flavor. Bittersweet chocolates typically have the highest cacao percentages, above 60 percent; followed by semi-sweet (plain), above 50 percent; and milk chocolate, below 50 percent.

DOUBLE-CHOCOLATE AND ORANGE TRUFFLES

For an extra-special touch, coat these confections with melted milk chocolate instead of dusting with cocoa. Set them out in paper candy cups on a silver tray. These truffles also make perfect thank-you gifts, as they will keep in an airtight container for a few weeks.

12 oz (375 g) milk chocolate, chopped

½ cup (4 fl oz/125 ml) thawed, frozen orange juice concentrate

2 tablespoons unsalted butter, at room temperature

Unsweetened cocoa powder for dusting

12 oz (375 g) bittersweet or semisweet (plain) chocolate, finely chopped

MAKES ABOUT 18 TRUFFLES

In a heavy saucepan over medium-low heat, combine the milk chocolate and orange juice concentrate and heat, stirring constantly, until smooth. Add the butter and stir until incorporated. Pour into a bowl; this mixture is the truffle filling. Cover and freeze until firm enough to mound in a spoon, about 40 minutes.

Line a baking sheet with aluminum foil. Using a tablespoon, scoop out rounded spoonfuls of the filling and drop onto the prepared pan, spacing them evenly. Cover and freeze until almost firm but still pliable, about 30 minutes.

Place the cocoa powder in a shallow bowl. Roll each chocolate mound between your palms into a smooth ball, then roll in the cocoa to coat evenly. Return to the baking sheet and freeze while you prepare the coating.

Line another baking sheet with foil. Place the bittersweet chocolate in the top pan of a double boiler or in a heatproof bowl. Place over (but not touching) barely simmering water, and heat, stirring occasionally, until melted and smooth. Remove from the heat and let cool slightly.

Drop 1 truffle ball into the melted chocolate and tilt the pan if necessary to coat the ball completely. Slip a fork under the truffle, lift it from the chocolate, and tap the fork gently against the side of the pan to allow any excess chocolate to drip off. Using a knife, gently slide the truffle off the fork and onto the prepared pan. Repeat with the remaining truffles.

Refrigerate the truffles, uncovered, until firm, about 1 hour. Store in a single layer in an airtight container in the refrigerator for up to 3 weeks.

The naming game

Chocolate truffles are so-named because their irregular spherical forms mimic the appearance of a black truffle. Truffles with a dusting of cocoa powder only heighten their resemblance to the fungus with its coating of earth.

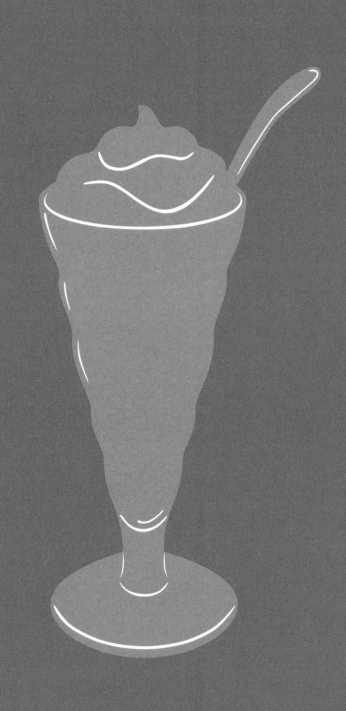

Puddings, MOUSSES & CUSTARDS

Puddings, Mousses & Custards

When people are asked what their favorite comfort-food desserts are, puddings, custards, and mousses are often the answer. Whether you're planning a traditional crème brûlée for a special-occasion meal or a homey bread pudding as the last course for a casual family supper, the tips on these pages and the recipes that follow will put a crowd-pleasing dessert on your table.

Pudding Types

Stove-top puddings
Use a heavy-bottomed saucepan to prevent cornstarch-thickened puddings from sticking and scorching. Stir and scrape the bottom and sides of the pan constantly with a wooden spoon to prevent lumps from forming.

Bread pudding variations
When making bread puddings, feel free to experiment with a different type of bread than what is called for in the recipe. You can even substitute cubes or chunks of stale pound cake or quick breads for yeast-leavened breads. Also, you can usually substitute milk for cream with good results.

Steamed pudding savvy
When making traditional steamed puddings, put the pudding mold on top of a trivet in the pot, to keep the bottom of the pudding from overcooking. Be sure to replenish the pot with more boiling water to maintain the original level specified in the recipe.

Many different kinds of desserts fall under the general heading of puddings. What they all usually have in common is a richness and smoothness that comes from using eggs and/or milk or cream. Here are some of the main subcategories of this satisfying family of desserts.

PUDDINGS   In the United States, this term applies to thick, creamy, cornstarch-thickened milk puddings, such as the Dark Chocolate Pudding on page 584.

BREAD PUDDINGS   These desserts (pages 582–83) start with firm-textured, sometimes stale bread, which is soaked and bound with milk or cream and eggs, sweetened with sugar or other sweeteners, and flavored or embellished in a variety of ways. Most bread puddings are baked in the oven, usually in a water bath (*opposite*).

STEAMED PUDDINGS   A cakelike dessert traditional to the English kitchen, a steamed pudding is a rich and flavorful batter based on flour or bread crumbs, enclosed in a decorative ceramic or metal mold, and gently cooked in a large pot of simmering water. The results are incomparably moist and flavorful, from the Steamed Chocolate Pudding on page 584, made from only a handful of ingredients, to the classic Christmas Steamed Fig Pudding with Caramel Cream on page 584, redolent of dried fruit and warm spices.

RICE PUDDINGS   Among the most time-honored of the pudding family, rice puddings, usually made from white rice, are typically thickened custard style with eggs, as in Warm Lemon Rice Custards (page 590), or simply by the starch in the rice itself as in Cinnamon Rice Pudding (page 591). The same description applies to tapioca-based puddings (page 593), which feature the pearly granules of the cassava root.

MOUSSES   The word *mousse* means "foam" in French, an apt term for these airy, rich desserts. Their texture comes from whipped cream alone or whipped cream and eggs, as in Chocolate Mousse or Mango Mousse (page 586).

CUSTARDS   A mixture of eggs and milk or cream cooked just until the proteins in the ingredients thicken to form a soft, smooth, satiny consistency that slides easily over the tongue, custard is among the world's most enduring comfort foods. Baked custards can be as simple as Chocolate Pots de Crème (page 588) or as elegant as a classic Crème Caramel (page 595).

CRÈME BRÛLÉES   This subcategory of custards (pages 596–97) takes its name from the French word for "burnt," a reference to the brittle, flavorful layer of caramelized sugar that is formed on each cooked custard just before it is served. The crisp coating is a pleasing textural contrast to the silky custard.

Basic Techniques

The basic techniques explained below will help you achieve the signature smooth, sometimes delicate consistency of the desserts in this chapter. For more essential dessert techniques, see pages 442–45.

USING A DOUBLE BOILER A double boiler is a set of two pans, one nested on top of the other, with room for water to simmer in the pan below. Delicate foods such as chocolate, custards, mousses, and cream sauces are placed in the top pan to heat them gently—or, in the case of chocolate, to melt (see page 566). The top pan should not touch the water beneath it, and the water should simmer gently, not boil. A tight fit between the pans ensures that no water or steam mixes with the ingredients—which, in the case of chocolate, can cause it to stiffen, or seize.

To make your own double boiler: Rest a heat-resistant glass or metal bowl inside the rim of a saucepan that can be used for the simmering water. Make sure the bowl is large enough so that it rests securely in the rim of the pan, with its bottom above—not touching—the simmering water.

USING A WATER BATH Sometimes referred to by the French term *bain-marie*, a water bath provides a moist environment for baking delicate custards, mousses, puddings, and cheesecakes. Although specialty water baths are available, it is easy to fashion one from pans you already have on hand.

To make a water bath for oven cooking: Select a baking pan or roasting pan large enough to hold the item to be baked along with a substantial amount of water, or the water will evaporate too quickly. If you are baking several small containers, such as custard cups, they should fit in the pan without touching. You can line the bottom of the pan with a folded kitchen towel to prevent small containers from rattling as they bake and to insulate delicate foods from the hot pan bottom. Place the dish or dishes holding the food inside the pan, and then pull out the center rack of the oven and place the pan on it. Carefully pour very hot tap water or boiling water, depending on the recipe, into the pan until it reaches about halfway up the sides of the dish or dishes, or as directed in individual recipes. (If you are using a springform pan inside the water bath, wrap the pan in aluminum foil before you set it in the water to prevent any leakage.) Finally, smoothly slide the rack into the oven, taking care to avoid splashing the hot water. It is advisable to check the water level in the water bath at regular intervals during cooking, pouring in more hot water as necessary to maintain the same level.

WORKING WITH GELATIN Many puddings, mousses, custards, and molded desserts would lose their shape without gelatin, an odorless, colorless, flavorless thickening agent derived from collagen, a protein extracted from the bones, cartilage, and tendons of animals. Look for powdered unflavored gelatin packaged in small paper envelopes in the baking section of your supermarket. Many pastry chefs favor gelatin sheets, but these are hard to find and more difficult to use in the home kitchen.

To use unflavored powdered gelatin: Sprinkle it over a little cold liquid and let it soften for a few minutes, without stirring. Stir the mixture directly into hot liquid. Before stirring the mixture into cold liquid, heat the softened gelatin in a double boiler (above) over hot water or in a small, heavy saucepan over low heat and stir until completely dissolved. Do not allow to boil. Proceed as directed in individual recipes. One envelope (1 tablespoon) powdered gelatin will jell 2 cups (16 fl oz/500 ml) liquid.

Baked custard basics
Because milk can develop a skin on its surface if it boils, do not let the milk for a custard even reach a simmer. Cook the milk or cream and sugar only until the sugar dissolves and the liquid is hot.

Testing custards for thickness
Many custard recipes call for cooking the mixture until it is thick enough to "coat the back of a spoon." To test if the density is correct, run your finger along the custard coating the back of the spoon. If it forms a path that remains for a few seconds before it begins to flow together, the custard is ready to be removed from the heat.

Torching crèmes brûlées
Modern cooks either slip the sugar-topped crèmes brûlées under a hot broiler (grill) to caramelize, or they use a handheld culinary torch fueled by a canister of butane gas inserted into its handle. The nozzle of the torch produces a small but intense flame that quickly and precisely caramelizes the sugar topping, forming a glossy, golden crust.

CUSTARDY BREAD PUDDING WITH BERRIES

Bread for pudding

The type of bread you choose for your pudding will lend its flavor and texture to the dessert. For example, egg-rich challah and butter-laden brioche will both add extra richness to the pudding. Choose a lean baguette, and the other flavors in the recipe will shine through.

The silky texture of this bread pudding mimics several sweet wines, making it a perfect dish to serve alongside a favorite dessert wine. Choose one with high acidity to cut the richness. If desired, serve the pudding with a pitcher of heavy (double) cream in place of the berries.

In a saucepan, combine the half-and-half, heavy cream, granulated sugar, and orange zest and bring to a boil over high heat, stirring to dissolve the sugar. Remove from the heat and let steep for 1 hour. Pour through a fine-mesh sieve placed over a clean saucepan.

Preheat the oven to 350°F (180°C).

Spread one side of the bread triangles with the butter. Arrange them, overlapping, in a 2-qt (2-l) baking dish.

Return the cream mixture to medium heat until small bubbles appear around the edge of the pan. Remove from the heat. In a bowl, whisk together the eggs and egg yolks until blended. Slowly add the hot cream mixture to the eggs while whisking constantly. Whisk in the vanilla. Holding the sieve over the bread-lined baking dish, strain the cream-egg mixture into the dish to immerse the bread.

Place the baking dish in a baking pan. Pour hot water into the baking pan to reach halfway up the sides of the dish. Bake until the top is golden brown and just set but the center still moves slightly when the dish is shaken, 30–40 minutes. Transfer to a wire rack. Using the fine-mesh sieve, dust the top with the confectioners' sugar. Let cool to lukewarm or room temperature before serving. Scoop onto individual plates and scatter some of the berries over each portion.

2 cups (16 fl oz/500 ml) half-and-half (half cream)

1 cup (8 fl oz/250 ml) heavy (double) cream

½ cup (4 oz/125 g) granulated sugar

2 orange zest strips, each about 2 inches (5 cm) long

6 slices fine-textured white bread, crusts removed and cut on the diagonal into triangles

4–5 tablespoons (2–2½ oz/ 60–75 g) unsalted butter, at room temperature

4 eggs, plus 2 egg yolks

1 tablespoon pure vanilla extract

¼ cup (1 oz/30 g) confectioners' (icing) sugar

1 cup (4 oz/125 g) sliced strawberries or whole raspberries or blueberries

MAKES 6 SERVINGS

RUM-RAISIN BREAD PUDDING

Let it soak

Don't skimp on the soaking time when making bread puddings. Bread that isn't allowed to soak up the custard will turn out dry and less appealing.

Raisins plumped in rum contribute their signature flavor to this custardy pudding. You can reinforce the flavor by accompanying the pudding with rum-raisin ice cream. Pitted dried sweet or sour cherries or cranberries can be used in place of the raisins.

In a small bowl, combine the raisins and rum and let stand for 30 minutes. While the raisins are soaking, preheat the oven to 325°F (165°C). Butter an 8-inch (20-cm) square baking dish or 4–6 custard cups.

Spread the bread cubes on a rimmed baking sheet and bake until lightly toasted, about 10 minutes. Remove the sheet from the oven and set aside.

In a large bowl, beat together the sugar, butter, eggs, milk, vanilla extract, and cinnamon until well blended. Stir in the bread cubes, apple, and the raisins and rum. Let stand until the bread cubes soak up most of the liquid, about 5 minutes.

½ cup (3 oz/90 g) golden raisins (sultanas)

¼ cup (2 fl oz/60 ml) dark rum or brandy

4 cups (8 oz/250 g) day-old bread cubes

½ cup (4 oz/125 g) sugar

⅓ cup (3 oz/90 g) unsalted butter, melted and cooled

3 eggs, lightly beaten

1½ cups (12 fl oz/
375 ml) milk

1½ teaspoons pure
vanilla extract

½ teaspoon ground
cinnamon

1 tart apple, unpeeled,
cored and cubed

MAKES 4–6 SERVINGS

Stir again and pour into the baking dish or divide evenly
among the custard cups.

Bake until a knife inserted into the center comes out clean,
30–40 minutes for custard cups or 50–60 minutes for a baking
dish. Serve hot, warm, or at room temperature.

PEAR AND DRIED CRANBERRY BREAD PUDDING

A scoop of vanilla ice cream or frozen yogurt makes a splendid partner for this fruit-laced bread
pudding that is big enough to serve a crowd. The baked pudding can rest at room temperature
for up to 2 hours and then be reheated in a 350°F (180°C) oven until warmed through.

7 tablespoons (3½ oz/
105 g) unsalted butter

4 firm, full-flavored pears
such as Anjou, peeled,
quartered, cored, and
sliced ⅛ inch (3 mm) thick

1 cup (7 oz/220 g) firmly
packed light brown sugar

1 teaspoon ground
cinnamon

4 day-old baguettes, each
about 18 inches (45 cm)
long, crusts removed, and
bread cut into ½-inch
(12-mm) cubes (about
10 cups/scant 2 lb/
scant 1 kg)

¾ cup (3 oz/90 g)
dried cranberries

6 eggs

1 teaspoon pure
almond extract

¼ teaspoon freshly
grated nutmeg

⅛ teaspoon salt

4 cups (32 fl oz/1 l)
half-and-half (half cream)

MAKES 12 SERVINGS

Butter a 9-by-13-inch (23-by-33-cm) baking dish with 2-inch
(5-cm) sides or similar 3-qt (3-l) baking dish.

In a large, heavy frying pan over medium-high heat, melt
4 tablespoons (2 oz/60 g) of the butter. Add the pear slices,
¼ cup (2 oz/60 g) of the brown sugar, and the cinnamon and
sauté, stirring constantly, until the pears are softened, about
8 minutes. Remove from the heat and set aside.

In a small saucepan over low heat, melt the remaining
3 tablespoons butter. Spread half of the bread cubes evenly
in the prepared baking dish. Brush with half of the melted
butter. Pour the pear mixture, including the pan juices, over
the bread cubes, spreading evenly. Scatter the dried cranberries
over the pears. Spread the remaining bread cubes over the
top, and brush with the remaining melted butter.

In a large bowl, whisk the eggs until blended. Whisk in ½ cup
(3 oz/100 g) of the brown sugar, the almond extract, nutmeg,
and salt. Add the half-and-half and mix thoroughly to
incorporate the sugar into the liquid. Ladle the egg mixture
evenly over the bread and pears.

Cover the top of the pudding with a sheet of waxed paper and
place 2 heavy plates or another baking dish on top to weight
down the contents. Let stand for 10 minutes. Remove the
weight(s) and waxed paper and cover the dish with plastic
wrap. Refrigerate for at least 4 hours or for up to overnight.

Preheat the oven to 350°F (180°C). Sprinkle the top of the
pudding with the remaining ¼ cup (2 oz/60 g) brown sugar.
Bake the pudding until the top is golden brown and a knife
inserted into the center comes out clean, about 1 hour. Remove
from the oven and let cool for 5–10 minutes. The pudding
will have puffed up during baking, but will settle as it cools.
Cut the warm pudding into portions, transfer to individual
plates, and serve.

Make it your own

*Bread puddings are
easy to vary. Here,
you can substitute
apples for the pears
and vanilla extract
for the almond
extract. Or, replace
the dried cranberries
with raisins, dried
sour cherries, diced
dried apricots,
or dried currants.*

583

DARK CHOCOLATE PUDDING

Buy the best

Because puddings and custards typically call for relatively few ingredients, always buy the best that your budget can afford, whether it be farm-fresh organic dairy products, the finest domestic or imported chocolate, or other ingredients.

Old-fashioned chocolate pudding never fails to delight the child in all of us, especially when it is topped with a dollop of softly whipped cream. This recipe takes just minutes to prepare and about 30 minutes to cool, so it's an ideal dessert on any day of the week.

In a heatproof bowl, whisk together the sugar, cornstarch, and salt. Set aside.

In a saucepan over medium heat, warm the milk until small bubbles appear around the edge of the pan. Add the chocolate and stir until melted, about 1 minute. Remove from the heat and stir in the vanilla.

Carefully ladle about one-fourth of the chocolate mixture into the sugar mixture and whisk until smooth. Add the remaining chocolate mixture and again whisk until smooth. Pour the combined mixtures back into the saucepan and place over medium heat. Cook, stirring constantly, until the pudding begins to thicken, scraping the pan well with a heat-resistant spatula to make sure it doesn't burn. Continue to cook, stirring constantly, until very thick, about 2 minutes.

Ladle the pudding into bowls, place a piece of plastic wrap directly on top, and let cool for at least 30 minutes. Serve right away, or cover and refrigerate for up to 4 hours. Top each serving with whipped cream and chocolate shavings.

¾ cup (6 oz/185 g) sugar

⅓ cup (1½ oz/45 g) cornstarch (cornflour)

¼ teaspoon salt

4 cups (32 fl oz/1 l) milk

3 oz (90 g) unsweetened chocolate, chopped4

1 teaspoon pure vanilla extract

Whipped Cream (page 454)

Shaved chocolate for garnish (see page 566)

MAKES 2 SERVINGS

STEAMED FIG PUDDING WITH CARAMEL CREAM

All bread crumbs are not the same

Do not substitute dried bread crumbs for the fresh ones called for here, or the pudding will have the wrong temperature. To make fresh bread crumbs, process large pieces of slightly stale, crustless bread in a food processor until very fine.

Steamed puddings such as this one are classic winter holiday desserts in England. For this festive version, use dried Black Mission or Calimyrna figs. Although this pudding is cakelike, scoop it out with a spoon for serving.

Trim the hard stems from the whole dried figs, then halve the fruit through the stem end. In a small bowl, combine the halved figs and liqueur, cover, and let stand for at least 1 hour or up to overnight.

Butter a 1-qt (1-l) pudding mold with a lid. Arrange the fig halves, rounded sides down, on the bottom. In a bowl, combine the minced figs, raisins, the 1 tablespoon flour, and the orange zest. Toss to combine. In a large bowl, beat together the butter and brown sugar until creamy. Add the eggs and beat just until blended. In another small bowl, stir together the ½ cup (2½ oz/75 g) flour and the baking powder. Stir into the butter mixture, mixing well. Stir in the bread crumbs, again mixing well. Mix in the orange juice and vanilla. Fold in the fig-raisin mixture. Spoon into the prepared pudding mold. Cover with a piece of buttered waxed paper, buttered side down. Secure the lid on the mold.

Set the mold on a trivet or small wire rack in a pot large enough to accommodate it comfortably. Pour in hot water

6 whole dried figs plus ½ cup (3 oz/90 g) minced

3 tablespoons orange liqueur

¾ cup (4½ oz/140 g) raisins

1 tablespoon plus ½ cup (2½ oz/75 g) all-purpose (plain) flour

1 teaspoon grated orange zest

½ cup (4 oz/125 g) unsalted butter, at room temperature

½ cup (3½ oz/105 g) firmly packed light brown sugar

3 eggs, lightly beaten

1 teaspoon baking powder

¾ cup (1½ oz/45 g) fine
fresh white bread crumbs

½ cup (4 fl oz/125 ml)
fresh orange juice

1 teaspoon pure
vanilla extract

FOR THE SAUCE

½ cup (4 oz/125 g)
granulated sugar

¼ cup (2 fl oz/60 ml)
orange juice

1¼ cups (10 fl oz/310 ml)
heavy (double) cream

½ teaspoon grated
orange zest

1 teaspoon pure
vanilla extract

MAKES 6 SERVINGS

to reach halfway up the sides of the mold. Cover the pot
and place over medium heat until the water starts to simmer,
then reduce the heat so the water is barely simmering. Steam
the pudding until set, about 2 hours, adding hot water to the
pot as needed to maintain the original level.

Meanwhile, make the sauce. In a heavy frying pan over
medium heat, melt the granulated sugar until it turns dark
amber. Add the orange juice all at once, then the cream.
The sugar will harden and turn gummy immediately, but
continue to cook, pushing gently at the sugar with a wooden
spoon, until the cream boils and the sugar melts again, about
10 minutes. Bring to a rolling boil and remove from the heat.
Stir in the orange zest and vanilla. Set aside.

Remove the mold from the pot and let stand, covered, for
15 minutes. Uncover and unmold onto a serving plate. Serve
warm or at room temperature. To serve, pour a pool of the
sauce onto each individual plate and, using a large spoon,
divide the pudding among the plates.

STEAMED CHOCOLATE PUDDING

This traditional-style English steamed pudding can be served hot or at room temperature.
If serving hot, try topping it with a dollop of White Chocolate Cream (page 453). If serving
at room temperature, serve with Whipped Cream (page 454) or Raspberry Sauce (page 462).

4 oz (125 g) semisweet
or bittersweet chocolate,
chopped

½ cup (4 oz/125 g)
unsalted butter

1 extra-large egg

½ cup (4 oz/125 g) sugar

1 cup (4 oz/125 g) sifted
all-purpose (plain) flour

1½ teaspoons
baking powder

½ cup (4 fl oz/125 ml) milk

1 tablespoon pure
vanilla extract

MAKES 6–8 SERVINGS

Generously butter a 1-qt (1-l) pudding mold with a lid.

Place the chocolate and butter in the top pan of a double
boiler. Place over (not touching) barely simmering water and
heat, stirring occasionally, until melted and smooth. Remove
from the heat and let cool slightly.

In a small bowl, mix together the egg and sugar with a fork.
Stir the egg mixture into the chocolate.

Sift together the sifted flour and baking powder directly onto
the chocolate mixture. Gently fold the flour mixture into the
chocolate mixture, mixing just until incorporated. Stir in
the milk and vanilla. Pour and scrape the mixture into the
prepared mold. Secure the lid on the mold

Set the mold on a trivet or small wire rack in a pot large
enough to accommodate it comfortably. Pour in hot water
to reach halfway up the sides of the mold. Cover the pot and
place over medium heat until the water starts to simmer,
then reduce the heat so the water is barely simmering. Steam
until the pudding is set, about 1½ hours, adding hot water
to the pot as needed to maintain the original level.

Carefully remove the mold from the pot and uncover.
Invert the pudding onto a serving plate and lift off the
mold. Serve hot or at room temperature.

**Steamed-pudding
molds**

*Made especially for
the job, steamed-
pudding molds often
look similar to Bundt
pans, with decorative
ribbed sides and
bottoms and center
tubes for even heat
distribution. The
molds come with
a tight-fitting lid to
prevent the steaming
water from spoiling
the pudding. Look
for the molds in
kitchenware stores.*

MANGO MOUSSE

Change the fruits

You can easily vary this dessert by substituting other fruits for the raspberries. If you particularly like mangoes, use more of them. Other delicious options include blueberries, sliced strawberries, or diced stone fruit of any kind.

For maximum flavor in this light and refreshing dessert, choose only ripe, sweet mangoes. They should be soft but not shriveled, and resemble the juiciest of peaches when sliced. The mousse will keep for a day in the refrigerator without losing its volume.

Peel the mangoes. Slice as much of the flesh off the pits as possible. Be careful to capture any juices. Pass the mango pieces through a food mill held over a bowl to create a smooth purée. (Alternatively, press the mango flesh through a sieve into a bowl.) Add any captured juice to the bowl. Add the sugar and set aside, stirring occasionally, until the sugar dissolves completely in the juices.

In a small saucepan, sprinkle the gelatin over 3 tablespoons water and let soften for a few minutes. Place over low heat and stir just until dissolved. Do not allow to boil. Remove from the heat and let cool for 2–3 minutes, then stir into the mango purée until blended.

In a large chilled bowl, using a whisk or an electric mixer on medium-high speed, whip the cream until stiff peaks form. Fold one-fourth of the mango purée into the cream to lighten it. Then gently fold in the remaining mango purée just until combined with no streaks remaining.

Spoon alternating layers of raspberries and mango mousse into individual bowls or a 1½-qt (1.5-l) serving bowl. Refrigerate for at least 1 hour before serving.

1 lb (500 g) mangoes

½ cup (4 oz/125 g) sugar

1 envelope (1 tablespoon) unflavored gelatin

1 cup (8 fl oz/250 ml) heavy (double) cream

3 cups (12 oz/375 g) raspberries

MAKES 4 SERVINGS

CHOCOLATE MOUSSE

Copper bowls for whipping

If you own a copper bowl, you can use it to whip egg whites without the addition of cream of tartar. The copper reacts chemically with the egg protein to produce tall, fluffy, stable whites with a satiny finish.

This twist on a classic recipe adds just a hint of cardamom for an exotic touch. Look for bittersweet chocolate with a high cacao percentage for the most intense chocolate flavor. This recipe uses raw egg whites; for more information, see page 37.

In a cup, dissolve the espresso powder in the boiling water, stir in the cardamom, and set aside.

Combine the chocolate and butter in the top pan of a double boiler or in a heatproof bowl. Place over (not touching) barely simmering water and heat, stirring occasionally, until melted and smooth. Add the espresso mixture and stir until blended. Remove from the heat.

In a separate bowl, combine the egg yolks and sugar. Whisk until increased in volume and very light, 3–4 minutes. While stirring the melted chocolate with a wooden spoon, gradually add the yolk mixture, then beat until the chocolate thickens.

In a bowl, using a clean whisk or an electric mixer on medium-high speed, beat together the egg whites and cream of tartar until stiff, glossy peaks form. Add about one-fourth of the beaten whites to the chocolate mixture and, using a rubber

½ teaspoon instant espresso powder

1 tablespoon boiling water

⅛ teaspoon ground cardamom or cinnamon

4 oz (125 g) bittersweet chocolate, finely chopped

2 tablespoons unsalted butter

4 eggs, separated

1 tablespoon sugar

⅛ teaspoon cream of tartar

Candied orange peel strips (page 464) for garnish

MAKES 4 SERVINGS

spatula, stir gently to blend. Add the remaining egg whites and fold gently just until no white streaks remain. Pour into a serving bowl. Cover the bowl with paper towels (this absorbs any condensation that forms), making sure they do not touch the mousse. Refrigerate the mousse for several hours until the mousse is well set.

To serve, spoon the mousse into individual shallow bowls. Place the candied orange peel alongside each serving.

LEMON-RASPBERRY MOUSSE

For an elegant presentation, garnish this cool, tangy dessert with whole fresh raspberries, thin slivers of lemon zest, and mint leaves. It's perfect for a hot-weather dinner party. This recipe uses uncooked egg whites; for more information, see page 37.

1 envelope (1 tablespoon) unflavored gelatin

⅓ cup (3 fl oz/80 ml) fresh lemon juice

1 cup (8 oz/250 g) sugar

4 egg whites

2 teaspoons grated lemon zest

1 cup (8 fl oz/250 ml) heavy (double) cream

Raspberry Sauce (page 462)

MAKES 6 SERVINGS

In a small bowl, sprinkle the gelatin over 3 tablespoons water and let stand for a few minutes to soften. Meanwhile, in a small saucepan over low heat, combine the lemon juice and sugar and heat, stirring, until the sugar dissolves. Add the softened gelatin and stir until dissolved. Do not allow to boil. Remove from the heat and let cool to room temperature.

In a large bowl, using an electric mixer on medium-high speed, beat the egg whites until soft peaks form. With the mixer still on medium-high speed, add the gelatin mixture in a thin, steady stream, and then continue to beat until stiff peaks form. Using a rubber spatula, fold in the lemon zest just until evenly distributed. Set aside.

In a chilled bowl, using a whisk or the mixer on medium-high speed, beat the cream until stiff peaks form. Fold the cream into the egg white mixture just until combined.

Spoon half of the Raspberry Sauce in the bottom of individual bowls. Top with half of the mousse. Repeat the layers, then serve right away.

Quick-and-easy juicing

When you need a relatively small amount of citrus juice for a recipe, a handheld citrus reamer is a great tool. When citrus halves are pressed and twisted against the ridged, cone-shaped surface of the wooden or metal tool, the membranes are loosened, releasing the juice from the pulp.

587

STRAWBERRY PARFAIT

Fraises des bois parfait

If you see the small, perfumed wild strawberries, called fraises des bois, in springtime farmers' markets, buy them and use them in this recipe for a special-occasion meal. Stem them and cut them in half, rather than slice them, and layer with the sabayon.

Sabayon, a Marsala-flavored egg custard, is made light and airy here by the last-minute addition of beaten egg whites. In this version, strawberries are folded in as well. This recipe uses uncooked egg whites; for more information, see page 37.

In a small bowl or cup, sprinkle the gelatin over 2 teaspoons water and let soften for a few minutes.

Meanwhile, in a bowl, whisk together the egg yolks, Marsala, and 3 tablespoons of the sugar. Place over (not touching) simmering water in a saucepan and heat, stirring constantly with a spoon, until a thick custard forms, 5–7 minutes. To test, draw your finger across the back of the spoon. If it forms a path that remains for a few seconds before it begins to flow together, the custard is ready. Stir in the gelatin mixture. Remove from the heat and press a piece of plastic wrap directly onto the surface. Set aside to cool.

Reserve ⅓ cup (1½ oz/45 g) of the strawberries to use for garnish. Add the remaining 1 tablespoon sugar to the remaining strawberries and mash with a fork to make a purée. Cover and refrigerate the puréed berries until needed.

When the custard is cool, place the egg whites in a bowl. Using a whisk or an electric mixer on medium-high speed, beat until stiff peaks form. Using a rubber spatula, stir one-fourth of the egg whites into the custard to lighten it, then fold in the remaining egg whites just until no white streaks remain. Fold in the puréed berries. (At this point, the mixture can be covered and refrigerated for at least 2 hours and served chilled; stir well before serving.)

Spoon into individual bowls, garnish with the reserved strawberries, and serve.

¼ teaspoon unflavored gelatin

3 eggs, separated

¼ cup (2 fl oz/60 ml) sweet Marsala

4 tablespoons (2 oz/60 g) sugar

2 cups (8 oz/250 g) strawberries, stemmed and thinly sliced

MAKES 4 SERVINGS

CHOCOLATE POTS DE CRÈME

Watch custards closely

It is important not to overcook custards, particularly chocolate ones, or they will become grainy and curdled and the ingredients may separate, resulting in a watery consistency.

These chocolate custards are among the most elegant of desserts, with a deep, rich chocolate flavor and minimalist presentation. Pot de crème pots or cups are small, lidded porcelain vessels, with a single curved handle. Custard cups can be substituted.

Combine the cream, chocolate, brown sugar, and salt in a heatproof bowl. Place over (not touching) simmering water in a saucepan and heat, stirring occasionally, until the chocolate is melted and small bubbles begin to appear around the edge of the bowl.

In a small bowl, whisk the egg yolks until blended, then whisk in a few tablespoons of the hot chocolate cream to warm them. Gradually stir the combined mixture into the chocolate cream and cook over the simmering water, stirring occasionally, until thickened, about 10 minutes.

1⅓ cups (11 fl oz/330 ml) heavy (double) cream

4 oz (125 g) semisweet (plain) chocolate, grated

1 tablespoon plus 1 teaspoon firmly packed light brown sugar

Pinch of salt

4 egg yolks

1 teaspoon pure
vanilla extract

Sugared Flowers,
homemade (page 465)
or purchased

MAKES 4 SERVINGS

Remove the pan from the heat, stir in the vanilla, and pour into pot de crème pots or small custard cups, dividing evenly. Let cool uncovered, then cover and refrigerate until cold, about 2 hours or up to overnight. Remove from the refrigerator 30 minutes before serving.

To serve, garnish the pots de crème with the sugared flowers. Serve at room temperature.

ALMOND CUSTARD IN FILO LAYERS

For this impressive dessert, filo sheets are sandwiched with a flavorful almond custard for a dish that will remind you at once of both a napoleon and baklava. It makes a great dish for a tea party or luncheon, arranged on a pretty platter for guests to help themselves.

1 lb (500 g) almond paste,
at room temperature

½ cup (4 oz/125 g) sugar

8 eggs

2 teaspoons all-purpose
(plain) flour

1½ teaspoons
baking powder

½ teaspoon ground
cinnamon

3 tablespoons brandy

1 tablespoon grated
orange zest

16 filo sheets (about
12 oz/375 g), thawed
according to package
instructions if frozen

½ cup (4 oz/125 g)
Clarified Butter (page 28),
melted and kept warm

FOR THE SYRUP

2 cups (1 lb/500 g) sugar

2 tablespoons fresh
lemon juice

1 orange zest strip,
3 inches (7.5 cm) long
and ½ inch (12 mm) wide

1 cinnamon stick,
about 2 inches (5 cm)

MAKES 16–24 PIECES

Preheat the oven to 325°F (165°C).

In a bowl, using an electric mixer on medium speed, beat together the almond paste and sugar until well combined, about 5 minutes. Beat in the eggs, one at a time, beating well after each addition. Add the flour, baking powder, cinnamon, brandy, and grated orange zest and beat until the mixture is creamy, about 5 minutes.

Place the filo sheets flat on a work surface and cover with a sheet of plastic wrap topped with a lightly dampened kitchen towel to prevent the filo from drying out. Brush the bottom of an 11-by-16-by-2½-inch (28-by-40-by-6-cm) baking pan with a little of the warm clarified butter. Lay 1 filo sheet in the pan and brush lightly with butter. Top the sheet with 7 more sheets, brushing each with butter. If necessary, cut the sheets to fit. Pour in the almond mixture, spreading it evenly. Layer the remaining 8 filo sheets on top, again brushing each with butter. Using a sharp knife, score the top few layers of filo into 16–24 diamonds or squares.

Bake until golden, 45–50 minutes.

Meanwhile, make the syrup. In a heavy saucepan, combine the sugar, 1 cup (8 fl oz/250 ml) water, lemon juice, orange zest strip, and cinnamon stick. Bring to a boil over high heat, stirring to dissolve the sugar completely. Reduce the heat to medium-low and simmer until the syrup is slightly thickened, 8–10 minutes. Let cool completely, then remove and discard the orange zest and cinnamon stick.

When the pastry is done, remove from the oven and immediately pour the cooled syrup evenly over the top. Return to the oven for 2–3 minutes longer. Remove from the oven again and let stand for a few hours before serving. Using a sharp knife, cut the pastry into pieces along the scored lines, being careful to cut all the way through to the pan bottom. Serve at room temperature. Store leftover pastries in an airtight container at room temperature for up to 2 days.

Keep it covered

When working with filo dough, always keep the tissue-thin sheets covered with plastic wrap topped with a lightly dampened kitchen towel, or they will dry out and tear easily. You can purchase frozen filo at most supermarkets. Look for fresh filo sheets at some Middle Eastern markets.

589

SIMPLE LEMON CUSTARD

Custard cups

These small, round porcelain baking dishes, typically 3–4 inches (7.5–10 cm) in diameter, are used for cooking and serving custards, puddings, and other baked dishes. Unlike ramekins, which have angled bottoms, custard cups often feature rounded bottoms. Ramekins can usually be used in place of custard cups in recipes.

A soft baked custard is always a welcome sight at the end of a meal. This recipe makes enough for a special dessert for two. Double the ingredients to make dessert for four, or save the extra servings for an indulgent breakfast the next morning.

Preheat the oven to 350°F (180°C).

In a small saucepan over medium heat, combine the milk, sugar, lemon zest, and salt and heat, stirring to dissolve the sugar, until bubbles appear around the edge of the pan, about 5 minutes. Remove from the heat.

In a bowl, whisk the egg yolks just until blended. Gradually whisk in the hot milk mixture. Pour the mixture through a fine-mesh sieve into a large measuring pitcher. Divide between two ¾-cup (6–fl oz/180-ml) custard cups.

Place the custard cups in a baking pan just large enough to hold them without touching. Carefully add hot water to the pan to reach halfway up the sides of the cups. Bake until the custard looks set when you jiggle a cup gently, about 30 minutes. Remove the cups from the water bath, let cool, and cover and chill before serving.

1 cup (8 fl oz/250 ml) milk

2½ tablespoons sugar

3 lemon zest strips

Pinch of salt

2 egg yolks

MAKES 2 SERVINGS

WARM LEMON RICE CUSTARDS

Short-grain rice

Because they are high in starch, the almost-spherical kernels of short-grain rice yield slightly sticky, moist results when cooked. That quality helps create the desired firm, creamy texture in these rice custards and other rice-based custards and puddings.

A cross between rice pudding and a baked custard, these desserts can be served warm, or you can bake them several hours in advance and serve them at room temperature. Let the custards cool completely, cover, and refrigerate; remove about 20 minutes before serving.

Preheat the oven to 400°F (200°C). Butter twelve ⅔-cup (5–fl oz/160-ml) ramekins. Bring a 2-qt (2-l) saucepan three-fourths full of water to a boil. Add the rice, bring back just to a boil, reduce the heat to medium, and simmer for 5 minutes. Drain and transfer to a bowl.

Pour the milk into the same pan and bring to a boil over medium heat. Return the rice to the pan and add the lemon zest. Cook the mixture, stirring occasionally, until the rice is tender and the milk is absorbed, about 20 minutes. Remove the rice from the heat. Add the granulated sugar and butter and stir until the sugar is completely dissolved.

In a large bowl, whisk together the eggs, egg yolks, and lemon juice until blended. Slowly add one-fourth of the hot rice to the eggs while stirring constantly. Continue to add the rice slowly, stirring constantly, until all of the rice has been added. Do not add the hot rice too quickly or the eggs will scramble. Spoon the mixture into the prepared ramekins, dividing it evenly. (The custards can be prepared up to this point 1 day in advance, covered, and refrigerated. About 20 minutes before you are ready to bake the custards, remove them from the refrigerator.)

1 cup (7 oz/220 g) short-grain white rice

3 cups (24 fl oz/750 ml) milk

1 tablespoon grated lemon zest

¾ cup (6 oz/185 g) granulated sugar

2 tablespoons unsalted butter

3 eggs, plus 3 egg yolks

1 tablespoon fresh lemon juice

Confectioners' (icing) sugar for dusting

MAKES 12 SERVINGS

Place the ramekins in a baking pan just large enough to hold them without touching. Carefully add hot water to the pan to reach halfway up the sides of the ramekins, then cover the pan with aluminum foil and bake until a skewer inserted into the center of a custard comes out clean, 30–35 minutes. Remove the ramekins from the water bath and let them cool for 10–20 minutes. Using a fine-mesh sieve, dust the tops with confectioners' sugar and serve right away.

CINNAMON RICE PUDDING

For the most delicate flavor and the creamiest texture, serve this rice pudding cool, not chilled. Here, a good measure of cinnamon infuses the pudding and provides an attractive and flavorful garnish. Use a rasp grater for grating the cinnamon over the top of the finished pudding.

4½ cups (36 fl oz/1.1 l) milk

⅔ cup (5 oz/155 g) sugar

1 tablespoon grated lemon zest

1 cinnamon stick, 3 inches (7.5 cm), plus 1 stick for garnish, optional

½ vanilla bean, split lengthwise

1 cup (7 oz/220 g) Spanish Bomba or Italian Arborio rice

MAKES 6–8 SERVINGS

In a saucepan, stir together the milk, 1½ cups (12 fl oz/375 ml) water, the sugar, lemon zest, and 1 cinnamon stick. Using the tip of a small, sharp knife, scrape the seeds from the vanilla pod into the mixture and then add the pod. Stir in the rice and bring to just below a boil over medium-high heat. Reduce the heat to maintain a brisk simmer and cook, stirring often, until the rice is tender but some liquid remains, 35–45 minutes. The pudding should have the consistency of thin oatmeal.

Remove the vanilla pod and cinnamon stick and discard. Spoon the pudding into individual dessert glasses or into a 2-qt (2-l) serving dish. Let cool to room temperature and then cover and refrigerate until cool, at least 1 hour or up to 1 day. If desired, grate the cinnamon stick over the top of each dessert just before serving.

Rice types for pudding

Do not substitute long-grain rice in this recipe, as it will not provide the requisite starch to achieve the classic desired texture in the pudding. Both types suggested here are easy to find in specialty-foods stores, as each one is used for a popular savory dish, Bomba for paella and Arborio for risotto.

591

COEURS À LA CRÈME

These individual cream cheese–based desserts are made in special heart-shaped molds. They are classically accompanied by berries or a berry sauce, but you can substitute any fruits you wish. This recipe uses uncooked egg whites; for more information, turn to page 37.

Coeur à la crème molds

These heart-shaped molds, made of porcelain, can be found in small or large sizes. They feature several evenly spaced holes in the bottom of the molds to drain off excess moisture and produce the desired texture in the classic French dessert.

Line six 1-cup (8–fl oz/250-ml) heart-shaped coeur à la crème molds with cheesecloth (muslin). Allow about 2 inches (5 cm) of cheesecloth to overhang the edges.

Using a large chilled bowl and chilled beaters, whip the cream on medium-high speed until it holds soft peaks. Beat in the cream cheese until the mixture is smooth.

In another bowl, using a whisk, beat together the egg whites and sugar until stiff, glossy peaks form. Fold the beaten egg whites into the cream mixture. Divide the mixture evenly among the prepared molds. Gently press down on the tops to pack each mold well. Set the molds in a large baking pan or roasting pan and cover the pan with plastic wrap. Place in the refrigerator to drain for at least 4 hours or up to 12 hours.

To serve, for each mold, invert an individual plate over the mold, then, holding the plate and mold together firmly, invert. Lift off the mold and peel off the cheesecloth. Repeat for all the molds, then spoon the sauce over the hearts and garnish with the berries, if using.

1 cup (8 fl oz/250 ml) heavy (double) cream

¾ lb (375 g) cream cheese, at room temperature

2 egg whites

¼ cup (2 oz/60 g) superfine (caster) sugar

Blueberry Sauce (page 463), chilled

6 strawberries, optional

MAKES 6 SERVINGS

PANNA COTTA WITH STRAWBERRIES

This extravagantly rich, quivery dessert, literally "cooked cream," is the perfect companion to summer fruits. Serve on individual dessert plates, surrounded by lightly sweetened ripe berries. A small portion is satisfying, especially if you use the very best ingredients.

High-flavor cream

For this dessert, it's worth it to seek out cream that has not been ultrapasturized, a process that involves heating the cream to 300°F (150°C) to extend shelf life. This means buying cream from a natural- or specialty-foods store, instead of the supermarket.

To make the cream, place the milk in a small bowl, sprinkle the gelatin over the top, and let stand for 5 minutes to soften.

Meanwhile, in a saucepan, combine the cream and sugar. Using the tip of a small, sharp knife, scrape the seeds from the vanilla pod into the cream mixture and then add the pod. Place over medium heat and stir until the cream just begins to simmer. Remove from the heat. Add the gelatin-milk mixture and stir to dissolve completely. Let cool for 10 minutes, then stir in the rum. Remove and discard the vanilla pod. Divide the mixture among twelve ½-cup (4–fl oz/ 125-ml) custard cups. Cover the cups with plastic wrap and refrigerate until set, about 8 hours.

About 1 hour before serving, prepare the fruit. In a large bowl, combine half of the strawberries and the sugar and crush with a fork. Slice the remaining strawberries (or leave whole if using small berries of another type) and add to the

FOR THE CREAM

½ cup (4 fl oz/125 ml) milk

1 envelope (1 tablespoon) unflavored gelatin

4 cups (32 fl oz/1 l) heavy (double) cream

¾ cup (6 oz/185 g) sugar

1 piece vanilla bean, 2 inches (5 cm) long, split lengthwise

3 tablespoons light rum

FOR THE FRUIT

4 cups (1 lb/500 g) strawberries or other berries

¼ cup (2 oz/60 g) sugar, or as needed

MAKES 12 SERVINGS

bowl. Toss to combine, then taste and add more sugar if needed. Cover, and refrigerate until serving.

To unmold the creams, set each custard cup in warm water to reach about halfway up the sides. Let stand for about 20 seconds. Remove from the water, wipe dry, then invert a serving plate over the cup and invert the serving plate and cup together. Shake gently until the cream comes loose. If it doesn't come loose easily, run a small knife around the inside edge of the cup to loosen the cream, then invert again.

Spoon the berries around the unmolded creams, dividing them evenly. Serve right away.

TAPIOCA BRÛLÉE WITH DRIED BLUEBERRIES

This version of crème brûlée is a riff on a treasured comfort-food dish: tapioca pudding. Here, it is studded with tangy dried blueberries and then topped with a caramelized topping for a modern take on the classic. Make the topping just before serving to preserve its crunch.

2 eggs, lightly beaten

6 tablespoons (1½ oz/45 g) instant tapioca

1 can (14 fl oz/430 ml) condensed milk

2 cups (16 fl oz/500 ml) milk

1 teaspoon grated lemon zest

⅔ cup (3 oz/90 g) dried blueberries

1 cup (7 oz/220 g) firmly packed dark brown sugar

MAKES 8 SERVINGS

In a saucepan, whisk together the eggs, tapioca, condensed milk, and milk until blended. Let stand for 5 minutes. Place over medium heat and stir slowly until the mixture comes to a full boil, 5–7 minutes. Cook, stirring constantly, until the mixture thickens considerably, about 1 minute longer. Stir in the lemon zest and blueberries. Pour the mixture into a shallow 1½–2-qt (1.5–2-l) flameproof dish. Refrigerate, uncovered, until very cold.

Just before serving, position a rack as close as possible to the heat source in the broiler (grill) and preheat the broiler. Place the brown sugar in a small bowl and stir in 2 tablespoons hot water to make a very thick paste free of lumps. Using the back of a spoon, spread a thin layer of the sugar paste over the top of the chilled pudding. Broil (grill) until the sugar melts and starts to bubble, 1–2 minutes. Watch carefully as it can burn easily. Remove from the oven and let stand until the sugar hardens into a shiny crust, 5–10 minutes.

Spoon onto small individual plates and serve right away.

593

Tapioca types

Tapioca comes in three basic forms, pearl (small dried balls of tapioca starch), granulated (coarsely broken-up pearl tapioca), and instant (finely granulated pearl tapioca). Be sure to use the form that is called for in the recipe you are using, as they are not interchangeable.

CARAMELIZED PUMPKIN FLANS

Sweet potato flan

Cooked and mashed orange-fleshed sweet potatoes can be used here in place of the pumpkin. To quickly cook the potatoes, prick them in several places with a fork and then cook in a microwave until very soft, 7–8 minutes. Let cool slightly, cut in half lengthwise, scoop out the flesh with a spoon, and mash the flesh well with a fork.

Some of the iconic flavors of the fall and winter holidays—pumpkin purée and a trio of warm pie spices—are in these rich custards. They are gilded with a dark, sweet layer of caramel, which becomes a complementary sauce after they are unmolded.

Preheat the oven to 325°F (165°C). Place four ½-cup (4–fl oz/ 125-ml) custard cups or ceramic ramekins in a baking pan just large enough to hold them without touching.

In a small saucepan over low heat, combine ½ cup (4 oz/125 g) of the sugar and 1½ tablespoons water and stir until the sugar dissolves. Raise the heat to high and cook, without stirring, until the liquid is caramel colored and has a faintly burnt aroma, 6–8 minutes; do not allow it to burn. Remove from the heat and carefully pour into the custard cups, tilting them to coat the bottoms and sides. Return to the pan.

In a saucepan over medium heat, warm the cream until small bubbles appear around the edge of the pan. Remove the pan from the heat. In a bowl, combine the pumpkin, the remaining ¼ cup (2 oz/60 g) sugar, the orange zest, cinnamon, ginger, nutmeg, and salt and mix well. Stir in the eggs until blended. Slowly add the hot cream while stirring constantly. Stir in the vanilla, and pour the mixture into the prepared custard cups.

Pour hot water into the pan to reach halfway up the sides of the cups. Cover the pan with aluminum foil. Bake until just set and a knife inserted into the center of a flan comes out clean, about 45 minutes. Carefully remove from the water bath and let rest on a wire rack for about 30 minutes, then cover and refrigerate until well chilled.

At serving time, run a knife around the inside edge of each dish and invert each flan onto a small individual plate or into a shallow bowl, allowing the caramel at the bottom of the cup to drizzle over the top of the flan. Serve right away.

¾ cup (6 oz/185 g) sugar

¾ cup (6 fl oz/180 ml) light (single) cream

½ cup (4 oz/125 g) pumpkin purée

Grated zest of 1 small orange

½ teaspoon ground cinnamon

¼ teaspoon ground ginger

Pinch of freshly grated nutmeg

Pinch of salt

2 eggs, lightly beaten

½ teaspoon pure vanilla extract

MAKES 4 SERVINGS

CRÈME CARAMEL

This favorite dessert can be found in many countries, either plain or flavored with various local ingredients. Flan is an example of the Spanish version, but this one reflects the French classic, with its particularly creamy, rich texture and flavor. It can be prepared well in advance.

1¼ cups (10 oz/315 g) sugar

1½ cups (12 fl oz/ 375 ml) milk

1½ cups (12 fl oz/375 ml) half-and-half (half cream)

3 eggs, plus 3 egg yolks

1 teaspoon pure vanilla extract

MAKES 8 OR 10 SERVINGS

Preheat the oven to 325°F (165°C). Place eight 1-cup (8–fl oz/ 250-ml) or ten ¾-cup (6–fl oz/180-ml) custard cups in a baking pan just large enough to hold them without touching.

In a small, heavy saucepan over low heat, combine ½ cup (4 oz/125 g) of the sugar and 3 tablespoons water and stir to dissolve the sugar. Raise the heat to high and cook, without stirring, until the liquid is caramel colored and has a faintly burnt aroma, 6–8 minutes; do not allow the mixture to burn. Remove from the heat and carefully pour the caramel into the custard cups, tilting them to coat the bottoms and sides. Return to the baking pan.

To make the custard, in a saucepan over medium heat, combine the milk, half-and-half, and the remaining ¾ cup (6 oz/185 g) sugar and heat, stirring to dissolve the sugar, until small bubbles appear around the edge of the pan. Meanwhile, in a bowl, lightly whisk together the eggs and egg yolks until blended. Very gradually add the hot milk mixture to the eggs while whisking constantly. Whisk in the vanilla. Pour the mixture through a fine-mesh sieve into a pitcher, and then pour into the prepared custard cups.

Pour hot water into the baking pan to reach halfway up the sides of the cups. Cover the pan with aluminum foil. Bake until just set and a knife inserted in the center of one of the custards comes out clean, about 50 minutes. Remove the custards from the water bath, let cool to room temperature, and refrigerate, uncovered, for 3 hours. You can then cover the custards and refrigerate for up to 2 days, if desired.

At serving time, run a knife around the inside edge of each custard cup and invert each custard onto a small individual plate or into a shallow bowl. Allow the caramel at the bottom of the cup to drizzle over the top of the custard and then remove the cups. Serve right away.

Orange crème caramel

To give this custard an orange flavor, stir 1 tbsp grated orange zest and 2 tbsp orange liqueur into the custard before pouring it into the custard cups.

595

CLASSIC CRÈME BRÛLÉE

Another way to caramelize

If you don't have a culinary torch for caramelizing the topping, place an oven rack 3–4 inches (7.5–10 cm) below the heating element and preheat the broiler (grill). Place the ramekins on a rimmed baking sheet and broil until the sugar bubbles and caramelizes, 1–2 minutes.

The name for this popular custard translates as "burnt cream" and the name fits. Crème brûlée has a silky richness that is perfectly complemented by a crisp topping of caramelized sugar. Properly prepared, the topping should crack audibly when you break into it with a spoon.

Preheat the oven to 325°F (165°C). Place six ¾-cup (6–fl oz/180-ml) ramekins in a baking pan just large enough to hold them without touching.

In a saucepan over medium heat, combine the cream, the ½ cup (3½ oz/105 g) sugar, vanilla bean, and salt and bring to a boil, stirring occasionally. Remove from the heat, cover, and let stand for 15 minutes to blend the flavors. Remove the vanilla pod from the cream and, using the tip of a small, sharp knife, scrape the seeds into the cream. Discard the pod.

In a large bowl, whisk the egg yolks until blended. Very gradually add the hot cream to the egg yolks while whisking constantly. Pour the mixture through a fine-mesh sieve into a pitcher, and then pour into the prepared ramekins.

Pour hot water into the baking pan to reach halfway up the sides of the ramekins. Bake until the custards jiggle just slightly in the centers when the ramekins are gently shaken, 30–35 minutes. Carefully remove the baking pan from the oven and let the custards cool in the water bath for 30 minutes. Remove the ramekins from the pan and let cool to room temperature. Wrap each ramekin in plastic wrap. Refrigerate for at least 4 hours or up to 3 days.

Unwrap the custards and sprinkle the 2 tablespoons sugar evenly over the tops. Tilt and tap each ramekin to distribute the sugar evenly on the surface of the custard. Using a culinary torch, caramelize the sugar by moving the torch in a figure-eight motion until the sugar is evenly browned and melted. Serve right away.

2½ cups (20 fl oz/625 ml) heavy (double) cream

½ cup (3½ oz/105 g) plus 2 tablespoons sugar

½ vanilla bean, split lengthwise

Pinch of salt

8 egg yolks

MAKES 6 SERVINGS

CRANBERRY CRÈME BRÛLÉE

Cranberries provide a tart surprise in this creamy-crisp autumn dessert. In other seasons, substitute your favorite fresh fruits—try berries or diced peaches—adjusting the amount of sugar according to the sweetness of the fruit.

Unsalted butter
for ramekins

2 cups (8 oz/250 g)
cranberries, halved

½ cup (4 oz/120 g)
granulated sugar

3 cups (24 fl oz/750 ml)
heavy (double) cream

1 piece vanilla bean,
2 inches (5 cm) long,
split lengthwise

8 egg yolks

½ cup (3½ oz/105 g) firmly
packed brown sugar

MAKES 8 SERVINGS

Preheat the oven to 350°F (180°C). Lightly butter the bottoms of eight ½-cup (4–fl oz/125-ml) ramekins and place in a baking pan just large enough to hold them without touching.

In a bowl, toss the cranberries with ¼ cup (2 oz/60 g) of the granulated sugar. Divide the sugared cranberries evenly among the prepared ramekins.

Pour the cream into a heavy saucepan. Using the tip of a small, sharp knife, scrape the seeds from the vanilla bean into the cream and then add the pod. Place over medium heat and heat until small bubbles appear around the edge of the pan. Remove from the heat.

In a bowl, whisk together the egg yolks and the remaining ¼ cup granulated sugar until pale yellow and thickened. Remove and discard the vanilla pod from the cream. Very gradually add the hot cream to the egg yolks while whisking constantly. Return the mixture to the saucepan, place over low heat, and cook, stirring constantly, until the mixture coats the back of a wooden spoon, 7–10 minutes. Remove the custard from the heat and pour through a fine-mesh sieve into the prepared ramekins.

Pour hot water into the baking pan to reach halfway up the sides of the ramekins. Bake until the custards jiggle just slightly in the centers when the ramekins are gently shaken, 20–25 minutes. Remove the ramekins from the baking dish and let cool to room temperature. Wrap each ramekin in plastic wrap. Refrigerate for at least 4 hours or up to 2 days.

Unwrap the custards and sprinkle the brown sugar evenly over the tops of the ramekins. Tilt and tap each ramekin to distribute the sugar evenly on the surface of the custard. Using a culinary torch, caramelize the sugar by moving the torch in a figure-eight motion until the sugar is evenly browned and melted. Serve right away.

Testing custards for doneness

When baking custards, don't let the center of the custard set fully in the oven, or it will turn out tough. The custard should still wiggle slightly when the dish is gently shaken, or a knife inserted into the center should come out clean but moist.

597

Frozen DESSERTS

Frozen Desserts

A scoop of ice cream or sorbet is one of summer's most welcome delights. Many of us think of frozen desserts as warm-weather treats. But as the guidelines on these pages and the the wide range of recipe styles and flavors that follow demonstrate, ice creams, gelati, sorbets, and other frozen desserts can be enjoyed year-round—any time you want to end a meal or perk up your afternoon with a cold, flavorful dessert.

Frozen Dessert Types and Techniques

Allow time to chill
Most frozen dessert bases benefit from being refrigerated until well chilled before you pour them into an ice cream maker. Chilling them helps bring together the flavors and prevents ice crystals from forming during churning, improving the final texture. Also, if you're using a machine that calls for ice, less ice will be needed later to cool the base, thus reducing the churning time.

Start sorbets with fresh fruit
When making fruit-flavored sorbets, use only fresh fruit. Sorbets made with cooked or canned fruits will not have the desired refreshing quality.

Successful scooping
A couple of simple tips will help you scoop ice cream like a pro. First, remove most frozen desserts from the freezer a short time before serving, so they can soften slightly at room temperature. Next, dip your ice cream scoop into a cup or bowl filled with hot water for several seconds, then shake off any water before scooping. The hot scoop will glide through the frozen mixture effortlessly.

Say "frozen dessert" and the first thing that comes to mind is generally some form of ice cream. But, as the wide range of recipes on the following pages demonstrate, frozen desserts come in many forms. Here are the seven main categories of frozen desserts in this book.

ICE CREAMS Two basic types of ice cream exist, one literally what the name implies, and the other a richer frozen dessert based on custard.

In its most basic and subtle-tasting version, sometimes referred to as Philadelphia-style ice cream because of its popularity in that city, ice cream is a mixture of heavy (double) cream or half-and-half (half cream), sugar, and flavorings, cooked until the sugar dissolves and then frozen in an ice cream maker. More complicated to make, and yielding richer results, are classic ice creams based on a custard mixture, sometimes called French-style ice cream, such as the Classic Vanilla Bean Ice Cream on page 604.

To make a classic custard-based ice cream: Heat cream or half-and-half, combined with any flavorings, following the recipe instructions. Meanwhile, in a bowl, whisk together sugar and egg yolks until smooth. While whisking continuously, slowly pour in the hot cream or half-and-half to form a custard mixture. Return the mixture to the saucepan, place over gentle heat, and cook, stirring continuously with a spatula or wooden spoon, until the custard thickens sufficiently to leave a path when you draw your finger across the back of the spatula or spoon, usually about 5 minutes. Set a sieve over a clean bowl and pour the custard through it to remove any lumps or bits of flavoring. Refrigerate the custard until very cold. Transfer to an ice cream maker and freeze according to the manufacturer's instructions, then transfer to an airtight freezer container and freeze until firm. To serve, remove from the freezer and, if necessary to ease scooping, let soften slightly at room temperature. Serve with an ice cream scoop.

GELATI These Italian-style frozen treats differ from ice cream in more than just name. Gelato is typically based on milk and sugar, with a wide range of different flavorings but without the use of eggs. Although it is lower in fat than ice cream, it also has a richer, denser consistency that is prized by its partisans. In commercial settings, this dense character is a result of being churned more slowly than ice cream, which means less air is beaten into the mixture as it freezes, although at home there is no way to alter the churning speed of the ice cream maker.

GRANITAS The Italian term *granita* refers to the granular texture of this variation on sorbet. Granitas such as Lemon-Lime Granita (page 612) are made without the aid of an ice cream maker, using only a metal bowl, freezer, whisk and/or fork to achieve the refreshingly icy result.

To make a granita: First pour the granita mixture, prepared according to the recipe instructions, into a shallow metal bowl or pan. Put the bowl in the freezer and freeze until the mixture is semifirm, whisking it every 15 to 30 minutes to promote even freezing, depending on the recipe. Then freeze until solid. Remove from the freezer and, using the tines of a table fork, firmly scrape the surface of the frozen mixture to form icy crystals. Scoop into serving dishes or glasses and serve right away.

SORBETS Characterized by their dense, smooth texture and wonderfully intense flavor, sorbets (pages 613–15) are usually based on pulverized fruit and are sweetened with either simple syrup or corn syrup, or a mixture. Sherbets, a close cousin, usually contain a little milk or half-and-half (half cream), while traditional sorbets are dairy free.

To make a sorbet: First combine the ingredients and blend thoroughly to form a purée, following the recipe instructions. Transfer to a bowl, cover, and refrigerate until very cold. Place the purée in an ice cream maker and process according to the manufacturer's instructions. Transfer to a freezer container and freeze until firm. To serve, remove the sorbet from the freezer and, if necessary to ease scooping, let it soften slightly at room temperature. Serve with an ice cream scoop.

FROZEN MOUSSES These frozen desserts are based on a light yet rich mixture of whipped cream or sometimes beaten egg whites, sugar, and flavorings. Sometimes beaten egg yolks are also incorporated. Because they are already stable when prepared and do not require the churning action of an ice cream maker to achieve a smooth consistency, frozen mousses are typically spooned into large or individual molds and slipped directly into the freezer. Large frozen mousses are usually unmolded to make an impressive presentation, as in Frozen Lemon Mousse with Blueberries (page 616); individual versions, such as Frozen Eggnog Mousse (page 616), are usually served in the containers in which they were frozen.

To freeze and unmold a mousse: Line the mold with plastic wrap, overhanging the edges by about 3 inches (7.5 cm). After filling the mold with the mousse mixture, fold the overhang over the mousse and then freeze until solid. About 1 hour before serving, place a serving platter in the freezer to chill. At serving time, uncover the mousse. Invert the chilled platter over the mold and then, holding the mold and platter firmly together with both hands, invert them. Lift off the mold and peel off the plastic wrap.

FROZEN YOGURTS A softer, tangier version of ice cream, frozen yogurt is a popular treat. It is easy to achieve frozen yogurt–shop results at home, such as in Raspberry Frozen Yogurt (page 615).

To make frozen yogurt: In a bowl, stir together plain yogurt, sweeteners, and flavorings. Cover and refrigerate until very cold, then transfer to an ice cream maker to churn as you would ice cream. Transfer to a freezer container and freeze until firm. Serve with an ice cream scoop, as you would ice cream.

PIES AND TORTES A wide variety of frozen desserts use ice cream, gelato, sorbet, or frozen mousse as the starting point for a more elaborate construction: an ice cream pie, cake, or torte.

In general, an ice cream pie such as Frozen Chocolate-Cream Cheese Pie (page 617) begins with a crumb crust (page 446), into which a softened frozen mixture is packed and smoothed. Before it is frozen solid, the pie can be topped with a layer of sweet sauce or some other embellishments or decorations, or the pie can be garnished with them after it is cut into wedges.

SERVING VESSELS

Frozen desserts can be attractively presented in a wide array of different types of containers.

Bowls and dishes
Whether small cups or bowls, elongated boats for holding multiscoop banana splits, or tall, fluted glasses ideal for sundaes or layered parfaits, many people like to put these containers in the freezer to chill shortly before serving time, so the desserts will stay colder longer.

Cones
Most supermarkets stock both types of classic cones: light and airy, pale tan "cake" cones and thinner, crispier, long, conical waffle-patterned "sugar" cones.

Filo cups
To make delicate, crisp cups, preheat an oven to 325°F (165°C). Butter 12 standard muffin cups. Melt 4 tbsp (2 oz/60 g) unsalted butter. Lay 1 filo sheet, about 12 by 16 inches (30 by 40 cm), on a sheet of waxed paper. Brush with some of the butter. Top with 3 more filo sheets, brushing each one with butter. Cut the stack into 12 pieces, each about 4 inches (10 cm) square, and gently press each piece into a prepared muffin cup. Bake until crisp and golden, about 10 minutes. Remove from the oven and let cool completely.

Tuile cups
Prepare the recipe for Pecan Tuiles (page 484), but gently press the still-warm cookies into individual muffin cups or onto overturned small ramekins to form cups. Let cool completely before using.

Mix-in techniques

Add ingredients toward the end of churning, when the ice cream is well frozen but still soft enough to stir or mold, or swirl them in by hand. You can alternate the ingredients with two or more layers of ice cream when you pack it.

Candies

Homemade or purchased candies make great additions. Try crushed red-and-white-striped peppermints; chunks of creamy chocolate truffle (pages 576–77); bits of marshmallow; or nuggets of nut brittle.

Chocolate Pieces

Whether you prefer bittersweet, semisweet, milk, or white chocolate, it makes a welcome addition to ice creams in the form of chips, chopped chunks, or shavings.

Cookies

Many people find the pairing of ice cream and cookies irresistible. Try sandwich, chocolate chip, gingersnap, or oatmeal raisin cookies.

Fruit

Mix in bite-size chunks of fresh fruits such as berries; dried fruits such as raisins; candied citrus peel; or a swirl of fruit syrup or your favorite jelly or jam.

Nuts

Use any shelled, toasted whole or coarsely chopped nuts, including almonds, hazelnuts (filberts), walnuts, pecans, macadamias, cashews, and peanuts.

Basic Frozen Dessert Techniques

USING AN ICE CREAM MAKER There are two basic kinds of ice cream makers. Both deliver good results and differ primarily in their cooling process and the amount of effort required.

Traditional ice cream makers: In its most basic form, a traditional ice cream maker consists of a hand crank, a bucket with a smaller canister inside, and a dasher, or stirrer. A combination of ice and rock salt is used to fill the gap between the bucket and the canister to chill down the ice cream base while you turn the crank, which rotates the dasher inside the canister. A popular variation replaces the ice and salt with liquid coolant concealed between the walls of a double-walled canister. The disadvantage is that you need to prefreeze the canister for up to 24 hours before you use it. Electric versions feature motors that turn the dasher for you.

Refrigeration ice cream makers: These self-contained, more costly—but exceedingly convenient—counter top appliances feature small electric freezing units that surround the tub into which you put the frozen dessert mixture, which is churned automatically.

SCOOPING ICE CREAM INTO CONES You can use almost any ice cream flavor that goes well with chocolate to make chocolate-dipped cones. However, avoid using ice creams that contain wine or liqueur, as they have a softer consistency that makes eating from a cone difficult.

To fill ice cream cones: First spoon a small amount of ice cream into a sugar cone, packing it gently. Then, dip a large ice cream scoop into hot water, shaking off the excess water; scoop a large ball of ice cream and place the ball on top of the cone, pressing down gently. Stand the cone upright in a small glass and place in the freezer. Repeat until you have as many servings as you like. Freeze until firm, about 2 hours.

PRESENTING FROZEN MOUSSES Mousse mixtures can be frozen into shapes that visually highlight their light and airy consistency.

To create individual frozen mousse soufflés: First make foil collars for individual ramekins. For each ¾-cup (6-fl oz/180-ml) ramekin, cut a 12-by-6-inch (30-by-15-cm) piece of aluminum foil. Fold in half lengthwise and wrap around the ramekin, forming a collar that extends from the base to above the rim. Fold and crimp the ends to seal. Spoon in the mousse, filling almost to the top of the foil. Freeze until solid. Just before serving, dip a small, thin, sharp knife blade in hot water, dry it, and run it between the mousse and the collar. Then, carefully unwrap the collar. Using the knife, smooth the sides of each mousse, if necessary.

To make and fill citrus cups: Cut a slice 1 inch (2.5 cm) thick from the stem end of a citrus fruit. Using a paring knife, cut around the pulp, then scoop it out with a small spoon. Cut a thin slice from the blossom end of the fruit so the cup will stand upright. For each cup, cut an 8-by-1-inch (20-by-2.5-cm) strip of parchment paper or aluminum foil and form a collar inside the shell, extending it about ¾ inch (2 cm) above the rim. Secure with tape and freeze. Spoon in the mousse (or softened ice cream or sorbet), filling to within ¼ inch (6 mm) of the top of the collar. Freeze overnight, or until solid. Just before serving, cut the tape. Dip a small, thin, sharp knife blade in hot water, dry it, and run it between the mousse and collar. Then, carefully remove the collar, lifting it up and away from the mousse. Using the knife, smooth the sides of each mousse, if necessary.

MAKING ICE CREAM SANDWICHES

Easy and appealing to pick up and eat out of hand, ice cream sandwiches are among the most popular frozen desserts. And they're so easy to make: Use any flavor ice cream you like, whether homemade or purchased; prepare or buy your favorite cookies, making sure they are of uniform size and ideally at least 3 inches (7.5 cm) in diameter.

To make ice cream sandwiches, remove the ice cream from the freezer and leave it at room temperature just until it has softened slightly. Scoop or spoon the ice cream onto the flat side of one cookie, using about ⅓ cup (3 fl oz/80 ml) for a 3-inch (7.5-cm) sandwich. Top with another cookie, flat side down. Press gently to spread the ice cream to the edge, smoothing the edge of the ice cream, if necessary, with the spoon or the edge of a table knife. If you like, roll the edge of the ice cream in nuts, chocolate chips, jimmies, sprinkles, or another embellishment. Wrap each sandwich in plastic wrap or foil and freeze until firm, about 2 hours.

Once you've mastered the method, it's easy to come up with all sorts of creative ice cream sandwich variations. Here are a few suggestions based on some of the recipes in this book.

Chocolate-Mint Ice Cream Sandwiches

Use Mint-Chocolate Chip Ice Cream (page 605) and your favorite chocolate cookies. If you like, chop chocolate-covered after-dinner mints and roll the edge of each ice cream sandwich in the pieces.

Triple-Chocolate Ice Cream Sandwiches

Use Chocolate Ice Cream with Fudge Swirl (page 604) and Chocolate-Chunk Cookies (page 471). If you like, roll the edge of each ice cream sandwich in chocolate chips, chocolate sprinkles, or grated chocolate (page 566) before freezing the sandwich solid.

Oatmeal-Nut Ice Cream Sandwiches

Use Classic Vanilla Bean Ice Cream (page 604) and Crisp Oatmeal Cookies (page 479). If you like, roll the edge of each sandwich in chopped walnuts, raisins, or trail mix before freezing the sandwich solid.

Peanut Butter and Berry Ice Cream Sandwiches

Use Strawberry Ice Cream (page 607) and Double-Peanut Peanut Butter Cookies (page 473). If you like, roll the edge of each ice cream sandwich in chopped peanuts before freezing the sandwich solid.

Peach and Pecan Ice Cream Sandwiches

Use Fresh Peach Ice Cream (page 606) and Snickerdoodles (page 474). If you like, roll the edge of each ice cream sandwich in chopped toasted pecans before freezing the sandwich solid.

Pumpkin Ginger Ice Cream Sandwiches

Use Pumpkin Spice Ice Cream (page 608) and Chewy Ginger Cookies (page 474). If you like, roll the edge of each ice cream sandwich in toasted shredded coconut before freezing the sandwich solid.

Coconut–White Chocolate Ice Cream Sandwiches

Use Coconut Ice Cream (page 608) and store-bought Chinese-style almond cookies. If you like, roll the edge of each ice cream sandwich in toasted shredded coconut or white chocolate chips before freezing the sandwich solid.

TOPPINGS AND GARNISHES

Adding a sauce, topping, or garnish to a frozen dessert makes an already welcome treat even more festive. Here are some ideas.

Chocolate
Sprinkle with chopped, shaved, curled, or grated chocolate (page 566).

Citrus zest
Especially good for fruit sorbets. Draw a citrus zester across the peel of a citrus fruit to remove its colorful, flavorful zest in long strips.

Chopped nuts and candies
Strew with toasted nuts, chopped brittle (page 568), or crumbled pralines (page 570) for a tasty crunch.

Sauces
Drizzle with your favorite store-bought sauce or a sweet sauce from this book, such as Hot Fudge Sauce (page 460), Butterscotch Sauce (page 461), or Raspberry Sauce (page 462).

Store-bought garnishes
Check the baking or ice cream sections of your market for chocolate jimmies, rainbow sprinkles, pastel candy confetti, or other similar decorations.

Sugared flowers
Use the recipe on page 465, or purchase sugared petals from a specialty-foods store. Violets and rose petals are common finds.

Whipped cream
Top nearly any frozen dessert with a spoonful of Whipped Cream (page 454).

CLASSIC VANILLA BEAN ICE CREAM

Read before you churn

Every ice cream maker is different. Before starting a recipe, be sure to read the instruction manual that came with your ice cream maker so that you know how it works and how to clean it thoroughly.

The best vanilla ice cream is made with vanilla beans that have been steeped in custard to release their maximum flavor. If vanilla beans are unavailable, omit the steeping and add 2 teaspoons pure vanilla extract to the chilled custard before freezing.

Pour the half-and-half into a heavy saucepan. Scrape the seeds from the vanilla pod into the pan and add the pod. Bring to a simmer over medium-high heat. Remove from the heat, cover, and let stand for 30 minutes.

Return the saucepan to the stove top over medium-high heat and again bring to a simmer. Meanwhile, in a bowl, whisk the sugar and egg yolks until blended. Very gradually add the hot half-and-half to the yolk mixture while whisking constantly. Return the mixture to the saucepan and place over medium-low heat. Cook, stirring slowly and constantly with a heat-resistant spatula, until the custard thickens and leaves a path on the back of the spatula when a finger is drawn across it, about 5 minutes. Do not allow to boil.

Pour the custard through a medium-mesh sieve into a clean bowl. Let cool, cover, and refrigerate until very cold, at least 3 hours or up to 24 hours.

Pour the custard into an ice cream maker and freeze according to the manufacturer's instructions. Transfer to a tightly covered container and place in the freezer until firm, at least 3 hours or up to 24 hours.

3 cups (24 fl oz/750 ml) half-and-half (half cream)

1 vanilla bean, split lengthwise

¾ cup (6 oz/185 g) sugar

6 egg yolks

MAKES ABOUT 5 CUPS (40 FL OZ/1.25 L)

604

CHOCOLATE ICE CREAM WITH FUDGE SWIRL

Layering flavors

Milk or cream, sugar, and eggs are the "body" of ice creams, but flavorings form the fashionable dress that gives them a personality. Like good clothing, flavors should be added with care, at the correct time, and often in different layers. And like too many pieces in an outfit, too many different flavors can overwhelm an ice cream.

In this chocolate lover's dream, large pockets of fudge are hidden inside a rich chocolate base for a surprise in every spoonful. For a pretty presentation, garnish scoops of the ice cream with sugared edible flowers or rose petals (page 465).

In a heavy saucepan over medium-high heat, warm 1½ cups (12 fl oz/375 ml) of the half-and-half until it comes to a simmer. Remove from the heat.

In a bowl, whisk together the egg yolks, sugar, and corn syrup until blended. Very gradually add the hot half-and-half to the yolk mixture while whisking constantly. Return the mixture to the saucepan and place over medium-low heat. Cook, stirring slowly and constantly with a heat-resistant spatula, until the custard thickens and leaves a path on the back of the spatula when a finger is drawn across it, about 5 minutes. Do not allow to boil.

Pour the custard through a medium-mesh sieve into a clean bowl. Add the chocolate and stir until melted. Stir in the vanilla and the remaining ½ cup (4 fl oz/125 ml) half-and-half. Let cool, cover, and refrigerate until very cold, at least 3 hours or up to 24 hours.

2 cups (16 fl oz/500 ml) half-and-half (half cream)

3 egg yolks

½ cup (4 oz/125 g) sugar

2 tablespoons light corn syrup

5 oz (155 g) bittersweet chocolate, finely chopped

½ teaspoon pure vanilla extract

4 tablespoons Hot Fudge Sauce, cooled to lukewarm (page 460)

MAKES ABOUT 3½ CUPS (28 FL OZ/875 ML)

Pour the custard into an ice cream maker and freeze according to the manufacturer's instructions.

Transfer half of the ice cream to a 1½-qt (1.5-l) rectangular container. Drizzle 2 tablespoons of the sauce over the ice cream. Top with the remaining ice cream, smoothing the top gently. Drizzle the remaining 2 tablespoons fudge sauce over the ice cream. Cover and place in the freezer until firm, at least 3 hours or up to 24 hours.

MINT–CHOCOLATE CHIP ICE CREAM

The potency of the mint leaves and the length of time that they are left to steep in the milk will determine the depth of the mint flavor. The ice cream will be a pale green, rather than the artificially created neon green of many commercial mint ice creams.

1½ cups (12 fl oz/ 375 ml) milk

1½ cups (12 fl oz/375 ml) heavy (double) cream

⅔ cup (5 oz/150 g) sugar

1 cup (1 oz/30 g) fresh mint leaves, from about 1 bunch

4 egg yolks

½ teaspoon pure vanilla extract

4 oz (125 g) bittersweet or semisweet (plain) chocolate, coarsely chopped

2 teaspoons canola oil

MAKES ABOUT 1 QT (1 L)

In a saucepan over medium heat, combine the milk, 1 cup (8 fl oz/250 ml) of the cream, ⅓ cup (2½ oz/75 g) of the sugar, and the mint leaves. Heat, stirring frequently, until small bubbles appear around the edge of the pan and the sugar is dissolved, 4–5 minutes. Do not allow to boil. Remove from the heat and let stand for 15–20 minutes.

In a bowl, whisk together the egg yolks and the remaining ⅓ cup sugar and ½ cup (4 fl oz/125 ml) cream until blended.

Return the saucepan to medium heat and heat, stirring frequently until bubbles again form around the edge of the pan, 2–4 minutes. Remove from the heat. Gradually add the hot milk mixture to the yolk mixture while whisking constantly. Return the mixture to the saucepan and place over medium-low heat. Cook, stirring slowly and constantly with a heat-resistant spatula, until the custard thickens and leaves a path on the back of the spatula when a finger is drawn across it, about 5 minutes. Do not allow to boil.

Pour the custard through a medium-mesh sieve into a clean bowl, pressing on the mint to release as much liquid as possible. Discard the mint leaves. Stir in the vanilla. Let cool, cover, and refrigerate for at least 3 hours or up to 24 hours.

In a heatproof bowl, combine the chocolate and oil. Set the bowl over (but not touching) simmering water in a saucepan (see page 566). Heat, stirring occasionally, just until the chocolate melts and the mixture becomes smooth. Remove from the heat and let cool to room temperature.

Pour the custard into an ice cream maker and freeze according to the manufacturer's instructions. About 2 minutes before the end of churning, drizzle the cooled melted chocolate into the mixing container. Transfer to a tightly covered container and place in the freezer until firm, at least 4 hours or up to 3 days.

Double the mint

For a deeper green and a more minty flavor, add 2 tbsp green crème de menthe while the ice cream is churning. If you have only white crème de menthe, it can be added for flavor only.

605

ORANGE ICE CREAM WITH TRUFFLES

Ice cream safety

Undercooked eggs can carry bacteria, but ice creams that employ a cooked custard base will all but eliminate this risk. If you are in doubt, test the cooked custard with an instant-read thermometer. The bacteria will be killed at 160°F (71°F).

In this creative ice cream, chocolate truffles are added to orange ice cream for a delicious and eye-catching treat. The number of truffles you add is up to you. If you have leftovers, coat them according to the recipe and give them as gifts.

Using a vegetable peeler, remove the zest from the oranges in long, wide strips and place in a heavy saucepan. Add 1 cup (8 fl oz/250 ml) of the cream and the half-and-half and bring to a simmer over medium-high heat. Remove from the heat.

In a bowl, whisk together the egg yolks and sugar until blended. Gradually add the hot cream mixture to the yolk mixture while whisking constantly. Return the mixture to the saucepan and place over medium-low heat. Add the orange juice and cook, stirring slowly and constantly with a heat-resistant spatula, until the custard thickens and leaves a path on the back of the spatula when a finger is drawn across it, about 5 minutes. Do not allow to boil.

Pour the custard through a medium-mesh sieve set over a clean bowl. Stir in the remaining 1 cup cream and the orange zest. Let the custard cool, cover, and refrigerate for at least 3 hours or up to 24 hours.

Pour the custard into an ice cream maker and freeze according to the manufacturer's instructions.

Transfer half of the ice cream to a 1½–2-qt (1.5–2-l) rectangular container; top with a layer of truffles, spacing them slightly apart. Cover with the remaining ice cream. Top with more truffles in the same manner, pressing them gently into the ice cream. Cover and place in the freezer until firm, at least 4 hours or up to 3 days.

2 small oranges

2 cups (16 fl oz/500 ml) heavy (double) cream

1 cup (8 fl oz/250 ml) half-and-half (half cream)

6 egg yolks

⅔ cup (5 oz/155 g) sugar

1 cup (8 fl oz/250 ml) fresh orange juice

2 teaspoons grated orange zest

Double-Chocolate and Orange Truffles (page 577), uncoated, well chilled

MAKES ABOUT 5 CUPS (40 FL OZ/1.25 L)

FRESH PEACH ICE CREAM

Fresh fruit ice creams

When adding fresh fruit to an ice cream base, whether before the base goes into the ice cream maker or while it is churning, be sure it is cut into small pieces. Large pieces tend to freeze too hard and become tasteless and unappealing.

For the best possible flavor, use only the ripest, juiciest peaches for this summertime treat, ideally organic peaches purchased at a farmers' market. The flavor of white peaches is too delicate for this ice cream; choose the more robust yellow varieties.

In a heavy saucepan over medium heat, combine the peaches, ¼ cup (2 oz/60 g) of the sugar, and the corn syrup. Stir until the sugar melts and the peaches are heated throughout, about 4 minutes. Pour into a large bowl and set aside. Pour the half-and-half and ½ cup (4 fl oz/125 ml) of the cream into the same saucepan and bring to a simmer over medium-high heat. Remove from the heat.

In a bowl, whisk together the egg yolks and the remaining ¼ cup sugar until blended. Gradually add the hot half-and-half mixture to the yolk mixture while whisking constantly. Return the mixture to the saucepan and place over medium-

2 cups (12 oz/375 g) peeled, finely chopped ripe peaches

½ cup (4 oz/125 g) sugar

¼ cup (2½ oz/75 g) light corn syrup

1½ cups (12 fl oz/375 ml) half-and-half (half cream)

1 cup (8 fl oz/250 ml) heavy (double) cream

4 egg yolks

½ teaspoon pure
vanilla extract

**MAKES ABOUT 5 CUPS
(40 FL OZ/1.25 L)**

low heat. Cook, stirring slowly and constantly with a heat-resistant spatula, until the custard thickens and leaves a path on the back of the spatula when a finger is drawn across it, about 5 minutes. Do not allow the mixture to boil.

Pour the custard through a medium-mesh sieve into the peach mixture. Transfer three-fourths of the peach mixture to a food processor or blender and process until smooth. Pour the purée back into the remaining peach mixture. Whisk in the vanilla and the remaining ½ cup cream until blended. Let the mixture cool, cover, and refrigerate for at least 3 hours or up to 24 hours.

Pour the custard into an ice cream maker and freeze according to the manufacturer's instructions. Transfer to a tightly covered container and place in the freezer until firm, at least 4 hours or up to 3 days.

STRAWBERRY ICE CREAM

The secret to making the best strawberry ice cream is to start with the juiciest, ripest, and most flavorful fruits. When added to the rich custard base during the last few minutes of churning, the chopped berries retain their texture and intensely fruity flavor.

Using frozen berries

When strawberries are out of season in your area, you can use high-quality unsweetened or lightly sweetened frozen sliced or whole berries.

2 cups (8 oz/250 g)
stemmed, coarsely
chopped strawberries

2 tablespoons plus ½ cup
(4 oz/125 g) sugar

1 cup (8 fl oz/250 ml) milk

1 cup (8 fl oz/250 ml)
heavy (double) cream

3 egg yolks

1 teaspoon pure vanilla
extract

MAKES ABOUT 1 QT (1 L)

In a food processor, process half of the strawberries with the 2 tablespoons sugar; set aside.

In a saucepan over medium heat, combine the milk, ¾ cup (6 fl oz/180 ml) of the cream, and the ½ cup (4 oz/125 g) sugar. Heat, stirring frequently, just until bubbles appear around the edge of the pan and the sugar is dissolved, 4–5 minutes. Remove the pan from the heat.

In a bowl, whisk together the egg yolks and the remaining ¼ cup (2 fl oz/60 ml) cream until blended. Gradually add the hot milk mixture to the yolk mixture while whisking constantly. Return the mixture to the saucepan and place over medium-low heat. Cook, stirring slowly and constantly with a heat-resistant spatula, until the custard thickens and leaves a path on the back of the spatula when a finger is drawn across it, about 5 minutes. Do not allow to boil.

Remove from the heat and stir in the puréed strawberries and vanilla. Pour through a fine-mesh sieve into a bowl. Let the mixture cool, cover, and refrigerate for at least 3 hours or up to 24 hours.

Pour the custard into an ice cream maker and freeze according to the manufacturer's instructions. During the last few minutes of churning, add the reserved coarsely chopped strawberries and churn just until incorporated. Transfer to a covered container and place in the freezer until firm, at least 4 hours or up to 3 days.

PUMPKIN SPICE ICE CREAM

**Freeze for
full flavor**

*Ice creams served
right after churning
tend to have a mild
taste. For the best
results, transfer
the ice cream to a
container and place
in the freezer for a
few hours to "ripen"
and develop a good,
deep flavor and
optimal texture.*

This rich and creamy ice cream is perfect for the fall and winter holiday season. Try serving it with warm Gingerbread (page 496), or use it for making a sundae with Butterscotch Sauce (page 461), Whipped Cream (page 454), and chopped toasted nuts.

In a heavy saucepan over medium-high heat, warm 1⅓ cups (11 fl oz/340 ml) of the cream and bring to a simmer. Remove from the heat.

In a bowl, whisk together the sugar, corn syrup, egg yolks, ginger, cinnamon, and nutmeg until blended. Gradually add the hot cream to the yolk mixture while whisking constantly. Return the mixture to the saucepan and place over medium-low heat. Cook, stirring slowly and constantly with a heat-resistant spatula, until the custard thickens and leaves a path on the back of the spatula when a finger is drawn across it, about 5 minutes. Do not allow the mixture to boil.

Pour the custard through a medium-mesh sieve set over a clean bowl. Whisk in the pumpkin, vanilla extract, and the remaining ⅔ cup (5 fl oz/160 ml) cream until blended. Let the custard cool, then cover, and refrigerate until very cold, at least 3 hours or up to 24 hours.

Pour the custard into an ice cream maker and freeze according to the manufacturer's instructions. Transfer to a covered container and place in the freezer until firm, at least 4 hours or for up to 3 days.

2 cups (16 fl oz/500 ml) heavy (double) cream

⅔ cup (5 oz/155 g) sugar

½ cup (5 fl oz/155 ml) light corn syrup

6 egg yolks

1 teaspoon ground ginger

½ teaspoon ground cinnamon

¼ teaspoon freshly grated nutmeg

⅔ cup (5 oz/155 g) canned pumpkin purée

1 teaspoon pure vanilla extract

MAKES ABOUT 1 QT (1 L)

COCONUT ICE CREAM

Storing your treats

*Store frozen
desserts in the part
of the freezer that
is consistently the
coldest. Do not keep
them near the freezer
door, where they
may thaw partially
each time the door
is opened. Place a
piece of plastic wrap
directly on the surface
of the dessert to help
prevent freezer burn.*

For a double coconut treat, stir ½ cup (1½ oz/45 g) toasted shredded coconut into the ice cream during the final minute of processing. To make a colorful parfait, layer the ice cream in tall footed glasses with diced tropical fruit.

In a heavy saucepan over medium-high heat, stir the flaked coconut until it begins to brown, about 7 minutes. Add the half-and-half and bring to a simmer. Remove from the heat. Cover and let stand for 30 minutes.

Pour the coconut mixture through a medium-mesh sieve set over a bowl. Press firmly on the coconut to extract as much liquid as possible; discard the coconut. Return the coconut milk to the saucepan and place over medium-high heat. Add the cream of coconut and bring to a simmer. Remove from the heat.

In a bowl, whisk together the egg yolks and sugar until blended. Gradually add the hot coconut-milk mixture into the yolk mixture while whisking constantly. Return the mixture to the saucepan and place over medium-low heat. Cook, stirring slowly and constantly with a heat-resistant spatula, until the custard thickens and leaves a path on the

1¼ cups (5 oz/155 g) firmly packed sweetened flaked dried coconut

1½ cups (12 fl oz/375 ml) half-and-half (half cream)

¾ cup (6 fl oz/180 ml) canned sweetened cream of coconut

6 egg yolks

⅓ cup (3 oz/90 g) sugar

1½ cups (12 fl oz/375 ml) heavy (double) cream

MAKES ABOUT 4½ CUPS (36 FL OZ/1.1 L)

back of the spatula when a finger is drawn across it, about 5 minutes. Do not allow to boil.

Pour the custard through the medium-mesh sieve set over a clean bowl. Add the cream and stir well. Let cool, cover, and refrigerate until very cold, at least 3 hours or up to 24 hours.

Pour the custard into an ice cream maker and freeze according to the manufacturer's instructions. Transfer to a covered container and place in the freezer until firm, at least 4 hours or for up to 3 days.

TOASTED ALMOND ICE CREAM

Sautéing the nuts in butter before incorporating them into the ice cream base intensifies the almond flavor of this simple ice cream. You can determine the final texture based on what you prefer: strain out the almonds for a smooth ice cream, leave them in for a crunchy one.

2 tablespoons
unsalted butter

¼ cup (2½ oz) coarsely
chopped almonds

3 cups (24 fl oz/750 ml)
half-and-half (half cream)

1 vanilla bean, or 1 teaspoon
pure vanilla extract

6 egg yolks

¾ cup (6 oz/185 g) sugar

2 tablespoons light
corn syrup

½ teaspoon pure
almond extract

MAKES ABOUT 5 CUPS
(40 FL OZ/1.25 L)

In a heavy saucepan over medium-high heat, melt the butter. Add the almonds and sauté, stirring often, until the almonds are golden and the butter browns, about 5 minutes. Do not allow to burn. Add the half-and-half and the vanilla bean, if using, and bring to a simmer. Remove from the heat.

In a bowl, whisk together the egg yolks, sugar, and corn syrup until blended. Gradually add the hot half-and-half mixture to the yolk mixture while whisking constantly. Return the mixture to the saucepan and place over medium-low heat. Cook, stirring slowly and constantly with a heat-resistant spatula, until the custard thickens and leaves a path on the back of the spatula when a finger is drawn across it, about 5 minutes. Do not allow the mixture to boil.

For a smooth-textured ice cream, pour the custard through a medium-mesh sieve into a clean bowl. For a crunchy texture, do not strain. Stir in the vanilla extract, if using, and almond extract. Let cool, cover, and refrigerate until very cold, at least 3 hours or up to 24 hours.

Pour the custard into an ice cream maker and freeze according to the manufacturer's instructions. Transfer to a covered container and place in the freezer until firm, at least 4 hours or for up to 3 days.

Sweet-smelling cutting boards

This advice might sound strange to you, but it is always a good idea to do it. Before you work with sweet ingredients, smell your cutting board to make sure it carries no odors from onions, garlic, or the like. Better yet, designate a cutting board for dessert making only.

609

LEMON–CRÈME FRAÎCHE ICE CREAM

The pleasantly tart, refreshing flavor of lemon is always welcome, but especially so after a rich meal. In this velvety ice cream, crème fraîche contributes richness and a flavor reminiscent of cheesecake. Serve accompanied by thin, crisp cookies.

In a heavy saucepan, combine the half-and-half and cream. Using a vegetable peeler, remove the zest of 1 lemon in long strips. Add the zest to the cream mixture, place over medium heat, and bring to a simmer. Remove from the heat.

Meanwhile, grate the zest from the remaining 2 lemons. In a food processor, combine the sugar and grated lemon zest and process until well mixed. In a bowl, whisk together the egg yolks and lemon sugar until blended. Gradually add the hot cream mixture to the yolk mixture while whisking constantly. Return the mixture to the saucepan and cook, stirring slowly and constantly with a heat-resistant spatula, until the custard thickens and leaves a path on the back of the spatula when a finger is drawn across it, about 5 minutes. Do not allow the mixture to boil.

Remove from the heat and stir for 1 minute. Let cool for 15 minutes, then whisk in the crème fraîche. Let cool, cover, and refrigerate until thoroughly chilled and the flavors have blended, about 8 hours.

Strain the mixture through a medium-mesh sieve into an ice cream maker and freeze according to the manufacturer's instructions. Transfer to a covered container and place in the freezer for at least 4 hours or up to 3 days.

1 cup (8 fl oz/250 ml) half-and-half (half cream)

1 cup (8 fl oz/250 ml) heavy (double) cream

3 lemons

¾ cup (6 oz/185 g) sugar

6 egg yolks

1 cup (8 fl oz/250 ml) crème fraîche

MAKES ABOUT 1½ QT (1.5 L)

CARAMEL GELATO

Because of its dense texture and full flavor, this gelato needs little embellishment. If you like, serve it with your favorite dessert sauce or with fresh fruit such as berries, peaches, or plums. Or, sprinkle portions with a tiny pinch of flaky sea salt, which will bring out the caramel flavor.

In a heavy saucepan over medium-low heat, combine the sugar and ¼ cup (2 fl oz/ 60 ml) water. Stir until the sugar dissolves, about 5 minutes. Using a pastry brush dipped in water, brush down the sides of the pan to prevent sugar crystals from forming. Raise the heat to medium-high, bring to a boil, and boil, without stirring, until the syrup is a deep caramel color, about 10 minutes (the timing will depend on the size and weight of the pan and the intensity of the heat). Gently swirl the pan occasionally to ensure the syrup caramelizes evenly. Gradually add the milk; the mixture will bubble vigorously. Reduce the heat to medium-low and stir until all the hard bits of caramel melt, about 5 minutes. Remove from the heat.

In a bowl, whisk together the egg yolks and corn syrup until blended. Gradually add the hot caramel to the yolk mixture

¾ cup (6 oz/185 g) sugar

2 cups (16 fl oz/500 ml) milk

5 egg yolks

2 tablespoons light corn syrup

½ teaspoon pure vanilla extract

MAKES ABOUT 2¾ CUPS (22 FL OZ/680 ML)

while whisking constantly. Return the mixture to the saucepan and place over medium-low heat. Cook, stirring slowly and constantly with a heat-resistant spatula, until the custard thickens and leaves a path on the back of the spatula when a finger is drawn across it, about 6 minutes. Do not allow the mixture to boil.

Pour the custard through a medium-mesh sieve set over a clean bowl. Stir in the vanilla. Let cool, cover, and refrigerate until very cold, at least 3 hours or up to 24 hours.

Pour the custard into an ice cream maker and freeze according to the manufacturer's instructions. Serve the gelato right away. Or, transfer to a covered container and place in the freezer for up to 3 days (the longer you freeze the gelato, the more it develops the texture of ice cream).

DARK CHOCOLATE GELATO

Using both semisweet chocolate and unsweetened cocoa powder gives this gelato an intense chocolate flavor. The vanilla extract softens the natural bitterness of the chocolate, making it rounder and fuller. Serve it plain or topped with semisweet or white chocolate shavings.

2 cups (16 fl oz/500 ml) milk

5 egg yolks

¾ cup (6 oz/185 g) sugar

2 tablespoons light corn syrup

4 oz (125 g) semisweet (plain) chocolate, chopped

¼ cup (¾ oz/20 g) unsweetened cocoa powder

1 teaspoon pure vanilla extract

MAKES ABOUT 1 QT (1 L)

In a heavy saucepan over medium-high heat, bring the milk to a simmer. Remove from the heat.

In a bowl, whisk together the egg yolks, sugar, and corn syrup until blended. Gradually add the hot milk to the yolk mixture while whisking constantly. Return the mixture to the saucepan and place over medium-low heat. Cook, stirring slowly and constantly with a heat-resistant spatula, until the custard thickens and leaves a path on the back of the spatula when a finger is drawn across it, about 6 minutes. Do not allow the mixture to boil.

Pour the custard through a medium-mesh sieve set over a clean metal bowl. Add the chocolate and cocoa powder and stir until the chocolate melts. Stir in the vanilla. Let the mixture cool, cover, and refrigerate until cold, at least 3 hours or up to 24 hours.

Pour the custard into an ice cream maker and freeze according to the manufacturer's instructions. Serve the gelato right away. Or, transfer to a covered container and place in the freezer for up to 3 days (the longer you freeze the gelato, the more it develops the texture of ice cream).

Serving frozen desserts

Since intense cold mutes flavors, most frozen desserts benefit from sitting for a few minutes at room temperature before serving. Five minutes or so on the countertop is usually sufficient for ice creams.

611

LEMON-LIME GRANITA

Granita parfait

Layer scoops of any flavor granita with large dollops of Whipped Cream (page 454) in footed parfait glasses. Serve with long spoons and a crisp cookie on the side.

Offer this refreshing treat after a spicy meal. For a festive presentation, serve it in chilled margarita or martini glasses. To intensify the citrus aroma, heat the zests of 1 lime and 1 lemon, cut into strips, with the sugar syrup, then strain before continuing.

In a heavy saucepan over medium heat, combine 2 cups (16 fl oz/500 ml) water and the sugar and stir until the sugar dissolves, about 2 minutes. Raise the heat to high and bring to a boil. Remove from the heat and let cool completely.

Stir in the lemon and lime juices, and pour the mixture into a shallow metal bowl or pan. Place in the freezer and freeze, whisking every 30 minutes, until semifirm, about 3 hours. Cover and return to the freezer without stirring until frozen solid, at least 8 hours or up to 24 hours.

At least 1 hour before serving, place 4 margarita glasses or wineglasses in the freezer.

To serve, using a fork, scrape the surface of the granita to form ice crystals. Scoop into the frozen glasses. Place a lime slice on the rim of each glass and serve right away.

1 cup (8 oz/250 g) sugar

⅓ cup (3 fl oz/80 ml) fresh lemon juice

⅓ cup (3 fl oz/80 ml) fresh lime juice

4 lime slices, each ⅛ inch (3 mm) thick and slit halfway

MAKES 4 SERVINGS

PINEAPPLE GRANITA WITH POMEGRANATE SEEDS

Granita in a hurry

To speed up the granita-making process, chill the metal bowl or pan in the freezer for up to an hour before adding the fruit purée to it.

Fresh pineapple is the best choice here, but if you cannot find a sweet, ripe fruit, you can substitute frozen pineapple. You can often find packages of pomegranate seeds at natural-foods stores, which lend a contrasting peppery flavor and crisp texture to the dessert.

In a small saucepan over medium heat, combine the pineapple juice and sugar and stir until the sugar dissolves, about 2 minutes. Raise the heat to high and bring to a boil. Remove from the heat and let cool for 15 minutes.

In a food processor or blender, combine the cooled syrup and the pineapple and process until smooth. Pour the mixture into a shallow metal bowl or pan. Place in the freezer and freeze, whisking every 30 minutes, until semifirm, about 3 hours. Cover and return to the freezer without stirring until frozen solid, at least 8 hours or up to 24 hours.

To serve, using a fork, scrape the surface of the granita to form ice crystals. Scoop into individual bowls and sprinkle with the pomegranate seeds.

1 cup (8 fl oz/250 ml) unsweetened pineapple juice

1 cup (8 oz/250 g) sugar

2 cups (12 oz/375 g) chopped fresh pineapple

Pomegranate seeds for garnish

MAKES 6 SERVINGS

COFFEE GRANITA WITH BRANDIED WHIPPED CREAM

Made with strong coffee, this Italian-style flavored ice makes a particularly appealing finale to a pasta meal. If you like, add up to 2 tablespoons Sambuca or other complementary liqueur to the granita mixture and omit the brandy in the whipped cream.

4 cups (32 fl oz/1 l) hot strong brewed coffee

¾ cup (6 oz/185 g) sugar, or as needed

¾ cup (6 fl oz/180 ml) heavy (double) cream

Brandy

Sweetened cocoa powder for garnish

MAKES 6 SERVINGS

In a pitcher or bowl, combine the coffee and the sugar and stir until the sugar dissolves. Pour the mixture into a shallow metal bowl or pan. Place in the freezer and freeze, whisking every 30 minutes, until semifirm, about 3 hours. Cover and return to the freezer without stirring until frozen solid, at least 8 hours or up to 24 hours.

In a chilled bowl, using a whisk or an electric mixer on medium-high speed, whip the cream until soft peaks form. Whip in sugar and brandy to taste.

To serve, spoon into individual bowls and top with the whipped cream, dividing it evenly. Using a fine-mesh sieve, lightly dust each serving with cocoa.

Make it strong

Brew the coffee very strong so the flavor will come through when the mixture is frozen. Although any roast can be used, an Italian or espresso roast will deliver the most authentic taste.

RUBY RED GRAPEFRUIT SORBET

Peak season for these huge, sweet grapefruits is winter through early spring. This sorbet can be made either in your freezer or in an ice cream maker. The hand method will result in a sorbet with larger ice crystals. Either way, it is a delicious treat.

¾ cup (6 oz/185 g) sugar

3 tablespoons fresh lemon juice

Grated zest of 1 Ruby Red grapefruit

1¼ cups (10 fl oz/310 ml) Ruby Red grapefruit juice, including the pulp but not the white membrane

MAKES ABOUT 2 CUPS

In a small saucepan over medium heat, combine the sugar, ⅔ cup (5 fl oz/160 ml) water, and the lemon juice. Bring to a simmer, stirring constantly until the sugar dissolves, and then simmer for 5 minutes. Remove the mixture from the heat and let cool completely.

In a bowl, combine the cooled syrup and the grapefruit zest and juice with its pulp. Cover the bowl and refrigerate until very cold, about 3 hours.

Pour the grapefruit mixture into a shallow metal bowl or pan, cover with aluminum foil, and place in the freezer for 20 minutes. Stir with a whisk or fork to aerate; re-cover and return to the freezer. Continue to stir every 20 minutes until the sorbet is frozen. It should take a total of 2 hours to achieve the right texture. Alternatively, pour the chilled mixture into an ice cream maker and freeze according to the manufacturer's instructions. Serve right away in individual bowls or wineglasses.

Grapefruit soda

Put 2 scoops of the sorbet in a tall glass. Fill the glass with club soda and stir well. Let stand for about 2 minutes and serve. For an adult treat, stir in an ounce (30 ml) or so of Campari.

SPICED PEAR AND SWEET WINE SORBET

Scoop types

Whether you prefer a round or paddle-shaped scoop for serving ice cream, be sure to buy a high-quality one that won't break or buckle when used for items that are frozen solid.

Gewürztraminer is known for its spicy aromas and flavors, often compared to a mixture of roses, cinnamon, and cloves. Here, it forms the base for a refreshing spiced pear sorbet accented with hints of cardamom. For the best flavor, use only very ripe fruits.

Wrap the cardamom pods in a small square of triple-thick cheesecloth (muslin) and tie in a tight bundle with kitchen string. In a heavy saucepan over medium heat, combine the cardamom bundle, pears, and 1 cup (8 fl oz/250 ml) of the wine. Bring to a simmer, cover, and cook, stirring occasionally, until the pears are tender, about 10 minutes. Remove the bundle and discard. Add the sugar and corn syrup and stir over medium heat until the sugar dissolves, about 3 minutes. Remove from the heat and let cool slightly.

Transfer the mixture to a food processor or blender and process until smooth. Pour into a bowl and stir in the remaining ¾ cup (6 fl oz/180 ml) wine. Cover and refrigerate until very cold, about 1 hour.

Transfer the mixture to an ice cream maker and freeze according to the manufacturer's instructions. Transfer to a covered container and place in the freezer until firm, at least 4 hours or up to 3 days.

4 cardamom pods, lightly crushed

2¼ lb (1.1 kg) ripe pears such as Bartlett (Williams') or Comice, peeled, quartered, and cored

1¾ cups (14 fl oz/430 ml) Gewürztraminer, Riesling, or other off-dry white wine

¾ cup (6 oz/185 g) sugar

2 tablespoons light corn syrup

MAKES ABOUT 4½ CUPS (36 FL OZ/1.1 L)

MANGO-LIME SORBET

Help things along

If you have underripe mangoes (mangoes that are firm to the touch), place them in a paper bag and keep at room temperature for 2 to 3 days to encourage ripening.

This tropical dessert makes a memorable end to a causal summer meal, or an interesting palate cleanser between courses of a formal dinner. Use only ripe mangoes to ensure the fullest flavor, and be sure to rinse the limes well before you grate the zest.

Peel the mangoes. Slice as much of the flesh off the pits as possible, coarsely chop, and place in a food processor.

In a small, heavy saucepan over medium-high heat, combine the sugar and mango nectar and bring to a boil, stirring occasionally, 3–4 minutes. Continue to boil, stirring the mixture frequently, until a clear syrup forms and no grains of sugar are visible, 1–2 minutes. Remove the syrup from the heat and let cool slightly.

Add the warm syrup and the lime zest and juice to the food processor and process until a smooth purée forms, about 1 minute. Pour the purée into a bowl, cover, and refrigerate until very cold, about 3 hours.

Transfer the mixture to an ice cream maker and freeze according to the manufacturer's instructions. Transfer to a covered container and place in the freezer until firm, at least 4 hours or up to 3 days.

2 large, ripe mangoes, about 2 lb (1 kg) total weight

⅔ cup (5 oz/155 g) sugar

¾ cup (6 fl oz/180 ml) mango nectar

1 teaspoon grated lime zest

1½ tablespoons fresh lime juice

MAKES ABOUT 1 QT (1 L)

GREEN APPLE SORBET

This fat-free treat is simple to make and has a light, refreshing flavor. The apple purée that forms the sorbet base will not be completely smooth, so the sorbet will have coarser texture than other homemade versions. Tart apples, such as Granny Smith, are the best choice.

1 cup (8 oz/250 g) sugar

1¼ cups (10 fl oz/310 g) apple cider

1 lb (500 g) tart green apples, peeled, cored, and coarsely chopped

1 tablespoon fresh lemon juice

MAKES ABOUT 1 QT (1 L)

In a heavy saucepan over medium heat, combine the sugar and apple cider and bring to a boil, stirring occasionally, 3–4 minutes. Continue to boil, stirring frequently, until a clear syrup forms and no grains of sugar are visible, 1–2 minutes. Add the apples and return the mixture to a boil. Reduce the heat to medium-low and cook, stirring constantly, until the apples are soft and mushy, 3–5 minutes. Remove from the heat and let cool for 10–15 minutes.

Using a slotted spoon, transfer the apples to a food processor. Add 1 cup (8 fl oz/250 ml) of the cooking liquid and the lemon juice and process until a fairly smooth purée forms, about 30 seconds. Pour into a bowl, add the remaining cooking liquid, and stir well. Cover the bowl and refrigerate until very cold, about 3 hours.

Transfer the mixture to an ice cream maker and freeze according to the manufacturer's instructions. Transfer to a covered container and place in the freezer until firm, at least 4 hours or up to 3 days.

Punch it up

If desired, add 1 tbsp Calvados or brandy to the ice cream maker near the end of the churning process. Don't add more than that or the sorbet may not freeze properly.

RASPBERRY FROZEN YOGURT

This recipe combines high-quality plain yogurt with fresh-from-the-farm berries for a flavor you can only achieve at home. The seeds from the berries lend an appealing crunchy texture. For the best texture and flavor, choose natural yogurt with no additives or stabilizers.

4 cups (2 lb/1 kg) plain whole-milk yogurt

⅔ cup (5 oz/155 g) plus 2 tablespoons sugar

¼ cup (2 fl oz/60 ml) light corn syrup

2 teaspoons pure vanilla extract

Pinch of salt

1½ cups (6 oz/185 g) fresh raspberries

1 teaspoon fresh lemon juice

MAKES ABOUT 1½ QT (1.5 L)

In a bowl, stir together the yogurt, the ⅔ cup sugar, the corn syrup, vanilla, and salt. Cover the bowl and refrigerate until very cold, about 1 hour.

Meanwhile, in another bowl, combine the raspberries, the remaining 2 tablespoons sugar, and the lemon juice. Using a fork, lightly crush the berries to release some of their juices. Cover and refrigerate with the yogurt mixture.

Transfer the yogurt mixture to an ice cream maker and freeze according to the manufacturer's instructions. About 1 minute before the yogurt is done churning, pour in the raspberry mixture and continue to churn. Transfer to a covered container and place in the freezer until firm, at least 2 hours or up to 3 days.

Yogurt types

The best frozen yogurt is made from natural yogurt without stabilizers or gelatin. Frozen desserts made with additives turn out slightly gummy.

FROZEN EGGNOG MOUSSE

Buying extracts

Vanilla, almond, or other extracts provide a little sweetness along with a unique flavor to frozen desserts and other recipes. Always buy extracts that are labeled "pure," rather than less-expensive imitation products that are synthetically flavored.

Frozen in individual soufflé dishes, these rich desserts make a lovely ending for a formal holiday meal. They are an especially good choice when you want to make your dessert ahead of time, as they can be stored in the freezer for up to 1 week.

Outfit each of six ¾-cup (6-fl oz/180-ml) ramekins with a foil collar (see page 602). Set aside.

In a heatproof bowl, whisk together the egg yolks, sugar, and ¼ cup (2 fl oz/60 ml) water until blended. Place over (not touching) simmering water in a saucepan and whisk constantly until the mixture registers 170°F (77°C) on a candy thermometer, about 10 minutes.

Remove the bowl from the heat. Using an electric mixer on high speed, beat the yolk mixture until it is cool and thickened, about 6 minutes.

In a chilled bowl, combine the cream, rum, brandy, vanilla, and nutmeg. Using the electric mixer fitted with clean, dry beaters, beat on medium-high speed until stiff peaks form. Using a rubber spatula, carefully fold the cream into the cooled yolk mixture just until no white streaks remain. Spoon into the prepared ramekins, dividing it equally. Freeze the mousses uncovered overnight.

Carefully unwrap the foil collars from the dishes, using a small, sharp knife dipped in hot water and dried as an aid, if necessary. Smooth the sides of each mousse with the knife, if necessary. Sprinkle with nutmeg and serve at once.

6 egg yolks

1 cup (8 oz/250 g) sugar

2 cups (16 fl oz/500 ml) cold heavy (double) cream

3 tablespoons dark rum

3 tablespoons brandy

1½ teaspoons pure vanilla extract

¼ teaspoon freshly grated nutmeg, plus more for garnish

MAKES 6 SERVINGS

FROZEN LEMON MOUSSE WITH BLUEBERRIES

Clean out the freezer

If you are planning to serve a frozen dessert at a dinner party, consider taking the time to clean and/or defrost the freezer in advance of the event. Some foods stored in the freezer can impart off odors or flavors into newly placed foods.

Lemons and blueberries have complementary flavors. Here, the berries are arranged inside a lemony molded frozen mixture, to create the perfect dessert for serving at the height of the summer blueberry season. The mousse can be made up to 3 days in advance of serving.

Line a 2-qt (2-l) ring mold with plastic wrap, overhanging the edges by about 3 inches (7.5 cm).

In a large heatproof bowl, whisk together the egg yolks, sugar, lemon juice, corn syrup, and lemon zest until blended. Place over (not touching) simmering water in a saucepan and whisk constantly until the mixture registers 170°F (77°C) on a candy thermometer, about 10 minutes.

Remove the bowl from the heat. Using an electric mixer on high speed, beat the yolk mixture until it is cool and thickened, about 6 minutes.

In a chilled bowl, using the electric mixer fitted with clean, dry beaters, beat the cream on medium-high speed until stiff peaks form. Using a rubber spatula, fold the cream into the cooled yolk mixture just until no white streaks remain.

8 egg yolks

1 cup (8 oz/250 g) sugar

⅔ cup (5 fl oz/160 ml) fresh lemon juice

¼ cup (2 fl oz/60 ml) light corn syrup

2 teaspoons grated lemon zest

2 cups (16 fl oz/500 ml) cold heavy (double) cream

½ cup (5 oz/155 g) seedless raspberry jam

4 cups (1 lb/500 g)
blueberries

Fresh mint sprigs for
garnish, optional

MAKES 10–12 SERVINGS

Spoon the mousse mixture into the prepared mold. Cover
tightly with the overhanging plastic wrap and freeze
overnight or for up to 3 days.

About 1 hour before serving, place a round platter in the
freezer. In a large, heavy frying pan over medium heat, stir
the jam just until melted. Remove the pan from the heat
and add the blueberries. Toss the berries to coat them thinly
with the jam. Let cool completely, about 1 hour.

Uncover the mousse. Invert the chilled platter over the mold
and then, holding the mold and platter firmly together with
both hands, invert them. Lift off the mold and peel off the
plastic wrap. Spoon enough of the blueberries into the center
of the ring to fill nicely. Garnish with mint sprigs, if using,
and serve. Pass the remaining berries at the table.

FROZEN CHOCOLATE–CREAM CHEESE PIE

This kid-friendly ice cream pie has all the flavors of cheesecake—a chocolate crumb crust,
a sweet and rich cream cheese filling, and a chocolaty topping—in an easy-to-make frozen pie.
And because only the crust requires baking, it's the ideal dessert for a warm summer evening.

Chocolate Crumb
Crust (page 446)

8 oz (250 g) semisweet
or bittersweet chocolate,
chopped, plus 1 block
for topping, optional

6 oz (185 g) cream cheese,
at room temperature

⅔ cup (5 oz/155 g) sugar

1 teaspoon pure
vanilla extract

½ cup (4 fl oz/125 ml) milk

2 cups (16 fl oz/500 ml)
cold heavy (double) cream,
whipped to soft peaks

MAKES ONE 10-INCH
(25-CM) PIE

Prepare the crumb crust and press onto the bottom and up
the sides of a 10-inch (25-cm) pie dish. Prebake as directed,
then let cool completely.

Place the chopped chocolate in the top pan of a double boiler
or a heatproof bowl. Place over (not touching) barely simmering
water and heat, stirring occasionally, until melted and smooth.
Remove from the heat and let cool to lukewarm.

In a bowl, using an electric mixer on medium speed, beat
together the cream cheese, sugar, vanilla, and milk until
mixed. Using a rubber spatula, gently fold in the whipped
cream and cooled chocolate, taking care not to deflate the
mixture too much.

Pour and scrape the mixture into the prepared crust, evenly
smoothing the top with the spatula. Cover with aluminum
foil and freeze for at least 4 hours or up to overnight.

Using a vegetable peeler, shave chocolate curls from the
block of chocolate, if using, and arrange on top.

Dress it up

*If you like, decorate
the top of this
decadent frozen
dessert with whipped
cream rosettes just
before serving. Fit a
pastry (piping) bag
with a star tip, and
spoon the whipped
cream into the bag
(see page 493).
Squeeze gently to
form rosettes.*

617

THE ULTIMATE BANANA SPLIT

Chocolate malt

Here's another soda-shop staple: In a blender, combine 2 scoops Dark Chocolate Gelato (page 611), ¼ cup (2 fl oz/60 ml) Homemade Chocolate Syrup (page 460), ¾ cup (6 fl oz/180 ml) milk, ¼ cup (¾ oz/ 20 g) malted milk powder, and a large handful of crushed ice cubes and blend until smooth. Pour into a tall glass and serve right away. Makes 1 large shake.

The soda-fountain favorite can be easily replicated at home. Made with homemade ice creams and toppings, these deluxe sundaes are even better than the ones you buy, but you can use purchased elements to save time. Make it your own by varying the ice creams and toppings.

Pour the fudge and butterscotch sauces into separate small saucepans, place over very low heat, and heat gently until they are just warm to the touch and pourable.

Peel the bananas and cut each in half lengthwise. If the dish you will be using is not long enough to accommodate the banana, cut the halves in half crosswise.

Put 1 scoop of the vanilla ice cream in the center of each of 2 serving dishes, ideally elongated oval banana-split dishes. Add a scoop each of the strawberry ice cream and chocolate gelato to either side of the vanilla ice cream.

Lay the banana halves along either side of the ice cream scoops. Spoon the raspberry sauce over the strawberry ice cream, the hot fudge sauce over the vanilla ice cream, and the butterscotch sauce over the chocolate gelato, dividing the sauces evenly between the 2 dishes.

Fit a pastry (piping) bag with a small star tip, and then spoon the whipped cream into the bag (see page 493). Pipe a swirl of whipped cream on top of each scoop of ice cream. (Or, use a spoon to top each scoop with a dollop of whipped cream.) Sprinkle the tops of the whipped cream mounds with the nuts. Set a cherry, stem side up, into each dollop of cream.

Set the banana split dishes onto plates for catching drips and serve right away, each with 1 or 2 long spoons.

6 tablespoons (3 fl oz/ 90 ml) Hot Fudge Sauce (page 460)

6 tablespoons (3 fl oz/ 90 ml) Butterscotch Sauce (page 461)

2 firm yellow bananas

2 large scoops Classic Vanilla Bean Ice Cream (page 604)

2 large scoops Strawberry Ice Cream (page 607)

2 large scoops Dark Chocolate Gelato (page 611)

¼ cup (2½ oz/75 g) Orange Marmalade–Raspberry Sauce (page 463)

½ cup (4 fl oz/125 ml) Whipped Cream (page 454)

¼ cup (1 oz/30 g) chopped peanuts or walnuts

6 maraschino cherries with stems

MAKES 2 LARGE SPLITS; 2–4 SERVINGS

INDIVIDUAL BAKED ALASKAS

Putting ice cream into a hot oven sounds daring, and only adds to the allure of this special-occasion dessert. The contrast of textures, temperatures, and flavors—airy, slightly charred sweet meringue; cold, creamy ice cream; a rich cake base—is the appeal of this showy classic.

4 slices pound cake, each 1 inch (2.5 cm) thick

2 tablespoons raspberry liqueur

1 pt (16 fl oz/500 ml) Strawberry Ice Cream (page 607), slightly softened

4 egg whites

½ cup (4 oz/125 g) sugar

¼ teaspoon cream of tartar

MAKES 4 SERVINGS

Line a baking sheet with parchment (baking) paper.

Using a 3-inch (7.5-cm) round cookie cutter, cut a circle from each cake slice. Arrange the circles on the prepared baking sheet, leaving at least 3 inches (7.5 cm) between the slices. Brush the cake slices lightly with the liqueur, then place the baking sheet in the freezer and freeze until the cake circles are firm, about 15 minutes.

Dip an ice cream scoop into hot water to warm briefly (for the best appearance, the scoop should be the same diameter as the cake circles). Pull the scoop across the ice cream to form a rounded scoop. Release the scoop onto the pound cake circle. Repeat with the remaining ice cream and cake circles. Place the baking sheet in the coldest part of the freezer until the ice cream is very firm, about 1 hour.

Using an electric mixer on medium speed, beat together the egg whites, 2 tablespoons of the sugar and the cream of tartar until foamy, about 1 minute. On medium speed, beat the egg whites until they begin to thicken, 2–3 minutes. On medium-high speed, beat until soft peaks form. On high speed, sprinkle in the remaining 6 tablespoons (3 oz/90 g) sugar, 1 tablespoon at a time, beating the egg whites for about 15 seconds after each addition. When all of the sugar has been added, continue to beat until the egg whites form stiff peaks, about 1 minute longer.

Take the baking sheet from the freezer. Working quickly, use a thin offset spatula to cover all of the ice cream–topped cake rounds completely with the meringue, dividing the meringue evenly. Use the spatula to make little swirls and points in the meringue. Return the baking sheet, uncovered, to the freezer for at least 10 minutes or up to 1 hour.

Position a rack in the center of the oven and preheat to 450°F (230°C). When the oven is hot, take the baking sheet directly from the freezer and place in the preheated oven. Bake until the meringue is pale gold and the tips of the swirls are browned, 4–5 minutes.

Transfer to individual plates and serve right away.

Quick softening

You can use a microwave to soften sorbet or ice cream for molding into composed desserts. Blast the ice cream in 10-second intervals and stir gently after each interval to preserve its texture.

619

Index

A

621

623

625

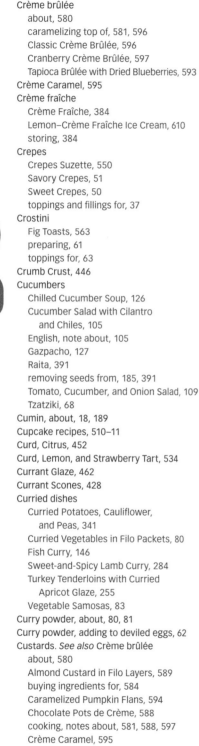

627

629

632

634

635

637

639

weldon**owen**

415 Jackson Street, Suite 200, San Francisco, CA 94111
Telephone: 415 291 0100 Fax: 415 291 8841
www.wopublishing.com

Weldon Owen is a division of:

BONNIER

WILLIAMS-SONOMA, INC.
Founder and Director Emeritus Chuck Williams

WELDON OWEN, INC.
CEO and President Terry Newell
Senior VP, International Sales Stuart Laurence
VP, Sales and New Business Development Amy Kaneko
Director of Finance Mark Perrigo

VP and Publisher Hannah Rahill
Executive Editor Jennifer Newens
Managing Editor Karen Templer
Text Writer Norman Kolpas
Editorial Assistant Becky Duffett

Associate Creative Director Emma Boys
Designer Lauren Charles
Junior Designer Anna Grace
Production Editor Linda Bouchard
Illustrator Tina Cash

Production Director Chris Hemesath
Production Manager Michelle Duggan
Color Manager Teri Bell

COOKING AT HOME
Conceived and produced by Weldon Owen, Inc.
In collaboration with Williams-Sonoma, Inc.
3250 Van Ness Avenue, San Francisco, CA 94109

A WELDON OWEN PRODUCTION
Copyright © 2010 Weldon Owen Inc. and Williams-Sonoma, Inc.
All rights reserved, including the right of reproduction
in whole or in part in any form.

Color separations by Mission Productions in Hong Kong
Printed and bound by Toppan Leefung Printing Limited in China

First printed in 2010
10 9 8 7 6 5 4 3 2 1

Library of Congress Cataloging-in-Publication
data is available.

ISBN-13: 978-1-74089-977-2
ISBN-10: 1-74089-977-6

The Editors of Williams-Sonoma
Donita Boles, Becky Duffett, Julia Humes, Kim Laidlaw, Amy Marr,
Julie Nelson, Jennifer Newens, and Hannah Rahill

ACKNOWLEDGMENTS
Weldon Owen wishes to thank Gaye Allen, Sarah Clegg, Leslie Evans, Michel Gadwa,
Elizabeth Parson, and Sharon Silva for their generous support in producing this book.

The content for this book was adapted from original recipes by Brigit Binns, Georgeanne Brennan, Lora Brody,
John Phillip Carroll, Emalee Chapman, Lane Crowther, Heidi Haughy Cusick, Abigail Johnson Dodge, Janet Fletcher,
Joyce Goldstein, Beth Hensperger, Dana Jacobi, Shelly Kaldunski, Sybil Kapoor, Susan Manlin Katzman, Denis Kelly,
Jeanne Thiel Kelley, Kiristine Kidd, Shirley King, Farina Wong Kingsley, Elinor Klivans, Norman Kolpas, Annabel Langbein,
Lorenza de' Medici, Jacqueline Mallorca, Susanna Palazuelos, Charles Pierce, Emanuala Stucchi Prinetti, Paul Richardson,
Rick Rodgers, Betty Rosbottom, Janeen Sarlin, Michele Scicolone, Phillip Stephen Schulz, The Scotto Sisters, Marie
Simmons, Marilyn Tausend, Sarah Tenaglia, Jan Weimer, Joanne Weir, Chuck Williams, and Diane Rossen Worthington.